RECORD OF PROCEEDINGS

INTERNATIONAL LABOUR
CONFERENCE

NINETY-THIRD SESSION
GENEVA, 2005

RECORD OF PROCEEDINGS

VOLUME II: COMMITTEE REPORTS
AUTHENTIC TEXTS
RESOLUTIONS

INTERNATIONAL LABOUR OFFICE
GENEVA

ISBN 92-2-115378-9
ISSN 0074-6681

First published 2005

The designations employed in ILO publications, which are in conformity with United Nations practice, and the presentation of material therein do not imply the expression of any opinion whatsoever on the part of the International Labour Office concerning the legal status of any country, area or territory or of its authorities, or concerning the delimitation of its frontiers.

The responsibility for opinions expressed in signed articles, studies and other contributions rests solely with their authors, and publication does not constitute an endorsement by the International Labour Office of the opinions expressed in them.

Reference to names of firms and commercial products and processes does not imply their endorsement by the International Labour Office, and any failure to mention a particular firm, commercial product or process is not a sign of disapproval.

ILO publications can be obtained through major booksellers or ILO local offices in many countries, or direct from ILO Publications, International Labour Office, CH-1211 Geneva 22, Switzerland. Catalogues or lists of new publications are available free of charge from the above address, or by email: pubvente@ilo.org

Visit our web site: www.ilo.org/publns

Formatted by TTE: ref. ILC93(2005)-Record of Proceedings
Printed by the International Labour Office, Geneva, Switzerland

Corrigenda

93rd Session of the International Labour Conference, June 2005

List of Records of Proceedings where requested changes have been made

RP No. 5-2

Page 16, paragraph 81.

RP No. 8

Page 8/5, speech by the Secretary-General.

RP No. 9

Page 9/2, the Workers' group.

RP No. 11

Page 11/2, speech by Mr. Togari.

Page 11/23, speech by Ms. Sasso Mazzufferi.

Page 11/29, speech by Ms. Flumian.

Page 11/33, speech by Mr. Rodríguez Barrera.

RP No. 12

Page 12/14, speech by Mr. Simeonov.

Page 12/22, speech by Mr. Richards.

RP No. 16

Page 16/6, speech by Mr. Djemam.

RP No. 17

Page 17/13, speech by Mr. Zharikov.

RP No. 22 Part two

Page 22, Part 2/17.

RP No. 24

Page 24/5, speech by Mr. Ribeiro Lopes.

Page 24/33, speech by Mr. Anand.

Page 24/33, speech by Ms. Awassi Atsimadja.

CONTENTS

Detailed contents of the Record of Proceedings

RP No.	Volume		Page
1	I	*Report of the Chairperson of the Governing Body to the Conference for the year 2004-05*	1
2	II	*Reports of the Selection Committee: First report*	1
3	II	*Reports of the Selection Committee: Composition of committees*	1
4	II	*Reports of the Credentials Committee*	1
5-1	II	*Second item on the agenda: Programme and Budget proposals for 2006-07 and other questions*	1
		First report of the Finance Committee of Government Representatives	1
		Resolutions submitted to the Conference	7
5-2	II	*Second item on the agenda: Programme and Budget proposals for 2006-07 and other questions*	1
		Second report of the Finance Committee of Government Representatives	1
		Resolutions submitted to the Conference	19
6	I	*First sitting:*	
		Opening of the session	1
		Speaker: Mr. Trotman *(Worker Vice-Chairperson of the Governing Body of the International Labour Office)*	
		Election of the President of the Conference	1
		Speakers: Mr. Yimer, Mr. Funes de Rioja, Mr. Sidi Saïd	
		Presidential address	2
		Election of the Vice-Presidents of the Conference	2
		Nomination of the Officers of the groups	2
		Constitution and composition of Conference committees	3
		Composition of the Selection Committee	3
		Suspension of certain provisions of the Standing Orders of the Conference	3

RP No.	Volume		Page
		Preliminary discussion of the Programme and Budget proposals for 2006-07	4
		Speakers: Mr. Botha, Mr. Funes de Rioja, Mr. Blondel, Mr. Trotman	
		Delegation of authority to the Officers of the Conference	6
7	I	*Follow-up activities by the Office under the Declaration on Fundamental Principles and Rights at Work: Freedom of association and collective bargaining, forced or compulsory labour, discrimination*	1
		A. Freedom of association and collective bargaining	1
		B. Forced and compulsory labour	2
		C. Discrimination: Employment and occupation	2
		Addressing racial/ethnic discrimination	2
		Strengthening the capacity of trade unions to address discrimination	2
		Promoting gender equality in employment policies	3
8	I	*Second sitting:*	
		Record vote on the resolutions concerning the arrears of contributions of Armenia and the Republic of Moldova	1
		Presentation of the report of the Chairperson of the Governing Body .	2
		Speaker: Mr. Séguin	
		Presentation of the Reports of the Director-General	4
		Speaker: The Secretary-General of the Conference	
		Reports of the Chairperson of the Governing Body and of the Director-General: Discussion	8
		Speakers: Mr. Funes de Rioja, Mr. Trotman, Mr. El Amawy, Mr. Morales Cartaya, Mr. Berzoini, Mr. Al Alawi, Mr. Wang, Mr. Kyrylenko, Mr. Mendoza, Mr. Méndez, Mr. Polančec, Mr. Hjort Frederiksen, Mr. Mdladlana, Mr. Burayzat	
		First report of the Selection Committee: Submission and noting	18
		Speaker: Mr. Razzouk	

RP No.	Volume		Page
		Record vote on the resolution concerning the arrears of contributions of Armenia: Results	19
		Record vote on the resolution concerning the arrears of contributions of the Republic of Moldova: Results	24
9	I	*Result of the elections to the Governing Body of the International Labour Office for the period 2005-08*	1
10	I	*Third (special) sitting:*	
		Address by His Excellency Mr. Abdelaziz Bouteflika, President of the People's Democratic Republic of Algeria	1
		Speakers: The President, the Secretary-General, Mr. Abdelaziz Bouteflika	
11	I	*Fourth sitting:*	
		Reports of the Chairperson of the Governing Body and of the Director-General: Discussion *(cont.)*	1
		Speakers: Mr. de Alba, Mr. Ng, Mr. Togari, Mr. Nkili, Mr. Goche, Mr. Mansouri, Mr. Boxall, Mr. Andres, Mr. Khaleghi, Ms. Blinkeviciute, Mr. Syed Shahir, Mr. Sanjeeva Reddy, Mr. Atwoli, Mr. Ferreira do Prado, Mr. Matulis, Mr. Sánchez Mesa	
		Fifth sitting:	
		Reports of the Chairperson of the Governing Body and of the Director-General: Discussion *(cont.)*	13
		Speakers: Mr. Lepik, Mr. Vazirov, Mr. Potter, Mr. De Geus, Mr. Gawanas, Ms. Levitskaya, Mr. Dahlan, Mr. Nordmann, Ms. Dyson, Ms. Filatov, Mr. Ryder, Mr. Petocz, Mr. Espinal Escobar, Mr. Thys, Ms. Sasso-Mazzufferi, Mr. Pheto, Mr. Basesgioglu, Mr. Teljebäck, Mgr. Tomasi, Mr. Kilic, Mr. Eremeev, Ms. Kolos, Mr. Lima Godoy, Ms. Flumian, Mr. Plaskitt, Mr. Guider, Ms. Taípo, Mr. Rodríguez Barrera, Mr. Kim, Mr. De Payva, Mr. Seneviratne, Mr. Yitzhaky, Mr. Mordant, Mr. Gryshchenko, Mr. Thailuan, Mr. Shcherbakov, Mr. Dowla, Mr. Lalovic, Mr. Salimian, Mr. Bejtaj, Mr. Sen	
12	I	*Sixth sitting:*	
		Global Report under the follow-up to the ILO Declaration on Fundamental Principles and Rights at Work: Interactive sitting	1
		Speakers: The President, Mr. Tabani, Mr. Trotman, Mr. Al Alawi, Mr. Eide, Mr. Pender, Mr. El Amawy, Mr. Buwalda, Ms. Goldberg, Mr. Hayat, Mr. Amin, Mr. Kpokolo, Mr. Funes de Rioja, Ms. Romero, Mr. Richards Mr. Simeonov, Mr. Shepard, Mr. Lima Godoy, Mr. Volynets	

RP No.	Volume		Page
		Seventh sitting:	
		Global Report under the follow-up to the ILO Declaration on Fundamental Principles and Rights at Work: Interactive sitting *(cont.)*	19

Speakers: Mr. Tambusai, Ms. Bakoru Zoe, Ms. Zhang, Mr. Sobashima, Ms. Taylor, Mr. Richards, Mr. Saldanha, Mr. Lambert, Ms. Yacob, Mr. Elmufti, Mr. De Vadder, Mr. Lawal, Mr. Salmenperä, Mr. Oni, Ms. Franco, Mr. Parrot, Mr. Tabani, Ms. Kirui, Mr. Lohia, Mr. Dzviti, Mr. Ahmed, Ms. Saab, Ms. Amadu, Ms. De Buitrago Arango, Ms. Maphanga, Mr. Chikuni, Mr. Servat Pereira de Sousa, Mr. Tibu, Mr. Mattar Alkaabi, Mr. Sankar Saha, Ms. Arshad, Mr. Gryshchenko, Mr. Page, Mr. Trotman, Mr. Tabani

13	I	*Eighth sitting:*	
		Ratification of international labour Conventions by Uganda, Saint Kitts and Nevis and Kyrgystan	1
		Reports of the Chairperson of the Governing Body and of the Director-General: Discussion *(cont.)*	1

Speakers: Mr. Da Costa Pitra Neto, Mr. Dkhil, Mr. Wagstaff, Mr. Biltgen, Mr. Fonseca Vieira Da Silva, Mr. Caldera Sánchez-Capitán, Ms. Chao, Mr. Spidla, Mr. Boisson, Mr. Gallardo Flores, Mr. Csizmar, Ms. Sto. Tomas, Mr. Jiménez Aguilar, Mr. Barbu, Mr. Rosso, Mr. Singh, Mr. Tateisi, Ms. Bakoru Zoe, Mr. N'Kolo Balamage, Mr. Peet, Mr. Ndiaye, Ms. Brighi, Mr. Dorado Cano, Mr. Tomada, Mr. Halkin, Ms. Mahase-Moiloa

Ninth sitting:

Reports of the Chairperson of the Governing Body and of the Director-General: Discussion *(cont.)* 21

Speakers: Mr. Bartenstein, Mr. Biyama, Mr. Abu-Libdeh, Mr. Klinpratoom, Mr. Aman, Mr. Somany, Mr. Ljubetic Godoy, Mr. Bayarsaikhan, Mr. Yurkin, Mr. Zellhoefer, Mr. Farrugia, Mr. Shmakov, Mr. Nakajima, Mr. Martínez Molina, Mr. Trejos Ballestero, Mr. Hayat, Mr. Zarb, Mr. Djilani, Mr. Marica, Mr. Lee, Mr. Aksam, Ms. Escoto Abreu, Mr. Akouete, Mr. Steyne, Mr. Larcher, Mr. Abdella, Mr. Al Manaa, Mr. Kim, Ms. Lucero, Mr. De la Haye, Mr. Bonmatí, Mr. Calixte, Ms. Muganza, Ms. Menkerios, Mr. Jrad, Mr. Ranjivason, Ms. Mint Bilal Ould Yamar, Mr. Nicolescu, Mr. Khammas, Mr. Alragheb

RP No.	Volume		Page
14	I	*Tenth sitting:*	

        Ratification of an international labour Convention and a Protocol by Bulgaria 1

        Reports of the Chairperson of the Governing Body and of the Director-General: Discussion *(cont.)* 1

            Speakers: Mr. Saktor, Mr. Killeen, Mr. Fong, Mr. Idris, Ms. Theodorsen, Mr. Monteiro, Mr. Soufan, Mr. Taliadoros, Mr. Jurca, Mr. Blondel, Mr. Mecina, Mr. Galea, Mr. Dalley, Mr. Chanpornpong, Mr. Kapuya, Mr. Hadi, Mr. Kuti, Mr. Simeonov, Mr. Abreu, Mr. Chen, Mr. Bouzia, Mr. Al-Mahfoodh, Mr. Mussa Baldé, Mr. Naruseb, Mr. Adda

    Twelfth sitting:

        Ratification of an international labour Convention by Tajikistan 21

        Reports of the Chairperson of the Governing Body and of the Director-General: Discussion *(cont.)* 21

            Speakers: Mr. Gosnar, Ms. Nguyen, Mr. Namuyamba, Mr. Naghiyev, Mr. Magaya, Mr. Trabelsi, Mr. Trenchev, Mr. Mammadov, Ms. Sigmund, Mr. Matugh Mohamed, Mr. Rosa Lança, Mr. Gómez Esguerra, Mr. Masoomi, Mr. El Azali, Mr. Paixão Bano, Mr. Xu, Mr. Parra Rojas, Mr. Habab, Mr. Al-Kuhlani, Mr. Singh, Mr. Sajda, Mr. Nguyen, Ms. Triana Alvis, Mr. Kearney, Mr. Rachman, Mr. Ahmed, Mr. Echavarría Saldarriaga, Mr. Sodnomdorj, Mr. Mailhos

| 15 | I | *Eleventh (special) sitting:* | |

        Address by His Excellency Mr. Olusegun Obasanjo, President of the Federal Republic of Nigeria.. 1

            Speakers: The President, the Secretary-General, Mr. Olusegun Obasanjo

| 16 | I | *Thirteenth sitting:* | |

        Reports of the Chairperson of the Governing Body and of the Director-General: Discussion *(cont.)* 1

            Speakers: Mr. Fanheiro, Mr. Zorigtbaatar, Mr. Mohbaliyev, Mr. Keira, Mr. Zinck, Mr. Yesayan, Mr. Martínez, Mr. Soriano, Mr. Djemam, Mr. Tarverdyan, Mr. Farah, Ms. Lanara-Tzotze, Mr. Abdo, Mr. Alemayehu, Mr. Mahmoud Mustapha, Mr. Sunmonu, Mr. Yanez Pol, Mr. Raut, Mr. Zawde, Ms. Ndong, Mr. Hasan

RP No.	Volume		Page
17	I	*Fourteenth sitting:*	
		Reports of the Chairperson of the Governing Body and of the Director-General: Discussion *(cont.)*..	1

Speakers: Mr. Bonomi, Mr. Szirmai, Ms. Arif, Mr. Arnold, Mr. George, Mr. Lambert, Ms. Awassi Atsimadja, Mr. Sukkar, Mr. Kulundu, Mr. Chiriboga, Ms. Toth Mucciacciaro, Mr. Kakanya, Mr. Otaredian, Mr. Servat Pereira de Sousa, Mr. Hoskins, Mr. Awira, Mr. Zharikov, Mr. Jouen, Mr. Abrantes, Mr. Leather, Mr. Edström, Ms. Almeus, Mr. Vongdara

Fifteenth sitting:

		Second report of the Finance Committee of Government Representatives: Submission, discussion and approval......................	19

Speakers: Mr. Elmiger *(Chairperson and Reporter of the Committee)*

		Ratification of an international labour Convention by the Lao People's Democratic Republic	20
		Reports of the Chairperson of the Governing Body and of the Director-General: Discussion *(cont.)*..	20

Speakers: Mr. Ledouble, Mr. Flores Flores, Ms. Kanda, Ms. Valkonen, Mr. Fernandez, Mr. Van Vuuren, Mr. Kane, Mr. Rambharat, Mr. Mena Quintana, Mr. Dinis, Ms. Poncini, Mr. Yovel, Mr. Ghandour, Mr. González González, Mr. Kuppan, Mr. Matheys, Mr. Giuseppi, Mr. Lucas Gómez, Mr. Arciniega, Mr. Boti, Ms. Bastos Duarte, Mr. Chikuni, Mr. Eytle, Mr. Jiménez

18	II	*Fourth item on the agenda: Occupational safety and health*	
		Report of the Committee on Safety and Health................................	1
		Proposed Conclusions..	63
		Resolution to place on the agenda of the next ordinary session of the Conference an item entitled "Occupational safety and health"	69
19	II	*Fifth item on the agenda: Work in the fishing sector (second discussion)*	
		Report of the Committee on the Fishing Sector	1
		A. Proposed Convention concerning work in the fishing sector ..	96
		B. Proposed Recommendation concerning work in the fishing sector...	122

RP No.	Volume		Page
19A	II	*Text of the Convention concerning work in the fishing sector submitted by the Drafting Committee*	1
19B	II	*Text of the Recommendation concerning work in the fishing sector submitted by the Drafting Committee*	1
20	II	*Sixth item on the agenda: Promoting youth employment (general discussion based on an integrated approach)*	
		Report of the Committee on Youth Employment	1
		Resolution concerning youth employment	65
		Conclusions on promoting pathways to decent work for youth	66
21	I	*Sixteenth sitting:*	
		Reports of the Chairperson of the Governing Body and of the Director-General: Discussion *(concl.)*	1
		Speakers: Mr. Celi Vegas, Mr. Eastmond, Mr. Dugasse, Mr. Malabag, Mr. Alfarargi, Mr. Díaz, Mr. Parra Gaona, Mr. Kaluat, Mr. Barak, Mr. Siriwardane, Mr. Assadallah, Ms. Bang Onsengdet, Mr. Cabezas Badilla, Mr. Gutiérrez Madueño, Mr. Trogen, Mr. Puri, Mr. Salmon, Mr. Funes de Rioja	
22	II	*Third item on the agenda: Information and reports on the application of Conventions and Recommendations*	
		Report of the Committee on the Application of Standards	1
23	I	*Reply by the Director-General to the discussion of his Report*	1
24	I	*Seventeenth sitting:*	
		Report of the Committee on the Fishing Sector: Submission, discussion and approval	1
		Speakers: Mr. Boumbopoulos *(Reporter)*, Ms. Anang, Mr. Sand Mortensen, Mr. Ribeiro Lopes, Mr. Endo, Mr. Smefjell, Ms. Ssenabulya, Mr. Todi, Mr. Vidaut Márquez, Mr. Masemola, Mr. Sandrasekera, Mr. Mathew, Mr. Zhang, Mr. Potter, Mr. Blonk, Mr. Okazaki	
		Proposed Convention concerning work in the fishing sector: Adoption	11
		Proposed Recommendation concerning work in the fishing sector: Adoption	11

RP No.	Volume		Page
		Report of the Committee on Safety and Health: Submission, discussion and approval...	11
		Speakers: Mr. Annakin *(Reporter)*, Mr. Lötter, Ms. Rantsolase, Mr. Békés, Ms. Pujadas, Mr. Erikson, Mr. Mahadevan, Ms. Moure, Mr. Abu Bakar, Mr. Edström, Mr. Potter	
		Proposed Conclusions with a view to a Convention and Recommendation: Adoption..	18
		Resolution to place on the agenda of the next ordinary session of the Conference an item entitled "Occupational safety and health": Adoption..	19
	Eighteenth sitting:		
		Record vote on the resolution concerning the arrears of contributions of Georgia...	21
		Record vote on the resolution concerning the arrears of contributions of Iraq...	21
		Record vote on the resolution concerning the arrears of contributions of Togo...	21
		Record vote on the resolution concerning the adoption of the Programme and Budget for 2006-07 and the allocation of the budget of income among member States..	21
		Speakers: Mr. Shepard, Mr. Richards, Mr. Fujisaki, Mr. Blondel	
		Resolution concerning the flag of the International Labour Organization: Adoption..	22
		Report of the Committee on Youth Employment: Submission, discussion and approval...	22
		Speakers: Ms. Imperial *(Reporter)*, Mr. Anderson, Ms. Moore, Mr. Abdelmoumene, Ms. Saab, Ms. Toth Mucciacciaro, Ms. Sonntag, Mr. Lambert, Mr. Cunha Dias, Ms. Lloyd, Mr. Anand, Ms. Awassi Atsimadja, Mr. Renique	
		Conclusions on promoting pathways to decent work for youth: Adoption..	34
		Resolution concerning youth employment: Adoption........................	34
		Record vote on the resolution concerning the arrears of contributions of Georgia: Results...	35
		Record vote on the resolution concerning the arrears of contributions of Iraq: Results..	40
		Record vote on the resolution concerning the arrears of contributions of Togo: Results..	45

RP No.	Volume		Page
		Record vote on the resolution for the adoption of the Programme and Budget for 2006-07 and the allocation of the budget of income among member States: Results	50
25	I	*Nineteenth sitting:*	

Second and third reports of the Credentials Committee: Submission and noting 1

> *Speakers:* Mr. Oni *(Chairperson and Reporter)*, Mr. Chipaziwa, Mr. Jiménez

Final record vote on the proposed Convention concerning work in the fishing sector: Adoption 3

Final record vote on the proposed Recommendation concerning work in the fishing sector: Adoption 3

> *Speakers:* Mr. Trotman, Mr. Funes de Rioja, Ms. Robinson, Mr. Smefjell, Mr. Thierry, the Legal Adviser

Report of the Committee on the Application of Standards: Submission, discussion and approval 5

> *Speakers:* Ms. Parra *(Reporter)*, Mr. Potter, Mr. Cortebeeck, Mr. Paixão Pardo *(Chairperson)*, Mr. MacPhee, Mr. Dorado Cano, Mr. Shein, Mr. Ould Mohamed Lemine, Mr. Chipaziwa, Mr. Nkhambule, Ms. Lu, Mr. Starovoytov, Mr. Chibebe, Mr. Ndoye, Ms. Brighi, Mr. Rodríguez Díaz, Mr. Ahmed, Mr. Salimian, Mr. Sankar Saha

Closing speeches 20

> *Speakers:* Mr. Finlay, Ms. Anderson, the Secretary-General, the President

Final record vote on the adoption of the Work in Fishing Convention, 2005: Results 24

Final record vote on the adoption of the Work in Fishing Recommendation, 2005: Results 30

Discussion in plenary sitting (Volume I)	RP No./Page
Global Report under the follow-up to the ILO Declaration on Fundamental Principles and Rights at Work: Interactive sitting	12/1
Examination of the second report of the Finance Committee of Government Representatives	17/19
Examination of the report of the Committee on the Fishing Sector	24/1
Examination of the report of the Committee on Safety and Health	24/11

	RP No./Page
Examination of the report of the Committee on Youth Employment.......	24/22
Examination of the second and third reports of the Credentials Committee	25/1
Examination of the report of the Committee on the Application of Standards	25/5

Governing Body (Volume I)

	RP No./Page
Report of the Chairperson of the Governing Body to the Conference for the year 2004-05	1/1

Record votes (Volume I)

	RP No./Page
Resolution concerning the arrears of contributions of Armenia................	8/1, 8/19
Resolution concerning the arrears of contributions of the Republic of Moldova..	8/1, 8/24
Resolution concerning the arrears of contributions of Georgia.................	24/21, 24/35
Resolution concerning the arrears of contributions of Iraq	24/21, 24/40
Resolution concerning the arrears of contributions of Togo	24/21, 24/45
Resolution concerning the adoption of the Programme and Budget for 2006-07 and the allocation of the budget of income among member States	24/21, 24/50
Work in Fishing Convention, 2005	25/3, 25/24
Work in Fishing Recommendation, 2005..	25/3, 25/30

Index of speakers in plenary sitting (Volume I)

Delegations (Volume I)

Committee reports (Volume II)

RP No./Page

Selection Committee

First report	2/1
Composition of committees...	3/1

RP No./Page

Credentials Committee

> Brief report presented on behalf of the Chairperson of the
> Governing Body 4/1
> First report 4/5
> Second report 4/11
> Third report 4/23

Finance Committee of Government Representatives

> First report 5-1/1
> Resolutions submitted to the Conference 5-1/7
> Second report 5-2/1
> Resolutions submitted to the Conference 5-2/19

Committee on Safety and Health

> Report 18/1
> Proposed Conclusions 18/63
> Resolution to place on the agenda of the next ordinary session
> of the Conference an item entitled "Occupational safety
> and health" 18/69

Committee on the Fishing Sector

> Report 19/1
> A. Proposed Convention concerning work in the
>   fishing sector 19/96
> B. Proposed Recommendation concerning work in the
>   fishing sector 19/122

Committee on Youth Employment

> Report 20/1
> Resolution concerning youth employment 20/65
> Conclusions on promoting pathways to decent work for youth 20/66

Committee on the Application of Standards

> Part One: General report 22/1
> Part Two: Observations and information concerning
> particular countries .... 22 Part 2/1
> Part Three: Special sitting to examine developments concerning
> the question of the observance by the Government of Myanmar
> of the Forced Labour Convention, 1930 (No. 29) .... 22 Part 3/1

Authentic texts adopted by the Conference (Volume II)   Page

Recommendation concerning work in the fishing sector 2

Resolutions adopted by the Conference (Volume II) — Page

I.	Resolution concerning youth employment...	1
II.	Resolution to place on the agenda of the next ordinary session of the Conference an item entitled "Occupational safety and health".............................	12
III.	Resolution concerning the flag of the International Labour Organization.............	12
IV.	Resolution concerning the adoption of the Programme and Budget for 2006-07 and the allocation of the budget of income among member States	17
V.	Resolution concerning the arrears of contributions of Armenia	17
VI.	Resolution concerning the arrears of contributions of the Republic of Moldova ..	18
VII.	Resolution concerning the arrears of contributions of Togo.................................	18
VIII.	Resolution concerning the arrears of contributions of Georgia	19
IX.	Resolution concerning the arrears of contributions of Iraq...................................	19
X.	Resolution concerning the composition of the Administrative Tribunal of the International Labour Organization...	20
XI.	Resolution concerning the assessment of contributions of new member States	20
XII.	Resolution concerning the scale of assessments of contributions to the budget for 2006..	20

COMMITTEE REPORTS

International Labour Conference

Record of Proceedings   2

Ninety-third Session, Geneva, 2005

Reports of the Selection Committee

First report

1. Election of the Officers of the Committee

The secretariat reconfirmed the membership of the Committee as that described in *Provisional Record* No. 3. So as to proceed with the election of the Chairperson, the regional coordinator for the Asia and Pacific group of governments informed the secretariat of the Government of Japan's intention to nominate the Government of Lebanon to replace it as a regular member. On this basis the Selection Committee subsequently elected its Officers as follows:

Chairperson:	Mr. A. Razzouk (Lebanon)
Employer Vice-Chairperson:	Mr. A. M'Kaissi (Tunisia)
Worker Vice-Chairperson:	Mr. L. Trotman (Barbados)

2. Reminder of the Selection Committee's authority under the Standing Orders

The Selection Committee was reminded that, at its 90th Session (2002), the Conference adopted a set of amendments to its Standing Orders aimed at streamlining a number of Conference procedures.[1]

For the Selection Committee, these amendments have resulted in two important changes. Firstly, under article 4, paragraph 2, of the Standing Orders, the Selection Committee, in addition to its traditional authority to fix the time and agenda of the plenary sittings, is now responsible for acting on behalf of the Conference with respect to decisions on non-controversial questions of a routine nature. Thus, except where consensus cannot be reached in respect of any particular question requiring a decision for the proper conduct of business, the Selection Committee can now decide on its own authority and its decisions no longer need to be endorsed by the Conference. Secondly, under article 9(a) of the Standing Orders, the Committee is no longer responsible for approving changes in the composition of committees, once their initial membership has been determined by the Conference. This responsibility is now exercised by each group.

---

[1] See 90th ILC, *Provisional Record* No. 2.

3. Discussion of the Reports of the Chairperson of the Governing Body and the Director-General: Opening date for the discussion and closing date for the list of speakers

The Selection Committee has decided that the discussion of the Reports of the Chairperson of the Governing Body and the Director-General will begin on Monday, 6 June, at 10 a.m., and to decide that the list of speakers will be closed on Wednesday, 8 June, at 6 p.m., under the usual conditions.

4. Discussion of the Global Report under the follow-up to the ILO Declaration on Fundamental Principles and Rights at Work

At its 292nd Session (March 2005), the Governing Body invited the Conference to adopt a set of provisional ad hoc arrangements for the discussion of the Global Report under the follow-up to the Declaration, which are reproduced in Appendix I.

On the basis of those proposed arrangements and subject to the Conference's approval of the necessary suspension of the Standing Orders, the Selection Committee decided that the Global Report under the follow-up to the Declaration be dealt with separately from the Reports of the Chairperson of the Governing Body and of the Director-General, in a maximum of two plenary sittings entirely devoted to it, on the same day.

The Selection Committee decided that the two sittings be held on Wednesday, 8 June.

5. Plan of work of Conference committees

The Selection Committee endorsed a draft plan of work for committees, which is not binding but would enable them, in organizing their work, to take maximum possible account of the overall needs and possibilities of the Conference, is attached in tabular form for the information of the Conference (Appendix V).

6. Governing Body elections

The Selection Committee has decided that the meetings of the electoral colleges be held in the afternoon of Monday, 6 June. According to the provision of article 52, paragraph 3, of the Standing Orders, and at the request of both the Government group and the Workers' group, the electronic voting system for the elections will be used. [2]

As regards the Government electoral college, it may be recalled that, when the Conference in 1995 approved an amendment to its Standing Orders increasing the number of Government deputy members from 18 to 28, it endorsed the principle that the ballot papers for the Government group should be drawn up and dealt with by the latter in such a manner as to guarantee an overall distribution of regular and deputy seats among the regions corresponding to that envisaged in the Instrument for the Amendment of the Constitution of the ILO, 1986.

---

[2] A description of the electronic voting system is attached in Appendix IV.

7. Suggestions to facilitate the work of the Conference

As in previous years, the Selection Committee invites the Conference to confirm the following principles:

(a) Quorum

(i) The quorum will be fixed provisionally, on the basis of the credentials received, in the brief report of the Chairperson of the Governing Body on the day before the opening of the Conference; the said report is published as a *Provisional Record*. This provisional quorum will remain unchanged until the Credentials Committee determines the quorum on the basis of registrations, it being understood that, if an important vote were to take place in the initial stages of the Conference (once the Credentials Committee has been appointed), the Conference might request the Credentials Committee to determine the quorum in an urgent report.

(ii) Thereafter, the quorum will be adjusted, under the authority of the Credentials Committee, so as to take into account new registrations and notices of departure from delegates leaving the Conference.

(iii) Delegates should register personally, immediately on arrival, as the quorum is calculated on the basis of the number of delegates registered.

(iv) Acceptance of appointment as a delegate implies an obligation to be available in Geneva personally, or through an adviser authorized to act as a substitute for the work of the Conference until its end, as important votes often take place on the last day.

(v) Delegates who are nevertheless obliged to leave the Conference before it finishes should give notice of their forthcoming departure to the secretariat of the Conference. The form utilized to indicate their date of departure also enables them to authorize an adviser to act and to vote in their place. At group meetings held during the second half of the Conference the attention of members of the groups will be drawn to the importance of completing and handing in this form.

(vi) In addition, one Government delegate of a country may report the departure of the other Government delegate, and the secretaries of the Employers' and Workers' groups may also give notice of the final departure of members of their groups, who have not authorized advisers to act in their place.

(vii) When a record vote is taken in plenary while committees are sitting, delegates are both entitled and expected to leave committees to vote unless they are replaced by a substitute in plenary. Announcements are made in the committees to ensure that all delegates are aware that a record vote is about to take place. Appropriate arrangements will be made for committees meeting in the ILO building.

(b) Punctuality

The Selection Committee would encourage committee chairpersons to start proceedings punctually, irrespective of the number of persons present, but on condition that votes will not be taken unless a quorum is clearly present.

(c) Negotiations

In order to facilitate more continuous negotiation in committees between the different groups, representatives of each group should meet with the chairperson and reporter of the committee and with the representative of the Secretary-General, whenever this is desirable, to ensure that the leaders of each group know fully the minds of their colleagues in the other groups; normally such meetings are held before each group has committed itself to a definite position. The function of these informal meetings is to afford opportunities for a fuller understanding of differences of view before definite positions have crystallized.

8. Participation in Conference committees by Members having lost the right to vote

At its 239th Session (February-March 1988), the Governing Body considered the implications of the appointment, as regular members of Conference committees, of representatives of a member State which had lost the right to vote under article 13, paragraph 4, of the Constitution of the ILO. It noted that, while the appointment of Employer and Worker representatives from such a State had no practical implications, because the Employers' and Workers' groups operated an effective system under article 56, paragraph 5(b), of the Conference Standing Orders for ensuring that deputy members of a committee voted in the place of regular members deprived of the right to vote, the same was not true of the Government group. As a result, if a Government that has lost the right to vote is appointed as a regular member of a committee, the distribution of votes between the three groups is distorted because the weighting of votes is based on the full regular membership and in practice the Government regular members of committees who are unable to vote do not make use of the possibility afforded by article 56, paragraph 5(a), of appointing a deputy member to vote in their place.

The Governing Body accordingly recommended that, in order to avoid such distortions, members of the Government group should not apply for regular membership of committees if they were not at the time in question entitled to vote. Should this practice, which has been maintained at all sessions of the Conference since 1987, for any reason not be fully respected, the weighting coefficients in committees should be calculated on the basis of the number of Government members entitled to vote.

The Selection Committee accordingly confirms that the calculation of weighting coefficients for votes in committees should be based on the number of regular Government members entitled to vote.

9. Requests for representation in Conference committees submitted by international non-governmental organizations

In accordance with article 2, paragraph 3(j), of the Standing Orders of the Conference, the Officers of the Governing Body have invited on its behalf certain international non-governmental organizations to be represented at the present session of the Conference, it being understood that it would be for the Selection Committee of the Conference to consider their requests to participate in the work of the committees dealing with items on the agenda in which they have expressed a particular interest.

The Committee noted the number of INGOs proposed by the Governing Body for participation in the various committees at this session and asked that the Governing Body be conscientious in its application of the participation criteria.

The provision of the Standing Orders of the Conference, which is relevant to such requests, is article 56, paragraph 9. In accordance with that article, the Selection Committee invited the following organizations to be represented in the committees stated:

Committee on the Application of Standards

African Commission of Health and Human Rights Promoters

Amnesty International

Anti-Slavery International

Education International

Federation of International Civil Servants' Associations

Friends World Committee for Consultation

General Confederation of Trade Unions

International Alliance of Women

International Centre for Trade Union Rights

International Confederation of Arab Trade Unions

International Confederation of Public Servants

International Council of Nurses

International Energy and Mines Organization

International Federation of Building and Wood Workers

International Federation of Employees in Public Services

International Federation of Trade Unions of Transport Workers

International Federation of University Women

International Federation of Women in Legal Careers

International Federation Terre des Hommes

International Metalworkers' Federation

International Textile, Garment and Leather Workers' Federation

International Union of Food, Agricultural, Hotel, Restaurant, Catering, Tobacco and Allied Workers' Associations

Latin American Central of Workers

Latin American Union of Municipal Workers

North-South XXI

Permanent Congress of Trade Union Unity of Latin American Workers

Southern African Trade Union Co-ordination Council

Trade Unions International of Public and Allied Employees

Union of International Associations

World Confederation of Teachers

World Federation of Personnel Management Associations

World Movement of Christian Workers

World Organisation against Torture

Committee on Occupational Safety and Health

African Commission of Health and Human Rights Promoters

Brotherhood of Asian Trade Unions

Democratic Organization of African Workers' Trade Unions

Exchange and Cooperation Centre for Latin America

Friends World Committee for Consultation

General Confederation of Trade Unions

International Alliance of Women

International Arts and Entertainment Alliance

International Association of Agricultural Medicine and Rural Health

International Association of Labour Inspection

International Commission on Occupational Health

International Confederation of Arab Trade Unions

International Council of Nurses

International Energy and Mines Organization

International Federation of Building and Wood Workers

International Federation of Business and Professional Women

International Federation of Employees in Public Services

International Federation of Trade Unions of Transport Workers

International Federation of University Women

International Federation of Women in Legal Careers

International Metalworkers' Federation

International Textile, Garment and Leather Workers' Federation

International Union of Food, Agricultural, Hotel, Restaurant, Catering, Tobacco and Allied Workers' Associations

North-South XXI

Permanent Congress of Trade Union Unity of Latin American Workers

Soroptimist International

Trade Unions International of Workers in Agriculture, Food, Commerce, Textiles and Allied Industries

Trade Unions International of Workers of the Building, Wood and Building Materials Industries

Union Network International

Union of International Associations

World Federation of Building and Woodworkers Unions

World Federation of Industry Workers

World Federation of Personnel Management Associations

World Movement of Christian Workers

World Organisation against Torture

World Union of Catholic Women's Organisations

Committee on the Fishing Sector

African Commission of Health and Human Rights Promoters

Democratic Organization of African Workers' Trade Unions

General Confederation of Trade Unions

International Christian Maritime Association

International Collective in Support of Fishworkers

International Confederation of Arab Trade Unions

International Federation of Trade Unions of Transport Workers

International Metalworkers' Federation

International Transport Workers' Federation

International Union of Food, Agricultural, Hotel, Restaurant, Catering, Tobacco and Allied Workers' Associations

Permanent Congress of Trade Union Unity of Latin American Workers

Trade Unions International of Workers in Agriculture, Food, Commerce, Textiles and Allied Industries

World Movement of Christian Workers

World Organisation against Torture

Committee on Youth Employment

African Commission of Health and Human Rights Promoters

Democratic Organization of African Workers' Trade Unions

Education International

Friends World Committee for Consultation

General Confederation of Trade Unions

International Alliance of Women

International Association for Educational and Vocational Guidance

International Association of Universities of the Third Age

International Christian Union of Business Executives

International Confederation of Arab Trade Unions

International Coordination of Young Christian Workers

International Council of Nurses

International Council on Social Welfare

International Energy and Mines Organization

International Federation of Building and Wood Workers

International Federation of Business and Professional Women

International Federation of Trade Unions of Transport Workers

International Federation of University Women

International Federation of Women in Legal Careers

International Federation Terre des Hommes

International Metalworkers' Federation

International Textile, Garment and Leather Workers' Federation

International Young Christian Workers

Latin American Central of Workers

Permanent Congress of Trade Union Unity of Latin American Workers

Soroptimist International

Southern African Trade Union Co-ordination Council

Trade Union Advisory Committee to the Organisation for Economic Cooperation and Development

Union Network International

World Association for Small and Medium Enterprises

World Confederation of Teachers

World Federation of Personnel Management Associations

World Movement of Christian Workers

World Organisation against Torture

World Union of Catholic Women's Organisations

10. Flag of the International Labour Organization

At its 292nd Session (March 2005), the Governing Body approved: (a) a draft resolution concerning the flag of the International Labour Organization, with a view to adoption by the International Labour Conference; and (b) the code and regulations for the use of the flag of the International Labour Organization, subject to their coming into force after adoption by the Conference of its resolution concerning the flag of the International Labour Organization. [3]

The Selection Committee invites the International Labour Conference to adopt the draft resolution concerning the flag of the International Labour Organization (Appendix II) and to take note of the code and regulations for the use of the flag approved by the Governing Body (Appendix III).

11. Composition of the Credentials Committee

The Selection Committee elected the following Offices as the three members of the Credentials Committee:

---

[3] GB.292/10(Rev.).

Government member: Mr. J.M. Oni (Benin)

Employer member: Ms. L. Sasso-Mazzufferi (Italy)

Worker member: Mr. U. Edström (Sweden)

12. Appointment of the Conference Drafting Committee

The Selection Committee decided that, in accordance with the provisions of article 6, paragraph 1, of the Standing Orders, the Conference Drafting Committee should be composed as follows:

- The President of the Conference or his representative.
- The Secretary-General of the Conference or his representative.
- The Legal Adviser of the Conference and his deputy.
- The Director of the International Labour Standards Department or his representative.
- The members of the relevant committee's drafting committee.

13. Delegation of authority to the Officers of the Selection Committee

In accordance with the usual practice and by virtue of article 4, paragraph 2, of the Standing Orders, the Selection Committee decided to delegate to its Officers the authority to arrange the programme of the Conference and fix the time and agenda of plenary sittings as well as to decide on any non-controversial issues of a routine nature necessary for the running of the Conference.

The effect of this delegation of authority will be that the Selection Committee will only be called on to meet during the present session of the Conference if other substantive matters requiring a decision arise.

14. Other questions: Electronic voting system

A description of the electronic voting system, to be used in principle for all votes in plenary sittings and for the Governing Body elections in accordance with article 19, paragraph 15, of the Standing Orders, is attached in Appendix IV.

Geneva, 2 June 2005.

(Signed) A. Razzouk,
Chairperson.

Appendix I

Ad hoc arrangements for the discussion of the Global Report under the follow-up to the Declaration at the 93rd Session of the International Labour Conference [1]

Principle of the discussion

Having regard to the various options referred to in the annex to the Declaration, the Governing Body recommends that the Global Report submitted to the Conference by the Director-General should be dealt with by the Conference, separately from the Director-General's Reports under article 12 of the Conference Standing Orders.

Timing of the discussion

A maximum of two sittings on the same day should be convened for the thematic discussion of the Global Report, with the possibility, if necessary, of extending the sitting. In order to take account of the programme of work of the Conference and of the fact that a number of ministers who usually are present during the second week of the Conference may wish to take the floor, the discussion of the Global Report should be held during the second week of the Conference. The date will be determined by the Selection Committee.

Procedure for the discussion

The separate discussion of the Global Report recommended above implies in particular that the statements made during the discussion of the Global Report should not fall under the limitation concerning the number of statements by each speaker in plenary provided for in article 12, paragraph 3, of the Standing Orders, and that the discussion should not be governed by the provisions of article 14, paragraph 6, concerning the time limit for speeches. Furthermore, exchanges of views on the suggested points for thematic discussion should not be subject to the restrictions laid down in article 14, paragraph 2, concerning the order in which speakers are called. These provisions should accordingly be suspended under the procedure provided for in article 76 of the Standing Orders to the extent necessary for the discussion of the Global Report.

Organization of the discussion

Given that the thematic discussion is not intended to lead to the adoption of conclusions or decisions by the Conference, on the one hand, and in consideration of the abovementioned suspensions of the Standing Orders, on the other, the Selection Committee may decide that this discussion should be conducted as a plenary committee and be chaired by one of the Officers of the Conference. Should the need arise, the Chairperson might be assisted by a moderator appointed by the Officers of the Conference.

Report to the plenary

The Chairperson of the plenary committee would present a short oral report to the plenary of the Conference and the thematic discussion would be reproduced in the *Provisional Record*.

---

[1] Adopted by the Governing Body at its 292nd Session (March 2005).

Appendix II

Draft resolution concerning the flag of the International Labour Organization

The General Conference of the International Labour Organization,

Mindful of the necessity to allow the Organization to be given the visibility it might need,

Noting that other international organizations of the United Nations system have adopted, through their competent organs, flags carrying their respective emblems,

Considering that the emblem, approved by the Director-General in Instruction No. 325 of 1 September 1967, is universally recognized as the International Labour Organization's logo,

Noting that the Governing Body of the International Labour Office has adopted the code and the regulations for the use of the flag of the International Labour Organization under the reservation that they come into force after the adoption of this resolution,

1. decides that a flag of the International Labour Organization is adopted which bears the emblem symbolizing tripartism and approved by the Director-General in Instruction No. 325 of 1 September 1967;

2. takes note of the code and regulations for the use of the flag of the International Labour Organization adopted by the Governing Body.

Appendix III

(a) Flag code of the International Labour Organization

1. Design of flag

The flag of the International Labour Organization shall be the official emblem of the International Labour Organization centred on a United Nations blue background, as approved by the Director-General on 1 September 1967. Such emblem shall appear in white on both sides of the flag except where otherwise prescribed by the regulations. The flag shall be made in such sizes as may, from time to time, be prescribed by the regulations.

2. Dignity of flag

The flag shall not be subjected to any indignity.

3. Flag protocol

1. The flag of the International Labour Organization shall not be subordinated to any other flag.

2. The manner in which the flag of the International Labour Organization may be flown, in relation to any other flag, shall be prescribed in the regulations.

4. Use of flag by the International Labour Organization

1. The flag shall be flown:

(a) from all buildings, offices and other property occupied by the International Labour Organization;

(b) from any official residence when such residence has been so designated by regulation;

2. The flag shall be used by any unit acting on behalf of the International Labour Organization such as any committee or commission or other entity established by the International Labour Organization, in such circumstances not covered in this code as may become necessary in the interests of the International Labour Organization.

5. Use of flag generally

The flag may be used in accordance with this flag code by governments, organizations and individuals to demonstrate support of the International Labour Organization and to further its principles and purposes. The manner and circumstances of display shall conform, in so far as appropriate, to the laws and customs applicable to the display of the national flag of the country in which the display is made.

6. Prohibition

The flag shall not be used in any manner inconsistent with this code or its regulations. On no account shall the flag or a replica thereof be used for commercial purposes or in direct association with an article of merchandise. The Director-General, subject to the approval of the Officers of the Governing Body, may deviate from this principle in special circumstances, such as the celebration of an anniversary of the Organization.

7. Mourning

The Director-General shall prescribe by regulation or otherwise the cases in which the flag shall be flown at half mast as a sign of mourning.

8. Manufacture and sale of flag

1. The flag may be manufactured for commercial purposes only upon written consent of the Director-General.

2. Such consent shall be subject to the following condition:

The manufacturer shall ensure that every purchaser of the flag receives a copy of this code and the regulations for implementing it and is informed of the conditions, set out in this code and its regulations, on which the flag may be used.

9. Violation

Any violation of this flag code and its regulations shall be punished in accordance with the laws of the country in which it takes place.

10. Regulations and amendments

The Governing Body, upon the Director-General's proposal, is empowered to make or revise the regulations for implementing this code and to amend the code, as appropriate.

(b) Regulations for the use of the flag of the International Labour Organization

These regulations are issued in pursuance of article 10 of the International Labour Organization flag code.

I. DIMENSIONS OF FLAG

1. In pursuance to article 1 of the flag code the proportions of the International Labour Organization flag shall be:

(a) hoist (width) of the International Labour Organization flag – 2;
flag (length) of the International Labour Organization flag – 3;

or

(b) hoist (width) of the International Labour Organization flag – 3;
flag (length) of the International Labour Organization flag – 5;

or

(c) the same proportions as those of the national flag of any country in which the International Labour Organization flag is flown.

2. The emblem shall in all cases be one-half of the hoist of the International Labour Organization flag and entirely centred.

II. FLAG PROTOCOL

The International Labour Organization flag may be displayed as follows:

1. General provisions

(a) The International Labour Organization flag may be displayed alone or with one or more other flags.

(b) When the International Labour Organization flag is displayed with one or more other flags, all the flags must be displayed on the same level and be of approximately equal size.

(c) On no account may any flag displayed with the International Labour Organization flag be displayed on a higher level than the International Labour Organization flag or be larger than it.

(d) The International Labour Organization flag may be displayed on either side of any other flag without being deemed to be subordinated to any such flag within the meaning of article 3, paragraph 1, of the International Labour Organization flag code.

(e) The International Labour Organization flag should normally only be displayed on a building or flagstaff from sunrise to sunset. The International Labour Organization flag may also be displayed at night in exceptional cases.

(f) The International Labour Organization flag should never be used as drapery of any sort, never festooned, drawn back, nor up, in folds, but always allowed to fall free.

2. Closed circle of flags

Other than in a circle of the flags of the United Nations and other specialized agencies, the International Labour Organization flag should not, in principle, be made part of a circle of flags. When flags are placed in a circle, the flags, other than the International Labour Organization flag, should be displayed in the French alphabetical order of the countries represented reading clockwise. The International Labour Organization flag should always be displayed on the flagpole in the centre of the circle of flags or in an appropriate adjoining area.

3. Line, cluster or semicircle of flags

In line, cluster or semicircle groupings all flags other than the International Labour Organization flag shall be displayed in the French alphabetical order of the countries represented starting from the left. In such cases, the International Labour Organization flag should either be displayed separately in an appropriate area or in the centre of the line, cluster or semicircle or, in cases where two International Labour Organization flags are available, at both ends of the line, cluster or semicircle.

4. National flag of the country in which the International Labour Organization flag is displayed

(a) The national flag of the country should appear in its normal position according to the French alphabetical order of the countries.

(b) When the country concerned wishes to make a special display of its national flag, the flags should be arranged in a line, cluster or semicircle and the national flag placed at each end of the line, cluster or semicircle separated from the grouping by an interval of not less than one-fifth of the total length of the line.

III. USE OF FLAG GENERALLY

1. Under article 5 of the International Labour Organization flag code, the International Labour Organization flag may be used to demonstrate the support of the International Labour Organization and to further its principles and purposes.

2. It is considered especially appropriate that the International Labour Organization flag should be displayed on the following occasions:

   (a) on the national day of the country in which the flag is displayed;

   (b) on the occasion of any official event, particularly in honour of the International Labour Organization; and

   (c) on the occasion of any official event which might or is desired to be related in some way to the International Labour Organization.

IV. Prohibitions

1. In accordance with article 6 of the International Labour Organization flag code, on no account shall the International Labour Organization flag or replica thereof be used for commercial purposes or in direct association with an article of merchandise.

2. Furthermore, neither the International Labour Organization flag nor any replica thereof shall be stamped, engraved or otherwise affixed on any stationery, books, magazines, periodicals or other publications of any nature whatsoever in a manner such as could imply that any such stationery, books, magazines, periodicals or other publications were published by or on behalf of the International Labour Organization unless such is in fact the case or in a manner such as has the effect of advertising a commercial product.

3. Subject to the provisions of paragraph 2 of this section, and with the exception of articles manufactured for presentation or sale to participants in the various meetings of the International Labour Organization, neither the International Labour Organization flag nor any replica thereof should be affixed in any manner on any article of any kind. Subject to the same exceptions, the International Labour Organization flag should not be reproduced on articles made of cloth, leather, material, synthetic material, etc. The International Labour Organization flag may be manufactured in the form of a lapel button.

4. Subject to the special cases mentioned in paragraphs 2 and 3, no mark, insignia, letter, word, figure, design, picture or drawing of any nature shall ever be placed upon or attached to the International Labour Organization flag or placed upon any replica thereof.

V. Mourning

1. In accordance with article 7 of the International Labour Organization flag code, whenever the Director-General of the International Labour Organization proclaims that the International Labour Organization is in official mourning, the International Labour Organization flag, wherever displayed, shall mark such an event by being flown at half mast during the period of official mourning.

2. Heads of offices and heads of International Labour Organization missions away from headquarters are authorized by the Director-General to lower the International Labour Organization flag to half mast in cases where they wish to follow official mourning in the country in which such offices or missions have their headquarters.

3. The International Labour Organization flag when displayed at half mast should first be hoisted to the peak for an instant and then lowered to the half-mast position. The flag should again be raised to the peak before it is lowered for the day. By "half mast" is meant lowering the flag to one-half the distance between the top and bottom of the mast.

4. Crepe streamers may be affixed to flagstaffs flying the International Labour Organization flag in a funeral procession only by order of the Director-General of the International Labour Organization.

5. When the International Labour Organization flag is used to cover a casket, it should not be lowered into the grave or allowed to touch the ground.

Appendix IV

The electronic voting system

The electronic system provides for votes (in most cases: yes, no, abstention) to be expressed by means of a "voting station" that will be made available to all delegates or persons empowered to vote on their behalf.

Where the electronic system is used, the subject and question to be voted on will be displayed and the President or Chairperson will announce the beginning of the vote. After the President or Chairperson has made sure that all delegates have been given sufficient opportunity to record their vote in one of the voting stations available to them, the President or Chairperson will announce the closure of the vote.

Where the method of vote is by show of hands, once all votes have been registered the final voting figures will be immediately displayed and subsequently published with the following indications: total number of votes in favour, total number of votes against, total number of abstentions and the quorum as well as the majority required.

Where a record vote is taken, once all votes have been registered the final voting figures will be immediately displayed with the following indications: total number of votes in favour, total number of votes against, total number of abstentions and the quorum as well as the majority required. These indications will subsequently be published together with a list of the delegates who have voted, showing how they have voted.

In the case of a secret ballot, once all votes have been registered the final voting figures will be immediately displayed and subsequently published with the following indications: total number of votes in favour, total number of votes against, total number of abstentions and the quorum as well as the majority required. There will be absolutely no access possible to individual votes nor any record of how the delegates have voted.

It is important that delegates should already have decided whether they or another member of their delegation will exercise their right to vote in a given case. Where more than one vote is nevertheless cast on behalf of a delegate at two different moments, or from two different places, only the first vote will be recognized, whether made by a delegate, by a substitute delegate or by an adviser who has received a specific written authorization to that end. Such specific authorizations must reach the secretariat sufficiently before the opening of voting is announced, so as to be duly recorded.

Appendix V

93rd Session (June 2005) of the International Labour Conference – Tentative plan of work

	M 30	T 31	W 1	Th 2	F 3	S 4	M 6	T 7	W 8	Th 9	F 10	S 11	M 13	T 14	W 15	Th 16	F 17
Group meetings	■																
GB elections							▬										
Plenary sittings		▬*					■	■	■[1]	■	■	□	■	■	■	■	
Finance Committee										A			Pl		V		
Application of Standards		■	■	■	■	■	■	■	■	■	■	■	A	A	Pl	Pl	
Committee on Safety and Health *(development of a new instrument)*		■	■	■	■	■	■	■	■	■	■	DC	A	A	Pl	Pl	
Committee on the Fishing Sector *(second discussion, standard setting)*		■	■	■	■	■	■	■	■	■	■	DC	A			V	
Committee for Promoting Youth Employment *(general discussion based on an integrated approach)*		■	■	■	■	■	■	■	■	■	■			A	Pl	Pl	
Selection Committee		▬															
Governing Body																	■

* Opening sitting and preliminary discussion on the Programme and Budget for 2006-07

[1] Discussion of the Global Report under the follow-up to the ILO Declaration

DC Drafting Committee
A Adoption by the Committee of its report
Pl Adoption of the report by the Conference in plenary sitting
V Record vote in plenary sitting of the Conference

▬ Half-day sitting
■ All day sitting
□ Sitting if necessary

CONTENTS

Page

Reports of the Selection Committee

First report 1

1. Election of the Officers of the Committee 1
2. Reminder of the Selection Committee's authority under the Standing Orders 1
3. Discussion of the Reports of the Chairperson of the Governing Body and the Director-General: Opening date for the discussion and closing date for the list of speakers 2
4. Discussion of the Global Report under the follow-up to the ILO Declaration on Fundamental Principles and Rights at Work 2
5. Plan of work of Conference committees 2
6. Governing Body elections 2
7. Suggestions to facilitate the work of the Conference 3
   (a) Quorum 3
   (b) Punctuality 3
   (c) Negotiations 4
8. Participation in Conference committees by Members having lost the right to vote 4
9. Requests for representation in Conference committees submitted by international non-governmental organizations 4
   Committee on the Application of Standards 5
   Committee on Occupational Safety and Health 6
   Committee on the Fishing Sector 7
   Committee on Youth Employment 8
10. Flag of the International Labour Organization 9
11. Composition of the Credentials Committee 9
12. Appointment of the Conference Drafting Committee 10
13. Delegation of authority to the Officers of the Selection Committee 10
14. Other questions: Electronic voting system 10

Appendices

Page

I. Ad hoc arrangements for the discussion of the Global Report under the follow-up to the Declaration at the 93rd Session of the International Labour Conference 11

II. Draft resolution concerning the flag of the International Labour Organization 12

III. (a) Flag code of the International Labour Organization 13

    (b) Regulations for the use of the flag of the International Labour Organization 14

IV. The electronic voting system 17

V. 93rd Session (June 2005) of the International Labour Conference – Tentative plan of work 18

International Labour Conference

Record of Proceedings

Ninety-third Session, Geneva, 2005

Composition of committees

The list of the composition of the committees of the Conference are appended.

Geneva, 1 June 2005

Composition des commissions
Composition of committees
Composición de las comisiones

(Note: Names of countries are given in French; los nombres de los paises figuran en frances.)

COMMISSION DE L'APPLICATION DES NORMES
COMMITTEE ON THE APPLICATION OF STANDARDS
COMISIÓN DE APLICACIÓN DE NORMAS

Membres gouvernementaux - Government members - Miembros gubernamentales

AFRIQUE DU SUD	ALGERIE	ALLEMAGNE
ANGOLA	ARABIE SAOUDITE	ARGENTINE
AUSTRALIE	AUTRICHE	BAHREIN
BARBADE	BELARUS	BELGIQUE
BENIN	BOLIVIE	BRESIL
BULGARIE	CAMEROUN	CANADA
REP. CENTRAFRICAINE	CHINE	COLOMBIE
REPUBLIQUE DE COREE	COSTA RICA	COTE D'IVOIRE
CUBA	DANEMARK	REP. DOMINICAINE
EGYPTE	EL SALVADOR	EMIRATS ARABES UNIS
EQUATEUR	ESPAGNE	ETATS-UNIS
FINLANDE	FRANCE	GABON
GRECE	GUATEMALA	HAITI
HONDURAS	HONGRIE	INDE
INDONESIE	REP. ISLAMIQUE D'IRAN	ISLANDE
ISRAEL	ITALIE	JAMAIQUE
JAPON	JORDANIE	KENYA
KOWEIT	LESOTHO	LETTONIE
LIBAN	LITUANIE	LUXEMBOURG
MADAGASCAR	MALAISIE	MALAWI
MALI	MALTE	MAROC
MEXIQUE	MOZAMBIQUE	MYANMAR
NAMIBIE	NEPAL	NICARAGUA
NIGER	NIGERIA	NORVEGE
NOUVELLE-ZELANDE	PAKISTAN	PANAMA
PAPOUASIE-NOUVELLE-GUINEE	PAYS-BAS	PEROU
PHILIPPINES	POLOGNE	PORTUGAL
QATAR	REP. DEM. DU CONGO	ROUMANIE
ROYAUME-UNI	FEDERATION DE RUSSIE	SAINT-MARIN
SENEGAL	SERBIE ET MONTENEGRO	SLOVENIE
SRI LANKA	SUEDE	SUISSE
SWAZILAND	REP.-UNIE DE TANZANIE	REPUBLIQUE TCHEQUE
THAILANDE	TRINITE-ET-TOBAGO	TUNISIE
VENEZUELA	ZIMBABWE	

Membres gouv. adjoints - Govt. deputy members - Miembros gub.adjuntos

ARMENIE	ESTONIE	ETHIOPIE
GUINEE	SINGAPOUR	SLOVAQUIE
TURQUIE	URUGUAY	

S = suppléant; substitute; suplente

Membres employeurs - Employers' members - Miembros empleadores

Sr. **AIZPURÚA (Panama)**
  Sr. LINERO

Mr. **AL SALEH (Bahreïn)**
  Mr. SHRIF

Mr. **ANDERSON (Australie)**
  Mr. NOAKES

M. **BOISSON (France)**
  Mme ROILAND
  Mme GUY

Mr. **CHEN (Chine)**
  Ms. CHEN

Mr. **DREESEN (Danemark)**
  Mr. SCHILDER
  Mr. GADE
  Mr. TORBEN A.

Sr. **FERRER DUFOL (Espagne)**
  Sr. SUÁREZ SANTOS
  Sr. DEL PUEYO PÉREZ
  Sr. CESTER BEATOBE

Mrs. **GERSTEIN (Allemagne)**
  Mr. PRINZ

M. **JALAL (Maroc)**
  M. BOUDHAIM

Mr. **KONDITI (Kenya)**
  Mr. MBUI

Mr. **LIMA GODOY (Brésil)**
  Ms. RONDON LINHARES
  Ms. CERQUEIRA COIMBRA DUQUE

Sr. **MENDEZ (Argentine)**
  Sr. FUNES DE RIOJA
  Sr. SPAGHI

Sra. **MUÑOZ (Venezuela)**
  Sr. DE ARBELOA

Ms. **NONDE (Zambie)**
  Mr. KAPEZA

Sr. **PARRA ROJAS (Cuba)**
  Sr. MESA GARCÍA
  Sr. VIDAUT MÁRQUEZ
  Sr. GONZÁLEZ RODRÍGUEZ

Mr. **POTTER (Etats-Unis)**
  Ms. SPENCER

Mrs. **RIDDERVOLD (Norvège)**
  Mrs. EGEDE-NISSEN
  Mrs. BENONISEN

Mr. **AL KHAFAJI (Iraq)**
  Mr. AHMED

Mr. **AL-RUBAIAI (Oman)**
  Mr. AL-KHUNJI

Sr. **ARTHUR ERRAZURIZ (Chili)**
  Sr. HUMERES NOGUER

Mr. **CERESCU (République de Moldova)**
  Mr. AXENTI

M. **DE KOSTER (Belgique)**
  M. DA COSTA
  Mme STORM

Sr. **ECHAVARRIA SALDARRIAGA (Colombie)**
  Sr. OJALVO PRIETO
  Sr. CARDOZO GONZALEZ

Mr. **FINLAY (Canada)**
  Mr. COON
  Ms. REGENBOGEN

Sr. **HALKIN (Mexique)**
  Sr. GUTIÉRREZ
  Sr. DE REGIL
  Sr. MENA
  Sr. YLLÁNEZ
  Sra. MORALES
  Sr. GARCÍA

Mr. **KHAMMAS (Emirats arabes unis)**
  Mr. ALGAIZI

Mr. **LAMBERT (Royaume-Uni)**
  Mr. SYDER

Mrs. **MAPHANGA (Swaziland)**
  Mr. NKOSI

Mr. **MENSA (Ghana)**
  Ms. OWUSU
  Mr. KOOMSON

M. **NICOLESCU (Roumanie)**
  M. PARVAN
  M. SIMON

Mr. **OTAREDIAN (République islamique d'Iran)**
  Mr. HAGHBAYAN

Mr. **PIRLER (Turquie)**
  Mr. CENTEL

Mr. **RACHMAN (Indonésie)**
  Mr. GUNAWAN
  Mr. ABDULLAH

Mme **SASSO MAZZUFFERI (Italie)**
  M. FERRARA
  Mme ROSSI
  M. DI NIOLA

S = suppléant; substitute; suplente

Mr. SIMEONOV (Bulgarie) 　Mrs. PAVLOVA 　Mr. DANEV 　Mrs. GEORGIEVA 　Mr. NEDYALKOV	**Mr. SINJANI (Malawi)**
Mr. SOMANY (Inde) 　Mr. ANAND 　Mr. LOHIA 　Mr. PANT	**Ms. SSENABULYA (Ouganda)** 　Mrs. GIDONGO 　Mr. DHIKUSOOKA
M. YOUSFI (Algérie) 　M. MEGATELI 　Mme OUZROUT 　M. MEHENNI	

Membres employeurs adjoints - Employers' deputy members - Miembros empleadores adjuntos

M. ABRANTES (Portugal) 　M. BERNARDO	**Mr. AL-HAROUN (Koweït)** 　Mr. AL-RABAH
Mr. ALRAGHEB (Jordanie) 　Mr. AL-AYOUBE	**M. BARDE (Suisse)** 　M. PLASSARD
Mr. CLEARY (Nouvelle-Zélande) 　Mr. ARNOLD	**Mr. DASANAYAKE (Sri Lanka)**
Mr. DOWLA (Bangladesh) 　Mr. RAHMAN	**Mrs. GLOBOCNIK (Slovénie)** 　Mrs. JEREB
Mr. HILTON-CLARKE (Trinité-et-Tobago)	**Mr. HUNTJENS (Pays-Bas)**
M. KYRIAKOPOULOS (Grèce) 　M. CHARAKAS 　Mme BARDANI 　Mme KOUTSIVITOU 　Mme KAKALIOURA	**Ms. LAURENT (Suède)** 　Mr. TROGEN
Sr. MAILHOS (Uruguay) 　Sr. FOSTIK	**Mr. MBWANJI (République-Unie de Tanzanie)** 　Mr. MAENDA 　Mr. KABYEMERA
Mme MENICUCCI (Saint-Marin)	**Mr. NATHAN (Malaisie)** 　Mr. SHAMSUDDIN
M. N'DOUMI (Côte d'Ivoire) 　M. KACOU DIAGOU 　M. DIALLO	**Mr. NINKOVIC (Serbie et Monténégro)** 　Mr. RAICKOVIC
Mr. PARKHOUSE (Namibie)	**Sr. PIGNATARO PACHECO (Costa Rica)**
Mr. PILIKOS (Chypre) 　Mr. KARIDIS	**Mr. PRIOR (République tchèque)** 　Mrs. DRBALOVÁ
Mr. PROBERT (Fidji) 　Mr. WARADI	**Mr. RISKI (Finlande)** 　Ms. ETU-SEPPÄLÄ
Mr. ROLEK (Hongrie) 　Mr. SZABADKAI 　Mr. TÓTH	**Ms. STEFANSDOTTIR (Islande)**
Mr. TABANI (Pakistan)	**Mr. TATEISI (Japon)** 　Mr. SUZUKI 　Mr. TAKAZAWA
Sr. TERÁN (Equateur)	**Mr. TESFAY (Erythrée)**
Sr. TOMASINO HURTADO (El Salvador)	**Sr. URTECHO (Honduras)**
Mr. VAN VUUREN (Afrique du Sud) 　Ms. NDONI	

S = suppléant; substitute; suplente

Membres travailleurs - Workers' members - Miembros trabajadores

M. ABDOU (Niger)	Mr. ABDUL RAHMAN (Bahreïn)
Mr. ADAMY (Allemagne)	Mr. AHMED (Pakistan)
Mr. AL NAILI (Jamahiriya arabe libyenne)	Mr. AL-AZMI (Koweït)
Mr. ALEMAYEHU (Ethiopie)	Mr. AL-KUHLANI (Yémen)
Mr. ALMARZOOQI (Emirats arabes unis)	Mr. AL-NAHARI (Oman)
M. ALVES TRINDADE (Portugal)	M. AZOUA (Bénin)
Mr. BAIPIDI (Botswana)	M. BENMOUHOUB (Algérie)
Sr. BERNAL CAMERO (Cuba)	Sr. BONMATÍ (Espagne)
M. BOUZIA (Maroc)	Sr. CABEZAS BADILLA (Costa Rica)
Sr. CHIRINO (Venezuela)	M. CORTEBEECK (Belgique)
Mr. CRIVELLI (Brésil)	Mrs. CZUGLERNÉ-IVÁNY (Hongrie)
M. DALEIDEN (Luxembourg)	M. DASSIS (Grèce)
Mme DEL RIO (Italie)	M. DJIBRINE (Tchad)
Mr. DORKENOO (Ghana)	Mr. EL AZALI (Egypte)
Mr. ETTY (Pays-Bas)	Ms. FAN (Chine)
Mme FERNANDA CARVALHO FRANCISCO (Angola)	Sr. FERNANDEZ (Uruguay)
Mr. FISHMAN (Etats-Unis)	Mr. GHANDOUR (Soudan)
Mr. GOODLEIGH (Jamaïque)	Mr. HABAB (République arabe syrienne)
Mr. HASAN (Bangladesh)	Mr. HOVHANNISYAN (Arménie)
Mr. KALIMANJIRA (Malawi)	Ms. KASUNIC (Croatie)
Mr. KILIC (Turquie)	Mr. KOSAISOOK (Thaïlande)
Sra. LARIOS (Mexique)	Mr. LEE (République de Corée)
M. LEPORI (Suisse)	Sr. LUCAS GÓMEZ (Guatemala)
Mr. MACAEFA (Lesotho)	Mr. MAQEKENI (Afrique du Sud)
Mr. MATULIS (Bélarus)	Sr. MENA QUINTANA (Panama)
Mrs. MESTANOVÁ (Slovaquie)	Ms. MUSKAT-GORSKA (Pologne)
M. NTONE DIBOTI (Cameroun)	Ms. OKUBO (Japon)
Mr. OSHIOMHOLE (Nigéria)	Mr. PARROT (Canada)
M. POPESCU (Roumanie)	Sr. RODRIGUEZ DIAZ (Colombie)
M. ROMDHANE (Tunisie)	Mme SALIMATA (Côte d'Ivoire)
Mr. SALIMIAN (République islamique d'Iran)	Mr. SAMEK (République tchèque)
Mr. SANJEEVA REDDY (Inde)	Mr. SIDOROV (Fédération de Russie)
Mr. SITHOLE (Swaziland)	M. SITOE (Mozambique)
M. SOCK (Sénégal)	Mr. STEYNE (Royaume-Uni)
Mr. SUBASINGHE (Sri Lanka)	Mr. SVENNINGSEN (Danemark)
Mrs. TAMMELEHT (Estonie)	Ms. TATE (Australie)
Ms. THAPPER (Suède)	Mrs. THEODORSEN (Norvège)
Sr. VENTURINI (Argentine)	M. VEYRIER (France)
Mrs. YACOB (Singapour)	Mr. YURKIN (Ukraine)

S = suppléant; substitute; suplente

Membres travailleurs adjoints - Workers' deputy members - Miembreos trabajadores adjuntos

Mr. ABDULLAH (Bahreïn)
Mr. ADU-AMANKWAH (Ghana)
Mr. AKPATASON (Nigéria)
Mr. AL-ROWAITIE (Arabie saoudite)
Mr. AZKAHE (République arabe syrienne)
Mme BRIGHI (Italie)
Ms. BYERS (Canada)
M. DE CARVALHO (Portugal)
Sr. DÍAZ (Venezuela)
Mr. ERIKSON (Norvège)
Mr. GAN (Chine)
M. GEYBELS (Belgique)
Sr. GONZÁLEZ BOAN (Espagne)
M. GRUSELIN (Belgique)
Mr. GYÖRGY (Hongrie)
Sra. IBARRA (Honduras)
Mr. INOKUCHI (Japon)
Sr. JIMENÉZ (Espagne)
Mr. KOZIK (Bélarus)
Mr. LAMBERT (Canada)
Sr. LÓPEZ GODOY (Uruguay)
Ms. LYNCH (Irlande)
Sra. MÀSPERO (Venezuela)
Sr. MEGUIRA (Argentine)
Mr. MOORE (Barbade)
Mr. NAKAJIMA (Japon)
Ms. PARKER (Norvège)
Mme PEDRO GARCIA (Angola)
Sr. PIUMATO (Argentine)
Sra. PUJADAS (Argentine)
M. RETUREAU (France)
M. RUSU (Roumanie)
Mr. SAUER (Autriche)
Mr. SHEPEL (Fédération de Russie)
Mr. SHYLOV (Ukraine)
Mr. SÜKÜN (Turquie)
Mr. TAHA (Egypte)
Ms. TAYLOR (Royaume-Uni)
M. TRAUSCH (Luxembourg)
Mr. WIENE (Danemark)
Mr. YOON (République de Corée)
M. ZOUNON (Bénin)

M. ADJABI (Algérie)
Ms. AHOKAS (Finlande)
Mr. ALI (Soudan)
M. ATTIGBE (Bénin)
M. BEN SAÏD (Tchad)
Ms. BURROW (Australie)
M. CHENDOUL (Tunisie)
M. DE JESUS RODRIGUES DA COSTA (Angola)
Mr. EDSTRÖM (Suède)
Sr. FRADES (Espagne)
Mme GARRIDO (France)
Sr. GOMEZ ESGUERRA (Colombie)
Ms. GOULART (Brésil)
M. GUIRO (Sénégal)
Mr. HAMZEIE (République islamique d'Iran)
Sra. IGEREGI SAN MIGUEL (Espagne)
M. IOUY (Maroc)
Mr. KANG (République de Corée)
Mr. KRAVCHENKO (Fédération de Russie)
Mme LANARA-TZOTZE (Grèce)
Sr. LÓPEZ GÓMEZ (Cuba)
M. MAMADOU (Niger)
Sr. MEDINA (Mexique)
Sra. MOLINA (El Salvador)
Mr. MUFTAH ALI (Jamahiriya arabe libyenne)
Mr. NASHIR ALI (Yémen)
Mme PECHEROT (France)
Ms. PIMENTEL (Brésil)
Mr. PRUIM (Pays-Bas)
Ms. RANTSOLASE (Afrique du Sud)
Mr. RUSANEN (Finlande)
Mr. SANKAR SAHA (Inde)
M. SEHIMI (Tunisie)
Mr. SHMAKOV (Fédération de Russie)
Mr. SILVA THOMAZ (Brésil)
Mr. SYED SHAHIR (Malaisie)
Mr. TAKOR (Nigéria)
Mr. TENE-PERTHIK (Israël)
Mr. WAGSTAFF (Nouvelle-Zélande)
M. WOLFF (Luxembourg)
Mr. ZELLHOEFER (Etats-Unis)

S = suppléant; substitute; suplente

COMMISSION DE LA SECURITE ET DE LA SANTE
COMMITTEE ON SAFETY AND HEALTH
COMISIÓN DE LA SEGURIDAD Y SALUD

Membres gouvernementaux - Government members - Miembros gubernamentales

AFRIQUE DU SUD	ALGERIE	ALLEMAGNE
ARABIE SAOUDITE	ARGENTINE	AUSTRALIE
AUTRICHE	BAHREIN	BARBADE
BELARUS	BELGIQUE	BRESIL
BURKINA FASO	CAMEROUN	CANADA
CHINE	COLOMBIE	REPUBLIQUE DE COREE
COTE D'IVOIRE	DANEMARK	REP. DOMINICAINE
EGYPTE	EL SALVADOR	EMIRATS ARABES UNIS
EQUATEUR	ESPAGNE	ETATS-UNIS
FINLANDE	FRANCE	GABON
GRECE	GUATEMALA	HAITI
HONDURAS	HONGRIE	INDE
INDONESIE	REP. ISLAMIQUE D'IRAN	ITALIE
JAMAIQUE	JAPON	JORDANIE
KENYA	KOWEIT	LESOTHO
LIBAN	JAMAHIRIYA ARABE LIBYENNE	LITUANIE
LUXEMBOURG	MADAGASCAR	MALAISIE
MALAWI	MALI	MALTE
MAROC	MEXIQUE	MOZAMBIQUE
MYANMAR	NAMIBIE	NIGER
NIGERIA	NORVEGE	NOUVELLE-ZELANDE
PAKISTAN	PANAMA	PAPOUASIE-NOUVELLE-GUINEE
PAYS-BAS	PHILIPPINES	POLOGNE
PORTUGAL	REP. DEM. DU CONGO	ROUMANIE
ROYAUME-UNI	FEDERATION DE RUSSIE	SENEGAL
SLOVENIE	SRI LANKA	SUEDE
SUISSE	SURINAME	SWAZILAND
REP.-UNIE DE TANZANIE	REPUBLIQUE TCHEQUE	THAILANDE
TRINITE-ET-TOBAGO	TUNISIE	URUGUAY
VENEZUELA	ZIMBABWE	

Membres gouv. adjoints - Govt. deputy members - Miembros gub.adjuntos

ARMENIE	BENIN	COSTA RICA
CUBA	ESTONIE	ETHIOPIE
ISRAEL	LETTONIE	NICARAGUA
PEROU	SAINT-MARIN	SINGAPOUR
SLOVAQUIE	TURQUIE	

S = suppléant; substitute; suplente

Membres employeurs - Employers' members - Miembros empleadores

Mr. AL SALEH (Bahreïn)
Mr. AL KHOOR

Mr. ALLAM (Egypte)
Mr. ABDO

M. BARDE (Suisse)
M. TELEKI

Mr. CHEN (Chine)
Mr. YU

M. DE KOSTER (Belgique)
M. DE MEESTER

Mr. DREESEN (Danemark)
Mr. TORBEN A.
Mr. GADE
Mr. SCHILDER

Sr. FERRER DUFOL (Espagne)
Sr. GÓMEZ ALBO
Sr. CESTER BEATOBE

Mrs. GERSTEIN (Allemagne)
Mr. MIKSCHE

Sr. HALKIN (Mexique)
Sr. MENA
Sr. DE REGIL
Sra. BARONA
Sr. CARVAJAL

M. JALAL (Maroc)
M. CHAOUKI
M. AYOUCHE

Mr. KIM (République de Corée)
Mr. LIM
Mr. JEON

Ms. LAURENT (Suède)
Mr. JANNERFELDT
Mr. TROGEN

Mr. MAKEKA (Lesotho)

Mr. MENSA (Ghana)
Mr. ATTA PAIDOO
Mr. BONNA
Mr. DUODU
Mr. BOTCHWAY
Mrs. YEBOAH

M. NICOLESCU (Roumanie)
M. CEACALOPOL
Mme MANOLE
M. CATARGIU
M. PARVAN

Mr. NINKOVIC (Serbie et Monténégro)
Mr. ZOVIC

Mr. OTAREDIAN (République islamique d'Iran)
Mr. HAGHBAYAN

Mr. AL-HAROUN (Koweït)
Mrs. AL-MISHARI

Mr. ALRAGHEB (Jordanie)

M. BOISSON (France)
Mme FAUCHOIS
Mme BUET
M. JULIEN

Mr. CLEARY (Nouvelle-Zélande)
Mr. ARNOLD

M. DIOP (Sénégal)
M. THIAO

Sr. ECHAVARRIA SALDARRIAGA (Colombie)
Sr. DEL RIO MAYA
Sr. MOLINA

Mr. FINLAY (Canada)
Mr. TANG
Mr. COTE

M. GOMES (Angola)

Mr. HUNTJENS (Pays-Bas)
Mr. KONING

Mr. KHAMMAS (Emirats arabes unis)

Mr. LAMBERT (Royaume-Uni)
Ms. ASHERSON

Mrs. LLOYD (Jamaïque)
Mr. EYTLE

Sr. MENDEZ (Argentine)
Sr. HERMIDA MARTINEZ
Sr. ALDAO ZAPIOLA
Sr. MANTILLA

Mr. NATHAN (Malaisie)
Mr. SHAMSUDDIN

Mr. NIINEMÄE (Estonie)

Ms. NONDE (Zambie)
Mr. KAPEZA

S = suppléant; substitute; suplente

Sr. PARRA ROJAS (Cuba)
    Sr. MESA GARCÍA
    Sr. VIDAUT MÁRQUEZ
    Sr. GONZÁLEZ RODRÍGUEZ

Mr. RACHMAN (Indonésie)
    Mr. RUDIYANTO
    Mr. DENIS

Mr. RISKI (Finlande)
    Mr. KUIKKO
    Ms. ETU-SEPPÄLÄ

Mr. SOMANY (Inde)
    Mr. CHOPRA
    Mr. PATIL

Mr. SULTAN-BEAUDOUIN (Seychelles)

Sr. TERÁN (Equateur)

Mr. POTTER (Etats-Unis)
    Ms. CHENGALUR
    Mr. TAUBITZ
    Mr. SEMRAU

Mrs. RIDDERVOLD (Norvège)
    Mrs. BENONISEN
    Mr. BARSTAD

Mme SASSO MAZZUFFERI (Italie)
    M. DI NIOLA
    Mme ROSSI
    M. FERRARA

Mr. SORIANO (Philippines)
    Mr. VARELA

Mr. TATEISI (Japon)
    Mr. TAKEDA
    Ms. SANUI

Mr. VAN VUUREN (Afrique du Sud)
    Mr. LOTTER

S = suppléant; substitute; suplente

Membres employeurs adjoints - Employers' deputy members - Miembros empleadores adjuntos

M. ABRANTES (Portugal)
  M. FERNANDES SALGUEIRO
  Mme NAGY MORAIS
  Mme FREIRE
  Mme DE CARVALHO
  M. BERNARDO

Mr. AL-RUBAIAI (Oman)
  Mr. AL-KHUNJI

Mme BERTRAND-SCHAUL (Luxembourg)
  M. SCHMIT
  M. KIEFFER
  M. KOEHNEN

Mr. CHANPORNPONG (Thaïlande)
  Mr. WONGTHONGLUA

Mr. DASANAYAKE (Sri Lanka)

M. GLELE (Bénin)
  M. ZANOU
  Mme TOLI

Mr. HUSBANDS (Barbade)

M. KYRIAKOPOULOS (Grèce)
  M. CHARAKAS
  Mme BARDANI
  Mme KOUTSIVITOU
  Mme KAKALIOURA

Sr. MAILHOS (Uruguay)
  Sr. FOSTIK

Mr. MBWANJI (République-Unie de Tanzanie)
  Mr. MAENDA
  Mr. KABYEMERA

M. NACOULMA (Burkina Faso)

Mr. PARKHOUSE (Namibie)

Mr. PRIOR (République tchèque)
  Mr. HROBSKY

Mr. ROLEK (Hongrie)
  Mr. CSUPORT
  Mrs. BOROSNÉ-BARTHA
  Mrs. OLAY

Ms. SSENABULYA (Ouganda)
  Mr. BYENSI
  Mr. THENGE

Mr. TABANI (Pakistan)

M. TRAORE (Mali)
  M. BODJI TOURE

Mr. AL KHAFAJI (Iraq)
  Mr. AHMED

Sr. ARTHUR ERRAZURIZ (Chili)
  Sr. HUMERES NOGUER

Mr. CERESCU (République de Moldova)
  Mr. AXENTI

Mr. DAHLAN (Arabie saoudite)

M. DJILANI (Tunisie)
  M. M'KAISSI

Mrs. GLOBOCNIK (Slovénie)
  Mrs. JEREB

Mr. KONDITI (Kenya)
  Mr. MBUI

Mr. LIMA GODOY (Brésil)
  Ms. CANTÍDIO MOTA
  Mr. COLETTO

Mrs. MAPHANGA (Swaziland)
  Mr. NKOSI

Sra. MUÑOZ (Venezuela)
  Sr. DE ARBELOA

M. N'DOUMI (Côte d'Ivoire)
  M. KACOU DIAGOU

Mr. PIRLER (Turquie)
  Mr. BÜYÜKUSLU
  Mr. KOC

Mr. PROBERT (Fidji)

Mr. SINJANI (Malawi)

Ms. STEFANSDOTTIR (Islande)

Mr. TOMEK (Autriche)
  Mr. BRAUNER
  Ms. OBERHOFER
  Ms. KADLEC

Sr. URTECHO (Honduras)

S = suppléant; substitute; suplente

M. YOUSFI (Algérie)
    M. NAÏT ABDELAZIZ
    M. CHEIKH
    Mme SAHRAOUI

Membres travailleurs - Workers' members - Miembros trabajadores

Mr. ABDULLAH (Bahreïn)	Sr. ABREU (République dominicaine)
Sr. ACEVES (Mexique)	Mr. AL NAAMA (Qatar)
Mr. AL-AZMI (Koweït)	M. ALHAIQUE (Italie)
Mr. ALHAMMADI (Emirats arabes unis)	Ms. AL-HASHIMI (Oman)
Mr. ALI (Soudan)	Sr. ALVIS FERNANDEZ (Colombie)
M. BEN SAÏD (Tchad)	M. BOUZRIBA (Tunisie)
Mr. BRYSON (Royaume-Uni)	Mr. CANAK (Serbie et Monténégro)
M. DE CARVALHO (Portugal)	Mme DIALLO (Guinée)
Mr. EL WAHAB (République arabe syrienne)	M. GLELE KAKAÏ (Bénin)
M. GUIRO (Sénégal)	Mr. HAMZEIE (République islamique d'Iran)
Ms. HAN (République de Corée)	Sr. IBARRA (Venezuela)
M. ISSOUFOU (Niger)	Mr. JIN (Chine)
Mr. JONES (Jamaïque)	Mr. JUMA'H (Jordanie)
M. JURCA (Roumanie)	Mr. KARA (Israël)
Mr. KHALIFA SALEM (Jamahiriya arabe libyenne)	M. KOLEVENTIS (Grèce)
Mr. KOSIR (Slovénie)	M. LEEMANS (Belgique)
Sr. LÓPEZ GODOY (Uruguay)	Mr. MAHADEVAN (Inde)
Mr. MALABAG (Papouasie-Nouvelle-Guinée)	Mr. MELANDER (Suède)
M. MENSAH FRANCOIS (Côte d'Ivoire)	Sra. MOLINA (El Salvador)
M. MOUSSOLE (Cameroun)	Mr. NASHIR ALI (Yémen)
Mr. ODAH (Nigéria)	Mme PEDRO GARCIA (Angola)
M. PIZZAFERRI (Luxembourg)	Sra. PUJADAS (Argentine)
Mr. RADHWAN (Arabie saoudite)	Mr. RAMPÁSEK (Slovaquie)
Ms. RANTSOLASE (Afrique du Sud)	Mr. ROSTOM (Egypte)
Mme SALHI (Algérie)	Mrs. SCHRÖDER (Allemagne)
Ms. SEMINARIO (Etats-Unis)	Mr. SIRIWARDANE (Sri Lanka)
Mr. SKÁCELÍK (République tchèque)	Mr. SOUZA (Brésil)
Mr. SÜKÜN (Turquie)	Mr. TRUMEL (Fédération de Russie)
Ms. VAICAITYTE (Lituanie)	Mr. VALOIS (Canada)
Mr. VAN KRUININT (Pays-Bas)	Mr. WAGSTAFF (Nouvelle-Zélande)
Mr. WOJCIK (Pologne)	Mr. WOLDE MICHAEL (Ethiopie)
Mme ZAHI (Maroc)	

S = suppléant; substitute; suplente

Membres travailleurs adjoints - Workers' deputy members - Miembreos trabajadores adjuntos

Mr. ABD EL HAMID (Egypte)
Mr. AGG (Hongrie)
Mr. AL-MAHFOODH (Bahreïn)
Mr. AL-MUDAETH (Koweït)
M. BAUSCH (Luxembourg)
Mme BRIGHI (Italie)
Mme BRUNEL (France)
Sr. CARCOBA (Espagne)
M. COJOCARU (Roumanie)
Sr. DEL VALLE (Mexique)
M. DJIBRINE (Tchad)
Mr. DWEAER (République arabe syrienne)
Mr. ERIKSON (Norvège)
Mme FERNANDA CARVALHO FRANCISCO (Angola)
Mr. FREIRE NETO (Brésil)
Mme GAMBIA (Bénin)
Mr. GBADEBO (Nigéria)
Mr. GRAVESON (Royaume-Uni)
Mr. HANSEN (Norvège)
Ms. HEINÄNEN (Finlande)
M. JOUBIER (France)
Mrs. KOULINKOVITCH (Bélarus)
M. LECOIN (France)
M. MAKROUM (Maroc)
M. MELKMANS (Belgique)
Mr. MOHAMED EL SENUSSI (Jamahiriya arabe libyenne)
M. MORDASINI (Suisse)
Mr. NAKAGIRI (Japon)
Mr. OH (République de Corée)
Sr. PÉREZ (Mexique)
Mme PSAROYIANNI (Grèce)
Mr. RAHMAN (Bangladesh)
Mr. REINHOLD (Suède)
M. SALIFOU (Niger)
Mr. SANGYARUK (Thaïlande)
Mr. SENEVIRATNE (Sri Lanka)
M. SPAUTZ (Luxembourg)
Mr. STEYNE (Royaume-Uni)
Ms. TAYLOR (Royaume-Uni)
Ms. THOMSEN (Norvège)
Mrs. TOTH MUCCIACCIARO (Croatie)
Mr. TROTMAN (Barbade)
Mr. WIENE (Danemark)
Mr. ZHANG (Chine)

Mr. ADU-AMANKWAH (Ghana)
Mr. ALEMAYEHU (Ethiopie)
Mr. ALMOGHRABI (Arabie saoudite)
Mr. ANSARI (République islamique d'Iran)
Ms. BEI (Autriche)
M. BRIKI (Tunisie)
Ms. BYERS (Canada)
Mr. CHANDRASENA (Sri Lanka)
Sr. DEL RIO (République dominicaine)
Sr. DÍAZ (Venezuela)
Mr. DORKENOO (Ghana)
Mr. ELSIDDIG (Soudan)
Mr. ETTY (Pays-Bas)
Sr. FERNÁNDEZ-BRASO (Espagne)
Mr. FROHLICH (Israël)
Mr. GATARIC (Serbie et Monténégro)
Mr. GJERDING (Norvège)
Mr. GYÖRGY (Hongrie)
Mr. HASAN (Bangladesh)
Mr. HOTOVY (République tchèque)
Mme KONSTANTINAKOU (Grèce)
Mr. LAMBERT (Canada)
Mr. LUKOVIC (Serbie et Monténégro)
M. MEIRINHO DE JESUS (Portugal)
Mr. MIERZEJEWSKI (Pologne)
Sr. MONTES DE OCA (Colombie)

Sr. MUÑOZ ORREGO (Chili)
M. NEJI (Tunisie)
Ms. OMONDI (Kenya)
Sr. POMATTA (Uruguay)
Ms. QARHASH (Yémen)
Mr. RASHEED (Jordanie)
Sr. RODRÍGUEZ SOLÍS (Panama)
Sr. SALINAS (Argentine)
Mr. SCHØNING (Danemark)
Mr. SHEPEL (Fédération de Russie)
Ms. STEPHENS (Royaume-Uni)
Ms. TATE (Australie)
Mr. THOMAS (Inde)
Mr. TOLKACHEV (Bélarus)
M. TOURE (Guinée)
Ms. VALKONEN (Finlande)
Mme YAFA (Sénégal)

S = suppléant; substitute; suplente

COMMISSION DU SECTEUR DE LA PECHE
COMMITTEE ON THE FISHING SECTOR
COMISIÓN DEL SECTOR PESQUERO

Membres gouvernementaux - Government members - Miembros gubernamentales

AFRIQUE DU SUD	ALGERIE	ALLEMAGNE
ANGOLA	ARABIE SAOUDITE	ARGENTINE
AUSTRALIE	AUTRICHE	BAHREIN
BELGIQUE	BRESIL	BURKINA FASO
CAMEROUN	CANADA	CHINE
COLOMBIE	REPUBLIQUE DE COREE	COTE D'IVOIRE
CUBA	DANEMARK	REP. DOMINICAINE
EGYPTE	EMIRATS ARABES UNIS	EQUATEUR
ESPAGNE	ETATS-UNIS	FINLANDE
FRANCE	GABON	GRECE
HAITI	HONDURAS	INDE
INDONESIE	REP. ISLAMIQUE D'IRAN	ISLANDE
ITALIE	JAPON	JORDANIE
KENYA	KIRIBATI	KOWEIT
LIBAN	LITUANIE	MALAISIE
MALTE	MAROC	MEXIQUE
MOZAMBIQUE	MYANMAR	NAMIBIE
NICARAGUA	NIGER	NIGERIA
NORVEGE	PAKISTAN	PANAMA
PAYS-BAS	PEROU	PHILIPPINES
PORTUGAL	REP. DEM. DU CONGO	ROYAUME-UNI
FEDERATION DE RUSSIE	SRI LANKA	SUEDE
THAILANDE	TUNISIE	URUGUAY
VENEZUELA	ZIMBABWE	

Membres gouv. adjoints - Govt. deputy members - Miembros gub.adjuntos

COSTA RICA	ESTONIE	GUATEMALA
LETTONIE	LUXEMBOURG	MALAWI
MALI	ROUMANIE	SEYCHELLES
SUISSE	REP.-UNIE DE TANZANIE	TURQUIE

S = suppléant; substitute; suplente

Membres employeurs - Employers' members - Miembros empleadores

Mr. AL MANAA (Qatar)
    Mr. AL-HAIDAR

M. BOISSON (France)
    Mme HERVOUET/DION

Sr. ECHAVARRIA SALDARRIAGA (Colombie)
    Sra. MONSALVE CUELLAR
    Sr. ARANGO VALLEJO

Mr. FINLAY (Canada)
    Ms. PENNEY
    Mr. CHAPMAN

Mr. HUNTJENS (Pays-Bas)
    Mr. VAN DER ZWAN
    Mr. BLONK

Mr. JEFFERY (Papouasie-Nouvelle-Guinée)

Mr. LAMBERT (Royaume-Uni)
    Mr. PIGGOTT
    Ms. WISEMAN

Mr. MENSA (Ghana)
    Mrs. ANANG
    Ms. QUIST-ADDO

Mr. OTAREDIAN (République islamique d'Iran)
    Mr. TATHIRI-MOGHADDAM

Mr. POTTER (Etats-Unis)
    Ms. FRENCH
    Mr. SEMRAU

Mrs. RIDDERVOLD (Norvège)
    Mr. BARSTAD
    Mrs. BENONISEN

Ms. SSENABULYA (Ouganda)
    Mr. THENGE

Mr. TATEISI (Japon)
    Mr. KOSAKA
    Ms. YOSHIKAWA

Sr. ARTHUR ERRAZURIZ (Chili)
    Sr. PIZARRO MAASS

M. DJILANI (Tunisie)
    M. SELLINI

Sr. FERRER DUFOL (Espagne)
    Sr. MARÍN ANDRÉS
    Sr. CESTER BEATOBE

M. GOMES (Angola)
    M. ANDRÉ
    Mme DE ASSUNÇÁO PAULINA MÁRIO

M. JALAL (Maroc)
    M. BOUDHAIM

Mr. KIM (République de Corée)
    Mr. LEE

Sr. MENDEZ (Argentine)
    Sr. BARBER SOLER
    Sr. ETALA

M. NICOLESCU (Roumanie)
    M. MIHALACHE
    M. COSTACHE
    M. CEACALOPOL

Sr. PARRA ROJAS (Cuba)
    Sr. MESA GARCÍA
    Sr. VIDAUT MÁRQUEZ
    Sr. GONZÁLEZ RODRÍGUEZ

Mr. RACHMAN (Indonésie)
    Mr. SUPARWANTO

Mr. SOMANY (Inde)
    Mr. TODI

Ms. STEFANSDOTTIR (Islande)
    Mr. MAGNUSSON

Mr. VAN VUUREN (Afrique du Sud)
    Mr. MULLER

S = suppléant; substitute; suplente

Membres employeurs adjoints - Employers' deputy members - Miembros empleadores adjuntos

Sr. AIZPURÚA (Panama)
   Sr. DE SANCTIS

Mr. CHEN (Chine)
   Ms. LIU

M. GLELE (Bénin)
   Mme TOLI

Sr. HALKIN (Mexique)
   Sr. MENA
   Sr. DE REGIL
   Sr. GUTIÉRREZ

Mr. KONDITI (Kenya)
   Mr. MBUI

Mr. LIMA GODOY (Brésil)
   Mr. FATTORI COSTA
   Mr. SFOGGIA

Mr. NATHAN (Malaisie)
   Mr. SHAMSUDDIN

Ms. NONDE (Zambie)
   Mr. MUSENGE

Mr. PIRLER (Turquie)
   Mr. ARSLAN
   Mr. BAYAZIT

Mme SASSO MAZZUFFERI (Italie)

Mr. TABANI (Pakistan)

Mr. AL-RUBAIAI (Oman)
   Mr. AL-WUHAIBI

Mrs. GERSTEIN (Allemagne)
   Mr. LINDEMANN

Mrs. GLOBOCNIK (Slovénie)
   Mrs. JEREB

Mr. KABUBUKE (Kiribati)

M. KYRIAKOPOULOS (Grèce)
   M. CHARAKAS
   Mme BARDANI
   Mme KOUTSIVITOU
   Mme KAKALIOURA

Sra. MUÑOZ (Venezuela)
   Sr. DE ARBELOA

Mr. NINKOVIC (Serbie et Monténégro)
   Mr. MITROVIC
   Mr. MITROVIC

Mr. PARKHOUSE (Namibie)
   Mr. VAN ROOYEN

Mr. PROBERT (Fidji)
   Mr. WARADI

Mr. SORIANO (Philippines)
   Mr. TAN

Mr. VAN OMMEREN (Suriname)

S = suppléant; substitute; suplente

Membres travailleurs - Workers' members - Miembros trabajadores

Mr. ABD EL HALIM (Egypte)	Mr. ADYANTHAYA (Inde)
Mr. AFRIYIE (Ghana)	Mr. AL-RIZAIQI (Oman)
Mr. ANSTEY (Canada)	Ms. ARSHAD (République islamique d'Iran)
M. BISSALA (Cameroun)	Sra. CANO MORENO (Panama)
Ms. CEJOVIC (Serbie et Monténégro)	M. DELIYANNAKIS (Grèce)
M. DOS SANTOS CARDOSO MACEDO (Portugal)	Mr. DUBINSKI (Pologne)
Mr. DWEAER (République arabe syrienne)	M. FATHI (Maroc)
Mr. GÖK (Turquie)	Sr. GRAJALES (Mexique)
Mr. GRAVESON (Royaume-Uni)	Mr. GUAN (Chine)
M. HOUNSINOU (Bénin)	Mr. IBRAHIM (Soudan)
Mr. IRABOR (Nigéria)	Ms. KIM (République de Corée)
Sr. LÓPEZ GÓMEZ (Cuba)	Mr. MASEMOLA (Afrique du Sud)
M. MEDDAHI (Tunisie)	Sr. MORANTES ALFONSO (Colombie)
Mr. MOYSEOS (Chypre)	Mr. MUFTAH ALI (Jamahiriya arabe libyenne)
Sr. PERÉZ (El Salvador)	Mr. PETROV (Ukraine)
Sr. POMATTA (Uruguay)	M. RAHMA (Algérie)
M. RETUREAU (France)	Mr. ROBERTS (Jamaïque)
Mr. ROBINSON (Seychelles)	Mr. RODRIGUES LEITE PENTEADO (Brésil)
M. SALIFOU (Niger)	Mr. SAND MORTENSEN (Danemark)
Mr. SANDRASEKERA (Sri Lanka)	M. STAN (Roumanie)
Sr. SUAREZ (Argentine)	Mr. SULISTYANTO (Indonésie)
Mr. TEICHERT (Allemagne)	Mr. TOMASSON (Islande)
M. TORCHE (Suisse)	Mme YAFA (Sénégal)

S = suppléant; substitute; suplente

Membres travailleurs adjoints - Workers' deputy members - Miembreos trabajadores adjuntos

Sr. AGUILAR (Mexique)
Mr. AL NAILI (Jamahiriya arabe libyenne)
M. ALBU (Roumanie)
Sr. ANGRIMAN (Argentine)
M. BADREDDINE (Algérie)
Mr. BRYSON (Royaume-Uni)
Ms. CEJOVIC (Serbie et Monténégro)
Mr. CORTIZO (Brésil)
M. FALL (Sénégal)
Mr. FUKUMA (Japon)
M. GKOUTZAMANIS (Grèce)
Mr. GUNNARSSON (Islande)
Mr. HANSEN (Norvège)
Mr. IIJIMA (Japon)
Mr. KAPENDA (Namibie)
Mr. LAMBERT (Canada)
M. MEIRINHO DE JESUS (Portugal)
Mr. MILANI (Afrique du Sud)
M. NIAMKEY (Côte d'Ivoire)
Mr. OUYANG (Chine)
Mr. PARROT (Canada)
M. SAAD (Tunisie)
Sr. SALAZAR (Mexique)
Mr. SMIDT (Danemark)
Sr. SORIANO (El Salvador)
Mr. STEYNE (Royaume-Uni)
Ms. TAYLOR (Royaume-Uni)
Mr. THOMAS (Inde)
Mr. TROTMAN (Barbade)
Mr. VALOIS (Canada)
M. VICTOR (Belgique)
Mr. YEOM (République de Corée)

Ms. AHOKAS (Finlande)
Mr. AL-AZMI (Koweït)
Mr. AL-MAHFOODH (Bahreïn)
Mr. ANKRAH (Ghana)
Mr. BROWN (Jamaïque)
Ms. BYERS (Canada)
M. CLAES (Belgique)
Mr. ERIKSON (Norvège)
Sr. FERNANDEZ (Uruguay)
Mme GAMBIA (Bénin)
M. GODHBANI (Tunisie)
Mr. HABAB (République arabe syrienne)
M. HUTULEAC (Roumanie)
M. ISSOUFOU (Niger)
Mr. KONDO (Japon)
Ms. LYNCH (Irlande)
Mr. MELANDER (Suède)
Mr. NAGAITSEV (Fédération de Russie)
Mr. NORDDAHL (Islande)
Mr. OYERINDE (Nigéria)
Mr. REINHOLD (Suède)
Mr. SADEGHI (République islamique d'Iran)
Ms. SCHANTZ (Etats-Unis)
Ms. SONNTAG (Nouvelle-Zélande)
M. SOW (Sénégal)
Mr. SURIN (Fédération de Russie)
Mrs. THEODORSEN (Norvège)
Ms. THOMSEN (Norvège)
Ms. VAICAITYTE (Lituanie)
M. VEYRIER (France)
Mr. WOJTASIK (Pologne)

S = suppléant; substitute; suplente

COMMISSION DE L'EMPLOI DES JEUNES
COMMITTEE ON YOUTH EMPLOYMENT
COMISIÓN DELEMPLEO DE LOS JOVENES

Membres gouvernementaux - Government members - Miembros gubernamentales

AFRIQUE DU SUD	ALGERIE	ALLEMAGNE
ARABIE SAOUDITE	ARGENTINE	AUSTRALIE
AUTRICHE	BAHREIN	BARBADE
BELARUS	BELGIQUE	BENIN
BRESIL	BULGARIE	BURKINA FASO
CAMEROUN	CANADA	REP. CENTRAFRICAINE
CHINE	COLOMBIE	REPUBLIQUE DE COREE
COTE D'IVOIRE	DANEMARK	REP. DOMINICAINE
EGYPTE	EL SALVADOR	EMIRATS ARABES UNIS
EQUATEUR	ESPAGNE	ETATS-UNIS
FINLANDE	FRANCE	GABON
GRECE	GUATEMALA	HAITI
HONDURAS	HONGRIE	INDE
INDONESIE	REP. ISLAMIQUE D'IRAN	ITALIE
JAMAIQUE	JAPON	JORDANIE
KENYA	KOWEIT	LESOTHO
LIBAN	JAMAHIRIYA ARABE LIBYENNE	LITUANIE
LUXEMBOURG	MADAGASCAR	MALAISIE
MALI	MALTE	MAROC
MEXIQUE	MOZAMBIQUE	MYANMAR
NAMIBIE	NEPAL	NIGER
NIGERIA	NORVEGE	NOUVELLE-ZELANDE
PAKISTAN	PANAMA	PAPOUASIE-NOUVELLE-GUINEE
PAYS-BAS	PHILIPPINES	POLOGNE
PORTUGAL	QATAR	REP. DEM. DU CONGO
ROYAUME-UNI	FEDERATION DE RUSSIE	SENEGAL
SEYCHELLES	SLOVENIE	SRI LANKA
SUEDE	SUISSE	SURINAME
SWAZILAND	REP.-UNIE DE TANZANIE	REPUBLIQUE TCHEQUE
THAILANDE	TRINITE-ET-TOBAGO	TUNISIE
VENEZUELA	ZIMBABWE	

Membres gouv. adjoints - Govt. deputy members - Miembros gub.adjuntos

COSTA RICA	CUBA	ESTONIE
ETHIOPIE	GUINEE	ISRAEL
LETTONIE	MALAWI	NICARAGUA
PEROU	ROUMANIE	SLOVAQUIE
TURQUIE	URUGUAY	

S = suppléant; substitute; suplente

Membres employeurs - Employers' members - Miembros empleadores

M. ABRANTES (Portugal)
   M. FERNANDES SALGUEIRO
   Mme LEAL

Mr. AL KHAFAJI (Iraq)
   Mr. AHMED

Mr. AL-HAROUN (Koweït)
   Mr. AL-FALIJ

Mr. AL-RUBAIAI (Oman)
   Mr. AL-WUHAIBI

Sr. ARTHUR ERRAZURIZ (Chili)
   Sr. BRUNA VARGAS
   Sr. HUMERES NOGUER

Mr. BARAK (Israël)

Mr. CHANPORNPONG (Thaïlande)
   Mr. WONGTHONGLUA

Mr. CLEARY (Nouvelle-Zélande)
   Mr. ARNOLD

M. DABO (Guinée)

M. DIOP (Sénégal)
   M. WADE

Sr. ECHAVARRIA SALDARRIAGA (Colombie)
   Sr. MEJIA GIRALDO
   Sr. BOTERO ARANGO

Mr. FARRUGIA (Malte)
   Mr. TABONE

Mr. FINLAY (Canada)
   Mr. KELLY

M. GLELE (Bénin)
   M. ZANOU
   Mme TOLI

Sr. HALKIN (Mexique)
   Sr. DE REGIL
   Sr. MENA
   Sr. YLLÁNEZ
   Sr. GUTIÉRREZ
   Sr. CARVAJAL

M. JALAL (Maroc)
   M. AYOUCHE
   M. BOUDHAIM

Mr. KIM (République de Corée)
   Ms. HWANG
   Ms. HA

M. KYRIAKOPOULOS (Grèce)
   M. CHARAKAS
   Mme BARDANI
   Mme KOUTSIVITOU
   Mme KAKALIOURA

Sr. AIZPURÚA (Panama)
   Sr. LINERO

Mr. AL SALEH (Bahreïn)
   Mr. AL KHOOR

Mr. ALLAM (Egypte)
   Mrs. MOHAMED

Mr. ANDERSON (Australie)

Mme AWASSI ATSIMADJA (Gabon)

M. BOISSON (France)
   Mme ANDRIEU
   M. PATINET

Mr. CHEN (Chine)
   Mr. LIU

Ms. CRONIN (Irlande)
   Ms. MAGUIRE

M. DE KOSTER (Belgique)

Mr. DREESEN (Danemark)
   Mr. GADE
   Mr. TORBEN A.
   Mr. SCHILDER

Mr. EREMEEV (Fédération de Russie)
   Mr. POLUEKTOV

Sr. FERRER DUFOL (Espagne)
   Sr. SUÁREZ GARCÍA
   Sr. MENÉNDEZ VALDÉS
   Sra. ASENJO

Mr. GANBAATAR (Mongolie)
   Mr. ZORIGTBAATAR

M. GOMES (Angola)
   M. ANDRÉ

Mrs. HORVATIC (Croatie)
   Ms. KATIC

Mr. KHAMMAS (Emirats arabes unis)
   Mr. ALKAABI
   Mr. ALGAIZI

Mr. KONDITI (Kenya)
   Mr. MBUI

Mr. LAMBERT (Royaume-Uni)
   Ms. VAN DER LINDEN
   Mr. WARMAN

S = suppléant; substitute; suplente

Ms. LAURENT (Suède)
    Mr. CARLSTEDT
    Mr. TROGEN

Mr. MBWANJI (République-Unie de Tanzanie)
    Mr. MAENDA
    Mr. KABYEMERA

Mr. MENSA (Ghana)
    Ms. ARYEE
    Mr. MENSAH
    Mr. LARYEA
    Mr. GARSHONG

M. NACOULMA (Burkina Faso)
    Mme YAMEOGO-TOU

M. NICOLESCU (Roumanie)
    M. MIHALACHE
    Mme MANOLE
    M. KOVACS
    M. PARVAN

Ms. NONDE (Zambie)
    Mr. MUSENGE

Mr. OTAREDIAN (République islamique d'Iran)
    Mr. ATHARI

Mr. POTTER (Etats-Unis)
    Ms. GOLDBERG
    Mr. SEMRAU

Mr. RACHMAN (Indonésie)
    Mr. NOOR
    Mr. ABDULLAH

Mr. RISKI (Finlande)
    Mr. RÄSÄNEN
    Ms. ETU-SEPPÄLÄ

Mme SASSO MAZZUFFERI (Italie)
    Mme ROSSI
    M. FERRARA
    M. DI NIOLA

Mr. SOMANY (Inde)
    Mr. DEWAN
    Mr. PATIL
    Mr. BEHURIA
    Mr. ANAND

Ms. SSENABULYA (Ouganda)
    Mr. LAPENGA
    Mr. BANDEEBIRE

Mr. TATEISI (Japon)
    Mr. HIRATA

Sr. TOMASINO HURTADO (El Salvador)

Mr. VAN VUUREN (Afrique du Sud)
    Ms. MAILA

Mrs. LLOYD (Jamaïque)
    Mr. EYTLE

Sr. MENDEZ (Argentine)
    Sr. ETALA
    Sr. SCHAER
    Sr. MELIAN

Mr. MOLEELE (Botswana)

Mr. NATHAN (Malaisie)
    Mr. SHAMSUDDIN

Mr. NINKOVIC (Serbie et Monténégro)
    Ms. STOJSIC-STOJANOVSKA
    Mr. ATANASKOVIC

Mr. OSHINOWO (Nigéria)

Sr. PIGNATARO PACHECO (Costa Rica)

Mr. PROBERT (Fidji)
    Mr. WARADI

Mrs. RIDDERVOLD (Norvège)
    Mr. JOHANNESEN
    Mrs. BENONISEN
    Mrs. EGEDE-NISSEN

Mr. ROLEK (Hongrie)
    Mr. SZIRMAI
    Ms. VARGA
    Mr. MAGYAR
    Mr. SZÜCS

Mr. SIMEONOV (Bulgarie)
    Mrs. PAVLOVA

Mr. SORIANO (Philippines)

Mr. TABANI (Pakistan)

Mr. TIN (Myanmar)

M. TRAORE (Mali)
    M. BODJI TOURE

S = suppléant; substitute; suplente

M. YOUSFI (Algérie)
    M. MEGATELI
    Mme OUZROUT
    M. NAÏT ABDELAZIZ
    M. SIACI
    M. MEHENNI

Membres employeurs adjoints - Employers' deputy members - Miembros empleadores adjuntos

Mr. ALRAGHEB (Jordanie)
    Mr. ALWER
Mr. BONI (Pologne)
    Ms. PERNAL
    Ms. BRZEZINSKA
Mr. DASANAYAKE (Sri Lanka)

Mrs. GERSTEIN (Allemagne)

Mr. HILTON-CLARKE (Trinité-et-Tobago)
    Mr. RAMBHARAT
Mr. HUSBANDS (Barbade)
    Ms. CADOGAN
Mr. KABUBUKE (Kiribati)

Sr. MAILHOS (Uruguay)
    Sr. FOSTIK
Mrs. MAPHANGA (Swaziland)
    Mr. NKOSI

Sra. MUÑOZ (Venezuela)
    Sr. DE ARBELOA

Mr. PARKHOUSE (Namibie)
    Mr. VAN ROOYEN

Mr. PILIKOS (Chypre)
    Mrs. PANAYIOTOU
    Mr. ANTONIOU
Mr. PRIOR (République tchèque)
    Mr. KOHOUTEK
Mr. SULTAN-BEAUDOUIN (Seychelles)
Mr. TOMEK (Autriche)
    Mr. BRAUNER
    Ms. OBERHOFER
    Ms. KADLEC
Sr. ZAVALA COSTA (Pérou)

M. BARDE (Suisse)
    M. HEFTI
Mr. DAHLAN (Arabie saoudite)

Mr. DOWLA (Bangladesh)
    Mr. RAHMAN
Mrs. GLOBOCNIK (Slovénie)
    Mrs. JEREB
Mr. HUNTJENS (Pays-Bas)
    Mr. RENIQUE
Mr. JEETUN (Maurice)
    Mr. DURSUN
Mr. LIMA GODOY (Brésil)
    Mr. ASSIS BENEVIDES GADELHA
    Mr. OLIVEIRA DIAS
Mr. MAKEKA (Lesotho)

Mme MENICUCCI (Saint-Marin)
    M. BOFFA
    Mme DELLA BALDA
M. N'DOUMI (Côte d'Ivoire)
    M. DIALLO
    M. KACOU DIAGOU
Sr. PARRA ROJAS (Cuba)
    Sr. MESA GARCÍA
    Sr. VIDAUT MÁRQUEZ
    Sr. GONZÁLEZ RODRÍGUEZ
Mr. PIRLER (Turquie)
    Mr. BÖLÜKBASI
    Mr. ERSOY
Mr. SINJANI (Malawi)

Sr. TERÁN (Equateur)
Sr. URTECHO (Honduras)
    Sr. AGURCIA

S = suppléant; substitute; suplente

Membres travailleurs - Workers' members - Miembros trabajadores

Mr. ALEKOU (Chypre)
Mr. ALMOGHRABI (Arabie saoudite)
Mr. ANKRAH (Ghana)
Mr. ASSADALLAH (Oman)
M. ATTIGBE (Bénin)
Mr. BAYARD (Etats-Unis)
M. BRAHMA (Maroc)
Ms. BURROW (Australie)
Mr. CHO (République de Corée)
M. DE JESUS RODRIGUES DA COSTA (Angola)
M. EKEDI (Cameroun)
Mr. GJERDING (Norvège)
Mr. GREP (Suriname)
Ms. ILESANMI (Nigéria)
Mr. LAMBERT (Canada)
Sr. LOBO SAN JUAN (Espagne)
Ms. MANN (Suède)
Mr. MOHAMED EL SENUSSI (Jamahiriya arabe libyenne)
Mr. NORDDAHL (Islande)
Mr. PATEL (Afrique du Sud)
M. POPA (Roumanie)
Ms. QARHASH (Yémen)
Mr. RØNTVED ANDERSEN (Danemark)
Mr. SAMARASINGHE (Sri Lanka)
Mr. SEN (Inde)
Mr. SOUZA BENEDETTI (Brésil)
Ms. STRELA (Fédération de Russie)
Mr. TAHA (Egypte)
Mrs. TOTH MUCCIACCIARO (Croatie)
Sra. TRIANA ALVIS (Colombie)
M. YAACOUBI (Tunisie)
Mr. ZHANG (Chine)

Mr. AL-MAHFOODH (Bahreïn)
Mr. AL-MUDAETH (Koweït)
Mr. ANSARI (République islamique d'Iran)
Mr. ATALAY (Turquie)
Mr. AZKAHE (République arabe syrienne)
Mme BERETTA (Italie)
Mrs. BRSELOVÁ (Slovaquie)
Ms. CEJOVIC (Serbie et Monténégro)
M. CUNHA DIAS (Portugal)
M. DELCROIX (Belgique)
Sr. FLORES (Mexique)
Mme GOERGEN (Luxembourg)
Sra. IBARRA (Honduras)
Mrs. KOULINKOVITCH (Bélarus)
Mr. LEPIK (Pologne)
M. MAMADOU (Niger)
Mr. MICALLEF (Malte)
Mr. MOORE (Barbade)

Ms. PAPE (Allemagne)
Sr. PIUMATO (Argentine)
Mr. PRUIM (Pays-Bas)
Mme RAHMANI (Algérie)
Mr. SALIH (Soudan)
Mme SAMBA (Sénégal)
Sr. SORIANO (El Salvador)
Ms. STEPHENS (Royaume-Uni)
Mr. SYED SHAHIR (Malaisie)
M. TAIIMATZIDIS (Grèce)
M. TOURE (Guinée)
M. TRICOCHE (France)
Mr. YUMOTO (Japon)

S = suppléant; substitute; suplente

Membres travailleurs adjoints - Workers' deputy members - Miembreos trabajadores adjuntos

Mrs. ABD EL HADY (Egypte)
Mr. ABDUL RAHMAN (Bahreïn)
Mr. ADYANTHAYA (Inde)
Mr. AHMADI-PANJAKI (République islamique d'Iran)
Sra. ANDERSON (Mexique)
Mr. BENCINI (Malte)
Ms. BOEGNER (Autriche)
Ms. CEJOVIC (Serbie et Monténégro)
Sr. DEL RIO (République dominicaine)
Mr. DEVENDRA (Sri Lanka)
M. DURY (Luxembourg)
Mr. EL WAHAB (République arabe syrienne)
Mr. ERIKSON (Norvège)
Ms. FUTAKATA (Japon)
Mr. HASAN (Bangladesh)
M. HOSSU (Roumanie)
Mr. JUNG (République de Corée)
Ms. KASUNIC (Croatie)
Ms. KIM (République de Corée)
Mme KRATIMENOU (Grèce)
Mr. LARSSON (Suède)
Mr. MASEMOLA (Afrique du Sud)
Sr. MEDINA DUEÑAS (Colombie)
Mr. NASHIR ALI (Yémen)
Sr. OJEDA (Mexique)
Ms. PARKER (Norvège)
Mme PETCU (Roumanie)
Mrs. PILAVAKI (Chypre)
Mr. RAHMAN (Bangladesh)
Sra. RICO (Espagne)
Mr. SITHOLE (Swaziland)
Ms. SONNTAG (Nouvelle-Zélande)
Mr. STEYNE (Royaume-Uni)
Ms. TAYLOR (Royaume-Uni)
M. TODJINOU (Bénin)
Mr. TÓTH (Hongrie)
Mr. TROTMAN (Barbade)
Mme VALCICA (Roumanie)
Ms. VEDRERO (Philippines)
Mr. ZELLHOEFER (Etats-Unis)

M. ABDOU (Niger)
Mr. ADEYEMI (Nigéria)
Mr. AFRIYIE (Ghana)
Mr. AL-AZMI (Koweït)
Mrs. BAUEROVÁ (République tchèque)
Mme BENSHILI (Maroc)
Ms. BYERS (Canada)
Mme DEL RIO (Italie)
Sr. DEL VALLE (Mexique)
M. DOS SANTOS CARDOSO MACEDO (Portugal)
Mr. ECKL (Allemagne)
Mr. ELSIDDIG (Soudan)
Sr. FERNANDEZ (Uruguay)
Sr. GHILINI (Argentine)
Ms. HEINÄNEN (Finlande)
M. JULIA (France)
Mr. KARA (Israël)
Mr. KHALIFA SALEM (Jamahiriya arabe libyenne)
Mr. KOSIR (Slovénie)
Mr. KRAVCHENKO (Fédération de Russie)
M. MAJDI (Tunisie)
Mr. MATULIS (Bélarus)
Mr. MILANI (Afrique du Sud)
Mme NIELES (Luxembourg)
Mr. OYERINDE (Nigéria)
Mr. PARROT (Canada)
Mme PETROPOULOU (Grèce)
Mr. RADHWAN (Arabie saoudite)
Mr. REINHOLD (Suède)
M. SAMB (Sénégal)
Mr. SLOOTWEG (Pays-Bas)
Mme SOSSOU (Bénin)
Ms. TATE (Australie)
M. TAZRIBINE (Belgique)
M. TORCHE (Suisse)
M. TRABELSI (Tunisie)
M. TSARAMBOULIDIS (Grèce)
Ms. VALKONEN (Finlande)
Mr. WOLDE MICHAEL (Ethiopie)
Mr. ZHAO (Chine)

S = suppléant; substitute; suplente

COMMISSION DE PROPOSITION
SELECTION COMMITTEE
COMISIÓN DE PROPOSICIONES

Membres gouvernementaux - Government members - Miembros gubernamentales

AFRIQUE DU SUD	ALLEMAGNE	ARABIE SAOUDITE
ARGENTINE	BAHAMAS	BRESIL
BULGARIE	CHINE	REPUBLIQUE DE COREE
REP. DOMINICAINE	EQUATEUR	ETATS-UNIS
FRANCE	GABON	INDE
INDONESIE	ITALIE	LIBAN
JAMAHIRIYA ARABE LIBYENNE	LITUANIE	MALI
MEXIQUE	NIGERIA	NORVEGE
PAKISTAN	ROYAUME-UNI	FEDERATION DE RUSSIE
SOUDAN		

Membres gouv. adjoints - Govt. deputy members - Miembros gub.adjuntos

BANGLADESH	BARBADE	BELARUS
BELGIQUE	BURUNDI	CAMEROUN
CANADA	EL SALVADOR	ESPAGNE
ETHIOPIE	GHANA	REP. ISLAMIQUE D'IRAN
JORDANIE	KENYA	LUXEMBOURG
MALAWI	MAROC	NIGER
NOUVELLE-ZELANDE	OMAN	PHILIPPINES
ROUMANIE	SINGAPOUR	SLOVENIE
TURQUIE	URUGUAY	VENEZUELA
VIET NAM		

Membres employeurs - Employers' members - Miembros empleadores

M. BARDE (Suisse)	**Mr. CHEN (Chine)**
Mr. DAHLAN (Arabie saoudite)	**Sr. FUNES DE RIOJA (Argentine)**
Mr. JEETUN (Maurice)	**Mr. LAMBERT (Royaume-Uni)**
Mr. LIMA GODOY (Brésil)	**M. M'KAISSI (Tunisie)**
M. NACOULMA (Burkina Faso)	**Mr. POTTER (Etats-Unis)**
Mme SASSO MAZZUFFERI (Italie)	**Mr. SUZUKI (Japon)**
Mr. TABANI (Pakistan)	**Mr. TROGEN (Suède)**

Membres employeurs adjoints - Employers' deputy members - Miembros empleadores adjuntos

Mr. ANAND (Inde)	Mme AWASSI ATSIMADJA (Gabon)
Mr. CLEARY (Nouvelle-Zélande)	Sr. DE ARBELOA (Venezuela)
Mr. EREMEEV (Fédération de Russie)	Sr. FERRER DUFOL (Espagne)
Mr. FINLAY (Canada)	Mr. HILTON-CLARKE (Trinité-et-Tobago)
Mrs. HORVATIC (Croatie)	Mr. KONDITI (Kenya)
Mr. MAKEKA (Lesotho)	Mr. OSHINOWO (Nigéria)
Sr. RICCI MUADI (Guatemala)	Mr. SORIANO (Philippines)

S = suppléant; substitute; suplente

Membres travailleurs - Workers' members - Miembros trabajadores

Mr. AHMED (Pakistan)
Mr. ATWOLI (Kenya)
Mr. CORTIZO (Brésil)
Mrs. ENGELEN-KEFER (Allemagne)
Mr. NAKAJIMA (Japon)
Sra. TRIANA ALVIS (Colombie)
Mrs. YACOB (Singapour)

Sra. ANDERSON (Mexique)
Mme BRIGHI (Italie)
Mme DIALLO (Guinée)
Mr. GHANDOUR (Soudan)
Mr. SIDOROV (Fédération de Russie)
Mr. TROTMAN (Barbade)
Mr. ZELLHOEFER (Etats-Unis)

Membres travailleurs adjoints - Workers' deputy members - Miembreos trabajadores adjuntos

M. BLONDEL (France)
M. CORTEBEECK (Belgique)
Ms. SEMINARIO (Etats-Unis)

Ms. BURROW (Australie)
Mr. SAND MORTENSEN (Danemark)

S = suppléant; substitute; suplente

The changes in the composition of committees as supplied by the groups are herewith reproduced

Changements apportés le 2 juin 2005
Changes made on 2 June 2005
Cambios aportados el 2 de junio de 2004

COMMITTEE ON THE APPLICATION OF STANDARDS

COMMISSION DE L'APPLICATION DES NORMES

COMISIÓN DE APLICACIÓN DE NORMAS

	Previous status Statut antérieur Calidad anterior	New status [1] Nouveau statut Nueva calidad

Governments - Gouvernements - Gobiernos

add/ajouter/añadir

BAHAMAS	-	T
CHILI	-	T
GHANA	-	T
JAMAHIRIYA ARABE LIBYENNE	-	T
MAURICE	-	T
MAURITANIE	-	T
OMAN	-	T
OUGANDA	-	T
REP. ARABE SYRIENNE	-	T
SOUDAN	-	T
TOGO	-	A
YEMEN	-	T
ZAMBIE	-	T

changer/change/cambiar

GUINEE	A	T
TURQUIE	A	T

Employers - Employeurs - Empleadores

add/ajouter/añadir

Mr. AL DEBS (République arabe syrienne)	-	T
M. BALBOUL (Liban)	-	Suppléant de M. HAMADEH
M. BOFFA (Saint-Marin)	-	Suppléant de Mme MENICUCCI
Mr. BOTCHWAY (Ghana)	-	Suppléant de Mr. MENSA
M. HAMADEH (Liban)	-	T
M. OULD ABDALLAHI (Mauritanie)	-	T
Mr. SHAHEEN (République arabe syrienne)	-	Suppléant de Mr. AL DEBS

---

[1] T: Regular member / membre Titulaire / miembro titular   S: Substitute member / membre suppléant / miembro suplente
A: Deputy member / membre adjoint / miembro adjunto   O: Observer member / membre observateur / miembro observadore

changer/change/cambiar

Mr. ANDERSON (Australie)	T	A
Sr. ARTHUR ERRAZURIZ (Chili)	T	A
M. BOISSON (France)	T	A
M. BOUDHAIM (Maroc)	S	Suppléant de M. JALAL
Mr. COON (Canada)	S	Suppléant de Mr. FINLAY
M. DA COSTA (Belgique)	S	Suppléant de M. DE KOSTER
M. DE KOSTER (Belgique)	T	A
M. DI NIOLA (Italie)	S	Suppléant de Mme SASSO MAZZUFFERI
M. FERRARA (Italie)	S	Suppléant de Mme SASSO MAZZUFFERI
Mr. FINLAY (Canada)	T	A
Sr. FUNES DE RIOJA (Argentine)	S	Suppléant de Sr. MENDEZ
Mrs. GERSTEIN (Allemagne)	T	A
Mme GUY (France)	S	Suppléant de M. BOISSON
Sr. HUMERES NOGUER (Chili)	S	Suppléant de Sr. ARTHUR ERRAZURIZ
M. JALAL (Maroc)	T	A
Mr. KAPEZA (Zambie)	S	Suppléant de Ms. NONDE
Mr. LAMBERT (Royaume-Uni)	T	A
Sr. MENDEZ (Argentine)	T	A
Mr. NOAKES (Australie)	S	Suppléant de Mr. ANDERSON
Ms. NONDE (Zambie)	T	A
Mr. POTTER (Etats-Unis)	T	A
Mr. PRINZ (Allemagne)	S	Suppléant de Mrs. GERSTEIN
Ms. REGENBOGEN (Canada)	S	Suppléant de Mr. FINLAY
Mme ROILAND (France)	S	Suppléant de M. BOISSON
Mme ROSSI (Italie)	S	Suppléant de Mme SASSO MAZZUFFERI
Mme SASSO MAZZUFFERI (Italie)	T	A
Sr. SPAGHI (Argentine)	S	Suppléant de Sr. MENDEZ
Ms. SPENCER (Etats-Unis)	S	Suppléant de Mr. POTTER
Mme STORM (Belgique)	S	Suppléant de M. DE KOSTER
Mr. SYDER (Royaume-Uni)	S	Suppléant de Mr. LAMBERT

delete/supprimer/suprimir

Mr. DANEV (Bulgarie)	S	
Mrs. GEORGIEVA (Bulgarie)	S	
Mr. NEDYALKOV (Bulgarie)	S	
Mrs. PAVLOVA (Bulgarie)	S	
Mr. SIMEONOV (Bulgarie)	T	

---

[1] T: Regular member / membre Titulaire / miembro titular   S: Substitute member / membre suppléant / miembro suplente
A: Deputy member / membre adjoint / miembro adjunto   O: Observer member / membre observateur / miembro observadore

Workers - Travailleurs - Trabajadores

add/ajouter/añadir

Sr. ARCINIEGA (Equateur)	-	A
Mr. BRYSON (Royaume-Uni)	-	A
Mr. CABRERA (Trinité-et-Tobago)	-	A
Sra. CHACÓN BRAVO (Cuba)	-	A
Mr. CHIBEBE (Zimbabwe)	-	A
M. DIOUF (Sénégal)	-	A
M. DUNIA MUTIMANWA LUBULA (République dém. du Congo)	-	T
Mr. GIUSEPPI (Trinité-et-Tobago)	-	T
Mr. HAMUTENYA (Namibie)	-	A
Sr. IBARRA (Equateur)	-	A
M. KANE (Mauritanie)	-	T
M. KPOKOLO (République centrafricaine)	-	T
Mr. KUBAI (Kenya)	-	T
M. MONGO (Congo)	-	T
Sr. MORANTES ALFONSO (Colombie)	-	A
M. MULAMBA MBUMBA (République dém. du Congo)	-	A
Mrs. NGUYEN (Viet Nam)	-	A
Sr. PARRA GAONA (Paraguay)	-	T
Mr. SILABAN (Indonésie)	-	T
Mr. SINGH (Fidji)	-	T
Sr. TATAMUEZ (Equateur)	-	T
Mr. TEMBO (Zambie)	-	T
Mr. TRENCHEV (Bulgarie)	-	T
Sr. YAGUAL (Equateur)	-	A

---

[1] T: Regular member / membre Titulaire / miembro titular   S: Substitute member / membre suppléant / miembro suplente
A: Deputy member / membre adjoint / miembro adjunto   O: Observer member / membre observateur / miembro observadore

changer/change/cambiar

M. ABDOU (Niger)	T	A
Mr. AL-AZMI (Koweït)	T	A
Mr. ALEMAYEHU (Ethiopie)	T	A
Mr. AL-NAHARI (Oman)	T	A
Sr. BONMATÍ (Espagne)	T	A
Sr. CHIRINO (Venezuela)	T	A
Mr. CRIVELLI (Brésil)	T	A
Mr. EL AZALI (Egypte)	T	A
Ms. KASUNIC (Croatie)	T	A
Mr. KOSAISOOK (Thaïlande)	T	A
Ms. MUSKAT-GORSKA (Pologne)	T	A
Mr. OSHIOMHOLE (Nigéria)	T	A
Sr. RODRIGUEZ DIAZ (Colombie)	T	A
Mr. SANJEEVA REDDY (Inde)	T	A
Mr. SUBASINGHE (Sri Lanka)	T	A
Mr. SVENNINGSEN (Danemark)	T	A

delete/supprimer/suprimir

Sr. LÓPEZ GÓMEZ (Cuba)		A

---

[1] T: Regular member / membre Titulaire / miembro titular   S: Substitute member / membre suppléant / miembro suplente
A: Deputy member / membre adjoint / miembro adjunto   O: Observer member / membre observateur / miembro observadore

COMMITTEE ON SAFETY AND HEALTH

COMMISSION DE LA SECURITE ET DE LA SANTE

COMISIÓN DE LA SEGURIDAD Y SALUD

	Previous status Statut antérieur Calidad anterior	New status [1] Nouveau statut Nueva calidad

Governments - Gouvernements - Gobiernos

add/ajouter/añadir

CHILI	-	T
GHANA	-	T
GUINEE	-	T
MAURICE	-	T
MAURITANIE	-	T
OMAN	-	T
OUGANDA	-	T
REP. ARABE SYRIENNE	-	T
SOUDAN	-	T
TOGO	-	T
YEMEN	-	T
ZAMBIE	-	T

changer/change/cambiar

TURQUIE	A	T

Employers - Employeurs - Empleadores

add/ajouter/añadir

M. BSAT (Liban)	-	Suppléant de M. HAMADEH
Ms. DA COSTA RODRIGUES DE CARVALHO (Brésil)	-	Suppléant de Mr. LIMA GODOY
M. HAMADEH (Liban)	-	T
Ms. QUIST-ADDO (Ghana)	-	Suppléant de Mr. MENSA

---

[1] T: Regular member / membre Titulaire / miembro titular   S: Substitute member / membre suppléant / miembro suplente
A: Deputy member / membre adjoint / miembro adjunto   O: Observer member / membre observateur / miembro observadore

changer/change/cambiar

M. BARDE (Suisse)	T	A
Ms. CHENGALUR (Etats-Unis)	S	Suppléant de Mr. POTTER
Mr. JANNERFELDT (Suède)	S	Suppléant de Ms. LAURENT
Ms. LAURENT (Suède)	T	A
Mr. POTTER (Etats-Unis)	T	A
Mr. SEMRAU (Etats-Unis)	S	Suppléant de Mr. POTTER
Mr. TAUBITZ (Etats-Unis)	S	Suppléant de Mr. POTTER
M. TELEKI (Suisse)	S	Suppléant de M. BARDE
Sr. TERÁN (Equateur)	T	A
Mr. TROGEN (Suède)	S	Suppléant de Ms. LAURENT

delete/supprimer/suprimir

Sr. CARVAJAL (Mexique)	S

Workers - Travailleurs - Trabajadores

add/ajouter/añadir

Sra. AGUILAR TORRES (Chili)	-	T
Mr. BOONRAT (Thaïlande)	-	A
Mr. CABRERA (Trinité-et-Tobago)	-	A
Mr. GEERMAN (Pays-Bas)	-	T
Mr. IGNACIO (Pays-Bas)	-	A
Sr. INFANTE (Venezuela)	-	A
M. KABULO MBODYAWASHA (République dém. du Congo)	-	T
M. KANE (Mauritanie)	-	A
Ms. KASUNIC (Croatie)	-	T
Mr. KUPPAN (Maurice)	-	T
Mr. MUDENDA (Zambie)	-	T
Ms. PALANU (Thaïlande)	-	A
Sr. TATAMUEZ (Equateur)	-	A
Sr. VIDELA VILLALOBOS (Chili)	-	T
Sr. YAGUAL (Equateur)	-	T
M. ZOUNNADJALA (Togo)	-	T

---

1 T: Regular member / membre Titulaire / miembro titular S: Substitute member / membre suppléant / miembro suplente
A: Deputy member / membre adjoint / miembro adjunto O: Observer member / membre observateur / miembro observadore

changer/change/cambiar

Sr. ACEVES (Mexique)	T	A
Mr. AL-AZMI (Koweït)	T	A
Ms. AL-HASHIMI (Oman)	T	A
M. BEN SAÏD (Tchad)	T	A
M. BOUZRIBA (Tunisie)	T	A
Mr. BRYSON (Royaume-Uni)	T	A
M. ISSOUFOU (Niger)	T	A
Mr. JONES (Jamaïque)	T	A
Mr. JUMA'H (Jordanie)	T	A
Mr. KARA (Israël)	T	A
Mr. KHALIFA SALEM (Jamahiriya arabe libyenne)	T	A
M. KOLEVENTIS (Grèce)	T	A
M. LEEMANS (Belgique)	T	A
Mr. MAHADEVAN (Inde)	T	A
Mr. MALABAG (Papouasie-Nouvelle-Guinée)	T	A
Mr. MELANDER (Suède)	T	A
Sra. MOLINA (El Salvador)	T	A
M. PIZZAFERRI (Luxembourg)	T	A
Mr. RADHWAN (Arabie saoudite)	T	A
Mr. ROSTOM (Egypte)	T	A
Mrs. SCHRÖDER (Allemagne)	T	A
Mr. SÜKÜN (Turquie)	T	A
Ms. VAICAITYTE (Lituanie)	T	A
Mr. VALOIS (Canada)	T	A
Mr. WAGSTAFF (Nouvelle-Zélande)	T	A

---

[1] T: Regular member / membre Titulaire / miembro titular   S: Substitute member / membre suppléant / miembro suplente
A: Deputy member / membre adjoint / miembro adjunto   O: Observer member / membre observateur / miembro observadore

COMMITTEE ON THE FISHING SECTOR
COMMISSION DU SECTEUR DE LA PECHE
COMISIÓN DEL SECTOR PESQUERO

	Previous status Statut antérieur Calidad anterior	New status [1] Nouveau statut Nueva calidad

Governments - Gouvernements - Gobiernos

add/ajouter/añadir

CHILI	-	T
GHANA	-	T
JAMAHIRIYA ARABE LIBYENNE	-	T
MAURICE	-	T
MAURITANIE	-	T
OMAN	-	T
OUGANDA	-	T
REP. ARABE SYRIENNE	-	T
SOUDAN	-	T
YEMEN	-	T
ZAMBIE	-	T

changer/change/cambiar

AUTRICHE	T	A
GUATEMALA	A	T
TURQUIE	A	T

Employers - Employeurs - Empleadores

add/ajouter/añadir

Sr. CARVAJAL (Mexique)	-	Suppléant de Sr. HALKIN
Mr. OKAZAKI (Japon)	-	Suppléant de Mr. TATEISI

---

[1] T: Regular member / membre Titulaire / miembro titular   S: Substitute member / membre suppléant / miembro suplente
A: Deputy member / membre adjoint / miembro adjunto   O: Observer member / membre observateur / miembro observadore

changer/change/cambiar

M. ANDRÉ (Angola)	S	Suppléant de M. GOMES
M. BOISSON (France)	T	A
M. BOUDHAIM (Maroc)	S	Suppléant de M. JALAL
Mr. CHAPMAN (Canada)	S	Suppléant de Mr. FINLAY
Mme DE ASSUNÇÁO PAULINA MÁRIO (Angola)	S	Suppléant de M. GOMES
M. DJILANI (Tunisie)	T	A
Mr. FINLAY (Canada)	T	A
Ms. FRENCH (Etats-Unis)	S	Suppléant de Mr. POTTER
M. GOMES (Angola)	T	A
Mme HERVOUET/DION (France)	S	Suppléant de M. BOISSON
M. JALAL (Maroc)	T	A
Mr. KOSAKA (Japon)	S	Suppléant de Mr. TATEISI
Mr. LAMBERT (Royaume-Uni)	T	A
Ms. PENNEY (Canada)	S	Suppléant de Mr. FINLAY
Mr. PIGGOTT (Royaume-Uni)	S	Suppléant de Mr. LAMBERT
Mr. POTTER (Etats-Unis)	T	A
M. SELLINI (Tunisie)	S	Suppléant de M. DJILANI
Mr. SEMRAU (Etats-Unis)	S	Suppléant de Mr. POTTER
Mr. TATEISI (Japon)	T	A
Ms. WISEMAN (Royaume-Uni)	S	Suppléant de Mr. LAMBERT

delete/supprimer/suprimir

Sr. ARANGO VALLEJO (Colombie)	S
Ms. YOSHIKAWA (Japon)	S

Workers - Travailleurs - Trabajadores

add/ajouter/añadir

Sra. CHACÓN BRAVO (Cuba)	-	T
M. KANE (Mauritanie)	-	A
M. MEL DJEDJE-LI (Côte d'Ivoire)	-	A
Mr. MONTAÑO (Philippines)	-	T
Mr. NGULA (République-Unie de Tanzanie)	-	A
Sr. TATAMUEZ (Equateur)	-	A
Sr. YAGUAL (Equateur)	-	A

---

[1] T: Regular member / membre Titulaire / miembro titular   S: Substitute member / membre suppléant / miembro suplente
A: Deputy member / membre adjoint / miembro adjunto   O: Observer member / membre observateur / miembro observadore

changer/change/cambiar

Mr. ADYANTHAYA (Inde)	T	A
Mr. AFRIYIE (Ghana)	T	A
Mr. AL-RIZAIQI (Oman)	T	A
M. BISSALA (Cameroun)	T	A
Sra. CANO MORENO (Panama)	T	A
Ms. CEJOVIC (Serbie et Monténégro)	T	A
M. DELIYANNAKIS (Grèce)	T	A
Mr. DWEAER (République arabe syrienne)	T	a
M. FATHI (Maroc)	T	A
Mr. IBRAHIM (Soudan)	T	A
Mr. IRABOR (Nigéria)	T	A
Sr. MORANTES ALFONSO (Colombie)	T	A
Mr. MOYSEOS (Chypre)	T	A
Mr. MUFTAH ALI (Jamahiriya arabe libyenne)	T	A
Mr. PETROV (Ukraine)	T	A
M. RAHMA (Algérie)	T	A
M. RETUREAU (France)	T	A
Mr. ROBERTS (Jamaïque)	T	A
Mr. ROBINSON (Seychelles)	T	A
M. SALIFOU (Niger)	T	A
M. STAN (Roumanie)	T	A
Sr. SUAREZ (Argentine)	T	A
M. TORCHE (Suisse)	T	A
Mme YAFA (Sénégal)	T	A

delete/supprimer/suprimir

Sr. LÓPEZ GÓMEZ (Cuba)	T

---

[1] T: Regular member / membre Titulaire / miembro titular   S: Substitute member / membre suppléant / miembro suplente
A: Deputy member / membre adjoint / miembro adjunto   O: Observer member / membre observateur / miembro observadore

COMMITTEE ON YOUTH EMPLOYMENT

COMMISSION DE L'EMPLOI DES JEUNES

COMISIÓN DELEMPLEO DE LOS JOVENES

	Previous status Statut antérieur Calidad anterior	New status [1] Nouveau statut Nueva calidad

Governments - Gouvernements - Gobiernos

add/ajouter/añadir

BAHAMAS	-	T
CHILI	-	T
GHANA	-	T
MAURICE	-	T
MAURITANIE	-	T
OMAN	-	T
OUGANDA	-	T
REP. ARABE SYRIENNE	-	T
SOUDAN	-	T
TOGO	-	T
YEMEN	-	T
ZAMBIE	-	T

changer/change/cambiar

BULGARIE	T	A
GUINEE	A	T
TURQUIE	A	T

---

[1] T: Regular member / membre Titulaire / miembro titular   S: Substitute member / membre suppléant / miembro suplente

A: Deputy member / membre adjoint / miembro adjunto   O: Observer member / membre observateur / miembro observadore

Employers - Employeurs - Empleadores

add/ajouter/añadir

M. ABEGA (Cameroun)	-	Suppléant de M. AYANGMA AMANG
Mr. ALHUMAIDAN (Arabie saoudite)	-	Suppléant de Mr. DAHLAN
Sr. ARANGO VALLEJO (Colombie)	-	Suppléant de Sr. ECHAVARRIA SALDARRIA
M. AYANGMA AMANG (Cameroun)	-	T
M. BAXEVANIS (Grèce)	-	Suppléant de M. KYRIAKOPOULOS
Mr. DANEV (Bulgarie)	-	Suppléant de Mr. SIMEONOV
Mrs. DLAMINI (Swaziland)	-	Suppléant de Mrs. MAPHANGA
Sra. GARZA (Mexique)	-	Suppléant de Sr. HALKIN
Mrs. GEORGIEVA (Bulgarie)	-	Suppléant de Mr. SIMEONOV
M. HAMADEH (Liban)	-	T
Mme IOANNIDOU (Grèce)	-	Suppléant de M. KYRIAKOPOULOS
M. LASSEY (Togo)	-	Suppléant de M. NAKU
M. NAKU (Togo)	-	T
Mr. NEDYALKOV (Bulgarie)	-	Suppléant de Mr. SIMEONOV
Ms. OWUSU (Ghana)	-	Suppléant de Mr. MENSA
M. UINGE (Mozambique)	-	T
M. ZAGUI (République centrafricaine)	-	T
Ms. ZDRODOWSKA (Pologne)	-	Suppléant de Mr. BONI

---

1 T: Regular member / membre Titulaire / miembro titular   S: Substitute member / membre suppléant / miembro suplente
A: Deputy member / membre adjoint / miembro adjunto   O: Observer member / membre observateur / miembro observadore

changer/change/cambiar

Mr. ABDULLAH (Indonésie)	S	Suppléant de Mr. RACHMAN
Mr. AHMED (Iraq)	S	Suppléant de Mr. AL KHAFAJI
Mr. AL KHAFAJI (Iraq)	T	A
Mr. AL KHOOR (Bahreïn)	S	Suppléant de Mr. AL SALEH
Mr. AL SALEH (Bahreïn)	T	A
Mr. ALLAM (Egypte)	T	A
Ms. ARYEE (Ghana)	S	Suppléant de Mr. MENSA
Mr. CHEN (Chine)	T	A
M. DE KOSTER (Belgique)	T	A
Mr. GARSHONG (Ghana)	S	Suppléant de Mr. MENSA
Ms. GOLDBERG (Etats-Unis)	S	Suppléant de Mr. POTTER
Ms. HA (République de Corée)	S	Suppléant de Mr. KIM
Ms. HWANG (République de Corée)	S	Suppléant de Mr. KIM
Mr. KIM (République de Corée)	T	A
Mr. LARYEA (Ghana)	S	Suppléant de Mr. MENSA
Mr. LIU (Chine)	S	Suppléant de Mr. CHEN
M. MEGATELI (Algérie)	S	Suppléant de M. YOUSFI
M. MEHENNI (Algérie)	S	Suppléant de M. YOUSFI
Mr. MENSA (Ghana)	T	A
Mr. MENSAH (Ghana)	S	Suppléant de Mr. MENSA
Mrs. MOHAMED (Egypte)	S	Suppléant de Mr. ALLAM
Mr. MUSENGE (Zambie)	S	Suppléant de Ms. NONDE
M. NACOULMA (Burkina Faso)	T	A
M. NAÏT ABDELAZIZ (Algérie)	S	Suppléant de M. YOUSFI
Ms. NONDE (Zambie)	T	A
Mr. NOOR (Indonésie)	S	Suppléant de Mr. RACHMAN
Mme OUZROUT (Algérie)	S	Suppléant de M. YOUSFI
Mrs. PAVLOVA (Bulgarie)	S	Suppléant de Mr. SIMEONOV
Mr. POTTER (Etats-Unis)	T	A
Mr. RACHMAN (Indonésie)	T	A
Mr. SEMRAU (Etats-Unis)	S	Suppléant de Mr. POTTER
M. SIACI (Algérie)	S	Suppléant de M. YOUSFI
Mr. SIMEONOV (Bulgarie)	T	A
Mr. TABANI (Pakistan)	T	A
Mr. TIN (Myanmar)	T	A
Sr. TOMASINO HURTADO (El Salvador)	T	A
Mme YAMEOGO-TOU (Burkina Faso)	S	Suppléant de M. NACOULMA
M. YOUSFI (Algérie)	T	A

delete/supprimer/suprimir

M. BOFFA (Saint-Marin)	S	

---

[1] T: Regular member / membre Titulaire / miembro titular   S: Substitute member / membre suppléant / miembro suplente
A: Deputy member / membre adjoint / miembro adjunto   O: Observer member / membre observateur / miembro observadore

Workers - Travailleurs - Trabajadores

add/ajouter/añadir

Mr. AL-KUHLANI (Yémen)	-	A
Mr. ATWOLI (Kenya)	-	A
Mr. BROWN (Jamaïque)	-	A
Sr. CANALES HUENCHUAN (Chili)	-	T
Mr. CHAALA (Zambie)	-	T
Sr. DÍAZ ZAVALA (Chili)	-	A
Mr. GEERMAN (Pays-Bas)	-	A
Mr. HIDAYAT (Indonésie)	-	T
Mr. IGNACIO (Pays-Bas)	-	A
M. KANE (Mauritanie)	-	A
Mr. NAMUDU (Fidji)	-	A
M. NYAMIEN MESSOU (Côte d'Ivoire)	-	T
Mr. ROBERTS (Jamaïque)	-	A
Mr. SINGH (Fidji)	-	A
Sr. TATAMUEZ (Equateur)	-	A
Sr. YAGUAL (Equateur)	-	A
M. YRA (Burkina Faso)	-	A

SELECTION COMMITTEE
COMMISSION DE PROPOSITION
COMISIÓN DE PROPOSICIONES

Previous status	New status [1]
Statut antérieur	Nouveau statut
Calidad anterior	Nueva calidad

Employers - Employeurs - Empleadores

add/ajouter/añadir

M. BOISSON (France)	-	T
Mr. NOAKES (Australie)	-	T

changer/change/cambiar

Mr. CHEN (Chine)	T	A

delete/supprimer/suprimir

Mme SASSO MAZZUFFERI (Italie)	T	

---

[1] T: Regular member / membre Titulaire / miembro titular   S: Substitute member / membre suppléant / miembro suplente
A: Deputy member / membre adjoint / miembro adjunto   O: Observer member / membre observateur / miembro observadore

Changements apportés le 3 juin 2005
Changes made on 3 June 2005
Cambios aportados el 3 de junio de 2005

COMMITTEE ON THE APPLICATION OF STANDARDS

COMMISSION DE L'APPLICATION DES NORMES

COMISIÓN DE APLICACIÓN DE NORMAS

	Previous status Statut antérieur Calidad anterior	New status [1] Nouveau statut Nueva calidad

Governments - Gouvernements - Gobiernos

add/ajouter/añadir

BURKINA FASO	-	T
CONGO	-	T
FIDJI	-	T

delete/supprimer/suprimir

| BAHAMAS | T | |

Employers - Employeurs - Empleadores

add/ajouter/añadir

Mr. BORGULA (Slovaquie)	-	A
Sr. CASTILLO CAMINERO (République dominicaine)	-	Suppléant de Sra. ESCOTO ABREU
Mr. ELGORASHI (Soudan)	-	T
Sra. ESCOTO ABREU (République dominicaine)	-	A
Sr. FIGUEROA PÉREZ (Guatemala)	-	Suppléant de Sr. RICCI MUADI
Mr. OSMAN (Soudan)	-	Suppléant de Mr. ELGORASHI
Sr. RICCI MUADI (Guatemala)	-	A
Mr. VAN NIEKERK (Afrique du Sud)	-	Suppléant de Mr. VAN VUUREN
Mr. YEMER (Ethiopie)	-	Suppléant de Mr. ZAWDE
Mr. ZAWDE (Ethiopie)	-	T

---

[1] T: Regular member / membre Titulaire / miembro titular   S: Substitute member / membre suppléant / miembro suplente
A: Deputy member / membre adjoint / miembro adjunto   O: Observer member / membre observateur / miembro observadore

changer/change/cambiar

Mr. AHMED (Iraq)	S	Suppléant de Mr. AL KHAFAJI
Sr. AIZPURÚA (Panama)	T	A
Mr. AL KHAFAJI (Iraq)	T	A
Mr. AL SALEH (Bahreïn)	T	A
Mr. AXENTI (République de Moldova)	S	Suppléant de Mr. CERESCU
M. BALBOUL (Liban)	S	Suppléant de M. HAMADEH
Mr. CERESCU (République de Moldova)	T	A
Sr. CESTER BEATOBE (Espagne)	S	Suppléant de Sr. FERRER DUFOL
Sr. DEL PUEYO PÉREZ (Espagne)	S	Suppléant de Sr. FERRER DUFOL
Mr. DREESEN (Danemark)	T	A
Sr. FERRER DUFOL (Espagne)	T	A
Mr. GADE (Danemark)	S	Suppléant de Mr. DREESEN
M. HAMADEH (Liban)	T	A
Mr. KONDITI (Kenya)	T	A
Sr. LINERO (Panama)	S	Suppléant de Sr. AIZPURÚA
Mr. MBUI (Kenya)	S	Suppléant de Mr. KONDITI
M. OULD ABDALLAHI (Mauritanie)	T	A
Mr. SCHILDER (Danemark)	S	Suppléant de Mr. DREESEN
Mr. SHAHEEN (République arabe syrienne)	S	T
Mr. SHRIF (Bahreïn)	S	Suppléant de Mr. AL SALEH
Sr. SUÁREZ SANTOS (Espagne)	S	Suppléant de Sr. FERRER DUFOL
Mr. TORBEN A. (Danemark)	S	Suppléant de Mr. DREESEN

Workers - Travailleurs - Trabajadores

add/ajouter/añadir

Mrs. FREEMAN (Libéria)	-	A
M. LILIOU (Burkina Faso)	-	T
Sr. LÓPEZ GÓMEZ (Cuba)	-	A
Mr. MANEA (République de Moldova)	-	T
Sr. ORTIZ ARCOS (Chili)	-	A
Sra. ROZAS VELÁSQUEZ (Chili)	-	A
Mr. RUZIVE (Zimbabwe)	-	T
Mr. WILLIAMS (Libéria)	-	A

changer/change/cambiar

Mr. AL-AZMI (Koweït)	A	T
Mr. CRIVELLI (Brésil)	A	T
Ms. FAN (Chine)	T	A
M. KANE (Mauritanie)	T	A
Mr. SINGH (Fidji)	T	A

---

1 T: Regular member / membre Titulaire / miembro titular   S: Substitute member / membre suppléant / miembro suplente
   A: Deputy member / membre adjoint / miembro adjunto   O: Observer member / membre observateur / miembro observadore

COMMITTEE ON SAFETY AND HEALTH

COMMISSION DE LA SECURITE ET DE LA SANTE

COMISIÓN DE LA SEGURIDAD Y SALUD

	Previous status Statut antérieur Calidad anterior	New status [1] Nouveau statut Nueva calidad

Governments - Gouvernements - Gobiernos

add/ajouter/añadir

CAMBODGE	-	T

delete/supprimer/suprimir

SOUDAN	T	

Employers - Employeurs - Empleadores

add/ajouter/añadir

Mr. BORGULA (Slovaquie)	-	A
Mrs. KROMEROVÁ (Slovaquie)	-	Suppléant de Mr. BORGULA
Mr. OKONKWO (Nigéria)	-	Suppléant de Mr. OSHINOWO
Mr. OSHINOWO (Nigéria)	-	A
Sr. TOMASINO HURTADO (El Salvador)	-	A
Mr. ZAWDE (Ethiopie)	-	T

---

[1] T: Regular member / membre Titulaire / miembro titular   S: Substitute member / membre suppléant / miembro suplente
A: Deputy member / membre adjoint / miembro adjunto   O: Observer member / membre observateur / miembro observadore

changer/change/cambiar

Mr. CHEN (Chine)	T	A
Mr. COTE (Canada)	S	Suppléant de Mr. FINLAY
Mr. DENIS (Indonésie)	S	Suppléant de Mr. RACHMAN
M. DI NIOLA (Italie)	S	Suppléant de Mme SASSO MAZZUFFERI
M. FERRARA (Italie)	S	Suppléant de Mme SASSO MAZZUFFERI
Mr. FINLAY (Canada)	T	A
Sr. GONZÁLEZ RODRÍGUEZ (Cuba)	S	Suppléant de Sr. PARRA ROJAS
Mr. HAGHBAYAN (République islamique d'Iran)	S	Suppléant de Mr. OTAREDIAN
Mr. JEON (République de Corée)	S	Suppléant de Mr. KIM
Mr. KIM (République de Corée)	T	A
Mr. LIM (République de Corée)	S	Suppléant de Mr. KIM
Sr. MESA GARCÍA (Cuba)	S	Suppléant de Sr. PARRA ROJAS
Mr. NATHAN (Malaisie)	T	A
Mr. OTAREDIAN (République islamique d'Iran)	T	A
Sr. PARRA ROJAS (Cuba)	T	A
Mr. RACHMAN (Indonésie)	T	A
Mme ROSSI (Italie)	S	Suppléant de Mme SASSO MAZZUFFERI
Mr. RUDIYANTO (Indonésie)	S	Suppléant de Mr. RACHMAN
Mme SASSO MAZZUFFERI (Italie)	T	A
Mr. SHAMSUDDIN (Malaisie)	S	Suppléant de Mr. NATHAN
Mr. SORIANO (Philippines)	T	A
Mr. TANG (Canada)	S	Suppléant de Mr. FINLAY
Mr. VARELA (Philippines)	S	Suppléant de Mr. SORIANO
Sr. VIDAUT MÁRQUEZ (Cuba)	S	Suppléant de Sr. PARRA ROJAS
Mr. YU (Chine)	S	Suppléant de Mr. CHEN

Workers - Travailleurs - Trabajadores

add/ajouter/añadir

Mr. AL-HIARY (Jordanie)	-	A
Mr. BALAIS (Philippines)	-	A
Mr. FERREIRA DO PRADO (Brésil)	-	A
Mrs. FREEMAN (Libéria)	-	A
Mme PECHLIVANDIOU (Grèce)	-	A
M. TIENDREBEOGO (Burkina Faso)	-	A
Mr. WILLIAMS (Libéria)	-	T

---

1 T: Regular member / membre Titulaire / miembro titular   S: Substitute member / membre suppléant / miembro suplente
A: Deputy member / membre adjoint / miembro adjunto   O: Observer member / membre observateur / miembro observadore

changer/change/cambiar

Sr. ALVIS FERNANDEZ (Colombie)	T	A
Ms. HAN (République de Corée)	T	A
M. MENSAH FRANCOIS (Côte d'Ivoire)	T	A
M. MOUSSOLE (Cameroun)	T	A
Mr. MUDENDA (Zambie)	T	A
Mr. ODAH (Nigéria)	T	A
Sra. PUJADAS (Argentine)	T	A
Mr. SKÁCELÍK (République tchèque)	T	A
Mr. TRUMEL (Fédération de Russie)	T	A
Mr. WOJCIK (Pologne)	T	A
Sr. YAGUAL (Equateur)	T	A

COMMITTEE ON THE FISHING SECTOR

COMMISSION DU SECTEUR DE LA PECHE

COMISIÓN DEL SECTOR PESQUERO

Previous status / Statut antérieur / Calidad anterior   New status [1] / Nouveau statut / Nueva calidad

Governments - Gouvernements - Gobiernos

add/ajouter/añadir

BAHAMAS	-	T
CONGO	-	T

Employers - Employeurs - Empleadores

add/ajouter/añadir

Mr. MANDA (Afrique du Sud)	-	Suppléant de Mr. VAN VUUREN
Mr. ZAWDE (Ethiopie)	-	A

changer/change/cambiar

Mr. OTAREDIAN (République islamique d'Iran)	T	A
Mr. RACHMAN (Indonésie)	T	A
Mr. SUPARWANTO (Indonésie)	S	Suppléant de Mr. RACHMAN
Mr. TATHIRI-MOGHADDAM (République islamique d'Iran)	S	Suppléant de Mr. OTAREDIAN

---

[1] T: Regular member / membre Titulaire / miembro titular   S: Substitute member / membre suppléant / miembro suplente
A: Deputy member / membre adjoint / miembro adjunto   O: Observer member / membre observateur / miembro observadore

Workers - Travailleurs - Trabajadores

add/ajouter/añadir

Mr. AL-ZAID (Koweït)	-	T
M. FALL (Sénégal)	-	T
Mrs. FREEMAN (Libéria)	-	T
Mr. WILLIAMS (Libéria)	-	A

changer/change/cambiar

Mr. ABD EL HALIM (Egypte)	T	A
Ms. ARSHAD (République islamique d'Iran)	T	A
Sra. CHACÓN BRAVO (Cuba)	T	A
Sr. GRAJALES (Mexique)	T	A
Mr. GUNNARSSON (Islande)	A	T
M. HOUNSINOU (Bénin)	T	A
Ms. KIM (République de Corée)	T	A
Mr. RODRIGUES LEITE PENTEADO (Brésil)	T	A
Mr. SANDRASEKERA (Sri Lanka)	T	A
Mr. THOMAS (Inde)	A	T
Mr. TOMASSON (Islande)	T	A

delete/supprimer/suprimir

Ms. VAICAITYTE (Lituanie)	A

COMMITTEE ON YOUTH EMPLOYMENT
COMMISSION DE L'EMPLOI DES JEUNES
COMISIÓN DELEMPLEO DE LOS JOVENES

	Previous status Statut antérieur Calidad anterior	New status [1] Nouveau statut Nueva calidad

Governments - Gouvernements - Gobiernos

add/ajouter/añadir

CAMBODGE	-	T
FIDJI	-	T
TCHAD	-	T

---

[1] T: Regular member / membre Titulaire / miembro titular   S: Substitute member / membre suppléant / miembro suplente
A: Deputy member / membre adjoint / miembro adjunto   O: Observer member / membre observateur / miembro observadore

Employers - Employeurs - Empleadores

add/ajouter/añadir

M. ALI ABBAS (Tchad)	-	A
Mr. BONNA (Ghana)	-	Suppléant de Mr. MENSA
Mr. ELGORASHI (Soudan)	-	T
Sr. FALCHETTI (Uruguay)	-	Suppléant de Sr. MAILHOS
Mr. OSMAN (Soudan)	-	Suppléant de Mr. ELGORASHI
Mr. THENGE (Ouganda)	-	Suppléant de Ms. SSENABULYA
Mr. YEMER (Ethiopie)	-	Suppléant de Mr. ZAWDE
Mr. ZAWDE (Ethiopie)	-	A

---

[1] T: Regular member / membre Titulaire / miembro titular   S: Substitute member / membre suppléant / miembro suplente
A: Deputy member / membre adjoint / miembro adjunto   O: Observer member / membre observateur / miembro observadore

changer/change/cambiar

Mr. AL-RUBAIAI (Oman)	T	A
Mr. AL-WUHAIBI (Oman)	S	Suppléant de Mr. AL-RUBAIAI
M. ANDRÉ (Angola)	S	Suppléant de M. GOMES
Sra. ASENJO (Espagne)	S	Suppléant de Sr. FERRER DUFOL
Mr. ATANASKOVIC (Serbie et Monténégro)	S	Suppléant de Mr. NINKOVIC
Mr. ATHARI (République islamique d'Iran)	S	Suppléant de Mr. OTAREDIAN
Mr. BARAK (Israël)	T	A
Mr. CHANPORNPONG (Thaïlande)	T	A
Mr. FARRUGIA (Malte)	T	A
Sr. FERRER DUFOL (Espagne)	T	A
Mr. GANBAATAR (Mongolie)	T	A
M. GLELE (Bénin)	T	A
M. GOMES (Angola)	T	A
M. KOVACS (Roumanie)	S	Suppléant de M. NICOLESCU
M. LASSEY (Togo)	S	Suppléant de M. NAKU
Mme MANOLE (Roumanie)	S	Suppléant de M. NICOLESCU
Sr. MENÉNDEZ VALDÉS (Espagne)	S	Suppléant de Sr. FERRER DUFOL
M. MIHALACHE (Roumanie)	S	Suppléant de M. NICOLESCU
M. NAKU (Togo)	T	A
M. NICOLESCU (Roumanie)	T	A
Mr. NINKOVIC (Serbie et Monténégro)	T	A
Mr. OTAREDIAN (République islamique d'Iran)	T	A
M. PARVAN (Roumanie)	S	Suppléant de M. NICOLESCU
Ms. STOJSIC-STOJANOVSKA (Serbie et Monténégro)	S	Suppléant de Mr. NINKOVIC
Sr. SUÁREZ GARCÍA (Espagne)	S	Suppléant de Sr. FERRER DUFOL
Mr. TABONE (Malte)	S	Suppléant de Mr. FARRUGIA
Mme TOLI (Bénin)	S	Suppléant de M. GLELE
Mr. WONGTHONGLUA (Thaïlande)	S	Suppléant de Mr. CHANPORNPONG
M. ZAGUI (République centrafricaine)	T	A
M. ZANOU (Bénin)	S	Suppléant de M. GLELE
Mr. ZORIGTBAATAR (Mongolie)	S	Suppléant de Mr. GANBAATAR

[1] T: Regular member / membre Titulaire / miembro titular   S: Substitute member / membre suppléant / miembro suplente
A: Deputy member / membre adjoint / miembro adjunto   O: Observer member / membre observateur / miembro observadore

Workers - Travailleurs - Trabajadores

add/ajouter/añadir

Mr. BENKO (Croatie)	-	A
Mrs. FREEMAN (Libéria)	-	A
Mr. FUSE (Japon)	-	A
Mr. KALSAKAU (Vanuatu)	-	A
M. MANZI (Rwanda)	-	T
Ms. MATSUMOTO (Japon)	-	A
Ms. VAICAITYTE (Lituanie)	-	A
Mr. WILLIAMS (Libéria)	-	A

changer/change/cambiar

Mr. ALEKOU (Chypre)	T	A
Mr. CHAALA (Zambie)	T	A
M. EKEDI (Cameroun)	T	A
Mr. HIDAYAT (Indonésie)	T	A
Ms. ILESANMI (Nigéria)	T	A
Sr. LOBO SAN JUAN (Espagne)	T	A
M. MAMADOU (Niger)	T	A
Ms. PAPE (Allemagne)	T	A
Mr. PATEL (Afrique du Sud)	T	A
Ms. QARHASH (Yémen)	T	A
Mr. ROBERTS (Jamaïque)	A	T
Mme SAMBA (Sénégal)	T	A
Mr. TAHA (Egypte)	T	A
M. TOURE (Guinée)	T	A
Mr. ZHANG (Chine)	T	A

SELECTION COMMITTEE
COMMISSION DE PROPOSITION
COMISIÓN DE PROPOSICIONES

	Previous status	**New status** [1]
	Statut antérieur	**Nouveau statut**
	Calidad anterior	**Nueva calidad**

Employers - Employeurs - Empleadores

delete/supprimer/suprimir

Sr. RICCI MUADI (Guatemala)	A

---

[1] T: Regular member / membre Titulaire / miembro titular   S: Substitute member / membre suppléant / miembro suplente
A: Deputy member / membre adjoint / miembro adjunto   O: Observer member / membre observateur / miembro observadore

Changements apportés le 4 juin 2005
Changes made on 4 June 2005
Cambios aportados el 4 de junio de 2005

COMMITTEE ON THE APPLICATION OF STANDARDS

COMMISSION DE L'APPLICATION DES NORMES

COMISIÓN DE APLICACIÓN DE NORMAS

	Previous status Statut antérieur Calidad anterior	New status [1] Nouveau statut Nueva calidad

Governments - Gouvernements - Gobiernos

add/ajouter/añadir

BOTSWANA	-	T
DJIBOUTI	-	T
IRLANDE	-	T
LIBERIA	-	T
TCHAD	-	T

Employers - Employeurs - Empleadores

add/ajouter/añadir

Mr. BIMHA (Zimbabwe)	-	A
Mr. MUFUKARE (Zimbabwe)	-	Suppléant de Mr. BIMHA
M. ZOULA (Congo)	-	A

Workers - Travailleurs - Trabajadores

add/ajouter/añadir

Mr. ADEYEMI (Nigéria)	-	A
Sr. ALVIS FERNANDEZ (Colombie)	-	T
M. BEKALE (Gabon)	-	A
Mr. DZHULYK (Ukraine)	-	T
Mrs. ENGELEN-KEFER (Allemagne)	-	A
M. GAHE MAHAN (Côte d'Ivoire)	-	T
Sr. MARTINEZ (Argentine)	-	A
M. MEDDAHI (Tunisie)	-	T
Mme MOMBO MOUELET (Gabon)	-	T
M. NUMA (Haïti)	-	A
M. OULD BEYE (Mauritanie)	-	T
Mr. OYERINDE (Nigéria)	-	T
Mr. SUKHBAATAR (Mongolie)	-	A

---

[1] T: Regular member / membre Titulaire / miembro titular   S: Substitute member / membre suppléant / miembro suplente
A: Deputy member / membre adjoint / miembro adjunto   O: Observer member / membre observateur / miembro observadore

changer/change/cambiar

Mr. CHIBEBE (Zimbabwe)	A	T
Mr. RUZIVE (Zimbabwe)	T	A

delete/supprimer/suprimir

M. ROMDHANE (Tunisie)	T	

COMMITTEE ON SAFETY AND HEALTH

COMMISSION DE LA SECURITE ET DE LA SANTE

COMISIÓN DE LA SEGURIDAD Y SALUD

	Previous status Statut antérieur Calidad anterior	New status [1] Nouveau statut Nueva calidad

Governments - Gouvernements - Gobiernos

add/ajouter/añadir

BOTSWANA	-	T
CONGO	-	T
IRLANDE	-	T
LIBERIA	-	T
TCHAD	-	T

Employers - Employeurs - Empleadores

add/ajouter/añadir

Mr. ARNETT (Bahamas)	-	A
Sr. CABEZAS (El Salvador)	-	Suppléant de Sr. TOMASINO HURTADO

---

[1] T: Regular member / membre Titulaire / miembro titular   S: Substitute member / membre suppléant / miembro suplente
A: Deputy member / membre adjoint / miembro adjunto   O: Observer member / membre observateur / miembro observadore

changer/change/cambiar

Mr. ABDO (Egypte)	S	Suppléant de Mr. ALLAM
Mr. ALLAM (Egypte)	T	A
Ms. ASHERSON (Royaume-Uni)	S	Suppléant de Mr. LAMBERT
Mr. DREESEN (Danemark)	T	A
Ms. ETU-SEPPÄLÄ (Finlande)	S	Suppléant de Mr. RISKI
Mr. GADE (Danemark)	S	Suppléant de Mr. DREESEN
Mr. KAPEZA (Zambie)	S	Suppléant de Ms. NONDE
Mr. KUIKKO (Finlande)	S	Suppléant de Mr. RISKI
Mr. LAMBERT (Royaume-Uni)	T	A
Mr. NIINEMÄE (Estonie)	T	A
Mr. NINKOVIC (Serbie et Monténégro)	T	A
Ms. NONDE (Zambie)	T	A
Mr. RISKI (Finlande)	T	A
Mr. SCHILDER (Danemark)	S	Suppléant de Mr. DREESEN
Mr. TORBEN A. (Danemark)	S	Suppléant de Mr. DREESEN
Mr. ZOVIC (Serbie et Monténégro)	S	Suppléant de Mr. NINKOVIC

Workers - Travailleurs - Trabajadores

add/ajouter/añadir

Mme CLARA RAJAONARIVO (Madagascar)	-	T
M. MAYOMBO (Gabon)	-	A
Mme NGARI (Gabon)	-	A
Mr. SUKHBAATAR (Mongolie)	-	T

changer/change/cambiar

Mr. GEERMAN (Pays-Bas)	T	A
Mr. NASHIR ALI (Yémen)	T	A
Mr. SKÁCELÍK (République tchèque)	A	T
Mr. WOLDE MICHAEL (Ethiopie)	T	A

delete/supprimer/suprimir

M. NEJI (Tunisie)	A

---

[1] T: Regular member / membre Titulaire / miembro titular   S: Substitute member / membre suppléant / miembro suplente
A: Deputy member / membre adjoint / miembro adjunto   O: Observer member / membre observateur / miembro observadore

COMMITTEE ON THE FISHING SECTOR

COMMISSION DU SECTEUR DE LA PECHE

COMISIÓN DEL SECTOR PESQUERO

	Previous status Statut antérieur Calidad anterior	New status [1] Nouveau statut Nueva calidad

Governments - Gouvernements - Gobiernos

add/ajouter/añadir

IRLANDE	-	T
LIBERIA	-	T

Employers - Employeurs - Empleadores

changer/change/cambiar

M. CEACALOPOL (Roumanie)	S	Suppléant de M. NICOLESCU
M. COSTACHE (Roumanie)	S	Suppléant de M. NICOLESCU
Sr. ECHAVARRIA SALDARRIAGA (Colombie)	T	A
M. MIHALACHE (Roumanie)	S	Suppléant de M. NICOLESCU
Sra. MONSALVE CUELLAR (Colombie)	S	Suppléant de Sr. ECHAVARRIA SALDARRIA
M. NICOLESCU (Roumanie)	T	A

Workers - Travailleurs - Trabajadores

add/ajouter/añadir

M. BIGOT (France)	-	A
Mr. KALSAKAU (Vanuatu)	-	A
Mr. METWALLY (Egypte)	-	A
M. NEJI (Tunisie)	-	T

changer/change/cambiar

Mr. ABD EL HALIM (Egypte)	A	T
Sra. CHACÓN BRAVO (Cuba)	A	T
M. FALL (Sénégal)	T	A
Mrs. FREEMAN (Libéria)	T	A
Mr. GÖK (Turquie)	T	A
Mr. IBRAHIM (Soudan)	A	T
M. MEDDAHI (Tunisie)	T	A
Mr. MONTAÑO (Philippines)	T	A
Mr. RODRIGUES LEITE PENTEADO (Brésil)	A	T

---

[1] T: Regular member / membre Titulaire / miembro titular   S: Substitute member / membre suppléant / miembro suplente

A: Deputy member / membre adjoint / miembro adjunto   O: Observer member / membre observateur / miembro observadore

COMMITTEE ON YOUTH EMPLOYMENT

COMMISSION DE L'EMPLOI DES JEUNES

COMISIÓN DELEMPLEO DE LOS JOVENES

	Previous status	New status [1]
	Statut antérieur	Nouveau statut
	Calidad anterior	Nueva calidad

Governments - Gouvernements - Gobiernos

add/ajouter/añadir

BOTSWANA	-	T
CHYPRE	-	T
CONGO	-	T
DJIBOUTI	-	T
IRLANDE	-	T
LIBERIA	-	T

Employers - Employeurs - Empleadores

add/ajouter/añadir

Mr. BIMHA (Zimbabwe)	-	A
Mr. MUFUKARE (Zimbabwe)	-	Suppléant de Mr. BIMHA
M. ZOULA (Congo)	-	A

---

[1] T: Regular member / membre Titulaire / miembro titular   S: Substitute member / membre suppléant / miembro suplente
A: Deputy member / membre adjoint / miembro adjunto   O: Observer member / membre observateur / miembro observadore

changer/change/cambiar

M. ABEGA (Cameroun)	S	Suppléant de M. AYANGMA AMANG
M. ABRANTES (Portugal)	T	A
Mr. ANAND (Inde)	S	Suppléant de Mr. SOMANY
Sr. ARTHUR ERRAZURIZ (Chili)	T	A
M. AYANGMA AMANG (Cameroun)	T	A
Mr. BEHURIA (Inde)	S	Suppléant de Mr. SOMANY
Sr. BRUNA VARGAS (Chili)	S	Suppléant de Sr. ARTHUR ERRAZURIZ
Mr. CARLSTEDT (Suède)	S	Suppléant de Ms. LAURENT
Ms. CRONIN (Irlande)	T	A
Mr. DEWAN (Inde)	S	Suppléant de Mr. SOMANY
Mr. DREESEN (Danemark)	T	A
Mr. ELGORASHI (Soudan)	T	A
Mr. EREMEEV (Fédération de Russie)	T	A
M. FERNANDES SALGUEIRO (Portugal)	S	Suppléant de M. ABRANTES
Mr. GADE (Danemark)	S	Suppléant de Mr. DREESEN
Sr. HUMERES NOGUER (Chili)	S	Suppléant de Sr. ARTHUR ERRAZURIZ
Ms. LAURENT (Suède)	T	A
Mme LEAL (Portugal)	S	Suppléant de M. ABRANTES
Ms. MAGUIRE (Irlande)	S	Suppléant de Ms. CRONIN
Ms. MAILA (Afrique du Sud)	S	Suppléant de Mr. VAN VUUREN
Mr. OSMAN (Soudan)	S	Suppléant de Mr. ELGORASHI
Mr. PATIL (Inde)	S	Suppléant de Mr. SOMANY
Mr. POLUEKTOV (Fédération de Russie)	S	Suppléant de Mr. EREMEEV
Mr. SCHILDER (Danemark)	S	Suppléant de Mr. DREESEN
Mr. SOMANY (Inde)	T	A
Mr. SORIANO (Philippines)	T	A
Mr. TORBEN A. (Danemark)	S	Suppléant de Mr. DREESEN
Mr. TROGEN (Suède)	S	Suppléant de Ms. LAURENT
Mr. VAN VUUREN (Afrique du Sud)	T	A

Workers - Travailleurs - Trabajadores

add/ajouter/añadir

M. BEKALE (Gabon)	-	T
M. BOUAMBA (Gabon)	-	A
M. GUINDO (Mali)	-	A
Sr. MARCANO (Venezuela)	-	A
Sr. PARRA GAONA (Paraguay)	-	A
Mr. SUKHBAATAR (Mongolie)	-	A

---

1 T: Regular member / membre Titulaire / miembro titular   S: Substitute member / membre suppléant / miembro suplente
  A: Deputy member / membre adjoint / miembro adjunto   O: Observer member / membre observateur / miembro observadore

changer/change/cambiar

Mr. AL-MAHFOODH (Bahreïn)	T	A
Mr. ALMOGHRABI (Arabie saoudite)	T	A
Mr. AL-MUDAETH (Koweït)	T	A
Mr. ANKRAH (Ghana)	T	A
Mr. ANSARI (République islamique d'Iran)	T	A
Mr. ASSADALLAH (Oman)	T	A
Mr. ATALAY (Turquie)	T	A
M. ATTIGBE (Bénin)	T	A
Mr. AZKAHE (République arabe syrienne)	T	A
Mme BERRETTA (Italie)	T	A
M. BRAHMA (Maroc)	T	A
Mrs. BRSELOVÁ (Slovaquie)	T	A
Ms. CEJOVIC (Serbie et Monténégro)	T	A
Mr. CHO (République de Corée)	T	A
M. DE JESUS RODRIGUES DA COSTA (Angola)	T	A
M. DELCROIX (Belgique)	T	A
Sr. FLORES (Mexique)	T	A
Mr. GJERDING (Norvège)	T	A
Mme GOERGEN (Luxembourg)	T	A
Mr. GREP (Suriname)	T	A
Ms. HEINÄNEN (Finlande)	A	T
Sra. IBARRA (Honduras)	T	A
Ms. ILESANMI (Nigéria)	A	T
Mrs. KOULINKOVITCH (Bélarus)	T	A
Mr. LEPIK (Pologne)	T	A
Ms. MANN (Suède)	T	A
M. MANZI (Rwanda)	T	A
Mr. MICALLEF (Malte)	T	A
Mr. MOHAMED EL SENUSSI (Jamahiriya arabe libyenne)	T	A
Mr. NORDDAHL (Islande)	T	A
M. NYAMIEN MESSOU (Côte d'Ivoire)	T	A
Sr. PIUMATO (Argentine)	T	A
Mr. PRUIM (Pays-Bas)	T	A
Mme RAHMANI (Algérie)	T	A
Mr. ROBERTS (Jamaïque)	T	A
Mr. RØNTVED ANDERSEN (Danemark)	T	A
Mr. SALIH (Soudan)	T	A
Mr. SAMARASINGHE (Sri Lanka)	T	A
Sr. SORIANO (El Salvador)	T	A
Mr. SOUZA BENEDETTI (Brésil)	T	A
Ms. STRELA (Fédération de Russie)	T	A

[1] T: Regular member / membre Titulaire / miembro titular   S: Substitute member / membre suppléant / miembro suplente
A: Deputy member / membre adjoint / miembro adjunto   O: Observer member / membre observateur / miembro observadore

Mr. SYED SHAHIR (Malaisie)	T	A
M. TAIIMATZIDIS (Grèce)	T	A
M. TAZRIBINE (Belgique)	A	T
Sra. TRIANA ALVIS (Colombie)	T	A
M. TRICOCHE (France)	T	A
M. YAACOUBI (Tunisie)	T	A

delete/supprimer/suprimir

Ms. QARHASH (Yémen)	A
Mr. TAHA (Egypte)	A
M. YRA (Burkina Faso)	A

---

1 T: Regular member / membre Titulaire / miembro titular   S: Substitute member / membre suppléant / miembro suplente
   A: Deputy member / membre adjoint / miembro adjunto   O: Observer member / membre observateur / miembro observadore

Changements apportés le 6 juin 2005
Changes made on 6 June 2005
Cambios aportados el 6 de junio de 2005

COMMITTEE ON THE APPLICATION OF STANDARDS

COMMISSION DE L'APPLICATION DES NORMES

COMISIÓN DE APLICACIÓN DE NORMAS

	Previous status Statut antérieur Calidad anterior	New status [1] Nouveau statut Nueva calidad

Governments - Gouvernements - Gobiernos

add/ajouter/añadir

UKRAINE	-	T

Workers - Travailleurs - Trabajadores

add/ajouter/añadir

M. OULD BOUBOU (Mauritanie)	-	A
M. OULD MOHAMED (Mauritanie)	-	A

COMMITTEE ON SAFETY AND HEALTH

COMMISSION DE LA SECURITE ET DE LA SANTE

COMISIÓN DE LA SEGURIDAD Y SALUD

	Previous status Statut antérieur Calidad anterior	New status [1] Nouveau statut Nueva calidad

Workers - Travailleurs - Trabajadores

add/ajouter/añadir

M. OULD BOUBOU (Mauritanie)	-	A

changer/change/cambiar

M. MORDASINI (Suisse)	A	T

---

[1] T: Regular member / membre Titulaire / miembro titular   S: Substitute member / membre suppléant / miembro suplente
A: Deputy member / membre adjoint / miembro adjunto   O: Observer member / membre observateur / miembro observadore

COMMITTEE ON THE FISHING SECTOR

COMMISSION DU SECTEUR DE LA PECHE

COMISIÓN DEL SECTOR PESQUERO

	Previous status Statut antérieur Calidad anterior	New status [1] Nouveau statut Nueva calidad

Governments - Gouvernements - Gobiernos

add/ajouter/añadir

GUINEE	-	T
NOUVELLE-ZELANDE	-	T

Workers - Travailleurs - Trabajadores

add/ajouter/añadir

M. OULD MOHAMED (Mauritanie)	-	A

changer/change/cambiar

Mr. ABD EL HALIM (Egypte)	T	a
Mr. AL-ZAID (Koweït)	T	A
M. HOUNSINOU (Bénin)	A	T
M. NEJI (Tunisie)	T	A

---

[1] T: Regular member / membre Titulaire / miembro titular   S: Substitute member / membre suppléant / miembro suplente
A: Deputy member / membre adjoint / miembro adjunto   O: Observer member / membre observateur / miembro observadore

Changements apportés le 7 juin 2005
Changes made on 7 June 2005
Cambios aportados el 7 de junio de 2005

COMMITTEE ON THE APPLICATION OF STANDARDS

COMMISSION DE L'APPLICATION DES NORMES

COMISIÓN DE APLICACIÓN DE NORMAS

	Previous status Statut antérieur Calidad anterior	New status [1] Nouveau statut Nueva calidad

Employers - Employeurs - Empleadores

add/ajouter/añadir

Sr. ESPAÑA SMITH (Bolivie)	-	A
M. OUSMANE (Niger)	-	A
M. SEYBOU (Niger)	-	Suppléant de M. OUSMANE

delete/supprimer/suprimir

| Mr. PROBERT (Fidji) | A | |
| Mr. WARADI (Fidji) | S | |

Workers - Travailleurs - Trabajadores

add/ajouter/añadir

M. BECCARI (Saint-Marin)	-	T
M. CAMARA (Guinée)	-	A
Mme DIALLO BAH (Guinée)	-	T
Mr. KALSAKAU (Vanuatu)	-	A
Sr. LOPEZ FERNANDEZ (Paraguay)	-	A
Mr. NAMUDU (Fidji)	-	A
M. SCHWAAB (Suisse)	-	A
M. THOMMEN (Suisse)	-	A

changer/change/cambiar

M. OULD BEYE (Mauritanie)	T	A
M. OULD BOUBOU (Mauritanie)	A	T
Mme SALIMATA (Côte d'Ivoire)	T	A
Mr. SINGH (Fidji)	A	T

delete/supprimer/suprimir

| M. LEPORI (Suisse) | T | |

---

[1] T: Regular member / membre Titulaire / miembro titular   S: Substitute member / membre suppléant / miembro suplente
A: Deputy member / membre adjoint / miembro adjunto   O: Observer member / membre observateur / miembro observadore

COMMITTEE ON SAFETY AND HEALTH

COMMISSION DE LA SECURITE ET DE LA SANTE

COMISIÓN DE LA SEGURIDAD Y SALUD

	Previous status Statut antérieur Calidad anterior	New status [1] Nouveau statut Nueva calidad

Employers - Employeurs - Empleadores

add/ajouter/añadir

Sr. ANDINO GÓMEZ (El Salvador)	-	Suppléant de Sr. TOMASINO HURTADO
Sr. CHÁVEZ QUINTANILLA (El Salvador)	-	Suppléant de Sr. TOMASINO HURTADO
Sr. ESPAÑA SMITH (Bolivie)	-	A
M. OUSMANE (Niger)	-	A
M. SEYBOU (Niger)	-	Suppléant de M. OUSMANE

changer/change/cambiar

Mr. AL KHOOR (Bahreïn)	S	Suppléant de Mr. AL SALEH
Mr. AL SALEH (Bahreïn)	T	A
M. BSAT (Liban)	S	Suppléant de M. HAMADEH
M. HAMADEH (Liban)	T	A
Mr. ZAWDE (Ethiopie)	T	A

Workers - Travailleurs - Trabajadores

add/ajouter/añadir

M. BATOUM (Djibouti)	-	A
M. DIRIEH (Djibouti)	-	T
M. DURY (Luxembourg)	-	A
Ms. DWYER (Irlande)	-	A
M. FOFANA (Guinée)	-	A
Sr. HERNÁNDEZ GARCÍA (El Salvador)	-	A
Mr. NAMUDU (Fidji)	-	T
Mr. SINGH (Fidji)	-	A
M. THOMMEN (Suisse)	-	A
Sr. VÁSQUEZ JOVEL (El Salvador)	-	T
Sr. VILLALOBOS PASTÉN (Chili)	-	A

---

[1] T: Regular member / membre Titulaire / miembro titular   S: Substitute member / membre suppléant / miembro suplente
A: Deputy member / membre adjoint / miembro adjunto   O: Observer member / membre observateur / miembro observadore

changer/change/cambiar

Mr. ABDULLAH (Bahreïn)	T	A
Mme CLARA RAJAONARIVO (Madagascar)	T	A
Mr. GEERMAN (Pays-Bas)	A	T
M. GLELE KAKAÏ (Bénin)	T	A
Mr. KUPPAN (Maurice)	T	A
Mrs. SCHRÖDER (Allemagne)	A	T
Mr. SKÁCELÍK (République tchèque)	T	A
Mr. SOUZA (Brésil)	T	A
Mr. SUKHBAATAR (Mongolie)	T	A
Sr. VIDELA VILLALOBOS (Chili)	T	A

COMMITTEE ON THE FISHING SECTOR
COMMISSION DU SECTEUR DE LA PECHE
COMISIÓN DEL SECTOR PESQUERO

Previous status   New status [1]
Statut antérieur   Nouveau statut
Calidad anterior   Nueva calidad

Employers - Employeurs - Empleadores

delete/supprimer/suprimir

Mr. PROBERT (Fidji)	A	
Mr. WARADI (Fidji)	S	

Workers - Travailleurs - Trabajadores

add/ajouter/añadir

M. FOFANA (Guinée)	-	T
Sr. MONDRAGÓN (Mexique)	-	A
M. MUKALAY HANGA (République dém. du Congo)	-	A
Mr. NAMUDU (Fidji)	-	A
Sr. RODRÍGUEZ (Venezuela)	-	A
Mr. SINGH (Fidji)	-	A

changer/change/cambiar

Mr. GRAVESON (Royaume-Uni)	T	A
Mr. IBRAHIM (Soudan)	T	A
Mr. MASEMOLA (Afrique du Sud)	T	A
Mr. TEICHERT (Allemagne)	T	A
Mr. THOMAS (Inde)	T	A

---

[1] T: Regular member / membre Titulaire / miembro titular   S: Substitute member / membre suppléant / miembro suplente
A: Deputy member / membre adjoint / miembro adjunto   O: Observer member / membre observateur / miembro observadore

COMMITTEE ON YOUTH EMPLOYMENT

COMMISSION DE L'EMPLOI DES JEUNES

COMISIÓN DELEMPLEO DE LOS JOVENES

	Previous status	New status [1]
	Statut antérieur	Nouveau statut
	Calidad anterior	Nueva calidad

Employers - Employeurs - Empleadores

add/ajouter/añadir

M. BUKASA TSHIENDA (République dém. du Congo)	-	Suppléant de M. NTAMBWE KITENGE
M. NGUB'USIM MPEZ-NKA (République dém. du Congo)	-	Suppléant de M. NTAMBWE KITENGE
M. NTAMBWE KITENGE (République dém. du Congo)	-	A
M. OUSMANE (Niger)	-	A
M. SEYBOU (Niger)	-	Suppléant de M. OUSMANE

Workers - Travailleurs - Trabajadores

add/ajouter/añadir

M. CAMARA (Guinée)	-	T
Mme DIALLO BAH (Guinée)	-	A
Ms. DWYER (Irlande)	-	A
M. PIERMATTEI (Saint-Marin)	-	T
M. SCHWAAB (Suisse)	-	A
Ms. VRIELING (Pays-Bas)	-	T

---

[1] T: Regular member / membre Titulaire / miembro titular   S: Substitute member / membre suppléant / miembro suplente

A: Deputy member / membre adjoint / miembro adjunto   O: Observer member / membre observateur / miembro observadore

Changements apportés le 8 juin 2005
Changes made on 8 June 2005
Cambios aportados el 8 de junio de 2005

COMMITTEE ON THE APPLICATION OF STANDARDS
COMMISSION DE L'APPLICATION DES NORMES
COMISIÓN DE APLICACIÓN DE NORMAS

	Previous status Statut antérieur Calidad anterior	New status [1] Nouveau statut Nueva calidad

Employers - Employeurs - Empleadores

add/ajouter/añadir

M. PIERRE FRANCOIS (Haïti)	-	Suppléant de Mme VICTOR
Mr. SEMRAU (Etats-Unis)	-	Suppléant de Mr. POTTER
Mme VICTOR (Haïti)	-	A

Workers - Travailleurs - Trabajadores

add/ajouter/añadir

M. BISSALA (Cameroun)	-	A
Mr. CHIRIAC (République de Moldova)	-	A
Sr. GUTIÉRREZ MADUEÑO (Pérou)	-	T
M. LUYEYE NGONGITE (République dém. du Congo)	-	A
M. MINTSA MI-ESSONO (Gabon)	-	A
Sr. PINEDA (Mexique)	-	A
Sr. SALINAS (Argentine)	-	A
Sr. SILVA BERÓN (Chili)	-	A

---

[1] T: Regular member / membre Titulaire / miembro titular   S: Substitute member / membre suppléant / miembro suplente
A: Deputy member / membre adjoint / miembro adjunto   O: Observer member / membre observateur / miembro observadore

changer/change/cambiar

Mr. AL-AZMI (Koweït)	T	A
Mme DIALLO BAH (Guinée)	T	A
Mr. DZHULYK (Ukraine)	T	A
Mr. HASAN (Bangladesh)	T	A
Mr. HOVHANNISYAN (Arménie)	T	A
Mr. KALIMANJIRA (Malawi)	T	A
M. KPOKOLO (République centrafricaine)	T	A
M. NTONE DIBOTI (Cameroun)	T	A
M. OULD BOUBOU (Mauritanie)	T	A
Mr. OYERINDE (Nigéria)	T	A
Mr. SILABAN (Indonésie)	T	A
Mr. SINGH (Fidji)	T	A
M. SITOE (Mozambique)	T	A
Mr. TEMBO (Zambie)	T	A
Mr. YURKIN (Ukraine)	T	A

COMMITTEE ON SAFETY AND HEALTH
COMMISSION DE LA SECURITE ET DE LA SANTE
COMISIÓN DE LA SEGURIDAD Y SALUD

	Previous status Statut antérieur Calidad anterior	New status [1] Nouveau statut Nueva calidad

Governments - Gouvernements - Gobiernos

add/ajouter/añadir

REP. DE MOLDOVA	-	T

Employers - Employeurs - Empleadores

add/ajouter/añadir

M. ANDRÉ (Angola)	-	Suppléant de M. GOMES
Mlle BANG ONSENGDET (République dém. populaire lao)	-	A
Sra. ESCOTO ABREU (République dominicaine)	-	A
Mr. GUZAVICIUS (Lituanie)	-	A
Ms. MEAS (Cambodge)	-	A
M. PIERRE FRANCOIS (Haïti)	-	Suppléant de Mme VICTOR
Mrs. ROMCHATTONGH (Thaïlande)	-	Suppléant de Mr. CHANPORNPONG
Mme VICTOR (Haïti)	-	A

---

[1] T: Regular member / membre Titulaire / miembro titular   S: Substitute member / membre suppléant / miembro suplente
A: Deputy member / membre adjoint / miembro adjunto   O: Observer member / membre observateur / miembro observadore

changer/change/cambiar

M. AYOUCHE (Maroc)	S	Suppléant de M. JALAL
M. CHAOUKI (Maroc)	S	Suppléant de M. JALAL
M. JALAL (Maroc)	T	A

Workers - Travailleurs - Trabajadores

add/ajouter/añadir

Mme GHALI (Maroc)	-	A
Mr. HUTAPEA (Indonésie)	-	A
M. MAYALA WU MWESI MWANZA (République dém. du Congo)	-	A
Mr. PAJOBO (Ouganda)	-	T

changer/change/cambiar

Sr. ABREU (République dominicaine)	T	A
Sra. AGUILAR TORRES (Chili)	T	A
Mr. HOTOVY (République tchèque)	A	T
M. KABULO MBODYAWASHA (République dém. du Congo)	T	A
M. MORDASINI (Suisse)	T	A
Sr. VÁSQUEZ JOVEL (El Salvador)	T	A
Mme ZAHI (Maroc)	T	A

delete/supprimer/suprimir

Mr. SKÁCELÍK (République tchèque)	A	

COMMITTEE ON THE FISHING SECTOR
COMMISSION DU SECTEUR DE LA PECHE
COMISIÓN DEL SECTOR PESQUERO

	Previous status Statut antérieur Calidad anterior	New status [1] Nouveau statut Nueva calidad

Employers - Employeurs - Empleadores

changer/change/cambiar

Mr. AL MANAA (Qatar)	T	A
Mr. AL-HAIDAR (Qatar)	S	Suppléant de Mr. AL MANAA
Sr. ARTHUR ERRAZURIZ (Chili)	T	A
Mr. JEFFERY (Papouasie-Nouvelle-Guinée)	T	A
Mr. MAGNUSSON (Islande)	S	Suppléant de Ms. STEFANSDOTTIR
Sr. PIZARRO MAASS (Chili)	S	Suppléant de Sr. ARTHUR ERRAZURIZ
Ms. STEFANSDOTTIR (Islande)	T	A

---

[1] T: Regular member / membre Titulaire / miembro titular   S: Substitute member / membre suppléant / miembro suplente
A: Deputy member / membre adjoint / miembro adjunto   O: Observer member / membre observateur / miembro observadore

Workers - Travailleurs - Trabajadores

add/ajouter/añadir

Sr. JIMÉNEZ (Espagne)	-	A
M. MINTSA MI-ESSONO (Gabon)	-	T
Sr. VILLALOBOS PASTÉN (Chili)	-	A

changer/change/cambiar

Mr. ABD EL HALIM (Egypte)	A	T
Mr. AL-ZAID (Koweït)	A	T
Sra. CHACÓN BRAVO (Cuba)	T	A
M. DOS SANTOS CARDOSO MACEDO (Portugal)	T	A
M. FOFANA (Guinée)	T	A

delete/supprimer/suprimir

M. BISSALA (Cameroun)	A

COMMITTEE ON YOUTH EMPLOYMENT

COMMISSION DE L'EMPLOI DES JEUNES

COMISIÓN DELEMPLEO DE LOS JOVENES

Previous status   New status [1]
Statut antérieur   Nouveau statut
Calidad anterior   Nueva calidad

Governments - Gouvernements - Gobiernos

add/ajouter/añadir

REP. DE MOLDOVA	-	T

Employers - Employeurs - Empleadores

add/ajouter/añadir

M. MUTABUNGA (République dém. du Congo)	-	Suppléant de M. NTAMBWE KITENGE
M. VAN DAMME (Belgique)	-	Suppléant de M. DE KOSTER

---

[1] T: Regular member / membre Titulaire / miembro titular   S: Substitute member / membre suppléant / miembro suplente
    A: Deputy member / membre adjoint / miembro adjunto   O: Observer member / membre observateur / miembro observadore

changer/change/cambiar

Mr. AL-FALIJ (Koweït)	S	Suppléant de Mr. AL-HAROUN
Mr. AL-HAROUN (Koweït)	T	A
Mr. BANDEEBIRE (Ouganda)	S	Suppléant de Ms. SSENABULYA
Mme BARDANI (Grèce)	S	Suppléant de M. KYRIAKOPOULOS
M. BAXEVANIS (Grèce)	S	Suppléant de M. KYRIAKOPOULOS
M. CHARAKAS (Grèce)	S	Suppléant de M. KYRIAKOPOULOS
M. HAMADEH (Liban)	T	A
Mme IOANNIDOU (Grèce)	S	Suppléant de M. KYRIAKOPOULOS
Mme KAKALIOURA (Grèce)	S	Suppléant de M. KYRIAKOPOULOS
Mme KOUTSIVITOU (Grèce)	S	Suppléant de M. KYRIAKOPOULOS
M. KYRIAKOPOULOS (Grèce)	T	A
Mr. LAPENGA (Ouganda)	S	Suppléant de Ms. SSENABULYA
Mr. MAGYAR (Hongrie)	S	Suppléant de Mr. ROLEK
Mr. NATHAN (Malaisie)	T	A
Mr. ROLEK (Hongrie)	T	A
Mr. SHAMSUDDIN (Malaisie)	S	Suppléant de Mr. NATHAN
Ms. SSENABULYA (Ouganda)	T	A
Mr. SZIRMAI (Hongrie)	S	Suppléant de Mr. ROLEK
Mr. SZÜCS (Hongrie)	S	Suppléant de Mr. ROLEK
Mr. THENGE (Ouganda)	S	Suppléant de Ms. SSENABULYA
M. UINGE (Mozambique)	T	A
Ms. VARGA (Hongrie)	S	Suppléant de Mr. ROLEK

delete/supprimer/suprimir

Ms. CADOGAN (Barbade)	S	

---

[1] T: Regular member / membre Titulaire / miembro titular   S: Substitute member / membre suppléant / miembro suplente
A: Deputy member / membre adjoint / miembro adjunto   O: Observer member / membre observateur / miembro observadore

Changements apportés le 9 juin 2005
Changes made on 9 June 2005
Cambios aportados el 9 de junio de 2005

COMMITTEE ON THE APPLICATION OF STANDARDS

COMMISSION DE L'APPLICATION DES NORMES

COMISIÓN DE APLICACIÓN DE NORMAS

	Previous status Statut antérieur Calidad anterior	New status [1] Nouveau statut Nueva calidad

Governments - Gouvernements - Gobiernos

changer/change/cambiar

ISRAEL	T	A

Employers - Employeurs - Empleadores

changer/change/cambiar

Mr. ABDULLAH (Indonésie)	S	Suppléant de Mr. RACHMAN
Mr. AL-KHUNJI (Oman)	S	Suppléant de Mr. AL-RUBAIAI
Mr. AL-RUBAIAI (Oman)	T	A
Mr. ANAND (Inde)	S	Suppléant de Mr. SOMANY
Mr. BOTCHWAY (Ghana)	S	Suppléant de Mr. MENSA
Ms. CERQUEIRA COIMBRA DUQUE (Brésil)	S	Suppléant de Mr. LIMA GODOY
Mr. GUNAWAN (Indonésie)	S	Suppléant de Mr. RACHMAN
Mr. KOOMSON (Ghana)	S	Suppléant de Mr. MENSA
Mr. LIMA GODOY (Brésil)	T	A
Mr. LOHIA (Inde)	S	Suppléant de Mr. SOMANY
Mr. MENSA (Ghana)	T	A
Ms. OWUSU (Ghana)	S	Suppléant de Mr. MENSA
Mr. PANT (Inde)	S	Suppléant de Mr. SOMANY
Mr. RACHMAN (Indonésie)	T	A
Ms. RONDON LINHARES (Brésil)	S	Suppléant de Mr. LIMA GODOY
Mr. SINJANI (Malawi)	T	A
Mr. SOMANY (Inde)	T	A
Mr. YEMER (Ethiopie)	S	Suppléant de Mr. ZAWDE
Mr. ZAWDE (Ethiopie)	T	A

---

[1] T: Regular member / membre Titulaire / miembro titular   S: Substitute member / membre suppléant / miembro suplente
A: Deputy member / membre adjoint / miembro adjunto   O: Observer member / membre observateur / miembro observadore

Workers - Travailleurs - Trabajadores

add/ajouter/añadir

M. AIT ALI (Algérie)	-	T
Mme ALMEUS (Haïti)	-	T
Sra. CANO MORENO (Panama)	-	A
Mme COROSSACZ (Italie)	-	A
Sr. GONZÁLEZ GAITÁN (Nicaragua)	-	A
Sr. JIMÉNEZ (Nicaragua)	-	T
M. SOUZA (Congo)	-	A

changer/change/cambiar

Mr. MACAEFA (Lesotho)	T	A

delete/supprimer/suprimir

M. BENMOUHOUB (Algérie)	T	

COMMITTEE ON SAFETY AND HEALTH

COMMISSION DE LA SECURITE ET DE LA SANTE

COMISIÓN DE LA SEGURIDAD Y SALUD

	Previous status Statut antérieur Calidad anterior	New status [1] Nouveau statut Nueva calidad

Employers - Employeurs - Empleadores

add/ajouter/añadir

Mrs. APPIA-NKANSAH (Ghana)	-	Suppléant de Mr. MENSA

changer/change/cambiar

Sr. ALDAO ZAPIOLA (Argentine)	S	Suppléant de Sr. MENDEZ
Sr. HERMIDA MARTINEZ (Argentine)	S	Suppléant de Sr. MENDEZ
Sr. MANTILLA (Argentine)	S	Suppléant de Sr. MENDEZ
Sr. MENDEZ (Argentine)	T	A

Workers - Travailleurs - Trabajadores

add/ajouter/añadir

Sr. GONZÁLEZ GAITÁN (Nicaragua)	-	A
Sr. JIMÉNEZ (Nicaragua)	-	A
Sr. LOPEZ (Argentine)	-	A

---

[1] T: Regular member / membre Titulaire / miembro titular   S: Substitute member / membre suppléant / miembro suplente
A: Deputy member / membre adjoint / miembro adjunto   O: Observer member / membre observateur / miembro observadore

changer/change/cambiar

Mr. JIN (Chine)	T	A
Mr. NAMUDU (Fidji)	T	A
Mr. PAJOBO (Ouganda)	T	A
Mr. WILLIAMS (Libéria)	T	A

COMMITTEE ON THE FISHING SECTOR
COMMISSION DU SECTEUR DE LA PECHE
COMISIÓN DEL SECTOR PESQUERO

Previous status   New status [1]
Statut antérieur   Nouveau statut
Calidad anterior   Nueva calidad

Governments - Gouvernements - Gobiernos

delete/supprimer/suprimir

ISLANDE	T	

Employers - Employeurs - Empleadores

add/ajouter/añadir

Sr. SEGURA ESPINOZA (Nicaragua)	-	A

changer/change/cambiar

Ms. SSENABULYA (Ouganda)	T	A
Mr. THENGE (Ouganda)	S	Suppléant de Ms. SSENABULYA

Workers - Travailleurs - Trabajadores

add/ajouter/añadir

Ms. CABATINGAN (Philippines)	-	A

changer/change/cambiar

Mr. ABD EL HALIM (Egypte)	T	A
Mr. AL-ZAID (Koweït)	T	A
Mr. GUNNARSSON (Islande)	T	A
M. MINTSA MI-ESSONO (Gabon)	T	A
Mr. SULISTYANTO (Indonésie)	T	A

---

[1] T: Regular member / membre Titulaire / miembro titular   S: Substitute member / membre suppléant / miembro suplente
A: Deputy member / membre adjoint / miembro adjunto   O: Observer member / membre observateur / miembro observadore

COMMITTEE ON YOUTH EMPLOYMENT

COMMISSION DE L'EMPLOI DES JEUNES

COMISIÓN DELEMPLEO DE LOS JOVENES

	Previous status Statut antérieur Calidad anterior	New status [1] Nouveau statut Nueva calidad

Employers - Employeurs - Empleadores

add/ajouter/añadir

Mme DEMBO KATOHUKE (République dém. du Congo)	-	Suppléant de M. NTAMBWE KITENGE

changer/change/cambiar

Mr. ALGAIZI (Emirats arabes unis)	S	Suppléant de Mr. KHAMMAS
M. AYOUCHE (Maroc)	S	Suppléant de M. JALAL
Mrs. BENONISEN (Norvège)	S	Suppléant de Mrs. RIDDERVOLD
M. BOUDHAIM (Maroc)	S	Suppléant de M. JALAL
M. DI NIOLA (Italie)	S	Suppléant de Mme SASSO MAZZUFFERI
Mrs. EGEDE-NISSEN (Norvège)	S	Suppléant de Mrs. RIDDERVOLD
Ms. ETU-SEPPÄLÄ (Finlande)	S	Suppléant de Mr. RISKI
M. FERRARA (Italie)	S	Suppléant de Mme SASSO MAZZUFFERI
Mr. FINLAY (Canada)	T	A
M. JALAL (Maroc)	T	A
Mr. JOHANNESEN (Norvège)	S	Suppléant de Mrs. RIDDERVOLD
Mr. KELLY (Canada)	S	Suppléant de Mr. FINLAY
Mr. KHAMMAS (Emirats arabes unis)	T	A
Mr. LAMBERT (Royaume-Uni)	T	A
Mr. MATTAR ALKAABI (Emirats arabes unis)	S	Suppléant de Mr. KHAMMAS
Mr. PROBERT (Fidji)	T	A
Mr. RÄSÄNEN (Finlande)	S	Suppléant de Mr. RISKI
Mrs. RIDDERVOLD (Norvège)	T	A
Mr. RISKI (Finlande)	T	A
Mme ROSSI (Italie)	S	Suppléant de Mme SASSO MAZZUFFERI
Mme SASSO MAZZUFFERI (Italie)	T	A
Ms. VAN DER LINDEN (Royaume-Uni)	S	Suppléant de Mr. LAMBERT
Mr. WARADI (Fidji)	S	Suppléant de Mr. PROBERT
Mr. WARMAN (Royaume-Uni)	S	Suppléant de Mr. LAMBERT

---

[1] T: Regular member / membre Titulaire / miembro titular   S: Substitute member / membre suppléant / miembro suplente
A: Deputy member / membre adjoint / miembro adjunto   O: Observer member / membre observateur / miembro observadore

Workers - Travailleurs - Trabajadores

add/ajouter/añadir

Mr. DIOMEDOUS (Chypre)	-	A
M. EKANGA (Congo)	-	A
Sr. LOPEZ FERNANDEZ (Paraguay)	-	A
M. NGUIE (Congo)	-	T

changer/change/cambiar

M. BEKALE (Gabon)	T	A
M. CAMARA (Guinée)	T	A
Sr. CANALES HUENCHUAN (Chili)	T	A
Mr. SOUZA BENEDETTI (Brésil)	A	T

---

[1] T: Regular member / membre Titulaire / miembro titular   S: Substitute member / membre suppléant / miembro suplente
A: Deputy member / membre adjoint / miembro adjunto   O: Observer member / membre observateur / miembro observadore

Changements apportés le 10 juin 2005
Changes made on 10 June 2005
Cambios aportados el 10 de junio de 2005

COMMITTEE ON THE APPLICATION OF STANDARDS

COMMISSION DE L'APPLICATION DES NORMES

COMISIÓN DE APLICACIÓN DE NORMAS

	Previous status Statut antérieur Calidad anterior	New status [1] Nouveau statut Nueva calidad

Governments - Gouvernements - Gobiernos

add/ajouter/añadir

BANGLADESH	-	T

Employers - Employeurs - Empleadores

changer/change/cambiar

Sr. DE REGIL (Mexique)	S	Suppléant de Sr. HALKIN
Sr. GARCÍA (Mexique)	S	Suppléant de Sr. HALKIN
Sr. GUTIÉRREZ (Mexique)	S	Suppléant de Sr. HALKIN
Sr. HALKIN (Mexique)	T	A
Sr. MENA (Mexique)	S	Suppléant de Sr. HALKIN
Sra. MORALES (Mexique)	S	Suppléant de Sr. HALKIN
Sr. YLLANES (Mexique)	S	Suppléant de Sr. HALKIN

Workers - Travailleurs - Trabajadores

add/ajouter/añadir

Mr. DAVID (Indonésie)	-	A
Mr. MIKLIC (Slovénie)	-	A
M. MUKALAY HANGA (République dém. du Congo)	-	A
M. OULD ALY OULD SIDI OUMAR (Mauritanie)	-	A
M. PICANDET (France)	-	A
Mr. WOLDE MICHAEL (Ethiopie)	-	A

---

[1] T: Regular member / membre Titulaire / miembro titular   S: Substitute member / membre suppléant / miembro suplente
A: Deputy member / membre adjoint / miembro adjunto   O: Observer member / membre observateur / miembro observadore

COMMITTEE ON SAFETY AND HEALTH

COMMISSION DE LA SECURITE ET DE LA SANTE

COMISIÓN DE LA SEGURIDAD Y SALUD

	Previous status / **Statut antérieur** / **Calidad anterior**	**New status** [1] / **Nouveau statut** / **Nueva calidad**

Governments - Gouvernements - Gobiernos

add/ajouter/añadir

BANGLADESH	-	T

Employers - Employeurs - Empleadores

changer/change/cambiar

Mr. ABDO (Egypte)	S	A
Sra. BARONA (Mexique)	S	Suppléant de Sr. HALKIN
Sr. DE REGIL (Mexique)	S	Suppléant de Sr. HALKIN
Sr. HALKIN (Mexique)	T	A
Sr. MENA (Mexique)	S	Suppléant de Sr. HALKIN

Workers - Travailleurs - Trabajadores

add/ajouter/añadir

Mr. BALDZENS (Lettonie)	-	A
M. OLIVIER (France)	-	A
M. SEHIMI (Tunisie)	-	A

delete/supprimer/suprimir

M. LECOIN (France)	A	

COMMITTEE ON THE FISHING SECTOR

COMMISSION DU SECTEUR DE LA PECHE

COMISIÓN DEL SECTOR PESQUERO

	Previous status / **Statut antérieur** / **Calidad anterior**	**New status** [1] / **Nouveau statut** / **Nueva calidad**

Governments - Gouvernements - Gobiernos

add/ajouter/añadir

BANGLADESH	-	T

---

[1] T: Regular member / membre Titulaire / miembro titular   S: Substitute member / membre suppléant / miembro suplente
A: Deputy member / membre adjoint / miembro adjunto   O: Observer member / membre observateur / miembro observadore

Employers - Employeurs - Empleadores

changer/change/cambiar

Sr. GONZÁLEZ RODRÍGUEZ (Cuba)	S	Suppléant de Sr. PARRA ROJAS
Sr. MESA GARCÍA (Cuba)	S	Suppléant de Sr. PARRA ROJAS
Sr. PARRA ROJAS (Cuba)	T	A
Mr. SOMANY (Inde)	T	A
Mr. TODI (Inde)	S	Suppléant de Mr. SOMANY
Sr. VIDAUT MÁRQUEZ (Cuba)	S	Suppléant de Sr. PARRA ROJAS

Workers - Travailleurs - Trabajadores

changer/change/cambiar

Mr. ABD EL HALIM (Egypte)	A	T
Mr. AL-ZAID (Koweït)	A	T
Mr. DUBINSKI (Pologne)	T	A

delete/supprimer/suprimir

M. MUKALAY HANGA (République dém. du Congo)	A

COMMITTEE ON YOUTH EMPLOYMENT
COMMISSION DE L'EMPLOI DES JEUNES
COMISIÓN DELEMPLEO DE LOS JOVENES

	Previous status Statut antérieur Calidad anterior	New status [1] Nouveau statut Nueva calidad

Governments - Gouvernements - Gobiernos

add/ajouter/añadir

BANGLADESH	-	T

Employers - Employeurs - Empleadores

add/ajouter/añadir

Mr. ABDO (Egypte)	-	A

---

[1] T: Regular member / membre Titulaire / miembro titular   S: Substitute member / membre suppléant / miembro suplente
A: Deputy member / membre adjoint / miembro adjunto   O: Observer member / membre observateur / miembro observadore

changer/change/cambiar

Sr. AIZPURÚA (Panama)	T	A
Sr. ARANGO VALLEJO (Colombie)	S	Suppléant de Sr. ECHAVARRIA SALDARRIA
Mme AWASSI ATSIMADJA (Gabon)	T	A
Sr. BOTERO ARANGO (Colombie)	S	Suppléant de Sr. ECHAVARRIA SALDARRIA
Sr. CARVAJAL (Mexique)	S	Suppléant de Sr. HALKIN
Sr. DE REGIL (Mexique)	S	Suppléant de Sr. HALKIN
Sr. ECHAVARRIA SALDARRIAGA (Colombie)	T	A
Sra. GARZA (Mexique)	S	Suppléant de Sr. HALKIN
Sr. GUTIÉRREZ (Mexique)	S	Suppléant de Sr. HALKIN
Sr. HALKIN (Mexique)	T	A
Mrs. HORVATIC (Croatie)	T	A
Ms. KATIC (Croatie)	S	Suppléant de Mrs. HORVATIC
Sr. LINERO (Panama)	S	Suppléant de Sr. AIZPURÚA
Sr. MEJIA GIRALDO (Colombie)	S	Suppléant de Sr. ECHAVARRIA SALDARRIA
Sr. MENA (Mexique)	S	Suppléant de Sr. HALKIN
Mrs. MOHAMED (Egypte)	S	Suppléant de Mr. ABDO
Sr. PIGNATARO PACHECO (Costa Rica)	T	A
Sr. YLLANES (Mexique)	S	Suppléant de Sr. HALKIN

Workers - Travailleurs - Trabajadores

add/ajouter/añadir

M. DIOP (Sénégal)	-	A
Mr. LOW KONG SAN (Singapour)	-	A
M. OSSETE (Congo)	-	A
Ms. QARHASH (Yémen)	-	A
M. SAADE (Liban)	-	A
Mr. TAHA (Egypte)	-	A

changer/change/cambiar

Ms. ILESANMI (Nigéria)	T	A
M. NGUIE (Congo)	T	A
M. PIERMATTEI (Saint-Marin)	T	A
Mr. SOUZA BENEDETTI (Brésil)	T	A
Ms. VRIELING (Pays-Bas)	T	A

---

[1] T: Regular member / membre Titulaire / miembro titular   S: Substitute member / membre suppléant / miembro suplente
A: Deputy member / membre adjoint / miembro adjunto   O: Observer member / membre observateur / miembro observadore

Changements apportés le 11 juin 2005
Changes made on 11 June 2005
Cambios aportados el 11 de junio de 2005

COMMITTEE ON THE APPLICATION OF STANDARDS

COMMISSION DE L'APPLICATION DES NORMES

COMISIÓN DE APLICACIÓN DE NORMAS

	Previous status Statut antérieur Calidad anterior	New status [1] Nouveau statut Nueva calidad

Governments - Gouvernements - Gobiernos

add/ajouter/añadir

CAP-VERT	-	T
SAINT-VINCENT-ET-GRENADINES	-	T

Employers - Employeurs - Empleadores

add/ajouter/añadir

Sr. CAPURRO (Paraguay)	-	A
Mme CORADO (Cap-Vert)	-	A
M. HEMEDI (République dém. du Congo)	-	Suppléant de M. NTAMBWE KITENGE
M. NTAMBWE KITENGE (République dém. du Congo)	-	A
Mr. PROVIDENCE (Saint-Vincent et-les Grenadines)	-	A

changer/change/cambiar

Mrs. BENONISEN (Norvège)	S	Suppléant de Mrs. RIDDERVOLD
Sr. CARDOZO GONZÁLEZ (Colombie)	S	Suppléant de Sr. ECHAVARRÍA SALDARRIA
Mr. CENTEL (Turquie)	S	Suppléant de Mr. PIRLER
Sr. ECHAVARRÍA SALDARRIAGA (Colombie)	T	A
Mrs. EGEDE-NISSEN (Norvège)	S	Suppléant de Mrs. RIDDERVOLD
Mr. ELGORASHI (Soudan)	T	A
Sr. OJALVO PRIETO (Colombie)	S	Suppléant de Sr. ECHAVARRÍA SALDARRIA
Mr. OSMAN (Soudan)	S	Suppléant de Mr. ELGORASHI
Mr. PIRLER (Turquie)	T	A
Mrs. RIDDERVOLD (Norvège)	T	A

Workers - Travailleurs - Trabajadores

add/ajouter/añadir

Ms. MANDEVILLE (Saint-Vincent et-les Grenadines)	-	A
M. MBOU MBINE (Gabon)	-	A

---

[1] T: Regular member / membre Titulaire / miembro titular   S: Substitute member / membre suppléant / miembro suplente
A: Deputy member / membre adjoint / miembro adjunto   O: Observer member / membre observateur / miembro observadore

delete/supprimer/suprimir

    Mr. PRUIM (Pays-Bas)   A

COMMITTEE ON SAFETY AND HEALTH
COMMISSION DE LA SECURITE ET DE LA SANTE
COMISIÓN DE LA SEGURIDAD Y SALUD

	Previous status Statut antérieur Calidad anterior	New status [1] Nouveau statut Nueva calidad

Governments - Gouvernements - Gobiernos

add/ajouter/añadir

| CAP-VERT | - | T |
| SAINT-VINCENT-ET-GRENADINES | - | T |

Employers - Employeurs - Empleadores

add/ajouter/añadir

| Mme CORADO (Cap-Vert) | - | A |
| Mrs. MOHAMED (Egypte) | - | Suppléant de Mr. ABDO |

Workers - Travailleurs - Trabajadores

changer/change/cambiar

| Mr. NAMUDU (Fidji) | A | T |

COMMITTEE ON THE FISHING SECTOR
COMMISSION DU SECTEUR DE LA PECHE
COMISIÓN DEL SECTOR PESQUERO

	Previous status Statut antérieur Calidad anterior	New status [1] Nouveau statut Nueva calidad

Governments - Gouvernements - Gobiernos

add/ajouter/añadir

| SAINT-VINCENT-ET-GRENADINES | - | T |

---

[1] T: Regular member / membre Titulaire / miembro titular   S: Substitute member / membre suppléant / miembro suplente
    A: Deputy member / membre adjoint / miembro adjunto   O: Observer member / membre observateur / miembro observadore

Employers - Employeurs - Empleadores

add/ajouter/añadir

Mme CORADO (Cap-Vert)	-	A

Workers - Travailleurs - Trabajadores

add/ajouter/añadir

M. SKOULATAKIS (Grèce)	-	A
M. ZOUNNADJALA (Togo)	-	A

changer/change/cambiar

Mr. AL-ZAID (Koweït)	T	A
Mr. GUAN (Chine)	T	A

delete/supprimer/suprimir

Mr. KONDO (Japon)	A	
Mr. RODRIGUES LEITE PENTEADO (Brésil)	T	

COMMITTEE ON YOUTH EMPLOYMENT

COMMISSION DE L'EMPLOI DES JEUNES

COMISIÓN DELEMPLEO DE LOS JOVENES

	Previous status	**New status** [1]
	Statut antérieur	**Nouveau statut**
	Calidad anterior	**Nueva calidad**

Governments - Gouvernements - Gobiernos

add/ajouter/añadir

GUINEE EQUATORIALE	-	T
SAINT-VINCENT-ET-GRENADINES	-	T

Employers - Employeurs - Empleadores

add/ajouter/añadir

Sr. CAPURRO (Paraguay)	-	A
Mme CORADO (Cap-Vert)	-	A
M. KADER (Niger)	-	Suppléant de M. OUSMANE
Sr. MATZEN MACOSO (Guinée équatoriale)	-	A

---

[1] T: Regular member / membre Titulaire / miembro titular   S: Substitute member / membre suppléant / miembro suplente
A: Deputy member / membre adjoint / miembro adjunto   O: Observer member / membre observateur / miembro observadore

Workers - Travailleurs - Trabajadores

add/ajouter/añadir

M. BIRBILIS (Grèce)	-	A
M. BISSALA (Cameroun)	-	A
M. ELLA NTSONG (Gabon)	-	A
Ms. MANDEVILLE (Saint-Vincent et-les Grenadines)	-	T
Sr. MICHÁ MAYE (Guinée équatoriale)	-	A
M. MOUSSAVOU (Gabon)	-	A
M. SOW (Sénégal)	-	A
Mme WETI (Gabon)	-	A
M. YRA (Burkina Faso)	-	A

changer/change/cambiar

Ms. HEINÄNEN (Finlande)	T	A
M. POPA (Roumanie)	T	A
M. TAZRIBINE (Belgique)	T	A
Ms. VRIELING (Pays-Bas)	A	T

delete/supprimer/suprimir

Mr. PRUIM (Pays-Bas)	A

---

[1] T: Regular member / membre Titulaire / miembro titular   S: Substitute member / membre suppléant / miembro suplente
A: Deputy member / membre adjoint / miembro adjunto   O: Observer member / membre observateur / miembro observadore

International Labour Conference

Record of Proceedings 4

Ninety-third Session, Geneva, 2005

Reports of the Credentials Committee

Brief report presented on behalf of the Chairperson of the Governing Body of the International Labour Office on the credentials of the delegates and advisers to the 93rd Session of the International Labour Conference
(Geneva, 30 May 2005)

1. The composition of each delegation and the procedure for appointing delegates and advisers to sessions of the International Labour Conference are governed by article 3 of the Constitution of the International Labour Organization.

2. In accordance with paragraphs 8 and 9 of article 3 of the Constitution, it is for the governments to communicate the nominations to the International Labour Office. The Conference examines these nominations and decides, in the case of dispute, whether delegates and advisers have been nominated in accordance with this article.

3. The Conference exercises this power through the Credentials Committee in accordance with the procedure laid down in articles 5 and 26 of its Standing Orders.

4. In particular, paragraph 2 of article 26 of the Standing Orders of the Conference provides that: "A brief report upon these credentials, drawn up by the Chairman of the Governing Body, shall, with the credentials, be open to inspection by the delegates on the day before the opening of the session of the Conference and shall be published as an appendix to the record of the first sitting."

5. The present report serves to provisionally fix the quorum necessary to give validity to the votes taken, in accordance with paragraph 1(2) of article 20 of the Standing Orders of the Conference.

6. The table below, which was established on Monday, 30 May 2005, at 2:00 p.m., shows the numerical composition of the delegations to the Conference based on the credentials provided. In this regard, it should be noted that the persons who have been nominated both as substitute delegates and as advisers have been included in the table amongst the advisers.

7. To date, 162 member States have communicated the names of the members of their delegations. Eighty-seven countries (two more than last year) deposited their credentials on or before 16 May 2005, thus meeting the 15-day deadline before the date fixed for the opening of the Conference, in compliance with paragraph 1 of article 26 of the Standing Orders of the Conference. The *First Provisional List of Delegations*, which appears on the opening day of the Conference, contains the names of the accredited participants received as of Saturday, 28 May 2005, and therefore does not include nine member States (Argentina, Bahamas, Botswana, Cape Verde, France, Guinea, Kazakhstan, Lesotho and

Paraguay) whose credentials were received subsequent to this date until the completion of this report are not included in this Provisional List.

8. Furthermore, while the Conference and the Credentials Committee have previously insisted on the obligation which article 3 of the Constitution imposes on governments requiring them to send complete delegations to the Conference, seven States (Belize, Gambia, Kazakhstan, Kyrgyzstan, Paraguay, Somalia and Vanuatu) have accredited delegations exclusively composed of Government delegates and one member State (Myanmar) has appointed an Employers' delegate but no Workers' delegate.

9. In addition, five member States (Jordan, Lesotho, Mauritius, Democratic Republic of Timor-Leste and Togo) have not always mentioned in their communications the organizations to which their Employers' and Workers' delegates and advisers belong or their respective functions. These governments are urged to complete this information as soon as possible.

10. Fifty-two governments (nine less than last year) have not confirmed that they would cover their delegates' and advisers' travel and subsistence expenses in accordance with paragraph 2(a) of article 13 of the Constitution. In this regard, in order to ensure greater clarity in establishing the credentials, it is advisable that governments use the form enclosed with the letter of convocation to the Conference which the Office addresses every year to member States or the electronic version made available by the Office.

11. Finally, we urge all delegates and advisers to register in person at the Registration Desk that is located at the Pavilion, which is near the ILO building, since the daily quorum is calculated on the basis of the number of delegates actually registered.

Composition of the Conference and quorum

12. At present 321 Government delegates, 155 Employers' delegates and 154 Workers' delegates – a total of 630 delegates – are accredited to the Conference.

13. There are, in addition, 1,001 Government advisers, 444 Employers' advisers and 545 Workers' advisers – a total of 1,990 advisers.

14. A total of 2,620 delegates and advisers have been nominated to take part in the work of the Conference in conformity with the provisions of the Constitution of the Organization.

15. Amongst those member States currently accredited, 18 are in arrears in the payment of their contributions to the Organization. Those Members, under the terms of paragraph 4 of article 13 of the Constitution, may not at present participate in the voting of the Conference or any of its committees (Armenia, Azerbaijan, Cambodia, Cape Verde, Central African Republic, Democratic Republic of the Congo, Djibouti, Gambia, Georgia, Guinea, Guinea-Bissau, Iraq, Kyrgyzstan, Republic of Moldova, Sao Tome and Principe, Sierra Leone, Somalia and Togo). Therefore, 66 delegates are not taken into account in calculating the quorum, nor is one delegate who, in accordance with article 4, paragraph 2, of the Constitution, cannot vote owing to the incomplete nature of his respective delegation (see paragraph 8 above).

16. In conformity with article 17 of the Constitution of the Organization and article 20 of the Standing Orders of the Conference, the necessary quorum to give a vote validity is provisionally 282. [1]

Observers

17. At present the Holy See has accredited an observers' delegation to the Conference.

Liberation movement and organizations invited

18. The Conference is also attended by:

- a tripartite delegation from Palestine, as a liberation movement invited in conformity with article 2, paragraph 3(k), of the Standing Orders of the Conference;

- representatives of the United Nations and some of its bodies, invited by virtue of Article II, paragraph 1 – relating to reciprocal representation – of the Agreement between the United Nations and the International Labour Organization, which came into effect on 14 December 1946;

- representatives of specialized agencies and other official international organizations, invited in conformity with article 2, paragraph 3(b), of the Standing Orders of the Conference;

- representatives of non-governmental international organizations with which consultative relations have been established, invited in conformity with article 2, paragraph 3(j), of the Standing Orders of the Conference; and

- representatives of other non-governmental international organizations also invited in conformity with article 2, paragraph 3(j), of the Standing Orders of the Conference.

19. A list of these representatives is appended to the list of delegations published as a supplement to the *Provisional Record* of the Conference.

Geneva, 30 May 2005.

(Signed) Mr. Daniel Funes de Rioja,
Vice-Chairperson of the Governing Body.

(Signed) Mr. Roy Trotman,
Vice-Chairperson of the Governing Body.

---

[1] That is, half the number of accredited delegates (630) after subtraction of the number not entitled to vote on the account of arrears (66) and of the incomplete delegation of Employers and Workers.

1) Government delegates   4) Employers' Advisers
2) Government advisers   5) Workers' delegates
3) Employers' delegates   6) Workers' Advisers

List of accredited delegates and advisers

	1)	2)	3)	4)	5)	6)		1)	2)	3)	4)	5)	6)		1)	2)	3)	4)	5)	6)
Afghanistan	2	3	1	-	1	-	Dominican Republic	2	5	1	4	1	4	Liberia	2	1	1	1	1	8	Seychelles	2	-	1	-	1	-
Albania	2	3	1	1	1	3	Ecuador	2	5	1	1	1	3	Libyan Arab Jamahiriya	2	7	1	-	1	3	Sierra Leone	2	3	1	2	1	2
Algeria	2	13	1	8	1	8	Egypt	2	9	1	4	1	5	Lithuania	2	3	1	-	1	-	Singapore	2	10	1	1	1	6
Angola	2	1	1	2	1	2	El Salvador	2	3	1	4	1	4	Luxembourg	2	10	1	5	1	8	Slovakia	2	7	1	2	1	3
Antigua and Barbuda	-	-	-	-	-	-	Equatorial Guinea	-	-	-	-	-	-	Madagascar	2	3	1	-	1	1	Samoa	-	-	-	-	-	-
Argentina	2	8	1	8	1	8	Eritrea	1	1	-	-	-	1	Malawi	2	4	1	-	1	1	Slovenia	2	6	1	1	1	1
Armenia	2	3	1	-	1	-	Estonia	2	3	1	1	1	1	Malaysia	2	9	1	2	1	1	Solomon Islands	-	-	-	-	-	-
Australia	2	3	1	1	1	1	Ethiopia	2	2	1	1	1	1	Mali	2	5	1	1	1	2	Somalia	2	2	-	-	-	-
Austria	2	7	1	3	1	4	Fiji	2	-	1	2	1	1	Malta	2	5	1	4	1	6	South Africa	2	8	1	8	1	5
Azerbaijan	2	2	1	7	1	2	Finland	2	5	1	3	1	3	Mauritania	2	3	1	-	1	4	Spain	2	13	1	8	1	8
Bahamas	2	-	1	-	1	-	France	2	16	1	8	1	8	Mauritius	2	-	1	2	1	-	Sri Lanka	2	7	1	-	1	6
Bahrain	2	6	1	2	1	2	Gabon	2	7	1	2	1	8	Mexico	2	10	1	8	1	8	Sudan	2	6	1	2	1	5
Bangladesh	2	4	1	1	1	1	Gambia	-	-	-	-	-	-	Republic of Moldova	2	-	1	1	1	1	Suriname	2	-	1	-	1	-
Barbados	2	5	1	1	1	1	Georgia	2	1	1	7	1	1	Mongolia	2	1	1	-	1	-	Swaziland	2	6	1	2	1	1
Belarus	2	5	1	2	1	3	Germany	2	10	1	4	1	5	Morocco	2	8	1	6	1	8	Sweden	2	7	1	3	1	5
Belgium	2	15	1	4	1	8	Ghana	2	13	1	8	1	4	Mozambique	2	6	1	-	1	1	Switzerland	2	8	1	3	1	6
Belize	2	-	-	-	-	-	Greece	2	16	1	8	1	8	Myanmar	2	6	1	1	1	-	Syrian Arab Republic	2	5	1	4	1	3
Benin	2	6	1	2	1	8	Grenada	-	-	-	-	-	-	Namibia	2	5	1	1	1	2	Tajikistan	-	-	-	-	-	-
Bolivia	2	1	1	-	1	1	Guatemala	2	7	1	1	1	1	Nepal	2	1	1	1	1	1	United Republic of Tanzania	2	16	1	4	1	1
Bosnia and Herzegovina	2	2	1	-	1	1	Guinea	2	8	1	4	1	7	Netherlands	2	14	1	6	1	6	Thailand	2	15	1	4	1	5
Botswana	2	7	1	-	1	1	Guinea-Bissau	2	1	-	-	-	1	New Zealand	2	3	1	1	1	1	The FYR Macedonia	-	-	-	-	-	-
Brazil	2	6	1	7	1	8	Guyana	2	3	1	2	1	2	Nicaragua	2	3	1	2	1	2	Democratic Rep. of Timor-Leste	2	-	1	-	1	-
Bulgaria	2	7	1	4	1	2	Haiti	-	-	-	-	-	-	Niger	2	5	1	3	1	5	Togo	2	2	1	1	1	4
Burkina Faso	2	11	1	1	1	2	Honduras	2	6	1	1	1	-	Nigeria	2	16	1	8	1	8	Trinidad and Tobago	2	4	1	2	1	1
Burundi	2	2	1	-	1	2	Hungary	2	13	1	1	1	1	Norway	2	8	1	8	1	5	Tunisia	2	7	1	8	1	8
Cambodia	2	3	1	1	1	3	Iceland	2	3	1	1	1	2	Oman	2	7	1	4	1	3	Turkey	2	15	1	8	1	7
Cameroon	2	4	1	-	1	3	India	2	7	1	8	1	7	Pakistan	2	3	1	-	1	-	Turkmenistan	-	-	-	-	-	-
Canada	2	15	1	6	1	4	Indonesia	2	16	1	8	1	8	Panama	2	2	1	2	1	2	Uganda	2	6	1	6	1	1
Cape Verde	2	-	1	-	-	-	Islamic Republic of Iran	2	-	1	-	1	5	Papua New Guinea	2	2	1	-	1	-	Ukraine	2	2	1	3	1	5
Central African Republic	2	4	1	-	1	1	Iraq	2	4	1	1	1	1	Paraguay	2	3	-	-	-	1	United Arab Emirates	2	6	1	2	1	1
Chad	2	2	1	1	1	1	Ireland	2	6	1	1	1	1	Peru	2	4	1	1	1	3	United Kingdom	2	14	1	5	1	4
Chile	2	11	1	4	1	8	Israel	2	16	1	5	1	4	Philippines	2	3	1	2	1	3	United States	2	16	1	6	1	8
China	2	20	1	8	1	10	Italy	2	10	1	3	1	3	Poland	2	11	1	4	1	5	Uruguay	2	7	1	2	1	2
Colombia	2	9	1	8	1	8	Jamaica	2	5	1	-	1	7	Portugal	-	8	1	8	1	6	Uzbekistan	-	-	-	-	-	-
Comoros	-	-	-	-	-	-	Japan	2	16	1	8	1	8	Qatar	2	7	1	1	1	-	Vanuatu	2	1	-	-	-	-
Congo	2	8	1	-	1	8	Jordan	2	8	1	2	1	4	Romania	2	6	1	8	1	8	Venezuela	2	9	1	8	1	8
Costa Rica	2	4	1	-	1	-	Kazakhstan	2	1	-	-	-	-	Russian Federation	2	16	1	3	1	8	Viet Nam	2	5	1	3	1	2
Côte d'Ivoire	2	10	1	2	1	6	Kenya	2	11	1	1	1	1	Rwanda	2	-	1	-	1	3	Yemen	2	2	1	2	1	2
Croatia	2	2	1	3	1	3	Kiribati	2	-	1	-	1	-	Saint Kitts and Nevis	-	-	-	-	-	-	Zambia	2	7	1	4	1	2
Cuba	2	8	1	3	1	6	Republic of Korea	2	10	1	7	1	8	Saint Lucia	-	-	-	-	-	-	Zimbabwe	2	11	1	1	1	1
Cyprus	2	3	1	7	1	5	Kuwait	2	15	1	3	1	3	Saint Vincent and the Grenadines	2	-	1	-	1	-							
Czech Republic	2	14	1	3	1	5	Kyrgyzstan	2	1	-	-	-	-	San Marino	2	1	1	1	1	3		1)	2)	3)	4)	5)	6)
Democratic Republic of the Congo	2	15	1	8	1	8	Lao People's Dem. Republic	-	-	-	-	-	-	Sao Tome and Principe	2	-	1	-	1	-	Total	321	1001	155	444	154	545
Denmark	2	8	1	3	1	6	Latvia	2	-	1	1	1	2	Saudi Arabia	2	6	1	1	1	2							
Djibouti	2	-	1	-	-	-	Lebanon	2	4	1	5	1	6	Senegal	2	6	1	3	1	8							
Dominica	-	-	-	-	-	-	Lesotho	2	2	1	1	1	1	Serbia and Montenegro	2	5	1	6	1	5							

First report

1. The Credentials Committee of the 93rd Session of the Conference is composed of Mr. Jules Medenou Oni, Government delegate, Benin, Chairperson; Ms. Lucia Sasso Mazzufferi, Employers' delegate, Italy; and Mr. Ulf Edström, Workers' delegate, Sweden.

Composition of the Conference

2. Since the signing of the brief report presented on behalf of the Chairperson of the Governing Body of the International Labour Office (*Provisional Record* No. 4A), the composition of the Conference has been modified as follows.

3. Of the 178 member States of the International Labour Organization, 166 are represented at the Conference, that is, four more than were accredited at the time that the brief report was signed. These are Haiti, the Lao People's Democratic Republic, Tajikistan and Uzbekistan.

Accredited delegates and advisers

4. A total of 649 delegates, including 330 Government delegates, 159 Employers' delegates and 160 Workers' delegates, have been accredited.

5. A total of 2,035 advisers, including 1,038 Government advisers, 449 Employers' advisers and 548 Workers' advisers, have been accredited.

6. Therefore a total of 2,684 delegates and advisers have been accredited.

7. With regard to the resolution adopted by the Conference at its 67th Session in June 1981, concerning the participation of women in ILO meetings, 99 of the 649 delegates and 498 of the 2,035 advisers accredited to the Conference are women. Women delegates represent no more than 15.3 per cent of total delegates, against 15.5 per cent last year. Therefore a total of 597 women have been accredited to the Conference, which is 22.2 per cent of total delegates and advisers against 23.24 per cent last year. The Committee deeply deplores that this percentage is even less than the previous year's already low figure and represents a step backwards in the trend of a slight yearly improvement, since 2001, towards more equal representation.

8. The Committee takes note with satisfaction that an increased number of member States (87) have deposited their credentials within the time prescribed under article 26 of the

Standing Orders of the Conference. The Committee welcomes this trend and hopes that it will continue next year.

9. The Committee also urges the Governments to avail themselves of the possibility to submit their credentials online,[1] so as to expedite the accreditation process.

Registered delegates and advisers

10. The following is the current status of the registration of delegates, which is the basis for determining the quorum for voting (see attached table established Friday, 3 June 2005 at noon).

11. Currently 562 delegates, including 295 Government delegates, 133 Employers' delegates and 134 Workers' delegates are registered.

12. In addition, 1,721 advisers, including 927 Government advisers, 368 Employers' advisers and 426 Workers' advisers are registered.

Incomplete and non-accredited delegations

13. The Committee notes that, to date, 12 member States have not sent a delegation (Antigua and Barbuda, Comoros, Dominica, Equatorial Guinea, The former Yugoslav Republic of Macedonia, Grenada, Guyana, Saint Kitts and Nevis, Saint Lucia, Samoa, Solomon Islands, and Turkmenistan). It further notes that, at the present time, the accredited delegations of five countries (Belize, Gambia, Kyrgyzstan, Somalia and Uzbekistan) are exclusively governmental. Two countries (Paraguay and Tajikistan) have a Workers' delegate but no Employers' delegate, and one country (Myanmar) has an Employers' delegate but no Workers' delegate. The Committee regrets that so many delegations are either not accredited or incomplete and wishes to affirm once again the necessity for governments to comply with the requirement of article 3 of the Constitution to send a complete tripartite delegation to the Conference. The Committee recalls that, pursuant to a decision of the Governing Body, each year the Director-General requests the governments of all member States which did not send a delegation or only sent an incomplete delegation to the Conference to indicate the reasons for their failure to do so. It also recalls that the information received in reply to that request is duly forwarded by the Office to the Governing Body. The Committee would encourage those governments that have not done so to provide the relevant information.

14. The Committee also notes that the number of advisers in each group is not evenly balanced; in particular, there are fewer Employers' advisers (449) than Workers' advisers (548). It once again urges governments to pay more attention to the relative proportions of the various categories of delegation members when making nominations to the Conference, as envisaged in article 3, paragraphs 1 and 2, of the Constitution. The Committee further recalls the request contained in the resolution, adopted by the Conference at its 56th Session in 1971, concerning the strengthening of tripartism in the overall activities of the International Labour Organization and hopes that governments will accord equal treatment to each of the groups when appointing advisers to their country's delegation to the Conference, so as to permit them to effectively follow the work of the various committees of the Conference. The Committee recalls in this connection the

---

[1] The credentials online are available at <http://ilc.ilo.org/credentials/index.asp>.

Members' obligation under article 13, paragraph 2(a), of the Constitution, to pay the travelling and subsistence expenses of their delegates and advisers and trusts that this obligation will be respected for the duration of the Conference.

Quorum

15. Twenty-one advisers, who are also substitutes to delegates not registered, have been taken into account in calculating the voting strength of the Conference.

16. Seventeen member States, the same number as last year, represented at the Conference are in arrears in their financial contributions to the Organization under the terms of article 13, paragraph 4, of the Constitution and therefore may not, at present, participate in the voting in the Conference or its committees. These are Armenia, Azerbaijan, Cape Verde, Central African Republic, Djibouti, Gambia, Georgia, Guinea-Bissau, Iraq, Kyrgyzstan, Republic of Moldova, Sao Tome and Principe, Sierra Leone, Somalia, Tajikistan, Togo and Uzbekistan. Since publication in the brief report (*Provisional Record* No. 4A) of the list of countries not allowed to vote, the delegations of two have been accredited. Therefore 56 registered delegates have not been taken into account in fixing the quorum. Three delegates from countries entitled to vote (Paraguay, Myanmar and Tajikistan) are also excluded, in accordance with article 4, paragraph 2, of the ILO Constitution, because their national delegations are incomplete. According to this article "if one of the Members fails to nominate one of the non-Government delegates whom it is entitled to nominate, the other non-Government delegate shall be allowed to sit and speak at the Conference, but not to vote".

17. At the present time the quorum required to give a vote validity is 274. This number represents 584 registered delegates (see paragraph 11 above), plus 21 substitute delegates (paragraph 15 above) minus 56 registered delegates not entitled to vote (see paragraph 16 above), the total being divided by two. The Committee appeals to the delegates to the Conference to register in person upon their arrival and to give timely notice of their departure date, in order to ensure that the quorum is as accurate as possible and that they are not counted as present when they are in fact absent from the Conference.

18. The Committee still regrets the fact that so many member States are in arrears in their payments, thereby depriving the Employers' and Workers' delegations from exercising their right to vote.

Observer, organizations and liberation movement invited

19. The Conference is also being attended by:

- representatives of one observer delegation (the Holy See) invited by the Conference;

- a tripartite delegation of a liberation movement (Palestine) invited in conformity with article 2, paragraph 3(k), of the Standing Orders of the Conference;

- representatives of the United Nations and some of its bodies invited by virtue of Article II, paragraph (1), concerning reciprocal representation, of the Agreement between the United Nations and the International Labour Organization, which came into effect on 14 December 1946;

- representatives of specialized agencies and other official international organizations, invited in conformity with article 2, paragraph 3(b), of the Standing Orders of the Conference;

- representatives of non-governmental international organizations with which consultative relations have been established, invited in conformity with article 2, paragraph 3(j), of the Standing Orders of the Conference;

- representatives of other non-governmental international organizations also invited in conformity with article 2, paragraph 3(j), of the Standing Orders of the Conference.

20. A list of these representatives is appended to the *List of Delegations* published as a supplement to the *Provisional Record* of the Conference and will be updated in the *First Revised List of Delegations* to be issued on Tuesday, 7 June 2005.

Objections, complaints and communications

21. To date, the Committee has before it several objections, complaints and communications. It has forthwith commenced their examination. The Committee believes that its work was facilitated by the fact that a substantial number of credentials had reached the Office prior to the Conference. Further, it is important that governments utilize the credentials form enclosed with the letter of convocation to the Conference, which is sent to governments every year, or the electronic version made available by the Office. This year, however, 48 per cent of member States did not use the forms. In order to comply with article 3, paragraph 5, of the Constitution, governments should provide accurate information on the employers' and workers' organizations consulted in nominating Employers' and Workers' delegates and advisers, as well as on the organizations that have agreed to such nominations.

22. In order to permit it to fulfil its mandate, the Committee recalled that all governments are urged to indicate in their credentials the organizations to which each of the Employers' and Workers' delegates and advisers belong, as well as their functions within those organizations. However, despite the urgent call made on behalf of the Chairperson in the brief report, seven governments (Bahamas, Jordan, Kazakhstan, Lesotho, Mauritius, Democratic Republic of Timor-Leste and Togo) have not provided the required information for all of the Employers' and Workers' delegates and advisers. The Committee therefore urges these governments to complete this information as soon as possible and hopes that in future sessions of the Conference such information will be provided on time for publication in the *Provisional List of Delegations*, which in accordance with article 26bis, paragraph 1(a), of the Standing Orders,[2] serves as the basis for the submission of objections to credentials.

23. The Committee welcomes the new database[3] on the verification of credentials and urges all interested parties to make full use of it.

---

[2] Interim provisions concerning verification of credentials adopted by the Conference at its 92nd (June 2004) Session and effective from the 93rd (June 2005) Session to the 96th (June 2007) Session of the International Labour Conference.

[3] The database is available at <http://www.ilo.org/dyn/creds/credsbrowse.home>.

24. The Credentials Committee submits the present report to the Conference so that it may take note of it.

Geneva, 3 June 2005.   *(Signed)*   Mr. Jules Medenou Oni,
                                                                  Chairperson.

                                                          Ms. Lucia Sasso Mazzufferi.

                                                                  Mr. Ulf Edström.

List of registered delegates and advisers

1) Government delegates
2) Government advisers
3) Employers' delegates
4) Employers' Advisers
5) Workers' delegates
6) Workers' Advisers

	1)	2)	3)	4)	5)	6)
Afghanistan	2	4	1	-	1	-
Albania	2	3	1	1	1	3
Algeria	2	11	1	4	1	8
Angola	2	3	1	-	1	2
Antigua and Barbuda	-	-	-	-	-	-
Argentina	2	5	1	8	1	3
Armenia	1	2	1	-	1	-
Australia	2	3	1	1	1	1
Austria	1	6	1	2	1	2
Azerbaijan	2	2	1	7	1	2
Bahamas	2	-	1	-	1	-
Bahrain	2	6	1	2	1	2
Bangladesh	2	4	1	1	1	1
Barbados	1	5	1	1	1	1
Belarus	2	5	1	2	-	3
Belgium	-	10	1	4	1	7
Belize	2	-	-	-	-	-
Benin	2	1	1	2	1	7
Bolivia	2	1	1	-	1	-
Bosnia and Herzegovina	2	2	1	-	1	-
Botswana	2	7	1	-	1	-
Brazil	2	5	1	5	1	7
Bulgaria	2	7	1	4	1	1
Burkina Faso	2	11	1	1	1	2
Burundi	-	1	-	-	1	-
Cambodia	2	3	1	-	1	3
Cameroon	1	6	1	1	1	1
Canada	1	13	1	7	1	4
Cape Verde	2	-	1	-	1	-
Central African Republic	2	4	1	-	1	1
Chad	2	2	1	-	1	1
Chile	2	6	-	2	1	8
China	2	20	1	8	1	10
Colombia	2	9	1	7	1	4
Comoros	-	-	-	-	-	-
Congo	2	8	1	-	1	8
Costa Rica	2	4	1	-	1	-
Côte d'Ivoire	2	10	1	2	1	6
Croatia	2	3	1	-	1	2
Cuba	2	8	1	3	1	6
Cyprus	2	3	1	6	1	5
Czech Republic	2	14	1	2	1	4
Democratic Republic of the Congo	2	15	1	8	1	8
Denmark	2	8	1	3	1	4
Djibouti	1	-	-	-	-	-
Dominica	-	-	-	-	-	-

	1)	2)	3)	4)	5)	6)
Dominican Republic	2	6	-	1	1	1
Ecuador	2	5	1	1	1	1
Egypt	2	9	1	4	1	6
El Salvador	2	3	1	1	1	2
Equatorial Guinea	-	-	-	-	-	-
Eritrea	1	1	1	-	1	1
Estonia	2	3	1	1	1	1
Ethiopia	2	2	1	1	1	1
Fiji	2	-	1	1	1	1
Finland	2	5	1	3	1	3
France	1	9	1	7	1	8
Gabon	-	2	1	-	1	2
Gambia	2	1	1	7	1	1
Georgia	2	1	1	1	1	1
Germany	2	10	1	4	1	5
Ghana	2	13	1	8	1	1
Greece	2	16	-	7	1	8
Grenada	-	-	-	-	-	-
Guatemala	2	5	1	-	1	-
Guinea	2	10	1	2	1	6
Guinea-Bissau	-	-	-	-	-	-
Guyana	-	-	-	-	-	-
Haiti	2	6	1	2	1	2
Honduras	2	6	1	1	1	-
Hungary	2	14	-	8	1	8
Iceland	2	2	1	1	1	2
India	2	7	1	7	1	5
Indonesia	2	16	1	7	1	2
Islamic Republic of Iran	2	16	1	5	1	5
Iraq	2	4	1	-	1	-
Ireland	2	16	1	1	1	1
Israel	2	5	1	1	1	4
Italy	1	6	1	1	1	3
Jamaica	2	8	1	1	1	4
Japan	2	16	1	8	1	8
Jordan	2	8	1	2	1	4
Kazakhstan	2	2	1	1	1	3
Kenya	2	11	1	1	1	3
Kiribati	2	-	1	-	1	-
Republic of Korea	2	10	-	7	-	5
Kuwait	2	15	1	3	1	3
Kyrgyzstan	2	1	-	-	-	-
Lao People's Dem. Republic	-	-	-	-	-	-
Latvia	2	-	1	-	-	-
Lebanon	2	5	1	3	1	-
Lesotho	2	4	1	-	1	1

	1)	2)	3)	4)	5)	6)
Liberia	2	6	-	1	1	1
Libyan Arab Jamahiriya	2	5	1	1	1	3
Lithuania	2	3	1	-	1	1
Luxembourg	2	8	1	1	1	6
Madagascar	2	3	1	1	1	1
Malawi	1	1	1	-	1	1
Malaysia	2	9	1	2	1	1
Mali	2	8	1	1	1	1
Malta	2	5	1	4	1	1
Mauritania	2	3	1	-	1	3
Mauritius	1	-	1	2	1	-
Mexico	2	10	-	7	1	8
Republic of Moldova	2	-	1	1	1	1
Mongolia	2	1	1	-	1	1
Morocco	2	8	1	3	1	5
Mozambique	2	6	1	1	1	1
Myanmar	2	6	1	-	1	8
Namibia	2	3	1	1	1	1
Nepal	2	5	1	-	1	-
Netherlands	2	12	1	4	1	6
New Zealand	2	3	1	1	1	1
Nicaragua	2	3	-	-	-	-
Niger	2	5	-	1	1	3
Nigeria	1	4	1	-	1	4
Norway	2	8	1	8	1	4
Oman	2	7	1	4	1	3
Pakistan	2	4	1	-	1	-
Panama	2	2	1	2	1	2
Papua New Guinea	2	2	1	-	1	-
Paraguay	2	3	-	1	1	-
Peru	2	4	1	-	1	-
Philippines	2	5	1	1	1	4
Poland	1	6	1	1	1	3
Portugal	2	8	1	1	1	4
Qatar	2	7	1	5	1	8
Romania	2	6	1	8	1	6
Russian Federation	2	8	1	1	-	5
Rwanda	1	2	-	-	1	-
Saint Kitts and Nevis	2	-	1	-	1	-
Saint Lucia	2	-	1	-	1	-
Saint Vincent and the Grenadines	-	-	-	-	-	-
San Marino	2	1	-	-	1	3
Sao Tome and Principe	-	-	-	-	-	-
Saudi Arabia	2	6	1	1	1	-
Senegal	2	5	1	3	1	1
Serbia and Montenegro	2	5	1	6	1	5

	1)	2)	3)	4)	5)	6)
Seychelles	2	1	-	1	1	1
Sierra Leone	2	5	1	-	1	3
Singapore	2	3	1	-	1	-
Slovakia	2	8	1	1	1	6
Samoa	2	3	1	-	1	1
Slovenia	2	1	1	-	1	-
Solomon Islands	2	9	1	2	1	1
Somalia	2	8	1	1	1	2
South Africa	2	5	1	4	1	6
Spain	2	3	1	-	1	4
Sri Lanka	1	-	1	2	1	-
Sudan	2	10	-	7	-	8
Suriname	2	-	1	1	1	1
Swaziland	2	1	1	-	1	1
Sweden	2	8	1	3	1	5
Switzerland	2	6	1	1	1	1
Syrian Arab Republic	2	6	1	-	1	-
Tajikistan	2	3	1	1	1	1
United Republic of Tanzania	2	1	-	-	1	-
Thailand	2	15	1	4	1	5
The FYR Macedonia	2	3	1	1	1	1
Democratic Rep. of Timor-Leste	-	-	-	-	-	-
Togo	2	-	1	-	1	3
Trinidad and Tobago	2	4	1	2	1	4
Tunisia	2	7	1	8	1	8
Turkey	2	15	1	8	1	7
Turkmenistan	-	-	-	-	-	-
Uganda	2	6	1	6	1	3
Ukraine	2	2	1	3	1	5
United Arab Emirates	2	6	1	2	1	1
United Kingdom	2	14	1	5	1	4
United States	2	16	1	6	1	4
Uruguay	2	7	1	2	1	2
Uzbekistan	2	-	1	-	1	-
Vanuatu	1	-	-	-	-	-
Venezuela	1	7	1	6	1	4
Viet Nam	2	8	1	3	1	2
Yemen	2	2	1	-	1	2
Zambia	2	7	1	2	1	1
Zimbabwe	2	11	1	1	1	1
Total	**295**	**927**	**133**	**368**	**134**	**426**

  1)   2)   3)   4)   5)   6)

Second report

Composition of the Conference

1. Since 3 June 2005, when the Credentials Committee adopted its first report (*Provisional Record* No. 4B), new credentials had been received from Equatorial Guinea and The former Yugoslav Republic of Macedonia. Therefore, at present a total of 168 member States are represented at the Conference. There are two more incomplete delegations in addition to those mentioned in paragraph 13 of its first report, Afghanistan and The former Yugoslav Republic of Macedonia; both have a Workers' delegate but no Employers' delegate. Regarding the accredited Members without the right to vote mentioned in paragraph 16 of its first report, three, Armenia, Cape Verde and the Republic of Moldova, have recovered the right to vote.

2. The Committee observes that of the seven member States mentioned in paragraph 22 of its first report, Bahamas, Lesotho, Timor-Leste and Togo have replied to its request to complete the information regarding the organizations and the functions of each of the members of the Employers' and Workers' delegations, whereas Jordan, Kazakhstan and Mauritius have not.

Objections

3. The Committee has received 19 objections this year. The objections relate both to the credentials of delegates and their advisers who are already accredited to the Conference as reflected in the *Provisional List of Delegations* and to the failure to deposit credentials of an Employers' or Workers' delegate. The latter category of objections is based on the interim provisions of the Conference Standing Orders concerning verification of credentials adopted by the International Labour Conference at its 92nd Session (June 2004) (*Provisional Record* No. 16). The Committee has completed the examination of the following six, which are listed below in French alphabetical order of the member States concerned.

Objection concerning the nomination of the Workers' delegation of the Bahamas

4. The Committee had received an objection from the President, Mr. Ferguson, and the Secretary-General, Mr. Morris, of the Commonwealth of the Bahamas Trade Union Congress (CBTUC) challenging the Workers' delegation of the Bahamas. According to the authors of the objection, the Government had bypassed the CBTUC in nominating the

Workers' delegation. The CBTUC was a representative organization in comparable size to the one from which the Workers' delegate to this year's Conference had been nominated. It regrouped some 32 organized unions from all economic sectors and represented some 10,000 workers of the 23,000 organized workers nationwide. On the basis of its representativeness, the CBTUC explained that from 1996 until 2004 it had an agreement with the Government wherein the Workers' delegate and adviser had been rotated between itself and the National Congress of Trade Unions (NCTU), so that both the CBTUC and the NCTU could participate at the annual sessions of the Conference. The CBTUC's representative had been nominated as the Workers' delegate to the 92nd Session (June 2004) of the Conference, whereas the NCTU's representative had been nominated as the Workers' delegate to this year's Conference. The CBTUC objected that there had been no consultative process in designating the Workers' delegation to this year's session of the Conference which is in contradiction to the Constitution of the International Labour Organization. Moreover, there was only one workers' representative nominated by the Government, which was inconsistent with the workers' organizations' internal arrangement with the Government.

5. The Committee received an unsolicited communication dated 2 June 2005 from Mr. Robert Farquharson, President of the Bahamas Communications and Public Officers Union. Mr. Farquharson, who is also the General Secretary of the NCTU, explained that the Government had declared the NCTU to be the umbrella organization most representative of the workers in the Bahamas following submission of information by the representative workers' organizations, namely the CBTUC and the NCTU, to the Minister of Labour and Immigration. In early 2005, the Minister informed the NCTU of this decision and invited it to submit the name of a representative so that the individual could be nominated as the Workers' delegate to the Conference. The NCTU also advised that six of the affiliates listed by the CBTUC in the attachment to its objection were in reality its members and in this regard submitted a list of its affiliates.

6. In a written communication received in reply to the Committee's request, Mr. Vincent A. Peet, Minister of Labour and Immigration, who was heading the Government delegation, noted that the CBTUC had not brought the matter to his attention but rather had filed an objection. The Government had recognized the NCTU as the most representative workers' organization in the country when regard was taken into account for the overwhelming number of workers represented by the NCTU and the diversity of the sectors involved. Although the Government had recognized both the CBTUC and the NCTU as the representative workers' organizations for several years and nominated representatives from both organizations to the Workers' delegation to the Conference, it considered this to be a heavy expense on the taxpayers of the country for this year.

7. The Government conceded that it had endorsed a "gentlemen's agreement" whereby the NCTU and CBTUC were invited each year to name a Workers' delegate and an adviser to the Conference, each taking annual turns as Workers' delegate or adviser. However, in light of the objections raised in preceding years, the Government had proceeded to examine the representativeness of the workers' organizations involved and relying on the information in its possession had decided that the NCTU was the most representative workers' organization in the country, based both on the size of its membership and its diverse affiliates. The Government also questioned the list of affiliates annexed to the objection and deemed it to be erroneous and misleading: at least two were not affiliated with the CBTUC, but rather with the NCTU; one affiliate was defunct; another two were employers' associations, one being in the informal economy; and one was an association of retired persons. Lastly, it annexed both a communication of 21 February 2005 addressed to the CBTUC requesting whether it would support the nomination of a representative from the NCTU as Workers' delegate to the Conference and, also, a list of trade unions. The Government, therefore, considered the objection to be unfounded.

8. The Committee notes the Government's position to set aside the application of the system of rotation that had been agreed upon by the two organizations and which the Government had endorsed, since the NCTU has been declared by it to be the most representative workers' organization. The Committee recalls its conclusion reached at the 87th Session (June 1999) of the Conference when it considered that the Government should have up-to-date statistical information both with regard to membership and affiliation (*Provisional Record* No. 21, paragraph 8). The Government submits a list of trade unions for 2005 and, based on the information submitted to the Committee, it appears that the Workers' delegate is representative of the workers of the Bahamas. The Committee, however, questions whether the Government undertook consultations with both representative workers' organizations regarding its decision to discontinue the application of the system of rotation due to economic reasons. On this point, the Committee hopes that the Government will clarify its consultation and nomination procedure prior to next year's Conference so that a common agreement can be reached amongst the interested parties. The objecting organization does not seek the invalidation of the Workers' delegate and, therefore, no further action is called on the Committee's part.

Objection concerning the failure to deposit credentials of a Workers' delegate of Belize

9. The Committee had before it an objection submitted by the International Confederation of Free Trade Unions (ICFTU), which stated that the Government of Belize had failed to nominate a Workers' delegate to the Conference. In view of the new mandate under the interim provisions of the Conference Standing Orders concerning verification of credentials, the Committee now had the possibility of examining objections where a government failed to deposit credentials of either a Workers' or Employers' delegate. The *Provisional List of Delegations* indicated that Belize was exclusively a governmental delegation. However, the objecting organization indicated that it had one affiliate, the National Union Congress of Belize, which could have legitimately taken part in a tripartite delegation. An explanation from the Government was requested for this year, hoping that a full tripartite delegation would be accredited at future sessions of the Conference.

10. In a written communication addressed to the Committee in reply to its request, Ms. Alicia Hunt, Chargée d'Affaires, of the Permanent Mission of Belize in Geneva and Government delegate at the Conference explained that all travel expenditures relating to ministers and government officials had been suspended as part of budgetary restrictions. The Government believed that the Permanent Mission could fully represent it and the people of Belize at the Conference and that as soon as the budgetary restrictions were lifted, Belize would send tripartite delegations.

11. The Committee notes that since 2001 Belize has not been represented at the Conference by a tripartite delegation. Since then the delegation has consisted of only two representatives from the Permanent Mission of Belize in Geneva. The Committee expresses its deep concern that Belize is represented exclusively by a governmental delegation. It emphasizes that whereas a government has the ability to assure its representation through a diplomatic mission, the same cannot be said for employers' or workers' organizations. The Committee reminds member States of their obligations under article 3, paragraph 1, of the ILO Constitution to nominate complete delegations to the Conference. Respect for the principles of tripartism requires a balanced representation of employers and workers so as to permit their effective participation at meetings. Without the participation of government, employers' and workers' representatives the International Labour Conference cannot function properly or attain its objectives.

Objection concerning the nomination of a Workers' adviser of El Salvador

12. The Committee had received an objection concerning the nomination of a Workers' adviser of El Salvador, submitted by the *Comisión Intersindical de El Salvador*. The objecting organization had received on 22 March 2005 a written communication from the Vice-President of the workers' section of the Superior Council of Labour (CST) requesting it to nominate three representatives to the Workers' delegation to the Conference. Mr. René Pérez Castillo, who at the time was an interim coordinator for the *Comisión Intersindical de El Salvador*, also received a copy of this request. In response to this request, the six trade unions of the country proposed a member from the *Central Autónoma de Trabajadores Salvadoreños* (CATS), the *Coordinadora Sindical de Trabajadores Salvadoreños* (CSTS), and the *Central de Trabajadores Democráticos* (CTD), all three trade unions affiliates of the objecting organization. Disregarding the proposal, Mr. René Pérez was nominated as an adviser even though his name was not included in the proposal put forth by the *Comisión Intersindical de El Salvador*. He was charged with only transmitting the names to the Superior Council of Labour. The objecting organization considered that the nomination was the result of a manoeuvre by the Government in question, which was indifferent to the grave and continued transgression of the principles of freedom of association. The objecting organization recalled that, in this regard, El Salvador had not ratified Conventions Nos. 87 and 98, which were principal instruments relating to freedom of association and collective bargaining.

13. The objecting organization emphasized that Mr. Pérez did not represent the workers of the *Comisión Intersindical de El Salvador*, as he had betrayed its decisions and principles. This was demonstrated by the fact that the *Comisión Intersindical de El Salvador* had submitted an objection and was considering filing a case before the competent tribunal against Mr. Pérez for illicit acts committed against the organization. As a consequence, the objecting organization sought the invalidation of the credentials of Mr. Pérez, adviser, for the fraudulent manner in which his nomination had taken place.

14. In a written communication addressed to the Committee at its request, Mr. José Roberto Espinal Escobar, Minister of Labour and Social Prevention who was heading the Government delegation, affirmed that the Government had limited itself to respecting the nomination effectuated by the workers' section of the Superior Council of Labour. The Government had received a communication on 3 May 2005 from the workers' section of the Superior Council of Labour, signed by its Vice-President, Mr. José Huiza Cisneros. The Vice-President had forwarded a list dated 8 April 2005 that was signed by Mr. Perez on behalf of the *Comisión Intersindical de El Salvador*, which included his own name as one of the four representatives of the workers of El Salvador to the Conference. In a communication dated 12 May 2005, the Ministry of Labour and Social Prevention officially informed the *Comisión Intersindical de El Salvador* of its nomination. The Government annexed various documents with respect to the selection and official communications with the interested parties.

15. The Committee observes that the nomination of the Workers' delegate had taken place in agreement with the most representative workers' organizations of the country, since it was the *Comisión Intersindical de El Salvador* that had submitted the name of Mr. Perez on 8 April 2005 to the Government. The Government had accepted the nomination received by the Superior Council of Labour. It, therefore, appears that this case is due to a conflict internal to the objecting organization. The Committee considers that on the basis of the information submitted to it that the Government has acted in conformity with article 3, paragraph 5, of the ILO Constitution. Consequently, the Committee decided not to retain the objection.

Objection concerning the nomination of the Workers' delegate of Lesotho

16. The Committee had before it an objection concerning the nomination of the Workers' delegate of Lesotho, submitted by Mr. Daniel Maraisane, Secretary-General of the Lesotho Clothing and Allied Workers' Union. It contended that the Workers' delegate, Mr. Macaefa Billy, did not represent the textile and garment industry workers of Lesotho, since he was a Member of the Parliament elected in 2002 and as a representative of the Lesotho Workers' Party. As a Member of Parliament, he was paid by the Government and his registration as General-Secretary of the Factory Workers' Union was part of the government strategy aimed at weakening the trade union movement in Lesotho. The objection also alleged that consultations regarding the nomination of Mr. Billy had not been held. Consequently, an invalidation of his credentials was requested.

17. In a written communication addressed to the Committee in response to its request, Mr. L. Mandoro, Principal Secretary of the Ministry of Employment and Labour, stated that the Congress of Lesotho Trade Union (COLETU) to which the Factory Workers' Union represented by Mr. Billy was affiliated, was the most representative workers' organization. The second largest federation is the Lesotho Congress of Trade Unions (LESODU), to which the objecting organization was an affiliate. LESODU, however, did not object to the nomination of Mr. Billy. The Government further considered that the functions of a Member of Parliament were not incompatible with trade union representation, either under national law or under the ILO Constitution.

18. The Committee does not share the view that a representative of a workers' organization cannot be at the same time a Member of Parliament. Furthermore, it has not been contested that COLETU, from which the Workers' delegate has been nominated, is the most representative organization within the meaning of article 3, paragraph 5, of the ILO Constitution. In absence of any other indication, the Committee has decided not to retain the objection.

Objection concerning the nomination of the Employers' delegate of Serbia and Montenegro

19. The Committee had before it an objection submitted by Mr. Dragutin Zagorac, President of the Serbian and Montenegrin Employers' Association (SMEA), challenging the nomination of the Employers' delegate, Mr. Rato Ninkovic, President of the Serbian Employers' Association (accredited by the Government as a representative of the Employers' Union of Serbia). The objecting organization submitted that not only was there a provisional court order prohibiting the Employers' delegate from using the seal and name of the organization he claimed to represent, but that the nomination of the Employers' delegate was in direct contradiction of an agreement that was made during a preparatory meeting for the 93rd Session (June 2005) of the Conference that was held on 19 April 2005, wherein Messrs. Zagorac, Mitrovic and Josipovic were selected to represent the employers at this year's Conference. The meeting was tripartite and attended by representatives of the Ministry of Foreign Affairs of the Union of Serbia and Montenegro, the Serbian Ministry of Labour, Employment and Social Politics, the SMEA, the Serbian Independent Unions' Association, the Montenegrin Independent Unions' Association, the Serbian and Montenegrin Independent Unions' Association and the Association of Free and Independent Unions (ASNS). The agreement was subsequently changed unilaterally by the Minister of Labour of Serbia and this action constituted interference with the principles of freedom of association and the independence of the employers' organizations.

20. The author of the objection further elaborated that the SMEA was the sole legitimate representative employers' organization from Serbia and Montenegro, having been

established in 1994 and being comprised of 115,000 members, of both collectives and individuals. The SMEA was also the head of the Serbian Employers' Association, the Montenegrin Employers' Association and the Kosovo Employers' Association. In contrast, the organization from which the Employers' delegate was nominated, the Serbian Employers' Association, was one of the employers' organizations acting at the Republic level of Serbia which had not proven its representativeness, but was in fact closely tied with the Minister of Labour of Serbia. The objecting organization represented the Union of Serbia and Montenegro at both the national and international level. On this basis, the author of the objection contended that the SMEA was the most representative employers' organization for the Union of Serbia and Montenegro and sought the invalidation of the credentials of the Employers' delegate.

21. The Committee received on 2 June 2005 an unsolicited communication from Mr. Zarko Milisavljevic, Vice-President of the Serbian Employers' Association. He advised that the Union of Serbia and Montenegro did not have a Ministry of Labour at that level, but rather the Ministry of Foreign Affairs acted as a contact point between the two Republics' Labour Ministries. The objecting organization was merely a coordinating body, as it was comprised of employers' organizations from each Republic and its Management Board was constituted of ten members, five from each respective employers' organizations. Furthermore, the author of the objection had been dismissed from his function of President of the SMEA and its genuine leader was now Mr. Mitrovic who had been elected on 17 May 2005 and nominated as Employers' adviser and substitute delegate. The Serbian Employers' Association was the only representative employers' organization in Serbia, since it had been duly registered, had demonstrated its representativeness and was responsible for collective bargaining within this Republic. On the basis of the foregoing, the Serbian Employers' Association submitted that its President, Mr. Ninkovic, was the genuine employers' representative correctly nominated to act as the Employers' delegate of Serbia and Montenegro to the Conference and, as a consequence, that the objection should be rejected.

22. In another unsolicited communication received by the Committee on 2 June 2005 from the Secretariat of the SMEA, certain statistical data were provided. Specifically, it furnished the number of some of the collectives which comprised its 117,353 members or 641,739 employees: 375,000 members from the General Association of Entrepreneurs of Belgrade; 50,000 members from the Association of Bakers and Pastry Makers of Serbia; 10,000 members from the Association of Private Petrol Stations of Serbia; and 17,000 from the General Association of Entrepreneurs of Nis. It represented approximately 25 per cent of the employed people in Serbia and Montenegro. It added that its affiliate, the Serbian Employers' Association, had no authority to act on its own at the international level, as the SMEA was a full member of the International Organisation of Employers (IOE). The SMEA argued that employers from Serbia and Montenegro could not be represented by any organization other than by it, especially in light of the provisional order that prohibited the Serbian Employers' Association from using its seal, stamp and name.

23. In a written communication received in reply to the Committee's request, Mr. Dejan Sahovic, Ambassador and Permanent Representative of Serbia and Montenegro in Geneva and Government delegate to the Conference, indicated that the objection submitted by Mr. Zagorac was unfounded for the twofold reason: that the SMEA was constituted of the Serbian Employers' Association and the Employers' Association of Montenegro; and that the author of the objection had no authority to submit the objection following the replacement of the Serbian Employers' Association's representatives from the SMEA Management Board and the consequent dismissal of Mr. Zagorac as President of the SMEA. On 17 May 2005 the Governing Board of the SMEA amended its statute and elected new management, Mr. Mitrovic from the Employers' Association of Montenegro.

Mr. Zagorac was later excluded by the Serbian Employers' Association following certain conduct that was incompatible with its statutes.

24. Regarding the question of the name and seal that had been raised by the author of the objection and the subsequent communications, the Government argued that it was of no relevance for the nomination of the Employers' delegation to the Conference. What was relevant was whether the employers' organization from which the delegate had been nominated was representative. Notwithstanding, it stated that the use of the name and seal by the author of the objection was an abuse. Further, the Serbian Employers' Association had been registered by the Ministry of Labour, Employment and Social Affairs of the Republic of Serbia and had been recognized as a representative employers' organization. In contrast, the SMEA was included in an NGO's register with the Ministry for Human and Minority Rights of Serbia and Montenegro and this registration did not prove its representative character as an employers' organization. The Government stated that labour legislation and tripartite social dialogue did not exist on the level of the Union, but only within each of its Republics. The Serbian Employers' Association had provided evidence on the number of its members and, prior to its registration, its representativeness was examined by the Committee for the Establishment of Representation of Trade Unions and Employers' Associations in Serbia.

25. In a third unsolicited communication received on 7 June 2005, the Committee was advised that the SMEA had resolved on 17 May 2005 that henceforth it would be known as the Employers' Union of Serbia and Montenegro (EUSM). This communication was signed by its President, Mr. Mitrovic.

26. The Committee notes that the objection does not involve the issue of the most representative employers' organization within Serbia and Montenegro, but rather the issue of who is entitled to participate in the consultation process and to represent the employers of Serbia and Montenegro. In regard to the latter, the Committee remarks that the particular constitutional structure of Serbia and Montenegro has implications on the registration, consultation and nomination procedures of the employers' organizations of Serbia and Montenegro, as well as who is competent to represent the employers at the international level.

27. While these issues do not fall directly within its mandate, the Committee recalls that the full application of article 3, paragraph 5, of the ILO Constitution entails the respect for the principles of freedom of association. In the present case, the Government has nominated representatives from the employers' organizations of each respective Republic to the Employers' delegation of Serbia and Montenegro. What is at stake is their legitimacy to represent all employers of Serbia and Montenegro. From the information submitted to the Committee, it appears that there remain several unresolved legal issues on this point, one of them being the issue of the use of the seal and name.

28. The Committee observes that the author of the objection was the Employers' delegate to last year's session of the Conference while the person he is now contesting, Mr. Ninkovic, was the Employers' adviser. As the objection does not indicate any substantial change in the internal structures of the employers' organizations in Serbia and Montenegro that would lead to the conclusion that there has been a change in the representative character of the employers' organizations, the Committee concludes that the questions raised in the objection are essentially internal. What remains unclear is the consultation process that took place and was the subject of a tripartite meeting on 19 April 2005, as well as the matter of representation at the international level by an employers' organization. The Committee expresses its hope that all interested parties will endeavour to resolve their differences before the next session of the Conference.

Objection concerning the nomination of an Employers' adviser of Swaziland

29. The Committee had before it an objection submitted by the Employers' group of the Conference concerning one of the Employers' advisers of Swaziland. The Employers' group submitted that the principles and procedures stipulated in article 3, paragraph 5, of the ILO Constitution had not been respected by the Government concerned, since it had failed to undertake official consultations with the most representative employers' organization in the country, specifically the Federation of Swaziland Employers and Chamber of Commerce (FSE&CC), prior to the nomination of the Employers' adviser and substitute delegate, Ms. Thulsile Dlamini, Secretary-General of the Federation of Swaziland Business Community. The Federation of Swaziland Employers (FSE) is part of the FSE&CC, registered in 1946, with 475 members consisting of companies and associations employing 70 per cent of employees in the formal sector. The Federation of Swaziland Business Community was formed in 2003 and at the end of 2004 had approximately 40 affiliates. However, it was neither a member of any recognized employers' organization nor had it engaged in dialogue with the FSE. The Employers' group, therefore, esteemed that the nomination of Ms. Dlamini was an imposition by the Government of a sponsored organization and that such action constituted an infringement of the right of the most representative employers' organization in the country to nominate appropriate representatives to the Conference.

30. Though the employers of Swaziland are represented at the Conference by the FSE, as both its Chief Executive Officer, Ms. Treasure T. Maphanga, and its President, Mr. Zakes Nkosi, had been accredited to the Conference as the Employers' delegate and substitute delegate and adviser, respectively, the Government was requested to furnish an explanation regarding this violation of procedures and to remember its constitutional obligations when carrying out nominations in the future.

31. In a written communication received in reply to the Committee's request, the Commissioner of Labour, Mr. J.L. Nkhambule, and Government delegate to the Conference advised that the Minister of Enterprise and Employment intended on: discussing and finalizing the consultation process for the appointment of delegates with a view to formalizing it with the tripartite partners after the Conference; and, that the two employers' federations would continue with their bilateral discussions with a view to their finalizing their agreement/understanding. He further informed the Committee that consultations had taken place during the Conference and that a further understanding had been reached with all the parties concerned on the way forward.

32. The Committee notes that the representativeness of the employers' organization is not in dispute. What has been called into question is the lack of consultations with the representative employers' organization for the purpose of nominating the Employers' delegation to the Conference. Although the Committee welcomes the Government's immediate steps to consult the representative employers' organizations during the Conference and to formalize the consultation process for the appointment of future delegations to the Conference, the Committee recalls that article 3, paragraph 5, of the ILO Constitution requires governments to undertake official consultations with the most representative employers' and workers' organizations in the country prior to nominating the tripartite delegation to the Conference. It trusts that the Government will ensure that the consultation process is carried out for the purpose of future nominations to the Conference.

Complaints

33. The Committee had also received and dealt with the following two complaints, which are listed below in French alphabetical order of the member States concerned.

Complaint concerning the non-payment of travel expenses of a member of the Employers' delegation of Peru

34. On 3 June 2005, the Committee received a complaint submitted by the Employers' group of the Conference concerning the non-payment of travel expenses of a member of the Employers' delegation of Peru. It considered that the Government had not met its obligations under article 13, paragraph 2(a), of the ILO Constitution, since the Government was paying only the subsistence expenses of the Employers' delegate, Mr. Jaime Zavala Costa. The *Confederación Nacional de Instituciones Empresariales Privadas* (CONFIEP) of which the Employers' delegate was a member had requested that the travel expenses of the Employers' adviser and substitute delegate, Mr. Julio César Barrenechea, be paid instead. This request was ignored by the Government. The Government was called upon to provide a clear explanation in response to its failure to pay the travel expenses of the adviser concerned, to fulfil its obligation by paying the travel expenses of at least one of the two members of the delegation referred to above and, in the future, to comply with its obligations as stipulated under article 13, paragraph 2(a), of the ILO Constitution.

35. In a written communication addressed to the Committee in response to its request, Mr. Roberto Servat Pereira de Sousa, Vice-Minister of Labour and Government delegate, advised that the partial payment to Mr. Jaime Zavala Costa was due to the precarious socio-economic and financial situation of the country. He added that Mr. Zavila Costa had received ten days of per diem which was equivalent to the amount that had been received by the rest of the delegation. It expresses its availability to examine whatever method or specific recommendation that could assist Peru to overcome this problematic question.

36. If the reasons invoked by the Government are understandable, the Committee notes the discrepancy of information furnished to it by both parties. The Government does not dispute the information contained in the complaint with regard to the failure to pay the travel expenses, however, the Committee notes that the Government had indicated in the Form for Credentials of Delegations that it had covered the travel expenses. Furthermore, the Committee considers that the payment of only ten days of subsistence expenses does not permit the delegation to follow the work of the Conference from beginning to end. This is incompatible with the obligations foreseen under article 13, paragraph 2(a), of the ILO Constitution, which requires that expenses be covered for a tripartite delegation in conditions that would permit the members to participate in the work of the Conference until its conclusion. The Committee has reiterated this in the past and it, therefore, calls on the Government to meet its constitutional obligations.

Complaint concerning the non-payment of the travel and subsistence expenses of an Employers' adviser of Swaziland

37. On 1 June 2005, the Committee received a complaint submitted by the Employers' group of the Conference on behalf of one of the Employers' advisers and substitute delegates of Swaziland. The complaint stated that the Government had undertaken to meet the travel and subsistence expenses for the participation in the Conference of one of the Employers' advisers and substitute delegates, Ms. Thulsile Dlamini, Secretary-General of the Federation of Swaziland Business Community, whereas it had not for the other, Mr. Zakes

Nkosi, President of the Federation of Swaziland Employers (FSE). This impedes the latter from fully participating in the work of the Conference.

38. In a written communication received in reply to the Committee's request, Mr. J.L. Nkhambule, Commissioner of Labour and Government delegate to the Conference advised that the Government would meet the normal cost for sending Mr. Nkosi, President of the FSE, as Employers' adviser and substitute delegate of Swaziland to the Conference.

39. The Committee notes that, in so far as the Government has agreed to cover the necessary expenses to enable the Employers' adviser and substitute delegate to be present until the last day of the Conference, the complaint becomes moot and requires no further intervention by the Committee. The Committee trusts that the Government will honour its commitment prior to the end of this Session of the Conference.

Communication

40. The Committee also received the following communication.

Communication concerning the Workers' delegation of Serbia and Montenegro

41. The Committee had received from the International Confederation of Free Trade Unions (ICFTU), a communication regarding the credentials of the Serbia and Montenegro Workers' delegation. The ICFTU noted with appreciation that the Government of Serbia and Montenegro had appointed a Workers' delegate and two advisers to this year's session of the Conference representatives from the United Branch Trade Unions (Nezavisnost), thus recognizing the genuine representativeness of this organization. It was also welcomed that adequate representation had been accorded to the most representative workers' organization of Montenegro, the Association of Independent Trade Unions of Montenegro (CITUM), through the nominations of one adviser and substitute delegate, and one adviser. Clarification, however, was sought from the Government as to how the remainder of the Workers' delegation had been appointed, since there had been allegations concerning attempts to only consult small and non-representative trade union organizations for the purpose of nominating the Workers' delegation to this session of the Conference. An assurance that a clear understanding prevailed within Serbia and Montenegro regarding the rules governing the tripartite structure of delegations at the Conference in accordance with article 3 of the ILO Constitution was sought.

42. The Committee notes that the communication of the ICFTU had been drafted neither as an objection, nor was it aimed at challenging the credentials of the Workers' delegation of Serbia and Montenegro. The Committee notes the absence of any information or comment from the Government. In these circumstances, the Committee considers that this communication does not call as such for any action on its part, but it does recall that governments are obliged to consult the most representative workers' organizations that exist in the country.

* * *

43. The Credentials Committee adopts this report unanimously. It submits it to the Conference in order that the Conference may take note of it.

Geneva, 10 June 2005. *(Signed)* Mr. Jules Medenou Oni, Chairperson.

Ms. Lucia Sasso Mazzufferi.

Mr. Ulf Edström.

Third report

Composition of the Conference

1. Since 10 June 2005, when the Committee adopted its second report (*Provisional Record* No. 4C), there have been no significant changes in the composition of the Conference.

2. As of this day there are 4,315 persons accredited to the Conference (as compared to 4,180 last year), of whom 3,842 are registered (as compared to 3,696 last year). The attached list contains more details on the number of delegates and advisers registered for each Member.

3. In addition, the Committee wishes to indicate that 168 ministers or vice-ministers have been accredited (as compared to 156 last year) to the Conference.

Objections

4. The total number of objections received this year is 19, the highest number since 2000. In this report, the Committee has considered the following 13 objections. They appear in the French alphabetical order of the Members concerned.

Objection concerning the nomination of the Employers' delegate of Burundi

5. The Committee had before it an objection, submitted by the Employers' group of the Conference, challenging the nomination of the Employers' delegate of Burundi. Just as it did for the 92nd Session (June 2004) of the Conference, the Government had nominated the President of the *Centrale syndicale des employeurs du Burundi* (CESEBU) without consulting the *Association des employeurs du Burundi* (AEB), which was not even represented by an adviser as it had been last year. The Government refused to apply the Committee's recommendation from last year even though it acknowledged the AEB as the most representative employers' organization. It continued to nominate CESEBU as the sole representative of the employers in various tripartite international forums (Social Partners' Forum and Head of States' Summit in Ouagadougou, September 2004; Committee of Social Affairs and Labour of the African Union in Johannesburg, April 2005; meeting of experts on social dialogue organized by PRODIAF in Kigali, April 2005; meeting of the representatives of the employers and of the trade unions with the Head of State of Burundi, April 2005). However, the Government's attitude was not justified by any increased representativeness that the CESEBU may have acquired since the prior session of the Conference.

6. Several elements favouring the AEB were mentioned. The AEB was founded in 1964, whereas the CESEBU was created only in 2004. Furthermore, the AEB is independent from the Government. As regards the scope and nature of its activities, the AEB has a general secretariat endowed with a highly qualified staff and is well equipped, whereas the CESEBU has neither staff nor headquarters (its secretariat is joined with the office of the Minister of Labour) and has no activities of its own, except for its participation at a few meetings arranged by the Minister of Labour and Social Security. As regards membership, only one enterprise member has resigned from the AEB. Indeed, the AEB has been strengthened in that the membership dues of its members are up to date. By contrast, the CESEBU's membership includes a number of fictitious affiliates. The number of the AEB's affiliates had risen from 98 in June 2004 to 112 at the present time. This reflects the Government's general non-observance for the principles of freedom of association, which affect both the AEB's rights and those of the most representative workers' organization, the *Confédération des syndicats du Burundi* (COSYBU). Accordingly, it was requested that the credentials of the Employers' delegate be invalidated.

7. The Committee notes with regret that the Government had not replied to its request for information regarding the conditions of the nomination of the Employers' delegate. It deplores the lack of cooperation from the Government and notes that the situation is similar to last year and has even worsened since the 92nd Session (June 2004) of the Conference, as the Employers' delegation this year does not even include a member from AEB (see Credentials Committee, Third Report, *Provisional Record* No. 6D, 2004). The Committee once more denounces the lack of consultation with AEB. It reiterates its deep concern with respect to practices that clearly violate the obligations under article 3, paragraph 5, of the ILO Constitution. Such practices, together with the silence of the Government, appear to support the more general allegations of interference and disregard for the principles of freedom of association formulated in the objection. Recalling that it is the right of the most representative organizations to nominate their representatives to the Conference and that governments shall respect their choice without interfering, the Committee continues to be deeply concerned by the total lack of progress in this matter. It, therefore, wishes to express once again the hope that the Government will avail itself of ILO technical assistance in order to avoid a similar situation from reoccurring.

8. In view of the objections concerning the nomination of the Employers' delegation of Burundi, already submitted to the Committee, as well as similar objections concerning the nomination of the Workers' delegation, the Committee unanimously considers that the procedure relating to the composition of the Employers' delegation of Burundi to the Conference should be the subject of a follow-up. By virtue of article 26bis, paragraph 7, of the Interim provisions of the Conference Standing Orders concerning the verification of credentials adopted by the International Labour Conference at its 92nd Session (June 2004) (*Provisional Record* No. 16), the Committee proposes that the Conference request that the Government of Burundi submit to the next session of the Conference, at the same time that it submits its credentials for the delegation of Burundi, a detailed report on the procedure utilized to nominate the Employers' delegate and advisers. Specifically, the organizations that will have been consulted on the matter; the date, time and place of these consultations; and the names of the individuals nominated by the organizations during these consultations.

Objection concerning the nomination of the Workers' delegate of Burundi

9. The Committee had received an objection, submitted by Mr. Pierre Claver Hajayandi, President of the *Confédération des syndicats du Burundi* (COSYBU), challenging the nomination of the Workers' delegate of Burundi. Appended to his communication was a copy of a letter, dated 4 May 2005, addressed by the COSYBU to the Minister of Labour and Social Security of Burundi, whereby the COSYBU nominated Mr. Hajayandi as the Workers' delegate to the present session of the Conference and Mr. Célestin Nsavymana, its Treasurer, as adviser. The Government, alleging that Mr. Hajayandi's mandate had expired and that he no longer possessed the statutory competence to represent the COSYBU, nominated Mr. Nsavymana as the Workers' delegate. This decision of the Government constituted interference in the internal affairs of the COSYBU. Accordingly, he requested the Committee to invalidate the credentials of the Workers' delegate of Burundi and that he be included in the delegation as the Workers' delegate.

10. In a written communication addressed to the Committee in response to its request, the Minister of Labour and Social Security provided the Committee extracts of a note from the Minister dated 21 May regarding the "evaluation of the legality of the executive office of the President and legal representation of the COSYBU", as well as its reply to a communication from the members of the Confederation Committee of the COSYBU denouncing the interference of the public authorities in their trade union activities. Specifically, the Minister considers that the statutes of the COSYBU do not confer on the Confederation Committee the authority to extend the Executive Committee's term of office and, therefore, its leaders, including Mr. Hajayandi, no longer enjoy any legitimacy to exercise their mandate. In addition, the Government considers that Mr. Hajayandi can no longer be a member of the COSYBU, since he is the medical director of a clinic and, thus, in actuality is an employer. The Minister added that he has limited himself to noting that the COSYBU has failed to respect its statutes and that such a conclusion does not amount to an act of interference. Finally, the Government expressed its readiness to undertake a joint assessment of this matter with the ILO.

11. The Committee notes that the representativeness of the COSYBU is not called into question, but rather the person who has been named to represent it and their function. It observes that the decision not to nominate Mr. Hajayandi as Workers' delegate does not arise from an internal decision of the organization. In this respect, the Committee recalls that in the Governing Body's 335th Report of the Committee of Freedom of Association, that that Committee had emphasized in its conclusions that the Government had stated that it respected the choice of the workers within tripartite institutions as made by the most representative organization, and that it had undertaken to rectify any mistakes that might have been made, which corresponds to the requirements for independence, transparency and predictability under article 3, paragraph 5, of the ILO Constitution. Consequently, deploring that the Government, which has a seat on the Governing Body's Committee on Freedom of Association since 2002, has not met its commitments, the Committee urges the Government to meet its constitutional obligations in this regard and to refrain from any act of interference. The Committee reminds the Government of the possibility to avail itself of technical assistance from the ILO.

12. In view of the objections concerning the nomination of the Workers' delegation of Burundi, already submitted to the Committee, as well as similar objections concerning the nomination of the Employers' delegation, the Committee unanimously concludes that the procedure relating to the composition of the Workers' delegation of Burundi to the Conference should be the subject of a follow-up. By virtue of article 26bis, paragraph 7, of the Interim provisions of the Standing Orders of the Conference concerning the verification of credentials, the Committee proposes that the Conference request that the Government of Burundi submit to the next session of the Conference, at the same time that it submits its credentials for the delegation of Burundi, a detailed report on the procedure utilized to nominate the Workers' delegate and advisers. Specifically, the organizations that will have been consulted on the matter; the date, time and place of these consultations; and the names of the individuals nominated by the organizations during these consultations.

Objection concerning the nomination of the Workers' delegate of Cape Verde

13. The Committee had received an objection from the Chairperson, Mr. José Manuel Vaz, President of the *Confederação Caboverdiana dos Sindicatos Livres* (CCSL) challenging the nomination of the Workers' delegate, on the basis that there had been no consultations and that the delegate nominated was not representative of the workers of the country. The objecting organization explained that since 1992 there have been two trade union confederations co-existing in Cape Verde, the CCSL and the *União National dos Trabalhadores de Cabo Verde* (UNTC-CS). As the result of certain differences and misunderstandings affecting the relations between the two trade union confederations, the Government had decided to introduce a system whereby the Workers' delegate to the Conference would be nominated on a rotational basis. The objecting organization submitted that this arrangement had functioned until 2004 and that its representativeness is demonstrated by the fact that one of its members had been nominated as the Workers' delegate for the 89th Session (June 2001) and 91st Session (June 2003) of the Conference without challenge.

14. The CCSL submitted that it had adopted a critical position with regard to certain Government policies, which in turn had caused a deterioration in its relations with the Government. As a consequence the Government, at the request of the UNTC-CS, launched a study in 2004 to determine the representativeness of the trade unions. To this effect, it requested information regarding the number of affiliated trade unions and their members. The UNTC-CS advised that it was comprised of 20,000 members, 15 trade unions, one federation and two regional trade union federations versus the CCSL's approximate 19,000 members, 19 trade unions and one federation. The Government, allegedly not satisfied with this information, wished to consult the archives of each trade union in order to confirm the information. This request was rejected by the CCSL on the grounds that it constituted interference with internal trade union affairs. As a result, the Government decided not to take into account the information provided by the CCSL and declared the UNTC-CS to be the most representative trade union confederation of Cape Verde. It considered the Government's actions to be biased and discriminatory. It also challenged the information itself as, according to the 2000 census carried out by the National Institute of Statistics, the UNTC-CS had 20,000 members, only 10,000 of whom were active. Consequently, the Government could not argue that the UNTC-CS was the most representative trade union confederation. Moreover, there was no legislation that set out clear and objective criteria for determining the representativeness of workers' and employers' organizations. Finally, the Government failed to carry out prior consultations concerning the nomination of the Workers' delegate.

15. The objecting organization also pointed to the different manner in which the Workers' and Employers' delegates were nominated. For the Workers' delegate, the Government had recourse to the so-called study on trade union representativeness and, thus, favoured the UNTC-CS. For the Employers' delegate, the rotational method that had been the norm since 1993 was employed. The UNTC-CS, in this manner, had selected the Workers' delegate for two consecutive years (2004 and 2005).

16. The CCSL vehemently opposed the Government's decision to unilaterally nominate a representative from the UNTC-CS as the Workers' delegate, since it did not recognize the study carried out by the Government.

17. In a written communication addressed to the Committee in response to its request, the Government indicated that the situation had been ongoing since 1991, when the CCSL was founded. The two centres could not reach an agreement as to who would nominate a Workers' delegate to the Conference. In the absence of any national legislation with

respect to the determination of the most representative workers' organization the Government introduced a system of rotation.

18. As a result of two objections submitted to the Conference (85th Session (June 1997) and 87th Session (June 1999)), the Committee advised the Government that it needed to establish an evaluation system in order for it to fulfil its obligations under article 3, paragraph 5, of the ILO Constitution. In 2005, the Government decided, with the assistance of the ILO, and in agreement with the Counsel for Consultation, to commission an independent study to assess the representativeness of the trade unions. This study was presented to the social partners on 20 October 2004, and on 10 November 2004 the Counsel for Consultation examined the conclusions. According to the study, the overwhelming majority of unionized workers in the country, practically nine in every ten, were affiliated with the UNTC-CS. All the social partners approved these conclusions, except for the CCSL. Consequently, the Government had limited itself to fulfilling its constitutional obligations by nominating a Workers' delegate from the ranks of the UNTC-CS.

19. The Committee notes with satisfaction that the Government had responded to its advice and evaluated the representative character of the two trade union centres. The Committee notes that the CCSL continues to contest the results of the study with respect to representativeness, but that it has limited itself to making declarations without submitting adequate proof to the Committee. In these circumstances, and in view of the information at its disposal, the Committee has decided not to retain the objection.

Objection concerning the nomination of the Workers' delegation of Djibouti

20. The Committee had before it an objection concerning the Workers' delegation of Djibouti, submitted by Messrs. Adan Mohamed Abdou, Secretary-General of the *Union djiboutienne du Travail* (UDT) and Kamil Diraneh Hared, Secretary-General of the *Union generale des travailleurs djiboutiens* (UGTD). In a communication dated 2 June 2005 the International Confederation of Free Trade Unions (ICFTU) associated itself with the objection. The authors of the objection contended that the Government, despite the commitments that it had undertaken on several occasions, had still not applied any of the recommendations of the ILO concerning the reinstatement of the directors and trade union militants of the UDT and the UGTD that had been dismissed in September 1995. Freedom of association and trade union rights continue to be flouted. The Government nominated to ILO meetings false representatives instead of legitimate Workers' representatives. The authors of the objection denounced the ongoing refusal of the Government to apply the recommendations of the ILO to take into account the legitimate representatives of the UDT and the UGTD in the tripartite delegations to the Conference.

21. In a written communication received in reply to the Committee's request, Mr. Guedi Absieh Houssein, Director of Work and Relations with Social Partners, writing on behalf of the Minister of Labour and National Solidarity, informed the Committee that the position of the Government remained the same as presented in its correspondence addressed to the Committee during previous sessions of the Conference.

22. Clarifications requested by the Committee were provided orally: on 9 June 2005, by Messrs. Houssein and Kamil Ali Mohamed, Director of Employment, Training and Professional Insertion; and on 14 June 2005, by Mr. Houmed Mohamed Dini, Minister of Employment and National Solidarity. All three emphasized that the national legislation does not require the approval of the authorities to establish a trade union, to choose its leaders, or to organize a trade union congress. They also affirmed that the law does not contain any disposition concerning the incompatibility of political activities with trade

union activities. They did not deny that there was a recurring trade union problem in Djibouti and the Minister, who had been in office for less than two weeks, expressed his concern about this issue. He had already met with one of the authors of the objection before his arrival in Geneva and he remains available to continue dialogue in order to find, with the assistance of the ILO, if appropriate, a satisfactory solution to the problems raised in the objection. The Government has already prepared a draft labour code, which has been submitted to Parliament, to replace the present one that dates from 1952.

23. The Committee remains concerned by the matters raised in the objection. It, however, welcomes that the Minister is available to tackle the issues that have been brought to the attention of the Committee on several occasions. The Committee takes due note of the affirmations relating to the lack of legal obstacles to the exercise of freedom of association in Djibouti. It cannot but encourage the Government to avail itself of ILO technical assistance, so as to permit it to bring its national legislation into conformity with the relevant ILO instruments. Trusting that the efforts of the new Minister will bring about satisfactory solutions with regard to the nomination of the Workers' delegate to the next session of the Conference, the Committee decided not to propose any action this year.

Objection concerning the failure to deposit credentials of a Workers' delegate of Gambia

24. The Committee had before it an objection, submitted by the International Confederation of Free Trade Unions (ICFTU), which stated that the Government of Gambia had failed to nominate a Workers' delegate to the Conference. In view of the new mandate under the Interim provisions of the Conference Standing Orders concerning verification of credentials, the Committee now had the possibility of examining objections where a government failed to deposit credentials of either a Workers' or Employers' delegate. The *Provisional list of delegations* indicated that Gambia was exclusively a governmental delegation. However, the objecting organization indicated that it had one affiliate, the Gambia Workers' Union, which could have legitimately taken part in a tripartite delegation. An explanation from the Government was requested for this year, hoping that a full tripartite delegation would be accredited at future sessions of the Conference.

25. In a written communication addressed to the Committee in reply to its request, Mr. Karamo K. Bojang, Permanent Secretary of the Department of State for Trade, Industry and Employment, explained that three umbrella unions, namely the Gambia National Trade Union Congress, the Gambia Labour Union and the Gambia Workers' Confederation, were consulted in view of identifying a Workers' delegate for the present session of the Conference. They were, however, invited on 10 May 2005 to make their own financial arrangements for the Conference. Although the Government wished to finance a tripartite delegation, it was not able to finance more than two people due to the resource constraints it was presently facing. It was hoped that a full tripartite delegation would be able to attend the future sessions of the Conference.

26. The Committee notes that, since 2003, Gambia has not been represented at the Conference by a tripartite delegation. Since then the delegation has consisted of only two governmental representatives that have arrived from the capital, Banjul. The Committee expresses its deep concern that Gambia is represented exclusively by a governmental delegation. The Committee reminds member States of their obligations under article 3, paragraph 1, of the ILO Constitution to nominate tripartite delegations to the Conference. Respect for the principles of tripartism requires a balanced representation of employers and workers so as to permit their effective participation at meetings. Without the participation of Government, Employers' and Workers' representatives the Conference cannot function properly or attain its objectives.

Objection concerning the nomination of the Workers' delegation of Guatemala

27. The Committee had received an objection regarding the nomination of the Workers' delegation of Guatemala submitted by the *Unión Sindical de Trabajadores de Guatemala* (UNSITRAGUA).

28. The Committee takes notes that this objection was not signed and that its authors remain anonymous. The objection is therefore irreceivable, by virtue of the dispositions of article 26bis, paragraph 1(b), of the Interim provisions of the Conference Standing Orders concerning verification of credentials.

Objection concerning the nomination of the Workers' delegation of India

29. The Committee had received an objection from the trade union *Bharatiya Mazdoor Sangh* (BMS) that challenged the nomination of the Workers' delegation. The BMS declared that it had boycotted the present session of the Conference, since the Government had unilaterally decided to appoint, at the last moment, a representative of the Indian National Trade Union Congress (INTUC) as the Workers' delegate without consulting the BMS. By a letter dated 5 April 2005, the Government initially decided that the BMS would nominate one of its members as Workers' delegate and another as adviser. The Government even confirmed the travel arrangements for the BMS representatives. The objecting organization stated that it was the most representative workers' organization, as evidenced by the fact that for nearly a decade the Workers' delegate to the Conference had been a member of the BMS. This representativeness was confirmed through a membership verification system introduced by the Government. The BMS was ready to accept the nomination of the substitute delegate from the INTUC, but this attempt for a compromise failed. The Committee was requested to verify the credentials of the Workers' delegate and ensure that they were in strict conformity with the ILO Constitution and Standing Orders of the Conference.

30. In a written communication addressed to the Committee in response to its request, the Ministry of Labour advised that, according to the latest general verification of trade union membership in 1996, the difference in membership between the BMS and the INTUC was marginal. The next general verification had been delayed for five years by the BMS legal challenges. Other verifications, however, had taken place at the level of industrial units and showed that the BMS had been losing ground since 1996. The Government further indicated that the individual who had been appointed Workers' delegate was a widely accepted leader, even amongst organizations not affiliated to the INTUC and that its designation was therefore "judicious and equitable". Moreover, the BMS was not affiliated to any international trade union, whereas the INTUC was affiliated to the ICFTU.

31. The Committee notes, at the outset, that the Minister of Labour's letter inviting the BMS to propose two of its representatives as the Workers' delegate and adviser was subject to the approval of the Government and, thus, did not constitute a final decision concerning the nomination. The information about the membership of the representative workers' organizations in India is outdated, which appears to be partly due to the legal challenges of the BMS. During the written consultations that the Government had undertaken, the representative of the INTUC seemed to have obtained support from workers' organizations other than his own. In the absence of sufficient and reliable information on the situation in India, the Committee can come to no conclusion on this particular case. It wishes, however, to note for the future that article 3, paragraph 5, of the ILO Constitution imposes on governments in countries were there are two or more representative workers' organizations an obligation to actively seek an agreement between them for the purpose of nominating the Workers' delegation. This obligation is not fulfilled where a government extends a mere invitation to the largest organization in terms of membership, nor can organizations of comparable importance in good faith claim for themselves the right to appoint the Workers' delegate without even attempting to reach an agreement with the other workers' organizations. The Committee urges the Government to clarify the process of consultation aimed at arriving at a nomination of the Workers' delegation to the Conference. The Committee hopes that the Government will ensure the establishment of objective and transparent criteria for determining the most representative organizations and that the process of nominating the Workers' delegation to the next session of the Conference will be engaged in a spirit of cooperation by all the parties involved.

Objections concerning the nomination of the Workers' delegation of Nepal

32. The Committee had before it an objection, submitted by Mr. Binod Shrestha, Secretary-General of the General Federation of Nepalese Trade Unions (GEFONT), Mr. Achyut Pandey, Secretary-General of the Nepal Trade Union Congress (NTUC) and Mr. Khila Nath Dahal, General-Secretary of the Democratic Confederation of Trade Unions (DECONT), challenging the nomination of the Workers' delegate of Nepal. The objecting organizations stated that they were the only representative workers' unions in Nepal and that, as such, they were convened to a meeting with the Ministry of Labour and Transport Management in March 2005 in order to present candidates for the Workers' delegation. In accordance with the Trade Union Act, 1992, which provides for a system of rotation, these unions unanimously proposed a representative of DECONT as the Workers' delegate, while the two other organizations were to be represented by an adviser each.

33. The objecting organizations learned on 20 May 2005 that the Government had nominated the Workers' delegate from a newly created union, the Nepal Agriculture Workers' Organization, and that no advisers were included in the delegation. They contended that this new union had neither been created in accordance with Nepalese law nor was it affiliated with any national trade union centre. The objecting organizations considered that such a nomination was contrary to both the ILO Constitution and the Trade Union Act, 1992. They considered that, in general, following recent political incidents in Nepal, the rights of trade unions were being undermined and that the nomination of the Workers' delegate should be viewed in this context. They considered that the Nepalese delegation did not have a tripartite character and sought the invalidation of the Workers' delegate's credentials.

34. Following a series of consultations involving, inter alia, the ILO Office in Nepal, the Government deposited on 31 May 2005 new credentials for the Nepalese delegation. Mr. Rajendra Bahadur Raut, President of DECONT, was included as the Workers' delegate while Mr. Bam Bahadur Dewan from the Nepal Agriculture Workers' Organization became adviser in the Workers' delegation.

35. On 7 June 2005, the Committee received a second objection concerning the Workers' delegation, this time submitted by the International Confederation of Free Trade Unions (ICFTU). The second objection was based on the *First revised provisional list of delegations*, which listed Mr. Dewan as the Workers' adviser and reiterated that the Government was attempting to undermine the principles of freedom of association. For example, the three trade union centres had not been permitted to properly examine the membership lists of 12 "national federations"; and amendments of the Civil Service Act that were unfavourable to unionized government workers were being adopted without participation of the workers' organizations. The Government was accused of establishing fictitious trade unions. Considering that Mr. Dewan came from an unknown organization,

the ICFTU requested that the nominations of the representatives to the Worker's delegation correspond to those agreed upon by the GEFONT, NTUC and DECONT.

36. In a written communication sent to the Committee at its request, Mr. Purushottam Ojha, Acting Secretary of the Ministry of Labour and Transport Management and Government delegate at the Conference, indicated that the second objection was unfounded. He explained that the Government had respected the system of rotation and on this basis had nominated a representative of the Nepal Agriculture Workers' Organization who is also the President of the Independent National Democratic Confederation of Nepalese Trade Union (INDECONT), a duly registered confederation, as adviser to the Workers' delegation. The Government added that it had no intention of undermining the unions and union rights of workers. Similarly, the right to establish new unions should also be respected by all existing workers' organizations. It considered the allegations baseless and untrue.

37. To the extent that the credentials of the Workers' delegate have been modified as requested by the objecting organization, the first objection requires no action by the Committee. The Committee notes with satisfaction the readiness of the Government to rectify the matter.

38. With regard to the second objection, however, the Committee notes that the Workers' adviser included in the delegation comes from a trade union that had been registered two days before the deposit of its credentials and had not been included in the consultation process. The Committee expresses its doubt concerning the representativeness of this trade union. The Committee wishes to recall that, when there are several representative workers' organizations in a country, the government has an obligation pursuant to the ILO Constitution not only to hold consultations with the most representative ones, but also to accept the choice of those organizations concerning the nomination of the Worker's delegation. Although the manner in which the nomination process was applied was flawed, the Committee does not propose any particular action this year. It, nevertheless, expects that the spirit of cooperation shown by the modification of the credentials of the Workers' delegate will prevail and that the Government will fully respect the choice of the representative organizations in nominating the Workers' delegation for the next session of the Conference without any interference. The Committee, therefore, encourages the Government to continue availing itself of ILO technical assistance in this matter so as to avoid a similar situation in the future.

Objection concerning the nomination of the Workers' delegate of Nicaragua

39. The Committee had received an objection concerning the nomination of the Workers' delegate of Nicaragua submitted by Messrs. José Espinoza Navas, Secretary-General of the *Confederación de Unificación Sindical*; Nilo Salazar Aguilar, Secretary-General of the *Confederación General de Trabajadores* (CGT-Independiente); Antonio Jarquin Rodríguez, Secretary-General of the *Central de Trabajadores Nicaragüenses* (CNT-Autónoma); and Roberto Antonio Moreno, Secretary-General of the *Confederación Unitaria de Trabajadores* (CUT). These four confederations constitute the *Congreso Permanente de los Trabajadores* (CPT). The authors of the objection submitted that prior to 1990 the Workers' delegates were unilaterally nominated by the Government. Since 1990, the Workers' representatives to the Conference had been elected, either unanimously or by majority, by them. In 2002 the Minister of Labour, Mr. Virgilio Gurdián Castellón, attempted without success to impose a candidate from the *Central Nicaragüense de Trabajadores* (CNT), which is favourable to the Government. It was from this organization that an adviser, Mr. Edmond Pallais, was later selected to become Vice-Minister of Labour. In 2004, it was not possible to nominate a candidate from the CNT, since it was inactive due to the withdrawal of a large number of its members and it had not held a general assembly. With the agreement of the Minister of Labour and of the Presidency of

the Republic, the CNT was reorganized in a fraudulent manner. The Minister of Labour ordered the registration of the executive committees of the trade unions, despite the fact that the workers had not elected them as no general assemblies had been held.

40. This year the Minister of Labour sent a letter to the representative trade union organizations in the country, which had been recognized by the various governments during the preceding 15 years, reminding them that they should nominate their delegate. However, the Vice-Minister of Labour, who continues to be an adviser to the CNT, convoked the non-representative confederations and in agreement with them nominated someone who was not a representative of the workers of the country. Consultations were not even held with the most representative workers' organizations. The authors of the objection sought the invalidation of the credentials of the Workers' delegate and sought that Mr. Nilo Salazar Aguilar, Secretary-General of the CGT-Independiente and of the CTP, be named in his place.

41. In a written communication addressed to the Committee in response to its request, Mrs. Yadira Martínez Flores, Director of the International Labour Affairs at the Ministry of Labour and Government, delegate to the Conference, indicated that the objection did not refer to a question of representativeness, but rather the manner in which the Workers' delegate was nominated. The Government had complied with the obligations contained in the Tripartite Consultation (International Labour Standards) Convention, 1976 (No. 144), when it nominated the Workers' delegation. On the basis of the registry of workers' organizations that is maintained by the Ministry of Labour, 14 organizations were consulted, even though not all their information in the registry was up to date. Three of the four organizations that comprise the objecting confederation were consulted and that process permitted the main ideological trade union thinking to express itself. All the organizations were convoked to an information session on 22 April 2005, during which they were requested to nominate the person of their choice so that they could assume the functions as Workers' delegate to the Conference. No consensus was reached and the CST proposed a vote, during which the Ministry of Labour acted as secretariat. Mr. Frank Jiménez, Secretary-General of the CNT and Ms. Maritza Zamora, Secretary-General of the CNTD were elected, respectively, as delegate and adviser. The CNT-Autónoma and the CGT-Independiente requested that their opposition be recorded. The Government denied that it had interfered in the selection process of the Workers' delegation and considered that the difficulty in designating the Workers' delegate was a reflection of the internal difficulties among the interested organizations.

42. Contrary to the Government's view, the Committee considers that the objection is not only due to the nomination procedure, but also concerns the question of representativeness of the workers' organizations that were convoked to participate in the consultations. The Government admitted that it had not invited the organizations because of their respective representativeness, but rather for historical reasons. In addition, the Government had placed all the organizations on the same footing. In these circumstances, at the time of the vote, this worked in favour of the lesser representative organizations to the detriment of the most representative workers' organizations. The Committee considers that the system of evaluating the representativeness of each organization that is invited to participate in the consultations to nominate the Workers' delegate to the Conference should be based on objective and verifiable criteria. In the absence of this information, the Committee cannot verify which are the most representative organizations amongst those invited. Therefore, it cannot ascertain whether the nomination of the Workers' delegate is in conformity with article 3, paragraph 5, of the ILO Constitution. The Committee trusts that the Government will undertake without delay to establish objective criteria so as to permit it to evaluate the representativeness of the workers' organizations in Nicaragua.

Objection concerning the nomination of the Workers' delegation of Venezuela

43. The Committee had received an objection submitted by the *Confederación de Trabajadores de Venezuela* (CTV) concerning the nomination of the Workers' delegation of Venezuela. The objecting organization claims, for the third consecutive year, that the nomination of the Workers' delegation was in flagrant contravention of the ILO Constitution and in clear contradiction with the criteria that had been reiterated in this matter by the Committee last year. Although CTV remains the most representative workers' organization of the country, the Ministry of Labour had once again used this year an artifice to prevent CTV from exercising its rights by nominating a delegate from the *Confederación General de Trabajadores* (CGT), a minority union. Under the pretext of endeavouring to achieve an agreed structure for the Workers' delegation, the Ministry convened the five national union centres (CTV, CUTV, CODESA, CGT and UNT) to a meeting held on 12 May 2005, at which a system of rotation was proposed again. This method of nomination confirmed the utmost lack of impartiality by the Government in respect to CTV, which recalled in writing the criteria stated last year by the Committee in this matter and reaffirmed that the delegation should be nominated in accordance with the genuine representativeness of each trade union. Furthermore the fact that the UNT, an organization aligned with the Government, is a minority union that may not even have by-laws or a constitution, had been included in this process demonstrated that the Government had utilized once more the minority unions to continue its anti-union practices. Contrary to the tolerance shown towards the UNT, the Government had been more stringent with the CTV by expressly reminding it in the convocation letter of the criteria set forth in the Organic Labour Act regarding the representativeness of trade unions. The Government also contested the legitimate character of its representatives. Although both the Supreme Court and the National Electoral Council challenged, in their decisions of 17 June 2004 and 12 January 2005 respectively, the validity of the elections of the CTV's Executive Board, the CTV insisted that such a challenge did not affect in any manner its existence or its rights. Consequently, the CTV requested that the credentials of the Workers' delegation be invalidated.

44. In a written communication addressed to the Committee in response to its request, Mr. Ruben Darío Molina, Director of the Bureau of International Relations and ILO Liaison Office of the Ministry of Labour, and Government adviser and substitute delegate to the Conference, considered that the objection was unfounded. In 2003 and 2004, the CTV did not enjoy the numerical superiority required to make it the most representative organization given that the statistics that it relied on were obsolete as compared to the statistics gathered by the Ministry of Labour. The Ministry had brought its statistics up to date, as a result of an agreement between it and the UNDP that was signed in 2003 for this purpose. The representativeness of the workers' organizations was measured on the basis of the number of those participating in collective bargaining agreements, in particular the number of members represented by collective agreements concluded by trade unions affiliated with confederations that are legally registered and up to date; as well as those that participate in consultations with the social partners. In 2003 and 2004, respectively, the UNT had a higher number of collective bargaining agreements (74.4 per cent and 45 per cent) versus the CTV (25.1 per cent and 22 per cent). Despite the UNT's greater representativeness, the Government had not nominated a representative from its ranks as the Workers' delegate to either the 92nd Session (June 2004) or 93rd Session (June 2005) to the Conference given that the workers' organizations, with the exception of the CTV, had relied on the system of rotation that had been agreed on in 2003.

45. With reference to the consultations undertaken this year, the Government invited the five most representative centres to two sessions convoked by the Vice-Minister of Labour on 6 and 12 May 2005 so that each could put forth proposals for the Workers' delegation. The

CODESA, the UNT, the CUTV and the CTV sent written proposals, whereas the CGT submitted its proposal during the meeting of 12 May 2005. This meeting took place in the office of the Vice-Minister and, as a result of that dialogue, the CGT, the CODESA and the UNT arrived at an agreement concerning the Workers' delegation. The representative of the CTV withdrew from this meeting, having his withdrawal recorded.

46. Turning to the system of rotation agreed upon by the majority of confederations in 2003, when the CTV ceased to be the most representative workers' organization, the Government stated that this system had been institutionalized so as to address the disagreements concerning the representativeness amongst the workers' organizations from the integrated system of the Andean subregion community. This agreement has been rejected by the CTV.

47. Turning to the CTV's statement that it is the most representative workers' organization, the Government stated that no judicial organ had recognized this, even though the CTV stated that its representativeness was attested to in the registry of the National Electoral Council. Following the trade union elections of October 2001, convoked by all the trade union centres, the CTV did not communicate a certified copy of the Act regarding the composition of its Executive Board. Moreover, the numerical superiority of the CTV was not demonstrated in a referendum as required by article 430 of the Organic Labour Law. Instead, it declared itself to be the winner of the elections without presenting numbers that demonstrated this numerical superiority. Three of the six trade union centres and third-level unions that participated in these elections contested this proclamation and the results announced by the CTV. The Supreme Court, in a decision dated 17 June 2004, confirmed that, for it to demonstrate its representativity of workers, a referendum should take place that would permit the workers' organizations to determine which was the most representative and best qualified to undertake effective dialogue so as to conclude collective bargaining agreements and negotiations in the event of conflict. In a decision dated 10 November 2004, the National Electoral Council annulled the CTV elections. The CTV announced that it would undertake a referendum, but had not done so to date. Therefore, it could not be concluded that the CTV was the most representative workers' organization.

48. The Committee, in the first place, notes that it has not received sufficient information to permit it to evaluate the representativeness of the five centres considered to be the most representative in the country. As the Committee had emphasized last year, the number of workers covered by either collective bargaining agreements or their scope is but one element to be considered. The Government should make a serious effort to arrive at an agreement with the different trade union centres on the basis of reliable criteria that would permit it to determine their representativeness in an objective manner. The Committee reiterates its hope, once again, that the Government will avail itself of ILO technical assistance in this regard. In the present case, the Committee also notes, on the basis of the information that it has received this year from the Government, that in 2002 the CTV covered more than 50 per cent of workers under collective bargaining agreements; in 2003 this figure had descended to 25 per cent; and in 2004 to 22 per cent. As the Committee has already indicated in the past, such a decrease could be tied to the fact that the CTV's ability to negotiate could have been limited due to the persistent attacks on this centre and which the supervisory bodies of the ILO have denounced. In addition, the abovementioned statistics do not correspond entirely to those furnished by the Government last year.

49. With reference to the process of consultation, three of the four centres invited to the meeting of 12 May 2005 by the Government were marginally representative with comparison to the CTV. Notwithstanding they have managed to impose a system of rotation, despite the clear opposition of the objecting organization. With the participation of the minority organizations, the system of rotation has produced a paradoxical result.

Last year, the Workers' delegate was a member of a centre that represented 0.33 per cent of the workers of the country, according to the statistics furnished by the Government. Whereas this year the delegate comes from an organization that in 2004 represented only 0.23 per cent of these workers. Consequently, one organization that represents the public sector (UNT), along with three others who do not represent more than 1 per cent of the workers of Venezuela have impeded, through the system of rotation, the CTV from being adequately represented in the Workers' delegation to the Conference. With regard to the existence of the rotation agreement the Committee recalls, once again, that as per its practice for the agreement to be considered it must be accepted by the most representative workers' organizations. This does not appear to be the case as it has been systematically refused by the CTV, which considers itself to be the most representative workers' organization.

50. Finally, the Committee notes the decisions of the competent authorities at the national level: that the National Electoral Council annulled the elections of 2001, wherein the Executive Committee of the CTV was nominated; and that the Supreme Court could not pronounce itself as to whether the CTV was the most representative workers' organization of the country, as it does not have the necessary technical elements. These decisions indicate that the CTV is not in a situation to confirm, at the national level, that it is the most representative workers' organization nor has the Government demonstrated the contrary. In addition, the Government appears to have ignored the conclusions of the supervisory bodies of the ILO: that the authorities must not deprive the members of the executive committee of the CTV of legitimacy in the absence of a pronouncement by the judicial authority nullifying the elections (see ILO: *Committee on Freedom of Association, 330th Report,* Case No. 2067, para. 173). Furthermore, the Committee notes that the Committee of Experts on the Application of Conventions and Recommendations also commented on the role of the Executive Committee of the CTV (see ILO: *Report of the Committee of Experts on the Application of Conventions and Recommendations*, Report III (Part I(A)), ILC, 93rd Session, Geneva, 2005). Consequently, the Committee reiterates that the process for the nomination of the Workers' delegation has not been impartial, transparent or foreseeable as is required by article 3, paragraph 5, of the ILO Constitution. This lack of respect can be viewed in the larger context of the systematic attacks directed at the independence of the trade unions that has been denounced to the Committee on Freedom of Association and the Committee of Experts on the Application of Conventions and Recommendations at the Conference. The Committee regrettably recalls, once again, that the nomination of the Workers' delegation should be both in agreement with the most representative workers' organizations, on the basis of pre-established, objective and verifiable criteria; and undertaken in such a manner so as to respect the capacity of the workers' organizations to act in absolute independence from the Government.

Objections concerning the nomination of the Workers' delegate of Zimbabwe

51. The Committee had before it an objection submitted by the International Confederation of Free Trade Unions (ICFTU) concerning the nomination of the Workers' delegate of Zimbabwe. It explained that the Government had nominated the Workers' delegate from the Zimbabwe Congress of Trade Unions (ZCTU), an affiliate of the objecting organization. The individual that had been nominated as the Workers' delegate, Mr. Elias Mlotshwa, had been unilaterally selected by the Government in direct contradiction of the ZCTU's own proposal. The ZCTU had communicated the name of its President, Mr. Lovemore Matombo, and its Secretary-General, Mr. Wellington Chibebe, on 20 May 2005 to the Government for the purpose of those individuals being nominated as, respectively, Workers' delegate and adviser and substitute delegate to the Conference. However, the Government, instead of nominating the individuals freely selected by the ZCTU, nominated someone else from the same organization as the Workers' delegate. It

esteemed that the Government's actions, including demanding minutes of internal meetings, amounted to an interference with a workers' organization's ability to act independently and that it was an attempt to divide its affiliate, the ZCTU.

52. The individual nominated by the Government to act as the Workers' delegate, Mr. Mlotshwa, Second Vice-President of ZCTU, had written to the ILO on 31 May 2005, to explain that he would not be attending the Conference as the names of the ZCTU's representatives had already been communicated to the Government on 20 May 2005. Consequently, the objecting organization sought the invalidation of the credentials of the Workers' delegate and sought that the genuine ZCTU representative, Mr. Matombo, be named instead to represent his fellow workers.

53. In a written communication addressed to the Committee at its request, Mr. N.T. Goche, Minister of Public Service, Labour and Social Welfare, who was heading the delegation of Zimbabwe to the Conference, confirmed that the ZCTU had a higher membership based on affiliates than the Zimbabwe Federation of Trade Unions (ZFTU) and that the ZCTU had been consulted, via correspondence, for the purpose of nominating the Workers' delegate to the Conference, in accordance with article 3, paragraph 5, of the ILO Constitution. However, the Government stated that it had not interfered with the internal selection process of the ZCTU when it nominated the Second Vice-President, Mr. Mlotshwa, to be the Workers' delegate. More accurately, it contended that the ZCTU had first nominated as Workers' delegate the Second Vice-President, Mr. Mlotshwa, and then the Third Vice-President, Mr. Ruzive, since the Second Vice-President had declined the nomination.

54. The Government was informed by the ZCTU that the objecting organization's portended candidate, the "suspended" President of ZCTU, Mr. Matombo, was facing disciplinary charges and was under union investigation. In this regard, the Government annexed to its communication a document sent to the attention of the Permanent Secretary of the Ministry of Public Service, Labour and Social Welfare, that was signed by a spokesperson of the ZCTU, Mr. Nicholas Mazarura, with a date of 13 May 2005. The ZCTU communication sought to register its concern over the inclusion of the ZCTU leadership, namely Messrs. L. Matombo and W. Chibebe, and Mesdames L. Matibenga and T. Khumalo, since they were facing "serious allegations". Moreover, it was in this communication that the name of the Second Vice-President, Mr. Mlotshwa, was put forth by the ZCTU and demonstrated that the objecting organization's accusation was unfounded.

55. It added that the nomination of the Second Vice-President, Mr. Mlotshwa, was also raised during a meeting that was held on 19 May 2005 with Mr. Chibebe. During this meeting, the Government questioned whether Messrs. Chibebe and Matombo had actually been elected at any General Council meeting. Mr. Chibebe was requested to provide the Government with the minutes for the meeting that was supposedly held on 23 April 2005, but to date has not done so. The Government considered that it had complied with article 3, paragraph 5, of the ILO Constitution, which in its view required it to do more than "rubber stamp" an appointment, but provided room for consultation and agreement.

56. In a communication dated 23 May 2005 from the Government to the ZCTU, the Government confirmed that it had received the name of the Second Vice-President as the ZCTU's candidate given that Messrs. Matombo and Chibebe, and Mesdames Matibenga and Khumalo were facing serious allegations.

57. Lastly, the Government annexed a communication dated 26 May 2005 from the ZCTU signed again by Mr. Mazarura furnishing the name of its Third Vice-President, Mr. Ruzive, since the Second Vice-President had declined the nomination as Workers' delegate and that the ZCTU refused to convey the names of Messrs. Matombo and Chibebe, and

Mesdames Matibenga and Khumalo, as their representatives given that they were facing serious allegations.

58. The Government, therefore, refuted the genuineness of the communication annexed to the objection dated 31 May 2005 and signed by Mr. Mlotshwa given that he had personally applied for a Swiss visa through the Ministry of Public Service, Labour and Social Welfare.

59. On 9 June 2005, the Committee received a second objection concerning the Workers' delegate from the ICFTU. The second objection was based on the *First revised provisional list of delegations*, which listed Mr. Ruzive as the Workers' delegate. The Government continued to override the most representative workers' organization's decision regarding who would represent it at the Conference, by now nominating Mr. Ruzive instead of Mr. Matombo. It also submitted information indicating that there was an internal conflict within its affiliate, ZCTU, between Mr. Mazarura, on the one hand, and Messrs. Matombo and Chibebe, and Mesdames Matibenga and Khumalo, on the other hand. This conflict was the subject of a lawsuit in a magistrates court. It questions the authenticity of the communication submitted on behalf of the ZCTU by Mr. Mazarura as he had no authority to use ZCTU letterhead and, in this regard, points to certain distinguishing features from genuine ZCTU letterhead, as well as a reference to the "Aggrieved Affiliates Workers' Union". Finally, it adds that there has been grave intimidation in an effort to dissuade workers from freely organizing.

60. On 10 June 2005, the Committee received a late objection concerning the Workers' delegate, from the Concerned Zimbabweans Abroad who requested the invalidation of the credentials of the Workers' delegate, Mr. Ruzive, on the basis that he did not represent the workers of Zimbabwe and was in fact a government sympathizer.

61. Clarifications that were requested by the Committee were provided orally by Mr. Poem Mudyawabikwa, Director for International Relations in the Labour Administration. He was accompanied by Messrs. Kuziwa Nyamwanza, Director for Legal Services and Langton Ngorima, Senior Labour Officer. Mr. Mudyawabikwa provided very detailed information on the process that led to the nomination of two Worker's delegates. In support of the information that the Government had already furnished to the Committee, he repeated that Mr. Matombo had not been nominated as Workers' delegate as he was the subject of serious allegations regarding his role in ZCTU. He also presented allegations against several other members of the ZCTU's leadership, including Mr. Chibebe. The Government was still seeking the minutes of the ZCTU's meeting that had taken place on 23 April 2005, which would demonstrate who was elected by the ZCTU as the Workers' representatives to the present session of the Conference. He added that the withdrawal of Mr. Mlotshwa, who actually proposed himself as Workers' delegate, was under duress and that the nomination of the present Workers' delegate, Mr. Ruzive, was done correctly with the support of 19 affiliates of ZCTU. Mr. Mudyawabikwa was, however, not able to list the 19 trade unions that comprise the Aggrieved Affiliates Workers' Unions. The Government did not verify who supported the letter of nomination sent by Mr. Mazarura nor did it request the minutes of the meetings wherein the nominations of Mr. Mlotshawa and Mr. Ruzive were decided.

62. The Committee notes that the objection is based on the rejection by the Government of the written proposal made by the most representative workers' organization to nominate its representative as the Workers' delegate. The Government does not question the representativeness of the organization, but rather the individual nominated. The Committee notes that, in light of the information put at its disposal, it is not in a position to verify allegations regarding internal conflicts within ZCTU. The Committee, however, notes that the actions taken by the Government are inconsistent with the principles of freedom of association and amount to interference in the internal activities of a workers' organization. Specifically, the Government's insistence on obtaining the minutes of a ZCTU meeting that took place on 23 April 2005 represents unnecessary interference in internal matters of ZCTU. The fact that the Government has not made similar requests for the purpose of verifying the alternative proposals leaves some doubts about whether its treatment is impartial with respect to the two other nominations. Furthermore, the level of detail that Mr. Mudyawabikwa furnished to the Committee indicates the Government's manoeuvres to manipulate the choice of the most representative workers' organization through its deep involvement in the internal problems of the ZCTU. Consequently, the Committee considers that the procedure for nominating the Workers' delegation did not fulfil the conditions of impartiality, transparency and predictability required under article 3, paragraph 5, of the ILO Constitution. As the Committee has stressed in the past, governments must accept the most representative organizations' choice regarding the persons to be nominated as the Workers' delegates. The Committee urges the Government to strictly adhere to its constitutional obligations while nominating the Workers' delegation for the next Conference.

Complaints

63. Following are the seven complaints that were not covered in the Committee's second report. They are listed below in the French alphabetical order of the member States concerned.

Complaint concerning the non-payment of the travel and subsistence expenses of the Employers' delegate of Guinea

64. On 3 June 2005, the Committee received a complaint submitted by the Employers' group of the Conference. The complaint stated that the Government had not made any arrangements to pay the travel and subsistence expenses of Mr. Abdoulaye Dabo, the Employers' delegate. It considers that this failure to comply with article 13, paragraph 2 (a), of the ILO Constitution was discriminatory as the Government was meeting the expenses of the other members of the delegation. The Government was requested to fulfil its obligation by paying the travel and subsistence expenses of Mr. Dabo and, in the future, to comply with its constitutional obligations in this respect.

65. The Committee was informed on 13 June 2005 by Mr. Dabo that his travel and subsistence expenses were paid by the Government. The Committee notes that, in so far as the Government has agreed to cover the necessary subsistence expenses to enable the Employers' delegate to be present until the last day of the Conference, the complaint becomes moot and requires no further intervention by the Committee.

Complaint concerning the non-payment of the travel and subsistence expenses of the Employers' delegation of Iraq

66. On 3 June 2005, the Committee received a complaint submitted by the Employers' group of the Conference. The complaint stated that the Government of Iraq had not made any arrangements to pay the travel and subsistence expenses of its Employers' delegation. The Government was requested to fulfil its obligation by making the necessary arrangements and, in the future, to comply with its constitutional obligations in this respect.

67. The Committee regrets that it has neither received any reply nor any information as to the reason for the absence of replies. Therefore, the Committee could imply that the allegations are accurate. To the extent that the complaint concerns the travel and subsistence expenses of the Employers' delegate, the Committee could find that a violation of the obligations contained in article 13, paragraph 2(a), of the ILO Constitution has been committed and it trusts that the Government will cover the travel and subsistence expenses of the Employers' delegate. It also trusts that in the future the Government will comply with its constitutional obligations in this respect.

68. The Committee recalls that article 13, paragraph 2(a), of the ILO Constitution imposes on its Members an obligation to pay the travel and subsistence expenses of the delegates and their advisers nominated to the Conference. The competence of the Committee to examine complaints on the non-respect of that provision is limited, however, to the situations envisaged in article 26ter, paragraph 1(a) and (b) of the Standing Orders. Consequently, the Committee has decided not to retain this part of the complaint.

Complaint concerning the non-payment of the travel and subsistence expenses of the Workers' adviser of Kazakhstan

69. The Committee had received a complaint submitted by Mr. L. Solomin, Vice-President of the Kazakhstan Confederation of Labour (KCL) and Workers' adviser of Kazakhstan to the Conference, alleging that, under the provisions of Order No. 145-p of 27 May 2005, the Government had undertaken to meet the travel and subsistence expenses of only the Workers' and Employers' delegates, thus, not covering his expenses.

70. The Government has not provided information regarding the allegations, nor has the Committee received any reply or any information as to the reason for the absence of a reply. The Committee recalls that article 13, paragraph 2(a), of the ILO Constitution imposes on its Members an obligation to pay the travel and subsistence expenses of the delegates and their advisers nominated to the Conference. The competence conferred to the Committee in 1997 to examine complaints on the non-respect of that provision is limited, however, to the situations envisaged in article 26ter, paragraph 1(a) and (b), of the Standing Orders, i.e. failure to cover the expenses of at least a tripartite delegation comprising two Government delegates, an Employers' delegate and a Workers' delegate, and cases of serious and manifest imbalance as between the number of Employer and Worker advisers whose expenses have been covered in the delegation and the number of advisers appointed for the Government delegates. Having found no serious and manifest imbalance as between the number of Government advisers and Workers' advisers, the Committee has decided not to retain the complaint.

Complaint concerning the non-payment of subsistence expenses of the Workers' delegate of Liberia

71. The Committee had before it a complaint submitted by the Liberia Federation of Labour Unions (LFLU), alleging the non-payment of expenses of the Workers' delegate of Liberia to the Conference. According to the complaint, the Government stated that it did not have money to sponsor him.

72. The Committee notes that the complaint had been received by the Committee's secretariat on 10 June 2005 at 10.45, that is, three days after the expiration of the deadline established by article 26ter, paragraph 2(a), of the Interim provisions of the Standing Orders of the Conference concerning verification of credentials. On this basis, the complaint is irreceivable.

Complaint concerning the non-payment of the subsistence expenses of the Workers' delegation of the Democratic Republic of the Congo

73. The Committee had before it a complaint, submitted by the International Confederation of Free Trade Unions (ICFTU) on behalf of Mr. Agustin Kabulo, Workers' delegate of the Democratic Republic of the Congo, alleging that his Government had failed to pay the subsistence expenses of the Workers' delegate and two advisers. It requested that the Government provide as soon as possible such subsistence expenses, as it should have done pursuant to article 13, paragraph 2(a), of the ILO Constitution.

74. Despite the Government concerned having been requested to provide information regarding the allegations, the Committee has neither received any reply nor any information as to the reason for the absence of such a reply. The Committee could, in these circumstances, imply that the allegations are accurate and conclude that a violation of the obligations contained in article 13, paragraph 2(a), of the ILO Constitution has been committed. This article obliges governments to bear the expenses of, at least, a complete tripartite delegation so as to permit them to participate for the entire duration of the Conference. The Committee also notes that the Form for Credentials submitted by the Government on 10 May 2005 stated that all the expenses of the ten members of the Workers' delegation had been covered by it. The Committee expects that this is the case and, therefore, does not propose any action at the present session of the Conference.

Second complaint concerning the partial payment of the subsistence expenses of the Workers' delegation of the Democratic Republic of the Congo

75. The Committee had before it a complaint, submitted by Mr. Leyeye-Ngongite, President of the *Intersyndicale des services publics de l'Etat national* (ISPEN) and Mr. Célestin Mayala Wumwesi, President of the *Intersyndical de l'Administration publique* (IAP), alleging that the Government had paid only ten days of subsistence expenses.

76. Under article 26ter, paragraph 2(b), of the Interim provisions of the Conference Standing Orders concerning verification of credentials, a complaint is irreceivable if the author is neither an accredited delegate or adviser nor someone acting on their behalf. The Committee observes that the authors of the objection have been nominated to the Workers' delegation, as persons to occupy advisers' posts that may fall vacant in their delegations designated in accordance with article 2, paragraph 3(i), of the Standing Orders of the Conference. The authors of the complaint, therefore, do not have standing to submit the complaint and, as a consequence, it is irreceivable. In addition, the Committee notes that the complaint had not been received by the secretariat of the Committee until 9 June 2005 at 11.25 a.m., which is to say after the expiration of the time delay provided in article 26ter, paragraph 2(a), of the Interim provisions of the Conference Standing Orders concerning verification of credentials.

Complaint concerning the non-payment of the travel and subsistence expenses of the Employers' delegation of Venezuela

77. The Committee had received a complaint submitted by the Employers' group of the Conference submitted on behalf of the Employers' delegate of Venezuela. The complaint stated that only the delegate and adviser of FEDECAMARAS were paid their expenses by the Government. It was recalled that for 50 years FEDECAMARAS had been the most representative employers' organization in Venezuela, which was confirmed by the

Committee in 2004. Three other organizations that sent representatives to the Conference, namely EMPREVEN, CONFAGAN and FEDEINDUSTRIA, cannot be considered as the most representative employers' organizations under the conditions set forth by the ILO. These organizations were included in the Employers' delegation in contravention of article 3, paragraph 5, of the ILO Constitution, as their nomination was done without the agreement of FEDECAMARAS. Consequently, these organizations should not be part of the Employers' delegations to future Conferences. Finally, the complaint requests that the travel and subsistence expenses of all advisers of FEDECAMARAS be covered by the Government.

78. In a written communication addressed to the Committee at its request, Mr. Ruben Darío Molina, Director of the Bureau of International Relations and ILO Liaison Office of the Ministry of Labour, and Government adviser and substitute delegate to the Conference, considered that the complaint was unfounded. The Employers' representatives were treated in the same manner as the Workers' representatives. It is surprising that the latter were silent about the treatment and were able to ensure financing of their representatives through the contributions of their respective organizations, while the Employers' representatives could not arrive at the same result. The employers' organizations agreed during the meeting of 11 May 2005 on the system of financing of their representatives to the Conference. FEDECAMARAS was apportioned, in addition to the expenses for an adviser as had been done for the other organizations, also the expenses for the Employers' delegate. As for the agreement itself, the Government rejected any allegations of pressure exerted on the representative of FEDECAMARAS. The fact that he signed the agreement following consultations by telephone with the President of FEDECAMARAS and that FEDECAMARAS alleged the pressure on its representatives only two weeks later, reflect conflicts internal to the organization. The meeting in question was only one in a series of meetings between the Government and employers' organizations held since November 2004 on labour-related issues. A copy of the 11 May 2005 agreement appended to the Government's submission reflects the Government's undertaking to cover the travel and subsistence expenses for the Employers' delegate as well as one adviser from each organization represented in the delegation.

79. It is not necessary to repeat the Committee's comments reflected in reports from previous years regarding the fact that FEDECAMARAS is the most representative employers' organization in Venezuela (see Credentials Committee, Third Report, *Provisional Record* No. 6D, 2004). The Committee notes that the position of the Government favours again the minority employers' organizations even on the issue of expenses. While article 13, paragraph 2(a), of the ILO Constitution imposes on all governments the obligation to pay the expenses of their tripartite delegations to the Conference, so that the payment of expenses of the Employer's delegate cannot be understood as a favour, the Government's decision to cover expenses of one adviser of each employers' organization included in the delegation clearly favours CONFAGAN and EMPREVEN, and punishes FEDECAMARAS. The Committee expresses its hopes that the relevant Government decisions for future Conferences will give due consideration to the level of representativeness of each organization not only in the distribution of posts within the Employers' delegation, but also on the issue of covering their expenses.

Communication

80. The Committee had received the following communication.

Communication concerning the Workers' delegation of Burundi

81. The Committee had received on 4 June 2005 a communication submitted by the International Confederation of Free Trade Unions (ICFTU), reporting actions of the Government against Mr. Pierre Claver Hajayandi, Secretary-General of the *Confédération des syndicates du Burundi* (COSYBU). Mr. Hajayandi is the author of an objection that the Committee examined in this report (Supra, paragraphs 9 to 12). The Committee takes note of the information contained in the communication submitted by the ICFTU. It considers that the subject of the communication does not call for any action on its part.

* * *

82. The Committee was advised of a certain number of communications sent by electronic mail to the International Labour Office and the secretariat of the Conference. To the extent that these communications do not contain any signatures and, therefore, their authenticity cannot be verified the Committee had decided to neither consider them nor include them in its report.

83. The Credentials Committee adopts this report unanimously. It submits it to the Conference so it may take note of it.

Geneva, 14 June 2005. *(Signed)* Mr. Jules Medenou Oni, Chairperson.

Ms. Lucia Sasso Mazzufferi.

Mr. Ulf Edström.

List of registered delegates and advisers

1) Government delegates
2) Government advisers
3) Employers' delegates
4) Employers' Advisers
5) Workers' delegates
6) Workers' Advisers

Country	1)	2)	3)	4)	5)	6)
Afghanistan	2	5	-	-	1	-
Albania	2	3	1	1	1	3
Algeria	1	12	1	6	1	8
Angola	2	3	1	2	1	2
Antigua and Barbuda	-	-	-	-	-	-
Argentina	1	7	-	8	1	7
Armenia	2	2	1	-	1	-
Australia	2	3	1	1	1	1
Austria	2	6	1	3	-	2
Azerbaijan	2	2	1	7	1	2
Bahamas	2	-	1	-	1	-
Bahrain	2	6	1	2	1	2
Bangladesh	2	4	1	1	1	1
Barbados	2	5	1	1	1	1
Belarus	2	6	1	2	-	3
Belgium	2	15	1	3	-	8
Belize	2	-	-	-	-	-
Benin	2	4	-	1	1	8
Bolivia	2	1	1	-	1	-
Bosnia and Herzegovina	2	2	1	-	1	-
Botswana	2	7	1	-	1	1
Brazil	2	6	1	6	1	7
Bulgaria	2	7	1	4	1	1
Burkina Faso	2	11	1	1	1	2
Burundi	1	1	-	-	1	2
Cambodia	2	3	1	1	1	3
Cameroon	2	9	1	1	1	3
Canada	2	13	1	7	1	4
Cape Verde	2	-	1	-	1	-
Central African Republic	2	4	1	-	1	-
Chad	2	2	1	-	1	1
Chile	2	8	1	4	-	8
China	2	20	1	8	1	10
Colombia	2	9	1	8	1	7
Comoros	-	-	-	-	-	-
Congo	2	8	1	-	1	6
Costa Rica	2	4	1	-	1	-
Côte d'Ivoire	2	10	-	2	1	6
Croatia	2	3	-	1	1	2
Cuba	2	8	1	3	1	6
Cyprus	2	3	1	6	1	5
Czech Republic	2	8	1	3	1	5
Democratic Republic of the Congo	1	15	1	8	1	8
Denmark	2	8	-	3	1	5
Djibouti	2	-	1	-	1	1
Dominica	-	-	-	-	-	-

Country	1)	2)	3)	4)	5)	6)
Dominican Republic	2	6	1	2	1	1
Ecuador	2	5	1	1	1	3
Egypt	2	9	1	3	1	6
El Salvador	2	3	1	3	1	4
Equatorial Guinea	2	-	-	-	-	-
Eritrea	1	1	1	-	1	1
Estonia	2	3	1	-	1	-
Ethiopia	2	2	1	1	1	1
Fiji	2	-	1	1	1	1
Finland	2	5	1	3	1	3
France	2	11	1	8	1	8
Gabon	2	5	1	2	1	5
Gambia	2	-	-	-	-	-
Georgia	2	1	1	7	1	1
Germany	2	10	1	4	1	5
Ghana	2	13	1	8	1	4
Greece	2	16	-	7	1	1
Grenada	-	-	-	-	-	-
Guatemala	2	6	1	-	1	-
Guinea	2	12	1	4	1	8
Guinea-Bissau	2	1	-	-	-	-
Guyana	-	-	-	-	-	-
Haiti	2	6	1	2	1	2
Honduras	2	6	1	1	1	1
Hungary	2	14	-	8	1	8
Iceland	2	3	1	1	1	2
India	2	7	-	7	1	5
Indonesia	2	16	1	7	1	4
Islamic Republic of Iran	2	16	1	5	1	5
Iraq	2	6	-	1	1	1
Ireland	2	16	1	1	1	1
Israel	2	5	-	1	1	4
Italy	2	6	1	1	1	3
Jamaica	2	8	1	1	1	4
Japan	2	16	1	8	1	8
Jordan	2	8	1	2	1	4
Kazakhstan	2	1	1	1	1	1
Kenya	2	11	1	1	1	3
Kiribati	-	-	-	-	-	-
Republic of Korea	-	10	1	-	6	8
Kuwait	2	15	1	3	1	3
Kyrgyzstan	2	1	-	-	-	-
Lao People's Dem. Republic	2	-	1	-	1	-
Latvia	2	-	1	1	1	-
Lebanon	2	5	1	3	1	5
Lesotho	2	4	1	-	1	-

Country	1)	2)	3)	4)	5)	6)
Liberia	2	1	-	-	-	1
Libyan Arab Jamahiriya	2	6	1	-	1	3
Lithuania	2	3	1	-	1	6
Luxembourg	2	10	1	5	-	8
Madagascar	2	3	1	1	1	1
Malawi	2	-	1	-	1	1
Malaysia	1	8	1	2	1	1
Mali	2	9	1	1	1	2
Malta	2	5	1	4	1	6
Mauritania	2	4	1	-	1	4
Mauritius	2	-	1	2	1	-
Mexico	2	9	1	7	1	8
Republic of Moldova	2	-	1	1	1	1
Mongolia	2	1	1	1	1	1
Morocco	2	8	1	5	-	6
Mozambique	2	6	1	-	1	1
Myanmar	2	6	1	-	1	1
Namibia	2	3	1	1	1	1
Nepal	2	1	-	1	-	1
Netherlands	2	12	1	1	1	5
New Zealand	2	3	1	1	1	1
Nicaragua	2	3	1	1	1	1
Niger	2	5	1	2	1	3
Nigeria	2	11	1	5	1	6
Norway	2	9	1	8	1	5
Oman	2	7	-	4	1	3
Pakistan	2	4	-	1	-	-
Panama	2	3	1	2	1	2
Papua New Guinea	2	2	1	-	1	-
Paraguay	1	3	1	2	1	1
Peru	2	4	1	-	1	-
Philippines	2	3	1	2	1	3
Poland	2	10	1	3	-	5
Portugal	2	8	1	7	1	5
Qatar	2	7	-	1	1	-
Romania	2	6	1	8	1	7
Russian Federation	2	13	1	2	1	5
Rwanda	1	2	-	1	-	3
Saint Kitts and Nevis	-	-	-	-	-	-
Saint Lucia	-	-	-	-	-	-
Saint Vincent and the Grenadines	2	-	-	-	-	-
San Marino	2	1	1	3	1	1
Sao Tome and Principe	1	-	1	-	1	-
Saudi Arabia	2	6	1	1	1	2
Senegal	2	5	1	3	1	3
Serbia and Montenegro	2	5	1	6	1	5

Country	1)	2)	3)	4)	5)	6)
Seychelles	2	-	1	-	1	-
Sierra Leone	1	-	-	1	-	3
Singapore	2	10	1	1	1	6
Slovakia	2	6	1	2	1	3
Samoa	-	-	-	-	-	-
Slovenia	2	6	1	1	1	1
Solomon Islands	-	-	-	-	-	-
Somalia	2	1	-	-	-	2
South Africa	2	9	1	8	1	6
Spain	2	11	1	7	1	8
Sri Lanka	2	7	1	-	1	5
Sudan	2	6	1	2	1	5
Suriname	2	-	-	-	-	-
Swaziland	2	3	1	2	-	1
Sweden	2	7	1	3	1	5
Switzerland	2	8	1	3	-	6
Syrian Arab Republic	2	5	1	2	1	3
Tajikistan	2	-	-	-	-	-
United Republic of Tanzania	2	14	1	2	1	1
Thailand	2	15	1	4	1	4
The FYR Macedonia	2	4	-	-	-	-
Democratic Rep. of Timor-Leste	2	1	-	1	-	-
Togo	2	-	1	1	1	4
Trinidad and Tobago	2	4	1	1	1	1
Tunisia	2	7	1	8	1	8
Turkey	2	15	1	8	1	7
Turkmenistan	-	-	-	-	-	-
Uganda	2	6	1	5	1	1
Ukraine	2	2	1	3	1	5
United Arab Emirates	1	6	1	2	1	1
United Kingdom	2	14	1	5	1	4
United States	2	15	1	6	1	6
Uruguay	2	7	1	3	1	2
Uzbekistan	2	-	-	1	-	-
Vanuatu	1	-	-	-	-	-
Venezuela	2	11	1	7	1	4
Viet Nam	2	8	1	3	1	2
Yemen	2	2	1	-	1	2
Zambia	2	9	1	2	1	1
Zimbabwe	2	12	1	1	1	1

	1)	2)	3)	4)	5)	6)
Total	322	989	142	404	146	480

International Labour Conference

Record of Proceedings   5-1

Ninety-third Session, Geneva, 2005

Second item on the agenda: Programme and Budget proposals for 2006-07 and other questions

First report of the Finance Committee of Government Representatives

1. The Finance Committee of Government Representatives met on 1 June 2005 with Mr. J-J. Elmiger (Switzerland) as Chairperson and Reporter and Ambassador Burayzat (Jordan) as Vice-Chairperson.

Request of the Government of Armenia, under paragraph 4 of article 13 of the Constitution of the International Labour Organization, for permission to vote

2. The Committee had before it a request (document C.F./D.2) from the Government of Armenia for permission to vote at the Conference. This request was referred to the Finance Committee as a matter of urgency in accordance with paragraph 1 of article 31 of the Standing Orders of the Conference. The text of the request, received on 16 May 2005, is as follows:

Permanent Representative of
the Republic of Armenia
Geneva, Switzerland

Dear Director-General,

I have the honour to inform you that the Government of Armenia wishes to regularize the arrears of contributions due by it to the International Labour Organisation and regain its right to vote and participate actively in the Organisation.

Careful consideration of the history and structure of Armenia's arrears accumulated over the previous years would provide explanation behind the situation. In particular, Armenia's total amount of accumulated arrears in the period 1992-1998 amounts to CHF 1,833,044. In average for the above seven years the assessed contribution stood at CHF 261,863 p.a. The present amount of contributions at CHF 7,097 represents only 2.7% of the expected average per annum contributions for the years 1992-1998. Of the overall amount of Armenia's unpaid contributions of CHF 1,935,666 those 94.6% of total arrears, which were accumulated in 1992-1998 represent the assessment of contributions far in excess of Armenia's actual capabilities. Review and analyses of Armenia's actual economic performance in the years 1992-1998 and state budget allocations would illustrate the unrealistic approach to expectations with regard to Armenia's financial obligations to the ILO. Armenia's failure to pay was due to conditions beyond its control.

I would therefore kindly request that you submit the following proposal for the settlement of Armenia's arrears of contribution to the competent authorities of the International Labour Organisation:

(a) Armenia will continue to regularly pay in full its assessed contribution in the year in which they become due.

(b) Armenia will settle the arrears of contribution that have accumulated up to the end of 2004, covering contributions from 1992 and amounting in total to CHF 1,935,666 by 20 annual instalments in accordance with the following schedule:

Total arrears to regular budget CHF 1,935,666
Scheduled payments of the arrears (20 years)

Year	Currency	Amount
2005	CHF	48,000
2006	CHF	48,000
2007	CHF	48,000
2008	CHF	48,000
2009	CHF	72,000
2010	CHF	72,000
2011	CHF	72,000
2012	CHF	72,000
2013	CHF	96,000
2014	CHF	96,000
2015	CHF	96,000
2016	CHF	96,000
2017	CHF	120,000
2018	CHF	120,000
2019	CHF	120,000
2020	CHF	120,000
2021	CHF	144,000
2022	CHF	144,000
2023	CHF	144,000
2024	CHF	159,666

Total payments of the arrears CHF 1,935,666

I would further request that you transmit to the 93rd International Labour Conference my Government's request that it be permitted to vote and enjoy other rights in the Organisation in accordance with article 13, paragraph 4 of the Constitution of ILO.

Yours sincerely,
(Signed) Zohrab MNATSAKANIAN.

3. The Committee noted the provisions of paragraph 4 of article 13 of the Constitution of the ILO, also articles 31 and 32 of the Standing Orders of the Conference, the texts of which appear in the Appendix to this report.

4. Armenia became a member of the ILO on 26 November 1992. In examining the financial relations between Armenia and the ILO during the period of membership, the Committee noted that the following payments in respect of assessed contributions had been made to the ILO:

Date of payment	Amount in Swiss francs	Details of payment
9 October 2003	7 683	Part 1992 contribution – equivalent to the 2003 assessment
8 November 2004	7 097	Part 1992 contribution – equivalent to the 2004 assessment

Contributions outstanding at 31 December 2004 amounted to 1,953,666 Swiss francs, covering the assessed contributions from 1992 to 2004. The 2005 contribution of 7,097 Swiss francs had also not been paid.

5. The representative of Armenia thanked the member States for their support and understanding and reaffirmed his country's commitment to the principles of the ILO.

6. *The Committee, being satisfied that the failure of Armenia to pay its arrears was due to conditions beyond its control, in accordance with the provisions of paragraph 4 of article 31 of the Standing Orders of the Conference, reports to the Conference as follows:*

    (a) that the failure of Armenia to pay in full the amounts owing was due to conditions beyond its control as explained in the letter in paragraph 2 above;

    (b) that the financial relations between Armenia and the Organization have been set out in paragraph 4 above.

7. *The Committee accordingly recommends the adoption by the Conference of the resolution concerning the granting to Armenia of permission to vote under paragraph 4 of article 13 of the Constitution of the International Labour Organization, the text of which appears at the end of this report.*

Request of the Government of the Republic of Moldova, under paragraph 4 of article 13 of the Constitution of the International Labour Organization, for permission to vote

8. The Committee had before it a request (document C.F./D.3) from the Government of the Republic of Moldova for permission to vote at the Conference. This request was referred to the Finance Committee as a matter of urgency in accordance with paragraph 1 of article 31 of the Standing Orders of the Conference. The text of the request, received on 3 May 2005, is as follows:

Ministry of Economics and Trade
of the Republic of Moldova

Mr. Juan Somavia
Director-General of the
International Labour Office

Dear Mr. Somavia,

I am pleased to inform you that the Government of the Republic of Moldova is very anxious to restore its voting rights within the International Labour Organization and at the same time to put forward a proposal regarding payment of its arrears of contributions.

The Government of the Republic of Moldova reaffirms its commitment to the principles and objectives of the ILO, and wishes in future to participate as a full member in the activities of the Organization.

I should like to draw your attention to the fact that the Republic of Moldova's ability to honour its financial obligations was seriously impaired by the grave economic crisis brought about by the collapse of the Soviet Union and by the considerable economic and social changes which affected the country.

Consequently, the economic problems experienced during the transition period have made it impossible for us to pay the accumulated arrears through one immediate transaction. I thus respectfully request your assistance with regard to submitting the following proposals to the Finance Committee of the 93rd Session of the International Labour Conference:

– On 27 April 2005, the Republic of Moldova transferred its 2005 member state contribution (3,548 CHF).

– The arrears accumulated during the 1992-2004 period of 2,729,346 Swiss francs will be paid over the course of 20 years, beginning in 2006, in line with the multi-annual payment plan included in the annex.

On behalf of the Government of the Republic of Moldova, I would ask you to pass on to the 93rd Session of the International Labour Conference my Government's request that approval be given for my country to have its voting and other rights restored, in accordance with article 13, paragraph 4, of the ILO Constitution.

I would like to take this opportunity, Sir, to renew the assurances of my highest consideration.

(Signed) Valeriu LAZĂR,
Minister.

Annex to the letter

Multi-year payments plan (2006-2025)

The purpose of the present plan is to eliminate Moldova's arrears within a period of 20 years. It provides for payment each year of the Republic of Moldova's current year assessment and a part of its arrears.

2006 – 136,473*	2016 – 136,467*
2007 – 136,467*	2017 – 136,467*
2008 – 136,467*	2018 – 136,467*
2009 – 136,467*	2019 – 136,467*
2010 – 136,467*	2020 – 136,467*
2011 – 136,467*	2021 – 136,467*
2012 – 136,467*	2022 – 136,467*
2013 – 136,467*	2023 – 136,467*
2014 – 136,467*	2024 – 136,467*
2015 – 136,467*	2025 – 136,467*

Total amount pending: 2,729,346 CHF

_____

* Plus contributions for the current year.

9. The Committee noted the provisions of paragraph 4 of article 13 of the Constitution of the ILO, also articles 31 and 32 of the Standing Orders of the Conference, the texts of which appear in the Appendix to this report.

10. The Republic of Moldova became a member of the Organization on 8 June 1992. During the period 1992-2004 the Republic of Moldova had made no payments to the ILO in respect of its assessed contributions. A payment of 3,548 Swiss francs was received on 28 April 2005, which, as indicated in the letter from the Government of the Republic of Moldova in paragraph 8 above, had been intended as a payment against its contribution corresponding to the year 2005. Contributions outstanding at 31 December 2004 amounted to 2,729,346 Swiss francs, covering the assessed contributions from 1992 to 2004.

11. There were no statements by Committee members concerning this item.

12. *The Committee, being satisfied that the failure of the Republic of Moldova to pay its arrears was due to conditions beyond its control, in accordance with the provisions of paragraph 4 of article 31 of the Standing Orders of the Conference, reports to the Conference as follows:*

    (a) that the failure of the Republic of Moldova to pay in full the amounts owing was due to conditions beyond its control as explained in the letter in paragraph 8 above;

    (b) that the financial relations between the Republic of Moldova and the Organization have been set out in paragraph 10 above.

13. *The Committee accordingly recommends the adoption by the Conference of the resolution concerning the granting to the Republic of Moldova of permission to vote under paragraph 4 of article 13 of the Constitution of the International Labour Organization, the text of which appears at the end of this report.*

Appendix

14. The provisions of paragraph 4 of article 13 of the Constitution of the ILO, also articles 31 and 32 of the Standing Orders of the Conference, are reproduced in the appendix to this report.

Geneva, 2 June 2005.

(Signed) J.-J. Elmiger,
Chairperson and Reporter.

Resolutions submitted to the Conference

Resolution concerning the arrears of contributions of Armenia

The General Conference of the International Labour Organization,

Having regard to paragraph 7 of article 10 of the Financial Regulations,

Accepts the arrangement proposed by the Government of Armenia for the settlement of its arrears of contributions due for the period 1992-2004 to the effect that:

(a) in 2005, the Government of Armenia will pay in full its contribution for the year 2005;

(b) in subsequent years, the Government of Armenia will continue to pay its current contribution in full in the year for which it is due;

(c) the Government of Armenia will settle arrears that have accumulated up to and including 31 December 2004, amounting to 1,935,666 Swiss francs, by payment, beginning in 2005, of 20 annual instalments in accordance with the following schedule:

Years		Annual instalment (in Swiss francs)	Total
2005-08	4 years	48 000	192 000
2009-12	4 years	72 000	288 000
2013-16	4 years	96 000	384 000
2017-20	4 years	120 000	480 000
2021-23	3 years	144 000	432 000
2024	1 year	159 666	159 666
Total			1 935 666

Decides that Armenia shall be permitted to vote, in accordance with paragraph 4 of article 13 of the Constitution of the International Labour Organization, after the conclusion of the present business.

Resolution concerning the arrears of contributions of the Republic of Moldova

The General Conference of the International Labour Organization,

Having regard to paragraph 7 of article 10 of the Financial Regulations,

Accepts the arrangement proposed by the Government of the Republic of Moldova for the settlement of its arrears of contributions due for the period 1992-2004 to the effect that:

(a) the payment of 3,548 Swiss francs made by the Government of the Republic of Moldova in April 2005 will be applied against its full contribution for the year 2005;

(b) in subsequent years, the Government of the Republic of Moldova will continue to pay its current contribution in full in the year for which it is due;

(c) the Government of the Republic of Moldova will settle arrears that have accumulated up to and including 31 December 2004, amounting to 2,729,346 Swiss francs, by payment, beginning in 2006, of first instalment of 136,473 Swiss francs and 19 annual instalments of 136,467 Swiss francs;

Decides that the Republic of Moldova shall be permitted to vote, in accordance with paragraph 4 of article 13 of the Constitution of the International Labour Organization, after the conclusion of the present business.

Appendix

Relevant provisions of the Constitution of the International Labour Organization and the Standing Orders of the International Labour Conference

1. Paragraph 4 of article 13 of the Constitution of the Organization provides as follows:

    4. A Member of the Organization which is in arrears in the payment of its financial contribution to the Organization shall have no vote in the Conference, in the Governing Body, in any committee, or in the elections of members of the Governing Body, if the amount of its arrears equals or exceeds the amount of the contributions due from it for the preceding two full years: Provided that the Conference may by a two-thirds majority of the votes cast by the delegates present permit such a Member to vote if it is satisfied that the failure to pay is due to conditions beyond the control of the Member.

2. Articles 31 and 32 of the Standing Orders of the Conference provide as follows:

ARTICLE 31

Procedure where proposal is made to permit Member in arrears to vote

1. Any request or proposal that the Conference should nevertheless permit a Member which is in arrears in the payment of its contributions to vote in accordance with article 13, paragraph 4, of the Constitution shall be referred in the first instance to the Finance Committee of the Conference, which shall report thereon as a matter of urgency.

2. Pending a decision on the request or proposal by the Conference, the Member shall not be entitled to vote.

3. The Finance Committee shall submit to the Conference a report giving its opinion on the request or proposal.

4. If the Finance Committee, having found that the failure to pay is due to conditions beyond the control of the Member, thinks fit to propose to the Conference that the Member should nevertheless be permitted to vote in accordance with article 13, paragraph 4, of the Constitution, it shall in its report:

(a) explain the nature of the conditions beyond the Member's control;

(b) give an analysis of the financial relations between the Member and the Organization during the preceding ten years; and

(c) indicate the measures which should be taken in order to settle the arrears.

5. Any decision which may be taken by the Conference to permit a Member which is in arrears in the payment of its contributions to vote notwithstanding such arrears may be made conditional upon the Member complying with any recommendations for settling the arrears which may be made by the Conference.

ARTICLE 32

Period of validity of a decision to permit Member in arrears to vote

1. Any decision by the Conference permitting a Member which is in arrears in the payment of its contributions to vote shall be valid for the session of the Conference at which the decision is taken. Any such decision shall be operative in regard to the Governing Body and committees until the opening of the general session of the Conference next following that at which it was taken.

2. Notwithstanding the provisions of paragraph 1 of this article, after the Conference has approved an arrangement under which the arrears of a Member are consolidated and are payable in annual instalments over a period of years, the Member shall be permitted to vote provided that, at the time of the vote concerned, the Member has fully paid all instalments under the arrangement, as well as all financial contributions under article 13 of the Constitution that were due before the end of the previous year. For any Member which, at the close of the session of the Conference, has not fully paid all such instalments and contributions due before the end of the previous year, the permission to vote shall lapse.

CONTENTS

Page

Second item on the agenda: Programme and Budget proposals for 2006-07 and other questions

First report of the Finance Committee of Government Representatives 1

Resolutions submitted to the Conference 7

Appendix 9

International Labour Conference

Record of Proceedings

5-2

Ninety-third Session, Geneva, 2005

Second item on the agenda: Programme and Budget proposals for 2006-07 and other questions

Second report of the Finance Committee of Government Representatives

1. The Finance Committee of Government Representatives met on 1, 2, 3 and 9 June 2005 with Mr. J.-J. Elmiger (Switzerland) as Chairperson and Reporter and Ambassador Burayzat (Jordan) as Vice-Chairperson.

Request of the Government of Togo, under paragraph 4 of article 13 of the Constitution of the International Labour Organization, for permission to vote

2. The Committee had before it a request (document C.F./D.8) from the Government of Togo for permission to vote at the Conference. This request was referred to the Finance Committee as a matter of urgency in accordance with paragraph 1 of article 31 of the Standing Orders of the Conference. The text of the request, dated 2 June 2005, is as follows:

Ministry of the Public Service,
Labour and Employment,
Office of the Minister,
Lomé, Republic of Togo.

2 June 2005

Dear Mr. Somavia,

I have the honour to inform you that the Government of Togo wishes to settle the arrears in contributions due to the International Labour Organization and to recover its right to vote in order to participate actively in the work of the Organization.

My country paid its contributions regularly until 1990, when a period of social and economic disruption began which hampered its development efforts.

Since 2003, however, the Government has decided to settle its arrears, and in June 2004 it paid an initial instalment, to be followed by others.

I would therefore appreciate it if you would submit the following proposal for the settlement of arrears in contributions owed by Togo to the competent department of the International Labour Office.

(a) For 2005, Togo will settle the full amount of its contribution, assessed at 3,548 Swiss francs, as a token of the Government's willingness to regularize its situation.

(b) Togo will settle the arrears in contributions that have accumulated up to the end of 2004, i.e. the contributions due for the period 1992-2004, totalling 213,453 Swiss francs, in seven annual instalments of 27,924 Swiss francs each, plus a final instalment of 17,985 Swiss francs.

(c) Togo will pay its subsequent years' contributions in the year in which they become due.

I would be grateful if you would transmit to the 93rd Session of the International Labour Conference my Government's request to be authorized to vote and to enjoy its other rights in the Organization, in accordance with article 13, paragraph 4, of the Constitution of the ILO.

Please accept the assurance of my highest consideration.

(Signed and stamped) Rodolphe Kossivi Osseyi, Minister.

3. The Committee noted the provisions of paragraph 4 of article 13 of the Constitution of the ILO, also articles 31 and 32 of the Standing Orders of the Conference, the texts of which appear in Appendix 1 to this report.

4. In examining the financial relations between Togo and the ILO, the Committee noted that the last payments made by Togo to the ILO in respect of its assessed contributions were the following:

Date of payment	Amount in Swiss francs	Details of payment
19 March 1991	32 438	Balance of 1989 and part of 1990 contribution
2 September 1992	29 499	Balance of 1990, full 1991 and part of 1992 contribution
7 June 2004	27 924	Part of 1992 contribution

Contributions outstanding at 31 December 2004 amounted to 213,453 Swiss francs, covering the assessed contributions from 1992 to 2004. The 2005 contribution of 3,548 Swiss francs had also not been paid.

5. *The Committee, being satisfied that the failure of Togo to pay its arrears was due to conditions beyond its control, in accordance with the provisions of paragraph 4 of article 31 of the Standing Orders of the Conference, reports to the Conference as follows:*

(a) that the failure of Togo to pay in full the amounts owing was due to conditions beyond its control as explained in the letter in paragraph 2 above;

(b) that the financial relations between Togo and the Organization have been set out in paragraph 4 above.

6. *The Committee accordingly recommends the adoption by the Conference of the resolution concerning the granting to Togo of permission to vote under paragraph 4 of article 13 of the Constitution of the International Labour Organization, the text of which appears at the end of this report.*

Request of the Government of Georgia, under paragraph 4 of article 13 of the Constitution of the International Labour Organization, for permission to vote

7. The Committee had before it a request (document C.F./D.9) from the Government of Georgia for permission to vote at the Conference. This request was referred to the Finance Committee as a matter of urgency in accordance with paragraph 1 of article 31 of the Standing Orders of the Conference. The text of the request, dated 18 May 2005, is as follows:

Minister of Foreign Affairs of Georgia

Tbilisi, May 18, 2005

Your Excellency,

I have the honour to inform you that the Government of Georgia wishes to regularize the arrears of contributions due by it to the International Labour Organization (ILO) and regain its right to vote, and at the same time would like to make a proposal to settle its arrears of contributions.

I would like to point out that the non-payment of contributions by the previous Government of Georgia was due to the following reasons:

- Economic crisis caused by the dissolution of the former USSR; Georgia is among the transition economies that have suffered most during the past decade.

- Civil unrest and conflicts in Abkhazia and Tskhinvali region in early 1990's.

- Georgia has 300,000 refugees and internally displaced persons from the "frozen conflicts" in Abkhazia and Tskhinvali region that are still heavy burdens for our budget.

- A number of external shocks did in fact greatly influence the economic development of Georgia in 1998-2001. Among them the most negative impacts on Georgian economy have Russian and Turkish financial crises.

- Severe droughts in 1998 and in 2000 affected almost all of the country and created energy shortages by limiting hydroelectric power generation.

- The increase in the price of energy imports, as well as some other additional negative facts, also had a considerable adverse impact on the country's development.

Thus, the abovementioned problems during the time of the transition period did not permit the previous Government of Georgia to settle the arrears of contribution.

Measures provided by the new Government of Georgia directed for generating economic development and increasing of tax collection allow Georgia to begin settlement of outstanding arrears of contributions with major International Organizations. The Government of Georgia hereby reaffirms its commitment to the goals and principles of ILO and would like further to take its full part in the activities of the Organization.

I would therefore kindly request that you submit the following proposal for the settlement of Georgia's arrears of contribution to the Finance Committee of the International Labour Conference at its 93rd session.

(a) For 2005, Georgia will pay in full its assessed contribution of 10,645 Swiss francs in order to demonstrate our commitment.

(b) Georgia will settle, up to the end of 2019, the arrears of contribution that have accumulated, amounting in total to 3,071,902 Swiss francs, by 14 annual instalments in accordance with the following schedule.

Years	% of arrears	Amount (in Swiss francs)
2006	1.5	46 079
2007	2.0	61 438
2008	2.0	61 438
2009	2.0	61 438
2010	2.0	61 438
2011	4.0	122 876
2012	5.0	153 595
2013	5.0	153 595
2014	10.0	307 190
2015	12.0	368 628
2016	12.0	368 628
2017	14.0	430 066
2018	14.0	430 066
2019	14.5	445 427
	Total	3 071 902

(c) Georgia also will settle subsequent years' contributions in the year in which they become due.

On behalf of the Government of Georgia, I would further request that you transmit to the 93rd session of International Labour Conference my Government's request that it be permitted to vote and enjoy other rights in the Organization in accordance with article 13, paragraph 4 of the ILO.

In the hope that this proposal will receive favourable consideration, I assure you, Mr. Director-General, of my highest consideration.

Yours sincerely,

[Signed]

Salome Zourabishvili.

8. The Committee noted the provisions of paragraph 4 of article 13 of the Constitution of the ILO, also articles 31 and 32 of the Standing Orders of the Conference, the texts of which appear in Appendix 1 to this report.

9. Georgia became a Member of the Organization on 22 June 1993 since which it had made no payments to the ILO in respect of its assessed contributions. Contributions outstanding at 31 December 2004 amounted to 3,071,902 Swiss francs, covering the assessed contributions from 1993 to 2004. The 2005 contribution of 10,645 Swiss francs had also not been paid.

10. *The Committee, being satisfied that the failure of Georgia to pay its arrears was due to conditions beyond its control, in accordance with the provisions of paragraph 4 of article 31 of the Standing Orders of the Conference, reports to the Conference as follows:*

   (a) that the failure of Georgia to pay in full the amounts owing was due to conditions beyond its control as explained in the letter in paragraph 7 above;

   (b) that the financial relations between Georgia and the Organization have been set out in paragraph 9 above.

11. *The Committee accordingly recommends the adoption by the Conference of the resolution concerning the granting to Georgia of permission to vote under paragraph 4 of article 13 of the Constitution of the International Labour Organization, the text of which appears at the end of this report.*

Request of the Government of Iraq, under paragraph 4 of article 13 of the Constitution of the International Labour Organization, for permission to vote

12. The Committee had before it a request (document C.F./D.10) from the Government of Iraq for permission to vote at the Conference. This request was referred to the Finance Committee as a matter of urgency in accordance with paragraph 1 of article 31 of the Standing Orders of the Conference. The text of the request, dated 8 June 2005, is as follows:

Republic of Iraq,
Ministry of Labour and Social Affairs,
Baghdad, Iraq.

8 June 2005

Dear Director-General of the International Labour Organization,

Reference is made to our meeting on Tuesday, 7 June 2005 with Ms. Patricia O'Donovan, Executive Director Management and Administration, and Mr. Greg Johnson, Treasurer and Financial Comptroller. We explained in that meeting that for reasons beyond the control of our Government, in particular, the significant reduction in Iraqi oil exports due to the terrorist acts against our oil pipelines and other installations, our Government has not had the financial means to pay its arrears of contribution to the International Labour Organization nor its annual contributions.

To enable us to honour our commitments to your Organization, we kindly request that the settlement of arrears be over a period of twenty years instead of the present 10 year period.

We will take immediate measures to pay the 2005 contribution of 56,772 Swiss francs and the new instalment amount of 306,390 Swiss francs.

Thank you for your kind cooperation.

(Signed)	*(Signed)*
Dr. Idris Hadi Salih,	Baha Al Shibib,
Minister of Labour and Social Affairs	Ambassador,
of Iraq.	Permanent Representative of Iraq.

13. The Committee noted the provisions of paragraph 4 of article 13 of the Constitution of the ILO, also articles 31 and 32 of the Standing Orders of the Conference, the texts of which appear in Appendix I to this report.

14. In examining the financial relations between Iraq and the ILO, the Committee noted that the last payment made by Iraq to the ILO in respect of its assessed contributions was the following:

Date of payment	Amount in Swiss francs	Details of payment
28 February 1990	116 399	Part 1988 contribution

At its 92nd (2004) Session of the International Labour Conference adopted an arrangement proposed by the Government of Iraq for the settlement of arrears of contribution due for the period of 1988-2003 of 5,652,327 Swiss francs. Under the terms of the agreement, Iraq was to pay in full its contribution for the year 2004 and an amount of 657,327 Swiss francs in

2004 and to settle its arrears in ten annual instalments, beginning in 2005. No payments had been received. Contributions outstanding at 31 December 2004 amounted to 6,127,793 Swiss francs, covering the assessed contributions from 1988 to 2004. The 2005 contribution of 56,772 Swiss francs had also not been paid.

15. *The Committee, being satisfied that the failure of Iraq to pay its arrears was due to conditions beyond its control, in accordance with the provisions of paragraph 4 of article 31 of the Standing Orders of the Conference, reports to the Conference as follows:*

   (a) that the failure of Iraq to pay in full the amounts owing was due to conditions beyond its control as explained in the letter in paragraph 12 above;

   (b) that the financial relations between Iraq and the Organization have been set out in paragraph 14 above.

16. *The Committee accordingly recommends the adoption by the Conference of the resolution concerning the granting to Iraq of permission to vote under paragraph 4 of article 13 of the Constitution of the International Labour Organization, the text of which appears at the end of this report.*

Status of collection of member States' contributions

17. The Committee had before it document C.F./D.4 containing information on the status of collection of member States' contributions as at 27 May 2005.

18. The Treasurer and Financial Comptroller reported that, in addition to the information contained in the Office paper, contributions had since been received from the following member States:

Country	Swiss francs
Democratic Republic of Congo	49 164
Paraguay	42 579
Morocco	166 582
Total	258 325

19. *The Committee took note of the information in the document.*

Composition of the Administrative Tribunal of the International Labour Organization

20. The Committee had before it Report II: Draft Programme and Budget 2006-07 and other financial questions, containing a draft resolution concerning appointments to the Administrative Tribunal of the ILO. The Chairperson explained that there had been no further nominations of a replacement for the judge whose term of office expired in June 2005 and that this issue would be taken up at the November session of the Programme, Financial and Administrative Committee.

21. *The Committee recommends that the Conference adopt the resolution, the text of which appears at the end of this report.*

Assessment of contributions of new member States

22. The Committee had before it Report II: Draft Programme and Budget 2006-07 and other financial questions, containing details of the proposed rate of assessment of the contribution of Samoa.

23. *The Committee recommends that the Conference adopt the resolution, the text of which appears at the end of this report.*

Scale of assessments of contributions to the budget for 2006

24. The Committee had before it Report II: Draft Programme and Budget 2006-07 and other financial questions, containing a draft scale of assessments for 2006.

25. *The Committee recommends that the Conference adopt the resolution, the text of which appears at the end of this report.*

Other questions

26. There were no papers under this item.

Programme and Budget proposals for 2006-07

27. The Committee had before it the Director-General's programme and budget proposals for the biennium 2006-07 first considered by the Governing Body at its 292nd Session (March 2005). The Committee also had before it Report II: Draft Programme and Budget 2006-07 and other financial questions, containing a report on the consideration of the Director-General's original and revised proposals as approved by the Governing Body.

28. The Director-General submitted to the Finance Committee the programme and budget proposals for the biennium 2006-07 with a proposed expenditure of US$568.6 million. His remarks accompanying the proposals are attached as Appendix II to this report.

29. Mr. Botha, speaking on behalf of the Employer Vice-Chairperson of the Governing Body, reminded the Committee that the report before them represented a consensus arrived at through a tripartite discussion and that he did not wish to reopen the debate. The process of discussing the programme and budget should be reviewed. The Employers had several improvements to suggest with the aim of making the process more transparent.

30. The programme and budget did not respond to all of the Employers' priorities, but such was the nature of negotiation. However, he supported the development of the decent work country programmes proposed in the Director-General's Report to the Conference and the emphasis on youth employment. He regretted that the document did not prioritize activities according to constituents' needs and that more rationalization and associated savings had not been achieved by eliminating overlaps in departments. Although the level of activities in the regions was being maintained, many activities undertaken in headquarters were to be

decreased which gave cause for concern. The ILO had to maintain its competencies and expertise in issues related to the world of work and should not broaden its activities or shift its focus to other fields outside its mandate. The decrease in the resources of the technical departments was due to heavy investments in three areas: accommodation; security; and new technology. He suggested clearer and better monitoring by the Governing Body, or by specialized tripartite experts, to keep expenditures within budget and to avoid unforeseen expenditure. The proposed programme and budget represented 1.1 per cent real growth. This was a welcome increase but insufficient to cover all investments and, consequently, departments had had to decrease their budgets, including ACT/EMP.

31. Several governments had not been satisfied with the programme and budget proposals. While the Employers understood the need for tighter budgetary policy and more savings, they supported the current programme and budget as a compromise between the need to modernize the ILO and maintain the level of activities for constituents.

32. Mr. Blondel, speaking on behalf of the Worker Vice-Chairperson of the Governing Body, thanked all those countries that paid their contributions regularly. The issue was of great importance for the Workers, who kept abreast of developments during every session of the Governing Body, since delays in the payment of contributions had serious consequences for the Organization's work. He welcomed the fact that contributions to the ILO were based on the United Nations scale of contributions, and hoped that the practice would continue.

33. With regard to the programme and budget proposals, he wished to emphasize three points. First, the budget was a response to the growing demand from various bodies and meetings working for the world of work. Second, it could not be the sole purpose of the budget to pay for staff; a proper balance had to be constantly sought between efficiency and staffing levels. Third, as the Workers had already noted, the principle of zero-growth had resulted in an erosion of 15 per cent of the Organization's resources since 1978. For that reason, the Workers had welcomed the original budget proposals, which had provided for a 4.3 per cent increase, even if that increase meant an additional burden on States including developing countries. After numerous consultations, a consensus had been reached on a 1.1 per cent budget increase. Although that amount was not sufficient, it showed that there was a willingness to accord the world of work its rightful place. It meant, however, that choices would have to be made with regard to activities. While the Workers had regretfully supported such a small budget increase, some countries still expressed reservations. Trade union organizations from these countries shared the view of the Workers' group. It was also important to note that these industrialized countries were in many cases donors of extra-budgetary resources. Failure to implement programmes that had been defined jointly, while funding certain activities on the side, was tantamount to calling tripartism into question.

34. In conclusion, he recalled that the ILO was a source of hope for the world of work, and invited the members of the Committee to adopt the draft resolution submitted by the Governing Body.

35. Speaking on behalf of the Africa group, the Government representative of South Africa believed that the consensus reached in the March 2005 Governing Body would go a long way to promoting decent work in Africa. The International Labour Conference had the responsibility to ensure that Africa was not marginalized. In view of the high rate of ratification of fundamental standards by Africa, Africa needed adequate technical cooperation funds to assist member States to put in place appropriate legislation. Furthermore, the three labour administration centres in Africa needed support from the ILO. The proposed budget was a step in the right direction in the struggle to reduce the decent work deficit and she supported the programme and budget proposals.

36. The Government representative of El Salvador, speaking on behalf of GRULAC, reiterated his group's statements made at the Governing Body in March 2005. He acknowledged the Office's efforts to adjust the programme to the needs and priorities of constituents when many countries were experiencing economic difficulties. In the revised programme and budget, GRULAC members appreciated the proposed strengthening of the field structure and the strategic objective to strengthen employment, particularly youth employment. They also appreciated the efforts made to reduce the overall budget level. Although these had not completely eliminated the need for increased contributions from member States, the revised level was acceptable. GRULAC was willing to support the budget but stressed that this should not be interpreted as a precedent for other United Nations bodies.

37. The Government representative of Norway, speaking on behalf of the Nordic States (Denmark, Finland, Iceland, Norway and Sweden), stated that the Nordic countries normally supported a zero real growth budget. They had always been strong supporters of the ILO and did not wish to weaken the ILO's ability to meet its goals. The Programme and Budget for 2006-07 proposed an increase of 1.1 per cent in real terms. The Nordic States could accept this but stressed that this could not be a precedent for the future. Nordic countries were still concerned about the distribution of resources between the regions and headquarters and believed that more resources should be shifted to the regions. He was concerned that ILO activities were increasingly dependent on extra-budgetary funding which meant that donors had increased influence over ILO projects. The relationship between regular budget and extra-budgetary resources should be addressed by the Governing Body. He urged the ILO to improve efficiencies and cost-effectiveness and recommended that the ILO take an active part in the wider United Nations process, making better use of the resources of the multilateral system.

38. The Government representative of Saudi Arabia, speaking on behalf of the Gulf States, expressed his concerns regarding the increased budget which was meant to cover the cost of inflation and exchange rate changes. The Gulf States believed that the priorities of the ILO should be reviewed and that the budget should be based on core activities. It should avoid non-urgent activities and there should be better planning regarding recurring costs. This would bring the budget into line with 2004-05 levels. There would be difficult decisions to make but this would be preferable to having to increase assessments every biennium. The Gulf States were prepared to approve the budget but wished to see resources channelled into training activities.

39. The Government representative of Belgium recalled that her Government had supported the proposed 1.1 per cent increase in expenditure at the Governing Body's March 2005 session, and that was still its position. She nevertheless wished to express her concern at the way in which the budget was divided up between the different items, and drew attention to the following points. First, there was a conflict between the ever growing number of requests for assistance received by the Office – justifiably, given the leading role which the Office might play in efforts to combat certain serious problems – and the budget cuts that had been requested. Second, since certain countries gave preference to the use of extra-budgetary resources, there was a risk that that guiding and monitoring role of the Office might be undermined. She noted that the extra-budgetary resources allocated to some of the ILO's sectors of activity amounted to double those from the regular budget. Third, it would not in her view be justified to shorten the Conference and the regional and technical meetings, given their usefulness. Lastly, as institutional expenditure was unavoidable, the ILO needed to provide for the necessary medium- and long-term investment.

40. Speaking on behalf of the governments of the United Kingdom, Canada, the Czech Republic, Hungary, the Netherlands, Japan and the United States, the Government representative of the United Kingdom expressed strong support for the introduction of

results-based management in the ILO. However, she was disappointed that strategic information from IRIS had not been incorporated to a greater extent in the budget. The ILO should further implement results-based budgeting principles, including improving existing indicators. She welcomed the overall aim of Making Decent Work a Global Goal the integrating theme for the period 2006-07, the emphasis on standards and employment creation and the focus on decentralization, provided that this would not involve a net budget increase. The governments she represented felt strongly that the ILO should keep pace with wider United Nations reforms and meet the high standards set by the multilateral system. The ILO would require dynamic leadership, including a well-trained and motivated staff, which would be important in meeting the objectives of the Organization. Clearer results-based budgeting would help make informed decisions about the impact on constituents. She expressed concern that accommodation, staff health and security had been managed in such a way that they now required emergency action. These problems should have been foreseen and she recommended that these priorities be fully integrated into the ILO budget. Measures to ensure the health and safety of staff should not be postponed. There was an urgent need for a review of the whole field structure. Moreover, the ILO should take advantage of common United Nations premises, with the aim of providing more focused ILO assistance to constituents with the greatest need. The ILO should also reconsider the value of holding a three-week annual conference at a cost of US$5 million. She would welcome a more efficient Conference on timely themes and felt that the International Labour Conference and the Governing Body could make better use of their time. It was difficult to identify the continuing relevance of sectoral activities work and she wondered whether this was a good use of US$10 million. The issue of over-grading was a problem that needed to be addressed immediately. The schedule of established posts for 2006-07 showed no change over 2004-05 and she sought clarification on this point. The reductions in travel costs were welcomed and she recommended that travel in economy class should be a requirement for ILO staff at all levels and Worker and Employer delegates when travelling at the expense of the ILO, except in extenuating circumstances. On-the-spot reviews by technical cooperation committee members should be discontinued. The IRIS project should not be run as a constant drain on resources but should rather be used as a tool to allow the Office to take advantage of efficiency savings. She encouraged the Office to focus on its strategic objectives and eliminate programmes that were no longer a priority. She urged the Director-General to consult governments at the earliest possible stage in the preparations of the 2008-09 programme and budget.

41. The Government representative of Brazil supported the statement made by El Salvador on behalf of GRULAC. Although his Government considered that the budget was not ideal, it was a good compromise and it would not be appropriate to re-open the debate. Brazil approved the proposed budget.

42. The Government representative of Italy welcomed the focus on results-based budgeting. His Government had hoped to see greater savings from the IRIS project. Cost increases were higher at the ILO than at other United Nations agencies in Geneva. He hoped that the Director-General would show leadership in such difficult budgetary times and wished to see positive changes in the proposals for the next biennium.

43. The Government representative of Switzerland considered that the ILO should have sufficient resources to carry out its activities effectively. She supported the revised programme and budget proposals and called on the constituents to do likewise.

44. The Government representative of the Netherlands supported the statement made by the United Kingdom on behalf of various IMEC members. At the March 2005 Governing Body session, the Netherlands had been unable to support the adjusted programme and budget. He considered examining the programme and budget proposals in the context of the UN reform process, to be a window of opportunity for ensuring the ILO's relevance in the UN family. He believed it to be essential for the Organization to keep pace with the wider UN reform process. It was in the best interest of all constituents, and not least the ILO itself, to optimize the efficiency and cost-effectiveness, and hence the comparative strength of the ILO. The Netherlands did not see itself engaged in a budget-cutting exercise. The Netherlands could support a "zero real growth plus" budget, provided that the Office offered full transparency in shaping its budget proposals, showed commitment to apply modern management principles and undertook appropriate management reform. The Netherlands, evidently a strong supporter of the ILO and its unique tripartite features, stressed that the ILO should apply sound practices of results-based management and reflect the will to join the UN reform process. He was encouraged by the planned management reforms that were presented to the Finance Committee by the Director-General. His Government would work with others to find a consensus on the budget level.

45. The Government representative of the United States, supporting the statement made by the United Kingdom, expressed his wish to see a budget that was acceptable to all governments. He expressed concern over non-programme expenditures and stressed that significant savings could be made in this area without affecting the ability of the Organization to carry out its programmes. An inability to change would place the ILO out of line with other United Nations organizations and this would affect the support given by some governments. The United States could not accept the revised budget and therefore proposed two changes. First, over-grading was costing the Organization US$6-10 million per biennium. There were 90 senior positions that could be regraded upon retirement of the incumbents. The ILO was aware of the problem but he believed that more could and should be done immediately or the opportunity to make significant savings would be lost. A reduction of US$3 million in staff costs should be made. Secondly, he urged the ILO to address the problem of travel costs. These were excessive and a further US$3 million reduction was possible. There was no lack of support for the ILO activities but his Government felt that the ILO should prioritize and make difficult decisions.

46. The Government representative of France welcomed the fact that the ILO's constituents had decided to reject the unjustified practice of assuming zero budget growth which, because of its artificial and arbitrary nature, made it impossible to formulate a budget that would allow the Organization to carry out its mandate and cope with non-compressible expenditure. In that respect, he endorsed what Mr. Blondel had said about zero growth. He also noted that the revised proposals were the result of a consensus to which France was party, although it was more supportive of the Director-General's original proposal, and all States needed to make efforts to that end. Lastly, with regard to the use – all too frequent in his view – of extra-budgetary resources, he had spoken against the practice, which could potentially distort the overall thrust of the Organization's activities. He therefore supported the revised programme and budget proposals.

47. The Government representative of Jordan explained that he wished to see a budget which effectively met constituents' needs at the lowest possible cost. Such a budget should have sufficient resources to fund technical assistance programmes, especially in South West Asia and Palestine. The ILO could play a role in the peace process in Palestine by establishing technical programmes which would ensure social justice for all in the region.

48. The Government representative of Lebanon requested information on the final level of the budget and on the Swiss franc/US dollar exchange rate that would be adopted. The budget should give more priority to youth employment and employment creation. Regional programmes for the Arab States would account for only 1.3 per cent of resources. This was insufficient to meet their needs with regard to human resources development and employment, programmes relating to the informal economy and countering the negative impacts of globalization. Far more should be given to technical cooperation in the region for it to remain sustainable and she called for an equitable distribution of allocations for technical assistance programmes. Such programmes should receive increased regular budget funding. More resources were required for the Arab Centre for Employment and Training in Tunisia and posts which remained vacant in Beirut should be filled urgently. She called for more publications to be available in Arabic, increased representation of the Arabic States amongst the ILO's senior managers and support for the Palestinian Fund for Employment and Social Protection. She also asked that the funding of the Turin Centre be increased.

49. The Government representative of Japan supported the statements made by the Government representatives of the United States and the United Kingdom. There was no lack of confidence in the ILO's activities; rather he wished to see more effective activities within the ILO's mandate. However, the budget structure of the Organization lacked flexibility because of an increase in administrative costs, such as personnel and travel. Action was needed before such inflexibility had an impact on the funding of programmes. The Director-General had mentioned reforms but no concrete proposals had been presented. The use of any future surplus should be decided by constituents and he believed that it should be appropriated for the Building Accommodation Fund and effective technical programmes in the developing countries. He asked that the Office provide a clear vision of savings in order for Japan to support the budget.

50. The Government representative of Portugal supported the programme and budget proposals which had very clear strategic objectives.

51. The Government representative of Spain expressed his country's commitment to the ILO and its four strategic objectives and urged that the ILO should strengthen its role in debates on globalization. He appreciated the effort made by the Office to rationalize certain areas of activity.

52. The Government representative of Senegal endorsed the statement made by the Government representative of South Africa on behalf of the Africa group, and emphasized that the ILO needed to be given the necessary resources for action. An organization's budget was the basis of its activities and thus of its very credibility. He emphasized that in order to achieve a consensus, all the parties had to compromise. Senegal had done so by accepting a reduction in expenditure. He highlighted the crucial role of the ILO in implementing the decisions adopted at the African Union Extraordinary Summit on Employment and Poverty Alleviation in Africa (held in Ouagadougou, Burkina Faso, in September 2004). Lastly, he emphasized that the ILO's activity, in order to have legitimacy, had to be based on the decisions of the ILO's constituent bodies, and that there had to be a balance between regular budget and extra-budgetary resources. In the light of these considerations, he supported the programme and budget proposals that had been submitted.

53. The Government representative of Benin welcomed the ILO's efforts, in particular its programmes aimed at mitigating the damaging effects of globalization and promoting decent work. He said he was in favour of the programme and budget proposals that had been submitted to the Committee.

54. The Government representative of Ukraine gave his full support to the Decent Work Agenda and the need to make decent work a global goal. Whilst implementing the 2006-07 programme, there should be increased focus on social protection, occupational health and safety programmes, the impact of HIV in the workplace, protection of migrant workers and prevention of human trafficking. The revised budget proposals were acceptable and he could join the consensus.

55. The Government representative of Pakistan commented that the ILO had seen a 15 per cent decline in its regular budget resources since 1978, despite a steady expansion of its role. Zero growth budgets had hampered implementation of programmes, and extra-budgetary funding, that essentially kept the ILO afloat, distorted priorities. The ILO needed to assist countries in employment creation by sharing experiences and giving policy advice. She supported the fact that five areas had been identified as priorities by the Director-General: globalization; poverty alleviation; gender equality; tripartism; and labour standards. Her Government supported the revised budget proposals recommended by the Governing Body.

56. The Government representative of Canada supported the statement made by the United Kingdom. His country remained committed to results-based management and he acknowledged that much had been achieved in this regard by the ILO. However, there still remained much to do and Canada would continue to seek improvements in the identification of priorities and in obtaining maximum value for money. He would support the revised programme and budget proposals if a consensus emerged.

57. The Government representative of Argentina supported the statement made by El Salvador on behalf of GRULAC. He reminded the Committee that Argentina had supported the original programme and budget proposals presented in March 2005 but had then been willing to support the revised proposals on the understanding that these met the concerns raised and that basic objectives would not be altered.

58. The Government representative of Germany recognized the effort that had been made to revise the original programme and budget proposals in order to achieve a reduction in costs. Germany had asked for greater reductions and she still felt that these could be considered. Further savings in specific areas as highlighted by other delegations could be pursued in the course of the next two years. Her country was faced with major budget constraints but it remained a priority for Germany to achieve a consensus and she could accept the revised proposals.

59. The Government representative of Cameroon associated himself with the statement made by the Government representative of South Africa on behalf of the Africa group. He had observed that other UN agencies whose membership was broadly the same as that of the ILO had obtained budget increases larger than the 1.1 per cent which was under discussion for the ILO. The budget cuts included in the revised proposals were regrettable and would have detrimental results in Africa.

60. The Government representative of Chile supported the statements made on behalf of GRULAC. He believed that a real effort had been made to meet the needs of all parties but was concerned about the long-term consequences of budget cuts, particularly with regard to staff reductions. The relative importance of voluntary contributions to the ILO was also a concern as it could add to the administrative burden and distort priorities.

61. The Government representative of Australia commended the Director-General for his strong statements of commitment to efficiency and productivity and urged that the next step be to establish targets and performance indicators. He observed that the intention to absorb around US$35 million in projected costs for 2006-07 was not yet actual savings and requested the ILO to report back over the course of the biennium, especially on the progress of IRIS. He was disappointed that little progress had been made on the problem of over-grading which required a concerted effort on the part of the Office. Referring to the decision to engage JIU on a review of the ILO's results-based management framework, he looked forward to discussing the outcome. Strategies to manage the impact of inflation and currency fluctuations were also important. Such costs could not be automatically absorbed by Members. Finally, there was a strong need for the ILO to provide a clearer and more

comprehensive picture of the cost, timeliness and quality of ILO outputs. The role of IRIS was an important part of this as were strategies such as benchmarking, total quality management, or the development and application of a balanced score card.

62. The Government representative of Mexico supported the statements made by GRULAC and the global objectives of the Decent Work Agenda. The programme and budget proposals continued to fund decent work country programmes and this, together with the fact that her Government's concerns regarding unforeseen expenditures and the expenditure levels in various items included in Part IV of the budget had been taken into account, meant that she fully endorsed the budget level recommended by the Governing Body. She shared concerns that an increase in extra-budgetary resources could distort the priorities of the ILO.

63. The Government representative of Tunisia supported the Decent Work Agenda and earlier comments made on behalf of the Africa group. Revisions to the programme and budget should not be allowed to negatively impact upon technical cooperation projects in African and Arab countries where they were vital. She looked forward to ILO support for the Arab Center for Employment and Training in Tunisia and hoped for more ILO assistance for the Palestinian Authority in the occupied territories.

64. The Government representative of New Zealand supported the Programme and Budget for 2006-07 and acknowledged the efforts made by the Director-General to produce revised proposals. She encouraged the Office to implement measures so that extraordinary items could be better anticipated.

65. The Government representative of the United Kingdom supported the proposals of the United States and reiterated that, although the ILO had the full support of the United Kingdom, financial restraints were necessary. He stated that his country's extra-budgetary contributions were designed to be targeted on ILO priorities within an agreed framework.

66. The Government representative of Uruguay, associating himself with the remarks made by the Government representative of El Salvador, supported the Programme and Budget proposals for 2006-07. His country, suffering from economic difficulties, could not easily back the programme and budget proposals, but understood that they were justified.

67. The Government representative of Nigeria supported comments made on behalf of the Africa group. She observed that the ILO's budget had remained almost the same over several years and was grateful for the extra-budgetary funds received from the United States, the United Kingdom, the European Union and the IMEC countries. The ILO, as the only tripartite agency in the United Nations, deserved the support of all governments for its programme and budget proposals.

68. The Government representative of the Democratic Republic of the Congo welcomed the fact that the ILO programme and budget proposals aimed to ensure the resources needed to attain the global goal of decent work and help member States by incorporating their regional priorities (employment creation, combating poverty, reintegration of child soldiers, support for children working in mines). He therefore supported the revised programme and budget proposals.

69. The Government representative of Namibia associated herself with the comments made on behalf of the Africa group. She believed that the programme and budget was realistic and supported further decentralization in order to build capacity at regional and national levels.

70. The Government representative of Hungary welcomed the four principal goals of the programme and budget and appreciated the emphasis on results-based management and savings.

71. The Government representative of Burkina Faso said that the projects launched following the Ouagadougou Summit in September 2004 required significant resources which the countries concerned did not have, and that as a result the grave problems that afflicted the least developed countries were now spilling over into the others. For that reason, since it had not been possible to adopt the original budget proposals, it was important now to support the revised proposals before the Committee.

72. The Government representative of Zimbabwe agreed with the views presented by the Government representative of South Africa on behalf of the Africa group. He reminded delegates that a 1.1 per cent increase in the budget was the result of tripartite deliberation and urged Members to adopt the budget as proposed.

73. The Government representative of Uganda supported the position of the Africa group. Many countries such as his, struggling with structural adjustment, were faced with competing ideas of how to improve their processes. Some people would argue that growth and development could be achieved without reference to sound labour law and the only body that countered this argument was the ILO. In East Africa, where countries were trying to integrate employment policies into new labour laws, technical support received from the ILO was invaluable. The ILO spearheaded studies on the elimination of the worst forms of child labour and reduction of HIV/AIDS which helped to reduce the incidence of HIV/AIDS among youth and vulnerable groups in the region. He argued that any reduction in the ILO budget would have a direct impact on his country and it would be the most vulnerable who would suffer.

74. The Government representative of the Syrian Arab Republic stated that, contrary to the views expressed by some member States, his country understood the term rationalizing to mean increasing capacity by better utilizing resources and thus not reducing the budget. His Government believed that resources should be decentralized at headquarters and that certain activities should be reviewed. He supported the revised budget as proposed with a 1.1 per cent increase.

75. The Government representative of the Czech Republic endorsed the statements made by the United Kingdom and the proposal for rationalization. His Government, although willing to join the consensus on the revised proposals, would have preferred a zero real growth budget and believed that better solutions could have and should have been found.

76. The Government representatives of the Republic of Korea and Ireland supported the revised Programme and Budget for 2006-07. Both countries welcomed the focus on results-based budgeting and the Office's commitment to continue its cost-saving efforts. The Government of Ireland hoped that improved planning and reporting would result from IRIS. The Government representative of the Bahamas also endorsed the revised budget proposals although the cuts made had proved difficult to accept. He supported the statement made on behalf of GRULAC by the Government representative of El Salvador. The Government representative of China also gave his support to the revised budget proposals.

77. The Government representatives of Malawi, Kenya and Senegal echoed the views expressed by the Government representative of South Africa on behalf of the Africa group. The Government representative of Malawi believed that the revised budget was a well thought out document, the result of long deliberations. Many of the least developed countries saw hope in the strategies incorporated in the proposed Programme and Budget

for 2006-07. In developing countries, there was a need to create decent employment and to empower youth which required action, not talk. For Africa to be able to attain the ideals of NEPAD and the Millennium Development Goals, the least the Committee could do, would be to accept the proposed budget with its increase of 1.1 per cent. The Government representatives of Malawi, Kenya and Senegal endorsed the revised budget proposals.

78. Replying to the discussion, the Director-General stated that he believed that the budget debate had been a valuable experience and thanked the Committee for supporting the Governing Body and the Organization. Several themes had recurred during the discussions: there was strong support for the ILO's work in the regions and many had argued for further decentralization; there was wide support for decent work country programmes as a means to more focused action in countries and to link the ILO's work with the rest of the UN system and the Millennium Development Goals; the initiatives on decent work for youth had been well received; and many governments had endorsed the budget recommended by the Governing Body.

79. He thanked the Committee for discussing frankly and constructively those areas in which the ILO could do better. Some key points had emerged: first, the need to improve results-based management systems with an emphasis on measurement of results and linking outcomes to resources; second, the application of modern management principles and practices directed at efficiency and productivity; third, the use of strategic analysis to anticipate and plan investments and, finally, the use of IRIS to streamline processes, improve efficiency and make management, performance and reporting more transparent. He was keen to work with the Committee in all of these areas. Indeed, when the idea of strategic budgeting had been proposed six years ago, it had become a joint exercise between the Office and the Governing Body.

80. Governments had a great wealth of experience in areas such as results-based management, organizational change and innovation, public sector management, management of information and communication technology and the ILO was keen to draw on this expertise. This would enable the Organization to submit the best possible strategic analysis and policy options to the Governing Body.

81. Many Committee members had asked about increased savings in areas such as grade structure, travel and the field structure. This was an ongoing process and savings in these and other areas would be vigorously pursued to free resources for the priorities that had been agreed upon, particularly the ILO's work in the regions. The targets for rebalancing the grade structure would be part of the wider discussions of the Human Resources Strategy during the November 2005 Governing Body. In this respect, he welcomed the statement by the Government representative of the United Kingdom, on behalf of the United States and other countries, that had constructively suggested areas where the ILO should work to achieve savings. The ILO needed to be managed professionally, with efficient programme implementation and a heightened appreciation of its sources of funding. The ILO needed to be a good custodian of the budget and he was committed to accelerate work on savings as a major priority so that the many needs identified in the debate could be better met.

82. The Director-General had been touched by the statement made by the Government representative of Uganda which had served to demonstrate the relevance of what the ILO was doing. This feeling of relevance was precisely what motivated him and other ILO officials in their work. He respected the opinion of those members that felt that resources should be reduced and reiterated that the ILO would work within its budget.

83. The Chairperson thanked the Director-General for his reply. There had been a constructive debate and there appeared to be broad support for the Programme and Budget proposals for

2006-07. Several countries had requested additional savings and this had been fully acknowledged by the Director-General. Other countries had requested that the budget be increased. However, the budget which had been recommended by the Governing Body in March 2005 constituted a fair compromise of the views expressed and he asked if the Committee was prepared to accept the recommendation concerning the Programme and Budget for 2006-07 contained in paragraph 6 on page 2 of Report II.

84. The Government representative of the United States stated that his country was a strong supporter of the ILO and commended the commitment of the Director-General to pursue efforts to increase efficiency. The United States did not want the ILO to be left behind in the wave of reforms sweeping through the UN system. In March 2005, his Government had moved away from its wish for zero nominal growth but, as in March, it remained unable to accept the revised budget level. He regretted that the United States could not join in the consensus and called for a vote on the proposed budget.

85. After a short recess, a vote was taken by show of hands. Of the 83 members voting, 80 voted in favour of the proposed budget level, 2 against and there was 1 abstention. The two-thirds majority required for the Committee to accept the Programme and Budget for 2006-07 was therefore achieved.

Resolution for the adoption of the Programme and Budget for 2006-07 and the allocation of the budget of income among member States

86. The Committee had before it document C.F./D.6 which contained summarized financial details of the Programme and Budget proposals for 2006-07 and a draft resolution for submission to the Conference. Following the decision in favour of the Governing Body's recommendation concerning the programme and budget, the Office had carried out the forward exchange contracts for the ILO's US dollar requirements for the 2006-07 biennium. The appropriate figures now to be inserted in the formal resolution were:

Budget of expenditure	US$594 310 000
Budget of income	US$594 310 000
Budget rate of exchange	1.25
Equivalent budget total in Swiss francs	CHF742 887 500

87. The Treasurer and Financial Comptroller explained that the forward exchange contracts would ensure that member States assessments would not rise as a result of further fluctuations in the exchange rate during 2006-07. The Office had also been able to take advantage of interest rate differentials, which should allow a premium of 11 million Swiss francs to be earned in the 2006-07 biennium. The net premium at the end of the biennium would be returned to member States. In accordance with article 11 of the Financial Regulations one half would be distributed to the incentive fund for early payment of contributions and one half would be returned to all member States once their contributions for the 2006-07 biennium had been paid.

88. Mr. Blondel, speaking on behalf of the Worker Vice-Chairperson of the Governing Body, welcomed the fact that the great majority of Governments had supported the programme and budget proposals. It was essential to continue to seek optimal efficiency within the framework of the policy defined on a tripartite basis. The ILO could not, however, be run like a commercial enterprise; its role was to encourage societies to evolve towards greater democracy and freedom, and to defend workers' right to decent work. He hoped that it

would be possible to reach consensus when it came to adopting the budget in plenary; that would enhance the ILO's credibility and authority.

89. Mr. Botha, speaking on behalf of the Employer Vice-Chairperson of the Governing Body, expressed his full agreement with the statement by Mr. Blondel.

90. *The Committee recommends that the Conference adopt the resolution, the text of which appears at the end of this report.*

Appendices

91. The provisions of paragraph 4 of article 13 of the Constitution of the ILO, also articles 31 and 32 of the Standing Orders of the Conference, are reproduced in Appendix I to this report.

92. The address of the Director-General regarding the Programme and Budget proposals for 2006-07 is attached as Appendix II to this report.

93. The draft scale for the assessment of contributions for the year 2006 is attached as Appendix III.

94. A table showing the proposed summarized budget of expenditure and income for 2006-07 is attached to this report (Appendix IV), together with a summary of the proposed expenditure budget for 2006-07 by appropriation line (Appendix V).

95. A statement showing the contributions due from each member State for 2006 is also attached as Appendix VI.

Geneva, 9 June 2005.

(Signed) J.-J. Elmiger,
Chairperson and Reporter.

Resolutions submitted to the Conference

Resolution concerning the arrears of contributions of Togo

The General Conference of the International Labour Organization,

Having regard to paragraph 7 of article 10 of the Financial Regulations,

Accepts the arrangement proposed by the Government of Togo for the settlement of its arrears of contributions due for the period 1992-2004 to the effect that:

(a) in 2005, the Government of Togo will pay in full its contribution for the year 2005;

(b) in subsequent years, the Government of Togo will continue to pay its current contribution in full in the year for which it is due;

(c) the Government of Togo will settle arrears that have accumulated up to and including 31 December 2004, amounting to 213,453 Swiss francs, by payment, beginning in 2006, of seven annual instalments of 27,924 Swiss francs and one final instalment of 17,985 Swiss francs.

Decides that Togo shall be permitted to vote, in accordance with paragraph 4 of article 13 of the Constitution of the International Labour Organization, after the conclusion of the present business.

Resolution concerning the arrears of contributions of Georgia

The General Conference of the International Labour Organization,

Having regard to paragraph 7 of article 10 of the Financial Regulations,

Accepts the arrangement proposed by the Government of Georgia for the settlement of its arrears of contributions due for the period 1993-2004 to the effect that:

(a) in 2005, the Government of Georgia will pay in full its contribution for the year 2005;

(b) in subsequent years, the Government of Georgia will continue to pay its current contribution in full in the year for which it is due;

(c) the Government of Georgia will settle arrears that have accumulated up to and including 31 December 2004, amounting to 3,071,902 Swiss francs, by payment, beginning in 2006, of 14 annual instalments in accordance with the following schedule:

Years	Amount (in Swiss francs)
2006	46 079
2007	61 438
2008	61 438
2009	61 438
2010	61 438
2011	122 876
2012	153 595
2013	153 595
2014	307 190
2015	368 628
2016	368 628
2017	430 066
2018	430 066
2019	445 427
Total	3 071 902

Decides that Georgia shall be permitted to vote, in accordance with paragraph 4 of article 13 of the Constitution of the International Labour Organization, after the conclusion of the present business.

Resolution concerning the arrears of contributions of Iraq

The General Conference of the International Labour Organization,

Having regard to paragraph 7 of article 10 of the Financial Regulations,

Accepts the arrangement proposed by the Government of Iraq for the settlement of its arrears of contributions due for the period 1988-2004 to the effect that:

(a) in 2005, the Government of Iraq will pay in full its contribution for the year 2005;

(b) in subsequent years, the Government of Iraq will continue to pay its current contribution in full in the year for which it is due;

(c) the Government of Iraq will settle arrears that have accumulated up to and including 31 December 2004, amounting to 6,127,793 Swiss francs, by payment, beginning in 2005, of 19 annual instalments of 306,390 Swiss francs and a final instalment of 306,383 Swiss francs,

Decides that Iraq shall be permitted to vote, in accordance with paragraph 4 of article 13 of the Constitution of the International Labour Organization, after the conclusion of the present business.

Resolution concerning the composition of the Administrative Tribunal of the International Labour Organization

The General Conference of the International Labour Organization,

Decides, in accordance with article III of the Statute of the Administrative Tribunal of the International Labour Organization, to renew the term of office of Ms. Geneviève Gaudron for three years,

Expresses its appreciation to Ms. Flerida Ruth P. Romero for her contribution over the last five years to the work of the Administrative Tribunal of the International Labour Organization.

Resolution concerning the assessment of contributions of new member States

The General Conference of the International Labour Organization,

Decides, in accordance with the established practice of harmonizing the rates of assessment of ILO member States with their rates of assessment in the United Nations, that the contribution of Samoa to the ILO budget for the period of its membership in the Organization in 2005 be based on an annual assessment rate of 0.001 per cent.

Resolution of scale of assessments of contributions to the budget for 2006

The General Conference of the International Labour Organization,

Decides, in accordance with article 9, paragraph 2, of the Financial Regulations, to adopt the draft scale of assessments for the year 2006 based on the scale adopted by the United Nations General Assembly in December 2003 as set out in column 3 of Appendix III to this document.

Resolution concerning the adoption of the Programme and Budget for 2006-07 and the allocation of the budget of income among member States

The General Conference of the International Labour Organization,

In virtue of the Financial Regulations, adopts for the 70th financial period, ending 31 December 2007, the budget of expenditure of the International Labour Organization amounting to US$594,310,000 and the budget of income amounting to US$594,310,000, which, at the budget rate of exchange of 1.25 Swiss francs to the US dollar, amounts to 742,887,500 Swiss francs, and resolves that the budget of income, denominated in Swiss francs, shall be allocated among member States in accordance with the scale of contributions recommended by the Finance Committee of Government Representatives.

Appendix I

Relevant provisions of the Constitution of the International Labour Organization and the Standing Orders of the International Labour Conference

1. Paragraph 4 of article 13 of the Constitution of the Organization provides as follows:

> 4. A Member of the Organization which is in arrears in the payment of its financial contribution to the Organization shall have no vote in the Conference, in the Governing Body, in any committee, or in the elections of members of the Governing Body, if the amount of its arrears equals or exceeds the amount of the contributions due from it for the preceding two full years: Provided that the Conference may by a two-thirds majority of the votes cast by the delegates present permit such a Member to vote if it is satisfied that the failure to pay is due to conditions beyond the control of the Member.

2. Articles 31 and 32 of the Standing Orders of the Conference provide as follows:

ARTICLE 31

Procedure where proposal is made to permit Member in arrears to vote

1. Any request or proposal that the Conference should nevertheless permit a Member which is in arrears in the payment of its contributions to vote in accordance with article 13, paragraph 4, of the Constitution shall be referred in the first instance to the Finance Committee of the Conference, which shall report thereon as a matter of urgency.

2. Pending a decision on the request or proposal by the Conference, the Member shall not be entitled to vote.

3. The Finance Committee shall submit to the Conference a report giving its opinion on the request or proposal.

4. If the Finance Committee, having found that the failure to pay is due to conditions beyond the control of the Member, thinks fit to propose to the Conference that the Member should nevertheless be permitted to vote in accordance with article 13, paragraph 4, of the Constitution, it shall in its report:

(a) explain the nature of the conditions beyond the Member's control;

(b) give an analysis of the financial relations between the Member and the Organization during the preceding ten years; and

(c) indicate the measures which should be taken in order to settle the arrears.

5. Any decision which may be taken by the Conference to permit a Member which is in arrears in the payment of its contributions to vote notwithstanding such arrears may be made conditional upon the Member complying with any recommendations for settling the arrears which may be made by the Conference.

ARTICLE 32

Period of validity of a decision to permit Member in arrears to vote

1. Any decision by the Conference permitting a Member which is in arrears in the payment of its contributions to vote shall be valid for the session of the Conference at which the decision is taken. Any such decision shall be operative in regard to the Governing Body and committees until the opening of the general session of the Conference next following that at which it was taken.

2. Notwithstanding the provisions of paragraph 1 of this article, after the Conference has approved an arrangement under which the arrears of a Member are consolidated and are payable in annual instalments over a period of years, the Member shall be permitted to vote provided that, at the time of the vote concerned, the Member has fully paid all instalments under the arrangement, as well as all financial contributions under article 13 of the Constitution that were due before the end of the previous year. For any Member which, at the close of the session of the Conference, has not fully paid all such instalments and contributions due before the end of the previous year, the permission to vote shall lapse.

Appendix II

International Labour Conference – 93rd Session

Address by Mr. Juan Somavia, Director-General, to the Finance Committee of Government Representatives on the Programme and Budget proposals for 2006-07 – 1 June 2005

Monsieur le Président,

Excellences, Honorables Délégués, Mesdames, Messieurs,

Your Committee has before it a recommendation forwarded by the Governing Body to the Conference to adopt a Programme and Budget for the biennium 2006-07 with a proposed expenditure of US$568.6 million.

The full tripartite flavour of that discussion and the adjustments made to the initial budget proposal are in the documentation available. But I think that before you begin your discussion, it might be useful for me to synthesize the way the budget was developed and modified, as the majority of you did not participate in the process as Members of the ILO Governing Body.

In our Organization, the Governing Body has the constitutional role of determining the level and content of the budget recommendation made to the International Labour Conference, based on their governance role and their in-depth knowledge of the Office and its programmes.

I have included extensive adjustments to my initial proposals based on the Governing Body's guidance. I urge that you approve the proposed budget resolution. This has also been requested by the spokespersons of the employers' and the workers' groups in yesterday's plenary.

Let me begin by commending all those who were directly involved in preparing the proposals before you, in particular, the members of the PFAC, as well as the Governing Body for assuming its mandated responsibilities – and beyond divergences – submitting to you a clear recommendation.

Our tripartite governance system performed extremely well. Your Committee can be satisfied with the excellent professional work accomplished in your name.

A special thanks to the President of the PFAC and the Governing Body – Monsieur Philippe Séguin, the spokesperson of the Employers' group, Mr. Bokkie Botha, and, the Workers' group, Monsieur Marc Blondel. They, together with many coordinators of regional groups, played a very important consensus-building role that led to the balanced proposal before you.

For our part, I wanted to ensure that the process by the Office of putting together the proposals to the PFAC was open and transparent. In fact, I want to thank so many of you who were deeply involved in the different consultations and who stated that this has been a clearly transparent budget process.

The proposals were the product of a long gestation with intensive consultations, starting with a discussion in November 2003, on the new Strategic Policy Framework for 2006-09. Formal and informal discussions continued from that time, including detailed analysis by the Governing Body in November 2004 and in March 2005.

Throughout the period, the Office met with employers and workers, with all regional government groups and was available for a significant number of individual governments. This brought clarity to the process and reduced the levels of uncertainty.

This process delivered a remarkable degree of convergence on the future direction for the ILO. Let me synthesize the substantive building blocks of the proposals:

- The focus is on decent work as a global goal with an emphasis on continuity – reinforcing, deepening and interrelating the four strategic objectives under the Decent Work Agenda.

- Decent work country programmes provide the structural framework for the delivery of ILO services to our constituents at the country level.

- Five mainstream strategies are interwoven through the strategic objectives to reinforce the integrating nature of decent work: globalization, poverty, gender equality, tripartism, and standards.
- InFocus initiatives are proposed in three areas of particular interest to constituents; corporate social responsibility; export processing zones; and the informal economy.
- More emphasis is placed on improving our knowledge base and service capacity.
- And, there was universal support for strengthening our action in the regions where we are closest to constituents.

The first round of discussions also gave strong support by countries in all regions to my original financial proposals amounting to expenditures of around US$23 million higher than the recommendation before you.

I am fully aware that the support for that budget level implied a real economic sacrifice on the part of all those governments that backed it. I was touched by the confidence in the value of our Organization's work and the disposition to take on a greater financial burden. I thanked all of them for their commitment.

At the same time, two of the largest contributors as well as some other countries, made clear that their national situations did not permit them to support the proposed budget level – and that substantial cuts were necessary.

Even in these cases, the comments on the work of our Organization were supportive, and the proposals that were made were directed at protecting and even strengthening our core substantive programmes. I understood the financial difficulties, and I valued the positive approach taken by them, which I would like to preserve to the greatest possible extent.

I engaged in intense consultations both with constituents and within the Office to find the appropriate balance between the demand to protect and increase resources for certain activities and the demand for substantial cuts. As you can imagine, this has not been an easy exercise. I hope this Committee appreciates the honest effort the Office made to present to the PFAC a revised workable proposal, which is now the recommendation of the Governing Body before you.

I would like to zero in on three priority points:

First, the recommended budget level is a fair balance of the diverse interests of member States that includes *significant and painful reductions*.

Second, the Governing Body recommendation continues and reinforces *improvements in results-based management, budgeting and efficiencies*.

Third, this budget is a balanced effort that includes *extensive savings measures*.

First, the budget level and reductions.

Naturally, and understandably, this is always a contentious issue. But I have always been committed to finding a reasonable balance and confronting the difficult and often competing challenges head-on.

Let me address adjustments that I made in order to respond to major priorities identified. This budget provides full funding for the regions. In other words, at a time when ILO activities are squeezed, we are continuing our commitment to decentralization and ensuring resources to service our constituents at the national and regional levels.

You know well that this has always been my priority. We need to make sure that we systematically reinforce the delivery capacity of our activities in the field and that resources do not get stuck in the process. Decent work country programmes will help to integrate better and rationalize our work with constituents at the national level.

This budget also takes note of the breadth of support in our discussions for employment issues, and in particular, ensures resources for tripartite initiatives at the national and local level to expand decent work for young people. Another central demand was the need to ensure funding of the Maritime Session of the Conference. That was done.

I must now come to the difficult issue of how we proceeded in the Office to reduce the budget level in order to meet the demand for "substantial cuts". In making our proposals in this area, we have been guided by many of the ideas for savings put forward in your discussions. All of this while protecting and, where possible, enhancing our core capacities to serve our constituents.

Consequently, we reduced Part IV of the budget – that is, funding for institutional investments – by a full US$15.9 million.

Essential investments in maintenance of buildings have been postponed until a comprehensive review of the total investment needs is carried out and submitted to the Building Subcommittee.

Significant resources to rebuild the Information Technology Systems Fund are also postponed.

The resources requested for security of staff have been absorbed within the existing budget level.

Staff training resources have been reduced.

We also made adjustments to the provision for cost increases.

In essence, we have eliminated or sharply decreased all cost increase provisions which do not result from obligations under the Staff Regulations, General Assembly decisions or other contractual or constitutional obligations.

In practice, this means that we will absorb cost increases of US$6.1 million, although we had fully justified them through prudent and objective consideration of inflation and related factors.

The global budget reduction for staff turnover was reinstated, adding a savings requirement of US$4.5 million to the US$6.1 million in savings we need to find to compensate for the reduction in cost adjustments.

The implication of these two measures is that we will start the 2006-07 biennium with an in-built requirement for savings of US$10.5 million.

Finally, based on requests from several members of the Governing Body, I withdrew the proposed increase in the reserve for Governing Body decisions during the biennium, shown under Part II of the budget. This will result in programme cuts if any Constitutional obligations or emergencies arise during the biennium exceeding the small provision for unforeseen expenditure.

The Governing Body approved these adjustments and recommended the draft resolution in front of you.

The net result of these changes is that the Governing Body recommendation to this Committee is now US$23.2 million below the initial budget proposal. This is in addition to the US$5.4 million that I had already removed from the proposals prior to their presentation to the PFAC based on the extensive consultations at the end of last year.

Second, as I did in previous budgets, I will continue to seek improvements in results-based management and budgeting. We must continue to make our performance more measurable, better linked to budgets and more clearly planned in terms of major outputs and activities.

On the issue of measurements of performance and the many suggestions for more precise indicators to respond to your concerns, I will ask all ILO programmes to establish, as part of their implementation planning for 2006-07, quantitative and qualitative criteria for measuring progress under each operational outcome. This measurement will be linked to the DWCPs, and will be reported to you in the interim Programme Implementation Report for 2006.

The new IRIS technology will support these improvements; 2006-07 will be the first biennium in which IRIS budgeting is fully applied and ILO management will seek to ensure that it results in better planning and reporting. This will include more complete information on spending patterns as part of the biennial Programme Implementation Report. The proposed Information and Communications Technology Subcommittee of the PFAC would oversee the contributions of IRIS to improve efficiency.

In November, the PFAC will discuss the external evaluation of results-based management and budgeting in the ILO. I believe external evaluations, together with our normal auditing process, which also covers management issues, are key components to guide our programmes. I know that external eyes help us see better.

The Governing Body will also address our overall evaluation policy and the role of the new internal evaluation unit. I am confident that the results of these discussions, together with the role of our Internal Auditor, will permit a further strengthening of our results-based management systems, including oversight, transparency and early response to the first signs of any management problem.

Third, the emphasis I have placed on savings is continued in the proposed budget. Starting in 2000-01, I have transferred resources from administrative work to the technical sectors and regions that deliver the ILO's products.

These transfers now mean that some US$15 million more is available for technical work each biennium, despite a static budget level. It also means that it costs 9 per cent less to administer the Office than when I took office.

The current proposals contain a number of savings measures for both the short and the longer term that are once again the product of listening and taking action.

The United States, for example, among other issues, has expressed its concerns about travel expenses. We have taken action. The proposed resources for travel are some 25 percent less than the 2004-05 level. This continues a systematic management practice we have been implementing progressively. For 2006-07, travel costs represent some 2.59 per cent of the total budget compared with 3.75 per cent in 2004-05 and 4.02 per cent in 2002-03. And Executive Directors have been charged with the responsibility of analysing travel in their own sectors and finding ways to further reduce costs.

IMEC countries have expressed concerns about the field structure. We are taking action. We will carry out a comprehensive review of our field structure, with a view to more efficient as well as more effective performance. The review itself will no doubt be a difficult process and I will count on the Governing Body's guidance.

Among other important contributions, Japan has taken the leadership in requesting a more balanced grade structure of the Office. Thank you for that. We are taking action. We have taken measures to begin rebalancing that structure. In my own decisions on senior appointments, for example, I have reduced grade levels of posts where possible and merged programmes in order to reduce senior positions and will continue to do so.

More importantly, to respond to this need, we already built in US$2 million in savings for reduced grade structure in calculating the budget proposals for staff costs. We will take additional measures to rationalize the structure of the Office, resulting in savings both directly and through the need for fewer managers in a streamlined operation. The Governing Body will review this more thoroughly in November when considering the human resource strategy.

You will have noticed that I have emphasized the Governing Body's role in overseeing policy related to enhancing the overall efficiency of the Office through the Building Subcommittee, the proposed ICT Subcommittee and PFAC discussions on human resource strategy and the field structure.

Let me add that what I am saying today to this Committee about future action is also the approach which I have instructed managers and staff to take. Let me quote from my recent staff address on 25 May 2005:

"The recent struggle over the budget reflects continued pressures from major funders – regular and extra-budgetary – legitimate demands I would add – to insist on increasingly better management practices, greater impact and more policy coordination within the multilateral system. … Things are already tight and will continue to be so. This is the reality. We will need to continue developing a mentality of efficiency and effectiveness, of savings and careful use of resources. We all need to be good custodians of the budget."

* * *

These proposals are, for differing reasons, difficult for all of us. Many of us are reasonably concerned that we will not invest prudently in our future and that we will respond to even less of the total demand for our services. At the same time, I cannot ignore the difficult economic situation in many of your countries.

I want to assure you that I am committed to continuing our track record of finding savings and efficiencies.

I have outlined a number of saving measures that I intend to pursue in the course of the next two years, in particular in the areas of rebalancing grade structure, review of the field network of offices, and travel.

These savings would be used for priorities such as investments in building and accommodation, support to ILO action in developing countries, and staff rejuvenation including recruitment of young officials from under-represented countries.

I genuinely hope that each and every member of this Committee can support the resolution before you. It reflects an exceptional level of consultation. They offer, I am convinced, a balanced response to the need for consensus in difficult circumstances.

The way forward is in your hands. The recommendation of the Governing Body and my comments today express an honest effort to respond to your conflicting demands. I hope that the spirit that produced such a high level of consensus around our programme activities can express itself now on financial issues, both in this Committee and in the plenary vote of the Conference.

I commend the budget resolution submitted to you by the Governing Body for adoption.

Thank you for your attention.

Appendix III

Scale of assessments

	State	ILO assessments 2005 Col.1 %	UN assessments 2006 Col.2 %	Draft scale of ILO assessments 2006 Col.3 %	Increase (Decrease) (Diff. between cols 3 and 1) Col.4 %
1	Afghanistan	0.002	0.002	0.002	-
2	Albania	0.005	0.005	0.005	-
3	Algeria	0.076	0.076	0.076	-
4	Angola	0.001	0.001	0.001	-
5	Antigua and Barbuda	0.003	0.003	0.003	-
6	Argentina	0.957	0.956	0.957	-
7	Armenia	0.002	0.002	0.002	-
8	Australia	1.593	1.592	1.593	-
9	Austria	0.860	0.859	0.860	-
10	Azerbaijan	0.005	0.005	0.005	-
11	Bahamas	0.013	0.013	0.013	-
12	Bahrain	0.030	0.030	0.030	-
13	Bangladesh	0.010	0.010	0.010	-
14	Barbados	0.010	0.010	0.010	-
15	Belarus	0.018	0.018	0.018	-
16	Belgium	1.070	1.069	1.070	-
17	Belize	0.001	0.001	0.001	-
18	Benin	0.002	0.002	0.002	-
19	Bolivia	0.009	0.009	0.009	-
20	Bosnia and Herzegovina	0.003	0.003	0.003	-
21	Botswana	0.012	0.012	0.012	-
22	Brazil	1.524	1.523	1.524	-
23	Bulgaria	0.017	0.017	0.017	-
24	Burkina Faso	0.002	0.002	0.002	-
25	Burundi	0.001	0.001	0.001	-
26	Cambodia	0.002	0.002	0.002	-
27	Cameroon	0.008	0.008	0.008	-
28	Canada	2.816	2.813	2.816	-
29	Cape Verde	0.001	0.001	0.001	-
30	Central African Republic	0.001	0.001	0.001	-
31	Chad	0.001	0.001	0.001	-
32	Chile	0.223	0.223	0.223	-
33	China	2.055	2.053	2.055	-
34	Colombia	0.155	0.155	0.155	-
35	Comoros	0.001	0.001	0.001	-
36	Congo	0.001	0.001	0.001	-
37	Costa Rica	0.030	0.030	0.030	-
38	Côte d'Ivoire	0.010	0.010	0.010	-
39	Croatia	0.037	0.037	0.037	-
40	Cuba	0.043	0.043	0.043	-
41	Cyprus	0.039	0.039	0.039	-
42	Czech Republic	0.183	0.183	0.183	-

	State	ILO assessments 2005 Col.1 %	UN assessments 2006 Col.2 %	Draft scale of ILO assessments 2006 Col.3 %	Increase (Decrease) (Diff. between cols 3 and 1) Col.4 %
43	Democratic Republic of the Congo	0.003	0.003	0.003	-
44	Denmark	0.719	0.718	0.719	-
45	Djibouti	0.001	0.001	0.001	-
46	Dominica	0.001	0.001	0.001	-
47	Dominican Republic	0.035	0.035	0.035	-
48	Ecuador	0.019	0.019	0.019	-
49	Egypt	0.120	0.120	0.120	-
50	El Salvador	0.022	0.022	0.022	-
51	Equatorial Guinea	0.002	0.002	0.002	-
52	Eritrea	0.001	0.001	0.001	-
53	Estonia	0.012	0.012	0.012	-
54	Ethiopia	0.004	0.004	0.004	-
55	Fiji	0.004	0.004	0.004	-
56	Finland	0.533	0.533	0.533	-
57	France	6.036	6.030	6.036	-
58	Gabon	0.009	0.009	0.009	-
59	Gambia	0.001	0.001	0.001	-
60	Georgia	0.003	0.003	0.003	-
61	Germany	8.670	8.662	8.670	-
62	Ghana	0.004	0.004	0.004	-
63	Greece	0.530	0.530	0.530	-
64	Grenada	0.001	0.001	0.001	-
65	Guatemala	0.030	0.030	0.030	-
66	Guinea	0.003	0.003	0.003	-
67	Guinea-Bissau	0.001	0.001	0.001	-
68	Guyana	0.001	0.001	0.001	-
69	Haiti	0.003	0.003	0.003	-
70	Honduras	0.005	0.005	0.005	-
71	Hungary	0.126	0.126	0.126	-
72	Iceland	0.034	0.034	0.034	-
73	India	0.421	0.421	0.421	-
74	Indonesia	0.142	0.142	0.142	-
75	Iran, Islamic Republic of	0.157	0.157	0.157	-
76	Iraq	0.016	0.016	0.016	-
77	Ireland	0.350	0.350	0.350	-
78	Israel	0.467	0.467	0.467	-
79	Italy	4.890	4.885	4.890	-
80	Jamaica	0.008	0.008	0.008	-
81	Japan	19.485	19.468	19.485	-
82	Jordan	0.011	0.011	0.011	-
83	Kazakhstan	0.025	0.025	0.025	-
84	Kenya	0.009	0.009	0.009	-
85	Kiribati	0.001	0.001	0.001	-
86	Korea, Republic of	1.798	1.796	1.797	(0.001)
87	Kuwait	0.162	0.162	0.162	-
88	Kyrgyzstan	0.001	0.001	0.001	-

	State	ILO assessments 2005 Col.1 %	UN assessments 2006 Col.2 %	Draft scale of ILO assessments 2006 Col.3 %	Increase (Decrease) (Diff. between cols 3 and 1) Col.4 %
89	Lao People's Democratic Republic	0.001	0.001	0.001	-
90	Latvia	0.015	0.015	0.015	-
91	Lebanon	0.024	0.024	0.024	-
92	Lesotho	0.001	0.001	0.001	-
93	Liberia	0.001	0.001	0.001	-
94	Libyan Arab Jamahiriya	0.132	0.132	0.132	-
95	Lithuania	0.024	0.024	0.024	-
96	Luxembourg	0.077	0.077	0.077	-
97	Madagascar	0.003	0.003	0.003	-
98	Malawi	0.001	0.001	0.001	-
99	Malaysia	0.203	0.203	0.203	-
100	Mali	0.002	0.002	0.002	-
101	Malta	0.014	0.014	0.014	-
102	Mauritania	0.001	0.001	0.001	-
103	Mauritius	0.011	0.011	0.011	-
104	Mexico	1.885	1.883	1.885	-
105	Moldova, Republic of	0.001	0.001	0.001	-
106	Mongolia	0.001	0.001	0.001	-
107	Morocco	0.047	0.047	0.047	-
108	Mozambique	0.001	0.001	0.001	-
109	Myanmar	0.010	0.010	0.010	-
110	Namibia	0.006	0.006	0.006	-
111	Nepal	0.004	0.004	0.004	-
112	Netherlands	1.691	1.690	1.691	-
113	New Zealand	0.221	0.221	0.221	-
114	Nicaragua	0.001	0.001	0.001	-
115	Niger	0.001	0.001	0.001	-
116	Nigeria	0.042	0.042	0.042	-
117	Norway	0.680	0.679	0.680	-
118	Oman	0.070	0.070	0.070	-
119	Pakistan	0.055	0.055	0.055	-
120	Panama	0.019	0.019	0.019	-
121	Papua New Guinea	0.003	0.003	0.003	-
122	Paraguay	0.012	0.012	0.012	-
123	Peru	0.092	0.092	0.092	-
124	Philippines	0.095	0.095	0.095	-
125	Poland	0.461	0.461	0.461	-
126	Portugal	0.470	0.470	0.470	-
127	Qatar	0.064	0.064	0.064	-
128	Romania	0.060	0.060	0.060	-
129	Russian Federation	1.101	1.100	1.101	-
130	Rwanda	0.001	0.001	0.001	-
131	Saint Kitts and Nevis	0.001	0.001	0.001	-
132	Saint Lucia	0.002	0.002	0.002	-
133	Saint Vincent and the Grenadines	0.001	0.001	0.001	-
134	Samoa	-	0.001	0.001	0.001

	State	ILO assessments 2005 Col.1 %	UN assessments 2006 Col.2 %	Draft scale of ILO assessments 2006 Col.3 %	Increase (Decrease) (Diff. between cols 3 and 1) Col.4 %
135	San Marino	0.003	0.003	0.003	-
136	Sao Tome and Principe	0.001	0.001	0.001	-
137	Saudi Arabia	0.714	0.713	0.714	-
138	Senegal	0.005	0.005	0.005	-
139	Serbia and Montenegro	0.019	0.019	0.019	-
140	Seychelles	0.002	0.002	0.002	-
141	Sierra Leone	0.001	0.001	0.001	-
142	Singapore	0.388	0.388	0.388	-
143	Slovakia	0.051	0.051	0.051	-
144	Slovenia	0.082	0.082	0.082	-
145	Solomon Islands	0.001	0.001	0.001	-
146	Somalia	0.001	0.001	0.001	-
147	South Africa	0.292	0.292	0.292	-
148	Spain	2.523	2.520	2.523	-
149	Sri Lanka	0.017	0.017	0.017	-
150	Sudan	0.008	0.008	0.008	-
151	Suriname	0.001	0.001	0.001	-
152	Swaziland	0.002	0.002	0.002	-
153	Sweden	0.999	0.998	0.999	-
154	Switzerland	1.198	1.197	1.198	-
155	Syrian Arab Republic	0.038	0.038	0.038	-
156	Tajikistan	0.001	0.001	0.001	-
157	Tanzania, United Republic of	0.006	0.006	0.006	-
158	Thailand	0.209	0.209	0.209	-
159	The former Yugoslav Republic of Macedonia	0.006	0.006	0.006	-
160	Timor-Leste, Democratic Republic of	0.001	0.001	0.001	-
161	Togo	0.001	0.001	0.001	-
162	Trinidad and Tobago	0.022	0.022	0.022	-
163	Tunisia	0.032	0.032	0.032	-
164	Turkey	0.372	0.372	0.372	-
165	Turkmenistan	0.005	0.005	0.005	-
166	Uganda	0.006	0.006	0.006	-
167	Ukraine	0.039	0.039	0.039	-
168	United Arab Emirates	0.235	0.235	0.235	-
169	United Kingdom	6.133	6.127	6.133	-
170	United States	22.000	22.000	22.000	-
171	Uruguay	0.048	0.048	0.048	-
172	Uzbekistan	0.014	0.014	0.014	-
173	Vanuatu	0.001	0.001	0.001	-
174	Venezuela	0.171	0.171	0.171	-
175	Viet Nam	0.021	0.021	0.021	-
176	Yemen	0.006	0.006	0.006	-
177	Zambia	0.002	0.002	0.002	-
178	Zimbabwe	0.007	0.007	0.007	-
		100.000	99.935	100.000	0.000

Appendix IV

Proposed summarized budget of expenditure and income for 2006-07

Expenditure	2004-05 budget US$	2006-07 estimates US$	Income	2004-05 budget US$	2004-05 budget SF	2006-07 estimates US$	2006-07 estimates SF
Part I Ordinary budget	528,715,000	587,253,275	Contributions from member States	529,590,000	709,650,600	594,310,000	742,887,500
Part II Unforeseen expenditure	875,000	875,000					
Part III Working Capital Fund	-	-					
Part IV Institutional investments and extraordinary items	-	6,181,725					
Total budget	529,590,000	594,310,000		529,590,000	709,650,600	594,310,000	742,887,500

Appendix V

Proposed expenditure budget by appropriation line (in US dollars)

Item	2004-05 Budget (US$)	2006-07 Estimates (in constant 2004-05 US$)	2006-07 Estimates (recosted) 1.34 to 1.25
Part I Ordinary budget			
A. Policy-making organs	**65,078,793**	**61,064,424**	**67,267,536**
B. Strategic objectives	**397,926,949**	**403,139,901**	**443,939,354**
Standards and fundamental principles and rights at work	*70,766,259*	*78,344,449*	*86,227,715*
Employment	*125,931,103*	*125,114,738*	*137,532,087*
Social protection	*72,717,717*	*86,221,934*	*95,340,336*
Social dialogue	*128,511,870*	*113,458,780*	*124,839,216*
C. Management services	**45,791,102**	**44,555,128**	**49,390,928**
D. Other budgetary provisions	**24,459,087**	**24,393,117**	**31,708,184**
Adjustment for staff turnover	*(4,540,931)*	*(4,540,931)*	*(5,052,727)*
Total Part I	**528,715,000**	**528,611,639**	**587,253,275**
Part II Unforeseen expenditure			
Unforeseen expenditure	875,000	875,000	875,000
Part III Working capital fund			
Working capital fund	-	-	-
Total (Parts I - III)	**529,590,000**	**529,486,639**	**588,128,275**
Part IV Institutional investments and extra-ordinary items			
Institutional investments and extra-ordinary items	-	5,810,000	6,181,725
TOTAL (Parts I - IV)	**529,590,000**	**535,296,639**	**594,310,000**

Appendix VI

INCOME BUDGET FOR 2006-2007
STATEMENT OF CONTRIBUTIONS DUE FROM MEMBER STATES FOR 2006
(In Swiss francs)

	Member States	Assessed Contribution for 2006 %	Assessed Contribution for 2006 Amount	2004 Incentive Scheme	2002-03 50% Net Premium	Prior years 50% Net Premium	Prior years Cash Surplus	Total Credits	Net Contribution for 2006
1	Afghanistan	0.002	7,429	9	-	-	-	9	7,420
2	Albania	0.005	18,572	-	-	-	1,102	1,102	17,470
3	Algeria	0.076	282,297	51	-	-	-	51	282,246
4	Angola	0.001	3,714	2	-	-	-	2	3,712
5	Antigua and Barbuda	0.003	11,143	-	-	-	-	-	11,143
6	Argentina	0.957	3,554,717	-	-	69,669	109,956	179,625	3,375,092
7	Armenia	0.002	7,429	-	-	-	-	-	7,429
8	Australia	1.593	5,917,099	1,573	-	-	-	1,573	5,915,526
9	Austria	0.860	3,194,416	893	-	-	-	893	3,193,523
10	Azerbaijan	0.005	18,572	-	-	-	-	-	18,572
11	Bahamas	0.013	48,288	12	-	-	-	12	48,276
12	Bahrain	0.030	111,433	18	-	-	-	18	111,415
13	Bangladesh	0.010	37,145	9	32	-	-	41	37,104
14	Barbados	0.010	37,145	-	29	-	-	29	37,116
15	Belarus	0.018	66,860	16	61	-	-	77	66,783
16	Belgium	1.070	3,974,448	56	-	-	-	56	3,974,392
17	Belize	0.001	3,714	-	-	-	-	-	3,714
18	Benin	0.002	7,429	-	6	-	-	6	7,423
19	Bolivia	0.009	33,430	-	-	-	-	-	33,430
20	Bosnia and Herzegovina	0.003	11,143	1	-	-	-	1	11,142
21	Botswana	0.012	44,573	8	-	-	-	8	44,565
22	Brazil	1.524	5,660,803	-	-	92,956	146,710	239,666	5,421,137
23	Bulgaria	0.017	63,146	11	-	-	-	11	63,135
24	Burkina Faso	0.002	7,429	2	-	-	-	2	7,427
25	Burundi	0.001	3,714	-	-	-	-	-	3,714
26	Cambodia	0.002	7,429	-	-	-	551	551	6,878
27	Cameroon	0.008	29,716	-	29	-	-	29	29,687
28	Canada	2.816	10,459,856	2,494	-	-	-	2,494	10,457,362
29	Cape Verde	0.001	3,714	-	-	-	-	-	3,714
30	Central African Republic	0.001	3,714	-	-	-	-	-	3,714
31	Chad	0.001	3,714	-	-	-	-	-	3,714
32	Chile	0.223	828,320	-	635	-	-	635	827,685
33	China	2.055	7,633,169	115	4,894	-	-	5,009	7,628,160
34	Colombia	0.155	575,738	-	591	-	-	591	575,147
35	Comoros	0.001	3,714	-	-	-	-	-	3,714
36	Congo	0.001	3,714	-	-	-	-	-	3,714
37	Costa Rica	0.030	111,433	-	-	-	-	-	111,433
38	Côte d'Ivoire	0.010	37,145	-	29	-	-	29	37,116
39	Croatia	0.037	137,434	-	-	-	-	-	137,434
40	Cuba	0.043	159,721	-	94	-	-	94	159,627
41	Cyprus	0.039	144,863	35	-	-	-	35	144,828
42	Czech Republic	0.183	679,742	186	-	-	-	186	679,556
43	Democratic Republic of the Congo	0.003	11,143	-	-	89	-	89	11,054
44	Denmark	0.719	2,670,681	731	-	-	-	731	2,669,950
45	Djibouti	0.001	3,714	-	-	-	-	-	3,714
46	Dominica	0.001	3,714	1	-	-	-	1	3,713
47	Dominican Republic	0.035	130,006	18	-	-	247	265	129,741
48	Ecuador	0.019	70,574	18	78	-	-	96	70,478
49	Egypt	0.120	445,733	-	-	-	-	-	445,733
50	El Salvador	0.022	81,718	-	58	-	-	58	81,660
51	Equatorial Guinea	0.002	7,429	-	-	-	-	-	7,429
52	Eritrea	0.001	3,714	1	-	-	-	1	3,713
53	Estonia	0.012	44,573	10	-	-	-	10	44,563
54	Ethiopia	0.004	14,858	4	-	-	-	4	14,854

INCOME BUDGET FOR 2006-2007
STATEMENT OF CONTRIBUTIONS DUE FROM MEMBER STATES FOR 2006
(In Swiss francs)

	Member States	Assessed Contribution for 2006 %	Assessed Contribution for 2006 Amount	Earned Credits: 2004 Incentive Scheme	Earned Credits: 2002-03 50% Net Premium	Earned Credits: Prior years 50% Net Premium	Earned Credits: Prior years Cash Surplus	Total Credits	Net Contribution for 2006
55	Fiji	0.004	14,858	3	-	-	-	3	14,855
56	Finland	0.533	1,979,795	505	-	-	-	505	1,979,290
57	France	6.036	22,420,345	1,262	-	-	-	1,262	22,419,083
58	Gabon	0.009	33,430	-	-	-	-	-	33,430
59	Gambia	0.001	3,714	-	-	-	-	-	3,714
60	Georgia	0.003	11,143	-	-	-	-	-	11,143
61	Germany	8.670	32,204,173	5,388	-	-	-	5,388	32,198,785
62	Ghana	0.004	14,858	5	16	449	709	1,179	13,679
63	Greece	0.530	1,968,652	20	1,722	-	-	1,742	1,966,910
64	Grenada	0.001	3,714	1	-	-	-	1	3,713
65	Guatemala	0.030	111,433	18	-	-	-	18	111,415
66	Guinea	0.003	11,143	-	-	-	-	-	11,143
67	Guinea-Bissau	0.001	3,714	-	-	-	-	-	3,714
68	Guyana	0.001	3,714	-	-	-	-	-	3,714
69	Haiti	0.003	11,143	-	6	128	202	336	10,807
70	Honduras	0.005	18,572	4	-	-	-	4	18,568
71	Hungary	0.126	468,019	13	-	-	-	13	468,006
72	Iceland	0.034	126,291	31	-	-	-	31	126,260
73	India	0.421	1,563,778	333	-	-	-	333	1,563,445
74	Indonesia	0.142	527,450	9	638	-	-	647	526,803
75	Iran, Islamic Republic of	0.157	583,167	-	-	-	-	-	583,167
76	Iraq	0.016	59,431	-	-	-	-	-	59,431
77	Ireland	0.350	1,300,053	226	-	-	-	226	1,299,827
78	Israel	0.467	1,734,643	-	-	22,132	34,931	57,063	1,677,580
79	Italy	4.890	18,163,600	1,175	16,172	-	-	17,347	18,146,253
80	Jamaica	0.008	29,716	1	-	-	-	1	29,715
81	Japan	19.485	72,375,815	14,917	62,317	-	-	77,234	72,298,581
82	Jordan	0.011	40,859	6	-	-	-	6	40,853
83	Kazakhstan	0.025	92,861	25	-	-	-	25	92,836
84	Kenya	0.009	33,430	6	-	-	-	6	33,424
85	Kiribati	0.001	3,714	1	-	-	-	1	3,713
86	Korea, Republic of	1.797	6,674,844	206	-	-	-	206	6,674,638
87	Kuwait	0.162	601,739	140	-	-	-	140	601,599
88	Kyrgyzstan	0.001	3,714	-	-	-	-	-	3,714
89	Lao People's Democratic Republic	0.001	3,714	1	3	692	291	987	2,727
90	Latvia	0.015	55,717	10	32	-	-	42	55,675
91	Lebanon	0.024	89,147	4	39	-	-	43	89,104
92	Lesotho	0.001	3,714	1	-	-	-	1	3,713
93	Liberia	0.001	3,714	1	-	-	-	1	3,713
94	Libyan Arab Jamahiriya	0.132	490,306	-	213	7,827	12,352	20,392	469,914
95	Lithuania	0.024	89,147	1	55	-	-	56	89,091
96	Luxembourg	0.077	286,012	77	-	-	-	77	285,935
97	Madagascar	0.003	11,143	-	-	-	-	-	11,143
98	Malawi	0.001	3,714	-	-	-	-	-	3,714
99	Malaysia	0.203	754,031	220	-	-	-	220	753,811
100	Mali	0.002	7,429	2	6	-	-	8	7,421
101	Malta	0.014	52,002	15	-	-	-	15	51,987
102	Mauritania	0.001	3,714	-	3	-	-	3	3,711
103	Mauritius	0.011	40,859	11	-	-	-	11	40,848
104	Mexico	1.885	7,001,715	271	-	-	-	271	7,001,444
105	Moldova, Republic of	0.001	3,714	-	-	-	-	-	3,714
106	Mongolia	0.001	3,714	-	-	128	202	330	3,384
107	Morocco	0.047	174,579	12	-	-	-	12	174,567
108	Mozambique	0.001	3,714	-	3	-	-	3	3,711
109	Myanmar	0.010	37,145	7	-	-	-	7	37,138
110	Namibia	0.006	22,287	-	-	-	-	-	22,287

INCOME BUDGET FOR 2006-2007
STATEMENT OF CONTRIBUTIONS DUE FROM MEMBER STATES FOR 2006
(In Swiss francs)

	Member States	Assessed Contribution for 2006 %	Assessed Contribution for 2006 Amount	2004 Incentive Scheme	2002-03 50% Net Premium	Prior years 50% Net Premium	Prior years Cash Surplus	Total Credits	Net Contribution for 2006
111	Nepal	0.004	14,858	-	13	-	-	13	14,845
112	Netherlands	1.691	6,281,114	1,569	-	-	-	1,569	6,279,545
113	New Zealand	0.221	820,891	231	-	-	-	231	820,660
114	Nicaragua	0.001	3,714	-	3	-	-	3	3,711
115	Niger	0.001	3,714	66	-	128	202	396	3,318
116	Nigeria	0.042	156,007	-	-	-	-	-	156,007
117	Norway	0.680	2,525,818	549	-	-	-	549	2,525,269
118	Oman	0.070	260,011	57	-	-	-	57	259,954
119	Pakistan	0.055	204,294	-	194	-	-	194	204,100
120	Panama	0.019	70,574	-	-	-	-	-	70,574
121	Papua New Guinea	0.003	11,143	-	-	-	-	-	11,143
122	Paraguay	0.012	44,573	12	-	-	1,017	1,029	43,544
123	Peru	0.092	341,728	-	-	6,223	9,821	16,044	325,684
124	Philippines	0.095	352,872	-	318	-	-	318	352,554
125	Poland	0.461	1,712,356	347	-	-	-	347	1,712,009
126	Portugal	0.470	1,745,786	26	-	-	-	26	1,745,760
127	Qatar	0.064	237,724	30	-	-	-	30	237,694
128	Romania	0.060	222,866	52	-	-	-	52	222,814
129	Russian Federation	1.101	4,089,596	-	3,818	-	-	3,818	4,085,778
130	Rwanda	0.001	3,714	-	-	-	-	-	3,714
131	Saint Kitts and Nevis	0.001	3,714	-	-	-	-	-	3,714
132	Saint Lucia	0.002	7,429	-	6	-	-	6	7,423
133	Saint Vincent and the Grenadines	0.001	3,714	1	3	-	-	4	3,710
134	Samoa	0.001	3,714	-	-	-	-	-	3,714
135	San Marino	0.003	11,143	2	-	-	-	2	11,141
136	Sao Tome and Principe	0.001	3,714	-	-	-	-	-	3,714
137	Saudi Arabia	0.714	2,652,109	482	-	-	-	482	2,651,627
138	Senegal	0.005	18,572	-	-	-	-	-	18,572
139	Serbia and Montenegro	0.019	70,574	-	-	-	-	-	70,574
140	Seychelles	0.002	7,429	-	6	128	202	336	7,093
141	Sierra Leone	0.001	3,714	-	-	-	-	-	3,714
142	Singapore	0.388	1,441,202	333	-	-	-	333	1,440,869
143	Slovakia	0.051	189,437	40	-	-	-	40	189,397
144	Slovenia	0.082	304,584	77	-	-	-	77	304,507
145	Solomon Islands	0.001	3,714	-	-	-	-	-	3,714
146	Somalia	0.001	3,714	-	-	-	-	-	3,714
147	South Africa	0.292	1,084,616	368	-	-	-	368	1,084,248
148	Spain	2.523	9,371,526	2,181	-	-	-	2,181	9,369,345
149	Sri Lanka	0.017	63,146	15	-	-	-	15	63,131
150	Sudan	0.008	29,716	-	-	449	709	1,158	28,558
151	Suriname	0.001	3,714	-	6	257	405	668	3,046
152	Swaziland	0.002	7,429	2	-	-	-	2	7,427
153	Sweden	0.999	3,710,723	969	-	-	-	969	3,709,754
154	Switzerland	1.198	4,449,896	1,224	-	-	-	1,224	4,448,672
155	Syrian Arab Republic	0.038	141,149	60	-	-	-	60	141,089
156	Tajikistan	0.001	3,714	-	-	-	-	-	3,714
157	Tanzania, United Republic of	0.006	22,287	3	13	-	-	16	22,271
158	Thailand	0.209	776,318	287	-	-	-	287	776,031
159	The form.Yug. Rep. of Macedonia	0.006	22,287	-	20	1,056	647	1,723	20,564
160	Timor-Leste, Dem. Rep of (1)	0.001	3,714	-	-	-	-	-	3,714
161	Togo	0.001	3,714	-	-	-	-	-	3,714
162	Trinidad and Tobago	0.022	81,718	15	52	-	-	67	81,651
163	Tunisia	0.032	118,862	-	95	-	-	95	118,767
164	Turkey	0.372	1,381,771	345	-	-	-	345	1,381,426
165	Turkmenistan	0.005	18,572	-	-	-	-	-	18,572
166	Uganda	0.006	22,287	-	-	-	-	-	22,287

INCOME BUDGET FOR 2006-2007
STATEMENT OF CONTRIBUTIONS DUE FROM MEMBER STATES FOR 2006
(In Swiss francs)

	Member States	Assessed Contribution for 2006 %	Assessed Contribution for 2006 Amount	2004 Incentive Scheme	2002-03 50% Net Premium	Prior years 50% Net Premium	Prior years Cash Surplus	Total Credits	Net Contribution for 2006
167	Ukraine	0.039	144,863	2	-	-	-	2	144,861
168	United Arab Emirates	0.235	872,893	174	-	-	-	174	872,719
169	United Kingdom	6.133	22,780,645	2,227	-	-	-	2,227	22,778,418
170	United States	22.000	81,717,625	-	71,059	-	-	71,059	81,646,566
171	Uruguay	0.048	178,293	-	-	-	-	-	178,293
172	Uzbekistan	0.014	52,002	-	-	-	-	-	52,002
173	Vanuatu	0.001	3,714		-	-	-	-	3,714
174	Venezuela	0.171	635,169	-	666	10,072	15,896	26,634	608,535
175	Viet Nam	0.021	78,003	5	-	-	-	5	77,998
176	Yemen	0.006	22,287	-	21	-	-	21	22,266
177	Zambia	0.002	7,429	-	-	-	-	-	7,429
178	Zimbabwe	0.007	26,001	6	26	-	-	32	25,969
	TOTAL	100.000	371,443,750	42,959	164,080	212,383	336,152	755,574	370,688,176

CONTENTS

Page

Second item on the agenda: Programme and Budget proposals for 2006-07 and other questions

Second report of the Finance Committee of Government Representatives 1

Resolutions submitted to the Conference 19

Appendices 23

International Labour Conference

Record of Proceedings

Ninety-third Session, Geneva, 2005

18

Fourth item on the agenda: Occupational safety and health

Report of the Committee on Safety and Health

1. The Committee on Occupational Safety and Health met for its first sitting on 31 May 2005. Initially, it consisted of 192 members (73 Government members, 48 Employer members and 71 Worker members). To achieve equality of voting strength, each Government member was allotted 3,408 votes, each Employer member 5,183 votes and each Worker member 3,504 votes. The composition of the Committee was modified nine times during the session, and the number of votes attributed to each member was adjusted accordingly.[1]

2. The Committee elected its Officers as follows:

Chairperson: Mr. A. Békés (Government member, Hungary)

Vice-Chairpersons: Mr. C. Lötter (Employer member, South Africa) and
Ms. P. Seminario (Worker member, United States)

Reporter: Mr. A. Annakin (Government member, New Zealand)

---

[1] The modifications were as follows:

(a) 1 June: 197 members (89 Government members with 315 votes each, 45 Employer members with 623 votes each and 63 Worker members with 445 votes each);

(b) 2 June: 190 members (101 Government members with 1,974 votes each, 42 Employer members with 4,747 votes each and 47 Worker members with 4,242 votes each);

(c) 3 June: 172 members (101 Government members with 1,258 votes each, 34 Employer members with 3,737 votes each and 37 Worker members with 3,434 votes each);

(d) 4 June: 170 members (106 Government members with 999 votes each, 27 Employer members with 3,922 votes each and 37 Worker members with 2,862 votes each);

(e) 6 June: 171 members (106 Government members with 513 votes each, 27 Employer members with 2,014 votes each and 38 Worker members with 1,431 votes each);

(f) 7 June: 165 members (106 Government members with 420 votes each, 24 Employer members with 1,855 votes each and 35 Worker members with 1,272 votes each);

(g) 8 June: 161 members (107 Government members with 713 votes each, 23 Employer members with 3,317 votes each and 31 Worker members with 2,461 votes each);

(h) 9 June: 156 members (107 Government members with 594 votes each, 22 Employer members with 2,889 votes each and 27 Worker members with 2,354 votes each);

(i) 13 June: 159 members (110 Government members with 42 votes each, 21 Employer members with 220 votes each and 28 Worker members with 165 votes each).

3. At its ninth sitting, the Committee appointed a Drafting Group composed of the following members:

Government member: Ms. N. Kocherhans (Switzerland)

Employer member: Mr. N. Cote (Canada)

Worker member: Mr. M. Leemans (Belgium)

4. The Committee had before it Reports IV(1) and IV(2), entitled *Promotional framework for occupational safety and health*, prepared by the Office for a first discussion of the fourth item on the agenda of the Conference: "Occupational Safety and Health – Development of a new instrument establishing a promotional framework in this area". The proposed Conclusions submitted by the Office were contained in Report IV(2).

5. The Committee held 13 sittings.

Introduction

6. The representative of the Secretary-General, Dr. Jukka Takala, welcomed the delegates, reminding them of the global burden of occupational accidents and diseases. The Committee then proceeded to elect its officers. The Chairperson thanked the Committee for his election, which he saw as a great honour for him and his country. He looked forward to working with the Vice-Chairpersons and members of the Committee in a constructive spirit of cooperation, and was confident of the Committee's success. The Vice-Chairpersons likewise pledged their commitment to effective collaboration and a successful outcome.

General discussion

7. The representative of the Secretary-General introduced the subject for discussion by the Committee. In June 2003, the International Labour Conference had adopted a global strategy for occupational safety and health (OSH), the aim of which was to build and maintain a preventative safety and health culture, and this focused on the right to a safe and healthy environment, the principle of prevention and a systems approach to managing occupational safety and health. The strategy included: (1) the promotion of occupational safety and health through awareness raising and advocacy; (2) ILO instruments such as standards (the subject for this Committee), codes of practice and guides; (3) technical assistance and cooperation on occupational safety and health; (4) knowledge development, management and dissemination; and (5) international collaboration.

8. In July 2004, the Office produced Report IV(1), entitled *Promotional framework for occupational safety and health*, which provided much of the technical background and proposals for a new instrument on a promotional framework for occupational safety and health. The same report included a questionnaire about the way forward, and replies to this questionnaire were summarized in Report IV(2), also entitled *Promotional framework for occupational safety and health*. The second report included a commentary prepared by the Office, together with proposed Conclusions for discussion by this Committee.

9. The proposed instrument was designed so as to promote safer and healthier working environments through a management systems approach and the development of national occupational safety and health programmes and the continual improvement of national occupational safety and health systems. The former were medium-term strategic programmes that aimed to place occupational safety and health high on national agendas,

with set targets and time frames. National occupational safety and health systems comprised relevant legislation, tripartite consultation and compliance assurance mechanisms such as inspection, as well as occupational safety and health services, data collection, training and information. National occupational safety and health programmes and systems should be mutually supportive, and ILO Conventions, Recommendations, codes of practice, etc., provided the basis for both.

10. As for the form of the instrument, there had been a mixed response from the 92 countries that replied to the above questionnaire. Most countries favoured either a Convention or a Convention and a Recommendation, as did most workers' organizations. Some countries favoured a Recommendation (only) or a Declaration, as did most employers' organizations. In Report IV(2), the Office proposed a Convention with an accompanying Recommendation as a basis for discussion by the Committee. However, the representative of the Secretary-General emphasized that it was the Committee that would decide on what form the instrument would take.

11. The Employer Vice-Chairperson, speaking on behalf of the Employers' group, congratulated both the Chairperson and the Worker Vice-Chairperson on their appointments and also looked forward to working with the Government members of the Committee. The work done by the Office in producing the report for this Committee was much appreciated. The Committee had an enormous responsibility to ensure a successful conclusion to its deliberations but, to do so, it would be necessary to be open to new approaches. The Governing Body, in 2000, decided to adopt an integrated approach to the ILO's standards-related activities, the first area of which was to be in the area of occupational safety and health, so there was precedent for thinking beyond the norm. He reminded the Committee of the strong consensus reached in 2003 for a new instrument establishing a promotional framework for occupational safety and health.

12. The purpose of this instrument was to ensure that priority be given to occupational safety and health in national agendas and to foster political commitment to developing national strategies for the improvement of occupational safety and health. These strategies were to be based on a preventative safety and health culture and the management systems approach. Further, it was to function as an overarching instrument with a promotional rather than a prescriptive content. The Employers' group was therefore disappointed to find that the basis for this Committee's discussion was a proposal for yet another Convention and Recommendation. It strongly supported a Declaration as the instrument best suited to making a difference, to making a real contribution to safety and health in the workplace.

13. The Worker Vice-Chairperson congratulated the Chairperson and the Employer Vice-Chairperson on their elections and thanked the Office for the preliminary discussions that the Office had organized in March 2005. She noted that protecting workers' safety and health had always formed part of the core mandate of the ILO, yet problems still persisted with over 2 million women and men dying annually from work-related accidents and diseases. New employment practices also increased workers' exposure to occupational hazards and risks. New hazards were also emerging. Preventing occupational accidents and diseases should therefore be given the highest priority. However, the Workers' group thought that the Office's proposals did not deal adequately with some of the elements agreed in 2003, namely: the rights of workers to a safe and healthy working environment, the respective responsibilities of governments, employers and workers, and the establishment of tripartite consultative mechanisms on occupational safety and health, workers' participation and representation at all levels, and measures for enforcement. The Workers' group considered that the new instrument should also take account of, build on and integrate existing key ILO instruments, such as the Occupational Safety and Health Convention, 1981 (No. 155), and should not be confined to the promotion of national

programmes and systems. Without the link to existing ILO instruments on occupational safety and health, the new instrument would weaken the rights and principles entailed in these instruments. However, she stressed that the goal should not be to impose new obligations on member States and employers, and that therefore the Convention should be easy to ratify.

14. The Workers' group supported the proposal to have a new instrument in the form of a Convention supplemented by a Recommendation. The basic principles to be taken into account in the new instrument were for the working environment to be safe and healthy, for occupational safety and health policies and programmes to be established at the national as well as at the enterprise level and for occupational safety and health to be given high priority. The responsibilities, duties and rights of employers, governments and workers needed to be defined at national and enterprise levels, and occupational safety and health information and training provided. Participation and representation of workers and their representatives should be included at all levels, in particular with respect to prevention initiatives. The promotional framework should include and link policy and key principles to both the national system of laws and regulations and to a national programme that sets priorities, goals and benchmarks in order to improve workplace safety and health. Other ILO instruments serve as the foundation of this framework. She emphasized that the new instrument should improve occupational safety and health at national levels and should contribute to the objectives set forth in the Decent Work Agenda.

15. The Government member of Egypt described the tasks of the National Institute for Occupational Safety and Health, which he represented. It had been established in 1969 and its task was to assist enterprises at all levels in the area of occupational safety and health and to carry out field studies and research to identify and solve occupational safety and health problems. The Institute was also involved in the training of experts and in occupational safety and health awareness-raising activities, in developing standards and data collection. Promotional activities required strategic planning and the involvement of all parties, and a good national framework for the promotion of occupational safety and health required everyone to be involved, including NGOs and especially the media (press and television).

16. The Government member of Japan said that the country had instituted its first Industrial Accident Prevention Plan 50 years ago, and that having a national programme for occupational safety and health had proved to be very effective. In order to take into account national differences, however, the new instrument discussed by the Committee should have minimum requirements and be simple and flexible so that all member States were able to apply it. Japan had already formulated guidelines on occupational safety and health management systems, and industrial occupational safety and health associations had also formulated their own systems based on national guidelines. He commended the ILO guidelines on this subject as a most useful document. He also highlighted the fact that his Government was on the verge of ratifying the Asbestos Convention, 1986 (No. 162), and thanked the Office for the help that it had offered during this process.

17. The Government member of Switzerland reaffirmed her Government's position in 2003, where a mechanism was sought to promote occupational safety and health. Her Government was against the idea of having a new Convention and Recommendation, since there were already many instruments dealing with occupational safety and health, and most had very low ratifications, preferring new mechanisms that provided practical protective measures. She expressed her disappointment that the Office had not studied more innovative ways to provide a promotional framework for occupational safety and health. Her Government would support a new instrument in the form of a Declaration, enhanced with practical protective measures.

18. The Government member of the Netherlands endorsed the need for a promotional framework for occupational safety and health, stressing the need for flexibility. He expressed his disappointment that the Committee was not discussing a consolidated Convention on occupational safety and health. Taking this into account, as well as the need for flexibility, his Government could only support a new instrument in the form of a Recommendation or Declaration.

19. The Government member of Australia stated that securing better occupational safety and health was of great importance to her Government. The Committee had a unique opportunity to develop a new promotional instrument for occupational safety and health as a basic principle, and it was important to be aware of the desired outcomes. However, since occupational safety and health Conventions were so poorly ratified, she questioned the Office proposal of a new Convention and Recommendation, as this would be unlikely to promote improvements in occupational safety and health. She said that the new instrument should be given the greatest chance to be ratified and, with this in mind, her Government proposed it take the form of a Declaration, to underpin the ILO's global objective of achieving decent work that is safe work. Such a Declaration should provide for accountability and reporting arrangements equivalent to those applicable under the follow-up to the Declaration on Fundamental Principles and Rights at Work. It should also promote compliance with the principles contained in Convention No. 155 and, as a minimum, should provide for the development and implementation in all member States of a national occupational safety and health policy in consultation with employers' and workers' organizations, periodic review of the policy, guidance to employers and workers on their legal obligations, the right of workers to remove themselves from dangerous work situations, and promotion of sound safety and health practices through education and awareness raising. A promotional campaign for Convention No. 155 should be launched and member States not ratifying it should be asked to report on progress annually. An occupational safety and health Declaration should incorporate a reporting mechanism on the efforts taken to implement the Declaration's principles. This follow-up process should be sufficiently flexible to allow member States to achieve the Declaration's principles within a reasonable time period. She said that this would hold all member States accountable for their efforts in improving occupational safety and health, not just those that had ratified Conventions.

20. The Government member of New Zealand expressed his Government's support for the development of a promotional instrument for occupational safety and health and that the new instrument should provide an overarching framework for programmes of action at the international, national and enterprise level. He described his Government's efforts, in collaboration with workers and employers, to develop a workplace health and safety strategy for New Zealand until 2015. Part of this also included the establishment of an expert national occupational health and safety advisory committee. While developing the strategy, he said that his Government had learned four lessons, which could be kept in mind by the Committee: (1) an inclusive process of consultation was essential for the new instrument to be accepted by all; (2) a comprehensive framework for action should be provided identifying priority areas, without actually prescribing the balance of interventions; (3) there should be an awareness-raising element; and (4) progress should be monitored. Active employee participation, a strong emphasis on good occupational safety and health practice as well as highlighting the link between good occupational safety and health practice and productivity were essential. He said that it was most important for occupational safety and health not to be seen as a stand-alone element, but as a key contributor to workplace productivity. His Government supported the new instrument taking the form of a Convention and a Recommendation.

21. The Government member of Argentina, speaking on behalf of the Government members of the Committee member States of MERCOSUR, said that his Government was extremely

active in promoting occupational safety and health and that they had undertaken numerous programmes, including the training of teachers, accident research and reduction, and special programmes for small and medium-sized enterprises. The Government of Argentina established an occupational safety and health week, that takes place every year between 21 and 28 April. His Government had signed an agreement adopting the ILO guidelines on occupational safety and health management systems, which will result in his agency becoming the main certification body for certifying companies. His Government supported the new instrument taking the form of a Convention and a Recommendation.

22. The Government member of South Africa described the situation in his country, where a study undertaken in 2004 identified four high-risk sectors and three secondary-risk sectors; the former would be a priority for the next five years. South Africa had already established an accord on safety and health at work – a policy document – signed by the three social partners. With regard to the proposed new instrument, it was very important for it to promote continual improvement. With this in mind, his country supported the idea of a promotional framework for occupational safety and health that progressively improved the national programme and systems. The new instrument should also be flexible, thus allowing for wide-scale adoption, so his Government supported it taking the form of a Convention and a Recommendation.

23. The Government member of India said that his country relied extensively on ILO instruments, especially when drawing up national legislation, and some of the more recent ones on occupational safety and health had had a strong bearing on emerging occupational safety and health legislation in India. On the question of ratifying ILO Conventions, this was only possible when there was consensus between all stakeholders, and he mentioned Convention No. 155 as an example. India realized that economic prosperity could only be achieved by having high standards of safety and health at the workplace, thereby improving the quality of work life. India favoured the new instrument to take the form of a Convention and a Recommendation.

24. The representative of the International Commission on Occupational Health (ICOH) explained that ICOH was a professional organization with members in approximately 100 countries. He expressed the support of ICOH for the proposed instruments, suggesting that the Convention should take into account the Occupational Health Services Convention, 1985 (No. 161), and its accompanying Recommendation (No. 171). These two instruments, and the proposed Convention and Recommendation, should mutually support each other. He emphasized the importance of occupational health services in workplaces, including small workplaces and those within the informal economy and agriculture, as such services supplemented the inspection system. He urged that occupational health services be developed in parallel with labour inspection. He was pleased to note that the proposed Convention specifically referred to consultations with professional associations on occupational safety and health and mentioned in this connection the national institutes for occupational health as consultative partners.

25. In response to the services needed by 3 billion workers, ICOH, in collaboration with the ILO and WHO, had developed a concept for basic occupational health services, which in a cost-effective manner would provide competent occupational health services to the underserved. This concept emphasized the principle of prevention, but would also address the need for curative service, as a reduction of the burden caused by injuries and diseases would result in more resources for the preventive aspect. The guidelines for basic occupational health services would provide countries practical guidance and tools on how to apply this service. While stressing the importance of employers' and workers' participation in implementing occupational safety and health programmes, he also called for the involvement of experts to help the implementation. He concluded by mentioning that development of occupational safety and health was a continuing process and he made

reference to the 34 committees, established under ICOH, as sources of information and help.

26. The representative of the International Association of Labour Inspection (IALI) explained that the Association was established in 1972 in order to provide professional support to labour inspection services. The aims of the Association were to promote professionalism of IALI members, provide opportunities for exchange of experience, to disseminate information through its web site and other publications, and to promote closer cooperation between members. The Association, now with more than 100 members from all over the world, had worked in close partnership with the ILO and was, in 1978, granted the status of a non-governmental international consultative organization. In its last three-year programme, IALI had implemented a range of activities including conferences and symposia, publication of newsletters and other supporting activities to the members. Particular emphasis was now placed on regional activities. IALI would be holding its triennial Congress and Assembly in the ILO building from 13 to 15 June 2005, addressing new challenges facing labour inspectorates, national occupational safety and health programmes and their implementation, and strategies for specific risks and sectors. While IALI welcomed a promotional framework instrument, the Association had not yet formed its views on the form of the instrument.

27. The representative of the International Federation of Building and Wood Workers (IFBWW) explained that workers in the trades represented by the IFBWW were among those having the most dangerous jobs. Workers in the building and woodworking sectors were often exposed to dust and chemicals, including asbestos; nearly 300 people died every day due to diseases caused by asbestos exposure and nearly all of them were from the building trades. She expressed concern that asbestos was still being used in the building sector, mainly in the form of asbestos-cement products in developing countries, while the material was banned in industrialized countries.

28. The IFBWW considered the ILO Conventions to be relevant and up to date, but called for more effective implementation of them, and supported the proposal for a Convention supplemented by a Recommendation. The new Convention should lay down the basic principles of safety and health at work and outline the defined rights, responsibilities and duties, highlighting the right to a safe and healthy working environment, the right to get information and training about the hazards and their prevention, the right to participation and representation on matters of safety and health, and the right to refuse dangerous work. The participation of workers in occupational safety and health was seen as essential. Joint employer-worker committees had proved useful and were required by law in many countries, at least for larger companies. The IFBWW had called for support to the system of regional safety representatives targeting especially the small companies. This system had been in operation in Sweden since 1947 for the forestry sector and since 1974 for all sectors. More such innovative schemes were called for.

29. The Government member of China supported the adoption of a new instrument. Her Government encouraged all countries to formulate and implement national policies and programmes. She spoke of some of the measures taken or planned in China between 2003 and 2010, and stressed the importance of harmonizing the development of her country's society and its economy. A new instrument would be easier for governments to adopt if it were not prescriptive but focused on principles, because the countries of the world were at such different levels of development while experiencing constant technological, social and economic change.

30. The Government member of Jordan recalled his country's extensive collaboration with the ILO and other organizations active in occupational safety and health. A number of Conventions relevant to labour protection had been ratified, for example the Labour

Inspection Convention, 1947 (No. 81). Dissemination of occupational safety and health information to workers was a high priority for his country, and the Government's Occupational Health and Safety Institute had been recognized by the ILO for its capacity to serve as a resource centre for other countries in the region. The institution of an occupational safety and health week was another sign of Jordan's new commitment in this area.

31. The Government member of Mexico affirmed his country's commitment to occupational safety and health as a high priority in its labour policy and in its public policy in general. He felt that the work accomplished between the 91st and the 93rd Sessions of the International Labour Conference reflected an important convergence of views among the ILO's constituents on the importance of raising the priority of occupational safety and health in public policy, on involving employers and workers in the formulation of that policy, on the promotion of a preventative safety and health culture, on the construction of more effective normative frameworks at the national and international levels and on the importance of an integrated approach and a global strategy. However, there were several things to be avoided: a Convention that was ineffective because it could not be ratified or implemented; fragmentation of standards; an approach that did not take account of the different levels of development of the countries of the world; creation of new bureaucracies; and adoption of an instrument that was prescriptive rather than promotional in nature. For all these reasons, the Government of Mexico would support that form of instrument that represented the consensus or majority view of the Committee.

32. The Government member of Senegal, speaking on behalf of the African Government members of the Committee,[2] pointed out that, since a summit meeting in Johannesburg in April 2005, the African countries had agreed to adopt an instrument on occupational safety and health that was geared to the needs of the informal sector and small and medium-sized enterprises. The instrument should give a high priority to the training of workers, and such training should be part of an overall national programme. This programme should be formulated in consultation with the social partners; it should also be implemented in a progressive manner, to ensure its permanence. The programme should be centred on occupational health services, but should not neglect the elimination or reduction of major industrial hazards. Furthermore, it was impossible to talk of workplace health without considering HIV/AIDS. All of these considerations led to the conclusion that occupational safety and health had to be taken as seriously as possible by the member States, so that the most appropriate form of an instrument would be a Convention supplemented by a Recommendation.

33. The Government member of Brazil, speaking on behalf of the Government members of the Committee member States of MERCOSUR, explained that in her country labour relations were part of a complex system wherein many different institutions had roles defined by law; the State was called on to resolve any conflicts; the Ministry of Labour ensured that labour rights were properly respected and implemented; working conditions may be determined by collective bargaining. She reviewed the evolution of occupational safety and health policy and regulations from 1943 to 2005. Workers were assumed to have a collective right to safe and healthy working conditions. Labour inspection was changing from a system of random inspections with little impact to a more consultative system, with unions having an active role. It was now clear that the formulation of occupational safety and health policy had to be intersectoral and multidisciplinary. Regulations should be

---

[2] Algeria, Benin, Burkina Faso, Cameroon, Côte d'Ivoire, Democratic Republic of the Congo, Egypt, Ethiopia, Gabon, Kenya, Lesotho, Libyan Arab Jamahiriya, Madagascar, Malawi, Mali, Morocco, Mozambique, Namibia, Niger, Nigeria, Senegal, South Africa, Swaziland, United Republic of Tanzania, Tunisia and Zimbabwe.

harmonized and prevention favoured over protection and compensation. The goal was a culture in which jobs were generated; employers saw workplace safety and health as an investment that added value to their products and workers gained more job satisfaction from improved working conditions. Her delegation favoured an instrument which took the form of a Convention supplemented by a Recommendation and which provided an integrating context for all the pre-existing occupational safety and health instruments.

34. The Government member of Lebanon reiterated the position that his Government had taken when replying to the Office's questionnaire, that they saw no drawback in the formulation of a new Convention and Recommendation. He stated that member States attached great importance to occupational safety and health, and this was reflected by the numerous laws in each country on the various aspects of the matter. His Government attached great importance to occupational safety and health, on the principle that it was better to prevent than to cure. Their labour code contained a whole chapter on occupational safety and health that applied to all workers, including women and adolescents; it included a list of occupational diseases. The Ministry of Labour had a labour inspection unit, in addition to one that monitored compliance with international labour standards in the field of occupational safety and health. It had to be admitted that some parties in Lebanon had not always shouldered their responsibilities, and implementation of international standards was slow and laborious. With this in mind, his Ministry had drafted a national occupational safety and health plan. In this system, employers were obliged to provide occupational safety and health for their workers as well as adequate supervision so that the workers could comply with occupational safety and health rules; workers were obliged to follow the rules, but also to make sure that employers followed them as well; the role of labour inspection had been strengthened. His Government's commitment to implementing international standards applied not only to the native workforce but also to migrant workers. A major contribution to ensuring decent working conditions was made by workplace occupational safety and health committees. Finally, he urged the Committee to take note of the strong role the media could play in raising public awareness of the importance of occupational safety and health.

35. The Government member of Uruguay, speaking on behalf of the Government members of the Committee member States of MERCOSUR, observed that ILO statistics showed how important it was for governments to take action to improve the situation, and expressed support for a Convention supplemented by a Recommendation. Clear standards and instruments were needed to advance occupational safety and health in member States. Complementary promotional activities should be held, such as the World Day for Occupational Safety and Health. Improved working conditions would improve labour relations. The new Government of Uruguay had created a tripartite labour relations committee with a mandate that included occupational safety and health.

36. The Government member of Canada stated that his country supported the development of a promotional instrument for occupational safety and health and that his Government remained committed to improve occupational safety and health through its national laws and regulations. He said that his Government preferred that a new instrument take the form of a Declaration, but would support the Committee's decision if another form of instrument were chosen, provided that it was an overarching instrument with promotional rather than prescriptive content; consensus was important. The new instrument should be clear and simple, so as to be easily understandable by everyone, and should serve as a focal point for global awareness raising and promotion.

37. The Government member of the United States noted the importance given to occupational safety and health by the ILO in its Constitution, and said that the development of a new instrument outlining a promotional framework would be very important, as this would enable the ILO to assist member States in developing their own national systems.

However, the proposed Conclusions seemed to include provisions already covered in other instruments, particularly the Occupational Safety and Health Convention, 1981 (No. 155), and its accompanying Recommendation (No. 164), as could be seen in the comparative analysis of occupational safety and health instruments provided by the Office. Therefore, her Government preferred that the new instrument take the form of a Declaration. She said that the ILO had employed the use of a Declaration on two occasions, namely the Declaration of Philadelphia in 1944 and the Declaration of Fundamental Principles and Rights at Work in 1998. She said that these Declarations helped promote awareness of the core international labour Conventions as well as workers' rights, and that the same model could be equally successful in the field of occupational safety and health.

38. The Government member of the Bolivarian Republic of Venezuela informed the Committee that in 2002 his country had created a new body for occupational safety and health, National Institute for Occupational Safety and Health (IMPSASALS) and that great progress had been made. For example, occupational safety and health had been defined legally and a new occupational safety and health law was under study in Parliament. He described the functions of this body, which included drafting laws and regulations, coordinating inspection services and developing technical programmes for information and training. He said that four main areas had been given priority status, namely occupational medicine, occupational safety and health and ergonomics, epidemiology and investigation, and communication and research. The integral parts of the national programme were health promotion, the reduction of occupational accidents and diseases, as well as the education and involvement of workers and employers. Six sectors had priority as objects of the programme: basic industries (oil, electricity, iron and steel, and aluminium), construction, health services, manufacturing, agriculture and education. His Government would prefer to have a Convention as the new instrument for a promotional framework in the area of occupational safety and health.

39. The Government member of Trinidad and Tobago, speaking on behalf of the Government members of the Committee member States of CARICOM,[3] pointed out the commitment of his group to ILO Conventions, and highlighted his group's high ratification of the core international labour Conventions. He said that his group was committed to improving occupational safety and health, and that an integrated approach was needed. Unfortunately, no country in his group had ratified Convention No. 155. Nonetheless, the group still considered occupational safety and health to be a priority and a fundamental right. With the help of the ILO Office in Port-of-Spain and the regional CARICOM secretariat, model legislation for occupational safety and health had been produced which had been passed into law in the Bahamas in 2001, and Trinidad and Tobago had passed an Act on occupational safety and health in 2004. The Barbadian Parliament was also discussing a new occupational safety and health bill. He explained that, in the case of Suriname, legislation was being continually modified and that the List of Occupational Diseases had already been embodied in the legislation. In the case of Jamaica, a new Occupational Safety and Health Act has been drafted and will be submitted to Parliament shortly. He drew the Committee's attention to the fact that the Occupational Safety and Health Act of 2004 for Trinidad and Tobago had not been proclaimed, as the provisions could not be enforced. He highlighted the prohibitive costs of transforming workplaces to meet the new standards as one of the causes of this non-proclamation. For example, even the facilities in the Ministry of Labour did not satisfy an occupational safety and health audit under the new Act. All the relevant legislation in CARICOM member States contained the essential elements for promoting occupational safety and health, but in the case of small States these could only be implemented if supported by a campaign, and if there were sufficient

---

[3] Bahamas, Barbados, Jamaica, Suriname and Trinidad and Tobago.

technical cooperation to establish the institutions necessary to enforce the laws. He suggested that the campaign should have provisions for compiling national profiles, gathering data and training appropriate human resources that could work together with the tripartite stakeholders to bring workplaces up to the applicable standards. He added that the campaign should be supported by research and guidance that could ensure the effective implementation of legislation. He feared that, without this support, any new instrument that would be adopted would suffer the same low rate of ratification as other ILO occupational safety and health instruments.

40. The Government member of El Salvador drew attention to his country's efforts in improving occupational safety and health. He noted the formation of a national tripartite committee on occupational safety and health, the drafting of new occupational safety and health legislation, the ratification of Convention No. 155, as well as a national programme to reduce occupational accidents and diseases with short-, medium- and long-term targets. He mentioned that Central America and the Dominican Republic had also taken measures on a tripartite basis to improve occupational safety and health. He felt that a Convention and Recommendation would be the most suitable form for a new instrument, as this would help in the establishment of a preventative occupational safety and health culture.

41. The Government member of Indonesia said that the Indonesian Government supported a Convention as the form for a new instrument for three reasons. First, a Convention would give occupational safety and health a higher priority in national policies, which were developed through tripartite cooperation. Therefore, all three parties would be responsible for the implementation of occupational safety and health at both the national and enterprise levels. Second, Indonesia had made it obligatory to implement the ILO's occupational safety and health management system guidelines at the enterprise level through the Manpower Law No. 13 of 2003. Hence, it would be easier to implement policies and programmes because they would be based on the integrated management system, which was one of the important pillars of the promotional framework. Third, a Convention would support collaboration between the national occupational safety and health system and the employment injury benefit schemes.

42. The Government member of Kenya mentioned that his Government was committed to developing and implementing effective occupational safety and health programmes to reduce accidents and diseases and thereby to increase productivity. He listed several occupational safety and health initiatives taken by the country, such as the maintenance of an information centre that was a National Centre in the network of the ILO's International Occupational Safety and Health Information Centre (CIS), and the setting up of a division for the coordination of training and dissemination of information. A guide to be used by approved training institutions had been developed to support training activities. Moreover, the Government had issued a code on the auditing of companies by approved experts, and had endorsed rules concerning safety and health committees, medical examinations of workers of certain industries, and prevention and control of noise. The Government had also drafted a new occupational safety and health bill, so as to have new developments reflected in the national legislation. He noted that all the above activities were implemented through a tripartite committee. He emphasized that the present legislation was developed with due regard to the principles of existing occupational safety and health Conventions and Recommendations. He stated that the Government of Kenya supported the adoption of a new instrument, but cautioned that this should take into account the vast challenges individual member countries were facing. Hence the instrument, in the form of a Convention supplemented by a Recommendation, should be simple to implement and appropriate for creation of a safety culture. For the instrument to be implemented, certain objectives should be considered: the creation of awareness among workers and employers, the development of programmes for combating accidents and diseases, the establishment of appropriate auditing procedures and the establishment of schemes for workers' medical examination.

43. The Government member of Tunisia informed the Committee that his Government placed special importance on occupational safety and health and thus had taken a number of initiatives including the development of a labour code that took into account international Conventions, the establishment of an advisory body and an inspectorate, and finally a fund for social solidarity. Tunisia celebrated a national day for occupational safety and health. Occupational safety and health was taught in schools. He mentioned that Tunisia was pleased with the promotional framework and suggested that it should take into account the present trend toward privatization. There should be provision for specific assistance programmes, including assistance to the Palestinian Authority. He hoped that the promotional framework would keep occupational safety and health high on the ILO's agenda, because of the low rate of ratification of the relevant Conventions so far.

44. The Government member of Thailand said that his country had given special emphasis to occupational safety and health in recent years, strengthening its national occupational safety and health system to cover all workers and providing quality occupational safety and health services. Thailand's five-year national occupational safety and health plan had set priorities that included developing new legislation and guidance, strengthening the labour inspectorate, better enforcement, improving the system for the reporting of accidents and diseases and promoting the better management of occupational safety and health and a wider safety culture through national campaigns. ILO standards such as Convention No. 155, as well as the Guidelines on Occupational Safety and Health Management Systems and the Global Occupational Safety and Health Strategy, had all provided useful advice in this process. The promotional framework instrument should commit governments to placing occupational safety and health higher on their national agendas, supporting mechanisms for tripartite cooperation and facilitating progressive improvements of national occupational safety and health systems and programmes. Thailand favoured the instrument being a Convention supplemented by a Recommendation.

45. The Government member of the United Kingdom, referring to the country's long history of occupational safety and health legislation and enforcement, said that the current national occupational safety and health strategy was based on the principle that good occupational safety and health standards were a cornerstone of civilized society. He welcomed the proposal for a new promotional framework instrument, adding that it needed to be sufficiently flexible to accommodate different cultures in a rapidly changing world. However, the ratification of ILO Conventions on occupational safety and health was poor and he doubted whether having another Convention, with or without a Recommendation, would be the way forward for this new instrument, which needed to be widely accepted. The United Kingdom therefore favoured adopting a Declaration or a Recommendation, but would be willing to cooperate in the development of a Convention should the Committee so agree.

46. The Government member of Algeria focused on the need for prevention, mentioning that Algeria had already introduced legislation on occupational safety and health and occupational medicine. Their recently opened Institute for Prevention of Occupational Risks supported all sectors of industry – especially the high-risk ones such as construction – providing advice on the prevention of occupational risks and working in collaboration with the labour inspectorate. Their tripartite National Council for Safety and Health at Work provided a forum for social partners to reach consensus on occupational safety and health legislation and other matters. Algeria supported the proposal for the new instrument to be a Convention supplemented by a Recommendation.

47. The Government member of Morocco referred to the country's national occupational safety and health strategy, which was being implemented by means of a new labour code based on international Conventions, awareness-raising campaigns and the training of specialists. Morocco agreed to the proposal for the new instrument to be a Convention supplemented by a Recommendation.

48. The Government member of the United Arab Emirates said that his country attached great importance to occupational safety and health and had much respect for relevant international standards. The Government's concern was to provide training and to ensure that there was adequate compliance with the law.

49. The Government member of Luxembourg, speaking on behalf of the Government members of the Committee Member States of the European Union [4] and Norway, supported the need to promote occupational safety and health at national and international levels. The current EU strategy, 2002-06, for occupational safety and health included binding and non-binding instruments, and this strategy could be a useful background for the ILO's proposals for a promotional framework, which needed to be acceptable to a much larger number of ILO member States. As far as the form of the promotional instrument was concerned, most of the Government members of the Committee Member States of the European Union [5] and Norway, supported a Convention supplemented by a Recommendation.

50. The Government member of Turkey said that his country was committed to the promotion of occupational safety and health as an important component of decent work and had ratified several international instruments including Convention No. 155 and the Occupational Health Services Convention, 1985 (No. 161). Awareness-raising activities included seminars in several provinces and a national occupational safety and health week during the first week of May, which had been held annually for the past 19 years with the participation of social partners. Social dialogue was very important for achieving advances in occupational safety and health, and the National Occupational Safety and Health Council had been recently established to facilitate the collaboration and participation of social partners. His country would contribute to the efforts of this Committee in devising a new promotional framework for occupational safety and health, one that was flexible and that could be readily implemented.

51. The Government member of Papua New Guinea emphasized the importance of occupational safety and health for national development, labour productivity and social welfare. However, although his country had had basic occupational safety and health legislation for many years, it lacked policy development, strategic planning and promotion of compliance. The Government now recognized that a strong and healthy workforce was a cornerstone to economic and social development, so occupational safety and health had become a priority. Papua New Guinea strongly supported the concept of the promotional framework, but as a small country it lacked the capacity and technical expertise and would look to the ILO for technical support for the promotion and improvement of occupational safety and health.

---

[4] Austria, Belgium, Czech Republic, Denmark, Estonia, Finland, France, Germany, Greece, Ireland, Italy, Lithuania, Luxembourg, Netherlands, Poland, Portugal, Slovenia, Spain, Sweden and United Kingdom.

[5] Austria, Belgium, Czech Republic, Denmark, Estonia, Finland, France, Greece, Ireland, Italy, Lithuania, Luxembourg, Poland, Portugal, Slovenia, Spain and Sweden.

52. The Worker Vice-Chairperson was heartened by the broad consensus so far on the goal of making occupational safety and health a higher priority at national, international and enterprise levels, and that a promotional framework was needed to achieve that. All were concerned to see work-related accidents and ill-health reduced and to improve the capacity of governments, working in a tripartite manner, to achieve this goal. She restated her firm belief that the form of the instrument should be a Convention supplemented by a Recommendation, and it should have an value for all involved. Referring to points raised previously by the Employer Vice-Chairperson about the need for a new approach, she said that the integrated approach for occupational safety and health was indeed a new approach and that legislation was an integral part of this. Legislation enshrined workers' rights at work and the Workers' group did not support the idea of replacing legislation with voluntary approaches, such as a Declaration.

53. She took the opportunity to refer to the World Day for Occupational Safety and Health, which had been mentioned by several members of the Committee, and reminded them of its origins. The date of 28 April had first been chosen by Canadian trade unionists as an annual day to commemorate those who had died at work, and the date had also been observed in the United States since 1989, where it was known as Workers' Memorial Day. This day was subsequently expanded into a World Day by the ILO and now focused on prevention, but she felt that the original purpose of the day – namely to remember those individuals who had died because of their work – should not be forgotten.

54. The Employer Vice-Chairperson was also encouraged that so many Committee members wanted to see positive improvements in occupational safety and health, but thought that the real issue for the Committee was about how such improvements could be achieved. He referred to comments made by the Worker Vice-Chairperson that the Workers' group did not wish to see any new obligations imposed, but said that if the promotional framework took the form of a Convention this would impose new obligations on those member States that ratified it. He questioned whether the Convention would then not become an instrument with only a few ratifications. He also said that the integrated approach was a much broader concept than the promotional framework and that it included technical cooperation, awareness raising, etc. If the Committee favoured moving towards yet another Convention, this would be maintaining the status quo, which would not ultimately bring about the improvements that were desired.

55. The representative of the Secretary-General informed the Committee of the International Occupational Hygiene Association's support for a promotional framework instrument.

Examination of the proposed Conclusions

Point 1

56. No amendments were submitted, so point 1 was adopted.

Point 2

57. Three amendments were submitted. Two of these were identical, one of which was submitted by the Government members of Australia, Canada, United States and Switzerland, and the other by the Employer members. Both amendments proposed that the words "a Convention supplemented by a Recommendation" should be replaced by "a Declaration".

58. The Employer Vice-Chairperson, speaking on behalf of the Employer members, spoke to the two above amendments. Ratification levels of occupational safety and health Conventions were generally low. This was particularly unfortunate in the case of Convention No. 155 because it was an important Convention in this area. Low ratification rates were due, on the one hand, to the prolonged process of ratification and, on the other, to the fact that although most Conventions had global application, not all Conventions were relevant to all countries. Conventions that were not ratified carried little impact, and it was likely that yet another occupational safety and health Convention would suffer the same fate. The adoption of a Convention did not foster political will, and he queried how a new Convention would promote the ratification of other Conventions. Conversely, the promotional framework envisaged by the Committee on Occupational Safety and Health in 2003 called for greater political commitment and increased awareness of occupational safety and health problems, and he considered that this call would be best served by a Declaration. He said that the Employers' group wanted the instrument to make an appreciable as well as an immediate difference and contested the notion put forward by the Worker Vice-Chairperson that a Declaration was the weakest form of instrument. A Declaration would enable all countries to develop their own national systems and programmes and to improve their occupational safety and health conditions, in accordance with their own conditions and practices.

59. The Government member of Canada, speaking also on behalf of the Government members of Australia, Switzerland and United States, spoke in support of the same amendment. The objective of this Committee was for as many countries as possible to accept the new instrument, which, given the poor ratification levels of occupational safety and health Conventions, pointed to it taking the form of a Declaration. Moreover, since the global occupational safety and health strategy adopted in 2003 called for greater political commitment to occupational safety and health, he considered that a promotional rather than a prescriptive instrument, such as a Convention, was needed. Many promotional frameworks had already been successfully set up and he considered that there was now a need for a promotional framework that could effectively promote occupational safety and health, and that a Declaration was the best means of achieving this.

60. The Worker Vice-Chairperson reiterated the view of the Workers' group, which was that the instrument should be a Convention supplemented by a Recommendation. She too was concerned about the low ratification levels of existing occupational safety and health Conventions, but also felt that the ILO had not promoted such Conventions adequately, adding that the new promotional framework should address this issue. In the 1990s, the ILO had run a successful campaign to increase ratification of the core Conventions; something similar could be done for occupational safety and health Conventions. She thought that this new instrument should be more promotional than prescriptive, encouraging high-level commitment at the national and enterprise levels. She referred to the remarks of the Employer Vice-Chairperson that the instrument should be symbolic, saying that she hoped that it would be much more than that; what was needed was an instrument that would make a real difference.

61. The Government member of Senegal spoke on behalf of the African Government members of the Committee. [6] She considered that the low rate of ratifications of occupational safety and health Conventions did not necessarily mean a low ratification rate of a new promotional framework Convention. In addition, the best way to demonstrate political commitment to occupational safety and health issues would be through adoption and

---

[6] The following Governments joined the African Government members of the Committee: Botswana, Ghana, Guinea, Uganda and Zambia.

ratification. A Convention rather than a Declaration was the better option for achieving this commitment, and the African Government members of the Committee favoured a Convention supplemented by a Recommendation.

62. The Government member of Argentina, speaking on behalf of the Government members of the Committee member States of MERCOSUR, emphasized that the right to safety and health at work was a fundamental right, and that ratification levels of occupational safety and health Conventions were not indicators of national concern for occupational safety and health. For example, two of the countries that he represented had abolished the use of asbestos without ratification of the Asbestos Convention, 1986 (No. 162). The Governments of the three countries nevertheless supported the adoption of a Convention supplemented by a Recommendation.

63. The representative of the Palestinian Authority called for a promotion of occupational safety and health for workers in occupied territories and countries. Working conditions in Palestine comprised many risks and these related to the employment policies of the occupier. He considered that workers in Palestine were victims of the occupier's policy and called for the burden to be lifted. The Palestinian Authority was in favour of the adoption of a Convention.

64. The Government member of the Libyan Arab Jamahiriya said that his country was concerned to provide good standards of occupational safety and health and had instituted training centres in all its provinces so as to bring their occupational safety and health standards into line with international practice. A council had been established to promote occupational safety and health, and implement promotional programmes. The Libyan Arab Jamahiriya favoured the adoption of a Convention.

65. The Government member of Luxembourg spoke also on behalf of the Government members of Austria, Belgium, Czech Republic, Estonia, Finland, France, Greece, Ireland, Italy, Lithuania, Norway, Poland, Portugal, Slovenia, Spain and Sweden. The Governments of these countries all supported the adoption of a "framework Convention" supplemented by a Recommendation.

66. The Government member of Chile highlighted the value of national tripartite agreements in making a real difference to improving occupational safety and health. The Government had made agreements with their social partners to work together to achieve significant reductions in numbers of accidents nationally, and their targets had been exceeded. New tripartite agreements had been recently made, and the promotional framework would further support such efforts. The agreements had their effect even when ILO Conventions had not been ratified, however, as was the case for Convention No. 155. Chile nevertheless supported the proposal for a Convention supplemented by a Recommendation.

67. The Government member of New Zealand expressed support for a Convention supplemented by a Recommendation. As in 2003, the underlying message was that these needed to act as an overarching instrument for existing ILO law, policy and practice, allowing a level of further specification to be included in a less binding manner. The instrument needed to be based on high-level principles, and a Convention supplemented by a Recommendation fitted well with New Zealand's outcome-focused strategies. However, he requested clarification of the legal status of a Declaration and a "framework Convention" before affirming his country's position.

68. The Government member of the Bolivarian Republic of Venezuela reiterated his support for a Convention supplemented by a Recommendation.

69. The Government member of Tunisia strongly affirmed the need for the promotional framework to be in the form of a Convention supplemented by a Recommendation, otherwise it would be seen as mere good intention. He added that it was also important for the instrument to take different country cultures into account.

70. The Legal Adviser then responded to the question raised by the Government member of New Zealand. He explained that Conventions were multilateral treaties that conferred rights and responsibilities on member States that ratified them, and that there was a mechanism for supervising their implementation. Recommendations were non-binding instruments that recommended practices, monitoring and so on. Unlike Conventions and Recommendations, Declarations were not mentioned in the ILO Constitution and were not legal instruments. They did not create legal obligations but could recall existing ones. Declarations were more political than other instruments and the ILO had not adopted many. Some, such as the Declaration of Philadelphia, were subsequently included in the ILO Constitution, so that when a country became an ILO member it subscribed to the Declaration as well. Others were the Declaration on Apartheid, 1964; the Declaration of Principles Concerning Multinational Corporations and Social Policy, 1977; and the Declaration on Fundamental Principles and Rights at Work, 1998. The last mentioned had an ad hoc follow-up mechanism, an expensive one and outside the usual practices for Conventions.

71. The Government member of Malaysia, speaking also on behalf of the Government members of Indonesia and Thailand, expressed support for a Convention supplemented by a Recommendation.

72. The Employer Vice-Chairperson asked for a record vote to be taken on the amendment to replace the words "Convention supplemented by a Recommendation" by the words "Declaration". If the amendment were adopted, the text in point 2 of the Conclusions would read: "The instrument should take the form of a Declaration".

73. Put to a vote, the amendments concerning the form of the instrument were rejected by 221,088 votes in favour and 335,580 votes against. [7]

---

[7] The Employer members requested that the details of the record vote be included in the report. The results were as follows:

For: Germany, Australia, Canada, Republic of Korea, United Arab Emirates, United States, Honduras, Mexico, Netherlands, United Kingdom, Switzerland. 42 Employer members voted for the amendment.

Against: South Africa, Algeria, Saudi Arabia, Argentina, Austria, Bahrain, Barbados, Belgium, Brazil, Burkina Faso, Cameroon, Chile, China, Côte d'Ivoire, Denmark, Dominican Republic, Egypt, El Salvador, Spain, Finland, France, Ghana, Greece, Guatemala, Guinea, India, Indonesia, Islamic Republic of Iran, Italy, Jamaica, Japan, Kenya, Kuwait, Lesotho, Lebanon, Libyan Arab Jamahiriya, Luxembourg, Madagascar, Malaysia, Malawi, Morocco, Mozambique, Namibia, Niger, Norway, New Zealand, Uganda, Pakistan, Panama, Papua New Guinea, Poland, Portugal, Democratic Republic of the Congo, Romania, Russian Federation, Senegal, Sri Lanka, Sweden, Swaziland, Syrian Arab Republic, United Republic of Tanzania, Czech Republic, Thailand, Trinidad and Tobago, Tunisia, Uruguay, Bolivarian Republic of Venezuela, Zambia, Zimbabwe. 47 Worker members voted against the amendment.

Abstentions: Hungary.

Absent: Belarus, Colombia, Ecuador, Gabon, Haiti, Jordan, Lithuania, Mali, Malta, Mauritius, Mauritania, Myanmar, Nigeria, Oman, Philippines, Slovenia, Sudan, Suriname, Turkey, Yemen.

74. The Government members of France and Luxembourg submitted an amendment to insert the words "subtitled Framework Convention" after the word "Convention" in the statement of the form of the proposed instrument in point 2 of the proposed Conclusions. The amendment reflected the position of the 17 Committee member States that had been enunciated earlier. It was important for the instrument to be a Convention in order for it to have the highest possible visibility and impact, but it should be as widely ratifiable as possible, and provide a solid foundation for the implementation of existing instruments. It was hoped that the word "framework" would provide a bridge, and a link to an "integrated approach", between those who favoured a binding instrument and those who did not, although even with the subtitle the instrument would be a binding Convention.

75. At the request of the Worker members, the Legal Adviser reminded the Committee that there were only two international labour standards recognized by the ILO legal system, Conventions and Recommendations. Although certain Conventions had been declared by the Governing Body or Conference to be "fundamental" or "priority" Conventions, the terms did not appear either in the text or in the titles of the instruments. Thus, a "framework" Convention would likewise not differ from any others in the way its ratification and implementation were monitored by the Organization. However, just as applying the term "fundamental" to some Conventions showed that the Organization felt that there was something special about them, using the word "framework" as proposed in the amendment would also lead readers to expect an instrument that was different in some way. If the Committee wished to use "framework", Members should be clear as to whether the word implied that the proposed Convention provided a frame for Conventions adopted in the past, a framework on which future Conventions could be built, or a framework to support member States' actions in implementing other Conventions.

76. The Employer Vice-Chairperson observed that, although the content of a text was more important than its title, the latter could communicate a message by itself. He pointed out that the word "framework" had already been used in discussions of a possible consolidated maritime Convention that would be radically different from the instrument in the present proposed Conclusions; this was likely to cause confusion. He offered a subamendment to replace the word "framework" with "promotional" in the subtitle proposed in the original amendment.

77. The Worker Vice-Chairperson opposed the subamendment: while a discussion of the wording of the title would be welcome, it should be undertaken when the title or the preamble of the proposed instrument were debated, not in the present consideration of the form of the instrument. She said that "promotional" reflected the objective of the Convention, and should not be included in its title.

78. The Government member of Senegal, speaking also on behalf of the African Government members of the Committee, felt that the Legal Adviser's opinion revealed a risk of confusion if a subtitle were applied to the proposed instrument, and opposed both the subamendment and the original amendment. The Government member of Argentina, speaking also on behalf of the Government members of Brazil, Chile, El Salvador, Dominican Republic and Uruguay, agreed, noting that the introduction of a subtitle could suggest to readers that the instrument was something different from either of the two types currently recognized in the ILO legal system.

79. The Employer members withdrew their subamendment and opposed the original amendment.

80. In response to the tripartite consensus, the Government members of France and Luxembourg withdrew their amendment. In doing so, the Government member of France called attention to European Union practice, in which the word "framework" was attached

to several directives without changing their nature or legal status. He hoped that the ideas exchanged in the discussion of the amendment would prove useful during the debates on other parts of the instrument, as suggested by the Worker Vice-Chairperson.

81. Point 2 was adopted without amendment.

Point 3

82. The Employer members withdrew an amendment that was intended to refer to a Declaration instead of a Convention.

83. The Government members of Argentina, Brazil, Chile, Dominican Republic, El Salvador, Panama and Uruguay submitted an amendment to add the following words after the first line of clause 3: "(a) the Constitution of the ILO;". The Government member of Uruguay introduced the amendment, saying that a new clause needed to be added to the Preamble with specific mention of the ILO's Constitution, bearing in mind the aim of this instrument. Both the Worker Vice-Chairperson and the Employer Vice-Chairperson supported the amendment. The Government member of Senegal, speaking on behalf of the African Government members of the Committee, also supported the amendment. The amendment was adopted.

84. The Worker Vice-Chairperson submitted an amendment to insert a new clause after the original clause 3(a), as follows: "the fundamental principles to be found in international labour Conventions, in particular, the core Conventions of the ILO". The Worker members considered that, in setting out a broad framework, there was a need to refer specifically to principles, in particular the fundamental principles and rights in core Conventions. The Employer Vice-Chairperson opposed the amendment because the core Conventions were not to do with occupational safety and health and he believed that such a clause moved the focus of the instrument away from occupational safety and health towards other areas of concern, thus weakening it. There were no views for or against the amendment from the Government members, and the Worker Vice-Chairperson withdrew it.

85. The Worker members submitted an amendment to include in clause 3 (the Preamble) references to several additional occupational safety and health Conventions and Recommendations. These were the: Occupational Health Services Convention, 1985 (No. 161), and the Occupational Health Services Recommendation, 1985 (No. 171); the Labour Inspection Convention, 1947 (No. 81), and the Labour Inspection Recommendation, 1947 (No. 81); the Safety and Health in Construction Convention, 1988 (No. 167), and the Safety and Health in Construction Recommendation, 1988 (No. 175); the Safety and Health in Mines Convention, 1995 (No. 176), and the Safety and Health in Mines Recommendation, 1995 (No. 183); the Safety and Health in Agriculture Convention, 2001 (No. 184), and the Safety and Health in Agriculture Recommendation, 2001 (No. 192). The Worker Vice-Chairperson explained that these Conventions and Recommendations were important because of their general application and that they needed to be promoted. The majority of countries had construction, mining and agricultural sectors, and these were the most hazardous.

86. The Employer members could not support the amendment. The Employer Vice-Chairperson was concerned that member States might be inhibited from ratifying a Convention that contained a list of several other Conventions and Recommendations in its Preamble, especially since many of the listed Conventions had not been ratified by most member States. There was also a danger that some important Conventions and Recommendations would be left out of the list. The Government member of the United

Kingdom spoke on behalf of the Government members of the Group of Industrialized Market Economies (PIEM) present in the Committee.[8] He said that the IMEC group agreed with the views of the Employer members, particularly that such a list of Conventions and Recommendations in the Preamble to a new Convention might deter member States from ratifying it. The group opposed the amendment.

87. The Worker Vice-Chairperson said that the intention of the amendment was to provide a note of some of the important occupational safety and health Conventions and Recommendations, and that she had understood that a Preamble to a Convention was not legally binding, but requested clarification from the Legal Adviser on this point. After consultation, a spokesperson for the secretariat confirmed that Preambles of Conventions were non-binding, and she referred to the Manual for drafting ILO instruments (2005).

88. The Government member of Senegal, speaking on behalf of the African Government members of the Committee, remarked that the amendment would overburden the Preamble unnecessarily. She also observed that all relevant occupational safety and health Conventions and Recommendations were listed in an annex to the Office Report IV(2), and they could be again listed in a future instrument. The African Government members of the Committee opposed the amendment. Noting the lack of support for the amendment, the Worker Vice-Chairperson withdrew it.

89. The Government member of Argentina, speaking also on behalf of the Government members of Brazil and Uruguay, introduced an amendment to include in the Preamble a reference to the Occupational Health Services Convention, 1985 (No. 161). He referred to clause 7(3)(c) of the proposed Conclusions, which specifically mentioned occupational health services, saying that it would be appropriate to refer to the relevant Convention in the Preamble. The Worker members supported the amendment but the Employer members did not, both of them for the same reasons that they respectively supported and opposed the previous amendment. The Government member of the United Kingdom, speaking on behalf of the Government members of the IMEC group present in the Committee, also opposed the amendment. The Government member of Argentina then withdrew it.

90. The Worker members submitted an amendment to add a new clause after clause 3(b): "the realization of decent work for all as a core objective of the International Labour Organization". The Worker Vice-Chairperson referred to the Director-General's Report in 1999 and the notion that decent work must be safe work. The Employer Vice-Chairperson agreed with the reasoning of the Worker members but wanted to focus specifically on occupational safety and health. He therefore submitted a subamendment to replace the proposed new clause in the amendment with the wording "the promotion of occupational safety and health in support of the realization of the ILO's core objective of decent work". The Worker Vice-Chairperson then put forward a sub-subamendment, proposing instead the clause: "the promotion of occupational safety and health as part of the ILO's core objective of decent work for all". The Employer Vice-Chairperson supported the sub-subamendment, as did the Government member of the United Kingdom, speaking on behalf of the Government members of the IMEC group present in the Committee. The amendment, as subamended, was then adopted.

91. The Government member of the United States, speaking also on behalf of the Government member of Canada, introduced an amendment to replace clause 3(d) with a new text: "the priority to be given to occupational safety and health in national agendas included in the

---

[8] Australia, Austria, Belgium, Canada, Czech Republic, Denmark, France, Germany, Hungary, Ireland, Italy, Japan, Luxembourg, Netherlands, New Zealand, Poland, San Marino, Switzerland, United Kingdom and United States.

Conclusions adopted by the 91st Session (2003) of the International Labour Conference concerning occupational safety and health". He explained that the rationale for the amendment was to focus on giving priority to occupational safety and health in national agendas. The Worker Vice-Chairperson opposed the amendment, saying that all of the Conclusions adopted by the International Labour Conference in 2003 were important and that there was a need to refer back to all of them in the new Convention. The Employer Vice-Chairperson, having initially supported the amendment, agreed with the Worker Vice-Chairperson and withdrew his support for it. The Government member of the United States then withdrew the amendment.

92. The Worker Vice-Chairperson then submitted an amendment to delete the words "in particular the priority to be given to occupational safety and health in national agendas" after the word "health" in line 2 of clause 3(d). She was concerned that, if the focus was only on national agendas, the international and workplace agendas might be forgotten. The Employer Vice-Chairperson opposed the amendment, saying that the Conclusions in 2003, as well as the current discussions, called for occupational safety and health to be given a higher priority at national level. He said that the international agenda had already been well covered in the global occupational safety and health strategy and that the national focus now needed to be sharpened. The Worker Vice-Chairperson withdrew the amendment.

93. The Worker members withdrew an amendment that would have replaced "occupational safety and health" by "a global strategy on occupational safety and health" in point 3(d).

94. The Worker members then submitted an amendment to delete clause 3(e) of the Preamble, which referred to "the importance of the promotion of a national preventative safety and health culture". The Committee agreed to postpone discussion of the amendment until the definitions in point 4 of the Office text had been debated. After adoption of an amended point 4 (see below), the Worker members withdrew the amendment.

95. The Government members of Indonesia, Malaysia and Thailand submitted an amendment to insert the word "continuous" before "promotion" in the clause cited above, on the grounds that the establishment of a preventative safety and health culture was a very long process. The Employer members, Worker members and many Government members supported the amendment, and it was adopted.

96. The Employer members withdrew an amendment to replace "Convention" with "Declaration" in the heading above point 3 in the proposed Conclusions, in light of the Committee's earlier decision on the form of the proposed instrument.

97. Point 3 was adopted as amended.

Point 4

98. The Government members of Canada and the United States submitted an amendment to delete point 4, which defined the terms "national programme on occupational safety and health" and "national system for occupational safety and health", because point 6 made their meaning clear enough. The Worker members opposed the amendment, saying that the definitions would help countries understand that a "programme" was a component of a "system". The Employer members, although sharing the Government members' desire to be as succinct as possible, agreed that definitions were necessary, and asserted that if they were removed from this part of the proposed instrument they would have to be introduced elsewhere. The amendment was withdrawn.

99. The Worker members submitted an amendment to insert the following statement of scope before the definitions: "This Convention should apply to all branches of economic activity

in which workers are employed". They wished the proposed instrument to be as inclusive as possible. The Employer Vice-Chairperson observed that the amendment seemed incompatible with that desire, since it did not seem to include the self-employed. The Government member of Brazil, speaking on behalf of the Government members of the Committee member States of MERCOSUR agreed, and noted that the informal economy also seemed to be excluded by the Worker members' formulation. The Government member of the United Kingdom, speaking on behalf of the Government members of the IMEC group present in the Committee, and the Government member of Malaysia, sympathized with the intention of the Worker members, but felt that the wording would bring the proposed instrument into conflict with national regulations and thus jeopardize its ability to be ratified. The Worker Vice-Chairperson withdrew the amendment, as well as an associated amendment to insert the words "scope and" before "definitions" in the title of point 4.

100. The Employer members withdrew an amendment to replace "Convention" by "Declaration" in point 4.

101. The Government members of Argentina, Brazil and Uruguay, and separately the Worker members, submitted very similar amendments to add a new clause at the beginning of point 4, to define the term "national policy" as in Convention No. 155. Discussion began with the Worker members' version: "'national policy' refers to the national policy on occupational safety, occupational health and the working environment developed in accordance with Article 4 of the Occupational Safety and Health Convention, 1981 (No. 155)". All were motivated by the feeling that the promotional framework had three components, not two, and that policies were as necessary as systems and programmes. The Government member of the United Kingdom, speaking on behalf of the Government members of the IMEC group present in the Committee, expressed sympathy with this position, but feared that citation of other Conventions might hinder ratification. The Government members of India, Uganda and Bolivarian Republic of Venezuela did not share this reservation, and supported the amendment. The Worker Vice-Chairperson reminded the Committee that the amendment was not importing all of Convention No. 155 into the proposed instrument, but was rather attempting to integrate the latter into the body of existing Conventions. The Government member of Uruguay noted that the lack of an occupational safety and health policy seemed to prevent ratification of Conventions by many countries, which made it important to mention policy explicitly in the proposed instrument.

102. The Government member of the United Kingdom offered a subamendment to insert "the principles of" before "Article 4" in the Worker members' amendment, to avoid making the ratification of the proposed instrument dependent on countries' acceptance of the wording of the existing Convention. The Worker members supported this subamendment, but the Employer members felt that it was confusing to have material from other Conventions incorporated by reference, since the reader could not see the exact wording of the cited text, and opposed both the subamendment and original amendment. The Employer Vice-Chairperson did, however, recall that the Committee on Occupational Safety and Health of the 91st Session of the International Labour Conference had rejected the repetition of text from one Convention to another. Although the Government member of Switzerland nonetheless felt it preferable to quote the cited definition in full from the existing Convention and opposed the amendment as subamended, the Government member of Senegal, speaking on behalf of the African Government members of the Committee, the Government member of Luxembourg, speaking on behalf of the Government members of the Committee Member States of the European Union, and many individual Government members, supported the amendment as subamended. The amendment was adopted as subamended.

103. As a result, the Government member of Brazil withdrew the similar amendment submitted by the Government members of Argentina, Brazil and Uruguay.

104. The Government members of Argentina, Brazil and Uruguay then submitted an amendment to change the order of clauses in point 4 so that "national system" preceded "national programme", on the grounds that there was a logical progression from policy to system to programme. The Worker members agreed, and supported the amendment. The Employer Vice-Chairperson opposed it, asserting that policy influenced programmes, and programmes influenced systems. The Government members of the African and IMEC groups supported the amendment; the Government member of the United Kingdom observed that his country had had a policy since 1833, but had developed programmes only more recently. The amendment was adopted.

105. The Worker members submitted an amendment to change "national programme" to "national action programme" in clause 4(a), in order to reinforce the promotional nature of the instrument and respond to the Employer members' call for action. The Employer members opposed the amendment, noting that the idea was implicit in the "means of action" already in the definition. The Government member of Senegal, speaking on behalf of the African Government members of the Committee, opposed the amendment, declaring that the concept of "action programme" was very restrictive, and difficult to render gracefully in French. The Worker members acknowledged the problems and withdrew the amendment. They also withdrew another amendment that would have added "action" to "programme" in a different part of point 4.

106. The Worker members then submitted an amendment to the definition of "national programme" that would insert the following phrase after "programme": "on occupational safety and health and the working environment developed to implement the national policy". They wished to clarify the link between programmes and policies. The Employer members opposed the amendment because it made the full definition very complex. The African Government members of the Committee, the Government members of the Committee Member States of the European Union, and the Government members of Canada and Switzerland, all agreed that the amended text was less clear than the original, and the Worker members withdrew the amendment.

107. The Government members of Indonesia, Malaysia and Thailand submitted an amendment to modify the definition of a national programme from one that included "objectives, priorities and means of action in the area of occupational safety and health to be achieved in a predetermined time frame" to one that had "been formulated to improve occupational safety and health within a predetermined time frame". They felt that the definition of "national programme" should be linked to outcomes. The Employer members felt that the amendment made the definition more vague and opposed it. The Worker members proposed a subamendment to restore the original text and then replace "to be achieved" by "formulated". The Employer members supported the subamendment, but wished to sub-subamend it, to keep the idea of achievement. With an adjustment of punctuation proposed by the Chairperson, the Employer and Worker members agreed on the text of the amendment as subamended and sub-subamended, and it was adopted.

108. The Government members of Cameroon, Côte d'Ivoire and Senegal submitted an amendment to replace the words "and means of action" in the definition of a national programme by ", means of action, strategies and indicators". The Government member of Senegal, noting that the African Government members of the Committee supported the amendment, explained that strategies were a precondition for actions, and indicators were necessary for monitoring achievement. The Worker members supported the amendment, while the Employer members opposed it. The Employer Vice-Chairperson asserted that there was no definition of "strategy", but in any case policies and programmes could

constitute strategies; furthermore, indicators were already referred to in clause 6(2)(c). Although the Government member of Senegal argued that the reference to indicators elsewhere in the proposed instrument was in a much different context, and that it was up to every programme to define its strategy, some 20 countries opposed the amendment, and it was withdrawn.

109. The Employer members withdrew an amendment that had been predicated on the choice of a Declaration as the form of the proposed instruments.

110. The Worker members withdrew an amendment to attach the word "action" to "programme" in clause 4(b), because the expression "action programme" had been rejected in the discussion of earlier amendments.

111. The Worker members submitted an amendment to add a new clause at the end of point 4, to define a national preventative safety and health culture as "one in which the right to a safe and healthy working environment is respected at all levels, where governments, employers and workers actively participate in securing a safe and healthy working environment through a system of defined rights, responsibilities and duties, and where the principle of prevention is accorded the highest priority". The Worker Vice-Chairperson recalled the extensive discussions of the concept at the 91st Session (2003) of the International Labour Conference, and the insistence of the Worker members that the simple term "safety culture" could be construed as meaning "modification of workers' behaviour". She felt that it would be useful to include the definition of the broader term in the proposed instrument. The Employer members supported the amendment on the basis of the 2003 consensus. There was no opposition from Government members, and the amendment was adopted.

112. Point 4 was adopted as amended.

Point 5

113. The Worker Vice-Chairperson introduced an amendment to replace the original text of point 5, which was headed "Objective", with the following text:

> The purpose of the Convention should be to:
>
> (a) ensure that each Member gives priority to improving occupational safety and health;
>
> (b) promote the ratification of occupational safety and health Conventions and effective implementation of ILO occupational safety and health instruments;
>
> (c) promote the development of a national preventative safety and health culture, based on principles of assessment and management of hazards in the workplace;
>
> (d) complement existing ILO occupational safety and health instruments, in particular the Occupational Safety and Health Convention, 1981 (No. 155), and its Protocol, 2002.

114. The Worker Vice-Chairperson explained the reasons for the amendment, namely that stating these items in particular would help to clarify the objectives of the Convention. The Employer Vice-Chairperson opposed the amendment, saying that it would make the objectives of the Convention less clear, that the inclusion of references to other occupational safety and health instruments would inhibit ratification of this one, and that the linking of "a national preventative safety and health culture" to assessing and managing hazards in the workplace ran contrary to the compromise already reached by the Committee on the definition of the term. The Government member of the United Kingdom, speaking on behalf of the Government members of the IMEC group present in the Committee, also opposed the amendment, as did the Government members of Egypt,

Lebanon and Senegal, speaking on behalf of the African Government members of the Committee.

115. The Worker Vice-Chairperson thought that it was the Committee's task to ensure occupational safety and health became a high priority on national agendas and that the objective should be to increase ratifications of occupational safety and health Conventions. Given the lack of support for the amendment, however, she subamended it by deleting clauses (c) and (d). The Employer Vice-Chairperson opposed the amendment as subamended, for the above reasons, as did the Government members of Namibia, Luxembourg, speaking on behalf of the Government members of the Committee Member States of the European Union, Argentina, speaking on behalf of the Government members of the Committee member States of MERCOSUR, and the United Kingdom, speaking on behalf of the Government members of the IMEC group present in the Committee. The Government member of Trinidad and Tobago, speaking also on behalf of the Government members of the Bahamas, Barbados, Jamaica and Suriname, also opposed the amendment as subamended, as did the Government member of China. The Worker Vice-Chairperson requested an indicative show of hands from Government members for or against her group's amendment, after which she withdrew the amendment in its entirety.

116. The Government member of Argentina, also speaking on behalf of the Government members of Brazil, Chile, Uruguay and Bolivarian Republic of Venezuela, submitted an amendment to replace all of the text after the words "should undertake" with the following: "to improve occupational safety and health in all work activities and progressively to ratify all the international labour standards listed in the annex to the Recommendation that accompanies this Convention, with a view to achieving a safe and healthy working environment. Member States that ratify this Convention also undertake to develop a preventative occupational safety and health culture." The Government member of Argentina explained that this amendment would help to define the objectives of this Convention and progressively improve preventative safety and health culture through the ratification of occupational safety and health Conventions. The Worker Vice-Chairperson supported the amendment. The Employer Vice-Chairperson opposed it for the same reasons that he opposed the previous amendment, as did the Government member of Luxembourg, speaking on behalf of the Government members of the Committee Member States of the European Union, Norway and Romania. The Government member of the United Kingdom, speaking on behalf of the Government members of the IMEC group present in the Committee, also opposed the amendment, as did the Government members of Egypt and Lebanon, on the grounds that it would make ratification of this Convention harder. The Government member of Uganda also opposed the amendment. The Government member of Argentina then withdrew the amendment.

117. The Employer Vice-Chairperson introduced an amendment to replace the words "undertake to take steps with a view to" with the words "take active steps towards". The amendment was intended to strengthen the text, not to change its content. The Worker Vice-Chairperson supported the proposal, as did the Government member of Luxembourg, speaking on behalf of the Government members of the Committee Member States of the European Union, and the Government member of the United Kingdom, speaking on behalf of the Government members of the IMEC group present in the Committee. The Government member of Argentina, speaking on behalf of the Government members of the Committee member States of MERCOSUR, also supported the amendment, but requested that the Spanish version of the amendment be checked. The amendment was accepted.

118. The Employer Vice-Chairperson submitted an amendment to delete the words "with due regard to relevant ILO instruments on occupational safety and health". He thought that referring to other ILO instruments at this point might inhibit governments from ratifying the Convention. He accepted that the reference was a valid one, but suggested that it could

be placed elsewhere, such as in the Recommendation. The Worker Vice-Chairperson opposed the proposed amendment, since other ILO instruments were very important and a helpful reference point in the Convention. She felt that it was important for this Convention to be integrated within the framework of all other occupational safety and health instruments, so the connection between them needed to be made.

119. The Government member of Luxembourg, speaking on behalf of the Government members of the Committee Member States of the European Union, Norway and Romania, opposed the amendment, referring to the arguments from the Worker Vice-Chairperson. The Government member of Tunisia considered that the amendment would conflict with the text of the Preamble and opposed it. The Government member of Argentina, speaking on behalf of the Government members of the Committee member States of MERCOSUR, strongly opposed the amendment because he felt it went against what the ILO stood for and did. The Government member of Senegal, speaking on behalf of the African Government members of the Committee, also opposed the amendment. The Employer Vice-Chairperson recalled the potential legal difficulties, but in light of the discussion, withdrew the amendment.

120. The Government member of the United Kingdom, speaking on behalf of the Government members of the IMEC group present in the Committee, introduced an amendment to replace the words "with due regard to" by the words "by taking into account the principles in". It was suggested that this wording would enable as many countries as possible to ratify the Convention. The Worker Vice-Chairperson subamended the phrase so as to delete the words "principles in" in the amendment. The Government member of the United Kingdom, speaking on behalf of the Government members of the IMEC group present in the Committee, opposed this subamendment, as did the Employer Vice-Chairperson, and the Worker Vice-Chairperson withdrew the subamendment.

121. The Worker Vice-Chairperson opposed the amendment as originally submitted. The Employer Vice-Chairperson considered that the amendment would be a sensible way forward and supported it. The Government member of Bahrain, speaking also on behalf of the Government members of Saudi Arabia and United Arab Emirates, all supported the amendment, as did the Government members of Ecuador, Libyan Arab Jamahiriya and Romania. Within the spirit of trying to reach a consensus, the Worker Vice-Chairperson then supported the amendment. The amendment was accepted.

122. The Government members of the Bahamas, Barbados, Jamaica, Suriname, and Trinidad and Tobago had submitted an amendment to insert "national law and" after "due regard to", but after the discussion on the previous amendment, this one was withdrawn.

123. The Worker Vice-Chairperson submitted an amendment to insert a new paragraph after the existing point 5 as follows: "Each Member should promote the right to a safe and healthy working environment as established in the Principles of National Policy in the Occupational Safety and Health Convention, 1981 (No. 155), and its Protocol, 2002." She explained that this amendment was one of several amendments from the Workers' group aimed at addressing national policy on occupational safety and health, a topic that was absent from the text now being considered. The intention of this amendment was to fill a gap concerning a basic element, namely the right to a safe and healthy working environment, considered to be a fundamental principle of a national policy. The Employer Vice-Chairperson strongly opposed the amendment, claiming that it was not the intention of this instrument to promote workers' rights, but rather to promote a preventative safety and health culture. He said that the correct context for dealing with rights was the ILO Declaration on Fundamental Principles and Rights at Work. The Government member of Argentina, speaking on behalf of the Government members of all the Latin American countries present, asked for further clarification of the amendment. The Worker Vice-

Chairperson referred back to the Conclusions of the 91st Session (2003) of the International Labour Conference, which mentioned the new promotional instrument and stated: "such a practical and constructive instrument should promote, inter alia, the right of workers to a safe and healthy working environment".

124. The Government member of Luxembourg supported the amendment, but the Government members of Morocco, Switzerland and United States all opposed it. After a show of hands from the Government members indicating general opposition to the amendment, the Worker Vice-Chairperson withdrew the amendment.

125. The Government member of Argentina, speaking also on behalf of the Government members of Brazil, Chile, Uruguay and Bolivarian Republic of Venezuela, submitted an amendment to add a new paragraph after point 5, as follows:

> (1) Each Member should promote a safe and healthy working environment by formulating a national policy to that end within the terms of reference of the Occupational Safety and Health Convention, 1981 (No. 155), and its Protocol of 2002.

The Employer Vice-Chairperson opposed the amendment because of its reference to Convention No. 155. The Worker Vice-Chairperson strongly supported the amendment, as she believed that it would promote a safe and healthy working environment.

126. The Government member of the United Kingdom proposed a subamendment to replace the phrase "within the terms of reference of" with "by taking into account the principles in". The amendment, as subamended, read:

> (1) Each Member should promote a safe and healthy working environment by formulating a national policy to that end by taking into account the principles in the Occupational Safety and Health Convention, 1981 (No. 155), and its Protocol of 2002.

The Government members of Switzerland and the United States both opposed the subamendment, but the Government member of Luxembourg, speaking on behalf of the Government members of the Committee Member States of the European Union, Norway and Romania, supported it. The Government member of the United Kingdom recalled that the Committee had already agreed to define "national policy" with reference to Convention No. 155. The Government member of Argentina supported the text as subamended, as did the Worker Vice-Chairperson.

127. The Government member of Uganda expressed concern that the heading above point 5 was "Objective", but the amendment being discussed seemed to reflect strategies. The Government member of Brazil, speaking for the same group of countries as had proposed the original amendment, said that her group would be proposing a new heading "National policy". The Government member of Norway indicated support for the amendment as subamended, as did the Government member of Lesotho who also asked for further clarification of the term "national policy". The Government member of Senegal, speaking on behalf of the African Government members of the Committee, also supported the amendment, adding that each member State should promote a safe and healthy working environment and that national policy should support this. The Government member of the Bahamas, speaking also on behalf of the Government members of Jamaica and Suriname, supported the amendment as subamended, as did the Government member of Ecuador.

128. The Government member of the United States recalled that the Committee had earlier defined national policy in accordance with Article 4 of Convention No. 155, and he considered that the amendment now being discussed was defining national policy in broader terms taking into account the whole of Convention No. 155 and its Protocol of 2002. He confirmed his opposition to the text as subamended. The Employer Vice-

Chairperson remarked that the Government member of the United States had raised a valid point, and submitted a second subamendment that would delete the text after the word "policy". The amendment as subamended now read:

(1) Each Member should promote a safe and healthy working environment by formulating a national policy.

The Worker Vice-Chairperson opposed the amendment as subamended. After a show of hands from the Government members indicating general support for the amendment as sub-subamended, the Worker Vice-Chairperson also supported it.

129. The Worker members submitted an amendment to insert a new third paragraph as follows: "Each Member should ensure continuous improvement of occupational safety and health by the development, in a tripartite context, of an effective policy, national system and national programme." The intent was to emphasize tripartism and to make continuous improvement a policy goal. The Employer Vice-Chairperson expressed doubt that continuous improvement could be ensured, or that "effective" was meaningful without a definition. The Government member of Luxembourg submitted a subamendment to replace "ensure" by "promote" and "effective" by "national". The Worker members, Employer members and the African Government members of the Committee all supported the amendment as subamended, and it was accepted.

130. As a result, the Government member of Argentina withdrew a very similar amendment submitted by the Government members of Argentina, Brazil, Chile, Uruguay and Bolivarian Republic of Venezuela.

131. The Worker members submitted an amendment to insert a new second paragraph after point 5 that encouraged member States to give occupational safety and health a high priority, to adopt a national policy in accordance with Convention No. 155 even if they had not ratified it, and to consider ratification of that and other important occupational safety and health Conventions. The Worker Vice-Chairperson immediately proposed a subamendment to delete the phrase about alignment of policy with Convention No. 155, because this principle had already been captured in a previously accepted amendment. The Employer members opposed the amendment, with or without the subamendment, on the grounds that it was both confusing and legally untenable for the proposed instrument to impose obligations on member States that they had refused by not ratifying the earlier Convention. The Government members of the Committee Member States of the European Union, the IMEC group, the Africa group, Norway and Tunisia all agreed with the Employer members and opposed the amendment as subamended. The Worker members expressed doubt that the proposed amendment would impose any such obligations, and suggested that the Legal Adviser be called. This was opposed by the Employer members and many Government members. Consequently, the Legal Adviser's opinion could not be heard in the Committee. The Worker members withdrew the amendment and subamendment.

132. The Worker members submitted an amendment that would insert a new fourth paragraph after point 5, enumerating five rights of workers that should be promoted and enhanced by member States. The amendment was opposed by the Employer members: these rights were stated in other Conventions, so to list them in the proposed instrument would be redundant for the countries that had ratified the relevant Conventions and a barrier to ratification for those that had not. The Government member of the United Kingdom agreed, observing that all members of the Committee had agreed that the instrument under consideration was not to be prescriptive. No one could deny that workers had the stated rights, but the proposed amendment was not appropriate to a framework instrument. The Government members of the Bahamas, Barbados, Jamaica, Lesotho, Libyan Arab Jamahiriya, Suriname, Trinidad and Tobago and the IMEC group present in the Committee all likewise opposed the amendment.

133. The Worker Vice-Chairperson stated that this was the most important issue for the Worker members. She feared that the positions reached during the 91st Session (2003) of the International Labour Conference were not being honoured, because paragraph 6 of the Conclusions of that Conference clearly stated that a promotional framework should promote workers' right to a safe and healthy working environment. This discussion was then suspended. In the subsequent session, she continued by saying that she did not see how the International Labour Organization could produce a document that did not assert that right. The Employer Vice-Chairperson replied that workers' rights were already covered in the definition of a preventative safety and health culture, and that it was in fact the Worker members' amendment that threatened the delicate balance achieved in 2003. He repeated his concern that the proposed instrument incorporated wording that had prevented member States from ratifying this and other occupational safety and health Conventions, and that it mentioned rights without mentioning the corresponding responsibilities of workers.

134. The Government member of Luxembourg, speaking on behalf of the Government members of the Committee Member States of the European Union and Romania, submitted a subamendment to delete the enumeration of specific rights and leave the proposed new fourth paragraph reading: "Each Member should promote and advance, at all relevant levels, the right of workers to a safe and healthy working environment". The subamendment was supported by the Government members of Norway and Switzerland, as well as the Government members of the Committee member States of MERCOSUR. The Employer members submitted a sub-subamendment to add to the end of the previously cited text, "as well as promote awareness of the responsibilities of all parties", but withdrew it in response to opposition from the Worker members and a number of Government members. The Worker members expressed support for the amendment as subamended by the Government member of Luxembourg, and the amendment was accepted.

135. The Worker members withdrew an amendment to insert a new heading "Promoting the principles of a national policy" that was identical in effect to an amendment submitted by the Government members of Argentina, Brazil, Chile, Uruguay and Bolivarian Republic of Venezuela. This latter amendment, to insert the heading "IV. National policy" after point 5 and before the previous Part "IV. National programme" in the Office text, was widely supported and accepted.

136. Point 5 was adopted as amended.

Point 6

137. Amendments to reverse the order of section IV, "National programme" and section V, "National system", were submitted by (1) the Government members of Botswana, Côte d'Ivoire, Namibia, Senegal, South Africa and Zambia; (2) the Worker members; and (3) the Government members of Argentina, Brazil, Chile, Uruguay and Bolivarian Republic of Venezuela. The Worker Vice-Chairperson pointed out that this brought the sections into line with the order of precedence "policy – system – programme" on which the Committee had agreed. The three amendments were accepted.

138. The Worker members withdrew an amendment to insert "action" before "programme" in the title of Part IV.

139. The Government members of Botswana, Côte d'Ivoire, Lesotho, Namibia, Senegal, South Africa and Zambia submitted an amendment to insert the word "monitor" after "implement" in the phrase "Each Member should formulate, implement and periodically review a national programme". The Government member of Namibia explained that monitoring would be necessary to gather the information for periodic reviews, to determine that the programme was in fact effective. The Employer and Worker members supported the amendment and it was accepted, on the understanding that the Drafting Committee would ensure that the French text included the best equivalent of the English "monitoring".

140. The Worker members withdrew two amendments to insert the word "action" before "programme" in points 6(1) and 6(2).

141. The Worker members submitted an amendment to add a new clause (a) to point 6(2), and immediately subamended it to read as follows: "contribute to the protection of workers from hazards and with the goal of eliminating work-related death, injuries and diseases", to reinforce the statement of purpose of national programmes. The Employer Vice-Chairperson objected that, in countries where commuting accidents were held to be occupational, the amendment would impose an impossible goal. Furthermore, this purpose was stated in the definition of national policy, on which national programmes were supposed to be based.

142. The Government member of the Libyan Arab Jamahiriya proposed a sub-subamendment, to replace "with the goal of eliminating" by "in order to limit". The Worker Vice-Chairperson appreciated the attempt at compromise, but insisted that elimination should be the goal; she recalled that the Employer Vice-Chairperson had said in his opening remarks that one death or injury was one too many. She opposed the sub-subamendment. The Employer Vice-Chairperson insisted that there was no inconsistency between denying the existence of workplace casualties and setting achievable goals, and supported the sub-subamendment. The Government member of Senegal, speaking on behalf of the African Government members of the Committee, supported the sub-subamendment, but asked if "limit" could be rendered by "reduire" in the French version of the clause. The Chairperson asked the Committee if "reduce" could be used in the English version instead of "limit" to translate the word used in Arabic by the Government member of the Libyan Arab Jamahiriya. This proposal was accepted without qualification by the Worker and Employer members and by the Government member of India, whereas the Government members of Bahrain, Jordan, Kuwait, Saudi Arabia and United Arab Emirates accepted "reduce" but would have preferred "limit".

143. The Government member of Luxembourg, speaking on behalf of the Government members of the Committee Member States of the European Union, submitted a subamendment to replace "hazards" with "work-related risks". The Employer members supported this subamendment but the Worker members opposed it. The Government member of Uganda reminded the Committee that hazards were intrinsic to substances or circumstances, whereas risk expressed the likelihood of a worker suffering from exposure to a hazard; he felt that "hazard" was the better word in the current context.

144. The Government member of Senegal, speaking on behalf of the African Government members [9] of the Committee, proposed a sub-subamendment to insert "hazards and" between "work-related" and "risks". This was supported by the Worker members, but the Employer members opposed it. The Government member of Luxembourg asserted that

---

[9] The following Government joined the African Government members of the Committee: Mauritania.

governments could expect to reduce risks, but could not necessarily eliminate hazards, because by definition they were intrinsic properties, and that mentioning the elimination of hazards would make the proposed Convention very difficult for many countries to ratify. The Government member of Senegal pointed out that the text itself spoke of protection from hazards rather than their elimination, which was perfectly feasible. Opinion was divided among the Government members of the Committee as to the appropriateness of naming "risks", "hazards" or both as the object of worker protection in national programmes. The Government member of Mauritania felt that it should be up to each member State to interpret the terms. The representative of the Secretary General reminded the Committee that several ILO codes of practice used "risk" and "hazard" together, and that it was possible to protect against hazards even if they could not be eliminated; Convention No. 155, indeed, used the term "hazard". The Worker Vice-Chairperson observed that the problem might be related to the fact that in some member States legislation was risk based, whereas in others it seemed to be hazards based. She proposed that, in order to progress, both terms be used, with note being taken of the problem here and a broadly acceptable solution found that could be brought into the second discussion of the Convention at the next International Labour Conference. The Chairperson suggested that it would be preferable to suspend debate on the amendment as sub-subamended overnight for reflection and consultation.

145. As a result of consultations among the Employer, Worker and Government members, the Worker Vice-Chairperson proposed a sub-sub-subamendment that would produce the following wording for the new clause: "contribute to the protection of workers by minimizing work-related hazards or risks in accordance with national law and practice in order to reduce work-related death, injuries and diseases". The Employer members supported the proposed text. The Government member of Luxembourg, speaking on behalf of the Government members of the Committee Member States of the European Union, submitted a sub-sub-sub-subamendment, to replace "hazards or risks" by "hazards and risks". The Government member of the United Kingdom, speaking on behalf of the Government members of the IMEC group present in the Committee, supported the amendment as most recently subamended, as did the Government member of Egypt. The Government member of Senegal, speaking on behalf of the African Government members of the Committee, did not oppose the amendment, but expressed concern over the inelegance of the French version of the text. The amendment was accepted as sub-sub-sub-subamended.

146. The Government member of Senegal, speaking also on behalf of the Government members of Botswana, Côte d'Ivoire, Lesotho, Namibia, South Africa and Zambia, submitted an amendment to insert the word "monitored" after the word "formulated" in paragraph 2(a). It was said that the amendment was needed to ensure that the national programme was monitored before the final "review"; the French version of the text implied monitoring, but the English text did not. The Employer Vice-Chairperson doubted whether the amendment was needed, but the Worker Vice-Chairperson supported it.

147. The Government member of the United Kingdom clarified that a "review" required ongoing monitoring and analysis before final revision, and so the text already implied monitoring. He opposed the amendment, as did the Government member of New Zealand, who also made reference to paragraph 2(c), which mentioned targets and indicators of progress. The Government member of Kenya supported the amendment. The Government member of Algeria suggested that the words "periodically evaluated" could be more appropriate than "monitored", and the Worker Vice-Chairperson submitted a subamendment to this effect, but withdrew it when it was pointed out that these words already appeared in point 6(1). The Government member of Luxembourg, speaking on behalf of the Government members of the Committee Member States of the European Union, opposed the amendment, since the amended point 6(1) already referred to "monitoring", and the Government member of Argentina, speaking on behalf of the Government members of the Committee member States of MERCOSUR, also thought that the amendment was not needed. With the assurances that the word "reviewed" had a broader meaning than just "revised", the amendment was withdrawn.

148. The Worker Vice-Chairperson submitted an amendment to add a new clause 2(b): "be based on principles of prevention, assessment and management of hazards at the workplace level", reasoning that there was a need to relate national action to the workplace level and that this was consistent with the Conclusions adopted by the 91st Session (2003) of the International Labour Conference. She immediately subamended the amendment so that it referred to "risks" as well as "hazards". The Employer Vice-Chairperson opposed the principle of the amendment, on the grounds that the proposed Convention was becoming too complex and was repeating what was covered in other standards. Furthermore, the matter of the proposed amendment was already included in Paragraph 13 of the proposed Recommendation that the Committee would be considering in due course. The Government member of Tunisia opposed the amendment, as he considered that it did not add any value to the Convention, but the Government member of Argentina, speaking on behalf of the Government members of the Committee member States of MERCOSUR, supported the amendment as indispensable. It likewise found support from the Government members of India, the Philippines and the African Government members of the Committee. The amendment was opposed by the Government members of Romania, Switzerland and the Committee Member States of the European Union.

149. After an overnight suspension of discussion for consultation, the Worker members proposed a sub-subamendment that yielded the following text: "promote the principles of prevention, assessment and management of hazards and risks at the workplace level, in accordance with national law and practice". The Employer Vice-Chairperson opposed the amendment in its latest version, asserting that the principles of prevention, assessment and management were amply covered in other Conventions, in the ILO *Guidelines on occupational safety and health management systems, ILO-OSH 2001* and even in point 13 of the proposed Conclusions currently under discussion; furthermore, it was not clear what was meant by promoting the principles in accordance with national law and practice. The Worker Vice-Chairperson replied that the revised language was an attempt to ensure that national programmes had some content and did not focus exclusively on process. All the instruments cited by the Employer Vice-Chairperson bore on systems, not programmes. The Government members of Egypt, Papua New Guinea and Uganda supported the amendment in its latest form as making the evolving instrument more concrete, but it was opposed as redundant by the Government members of Indonesia, Norway, Philippines, Romania, United States and the Committee Member States of the European Union. The Worker Vice-Chairperson withdrew the amendment with its sub- and sub-subamendments, while maintaining that it did not violate the concept of a framework instrument to include wording that would link it to existing Conventions, but rather reflected the integrated approach favoured by the ILO.

150. The Worker members submitted an amendment to insert the words "initiatives fostering" before "the development" in clause 6(2)(b), on the grounds that it would underline the active nature of national programmes, make the clause more concrete and bring in wording agreed on in 2003. The Employer members felt that the additional words made the statement weaker, not stronger. The Government member of Senegal, speaking on behalf of the African Government members of the Committee, agreed, and the amendment was withdrawn.

151. The Worker Vice-Chairperson submitted an amendment to insert a new clause after clause 6(2)(b), to say that a national programme should "ensure worker participation and representation at all levels". She said that paragraph 6(1) called for worker participation only in the development of programmes. The Employer members opposed the amendment, pointing out that the issue was dealt with extensively in Article 19 of Convention No. 155, and that such a clause was too prescriptive for a framework instrument. The Government members of Egypt, Norway, Romania, the Committee Member States of the European Union, the African Government members of the Committee and the Government members of the IMEC group present in the Committee all agreed, and the amendment was withdrawn.

152. The Government member of Luxembourg introduced an amendment, proposed also by the Government members of Austria, Belgium, Czech Republic, Denmark, Estonia, Finland, France, Germany, Greece, Ireland, Italy, Netherlands, Norway, Poland, Portugal, Slovenia, Spain, Sweden and United Kingdom, to insert the words "where appropriate" after the words "of progress" at the end of clause 6(2)(c). This would make the clause more flexible and easier for countries to implement. The Worker members sympathized with the desire for flexibility, but felt that the amendment would allow national programmes to be in conformity with the proposed Convention without having any monitoring mechanism at all. The Worker Vice-Chairperson proposed a subamendment to move the word "appropriate" to the second position in the clause, so that it would read "include appropriate targets and indicators of progress". This was opposed by the proposers and by the Employer members, and was withdrawn. The Government member of the United Kingdom explained that it was important for targets to reflect outcomes, relating to the reduction of accidents and ill health, and not just outputs, for example, relating to numbers of leaflets distributed. "Appropriate" targets should therefore be related to outcomes, if possible. The Government member of Argentina, speaking on behalf of the Government members of the Committee member States of MERCOSUR, Chile, Ecuador and Bolivarian Republic of Venezuela, opposed the amendment: it seemed to admit the possibility of national programmes without targets or indicators of progress, while in fact a country could not have a meaningful programme without them. The African Government members of the Committee agreed. The Worker members and the Government members of the Bahamas, Bahrain, Barbados, Jamaica, Jordan, Lebanon, Saudi Arabia, Suriname, Trinidad and Tobago, and United Arab Emirates likewise opposed the amendment. The Government members of Canada, New Zealand, Papua New Guinea and Switzerland supported it. In view of the balance of opinion against the amendment, it was withdrawn by its proposers.

153. The Government member of Argentina, speaking on behalf of the Government members of the member States of MERCOSUR, introduced an amendment to replace the word "include" with the words "establish priorities" in clause (c), explaining that the establishment of priorities was very important in national programmes. The Employer Vice-Chairperson opposed the amendment because priorities were already included in the definition of "national programme for occupational safety and health". The Worker Vice-Chairperson supported the amendment because it was an important concept that needed emphasizing. The Government member of New Zealand submitted a subamendment to amplify the text further to read "establish objectives, priorities, means of action", as set out in section II, Definitions. The Worker Vice-Chairperson supported the subamendment, but the Employer Vice-Chairperson opposed it, as did most Government members, because the amendment was seen as repetitive. The subamendment was withdrawn. Several Government members opposed the original amendment, as did the Employer Vice-Chairperson, on the grounds that it was superfluous, and the amendment was withdrawn.

154. The Government member of Senegal, speaking on behalf of the African Government members of the Committee, introduced an amendment to insert the word "strategies" after the word "include" in clause (c). She considered that strategies were needed within national programmes, since they provided the guidance on how the targets would be achieved. The Worker Vice-Chairperson supported the amendment, but the Employer Vice-Chairperson opposed it because he believed that strategies were a much broader

concept than this, and their inclusion in the text in this way made them less significant, as well as making the text more complicated. The Government member of Luxembourg, on behalf of the Government members of the Committee Member States of the European Union, and the Government member of the United Kingdom, speaking on behalf of the Government members of the IMEC group present in the Committee, also opposed the amendment because it was considered that the additional wording was not needed and that strategies were already included in national systems. The Government member of Jordan also opposed the amendment, which was then withdrawn.

155. The Government member of France, speaking also on behalf of the Government member of Luxembourg, introduced an amendment to add a new clause after (c) that read: "be supported, where possible, by other complimentary national programmes and plans which will assist in achieving the objective of a safer and healthier working environment". The Safety and Health Committee at the International Labour Conference in 2003 had considered it important to "mainstream" occupational safety and health as part of other programmes, and the amendment would help foster synergies between different national programmes, so progressing occupational safety and health higher up national agendas. There was no equivalent word in French for "mainstreaming", which is why the amendment was worded in the way that it was. The Employer Vice-Chairperson supported the amendment, as did the Worker Vice-Chairperson and the Government member of Argentina, speaking on behalf of the Government members of the Committee member States of MERCOSUR. The amendment was accepted.

156. The Worker Vice-Chairperson withdrew an amendment to insert the word "action" after "national" in paragraph (3).

157. The Government member of Senegal, speaking also on behalf of the Government members of Botswana, Côte d'Ivoire, Lesotho, Namibia, South Africa and Zambia, submitted an amendment to delete the words "to the extent possible" in the first line of paragraph (3), since they believed that the endorsement and launching of a national programme by the highest national authorities was essential and not optional. The amendment was supported by the other African Government members of the Committee. The Worker Vice-Chairperson supported the amendment, but the Employer Vice-Chairperson opposed it, as did the Government member of Luxembourg, speaking on behalf of the Government members of the Committee Member States of the European Union, Norway and Romania, and the Government member of the United Kingdom, speaking on behalf of the Government members of the IMEC group present in the Committee, because it was felt to be impracticable to expect national programmes to be endorsed at the highest political level in every country. The Government member of Jordan also opposed the amendment, but the Government member of Argentina, speaking on behalf of the Government members of the Committee member States of MERCOSUR, Chile and Bolivarian Republic of Venezuela, supported it. However, the amendment was withdrawn.

158. Point 6 was adopted as amended.

Point 7

159. The Worker members submitted an amendment to replace the words "progressively develop" by the words "periodically review" in the first line of paragraph (1), then subamended it by combining both sets of words so as to read: "progressively develop and periodically review". She explained that the periodic review would be a new concept to the national system, but like the national programme, it was necessary both to develop and periodically to review the system to ensure that it was up to date and relevant. The Employer Vice-Chairperson supported this subamendment, as did many Government members and the amendment was accepted as subamended.

160. The Worker Vice-Chairperson submitted an amendment to include the words "inter alia" after the word "include" in paragraph (2), to clarify that the national system should not be limited to the items mentioned in clauses (a), (b) and (c). The Employer Vice-Chairperson supported the intention of the amendment, but questioned whether it was necessary, since the word "include" implied that the list was not exhaustive. The Government member of the United Kingdom also supported the intention of the amendment, but objected to the use of a Latin phrase instead of an English one, suggesting "among others" instead. The Government member of Luxembourg, speaking on behalf of the Committee Member States of the European Union, Norway and Romania, supported the amendment, provided that the English words were used instead of the Latin ones. The Employer Vice-Chairperson and the Worker Vice-Chairperson both approved of the new version, so the amendment was accepted with "among others" instead of "inter alia".

161. The Government member of Luxembourg, speaking on behalf of the Committee Member States of the European Union, Norway and Romania, introduced an amendment to replace paragraph (2)(a) with the phrase: "laws, regulations, other non-binding instruments on occupational safety and health". He then subamended the phrase to replace the word "instruments" with "agreements", explaining that in the European Union many other agreements were used as part of national systems for occupational safety and health. The Worker Vice-Chairperson supported the text as subamended, but the Employer Vice-Chairperson opposed it because he said that in principle all such agreements were binding. The Government member of Luxembourg then subamended the phrase further by adding "collective" before "agreements". The Government member of Argentina, speaking on behalf of the Government members of the Committee member States of MERCOSUR, opposed both the subamendments, since all collective agreements were binding in their countries and they would be unable to ratify the Convention if it included non-binding collective agreements in the text.

162. The Employer Vice-Chairperson subamended the text further so that the whole phrase just read: "laws, regulations and other relevant instruments". The Government member of Luxembourg, after consulting with the Government members of the Committee Member States of the European Union, opposed the new text, as it was necessary to have the term "collective agreement" in the Convention for it to be ratified by European Union Member States. The Worker Vice-Chairperson then proposed a sub-sub-sub-subamendment, with the following text: "laws, regulations, collective agreements and other relevant instruments on occupational safety and health". The Employer Vice-Chairperson supported this, as did the Government member of Luxembourg, and the amendment as finally subamended was accepted.

163. The Government member of Luxembourg, speaking on behalf of the Government members of the Committee Member States of the European Union, Norway and Romania, submitted an amendment to insert the words "or body" after the word "authority" and insert the words "or bodies" after the word "authorities" in paragraph (2)(b). He then subamended the text by adding "in accordance with national laws and practice" after the word "bodies". He explained that the national occupational safety and health systems in European Union countries involved both designated authorities and non-public bodies, but that some of these bodies needed to work within the legal framework, hence the wording about national laws and practice. The Government member of Morocco voiced her support for the subamended text, and both the Worker Vice-Chairperson and the Employer Vice-Chairperson accepted it, so the amendment as subamended was accepted.

164. The Government member of Senegal, speaking on behalf of the African Government members of the Committee, introduced their amendment to delete the words "including systems of inspections" in paragraph (2)(c). She explained that it was unnecessary to specify inspection systems here, as they already formed an integral part of national

mechanisms for ensuring compliance with laws and regulations. The Employer Vice-Chairperson supported the amendment, but the Worker Vice-Chairperson opposed it on the grounds that, if inspection systems were not mentioned, the task of ensuring compliance could be given to private organizations, with third-party audits by private companies replacing government inspections. The Government member of Luxembourg, speaking on behalf of the Government members of the Committee Member States of the European Union and Norway, opposed the amendment, as did the Government member of the United Kingdom, speaking on behalf of the Government members of the IMEC group present in the Committee. The latter added that, although numbers of inspectors were usually quite low and that other methods were used to ensure compliance, the IMEC group did not want to lose the concept of inspection. The Government member of Jordan also rejected the amendment, as did the Government member of Indonesia. After it became clear that most Government members did not support the amendment, the Government member of Senegal withdrew it.

165. The Worker Vice-Chairperson withdrew an amendment to insert the words "adequate and appropriate" after the word "including" in paragraph (2)(c).

166. The Worker Vice-Chairperson withdrew an amendment to insert the words "and monitoring of remedial actions" after the word "inspection" in paragraph (2)(c).

167. The Government member of Uruguay, speaking also on behalf of the Government members of Argentina, Brazil, Chile and Bolivarian Republic of Venezuela, submitted an amendment to add a new clause after paragraph (2)(c): "mechanisms for inter-institutional coordination between the government bodies concerned". She explained that the aim of this amendment was to promote consultation between relevant government bodies on occupational safety and health matters. The Employer Vice-Chairperson opposed the amendment because he considered that a Convention was not an appropriate means to ensure such consultation, but the Worker Vice-Chairperson supported it. The Government member of Luxembourg, speaking on behalf of the Government members of the Committee Member States of the European Union, Norway and Romania, opposed the amendment for the same reasons, as did the Government member of the United Kingdom, speaking on behalf of the Government members of the IMEC group present in the Committee, saying that it would be an obstacle to ratification. The Government member of Algeria supported the amendment, but the Government member of Lebanon opposed it, as did the Government member of Bahrain, speaking also on behalf of the Government members of Saudi Arabia and the United Arab Emirates. The Government member of Uruguay explained that the Labour Inspection Convention, 1947 (No. 81), established the need for coordination and it was with this in mind that they wished to extend coordination, but, given the views expressed by Committee members, the amendment was withdrawn.

168. The Worker Vice-Chairperson submitted an amendment to insert a new clause: "arrangements at the level of the undertaking to ensure cooperation between management, workers and their representatives as an essential element of organizational prevention measures" after paragraph (2)(c). She argued that the amendment was needed to ensure that there was good connection between the national occupational safety and health system and local enterprises, where accidents and ill health actually occurred, and that national systems could only have an impact if they promoted cooperation between managers and workers at the enterprise level. The concept existed in other ILO instruments. The Employer Vice-Chairperson opposed the amendment because he believed it took the discussion to an enterprise level, whereas this section of the Convention dealt with the national level. He added that this idea was already contained in Article 20 of Convention No. 155 and in point 14(2) of this Convention. The Government member of Senegal, speaking on behalf of the African Government members of the Committee, also opposed the amendment, as did the Government member of Thailand, saying that such cooperation

was to some extent already required under existing national law. The Government member of Uruguay, speaking on behalf of the Government members of the Committee member States of MERCOSUR, Ecuador and Bolivarian Republic of Venezuela, supported the amendment, as it would be the only paragraph actually requiring workplace level cooperation.

169. The Government member of Luxembourg submitted a subamendment to replace "ensure" by "promote". The Worker Vice-Chairperson supported the subamendment, but the Employer Vice-Chairperson opposed it, saying that he could not accept that a national system could deal with arrangements at enterprise level. The Government member of Luxembourg submitted a further subamendment to replace the word "organizational" by "workplace-related". The Worker Vice-Chairperson accepted the sub-subamendment, but the Employer Vice-Chairperson opposed it.

170. The Employer Vice-Chairperson then submitted a sub-sub-subamendment to replace the existing text with "promotion of cooperation between management, workers and their representatives". The Worker Vice-Chairperson opposed this latest subamendment, as there was no mention of the workplace. The Government member of Argentina, speaking on behalf of the Government members of the Committee member States of MERCOSUR, Ecuador and Bolivarian Republic of Venezuela, and also the Government member of Papua New Guinea opposed the latest subamendment on the grounds that it was vital to ensure a linkage between the national system and enterprise. The Government member of Lebanon also opposed it, saying that this type of cooperation needed to be mandatory and not voluntary. The Employer Vice-Chairperson withdrew the sub-sub-subamendment.

171. The Government member of the United States opposed the amendment, even as sub-subamended. He pointed out that there was a whole section of Convention No. 155 devoted to this topic, and that the language of the amendment was very close to that of Article 20 of that Convention, so he felt that the amendment violated the principle of not repeating the content of other Conventions. The Government member of Senegal, speaking on behalf of the African Government members of the Committee, also opposed the amendment as sub-subamended. The Government member of New Zealand expressed discomfort with the wording, but supported the amendment as sub-subamended because employee participation was such a key part of a national system.

172. The Government member of the United Kingdom proposed a sub-sub-subamendment to move the phrase "at the level of the undertaking" to follow "workers and their representatives". The Employer members opposed the amendment in its latest form, asserting that its substance would be covered by point 14 of the proposed Conclusions. The Worker members did support the sub-sub-subamendment, as did 14 Government members of the Committee. In recognition of this breadth of support, the Employer members dropped their opposition and the amendment was accepted as sub-sub-subamended.

173. Two amendments of different wording but similar effect were submitted by the Government members of Botswana, Cameroon, Côte d'Ivoire, Lesotho, Namibia, Senegal, South Africa and Zambia, on one hand, and the Worker members, on the other. The former amendment proposed to delete the introductory phrase of paragraph 7(3) and renumber its individual clauses as a continuation of paragraph 2. They felt that the words "where appropriate" in the introductory phrase would enable countries to avoid including important elements in their national systems. The Employer Vice-Chairperson expressed surprise that any governments would willingly make things more difficult for themselves by reducing the flexibility of the proposed instrument, and opposed the amendment. The Government member of Luxembourg, speaking on behalf of the Government members of the Committee Member States of the European Union, Norway and Romania, indeed opposed the amendment for this reason, as did the Government members of the Bahamas,

Barbados, Jamaica, Suriname, Trinidad and Tobago, and the Government member of the United Kingdom, speaking on behalf of the Government members of the IMEC group present in the Committee. The Government members of Algeria, Egypt, Lebanon and Morocco supported the amendment. The Government member of the United States felt that the purpose of separate paragraphs 7(2) and 7(3), with "where appropriate" in the latter, was not to dispense countries of obligations but to allow different solutions in different countries. The Government member of Côte d'Ivoire, speaking for the proposers, withdrew the amendment.

174. The Worker members' amendment proposed to move clauses (a), (b) and (d) from paragraph 7(3) to paragraph 7(2), so that the phrase "where appropriate" would not apply to them. Given the similarity of the two amendments, the Employer Vice-Chairperson invited the Worker members to withdraw their amendment, in keeping with the principle that a framework instrument should be as flexible as possible. The Government member of the United Kingdom, speaking on behalf of the Government members of the IMEC group present in the Committee, opposed the amendment for the same reasons as in the case of the amendment of the eight African Government members of the Committee. The Government member of Senegal, speaking on behalf of the African Government members of the Committee, also opposed the amendment, and it was withdrawn.

175. The Worker members submitted an amendment to insert the words "the provision of" before "occupational safety and health training" where this was mentioned as an element of a national system. The Employer members supported the amendment and, in the absence of objections from the Government members, the amendment was accepted.

176. The Government members of Austria, Belgium, Czech Republic, Estonia, Finland, France, Germany, Greece, Ireland, Luxembourg, Norway, Netherlands, Poland, Portugal, Slovenia, Spain, Sweden and United Kingdom submitted an amendment to insert the words "in accordance with national law and practice" after "occupational health services" where they were named as another element of a national system. The Government member of Luxembourg explained that this was intended to make the proposed instrument more flexible and thus more easily ratified. The amendment was accepted with the support of the Worker and Employer members.

177. The Government members of Austria, Belgium, Czech Republic, Estonia, Finland, France, Germany, Greece, Ireland, Luxembourg, Norway, Netherlands, Poland, Portugal, Slovenia, Spain, Sweden and United Kingdom submitted an amendment to insert a new clause, to add "scientific bodies conducting research in the area of occupational safety and health" as an element of a national system. The Government member of Luxembourg reminded the Committee that European countries believed strongly in the importance of research, as witnessed by the European Union's maintenance of the European Foundation for Living and Working Conditions in Dublin and the European Agency for Safety and Health at Work in Bilbao. The Employer member observed that some countries funded activities, not bodies, and proposed a subamendment to shorten the clause to "research on occupational safety and health". The Government member of Luxembourg, speaking on behalf of the proposers of the original amendment, supported the subamendment, as did the Worker members, and the amendment was accepted as subamended.

178. The Government members of Argentina, Brazil, Chile, Uruguay and Bolivarian Republic of Venezuela submitted an amendment to reword a clause that named another element of a national system, the amended clause to read "a mechanism for reporting, recording and investigating all work-related accidents, incidents and diseases". In introducing the amendment, the Government member of Argentina immediately subamended it to insert "data analysis" before "investigating" for the sake of completeness. He insisted on the importance of investigating incidents as well as more serious events, in order for serious

accidents to be avoided. The Employer members opposed the amendment because of the burden on governments of investigating all incidents. The Worker members proposed a sub-subamendment to remove the word "all" from the clause and to better render in English the sense of the Spanish amendment: "a mechanism for reporting, recording, collecting and analysing data on, and investigating work-related accidents, incidents and diseases". The Employer members objected to this inclusion, because it was already the object of a Protocol to Convention No. 155. The Government member of Luxembourg, speaking on behalf of the Government members of the Committee Member States of the European Union, Norway and Romania, supported the sub-subamendment because it was compatible with European legislation. He cautioned the Employer members that, in Europe, much of the burden of data collection and reporting fell on enterprises rather than governments. The Government member of Lebanon remarked that, in his country, too, enterprises were responsible for declaring all accidents. He felt that the wording of the clause was less important than that it be binding, but supported the amendment as sub-subamended. The African Government members of the Committee also supported it, but it was opposed by the Government members of Canada, India, Japan, Jordan, New Zealand and Switzerland. The Government member of Switzerland pointed out that "work-related" accidents and diseases was a much broader category than "occupational" accidents and diseases. This latter term was the one on which Swiss recording and notification were based, so a Convention that contained the text of the amendment would be very difficult for her country to ratify. She further demonstrated to the Committee that incidents could be trivial, and that recording and analysing them would be an overwhelming task. The Worker Vice-Chairperson observed that the recording and investigation of accidents and diseases would not be the responsibility of governments alone just because it was inscribed in a national occupational safety and health system, and the words "where appropriate" in the introductory phrases of paragraph 7(3) made the clause non-binding. Nonetheless, the sub- and sub-subamendments, as well as the original amendment, did not find wide support in the Committee and were withdrawn by their respective proposers.

179. The Worker Vice-Chairperson introduced an amendment to insert the words "complete and accurate" before "data" in the Office text of the clause under discussion, to give "a mechanism for the collection and analysis of complete and accurate data on occupational accidents and diseases". She immediately subamended the text to delete "complete and". The amendment was motivated by the problems of data quality currently experienced in her country and elsewhere, and by the importance of accurate data for meaningful targets and indicators. The Government member of the United Kingdom opposed the amendment as subamended, because investigators always tried to get the best data possible. The Employer members agreed, noting that the accuracy of data could not be known at the time of collection, but only after analysis. The Government member of Senegal, speaking on behalf of the African Government members of the Committee, also opposed the amendment as subamended, and it was withdrawn.

180. The Government members of Austria, Belgium, Czech Republic, Estonia, Finland, France, Germany, Greece, Ireland, Luxembourg, Norway, Netherlands, Poland, Portugal, Slovenia, Spain, Sweden and United Kingdom submitted an amendment to add the words "according to relevant ILO references" after the word "diseases" at the end of the clause (7(3)(d)). The Government member of Luxembourg, in introducing the amendment, immediately subamended it to improve the readability of the amended clause by modifying the qualifying phrase and placing it elsewhere in the clause, to give "a mechanism, taking into account relevant ILO references, for the collection and analysis of data on occupational accidents and diseases". In response to a question from the Worker Vice-Chairperson, he indicated that "relevant ILO references" meant documents such as the Protocol of 2002 to Convention No. 155, which dealt with recording, notification and national statistics. The Employer members supported the amendment as subamended. The Worker members felt uncomfortable with the term "references" and proposed a sub-subamendment to replace the word with "instruments". On being assured by the representative of the Secretary-General that "instruments" would be an appropriate term, the Government member of Luxembourg supported the sub-subamendment on behalf of the proposers of the original amendment.

181. The Employer Vice-Chairperson supported the text as further subamended, as did the Government members of Argentina, speaking on behalf of the Government members of the Committee member States of MERCOSUR, Ecuador, India, Russian Federation and Thailand. The amendment was accepted as sub-subamended.

182. The Worker Vice-Chairperson submitted an amendment to insert "provisions for" before "collaboration" in paragraph (3)(e), explaining that these were only for editorial reasons. The Employer Vice-Chairperson and several Government members supported the amendment, and it was accepted.

183. The Employer Vice-Chairperson submitted an amendment to replace the words "employment injury insurance scheme" in paragraph (7)(e) with the words "insurance schemes covering occupational safety and health", saying that this addition would help to cover all insurance schemes dealing with occupational safety and health. The Government member of Luxembourg, speaking on behalf of the Government members of the Committee Member States of the European Union and Norway, subamended the text by adding the word "relevant" before "insurance schemes covering occupational safety and health". This text as subamended was supported by the Employer Vice-Chairperson and the Worker Vice-Chairperson and was accepted.

184. The Government member of Luxembourg withdrew an amendment that covered the same issue as the previous one.

185. The Government member of the Republic of Korea, seconded by the Government member of Thailand, introduced an amendment to insert a new clause after paragraph (3)(e), as follows: "support mechanisms for a progressive improvement of occupational safety and health conditions in small-and medium-sized enterprises." He explained that it was necessary to pay particular attention to small-and medium-sized enterprises, since the majority of accidents occurred in such enterprises, their numbers were increasing, and they lacked a systematic approach to managing occupational safety and health. The Employer Vice-Chairperson proposed a subamendment to insert the word "micro" before "small", since all three terms were in common usage. The Worker Vice-Chairperson and several Government members supported the amendment as subamended and it was accepted.

186. A second amendment submitted by the Government of the Republic of Korea, seconded by the Government member of Thailand, was withdrawn.

187. The Worker Vice-Chairperson introduced an amendment to insert, after point 7, an annex with the same content as the present annex to the Recommendation. She explained that if one of the aims of the Convention were to promote greater levels of ratification of occupational safety and health Conventions, it would be helpful to list relevant instruments in an annex to the Convention. She considered that Governments ratifying this Convention would not be bound to ratifying the listed Conventions because they were contained in an annex. The Employer Vice-Chairperson opposed the amendment, saying that the main purpose of having annexes in Conventions was to place text there that would otherwise make the Conventions too cumbersome. He also considered that annexes were integral parts of Conventions and therefore there would be an obligation on governments ratifying this Convention to also ratify the other listed Conventions. The Worker Vice-Chairperson clarified that the intention was not to create binding obligations on the governments but to

be helpful. Given that there might be legal consequences from having such a list in an annex to the Convention, she withdrew the amendment.

188. Point 7 was adopted as amended.

Point 8

189. The Worker Vice-Chairperson introduced an amendment to insert, after the new heading I, a new first point, as follows: "In giving effect to the measures to promote the national policy for occupational safety and health referred to in points ... above, Members should consult with and promote the active participation of employers, workers and their representatives and relevant government authorities and bodies." She explained that this amendment was one of three which the Workers' group were submitting so as to insert elements of national policy in the Recommendation. She recalled the agreement at earlier sittings to include provisions for a national policy in the Convention and considered that parallel aspects should be included in the Recommendations. The amendment underlined the need for broad consultations with employers, workers and other authorities and bodies when drafting the policy. The Employer Vice-Chairperson opposed the amendment, saying that provisions for such consultation were adequately covered in the Convention and did not need repeating in the Recommendation. The Government member of the United States also opposed the amendment, recalling the provisions on national policy in Convention No. 155, and those on tripartite involvement in Recommendation No. 164. The Government member of Luxembourg speaking on behalf of the Government members of the Committee Member States of the European Union, Norway and Romania, also opposed the amendment for similar reasons, as did the Government member of Senegal, speaking on behalf of the African Government members of the Committee. The Worker Vice-Chairperson withdrew the amendment, but added that she would still encourage the inclusion of elements on national policy in the Recommendation.

190. The Worker Vice-Chairperson submitted an amendment to insert, after the new heading I, a new second point, as follows: "In taking steps referred to in point ... above, to promote and advance at all levels the rights of workers to a safe and healthy working environment, Members should ensure that promotional activities are developed with the participation of representative organizations of employers and workers and are directed, in particular, to promotion of occupational safety and health at the level of the workplace." She explained that this amendment also aimed at introducing elements of national policy in the Recommendation, in particular the rights of workers to a safe and healthy working environment. The Employer Vice-Chairperson opposed the amendment for the same reasons that the previous amendment was opposed. The Government member of Luxembourg, speaking on behalf of the Government members of the Committee Member States of the European Union, Norway and Romania, opposed the amendment for the same reasons as before, as did the Government member of the United Kingdom speaking on behalf of the Government members of the IMEC group present in the Committee, and the Government member of Senegal, speaking on behalf of the African Government members of the Committee. The Worker Vice-Chairperson then withdrew the amendment.

191. The Worker Vice-Chairperson introduced an amendment to insert, after the new heading I, a new third point, as follows:

> The policy should be based on the responsibilities, duties and rights of governments, employers and workers, inter alia:
>
> (a) governments' responsibility to ensure enforcement of legislation;
>
> (b) employers' responsibility to ensure a healthy and safe working environment, carry out appropriate risk assessments in relation to safety and health, ensure adequate and

appropriate training, provide workers with protective personal equipment when there is no other way to ensure their safety and health and to take immediate steps to stop any operation where there is an imminent and serious danger to safety and health and to evacuate workers as appropriate;

(c) workers and their representatives rights:

(i) to be informed and consulted on safety and health matters;

(ii) to participate in the application, review and development of safety and health matters;

(d) workers' duty to comply with prescribed safety and health measures and to cooperate with employers in order for employers to comply with their own duties and responsibilities.

192. The Worker Vice-Chairperson explained that the amendment aimed at including the basis for a national policy and giving more guidance to the member States on the issues. Acknowledging the duplication, she felt that this was needed to highlight the links between the two instruments, and to amplify point 6 of the Convention. The Employer Vice-Chairperson opposed the amendment, pointing out the duplication and saying that other aspects of the amendment were inappropriate – for example, the responsibility of Governments was more than just ensuring the enforcement of legislation. Further, responsibilities, duties and rights were already covered in other Conventions. The Government member of Luxembourg, speaking on behalf of the Government members of the Committee Member States of the European Union, Norway and Romania, opposed the amendment, as did the Government member of the United Kingdom, speaking on behalf of the rest of the Government members of the IMEC group. The Government member of China said that the Convention and the Recommendation were part of an integrated approach and that repetition between them was not necessary, and he opposed the amendment. The Worker Vice-Chairperson was surprised to see so much opposition to including guidance about such an important matter in the Recommendation, but accepted it and withdrew the amendment.

193. The Worker Vice-Chairperson withdrew the amendment, objecting that the Committee's rejection of amendments to the Convention text on the grounds that it was binding on member States was no reason to reject amendments to the text of the projected Recommendation.

194. The Government members of Argentina, Brazil, Chile, Dominican Republic, El Salvador, Panama, Uruguay and Bolivarian Republic of Venezuela submitted an amendment to insert a new point after a new heading C.I, to read: "In formulating their national policies, member States should take into account the provisions of Article 4 of the Occupational Safety and Health Convention, 1981 (No. 155), and take steps towards ratifying the instrument." In introducing the amendment, the Government member of Uruguay thought that it was for the Recommendation to include details on how policy was to be put into practice, as stated earlier by the Worker members. The Employer members opposed the amendment as redundant, arguing that the proposed Convention already contained stronger wording in the sense of the amendment, and that it was already part of the definition of a national policy. The Worker members felt that the amendment was good and provided a sound basis for the implementation of national policy. The encouragement to ratify Convention No. 155 was important in view of the low number of ratifications of this central Convention. The African Government members of the Committee, as well as Government members of the Committee Member States of the European Union, India, Norway, Romania and the IMEC group all opposed the amendment; the Government member of Luxembourg felt that the reference to Article 4 of Convention No. 155 was redundant, as many countries could not respond to the insistence on taking steps to ratify that Convention. The Government member of Uruguay withdrew the amendment,

expressing regret at the Committee's failure to give the proposed instrument more substance.

195. The Worker Vice-Chairperson reported that consultations with the Legal Adviser had provided reassurance that referring to other instruments in a Convention or Recommendation posed no legal problem, nor did including in an instrument an encouragement to ratify Conventions.

196. The Worker members withdrew an amendment that would have inserted a new heading: "I. Promoting the principles of national policy"; nothing remained to which the heading would have applied.

197. The Government member of Brazil withdrew a similar amendment to insert a "policy" heading, as submitted by the Government members of Argentina, Brazil, Chile, Dominican Republic, El Salvador, Panama, Uruguay and Bolivarian Republic of Venezuela. She reminded the Committee that the proposed Recommendation was now inconsistent with the proposed Convention, because a new heading and paragraph on policy had been adopted in the latter while there was nothing in the former. She hoped that some attention could be given to filling this gap before the second reading of the proposed instruments at the next International Labour Conference.

198. The Government members of Argentina, Brazil, Chile, Dominican Republic, Panama, Uruguay and Bolivarian Republic of Venezuela submitted an amendment to invert the order of the sections of the proposed Recommendation so that "National System" preceded "National Programme". This reflected the consensus on the structure of the proposed Convention. The amendment was accepted without discussion.

199. To be consistent with previous decisions, the Worker members withdrew two amendments to insert the word "action" before "programme" in the expression "national programme" in the title and first line of point 8.

200. The Government members of Argentina, Brazil, Chile, El Salvador, Panama, Uruguay and Bolivarian Republic of Venezuela withdrew an amendment to delete point 8 entirely, in favour of a less radical amendment submitted by the Government member of Norway and the Government members of the Committee Member States of the European Union.

201. The Government members of Austria, Belgium, Czech Republic, Denmark, Estonia, Finland, France, Germany, Greece, Ireland, Italy, Luxembourg, Norway, Netherlands, Poland, Portugal, Slovenia, Sweden, Spain and United Kingdom, introduced an amendment which would delete the text "such as professional associations of occupational safety and health", that followed "interested parties". The proposers wished to avoid constraining the interpretation of "interested parties" with an example. The amendment was supported by the Employer and Worker members, and was adopted.

202. As a result, two amendments bearing on the deleted text fell; one had been submitted by the Government members of the Bahamas, Barbados, Jamaica, Suriname, and Trinidad and Tobago, the other by the Worker members.

203. The Worker members submitted an amendment to insert a new point after point 8, enumerating workplace prevention activities that could be part of a national programme. They were motivated by a desire to give more substance to the proposed instrument. The Employer Vice-Chairperson opposed the amendment on the grounds that it repeated elements of Recommendation No. 164, and could be difficult for some countries to implement. The Government member of Luxembourg, speaking on behalf of the Government members of the Committee Member States of the European Union, Norway and Romania, also opposed the amendment as weighing down the proposed instrument with specifics when the relevant idea had already been expressed in point 10 of the proposed Conclusions. The Government member of the United Kingdom, speaking on behalf of the Government members of the IMEC group present in the Committee, agreed that the issue of workplace promotion had been dealt with adequately in the proposed Convention, and opposed the amendment. The Worker Vice-Chairperson withdrew the amendment, protesting that the Committee's refusal to include more substantive provisions would leave the proposed instrument an empty shell.

204. Point 8 was adopted as amended.

Point 9

205. To be consistent with previous decisions, the Worker members withdrew an amendment to insert the word "action" before "programme" in the expression "national programme" in the first line of point 9.

206. The Government members of Cameroon, Côte d'Ivoire, Guinea, Kenya, Lesotho, Malawi, Namibia, Niger, Senegal and South Africa submitted an amendment to replace the words "associated, where appropriate" with "harmonized" in point 9, to give: "National programmes on occupational safety and health should be harmonized with other national programmes and plans, such as those relating to economic development." They felt that this strengthened the provision. The Worker members proposed a subamendment, to replace "harmonized" by "coordinated", because in many places "harmonized" implied a very close alignment that might not be appropriate in the present context. The Employer members proposed a sub-subamendment to restore the words "where appropriate" after "coordinated". Both proposals were supported by the African Government members of the Committee, and in the absence of opposition from other members of the Committee the amendment as sub- and sub-subamended was accepted.

207. The Government members of Austria, Belgium, Czech Republic, Denmark, Estonia, Finland, France, Germany, Greece, Ireland, Italy, Luxembourg, Norway, Netherlands, Poland, Portugal, Slovenia, Spain, Sweden and United Kingdom submitted an amendment to delete the rest of the text after the word "plans", again to avoid constraining the interpretation of the point by giving an example. The Employer members opposed the amendment, because economic development was such an important issue, particularly for developing countries. The Worker members agreed and likewise opposed the amendment. It was withdrawn by the Government member of Luxembourg.

208. The Worker members submitted an amendment to expand the linkage of occupational safety and health with other programmes and plans by inserting the words "public health and" before "economic development". This was supported by the Employer members, and in the absence of objection by Government members was accepted.

209. Point 9 was adopted as amended.

Point 10

210. To be consistent with previous decisions, the Worker members withdrew an amendment to insert the word "action" before "programme" in the expression "national programme" in the first line of point 10.

211. The Employer members submitted an amendment to replace the words ", and without prejudice to their obligations under Conventions which they have ratified, Members should

take into account the international labour Conventions and Recommendations listed in the annex." with the words: "Members should, as appropriate, give due regard to relevant ILO instruments on occupational safety and health." On introducing the amendment, the Employer Vice-Chairperson immediately subamended it to insert "the principles of the" before "relevant". This was felt to be in harmony with previous decisions, and to eliminate legalistic wording. The Worker members strongly opposed the amendment, on the grounds that it diluted the Office text. They held that it was not just legal jargon to recall countries' obligations, and the annex provided important guidance.

212. The Government member of Canada supported the amendment as subamended. The Government member of Luxembourg suggested a compromise sub-subamendment: to add "listed in the annex" to the end of the amended text. The Employer members supported the sub-subamendment. The Worker members proposed a sub-sub-subamendment, to restore the words ", and without prejudice to their obligations under Conventions which they have ratified", to give due attention to the rights of workers.

213. The Employer Vice-Chairperson opposed the sub-sub-subamendment, firstly because the introduction of "rights" was inappropriate as this was just a repetition, and secondly because he questioned the basis of reintroducing the "without prejudice" part. He asked how it was possible for governments not to fulfil the obligations of a Convention that they had ratified. The Government member of Luxembourg, speaking on behalf of the Government members of the Committee Member States of the European Union and Romania, also opposed the text as most recently amended, as did the Government member of Canada, but the Government member of Argentina, speaking on behalf of the Government members of the Committee member States of MERCOSUR and the Bolivarian Republic of Venezuela, supported it. After some further clarification of Government members' views, the sub-sub-subamendment was withdrawn.

214. The text as sub-subamended was still unacceptable to the Worker Vice-Chairperson, who preferred the original Office text, as did the Government member of Senegal, speaking on behalf of the African Government members of the Committee. The Government member of Argentina, speaking also on behalf of the Government members of the Committee member States of MERCOSUR and the Bolivarian Republic of Venezuela, also opposed the sub-subamendment, preferring the original Office text, as did the Government members of Thailand and Lebanon. The Government member of Luxembourg, speaking on behalf of the Government members of the Committee Member States of the European Union and Romania, supported the sub-subamended text, as did the Government member of the United Kingdom, speaking also on behalf of the Government members of the IMEC group present in the Committee. The Government member of the United Kingdom proposed to amend the text again by adding the words "and content of" after the word "principles". After some discussion, it became clear that this further amendment had no support because it added little to the original text, and it was withdrawn. More and more support was eventually given to the original Office text and the subamendments and the original amendment were withdrawn.

215. The Government member of the United States, speaking on behalf of the Government members of Australia, Canada, Netherlands, Switzerland and United Kingdom, introduced an amendment to delete the words "listed in the annex" in the fourth line of point 10, on the grounds that a list of Conventions and Recommendations would be often amended or augmented, and that the phrase was superfluous. The Government member of Switzerland supported the amendment for the same reasons, adding that updated Conventions and Recommendations were available through the ILO web site. The Worker Vice-Chairperson opposed the amendment, saying that the annex would usefully indicate the major occupational safety and health Conventions and Recommendations and that their updating should not cause difficulties for governments since the list was in a Recommendation. The

Government member of Senegal, speaking on behalf of the African Government members of the Committee, agreed and opposed the amendment, preferring the original Office text. The Government member of Luxembourg, speaking on behalf of the Government members of the Committee Member States of the European Union and Romania, opposed the amendment for the same reasons, as did the Government member of Brazil, speaking on behalf of the Government members of the Committee member States of MERCOSUR and the Bolivarian Republic of Venezuela. The Employer Vice-Chairperson agreed that the original Office text was helpful and therefore opposed the amendment. The amendment was withdrawn.

216. The Government member of the United Kingdom, speaking also on behalf of the Government members of Australia, Belgium, Canada, Czech Republic, France, Germany, Hungary, Ireland, Italy, Japan, Luxembourg, Netherlands, New Zealand, San Marino, Switzerland and United States, submitted an amendment to insert the words "principles of the relevant" after the words "take into account the" in the third line of point 10. The amendment had the support of the Government members of Austria, Poland, Spain and Sweden, and the remaining Committee Member States of the European Union and the IMEC group present in the Committee. The Government member of the United Kingdom explained that these words were needed so as to give more flexibility in the text of the Recommendation and to make ratification of the Convention easier. The Government member of Mexico supported the amendment for the same reasons, as did the Employer Vice-Chairperson. The Worker Vice-Chairperson opposed the amendment, however, preferring the Office text, which she considered to be stronger, adding that this point related to formulating national occupational safety and health programmes and not to ratifying the Convention. The Government member of the Russian Federation also opposed the amendment, preferring the Office text, as did the Government member of Senegal, speaking on behalf of the African Government members of the Committee, for the same reasons. The Government member of Brazil, speaking on behalf of the Government members of the Committee member States of MERCOSUR, Ecuador and Bolivarian Republic of Venezuela, also opposed the amendment, preferring the Office text, as did the Government members of China, Lebanon and Thailand. The amendment was withdrawn.

217. The Worker Vice-Chairperson withdrew an amendment to insert the words "and relevant reports of other UN agencies, such as the World Health Organization" after the word "annex" at the end of point 10.

218. Point 10 was adopted as amended.

Point 11

219. The Worker Vice-Chairperson submitted an amendment to replace the words "maintaining and progressively developing" with the words "maintaining, progressively developing and periodically reviewing" in the first line of point 11, so as to be consistent with the Convention. The Employer Vice-Chairperson supported the amendment as did several governments, and the amendment was accepted.

220. The Worker Vice-Chairperson submitted an amendment to delete the text after "Members" in the second line, and to insert the following text:

should:

(1) consult with, and promote the active participation of, employers, workers and their representatives and relevant governmental institutions, including public health authorities;

(2) ensure compliance with national laws and regulations, including adequate and appropriate systems of inspection;

(3) take steps to ratify and promote the effective implementation of the Occupational Safety and Health Convention, 1981 (No. 155), and other ILO Conventions listed in the Annex to this Recommendation;

(4) periodically review and, as appropriate, update, on a tripartite basis, national laws and regulations on occupational safety and health giving priority to emerging hazards such as ergonomic, biological and work-related psychosocial hazards.

221. The Worker Vice-Chairperson then subamended the text in paragraph (2) above to read: "ensure that mechanisms of compliance referred to in point 7(2)(c) include" instead of "ensure compliance with national laws and regulations, including", and the text in paragraph (3) above to delete "take steps to ratify and", and again in paragraph (3) to insert "relevant" before the words "ILO Conventions". She explained that the intention was to provide further guidance on the above matters and to give priority to emerging hazards such as those mentioned above. The Employer Vice-Chairperson opposed the amendment as subamended, stating that it was repetitive and inappropriate, and that the reference to Convention No. 155 was tantamount to recommending its ratification. While reviewing legislation on a tripartite basis could be appropriate to most countries, updating legislation on such a basis might not be. There was also much debate as to what emerging hazards actually were in each country and this should not be resolved at a global level. The Government member of China also opposed the amendment, preferring the Office text, and the Government member of Senegal, speaking on behalf of the African Government members of the Committee, also opposed it, saying that it would make obligations on governments heavier and make the instrument harder to ratify. The Government member of the United Kingdom, speaking on behalf of the Government members of the Committee Member States of the European Union and of the IMEC group present in the Committee, opposed the amendment and pointed out that the European Union had recently adopted a non-binding agreement on psychosocial hazards. The Government member of Lebanon also opposed the amendment, preferring the Office text. The Worker Vice-Chairperson withdrew the amendment, hoping that it would be possible to return to these issues at the next meeting of the Committee on Safety and Health in 2006, and that discussions would address the issue of how to promote occupational safety and health and relevant ILO instruments.

222. The Government member of Uruguay, speaking also on behalf of the Government members of Argentina, Brazil, Chile, Dominican Republic, Panama and Bolivarian Republic of Venezuela, withdrew an amendment to replace the text that follows the words "Members may" with "create mechanisms for coordinating the competent government bodies, and the conditions needed for them to function effectively, in order to enhance their combined action".

223. The Government member of Luxembourg, speaking also on behalf of the Government members of Austria, Belgium, Czech Republic, Denmark, Estonia, Finland, France, Germany, Greece, Ireland, Italy, Netherlands, Norway, Poland, Portugal, Slovenia, Spain, Sweden and United Kingdom, introduced an amendment to delete the rest of the sentence after the words "interested parties" in the third line. He said that their intention was to ensure that the process of consultation referred to here remain as open as possible, and was not just focused on professional associations of occupational safety and health. The Employer Vice-Chairperson supported the amendment, as did the Worker Vice-Chairperson. The Government member of Senegal, speaking on behalf of the African Government members of the Committee, Brazil, speaking on behalf of the Government members of the Committee member States of MERCOSUR, and China, all supported the amendment for the same reasons, and it was accepted.

224. Point 11 was adopted as amended.

New point after point 11

225. The Worker Vice-Chairperson introduced an amendment so as to insert a new point after point 11, to read as follows: "With a view to reducing occupational accidents, diseases and deaths, the national system should provide appropriate measures for the protection of workers in high-risk sectors and of vulnerable workers including workers in the informal economy, migrant and young workers." She said that their intention was to focus on those sectors and groups which faced specific risks and had high rates of fatalities, injuries and illness, and to recommend that national systems focus on these high-risk sectors, particularly construction, mining and agriculture, in order to reduce injuries and deaths. The Employer Vice-Chairperson remarked that the definition of "vulnerable workers" varied from one country to another, but he supported the concept of the amendment.

226. The Government member of Argentina, speaking on behalf of the Government members of the Committee member States of MERCOSUR and the Bolivarian Republic of Venezuela, supported the amendment, observing that the informal economy accounted for over 50 per cent of workers in many ILO member States, including Latin American ones. The informal economy, migrant workers and those in high-risk sectors were indeed a priority for national occupational safety and health systems. The Government member of India agreed and also supported the amendment, as did the Government members of Mexico and the Philippines, both of whom mentioned the plight of migrant workers in particular. The Government member of Senegal, speaking on behalf of the African Government members of the Committee, strongly supported the amendment. The Government member of Luxembourg, speaking on behalf of the Government members of the Committee Member States of the European Union, was also concerned about workers in high-risk sectors, but thought that such a list could not be comprehensive, so he proposed a subamendment to delete all the text after the words "vulnerable workers". However, the Worker Vice-Chairperson considered it very important to include these groups, so she subamended the text by adding "such as workers in the informal economy, migrant and young workers". This was acceptable to the Committee Member States of the European Union, but the Employer Vice-Chairperson was concerned that regular workers were excluded. He therefore submitted a sub-subamendment to insert, after the words "the protection of" in the second line, the words "all workers, in particular". The Worker Vice-Chairperson supported this sub-subamendment, as did several Government members.

227. The new point after point 11 was adopted as amended.

Point 12

228. The Worker members submitted an amendment to insert the words "awareness in the workplace and" after the word "raise" in clause (a) of point 12, because the Office text spoke only of raising public awareness, while it was essential to raise awareness of occupational safety and health issues in the workplace as well. The Employer members opposed the amendment. They agreed with the need for occupational safety and health awareness in the workplace, but did not feel that national authorities should be held responsible for it. The Worker members replied that the text spoke of national campaigns, and reminded the Committee that, although public awareness was important for building support for occupational safety and health programmes, the workplace was where accidents happened and so should be of the greatest importance for awareness raising.

229. The amendment was then supported by the Employer members and by the Government members of Bahrain, Lebanon, Saudi Arabia and United Arab Emirates. The Government

member of Senegal, speaking on behalf of the African Government members of the Committee, also supported the amendment on the grounds that both workers and their families needed to be made aware of risks and preventative measures. The Government member of Thailand added that public awareness campaigns were important for building the safety consciousness of students as future members of the labour force. The amendment was accepted.

230. The Government members of Austria, Belgium, Czech Republic, Denmark, Estonia, Finland, France, Germany, Greece, Ireland, Italy, Luxembourg, Norway, Netherlands, Poland, Portugal, Slovenia, Spain, Sweden and United Kingdom submitted an amendment to replace the word "as" by the word "where" before "appropriate" in the English and Spanish versions of clause 12(a). The amendment was accepted without debate.

231. The Worker members submitted an amendment to insert a new clause after 12(a), with the text: "to ensure that there are recognized mechanisms for delivery of occupational safety and health education and training, in particular for management, supervisors, workers and their representatives and government officials responsible for safety and health". The Worker Vice-Chairperson pointed out that clause 12(b) in the Office text referred to the inclusion of certain concepts in training programmes, but nowhere did the text explicitly propose the establishment of education and training programmes in the first place. In response to a question from the Chairperson about the definition of "recognized mechanisms", she subamended the amendment to delete "recognized", so that there would be no implication that some sort of obligatory certification process would be applicable to the education and training programmes. The Employer Vice-Chairperson recalled that on several occasions the Committee had shown a preference for "promote" over "ensure", and sub-subamended the clause to replace "to ensure that there are" by "to promote". This was supported by the Government member of the United Kingdom, speaking on behalf of the Government members of the IMEC group present in the Committee, China and Mexico, and finally by the Worker members. The amendment was accepted as sub-subamended.

232. The Government members of Austria, Belgium, Czech Republic, Denmark, Estonia, Finland, France, Germany, Greece, Hungary, Ireland, Italy, Luxembourg, Norway, Netherlands, Poland, Portugal, Slovenia, Spain, Sweden and United Kingdom submitted an amendment to replace the words "hazard, risk and prevention" by "occupational safety and health" in clause 12(b), to both broaden and simplify the clause. The amendment was supported by the Worker and Employer members, and accepted without debate.

233. The Worker members submitted an amendment to add four clauses after the existing clause (b). The first, "to ensure exchange of occupational safety and health statistics and data between relevant authorities, employers, workers and their representatives", was subamended by the Employer members to replace "ensure" by "facilitate" and sub-subamended by the Government member of the United Kingdom to insert "the" before exchange. The resulting text was accepted by the Committee.

234. The second clause, "to provide information and advice to employers and workers and promote or facilitate cooperation between them and their organizations with a view to eliminating hazards or reducing them", was accepted without modification.

235. The third clause, "to promote the establishment of health and safety policies and of joint safety and health committees and workers' safety representatives at the level of the workplace", was opposed by the Employer members and the Government members of India, Switzerland and United States, on the grounds that it was too prescriptive and conflicted with existing national legislation. The text was supported by the Government members of Dominican Republic, Ecuador, Norway, Romania, Bolivarian Republic of Venezuela, the Committee Member States of the European Union and the Committee

member States of MERCOSUR. The Worker Vice-Chairperson reminded the Committee that the text under discussion was a proposed Recommendation, and so as a non-binding instrument incapable of conflicting with national laws. However, she offered a subamendment to add "in accordance with national law and practice" at the end of the clause if it would make it more widely acceptable. The Government members of the African Government members of the Committee, the Bahamas, Barbados, India, Lebanon, Mexico, Jamaica, Russan Federation, Suriname, and Trinidad and Tobago, as well as the Employer members, supported the subamendment and the resulting text was accepted.

236. The fourth clause, "to address the constraints of small- and medium-sized enterprises and contractors in the monitoring of occupational safety and health policies and regulations, by establishing a system of regional safety representatives", was opposed by the Employer members as being out of place in a point that was supposed to deal with the promotion of a national preventative safety and health culture. The Government member of France offered a subamendment by way of a compromise, to replace "monitoring" by "implementation", to delete "by establishing a system of regional safety representatives" and to insert "in accordance with national law and practice". The Worker members were unwilling to abandon the concept of roving safety representatives, and sub-subamended the text to read: "to address the constraints of small- and medium-sized enterprises and contractors in the monitoring of occupational safety and health policies and regulations, by establishing a system of regional safety representatives, according to national law and practice". The Employer members could not support such a controversial concept. The Government member of the United Kingdom, speaking on behalf of the Government members of the IMEC group present in the Committee, remarked that the concept was being tested in his country, but that it would be premature to include it in the proposed instrument. He felt that in any case the subamendment of the Government member of France did not exclude a role for regional safety representatives in the promotion of a preventative safety and health culture, even if they were not mentioned explicitly. The Government member of Mexico stated that regional safety representatives were incompatible with the Mexican occupational safety and health system. After the Worker members withdrew their sub-subamendment, the Employer members agreed to support the clause proposed by the Government member of France. The Worker Vice-Chairperson then proposed a subamendment, to insert "micro-," before "small-" in recognition of the importance of this category of enterprise, as acknowledged earlier by the Committee. This met with general agreement. The Employer members proposed a subamendment to delete "and contractors", on the grounds that these could be very large enterprises. The Worker members opposed the subamendment because the proposed clause focused specifically on smaller enterprises, and it was withdrawn. The clause was accepted as subamended, and the amendment as a whole was accepted.

237. Point 12 was adopted as amended.

Point 13

238. The Government members of Australia, Austria, Belgium, Canada, Czech Republic, Denmark, Finland, France, Germany, Greece, Ireland, Italy, Japan, Luxembourg, New Zealand, Netherlands, Poland, San Marino, Spain, Sweden, Switzerland, United Kingdom and United States submitted an amendment to replace the words "based on" with "such as that set out in", referring to the Guidelines on occupational safety and health management systems, ILO-OSH 2001, in the English and Spanish texts, and insert the word "notamment" after "en se fondant" in the French text of point 13. The Government member of the United Kingdom explained that ILO-OSH 2001 was cited only as an example. The amendment was supported by the Worker and Employer members, and by the African Government members of the Committee, and was accepted.

239. The Government member of Luxembourg, speaking on behalf of the Government members of the Committee Member States of the European Union and Norway, withdrew an amendment that would have had the same effect as that just accepted.

240. Point 13 was adopted as amended.

Point 14

241. The Worker Vice-Chairperson introduced an amendment to replace the words "national systems" in the second line of paragraph 14(1) with the words "the national system, policy and programme, and the progress that has been made in achieving a safer and healthier working environment". The intention was twofold: to include the concepts of national policy and national programmes in the profile for review to be consistent with the structure of the instrument; and, through the profile, to look at progress made in occupational safety and health. She pointed out that the language used was the same as that in the Convention. The Employer Vice-Chairperson did not object to the amendment, but preferred the wording of a similar but broader one submitted by a number of European Government members and scheduled for discussion later. The Worker Vice-Chairperson responded with a subamendment to replace "the national system, policy and programme" by the relevant phrase from the amendment cited by the Employer Vice-Chairperson: "the existing situation on occupational safety and health". The Employer Vice-Chairperson supported the amendment as subamended, as did the Government members of Brazil (speaking on behalf of the Government members of the Committee member States of MERCOSUR), China, Lebanon, Luxembourg (speaking on behalf of the Government members of the Committee Member States of the European Union, Norway and Romania), Namibia (speaking on behalf of the African Government members of the Committee), Papua New Guinea and Thailand. The amendment was thus adopted as subamended.

242. The Government member of Luxembourg withdrew an amendment submitted by the Government members of Austria, Belgium, Czech Republic, Denmark, Estonia, Finland, France, Germany, Greece, Hungary, Ireland, Italy, Luxembourg, Norway, Netherlands, Poland, Portugal, Slovenia, Spain, Sweden and United Kingdom, because its content had been taken over in the amendment just adopted.

243. The Government member of Luxembourg, speaking also on behalf of the Government members of Austria, Belgium, Czech Republic, Denmark, Estonia, Finland, France, Germany, Greece, Hungary, Ireland, Italy, Norway, Netherlands, Poland, Portugal, Slovenia, Spain, Sweden and United Kingdom, introduced an amendment to replace the word "regularly" in the first line of paragraph 14(1) by the words "when necessary". He explained that "regularly" could mean every week or every ten years, and that frequent regular updates could be unnecessary. The Worker Vice-Chairperson opposed the amendment, even if no periodicity was stated in the Office text. "Regularly" implied a systematic approach, and emphasized the ongoing nature of the updates. The Employer Vice-Chairperson supported the amendment; "when necessary" could imply "regularly", but not vice versa. The Government member of Luxembourg subamended the amendment by adding the word "systematically" before "when necessary", in deference to the Worker members' concerns. The Worker Vice-Chairperson continued to prefer "regularly", feeling that an appropriate periodicity could be determined on a tripartite basis in any given country; the Worker members agreed with the rest of the Committee that the proposed instrument should not authorize unnecessary updates. However, she hoped to find compromise wording, and proposed to sub-subamend the text by replacing "systematically" by "periodically"

244. The Employer Vice-Chairperson thereupon proposed a sub-sub-subamendment: "when necessary, on a regular basis,". The Worker Vice-Chairperson objected that this

formulation did not require a national profile to be prepared or updated at all, and the sub-sub-subamendment was withdrawn. After the Government member of Lebanon expressed a preference for the Office text, the Government member of Luxembourg withdrew the amendment.

245. The Government member of Luxembourg, speaking also on behalf of the Government members of Austria, Belgium, Czech Republic, Denmark, Spain, Estonia, Finland, France, Germany, Greece, Ireland, Italy, Norway, Netherlands, Poland, Portugal, Slovenia, Sweden and United Kingdom, submitted an amendment which proposed in point 14(2) to delete the entire paragraph following the word "information" in the second line and to replace it by the following words "based on guidelines issued by the ILO. A national occupational safety and health profile could:" followed by five new clauses:

 (a) be prepared at the country level through a process that involves all the national competent and other designated authorities concerned with the various aspects of OSH, and more importantly the most representative organizations of employers and workers;

 (b) include basic data on all parameters that may affect the sound management of OSH, at both the national and enterprise levels, including available legislative framework, enforcement and implementation mechanisms and infrastructures, workforce distribution, human and financial resources devoted to OSH, OSH initiatives at the enterprise level and level of protection;

 (c) provide practical information on ongoing activities at the country level (e.g. activities related to the implementation of international agreements, ongoing and planned technical assistance projects);

 (d) enable a country to identify gaps in and needs for further development of existing legal, institutional, administrative and technical infrastructure related to the sound management of OSH, taking into account relevant ILO Conventions, Recommendations and codes of practice;

 (e) provide a means for improved coordination among all parties interested in OSH. The process of preparing the profile itself may serve as a starting point for improved coordination and should facilitate communications and an improved understanding of the potential problems and activities being undertaken within the country.

246. He immediately subamended the amendment in its French version for better correspondence with the English version: "les directives" was replaced by "des directives" and "devrait" was replaced by "pourrait". The first two lines of point 14(2) would thus read "basées sur des directives du BIT. Un profil national de la sécurité et de la santé au travail pourrait:". He then subamended the contents of the amendment by deleting its five clauses and adding after the word "could" the words "include the elements of paragraph 44 of Report IV(1) of the ILO". As a result, point 14(2) as subamended read: "In addition to the elements provided for in point 7(2) and (3), the national profile on occupational safety and health should include information based on guidelines issued by the ILO. A national occupational safety and health profile could include the elements of paragraph 44 of Report IV(1) of the ILO."

247. The Government member of Luxembourg explained that the five clauses in the amendment as originally submitted had been taken from paragraph 44 of the report that had been circulated to member States with a questionnaire prior to the drafting of the present proposed Conclusions. He said that the original Office text with nine clauses had seemed long and tedious, but still not complete. The subamendment simplified the text and made it more readable by simply referring to the report rather than quoting it.

248. The Worker Vice-Chairperson objected to the reference to an ILO report to which many people might not have access. She reminded the Committee members that previous discussions on references to ILO Conventions and Recommendations had met with

resistance, and opposed the amendment as subamended. She asked the secretariat how the ILO could provide the guidelines referred to in the amendment. The representative of the Secretary-General replied that the question should be directed to the Government members who submitted the amendment, to know whether they were thinking of some existing reference, such as the Protocol to Convention No. 155 or a code of practice, or something to be produced in the future; as a matter of principle, an instrument should not refer to something that did not yet exist. For example, the Office could provide guidance on an Internet site, but that site did not exist yet and the Committee should not make reference to it in the proposed instrument.

249. The Employer Vice-Chairperson also did not think that it was appropriate for a Recommendation to refer to a report. He noted that the amendment and subamendment had eliminated the words "where appropriate", which the Worker members also favoured.

250. With both the Worker and Employer members preferring the Office text, the Government member of Luxembourg withdrew the amendment.

251. The Government members of Argentina, Brazil, Chile, Dominican Republic, Panama, Uruguay and Bolivarian Republic of Venezuela withdrew an amendment to delete "and enterprise" from clause (a) of point 14(2).

252. The Government member of the Dominican Republic introduced an amendment submitted by the Government members of Argentina, Brazil, Chile, Dominican Republic, Panama, Uruguay and Bolivarian Republic of Venezuela, which proposed to insert a new clause after point 14(2)(b): "updating of the list of occupational and work-related diseases;". She indicated that the proposers wished to have a constant process of updating, to facilitate research, and felt that the amendment complemented the clauses of the Office text. The Worker Vice-Chairperson supported the amendment. The Employer Vice-Chairperson questioned the expression "the list". He noted that some countries had lists of occupational diseases and some others did not. In any case, a list of occupational diseases seemed more appropriate as a component of a national programme, not part of a national profile.

253. The Government member of Tunisia, in support of the proposed amendment, said that in his country national legislation required that such an updated list exist. Updating was important because new occupational diseases were being identified, and workers were being exposed to new toxic substances. The Government member of Senegal supported the amendment, speaking on behalf of the African Government members of the Committee. She expressed appreciation for the fact that the words "where appropriate" would cover the case of countries without official lists of occupational diseases, but asked the proponents of the amendment how occupational diseases were different from work-related diseases.

254. The Chairperson requested clarification as to how a process or activity like updating a list could be considered a part of a national profile.

255. The Government member of the Dominican Republic replied to the Government member of Senegal that the term "occupational disease" was used when referring to those diseases on the official lists of occupational diseases in countries. She said that there were many other diseases that might be caused by work but that were not on such lists. She gave the example of backache, which was not on her country's list of occupational diseases but which could be work-related.

256. In response to the Chairperson's question, the Government member of Brazil, speaking on behalf of the Government members of the Committee member States of MERCOSUR, subamended the amendment. The new text read: "lists of occupational diseases and work-related diseases". She said that the updating process was already covered in point 14(1).

257. The Government member of the United Kingdom, speaking on behalf of the Government members of the IMEC group present in the Committee, opposed the amendment as subamended. He asserted that it was redundant in view of the reference to statistics in clause (f), since the compilation of statistics implied the existence of lists. The Worker Vice-Chairperson supported the amendment as subamended. She pointed out that (f) referred only to statistics for occupational diseases, but they might or might not include information on other work-related diseases. She reminded the Committee that such lists were also very important as a basis for compensation. The Employer Vice-Chairperson opposed the amendment as subamended because it made point 14(2) say that a national profile should contain information on lists of diseases, which did not seem sensible. The Government member of Mexico also opposed the amendment as subamended. He explained that no distinction was made in his country's legislation between occupational and work-related diseases, and that making a distinction in this instrument would engender a long political process. The Government member of Senegal, speaking on behalf of the African Government members of the Committee, insisted that lists were different from statistics, and supported the amendment as subamended. The Government member of China explained that in his country the occupational diseases list does not include all diseases related to work. He reminded the Committee that the ILO had updated its list of occupational diseases in 2002, and that member States, depending on their economic and social development, could do the same. The list was used both for compensation and for compilation of statistics. He supported the amendment as subamended.

258. A straw poll showed that most Government members were not in favour of the amendment as subamended, and the Government member of the Dominican Republic withdrew the amendment.

259. The Employer Vice-Chairperson introduced an amendment to insert the words "including promotional initiatives" after the word "structure" in paragraph (2)(c), because such initiatives were important and it would be helpful to hear of progress in national profiles. The Worker Vice-Chairperson supported the amendment, there were no objections from Government members, and it was adopted.

260. The Worker Vice-Chairperson submitted an amendment to insert the words "safety and health officers, physicians, hygienists and safety and health representatives" instead of the words "officers, occupational physicians and hygienists" in the second line of paragraph (2)(e). She subsequently subamended the text to refer to "occupational physicians". She explained that the amendment would clarify the Office text and include safety and health representatives who played a very important role at the workplace. The Employer Vice-Chairperson opposed it because he considered that the term "safety and health representatives" was too vague and that it would not practicable to provide national estimates of their numbers. The Government member of the United Kingdom, speaking on behalf of the Government members of the IMEC group present in the Committee, opposed the amendment for the same reasons, adding that one could extend the list to other specialists, such as ergonomists, occupational psychologists and safety engineers, and that the professions listed were only indicative. The Government member of Senegal, speaking on behalf of the African Government members of the Committee, also opposed the amendment for the same reasons, and it was withdrawn.

261. The Government member of Brazil, speaking also on behalf of the Government members of Argentina, Chile, Dominican Republic, Panama, Uruguay and Bolivarian Republic of Venezuela, withdrew an amendment to replace clause (f) in paragraph (2) with the words: "statistics on incidents, occupational accidents and work-related diseases".

262. The Employer Vice-Chairperson submitted an amendment to insert the words "in the field of occupational safety and health" after the words "policies and programmes" in

paragraph (2)(g). He immediately subamended it so as to refer only to "occupational safety and health". The Worker Vice-Chairperson supported the amendment as subamended, as did Government members, and it was adopted.

263. The Government member of Barbados, speaking also on behalf of the Government members of the Bahamas, Jamaica, Suriname, and Trinidad and Tobago, submitted an amendment to insert a new clause "financial and budgetary resources" after clause (2)(i). He considered that such information was important and should be included in a national profile. The Worker Vice-Chairperson agreed with the amendment but subamended it to read "financial and budgetary resources with regard to occupational safety and health", adding that such resources were an important indicator of national commitment to occupational safety and health. The Government member of Senegal, speaking on behalf of the African Government members of the Committee, supported the subamended text for the above reasons, as did the Government member of Brazil, speaking on behalf of the Government members of the Committee member States of MERCOSUR, adding that the information was also useful in sensitizing public opinion.

264. The Government members of Lebanon and Bahrain opposed the subamended text and so did the Government member of Indonesia, speaking also on behalf of the Government member of the Philippines, who said that financial resources for occupational safety and health often came from several government ministries and the private sector, and this would make them difficult to estimate. The latter speaker also referred to the words "any other relevant information" in paragraph (2)(i), which she considered sufficient to cover financial resources as well. The Government member of Bahrain, speaking also on behalf of the Government members of Saudi Arabia and the United Arab Emirates, also opposed the text as subamended.

265. The Government member of Namibia reiterated the support of the African Government members of the Committee for the amended text, and the Government member of Papua New Guinea also supported it, saying that government claims to give priority to occupational safety and health should be complemented by resource allocation. The Government member of the United Kingdom, speaking on behalf of the Government members of the IMEC group present in the Committee, said that their group members already published such information so the inclusion of the clause would not create any difficulties for them, but they were concerned only about other countries for which the clause might cause problems. However, he added that having to publish such information could act as a spur to increasing resources for occupational safety and health. Having listened to the views of the Government members, the Employer Vice-Chairperson supported the subamended text; a show of hands amongst Government members also indicated strong support for it, and it was adopted.

266. The Worker Vice-Chairperson submitted an amendment to add a new clause "mechanisms for the provision of occupational health services and the number of workers covered by such services" after clause (2)(i). She said that occupational health services were important and that it would be useful for their coverage to be articulated in national profiles. The Employer Vice-Chairperson thought that stating the number of workers covered by such services was meaningless in itself and he subamended the text to read simply "occupational health services". The Worker Vice-Chairperson subamended the text again so as to read "mechanisms for the provision of occupational health services and the coverage of workers by such services", and the Employer Vice-Chairperson supported this.

267. The Government member of the United Kingdom, speaking on behalf of the Government members of the IMEC group present in the Committee, opposed the amendment as subamended, since national profiles already had to refer to occupational health services because the latter were included in point 7(3) to which point 14 referred. Moreover, he

considered that measuring the coverage of such services was very time-consuming and did not in itself contribute to the reduction of accidents and diseases. For the same reasons, the Government member of Senegal, speaking on behalf of the African Government members of the Committee, opposed the subamended text, as did the Government member of Tunisia. The Government member of the Philippines thought that a review of the occupational health services and their coverage in her country could be useful, so she supported the text as subamended.

268. The Government member of Mexico queried how it would be possible to establish the coverage of occupational health services within the informal economy. The Worker Vice-Chairperson explained that the intention of the amendment was to provide useful information about the provision and coverage of occupational health services, and that it was only relevant for those countries where such services existed. The proposed new clause would not place further obligations on governments, as it did not require such services to be provided. However, given that the amendment would cause problems for some governments, the Employer Vice-Chairperson withdrew his support for the text as subamended, and the Worker Vice-Chairperson, also in light of the discussion, withdrew the original amendment and subamended versions.

269. Point 14 was adopted as amended.

Point 15

270. The Worker members submitted an amendment to replace the Office text of point 15 by the following:

> 15. The International Labour Organization should:
>
> (1)(a) facilitate the exchange of information on national policies, systems and programmes on occupational safety and health, including best practices and innovative approaches, and the identification of new and emerging hazards and risks in the workplace; and
>
> (b) assess the progress that has been made in achieving a safer and healthier working environment.

271. The Worker Vice-Chairperson explained that the expanded point 15 would reflect the "policy – system – programme" structure found elsewhere in the proposed instruments. The Worker members preferred "best" practices to those that were merely "good". New and emerging hazards and risks merited inclusion, and the ILO could play a valuable role in their identification. The Worker Vice-Chairperson subamended the text, to insert "and report on" after "assess" in clause (b), in order to further facilitate the sharing of information. The Organization already engaged in these activities, but the fact deserved to be put in writing.

272. In response to the question from the Chairperson, the representative of the Secretary-General confirmed that "Organization" was the appropriate word in this context, rather than "Office".

273. The Employer members opposed the amendment on the basis that a reference to "best" practice is a narrower concept than that proposed by the Office – i.e. good practices. It seemed inappropriate to give instructions to the ILO by way of a Recommendation.

274. The representative of the Secretary-General informed the Committee that there was no prohibition against including instructions to the Organization in a Recommendation, citing the Prevention of Major Industrial Accidents Recommendation, 1993 (No. 181). However, the carrying out of the instructions depended on the funding accorded by the Governing

Body of the International Labour Office and ultimately by the International Labour Conference. An alternative way to give instructions to the Organization and others was the adoption of resolutions, for which there was a well-established mechanism.

275. The Employer Vice-Chairperson expressed reassurance as to the propriety of the amendment, but remained opposed on the basis of its content, even after the Worker members submitted a subamendment to replace "best practices" with "good practices". The Government member of the United States also opposed the amendment. He noted that the competent authorities in his country were already subject to many reporting requirements, and that the amendment represented a considerable additional burden. Furthermore, the word "assess" implied that the ILO would be making value judgements about the ways different countries went about implementing the provisions of the Convention, which was unacceptable. Finally, unless some new mechanism were created the ILO had no way to assess the performance of countries that had not ratified the proposed Convention.

276. In response to a proposal from the Chairperson to discuss the two clauses of the amendment separately, the Government members of Brazil (speaking on behalf of the Government members of the Committee member States of MERCOSUR and the Bolivarian Republic of Venezuela), China, India, Luxembourg (speaking on behalf of the Government members of the Committee Member States of the European Union, Norway and Romania), Libyan Arab Jamahiriya, Russan Federation and United Kingdom (speaking on behalf of the Government members of the IMEC group present in the Committee) supported clause (a) as subamended. In view of the widespread support, the Employer members dropped their opposition and the amendment was adopted.

277. Clause (b) was supported by the Government members of the Committee Member States of the European Union, and the Government member of Lebanon, but opposed as redundant by the Government member of New Zealand. The Government member of Brazil, speaking on behalf of the Government members of the Committee member States of MERCOSUR, subamended the clause to replace "assess" by "inform on". This was supported by the Worker members, who testified that they had not intended for their original amendment to impose a new assessment mechanism. The Employer members opposed the subamendment because it did not say who was to be informed. The Government member of Switzerland opposed the clause as imposing new costs on the ILO; having chaired discussions on the Organization's budget in the Governing Body, Switzerland was fully aware of the financial constraints on the Office's activities. She also endorsed the objections of other speakers. The Government member of the United Kingdom agreed with the Government member of Switzerland in opposing the clause, asserting that money was better spent on activities than reports. The Government member of Argentina, speaking on behalf of the Government members of the Committee member States of MERCOSUR and the Bolivarian Republic of Venezuela, supported the clause, declaring that the occupational safety and health-related Conventions guaranteed workers' lives, and that monitoring their implementation should thus have high priority. The Government member of Sweden also supported the clause as subamended, although he noted that the ILO's occupational safety and health programme was already engaged in disseminating information. The Government member of France recalled the widespread support for the monitoring of programme performance that had been expressed earlier in the Committee's discussions. The African Government members of the Committee, the Government members of the Committee Member States of the European Union, except the United Kingdom, and the Government member of Algeria added their support. The Employer members thereupon withdrew their opposition, and the remainder of the amendment was adopted as subamended.

278. The Worker members submitted an amendment to add a further paragraph to point 15:

> (2) In addition, the International Labour Organization should:
>
> (a) promote the ratification and effective implementation of ILO instruments on occupational safety and health, in particular the Occupational Safety and Health Convention, 1981 (No. 155), the Occupational Health Services Convention, 1985, (No. 161), the Labour Inspection Convention, 1947 (No. 81), the Safety and Health in Construction Convention, 1988 (No. 167), the Safety and Health in Mines Convention, 1995 (No. 176), and the Safety and Health in Agriculture Convention, 2001 (No. 184);
>
> (b) give due attention to the provision of technical assistance to member States to assist them with the ratification and effective implementation of these and other Conventions listed in the Annex below.

279. The Worker Vice-Chairperson explained that the amendment was motivated by the recurring insistence of Committee members on the necessity of ratifying and implementing existing Conventions. The Employer Vice-Chairperson opposed the amendment on the grounds that it simply repeated the "job description" of the International Labour Office. The Government member of the United States objected that the International Labour Office already had a unit dedicated to monitoring ratification, and that this amendment appeared to be aimed at giving them instructions. The African Government members of the Committee, the Government members of the Committee Member States of the European Union and the Government members of Jordan, Libyan Arab Jamahiriya, Norway and Romania all opposed the amendment as an unnecessary restatement of basic tasks of the International Labour Office. The Worker members withdrew the amendment.

280. Point 15 was adopted as amended.

New point after point 15

281. The Government member of Uruguay introduced an amendment submitted by the Government members of Argentina, Brazil, Chile, Dominican Republic, Panama, Uruguay and Bolivarian Republic of Venezuela, to insert a new point after point 15, as follows:

> V. PROMOTION OF OCCUPATIONAL SAFETY AND HEALTH
> AT THE INTERNATIONAL LEVEL
>
> 16. The ILO and its constituents shall make very effort to ensure that the right to life enshrined in the ILO's international Conventions on occupational safety and health is included in the fundamental rights.

282. She recalled the presentation on the global toll of accidents and diseases that had been presented at the opening of the Committee's deliberations. She declared that it was unacceptable for workers to risk their lives in the creation of wealth, and incompatible with the ILO's concept of decent work as reflected in the Declaration on Fundamental Principles and Rights at Work (1998). The Employer Vice-Chairperson objected that the expression "right to life" had wide-ranging implications and different meanings in different countries that made it inadvisable to incorporate it in the present text. Further, after the Committee's insistence on casting that text in the form of a Convention supplemented by a Recommendation rather than a Declaration, it was inappropriate to now raise issues that could only be accommodated in a Declaration. The Worker Vice-Chairperson supported the amendment as a contribution to raising the profile of occupational safety and health in the International Labour Organization. The Government members of Algeria, Lebanon and Morocco likewise supported the amendment. The Government member of the United States strongly opposed the amendment because: the word "ensure" was inconsistent with decisions taken earlier by the Committee; the expression "international Conventions"

raised the question of what other kinds there were; "fundamental rights" were undefined and the term "right to life" was subject to many interpretations. The Government member of Luxembourg proposed a subamendment to delete "international" before "Conventions" and to add the phrase "as described in the core Conventions of the ILO" after "fundamental rights". A technical expert from the secretariat observed that the right to life was not articulated in any ILO instruments, nor did the notion of "core Conventions" appear in ILO standards.

283. The Worker Vice-Chairperson submitted a sub-subamendment to refer to "a right to a safe and healthy working environment" instead of "a right to life". The Employer Vice-Chairperson said that referring health and safety as a fundamental right contradicted earlier agreement in the Committee on the concept of a national preventative safety and health culture, which referred to rights in the context of corresponding responsibilities and duties, and he opposed this sub-subamendment. The Government member of Luxembourg, speaking on behalf of the Government members of the Committee Member States of the European Union, requested the Office's advice about the terms "fundamental rights" and "core Conventions". The ILO Legal Adviser explained that the terms had no agreed legal significance but had been articulated by the Office and approved by the International Labour Conference in 1998, when it adopted the ILO Declaration on Fundamental Principles and Rights at Work. At that time it was understood that the rights and principles contained in the so-called ILO core Conventions were "fundamental" only insofar as their protection was necessary for the enjoyment of the rights contained in the other ILO instruments. However, fundamental human rights had been laid down in other documents such as the Universal Declaration of Human Rights and the International Covenant on Economic, Social and Cultural Rights, rather than in ILO "core Conventions". The right to a safe and healthy working environment, encompassed in the right to life, could be inferred from these other instruments. It would therefore be meaningless to relate the right to a safe and healthy working environment, as proposed in the above sub-subamendment, to the fundamental principles and rights at work or to so-called ILO core Conventions.

284. Having heard the legal advice, the Government member of Luxembourg, speaking on behalf of the Government members of the Committee Member States of the European Union, withdrew his subamendment, but the Worker Vice-Chairperson reintroduced her sub-subamendment as a subamendment so as to refer to "a right to a safe and healthy working environment" instead of "a right to life". The Employer Vice-Chairperson agreed with the concept but considered it inappropriate to introduce it in the Recommendation, reiterating the need to have such a concept supported by corresponding responsibilities and duties. He opposed the amendment as subamended. The Government member of Tunisia also opposed it, believing that it would have been better to place such a text in the Preamble. Agreeing with this, the Government member of Senegal, speaking on behalf of the African Government members of the Committee, also opposed the amendment as subamended. The Government member of Switzerland also opposed it, adding that if member States ratified the occupational safety and health Conventions, the right to a safe and healthy working environment would be enshrined in national legislation. The Government member of Luxembourg, speaking on behalf of the Government members of the Committee Member States of the European Union, also opposed the amendment for legal reasons, as did the Government member of Lebanon.

285. The Government member of Argentina, speaking also on behalf of the Government members of Brazil, Chile, Dominican Republic, Panama, Uruguay and Bolivarian Republic of Venezuela, was surprised at the degree of opposition to the amendment. He agreed that the wording of the text and its position in the instruments could be improved, but he hoped that there was no doubt about the need to attach to occupational safety and health the same degree of importance within ILO circles as was given to subjects covered

by the core Conventions. However, in view of the discussion he withdrew the amendment, noting that the issue would be brought up next year.

286. The new point after point 15 was withdrawn.

Point 16

287. The Government member of Canada, speaking also on behalf of the Government members of Australia, Netherlands, United Kingdom, Switzerland and United States, withdrew an amendment to delete point 16.

288. The Employer Vice-Chairperson submitted an amendment to replace the word "shall" in the second line with the word "may", because he considered that the former wording imposed too strong a requirement on the Governing Body. The Worker Vice-Chairperson opposed the amendment, preferring the Office text, which she understood meant that the Governing Body would adopt any list that they had reviewed and updated. The Employer Vice-Chairperson subamended his amendment to replace "shall" with "should", in keeping with the language of a Recommendation; the Worker Vice-Chairperson supported the subamended text. The representative of the Secretary-General said that the Office text reflected the usual sequence of wording in Recommendations, namely that the first word in a Paragraph was "should", followed by "shall" in following sentences. With this assurance, the Employer Vice-Chairperson withdrew his amendment.

289. Point 16 was adopted as amended.

Annex

290. The Employer Vice-Chairperson submitted an amendment to insert, after the list of Recommendations in the annex, a new section headed "III. Codes of practice", to contain the complete list of ILO codes of practice on occupational safety and health. He also submitted a subamendment to correct two errors concerning dates of publication. He stated that it would be useful to have a list of all occupational safety and health instruments together in one annex, particularly as some codes of practice were more useful than some of the older Conventions. The Worker Vice-Chairperson opposed the amendment, saying that it was inappropriate to include codes of practice, since this instrument was about national action whereas codes of practice were more relevant at the enterprise level. Moreover, the list of Conventions and Recommendations in the annex contained only those that had been deemed up to date, whereas the proposed list of codes of practice was comprehensive. The Government member of the United States opposed the amendment for the same reasons, expressing concern about the length of the annex if the amendment were adopted. The Employer Vice-Chairperson accepted that codes of practice focused on the workplace, and since the addition of such codes to the annex was not a vital matter for the Employers' group, the amendment was withdrawn.

291. The annex was adopted.

292. At its 13th sitting, the Committee adopted its report, subject to changes requested by several members, as well as the proposed Conclusions as presented at the end of the report. The Committee also adopted a resolution to place on the agenda of the next ordinary session of the International Labour Conference an item entitled "Occupational safety and health" for a second discussion with a view to the adoption of a Convention and a Recommendation.

293. Changes requested by the Employer members, the Worker members and the Government members of Argentina (on behalf of the Government members of the Committee member States of MERCOSUR), Brazil, China, El Salvador, Senegal (on behalf of the African Government members of the Committee), Switzerland, Trinidad and Tobago (on behalf of the Government members of CARICOM), the United Kingdom (on behalf of the Government members of the Group of Industrialized Market Economies [IMEC] present in the Committee and the Government members of the Committee Member States of the European Union), Uruguay and the Bolivarian Republic of Venezuela were noted and incorporated in the report. The statements attributed to the Legal Advisor in the report were verified.

294. The Director-General of the ILO, Secretary-General of the Conference, congratulated the Committee on its efficiency and productivity, and thanked the secretariat and support staff for their contribution. He particularly saluted the spirit of consensus that was shown by the holding of only one vote during two weeks of work. He declared that safety and health constituted a core element of the Decent Work Agenda, that decent work must be safe work. He recalled that occupational safety and health had been the first topic to be discussed in the context of an integrated approach to international labour standards, and that the Committee and its promotional framework Convention and Recommendation were a direct result of those discussions. He congratulated the Committee for its openness in exploring this new type of Convention, and felt that it would contribute greatly to raising public awareness of the need to put occupational safety and health higher on the world's agenda.

295. The Government member of Senegal, speaking on behalf of the African Government members of the Committee, thanked the Chairperson and the secretariat for their support to the work of the Committee, the Employer and Worker members for their spirit of collaboration, and the members of her group for their contribution. The Government member of the United Kingdom, speaking on behalf of the Government members of the Group of Industrialized Market Economies (IMEC) present in the Committee and the Government members of the Committee Member States of the European Union, echoed these sentiments, acknowledging that certain Committee members had wanted a different form of instrument while others had wanted more detailed content, but all had put the highest value on reaching consensus and moving the work of the Committee forward. The Government member of the Bolivarian Republic of Venezuela emphasized the importance of the Committee's work for improving the quality of information and training in the area of occupational safety and health, and for making everyone an active participant in the development of a preventative safety and health culture.

296. The Employer Vice-Chairperson thanked the Committee, his Government and Worker counterparts, as well as the Employer members, and expressed particular satisfaction with the Chairperson's contribution to the success of the Committee.

297. The Worker spokesperson associated himself, personally and on behalf of the Vice-Chairperson, with the foregoing speakers' remarks, particularly paying tribute to the Chairperson's ability to keep the Committee on track with skill and good humour. He expressed gratitude to the Worker members for their hard work and support.

298. The representative of the Secretary-General thanked all the participants. He remarked that the International Labour Conference was sometimes likened to a circus, where every Committee was a ring. If one pursued that analogy, it came naturally to liken the groups of Government members to the elephants, for their intelligence and their ability to move things. He called on the Committee members and the Office to work over the next 12 months to refine the instruments that had been approved.

299. The Chairperson wanted his closing remarks to be distinguished by mentioning the crucial role of the interpreters first, rather than later in his acknowledgements, as previous speakers had done. He thanked everyone for the pleasure that he had in chairing a meeting that had been widely recognized as a success, and looked forward to an equally successful meeting in a year's time.

300. The report of the Committee, the proposed Conclusions and the resolution to place on the agenda of the next ordinary session of the Conference an item entitled "Occupational safety and health" are submitted for consideration.

Geneva, 13 June 2005. *(Signed)* Mr. A. Békés,
Chairperson.

Mr. A. Annakin,
Reporter.

Proposed Conclusions

A. Form of the instrument

1. The International Labour Conference should adopt an instrument establishing the promotional framework on occupational safety and health.

2. The instrument should take the form of a Convention supplemented by a Recommendation.

B. Proposed Conclusions with a view to a Convention

I. Preamble

3. The Convention should include a Preamble referring to:

    (a) the Constitution of the International Labour Organization;

    (b) Paragraph III(g) of the Philadelphia Declaration which provides that the International Labour Organization has the solemn obligation to further among the nations of the world programmes which will achieve adequate protection for the life and health of workers in all occupations;

    (c) the Occupational Safety and Health Convention, 1981 (No. 155), and the Occupational Safety and Health Recommendation, 1981 (No. 164);

    (d) the promotion of occupational safety and health as part of the International Labour Organization's core objective of decent work for all;

    (e) the Conclusions concerning occupational safety and health adopted by the 91st Session (2003) of the International Labour Conference, in particular the priority to be given to occupational safety and health in national agendas;

    (f) the importance of the continuous promotion of a national preventative safety and health culture.

II. Definitions

4. For the purpose of this Convention:

    (a) "national policy" refers to the national policy on occupational safety and health and the working environment developed in accordance with the principles of Article 4 of the Occupational Safety and Health Convention, 1981 (No. 155);

    (b) "national system for occupational safety and health" refers to the infrastructure which provides the main framework for implementing national programmes on occupational safety and health;

    (c) "national programme on occupational safety and health" refers to any national programme that includes objectives, priorities and means of action formulated to improve occupational safety and health, to be achieved in a predetermined time frame;

(d) "a national preventative safety and health culture" refers to a culture in which the right to a safe and healthy working environment is respected at all levels, where governments, employers and workers actively participate in securing a safe and healthy working environment through a system of defined rights, responsibilities and duties, and where the principle of prevention is accorded the highest priority.

III. Objective

5. Each Member which ratifies this Convention should take active steps towards achieving progressively a safer and healthier working environment through national programmes on occupational safety and health by taking into account the principles in relevant ILO instruments on occupational safety and health.

IV. National policy

6. Each Member should promote a safe and healthy working environment by formulating a national policy.

7. Each Member should promote continuous improvement of occupational safety and health by the development, in a tripartite context, of a national policy, national system and national programme.

8. Each Member should promote and advance, at all relevant levels, the right of workers to a safe and healthy working environment.

V. National system

9. (1) Each Member should establish, maintain, progressively develop and periodically review a national system for occupational safety and health, in consultation with representative organizations of employers and workers.

(2) The national system for occupational safety and health should include among others:

(a) laws, regulations, collective agreements and other relevant instruments on occupational safety and health;

(b) an authority or body, or authorities or bodies responsible for occupational safety and health, designated in accordance with national law and practice;

(c) mechanisms for ensuring compliance with national laws and regulations, including systems of inspection;

(d) arrangements to promote, at the level of the undertaking, cooperation between management, workers and their representatives as an essential element of workplace-related prevention measures.

(3) The national system for occupational safety and health should include, where appropriate:

(a) information and advisory services on occupational safety and health;

(b) the provision of occupational safety and health training;

(c) occupational health services in accordance with national law and practice;

(d) research on occupational safety and health;

(e) a mechanism for the collection and analysis of data on occupational accidents and diseases, taking into account relevant ILO instruments;

(f) provisions for collaboration with relevant injury insurance schemes covering occupational accidents and diseases;

(g) support mechanisms for a progressive improvement of occupational safety and health conditions in micro, small and medium-sized enterprises.

VI. *National programme*

10. (1) Each Member should formulate, implement, monitor and periodically review a national programme on occupational safety and health in consultation with representative organizations of employers and workers.

   (2) The national programme should:

   (a) contribute to the protection of workers by minimizing work-related hazards and risks, in accordance with national law and practice, in order to reduce work-related deaths, injuries and diseases;

   (b) be formulated and reviewed on the basis of analysis of the national situation on occupational safety and health, including the national system for occupational safety and health;

   (c) promote the development of a national preventative safety and health culture;

   (d) include targets and indicators of progress;

   (e) be supported, where possible, by other complementary national programmes and plans which will assist in achieving the objective of a safer and healthier working environment.

   (3) The national programme should be widely publicized and, to the extent possible, endorsed and launched by the highest national authorities.

C. Proposed Conclusions with a view to a Recommendation

I. *National system*

11. In establishing, maintaining, progressively developing and periodically reviewing the national system for occupational safety and health defined in point 4(b) above, Members may extend the consultations provided for in point 9(1) above to other interested parties.

12. With a view to reducing occupational accidents, diseases and deaths, the national system should provide appropriate measures for the protection of all workers, in particular workers

in high-risk sectors and of vulnerable workers such as those in the informal economy, migrant and young workers.

13. In promoting a national preventative safety and health culture, Members should seek:

    (a) to raise awareness in the workplace and public awareness on occupational safety and health through national campaigns linked, where appropriate, with international initiatives;

    (b) to promote mechanisms for delivery of occupational safety and health education and training, in particular for management, supervisors, workers and their representatives and government officials responsible for safety and health;

    (c) to introduce occupational safety and health concepts in educational and vocational training programmes;

    (d) to facilitate the exchange of occupational safety and health statistics and data between relevant authorities, employers, workers and their representatives;

    (e) to provide information and advice to employers and workers and promote or facilitate cooperation between them and their organizations with a view to eliminating or reducing hazards;

    (f) to promote, at the level of the workplace, the establishment of safety and health policies and joint safety and health committees and the designation of workers' safety representatives, in accordance with national law and practice;

    (g) to address the constraints of micro, small and medium-sized enterprises and contractors in the implementation of occupational safety and health policies and regulations in accordance with national law and practice.

14. Members should promote the management systems approach to occupational safety and health, such as that set out in the *Guidelines on occupational safety and health management systems, ILO-OSH 2001*.

II. National programme

15. In formulating and reviewing the national programme on occupational safety and health defined in point 4(c) above, Members may extend the consultations provided for in point 10(1) above to other interested parties.

16. The national programme on occupational safety and health should be coordinated, where appropriate, with other national programmes and plans, such as those relating to public health and economic development.

17. In formulating and reviewing the national programme on occupational safety and health, and without prejudice to their obligations under Conventions which they have ratified, Members should take into account the international labour Conventions and Recommendations listed in the annex.

III. National profile

18. (1) Members should prepare and regularly update a national profile which summarizes the existing situation on occupational safety and health and the progress that has been

made in achieving a safer and healthier working environment. The profile should be used as a basis for formulating and reviewing the national programme.

(2) In addition to information on the elements provided for in point 9(2) and (3) above, the national profile on occupational safety and health should include information on the following elements, where appropriate:

(a) coordination and collaboration mechanisms at national and enterprise levels, including national programme review mechanisms;

(b) technical standards, codes of practice and guidelines on occupational safety and health;

(c) educational and awareness-raising structures including promotional initiatives;

(d) specialized technical, medical and scientific institutions with linkages to various aspects of occupational safety and health, including research institutes and laboratories concerning occupational safety and health;

(e) human resources active in the area of occupational safety and health, such as inspectors, officers, occupational physicians and hygienists;

(f) occupational accident and disease statistics;

(g) occupational safety and health policies and programmes of organizations of employers and workers;

(h) regular or ongoing activities related to occupational safety and health, including international collaboration;

(i) related data addressing, for example, demography, literacy, economy and employment, as available, as well as any other relevant information;

(j) financial and budgetary resources with regard to occupational safety and health.

IV. International exchange of information

19. The International Labour Organization should:

(1) facilitate the exchange of information on national policies, systems and programmes on occupational safety and health, including good practices and innovative approaches, and the identification of new and emerging hazards and risks in the workplace;

(2) inform on progress made in achieving a safer and healthier working environment.

V. Updating of the annex

20. The list as annexed to this Recommendation should be reviewed and updated by the Governing Body of the International Labour Office. Any new list so established shall be adopted by the Governing Body and upon adoption shall replace the preceding list and shall be communicated to the Members of the International Labour Organization.

Annex

I. Conventions

    Labour Inspection Convention, 1947 (No. 81)

    Radiation Protection Convention, 1960 (No. 115)

    Hygiene (Commerce and Offices) Convention, 1964 (No. 120)

    Labour Inspection (Agriculture) Convention, 1969 (No. 129)

    Occupational Cancer Convention, 1974 (No. 139)

    Working Environment (Air Pollution, Noise and Vibration) Convention, 1977 (No. 148)

    Occupational Safety and Health (Dock Work) Convention, 1979 (No. 152)

    Occupational Safety and Health Convention, 1981 (No. 155)

    Occupational Health Services Convention, 1985 (No. 161)

    Asbestos Convention, 1986 (No. 162)

    Safety and Health in Construction Convention, 1988 (No. 167)

    Chemicals Convention, 1990 (No. 170)

    Prevention of Major Industrial Accidents Convention, 1993 (No. 174)

    Safety and Health in Mines Convention, 1995 (No. 176)

    Protocol of 1995 to the Labour Inspection Convention, 1947 (No. 81)

    Safety and Health in Agriculture Convention, 2001 (No. 184)

    Protocol of 2002 to the Occupational Safety and Health Convention, 1981 (No. 155)

II. Recommendations

    Labour Inspection Recommendation, 1947 (No. 81)

    Labour Inspection (Mining and Transport) Recommendation, 1947 (No. 82)

    Protection of Workers' Health Recommendation, 1953 (No. 97)

    Welfare Facilities Recommendation, 1956 (No. 102)

    Radiation Protection Recommendation, 1960 (No. 114)

    Workers' Housing Recommendation, 1961 (No. 115)

    Hygiene (Commerce and Offices) Recommendation, 1964 (No. 120)

    Labour Inspection (Agriculture) Recommendation, 1969 (No. 133)

    Occupational Cancer Recommendation, 1974 (No. 147)

    Working Environment (Air Pollution, Noise and Vibration) Recommendation, 1977 (No. 156)

    Occupational Safety and Health (Dock Work) Recommendation, 1979 (No. 160)

    Occupational Safety and Health Recommendation, 1981 (No. 164)

    Occupational Health Services Recommendation, 1985 (No. 171)

    Asbestos Recommendation, 1986 (No. 172)

    Safety and Health in Construction Recommendation, 1988 (No. 175)

    Chemicals Recommendation, 1990 (No. 177)

    Prevention of Major Industrial Accidents Recommendation, 1993 (No. 181)

    Safety and Health in Mines Recommendation, 1995 (No. 183)

    Safety and Health in Agriculture Recommendation, 2001 (No. 192)

    List of Occupational Diseases Recommendation, 2002 (No. 194)

Resolution to place on the agenda of the next ordinary session of the Conference an item entitled "Occupational safety and health"

The General Conference of the International Labour Organization,

Having adopted the report of the Committee appointed to consider the fourth item on the agenda,

Having in particular approved as general conclusions, with a view to the consultation of Governments, proposals for a Convention and a Recommendation concerning occupational safety and health,

Decides that an item entitled "Occupational safety and health" shall be included in the agenda of its next ordinary session for second discussion with a view to the adoption of a Convention and Recommendation.

CONTENTS

Page

Fourth item on the agenda: Occupational safety and health

Report of the Committee on Safety and Health 1

Proposed Conclusions 63

Resolution to place on the agenda of the next ordinary session of the
Conference an item entitled "Occupational safety and health" 69

International Labour Conference

Record of Proceedings   19

Ninety-third Session, Geneva, 2005

Fifth item on the agenda:
Work in the fishing sector
(second discussion)

Report of the Committee on the Fishing Sector

1. The Committee on the Fishing Sector held its first sitting on 31 May 2005. It was originally composed of 123 members (54 Government members, 21 Employer members and 48 Worker members). To achieve equality of voting strength, each Government member entitled to vote was allotted 56 votes, each Employer member 144 votes and each Worker member 63 votes. The composition of the Committee was modified ten times during the session and the number of votes attributed to each member adjusted accordingly.[1]

---

[1] The modifications were as follows:

(a) 1 June: 143 members (71 Government members entitled to vote with 598 votes each, 26 Employer members with 1,633 votes each and 46 Worker members with 923 votes each);

(b) 2 June: 124 members (83 Government members entitled to vote with 414 votes each, 18 Employer members with 1,909 votes each and 23 Worker members with 1,494 votes each);

(c) 3 June: 120 members (85 Government members entitled to vote with 304 votes each, 16 Employer members with 1,615 votes each and 19 Worker members with 1,360 votes each);

(d) 4 June: 120 members (87 Government members entitled to vote with 266 votes each, 14 Employer members with 1,653 votes each and 19 Worker members with 1,218 votes each);

(e) 6 June: 120 members (89 Government members entitled to vote with 238 votes each, 14 Employer members with 1,513 votes each and 17 Worker members with 1,246 votes each);

(f) 7 June: 116 members (89 Government members entitled to vote with 182 votes each, 14 Employer members with 1,157 votes each and 13 Worker members with 1,246 votes each);

(g) 8 June: 112 members (89 Government members entitled to vote with 130 votes each, 10 Employer members with 1,157 votes each and 13 Worker members with 890 votes each);

(h) 9 June: 105 members (88 Government members entitled to vote with 9 votes each, 9 Employer members with 88 votes each and 8 Worker members with 99 votes each);

(i) 10 June: 105 members (89 Government members entitled to vote with 63 votes each, 7 Employer members with 801 votes each and 9 Worker members with 623 votes each)

(j) 13 June: 103 members (90 Government members entitled to vote with 7 votes each, 7 Employer members with 90 votes each and 6 Worker members with 105 votes each.

2. The Committee elected its Officers as follows:

Chairperson: Mr. F. Ribeiro Lopes (Government member, Portugal) at its first sitting

Vice-Chairpersons: Ms. R. Karikari Anang (Employer member, Ghana) and Mr. P. Mortensen (Worker member, Denmark) at its first sitting

Reporter: Mr. G. Boumbopoulos (Government member, Greece) at its second sitting

3. At its second sitting the Committee appointed a Drafting Committee composed of the following members: Ms. M. Martyn (Government member, United Kingdom) and Mr. A. Moussat (Government member, France); Ms. T. French (Employer member, United States), Mr. R. Manda (Employer member, South Africa) and Mr. A Piggott (Employer member, United Kingdom); Ms. E. Lynch (Worker member, Ireland) and Mr. I. Victor (Worker member, Belgium); and the Reporter, Mr. G. Boumbopoulos (Government member, Greece) (ex officio).

4. At its second sitting, the Committee appointed a Working Party to consider Article 5 and Annex I. It was composed of the following members: Mr. N. Campbell (Government member, South Africa), Mr. J. Downie (Government member, United Kingdom), Mr. H. Endo (Government member, Japan), Mr. P. Livet (Government member, France), Mr. P. Mannion (Government member, Canada), Ms. V. Ribeiro Albuquerque (Government member, Brazil) and Mr. R. Sylvestersen (Government member, Denmark); Ms. M.-C. Hervouet-Dion (Employer member, France), Mr. Y. Okazaki (Employer member, Japan) and Ms. C. Penney (Employer member, Canada); Mr. H. Angriman (Worker member, Argentina), Mr. M. Claes (Worker member, Belgium), Mr. J. Hansen (Worker member, Norway), Mr. R. Kapenda (Worker member, Namibia), Mr. S. Kondo (Worker member, Japan) and assisted by Mr. R. Karavatchev (International Transport Workers' Federation). At its fifth sitting the mandate of the Working Party was extended to consider Articles 25-28 and Annex III. The members of the Working Party were Mr. N. Campbell (Government member, South Africa), Mr. J. Downie (Government member, United Kingdom), Mr. P. Livet (Government member, France), Mr. P. Mannion (Government member, Canada), Ms. V. Ribeiro Albuquerque (Government member, Brazil), Mr. R. Sylvestersen (Government member, Denmark) and Mr. Y. Takeba (Government member, Japan); Mr. C. Blonk (Employer member, Netherlands), Mr. B. Chapman (Employer member, Canada), Ms. M.-C. Hervouet-Dion (Employer member, France) and Mr. Y. Okazaki (Employer member, Japan); Mr. H. Angriman (Worker member, Argentina), Mr. M. Claes (Worker member, Belgium), Mr. J. Hansen (Worker member, Norway) and Mr. K. Masemola (Worker member, South Africa) assisted by Mr. R. Karavatchev (International Transport Workers' Federation).

5. The Committee held 16 sittings. The Committee had before it Reports V(2A) and V(2B), prepared by the office on the fifth item of the agenda of the Conference: Work in the fishing sector.

Introduction

6. The Chairperson thanked the Committee for his election and recalled that the goal of this Committee was to present the International Labour Conference with a Convention and Recommendation on work in the fishing sector for its consideration and adoption. The overarching objective was to ensure that the ILO's goal of decent work – promoting opportunities for men and women to obtain decent and productive work in conditions of

freedom, equity, security and dignity – could be achieved in the fishing sector. The challenge before the Committee was threefold: to develop a standard that provided protection for as much of the world's fishing population as possible; to develop a standard that could be widely ratified in order to have a real impact on the life of fishers; and to ensure that its implementation would improve matters not only for fishers working on small vessels close to shore, but also those working on distant-water vessels that would remain at sea for extended periods. During discussions on the draft consolidated maritime labour Convention, it had been decided to exclude fishers from the provisions of that Convention. It was therefore the task of this Committee to ensure that fishers were not left without protection. Fishers, like all other workers, had the right to decent work and were entitled to good living and working conditions. The Chairperson emphasized that due to the length of the proposed instruments, the Committee would have to work in a very focused and deliberate manner in order to complete its work.

7. The representative of the Secretary-General recalled the first discussion on this issue, held during the 92nd Session of the International Labour Conference. During that first discussion, the Committee was not able to consider all of the proposed text due to time constraints. In particular, Part V on accommodation and food; the provisions concerning social security; Annex I concerning fishers' work agreements; Annex II concerning accommodation; and the proposed Conclusions with a view to the Recommendation were not examined. The Committee agreed that the Office should enable consultation on Part V and Annex II of the Conclusions, both of which covered accommodation, between the end of the 92nd Session of the International Labour Conference and the beginning of its 93rd Session.

8. The Office accordingly held a Tripartite Meeting of Experts on the Fishing Sector. The purpose of that Meeting was to review and formulate provisions on accommodation and to handle any other pending issues identified by the Conference. The ILO Governing Body asked the Meeting of Experts also to consider provisions for larger vessels in order to assist the Office in drafting such provisions. The Meeting was also provided with copies of various amendments to Part V and to Annex II that had been submitted during the 92nd Session of the International Labour Conference but had not been considered due to lack of time. The report of the Meeting of Experts should be read in conjunction with Annex I entitled "Provisions for accommodation, large fishing vessels and social security discussed at the Tripartite Meeting of Experts on the Fishing Sector", both of which were included as an Appendix to Report V(2A).

9. The speaker then introduced the Office reports. Report V(1) contained the Conclusions adopted by the Committee last year in the form of a proposed Convention and Recommendation. Governments were sent copies of this report and were requested to consult with the most representative organizations of workers and employers and inform the Office of any amendments or comments on the proposed text. Report V(2A) contained a summary of the replies received from 43 member States. Report V(2B), which would be the main focus of the Committee's work, included the proposed text of a Convention and Recommendation concerning Work in the Fishing Sector.

10. The speaker highlighted certain significant changes to Report V(1) that had been introduced since the first discussion at the 92nd Session of the International Labour Conference. These included: the placement of provisions for "larger" vessels throughout the text rather than in a separate section; a new Annex I on equivalence in units of measurement; slight changes to length overall figures in light of IMO analysis; new proposed figures for equivalent units as concerned gross tonnage; the introduction of definitions for "length overall" and "international voyage"; and clarification to Part VII in the provisions on compliance and enforcement. These, as well as other changes, were noted in the commentary in Report V(2A).

11. In closing, the speaker drew attention to the significant potential impact an ILO Convention and Recommendation on work in the fishing sector could have, not only on fishers themselves, but also in a broader context encompassing related industries, families and coastal communities. The exclusion of fishers from the protection afforded by existing maritime labour Conventions and Recommendations, as a result of the development of the draft consolidated maritime labour Convention, highlighted the importance of the Committee's work.

12. The Legal Adviser recognized the challenge the Committee faced in examining a much longer text than was usually examined during standard setting discussions. To address this issue, the Meeting of Experts on the Fishing Sector had accepted the suggestion to have a standing drafting committee that would meet daily. This is fully in keeping with article 59 of the Standing Orders of the International Labour Conference, which does not contain any provisions as to when the drafting committee could meet or what its work should consist of. The Office therefore proposed holding daily meetings of the drafting committee to ensure that the provisions approved by the Committee say the same thing in the two authentic languages. The text adopted on a daily basis by the drafting committee will be, in principle, the final version submitted to the Committee for its approval. In addition, the drafting committee could also assist the Committee by drafting text for provisions on which there was consensus in the Committee, but for which exact wording needed to be formulated. These draft provisions could then be returned to the Committee for further deliberation and eventual adoption, further amendment, or rejection.

General discussion

13. The Employer Vice-Chairperson stated that the Committee was in a position either to develop a widely ratifiable Convention or one that would remain unratified and would leave the majority of fishers without standards. While fishers in developed countries were covered by existing Conventions, other fishers were not protected by international standards since developing countries had not been in a position to ratify the fishing instruments. It was thus essential for the Committee to develop an inclusive Convention that would strike a balance between developed member States with regulations and developing countries without regulations. Furthermore, the Convention should seek to establish minimum standards, not maximum standards, since individual member States could always increase protection if practicable in their national contexts. The Committee should also seek to develop a Convention that governments would enforce and that would maintain jobs in the sector. The challenge therefore was to develop an instrument providing both strong protection and enough flexibility to accommodate the diverse conditions in the fishing industry. Unfortunately, it appeared that the Committee was not heading towards a widely ratifiable instrument. Furthermore, given the diversity of the industry and the need for flexibility, vessel length or tonnage should not be used as a basis for additional requirements in areas such as minimum age, medical examination or accommodation. Fishers worldwide should enjoy the same protection, regardless of vessel size.

14. The Worker Vice-Chairperson noted the importance in striking a balance between existing standards and their possible improvement on the one hand, and the necessary flexibility for small-scale fisheries in developing countries and widespread ratification on the other. This balance also included the question of requirements for larger vessels. The Workers' group however, would find it difficult to agree to the removal of existing standards. This was especially true given the development of the draft consolidated maritime labour Convention, which, if adopted, would lead to the suspension of a number of maritime Conventions covering fishers. The disastrous consequences of the tsunami for fishers and fishing communities further strengthened the need for a meaningful Convention. The

Workers intended to table a resolution to that effect and invited Governments and Employers to assist in its drafting.

15. The Government member of Lebanon recalled the importance of the fishing industry and hoped that the standard under discussion would help to solve the problems of this sector. Questions that needed to be considered by the Committee included the scope of the instrument, as well as its consistency with other instruments. In particular, the Committee needed to ensure that the Convention would be in line with the Minimum Age Convention, 1973 (No. 138), and its provisions on the education and training of young workers. The Committee's goal was to develop a clear and flexible standard with provisions that were easily understood. Accordingly, a request was made that the Arabic translation be as simple as possible.

16. The Government member of Norway said that there was a strong need for a new and effective international standard on fishers' working and living conditions. There were, however, a few major obstacles to the successful adoption of the instrument, for example the attempt to regulate social security. It would be unacceptable to have regulations that would place heavy burdens on countries with developed social security systems and practically none on countries without such systems. It would likewise be unacceptable to confer rights in a contributory system to those who were not contributing, and to treat fishers who had chosen to be self-employed as employees. In order to safeguard the lives and health of fishers, the Committee needed to create a standard that would not force fishing vessel owners to adopt lower standards in order to remain competitive. Only a Convention aimed towards the highest common denominator could provide the best possible foundation for the future of the fishing industry.

17. The Government member of India stated that, given the hazardous nature of the fishing sector, the proposed instruments were crucial to provide a regulatory framework for large fishing operations. However, the draft provisions did not adequately address the concerns of small-scale fishers. In the case of subsistence fishing, provisions concerning minimum wage, medical examination, manning and hours of rest, fishers' work agreements, repatriation and similar issues, would be difficult to enforce. The new fishing instrument should be practicable and enforceable in countries with diverse ecologies and long coastlines.

18. The Government member of Turkey said the standard should provide stronger protection for workers, while being flexible enough to enable less-developed member States to ratify it. She described recently adopted national legislation covering the fishing sector that conformed with much of the draft text.

19. The Government member of Japan noted the number of ratifications of existing ILO fishing Conventions was low due to overly detailed and prescriptive requirements. It was therefore crucial that the new Convention and Recommendation be flexible enough to attain wide ratification. In this context, the issue of accommodation was of concern and there was a need for more flexibility in this area. The conversion of length into gross tonnage would have to be discussed to take into account the equal application of the Convention among member States.

20. The Government member of Greece stated that the adoption of the lengthy Convention and Recommendation in the time available would not be an easy task. However, he was optimistic that the spirit of tripartism would prevail and that a modern fishing standard maintaining the ILO's maritime tradition would be adopted.

21. The Government member of Canada stated the Committee's goal was to adopt a credible standard that provided appropriate protection for fishers worldwide. The new instruments

should be meaningful and practicable to accommodate a diverse industry and should avoid including prescriptive provisions that would impede widespread ratification and implementation. To this end, the Committee should consider the possibility of using other tools for providing detailed guidance, such as codes of practice.

22. The Government member of Brazil said that due to the over-exploitation of fishing grounds, small fishing vessels in many developing countries tended to operate in increasingly remote and unsafe areas. Fishers lacked social security and had unacceptable working conditions. This Convention offered the opportunity to improve this situation. Even though the Convention had not yet been adopted, the fishing sector had already benefited from the attention brought about by these discussions.

23. The Government member of the Bahamas noted the importance of the fishing sector for his country and expressed support in ensuring a productive outcome of the discussions.

24. The Government member of South Africa stated that the Convention should modernize the protection contained in the existing fishing instruments and provide sufficient flexibility. The provisions on social security could place a heavy burden on Members with respect to fishers not resident in their territories. The creation of separate provisions for different sizes of fishing vessel was another area for concern; the Convention should be a minimum standard.

25. The Government member of Australia welcomed the rationalization of standards as part of an integrated approach to ILO maritime and fishing instruments. The proposed Convention should specify broad principles focused on appropriate goals and protection, and be flexible enough to accommodate different national circumstances and levels of development. Prescriptive detail should be included in the Recommendation or in a code of practice. The definition of "fisher" should not include self-employed persons and the terms of genuine independent contracting arrangements should not become subject to the provisions of this Convention. Given the exclusion of fishers from the draft consolidated maritime labour Convention, it was essential to adopt a Convention covering the fishing sector.

26. The Government member of Namibia noted the importance of crafting an instrument that would be protective, but also widely ratifiable. In this regard, there were a number of critical areas such as accommodation, social security, and length and tonnage issues. It was important to avoid unnecessary duplication and to avoid deviating from established principles. This could be accomplished by cooperating with the work of organizations such as the IMO.

27. The Government member of China noted the fishing industry was very diverse. While sophisticated vessels were sometimes used, there was also much more smaller scale fishing. The Convention would need to take these varying levels of employment into consideration, as well as differences in national regulations. She added that the standard should not be overly detailed, in order to ensure that the rights of fishers could be protected.

28. The Government member of Indonesia stated that improved working conditions in the fishing sector would make the sector more attractive, reduce unemployment and contribute to sustainable development. The Convention needed to take into account local conditions and the fact that small-scale fisheries were often family businesses with limited financial resources. Financial implications should be taken into account so as to avert any loss of employment. While it was important to improve working conditions on fishing vessels, a Convention should not be too detailed so that member States could adapt its principles to local circumstances.

29. The Government member of the United Kingdom stated the goal was to create a ratifiable Convention that struck the right balance between detail and general principles. Even countries with well-developed standards would be unable to ratify the new Convention if one or two small provisions presented them with difficulties. Flexibility should not be seen as a weakness, rather a reflection of the diversity of the circumstances to be covered by the instrument.

30. The Government member of Nigeria urged the Committee to continue to consider the situation of developing countries, particularly in respect to issues such as accommodation, social protection and conditions of employment. The debt burden of many developing countries was huge and the instrument, therefore, needed to be flexible. The suggestions resulting from the Tripartite Meeting of Experts on the Fishing Sector were supported, in so far as these were all-embracing and integrated.

31. The Government member of the Bolivarian Republic of Venezuela described the situation in his country, providing information on the national system of labour inspection and emphasizing the importance of communication, training, education and prevention.

32. The representative of the Food and Agricultural Organization of the United Nations (FAO) stressed that fishing was a vital source of food, employment, trade and economic well-being and needed to be conducted in a reasonable manner. An important step towards this goal was the promotion of safety and health of fishers. The FAO/ILO/IMO Code of Safety for Fishermen and Fishing Vessels and the Voluntary Guidelines for the Design, Construction and Equipment of Small Fishing Vessels had recently been revised. These revisions had been approved by the FAO and the IMO and were pending approval by the ILO. On the issue of accommodation, it was emphasized that while provisions on this topic should be included in the new ILO instruments, it was important that any major conflicts with the aforementioned FAO/ILO/IMO instruments be avoided. The speaker supported the text of the proposed Recommendation requesting that competent authorities take into account relevant international guidance. He also agreed with the current draft on the scope of the Convention and equivalent units of measurement. Length (L) as defined in Article 1 was the main basis for the measurement of vessels in several international instruments. Alternative parameters should, as foreseen, be allowed to take into account the different traditions of some regions. The equivalent figures for length overall corresponded fairly well to length (L); the figures for gross tonnage might, however, need to be increased.

33. The representative of the International Christian Maritime Association (ICMA) suggested the medical care provisions should be amended in order to preserve the rights that fishers and other seafarers currently enjoyed. Shipowners were responsible for providing medical care for any illness or injury a fisher suffered while in service; however the proposed provisions on this topic shifted financial responsibility away from shipowners. Also, given the high risks of fishing, it was suggested that the minimum age for working on fishing vessels should be raised to 18 years.

34. The representative of the International Collective in Support of Fishworkers (ICSF) noted that certain types of fishing were excluded from the instrument, such as commercial beach fishing and diving. The provisions on health care, in particular, needed to be extended to cover workers in these areas. To this effect, the definition of fisher needed to be broadened to include persons employed in shore-based fishing operations who did not necessarily work on board a fishing vessel. Consultations with various fishers' organizations had indicated overwhelming support for the inclusion of social security. The Convention's provisions should be no less than those contained in the Social Security (Minimum Standards) Convention, 1952 (No. 102). The tsunami disaster had demonstrated the need for social security for small-scale fishers. The provisions covering small-scale fishers undertaking long voyages should be no different from those applicable to fishers on larger

vessels undertaking similar voyages. Concerning larger vessels, the protection afforded to fishers aboard those vessels should be at least equal to that provided by current ILO instruments. Finally, the ILO should also strive to create links with international standards on fishery management, particularly on regional levels.

Consideration of the proposed Convention concerning work in the fishing sector

Preamble

D.6

35. The Worker Vice-Chairperson proposed an amendment to insert a new paragraph after the fourth paragraph to read: "Noting that the International Labour Organization has designated fishing as an especially hazardous sector, and". This wording was based on the conclusions of the ILO Tripartite Meeting on Safety and Health in the Fishing Industry (1999).

36. The Employer Vice-Chairperson requested clarification from the Office as to the exact wording found in the conclusions of the Tripartite Meeting on Safety and Health in the Fishing Industry (1999) and questioned the implications of referring to fishing as especially hazardous.

37. The Government member of Norway, speaking on behalf of the Government group, shared the Employers' group's concerns.

38. The representative of the Secretary-General said the unanimously adopted conclusions of the Tripartite Meeting on Safety and Health in the Fishing Industry (1999), as contained in its *Note on the proceedings*, had been approved by the Governing Body and subsequently sent to all member States, who had been asked to circulate them to the most representative workers' and employers' organizations. The exact wording used in these conclusions was "Fishing is a hazardous occupation when compared to other occupations".

39. The Employer Vice-Chairperson opposed the amendment since it was not in line with the original wording, and since the addition of "especially" had further implications.

40. The Worker Vice-Chairperson proposed a subamendment to his group's amendment to read: "Noting that the International Labour Organization has designated fishing as a hazardous occupation when compared to other occupations,".

41. The Government members of Egypt and Lebanon and the Employers' group supported the subamendment.

42. The Government member of the United Kingdom pointed out that "designated" implied the ILO had given fishing a special status. Instead, the ILO had simply accepted that it was a hazardous profession. She proposed a further amendment to replace "designated" by "accepted".

43. The Government member of Namibia agreed since it would avoid creating any unwanted implications.

44. The Committee agreed to send the amendment as subamended to the Drafting Committee with the request that it provide an alternative formulation for "designated" that would reflect the Committee's concerns.

New preambular paragraphs

C.R./D.1(C.S.P.)

45. The Drafting Committee proposed the following wording: "Recognizing that the International Labour Organization considers fishing as a hazardous occupation when compared to other occupations, and", which was accepted by the Committee.

D.20, D.22

46. The Government member of Denmark introduced two amendments that had been submitted by the Government members of Austria, Belgium, Denmark, Finland, France, Germany, Greece, Ireland, Malta, Netherlands, Norway, Portugal, Spain, Sweden and the United Kingdom. The first amendment deleted the words "and the Seafarers' Identity Documents Convention (Revised), 2003," at the end of the sixth paragraph, and inserted the word "and" after "1981,". The second amendment added a new paragraph after the sixth paragraph to read: "Noting also Article 1, paragraph 3, of the Seafarers' Identity Documents Convention (Revised), 2003, and". The purpose was to replace the general reference to the Seafarers' Identity Documents Convention (Revised), 2003 (No. 185), with a more specific reference to the Article contained therein that dealt with fishers.

47. The Employer and Worker Vice-Chairpersons supported both amendments.

48. The Government member of Norway, speaking on behalf of the Government group, also supported the amendments.

49. The two amendments were adopted.

50. Subsequent to the Committee's discussions on social security, the Drafting Committee proposed for the Committee's consideration a draft text C.R./D.4(C.S.P.) relating to the placement and wording of the reference to Convention No. 102 in the Preamble of the Convention. The words "the Social Security (Minimum Standards) Convention, 1952 notwithstanding the provisions of Article 77 of that Convention" had been deleted from the sixth preambular paragraph in which the Committee had placed them and a new preambular paragraph was added to read as follows: "Noting, in addition, the Social Security (Minimum Standards) Convention, 1952, and considering that the provisions of Article 77 of that Convention should not be an obstacle to protection extended by Members to fishers under social security schemes, and". The Chairperson invited the Legal Adviser to clarify the reasons for the revision of the text.

51. The Legal Adviser stated that the Committee had made its intentions clear, but the text adopted by the Committee had been unsound from a legal point of view. The Drafting Committee had proposed a revised text that would discourage member States that chose to ratify the new Convention from considering Article 77 of Convention No. 102 as an obstacle to the extension of protection to fishers under their social security schemes.

52. The Chairperson thanked the Drafting Committee for their excellent work and, noting there was no objection, declared the text in C.R./D.4(C.S.P.) adopted.

D.7

53. The Worker Vice-Chairperson introduced an amendment to add a new paragraph after the eighth paragraph: "Recalling that the United Nations Convention on the Law of the Sea, 1982, sets out a legal framework within which all activities in the oceans and seas must be carried out and is of strategic importance as the basis for national, regional and global

action and cooperation in the marine sector, and that its integrity needs to be maintained, and". The United Nations Convention on the Law of the Sea, 1982, was an important instrument that provided a global legal framework which had an impact on some of the provisions of the new Convention.

54. The Government members of Cameroon, Egypt and Mauritania supported the amendment.

55. The Government member of the Bolivarian Republic of Venezuela noted that the Preamble already covered the important aspects of safety and health. Also, while his Government was not opposed to the United Nations Convention on the Law of the Sea, 1982, States that were not contracting parties to that Convention were not bound by its provisions. He therefore proposed a subamendment to address these issues. The subamendment was not seconded and so was not discussed.

56. The Government member of the United States, while not opposed to referring to the United Nations Convention on the Law of the Sea, 1982, noted that the explanatory text proposed in the amendment gave this Convention greater emphasis than other instruments referred to in the Preamble.

57. The Government members of Japan and the Bolivarian Republic of Venezuela and the Employers' group supported the comment made by the Government member of the United States.

58. The Government member of Germany said the United Nations Convention on the Law of the Sea, 1982, should be referred to in the same succinct manner as the other instruments.

59. The Employer Vice-Chairperson proposed subamending the text to read: "Recalling the United Nations Convention on the Law of the Sea, 1982" in order to remove an unnecessary level of detail.

60. The Worker Vice-Chairperson accepted the subamendment.

61. The amendment was adopted as subamended.

D.3

62. The Worker Vice-Chairperson introduced an amendment to insert the following paragraph after the eighth paragraph: "Recalling that Article 94 of the United Nations Convention on the Law of the Sea, 1982, establishes the duties and obligations of a flag State with regard to, inter alia, labour conditions, crewing and social matters on vessels that fly its flag, and". The purpose was to provide guidance to the competent authorities on flag State responsibilities under the United Nations Convention on the Law of the Sea, 1982, with regard to labour conditions and social matters. This amendment was especially important given the Committee's decision on the previous amendment.

63. The Government member of Mauritania considered this amendment was unnecessary, given the adoption of the previous amendment.

64. The Government member of Portugal proposed further amending the previously discussed amendment to read: "Recalling the United Nations Convention on the Law of the Sea, 1982, in particular Article 94, which established the duties and obligations of a flag State with regard to, inter alia, labour conditions, crewing and social matters on vessels that fly its flag, and". This would address the concerns of the Workers' group.

65. The Government members of Egypt and Japan, as well as the Workers' group, supported this further amendment.

66. The Government member of Germany stated it was unnecessary to include a specific reference to Article 94. Any government that had ratified the United Nations Convention on the Law of the Sea, 1982, did not need a reminder of its responsibilities under that Convention.

67. The Employer Vice-Chairperson opposed the further amendment on both procedural and substantive grounds. The previous amendment had already been adopted and should therefore not be opened for further amendment. In addition, the reference already made to the United Nations Convention on the Law of the Sea, 1982, was sufficient.

68. The Government members of Cameroon, Côte d'Ivoire, Lebanon and Mozambique opposed the further amendment and the amendment.

69. The Worker Vice-Chairperson withdrew the amendment.

70. The Preamble was adopted as amended.

Part I. Definitions and scope

Definitions

Article 1

Subparagraph (a)

D.4

71. The Government member of Indonesia introduced an amendment submitted by the Government members of Indonesia and the Philippines to insert the words "fishing for research, fishing for training" in the second line of subparagraph (a) after the words "subsistence fishing". She noted that Article 4 provided guidance on exclusion from the scope of the Convention for ratifying member States, and fishing research and fishing training vessels should be included in the categories of excluded vessels.

72. The Worker Vice-Chairperson opposed the amendment.

73. The Employer Vice-Chairperson and the Government member of Egypt supported the amendment since the proposed Convention was aimed at commercial fishing.

74. The Government member of Norway, speaking on behalf of the Government group, indicated that a clear majority of Governments opposed the amendment.

75. The Government member of Namibia opposed the amendment, considering that Article 2, paragraph 1, and Article 3, paragraph 1, addressed the concerns of the Government members of Indonesia and the Philippines.

76. The Employer Vice-Chairperson stated that in light of the intervention of the Government member of Namibia, her group withdrew its support for the amendment.

77. The amendment was not adopted.

Subparagraph (e)

D.17

78. The Government member of Australia submitted an amendment, seconded by the Government member of India, to delete the words "or engaged in any capacity or carrying out an occupation" in subparagraph (e).

79. As the Government member of Australia was not present, the amendment was not discussed.

D.13

80. An amendment submitted by the Government member of Spain was not seconded and therefore not discussed.

D.24

81. The Workers' group withdrew an amendment.

82. On a point of order, the Government member of Lebanon, supported by the Government member of Egypt, stated that even though an amendment to Article 1(e) had not been discussed, the definition of fisher was very relevant and clarification from the secretariat was necessary.

83. The representative of the Secretary-General clarified that Article 1(e) had been adopted without amendment.

Subparagraph (h)

D.16

84. The Government member of Greece introduced an amendment submitted by the Government members of Belgium, Finland, France, Germany, Greece, Netherlands, Norway, Portugal, Spain, Sweden and the United Kingdom to insert, in clauses (i), (ii) and (iii) of subparagraph (h), the words "for the Member concerned" after the words "the entry into force of the Convention". The definition of the term "new fishing vessel", which was used for technical issues such as accommodation, entailed practical problems for member States that ratified the Convention some time after it had come into force. For example, in the period between the entry into force of the Convention and the entry into force of the Convention for a particular Member, said Member might have accepted a certain number of vessels into its register. However, after entry into force of the Convention for the Member concerned, those vessels would have to leave the register because of non-compliance with provisions they had not been required to comply with at the time of registration. Subparagraph (h) as found in the draft text would require parliaments to regulate retroactively.

85. The Government members of Canada, Denmark, Japan, Lebanon, Namibia and the United States, as well as the Employers' group, supported the amendment.

86. The Worker Vice-Chairperson expressed concerns about the amendment for control reasons, but did not oppose it.

87. The amendment was adopted.

Subparagraph (l)

D.2

88. The Government member of South Africa introduced an amendment submitted by the Government members of Iceland and South Africa to insert, in subparagraph (l), between the words "line" and "between", the words "parallel to the designated waterline". This was a technical amendment intended to bring the wording in line with the FAO/ILO/IMO Code of Safety for Fishermen and Fishing Vessels and the Voluntary Guidelines for the Design, Construction and Equipment of Small Fishing Vessels, and to reflect the wording of subparagraph (k).

89. The Employer and Worker Vice-Chairpersons supported the proposal.

90. The amendment was adopted.

Subparagraph (m)

D.18

91. The Government member of the United Kingdom introduced an amendment submitted by the Government members of Belgium, Finland, France, Germany, Greece, Netherlands, Norway, Portugal, Spain, Sweden and the United Kingdom to replace, in subparagraph (m), the words "in recruiting fishers on behalf of employers or placing fishers with employers" by the words "in recruiting or placing fishers on behalf of employers, fishing vessel owners or operators". This amendment sought to reflect the variety of employment and work relationships in the fishing sector.

92. The Worker Vice-Chairperson felt that, in the light of the definitions of "fishing vessel owner" in subparagraph (d) and "fisher's work agreement" in subparagraph (f), the amendment would be confusing. The Workers therefore opposed the amendment.

93. The Employer Vice-Chairperson opposed the amendment and proposed a subamendment to replace the words "in recruiting fishers on behalf of employers or placing fishers with employers" by the words "in recruiting or placing fishers respectively on behalf of or with employers, fishing vessel owners or operators, unless such service is provided within a group of connected legal entities". The purpose of the subamendment was twofold: (1) to reflect the fact that recruitment could be done on behalf of someone but placement could only be done with someone; and (2) to ensure that licences would not be required where a company providing recruitment services was part of a group of companies that owned a fishing vessel or fishing vessels and was providing those services to the other companies in the group.

94. The Worker Vice-Chairperson expressed concern at the words "operators" and "entities" and proposed an alternate subamendment to replace the words "in recruiting fishers on behalf of employers or placing fishers with employers" by the words "in recruiting or placing fishers on behalf of fishing vessel owners".

95. The Government members of Portugal, South Africa and the United Kingdom supported the Workers' group's subamendment.

96. The Government member of Greece also supported the Workers' group's subamendment, and suggested that the concern expressed by the Employers' group might be better dealt with in Article 22 on "Recruitment and placement".

97. The Employer Vice-Chairperson withdrew her group's subamendment and proposed a further amendment to the Workers' subamendment to read: "in recruiting or placing fishers, respectively on behalf of or with fishing vessel owners."

98. The Government member of Egypt supported this further amendment because it clarified that a fishing vessel owner must assume his or her responsibilities.

99. The Workers' Vice-Chairperson also agreed with the further amendment.

100. The amendment was adopted as subamended.

D.9

101. The Employer Vice-Chairperson withdrew an amendment in light of the adoption of the previous amendment.

Subparagraph (o)

D.15

102. The Government member of the United Kingdom introduced an amendment submitted by the Government members of Austria, Belgium, Denmark, Finland, France, Germany, Greece, Ireland, Malta, Netherlands, Norway, Portugal, Sweden and the United Kingdom to delete subparagraph (o). The Government group had tried to refine the definition of "international voyage" but it had proved too difficult given the number of occurrences throughout the text in which the term was used with different applications. It would therefore be more appropriate to delete the definition here and consider the application within each article where the term was mentioned.

103. The Government member of Norway, speaking on behalf of the Government group, expressed support for the amendment.

104. The Worker Vice-Chairperson sought assurances that appropriate wording would be introduced in the Articles where there was a reference to "international voyage". He suggested that paragraph (o) be put in square brackets until this issue was resolved.

105. The Employer Vice-Chairperson agreed to the Workers' proposal and suggested also postponing discussion of her group's amendment on subparagraph (o).

106. The Government members of Greece, Netherlands and Norway were in favour of the proposals of the Employers' and Workers' groups.

107. After subsequent discussions and decisions regarding the replacement or removal of the term "international voyage" wherever it had occurred in the Office text, the Chairperson drew the Committee's attention to the fact that it was no longer necessary to retain subparagraph (o) of Article 1, which defined international voyages. The Government members' amendment to delete it was therefore adopted.

D.14

108. The Employer members' amendment (D.14) fell as a result.

109. Article 1 was adopted as amended.

Scope

Article 2

Paragraph 1

D.10

> **110.** The Government member of Germany introduced an amendment to replace the words at the beginning of paragraph 1 "Except as provided otherwise, the Convention" by the words "Except as provided otherwise in this Convention, it" in order to lend greater precision to the text.
>
> **111.** The Government member of Greece supported the amendment, as did the Government member of Namibia, speaking on behalf of the Government members of Cameroon, Côte d'Ivoire, Mauritania, Mozambique, Nigeria and South Africa.
>
> **112.** The Government member of the United Kingdom, in supporting the amendment, suggested that it be referred to the Drafting Committee to make it more precise.
>
> **113.** The Worker Vice-Chairperson and the Employer Vice-Chairperson also expressed support.
>
> **114.** The amendment was adopted and the text referred to the Drafting Committee.

Paragraph 3

D.5

> **115.** The Government member of Denmark introduced an amendment submitted by the Government members of Denmark, Germany and Norway to add in paragraph 3, after the words "on smaller vessels", the words "in whole or in part". The purpose was to enable the extension of protection to fishers working on smaller vessels as and when possible.
>
> **116.** The Workers' group supported the amendment.
>
> **117.** The Employers' group also supported the amendment, observing that the length of vessels concerned had not yet been decided and therefore the number 24 should remain in square brackets.
>
> **118.** The amendment was adopted.
>
> **119.** Article 2 was adopted as amended.

Article 3

> **120.** Article 3 was adopted without amendment.

Article 4

> **121.** Article 4 was adopted without amendment.

Article 5 and Annex I

> **122.** A Working Party was appointed to consider Article 5 in conjunction with Annex I and all relevant amendments thereto (D.8, 19, 11, 12, 21). The Government member of Brazil, who served as the Chairperson of the Working Party, introduced the conclusions of their

work, contained in document C.S.P./D.101. She noted the great difficulty encountered in forming a consensus on the use of gross tonnage as an alternative to length and length overall. Initially, discussion had focused on replacing the gross tonnage figure of 100 by 300 as an equivalent to a length of 24 metres, but then various alternative figures were discussed for 15 and 45 metres as well. The Working Party agreed that the primary impact of equivalency would be on crew accommodation. Some representatives believed that discussing gross tonnage equivalents for size limits contained in Annex III on accommodation might help resolve the issue in Annex I. After the Committee extended the Working Party's mandate to discuss the relevant figures for tonnage in Annex III, the Working Party was able to agree that the use of equivalent tonnage, as indicated in Annex I, could be used as an alternative to length and length overall, but that it would only be applicable to eight paragraphs in Annex III. Those paragraphs were 10, 31, 32, 34, 36, 39, 54 and 59. After much debate on which figures to apply, in an effort to achieve compromise, the Employers' group proposed the following equivalent measures of gross tonnage to length: a gross tonnage of 200 gt should be considered equivalent to a length of 24 metres; a gross tonnage of 55 gt should be considered equivalent to a length of 15 metres; and a gross tonnage of 700 gt should be considered equivalent to a length of 45 metres. These figures and the revised text for Annex I, paragraph 2, were to be considered as an integrated package. A majority of the Government members accepted this proposal, but the Workers could not agree, since, in their opinion, the figures proposed were not supported by sufficient evidence.

123. The Employer Vice-Chairperson recalled the divergent views expressed with regard to the figures proposed for Annex I, paragraph 2. Originally, the Employers had proposed greater gross tonnage equivalents, but in the course of discussion had agreed to those contained in the Working Party's report. She stressed the need for an all-inclusive, widely ratifiable Convention and asked Government members to express their views on the package proposed.

124. A Worker member from Argentina stressed that the issue of equivalence was highly sensitive for his group and could make or break the Convention. Initially, the Workers had supported the Office text. They wished to avoid coming up with tonnage equivalents that might result in the requirements for accommodation not being obtained. The International Commission for the Conservation of Atlantic Tunas had already reported that a fleet of vessels 23.9 metres in length was being built in an effort to avoid compliance with legislation on vessels of 24 metres or longer. The Workers' group offered a compromise proposal to have the values set at 150 gt as an equivalent to a length of 24 metres, 55 gt as an equivalent to a length of 15 metres, and 700 gt as an equivalent to a length of 45 metres.

125. The Government member of Norway, speaking on behalf of the Government group, pointed out that the Government group had considered the proposal contained in C.S.P./D.101 as a package deal and that the tonnage equivalents proposed were to be limited to the eight paragraphs mentioned. On that basis, a clear majority of governments supported the conclusions of the Working Party. The Government group had not had the opportunity to discuss the Workers' alternative proposal just presented.

126. The Government member of France would not comment on the gross tonnage figures proposed by the Workers' group, but noted that, of the eight paragraphs in Annex III which referred to tonnage, only six were still at issue, as paragraphs 32 and 59 referred to a tonnage that was agreed by all three groups. It might be possible to consider deleting paragraph 2(b) of Annex I, which referred to a gross tonnage equivalent length of 15 metres.

127. The Government member of Japan felt that the Committee should adopt a compromise that would be applicable to all countries. He preferred the larger gross tonnage figures that had

been discussed, but was willing to accept the Employers' figures, which should apply to all parts of the Convention and its annexes.

128. The Government member of Portugal in principle preferred the Office text. She could not agree with the Employers' proposal, but could support that of the Workers. She agreed with the proposal of the Government member of France.

129. The Government member of Brazil preferred the original text, but would support the Workers' proposal. She noted that two of the three figures were the same as those proposed by the Employers.

130. The Government member of Indonesia supported the compromise proposal of the Working Party. According to a study carried out in his country, 24 metres was equivalent to 200 gross tonnes for steel vessels and 150 gross tonnes for wooden ships.

131. The Government member of Norway expressed sympathy for the Workers' group's view, but stressed the importance of preserving the package deal.

132. The Government members of Germany, Namibia, South Africa and Turkey also supported the package deal. In response to a query from the Government member of South Africa, it was confirmed that only the figures in square brackets (and not the three subparagraphs) in Annex I, paragraph 2, would be replaced if the Working Party's conclusions were accepted by the Committee.

133. The Government member of Egypt asked for clarification as to how the figures contained in the Working Party's report had been determined.

134. The Government member of Brazil stated that the Working Party had examined statistical information from Argentina, Japan and the United Kingdom. The aim had been to arrive at widely acceptable, comparable figures, although it was clear that fishing vessels and fleets varied widely across different regions of the world. She pointed out that under Article 43, Annex III could be amended to take account of changes in the size and shape of vessels in the future as design and technology evolved.

135. The Employer Vice-Chairperson reported that, following consultations with the Workers' group and some Government members, a compromise had been reached to the effect that a gross tonnage of 175 gt should be deemed equivalent to a length of 24 metres.

136. The Worker Vice-Chairperson confirmed his group's acceptance of this.

137. The Government member of Norway supported the Employers' and Workers' proposal and pointed out that, although full consultation had not been possible, he had received positive feedback from a number of Government members.

138. The Government member of Japan expressed disappointment and grave concern with the outcome. He stated with regret that the lower compromise figure would pose an obstacle for the internal process of ratification in his country.

139. The Committee adopted Article 5 and Annex 1 as amended and referred the text to the Drafting Committee.

Article 5, Annex I and Annex III

140. The Legal Adviser presented changes to Article 5 and Annex III that had been made by the Drafting Committee when revising Article 5 and Annex I, as adopted by the Committee.

These proposed modifications did not change the intent behind the provisions but offered additional precision and ensured greater consistency and flexibility throughout the Convention.

141. In revising the adopted text, it seemed to the Drafting Committee that the equivalent units of measurement, referring to length overall, could apply to the whole Convention, whereas the others referring to gross tonnage were to apply only to the specified provisions of Annex III. Given that equivalence could be applied to all provisions after consultation, it was necessary to be more specific about regular tonnage. Also for reasons of monitoring and possible exceptions, there was a need to be clear that two types of exceptions could be subject to the reporting requirements of article 22 of the ILO Constitution. The Drafting Committee therefore proposed replacing Article 5 with the following text (C.R./D.2):

> 1. For the purpose of this Convention, the competent authority, after consultation, may decide to use length overall (LOA) in place of length (L) as the basis for measurement, in accordance with the equivalence set out in Annex I. In addition, for the purpose of the paragraphs specified in Annex III of this Convention, the competent authority, after consultation, may decide to use gross tonnage in place of length (L) or length overall (LOA) as the basis for measurement in accordance with the equivalence set out in Annex III.
>
> 2. In the reports submitted under article 22 of the Constitution, the Member shall communicate the reasons for the decision taken under this Article and any comments arising from the consultation.

142. In order to ensure consistency, it was also necessary to add a new paragraph to the general provisions of Annex III. Therefore, paragraph 2 was deleted from Annex I and the following paragraph was inserted after paragraph 5 of Annex III (C.R./D.3):

> The use of gross tonnage as referred to in Article 5 of this Convention is limited to the following specified paragraphs of this Annex: 10, 31, 32, 34, 36, 39, 54 and 59. For these purposes, where the competent authority, after consultation, decided to use gross tonnage (gt) as the basis of measurement:
>
> (a) a gross tonnage of 175 gt shall be considered equivalent to a length (L) of 24 metres or a length overall (LOA) of [26.5] metres;
>
> (b) a gross tonnage of 55 gt shall be considered equivalent to a length (L) of 15 metres or a length overall (LOA) of [16.5] metres;
>
> (c) a gross tonnage of 700 gt shall be considered equivalent to a length (L) of 45 metres or a length overall (LOA) of [50] metres.

This provided a clear view of the exceptions and scope of application of exceptions.

143. The Legal Adviser further noted that some minor consequent changes might be necessary as a result of these proposals, such as a change in the definition of gross tonnage so that it referred to Annex III and not Annex I.

144. In response to a query from the Government member of France, the Legal Adviser clarified that Annex I had been reduced to one paragraph to cover the provisions on length overall, which applied to the whole Convention.

145. Both the Employer and Worker Vice-Chairpersons accepted the proposed texts.

146. In order to take into account concerns expressed by the Government member of Japan, the Chairperson proposed the Committee accept the texts proposed by the Drafting Committee with the understanding that they could be adjusted in accordance with any subsequent changes agreed by the Committee. The Committee agreed and Article 5, the new paragraph in Annex III and the resulting changes in Annex I were adopted as amended by the Drafting Committee.

Part II. General principles

Implementation

Article 6

147. Article 6 was adopted without amendment.

Competent authority and coordination

Article 7

148. Article 7 was adopted without amendment.

Responsibilities of fishing vessel owners, skippers and fishers

Article 8

Subparagraph 2(a)

D.39

149. The Employer Vice-Chairperson introduced an amendment to replace the word "best" by the words "most appropriate" as "best" was too subjective.

150. The Worker Vice-Chairperson opposed the amendment.

151. The Government member of Norway, speaking on behalf of the Government group, opposed the amendment.

152. The Employer Vice-Chairperson withdrew the amendment.

Subparagraph 2(b)

D.36

153. The Employer Vice-Chairperson introduced an amendment to delete the words ", including prevention of fatigue" as the measurement and prevention of fatigue could not be quantified. Moreover, the respect for safety and health encompassed issues of fatigue, making the addition of a specific reference to that issue unnecessary.

154. The Government member of India supported the amendment.

155. The Worker Vice-Chairperson strongly opposed the amendment and noted that similar wording was used in IMO guidelines.

156. The Government member of Norway, speaking on behalf of the Government group, opposed the amendment.

157. The Government member of Turkey opposed the amendment and explained that a link existed between working hours and fatigue. Fatigue directly affected workers' health and needed to be included.

158. The Government member of Namibia, speaking on behalf of the Government members of Cameroon, Côte d'Ivoire, Mauritania, Mozambique, Nigeria and South Africa, opposed the amendment.

159. The Government member of Egypt said the legal aspects of the term "fatigue" required clarification. It was important for the Committee to identify what kind of work led to fatigue.

160. The Government member of Lebanon supported the statement of the Government member of Egypt.

161. The Employer Vice-Chairperson proposed a subamendment to read ", including the prevention of excessive fatigue".

162. The Worker Vice-Chairperson strongly opposed the subamendment, noting that fatigue was a well-defined term.

163. The Government member of Greece pointed out that the subamendment seemed to allow for certain levels of fatigue, as long as they were not excessive.

164. The Government member of Norway opposed the subamendment. Allowing certain levels of fatigue while disallowing others was unacceptable. Also, the issue had links to Article 14 on manning and hours of rest.

165. The Government member of Denmark opposed the subamendment. The Seafarers' Hours of Work and the Manning of Ships Convention, 1996 (No. 180), used the word "fatigue" in Article 11, demonstrating there were already ILO instruments addressing this issue.

166. The Government member of Germany agreed with the Government members of Denmark and Norway.

167. The Employer Vice-Chairperson withdrew the subamendment and the amendment.

Subparagraph 2(c)

D.37

168. The Employer Vice-Chairperson introduced an amendment to replace the text of subparagraph 2(c) by: "facilitating training in awareness of on-board occupational safety and health risks", in order to clarify the nature of the training.

169. The Worker Vice-Chairperson supported the amendment.

170. The Government member of Norway, speaking on behalf of the Government group, opposed the amendment and noted the link with Article 32, subparagraph 3(b). The original wording was reasonable as an obligation for a skipper. The wording suggested by the Employers' group seemed to describe an employer's obligation.

171. The Employer Vice-Chairperson stated that the amendment was not intended to detract from the responsibility of the skipper.

172. The Government member of Norway noted that the amendment was substantively different from the original draft, since the new wording no longer required on-board training. The skipper was responsible for on-board training, but not necessarily for training on safety and health on board which could be done ashore.

173. The Government member of France agreed with the Government member of Norway.

174. The Government member of Denmark said on-board training was an essential aspect of occupational safety and health training. The amendment suggested onshore training could suffice to comply with the provision, which was unacceptable.

175. The Government member of the Philippines opposed the amendment, preferring the broader, less restrictive nature of the original text.

176. The Government member of the United Kingdom, seconded by the Government member of Norway, proposed a subamendment to replace the text of subparagraph 2(c) by: "facilitating on-board occupational safety and health awareness training".

177. The Employer and Worker Vice-Chairpersons supported the subamendment.

178. The amendment was adopted as subamended.

Paragraph 4

D.40, D.43

179. The Committee considered two amendments to delete the words "and reasonable" in paragraph 4. The amendments had been submitted by the Employers' group and the Government members of Austria, Belgium, Denmark, Finland, France, Germany, Greece, Ireland, Netherlands, Norway, Portugal, Spain, Sweden and the United Kingdom. The Employer Vice-Chairperson introduced the amendments, stating "reasonable" was unnecessary in this context. Orders were required to be lawful, and it was the law that determined what was reasonable.

180. The Government member of Greece added that it was a maritime tradition to obey the orders of the skipper, who had specific rights and obligations on board a ship.

181. The Worker Vice-Chairperson supported the amendments.

182. The amendments were adopted.

D.34

183. The Government members of Belgium and France submitted an amendment which was a drafting change affecting only the French version of the text.

184. The amendment was adopted and sent to the Drafting Committee.

185. Article 8 was adopted as amended.

Part III. Minimum requirements for work on board fishing vessels

Minimum age

Article 9

Paragraph 2

D.25, D.28

186. The Committee considered two amendments to delete paragraph 2. The amendments were submitted respectively by the Government members of Brazil, Spain and the Bolivarian Republic of Venezuela, and Canada, Switzerland and the United States. The Government member of Switzerland introduced the amendments, which sought to address inconsistencies with the Minimum Age Convention, 1973 (No. 138), and Worst Forms of Child Labour Convention, 1999 (No. 182). The possibility for persons of the age of 15 to perform light work did not appear coherent with these labour standards. In a sector considered hazardous, it was difficult to categorize certain activities as light work. During the Government group's meeting, the Legal Adviser had noted that care was needed when sectoral Conventions dealt with subjects also covered by general and broadly ratified Conventions.

187. The Worker Vice-Chairperson recalled that the provisions agreed upon for Article 9 during the first discussion of the proposed standard were a "package" that balanced all the concerns expressed and should not be reopened.

188. The Employer Vice-Chairperson opposed the amendment, as it removed the flexibility introduced by paragraph 2.

189. The Government member of Norway, speaking on behalf of the Government group, stated the Government group was evenly divided on the amendments to Article 9 and had not reached a common position.

190. The Government member of Greece shared the concerns of the Government member of Switzerland, but agreed that Article 9 was a "package" solution complemented by the new paragraph 7. According to paragraph 2, persons of 15 years of age could only perform light work if authorized by the competent authority in accordance with national laws and practice and after consultation. Moreover, paragraph 1 already allowed persons of 15 years of age to work on board in the framework of vocational training. In addition to being flexible, paragraph 2 reflected maritime tradition and provided safeguards for continuing to attract new entrants into the industry. He opposed the amendments.

191. The Government members of Denmark, France and Nigeria supported the Government member of Greece and opposed the amendments, as did the Government members of Egypt, India, Mexico and Norway.

192. The Worker Vice-Chairperson opposed the amendments, noting that the wording of paragraph 2 was consistent with Article 7, paragraph 2, of Convention No. 138.

193. The Government member of Switzerland stated the Committee had addressed her concerns and withdrew the amendment, as well as amendments D.27, D.28, D.31 and D.32, which dealt with the same matter.

194. The other amendment (D.25) was not adopted.

Paragraph 3

D.41

195. The Government member of Norway introduced an amendment, submitted by the Government members of Austria, Belgium, Denmark, Finland, France, Germany, Greece, Ireland, Netherlands, Norway, Portugal, Spain, Sweden and the United Kingdom, to replace the text of Article 9, paragraph 3, by the following: "Fishers under the age of 18 shall not be required to perform tasks which are particularly hazardous in nature". Paragraph 3 implied that fishing was not an honest profession and that it was necessary to protect the morals of fishers under the age of 18 but not of fishers over that age. The amendment modernized the provision while retaining its intention.

196. The Government member of Switzerland stated that the original text reflected the wording of Conventions Nos. 138 and 182, which many countries had already ratified. The amendment introduced new concepts that had not been clearly defined in internationally accepted texts.

197. The Worker Vice-Chairperson opposed the amendment, agreeing with the Government member of Switzerland.

198. The Government member of Egypt felt the instrument should simply state that the minimum age for working on a fishing vessel should be 18.

199. The Government members of India, Lebanon and Namibia opposed the amendment.

200. The Employer Vice-Chairperson supported the amendment. The context of this draft Convention was different from that of Conventions Nos. 138 and 182. The issue of morals did not belong in a discussion on fishing. Also, paragraph 7 clearly stipulated that none of its provisions affected obligations arising from having ratified other Conventions.

201. The Government member of the United States said the original wording was designed to protect children. There was a danger that the use of different wording might suggest that the intention of the present Convention was different.

202. The Chairperson requested an indicative show of hands and noted that the majority of Governments opposed the amendment.

203. The Employer Vice-Chairperson requested a record vote.

204. After consultation, the Government member of Norway, on behalf of the Government members sponsoring the amendment, withdrew it.

Paragraph 5

D.26

205. The Government members of Brazil and Spain withdrew an amendment (D.26) prior to its discussion.

206. Article 9 was adopted without amendment.

Medical examination

Article 10

Paragraph 1

D.38

207. The Employer Vice-Chairperson introduced an amendment to replace the words "No fishers shall work on board a fishing vessel" by "Skippers and other fishers directly involved in navigation or the safe operation of the vessel, as determined by national laws or regulations or the competent authority, shall not work on board a vessel". A reference to national laws or regulations or the competent authority was necessary since a valid medical certificate might not be required for small-scale fishing,

208. The Worker Vice-Chairperson opposed the amendment and observed that the necessary flexibility was provided by paragraph 2 of the same Article.

209. The Government member of Norway, speaking on behalf of the Government group, stated a majority of the Government group opposed the amendment.

210. The Government member of Egypt stressed that medical fitness was essential to guard fishers and their catch from disease.

211. The Government member of Lebanon agreed that a valid medical certificate should be a prerequisite for any person working on a fishing vessel.

212. The Government member of Turkey opposed the amendment.

213. The Employer Vice-Chairperson withdrew the amendment.

Paragraph 3

D.33

214. The Employer Vice-Chairperson withdrew an amendment prior to its discussion.

D.45

215. The Government member of Greece introduced an amendment submitted by the Government members of Belgium, Denmark, Finland, France, Germany, Greece, Ireland, Netherlands, Norway, Portugal, Spain, Sweden and the United Kingdom, to replace the word "person" by the word "fisher" in the three instances in which it occurred in the paragraph. This was a drafting issue, since the Committee had already accepted a definition of the term "fisher".

216. The Worker and Employer Vice-Chairpersons supported the amendment and agreed that it be referred to the Drafting Committee.

217. The amendment was adopted and submitted to the Drafting Committee.

D.44

218. The Government member of Greece introduced an amendment submitted by the Government members of Belgium, Denmark, Finland, France, Germany, Greece, Ireland, Netherlands, Norway, Portugal, Spain, Sweden and the United Kingdom to replace the

words "or on an international voyage or" by the word "and". This amendment was concerned solely with Article 10, paragraph 3, which dealt with instances where exemptions from the requirement concerning medical certificates were not allowed. The amendment did not seek to address the issue of the definition of "international voyage" as dealt with in Article 1.

219. The Worker Vice-Chairperson strongly opposed the amendment.

220. The Employer Vice-Chairperson supported the amendment.

221. The Government member of Norway, speaking on behalf of the Government group, supported the amendment.

222. The Worker Vice-Chairperson proposed a subamendment to replace "and" with "or".

223. The Government members of Denmark, France, Greece, Namibia, Philippines, Portugal and Spain supported the subamendment.

224. The Government member of India and the Employer Vice-Chairperson were concerned that the subamendment would imply that small vessels remaining at sea for more than three days but staying close to shore would not be exempt from the requirement regarding medical certificates.

225. The Chairperson pointed out that the concern voiced by the Government member of India and the Employer Vice-Chairperson was covered by Article 3, paragraph 1, which stipulated that the competent authority might exclude limited categories of fishers or fishing vessels from the requirements of the Convention.

226. The amendment was adopted as subamended.

227. Article 10 was adopted as amended.

Article 11

Subparagraph (d)

D.30

228. The Government member of Norway introduced an amendment submitted by the Government members of Norway and Spain to add, after the word "certificates", the words ", which in no case shall exceed two years", in order to promote and improve safety and health on small vessels. The current formulation could be read to permit indefinite validity of medical certificates. Where required, Article 3 provided sufficient flexibility.

229. The Government member of Egypt pointed out that Article 10, paragraph 1, clearly indicated no fisher could work without a valid medical certificate. From a legal perspective, there was thus no need to mention the frequency of medical examinations and the period of validity as once certificates expired they had to be renewed.

230. The Government member of Norway, speaking on behalf of the Government group, stated a clear majority of the Government group opposed the amendment. The original text adequately reflected the need for flexibility regarding the period of validity.

231. The Employer Vice-Chairperson opposed the amendment.

232. The Government member of the Syrian Arab Republic stated that paragraphs 2 and 3 of Article 12 adequately addressed the issue of period of validity of medical certificates. The Government member of Lebanon agreed.

233. The Government members of Norway and Spain withdrew the amendment.

Subparagraph (e)

D.35

234. An amendment submitted by the Government member of Spain was not seconded and not discussed.

D.42

235. The Government member of Greece introduced an amendment submitted by the Government members of Belgium, Denmark, Finland, France, Germany, Greece, Ireland, Netherlands, Norway, Portugal, Spain, Sweden and the United Kingdom to replace the word "person" by the word "fisher" in subparagraph (e). This was a drafting issue.

236. The Employer Vice-Chairperson supported the amendment.

237. The Worker Vice-Chairperson opposed the amendment, noting that in this context "person" was correct, since a person seeking a medical certificate might not yet be a fisher.

238. The Government member of Greece underlined that the draft Convention dealt specifically with fishers and owners of fishing vessels, rather than members of the general public. The term "fishers" was more appropriate.

239. The Government member of Egypt stated there was need for clarification on the legal background of the terms "fisher" and "person".

240. The Government member of Lebanon preferred to keep the original text in order to remain consistent with the definition in Article 1(e).

241. The Government member of Namibia supported the amendment. Article 1(e) provided a definition for "fisher" which indicated that it included every person employed or engaged in any capacity or carrying out an occupation on board any fishing vessel.

242. The Employer Vice-Chairperson requested clarification from the secretariat as to what was meant by "Except as provided otherwise, the Convention applies to all fishers and all fishing vessels engaged in commercial fishing operations" in Article 2.1.

243. The deputy representative of the Secretary-General clarified the provision "Except as provided otherwise" in Article 2.1 could cover such cases as those of "persons" referred to in Article 11, subparagraph (e), that, for example, had applied for and were refused fishing licences or had failed to obtain medical certificates and thus were not, and perhaps would never become, fishers.

244. The Government member of Greece withdrew the amendment in light of the foregoing explanation.

245. Article 11 was adopted.

Medical examination

Article 12

D.148

246. The Employer Vice-Chairperson withdrew an amendment (D. 148) without discussion.

D.172

247. The Government member of Denmark introduced an amendment submitted by the Government members of the Bahamas, Belgium, Brazil, Côte d'Ivoire, Cuba, Denmark, Egypt, Finland, France, Germany, Greece, Ireland, Iceland, Kenya, Mauritania, Mexico, Mozambique, Namibia, Netherlands, Norway, Portugal, South Africa, Spain, Sweden, Syrian Arab Republic, Turkey, United Arab Emirates, United Kingdom and Uruguay to delete the words "or on an international voyage" from the introductory phrase of Article 12. He praised the cooperative spirit of the many Government members who had worked together to examine every provision that contained a reference to international voyages and to develop an alternative definition. The solution found for Article 10, paragraph 3, was equally applicable here.

248. The Worker Vice-Chairperson, the Employer Vice-Chairperson and the Government member of Norway, speaking on behalf of the Government group, all expressed support for the amendment, which was adopted.

D.149

249. The Employer Vice-Chairperson introduced an amendment to replace the text of paragraph 2 by the following: "Each Member shall adopt laws, regulations and other measures providing for the frequency of medical examinations and the period of validity of medical certificates." and immediately proposed a subamendment to insert "after consultations" after "shall". The purpose of the amendment was to increase flexibility to enable wide ratification. Reference to the frequency and the period of validity of medical certificates had been retained.

250. The Government member of Greece noted that these ideas were already covered in subparagraph (d) of Article 11 and Article 12 covered larger vessels. The subamendment offered nothing extra apart from the idea of "consultations" and that was not sufficient.

251. The Government member of Norway stated that the content of Article 12, paragraph 2, was crucial for safety aboard larger vessels. He would have preferred amending Article 11 to contain similar provisions.

252. The Worker Vice-Chairperson joined the Government members of Greece and Norway in rejecting the amendment, as did the Government members of Denmark, France and Germany.

253. The Employer Vice-Chairperson withdrew the amendment.

254. Article 12 was adopted as amended.

Part IV. Conditions of service

Manning and hours of rest

Article 13

D.132

255. The Government member of Denmark presented an amendment, submitted by the Government members of Denmark, Finland, France, Germany, Ireland, Netherlands, Norway, Portugal, Spain, Sweden and the United Kingdom, which was intended to replace the text of subparagraph (b) by the following text: "fishers are given regular periods of rest of sufficient length to ensure health and safety." Regularity of rest periods was essential for the health and safety of fishers.

256. The Worker Vice-Chairperson supported the amendment.

257. The Employer Vice-Chairperson requested clarification as to the intended meaning of "regular". The term seemed to imply "at fixed intervals" and this was not always practicable on fishing vessels. Vessels engaged in night fishing could not accord fishers rest periods at night, for example. She proposed a subamendment to replace the word "regular" by "appropriate".

258. The Worker Vice-Chairperson opposed the Employer members' subamendment.

259. The Government member of Denmark remarked that the Convention offered sufficient flexibility with regard to exceptional circumstances. In normal circumstances, however, it was important to maintain the regularity of rest periods as a matter of occupational safety and health. The timing of rest periods could vary according to the fishing operations being undertaken.

260. The Government member of Norway observed that there was a clear majority in the Government group in favour of the amendment. He could not, however, comment on the Employer members' subamendment.

261. The Government member of Lebanon noted that it was obvious that fishers should take rest periods that were regular and appropriate, and proposed that the phrase "regular periods of rest of sufficient length" be replaced by "sufficient daily rest periods".

262. The Government member of China seconded the subamendment of the Government member of Lebanon, which was supported by the Government members of Egypt, Japan and the Syrian Arab Republic.

263. The Government member of Belgium did not support either subamendment. The word "regular" was a flexible term, not a fixed one, and was better than the alternatives proposed.

264. The Government members of the Bahamas, Germany, Namibia, Norway, Philippines and Turkey also preferred the amendment to either of the proposed subamendments. The Government member of Germany noted that "regular" implied "on a daily basis", but not necessarily at a fixed time. The Government member of the Philippines observed that the regularity of rest periods could be discerned both in established work arrangements between employers and workers and in the policies of individual countries.

265. The Employer Vice-Chairperson noted the various understandings of what the term "regular" implied for various members of the Committee, in particular "not at an appointed time" and "based on established work arrangements". She asked for clarification as to the flexibility that the Convention offered with regard to the determination of rest periods.

266. The Government member of Denmark responded that the non-prescriptive chapeau of Article 13 provided sufficient flexibility, since it was for the competent authority to decide. As for the additional requirements in Article 14, its paragraphs 2 and 3, enabled the competent authority to make other arrangements as necessary in the light of circumstances.

267. The Government member of Germany noted that flexibility was also evident in the requirement that fishers have appropriate periods of rest within a 24-hour period, but not at a specific time each day.

268. The Employer member of the Netherlands felt that the interpretations of the term "regular" made by the Government members of Denmark and Germany were contradictory. Also, the flexibility granted in Article 14 only related to larger vessels. Therefore, countries like Egypt or the Syrian Arab Republic, where most fishing was carried out on small vessels, would not derive much benefit from it.

269. The Government member of Egypt affirmed that everybody agreed that fishers should be entitled to periods of rest specified in national laws or regulations and that details should be left to work arrangements between employers and workers taking into account the circumstances on board the vessel.

270. The Government member of South Africa supported the amendment and stated that the two subamendments could have unintended consequences. For example, the term "appropriate" might mean that periods of rest could be accumulated and given at the end of the voyage. International studies illustrated that irregular periods of rest had serious consequences for occupational safety and health. As to the query of the Employer Vice-Chairperson, there was sufficient flexibility because neither hours of work nor hours of rest were specified, and rest periods were not required at a specific time.

271. The Chairperson concluded that a sufficient majority of the Committee members supported the amendment, which was therefore adopted.

272. Article 13 was adopted as amended.

Article 14

D.177

273. The Government member of Denmark introduced an amendment, on behalf of the Government members of the Bahamas, Belgium, Brazil, Côte d'Ivoire, Cuba, Denmark, Egypt, Finland, France, Germany, Greece, Iceland, Ireland, Kenya, Mauritania, Mexico, Mozambique, Namibia, Netherlands, Norway, Portugal, South Africa, Spain, Sweden, Syrian Arab Republic, Turkey, United Arab Emirates, United Kingdom and Uruguay to replace paragraph 1 by the following paragraph:

> 1. In addition to the requirements set out in Article 13, the competent authority shall:
>
> (a) for vessels of [24] metres in length and over, establish a minimum level of manning for the safe navigation of the vessel, specifying the number and the qualifications of the fishers required;
>
> (b) for fishing vessels regardless of size remaining at sea for more than three days, after consultation and for the purpose of limiting fatigue, establish the minimum hours of rest

to be provided to fishers. Minimum hours of rest shall be no less than ten hours in any 24-hour period, and 77 hours in any seven-day period.

The speaker explained that subparagraph (a) dealt with manning, whilst subparagraph (b) dealt with rest hours. These two issues were too different to be covered by the same parameters. As a consequence, the amendment proposed to delete the reference to international voyages in (a) and to extend the notion of rest hours in (b) to cover all vessels which were at sea for more than three days, regardless of size.

274. The Employer Vice-Chairperson did not support the totality of the amendment. The Employer members had submitted their own amendments to delete the reference to international voyages from the introductory phrase and the number and qualifications of fishers from subparagraph (a) and to lessen the requirements in subparagraph (b). Overly prescriptive details would have a negative impact on the cost of operations as well as on the livelihoods of those whose earnings were derived from a share of the catch. She urged the Committee to take the Employer members' amendments into account.

275. The Worker Vice-Chairperson strongly supported the Government members' amendment, which was important in terms of fishers' safety and health.

276. The Government member of Norway, on behalf of the Government group, supported the proposed amendment.

277. The Government member of Canada commented that the second sentence of subparagraph (b) was too prescriptive and could be shifted to the Recommendation, an opinion shared by the Government members of Japan and the United States and the Employers' group.

278. The Government member of Denmark did not support the moving of subparagraph (b) to the Recommendation and added that paragraphs 2 and 3 of Article 14 of the Office text offered sufficient flexibility.

279. The Worker Vice-Chairperson observed that fatigue was the principal cause of many accidents and, for this reason, the specific requirements regarding minimum hours of rest should remain in the Convention.

280. The Government member of Norway supported that view, noting that only 10 hours of daily rest amounted potentially to 14 hours of work per day. This was a major safety concern.

281. The Government member of France noted that, while hours of work were difficult to regulate in the sector due to the nature of fishing, minimum hours of rest could be determined and it was vital to retain this provision in the Convention.

282. The Government members of Portugal, South Africa and the United Kingdom agreed.

283. The amendment was adopted. As a result, amendments D.173, D.181, D.108, D.109, D.152, D.154, D.180, and D.111 fell.

D.182

284. The Employer Vice-Chairperson introduced an amendment to replace the text of paragraph 2 by the following text: "In accordance with general principles of protection of health and safety of workers, and for objective or technical reasons or reasons concerning the organization of work, Members may allow exceptions from the provision laid down in

paragraph 1(b)." It was important to ensure flexibility. She noted that the notion of compensatory rest periods was included in the phrase "general principles of protection of health and safety".

285. The Worker Vice-Chairperson found the amendment undermined paragraph 1(b), which the Committee had just adopted. As a consequence, he could not support it.

286. The Government member of Norway indicated that the Government group did not support the amendment.

287. The Employer Vice-Chairperson withdrew the amendment.

D.113

288. The Worker Vice-Chairperson introduced an amendment in paragraph 2, to insert after the words "specified reasons" the words ", as set out in a collective agreement," stating that such a provision would increase the influence of the social partners.

289. The Government member of Norway, speaking on behalf of the Government group, did not support the amendment.

290. The Employer Vice-Chairperson did not support the amendment.

291. The Worker Vice-Chairperson therefore withdrew the amendment.

292. Article 14 was adopted as amended.

Crew list

Article 15

D.151

293. The Government member of Greece introduced an amendment submitted by the Government members of Denmark, Finland, France, Germany, Greece, Ireland, Netherlands, Norway, Portugal, Spain, Sweden and the United Kingdom, to add the words "and when" after the word "whom" in the second sentence. The proposal sought to ensure the proper handling of administrative procedures.

294. The Employer Vice-Chairperson, the Worker Vice-Chairperson and the Government member of Norway, speaking on behalf of the Government group, supported the amendment, which was thus adopted.

D.103

295. The Worker Vice-Chairperson introduced an amendment submitted by the Workers' group to add the words "and for what purpose(s)" at the end of the second sentence.

296. The Employer Vice-Chairperson supported the amendment.

297. The Government member of Norway, speaking on behalf of the Government group, reported that a clear majority of Governments opposed this amendment.

298. The Government members of Egypt, Germany and the Syrian Arab Republic preferred the Office text.

299. The Government member of Greece supported the amendment because crew lists contained fishers' personal data, and applicable legislation concerning the protection of personal data should be taken into account.

300. The Government member of Namibia supported the amendment, since it was logical that the Government should know the purpose before providing the crew list to anybody.

301. The Government member of India supported the amendment for security reasons.

302. The amendment was adopted.

D.127, D.128

303. The Employer Vice-Chairperson introduced an amendment to replace the word "*rôle*" by "*liste*" in the French version and "*un rol de tripulación*" by "*una lista de tripulantes*" and the words "*dicho rol*" by the words "*dicha lista*" in the Spanish version. The amendment did not concern the English text.

304. The Government member of Spain introduced an amendment to the same effect, submitted by the Government members of Belgium, France and Spain. This was not just a translation issue; there were substantive differences between the two types of lists.

305. The Worker Vice-Chairperson said that Spanish-speaking Worker members had pointed out that the terms were often used interchangeably.

306. The Government member of Spain explained that a "*rol*" and a "*lista*" were two different documents: a "*rol*" contained additional information on, inter alia, the vessel's characteristics, the duties of the crew members, and safety certificates. A "*lista*" was simply a list containing the crew members' names.

307. A member of the secretariat recalled the background and evolution of the provision. The proposed Conclusions discussed by the Committee in 2004 had referred to a "list of persons on board" and a subsequent Drafting Committee had replaced this formulation by the technical term "crew list". The intention of the provision was to ensure that authorities would be in a position to quickly assess the number and identity of crew members on board a specific ship, in the event of a maritime accident.

308. The Government member of Mexico, in the light of the explanation given by the Office, agreed that the word "*lista*" should be used instead of "*rol*" in the Spanish version.

309. The Government member of France also supported the amendments.

310. The Worker Vice-Chairperson agreed to the amendments, which were adopted.

311. Article 15 was adopted as amended.

Fisher's work agreement

Article 16

312. Article 16 was adopted without amendment.

Article 17

D.150, D.156

313. The Government member of Greece introduced an amendment, submitted by the Government members of Belgium, Denmark, Finland, France, Germany, Greece, Ireland, Netherlands, Norway, Portugal, Spain, Sweden and the United Kingdom, to delete subparagraph (b). The requirement to keep records concerning a fisher's work under a work agreement was an unnecessary bureaucratic burden. Article 15 ensured that authorities would know how many fishers were on board and Article 16 provided for the fisher to be given a work agreement in accordance with the Convention, making subparagraph (b) of Article 17 unnecessary.

314. The Government member of Egypt referred to Article 5 of the Fishermen's Articles of Agreement Convention, 1959 (No. 114), and supported the original draft text.

315. The Worker Vice-Chairperson said that the Worker members could not support the proposal to delete subparagraph (b), but signalled their support for an amendment (D.156) submitted by the Employer members.

316. The Employer Vice-Chairperson introduced an amendment to insert the words "where applicable," before the word "maintenance" in subparagraph (b). This proposal would offer governments discretion as to whether or not to keep such records. Both amendments before the Committee were acceptable to her group.

317. The Government member of Greece stated that his delegation, which had been one of the sponsors of the amendment to delete subparagraph (b), was willing to withdraw its support for that amendment in favour of the Employer members' proposal.

318. The Government members of Denmark, France, Norway and Portugal also withdrew support for their own amendment, which was then considered withdrawn with the tacit approval of all sponsors.

319. The Government members of Lebanon and the Syrian Arab Republic supported the Employers' amendment, which was adopted.

320. Article 17 was adopted as amended.

Article 18

D.158

321. The Employer Vice-Chairperson introduced an amendment, which would replace the text of Article 18 by the following: "A copy of the fisher's work agreement shall be provided to the fisher." Possession by the fisher of the work agreement was sufficient; any requirement that the agreement be carried on board the fishing vessel was superfluous.

322. The Worker Vice-Chairperson rejected the amendment. The Office text was preferable for compliance and inspection purposes.

323. The Government member of Namibia opposed the amendment. Article 18 rightfully addressed two issues: first, that the fisher should have a copy of the agreement; and second, that a copy should be kept on board the vessel.

324. The Government member of the Bahamas, speaking on behalf of the Government members of CARICOM, and the Government members of Egypt and Spain, also supported the Office text, citing the arguments presented by the Worker Vice-Chairperson and the Government member of Namibia.

325. The Government member of Spain suggested that the Drafting Committee be informed that the term used in Article 17 should also be used in Article 18.

326. The Employer Vice-Chairperson withdrew the Employer members' amendment.

327. Article 18 was adopted without amendment.

Article 19

D.147

328. The Government member of Greece introduced an amendment submitted by the Government members of Denmark, Greece and the Netherlands to add at the end of the Article the following sentence: "For fishing vessels of less than [24] metres in length, a Member may, after consultation, not apply Articles 16-18 and Annex II to fishers that are husband or wife, brothers or sisters, or children of the fishing vessel owner." The purpose of the amendment was to reflect a special cultural element. The key elements of the proposed amendment were to allow Members, should they so decide and only after consultation, to permit small fishing vessels on which members of the same family are working not to follow certain procedures. The aim was to reflect the real situation on many small vessels with small crews. Following consultations with the other Government members that had submitted the amendment, the speaker proposed a subamendment that would read as follows: "For fishing vessels with fewer than five fishers employed or engaged, a Member may, after consultation, not apply Articles 16-18 and Annex II to those who are husband or wife, brothers or sisters, or children of the fishing vessel owner."

329. The Government member of Egypt supported the subamendment, which was in compliance with Article 1, paragraph 2, of the Fishermen's Articles of Agreement Convention, 1959 (No. 114).

330. The Worker Vice-Chairperson stated that the Worker members could agree with the subamendment on condition that the [24] metre vessel length be kept in the text.

331. The Government member of Greece accepted the further subamendment submitted by the Worker members.

332. The Government member of Norway then proposed a further subamendment to replace the word "children" with the words "sons or daughters" because children would not be allowed to work on fishing vessels. This proposal was seconded by the Government member of Greece.

333. The Employer Vice-Chairperson pointed out that there might be cases in which more than five family members of the fishing vessel owner could be working on the fishing vessel and wondered whether the intention was not to apply the said Articles in such cases. She proposed to further subamend the text to remove the reference to "fewer than five fishers employed or engaged".

334. The Government member of China agreed there was no need for the reference to "fewer than five fishers".

335. The Worker Vice-Chairperson opposed the Employers' group's proposal to remove the reference to "fewer than five fishers".

336. The Government member of Spain preferred the original text. The amendment contradicted Spanish regulations and did not cover the possibility that family members could be living independently from the vessel owner.

337. The Government member of Portugal supported the comments of the Government member of Spain.

338. The Government member of Germany supported the amendment, but said it should be considered an exception, and that a limit of five fishers should be adopted.

339. The Government member of the Syrian Arab Republic opposed the amendment, stating that an overly detailed text would create difficulties in implementation.

340. In the interest of time, the Worker Vice-Chairperson suggested reverting to the original text.

341. The Committee agreed and the amendment was not adopted.

342. Article 19 was adopted.

Article 20

D.176

343. The Government member of Denmark introduced an amendment submitted by the Government members of the Bahamas, Belgium, Brazil, Côte d'Ivoire, Cuba, Denmark, Egypt, Finland, France, Germany, Greece, Iceland, Ireland, Japan, Kenya, Mauritania, Mexico, Mozambique, Namibia, Netherlands, Norway, Portugal, South Africa, Spain, Sweden, Syrian Arab Republic, Turkey, United Arab Emirates, United Kingdom and Uruguay to delete Article 20. He proposed an immediate subamendment, however, to retain the reference in Article 20 to a written and signed work agreement and to refer it to the Drafting Committee for redrafting and appropriate placement. As an aid to the Committee and purely for illustrative purposes, the sponsors had provided the text of Annex II which would result, should the amendment be adopted. Annex II would apply to all vessels regardless of size. The speaker assured the Committee that Annex II remained open to discussion.

344. The Worker Vice-Chairperson supported the amendment as subamended.

345. The Government group also supported the proposal.

346. The amendment was adopted as subamended.

D.178

347. The Employer Vice-Chairperson withdrew an amendment (D.178).

D.107

348. The Worker Vice-Chairperson introduced an amendment to replace paragraph 2 with the following text: "It shall be the responsibility of the fishing vessel owner to ensure that each fisher has a written work agreement signed by both the fisher and the fishing vessel owner

or an authorized representative of the fishing vessel owner." The intention was to make clear that both contracting parties needed to sign the agreement.

349. An Employer member from the Netherlands proposed a subamendment to replace the second mention of "fishing vessel owner" with "contracting party of the fisher". This subamendment would deal with cases where the fishing vessel owner, as defined in Article 1 of the Convention, was not party to the fisher's work agreement. Such situations were recognized in subparagraph 1(d) of Annex II of the Office text, which referred to "the employer, or fishing vessel owner, or other party to the agreement with the fisher".

350. The Worker Vice-Chairperson did not support the subamendment, since it was too detailed.

351. The Government member of the Syrian Arab Republic found the Office text complete and comprehensive and therefore opposed both the amendment and the subamendment.

352. The Government member of the United Kingdom felt that the wording proposed by the Employers was difficult to understand and wondered whether the definition of "fishing vessel owner" in Article 1 was not broad enough to cover the cases that were of concern to the Employers.

353. The Government member of Namibia rejected the Employer members' subamendment for the reasons cited by the Government member of the United Kingdom. The term "contracting party of the fisher" was not defined, nor did it appear elsewhere in the Convention.

354. The Government member of the Netherlands suggested that the wording found in subparagraph 1(d) of Annex II be used instead of the new term proposed by the Employer member from the Netherlands.

355. The Government member of Egypt stressed that it was important that the Article be drafted in a clear manner. The essential point was to ensure that there was a written contract signed by the two parties and that it was in conformity with the provisions of the Convention.

356. The Employer member from the Netherlands clarified that the definition of "fishing vessel owner" in Article 1 did not include employment services. These services were defined in Article 1, subparagraph 1(b), of the Private Employment Agencies Convention, 1997 (No. 181), as services a private employment agency might provide, including "services consisting of employing workers with a view to making them available to a third party, who may be a natural or legal person (referred to below as a 'user enterprise') which assigns their tasks and supervises the execution of these tasks". Employment services were not covered by the definition of "fishing vessel owner" in Article 1, although these businesses were legal enterprises operating in all countries. Such services were often used in the fishing industry to supply crew to fishing vessels. The subamendment would bring the Worker members' amendment into line with this reality. The Employer members therefore supported the proposal of the Government member of the Netherlands, which addressed these concerns.

357. The Government member of Norway believed that the wording "or an authorized representative of the fishing vessel owner", as contained in the Workers' amendment, took care of the concerns raised by the Employers. Fishing vessel owners could authorize employment services to sign the agreement on their behalf, while remaining responsible for ensuring that each fisher had a written and signed agreement.

358. The Worker Vice-Chairperson shared the view expressed by the Government member of Norway. The proposal of the Government member of the Netherlands would undermine the intent of their amendment.

359. Further support for the position of the Government member of Norway was expressed by the Government members of Algeria, Belgium, Denmark, France, Germany, Ireland, Namibia, Nigeria, Portugal and Tunisia.

360. The Government member of South Africa supported the subamendment of the Government member of the Netherlands. Outsourcing had become the predominant means of providing crew to fishing vessels. Workers thus engaged should be provided with the protection of the Convention.

361. The Government member of the Syrian Arab Republic believed that the concept of "fishing vessel owner" as it appeared in the Office text was sufficiently broad and balanced.

362. The Government member of the Philippines felt that the Office text was sufficient in form and substance, and consistent with the principle that the liability rested on the fishing vessel owners, regardless of their representation by another entity.

363. The Government member of Egypt agreed that, whether it was the fishing vessel owner or his or her representative who signed the agreement, the legal relationship and responsibilities of the fishing vessel owner remained the same.

364. As the majority of Committee members had expressed support for the Workers' amendment, it was adopted.

365. Article 20 was adopted as amended.

Repatriation

Article 21

D.183

366. The Employer Vice-Chairperson introduced an amendment to replace the text of paragraph 1 with the following text:

> Members shall ensure that fishers on a fishing vessel that flies their flag and that enters a foreign port are entitled to repatriation in the event that the fisher's work agreement has expired or has been terminated for justified reasons by the fisher or by the fishing vessel owner, or the fisher is no longer able to carry out the duties required under the work agreement or cannot be expected to carry them out in the specific circumstances. This also applies to fishers from that vessel who are transported from the vessel to the foreign port.

She then subamended it by adding "for the same reasons" after "transported" in the last line.

367. The Worker Vice-Chairperson supported the amendment as subamended.

368. The Government member of Norway, speaking on behalf of the Government group, preferred the Office text.

369. The Government member of Denmark remarked that an amendment (D.171) submitted by numerous Government members had the same intention as the Employers' proposal, which he supported

370. The Government members of Algeria, Egypt, Germany, Greece, India, Lebanon, Syrian Arab Republic and Tunisia also supported the amendment as subamended.

371. The amendment was adopted as subamended.

D.171

372. The Government member of Denmark withdrew an amendment (D.171).

D.146

373. The Government member of Denmark remarked that there could be situations where the cost of repatriation might be borne by the fisher himself. The draft consolidated maritime labour Convention had provided some guidance in this respect. The Government members of Denmark, Finland, Ireland, Netherlands, Portugal, Sweden and the United Kingdom therefore proposed an amendment to replace paragraph 2 by the following paragraph: "Members shall, after consultation, prescribe the circumstances where the fishers have a right to be repatriated at no cost to themselves."

374. The Employer Vice-Chairperson stated that the Employer members did not support this amendment. The phrase "or other measures" in the Office text would cover the Governments' concerns, as such measures could be prescribed by Members to take account of special circumstances.

375. The Worker Vice-Chairperson agreed and did not support the amendment.

376. The Government member of Norway said a clear majority of the Government group supported the amendment.

377. The Government member of Spain did not support the amendment. He preferred a clear definition of the circumstances under which a fisher would have to cover the costs of repatriation. These costs were high and should only be borne by a fisher who failed to meet his or her obligations.

378. The Government member of Egypt favoured the Office text because there was a reference to the obligations of the fishing vessel owner regarding the cost of repatriation. If, however, the fisher failed to respect his obligations, then the fishing vessel owner would not be liable for the cost of repatriation.

379. The Government members of Algeria, Japan, Lebanon, Syrian Arab Republic and Tunisia also preferred the Office text.

380. The amendment was not adopted.

D.179

381. The Employer Vice-Chairperson withdrew an amendment (D.179).

D.110

382. The Worker Vice-Chairperson introduced an amendment to insert in paragraph 3, after the words "entitled to repatriation" the words ", which shall not exceed nine months,". At present, no maximum duration of service was set after which a fisher would be entitled to see his or her family. He suggested inserting a maximum period of nine months of service for the entitlement to repatriation.

383. The Government member of Norway stated that the Government group did not support the amendment. The period of service which would give rise to an entitlement to repatriation was an issue to be agreed between the employer and the worker.

384. The Employer Vice-Chairperson endorsed this view.

385. The Worker Vice-Chairperson withdrew the amendment.

D.184

386. The Employer Vice-Chairperson withdrew an amendment (D.184).

387. Article 21 was adopted as amended.

Recruitment and placement

Article 22

Paragraph 2

D.134

388. The Government member of Denmark, speaking on behalf of the Government members of Denmark, Germany, Ireland and Sweden, proposed an amendment to replace the text of paragraph 2 by the following:

> Any private service providing recruitment and placement of fishers operating in its territory shall be operated in conformity with the general rules of the public employment service covering recruitment and placement of all workers and employers and/or the established practice of recruitment and placement of fishers. If there are no regulations or established practice in the member State in question or the employment conditions of fishers necessitate it, any private service providing recruitment and placement for fishers operating in its territory shall be operated in conformity with a standardized system of licensing or certification or other form of regulation, which shall be established, maintained or modified only after consultation.

The text of the existing paragraph 4 would be moved to the end of this new text. The purpose of this amendment was to make it possible for countries with established systems for shore-based recruitment and placement to continue using these systems after ratification.

389. In response to requests from the Employer and Worker Vice-Chairpersons, the deputy representative of the Secretary-General provided the following clarification on the relationship between the amendment and the Recruitment and Placement of Seafarers Convention, 1996 (No. 179), and the Private Employment Agencies Convention, 1997 (No. 181). The text of Article 22, paragraph 2, was similar to the second sentence of the amendment. Both were in line with the principles set out in Article 2, paragraph 2, of Convention No. 179 and in Article 3, paragraph 2, of Convention No. 181, save in so far as the amendment introduced the concept of a standardized system of licensing or certification or other form of regulation. The first sentence of the amendment, however, was not founded in either of these Conventions, and it was for the Committee to decide whether or not to include this sentence in the Convention.

390. The Government member of Denmark proposed a subamendment to replace the words ". If there are no regulations or established practice in the member State in question or the employment conditions of fishers necessitate it, any private service providing recruitment and placement for fishers operating in its territory shall be operated" by ", or".

391. The Worker Vice-Chairperson proposed an alternate subamendment to delete the words "and employers and/or the established practice of recruitment and placement of fishers."

392. The Government member of the Netherlands supported the subamendments of both the Government member of Denmark and the Workers' group.

393. The Government member of the United Kingdom said that, under the terms of the amendment, private services would have to operate under the same conditions as the public employment service, which seemed unreasonable. She therefore proposed a subamendment to delete the words "of the public employment service".

394. The Government members of France and Ireland supported the subamendment proposed by the Government member of the United Kingdom.

395. The Government member of Greece stated that often the general rules covering recruitment and placement were the rules that governed public employment services and so the subamendment proposed by the Government member of the United Kingdom would not free private services from having to operate under the same conditions as the public employment services.

396. The Worker Vice-Chairperson opposed the subamendment proposed by the Government member of the United Kingdom and supported the original text.

397. The Employer Vice-Chairperson also supported the original text.

398. The Chairperson concluded that a sufficient majority of the Committee members opposed the amendment and its subamendments, which were therefore not adopted.

D.160

399. The Employer Vice-Chairperson introduced an amendment to add the following new sentence at the end of Article 22, paragraph 2: "This shall not apply to a private service providing recruitment and placement solely within a legal group of companies to which it belongs."

400. The Worker Vice-Chairperson and the Government member of Norway, speaking on behalf of the Government group, opposed the amendment

401. The Employer Vice-Chairperson withdrew the amendment.

Paragraph 3

D.129

402. The Government member of the United Kingdom introduced an amendment submitted by the Government members of Belgium, Denmark, Finland, France, Germany, Greece, Ireland, Netherlands, Portugal, Spain, Sweden and the United Kingdom. Noting an error in

the original amendment she immediately proposed a subamendment to replace in subparagraph (c) the words "under which the licence, certificate or similar authorization" by the words "under which any licence, certificate or similar authorization". The purpose of this subamendment was to cover the circumstances under which there might not be a licence, certificate or authorization.

403. The Employer Vice-Chairperson, the Worker Vice-Chairperson and the Government member of Norway, speaking on behalf of the Government group, supported the subamendment, which was adopted.

D.145

404. The Government member of Greece introduced an amendment submitted by the Government members of Finland, Greece, Ireland, Netherlands, Norway, Spain and the United Kingdom to insert the word "private" before all instances of the word "recruitment" in subparagraph (c). The aim of the proposed amendment was to clarify that only private recruitment or placement services would require a licence, certificate or similar authorization and not public ones. The Government member of Ireland further clarified that the intention was that the word "private" would refer to both "recruitment" and "placement service".

405. The Employer Vice-Chairperson, the Worker Vice-Chairperson and the Government member of Norway, speaking on behalf of the Government group, supported the amendment, which was adopted.

Paragraph 4

D.159, D.144

406. The Committee considered two amendments submitted by the Employer members and by the Government members of Denmark, Finland, France, Germany, Greece, Ireland, Netherlands, Portugal Spain, Sweden and the United Kingdom to delete paragraph 4. The Employer Vice-Chairperson introduced the amendment and stated it did not appear logical that a fisher who would seek employment should be compensated if he or she did not succeed in getting that employment.

407. The Government member of the United Kingdom supported the amendment, noting that paragraph 4 was too prescriptive and might deter ratification.

408. The Worker Vice-Chairperson opposed the amendments and pointed out that paragraph 4 was taken from Article 4, subparagraph 2(f), of the Recruitment and Placement of Seafarers Convention, 1996 (No. 179). He proposed a subamendment to insert the word "private" before the phrase "recruitment or placement service".

409. The Chairperson stated the subamendment proposed by the Worker Vice-Chairperson was not valid and it was therefore not discussed.

410. The Government member of Norway, speaking on behalf of the Government group, supported the amendments.

411. The Government member of Uruguay opposed the amendment.

412. The Chairperson concluded that a sufficient majority of the Committee members supported the amendment, which was therefore adopted.

413. Article 22 was adopted as amended.

Payment of fishers

Article 23

Paragraph 1

D.143

> 414. The Government member of the United Kingdom introduced an amendment submitted by the Government members of Finland, France, Germany, Ireland, Netherlands, Portugal, Sweden and the United Kingdom to delete the second sentence of paragraph 1 because the original text was not clear as to what other fishers might be paid. The sentence was also too detailed for the Convention.
>
> 415. The Worker Vice-Chairperson opposed the amendment.
>
> 416. The Employer Vice-Chairperson and the Government member of Norway, speaking on behalf of the Government group, supported the amendment.
>
> 417. The Chairperson concluded that a sufficient majority of the Committee members supported the amendment, which was adopted.

Article 23

Paragraph 2

D.142

> 418. The Government member of the United Kingdom introduced an amendment submitted by the Government members of Belgium, Denmark, Finland, France, Germany, Greece, Ireland, Netherlands, Norway, Portugal, Spain, Sweden and the United Kingdom to delete paragraph 2 because it was too prescriptive and there would be practical difficulties in implementing its provisions.
>
> 419. The Employer Vice-Chairperson and the Government member of Norway, speaking on behalf of the Government group, supported the amendment.
>
> 420. The Worker Vice-Chairperson opposed the amendment.
>
> 421. The Chairperson concluded that a sufficient majority of Committee members supported the amendment, which was adopted.

New paragraph to follow paragraph 2

D.114

> 422. The Worker Vice-Chairperson withdrew an amendment before its discussion.
>
> 423. Article 23 was adopted as amended.

Payment of fishers

Article 24

D.175

424. The Government member of Denmark introduced an amendment submitted by the Government members of the Bahamas, Belgium, Brazil, Côte d'Ivoire, Cuba, Denmark, Egypt, Finland, France, Germany, Greece, Iceland, Ireland, Japan, Kenya, Mauritania, Mexico, Mozambique, Namibia, Netherlands, Norway, Portugal, South Africa, Spain, Sweden, Syrian Arab Republic, Turkey, United Arab Emirates, United Kingdom and Uruguay to delete the words "of [24] metres in length and over or engaged on international voyages". The provisions of this Article should apply to all fishing vessels.

425. The Worker Vice-Chairperson expressed support.

426. The Government member of Norway, speaking on behalf of the Government group, also supported the amendment, as did the Government members of Algeria, Lebanon and Tunisia.

427. The Employer Vice-Chairperson stated that the Employer members supported the amendment, but wished to bring to the attention of the Committee the contents of an amendment (D.192) that they had submitted, which added the words "normally remaining at sea for more than 14 days". If their amendment were adopted, then only very small boats that did not stay at sea for such a long period of time would in practice be exempted.

428. The Government-sponsored amendment was adopted.

D.192

429. The Employer Vice-Chairperson introduced an amendment, which she immediately subamended to insert only the words "normally remaining at sea for more than 14 days" after "vessels".

430. The Worker Vice-Chairperson did not support this proposal.

431. The Government member of Norway stated that the Government group did not support the Employer members' amendment, a view reiterated by the Government member of Argentina.

432. The Government member of India supported the amendment as subamended. It was important for countries like hers to have the opportunity to exempt small fishing vessels from the provisions of Article 24.

433. The amendment as subamended was not adopted.

D.116

434. The Worker Vice-Chairperson introduced an amendment to replace the words "payments received" by the word "earnings". The purpose was to make a clearer, more understandable text.

435. The Employer Vice-Chairperson requested clarification from the Worker members as to the difference in meaning between "earnings" and "payments received, including advances".

436. The Worker Vice-Chairperson explained that payment might take many forms. In order to ensure that all forms of payments, including share of catch, would be included, the term "earnings" was proposed.

437. The Employer Vice-Chairperson felt that the term "payments" included share of catch and preferred the Office text.

438. The Government member of Norway said that the Government group supported the amendment for the same reasons put forward by the Worker members. The term "earnings" included diverse methods of payments.

439. The Government member of Egypt, speaking also on behalf of the Government members of Algeria, Lebanon, Saudi Arabia, Syrian Arab Republic and Tunisia, said that the term "payments" was preferable to "earnings" as the discussion was about salaries paid to fishers.

440. The Employer Vice-Chairperson wondered why, if the aim of the Worker members was for a clearer, more inclusive text, they had deleted the word "received".

441. The Worker Vice-Chairperson withdrew the amendment.

D.117

442. The Worker Vice-Chairperson introduced an amendment to replace the words "reasonable cost" by the words "no cost". There had been frequent reports of occasions when fishers faced difficulties with some manning agencies when remitting payments to their families, especially when payments were to be made in different currencies.

443. The Employer Vice-Chairperson expressed her group's support for the amendment.

444. The Government member of Norway stated that the Government group did not support the amendment.

445. The Government member of France initially had reservations about the amendment but, in the light of the Employer members' support, also supported it.

446. The Government members of Argentina, Côte d'Ivoire, Japan, Portugal and Spain agreed with the Government member of France.

447. The amendment was therefore adopted.

448. Article 24 was adopted as amended.

Part V. Accommodation and food

Articles 25-28

449. The Committee agreed on a further mandate for the Working Party. It should examine all relevant amendments submitted to Articles 25-28 and Annex III and develop and propose text on the above provisions for consideration by the Committee.

450. Following the deliberations of the Working Party on Articles 25-28 and Annex III, the Government member of Brazil, who served as Chairperson, presented her report to the Committee. She recalled the terms of reference and stated that the Working Party had considered all amendments submitted on these items (D.46-D.93, D.95-D.100 and

C.S.P/WP/D.4-D.25), as well as other proposals and subamendments put forward by various Members. A document (C.S.P./D.221) was distributed to the Committee, which contained a list of paragraphs on which consensus had been reached and a list of those on which there had been no consensus.

451. The Chairperson of the Working Party then highlighted the substantive changes made by the Working Party.

452. In Article 25, there was some concern that the expression "potable water" was not universally understood and "drinking water" might be a better term (D.46). The Working Party suggested that the Drafting Committee should examine this issue, which was also relevant to Article 27(b) (D.49) and paragraph 70 (D.72) of Annex III.

453. In Article 26, subparagraph (g), it was agreed that the words "that does not meet the requirements of this Convention" (D.76) be added at the end.

454. In Article 27, subparagraph (c), it was agreed that a fishers' work agreement be added as an option to recover the cost of food and drinking water (D.51).

455. Regarding Article 28, some members had felt the provisions of Annex III were too prescriptive and that more flexibility was needed. After much debate, it was decided that a new paragraph should be added to this Article, to read: "A Member which is not in a position to implement the provisions of Annex III may, after consultation, adopt provisions in its laws and regulations or other measures which are substantially equivalent to the provisions set out in Annex III, with the exception of provisions related to Article 27." With the exception of one Government member, all members of the Working Party had supported this paragraph. Since there was not unanimous agreement by the Working Party, and as it was such a significant issue, it was decided that this suggestion would remain in square brackets for further consideration by the Committee.

456. As a result of a subamendment (D.78) to paragraph 1 of Annex III, the Working Party suggested that the competent authority "may, after consultation," apply requirements in this Annex to existing vessels.

457. Two new paragraphs were proposed to the general provisions of the Annex. The first was in response to various amendments to apply some of the provisions to working spaces, in addition to accommodation. It read as follows:

> Members may extend the requirements of this Annex regarding noise and vibration, ventilation, heating and air conditioning, and lighting to enclosed working spaces and spaces used for storage, if after consultation, such application is considered appropriate and will not have a negative influence on the function of the process or working conditions or the quality of the catches.

458. The second paragraph was agreed upon as a result of the conclusions of the Working Party on Annex I, which had been adopted by the Committee. The text was received by the Drafting Committee, which recommended in C.R./D.3(C.S.P.) the inclusion of the following wording in Annex III.

> The use of gross tonnage as referred to in Article 5 of this Convention is limited to the following specified paragraphs of this Annex: 10, 31, 32, 34, 36, 39, 54 and 59. For these purposes, where the competent authority, after consultation, decides to use gross tonnage (gt) as the basis of measurement:
>
> (a) a gross tonnage of 175 gt shall be considered equivalent to a length (L) of 24 metres or a length overall (LOA) of 26.5 metres;

(b) a gross tonnage of 55 gt shall be considered equivalent to a length (L) of 15 metres or a length overall (LOA) of 16.5 metres;

(c) a gross tonnage of 700 gt shall be considered equivalent to a length (L) of 45 metres or a length overall (LOA) of 50 metres."

Consequently, all references to tonnage elsewhere in the Annex were removed. The square brackets around the length limits throughout the Annex were also removed.

459. At the end of paragraph 12, a new sentence was added so as not to exclude the possibility of sanitary areas being shared by two cabins.

460. Consensus was reached to add "crew accommodation" to paragraph 14 (D.62).

461. The phrase "as far as practicable, in accordance with relevant international standards" was added to paragraph 16 (D.96).

462. Paragraph 19 was subamended (D.67) to allow for other measures besides ventilation to protect non-smokers from tobacco smoke on board.

463. Two amendments to paragraph 27 (D.97, D.95) were agreed upon to ensure that emergency lighting was provided in sleeping rooms.

464. Paragraph 44 was amended (D.70) to ensure that mess rooms would not be located forward of the collision bulkhead.

465. The square brackets around the word "four" were removed in paragraph 54 (D.91).

466. The word "adequate" was inserted in front of "facilities" in paragraphs 56 and 57 (D.77, D.71).

467. In paragraph 60, a reference to "other protective equipment" was inserted (D.92).

468. A sentence was added at the end of paragraph 61 to provide for cases where certain fishers bore the cost of bed linen, which could happen under certain collective agreements.

469. In paragraph 62, it was specified that mess rooms could be used for recreational activities.

470. In paragraph 63, it was underlined that the cost of communications should be reasonable and should not exceed the full cost to the vessel owner (D.73).

471. A reference to the protection needed for gas bottles on deck was inserted in paragraph 67 (D.94).

472. The Government member of Brazil concluded her intervention by recommending document C.S.P/D.219, which contained the Working Party's proposals for the text of Articles 25-28 and Annex III, to the Committee for the adoption of the text on which there was consensus and for further consideration of the remaining text, taking the Working Party's views into account.

473. After discussion between the Officers of the Committee and the Legal Adviser, the Chairperson announced that the proposals from the Working Party would be treated as a global amendment and were therefore open to subamendment. For the paragraphs on which the Working Party had not reached consensus, the Committee would consider each paragraph individually and members could present their proposals in the form of subamendments for consideration by the Committee. He hoped that the paragraphs on

which consensus had been achieved in the Working Party would not be subject to further subamendment by the Committee.

Articles 25, 26, 27, 28

474. On the basis of the consensus reached in the Working Party, the Committee adopted Articles 25, 26 and 27, as proposed by the Working Party.

475. The Government member of Japan did not believe the Working Party had achieved consensus on paragraph 1 of new Article 28. He thanked the Working Party for its hard work but regretted that the result did not provide sufficient flexibility. He presented a subamendment (D.81), submitted by the Government members of China, Indonesia, Japan and the Republic of Korea, to replace, in Article 28, the words "shall give full effect" by the words "shall give effect, as far as possible according to the condition of the Member,". His delegation's calculations indicated that the equivalency of a vessel of 24 metres in length should be 300 gt, rather than the 175 gt the Committee had agreed upon in Annex III. Given the Committee's decision, it had become even more crucial to ensure the Convention was sufficiently flexible. This was especially true for his Government. In Japan it was very difficult to increase the tonnage of fishing vessels because fishing resources were managed through the strict restriction of the number and tonnage of vessels. A vessel that was 23.95 metres long and 300 gt was obviously larger than one of 24.05 m and 176 gt. The former, larger vessel would not be subject to the stricter rules because of its length, whereas the latter would, despite being much smaller. He questioned this rationale, in terms of the equal and fair application of the Convention. The Accommodation of Crews (Fishermen) Convention, 1966 (No. 126), had few ratifications, yet the current draft of Annex III introduced stricter and more prescriptive provisions than those found in that Convention. This would unintentionally pose problems in terms of equal and fair application, and create serious obstacles for ratification for many countries, including Japan. Because of Japan's legal framework, these obstacles would not be removed by including the proposed new paragraph in Article 28. He urged the Committee to consider carefully the implications of rejecting the subamendment he had introduced.

476. The Committee agreed to examine this subamendment in conjunction with the Working Party's proposed additional paragraph for Article 28, as presented by the Chairperson of the Working Party.

477. The Government member of the United States emphasized that when the process of drafting the instruments had begun, he had understood that the intention was to address the interests of the most vulnerable workers. Thus, the aim had been not to be overly prescriptive, in order to adopt a Convention that could enjoy wide ratification. Nonetheless, too much prescription had been introduced into the text. The proposed new paragraph in Article 28 alleviated this problem, and he had no objection to the wording, which would help to encourage wider ratification.

478. The Government member of Norway, speaking on behalf of the Government group, stated there had been a clear majority in favour of the proposed new paragraph in Article 28.

479. The Employer and Worker Vice-Chairpersons supported this view.

480. The Government member of Japan supported the statement of the Government member of the United States, but as he had stated previously, the proposed new paragraph in Article 28 was not sufficient to allow his Government to find a way to ratify the Convention. He therefore opposed it.

481. The Government member of China strongly supported Japan's statement and agreed with the statement of the Government member of the United States. It was noteworthy that few Members had ratified the Accommodation of Crews (Fishermen) Convention, 1966 (No. 126), and other related Conventions. Perhaps these Conventions had been overly prescriptive. Since 80 per cent of fishing vessels were in Asia, the Convention ought to take Asian vessels into account. The key issue was to maximize the rights of fishers, especially the most vulnerable among them. The Working Party had introduced some flexibility into the text, but it was not sufficient. The text of the subamendment introduced by the Government member of Japan should be introduced into Article 28.

482. The Government member of Norway referred to Article 3, and felt that reference could also be made there to "substantial equivalence", to resolve some of the problems raised by the Government members of China and Japan with regard to compliance with Annex III.

483. The Government member of Japan requested confirmation on whether or not Article 3 would be applied to larger vessels of 24 m and over. The Chairperson replied that Article 3 had already been discussed, including explanations on the scope of its coverage. It was not possible to reopen discussion on a provision that had already been adopted.

484. The Government member of Japan reiterated his wish to have the subamendment included in Article 28.

485. The Chairperson concluded that a majority of the Committee members opposed the subamendment, which was therefore not adopted. A majority of Committee members supported the new paragraph in Article 28, which was adopted.

486. Article 28 was adopted, as proposed by the Working Party.

Part VI. Health protection, medical care and social security

Medical care

Article 29

487. Article 29 was adopted without amendment.

Article 30

D.170

488. The Government member of Denmark introduced an amendment submitted by the Government members of the Bahamas, Belgium, Brazil, Côte d'Ivoire, Cuba, Denmark, Egypt, Finland, France, Germany, Greece, Iceland, Ireland, Japan, Kenya, Mauritania, Mexico, Mozambique, Namibia, Netherlands, Norway, Portugal, South Africa, Spain, Sweden, Syrian Arab Republic, Turkey, United Arab Emirates, United Kingdom and Uruguay to replace, in the introductory phrase of Article 30, the words "or those engaged on international voyages or normally remaining at sea for more than three days" by the words "taking into account the number of fishers on board, the area of operation and the duration of the voyage". Since the Article concerned medical care and medical equipment, it would be best to use the same wording as in Article 29, subparagraph (a).

489. The Employer and Worker Vice-Chairpersons, the Government member of Argentina, and the Government member of Norway, speaking on behalf of the Government group, supported the amendment.

490. The amendment was adopted.

D.189

491. Due to the adoption of the previous amendment, the Employer Vice-Chairperson withdrew an amendment (D.189).

D.139

492. The Government member of the United Kingdom introduced an amendment submitted by the Government members of Denmark, Finland, France, Germany, Greece, Ireland, Netherlands, Norway, Portugal, Spain, Sweden and the United Kingdom, to add, at the end of subparagraph (c), the words "or the *International Medical Guide for Ships*". On the suggestion of the International Maritime Health Association, it was felt it was important to make a reference to this publication.

493. The Worker and Employer Vice-Chairpersons and the Government member of Norway, speaking on behalf of the Government group, supported the amendment.

494. The amendment was adopted.

495. Article 30 was adopted as amended.

Occupational safety and health and accident prevention

Article 31

D.140

496. The Government member of Denmark introduced an amendment submitted by the Government members of Denmark, Finland, France, Germany, Greece, Ireland, Netherlands, Norway, Portugal and Sweden to insert, at the beginning of subparagraph (b), before the word "training", the words "on board". The insertion aimed to ensure that laws, regulations or other measures provided for on-board training.

497. Both the Employers' and Workers' groups agreed that on-board training was important, but thought that the text of the Convention should refer to training in a more general sense and not be restricted to on-board training. They therefore did not support the proposed amendment.

498. The Government member of Denmark withdrew the amendment with the permission of the other sponsors.

D.138

499. The Government member of Greece presented an amendment submitted by the Government members of Denmark, Finland, Germany, Greece, Ireland, Netherlands, Norway, Spain, Sweden and the United Kingdom to insert the words "or, after consultation, of other appropriate bodies" after the word "committees". The proposal aimed at ensuring that, should bodies other than joint committees be set up to deal with occupational safety and health issues, this would be done only after consultation in accordance with Article 1.

500. Both the Employer and Worker Vice-Chairpersons expressed their groups' support for the amendment.

501. The Government member of Norway indicated that the Government group also supported the amendment.

502. Article 31 was thus adopted as amended.

Article 32

D.187

503. The Employer Vice-Chairperson withdrew an amendment (D.187).

D.174

504. The Government member of Denmark introduced an amendment submitted by the Government members of the Bahamas, Belgium, Brazil, Côte d'Ivoire, Cuba, Denmark, Egypt, Finland, France, Germany, Greece, Iceland, Ireland, Japan, Kenya, Mauritania, Mexico, Mozambique, Namibia, Netherlands, Norway, Portugal, South Africa, Spain, Sweden, Syrian Arab Republic, Turkey, United Arab Emirates, United Kingdom and Uruguay to replace, in paragraph 1, the words "or those engaged on international voyages" by the words "taking into account the number of fishers on board, the area of operation and the duration of the voyage". This was an occupational safety and health issue and could therefore use the wording found in Article 29(a), as had been done with Article 30.

505. The Employer Vice-Chairperson and the Government member of Norway, speaking on behalf of the Government group, supported the amendment.

506. The Worker Vice-Chairperson proposed a subamendment to add the words "normally remaining at sea for more than three days" at the end of the amendment text.

507. The Government members of Denmark, Egypt, Norway and the Philippines supported the subamendment.

508. The Government member of Namibia opposed the subamendment, as it would mean the duration could be indefinite.

509. The Government member of Uruguay considered the subamendment rendered the text unclear once the implications of the words "duration of the voyage" and "more than three days" were combined.

510. The Government member of Côte d'Ivoire, also speaking on behalf of the Government members of Congo and Guinea, opposed the subamendment.

511. The Government member of Lebanon, speaking on behalf of the Government members of Algeria, Egypt, Lebanon, Saudi Arabia, Syrian Arab Republic, Tunisia and the United Arab Emirates, supported the subamendment, but suggested the wording be clarified.

512. Numerous proposals were put forward as to the formulation and position of various elements contained within the subamendment.

513. The Government member of Uruguay enquired whether the intent of the subamendment was to have the provision cover all vessels or only vessels of [24] metres in length and over. If it was meant to refer only to vessels of [24] metres in length and over, then the subamendment was unnecessary as the time element was captured by the words "duration of the voyage". If the provision was meant to refer to all vessels, then the wording would need to be revised to make this clear.

514. A Worker member stated that the intent of the subamendment was to have the provision cover all fishing vessels of [24] metres in length and over irrespective of the length of the voyage, and all fishing vessels normally remaining at sea for more than three days irrespective of size. Moreover, the administration should take into consideration the number of fishers on board, the area of operation and the duration of voyages of less than three days, for the purposes of extending the application of the Article.

515. The Government member of South Africa said that, in the light of the clarifications provided, he could not support the subamendment. The proposal would change the intent of Article 32 by extending its application to all fishing vessels.

516. Following consultations, the Employer Vice-Chairperson introduced the following text: "The requirements of this Article shall apply to fishing vessels of [24] metres in length and over normally remaining at sea for more than three days and, after consultation, to other vessels, taking into account the number of fishers on board, the area of operation and the duration of the voyage." This proposal had the support of the social partners, although the Employer members had agreed to this text with great reluctance. The provision was overly prescriptive and the Committee risked drafting a Convention that would place too many burdens on small-scale fishers in less developed countries.

517. The Government member of Egypt asked for clarification on the meaning of "after consultations" and "other vessels".

518. The Government members of Cameroon, Côte d'Ivoire, Egypt, Germany, Japan, Mauritania, Mozambique, Namibia, Nigeria, Norway, Saudi Arabia, South Africa, Syrian Arab Republic and the United Arab Emirates all supported the social partners' proposal.

519. The amendment as subamended was adopted

D.112

520. The Worker Vice-Chairperson withdrew an amendment (D.112).

D.185

521. The Employer Vice-Chairperson introduced an amendment to replace the words "provide fishers" by the words "ensure that every fisher on board is provided" in subparagraph 3(a). Such wording would be clearer than the Office text.

522. The Government member of Norway noted that a clear majority of the Government group was in favour of the amendment.

523. The Worker Vice-Chairperson opposed the amendment as it would change the whole meaning of the Office text.

524. The Employer Vice-Chairperson reassured the Worker members that the definition of "fishing vessel owner" included any other organization or person who assumed the responsibility for the operation of the vessel and agreed to take over the duties and responsibilities of the fishing vessel owners. The aim was to make the subparagraph clearer and fairer than the original text. There was nothing hidden in the wording of the amendment.

525. The Worker Vice-Chairperson, in the light of the explanation, accepted the amendment.

526. The amendment was adopted.

D.130

527. The Government member of France introduced an amendment submitted by the Government members of Belgium, Denmark, Finland, France, Germany, Ireland, Netherlands, Norway, Portugal, Spain, Sweden and the United Kingdom to insert the word "personal" after the word "appropriate" in subparagraph 3(a). The word "personal" made clear what type of protective gear was to be provided.

528. The Worker Vice-Chairperson, the Employer Vice-Chairperson and the Government member of Norway, speaking on behalf of the Government group, all supported the amendment.

529. The amendment was adopted.

D.118

530. The Worker Vice-Chairperson introduced an amendment to delete the words "; the competent authority may grant written exemptions from this requirement for fishers who have demonstrated equivalent knowledge and experience" from subparagraph 3(b). Even fishers with vast experience could benefit from basic safety training.

531. The Government member of Norway stated that the Government group opposed the amendment by a clear majority.

532. The Employer Vice-Chairperson also opposed the amendment.

533. The Worker Vice-Chairperson withdrew the amendment.

534. Article 32 was adopted as amended.

New Article after Article 32

D.126

535. The Government member of Denmark introduced an amendment submitted by the Government members of Denmark, France, Norway and Spain to insert a new Article containing the provisions of Paragraph 44 of the proposed Recommendation. This idea had been discussed in the Meeting of Experts held in September 2003, and the Government of Denmark had proposed its inclusion in the Convention in 2004, but the text had been placed in the Recommendation. The involvement of the fisher in risk assessment was a vital aspect of the Convention. The fishers were the most knowledgeable about the risks and could contribute substantially to improving safety and health on board fishing vessels.

536. The Employer Vice-Chairperson asked whether this proposal presupposed that all ratifying States would also have to ratify the International Convention on Standards of Training, Certification and Watchkeeping for Fishing Vessel Personnel, 1995 (STCW-F Convention), when that standard had not yet come into force. Text on risk evaluation was more appropriate in the Recommendation.

537. The Government member of Denmark responded that the intention was not to oblige any country to ratify the STCW-F Convention, but rather to offer inspiration. The Government member of France agreed that including this text would involve no obligation for member States to ratify the STCW-F Convention.

538. The Government member of Norway stated that a clear majority of the Government group opposed the amendment. The Government member of Chile opposed the amendment.

539. The Government member of the United Kingdom was part of the Government group majority opposed to the amendment. She was not opposed to risk assessment, which was important, but noted that the general principle was already included in Article 32. The text of Paragraph 44 of the proposed Recommendation was inspirational, but also aspirational and would be better placed in the proposed Recommendation.

540. The Worker Vice-Chairperson considered risk assessment to be very important. Although the text could have been better formulated, he supported the amendment as proposed.

541. The Government member of Ireland remarked that many work-related accidents were due to the lack of risk assessment and risk management. He supported the inclusion of the text on risk assessment in the Convention as did the Government members of Argentina and Belgium.

542. The Government member of Norway said that risk assessment was crucial for fishers and vessel owners. It encouraged those with the best knowledge of the vessels and the risks to take preventive measures to avoid accidents. It was important to include the text in the Convention.

543. The Government member of Greece agreed with the Government member of the United Kingdom. Although he supported the principles that lay behind it, he could not support the amendment. Despite the views expressed by other Government members, the inclusion of the reference to the STCW-F Convention might be interpreted differently by the Committee of Experts on the Application of Conventions and Recommendations.

544. The Government member of Brazil felt that it was very important to take the views of the Government members of Greece and the United Kingdom into account. The text of the proposed Article was too detailed, and its proper place was in the Recommendation.

545. The Government member of Japan associated his delegation with the views expressed by the Government members of Brazil, Greece and the United Kingdom.

546. The Government member of Denmark asked for legal advice on the implications in relation to STCW-F. He suggested a subamendment to delete the text of Paragraph 44(1)(b) of the Recommendation after the word "training", which was seconded by the Government member of Norway.

547. The Government member of Greece appreciated the subamendment, but agreed with the Worker members that the text could have been better drafted. While he shared the concerns of the sponsors of the amendment and the subamendment, he could not support the proposals.

548. The Government member of South Africa, also speaking on behalf of the Government member of Namibia, expressed reservations about the inclusion of such a restrictive clause in the Convention. He did not support the subamendment.

549. The Worker Vice-Chairperson suggested a further subamendment to move just the introductory phrase of Paragraph 44(1) from the Recommendation to the Convention, to change "should" to "shall", and to have a full stop after "representatives", thereby deleting the last three words. The remainder of the text on risk assessment should be left in the Recommendation.

550. The Government member of Portugal supported the Workers' further subamendment.

551. The Employer Vice-Chairperson remarked that the notion of risk assessment was already present in Article 31(a), which included risk evaluation and management.

552. The Government member of the United Kingdom supported the Worker members' proposal. The inclusion of the reference to the participation of fishers or their representatives added an important element not found in Article 31.

553. The Government members of Argentina, Brazil, Denmark, Egypt, France, Greece, Japan, Mozambique, Namibia, Philippines and South Africa all supported the Workers' further subamendment.

554. The Government member of Mexico also supported the further subamendment, but suggested adding "as appropriate", a view also endorsed by the Government member of the Bolivarian Republic of Venezuela.

555. The Government member of China did not support the further subamendment.

556. The amendment was adopted as subamended.

557. The new Article after Article 32 was adopted.

Social security

Articles 33 to 36

D.105, D.196

558. The Government member of Norway submitted an amendment, seconded by the Government member of Spain, to replace the words "benefit from" by the words "participate in".

559. The Government member of Spain proposed a subamendment to retain "benefit from" following "participate in" to read, "participate in and benefit from". Participating in a social security system usually referred to making contributions; benefiting from the system was a separate concept. It was important to include both ideas.

560. The Government member of Norway seconded the subamendment and concurred with the comment of the Government member of Spain.

561. The Government member of South Africa favoured the wording "participate in". The concept of benefiting was implied in the concept of participation and seemed redundant.

562. The Employer Vice-Chairperson suggested examining amendments D.105 and D.196 together, in view of prior consultations.

563. The Government member of Norway, also speaking on behalf of the Government member of Spain, withdrew their amendment and subamendment in order to allow the Committee to focus on the results of prior consultations between governments and the social partners.

564. In reply to a request for clarification by the Government member of Norway, a member of the secretariat explained that Article 33 of the Office text did not prevent member States from concluding that fishers might need to make contributions for the acquisition of social security benefits arising from this Article. Fishers were entitled to benefit from national

schemes as dictated by the specificities of each system. In States where schemes were based on contributions, States could ask fishers to contribute; States that based the acquisition of rights purely on residency could not require such payments to be made.

565. The Government member of Egypt outlined Egypt's national system and emphasized the difference between the concepts of social security and social assistance. The meaning of social security should be clarified in the context of the draft Convention.

566. The Government member of the Netherlands summarized prior tripartite consultations, which had focused on three issues. First, in view of several amendments submitted by the Worker members to insert references to the Social Security (Minimum Standards) Convention, 1952 (No. 102), it had been decided to insert a general reference to Convention No. 102 in the Preamble. Secondly, amendment D.133, submitted by the Government members of Belgium, Denmark, Finland, France, Germany, Ireland, Netherlands, Portugal, Spain, Sweden and the United Kingdom, to replace Articles 33 and 34 by new text, had been the basis for compromise and had been subamended to address the groups' concerns. Thirdly, the amendment submitted by the Employers to add "comparable" after "other" in Article 33 had been examined by the groups in their separate group consultations.

567. The Employer Vice-Chairperson reported that, as a result of the consultations, her group suggested subamending D.196 to replace "comparable" with "to other workers with comparable employment status".

568. The Government member of Norway, as a result of the Government group's consultations, suggested a subamendment to replace "comparable" with "to other workers, including employed and self-employed, ordinarily resident in its territory".

569. A Worker member from Denmark explained that the Employer members' original amendment (D.196) had raised serious concerns in his group, since it was not possible to determine what fishers should be compared to. The Workers' group opposed the amendment because fishers should be treated no differently from other workers resident in a country. Since the newly proposed subamendments seemed to substantially change the amendment, he suggested that the Government and Employer members should elaborate on their reasoning behind these subamendments.

570. After further consultations among the groups, the Government member of the Netherlands was happy to report that agreement had been reached by a clear majority of Government members as well as the Employer and Worker members on the Articles on social security being included in the draft Convention. The first point on which there was agreement related to the sixth preambular paragraph, starting with "Noting the relevant instruments" where after the words "in particular" the following words should be inserted: "the Social Security (Minimum Standards) Convention, 1952, notwithstanding the provisions of Article 77 of that Convention,". The second issue on which agreement had been reached was Article 33 where, after the words "other workers" the following words should be inserted ", including employed and self-employed persons,". There were no changes to Article 34, but Article 35 was revised to read as follows: "Members shall cooperate through bilateral or multilateral agreements or other arrangements, in accordance with national laws, regulations or practice, to achieve progressively comprehensive social security protection for fishers, taking into account the principle of equality of treatment irrespective of nationality, and to ensure the maintenance of social security rights which have been acquired or are in the course of acquisition by all fishers regardless of residence." As Members had some concerns about the readability of the new text of Article 35, which was considered to be too long, there was a proposal that it be split into two sentences, but without changing the meaning. It was suggested that it be referred to the

Drafting Committee for this purpose. Finally, new wording was also proposed for Article 36 to read as follows: "Notwithstanding the attribution of responsibilities in Articles 33, 34 and 35, Members may determine, through bilateral and multilateral agreements and through provisions adopted in the framework of regional economic integration organizations, other rules concerning the social security legislation to which fishers are subject." These proposals were supported by a clear majority of Government members, as well as the Employers' and Workers' groups. Should the Committee as a whole accept and adopt them, there would be no need to deal with the individual amendments proposed on the Articles related to social security.

571. The Worker Vice-Chairperson confirmed that his group was in full accord with the statement of the previous speaker.

572. The Employer Vice-Chairperson indicated that Employers had participated in the discussions and agreed to the package. They nevertheless wished to have a clearer definition of the term "worker" in light of the reference in Article 33 to a worker also including employed and self-employed persons. Concerning the new wording in Article 35, the Employers' group subscribed to the view that the Drafting Committee should break the sentence into two parts, taking care with the references to bilateral and multilateral agreements or arrangements.

573. The Legal Adviser, responding to the Employer members' request, explained that the term "worker" had defied definition since the founding of the ILO in 1919. While there was as yet no definitive answer, elements of a definition could be inferred from an examination of international labour Conventions. Although unstated, the notion of a "waged" or "salaried" person was often implicit. In the Discrimination (Employment and Occupation) Convention, 1958 (No. 111), however, the concept of "worker" had been extended beyond a person who earns a wage or salary to encompass any person who works, even including an employer. In the current draft Convention, in the absence of a definition, the concept of worker would include not only waged workers, but also independent or self-employed fishers, who might be covered by their country's social security system, which applied to a wide range of people.

574. The Chairperson noted the Committee's acceptance of the text agreed by the majority of the Government group and the Employers' and Workers' groups on the sixth preambular paragraph, and Articles 33, 34, 35 and 36, as reported on by the Government member of the Netherlands and the sponsors' willingness to consider all other proposed amendments on social security to have been withdrawn. Those provisions were considered as adopted. Article 35 was being referred to the Drafting Committee as suggested by the Government member of the Netherlands in his report and similarly proposed by the Employers' group. The Chairperson thanked the Committee members for their excellent work.

575. Articles 33 to 36 were adopted as amended.

New Article after Article 37

D.123, D.124

576. The Worker Vice-Chairperson stated that the Article should cover all types of sickness, not just those that were work-related. The Workers' group was therefore proposing that, in the heading preceding Article 37 as well as in paragraph 1, the words "work-related" be deleted.

577. The Government member of Norway, speaking on behalf of the Government group, opposed the amendments. Article 37 aimed to offer fishers protection for work-related

sickness, injury or death. Non-work-related contingencies should be addressed through other, more general instruments covering wider population groups.

578. The Employer Vice-Chairperson agreed with the views expressed by the Government member of Norway. Her group did not support the amendments.

579. The Worker Vice-Chairperson withdrew both amendments.

580. Article 37 was adopted without amendment.

New Article after Article 37

D.141, subamended by D.220

581. A Worker member from Denmark presented his group's proposed amendment. Fishing vessel owners had the same liabilities regarding the costs of accident and illness as shore-based employers, and it was important that fishers working on vessels operating in foreign waters should be able to obtain medical care in foreign countries and that such care would be paid for. Having heard many comments in the Committee about the need to avoid being overly prescriptive, the Workers' group had decided to subamend their amendment to read as follows:

> 1. Each Member shall adopt laws and regulations requiring that the owners of fishing vessels that fly its flag are responsible for health protection and medical care of all fishers working on board their vessels, including all related costs, providing the same level of protection as applies to workers in shore-based industries.
>
> 2. Each Member shall adopt laws and regulations requiring fishing vessel owners to be liable for defraying the expense of medical care and related maintenance during medical treatment in a foreign country, at least until the fisher has been repatriated."

582. The Worker Vice-Chairperson said that following consultations, an agreement had been reached to add the following new Article after Article 37:

> 1. In the absence of national provisions for fishers, each member shall adopt laws, regulations or other measures to ensure that fishing vessel owners are responsible for the provision to fishers on vessels flying their flag, health protection and medical care while employed, engaged or working on a vessel at sea or in a foreign port. Such laws, regulations or other measures shall ensure that fishing vessel owners are responsible for defraying the expenses of medical care, including related material assistance and support, during medical treatment in a foreign country, until the fisher has been repatriated.
>
> 2. National laws or regulations may permit the exclusion of the liability of the fishing vessel owner if the injury occurred otherwise than on the service of the vessel or the sickness or infirmity was concealed during engagement or the injury or sickness was due to an wilful act, default or misbehaviour.

583. The Employer Vice-Chairperson and the Government member of Norway, speaking on behalf of the Government group, supported the text.

584. The Committee adopted the new Article to follow Article 37.

Part VII. Compliance and enforcement

Article 38

585. Article 38 was adopted without amendment.

Article 39

D.169

586. The Government member of Denmark introduced an amendment submitted by the Government members of the Bahamas, Belgium, Brazil, Côte d'Ivoire, Cuba, Denmark, Egypt, Finland, France, Germany, Greece, Iceland, Ireland, Japan, Kenya, Mauritania, Mexico, Mozambique, Namibia, Netherlands, Norway, Portugal, South Africa, Spain, Sweden, Syrian Arab Republic, Turkey, United Arab Emirates, United Kingdom and Uruguay to replace the words "or those engaged on international voyages" by the words "or those normally engaged in voyages to or from foreign ports". He explained that the guiding principle in the drafting of this amendment had been to find alternative wording for the notion of international voyages.

587. The Worker Vice-Chairperson, noting that port State control was a complex issue, subamended the amendment by replacing the phrase "those normally engaged in voyages to or from foreign ports" by the words "vessels on a voyage 200 nautical miles beyond the coastline of the flag State and remaining at sea for more than three days".

588. The Government member of Denmark responded that the sponsors of the amendment could accept the Worker members' subamendment.

589. The Government members of Argentina, Brazil, Germany, Mexico, Mozambique, Namibia and South Africa also supported the subamendment.

590. The Government member of China expressed her preference for the Office text.

591. The Government member of the Philippines asked what the justification was for selecting 200 nautical miles.

592. The Government member of Egypt responded that the distance of 200 nautical miles was the exclusive economic zone according to the United Nations Convention on the Law of the Sea.

593. The Employer Vice-Chairperson asked whether the subamendment was intended to cover vessels normally engaged on such voyages or those that were engaged on one occasion on such a voyage.

594. The Worker Vice-Chairperson indicated that if the Employer members wished to submit a further subamendment to add the word "normally", the Worker members would support it.

595. The Government member of Greece also expressed support.

596. The Employer Vice-Chairperson proposed a further subamendment which would result in the following text for Article 39:

> Members shall require that fishing vessels of [24] metres in length and over and all vessels normally on voyages 200 nautical miles beyond the coastline of the flag State or the outer edge of its continental shelf, whichever is greater, and remaining at sea for more than three days carry a valid document issued by the competent authority stating that the vessel has been inspected by the competent authority or on its behalf, for compliance with the provisions of this Convention concerning living and working conditions. Such a document shall be valid for a period of [three] years or, if issued on the same date as the International Fishing Vessel Safety Certificate, for the period of validity of that certificate.

597. The Worker Vice-Chairperson expressed support for the proposal.

598. The Government member of Ireland stated that, while he did not have any objection in principle to the proposed text, the wording seemed a bit vague and might therefore pose some difficulty for ratifying Members.

599. The Government members of Algeria and Saudi Arabia supported the further subamendment.

600. The amendment was adopted as subamended.

D.193

601. The Employer Vice-Chairperson withdrew an amendment (D.193).

D.125

602. The Government member of Denmark introduced an amendment submitted by the Government members of Denmark, Finland, Germany, Greece, Ireland, Netherlands, Norway, Portugal, Sweden and the United Kingdom to replace the word "[three]" by "five". He stressed the desirability of achieving harmonization regarding the validity of certificates with the different IMO Conventions, such as the MARPOL Convention, and reminded the Committee of the Global and uniform implementation of the harmonized system of survey and certification.

603. The Worker Vice-Chairperson pointed out that intermediate surveys were undertaken within the five-year period of validity.

604. The Government member of Denmark emphasized that the issue here was one of the validity of documents rather than the frequency of inspections. While there might indeed be some other frequency for inspections under other Conventions, he underlined the need for the validity of certificates under the Convention to be consistent with the five years specified under IMO Conventions.

605. The Employer Vice-Chairperson expressed support for the proposed amendment for the reasons given by the Government member of Denmark.

606. The Government member of Egypt preferred the Office text because the validity of documents was left to the prerogative of competent national authorities and three years' duration was more reasonable than five.

607. The Government member of Norway indicated that the Government group supported the amendment.

608. The Worker Vice-Chairperson expressed his group's support for the amendment as well.

609. The amendment was adopted.

610. Article 39 was adopted as amended.

Article 40

611. Article 40 was adopted without amendment.

Article 41

D.157

612. The Worker Vice-Chairperson introduced an amendment to replace the text of paragraph 2 by the following:

> If a Member, in whose port a fishing vessel calls in the normal course of its business or for operational reasons, receives a complaint or obtains evidence that such vessel does not conform to the standards of this Convention, it may prepare a report addressed to the Government of the country in which the vessel is registered, with a copy to the Director-General of the International Labour Office, and may take measures necessary to rectify any conditions on board which are clearly hazardous to safety or health.

The text was drawn from the Merchant Shipping (Minimum Standards) Convention, 1976 (No. 147), which had proven its worth. The proposal was editorial, rather than substantive in nature.

613. The Government member of Norway expressed the Government group's support for the proposed amendment.

614. The Employer Vice-Chairperson observed that a Member that had not ratified the Convention should not have its standards imposed on it. She therefore suggested subamending the proposal as follows: in the first line, add "that has ratified this Convention" after the word "Member" and "from the country of a Member that has also ratified this Convention" after "vessel" and in the third line replace "standards" with "requirements".

615. The Government member of Greece rejected the amendment on the grounds that it conflicted with the provisions of Article 42 on which the Employers had not proposed any amendment.

616. The Worker Vice-Chairperson agreed with the position of the Government member of Greece and did not support the subamendment.

617. The Government member of Norway also concurred. The Employers' proposed subamendment would be a disincentive for ratification and so could not be supported.

618. The Employer Vice-Chairperson withdrew the subamendment.

619. The amendment was adopted.

D.162

620. The Worker Vice-Chairperson proposed an amendment to replace the text of paragraph 4 by the following: "For the purpose of this Article, 'complaint' means information submitted by a fisher, a professional body, an association, a trade union or, generally, any person with an interest in the safety of the vessel, including an interest in safety or health hazards to the fishers on board". The text was adapted from Article 4 of the Merchant Shipping (Minimum Standards) Convention, 1976 (No. 147).

621. In answer to a query from the Government member of Egypt, a member of the secretariat stated that the relevant authority with whom a complaint could be filed were the flag State in relation to paragraph 1 and the port State in relation to paragraph 2.

622. The Government member of Norway observed that there was a clear majority in the Government group against adopting this amendment.

623. The Employer Vice-Chairperson also opposed the text. There was no need for a definition of complaints.

624. The Worker Vice-Chairperson withdrew the amendment.

625. Article 41 was adopted as amended.

Article 42

D.153

626. The Government member of Japan introduced an amendment, jointly sponsored with the Government member of Indonesia, to replace the words "apply the" by the words "implement its responsibility under this" [Convention]. This wording would be consistent with that adopted in the draft consolidated maritime labour Convention.

627. The Government member of Norway observed that there was a clear majority in the Government group against adopting this amendment.

628. The Government member of Ireland had reconsidered his original view after the explanation by the Government member of Japan, and now supported the amendment.

629. The Worker Vice-Chairperson felt that the proposal was more about drafting than substance and could support it.

630. The Employer Vice-Chairperson believed that the original wording was probably closer to ILO usage than the amendment and sought the advice of the secretariat.

631. The deputy representative of the Secretary-General stated that the term "apply" was the usual ILO term, while "implement its responsibility under this Convention" would be a novelty.

632. The Employer Vice-Chairperson preferred the Office text.

633. The amendment was rejected.

634. Article 42 was adopted without amendment.

Part VIII. Amendment of Annexes I and III

Article 43

D.155, D.161

635. The Worker Vice-Chairperson introduced two amendments the effect of which would be to include Annex II within the list of annexes in both the heading and the body of Article 43.

636. The Government member of Norway, speaking on behalf of the Government group, supported both amendments.

637. The Employer Vice-Chairperson also expressed support.

638. The amendments were adopted.

639. Article 43 was adopted as amended.

Bracketed figures

640. The Committee then turned to the question of the figures which remained in brackets.

641. The Employer Vice-Chairperson indicated that, at the outset of discussions, it had been considered fundamental to develop a Convention that did not make reference to vessel size. The Employers' group still considered this a vital issue and so proposed to replace the figure of 24 metres by 45 metres, throughout the Convention. Fishing vessels below 45 metres in length accounted for innumerable small fishing vessels and the majority of the world's fishing vessels in Asia, Africa and South America. The Convention should focus on the protection of those small-scale fishers who lived in unacceptable conditions, rather than fishers in developed countries who were already protected by relatively high standards. If the majority of the world's fishers did not benefit from the Convention, the Committee would not have fulfilled its mandate. If the figure of 45 metres replaced the figure of 24 metres, all the other provisions would still cover fishing vessels below 45 metres. Also, it should be noted that the previous Conventions and Recommendations on the fishing sector had received few ratifications as a result of being too prescriptive. Most member States who supported the figure of 24 metres, would later find it difficult to ratify the Convention.

642. The Government member of Japan supported the proposal of the Employers' group, since his delegation had great problems with the gross tonnage equivalent for 24 metres. He also stated that this amendment would facilitate worldwide ratification of the Convention.

643. The Worker Vice-Chairperson did not support the proposal of the Employers' group. The Workers' group supported removing the brackets and maintaining the figures as they appeared in the text.

644. The Government member of South Africa appreciated the sentiments of the Employers' group. However, modern fishing vessels of 45 metres in length could have at least 1,000 gross tons, and if these vessels flew a flag of convenience, fishers would suffer from exactly the conditions referred to by the Employers' group, despite working on board a large vessel.

645. The Government member of Brazil supported the position of the Workers' group. Fishing vessels below 24 metres would be covered by less stringent requirements, which would greatly facilitate ratification by developing countries.

646. The Government members of Algeria, Argentina, Cameroon, Mexico, Namibia, Portugal, Saudi Arabia, South Africa and the Bolivarian Republic of Venezuela, supported the deletion of the square brackets and the retention of the figures as they were in the text.

647. The Chairperson concluded that the majority of the Committee supported the deletion of the square brackets and the retention of the figures 24 and 45 metres, as they appeared throughout the text. It was so adopted.

648. The Employer Vice-Chairperson challenged the Governments that supported the inclusion of 24 metres throughout the Convention to ratify and apply the Convention.

Final provisions

649. The representative of the Legal Adviser provided clarification on the final provisions of the proposed Convention. Since the outset, the ILO had used standard final provisions that were not submitted to the standard-setting Committees. The Conference Drafting Committee added these standard final provisions to the proposed Convention as adopted by the standard-setting Committee. Nonetheless, certain parameters of the standardized final provisions were left open, such as the number of ratifications and the period of time required for the entry into force of the Convention and the time-span required for denunciation purposes. The standard final provisions usually provided that the Convention should come into force 12 months after the date on which the ratifications of two Members had been registered with the Director-General. The five fishing Conventions currently in force contained that standard provision. However, the number of months and of ratifications required constituted open parameters that the Committee could modify. In the framework of maritime Conventions, it was recognized that, in addition to the total number of ratifications required for a Convention's entry into force, a given number of these could be required to come from member States that fulfilled certain conditions, for example, member States whose merchant fleets represented a certain gross tonnage of shipping. In such cases, it was essential that any qualifying conditions concerning the necessary ratifications were based on objective criteria and easily applicable. If it so wished, the Committee could instruct the Drafting Committee as to the manner in which the open parameters should be fixed. This could be done at any time by means of a simple oral or written motion.

650. The Chairperson invited the Legal Adviser to shed light on the impact of the adoption of the new Convention under discussion on the status of other international labour standards related to the fishing sector.

651. The Legal Adviser noted that the Preamble of the draft Convention mentioned the need to revise the seven international instruments adopted specifically for the fishing sector to bring them up to date. Preambular paragraphs had no mandatory force, however. Should the Committee wish to decide that some or all of the Conventions listed in the Preamble were to be considered revised by the draft Convention, a provision to that effect would need to appear within the body of the Convention. The revised Conventions would be closed to further ratification once the new Convention came into force, although they would remain binding on those Members that had previously ratified them and did not ratify the new Convention. Only the new Convention would be open to ratification. The Committee would need to provide a clear indication as to which of the earlier Conventions had been revised by the new Convention and which, if any, were to remain open to ratification.

652. In response to a query from the Government member of Greece, the Legal Adviser explained that the ratification of the new Convention would also entail automatic denunciation of the revised Convention(s) by the ratifying Member, unless the Committee wished to have a clause that provided otherwise included in the new Convention. The Drafting Committee would need clear guidance from the Committee on whether or not the new Convention revised any or all of the earlier Conventions and whether the ratification of the new Convention would entail the automatic denunciation of the revised Conventions.

653. The Government member of Norway, speaking on behalf of the Government group, stated that the present Convention should revise all relevant Conventions and its ratification result in the denunciation of those Conventions for Members who had ratified them. However, the Fishermen's Competency Certificates Convention, 1966 (No. 125), should not figure on the list of those to be revised by the new Convention, as the issues covered in Convention No. 125 had not been covered by the proposed Convention.

654. The Worker Vice-Chairperson supported the view expressed by the Government member of Norway.

655. In the light of these suggestions, the Legal Adviser proposed, for the Committee's consideration, the following text to be submitted as a new Article following Article 45 of the Convention: "This Convention revises the Minimum Age (Fisherman) Convention, 1959, the Medical Examination (Fishermen) Convention, 1959, the Fisherman's Articles of Agreement Convention, 1959, and the Accommodation of Crews (Fishermen Convention), 1966." If this new Article were adopted, the Committee might also wish to instruct the Conference Drafting Committee on a consequential revision to the 13th paragraph in the Preamble of the Convention, to replace the words "the seven" by "the following" in the first line and to delete "the Fisherman's Competency Certificate Convention, 1966".

656. The Worker Vice-Chairperson supported the text proposed by the Legal Adviser. He noted however that the Vocational Training (Fishermen) Recommendation, 1966 (No. 126), should not be revised, since vocational training was not covered in the draft Convention.

657. The Employer Vice-Chairperson supported the text proposed by the Legal Adviser, as well as the views expressed by the Workers' group.

658. The Government member of Norway inquired whether it was appropriate to refer to Recommendations in the Preamble.

659. The Legal Adviser recommended that the Hours of Work (Fishing) Recommendation, 1920 (No. 7), be considered as revised since the issue of hours of work had been dealt with in the draft Convention through its provisions on hours of rest, and the Recommendation adopted in 1920 was obsolete. The Vocational Training (Fishermen) Recommendation, 1966 (No. 126), however, concerned an issue that was not addressed in the proposed Convention or Recommendation. It was for the Committee to decide whether it should be maintained, as it was the only ILO instrument on that subject, or whether it should be considered as revised.

660. The Government member of Norway stated that during its consultations, the Government group had not discussed whether the Accommodation of Crews (Fishermen) Convention, 1966 (No. 126), should be revised by the proposed Convention. It appeared logical, however, that it not be considered revised, given that the issue of vocational training was not covered in the proposed Convention.

661. The Committee therefore adopted the text proposed by the Legal Adviser, and further agreed that the reference to the Accommodation of Crews (Fishermen) Convention, 1966 (No. 126), the 13th preambular paragraph, be removed.

662. The Committee then considered the issue of entry into force of the proposed Convention.

663. The Government member of Japan introduced a motion submitted by the Government members of China, Japan and the Philippines, requesting the Committee to "invite the Conference Drafting Committee to modify the standard final article governing entry into force of the Convention in order to provide that the Convention shall come into force 12 months after the date on which there have been registered with the Director-General, the ratifications by at least 15 coastal States representing 50 per cent of the total number of fishing vessels registered in coastal States worldwide." It was important for the new Convention to be supported by enough countries with large fishing capacity. Share of

vessels should be used as a criterion for entry into force. The International Convention on Standards of Training, Certification and Watchkeeping for Fishing Vessel Personnel (STCW-F), 1995, required ratification by 15 coastal States to enter into force. The United Nations Convention on the Law of the Sea (UNCLOS) required ratification by 60 countries for entry into force. If the Committee wished the Convention to be a truly international instrument that could be effectively implemented, it should adopt the motion submitted by the Government members of China, Japan and the Philippines.

664. The Worker Vice-Chairperson said that it was not normal practice for ILO instruments to provide for entry into force in terms of a percentage. Moreover, the STCW-F Convention did not contain entry-into-force provisions based on percentages.

665. The Government member of Norway stated that the present Convention was very different from the draft consolidated maritime labour Convention and that the introduction of a percentage would impede the entry into force of the proposed Convention and was therefore not desirable.

666. In response to a query from the Employer Vice-Chairperson, the Legal Adviser said that the issue was not a legal one, but rather a matter for decision by the Committee, as there was no particular rule on entry into force of a Convention. Since standard final clauses were adopted in the 1920s, two member States had been considered to be a default number. Where there was no stipulation to the contrary, a Convention entered into force following its ratification by two member States. The Committee could choose whatever number it deemed appropriate. The Government member of Norway, speaking on behalf of the Government group, proposed that the Convention enter into force after ratification by ten countries, of which at least eight were coastal States.

667. The Worker Vice-Chairperson supported the proposal made by the Government group.

668. The Employer Vice-Chairperson supported the proposal of the Government members of China, Japan and the Philippines.

669. The Government member of Namibia, speaking on behalf of the Government members of Cameroon, Côte d'Ivoire, Mauritania, Mozambique, Nigeria and South Africa, supported the Government group's proposal. The figures proposed were a compromise with which most Governments felt comfortable.

670. The Government member of South Africa noted his country was emerging from an era of apartheid, and therefore fishers in that country were not covered by the older fishing instruments. As a result, his Government was very much committed to this process. He supported the proposal of the Government group.

671. The Government members of Argentina, Belgium, Denmark, France, Greece, Netherlands, Portugal, Spain and the United Kingdom also supported the proposal of the Government group.

672. The Government member of the Syrian Arab Republic said that, given the specificity of the fishing sector in Asian countries, his Government supported the motion presented by the Government members of China, Japan and the Philippines.

673. The Chairperson concluded that the motion had not carried. He further concluded that a sufficient majority of the Committee members supported the Government group's proposal, which was adopted.

Annex I

674. Annex I was discussed in conjunction with Article 5, and the summary of the discussions is found under Article 5 of this report.

Annex II

Fisher's work agreement

D.186, D.164

675. The Employer Vice-Chairperson proposed an amendment to the introductory phrase of paragraph 1, to add the words "or through collective agreement or by a written employment policy that is made available to the fisher", after the word "regulations". She then proposed a subamendment to replace the words "or through collective agreement or by a written employment policy that is made available to the fisher" by "or measures that are substantially equivalent, or through collective agreement, where applicable".

676. The Worker Vice-Chairperson proposed an amendment to insert the words "or a collective bargaining agreement", at the end of the introductory phrase of paragraph 1. This was intended to reflect the fact that in some countries these matters were regulated by collective agreement.

677. The Government member of Norway stated that the Government group supported the Workers' amendment. The Employers' initial proposal had raised some concern as to the implications of the phrase "written employment policy", but the group had not had a chance to discuss the Employers' subamendment.

678. The Employer Vice-Chairperson explained that the "measures" referred to in her group's subamendment would be measures regulated by government, not by industry. The Employers' subamendment had removed the wording that had been of concern to the Government group.

679. The Government member of France preferred the Workers' amendment.

680. The Employer Vice-Chairperson withdrew her group's amendment and proposed a subamendment to add the words "where applicable" at the end of the Workers' amendment.

681. The amendment was adopted as subamended.

D.168

682. The Government member of Denmark introduced an amendment submitted by the Government members of Denmark, Greece and Ireland to replace the last "and" in subparagraph 1(a) by "and/or". Denmark had a system for uniquely identifying each fisher, without needing to specify the fisher's birthplace.

683. The Employer Vice-Chairperson requested clarification from the Office about the use of the term "and/or" in Conventions.

684. A representative of the Legal Adviser confirmed that the term "and/or" should be avoided in ILO Conventions. It could usually be replaced by the simple "or", which had an inclusive meaning. When the context required alternatives, one should rather resort to "either … or".

685. The Worker Vice-Chairperson opposed the amendment as unnecessary.

686. The Government member of Norway stated that the Government group had agreed to support the amendment.

687. The Employer Vice-Chairperson stated that, in view of the explanation from the Office, it should be possible to retain the original text for subparagraph 1(a).

688. The Government member of the Bahamas noted that there had been much talk in the Committee relating to social security and problems related to the repatriation of social security income to the worker's country of origin. He expressed concern about how the proposed amendment might affect the payment of social security benefits if countries issued work agreements in which the place of birth of the fisher could not be identified.

689. The Government member of Spain suggested that the problem raised by the Government member of Denmark might be addressed by adding the words "as necessary" at the end of subparagraph 1(a).

690. The Worker Vice-Chairperson pointed out that within the introductory portion of paragraph 1, the phrase "except in so far as the inclusion of one or more of them is rendered unnecessary" might offer the flexibility being sought by the Government member of Denmark.

691. The Government member of Denmark agreed that paragraph 1 might indeed provide the solution and, in light of the explanation provided by the Office regarding the use of "and/or", he withdrew the amendment.

D.165

692. The Worker Vice-Chairperson introduced an amendment to insert the words "and the registration number of the vessel or vessels" before the words "on board" in subparagraph 1(c). He argued that vessel names were not unique, but registration numbers were.

693. The Government member of Norway stated that the Government group had agreed to support the amendment.

694. The Employer Vice-Chairperson asked for clarification as to which registration number should be used. Would fishers have to change their work agreements each time they changed vessels?

695. The Worker Vice-Chairperson said that it was important that the work agreement be changed in accordance with the vessel.

696. An Employer member from the Netherlands pointed out that there were several registration number systems, and indeed the same vessel could be registered in various countries under different numbers. He asked whether the Worker Vice-Chairperson was referring to IMO registration numbers.

697. The Worker Vice-Chairperson replied that IMO registration numbers were not valid for fishing vessels.

698. The amendment was adopted.

D.166

699. The Government member of the United Kingdom observed that in subparagraph 1(k) the current text referred to "insurance". She introduced an amendment submitted by the Government members of Finland, France, Germany, Greece, Ireland, Netherlands, Norway, Portugal, Spain, Sweden and the United Kingdom to replace the word "insurance" with the word "protection". The term "protection" was broader and provided other options for social security.

700. The Employer Vice-Chairperson supported the amendment for the same reasons stated by the Government member of the United Kingdom.

701. The Worker Vice-Chairperson preferred the original text, and felt that the term "protection" was too broad and vague. Financial security protection was the heart of the matter.

702. The Government member of Norway reported that the Government group had agreed to support the amendment.

703. The Government member of Egypt preferred the Office text. He believed that protection should in fact be provided through a social security system that covered all citizens.

704. The Government member of the United Kingdom observed that the title of Article 37 was "Protection in the case of work-related sickness, injury or death". Protection was the right word to use.

705. The Worker Vice-Chairperson, after hearing the comments of the Government member of the United Kingdom, proposed a subamendment to replace the word "insurance" by the words "financial security protection".

706. The Employer Vice-Chairperson opposed the subamendment.

707. The amendment was adopted.

D.191, D.188, D.190

708. The Employer Vice-Chairperson withdrew amendments D.191, D.188, and D.190 in light of the reorganization of Annex II, which had resulted from the adoption of Article 20 as amended. In her view, the reordered Annex II, which had been provided for illustrative purposes in amendment D.176, rather than the Office text, should be the basis for the current discussion.

709. To clarify the situation, the representative of the Secretary-General stated that through its adoption of Article 20 as amended, the Committee had made its intentions clear as to its objective for the second part of Annex II, which was to delete the chapeau of paragraph 2 and add the remaining subparagraphs to paragraph 1. The question was how to achieve it. The Committee agreed to continue discussions on this basis. That text and all subsequent agreed changes would be referred to the Drafting Committee for determination of the order of the subparagraphs.

D.167

710. The Government member of Greece presented an amendment submitted by the Government members of Belgium, Denmark, Finland, France, Germany, Greece, Ireland,

Netherlands, Norway, Portugal, Sweden and the United Kingdom to delete the words "or maximum hours of work per day and per week" in subparagraph 2(e).

711. The Worker Vice-Chairperson, the Employer Vice-Chairperson and the Government member of Norway, speaking on behalf of the Government group, all supported the amendment, which was adopted.

712. Annex II was adopted as amended.

Annex III

713. Discussion of Annex III was based on document C.S.P./219, which contained the recommended text of the Working Party on Articles 25-28 and Annex III. That text was treated as a global amendment open to subamendment by the Committee. The Chairperson observed that the Working Party had reached consensus on paragraphs 2-5, 7, 9, 11-16 and 18-22. The Committee adopted these paragraphs.

714. The Employer Vice-Chairperson noted that there was still an issue pending regarding paragraph 23. Referring to the report of the Chairperson of the Working Party, she stated that the Employers' group had understood there would no longer be any references to working areas and working spaces. Yet paragraph 23, as found in document C.S.P./D.219, maintained such a reference.

715. The Government member of the United Kingdom explained that the remaining reference was an oversight by the Working Party. To resolve the issue, he suggested subamending paragraph 23 by ending the sentence immediately after the words "control room". The words "where applicable" at the end of the paragraph did not need to be retained as they had only referred to the preceding words, "work areas".

716. The Government member of Brazil, as Chairperson of the Working Party, pointed out that there had been no amendment presented to the Working Party on paragraph 23. She noted that the only difference between the text agreed upon by the Working Party and the Office text was the removal of the reference to gross tonnage.

717. The Government member of Spain suggested subamending the text as follows: "For vessels of 24 metres in length and over, with the exception of those regularly engaged in areas where temperate climatic conditions do not require it, air conditioning shall be provided in accommodation spaces." Furthermore, the provision, as subamended by the Government member of the United Kingdom, still dealt with spaces other than accommodation spaces. Thus, it encroached upon the scope of Annex III, which referred only to accommodation.

718. The Government member of the United Kingdom noted that the paragraph on heating and air conditioning was meant to cover all areas, especially working spaces. The proposal from the Government member of Spain would have the effect of making heating and air conditioning optional in areas such as the bridge, the radio room and any centralized machinery control room, as well as in working spaces. The Working Party had not meant to change the intent of the paragraph in this manner.

719. The Worker Vice-Chairperson expressed his support for the proposal of the Government member of the United Kingdom. Clearly, air conditioning and heating should also be provided on the bridge, the radio room and any centralized machinery control room.

720. In view of the statements made, the Government member of Spain withdrew the subamendment he had proposed.

721. The Employer Vice-Chairperson and the Government members of Denmark, France, Namibia and South Africa supported the subamendment proposed by the Government member of the United Kingdom.

722. The Committee adopted the subamendment.

723. The Committee adopted paragraph 23, as subamended.

724. The Committee adopted paragraphs 24-30, 35, 37, 38, 40-42, 44-53, 55, 58, 60-69, 71, 73, 74, 76, and three new unnumbered paragraphs proposed by the Working Party.

725. In response to a question from the Government member of Japan, the Chairperson pointed out that the current discussion only concerned the placement of the provision on equivalences of tonnage and length. The discussion on the provision's substance could not be re-opened by the Committee, since it had already been addressed and decided upon.

726. The Committee then considered the paragraphs in Annex III on which there had not been consensus in the Working Party.

Paragraph 1

D.79

727. The Government member of Japan introduced a subamendment, submitted by China, Indonesia and Japan to insert the words ", as far as possible according to the condition of the Member," in paragraph 1, after the words "fishing vessels". The subamendment was intended to provide additional flexibility, thus allowing for wide ratification of the Convention.

728. The Government member of the United Kingdom reminded the Committee of the discussion on the subamendment to Article 28 and suggested that this subamendment should be rejected for the same reasons.

729. A Worker member from Argentina agreed with the Government member of the United Kingdom and opposed the subamendment. The text agreed upon by the Working Party should be retained.

730. The Government member of China insisted on the subamendment and hoped the Committee would consider it favourably.

731. The Chairperson concluded that a sufficient majority of the Committee members opposed the subamendment, which was not adopted.

732. The Committee adopted paragraph 1, as proposed by the Working Party.

Paragraph 6

733. An Employer member from Canada introduced a subamendment to delete the words "the crew accommodation of a vessel has been reconstructed or substantially altered" and replace the words "such vessel" by the words "such new vessel". This would effectively remove the requirement for existing fishing vessels to comply with the provisions of Annex III in case of reconstruction or substantial alteration of their crew accommodation. Paragraph 1 of Annex III still enabled the competent authority to apply the provisions of Annex III to existing vessels, when and in so far as it determined that this was reasonable and practicable. While paragraph 1 allowed such an extension, paragraph 6 imposed it,

thus limiting the market for such vessels and increasing costs. Paragraph 6 should, therefore, only relate to new fishing vessels.

734. A Worker member from Argentina disagreed with the proposed subamendment. Paragraph 1 established that Annex III would apply only to new fishing vessels, unless the competent authority extended it to existing fishing vessels. This extension could only be done in a limited manner, since imposing new requirements to vessels already in use involved substantial changes. However, in the case of rebuilding, fishing vessels should cater for the requirements of the Convention.

735. An Employer member from Canada agreed that, where possible, fishing vessels where the crew accommodation was reconstructed or substantially altered should be brought into conformity with the requirements of the Convention. However, to impose this in all cases was unacceptable. Fishing vessels were sometimes altered for commercial reasons, with the effect of the crew accommodation being altered, but this did not mean these fishing vessels were in a position to meet the requirements of the Convention. If compliance was possible, paragraph 1 enabled the competent authority to extend Annex III to these fishing vessels. A forced extension would increase costs and have the indirect effect that existing modified fishing vessels would not be available for use in developing countries.

736. The Government member of the United Kingdom appreciated the concerns raised but believed that the Employers referred to subsequent alterations of crew accommodation arising from other alterations, and not to "substantial alterations". It was common practice, in the case of real substantial alterations, to make every effort to meet the new requirements. This was a standard phrase in international legislation.

737. An Employer member from Canada indicated there was no commonly agreed upon definition of "substantial alteration". Some administrations considered the subsequent alterations of crew accommodation as a result of commercial alterations to be substantial alterations.

738. The Government member of Denmark stated that, in the context of the grandfather clause of the International Convention for the Safety of Life at Sea, the IMO had issued a circular describing the term "substantial alteration", which was used by most administrations.

739. The Government member of Egypt supported the subamendment, as the application of Annex III to existing fishing vessels would create practical difficulties.

740. The Government member of Germany felt the problem was resolved by the new paragraph in Article 28.

741. An Employer member from Canada found that the new paragraph in Article 28 did not address the Employer members' concerns, since the competent authority would have to interpret it and vessel operators were not necessarily aware of the requirements.

742. The Government member of the United Kingdom considered that there was scope in paragraph 6 to provide that the competent authority should take its decision after consultations. This would accommodate the Employers' concerns, since fishing vessel owners and the competent authority would decide to what extent compliance with the requirements was practicable.

743. Following consultations, an Employer member from Canada introduced a subamendment to replace paragraph 6 with:

> The competent authority shall satisfy itself that, on every occasion when a vessel is newly constructed or the crew accommodation of a vessel has been reconstructed, such a vessel complies with the requirements of this Annex. The competent authority shall, to the extent practicable, require compliance with this Annex for a vessel that changes the flag it flies to the flag of a Member, or when the crew accommodation is substantially altered.

744. The Worker Vice-Chairperson and the Government members of Algeria, France, Republic of Korea, Norway, Saudi Arabia and the United Kingdom expressed their support for the subamendment.

745. The subamendment was adopted.

746. Paragraph 6 was adopted as subamended.

Paragraph 8

747. In view of the adoption of paragraph 6, the Employer members supported the text of paragraph 8.

748. Paragraph 8 was adopted.

Paragraph 10

D.82

749. A subamendment (D.82) was not seconded and therefore not discussed.

750. The Employer Vice-Chairperson presented a subamendment to delete the word "limited" in the second sentence of paragraph 10 in order to meet some of the concerns of certain Asian countries.

751. The Worker Vice-Chairperson considered that the original text afforded ample leeway and did not support the subamendment.

752. The Government member of Norway believed that, taken in conjunction with the new paragraph in Article 28, paragraph 10 provided sufficient flexibility.

753. The Government member of Germany emphasized that the concept of "substantial equivalence" introduced in the new paragraph in Article 28 was of the utmost importance. If the headroom of 190 cm was sufficient for Japanese fishers, then the Convention should provide for the necessary flexibility for Japan and other countries to be able to ratify.

754. The Government member of Japan supported the subamendment presented by the Workers' group and recalled that paragraph 10 had not been unanimously agreed upon at the Tripartite Meeting of Experts in December 2004.

755. The Government member of Namibia opposed the subamendment, as the concept of substantial equivalence was sufficiently explicit in this provision.

756. The Government member of China thanked the Government member of Germany for stressing the need for flexibility and confirmed that the prescriptive paragraphs in the Convention relating to headroom and size of beds did not take into account the national contexts of certain Asian countries.

757. The Government member of Greece observed that the concept of substantial equivalence had been accepted by all member States that had ratified the Merchant Shipping (Minimum

Standards) Convention, 1976 (No. 147), among which figured Japan. Specific figures were contained in the Accommodation of Crews Convention (Revised), 1949 (No. 92), which appeared in the Appendix to Convention No. 147.

758. The Government member of the United Kingdom pointed out that the Government of Japan, in its comments on the proposed Convention and Recommendation reproduced in Report V(A), had urged the inclusion of the concept of substantial equivalence for the purpose of widespread ratification.

759. The representative of the Legal Adviser stated that the concept of substantial equivalence in Article 28 of the Convention only applied to Annex III. The concept appeared in Article 2 of Convention No. 147 under which each ratifying Member undertook to satisfy itself that its laws and regulations on safety standards, social security measures and shipboard conditions of employment and shipboard living arrangements were substantially equivalent to the Conventions or Articles of Conventions referred to in the Appendix to that Convention. In practice, that meant that the Member was permitted to achieve the goals of the Convention by means other than those specified within the detailed provisions of the Convention. The Member's compliance might be subject to monitoring, however, and it was for the Member to prove that the goals of the Convention had been achieved.

760. Paragraph 10 of Annex III was adopted without amendment.

Paragraph 17

D.84

761. A subamendment (D.84) was not seconded and therefore not discussed.

D.64

762. A Worker member from Argentina withdrew a subamendment (D.64), since text on working spaces had been included in the general clauses.

763. The Employer Vice-Chairperson introduced a subamendment to insert "develop and" after "the competent authority shall". Since no standards for vibration in accommodation spaces existed, these needed to be developed.

764. The Government member of Norway opposed the Employers' group's proposal. The resulting wording would put an obligation on competent authorities to develop standards themselves. The original wording allowed for the adoption of standards developed elsewhere but did not preclude the development of national standards.

765. The Government members of the Bahamas and the Syrian Arab Republic and a Worker member from Argentina supported the Norwegian position.

766. The Employer Vice-Chairperson withdrew her group's proposal.

767. Paragraph 17 was adopted.

Paragraph 31

D.93

768. The Government member of Japan introduced a subamendment (D. 93), seconded by the Government member of China, to delete the words "which are not less than [100] gt but which are less than [45] metres in length and less than [500] gt" after the word "over" from

paragraph 31 and at the end of the paragraph to add the following: "For vessels of less than [45] metres in length, the competent authority, after consultation, may permit some limited reduction in the floor area per person of sleeping rooms in particular cases if the size and type of intended service of the vessel make the requirements unreasonable or impracticable." The requirements currently envisaged in the Convention were too high and did not suit the conditions on Asian vessels. The subamendment would provide flexibility and thus help States to implement the Convention.

769. The subamendment was not adopted.

D.52

770. A Worker member from Argentina introduced a subamendment to replace "[1]" by "1.5". The aim was to increase the per person living space on board. This was a very sensitive and important issue for fishers. This subamendment reflected the considerable increase of area available on ships, following the prior decision on tonnages. The Committee had an opportunity to improve substantially the living and accommodation conditions of fishers.

771. The Government member of China opposed the subamendment, since the resulting requirements were not suitable for Asian vessels.

772. The Government members of Japan and the Republic of Korea supported the Chinese position. The proposed dimensions were much larger than those contained in the Accommodation of Crews (Fishermen) Convention, 1966 (No. 126). If adopted, they would create a major obstacle for ratification.

773. The Government member of Norway informed the Committee that a clear majority of Government members supported the subamendment.

774. The Government member of Lebanon supported the amendment. When considering human comfort in sleeping areas, no distinction could be made according to vessel size.

775. The subamendment was adopted.

776. Paragraph 31 was adopted as subamended.

Paragraph 32

D.100

777. A subamendment (D.100) was not seconded and therefore not discussed.

D.55

778. A Worker member from Argentina introduced a subamendment to replace "[1.5]" by "2". The reasons were the same as those stated for paragraph 31.

779. The Government member of Norway, speaking on behalf of the Government group, indicated that a clear majority of Government members supported the proposal.

780. An Employer member from Canada objected to the subamendment and referred to the previous intervention of the Government member of Lebanon. There should be no distinction as to comfort between fishing vessels of 24 m and fishing vessels of 45 m in length or over. The appropriate standard for smaller vessels was also suitable for the larger ones. Furthermore, larger rooms led to fishing vessels with greater gross tonnage but less fishing capacity. The speaker noted that various jurisdictions had rules and regulations

regarding fishing capacity in relation to gross tonnage. Moreover, the serious concerns raised by the Asian countries should be taken into account in order not to impede ratification.

781. The Government member of France considered that, according to the length-gross tonnage equivalents adopted, the gross tonnage of vessels of 45 m (700 gt) was four times greater than the gross tonnage of vessels of 24 m (175 gt), while the per person floor area on the larger vessels would only be increased by one third. The argument of the Employers' group was therefore not convincing.

782. The Government member of Lebanon opposed the subamendment reiterating his views regarding comfort.

783. The Government member of the Republic of Korea opposed the subamendment in light of the size of fishing vessels in his country.

784. The subamendment was adopted.

785. Paragraph 32 was adopted as subamended.

Paragraph 33

D.87

786. The Government member of Japan introduced a subamendment submitted by the Government members of Japan and the Republic of Korea to add, after the word "persons", the words "as far as practicable" in paragraph 33. The addition would make the provision more flexible and thus facilitate ratification.

787. The subamendment was not adopted.

788. Paragraph 33 was adopted without amendment.

Paragraph 34

D.86

789. A subamendment (D.86) was not seconded and therefore not discussed.

790. The Government member of Norway, speaking on behalf of the Government group, proposed a subamendment to delete the words "but which are less than 45 metres in length".

791. The Government member of the United Kingdom believed that the present wording of paragraph 34 was the result of a consequential amendment relating to gross tonnage that offered the possibility to choose between fishing vessels of 24 m and 45 m in length. The Government group had agreed to the deletion of the words "but which are less than 45 metres in length", since, otherwise, Annex III would contain no requirements concerning the number of persons per sleeping room for fishing vessels of 45 m in length and over.

792. In response to a request for clarification from an Employer member from Canada, the representative of the Secretary-General reminded the Committee that paragraph 34 of the Office text had not accurately reflected the results of the Meeting of Experts held in December 2004. The intention was to have two alternatives.

793. The subamendment was adopted.

D.56

794. A Worker member from Argentina introduced a subamendment to replace the words "not be more than four persons" by "generally be two persons and, at a maximum, four persons". The space required for two two-person cabins was not much more than that required for one four-person cabin, but such a provision would certainly improve the conditions.

795. An Employer member from Canada sought clarification from the Office as to the legal meaning of "shall generally be".

796. The representative of the Legal Adviser advised that this meant "in the absence of exceptional circumstances".

797. An Employer member from Canada, speaking on behalf of the Employers' group, opposed the subamendment on the basis that it would have a negative impact on the development of fisheries.

798. The Government members of Argentina, Brazil, Denmark, Philippines and Spain supported the amendment.

799. The Government members of Cameroon, France, Japan, Kenya, Republic of Korea, Mauritania, Mozambique, Namibia, Nigeria, South Africa and the Syrian Arab Republic preferred the text proposed by the Working Party.

800. The Government member of the United Kingdom, although sympathizing with the Worker members' subamendment, could not support it. He suggested that the provision be shifted to the Recommendation, a proposal supported by both the Workers' and the Employers' groups.

801. The subamendment was adopted and referred to the Drafting Committee for appropriate rewording and placement in the Recommendation.

D.57

802. A Worker member from Argentina withdrew a subamendment (D.57).

803. Paragraph 34 was adopted as amended.

Paragraph 36

D.58, D.59

804. A Worker member from Argentina withdrew two subamendments (D.58 and D.59).

805. Paragraph 36 was adopted without amendment.

Paragraph 39

D.90

806. A subamendment (D.90) was not seconded and therefore not discussed.

D.61, D.98

807. A Worker member from Argentina introduced a subamendment to replace "[190]" by "198" and replace "[68]" by "80". The aim of the subamendment was to increase the size of berths.

808. The Government member of Norway explained that a clear majority of the Government group had supported this subamendment as well as a similar subamendment (D.98) on the length of berths submitted by a number of Government members. The Government group favoured increasing berth sizes.

809. The Government member of Japan opposed the subamendment because the proposed dimensions were too large for Asian people. When ships rolled in rough seas, fishers would slide about in their berths. This sideways movement was uncomfortable and not desirable.

810. The Government member of China agreed.

811. The subamendment was adopted and that of the Government members withdrawn.

812. An Employer member from Canada, while acknowledging the majority support the subamendments had received, expressed his group's reservations with regard to this decision. He regretted that the needs of the Asian countries seemed to be ignored by the Committee and foresaw problems for the ratification of the Convention. The Employers' group had suggested shifting the provision to the Recommendation.

813. Paragraph 39 was adopted as amended.

Paragraph 43

D.99

814. The Government member of France introduced a subamendment, submitted by the Government members of Belgium, Denmark, Finland, France, Germany, Greece, Netherlands, Norway, Portugal, Sweden and the United Kingdom, to delete ", and shall be provided on vessels of [24] metres in length and over which are not less than [100] gt". The amendment sought to remove the proposed requirement for larger vessels to provide separate sleeping rooms for men and women fishers. Given the very limited number of women fishers, such a provision might lead to further discrimination against women fishers, something the sponsors of the subamendment strongly objected to.

815. The Government member of Norway said that the Government group supported the subamendment.

816. A Worker member from Argentina proposed a further subamendment to move the paragraph to the Recommendation with the following wording: "Separate sleeping rooms for men and women should be provided on vessels of 24 metres in length and over."

817. The Employer Vice-Chairperson supported the proposal.

818. The Government member of Norway, speaking on behalf of the Government group, was confident that Governments could support the proposal.

819. The subamendment was adopted.

820. Paragraph 43 was adopted as amended and moved to the Recommendation.

Paragraph 54

D.83

821. The Government member of Japan introduced a subamendment submitted by the Government members of Japan and the Republic of Korea to replace the existing text in Paragraph 54 of the conclusions of the Working Party by the following:

> On vessels of 24 metres in length and over, for all fishers who do not occupy rooms to which sanitary facilities are attached, there shall be provided at least one tub or shower or both and one toilet for every eight persons or fewer, and one washbasin for every six persons or fewer. The competent authority, after consultation, may establish alternative requirements to the above requirement in particular cases if the size and type of intended service of the vessel make the requirements impracticable.

822. The exceptions contained in the proposal corresponded to those adopted in the framework of the Accommodation of Crews (Fishermen) Convention, 1966 (No. 126), and the FAO/ILO/IMO Code of Safety for Fishermen and Fishing Vessels. The current wording of paragraph 54 imposed overly strict conditions without providing for exceptions. While paragraph 2 of Article 28 of the Convention allowed for substantial equivalence, it could not be applied in the case of paragraph 54 of Annex III. The frequency of visiting sanitary facilities was the same in all countries.

823. The subamendment was not adopted.

D.75

824. A Worker member of Argentina introduced a subamendment submitted by the Workers' group to add the sentence "Separate sanitary facilities shall be provided for woman fishers." at the end of paragraph 54. He suggested a further subamendment to move the sentence to the Recommendation using the word "should" instead of "shall".

825. The Employer Vice-Chairperson agreed with the proposal.

826. The Government member of Norway, speaking on behalf of the Government group, was confident that Governments could support the proposal, considering that paragraph 50 already provided that sanitary facilities used by women fishers should allow for reasonable privacy.

827. The subamendment was adopted.

828. Paragraph 54 was adopted as amended and moved to the Recommendation.

829. Paragraphs 56 and 57 were adopted.

Paragraph 59

830. An Employer member from Canada proposed a subamendment to replace "sick bay" with the phrase "cabin designated for fishers who suffer illness or injury" and to add the words "in accordance with national standards" after the words "properly equipped ". While the Employers' group did not disagree with the intent of the provision, there was a lack of clarity regarding the definition of "sick bay".

831. The Government member of France preferred the Working Party text. He also remarked that the Working Party text for paragraph 58 no longer contained the word "isolated" and the subamendment to paragraph 59 removed the word "separate".

832. The Government member of South Africa could not support the subamendment; there had to be a dedicated sick bay or hospital on large vessels, not a mere cabin.

833. The Government member of Brazil agreed with the Government member of South Africa. As Chairperson of the Working Party, she confirmed that the Working Party had decided to remove the word "isolated" from paragraph 58, but there had been no consensus on paragraph 59.

834. An Employer member from Canada drew a distinction between paragraphs 58 and 59. Paragraph 58 required that a cabin be made available to a fisher who suffered an illness or injury. This cabin did not necessarily need to be a designated sick bay. Paragraph 59 required that a separate sick bay be available. There was no dispute with the idea that a facility had to be available. What was unclear was the meaning of "sick bay". It was important to remember that the Convention sought to establish minimum standards. Some modern 60-70 metre long vessels did not have hospitals or sick bays, and could be run efficiently for health purposes. A designated cabin could be supplied with oxygen and first aid materials such as bandages. Medicines might be kept separately, for instance in the captain's cabin.

835. In reference to the comment of the previous speaker, the Government member of Greece noted these provisions would apply to new fishing vessels.

836. An Employer member from Canada requested a definition of "sick bay".

837. The Government member of the United Kingdom stated that a sick bay was a cabin that was used for no other purpose. This definition had long existed. Also, the issue of medical supplies was adequately covered in Article 29, subparagraph (c).

838. An Employer member from Canada noted that Article 29, subparagraph (c), could be interpreted as saying that medical supplies would be carried on board, but not necessarily in the sick bay or designated cabin.

839. The Government members of Argentina, France, South Africa, United Kingdom and Uruguay preferred the term "sick bay".

840. An Employer member from Canada said that the term "sick bay" as defined by the Government member of the United Kingdom was acceptable to his group.

841. The subamendment was not adopted.

842. Paragraph 59 was adopted.

Paragraph 70

843. Paragraph 70 was adopted, on the understanding that the question of "drinking water" as opposed to "potable water" would be referred to the Drafting Committee.

Paragraph 72

844. An Employer member from Canada stated that his group withdrew the objection it had formulated in the Working Party.

845. Paragraph 72 was adopted.

Paragraph 75

D.74

846. A Worker member from Argentina withdrew a subamendment before it was discussed.

847. An Employer member from Canada proposed deleting the last sentence of the paragraph, as it could entail unnecessary paperwork for owner-operated coastal vessels, where such inspections were carried out routinely and corrective steps taken before the vessel left the port.

848. The Government members of France and South Africa observed that the recording of inspections was standard practice in the majority of maritime acts and should not create undue administrative burdens.

849. In the absence of any statements of support for the subamendment, the Chairperson concluded that it was not adopted.

850. Paragraph 75 was adopted.

851. Annex III, as proposed by the Working Party and subamended by the Committee, was adopted.

Consideration of the proposed Recommendation concerning work in the fishing sector

Part I. Conditions for work on board fishing vessels

Protection of young persons

Paragraphs 1 to 5

852. Paragraphs 1 to 5 were adopted without amendment.

Medical examination

Paragraphs 6 to 10

853. Paragraphs 6 to 10 were adopted without amendment.

Competency and training

Paragraph 11

854. Paragraph 11 was adopted without amendment.

Paragraph 12

D.203

855. The Government member of the United Kingdom introduced an amendment submitted by the Government members of Finland, France, Germany, Greece, Ireland, Netherlands, Norway, Portugal, Spain, Sweden and the United Kingdom to delete Paragraph 12, because the matter was already adequately covered in the Convention.

856. The Worker Vice-Chairperson, the Employer Vice-Chairperson and a clear majority of the Government group supported the amendment.

857. The amendment was adopted and Paragraph 12 was deleted.

Part II. Conditions of service

Record of service

Paragraph 13

D.209

858. The Employer Vice-Chairperson introduced an amendment to replace the word "voyage" by "contract" both times it appeared in Paragraph 13. Fishers worked under contract and many voyages could be undertaken under a single contract. A record of service would be more appropriately established on the basis of the whole contractual period.

859. The Worker Vice-Chairperson could not agree with the proposal. A new term, "contract", was being introduced.

860. The Government member of Norway stated that a clear majority of the Government group supported the amendment.

861. The amendment was adopted.

862. Paragraph 13 was adopted as amended.

Special measures

Paragraph 14

863. Paragraph 14 was adopted.

Payment of fishers

New Paragraph before Paragraph 15

D.201

864. The Government member of France introduced an amendment jointly submitted with the Government member of Denmark to insert a new Paragraph before Paragraph 15 under the heading "Payment of fishers" to read as follows: "Collective agreements or measures adopted by the competent authority shall ensure advances against earnings for fishers under prescribed conditions." Irregular payment of wages was a problem in the sector. The speaker subamended the French version of the text.

865. The Worker Vice-Chairperson supported the amendment as subamended.

866. The Government member of Norway noted that the Government group had supported the intent of the amendment, but not the wording. Speaking on behalf of the Government group, he proposed a subamendment, which read as follows: "Fishers should have the right to advances against earnings under prescribed conditions."

867. The Employer Vice-Chairperson supported the Government group's subamendment as did the Worker Vice-Chairperson.

868. The amendment was adopted as subamended.

869. The new Paragraph before Paragraph 15 was adopted.

Paragraph 15

D.208

870. The Employer Vice-Chairperson introduced an amendment to add the words "If applicable" at the beginning of Paragraph 15.

871. The Worker Vice-Chairperson opposed the amendment as did the Government member of Norway, speaking on behalf of the Government group.

872. The Employer Vice-Chairperson withdrew the amendment.

D.207

873. The Employer Vice-Chairperson introduced an amendment to delete the words "or those engaged on international voyages". Since many countries would make use of the Recommendation as guidelines, the reappearance of the term "international voyage" could create problems. The original wording suggested that vessels of less than 24 metres length that undertook international voyages were also targeted by this provision. This needed to be rectified in order to protect workers on small fishing vessels, which might undertake international voyages.

874. The Worker Vice-Chairperson supported the amendment.

875. The Government member of Norway said that the Government group supported the amendment.

876. The amendment was adopted.

D.199

877. The Worker Vice-Chairperson noted that nowhere in the present text was the regularity of payments mentioned. Yet regular payments were important to fishers so that they could meet their obligations at home. He, therefore, proposed to insert the word "regular" after the word "minimum".

878. The Government member of Norway stated that the Government group did not support the amendment.

879. The Employer Vice-Chairperson also opposed the amendment.

880. The Worker Vice-Chairperson withdrew the amendment.

881. Paragraph 15 was adopted as amended.

Part III. Accommodation

Paragraphs 16 to 18

882. Paragraphs 16 to 18 were adopted without amendment.

Design and construction

Paragraphs 19 to 21

> **883.** Paragraphs 19 to 21 were adopted without amendment.

Noise and vibration

Paragraph 22

D.206

> **884.** The Employer Vice-Chairperson introduced an amendment to delete the word "and" after the word "workplace" and to delete the rest of the sentence after the words "where applicable". The reference to "specific protection" was unclear and needed to be explained
>
> **885.** The Government member of Norway said that a clear majority in the Government group was against the amendment. The IMO reference offered helpful guidance and should be kept.
>
> **886.** The Worker Vice-Chairperson agreed with the Government member of Norway and opposed the amendment.
>
> **887.** A member of the secretariat explained that during the Tripartite Meeting of Experts on the Fishing Sector held in December 2004, experts had raised the issue of noise and vibration and had suggested that IMO Resolution A.468(XII) – Code on Noise Levels on Board Ships was relevant and should be referred to in the recommendatory provisions.
>
> **888.** The amendment was not adopted.

D.205

> **889.** The Worker Vice-Chairperson stated that many fishers were regularly exposed to vibrations over long periods of time, with negative effects on their health, making it necessary to include this issue in the Recommendation. He therefore introduced an amendment to insert the following Paragraphs after Paragraph 22:
>
>> 1. The competent authority in each Member, in conjunction with the competent international bodies and with representatives of organizations of fishing vessel owners and fishers and taking into account, as appropriate, relevant international standards, should review on an ongoing basis the problem of vibration on board fishing vessels with the objective of improving the protection of fishers, as far as practicable, from the adverse effects of vibration.
>>
>> 2. Such review should cover the effect of exposure to excessive vibration on the health and comfort of fishers and the measures to be prescribed or recommended to reduce vibration on fishing vessels to protect fishers.
>>
>> 3. Measures to reduce vibration to be considered should include the following:
>>
>> (a) instruction of fishers in the dangers to their health of prolonged exposure to vibration;
>>
>> (b) provision of approved personal protective equipment to fishers where necessary;
>>
>> (c) assessment of risks and reduction of exposure in sleeping rooms, mess rooms, recreational accommodation and catering facilities and other fishers accommodation by adopting measures in accordance with the guidance provided by the ILO Code of practice on ambient factors in the workplace and subsequent revisions, taking into account the difference between exposure in the workplace and in the living space.

890. The Employer Vice-Chairperson supported the inclusion of a Paragraph on vibration, but felt that the suggested text was too detailed. She therefore suggested a subamendment to delete Paragraphs 2 and 3.

891. The Government member of Norway explained that the Government group had supported the amendment's intent, but their opinions were divided as to the actual content. Some felt that the wording was too prescriptive, others thought it provided the right amount of detail.

892. The Government member of the Bolivarian Republic of Venezuela opposed the subamendment, stating this issue was linked with the Committee's previous discussions on the protection of workers from occupational health problems and needed to be given due consideration. Paragraphs 2 and 3 highlighted the important issues of prevention and protection from risk, and so needed to be retained.

893. The Government member of Norway opposed the subamendment, noting that noise and vibration were concerns for the safety and health of fishers and for effective fishing. These recommendatory provisions provided important information on prevention measures.

894. The Government members of Denmark and Spain opposed the subamendment.

895. The Employer Vice-Chairperson withdrew the subamendment.

896. The amendment was adopted.

897. Paragraph 22 was adopted as amended.

Paragraph 23

D.202

898. The Worker Vice-Chairperson introduced an amendment to insert the following section after Paragraph 23:

Lighting

Methods of lighting should not endanger the health or safety of the fishers or the safety of the vessel.

The intent was to draw attention to the fact that some methods of lighting could be dangerous to the crew and to the vessel.

899. The Employer Vice-Chairperson and the Government member of Norway, speaking on behalf of the Government group, supported the amendment.

900. The amendment was adopted.

901. Paragraph 23 was adopted as amended.

New Paragraph before Paragraph 24

902. The Committee then examined a proposal by the Drafting Committee (C.R./D.5(C.S.P.)), relating to the Recommendation. The proposal was to insert the following new Paragraph after the title "Sleeping rooms" and before Paragraph 24: "For vessels of [24] metres in length and over, the number of persons allowed to occupy each sleeping room should not normally be more than two and, at a maximum, four persons."

903. The Legal Adviser stated that, as requested by the Committee, a new Paragraph was to be inserted in the Recommendation, rather than in the Convention. The provision was, therefore, not binding. The English text as it appeared in document C.R./D.5(C.S.P.) was correct, while the French and Spanish versions contained minor errors which would be corrected.

904. The Chairperson thanked the Drafting Committee for their excellent work and, noting there was no objection, declared the text in C.R./D.5(C.S.P.) adopted.

Paragraph 24

D.213, D.197

905. The Employer Vice-Chairperson introduced an amendment to delete the word "spring" in the first line of Paragraph 24, as springs were no longer widely used in mattresses, having been replaced by more modern materials.

906. The Government member of Norway stated that the Government group shared the concerns of the Employers' group. It had, however, favoured the amendment submitted by the Republic of Korea and the Philippines to replace the words "spring mattress of approved material, or with a spring base and a mattress" by the words "comfortable mattress with a cushioned bottom or a combined mattress, including a spring bottom, or a spring mattress. The cushioning material used should be made". This amendment was superior in wording.

907. The Worker Vice-Chairperson supported the statement of the Government member of Norway.

908. The Employer Vice-Chairperson supported the amendment favoured by the Government members and withdrew her group's amendment.

909. The amendment was adopted.

910. Paragraph 24 was adopted as amended.

Paragraphs 25 and 26

911. Paragraphs 25 and 26 were adopted without amendment.

Paragraph 27

D.198, D.212

912. The Government member of the Republic of Korea introduced an amendment (D.198), submitted by the Republic of Korea and the Philippines, to delete Paragraph 27. The Office text assumed that incompatibilities between crew and officers existed and threatened harmonious conviviality on board. Furthermore, divided mess rooms did not allow space to be used efficiently. A decision to require mess rooms to be divided should be left to the discretion of member States.

913. The Worker Vice-Chairperson opposed the amendment, but supported an amendment (D.212), submitted by the Employers to add the words "In accordance with national law and practice," to the beginning of the Paragraph.

914. The Government member of Norway, speaking on behalf of the Government group, stated that a clear majority of Government members favoured the amendment to delete the Paragraph.

915. The Employer Vice-Chairperson withdrew her group's amendment and supported the amendment to delete the Paragraph.

916. The amendment was adopted

917. Paragraph 27 was deleted.

Paragraphs 28 and 29

918. Paragraphs 28 and 29 were adopted without amendment.

Paragraph 30

D.204

919. The Worker Vice-Chairperson introduced an amendment to insert the following text at the end of Paragraph 30:

> Consideration should also be given to including the following facilities at no cost to the fishers, where practicable:
>
> (a) a smoking room;
>
> (b) television viewing and the reception of radio broadcasts;
>
> (c) projection of films or video films, the stock of which should be adequate for the duration of the voyage and, where necessary, changed at reasonable intervals;
>
> (d) sports equipment including exercise equipment, table games, deck games;
>
> (e) a library containing vocational and other books, the stock of which should be adequate for the duration of the voyage and changed at reasonable intervals;
>
> (f) facilities for recreational handicrafts;
>
> (g) electronic equipment such as radio, TV, video recorder, DVD/CD player, personal computer and software, cassette recorder/player.

The objects and facilities listed were already part of the daily life on board many fishing vessels to varying degrees. It was advisable, however, to draw the attention of national legislators to these measures, which would enrich leisure time on board.

920. The Government member of Norway, speaking on behalf of the Government group, supported the amendment.

921. The Employer Vice-Chairperson opposed the amendment. She proposed a subamendment to delete "at no cost" since in most cases, these facilities or items were not provided free of cost. In any case, this issue was subject to collective bargaining and was decided upon between employers and workers.

922. The Government members of Argentina, France and Spain did not support the subamendment.

923. The subamendment was not adopted.

924. The amendment was adopted.

925. Paragraph 30 was adopted as amended.

Paragraph 31

D.211

926. The Employer Vice-Chairperson introduced an amendment to delete Paragraph 31, since it seemed impracticable to separate mess and recreation areas.

927. The Government member of Norway, speaking on behalf of the Government group, supported the amendment.

928. The Committee adopted the amendment to delete Paragraph 31.

Paragraph 32

929. Paragraph 32 was adopted without amendment.

Part IV. Health protection, medical care and social security

Paragraph 33

930. Paragraph 33 was adopted without amendment.

Paragraph 34

D.210

931. The Employer Vice-Chairperson introduced an amendment to delete the words "and ordinarily engaged on international voyages of more than three days' duration". Vessels carrying 100 or more fishers required a qualified medical doctor on board, irrespective of the duration of the voyage.

932. The Worker Vice-Chairperson and the Government member of Norway, speaking on behalf of the Government group, supported the amendment.

933. The amendment was adopted.

934. Paragraph 34 was adopted as amended.

Paragraphs 35 to 37

935. Paragraphs 35 to 37 were adopted without amendment.

Occupational safety and health

Research, dissemination of information and consultation

Paragraphs 38 to 42

936. Paragraphs 38 to 42 were adopted without amendment.

Occupational safety and health management systems

Paragraph 43

D.216

937. The Employer Vice-Chairperson withdrew an amendment (D.216) prior to its discussion.

938. Paragraph 43 was adopted without amendment.

Risk evaluation

Paragraph 44

D.218

939. The Employer Vice-Chairperson submitted an amendment to add the words "as soon as it comes into force" at the end of subparagraph (1)(b). The reason was that the Paragraph currently referred to an international instrument that was not yet in force.

940. The Government member of Norway, speaking on behalf of the Government group, opposed the amendment. Although the International Convention on Standards of Training, Certification and Watchkeeping for Fishing Vessel Personnel had not come into force, it could provide useful guidance.

941. The Worker Vice-Chairperson agreed with the Government group and opposed the amendment.

942. The amendment was not adopted.

D.214

943. The Employer Vice-Chairperson submitted an amendment to delete subparagraph (2)(b) concerning an occupational safety and health management system, given that the issue of occupational safety and health was already dealt with in Paragraph 43.

944. The Government member of Norway, speaking on behalf of the Government group, opposed the amendment. While subparagraph (1)(a) provided that risk evaluation in relation to fishing should include risk assessment and management, subparagraph (2)(b) stipulated that, to give effect to subparagraph 1(a), Members should adopt laws, regulations or other measures requiring, inter alia, an occupational safety and health management system with certain recommended features. It was essential to keep this subparagraph.

945. The Employer Vice-Chairperson withdrew the amendment.

946. Paragraph 44 was adopted without amendment.

Technical specifications

Paragraph 45

D.215

947. The Employer Vice-Chairperson withdrew an amendment (D.215) prior to its discussion.

948. Paragraph 45 was adopted without amendment.

Paragraph 46

949. Paragraph 46 was adopted without amendment.

Establishment of a list of occupational diseases

Paragraph 47

950. Paragraph 47 was adopted without amendment.

Social security

Paragraphs 48 to 50

951. Paragraphs 48 to 50 were adopted without amendment.

Part V. Other provisions

Paragraph 51

D.217

952. The Employer Vice-Chairperson introduced an amendment to insert the words "which has ratified the Convention" after the word "Member". A coastal State that had not ratified the Convention could not require fishing vessels from other States to comply with the Convention when granting fishing licences.

953. The Government member of Norway, speaking on behalf of the Government group, opposed the amendment. The proposal did not serve the intent of the Employers' group, since only ratifying member States were bound by the Convention and would be called upon to take into consideration the Recommendation. Moreover, the amendment would impede on the sovereign right of member States that had not ratified the Convention to set requirements as they deemed fit within their territory.

954. The Government member of China supported the amendment and suggested adding a point concerning Members having signed bilateral fishing agreements.

955. The Worker Vice-Chairperson stated the amendment would support flag of convenience vessels and was therefore not acceptable.

956. In response to a request for clarification as to the meaning of the word "Member", the representative of the Legal Adviser stated that each Convention had a clause starting with the words "Each Member which ratifies this Convention shall …" and any subsequent mentions of Members were dictated by this clause. Since Recommendations could not be ratified and were addressed to all Members of the ILO, the word "Member" in a Recommendation did not refer to a ratifying State, but to all Members.

957. The Government member of Namibia therefore inferred that the term "Member" had two meanings. In Recommendations, it had to be understood in its broad sense of all ILO member States. Referring to the arguments of the Government member of Norway, he opposed the amendment.

958. The Employer Vice-Chairperson reiterated that it was perplexing why coastal ILO member States that had not ratified the Convention should require fishing vessels from other States to comply with the Convention.

959. The Chairperson concluded that a sufficient majority of the Committee members opposed the amendment, which was not adopted.

960. Paragraph 51 was adopted without amendment.

New Paragraph after Paragraph 51

D.200

961. The Government member of France, also speaking on behalf of the Government member of Denmark, introduced an amendment seeking to insert a new Paragraph after Paragraph 51. In light of the decision taken on Paragraph 51, he immediately subamended the text to read: "If such licences are issued by coastal States, these coastal States should take into account certificates or other valid documents stating that the vessel concerned has been inspected by the competent authority or on its behalf and has been in compliance with the provisions of the Convention concerning work in the fishing sector." This provision was essential to provide minimum objective guarantees for flag States.

962. The Government member of Denmark seconded the subamendment.

963. The Worker and Employer Vice-Chairpersons supported the subamendment.

964. The Government member of Norway, speaking on behalf of the Government group, opposed the amendment and invited individual Governments to comment on the subamendment.

965. The Government member of Norway proposed a further subamendment to add the word "found" before "in compliance" as the proposed wording seemed to indicate that the vessel had been in compliance but no longer was.

966. The representative of the Secretary-General informed the Committee this was most likely a translation issue.

967. The Government member of Greece recalled that Article 39 referred to "documents" and made specifications as to their use. The subamendment implied that all fishing vessels, irrespective of distance from flag State or of size, should have certificates or other valid inspection documents while fishing in the exclusive economic zone of another State. Since Article 39 made provisions for these documents, he could not support the amendment.

968. The Government members of Egypt, Japan and the United Kingdom agreed with the Government member of Greece.

969. The Government member of Ireland found the amendment too legalistic for a Recommendation. It contained implications regarding inspection and verification that his country found unacceptable.

970. The Chairperson concluded that a sufficient majority of the Committee members supported the amendment, which was adopted as subamended.

971. The new Paragraph following Paragraph 51 was adopted.

972. The Committee adopted the Recommendation as amended.

Adoption of the report

973. The Reporter congratulated the Committee on the spirit of cooperation and collaboration that it had demonstrated throughout its discussions. The Committee's goal had been to develop a Convention and a Recommendation that would reflect the changes in the fishing sector over the past 40 years, to achieve widespread ratification, to reach the greater portion of the world's fishers and to address such issues as safety and health, social security, compliance and enforcement. In doing so, the Committee had had to resolve some complex and sensitive technical issues, and the outcome had been a practical, comprehensive and ratifiable Convention and a Recommendation. Not a single vote had been necessary during the crucial second discussion. This fact demonstrated the Committee's commitment, its willingness to consult, its desire for consensus, its concern for the world's fishers and the clarity of the Office text. He wished to thank the Office for its unstinting efforts, and in particular Loic Picard, Norman Jennings, Joachim Grimsmann, Brandt Wagner, Dani Appave, Antoinette Juvet-Mir, Ann Herbert, Anamaria Vere, Martin Hahn, as well as Cleopatra Doumbia-Henry who had been as involved and committed behind the scenes as always. He also congratulated the Drafting Committee on its excellent work. He concluded by recommending the draft report (C.S.P./D.228) for adoption by the Committee.

974. The report was adopted with minor amendmentS.

Adoption of the proposed Convention and the proposed Recommendation

975. The Reporter thanked the Drafting Committee members for the excellent work done on behalf of the Committee under the able chairpersonship of the Legal Adviser. The text which had emerged from the Committee's deliberations, with 46 Articles in the proposed Convention, three annexes and an accompanying Recommendation, was probably the longest instrument ever discussed during an International Labour Conference. For this reason, the Committee's Drafting Committee had met on a daily basis to keep up with the text as developed by the Committee and to respond interactively to requests from the Committee by making suggestions and returning proposals to the Committee for consideration and adoption. The Drafting Committee had served in fact as a drafter of text referred to it by the Committee, when consensus had been reached on substance and intent, but the precise wording had yet to be worked out. This new method of working had proved effective and worthwhile. In closing, the speaker urged the Committee to adopt the proposed Convention and proposed Recommendation concerning work in the fishing sector.

976. The Government member of Japan expressed his gratitude to all those involved in the Committee's deliberations. He thanked, in particular, the members of the Working Party on accommodation and food, who through their hard work over a three-day period, had drafted provisions with a certain flexibility, by adding new paragraph 2 to Article 28. Despite this, however, the Convention did not offer sufficient flexibility for the purposes of widespread ratification. First, several paragraphs of Annex III, which prescribed new rules on accommodation and food, contained even stricter and more prescriptive provisions than the Accommodation of Crews (Fishermen) Convention, 1966 (No. 126). Second, the Committee had failed to select appropriate gross tonnage figures equivalent to the fishing vessel lengths of 15, 24 and 45 metres. For instance, the figure of 175 gross tonnes, which was adopted as equivalent to 24 metres in length, was much smaller than the figure proposed by Japan. As a result, major problems would arise in terms of ensuring equal and fair application of the Convention. Third, the Committee had failed to adopt appropriate conditions for the entry into force of the Convention. The required number of ten ratifications of which eight should be from coastal member States was too small when compared with other international instruments and thus inappropriate. All in all, the flexibility introduced in the proposed Convention did not accommodate the concerns expressed by the Government member of Japan. The speaker expressed concern as to whether or not the Convention could achieve widespread ratification and thus become a genuine international instrument. For these reasons, the Government of Japan could not support the adoption of the draft Convention and its annexes. This position should not, however, be interpreted as lack of care about decent work in the fishing sector. Japan would continue to make every effort to improve working conditions in the fishing sector, taking into account the results of the Committee.

977. The Employer Vice-Chairperson supported the adoption of the proposed instruments as a true reflection of the Committee's work. This should not be interpreted, however, as an indication of the Employers' group's position on the adoption of the Convention or the Recommendation at the Conference level.

978. The Chairperson declared the proposed Convention with its annexes and the proposed Recommendation to be adopted.

Consideration of draft resolutions

979. The Employer Vice-Chairperson noted that, due to time constraints, the Employers' group had not been able to examine the draft resolutions and could therefore not take part in a discussion on this subject.

980. The Worker Vice-Chairperson and the Government member of Norway, speaking on behalf of the Government group, stated that their groups were in a position to discuss the draft resolutions.

981. Following consultations, the Chairperson stated that, in light of the situation, the draft resolutions would be introduced and Committee members could express their views, but the Committee would not take a decision as to whether or not the resolutions should be adopted.

982. The Worker Vice-Chairperson introduced a draft resolution concerning the impact of the earthquake and tsunami disaster in the Indian Ocean, which he immediately subamended to read:

> The General Conference of the International Labour Organization,
>
> Having adopted the Convention concerning work in the fishing sector,
>
> Mindful of the core mandate of the Organization which is to promote decent conditions of work,
>
> Notes with grave concern the loss of life and the adverse impact the tsunami caused in the fishing sector in certain countries,
>
> Welcomes the prompt action taken by the Organization, in cooperation with other international organizations, to respond to the impact of the disaster, and
>
> Invites the Governing Body of the International Labour Office to request the Director-General to give due priority, in the use of resources, to ensuring that the Organization uses its special expertise to respond, through the promotion of social dialogue, to the labour market, employment and social protection needs of the affected countries, especially in the fishing sector and thereby contribute to the rehabilitation programmes.

983. The resolution aimed to lessen the negative impact on the Asian region of the earthquake and tsunami disaster.

984. The Government member of Norway noted that a clear majority of Government members had supported this resolution.

985. The Worker Vice-Chairperson introduced the following draft resolution concerning social security protection in the fishing sector:

> The General Conference of the International Labour Organization,
>
> Having adopted the Convention concerning work in the fishing sector,
>
> Taking into consideration that the Seafarers' Pensions Convention, 1946 (No. 71), and the Social Security (Seafarers) Convention (Revised), 1987 (No. 165), have received only a small number of ratification,
>
> Noting that Article 77 of the Social Security (Minimum Standards) Convention, 1952 (No. 102), expressly excludes sea fishers from the application of the Convention,
>
> Considers that, given the fact that sea fishing is considered by the Organization as a hazardous occupation when compared to other occupations, social security protection needs to be provided,
>
> Invites the Governing Body of the International Labour Office to request the Director-General to give due priority, in the use of resources, to promoting social security protection for sea fishers and, to facilitate the process, to have the Office prepare a global report on the provision of social security protection for sea fishers.

986. The resolution aimed to give effect to the decisions taken in regard to social security, by asking the Office to promote social security for fishers.

987. The Government member of Norway noted that a clear majority of Government members had supported the intent of this resolution.

988. The Worker Vice-Chairperson introduced a draft resolution concerning the impact on the globalization of the fishing sector, which aimed to ensure that the Office would continue making contributions to the international work in the sector. The draft resolution read:

> The General Conference of the International Labour Organization,
>
> Having adopted the Convention concerning work in the fishing sector,
>
> Noting the growth in world trade in fisheries products and the contribution fishing makes to the food security of many communities,
>
> Mindful of the core mandate of the Organization which is to promote decent conditions of work,
>
> Invites the Governing Body of the International Labour Office to request the Director-General to give due priority, in the use of resources, to examining the impact of globalization on the fishing sector, including the increasing employment or engagement on non-domiciled fishers.

989. The Government member of Norway stated that a clear majority of Government members had supported the intent of this draft resolution. The Government group would have preferred, however, to focus on fishers' living and working conditions.

990. The Government member of Japan stated that, during the discussion in the Government group, his delegation had suggested to amend the draft resolution by inserting "the effects of the growth in world trade in fisheries products on the fishing industry and" after "including" in the final paragraph. This addition reflected the adverse effects on the Japanese fishing industry of the growth in the world trade in fisheries products.

991. The Worker Vice-Chairperson introduced the following draft resolution concerning occupational diseases and injuries in the fishing sector:

> The General Conference of the International Labour Organization,
>
> Having adopted the Convention concerning work in the fishing sector,
>
> Notes that sea fishing is considered by the Organization as a hazardous occupation when compared to other occupations,
>
> Invites the Governing Body of the International Labour Office to request the Director-General to give due priority, in the use of resources, to examining, in cooperation with the World Health Organization, the occupational diseases and injuries affecting fishers and to examine their impact on both the fishing industry and on fishers and their dependants.

992. Given the hazardous nature of the fishing sector, the resolution aimed to improve the life of fishers worldwide by asking the Office to conduct additional work on occupational diseases and injuries.

993. The Government member of Norway stated that a clear majority of Government members had supported the draft resolution.

994. The Worker Vice-Chairperson introduced the following draft resolution concerning technical cooperation relating to work in the fishing sector, in order to help ratification of the instrument:

> The General Conference of the International Labour Organization,
>
> Having adopted the Convention concerning work in the fishing sector,
>
> Noting that the success of the Convention will depend upon the availability of the necessary expertise and material resources in the ratifying member States,
>
> Urges Members to agree among themselves on measures of cooperation which would enable them to share expertise and resources, where appropriate,
>
> Invites the Governing Body of the International Labour Office to request the Director-General to give due priority, in the use of resources allocated to the Organization's technical cooperation programme, to assisting countries in the sharing of their expertise.

995. The Government member of Norway stated that a clear majority of the Government group supported the draft resolution.

Closing remarks

996. The Secretary-General of the Conference stated that the adoption of a new instrument to protect the world's fishers represented the first fruits of the ILO's important programme to revise and consolidate old ILO standards. The Committee had managed to find the delicate balance between protecting the vast majority of small-scale fishers and not diluting the existing protection afforded to fishers on large ocean-going vessels or vessels at sea for long periods of time. Despite differing positions, the Committee had been able to find compromises, thanks to a spirit of tripartism and social dialogue. He concluded by noting that that much work remained; the Convention would need to be promoted, ratified and, once it entered into force, implemented. The ILO would do its best to assist in this process of making the new Convention a reality for the global fishing sector.

997. The Government member of Norway, speaking on behalf of the Government group, thanked all those on the Committee and in the secretariat for their tireless efforts to achieve positive results. He reserved particular thanks for the members of the Government group for their efforts to reach common positions on many issues. Their willingness to do so had made a crucial contribution to the Committee's work. He congratulated the Committee for having opted for a "positive spiral" in order to achieve the best possible living and working conditions for fishers, and urged all parties to maintain momentum on these issues.

998. The Employer Vice-Chairperson expressed her gratitude to the Committee's officers, members and the secretariat. Particularly warm thanks were conveyed to the Legal Adviser for the innovative role he and the Drafting Committee had played. Without his assistance, the Committee could not have successfully completed its work. She closed by reminding the Committee of her group's concerns with regard to the instrument, noting that posterity would judge their work.

999. The Worker Vice-Chairperson thanked the Chairperson and all members of the Committee, whose work was reflected in the new consolidated labour standards for the fishing sector, which improved upon existing standards and provided flexibility. He congratulated the Office on the excellent quality of the texts it had produced and thanked the secretariat for their long hours of work.

1000. The representative of the Secretary-General thanked the speakers for their kind words regarding the secretariat's hard work. It was good to see that the results of this work had proved to be satisfactory.

1001. The Chairperson also thanked the secretariat for their dedication and competence and for the excellence of the documents that had formed the basis of the discussion. The Committee reports were comprehensive and complex documents, which had been produced under very tight time constraints. The technical expertise that the members had demonstrated in the plenary as well as in the Drafting Committee and Working Party was highly appreciated. He noted the capacity of Committee members to listen to each other's concerns and to find common positions on some of the most important parts of the new instruments. The Employer and Worker Vice-Chairpersons had been excellent advocates for their groups' positions. The work of the Working Party and the Drafting Committee had been invaluable. Finally, the Chairperson thanked the interpreters, who had made it possible for him to speak in his mother tongue, Portuguese.

1002. The report of the Committee, and the texts of the proposed Convention and the proposed Recommendation are submitted to the Conference for consideration.

Geneva, 15 June 2005.

(Signed) F. Ribeiro Lopes,
Chairperson.

G. Boumbopoulos,
Reporter.

A. Proposed Convention concerning work in the fishing sector

The General Conference of the International Labour Organization,

Having been convened at Geneva by the Governing Body of the International Labour Office, and having met in its 93rd Session on 31 May 2005, and

Recognizing that globalization has a profound impact on the fishing sector, and

Noting the ILO Declaration on Fundamental Principles and Rights at Work, 1998, and

Taking into consideration the fundamental rights to be found in the following international labour Conventions: the Forced Labour Convention, 1930, the Freedom of Association and Protection of the Right to Organise Convention, 1948, the Right to Organise and Collective Bargaining Convention, 1949, the Equal Remuneration Convention, 1951, the Abolition of Forced Labour Convention, 1957, the Discrimination (Employment and Occupation) Convention, 1958, the Minimum Age Convention, 1973, and the Worst Forms of Child Labour Convention, 1999, and

Noting the relevant instruments of the International Labour Organization, in particular the Occupational Safety and Health Convention and Recommendation, 1981, and the Occupational Health Services Convention and Recommendation, 1985, and

Noting, in addition, the Social Security (Minimum Standards) Convention, 1952, and considering that the provisions of Article 77 of that Convention should not be an obstacle to protection extended by Members to fishers under social security schemes, and

Recognizing that the International Labour Organization considers fishing as a hazardous occupation when compared to other occupations, and

Noting also Article 1, paragraph 3 of the Seafarers' Identity Documents Convention (Revised), 2003, and

Mindful of the core mandate of the Organization, which is to promote decent conditions of work, and

Mindful of the need to protect and promote the rights of fishers in this regard, and

Recalling the United Nations Convention on the Law of the Sea, 1982, and

Taking into account the need to revise the following international instruments adopted by the International Labour Conference specifically concerning the fishing sector, namely the Hours of Work (Fishing) Recommendation, 1920, the Minimum Age (Fishermen) Convention, 1959, the Medical Examination (Fishermen) Convention, 1959, the Fishermen's Articles of Agreement Convention, 1959, and the Accommodation of Crews (Fishermen) Convention, 1966, to bring them up to date and to reach a greater number of the world's fishers, particularly those working on board smaller vessels, and

Noting that the objective of this Convention is to ensure that fishers have decent conditions of work on board fishing vessels with regard to minimum requirements for work on board; conditions of service; accommodation and food; occupational safety and health protection; medical care and social security, and

Having decided upon the adoption of certain proposals with regard to work in the fishing sector, which is the fifth item on the agenda of the session, and

Having determined that these proposals shall take the form of an international Convention;

adopts this   day of June of the year two thousand and five the following Convention, which may be cited as the Work in Fishing Convention, 2005.

PART I. DEFINITIONS AND SCOPE

DEFINITIONS

Article 1

For the purposes of the Convention:

(a) "commercial fishing" means all fishing operations, including fishing operations on rivers, lakes and canals, with the exception of subsistence fishing and recreational fishing;

(b) "competent authority" means the minister, government department or other authority having power to issue and enforce regulations, orders or other instructions having the force of law in respect of the subject matter of the provision concerned;

(c) "consultation" means consultation by the competent authority with the representative organizations of employers and workers concerned, and in particular the representative organizations of fishing vessel owners and fishers, where they exist, on the measures to be taken to give effect to the provisions of the Convention and with respect to any derogation, exemption or other flexible application as allowed under the Convention;

(d) "fishing vessel owner" means the owner of the fishing vessel or any other organization or person who has assumed the responsibility for the operation of the vessel from the owner or other organization or person and who, on assuming such responsibility, has agreed to take over the duties and responsibilities imposed on fishing vessel owners in accordance with the Convention;

(e) "fisher" means every person employed or engaged in any capacity or carrying out an occupation on board any fishing vessel, including persons working on board who are paid on the basis of a share of the catch but excluding pilots, naval personnel, other persons in the permanent service of a government, shore-based persons carrying out work aboard a fishing vessel and fisheries observers;

(f) "fisher's work agreement" means a contract of employment, articles of agreement or other similar arrangements or any other contract governing a fisher's living and working conditions on board a vessel;

(g) "fishing vessel" or "vessel" means any ship or boat, of any nature whatsoever, irrespective of the form of ownership, used or intended to be used for the purpose of commercial fishing;

(h) "new fishing vessel" means a vessel for which:

   (i) the building or major conversion contract is placed on or after the date of the entry into force of the Convention for the Member concerned; or

   (ii) the building or major conversion contract has been placed before the date of the entry into force of the Convention for the Member concerned, and which is delivered three years or more after that date; or

   (iii) in the absence of a building contract, on or after the date of the entry into force of the Convention for the Member concerned:

   – the keel is laid, or

   – construction identifiable with a specific vessel begins, or

   – assembly has commenced comprising at least 50 tonnes or 1 per cent of the estimated mass of all structural material, whichever is less;

(i) "existing vessel" means a vessel that is not a new fishing vessel;

(j) "gross tonnage" means the gross tonnage calculated in accordance with the tonnage measurement regulations contained in Annex I to the International Convention on Tonnage Measurement of Ships, 1969, or any instrument amending or replacing it;

(k) "length" (L) shall be taken as 96 per cent of the total length on a waterline at 85 per cent of the least moulded depth measured from the keel line, or as the length from the foreside of the stem to the axis of the rudder stock on that waterline, if that be greater. In vessels designed with rake of keel, the waterline on which this length is measured shall be parallel to the designed waterline;

(l) "length overall" (LOA) shall be taken as the distance in a straight line parallel to the designed waterline between the foremost point of the bow and the aftermost point of the stern;

(m) "recruitment and placement service" means any person, company, institution, agency or other organization, in the public or the private sector, which is engaged in recruiting fishers on behalf of, or placing fishers with, fishing vessel owners;

(n) "skipper" means the person having command of a fishing vessel.

SCOPE

Article 2

1. Except as otherwise provided herein, this Convention applies to all fishers and all fishing vessels engaged in commercial fishing operations.

2. In the event of doubt as to whether a vessel is engaged in commercial fishing, the question shall be determined by the competent authority after consultation.

3. Any Member, after consultation, may extend, in whole or in part, to fishers working on smaller vessels the protection provided in this Convention for fishers working on vessels 24 metres in length and over.

Article 3

1. The competent authority, after consultation, may exclude from the requirements of this Convention, or certain provisions thereof, where their application raises special and substantial problems in the light of the particular conditions of service of the fishers or the fishing vessels' operations:

(a) fishing vessels engaged in fishing operations in rivers, lakes and canals; and

(b) limited categories of fishers or fishing vessels.

2. In the case of exclusions under the preceding paragraph and, where practicable, this competent authority shall take measures, as appropriate, to extend progressively the requirements under the Convention to those categories of fishers and fishing vessels concerned.

Article 4

1. Each Member which ratifies the Convention shall, in the first report on the application of the Convention submitted under article 22 of the Constitution of the International Labour Organisation:

(a) list any categories of fishers or fishing vessels excluded under Article 3, paragraph 1;

(b) give the reasons for such exclusion, stating the respective positions of the representative organizations of employers and workers concerned, in particular the representative organizations of fishing vessel owners and fishers, where they exist; and

(c) describe any measures taken to provide equivalent protection to the excluded categories.

2. Each Member shall describe in subsequent reports submitted under article 22 of the Constitution the measures taken with a view to extending progressively the provisions of the Convention to the excluded fishers and fishing vessels.

Article 5

1. For the purpose of this Convention, the competent authority, after consultation, may decide to use length overall (LOA) in place of length (L) as the basis for measurement, in accordance with the equivalence set out in Annex I. In addition, for the purpose of the paragraphs specified in Annex III of this Convention, the competent authority, after consultation, may decide to use gross tonnage in place of length (L) or length overall (LOA) as the basis for measurement in accordance with the equivalence set out in Annex III.

2. In the reports submitted under article 22 of the Constitution, the Member shall communicate the reasons for the decision taken under this Article and any comments arising from the consultation.

Part II. General principles

Implementation

Article 6

1. Each Member shall implement and enforce laws, regulations or other measures that it has adopted to fulfil its commitments under this Convention with respect to fishers and fishing vessels under its jurisdiction. Other measures may include collective agreements, court decisions, arbitration awards, or other means consistent with national law and practice.

2. Nothing in this Convention shall affect any law, award or custom, or any agreement between fishing vessel owners and fishers, which ensures more favourable conditions than those provided for in the Convention.

Competent authority and coordination

Article 7

Each Member shall:

(a) designate the competent authority or authorities; and

(b) establish mechanisms for coordination among relevant authorities for the fishing sector at the national and local levels, as appropriate, and define their functions and responsibilities, taking into account their complementarities and national conditions and practice.

Responsibilities of fishing vessel owners, skippers and fishers

Article 8

1. The fishing vessel owner has the overall responsibility to ensure that the skipper is provided with the necessary resources and facilities to comply with the obligations of this Convention.

2. The skipper has the responsibility for the safety of the fishers on board and the safe operation of the vessel, including but not limited to the following areas:

(a) providing such supervision as will ensure that, as far as possible, fishers perform their work in the best conditions of safety and health;

(b) managing the fishers in a manner which respects safety and health, including prevention of fatigue;

(c) facilitating on-board occupational safety and health awareness training; and

(d) ensuring compliance with safety of navigation, watchkeeping and associated good seamanship standards.

3. The skipper shall not be constrained by the fishing vessel owner from taking any decision which, in the professional judgement of the skipper, is necessary for the safety of the vessel and its safe navigation and safe operation, or the safety of the fishers on board.

4. Fishers shall comply with the lawful orders of the skipper and applicable safety and health measures.

PART III. MINIMUM REQUIREMENTS FOR WORK ON BOARD FISHING VESSELS

MINIMUM AGE

Article 9

1. The minimum age for work on board a fishing vessel shall be 16 years. However, the competent authority may authorize a minimum age of 15 for persons who are no longer subject to compulsory schooling as provided by national legislation, and who are engaged in vocational training in fishing.

2. The competent authority, in accordance with national laws and practice, may authorize persons of the age of 15 to perform light work during school holidays. In such cases, it shall determine, after consultation, the kinds of work permitted and shall prescribe the conditions in which such work shall be undertaken and the periods of rest required.

3. The minimum age for assignment to activities on board fishing vessels, which by their nature or the circumstances in which they are carried out are likely to jeopardize the health, safety or morals of young persons, shall not be less than 18 years.

4. The types of activities to which paragraph 3 of this Article applies shall be determined by national laws or regulations, or by the competent authority, after consultation, taking into account the risks concerned and the applicable international standards.

5. The performance of the activities referred to in paragraph 3 of this Article as from the age of 16 may be authorized by national laws or regulations, or by decision of the competent authority, after consultation, on condition that the health, safety or morals of the young persons concerned are fully protected and that the young persons concerned have received adequate specific instruction or vocational training and have completed basic pre-sea safety training.

6. The engagement of fishers under the age of 18 for work at night shall be prohibited. For the purpose of this Article, "night" shall be defined in accordance with national law and practice. It shall cover a period of at least nine hours starting no later than midnight and ending no earlier than 5 a.m. An exception to strict compliance with the night work restriction may be made by the competent authority when:

(a) the effective training of the fishers concerned, in accordance with established programmes and schedules, would be impaired; or

(b) the specific nature of the duty or a recognized training programme requires that fishers covered by the exception perform duties at night and the authority determines, after consultation, that the work will not have a detrimental impact on their health or well-being.

7. None of the provisions in this Article shall affect any obligations assumed by the Member arising from the ratification of any other international labour Convention.

MEDICAL EXAMINATION

Article 10

1. No fishers shall work on board a fishing vessel without a valid medical certificate attesting to fitness to perform their duties.

2. The competent authority, after consultation, may grant exemptions from the application of paragraph 1 of this Article, taking into account the health and safety of fishers, size of the vessel, availability of medical assistance and evacuation, duration of the voyage, area of operation, and type of fishing operation.

3. The exemptions in paragraph 2 of this Article shall not apply to a fisher working on a fishing vessel of 24 metres in length and over or which normally remains at sea for more than three days. In urgent cases, the competent authority may permit a fisher to work on such a vessel for a period of a limited and specified duration until a medical certificate can be obtained, provided that the fisher is in possession of an expired medical certificate of a recent date.

Article 11

Each Member shall adopt laws, regulations or other measures providing for:

(a) the nature of medical examinations;

(b) the form and content of medical certificates;

(c) the issue of a medical certificate by a duly qualified medical practitioner or, in the case of a certificate solely concerning eyesight, by a person recognized by the competent authority as qualified to issue such a certificate; these persons shall enjoy full independence in exercising their professional judgement;

(d) the frequency of medical examinations and the period of validity of medical certificates;

(e) the right to a further examination by a second independent medical practitioner in the event that a person has been refused a certificate or has had limitations imposed on the work he or she may perform; and

(f) other relevant requirements.

Article 12

On a fishing vessel of 24 metres in length and over, or on a vessel which normally remains at sea for more than three days:

(1) The medical certificate of a fisher shall state, at a minimum, that:

   (a) the hearing and sight of the fisher concerned are satisfactory for the fisher's duties on the vessel; and

(b) the fisher is not suffering from any medical condition likely to be aggravated by service at sea or to render the fisher unfit for such service or to endanger the health of other persons on board.

(2) The medical certificate shall be valid for a maximum period of two years unless the fisher is under the age of 18, in which case the maximum period of validity shall be one year.

(3) If the period of validity of a certificate expires in the course of a voyage, the certificate shall remain in force until the end of that voyage.

PART IV. CONDITIONS OF SERVICE

MANNING AND HOURS OF REST

Article 13

Each Member shall adopt laws, regulations or other measures requiring that owners of fishing vessels flying its flag ensure that:

(a) their vessels are sufficiently and safely manned with a crew necessary for the safe navigation and operation of the vessel and under the control of a competent skipper; and

(b) fishers are given regular periods of rest of sufficient length to ensure health and safety.

Article 14

1. In addition to the requirements set out in Article 13, the competent authority shall:

(a) for vessels of 24 metres in length and over, establish a minimum level of manning for the safe navigation of the vessel, specifying the number and the qualifications of the fishers required;

(b) for fishing vessels regardless of size remaining at sea for more than three days, after consultation and for the purpose of limiting fatigue, establish the minimum hours of rest to be provided to fishers. Minimum hours of rest shall not be less than ten hours in any 24-hour period, and 77 hours in any seven-day period.

2. The competent authority may permit, for limited and specified reasons, temporary exceptions to the limits established in paragraph 1(b) of this Article. However, in such circumstances, it shall require that fishers shall receive compensatory periods of rest as soon as practicable.

3. The competent authority, after consultation, may establish alternative requirements to those in paragraphs 1 and 2 of this Article. However, such alternative requirements shall provide at least the same level of protection.

CREW LIST

Article 15

Every fishing vessel shall carry a crew list, a copy of which shall be provided to authorized persons ashore prior to departure of the vessel, or communicated ashore immediately after departure of the vessel. The competent authority shall determine to whom and when such information shall be provided and for what purpose or purposes.

FISHER'S WORK AGREEMENT

Article 16

Each Member shall adopt laws, regulations or other measures:

(a) requiring that fishers working on vessels flying its flag have the protection of a fisher's work agreement that is comprehensible to them and is consistent with the provisions of this Convention;

(b) specifying the minimum particulars to be included in fishers' work agreements in accordance with the provisions contained in Annex II.

Article 17

Each Member shall adopt laws, regulations or other measures regarding:

(a) procedures for ensuring that a fisher has an opportunity to review and seek advice on the terms of the fisher's work agreement before it is concluded;

(b) where applicable, the maintenance of records concerning the fisher's work under such an agreement; and

(c) the means of settling disputes in connection with a fisher's work agreement.

Article 18

The fisher's work agreement, a copy of which shall be provided to the fisher, shall be carried on board and be available to the fisher and, in accordance with national law and practice, to other concerned parties on request.

Article 19

Articles 16 to 18 and Annex II do not apply to a fishing vessel owner who is also single-handedly operating the vessel.

Article 20

It shall be the responsibility of the fishing vessel owner to ensure that each fisher has a written work agreement signed by both the fisher and the fishing vessel owner or an authorized representative of the fishing vessel owner.

Repatriation

Article 21

1. Members shall ensure that fishers on a fishing vessel that flies their flag and that enters a foreign port are entitled to repatriation in the event that the fisher's work agreement has expired or has been terminated for justified reasons by the fisher or by the fishing vessel owner, or the fisher is no longer able to carry out the duties required under the work agreement or cannot be expected to carry them out in the specific circumstances. This also applies to fishers from that vessel who are transferred for the same reasons from the vessel to the foreign port.

2. The cost of the repatriation referred to in paragraph 1 of this Article shall be borne by the fishing vessel owner, except where the fisher has been found, in accordance with national laws, regulations or other measures, to be in serious default of his or her work agreement obligations.

3. Members shall prescribe, by means of laws, regulations or other measures, the precise circumstances entitling a fisher covered by paragraph 1 of this Article to repatriation, the maximum duration of service periods on board following which a fisher is entitled to repatriation, and the destinations to which fishers may be repatriated.

4. If a fishing vessel owner fails to provide for the repatriation referred to in this Article, the Member whose flag the vessel flies shall arrange for the repatriation of the fisher concerned and shall be entitled to recover the cost from the fishing vessel owner.

Recruitment and placement

Article 22

1. Each Member that operates a public service providing recruitment and placement for fishers shall ensure that the service forms part of, or is coordinated with, a public employment service for all workers and employers.

2. Any private service providing recruitment and placement for fishers which operates in the territory of a Member shall do so in conformity with a standardized system of licensing or certification or other form of regulation, which shall be established, maintained or modified only after consultation.

3. Each Member shall, by means of laws, regulations or other measures:

(a) prohibit recruitment and placement services from using means, mechanisms or lists intended to prevent or deter fishers from engaging for work;

(b) require that no fees or other charges for recruitment and placement of fishers be borne directly or indirectly, in whole or in part, by the fisher; and

(c) determine the conditions under which any licence, certificate or similar authorization of a private recruitment or placement service may be suspended or withdrawn in case of violation of relevant laws or regulations; and specify the conditions under which private recruitment and placement services can operate.

PAYMENT OF FISHERS

Article 23

Each Member, after consultation, shall adopt laws, regulations or other measures providing that fishers who are paid a wage are ensured a monthly or regular payment.

Article 24

Each Member shall require that all fishers working on board fishing vessels shall be given a means to transmit all or part of their payments received, including advances, to their families at no cost.

PART V. ACCOMMODATION AND FOOD

Article 25

Each Member shall adopt laws, regulations or other measures for fishing vessels that fly its flag with respect to accommodation, food and potable water on board.

Article 26

1. Each Member shall adopt laws, regulations or other measures requiring that accommodation on board fishing vessels that fly its flag shall be of sufficient size and quality and appropriately equipped for the service of the vessel and the length of time fishers live on board. In particular, such measures shall address, as appropriate, the following issues:

(a) approval of plans for the construction or modification of fishing vessels in respect of accommodation;

(b) maintenance of accommodation and galley spaces with due regard to hygiene and overall safe, healthy and comfortable conditions;

(c) ventilation, heating, cooling and lighting;

(d) mitigation of excessive noise and vibration;

(e) location, size, construction materials, furnishing and equipping of sleeping rooms, mess-rooms and other accommodation spaces;

(f) sanitary facilities, including toilets and washing facilities, and supply of sufficient hot and cold water; and

(g) procedures for responding to complaints concerning accommodation that does not meet the requirements of this Convention.

Article 27

Each Member shall adopt laws, regulations or other measures requiring that:

(a) the food carried and served on board be of a sufficient nutritional value, quality and quantity;

(b) potable water be of sufficient quality and quantity; and

(c) the food and water shall be provided by the fishing vessel owner at no cost to the fisher. However, the cost can be recovered as an operational cost if the collective agreement governing a share system or a fisher's work agreement so provides.

Article 28

1. The laws, regulations or other measures to be adopted by the Member in accordance with Articles 25 to 27 shall give full effect to Annex III concerning fishing vessel accommodation. Annex III may be amended in the manner provided for in Article 45.

2. A Member which is not in a position to implement the provisions of Annex III may, after consultation, adopt provisions in its laws and regulations or other measures which are substantially equivalent to the provisions set out in Annex III, with the exception of provisions related to Article 27.

PART VI. MEDICAL CARE, HEALTH PROTECTION, AND SOCIAL SECURITY

MEDICAL CARE

Article 29

Each Member shall adopt laws, regulations or other measures requiring that:

(a) fishing vessels carry appropriate medical equipment and medical supplies for the service of the vessel, taking into account the number of fishers on board, the area of operation and the length of the voyage;

(b) fishing vessels have at least one person on board who is qualified or trained in first aid and other forms of medical care and who has the necessary knowledge to use the medical equipment and supplies for the vessel concerned, taking into account the number of fishers on board, the area of operation and the length of the voyage;

(c) medical equipment and supplies carried on board be accompanied by instructions or other information in a language and format understood by the person or persons referred to in subparagraph (b);

(d) fishing vessels be equipped for radio or satellite communication with persons or services ashore that can provide medical advice, taking into account the area of operation and the length of the voyage; and

(e) fishers have the right to medical treatment ashore and the right to be taken ashore in a timely manner for treatment in the event of serious injury or illness.

Article 30

For fishing vessels of 24 metres in length and over, taking into account the number of fishers on board, the area of operation and the duration of the voyage, each Member shall adopt laws, regulations or other measures requiring that:

(a) the competent authority prescribe the medical equipment and medical supplies to be carried on board;

(b) the medical equipment and medical supplies carried on board be properly maintained and inspected at regular intervals established by the competent authority by responsible persons designated or approved by the competent authority;

(c) the vessels carry a medical guide adopted or approved by the competent authority, or the (ILO/IMO/WHO) *International Medical Guide for Ships*;

(d) the vessels have access to a prearranged system of medical advice to vessels at sea by radio or satellite communication, including specialist advice, which shall be available at all times;

(e) the vessels carry on board a list of radio or satellite stations through which medical advice can be obtained; and

(f) to the extent consistent with the Member's national law and practice, medical care while the fisher is on board or landed in a foreign port be provided free of charge to the fisher.

OCCUPATIONAL SAFETY AND HEALTH AND ACCIDENT PREVENTION

Article 31

Each Member shall adopt laws, regulations or other measures concerning:

(a) the prevention of occupational accidents, occupational diseases and work-related risks on board fishing vessels, including risk evaluation and management, training and on-board instruction of fishers;

(b) training for fishers in the handling of types of fishing gear they will use and in the knowledge of the fishing operations in which they will be engaged;

(c) the obligations of fishing vessel owners, fishers and others concerned, due account being taken of the safety and health of fishers under the age of 18;

(d) the reporting and investigation of accidents on board fishing vessels flying its flag; and

(e) the setting up of joint committees on occupational safety and health or, after consultation, of other appropriate bodies.

Article 32

1. The requirements of this Article shall apply to fishing vessels of 24 metres in length and over normally remaining at sea for more than three days and, after consultation, to other vessels, taking into account the number of fishers on board, the area of operation, and the duration of the voyage.

2. The competent authority shall:

(a) after consultation, require that the fishing vessel owner, in accordance with national laws, regulations, collective bargaining agreements and practice, establish on-board procedures for the prevention of occupational accidents, injuries and diseases, taking into account the specific hazards and risks on the fishing vessel concerned;

(b) require that fishing vessel owners, skippers, fishers and other relevant persons be provided with sufficient and suitable guidance, training material, or other appropriate information on how to assess and manage risks to safety and health on board fishing vessels.

3. Fishing vessel owners shall:

(a) ensure that every fisher on board is provided with appropriate personal protective clothing and equipment;

(b) ensure that every fisher on board has received basic safety training approved by the competent authority; the competent authority may grant written exemptions from this requirement for fishers who have demonstrated equivalent knowledge and experience;

(c) ensure that fishers are sufficiently and reasonably familiarized with equipment and its methods of operation, including relevant safety measures, prior to using the equipment or participating in the operations concerned.

Article 33

Risk evaluation in relation to fishing shall be conducted, as appropriate, with the participation of fishers or their representatives.

SOCIAL SECURITY

Article 34

Each Member shall ensure that fishers ordinarily resident in its territory, and their dependants to the extent provided in national law, are entitled to benefit from social security protection under conditions no less favourable than those applicable to other workers, including employed and self-employed persons, ordinarily resident in its territory.

Article 35

Each Member shall undertake to take steps, according to national circumstances, to achieve progressively comprehensive social security protection for all fishers who are ordinarily resident in its territory.

Article 36

Members shall cooperate through bilateral or multilateral agreements or other arrangements, in accordance with national laws, regulations or practice:

(a) to achieve progressively comprehensive social security protection for fishers, taking into account the principle of equality of treatment irrespective of nationality; and

(b) to ensure the maintenance of social security rights which have been acquired or are in the course of acquisition by all fishers regardless of residence.

Article 37

Notwithstanding the attribution of responsibilities in Articles 34, 35 and 36, Members may determine, through bilateral and multilateral agreements and through provisions adopted in the framework of regional economic integration organizations, other rules concerning the social security legislation to which fishers are subject.

PROTECTION IN THE CASE OF WORK-RELATED SICKNESS, INJURY OR DEATH

Article 38

1. Each Member shall take measures to provide fishers with protection, in accordance with national laws, regulations or practice, for work-related sickness, injury or death.

2. In the event of injury due to occupational accident or disease, the fisher shall have access to:

(a) appropriate medical care; and

(b) the corresponding compensation in accordance with national laws and regulations.

3. Taking into account the characteristics within the fishing sector, the protection referred to in paragraph 1 of this Article may be ensured through:

(a) a system for fishing vessel owners' liability; or

(b) compulsory insurance, workers' compensation or other schemes.

Article 39

1. In the absence of national provisions for fishers, each Member shall adopt laws, regulations or other measures to ensure that fishing vessel owners are responsible for the provision to fishers on vessels flying its flag, of health protection and medical care while employed or engaged or working on a vessel at sea or in a foreign port. Such laws, regulations or other measures shall ensure that fishing vessel owners are responsible for defraying the expenses of medical care, including related material assistance and support, during medical treatment in a foreign country, until the fisher has been repatriated.

2. National laws or regulations may permit the exclusion of the liability of the fishing vessel owner if the injury occurred otherwise than on the service of the vessel or the sickness or infirmity was concealed during engagement, or the injury or sickness was due to a wilful act, default or misbehaviour.

PART VII. COMPLIANCE AND ENFORCEMENT

Article 40

Each Member shall exercise effective jurisdiction and control over vessels that fly its flag by establishing a system for ensuring compliance with the standards of this Convention including, as appropriate, inspections, reporting, monitoring, complaints procedures, appropriate penalties and corrective measures, in accordance with national laws or regulations.

Article 41

Members shall require that fishing vessels remaining at sea for more than three days, whether 24 metres in length and over or normally on voyages 200 nautical miles beyond the coastline of the flag State or the outer edge of its continental shelf, whichever is greater, carry a valid document issued by the competent authority stating that the vessel has been inspected by the competent authority or on its behalf, for compliance with the provisions of this Convention concerning living and working conditions. Such a document shall be valid for a period of five years or, if issued on the same date as the International Fishing Vessel Safety Certificate, for the period of validity of that certificate.

Article 42

1. The competent authority shall appoint a sufficient number of qualified inspectors to fulfil its responsibilities under Article 41.

2. In establishing an effective system for the inspection of living and working conditions on board fishing vessels, a Member, where appropriate, may authorize public institutions or other organizations that it recognizes as competent and independent to carry out inspections and issue documents. In all cases, the Member shall remain fully responsible for the inspection and issuance of the related documents concerning the living and working conditions of the fishers on fishing vessels that fly its flag.

Article 43

1. A Member which receives a complaint or obtains evidence that a fishing vessel that flies its flag does not conform to the requirements of this Convention shall take the steps necessary to investigate the matter and ensure that action is taken to remedy any deficiencies found.

2. If a Member, in whose port a fishing vessel calls in the normal course of its business or for operational reasons, receives a complaint or obtains evidence that such vessel does not conform to the standards of this Convention, it may prepare a report addressed to the government of the flag State of the vessel, with a copy to the Director-General of the International Labour Office, and may take measures necessary to rectify any conditions on board which are clearly hazardous to safety or health.

3. In taking the measures referred to in paragraph 2 of this Article, the Member shall notify forthwith the nearest representative of the flag State and, if possible, shall have such representative present. The Member shall not unreasonably detain or delay the vessel.

4. For the purpose of this Article, the complaint may be submitted by a fisher, a professional body, an association, a trade union or, generally, any person with an interest in the safety of the vessel, including an interest in safety or health hazards to the fishers on board.

5. This Article does not apply to complaints which a Member considers to be manifestly unfounded.

Article 44

Each Member shall apply the Convention in such a way as to ensure that the fishing vessels flying the flag of States that have not ratified the Convention do not receive more favourable treatment than fishing vessels that fly the flag of Members that have ratified it.

PART VIII. AMENDMENT OF ANNEXES I, II AND III

Article 45

1. Subject to the relevant provisions of this Convention, the International Labour Conference may amend Annexes I, II and III. The Governing Body of the International Labour Office may place an item on the agenda of the Conference regarding proposals for such amendments established by a tripartite meeting of experts. The decision to adopt the proposals shall require a majority of two-thirds of the votes cast by the delegates present at the Conference, including at least half the Members that have ratified this Convention.

2. Any amendment adopted in accordance with paragraph 1 of this Article shall enter into force, six months after the date of its adoption, for any Member that has ratified this Convention, unless such Member has given written notice to the Director-General that it shall not enter into force for that Member, or shall only enter into force at a later date upon subsequent written notification.

Article 46

This Convention revises the Minimum Age (Fisherman) Convention, 1959, the Medical Examination (Fishermen) Convention, 1959, the Fishermen's Articles of Agreement Convention, 1959, and the Accommodation of Crews (Fishermen's Convention), 1966.

ANNEX I

EQUIVALENCE IN MEASUREMENT

For the purpose of this Convention, where the competent authority, after consultation, decides to use length overall (LOA) rather than length (L) as the basis of measurement:

(a) a length overall (LOA) of 16.5 metres shall be considered equivalent to a length (L) of 15 metres;

(b) a length overall (LOA) of 26.5 metres shall be considered equivalent to a length (L) of 24 metres;

(c) a length overall (LOA) of 50 metres shall be considered equivalent to a length (L) of 45 metres.

ANNEX II

FISHER'S WORK AGREEMENT

The fisher's work agreement shall contain the following particulars, except in so far as the inclusion of one or more of them is rendered unnecessary by the fact that the matter is regulated in another manner by national laws or regulations, or a collective bargaining agreement where applicable:

(a) the fisher's family name and other names, date of birth or age, and birthplace;

(b) the place at which and date on which the agreement was concluded;

(c) the name of the fishing vessel or vessels and the registration number of the vessel or vessels on board which the fisher undertakes to work;

(d) the name of the employer, or fishing vessel owner, or other party to the agreement with the fisher;

(e) the voyage or voyages to be undertaken, if this can be determined at the time of making the agreement;

(f) the capacity in which the fisher is to be employed or engaged;

(g) if possible, the place at which and date on which the fisher is required to report on board for service;

(h) the provisions to be supplied to the fisher, unless some alternative system is provided for by national law or regulation;

(i) the amount of wages, or the amount of the share and the method of calculating such share if remuneration is to be on a share basis, or the amount of the wage and share and the method of calculating the latter if remuneration is to be on a combined basis, and any agreed minimum wage;

(j) the termination of the agreement and the conditions thereof, namely:

   (i) if the agreement has been made for a definite period, the date fixed for its expiry;

   (ii) if the agreement has been made for a voyage, the port of destination and the time which has to expire after arrival before the fisher shall be discharged;

   (iii) if the agreement has been made for an indefinite period, the conditions which shall entitle either party to rescind it, as well as the required period of notice for rescission, provided that such period shall not be less for the employer, or fishing vessel owner or other party to the agreement with the fisher;

(k) the protection that will cover the fisher in the event of sickness, injury or death in connection with service;

(l) the amount of paid annual leave or the formula used for calculating leave, where applicable;

(m) the health and social security coverage and benefits to be provided to the fisher by the employer, fishing vessel owner, or other party or parties to the fisher's work agreement, as applicable;

(n) the fisher's entitlement to repatriation;

(o) a reference to the collective bargaining agreement, where applicable;

(p) the minimum periods of rest, in accordance with national laws, regulations or other measures; and

(q) any other particulars which national law or regulation may require.

ANNEX III

FISHING VESSEL ACCOMMODATION

General provisions

1. The following shall apply to all new, decked fishing vessels, subject to any exclusions provided for in accordance with Article 3 of this Convention. The competent authority may, after consultation, also apply the requirements of this Annex to existing vessels, when and in so far as it determines that this is reasonable and practicable.

2. The competent authority, after consultation, may permit variations to the provisions of this Annex for fishing vessels normally remaining at sea for less than 24 hours where the fishers do not live on board the vessel in port. In the case of such vessels, the competent authority shall ensure that the fishers concerned have adequate facilities for resting, eating and sanitation purposes.

3. Any variations made by a Member under paragraph 2 of this Annex shall be reported to the International Labour Office under article 22 of the Constitution of the International Labour Organisation.

4. The requirements for vessels of 24 metres in length and over may be applied to vessels between 15 and 24 metres in length where the competent authority determines, after consultation, that this is reasonable and practicable.

5. Fishers working on board feeder vessels which do not have appropriate accommodation and sanitary facilities shall be provided with such accommodation and facilities on board the mother vessel.

6. Members may extend the requirements of this Annex regarding noise and vibration, ventilation, heating and air conditioning, and lighting to enclosed working spaces and spaces used for storage if, after consultation, such application is considered appropriate and will not have a negative influence on the function of the process or working conditions or the quality of the catches.

7. The use of gross tonnage as referred to in Article 5 of this Convention is limited to the following specified paragraphs of this annex: 12, 34, 35, 37, 39, 42, 56 and 61. For these purposes, where the competent authority, after consultation, decides to use gross tonnage (gt) as the basis of measurement:

(a) a gross tonnage of 55 gt shall be considered equivalent to a length (L) of 15 metres or a length overall (LOA) of 16.5 metres;

(b) a gross tonnage of 175 gt shall be considered equivalent to a length (L) of 24 metres or a length overall (LOA) of 26.5 metres;

(c) a gross tonnage of 700 gt shall be considered equivalent to a length (L) of 45 metres or a length overall (LOA) of 50 metres.

Planning and control

8. The competent authority shall satisfy itself that, on every occasion when a vessel is newly constructed or the crew accommodation of a vessel has been reconstructed, such vessel complies with the requirements of this annex. The competent authority shall, to the extent practicable, require compliance with this annex for a vessel that changes the flag it flies to the flag of the Member, or when the crew accommodation of a vessel is substantially altered.

9. For the occasions noted in paragraph 8 of this annex, for vessels of 24 metres in length and over, detailed plans and information concerning accommodation shall be required to be submitted for approval to the competent authority, or an entity authorized by it.

10. For vessels of 24 metres in length and over, on every occasion when the vessel changes the flag it flies to the flag of the Member or the crew accommodation of the fishing vessel has been reconstructed or substantially altered, the competent authority shall inspect the accommodation for

compliance with this Convention. The competent authority may carry out additional inspections of crew accommodation at its discretion.

Design and construction

Headroom

11. There shall be adequate headroom in all accommodation spaces. For spaces where fishers are expected to stand for prolonged periods, the minimum headroom shall be prescribed by the competent authority.

12. For vessels of 24 metres in length and over, the minimum permitted headroom in all accommodation where full and free movement is necessary shall not be less than 200 centimetres. The competent authority may permit some limited reduction in headroom in any space, or part of any space, in such accommodation where it is satisfied that such reduction is reasonable, and will not result in discomfort to the fishers.

Openings into and between accommodation spaces

13. There shall be no direct openings into sleeping rooms from fish rooms and machinery spaces, except for the purpose of emergency escape. Where reasonable and practicable, direct openings from galleys, storerooms, drying rooms or communal sanitary areas shall be avoided unless expressly provided otherwise.

14. For vessels of 24 metres in length and over, there shall be no direct openings, except for the purpose of emergency escape, into sleeping rooms from fish rooms and machinery spaces or from galleys, storerooms, drying rooms or communal sanitary areas; that part of the bulkhead separating such places from sleeping rooms and external bulkheads shall be efficiently constructed of steel or another approved material and shall be watertight and gas-tight. This provision does not exclude the possibility of sanitary areas being shared between two cabins.

Insulation

15. Accommodation spaces shall be adequately insulated; the materials used to construct internal bulkheads, panelling and sheeting, and floors and joinings shall be suitable for the purpose and shall be conducive to ensuring a healthy environment. Sufficient drainage shall be provided in all accommodation spaces.

Other

16. All practicable measures shall be taken to protect fishing vessels' crew accommodation against flies and other insects, particularly when vessels are operating in mosquito-infested areas.

17. Emergency escapes from all crew accommodation spaces shall be provided as necessary.

Noise and vibration

18. The competent authority shall take measures to limit excessive noise and vibration in accommodation spaces and, as far as practicable, in accordance with relevant international standards.

19. For vessels of 24 metres in length and over, the competent authority shall adopt standards for noise and vibration in accommodation spaces which shall ensure adequate protection to fishers from the effects of such noise and vibration, including the effects of noise- and vibration-induced fatigue.

Ventilation

20. Accommodation spaces shall be ventilated, taking into account climatic conditions. The system of ventilation shall supply air in a satisfactory condition whenever fishers are on board.

21. Ventilation arrangements or other measures shall be such as to protect non-smokers from tobacco smoke.

22. Vessels of 24 metres in length and over shall be equipped with a system of ventilation for accommodation, which shall be controlled so as to maintain the air in a satisfactory condition and to ensure sufficiency of air movement in all weather conditions and climates. Ventilation systems shall be in operation at all times when fishers are on board.

Heating and air conditioning

23. Accommodation spaces shall be adequately heated, taking into account climatic conditions.

24. For vessels of 24 metres in length and over, adequate heat shall be provided, through an appropriate heating system, except in fishing vessels operating exclusively in tropical climates. The system of heating shall provide heat in all conditions, as necessary, and shall be in operation when fishers are living or working on board, and when conditions so require.

25. For vessels of 24 metres in length and over, with the exception of those regularly engaged in areas where temperate climatic conditions do not require it, air conditioning shall be provided in accommodation spaces, the bridge, the radio room and any centralized machinery control room.

Lighting

26. All accommodation spaces shall be provided with adequate light.

27. Wherever practicable, accommodation spaces shall be lit with natural light in addition to artificial light. Where sleeping spaces have natural light, a means of blocking the light shall be provided.

28. Adequate reading light shall be provided for every berth in addition to the normal lighting of the sleeping room.

29. Emergency lighting shall be provided in sleeping rooms.

30. Where a vessel is not fitted with emergency lighting in mess rooms, passageways, and any spaces that are or may be used for emergency escape, permanent night lighting shall be provided in such spaces.

31. For vessels of 24 metres in length and over, lighting in accommodation spaces shall meet a standard established by the competent authority. In any part of the accommodation space available for free movement, the minimum standard for such lighting shall be such as to permit a person with normal vision to read an ordinary newspaper on a clear day.

Sleeping rooms

General

32. Where the design, dimensions or purpose of the vessel allow, the sleeping accommodation shall be located so as to minimize the effects of motion and acceleration but shall in no case be located forward of the collision bulkhead.

Floor area

33. The number of persons per sleeping room and the floor area per person, excluding space occupied by berths and lockers, shall be such as to provide adequate space and comfort for the fishers on board, taking into account the service of the vessel.

34. For vessels of 24 metres in length and over but which are less than 45 metres in length, the floor area per person of sleeping rooms, excluding space occupied by berths and lockers, shall not be less than 1.5 square metres.

35. For vessels of 45 metres in length and over, the floor area per person of sleeping rooms, excluding space occupied by berths and lockers, shall not be less than 2 square metres.

Persons per sleeping room

36. To the extent not expressly provided otherwise, the number of persons allowed to occupy each sleeping room shall not be more than six.

37. For vessels of 24 metres in length and over, the number of persons allowed to occupy each sleeping room shall not be more than four. The competent authority may permit exceptions to this requirement in particular cases if the size, type or intended service of the vessel makes the requirement unreasonable or impracticable.

38. To the extent not expressly provided otherwise, a separate sleeping room or sleeping rooms shall be provided for officers, wherever practicable.

39. For vessels of 24 metres in length and over, sleeping rooms for officers shall be for one person wherever possible and in no case shall the sleeping room contain more than two berths. The competent authority may permit exceptions to the requirements of this paragraph in particular cases if the size, type or intended service of the vessel makes the requirements unreasonable or impracticable.

Other

40. The maximum number of persons to be accommodated in any sleeping room shall be legibly and indelibly marked in a place in the room where it can be conveniently seen.

41. The members of the crew shall be provided with individual berths of appropriate dimensions. Mattresses shall be of a suitable material.

42. For vessels of 24 metres in length and over, the minimum inside dimensions of the berths shall not be less than 198 by 80 centimetres.

43. Sleeping rooms shall be so planned and equipped as to ensure reasonable comfort for the occupants and to facilitate tidiness. Equipment provided shall include berths, individual lockers sufficient for clothing and other personal effects, and a suitable writing surface.

44. For vessels of 24 metres in length and over, a desk suitable for writing, with a chair, shall be provided.

45. Sleeping accommodation shall be situated or equipped, as practicable, so as to provide appropriate levels of privacy for men and for women.

Mess rooms

46. Mess rooms shall be as close as possible to the galley, but in no case shall be located forward of the collision bulkhead.

47. Vessels shall be provided with mess room accommodation suitable for their service. To the extent not expressly provided otherwise, mess room accommodation shall be separate from sleeping quarters, where practicable.

48. For vessels of 24 metres in length and over, mess room accommodation shall be separate from sleeping quarters.

49. The dimensions and equipment of each mess room shall be sufficient for the number of persons likely to use it at any one time.

50. For vessels of 24 metres in length and over, a refrigerator of sufficient capacity and facilities for making hot and cold drinks shall be available and accessible to fishers at all times.

Sanitary accommodation

51. Sanitary facilities, which include toilets, washbasins, and tubs or showers, shall be provided for all persons on board, as appropriate for the service of the vessel. These facilities shall meet at least minimum standards of health and hygiene and reasonable standards of quality.

52. The sanitary accommodation shall be such as to eliminate contamination of other spaces as far as practicable. The sanitary facilities used by women fishers shall allow for reasonable privacy.

53. Cold fresh water and hot fresh water shall be available to all fishers and other persons on board, in sufficient quantities to allow for proper hygiene. The competent authority may establish, after consultation, the minimum amount of water to be provided.

54. Where sanitary facilities are provided, they shall be fitted with ventilation to the open air, independent of any other part of the accommodation.

55. All surfaces in sanitary accommodation shall be such as to facilitate easy and effective cleaning. Floors shall have a non-slip deck covering.

56. On vessels of 24 metres in length and over, for all fishers who do not occupy rooms to which sanitary facilities are attached, there shall be provided at least one tub or shower or both, one toilet, and one washbasin for every four persons or fewer.

Laundry facilities

57. Amenities for washing and drying clothes shall be provided as necessary, taking into account the service of the vessel, to the extent not expressly provided otherwise.

58. For vessels of 24 metres in length and over, adequate facilities for washing, drying and ironing clothes shall be provided.

59. For vessels of 45 metres in length and over, adequate facilities for washing, drying and ironing clothes shall be provided in a compartment separate from sleeping rooms, mess rooms and toilets, and shall be adequately ventilated, heated and equipped with lines or other means for drying clothes.

Facilities for sick and injured fishers

60. Whenever necessary, a cabin shall be made available for a fisher who suffers illness or injury.

61. For vessels of 45 metres in length and over, there shall be a separate sick bay. The space shall be properly equipped and shall be maintained in a hygienic state.

Other facilities

62. A place for hanging foul-weather gear and other personal protective equipment shall be provided outside of, but convenient to, sleeping rooms.

Bedding, mess utensils and miscellaneous provisions

63. Appropriate eating utensils, and bedding and other linen shall be provided to all fishers on board. However, the cost of the linen can be recovered as an operational cost if the collective agreement or the fisher's work agreement so provides.

Recreational facilities

64. For vessels of 24 metres in length and over, appropriate recreational facilities, amenities and services shall be provided for all fishers on board. Where appropriate, mess rooms may be used for recreational activities.

Communication facilities

65. All fishers on board shall be given reasonable access to communication facilities, to the extent practicable, at a reasonable cost and not exceeding the full cost to the fishing vessel owner.

Galley and food storage facilities

66. Cooking equipment shall be provided on board. To the extent not expressly provided otherwise, this equipment shall be fitted, where practicable, in a separate galley.

67. The galley, or cooking area where a separate galley is not provided, shall be of adequate size for the purpose, well lit and ventilated, and properly equipped and maintained.

68. For vessels of 24 metres in length and over, there shall be a separate galley.

69. The containers of butane or propane gas used for cooking purposes in a galley shall be kept on the open deck and in a shelter which is designed to protect them from external heat sources and external impact.

70. A suitable place for provisions of adequate capacity shall be provided which can be kept dry, cool and well-ventilated in order to avoid deterioration of the stores and, to the extent not expressly provided otherwise, refrigerators or other low-temperature storage shall be used, where possible.

71. For vessels of 24 metres in length and over, a provisions storeroom and refrigerator and other low-temperature storage shall be used.

Food and potable water

72. Food and potable water shall be sufficient, having regard to the number of fishers, and the duration and nature of the voyage. In addition, they shall be suitable in respect of nutritional value, quality, quantity and variety, having regard as well to the fishers' religious requirements and cultural practices in relation to food.

73. The competent authority may establish requirements for the minimum standards and quantity of food and water to be carried on board.

Clean and habitable conditions

74. Accommodation shall be maintained in a clean and habitable condition and shall be kept free of goods and stores which are not the personal property of the occupants.

75. Galley and food storage facilities shall be maintained in a hygienic condition.

76. Waste shall be kept in closed, well-sealed containers and removed from food-handling areas whenever necessary.

Inspections by the skipper or under the authority of the skipper

77. For vessels of 24 metres in length and over, the competent authority shall require frequent inspections to be carried out, by or under the authority of the skipper, to ensure that:

(a) accommodation is clean, decently habitable and safe, and is maintained in a good state of repair;

(b) food and water supplies are sufficient; and

(c) galley and food storage spaces and equipment are hygienic and in a proper state of repair.

The results of such inspections, and the actions taken to address any deficiencies found, shall be recorded and available for review.

Variations

78. The competent authority, after consultation, may permit derogations from the provisions in this annex to take into account, without discrimination, the interests of fishers having differing and distinctive religious and social practices, on condition that such derogations do not result in overall conditions less favourable than those which would result from the application of this annex.

B. Proposed Recommendation concerning work in the fishing sector

The General Conference of the International Labour Organization,

Having been convened at Geneva by the Governing Body of the International Labour Office, and having met in its 93rd Session on 31 May 2005, and

Taking into account the need to revise the Hours of Work (Fishing) Recommendation, 1920, and

Having decided upon the adoption of certain proposals with regard to work in the fishing sector, which is the fifth item on the agenda of the session, and

Having determined that these proposals shall take the form of a Recommendation supplementing the Work in Fishing Convention, 2005 (hereinafter referred to as "the Convention");

adopts this   day of June of the year two thousand and five the following Recommendation, which may be cited as the Work in Fishing Recommendation, 2005.

PART I. CONDITIONS FOR WORK ON BOARD FISHING VESSELS

Protection of young persons

1. Members should establish the requirements for the pre-sea training of persons between the ages of 16 and 18 working on board fishing vessels, taking into account international instruments concerning training for work on board fishing vessels, including occupational safety and health issues such as night work, hazardous tasks, work with dangerous machinery, manual handling and transport of heavy loads, work in high latitudes, work for excessive periods of time and other relevant issues identified after an assessment of the risks concerned.

2. The training of persons between the ages of 16 and 18 might be provided through participation in an apprenticeship or approved training programme, which should operate under established rules and be monitored by the competent authority, and should not interfere with the person's general education.

3. Members should take measures to ensure that the safety, lifesaving and survival equipment carried on board fishing vessels carrying persons under the age of 18 is appropriate for the size of such persons.

4. The working hours of fishers under the age of 18 should not exceed eight hours per day and 40 hours per week, and they should not work overtime except where unavoidable for safety reasons.

5. Fishers under the age of 18 should be assured sufficient time for all meals and a break of at least one hour for the main meal of the day.

Medical examination

6. When prescribing the nature of the examination, Members should pay due regard to the age of the person to be examined and the nature of the duties to be performed.

7. The medical certificate should be signed by a medical practitioner approved by the competent authority.

8. Arrangements should be made to enable a person who, after examination, is determined to be unfit for work on board fishing vessels or certain types of fishing vessels, or for certain types of work on board, to apply for a further examination by a medical referee or referees who should be independent of any fishing vessel owner or of any organization of fishing vessel owners or fishers.

9. The competent authority should take into account international guidance on medical examination and certification of persons working at sea, such as the (ILO/WHO) *Guidelines for Conducting Pre-sea and Periodic Medical Fitness Examinations for Seafarers*.

10. For fishers exempted from the application of the provisions concerning medical examination in the Convention, the competent authority should take adequate measures to provide health surveillance for the purpose of occupational safety and health.

Competency and training

11. Members should:

(a) take into account generally accepted international standards concerning training and competencies of fishers in determining the competencies required for skippers, mates, engineers and other persons working on board fishing vessels;

(b) address the following issues, with regard to the vocational training of fishers: national planning and administration, including coordination; financing and training standards; training programmes, including pre-vocational training and also short courses for working fishers; methods of training; and international cooperation;

(c) ensure that there is no discrimination with regard to access to training.

PART II. CONDITIONS OF SERVICE

Record of service

12. At the end of each contract, a record of service in regard to that contract should be made available to the fisher concerned, or entered in the fisher's service book.

Special measures

13. For fishers excluded from the scope of the Convention, the competent authority should take measures to provide them with adequate protection with respect to their conditions of work and means of dispute settlement.

Payment of fishers

14. Fishers should have the right to advances against earnings under prescribed conditions.

15. For vessels of 24 metres in length and over, all fishers should be entitled to minimum payment in accordance with national laws, regulations or collective agreements.

Part III. Accommodation

16. When establishing requirements or guidance, the competent authority should take into account relevant international guidance on accommodation, food, and health and hygiene relating to persons working or living on board vessels, including the most recent editions of the (FAO/ILO/IMO) *Code of Safety for Fishermen and Fishing Vessels* and the (FAO/ILO/IMO) *Voluntary Guidelines for the Design, Construction and Equipment of Small Fishing Vessels*.

17. The competent authority should work with relevant organizations and agencies to develop and disseminate educational material and on-board information and guidance concerning safe and healthy accommodation and food on board fishing vessels.

18. Inspections of crew accommodation required by the competent authority should be carried out together with initial or periodic surveys or inspections for other purposes.

Design and construction

19. Adequate insulation should be provided for exposed decks over crew accommodation spaces, external bulkheads of sleeping rooms and mess rooms, machinery casings and boundary bulkheads of galleys and other spaces in which heat is produced, and, as necessary, to prevent condensation or overheating in sleeping rooms, mess rooms, recreation rooms and passageways.

20. Protection should be provided from the heat effects of any steam or hot water service pipes. Main steam and exhaust pipes should not pass through crew accommodation or through passageways leading to crew accommodation. Where this cannot be avoided, pipes should be adequately insulated and encased.

21. Materials and furnishings used in accommodation spaces should be impervious to dampness, easy to keep clean and not likely to harbour vermin.

Noise and vibration

22. Noise levels for working and living spaces, which are established by the competent authority, should be in conformity with the guidelines of the International Labour Organization on exposure levels to ambient factors in the workplace and, where applicable, the specific protection recommended by the International Maritime Organization, together with any subsequent amending and supplementary instruments for acceptable noise levels on board ships.

23. The competent authority, in conjunction with the competent international bodies and with representatives of organizations of fishing vessel owners and fishers and taking into account, as appropriate, relevant international standards, should review on an ongoing basis the problem of vibration on board fishing vessels with the objective of improving the protection of fishers, as far as practicable, from the adverse effects of vibration.

(1) Such review should cover the effect of exposure to excessive vibration on the health and comfort of fishers and the measures to be prescribed or recommended to reduce vibration on fishing vessels to protect fishers.

(2) Measures to reduce vibration, or its effects, to be considered should include:

(a) instruction of fishers in the dangers to their health of prolonged exposure to vibration; and

(b) provision of approved personal protective equipment to fishers where necessary;

(c) assessment of risks and reduction of exposure in sleeping rooms, mess rooms, recreational accommodation and catering facilities and other fishers' accommodation by adopting measures in accordance with the guidance provided by the (ILO) code of practice *Ambient factors in the workplace* and any subsequent revisions, taking into account the difference between exposure in the workplace and in the living space.

Heating

24. The heating system should be capable of maintaining the temperature in crew accommodation at a satisfactory level, as established by the competent authority, under normal conditions of weather and climate likely to be met with on service, and should be designed so as not to endanger the health or safety of the fishers or the safety of the vessel.

Lighting

25. Methods of lighting should not endanger the health and safety of the fishers or the safety of the vessel.

Sleeping rooms

26. Each berth should be fitted with a comfortable mattress with a cushioned bottom or a combined mattress, including a spring bottom, or a spring mattress. The cushioning material used should be made of approved material. Berths should not be placed side by side in such a way that access to one berth can be obtained only over another. The lower berth in a double tier should not be less than 0.3 metres above the floor, and the upper berth should be fitted with a dust-proof bottom and placed approximately midway between the bottom of the lower berth and the lower side of the deck head beams. Berths should not be arranged in tiers of more than two. In the case of berths placed along the vessel's side, there should be only a single tier when a sidelight is situated above a berth.

27. Sleeping rooms should be fitted with curtains for the sidelights, as well as a mirror, small cabinets for toilet requisites, a book rack and a sufficient number of coat hooks.

28. As far as practicable, berthing of crew members should be so arranged that watches are separated and that no day worker shares a room with a watch keeper.

29. On vessels of 24 metres in length and over, separate sleeping rooms for men and women should be provided.

Sanitary accommodation

30. Sanitary accommodation spaces should have:

(a) floors of approved durable material which can be easily cleaned, and which are impervious to dampness and properly drained;

(b) bulkheads of steel or other approved material which should be watertight up to at least 0.23 metres above the level of the deck;

(c) sufficient lighting, heating and ventilation; and

(d) soil pipes and waste pipes of adequate dimensions which are constructed so as to minimize the risk of obstruction and to facilitate cleaning; such pipes should not pass through fresh water or drinking-water tanks, nor should they, if practicable, pass overhead in mess rooms or sleeping accommodation.

31. Toilets should be of an approved type and provided with an ample flush of water, available at all times and independently controllable. Where practicable, they should be situated convenient to, but separate from, sleeping rooms and washrooms. Where there is more than one toilet in a compartment, the toilets should be sufficiently screened to ensure privacy.

32. Separate sanitary facilities should be provided for women fishers.

Recreational facilities

33. Where recreational facilities are required, furnishings should include, as a minimum, a bookcase and facilities for reading, writing and, where practicable, games. Recreational facilities and services should be reviewed frequently to ensure that they are appropriate in the light of changes in the needs of fishers resulting from technical, operational and other developments. Consideration should also be given to including the following facilities at no cost to the fishers, where practicable:

(a) a smoking room;

(b) television viewing and the reception of radio broadcasts;

(c) projection of films or video films, the stock of which should be adequate for the duration of the voyage and, where necessary, changed at reasonable intervals;

(d) sports equipment including exercise equipment, table games, and deck games;

(e) a library containing vocational and other books, the stock of which should be adequate for the duration of the voyage and changed at reasonable intervals;

(f) facilities for recreational handicrafts; and

(g) electronic equipment such as radio, TV, video recorder, DVD/CD player, personal computer and software, and cassette recorder/player.

Food

34. Fishers employed as cooks should be trained and qualified for their position on board.

PART IV. MEDICAL CARE, HEALTH PROTECTION AND SOCIAL SECURITY

Medical care on board

35. The competent authority should establish a list of medical supplies and equipment appropriate to the risks concerned that should be carried on fishing vessels; such list should include women's sanitary protection supplies together with discreet, environmentally friendly disposal units.

36. Fishing vessels carrying 100 or more fishers should have a qualified medical doctor on board.

37. Fishers should receive training in basic first aid in accordance with national laws and regulations, taking into account applicable international instruments.

38. A standard medical report form should be specially designed to facilitate the confidential exchange of medical and related information concerning individual fishers between the fishing vessel and the shore in cases of illness or injury.

39. For vessels of 24 metres in length and over, in addition to the provisions of Article 32 of the Convention, the following elements should be taken into account:

(a) when prescribing the medical equipment and supplies to be carried on board, the competent authority should take into account international recommendations in this field, such as those contained in the most recent editions of the (ILO/IMO/WHO) *International Medical Guide for Ships* and the (WHO) *Model List of Essential Medicines*, as well as advances in medical knowledge and approved methods of treatment;

(b) inspections of medical equipment and supplies should take place at intervals of no more than 12 months; the inspector should ensure that expiry dates and conditions of storage of all medicines are checked, the contents of the medicine chest are listed and conform to the medical guide used nationally, and medical supplies are labelled with generic names in addition to any brand names used, and with expiry dates and conditions of storage;

(c) the medical guide should explain how the contents of the medical equipment and supplies are to be used, and should be designed to enable persons other than a medical doctor to care for the sick or injured on board, both with and without medical advice by radio or satellite communication; the guide should be prepared taking into account international recommendations in this field, including those contained in the most recent editions of the (ILO/IMO/WHO) *International Medical Guide for Ships* and the (IMO) *Medical First Aid Guide for Use in Accidents Involving Dangerous Goods*; and

(d) medical advice provided by radio or satellite communication should be available free of charge to all vessels irrespective of the flag they fly.

Occupational safety and health

Research, dissemination of information and consultation

40. In order to contribute to the continuous improvement of safety and health of fishers, Members should have in place policies and programmes for the prevention of accidents on board fishing vessels which should provide for the gathering and dissemination of occupational health and safety materials, research and analysis, taking into consideration technological progress and knowledge in the field of occupational safety and health as well as of relevant international instruments.

41. The competent authority should take measures to ensure regular consultations on safety and health matters with the aim of ensuring that all concerned are kept reasonably informed of national, international and other developments in the field and on their possible application to fishing vessels flying the flag of the Member.

42. When ensuring that fishing vessel owners, skippers, fishers and other relevant persons receive sufficient and suitable guidance, training material, or other appropriate information, the competent authority should take into account relevant international standards, codes, guidance and other information. In so doing, the competent authority should keep abreast of and utilize international research and guidance concerning safety and health in the fishing sector, including relevant research in occupational safety and health in general which may be applicable to work on board fishing vessels.

43. Information concerning particular hazards should be brought to the attention of all fishers and other persons on board through official notices containing instructions or guidance, or other appropriate means.

44. Joint committees on occupational safety and health should be established:

(a) ashore; or

(b) on fishing vessels, where determined by the competent authority, after consultation, to be practicable in light of the number of fishers on board the vessel.

Occupational safety and health management systems

45. When establishing methods and programmes concerning safety and health in the fishing sector, the competent authority should take into account any relevant international guidance concerning occupational safety and health management systems, including the *Guidelines on occupational safety and health management systems, ILO-OSH 2001*.

Risk evaluation

46. (1) Risk evaluation in relation to fishing should be conducted, as appropriate, with the participation of fishers or their representatives and should include:

(a) risk assessment and management;

(b) training, taking into consideration the relevant provisions of Chapter III of the International Convention on Standards of Training, Certification and Watchkeeping for Fishing Vessel Personnel, 1995 (STCW-F Convention) adopted by the IMO; and

(c) on-board instruction of fishers.

(2) To give effect to subparagraph (1)(a), Members, after consultation, should adopt laws, regulations or other measures requiring:

(a) the regular and active involvement of all fishers in improving safety and health by continually identifying hazards, assessing risks and taking action to address risks through safety management;

(b) an occupational safety and health management system that may include an occupational safety and health policy, provisions for fisher participation and provisions concerning organizing, planning, implementing and evaluating the system and taking action to improve the system; and

(c) a system for the purpose of assisting in the implementation of a safety and health policy and programme and providing fishers with a forum to influence safety and health matters; on-board prevention procedures should be designed so as to involve fishers in the identification of hazards and potential hazards and in the implementation of measures to reduce or eliminate such hazards.

(3) When developing the provisions referred to in subparagraph (1)(a), Members should take into account the relevant international instruments on risk assessment and management.

Technical specifications

47. Members should address the following, to the extent practicable and as appropriate to the conditions in the fishing sector:

(a) seaworthiness and stability of fishing vessels;

(b) radio communications;

(c) temperature, ventilation and lighting of working areas;

(d) mitigation of the slipperiness of deck surfaces;

(e) machinery safety, including guarding of machinery;

(f) vessel familiarization for fishers and fisheries observers new to the vessel;

(g) personal protective equipment;

(h) fire-fighting and lifesaving;

(i) loading and unloading of the vessel;

(j) lifting gear;

(k) anchoring and mooring equipment;

(l) safety and health in living quarters;

(m) noise and vibration in work areas;

(n) ergonomics, including in relation to the layout of workstations and manual lifting and handling;

(o) equipment and procedures for the catching, handling, storage and processing of fish and other marine resources;

(p) vessel design, construction and modification relevant to occupational safety and health;

(q) navigation and vessel handling;

(r) hazardous materials used on board the vessel;

(s) safe means of access to and exit from fishing vessels in port;

(t) special safety and health requirements for young persons;

(u) prevention of fatigue; and

(v) other issues related to safety and health.

48. When developing laws, regulations or other measures concerning technical standards relating to safety and health on board fishing vessels, the competent authority should take into account the most recent edition of the (FAO/ILO/IMO) *Code of Safety for Fishermen and Fishing Vessels, Part A*.

Establishment of a list of occupational diseases

49. Members should establish a list of diseases known to arise out of exposure to dangerous substances or conditions in the fishing sector.

Social security

50. For the purpose of extending social security protection progressively to all fishers, Members should maintain up-to-date information on the following:

(a) the percentage of fishers covered;

(b) the range of contingencies covered; and

(c) the level of benefits.

51. Every person protected under Article 34 of the Convention should have a right of appeal in the case of a refusal of the benefit or of an adverse determination as to the quality or quantity of the benefit.

52. The protections referred to in Articles 38 and 39 of the Convention should be granted throughout the contingency covered.

PART V. OTHER PROVISIONS

53. A Member, in its capacity as a coastal State, when granting licences for fishing in its exclusive economic zone, may require that fishing vessels comply with the standards of the Convention. If such licences are issued by coastal States, these States should take into account certificates or other valid documents stating that the vessel concerned has been inspected by the competent authority or on its behalf and has been found to be in compliance with the provisions of the Convention concerning work in the fishing sector.

CONTENTS

Page

Fifth item on the agenda: Work in the fishing sector (second discussion)

Report of the Committee on the Fishing Sector 1

A. Proposed Convention concerning work in the fishing sector 96

B. Proposed Recommendation concerning work in the fishing sector 122

International Labour Conference

Record of Proceedings

Ninety-third Session, Geneva, 2005

19A

Conférence internationale du Travail

Compte rendu des travaux

Quatre-vingt-treizième session, Genève, 2005

TEXT OF THE CONVENTION CONCERNING
WORK IN THE FISHING SECTOR
SUBMITTED BY THE DRAFTING COMMITTEE

TEXTE DE LA CONVENTION CONCERNANT
LE TRAVAIL DANS LE SECTEUR DE LA PÊCHE
PRÉSENTÉ PAR LE COMITÉ DE RÉDACTION

TEXT OF THE CONVENTION CONCERNING WORK IN THE FISHING SECTOR

The General Conference of the International Labour Organization,

Having been convened at Geneva by the Governing Body of the International Labour Office, and having met in its 93rd Session on 31 May 2005, and

Recognizing that globalization has a profound impact on the fishing sector, and

Noting the ILO Declaration on Fundamental Principles and Rights at Work, 1998, and

Taking into consideration the fundamental rights to be found in the following international labour Conventions: the Forced Labour Convention, 1930, the Freedom of Association and Protection of the Right to Organise Convention, 1948, the Right to Organise and Collective Bargaining Convention, 1949, the Equal Remuneration Convention, 1951, the Abolition of Forced Labour Convention, 1957, the Discrimination (Employment and Occupation) Convention, 1958, the Minimum Age Convention, 1973, and the Worst Forms of Child Labour Convention, 1999, and

Noting the relevant instruments of the International Labour Organization, in particular the Occupational Safety and Health Convention and Recommendation, 1981, and the Occupational Health Services Convention and Recommendation, 1985, and

Noting, in addition, the Social Security (Minimum Standards) Convention, 1952, and considering that the provisions of Article 77 of that Convention should not be an obstacle to protection extended by Members to fishers under social security schemes, and

Recognizing that the International Labour Organization considers fishing as a hazardous occupation when compared to other occupations, and

Noting also Article 1, paragraph 3 of the Seafarers' Identity Documents Convention (Revised), 2003, and

Mindful of the core mandate of the Organization, which is to promote decent conditions of work, and

Mindful of the need to protect and promote the rights of fishers in this regard, and

Recalling the United Nations Convention on the Law of the Sea, 1982, and

Taking into account the need to revise the following international instruments adopted by the International Labour Conference specifically concerning the fishing sector, namely the Hours of Work (Fishing) Recommendation, 1920, the Minimum Age

TEXTE DE LA CONVENTION CONCERNANT LE TRAVAIL DANS LE SECTEUR DE LA PÊCHE

La Conférence générale de l'Organisation internationale du Travail,

Convoquée à Genève par le Conseil d'administration du Bureau international du Travail, et s'y étant réunie le 31 mai 2005, en sa quatre-vingt-treizième session;

Reconnaissant que la mondialisation a un impact profond sur le secteur de la pêche;

Notant la Déclaration de l'OIT relative aux principes et droits fondamentaux au travail, 1998;

Tenant compte des droits fondamentaux énoncés dans les conventions internationales du travail suivantes: la convention sur le travail forcé, 1930, la convention sur la liberté syndicale et la protection du droit syndical, 1948, la convention sur le droit d'organisation et de négociation collective, 1949, la convention sur l'égalité de rémunération, 1951, la convention sur l'abolition du travail forcé, 1957, la convention concernant la discrimination (emploi et profession), 1958, la convention sur l'âge minimum, 1973, et la convention sur les pires formes de travail des enfants, 1999;

Notant les instruments pertinents de l'Organisation internationale du Travail, en particulier la convention et la recommandation sur la sécurité et la santé des travailleurs, 1981, ainsi que la convention et la recommandation sur les services de santé au travail, 1985;

Notant en outre la convention concernant la sécurité sociale (norme minimum), 1952, et considérant que les dispositions de l'article 77 de ladite convention ne devraient pas faire obstacle à la protection offerte aux pêcheurs par les Membres dans le cadre des systèmes de sécurité sociale;

Reconnaissant que l'Organisation internationale du Travail considère la pêche comme une activité dangereuse par rapport à d'autres;

Notant également le paragraphe 3 de l'article 1 de la convention sur les pièces d'identité des gens de mer (révisée), 2003;

Consciente que l'Organisation a pour mandat fondamental de promouvoir des conditions de travail décentes;

Consciente de la nécessité de protéger et de promouvoir les droits des pêcheurs en la matière;

Rappelant la Convention des Nations Unies sur le droit de la mer, 1982;

Tenant compte de la nécessité de réviser les instruments internationaux suivants adoptés par la Conférence internationale du Travail concernant spécifiquement le secteur de la pêche, à savoir la recommandation sur la durée du travail (pêche), 1920, la

(Fishermen) Convention, 1959, the Medical Examination (Fishermen) Convention, 1959, the Fishermen's Articles of Agreement Convention, 1959, and the Accommodation of Crews (Fishermen) Convention, 1966, to bring them up to date and to reach a greater number of the world's fishers, particularly those working on board smaller vessels, and

Noting that the objective of this Convention is to ensure that fishers have decent conditions of work on board fishing vessels with regard to minimum requirements for work on board; conditions of service; accommodation and food; occupational safety and health protection; medical care and social security, and

Having decided upon the adoption of certain proposals with regard to work in the fishing sector, which is the fifth item on the agenda of the session, and

Having determined that these proposals shall take the form of an international Convention;

adopts this day of June of the year two thousand and five the following Convention, which may be cited as the Work in Fishing Convention, 2005.

PART I. DEFINITIONS AND SCOPE

DEFINITIONS

Article 1

For the purposes of the Convention:

(a) "commercial fishing" means all fishing operations, including fishing operations on rivers, lakes and canals, with the exception of subsistence fishing and recreational fishing;

(b) "competent authority" means the minister, government department or other authority having power to issue and enforce regulations, orders or other instructions having the force of law in respect of the subject matter of the provision concerned;

(c) "consultation" means consultation by the competent authority with the representative organizations of employers and workers concerned, and in particular the representative organizations of fishing vessel owners and fishers, where they exist, on the measures to be taken to give effect to the provisions of the Convention and with respect to any derogation, exemption or other flexible application as allowed under the Convention;

convention sur l'âge minimum (pêcheurs), 1959, la convention sur l'examen médical des pêcheurs, 1959, la convention sur le contrat d'engagement des pêcheurs, 1959, et la convention sur le logement à bord des bateaux de pêche, 1966, afin de mettre à jour ces instruments et d'atteindre un plus grand nombre de pêcheurs dans le monde, en particulier ceux travaillant à bord de navires plus petits;

Notant que l'objectif de la présente convention est d'assurer que les pêcheurs bénéficient de conditions décentes pour travailler à bord des navires de pêche en ce qui concerne les conditions minimales requises pour le travail à bord, les conditions de service, le logement et l'alimentation, la protection de la santé et de la sécurité au travail, les soins médicaux et la sécurité sociale;

Après avoir décidé d'adopter diverses propositions relatives au travail dans le secteur de la pêche, question qui constitue le cinquième point à l'ordre du jour de la session;

Après avoir décidé que ces propositions prendraient la forme d'une convention internationale,

adopte, ce   jour de juin deux mille cinq, la convention ci-après, qui sera dénommée Convention sur le travail dans la pêche, 2005.

PARTIE I. DÉFINITIONS ET CHAMP D'APPLICATION

DÉFINITIONS

Article 1

Aux fins de la présente convention:

a) les termes «pêche commerciale» désignent toutes les opérations de pêche, y compris les opérations de pêche dans les cours d'eau, les lacs et les canaux, à l'exception de la pêche de subsistance et de la pêche de loisir;

b) les termes «autorité compétente» désignent le ministre, le service gouvernemental ou toute autre autorité habilités à édicter et à faire respecter les règlements, arrêtés ou autres instructions ayant force obligatoire dans le domaine visé par la disposition de la convention;

c) le terme «consultation» désigne la consultation par l'autorité compétente des organisations représentatives d'employeurs et de travailleurs intéressées, et en particulier les organisations représentatives d'armateurs à la pêche et de pêcheurs, lorsqu'elles existent, sur les mesures à prendre pour donner effet aux dispositions de la convention et en ce qui concerne toute dérogation, exemption ou autre forme d'application souple qui est permise par la convention;

(d) "fishing vessel owner" means the owner of the fishing vessel or any other organization or person who has assumed the responsibility for the operation of the vessel from the owner or other organization or person and who, on assuming such responsibility, has agreed to take over the duties and responsibilities imposed on fishing vessel owners in accordance with the Convention;

(e) "fisher" means every person employed or engaged in any capacity or carrying out an occupation on board any fishing vessel, including persons working on board who are paid on the basis of a share of the catch but excluding pilots, naval personnel, other persons in the permanent service of a government, shore-based persons carrying out work aboard a fishing vessel and fisheries observers;

(f) "fisher's work agreement" means a contract of employment, articles of agreement or other similar arrangements or any other contract governing a fisher's living and working conditions on board a vessel;

(g) "fishing vessel" or "vessel" means any ship or boat, of any nature whatsoever, irrespective of the form of ownership, used or intended to be used for the purpose of commercial fishing;

(h) "new fishing vessel" means a vessel for which:
   (i) the building or major conversion contract is placed on or after the date of the entry into force of the Convention for the Member concerned; or
   (ii) the building or major conversion contract has been placed before the date of the entry into force of the Convention for the Member concerned, and which is delivered three years or more after that date; or
   (iii) in the absence of a building contract, on or after the date of the entry into force of the Convention for the Member concerned:
      — the keel is laid, or
      — construction identifiable with a specific vessel begins, or
      — assembly has commenced comprising at least 50 tonnes or 1 per cent of the estimated mass of all structural material, whichever is less;

(i) "existing vessel" means a vessel that is not a new fishing vessel;

(j) "gross tonnage" means the gross tonnage calculated in accordance with the tonnage measurement regulations contained in Annex I to the International Convention on Tonnage Measurement of Ships, 1969, or any instrument amending or replacing it;

(k) "length" (L) shall be taken as 96 per cent of the total length on a waterline at 85 per cent of the least moulded depth measured from the

d) les termes «armateur à la pêche» désignent le propriétaire du navire ou toute autre entité ou personne à laquelle la responsabilité de l'exploitation du navire a été confiée et qui, en assumant cette responsabilité, a accepté de s'acquitter des tâches et obligations qui incombent aux armateurs à la pêche aux termes de la convention;

e) le terme «pêcheur» désigne toute personne employée ou engagée à quelque titre que ce soit ou exerçant une activité professionnelle à bord d'un navire de pêche, y compris les personnes travaillant à bord qui sont rémunérées à la part, mais à l'exclusion des pilotes, des équipages de la flotte de guerre, des autres personnes au service permanent du gouvernement, des personnes basées à terre chargées d'effectuer des travaux à bord d'un navire de pêche et des observateurs des pêches;

f) les termes «accord d'engagement du pêcheur» désignent le contrat d'emploi, le contrat d'engagement ou autre accord similaire ainsi que tout autre contrat régissant les conditions de vie et de travail du pêcheur à bord du navire;

g) les termes «navire de pêche» ou «navire» désignent tout bateau ou embarcation, quelles qu'en soient la nature et la forme de propriété, affecté ou destiné à être affecté à la pêche commerciale;

h) les termes «navire de pêche neuf» désignent un navire pour lequel:
   i) le contrat de construction ou de transformation importante est passé à la date d'entrée en vigueur de la convention pour le Membre concerné ou après cette date; ou
   ii) le contrat de construction ou de transformation importante a été passé avant la date d'entrée en vigueur de la convention pour le Membre concerné, et qui est livré trois ans ou plus après cette date; ou
   iii) en l'absence d'un contrat de construction à la date d'entrée en vigueur de la convention pour le Membre concerné ou après cette date:
      — la quille est posée; ou
      — une construction permettant d'identifier un navire particulier a commencé; ou
      — le montage a commencé, employant au moins 50 tonnes ou 1 pour cent de la masse estimée de tous les matériaux de structure, si cette dernière valeur est inférieure;

i) les termes «navire existant» désignent un navire qui n'est pas un navire de pêche neuf;

j) les termes «jauge brute» désignent le tonnage brut d'un navire évalué conformément aux dispositions de l'annexe I à la Convention internationale de 1969 sur le jaugeage des navires ou de tout instrument l'amendant ou la remplaçant;

k) le terme «longueur» (L) désigne 96 pour cent de la longueur totale à la flottaison située à une distance de la ligne de quille égale à 85 pour cent

keel line, or as the length from the foreside of the stem to the axis of the rudder stock on that waterline, if that be greater. In vessels designed with rake of keel, the waterline on which this length is measured shall be parallel to the designed waterline;

(l) "length overall" (LOA) shall be taken as the distance in a straight line parallel to the designed waterline between the foremost point of the bow and the aftermost point of the stern;

(m) "recruitment and placement service" means any person, company, institution, agency or other organization, in the public or the private sector, which is engaged in recruiting fishers on behalf of, or placing fishers with, fishing vessel owners;

(n) "skipper" means the person having command of a fishing vessel.

SCOPE

Article 2

1. Except as otherwise provided herein, this Convention applies to all fishers and all fishing vessels engaged in commercial fishing operations.

2. In the event of doubt as to whether a vessel is engaged in commercial fishing, the question shall be determined by the competent authority after consultation.

3. Any Member, after consultation, may extend, in whole or in part, to fishers working on smaller vessels the protection provided in this Convention for fishers working on vessels of 24 metres in length and over.

Article 3

1. The competent authority, after consultation, may exclude from the requirements of this Convention, or certain provisions thereof, where their application raises special and substantial problems in the light of the particular conditions of service of the fishers or the fishing vessels' operations:

(a) fishing vessels engaged in fishing operations in rivers, lakes and canals; and

(b) limited categories of fishers or fishing vessels.

2. In the case of exclusions under the preceding paragraph and, where practicable, the competent authority shall take measures, as appropriate, to extend progressively the requirements under this Convention to those categories of fishers and fishing vessels concerned.

du creux minimal sur quille, ou encore à la distance entre la face avant de l'étrave et l'axe de la mèche du gouvernail à cette flottaison, si cette valeur est supérieure. Pour les navires conçus pour naviguer avec une quille inclinée, la flottaison servant à mesurer cette longueur doit être parallèle à la flottaison en charge prévue;

l) les termes «longueur hors tout» (LHT) désignent la distance mesurée en ligne droite parallèlement à la flottaison en charge prévue de l'extrémité avant de la proue à l'extrémité arrière de la poupe;

m) les termes «service de recrutement et de placement» désignent toute personne, société, institution, agence ou autre organisation du secteur public ou privé exerçant des activités relatives au recrutement de pêcheurs pour le compte de, ou au placement de pêcheurs auprès d'armateurs à la pêche;

n) le terme «patron» désigne la personne chargée du commandement d'un navire de pêche;

CHAMP D'APPLICATION

Article 2

1. Sauf disposition contraire de la présente convention, celle-ci s'applique à tous les pêcheurs et à tous les navires de pêche engagés dans des opérations de pêche commerciale.

2. En cas de doute sur l'affectation d'un navire à la pêche commerciale, il appartient à l'autorité compétente de déterminer son type d'affectation après consultation.

3. Tout Membre peut, après consultation, étendre totalement ou en partie la protection prévue par la convention pour les pêcheurs travaillant sur des navires d'une longueur égale ou supérieure à 24 mètres à ceux travaillant sur des navires plus petits.

Article 3

1. L'autorité compétente peut, après consultation, exclure des prescriptions de la présente convention, ou de certaines de ses dispositions, lorsque leur application soulèverait des difficultés particulières et importantes compte tenu des conditions spécifiques de service des pêcheurs ou des opérations des navires de pêche considérés:

a) les navires de pêche engagés dans des opérations de pêche sur les cours d'eau, les lacs et les canaux;

b) des catégories limitées de pêcheurs ou de navires de pêche.

2. En cas d'exclusion visée au paragraphe précédent, et lorsque cela est réalisable, l'autorité compétente prend, si besoin est, des mesures pour étendre progressivement les prescriptions prévues par la présente convention à ces catégories de pêcheurs ou de navires de pêche.

Article 4

1. Each Member which ratifies the Convention shall, in the first report on the application of the Convention submitted under article 22 of the Constitution of the International Labour Organisation:

(a) list any categories of fishers or fishing vessels excluded under Article 3, paragraph 1;

(b) give the reasons for such exclusion, stating the respective positions of the representative organizations of employers and workers concerned, in particular the representative organizations of fishing vessel owners and fishers, where they exist; and

(c) describe any measures taken to provide equivalent protection to the excluded categories.

2. Each Member shall describe in subsequent reports submitted under article 22 of the Constitution the measures taken with a view to extending progressively the provisions of the Convention to the excluded fishers and fishing vessels.

Article 5

1. For the purpose of this Convention, the competent authority, after consultation, may decide to use length overall (LOA) in place of length (L) as the basis for measurement, in accordance with the equivalence set out in Annex I. In addition, for the purpose of the paragraphs specified in Annex III of this Convention, the competent authority, after consultation, may decide to use gross tonnage in place of length (L) or length overall (LOA) as the basis for measurement in accordance with the equivalence set out in Annex III.

2. In the reports submitted under article 22 of the Constitution, the Member shall communicate the reasons for the decision taken under this Article and any comments arising from the consultation.

PART II. GENERAL PRINCIPLES

IMPLEMENTATION

Article 6

1. Each Member shall implement and enforce laws, regulations or other measures that it has adopted to fulfil its commitments under this Convention with respect to fishers and fishing vessels under its jurisdiction. Other measures may include collective agreements, court decisions, arbitration awards, or other means consistent with national law and practice.

Article 4

1. Tout Membre qui ratifie la convention doit, dans le premier rapport sur l'application de celle-ci qu'il est tenu de présenter en vertu de l'article 22 de la Constitution de l'Organisation internationale du Travail:

a) indiquer les catégories de pêcheurs ou de navires de pêche qui sont exclues en application du premier paragraphe de l'article 3;

b) donner les motifs de ces exclusions en exposant les positions respectives des organisations représentatives d'employeurs et de travailleurs intéressées, en particulier des organisations représentatives d'armateurs à la pêche et de pêcheurs, s'il en existe;

c) décrire toute mesure prise pour octroyer une protection équivalente aux catégories exclues.

2. Tout Membre décrira, dans ses rapports ultérieurs présentés en vertu de l'article 22 de la Constitution, les mesures prises en vue d'étendre progressivement les dispositions de la convention aux catégories de pêcheurs et de navires exclues.

Article 5

1. Aux fins de la présente convention, l'autorité compétente peut, après consultation, décider d'utiliser la longueur hors tout (LHT) à la place de la longueur (L) comme critère de mesure, conformément à l'équivalence établie à l'annexe I. En outre, aux fins des paragraphes spécifiés à l'annexe III de la présente convention, l'autorité compétente peut, après consultation, décider d'utiliser la jauge brute à la place de la longueur (L) comme critère de mesure, conformément à l'équivalence établie à l'annexe III.

2. Dans les rapports présentés en vertu de l'article 22 de la Constitution, le Membre communiquera les raisons de la décision prise en vertu du présent article et les observations faites lors de la consultation.

PARTIE II. PRINCIPES GÉNÉRAUX

MISE EN ŒUVRE

Article 6

1. Tout Membre doit mettre en œuvre et faire respecter les lois, règlements ou autres mesures qu'il a adoptés afin de s'acquitter de ses obligations aux termes de la présente convention en ce qui concerne les pêcheurs et les navires de pêche relevant de sa compétence; les autres mesures peuvent comprendre des conventions collectives, des décisions judiciaires, des sentences arbitrales et autres moyens conformes à la législation et à la pratique nationales.

2. Nothing in this Convention shall affect any law, award or custom, or any agreement between fishing vessel owners and fishers, which ensures more favourable conditions than those provided for in the Convention.

COMPETENT AUTHORITY AND COORDINATION

Article 7

Each Member shall:

(a) designate the competent authority or authorities; and

(b) establish mechanisms for coordination among relevant authorities for the fishing sector at the national and local levels, as appropriate, and define their functions and responsibilities, taking into account their complementarities and national conditions and practice.

RESPONSIBILITIES OF FISHING VESSEL OWNERS, SKIPPERS AND FISHERS

Article 8

1. The fishing vessel owner has the overall responsibility to ensure that the skipper is provided with the necessary resources and facilities to comply with the obligations of this Convention.

2. The skipper has the responsibility for the safety of the fishers on board and the safe operation of the vessel, including but not limited to the following areas:

(a) providing such supervision as will ensure that, as far as possible, fishers perform their work in the best conditions of safety and health;

(b) managing the fishers in a manner which respects safety and health, including prevention of fatigue;

(c) facilitating on-board occupational safety and health awareness training; and

(d) ensuring compliance with safety of navigation, watch-keeping and associated good seamanship standards.

3. The skipper shall not be constrained by the fishing vessel owner from taking any decision which, in the professional judgement of the skipper, is necessary for the safety of the vessel and its safe navigation and safe operation, or the safety of the fishers on board.

4. Fishers shall comply with the lawful orders of the skipper and applicable safety and health measures.

2. Aucune des dispositions de la présente convention n'aura d'incidence sur les lois, décisions, coutumes ou sur les accords entre armateurs à la pêche et pêcheurs qui garantissent des conditions plus favorables que celles prévues par la convention.

AUTORITÉ COMPÉTENTE ET COORDINATION

Article 7

Tout Membre doit:

a) désigner l'autorité compétente ou les autorités compétentes;

b) établir des mécanismes de coordination entre les autorités concernées pour le secteur de la pêche aux niveaux national et local, selon le cas, et définir leurs fonctions et responsabilités en tenant compte de leur complémentarité ainsi que des conditions et de la pratique nationales.

RESPONSABILITÉS DES ARMATEURS À LA PÊCHE, DES PATRONS ET DES PÊCHEURS

Article 8

1. L'armateur à la pêche a la responsabilité globale de veiller à ce que le patron dispose des ressources et moyens nécessaires pour s'acquitter des obligations de la présente convention.

2. La responsabilité de la sécurité des pêcheurs à bord et du fonctionnement sûr du navire incombe au patron, notamment, mais non exclusivement, dans les domaines suivants:

a) la supervision, qui doit être réalisée de façon à ce que les pêcheurs puissent, dans la mesure du possible, exécuter leur travail dans les meilleures conditions de sécurité et de santé;

b) l'organisation du travail des pêcheurs, qui doit se faire en respectant la sécurité et la santé, y compris la prévention de la fatigue;

c) la mise à disposition à bord d'une formation de sensibilisation à la sécurité et à la santé au travail;

d) le respect des normes de sécurité de la navigation, de veille et de bonnes pratiques maritimes.

3. L'armateur à la pêche n'entravera pas la liberté du patron de prendre toute décision qui, de l'avis professionnel de ce dernier, est nécessaire pour la sécurité du navire, de sa navigation et de son exploitation, ou pour la sécurité des pêcheurs qui sont à bord.

4. Les pêcheurs doivent respecter les ordres légaux du patron et les mesures de sécurité et de santé applicables.

PART III. MINIMUM REQUIREMENTS FOR WORK ON BOARD FISHING VESSELS

MINIMUM AGE

Article 9

1. The minimum age for work on board a fishing vessel shall be 16 years. However, the competent authority may authorize a minimum age of 15 for persons who are no longer subject to compulsory schooling as provided by national legislation, and who are engaged in vocational training in fishing.

2. The competent authority, in accordance with national laws and practice, may authorize persons of the age of 15 to perform light work during school holidays. In such cases, it shall determine, after consultation, the kinds of work permitted and shall prescribe the conditions in which such work shall be undertaken and the periods of rest required.

3. The minimum age for assignment to activities on board fishing vessels, which by their nature or the circumstances in which they are carried out are likely to jeopardize the health, safety or morals of young persons, shall not be less than 18 years.

4. The types of activities to which paragraph 3 of this Article applies shall be determined by national laws or regulations, or by the competent authority, after consultation, taking into account the risks concerned and the applicable international standards.

5. The performance of the activities referred to in paragraph 3 of this Article as from the age of 16 may be authorized by national laws or regulations, or by decision of the competent authority, after consultation, on condition that the health, safety or morals of the young persons concerned are fully protected and that the young persons concerned have received adequate specific instruction or vocational training and have completed basic pre-sea safety training.

6. The engagement of fishers under the age of 18 for work at night shall be prohibited. For the purpose of this Article, "night" shall be defined in accordance with national law and practice. It shall cover a period of at least nine hours starting no later than midnight and ending no earlier than 5 a.m. An exception to strict compliance with the night work restriction may be made by the competent authority when:

(a) the effective training of the fishers concerned, in accordance with established programmes and schedules, would be impaired; or

(b) the specific nature of the duty or a recognized training programme requires that fishers covered by the exception perform duties at night and the authority determines, after consultation, that the work will not have a detrimental impact on their health or well-being.

PARTIE III. CONDITIONS MINIMALES REQUISES POUR LE TRAVAIL À BORD DES NAVIRES DE PÊCHE

ÂGE MINIMUM

Article 9

1. L'âge minimum pour le travail à bord d'un navire de pêche est de 16 ans. Toutefois, l'autorité compétente peut autoriser un âge minimum de 15 ans pour les personnes qui ne sont plus soumises à l'obligation de scolarité imposée par la législation nationale et suivent une formation professionnelle en matière de pêche.

2. L'autorité compétente peut, conformément à la législation et à la pratique nationales, autoriser des personnes âgées de 15 ans à exécuter des travaux légers lors des vacances scolaires. Dans ces cas, elle déterminera, après consultation, les types de travail autorisés et prescrira les conditions dans lesquelles ce travail sera entrepris et les périodes de repos requises.

3. L'âge minimum d'affectation à des activités à bord d'un navire de pêche qui, par leur nature ou les conditions dans lesquelles elles s'exercent, sont susceptibles de compromettre la santé, la sécurité ou la moralité des jeunes travailleurs ne doit pas être inférieur à 18 ans.

4. Les types d'activités visés au paragraphe 3 du présent article sont déterminés par la législation nationale ou l'autorité compétente, après consultation, en tenant compte des risques qu'ils comportent et des normes internationales applicables.

5. L'exécution des activités visées au paragraphe 3 du présent article dès l'âge de 16 ans peut être autorisée par la législation nationale ou par une décision de l'autorité compétente, après consultation, à condition que la santé, la sécurité ou la moralité des jeunes travailleurs soient pleinement garanties, qu'ils aient reçu une instruction spécifique et adéquate ou une formation professionnelle et qu'ils aient suivi intégralement une formation de base aux questions de sécurité préalable à l'embarquement.

6. Il est interdit d'engager un pêcheur de moins de 18 ans pour un travail de nuit. Aux fins du présent article, le terme «nuit» est défini conformément à la législation et à la pratique nationales. Il couvre une période de neuf heures consécutives au moins, commençant au plus tard à minuit et se terminant au plus tôt à 5 heures du matin. Une dérogation à la stricte observation de la restriction concernant le travail de nuit peut être décidée par l'autorité compétente quand:

a) la formation effective des pêcheurs concernés dans le cadre de programmes et plans d'études établis pourrait en être compromise; ou

b) la nature particulière de la tâche ou un programme de formation agréé exige que les pêcheurs visés par la dérogation travaillent la nuit et l'autorité décide, après consultation, que ce travail ne portera pas préjudice à leur santé ou à leur bien-être.

7. None of the provisions in this Article shall affect any obligations assumed by the Member arising from the ratification of any other international labour Convention.

MEDICAL EXAMINATION

Article 10

1. No fishers shall work on board a fishing vessel without a valid medical certificate attesting to fitness to perform their duties.

2. The competent authority, after consultation, may grant exemptions from the application of paragraph 1 of this Article, taking into account the health and safety of fishers, size of the vessel, availability of medical assistance and evacuation, duration of the voyage, area of operation, and type of fishing operation.

3. The exemptions in paragraph 2 of this Article shall not apply to a fisher working on a fishing vessel of 24 metres in length and over or which normally remains at sea for more than three days. In urgent cases, the competent authority may permit a fisher to work on such a vessel for a period of a limited and specified duration until a medical certificate can be obtained, provided that the fisher is in possession of an expired medical certificate of a recent date.

Article 11

Each Member shall adopt laws, regulations or other measures providing for:

(a) the nature of medical examinations;

(b) the form and content of medical certificates;

(c) the issue of a medical certificate by a duly qualified medical practitioner or, in the case of a certificate solely concerning eyesight, by a person recognized by the competent authority as qualified to issue such a certificate; these persons shall enjoy full independence in exercising their professional judgement;

(d) the frequency of medical examinations and the period of validity of medical certificates;

(e) the right to a further examination by a second independent medical practitioner in the event that a person has been refused a certificate or has had limitations imposed on the work he or she may perform; and

(f) other relevant requirements.

Article 12

On a fishing vessel of 24 metres in length and over, or on a vessel which normally remains at sea for more than three days:

7. Aucune des dispositions de cet article n'a d'incidence sur les obligations souscrites par le Membre en vertu de la ratification d'autres conventions internationales du travail.

EXAMEN MÉDICAL

Article 10

1. Aucun pêcheur ne doit travailler à bord d'un navire de pêche sans disposer d'un certificat médical valide attestant de son aptitude à exécuter ses tâches.

2. L'autorité compétente peut, après consultation, octroyer des dérogations à l'application du paragraphe 1 du présent article, compte tenu de la santé et de la sécurité des pêcheurs, de la taille du navire, de la disponibilité de l'assistance médicale et des moyens d'évacuation, de la durée du voyage, de la zone d'opération et du type d'activité de pêche.

3. Les dérogations visées au paragraphe 2 du présent article ne s'appliqueront pas à un pêcheur travaillant sur un navire de pêche d'une longueur égale ou supérieure à 24 mètres ou qui passe normalement plus de trois jours en mer. Dans les cas urgents, l'autorité compétente peut autoriser un pêcheur à travailler sur un tel navire pour une période d'une durée limitée et spécifiée en attendant qu'il puisse obtenir un certificat médical, sous réserve que ce pêcheur soit en possession d'un certificat médical expiré depuis peu.

Article 11

Tout Membre doit adopter des lois, règlements ou autres mesures concernant:

a) la nature des examens médicaux;

b) la forme et le contenu des certificats médicaux;

c) la délivrance du certificat médical par du personnel médical dûment qualifié ou, dans le cas d'un certificat concernant seulement la vue, par une personne habilitée par l'autorité compétente à délivrer un tel certificat; ces personnes doivent jouir d'une totale indépendance lorsqu'elles exercent leur jugement professionnel;

d) la fréquence des examens médicaux et la durée de validité des certificats médicaux;

e) le droit pour une personne d'être réexaminée par du personnel médical indépendant différent au cas où elle se verrait refuser un certificat ou imposer des limitations au travail qu'elle peut effectuer;

f) les autres conditions requises.

Article 12

Sur un navire de pêche d'une longueur égale ou supérieure à 24 mètres ou passant normalement plus de trois jours en mer:

1. The medical certificate of a fisher shall state, at a minimum, that:

(a) the hearing and sight of the fisher concerned are satisfactory for the fisher's duties on the vessel; and

(b) the fisher is not suffering from any medical condition likely to be aggravated by service at sea or to render the fisher unfit for such service or to endanger the health of other persons on board.

2. The medical certificate shall be valid for a maximum period of two years unless the fisher is under the age of 18, in which case the maximum period of validity shall be one year.

3. If the period of validity of a certificate expires in the course of a voyage, the certificate shall remain in force until the end of that voyage.

PART IV. CONDITIONS OF SERVICE

MANNING AND HOURS OF REST

Article 13

Each Member shall adopt laws, regulations or other measures requiring that owners of fishing vessels flying its flag ensure that:

(a) their vessels are sufficiently and safely manned with a crew necessary for the safe navigation and operation of the vessel and under the control of a competent skipper; and

(b) fishers are given regular periods of rest of sufficient length to ensure health and safety.

Article 14

1. In addition to the requirements set out in Article 13, the competent authority shall:

(a) for vessels of 24 metres in length and over, establish a minimum level of manning for the safe navigation of the vessel, specifying the number and the qualifications of the fishers required;

(b) for fishing vessels regardless of size remaining at sea for more than three days, after consultation and for the purpose of limiting fatigue, establish the minimum hours of rest to be provided to fishers. Minimum hours of rest shall not be less than ten hours in any 24-hour period, and 77 hours in any seven-day period.

2. The competent authority may permit, for limited and specified reasons, temporary exceptions to the limits established in paragraph 1(b) of

1. Le certificat médical du pêcheur doit au minimum indiquer:

a) que l'ouïe et la vue de l'intéressé sont satisfaisantes compte tenu de ses tâches sur le navire; et

b) que l'intéressé n'a aucun problème médical de nature à être aggravé par le service en mer ou qui le rend inapte à ce service ou qui comporterait des risques pour la santé d'autres personnes à bord.

2. Le certificat médical est valide pendant deux ans au maximum à moins que le pêcheur soit âgé de moins de 18 ans, auquel cas la durée maximale de validité sera d'un an.

3. Si la période de validité du certificat expire au cours d'un voyage, le certificat reste valide jusqu'à la fin du voyage.

PARTIE IV. CONDITIONS DE SERVICE

ÉQUIPAGE ET DURÉE DU REPOS

Article 13

Tout Membre doit adopter des lois, règlements ou autres mesures prévoyant que les armateurs de navires de pêche battant son pavillon veillent à ce que:

a) leurs navires soient dotés d'un équipage suffisant en nombre et en qualité pour assurer une navigation et un fonctionnement dans des conditions sûres et sous le contrôle d'un patron compétent;

b) des périodes de repos régulières d'une fréquence et d'une durée suffisantes pour préserver leur santé et leur sécurité soient octroyées aux pêcheurs.

Article 14

1. Outre les prescriptions énoncées à l'article 13, l'autorité compétente doit:

a) pour les navires d'une longueur égale ou supérieure à 24 mètres, fixer l'effectif minimal propre à garantir la sécurité de navigation du navire et préciser le nombre de pêcheurs requis et les qualifications qu'ils doivent posséder;

b) pour les navires de pêche restant en mer plus de trois jours, quelle que soit leur taille, fixer, après consultation et en vue de limiter la fatigue, une durée minimum de repos pour les pêcheurs. Cette durée ne doit pas être inférieure à dix heures par période de 24 heures, ni à 77 heures par période de sept jours.

2. L'autorité compétente peut, pour des raisons limitées et précises, autoriser qu'il soit dérogé temporairement aux durées de repos fixées à

this Article. However, in such circumstances, it shall require that fishers shall receive compensatory periods of rest as soon as practicable.

3. The competent authority, after consultation, may establish alternative requirements to those in paragraphs 1 and 2 of this Article. However, such alternative requirements shall provide at least the same level of protection.

CREW LIST

Article 15

Every fishing vessel shall carry a crew list, a copy of which shall be provided to authorized persons ashore prior to departure of the vessel, or communicated ashore immediately after departure of the vessel. The competent authority shall determine to whom and when such information shall be provided and for what purpose or purposes.

FISHER'S WORK AGREEMENT

Article 16

Each Member shall adopt laws, regulations or other measures:

(a) requiring that fishers working on vessels flying its flag have the protection of a fisher's work agreement that is comprehensible to them and is consistent with the provisions of this Convention; and

(b) specifying the minimum particulars to be included in fishers' work agreements in accordance with the provisions contained in Annex II.

Article 17

Each Member shall adopt laws, regulations or other measures regarding:

(a) procedures for ensuring that a fisher has an opportunity to review and seek advice on the terms of the fisher's work agreement before it is concluded;

(b) where applicable, the maintenance of records concerning the fisher's work under such an agreement; and

(c) the means of settling disputes in connection with a fisher's work agreement.

l'alinéa *b)* du paragraphe 1 du présent article. Dans ces cas, elle doit toutefois exiger que des périodes de repos compensatoires soient accordées aux pêcheurs dès que possible.

3. L'autorité compétente peut, après consultation, établir des prescriptions remplaçant celles fixées aux paragraphes 1 et 2 du présent article. Toutefois, le niveau de protection prévu par lesdites prescriptions ne doit pas être moindre.

LISTE D'ÉQUIPAGE

Article 15

Tout navire de pêche doit avoir à bord une liste d'équipage, dont un exemplaire est fourni aux personnes autorisées à terre avant le départ du navire ou communiqué à terre immédiatement après. L'autorité compétente doit déterminer à qui, à quel moment et à quelles fins cette information doit être fournie.

ACCORD D'ENGAGEMENT DU PÊCHEUR

Article 16

Tout Membre doit adopter des lois, règlements ou autres mesures:

a) prévoyant que les pêcheurs travaillant à bord des navires battant son pavillon soient protégés par un accord d'engagement qui soit conforme aux dispositions de la présente convention et qui leur soit compréhensible;

b) indiquant les mentions minimales à inclure dans les accords d'engagement des pêcheurs, conformément aux dispositions de l'annexe II.

Article 17

Tout Membre doit adopter des lois, règlements ou autres mesures concernant:

a) les procédures garantissant que le pêcheur a la possibilité d'examiner les clauses de son accord d'engagement et de demander conseil à ce sujet avant de le conclure;

b) s'il y a lieu, la tenue des états de service du pêcheur dans le cadre de cet accord;

c) les moyens de régler les différends relatifs à l'accord d'engagement du pêcheur.

Article 18

The fisher's work agreement, a copy of which shall be provided to the fisher, shall be carried on board and be available to the fisher and, in accordance with national law and practice, to other concerned parties on request.

Article 19

Articles 16 to 18 and Annex II do not apply to a fishing vessel owner who is also single-handedly operating the vessel.

Article 20

It shall be the responsibility of the fishing vessel owner to ensure that each fisher has a written work agreement signed by both the fisher and the fishing vessel owner or an authorized representative of the fishing vessel owner.

REPATRIATION

Article 21

1. Members shall ensure that fishers on a fishing vessel that flies their flag and that enters a foreign port are entitled to repatriation in the event that the fisher's work agreement has expired or has been terminated for justified reasons by the fisher or by the fishing vessel owner, or the fisher is no longer able to carry out the duties required under the work agreement or cannot be expected to carry them out in the specific circumstances. This also applies to fishers from that vessel who are transferred for the same reasons from the vessel to the foreign port.

2. The cost of the repatriation referred to in paragraph 1 of this Article shall be borne by the fishing vessel owner, except where the fisher has been found, in accordance with national laws, regulations or other measures, to be in serious default of his or her work agreement obligations.

3. Members shall prescribe, by means of laws, regulations or other measures, the precise circumstances entitling a fisher covered by paragraph 1 of this Article to repatriation, the maximum duration of service periods on board following which a fisher is entitled to repatriation, and the destinations to which fishers may be repatriated.

4. If a fishing vessel owner fails to provide for the repatriation referred to in this Article, the Member whose flag the vessel flies shall arrange for the repatriation of the fisher concerned and shall be entitled to recover the cost from the fishing vessel owner.

Article 18

L'accord d'engagement du pêcheur, dont un exemplaire lui est remis, est disponible à bord, à la disposition du pêcheur et, conformément à la législation et à la pratique nationales, de toute autre partie concernée qui en fait la demande.

Article 19

Les articles 16 à 18 et l'annexe II ne s'appliquent pas au propriétaire de navire qui exploite celui-ci seul.

Article 20

Il incombe à l'armateur à la pêche de veiller à ce que chaque pêcheur soit en possession d'un accord d'engagement écrit, signé à la fois par le pêcheur et l'armateur à la pêche, ou par un représentant autorisé de celui-ci.

RAPATRIEMENT

Article 21

1. Les Membres doivent veiller à ce que les pêcheurs à bord d'un navire de pêche battant leur pavillon et qui entre dans un port étranger aient le droit d'être rapatriés lorsque l'accord d'engagement du pêcheur a expiré, ou lorsque le pêcheur ou l'armateur à la pêche y a mis fin pour des raisons justifiées, ou lorsque le pêcheur n'est plus en mesure de s'acquitter des tâches qui lui incombent en vertu de l'accord d'engagement ou qu'on ne peut attendre de lui qu'il les exécute compte tenu des circonstances. La présente disposition s'applique également aux pêcheurs de ce navire qui sont transférés pour les mêmes raisons du navire vers un port étranger.

2. Les frais du rapatriement visé au paragraphe 1 du présent article doivent être pris en charge par l'armateur à la pêche, sauf si le pêcheur a été reconnu, conformément à la législation nationale ou à d'autres dispositions applicables, coupable d'un manquement grave aux obligations de son accord d'engagement.

3. Les Membres doivent déterminer, par voie de législation ou autre, les circonstances précises donnant droit à un rapatriement, la durée maximale des périodes d'embarquement au terme desquelles les pêcheurs visés au paragraphe 1 du présent article ont droit au rapatriement, et les destinations vers lesquelles ils peuvent être rapatriés.

4. Si l'armateur à la pêche omet de pourvoir au rapatriement visé au présent article, le Membre dont le navire bat pavillon doit organiser le rapatriement du pêcheur concerné et a le droit de recouvrer les frais auprès de l'armateur à la pêche.

RECRUITMENT AND PLACEMENT

Article 22

1. Each Member that operates a public service providing recruitment and placement for fishers shall ensure that the service forms part of, or is coordinated with, a public employment service for all workers and employers.

2. Any private service providing recruitment and placement for fishers which operates in the territory of a Member shall do so in conformity with a standardized system of licensing or certification or other form of regulation, which shall be established, maintained or modified only after consultation.

3. Each Member shall, by means of laws, regulations or other measures:
(a) prohibit recruitment and placement services from using means, mechanisms or lists intended to prevent or deter fishers from engaging for work;
(b) require that no fees or other charges for recruitment and placement of fishers be borne directly or indirectly, in whole or in part, by the fisher; and
(c) determine the conditions under which any licence, certificate or similar authorization of a private recruitment or placement service may be suspended or withdrawn in case of violation of relevant laws or regulations; and specify the conditions under which private recruitment and placement services can operate.

PAYMENT OF FISHERS

Article 23

Each Member, after consultation, shall adopt laws, regulations or other measures providing that fishers who are paid a wage are ensured a monthly or regular payment.

Article 24

Each Member shall require that all fishers working on board fishing vessels shall be given a means to transmit all or part of their payments received, including advances, to their families at no cost.

PART V.   ACCOMMODATION AND FOOD

Article 25

Each Member shall adopt laws, regulations or other measures for fishing vessels that fly its flag with respect to accommodation, food and potable water on board.

RECRUTEMENT ET PLACEMENT

Article 22

1. Tout Membre qui a mis en place un service public de recrutement et de placement de pêcheurs doit s'assurer que ce service fait partie du service public de l'emploi ouvert à l'ensemble des travailleurs et des employeurs ou qu'il agit en coordination avec celui-ci.

2. Les services privés de recrutement et de placement de pêcheurs qui sont établis sur le territoire d'un Membre doivent exercer leur activité en vertu d'un système de licence ou d'agrément normalisé ou d'une autre forme de réglementation, lesquels ne seront établis, maintenus ou modifiés qu'après consultation.

3. Tout Membre doit, par voie de législation ou autres mesures:

a) interdire aux services de recrutement et de placement d'avoir recours à des moyens, mécanismes ou listes visant à empêcher ou à dissuader les pêcheurs d'obtenir un engagement;

b) interdire que des honoraires ou autres frais soient supportés par les pêcheurs, directement ou indirectement, en tout ou en partie, pour le recrutement et le placement;

c) fixer les conditions dans lesquelles une licence, un agrément ou toute autre autorisation d'un service privé de recrutement et de placement peuvent être suspendus ou retirés en cas d'infraction à la législation pertinente et préciser les conditions dans lesquelles lesdits services privés peuvent exercer leurs activités.

PAIEMENTS DES PÊCHEURS

Article 23

Tout Membre adopte, après consultation, une législation ou d'autres mesures prescrivant que les pêcheurs qui perçoivent un salaire seront payés mensuellement ou à intervalles réguliers.

Article 24

Tout Membre doit exiger que tous les pêcheurs travaillant à bord de navires de pêche aient les moyens de faire parvenir à leur famille et sans frais tout ou partie des paiements reçus, y compris les avances.

PARTIE V. LOGEMENT ET ALIMENTATION

Article 25

Tout Membre doit adopter une législation ou d'autres mesures relatives au logement, à la nourriture et à l'eau potable à bord des navires de pêche battant son pavillon.

Article 26

Each Member shall adopt laws, regulations or other measures requiring that accommodation on board fishing vessels that fly its flag shall be of sufficient size and quality and appropriately equipped for the service of the vessel and the length of time fishers live on board. In particular, such measures shall address, as appropriate, the following issues:

(a) approval of plans for the construction or modification of fishing vessels in respect of accommodation;

(b) maintenance of accommodation and galley spaces with due regard to hygiene and overall safe, healthy and comfortable conditions;

(c) ventilation, heating, cooling and lighting;

(d) mitigation of excessive noise and vibration;

(e) location, size, construction materials, furnishing and equipping of sleeping rooms, mess rooms and other accommodation spaces;

(f) sanitary facilities, including toilets and washing facilities, and supply of sufficient hot and cold water; and

(g) procedures for responding to complaints concerning accommodation that does not meet the requirements of this Convention.

Article 27

Each Member shall adopt laws, regulations or other measures requiring that:

(a) the food carried and served on board be of a sufficient nutritional value, quality and quantity;

(b) potable water be of sufficient quality and quantity; and

(c) the food and water shall be provided by the fishing vessel owner at no cost to the fisher. However, the cost can be recovered as an operational cost if the collective agreement governing a share system or a fisher's work agreement so provides.

Article 28

1. The laws, regulations or other measures to be adopted by the Member in accordance with Articles 25 to 27 shall give full effect to Annex III concerning fishing vessel accommodation. Annex III may be amended in the manner provided for in Article 45.

2. A Member which is not in a position to implement the provisions of Annex III may, after consultation, adopt provisions in its laws and regulations or other measures which are substantially equivalent to the provisions set out in Annex III, with the exception of provisions related to Article 27.

Article 26

Tout Membre doit adopter une législation ou d'autres mesures prévoyant que le logement à bord des navires de pêche battant son pavillon sera d'une qualité et d'une taille suffisantes et qu'il sera équipé de façon adaptée au service du navire et à la durée du séjour des pêcheurs à bord. En particulier, ces mesures régleront, selon le cas, les questions suivantes:

a) approbation des plans de construction ou de modification des navires de pêche en ce qui concerne le logement;

b) maintien du logement et de la cuisine dans des conditions générales d'hygiène, de sécurité, de santé et de confort;

c) ventilation, chauffage, refroidissement et éclairage;

d) réduction des bruits et vibrations excessifs;

e) emplacement, taille, matériaux de construction, fournitures et équipement des cabines, réfectoires et autres espaces de logement;

f) installations sanitaires, comprenant des toilettes et des moyens de lavage, et fourniture d'eau chaude et froide en quantité suffisante;

g) procédures d'examen des plaintes concernant des conditions de logement qui ne satisfont pas aux prescriptions de la présente convention.

Article 27

Tout Membre doit adopter une législation ou d'autres mesures prévoyant que:

a) la nourriture transportée et servie à bord doit être d'une valeur nutritionnelle, d'une qualité et d'une quantité suffisantes;

b) l'eau potable doit être d'une qualité et d'une quantité suffisantes;

c) la nourriture et l'eau potable doivent être fournies par l'armateur à la pêche sans frais pour le pêcheur. Toutefois, les frais peuvent être recouvrés sous forme de coûts d'exploitation pour autant qu'une convention collective régissant un système de rémunération à la part ou que l'accord d'engagement du pêcheur le prévoie.

Article 28

1. La législation ou les autres mesures adoptées par le Membre conformément aux articles 25 à 27 doivent donner pleinement effet à l'annexe III concernant le logement à bord des navires de pêche. L'annexe III peut être amendée de la façon prévue à l'article 45.

2. Un Membre qui n'est pas en mesure d'appliquer les dispositions de l'annexe III peut, après consultation, adopter dans sa législation des dispositions ou d'autres mesures équivalentes dans l'ensemble aux dispositions énoncées à l'annexe III, à l'exception des dispositions se rapportant à l'article 27.

Part VI. Medical care, health protection, and social security

Medical care

Article 29

Each Member shall adopt laws, regulations or other measures requiring that:

(a) fishing vessels carry appropriate medical equipment and medical supplies for the service of the vessel, taking into account the number of fishers on board, the area of operation and the length of the voyage;

(b) fishing vessels have at least one person on board who is qualified or trained in first aid and other forms of medical care and who has the necessary knowledge to use the medical equipment and supplies for the vessel concerned, taking into account the number of fishers on board, the area of operation and the length of the voyage;

(c) medical equipment and supplies carried on board be accompanied by instructions or other information in a language and format understood by the person or persons referred to in subparagraph (b);

(d) fishing vessels be equipped for radio or satellite communication with persons or services ashore that can provide medical advice, taking into account the area of operation and the length of the voyage; and

(e) fishers have the right to medical treatment ashore and the right to be taken ashore in a timely manner for treatment in the event of serious injury or illness.

Article 30

For fishing vessels of 24 metres in length and over, taking into account the number of fishers on board, the area of operation and the duration of the voyage, each Member shall adopt laws, regulations or other measures requiring that:

(a) the competent authority prescribe the medical equipment and medical supplies to be carried on board;

(b) the medical equipment and medical supplies carried on board be properly maintained and inspected at regular intervals established by the competent authority by responsible persons designated or approved by the competent authority;

(c) the vessels carry a medical guide adopted or approved by the competent authority, or the (ILO/IMO/WHO) *International Medical Guide for Ships;*

Partie VI. Soins médicaux, protection de la santé et sécurité sociale

SOINS MÉDICAUX

Article 29

Tout Membre doit adopter une législation ou d'autres mesures prévoyant que:

a) les navires de pêche soient dotés de fournitures et d'un matériel médicaux adaptés au service du navire, compte tenu du nombre de pêcheurs à bord, de la zone d'opération et de la durée du voyage;

b) les navires de pêche aient à leur bord au moins une personne qualifiée ou formée pour donner les premiers secours et autres formes de soins médicaux, qui sache utiliser les fournitures et le matériel médicaux dont est doté le navire, compte tenu du nombre de pêcheurs à bord, de la zone d'opération et de la durée du voyage;

c) les fournitures et le matériel médicaux présents à bord soient accompagnés d'instructions ou d'autres informations dans une langue et une présentation compréhensibles à la personne ou aux personnes mentionnées à l'alinéa b);

d) les navires de pêche soient équipés d'un système de communication par radio ou par satellite avec des personnes ou services à terre pouvant fournir des consultations médicales, compte tenu de la zone d'opération et de la durée du voyage;

e) les pêcheurs aient le droit de bénéficier d'un traitement médical à terre et d'être débarqués à cet effet en temps voulu en cas de lésion ou de maladie grave.

Article 30

Pour les navires de pêche d'une longueur égale ou supérieure à 24 mètres, compte tenu du nombre de pêcheurs à bord, de la zone d'opération et de la durée du voyage, tout Membre doit adopter une législation ou d'autres mesures prévoyant que:

a) l'autorité compétente prescrive le matériel médical et les fournitures médicales à avoir à disposition à bord;

b) le matériel médical et les fournitures médicales disponibles à bord soient entretenus de façon adéquate et inspectés à des intervalles réguliers, fixés par l'autorité compétente, par des responsables désignés ou agréés par celle-ci;

c) les navires soient pourvus d'un guide médical de bord adopté ou approuvé par l'autorité compétente ou du *Guide médical international de bord* (OIT/OMI/OMS);

(d) the vessels have access to a prearranged system of medical advice to vessels at sea by radio or satellite communication, including specialist advice, which shall be available at all times;

(e) the vessels carry on board a list of radio or satellite stations through which medical advice can be obtained; and

(f) to the extent consistent with the Member's national law and practice, medical care while the fisher is on board or landed in a foreign port be provided free of charge to the fisher.

OCCUPATIONAL SAFETY AND HEALTH AND ACCIDENT PREVENTION

Article 31

Each Member shall adopt laws, regulations or other measures concerning:

(a) the prevention of occupational accidents, occupational diseases and work-related risks on board fishing vessels, including risk evaluation and management, training and on-board instruction of fishers;

(b) training for fishers in the handling of types of fishing gear they will use and in the knowledge of the fishing operations in which they will be engaged;

(c) the obligations of fishing vessel owners, fishers and others concerned, due account being taken of the safety and health of fishers under the age of 18;

(d) the reporting and investigation of accidents on board fishing vessels flying its flag; and

(e) the setting up of joint committees on occupational safety and health or, after consultation, of other appropriate bodies.

Article 32

1. The requirements of this Article shall apply to fishing vessels of 24 metres in length and over normally remaining at sea for more than three days and, after consultation, to other vessels, taking into account the number of fishers on board, the area of operation, and the duration of the voyage.

2. The competent authority shall:

(a) after consultation, require that the fishing vessel owner, in accordance with national laws, regulations, collective bargaining agreements and practice, establish on-board procedures for the prevention of occupational accidents, injuries and diseases, taking into account the specific hazards and risks on the fishing vessel concerned; and

d) les navires en mer aient accès, au moyen d'arrangements préalables, à des consultations médicales par radio ou par satellite, y compris à des conseils de spécialistes, à toute heure du jour ou de la nuit;

e) les navires conservent à bord une liste de stations de radio ou de satellite par l'intermédiaire desquelles des consultations médicales peuvent être obtenues;

f) dans une mesure conforme à la législation et à la pratique du Membre, les soins médicaux dispensés au pêcheur lorsqu'il est à bord ou débarqué dans un port étranger lui soient fournis gratuitement.

SANTÉ ET SÉCURITÉ AU TRAVAIL ET PRÉVENTION
DES ACCIDENTS DU TRAVAIL

Article 31

Tout Membre doit adopter une législation ou d'autres mesures concernant:

a) la prévention des accidents du travail, des maladies professionnelles et des risques liés au travail à bord des navires, notamment l'évaluation et la gestion des risques, la formation des pêcheurs et l'instruction à bord;

b) la formation des pêcheurs à l'utilisation des engins de pêche dont ils se serviront et à la connaissance des opérations de pêche qu'ils auront à effectuer;

c) les obligations des armateurs à la pêche, des pêcheurs et autres personnes intéressées, compte dûment tenu de la santé et de la sécurité des pêcheurs âgés de moins de 18 ans;

d) la déclaration des accidents survenant à bord des navires de pêche battant son pavillon et la réalisation d'enquêtes sur ces accidents;

e) la constitution de comités paritaires de santé et de sécurité au travail ou, après consultation, d'autres organismes qualifiés.

Article 32

1. Les prescriptions de cet article s'appliquent aux navires d'une longueur égale ou supérieure à 24 mètres qui restent habituellement en mer pour plus de trois jours et, après consultation, à d'autres navires, compte tenu du nombre de pêcheurs à bord, de la zone d'opération et de la durée du voyage.

2. L'autorité compétente doit:

a) après consultation, faire obligation à l'armateur à la pêche d'établir, conformément à la législation, aux conventions collectives et à la pratique nationales, des procédures à bord visant à prévenir les accidents du travail et les lésions et maladies professionnelles, compte tenu des dangers et risques spécifiques du navire de pêche concerné;

(b) require that fishing vessel owners, skippers, fishers and other relevant persons be provided with sufficient and suitable guidance, training material, or other appropriate information on how to assess and manage risks to safety and health on board fishing vessels.

3. Fishing vessel owners shall:

(a) ensure that every fisher on board is provided with appropriate personal protective clothing and equipment;

(b) ensure that every fisher on board has received basic safety training approved by the competent authority; the competent authority may grant written exemptions from this requirement for fishers who have demonstrated equivalent knowledge and experience; and

(c) ensure that fishers are sufficiently and reasonably familiarized with equipment and its methods of operation, including relevant safety measures, prior to using the equipment or participating in the operations concerned.

Article 33

Risk evaluation in relation to fishing shall be conducted, as appropriate, with the participation of fishers or their representatives.

SOCIAL SECURITY

Article 34

Each Member shall ensure that fishers ordinarily resident in its territory, and their dependants to the extent provided in national law, are entitled to benefit from social security protection under conditions no less favourable than those applicable to other workers, including employed and self-employed persons, ordinarily resident in its territory.

Article 35

Each Member shall undertake to take steps, according to national circumstances, to achieve progressively comprehensive social security protection for all fishers who are ordinarily resident in its territory.

Article 36

Members shall cooperate through bilateral or multilateral agreements or other arrangements, in accordance with national laws, regulations or practice:

b) exiger que les armateurs à la pêche, les patrons, les pêcheurs et les autres personnes concernées reçoivent suffisamment de directives et de matériel de formation appropriés ainsi que toute autre information pertinente sur la manière d'évaluer et de gérer les risques en matière de santé et de sécurité à bord des navires de pêche.

3. Les armateurs à la pêche doivent:

a) veiller à ce que tous les pêcheurs à bord reçoivent des vêtements et équipements de protection individuelle appropriés;

b) veiller à ce que tous les pêcheurs à bord aient reçu une formation de base en matière de sécurité, approuvée par l'autorité compétente; cette dernière peut cependant accorder une dérogation écrite dans le cas des pêcheurs qui démontrent qu'ils possèdent des connaissances et une expérience équivalentes;

c) veiller à ce que les pêcheurs soient suffisamment et convenablement familiarisés avec l'équipement et les opérations de pêche, y compris avec les mesures de sécurité s'y rapportant, avant d'utiliser cet équipement ou de participer auxdites opérations.

Article 33

L'évaluation des risques concernant la pêche est effectuée, selon le cas, avec la participation de pêcheurs ou de leurs représentants.

SÉCURITÉ SOCIALE

Article 34

Tout Membre veillera à ce que les pêcheurs résidant habituellement sur son territoire et, dans la mesure prévue par la législation nationale, les personnes à leur charge bénéficient de la sécurité sociale à des conditions non moins favorables que celles qui s'appliquent aux autres travailleurs, y compris les personnes salariées ou indépendantes, résidant habituellement sur son territoire.

Article 35

Tout Membre s'engage à prendre des mesures, en fonction de la situation nationale, pour assurer progressivement une protection complète de sécurité sociale à tous les pêcheurs résidant habituellement sur son territoire.

Article 36

Les Membres doivent coopérer, dans le cadre d'accords bilatéraux ou multilatéraux ou d'autres arrangements, en conformité avec la législation ou la pratique nationales, en vue:

(a) to achieve progressively comprehensive social security protection for fishers, taking into account the principle of equality of treatment irrespective of nationality; and

(b) to ensure the maintenance of social security rights which have been acquired or are in the course of acquisition by all fishers regardless of residence.

Article 37

Notwithstanding the attribution of responsibilities in Articles 34, 35 and 36, Members may determine, through bilateral and multilateral agreements and through provisions adopted in the framework of regional economic integration organizations, other rules concerning the social security legislation to which fishers are subject.

PROTECTION IN THE CASE OF WORK-RELATED SICKNESS, INJURY OR DEATH

Article 38

1. Each Member shall take measures to provide fishers with protection, in accordance with national laws, regulations or practice, for work-related sickness, injury or death.

2. In the event of injury due to occupational accident or disease, the fisher shall have access to:

(a) appropriate medical care; and

(b) the corresponding compensation in accordance with national laws and regulations.

3. Taking into account the characteristics within the fishing sector, the protection referred to in paragraph 1 of this Article may be ensured through:

(a) a system for fishing vessel owners' liability; or

(b) compulsory insurance, workers' compensation or other schemes.

Article 39

1. In the absence of national provisions for fishers, each Member shall adopt laws, regulations or other measures to ensure that fishing vessel owners are responsible for the provision to fishers on vessels flying its flag, of health protection and medical care while employed or engaged or working on a vessel at sea or in a foreign port. Such laws, regulations or other measures shall ensure that fishing vessel owners are responsible for defraying the expenses of medical care, including related material assistance and support, during medical treatment in a foreign country, until the fisher has been repatriated.

a) d'assurer progressivement une protection complète de sécurité sociale aux pêcheurs, sans considération de la nationalité, en tenant compte du principe d'égalité de traitement;

b) de garantir le maintien des droits en matière de sécurité sociale acquis ou en cours d'acquisition par tous les pêcheurs, indépendamment de leur lieu de résidence.

Article 37

Nonobstant l'attribution des responsabilités prévues aux articles 34, 35 et 36, les Membres peuvent déterminer, par des accords bilatéraux ou multilatéraux et par des dispositions adoptées dans le cadre d'organisations régionales d'intégration économique, d'autres règlements touchant à la législation en matière de sécurité sociale applicable aux pêcheurs.

PROTECTION EN CAS DE MALADIE,
LÉSIONS OU DÉCÈS LIÉS AU TRAVAIL

Article 38

1. Tout Membre prend des mesures en vue d'assurer aux pêcheurs une protection, conformément à la législation et à la pratique nationales, en cas de maladie, de lésion ou de décès liés au travail.

2. En cas de lésion provoquée par un accident du travail ou une maladie professionnelle, le pêcheur doit:

a) avoir accès à des soins médicaux appropriés;

b) bénéficier d'une indemnisation correspondante conformément à la législation nationale.

3. Compte tenu des caractéristiques du secteur de la pêche, la protection visée au paragraphe 1 du présent article pourra être assurée:

a) soit par un régime reposant sur la responsabilité de l'armateur à la pêche;

b) soit par un régime d'assurance obligatoire d'indemnisation des travailleurs ou d'autres régimes.

Article 39

1. En l'absence de dispositions nationales applicables aux pêcheurs, tout Membre adopte une législation ou d'autres mesures visant à garantir que les armateurs à la pêche assurent la protection de la santé et les soins médicaux des pêcheurs lorsque ces derniers sont employés ou engagés ou travaillent à bord d'un navire battant son pavillon, en mer ou dans un port étranger. Ladite législation ou les autres mesures doivent garantir que les armateurs à la pêche acquittent les frais des soins médicaux, y compris l'aide et le soutien matériels correspondants pendant la durée des traitements médicaux dispensés à l'étranger jusqu'au rapatriement du pêcheur.

2. National laws or regulations may permit the exclusion of the liability of the fishing vessel owner if the injury occurred otherwise than on the service of the vessel or the sickness or infirmity was concealed during engagement, or the injury or sickness was due to a wilful act, default or misbehaviour.

PART VII. COMPLIANCE AND ENFORCEMENT

Article 40

Each Member shall exercise effective jurisdiction and control over vessels that fly its flag by establishing a system for ensuring compliance with the standards of this Convention including, as appropriate, inspections, reporting, monitoring, complaints procedures, appropriate penalties and corrective measures, in accordance with national laws or regulations.

Article 41

Members shall require that fishing vessels remaining at sea for more than three days, whether 24 metres in length and over or normally on voyages 200 nautical miles beyond the coastline of the flag State or the outer edge of its continental shelf, whichever is greater, carry a valid document issued by the competent authority stating that the vessel has been inspected by the competent authority or on its behalf, for compliance with the provisions of this Convention concerning living and working conditions. Such a document shall be valid for a period of five years or, if issued on the same date as the International Fishing Vessel Safety Certificate, for the period of validity of that certificate.

Article 42

1. The competent authority shall appoint a sufficient number of qualified inspectors to fulfil its responsibilities under Article 41.

2. In establishing an effective system for the inspection of living and working conditions on board fishing vessels, a Member, where appropriate, may authorize public institutions or other organizations that it recognizes as competent and independent to carry out inspections and issue documents. In all cases, the Member shall remain fully responsible for the inspection and issuance of the related documents concerning the living and working conditions of the fishers on fishing vessels that fly its flag.

Article 43

1. A Member which receives a complaint or obtains evidence that a fishing vessel that flies its flag does not conform to the requirements of this

2. La législation nationale peut prévoir de décharger l'armateur à la pêche de sa responsabilité dans le cas où l'accident n'est pas survenu en service à bord du navire de pêche ou si la maladie ou l'infirmité a été dissimulée lors de l'engagement ou si l'accident ou la maladie est imputable à un acte intentionnel, une faute intentionnelle ou un écart de conduite du pêcheur.

PARTIE VII. RESPECT ET APPLICATION

Article 40

Tout Membre exerce une compétence et un contrôle effectifs sur les navires battant son pavillon en se dotant d'un système propre à garantir le respect des normes de la présente convention, notamment en prévoyant, s'il y a lieu, la conduite d'inspections, l'établissement de rapports, une procédure de règlement des plaintes, un suivi et la mise en œuvre de sanctions et mesures correctives appropriées conformément à la législation nationale.

Article 41

Les Membres doivent exiger que les navires de pêche qui restent en mer pour plus de trois jours et qui, soit ont une longueur égale ou supérieure à 24 mètres, soit naviguent habituellement à plus de 200 milles nautiques de la côte de l'Etat du pavillon ou du rebord externe du plateau continental, si celui-ci est plus éloigné, aient à bord un document valide délivré par l'autorité compétente, indiquant qu'ils ont été inspectés par l'autorité compétente ou en son nom, en vue de déterminer leur conformité aux dispositions de la convention concernant les conditions de vie et de travail. La durée de validité de ce document est de cinq ans ou identique à la durée de validité du certificat international de sécurité des navires de pêche s'il a été délivré à la même date.

Article 42

1. L'autorité compétente désignera un nombre suffisant d'inspecteurs qualifiés afin d'assumer les responsabilités qui lui incombent en vertu de l'article 41.

2. Aux fins de l'instauration d'un système efficace d'inspection des conditions de vie et de travail à bord des navires de pêche, un Membre peut, s'il y a lieu, autoriser des institutions publiques ou d'autres organismes dont il reconnaît la compétence et l'indépendance à réaliser des inspections et à délivrer des certificats. Dans tous les cas, le Membre demeurera entièrement responsable de l'inspection et de la délivrance des certificats correspondants relatifs aux conditions de vie et de travail des pêcheurs à bord des navires battant son pavillon.

Article 43

1. Un Membre qui reçoit une plainte ou qui acquiert la preuve qu'un navire battant son pavillon ne se conforme pas aux prescriptions de la

Convention shall take the steps necessary to investigate the matter and ensure that action is taken to remedy any deficiencies found.

2. If a Member, in whose port a fishing vessel calls in the normal course of its business or for operational reasons, receives a complaint or obtains evidence that such vessel does not conform to the standards of this Convention, it may prepare a report addressed to the government of the flag State of the vessel, with a copy to the Director-General of the International Labour Office, and may take measures necessary to rectify any conditions on board which are clearly hazardous to safety or health.

3. In taking the measures referred to in paragraph 2 of this Article, the Member shall notify forthwith the nearest representative of the flag State and, if possible, shall have such representative present. The Member shall not unreasonably detain or delay the vessel.

4. For the purpose of this Article, the complaint may be submitted by a fisher, a professional body, an association, a trade union or, generally, any person with an interest in the safety of the vessel, including an interest in safety or health hazards to the fishers on board.

5. This Article does not apply to complaints which a Member considers to be manifestly unfounded.

Article 44

Each Member shall apply the Convention in such a way as to ensure that the fishing vessels flying the flag of States that have not ratified the Convention do not receive more favourable treatment than fishing vessels that fly the flag of Members that have ratified it.

PART VIII. AMENDMENT OF ANNEXES I, II AND III

Article 45

1. Subject to the relevant provisions of this Convention, the International Labour Conference may amend Annexes I, II and III. The Governing Body of the International Labour Office may place an item on the agenda of the Conference regarding proposals for such amendments established by a tripartite meeting of experts. The decision to adopt the proposals shall require a majority of two-thirds of the votes cast by the delegates present at the Conference, including at least half the Members that have ratified this Convention.

2. Any amendment adopted in accordance with paragraph 1 of this Article shall enter into force six months after the date of its adoption for any Member that has ratified this Convention, unless such Member has given written notice to the Director-General that it shall not enter into force for that Member, or shall only enter into force at a later date upon subsequent written notification.

convention prend les dispositions nécessaires aux fins d'enquête et s'assure que des mesures sont prises pour remédier aux défaillances constatées.

2. Si un Membre dans le port duquel un navire de pêche fait escale dans le cours normal de son activité ou pour une raison inhérente à son exploitation reçoit une plainte ou acquiert la preuve que ce navire de pêche n'est pas conforme aux normes de la présente convention, il peut adresser un rapport au gouvernement de l'Etat du pavillon, avec copie au Directeur général du Bureau international du Travail, et prendre les mesures nécessaires pour redresser toute situation à bord qui constitue manifestement un danger pour la sécurité ou la santé.

3. S'il prend les mesures mentionnées au paragraphe 2 du présent article, le Membre doit en informer immédiatement le plus proche représentant de l'Etat du pavillon et demander à celui-ci d'être présent si possible. Il ne doit pas retenir ou retarder indûment le navire.

4. Aux fins du présent article, une plainte peut être soumise par un pêcheur, un organisme professionnel, une association, un syndicat ou, de manière générale, toute personne ayant un intérêt à la sécurité du navire, y compris un intérêt à la sécurité ou à la santé des pêcheurs à bord.

5. Cet article ne s'applique pas aux plaintes qu'un Membre considère manifestement infondées.

Article 44

Tout Membre appliquera la convention de manière à garantir que les navires de pêche battant pavillon d'Etats qui n'ont pas ratifié la convention ne bénéficient pas d'un traitement plus favorable que celui accordé aux navires battant pavillon des Membres qui l'ont ratifiée.

PARTIE VIII.   AMENDEMENTS DES ANNEXES I, II ET III

Article 45

1. Sous réserve des dispositions pertinentes de la présente convention, la Conférence internationale du Travail peut amender les annexes I, II et III. Le Conseil d'administration du Bureau international du Travail peut inscrire à l'ordre du jour de la Conférence des propositions d'amendements établies par une réunion tripartite d'experts. La majorité des deux tiers des voix des délégués présents à la Conférence, comprenant au moins la moitié des Membres ayant ratifié cette convention, est requise pour l'adoption d'amendements.

2. Tout amendement adopté conformément au paragraphe 1 du présent article entre en vigueur six mois après la date de son adoption pour tout Membre ayant ratifié la présente convention, à moins que le Membre en question n'ait adressé au Directeur général une notification écrite précisant que cet amendement n'entrera pas en vigueur à son égard ou n'entrera en vigueur qu'ultérieurement à la suite d'une nouvelle notification.

Part IX. Final Provisions

Article 46

This Convention revises the Minimum Age (Fishermen) Convention, 1959, the Medical Examination (Fishermen) Convention, 1959, the Fishermen's Articles of Agreement Convention, 1959, and the Accommodation of Crews (Fishermen) Convention, 1966.

Article 47

The formal ratifications of this Convention shall be communicated to the Director-General of the International Labour Office for registration.

Article 48

1. This Convention shall be binding only upon those Members of the International Labour Organization whose ratifications have been registered with the Director-General.

2. It shall come into force twelve months after the date on which the ratifications of ten Members, eight of which are coastal States, have been registered with the Director-General.

3. Thereafter, this Convention shall come into force for any Member twelve months after the date on which its ratification is registered.

Article 49

1. A Member which has ratified this Convention may denounce it after the expiration of ten years from the date on which the Convention first comes into force, by an act communicated to the Director-General of the International Labour Office for registration. Such denunciation shall not take effect until one year after the date on which it is registered.

2. Each Member which has ratified this Convention and which does not, within the year following the expiration of the period of ten years mentioned in the preceding paragraph, exercise the right of denunciation provided for in this Article, will be bound for another period of ten years and, thereafter, may denounce this Convention within the first year of each new period of ten years under the terms provided for in this Article.

Article 50

1. The Director-General of the International Labour Office shall notify all Members of the International Labour Organization of the registration of all ratifications and denunciations that have been communicated by the Members of the Organization.

PARTIE IX. DISPOSITIONS FINALES

Article 46

La présente convention révise la convention sur l'âge minimum (pêcheurs), 1959, la convention sur l'examen médical des pêcheurs, 1959, la convention sur le contrat d'engagement des pêcheurs, 1959, et la convention sur le logement à bord des bateaux de pêche, 1966.

Article 47

Les ratifications formelles de la présente convention sont communiquées au Directeur général du Bureau international du Travail aux fins d'enregistrement.

Article 48

1. La présente convention ne lie que les Membres de l'Organisation internationale du Travail dont la ratification a été enregistrée par le Directeur général du Bureau international du Travail.

2. Elle entre en vigueur douze mois après que les ratifications de dix Membres comprenant huit États côtiers ont été enregistrées par le Directeur général.

3. Par la suite, cette convention entre en vigueur pour chaque Membre douze mois après la date de l'enregistrement de sa ratification.

Article 49

1. Tout Membre ayant ratifié la présente convention peut la dénoncer à l'expiration d'une période de dix années après la date de la mise en vigueur initiale de la convention, par un acte communiqué au Directeur général du Bureau international du Travail aux fins d'enregistrement. La dénonciation ne prend effet qu'une année après avoir été enregistrée.

2. Tout Membre ayant ratifié la présente convention qui, dans l'année après l'expiration de la période de dix années mentionnée au paragraphe précédent, ne se prévaut pas de la faculté de dénonciation prévue par le présent article sera lié pour une nouvelle période de dix années et, par la suite, pourra dénoncer la présente convention dans la première année de chaque nouvelle période de dix années dans les conditions prévues au présent article.

Article 50

1. Le Directeur général du Bureau international du Travail notifie à tous les Membres de l'Organisation internationale du Travail l'enregistrement de toutes ratifications et de tous actes de dénonciation qui lui seront communiqués par les Membres de l'Organisation.

2. When notifying the Members of the Organization of the registration of the last of the ratifications required to bring this Convention into force, the Director-General shall draw the attention of the Members of the Organization to the date upon which the Convention will come into force.

Article 51

The Director-General of the International Labour Office shall communicate to the Secretary-General of the United Nations for registration in accordance with Article 102 of the Charter of the United Nations full particulars of all ratifications and denunciations that have been registered.

Article 52

At such times as it may consider necessary, the Governing Body of the International Labour Office shall present to the General Conference a report on the working of this Convention and shall examine the desirability of placing on the agenda of the Conference the question of its revision.

Article 53

1. Should the Conference adopt a new Convention revising this Convention, then, unless the new Convention otherwise provides:

(a) the ratification by a Member of the new revising Convention shall *ipso jure* involve the immediate denunciation of this Convention, notwithstanding the provisions of Article 49 above, if and when the new revising Convention shall have come into force; and

(b) as from the date when the new revising Convention comes into force, this Convention shall cease to be open to ratification by the Members.

2. This Convention shall in any case remain in force in its actual form and content for those Members which have ratified it but have not ratified the revising Convention.

Article 54

The English and French versions of the text of this Convention are equally authoritative.

2. En notifiant aux Membres de l'Organisation l'enregistrement de la dernière ratification nécessaire à l'entrée en vigueur de la convention, le Directeur général appelle l'attention des Membres de l'Organisation sur la date à laquelle la présente convention entre en vigueur.

Article 51

Le Directeur général du Bureau international du Travail communique au Secrétaire général des Nations Unies, aux fins d'enregistrement, conformément à l'article 102 de la Charte des Nations Unies, des renseignements complets au sujet de toutes ratifications et dénonciations enregistrées.

Article 52

Chaque fois qu'il le jugera nécessaire, le Conseil d'administration du Bureau international du Travail présentera à la Conférence générale un rapport sur l'application de la présente convention et examinera s'il y a lieu d'inscrire à l'ordre du jour de la Conférence la question de sa révision.

Article 53

1. Au cas où la Conférence adopte une nouvelle convention portant révision de la présente convention, et à moins que la nouvelle convention ne dispose autrement:

a) la ratification par un Membre de la nouvelle convention portant révision entraîne de plein droit, nonobstant l'article 49 ci-dessus, la dénonciation immédiate de la présente convention, sous réserve que la nouvelle convention portant révision soit entrée en vigueur ;

b) à partir de la date de l'entrée en vigueur de la nouvelle convention portant révision, la présente convention cesse d'être ouverte à la ratification des Membres.

2. La présente convention demeure en tout cas en vigueur dans sa forme et teneur pour les Membres qui l'auraient ratifiée et qui ne ratifieraient pas la convention portant révision.

Article 54

Les versions française et anglaise de la présente convention font également foi.

ANNEX I

EQUIVALENCE IN MEASUREMENT

For the purpose of this Convention, where the competent authority, after consultation, decides to use length overall (LOA) rather than length (L) as the basis of measurement:

(a) a length overall (LOA) of 16.5 metres shall be considered equivalent to a length (L) of 15 metres;

(b) a length overall (LOA) of 26.5 metres shall be considered equivalent to a length (L) of 24 metres;

(c) a length overall (LOA) of 50 metres shall be considered equivalent to a length (L) of 45 metres.

ANNEXE I

EQUIVALENCE POUR LE MESURAGE

Aux fins de la présente convention, lorsque l'autorité compétente, après consultation, décide d'utiliser la longueur hors tout (LHT) comme critère de mesure plutôt que la longueur (L):

a) une longueur hors tout (LHT) de 16,5 mètres sera considérée comme équivalente à une longueur (L) de 15 mètres;

b) une longueur hors tout (LHT) de 26,5 mètres sera considérée comme équivalente à une longueur (L) de 24 mètres;

c) une longueur hors tout (LHT) de 50 mètres sera considérée comme équivalente à une longueur (L) de 45 mètres.

Annex II

Fisher's work agreement

The fisher's work agreement shall contain the following particulars, except in so far as the inclusion of one or more of them is rendered unnecessary by the fact that the matter is regulated in another manner by national laws or regulations, or a collective bargaining agreement where applicable:

(a) the fisher's family name and other names, date of birth or age, and birthplace;

(b) the place at which and date on which the agreement was concluded;

(c) the name of the fishing vessel or vessels and the registration number of the vessel or vessels on board which the fisher undertakes to work;

(d) the name of the employer, or fishing vessel owner, or other party to the agreement with the fisher;

(e) the voyage or voyages to be undertaken, if this can be determined at the time of making the agreement;

(f) the capacity in which the fisher is to be employed or engaged;

(g) if possible, the place at which and date on which the fisher is required to report on board for service;

(h) the provisions to be supplied to the fisher, unless some alternative system is provided for by national law or regulation;

(i) the amount of wages, or the amount of the share and the method of calculating such share if remuneration is to be on a share basis, or the amount of the wage and share and the method of calculating the latter if remuneration is to be on a combined basis, and any agreed minimum wage;

(j) the termination of the agreement and the conditions thereof, namely:

  (i) if the agreement has been made for a definite period, the date fixed for its expiry;

  (ii) if the agreement has been made for a voyage, the port of destination and the time which has to expire after arrival before the fisher shall be discharged;

  (iii) if the agreement has been made for an indefinite period, the conditions which shall entitle either party to rescind it, as well as the required period of notice for rescission, provided that such period shall not be less for the employer, or fishing vessel owner or other party to the agreement with the fisher;

(k) the protection that will cover the fisher in the event of sickness, injury or death in connection with service;

Annexe II

Accord d'engagement du pêcheur

L'accord d'engagement du pêcheur devra comporter les mentions suivantes, sauf dans les cas où l'inclusion de l'une de ces mentions ou de certaines d'entre elles est inutile, la question étant déjà réglée d'une autre manière par la législation nationale ou, le cas échéant, par une convention collective:

a) les nom et prénoms du pêcheur, la date de naissance ou l'âge, ainsi que le lieu de naissance;

b) le lieu et la date de la conclusion du contrat;

c) la désignation du ou des navires de pêche et le numéro d'immatriculation du ou des navires de pêche à bord duquel ou desquels le pêcheur s'engage à travailler;

d) le nom de l'employeur ou de l'armateur à la pêche ou autre partie à l'accord;

e) le voyage ou les voyages à entreprendre, s'ils peuvent être déterminés au moment de l'engagement;

f) la fonction pour laquelle le pêcheur doit être employé ou engagé;

g) si possible, la date à laquelle et le lieu où le pêcheur sera tenu de se présenter à bord pour le commencement de son service;

h) les vivres à allouer au pêcheur, sauf si la législation nationale prévoit un système différent;

i) le montant du salaire du pêcheur ou, s'il est rémunéré à la part, le pourcentage de sa part et le mode de calcul de celle-ci, ou encore, si un système mixte de rémunération est appliqué, le montant du salaire, le pourcentage de sa part et le mode de calcul de celle-ci, ainsi que tout salaire minimum convenu;

j) l'échéance de l'accord et les conditions y relatives, soit:

   i) si l'accord a été conclu pour une durée déterminée, la date fixée pour son expiration;

   ii) si l'accord a été conclu au voyage, le port de destination convenu pour la fin de l'accord et l'indication du délai à l'expiration duquel le pêcheur sera libéré après l'arrivée à cette destination;

   iii) si l'accord a été conclu pour une durée indéterminée, les conditions dans lesquelles chaque partie pourra dénoncer l'accord ainsi que le délai de préavis requis, lequel n'est pas plus court pour l'employeur, l'armateur à la pêche ou autre partie que pour le pêcheur;

k) la protection en cas de maladie, de lésion ou de décès du pêcheur lié à son service;

(l) the amount of paid annual leave or the formula used for calculating leave, where applicable;

(m) the health and social security coverage and benefits to be provided to the fisher by the employer, fishing vessel owner, or other party or parties to the fisher's work agreement, as applicable;

(n) the fisher's entitlement to repatriation;

(o) a reference to the collective bargaining agreement, where applicable;

(p) the minimum periods of rest, in accordance with national laws, regulations or other measures; and

(q) any other particulars which national law or regulation may require.

l) le congé payé annuel ou la formule utilisée pour le calculer, le cas échéant;

m) les prestations en matière de protection de la santé et de sécurité sociale qui doivent être assurées au pêcheur par l'employeur, l'armateur à la pêche ou autre partie à l'accord d'engagement du pêcheur, selon le cas;

n) le droit du pêcheur à un rapatriement;

o) la référence à la convention collective, le cas échéant;

p) les périodes minimales de repos conformément à la législation nationale ou autres mesures;

q) toutes autres mentions que la législation nationale peut exiger.

ANNEX III

FISHING VESSEL ACCOMMODATION

General provisions

1. The following shall apply to all new, decked fishing vessels, subject to any exclusions provided for in accordance with Article 3 of this Convention. The competent authority may, after consultation, also apply the requirements of this Annex to existing vessels, when and in so far as it determines that this is reasonable and practicable.

2. The competent authority, after consultation, may permit variations to the provisions of this Annex for fishing vessels normally remaining at sea for less than 24 hours where the fishers do not live on board the vessel in port. In the case of such vessels, the competent authority shall ensure that the fishers concerned have adequate facilities for resting, eating and sanitation purposes.

3. Any variations made by a Member under paragraph 2 of this Annex shall be reported to the International Labour Office under article 22 of the Constitution of the International Labour Organisation.

4. The requirements for vessels of 24 metres in length and over may be applied to vessels between 15 and 24 metres in length where the competent authority determines, after consultation, that this is reasonable and practicable.

5. Fishers working on board feeder vessels which do not have appropriate accommodation and sanitary facilities shall be provided with such accommodation and facilities on board the mother vessel.

6. Members may extend the requirements of this Annex regarding noise and vibration, ventilation, heating and air conditioning, and lighting to enclosed working spaces and spaces used for storage if, after consultation, such application is considered appropriate and will not have a negative influence on the function of the process or working conditions or the quality of the catches.

7. The use of gross tonnage as referred to in Article 5 of this Convention is limited to the following specified paragraphs of this Annex: 12, 34, 35, 37, 39, 42, 56 and 61. For these purposes, where the competent authority, after consultation, decides to use gross tonnage (gt) as the basis of measurement:

(a) a gross tonnage of 55 gt shall be considered equivalent to a length (L) of 15 metres or a length overall (LOA) of 16.5 metres;

(b) a gross tonnage of 175 gt shall be considered equivalent to a length (L) of 24 metres or a length overall (LOA) of 26.5 metres;

Annexe III

Logement à bord des navires de pêche

Dispositions générales

1. Les dispositions suivantes s'appliquent à tous les nouveaux navires de pêche pontés, sauf exclusions autorisées aux termes de l'article 3 de la présente convention. L'autorité compétente peut également, après consultation, appliquer les prescriptions de la présente annexe aux navires existants, dès lors que et dans la mesure où elle décide que cela est raisonnable et réalisable.

2. L'autorité compétente peut, après consultation, autoriser des dérogations aux dispositions de la présente annexe pour des navires de pêche ne restant normalement en mer que pour des durées inférieures à 24 heures si les pêcheurs ne vivent pas à bord du navire lorsqu'il est au port. Dans le cas de tels navires, l'autorité compétente doit veiller à ce que les pêcheurs concernés aient à leur disposition des installations adéquates pour leurs repos, alimentation et hygiène.

3. Toute dérogation faite par un Membre en vertu du paragraphe 2 de la présente annexe doit être communiquée au Bureau international du Travail conformément à l'article 22 de la Constitution de l'Organisation internationale du Travail.

4. Les prescriptions valables pour les navires d'une longueur égale ou supérieure à 24 mètres peuvent s'appliquer aux navires d'une longueur comprise entre 15 et 24 mètres si l'autorité compétente décide, après consultation, que cela est raisonnable et réalisable.

5. Les pêcheurs travaillant à bord de navires nourrices dépourvus de logements et d'installations sanitaires appropriés pourront utiliser ceux du navire mère.

6. Les Membres peuvent étendre les dispositions de la présente annexe relatives au bruit et aux vibrations, à la ventilation, au chauffage et à la climatisation, à l'éclairage aux lieux de travail clos et aux espaces servant à l'entreposage si, après consultation, cette extension est considérée appropriée et n'influe pas négativement sur les conditions de travail ou sur le traitement ou la qualité des captures.

7. L'utilisation de la jauge brute visée à l'article 5 de la présente convention est limitée aux paragraphes de la présente annexe spécifiés ci-après: 12, 34, 35, 37, 39, 42, 56 et 61. A ces fins, lorsque l'autorité compétente, après consultation, décide d'utiliser la jauge brute comme critère de mesure:

a) une jauge brute de 55 sera considérée comme équivalente à une longueur (L) de 15 mètres, ou à une longueur hors tout (LHT) de 16,5 mètres;

b) une jauge brute de 175 sera considérée comme équivalente à une longueur (L) de 24 mètres, ou à une longueur hors tout (LHT) de 26,5 mètres;

(c) a gross tonnage of 700 gt shall be considered equivalent to a length (L) of 45 metres or a length overall (LOA) of 50 metres.

Planning and control

8. The competent authority shall satisfy itself that, on every occasion when a vessel is newly constructed or the crew accommodation of a vessel has been reconstructed, such vessel complies with the requirements of this Annex. The competent authority shall, to the extent practicable, require compliance with this Annex for a vessel that changes the flag it flies to the flag of the Member, or when the crew accommodation of a vessel is substantially altered.

9. For the occasions noted in paragraph 8 of this Annex, for vessels of 24 metres in length and over, detailed plans and information concerning accommodation shall be required to be submitted for approval to the competent authority, or an entity authorized by it.

10. For vessels of 24 metres in length and over, on every occasion when the vessel changes the flag it flies to the flag of the Member, or the crew accommodation of the fishing vessel has been reconstructed or substantially altered, the competent authority shall inspect the accommodation for compliance with this Convention. The competent authority may carry out additional inspections of crew accommodation at its discretion.

Design and construction

Headroom

11. There shall be adequate headroom in all accommodation spaces. For spaces where fishers are expected to stand for prolonged periods, the minimum headroom shall be prescribed by the competent authority.

12. For vessels of 24 metres in length and over, the minimum permitted headroom in all accommodation where full and free movement is necessary shall not be less than 200 centimetres. The competent authority may permit some limited reduction in headroom in any space, or part of any space, in such accommodation where it is satisfied that such reduction is reasonable, and will not result in discomfort to the fishers.

Openings into and between accommodation spaces

13. There shall be no direct openings into sleeping rooms from fish rooms and machinery spaces, except for the purpose of emergency escape. Where reasonable and practicable, direct openings from galleys, storerooms,

c) une jauge brute de 700 sera considérée comme équivalente à une longueur (L) de 45 mètres, ou à une longueur hors tout (LHT) de 50 mètres.

Planification et contrôle

8. L'autorité compétente doit vérifier que, chaque fois qu'un navire vient d'être construit, ou que le logement de l'équipage à bord du navire a été refait à neuf, ledit navire est conforme aux prescriptions de la présente annexe. L'autorité compétente doit, dans la mesure du possible, exiger qu'un navire qui remplace son pavillon par le pavillon du Membre ou qu'un navire dont le logement de l'équipage a été substantiellement modifié se conforme aux prescriptions de la présente annexe.

9. Dans les situations visées au paragraphe 8 de la présente annexe, pour les navires d'une longueur égale ou supérieure à 24 mètres, l'autorité compétente doit demander que les plans détaillés du logement de l'équipage et des informations à son sujet soient soumis pour approbation à l'autorité compétente ou à une entité qu'elle a habilitée à cette fin.

10. Pour les navires d'une longueur égale ou supérieure à 24 mètres, l'autorité compétente doit contrôler, chaque fois que le navire remplace son pavillon par le pavillon du Membre ou que le logement de l'équipage a été refait à neuf ou substantiellement modifié, que celui-ci est conforme aux prescriptions de la présente convention. L'autorité compétente peut réaliser, lorsqu'elle le juge opportun, des inspections complémentaires du logement de l'équipage.

Conception et construction

Hauteur sous plafond

11. Tous les logements doivent avoir une hauteur sous plafond adéquate. L'autorité compétente doit prescrire la hauteur sous plafond minimale des locaux où les pêcheurs doivent se tenir debout pendant de longues périodes.

12. Sur les navires d'une longueur égale ou supérieure à 24 mètres, la hauteur sous plafond minimale autorisée dans tous les logements où les pêcheurs doivent pouvoir jouir d'une entière liberté de mouvement ne doit pas être inférieure à 200 centimètres. L'autorité compétente peut autoriser une hauteur sous plafond légèrement inférieure dans tout logement ou partie de logement où elle s'est assurée qu'une telle diminution est raisonnable et ne causera pas d'inconfort aux pêcheurs.

Ouvertures donnant sur les locaux d'habitation et entre eux

13. Les ouvertures directes entre les postes de couchage et les cales à poissons et salles des machines doivent être proscrites, sauf lorsqu'il s'agit d'issues de secours. Dans la mesure où cela est raisonnable et réalisable, les

drying rooms or communal sanitary areas shall be avoided unless expressly provided otherwise.

14. For vessels of 24 metres in length and over, there shall be no direct openings, except for the purpose of emergency escape, into sleeping rooms from fish rooms and machinery spaces or from galleys, storerooms, drying rooms or communal sanitary areas; that part of the bulkhead separating such places from sleeping rooms and external bulkheads shall be efficiently constructed of steel or another approved material and shall be watertight and gas-tight. This provision does not exclude the possibility of sanitary areas being shared between two cabins.

Insulation

15. Accommodation spaces shall be adequately insulated; the materials used to construct internal bulkheads, panelling and sheeting, and floors and joinings shall be suitable for the purpose and shall be conducive to ensuring a healthy environment. Sufficient drainage shall be provided in all accommodation spaces.

Other

16. All practicable measures shall be taken to protect fishing vessels' crew accommodation against flies and other insects, particularly when vessels are operating in mosquito-infested areas.

17. Emergency escapes from all crew accommodation spaces shall be provided as necessary.

Noise and vibration

18. The competent authority shall take measures to limit excessive noise and vibration in accommodation spaces and, as far as practicable, in accordance with relevant international standards.

19. For vessels of 24 metres in length and over, the competent authority shall adopt standards for noise and vibration in accommodation spaces which shall ensure adequate protection to fishers from the effects of such noise and vibration, including the effects of noise- and vibration-induced fatigue.

Ventilation

20. Accommodation spaces shall be ventilated, taking into account climatic conditions. The system of ventilation shall supply air in a satisfactory condition whenever fishers are on board.

ouvertures directes entre les postes de couchage et les cuisines, cambuses, séchoirs ou installations sanitaires communes doivent être évitées, à moins qu'il n'en soit expressément disposé autrement.

14. Sur les navires d'une longueur égale ou supérieure à 24 mètres, il ne doit y avoir aucune ouverture reliant directement les postes de couchage aux cales à poissons, salles des machines, cuisines, cambuses, séchoirs ou installations sanitaires communes, sauf lorsqu'il s'agit d'issues de secours; la partie de la cloison séparant ces locaux des postes de couchage et des cloisons externes doit être convenablement construite en acier ou autre matériau homologué et être étanche à l'eau et aux gaz. La présente disposition n'exclut pas la possibilité d'un partage d'installations sanitaires entre deux cabines.

Isolation

15. L'isolation du logement de l'équipage doit être adéquate; les matériaux employés pour construire les cloisons, les panneaux et les vaigrages intérieurs, ainsi que les revêtements de sol et les joints doivent être adaptés à leur emploi et de nature à garantir un environnement sain. Des dispositifs d'écoulement des eaux suffisants doivent être prévus dans tous les logements.

Autres

16. Tous les moyens possibles doivent être mis en œuvre pour empêcher que les mouches et autres insectes ne pénètrent dans les locaux d'habitation de l'équipage des navires de pêche, en particulier lorsque ceux-ci opèrent dans des zones infestées de moustiques.

17. Tous les logements d'équipage doivent être dotés des issues de secours nécessaires.

Bruits et vibrations

18. L'autorité compétente doit prendre des mesures pour réduire les bruits et vibrations excessifs dans les locaux d'habitation, si possible en conformité avec les normes internationales pertinentes.

19. Sur les navires d'une longueur égale ou supérieure à 24 mètres, l'autorité compétente doit adopter des normes réglementant les niveaux de bruit et de vibrations dans les locaux d'habitation de manière à protéger adéquatement les pêcheurs des effets nocifs de ces bruits et vibrations, notamment de la fatigue qu'ils induisent.

Ventilation

20. Les locaux d'habitation doivent être ventilés en fonction des conditions climatiques. Le système de ventilation doit permettre une aération satisfaisante des locaux lorsque les pêcheurs sont à bord.

21. Ventilation arrangements or other measures shall be such as to protect non-smokers from tobacco smoke.

22. Vessels of 24 metres in length and over shall be equipped with a system of ventilation for accommodation, which shall be controlled so as to maintain the air in a satisfactory condition and to ensure sufficiency of air movement in all weather conditions and climates. Ventilation systems shall be in operation at all times when fishers are on board.

Heating and air conditioning

23. Accommodation spaces shall be adequately heated, taking into account climatic conditions.

24. For vessels of 24 metres in length and over, adequate heat shall be provided, through an appropriate heating system, except in fishing vessels operating exclusively in tropical climates. The system of heating shall provide heat in all conditions, as necessary, and shall be in operation when fishers are living or working on board, and when conditions so require.

25. For vessels of 24 metres in length and over, with the exception of those regularly engaged in areas where temperate climatic conditions do not require it, air conditioning shall be provided in accommodation spaces, the bridge, the radio room and any centralized machinery control room.

Lighting

26. All accommodation spaces shall be provided with adequate light.

27. Wherever practicable, accommodation spaces shall be lit with natural light in addition to artificial light. Where sleeping spaces have natural light, a means of blocking the light shall be provided.

28. Adequate reading light shall be provided for every berth in addition to the normal lighting of the sleeping room.

29. Emergency lighting shall be provided in sleeping rooms.

30. Where a vessel is not fitted with emergency lighting in mess rooms, passageways, and any spaces that are or may be used for emergency escape, permanent night lighting shall be provided in such spaces.

31. For vessels of 24 metres in length and over, lighting in accommodation spaces shall meet a standard established by the competent authority. In any part of the accommodation space available for free movement, the minimum standard for such lighting shall be such as to permit a person with normal vision to read an ordinary newspaper on a clear day.

21. Le système de ventilation doit être conçu ou d'autres mesures doivent être prises de manière à protéger les non-fumeurs de la fumée de tabac.

22. Les navires d'une longueur égale ou supérieure à 24 mètres doivent être équipés d'un système de ventilation réglable des emménagements, de façon à maintenir l'air dans des conditions satisfaisantes et à en assurer une circulation suffisante par tous les temps et sous tous les climats. Les systèmes de ventilation doivent fonctionner en permanence lorsque les pêcheurs sont à bord.

Chauffage et climatisation

23. Les locaux d'habitation doivent être chauffés de manière adéquate en fonction des conditions climatiques.

24. Sur les navires d'une longueur égale ou supérieure à 24 mètres, un chauffage adéquat fourni par un système de chauffage approprié doit être prévu sauf sur les navires de pêche opérant exclusivement en zone tropicale. Le système de chauffage doit fournir de la chaleur dans toutes les conditions, suivant les besoins, et fonctionner lorsque les pêcheurs séjournent ou travaillent à bord et que les conditions l'exigent.

25. Sur les navires d'une longueur égale ou supérieure à 24 mètres, à l'exception de ceux opérant dans des zones où les conditions climatiques tempérées ne l'exigent pas, les locaux d'habitation, la passerelle, les salles de radio et toute salle de contrôle des machines centralisée doivent être équipés d'un système de climatisation.

Eclairage

26. Tous les locaux d'habitation doivent bénéficier d'un éclairage adéquat.

27. Dans la mesure du possible, les locaux d'habitation doivent, outre un éclairage artificiel, être éclairés par la lumière naturelle. Lorsque les postes de couchage sont éclairés par la lumière naturelle, un moyen de l'occulter doit être prévu.

28. Chaque couchette doit être dotée d'un éclairage de chevet en complément de l'éclairage normal du poste de couchage.

29. Les postes de couchage doivent être équipés d'un éclairage de secours.

30. Si à bord d'un navire les réfectoires, les coursives et les locaux qui sont ou peuvent être traversés comme issues de secours ne sont pas équipés d'un éclairage de secours, un éclairage permanent doit y être prévu pendant la nuit.

31. Sur les navires d'une longueur égale ou supérieure à 24 mètres, les locaux d'habitation doivent être éclairés conformément à une norme établie par l'autorité compétente. En tous points du local d'habitation où l'on peut circuler librement, la norme minimale de cet éclairage doit être telle qu'une personne dotée d'une acuité visuelle normale puisse lire, par temps clair, un journal imprimé ordinaire.

Sleeping rooms

General

32. Where the design, dimensions or purpose of the vessel allow, the sleeping accommodation shall be located so as to minimize the effects of motion and acceleration but shall in no case be located forward of the collision bulkhead.

Floor area

33. The number of persons per sleeping room and the floor area per person, excluding space occupied by berths and lockers, shall be such as to provide adequate space and comfort for the fishers on board, taking into account the service of the vessel.

34. For vessels of 24 metres in length and over but which are less than 45 metres in length, the floor area per person of sleeping rooms, excluding space occupied by berths and lockers, shall not be less than 1.5 square metres.

35. For vessels of 45 metres in length and over, the floor area per person of sleeping rooms, excluding space occupied by berths and lockers, shall not be less than 2 square metres.

Persons per sleeping room

36. To the extent not expressly provided otherwise, the number of persons allowed to occupy each sleeping room shall not be more than six.

37. For vessels of 24 metres in length and over, the number of persons allowed to occupy each sleeping room shall not be more than four. The competent authority may permit exceptions to this requirement in particular cases if the size, type or intended service of the vessel makes the requirement unreasonable or impracticable.

38. To the extent not expressly provided otherwise, a separate sleeping room or sleeping rooms shall be provided for officers, wherever practicable.

39. For vessels of 24 metres in length and over, sleeping rooms for officers shall be for one person wherever possible and in no case shall the sleeping room contain more than two berths. The competent authority may permit exceptions to the requirements of this paragraph in particular cases if the size, type or intended service of the vessel makes the requirements unreasonable or impracticable.

Postes de couchage

Dispositions générales

32. Lorsque la conception, les dimensions ou l'usage même du navire le permet, les postes de couchage doivent être situés de telle manière que les mouvements et l'accélération du navire soient ressentis le moins possible mais ils ne doivent être situés en aucun cas en avant de la cloison d'abordage.

Superficie au sol

33. Le nombre de personnes par poste de couchage ainsi que la superficie au sol par personne, déduction faite de la superficie occupée par les couchettes et les armoires, doivent permettre aux pêcheurs de disposer de suffisamment d'espace et de confort à bord, compte tenu de l'utilisation du navire.

34. Sur les navires d'une longueur égale ou supérieure à 24 mètres, mais d'une longueur inférieure à 45 mètres, la superficie au sol par occupant d'un poste de couchage, déduction faite de la superficie occupée par les couchettes et les armoires, ne doit pas être inférieure à 1,5 mètre carré.

35. Sur les navires d'une longueur égale ou supérieure à 45 mètres, la superficie au sol par occupant d'un poste de couchage, déduction faite de la superficie occupée par les couchettes et les armoires, ne doit pas être inférieure à 2 mètres carrés.

Nombre de personnes par poste de couchage

36. Dans la mesure où il n'en est pas expressément disposé autrement, le nombre de personnes autorisées à occuper un poste de couchage ne doit pas être supérieur à six.

37. Sur les navires d'une longueur égale ou supérieure à 24 mètres, le nombre de personnes autorisées à occuper un poste de couchage ne doit pas être supérieur à quatre. L'autorité compétente peut accorder des dérogations à cette prescription dans certains cas si la taille et le type du navire ou son utilisation la rendent déraisonnable ou irréalisable.

38. Dans la mesure où il n'en est pas expressément disposé autrement, une ou plusieurs cabines séparées doivent être réservées aux officiers, lorsque cela est possible.

39. Sur les navires d'une longueur égale ou supérieure à 24 mètres, les postes de couchage réservés aux officiers doivent accueillir une seule personne dans la mesure du possible et ne doivent en aucun cas contenir plus de deux couchettes. L'autorité compétente peut accorder des dérogations aux prescriptions de ce paragraphe dans certains cas si la taille et le type du navire ou son utilisation les rendent déraisonnables ou irréalisables.

Other

40. The maximum number of persons to be accommodated in any sleeping room shall be legibly and indelibly marked in a place in the room where it can be conveniently seen.

41. The members of the crew shall be provided with individual berths of appropriate dimensions. Mattresses shall be of a suitable material.

42. For vessels of 24 metres in length and over, the minimum inside dimensions of the berths shall not be less than 198 by 80 centimetres.

43. Sleeping rooms shall be so planned and equipped as to ensure reasonable comfort for the occupants and to facilitate tidiness. Equipment provided shall include berths, individual lockers sufficient for clothing and other personal effects, and a suitable writing surface.

44. For vessels of 24 metres in length and over, a desk suitable for writing, with a chair, shall be provided.

45. Sleeping accommodation shall be situated or equipped, as practicable, so as to provide appropriate levels of privacy for men and for women.

Mess rooms

46. Mess rooms shall be as close as possible to the galley, but in no case shall be located forward of the collision bulkhead.

47. Vessels shall be provided with mess-room accommodation suitable for their service. To the extent not expressly provided otherwise, mess-room accommodation shall be separate from sleeping quarters, where practicable.

48. For vessels of 24 metres in length and over, mess-room accommodation shall be separate from sleeping quarters.

49. The dimensions and equipment of each mess room shall be sufficient for the number of persons likely to use it at any one time.

50. For vessels of 24 metres in length and over, a refrigerator of sufficient capacity and facilities for making hot and cold drinks shall be available and accessible to fishers at all times.

Sanitary accommodation

51. Sanitary facilities, which include toilets, washbasins, and tubs or showers, shall be provided for all persons on board, as appropriate for the

Autres

40. Le nombre maximal de personnes autorisées à occuper un poste de couchage doit être inscrit de manière lisible et indélébile à un endroit où il peut se lire facilement.

41. Les membres d'équipage doivent disposer d'une couchette individuelle de dimensions suffisantes. Les matelas doivent être d'un matériau adéquat.

42. Sur les navires d'une longueur égale ou supérieure à 24 mètres, les dimensions internes minimales des couchettes ne doivent pas être inférieures à 198 centimètres sur 80 centimètres.

43. Les postes de couchage doivent être conçus et équipés de manière à garantir aux occupants un confort raisonnable et à faciliter leur maintien en ordre. Les équipements fournis doivent comprendre des couchettes, des armoires individuelles suffisamment grandes pour contenir des vêtements et autres effets personnels et une surface plane adéquate où il est possible d'écrire.

44. Sur les navires d'une longueur égale ou supérieure à 24 mètres, un bureau pour écrire et une chaise adaptés doivent être fournis.

45. Les postes de couchage doivent, dans la mesure du possible, être situés ou équipés de telle manière que tant les hommes que les femmes puissent convenablement préserver leur intimité.

Réfectoires

46. Les réfectoires doivent être aussi proches que possible de la cuisine, mais en aucun cas en avant de la cloison d'abordage.

47. Les navires doivent posséder un réfectoire adapté à leur utilisation. Le local du réfectoire doit être si possible à l'écart des postes de couchage, dans la mesure où il n'en est pas expressément disposé autrement.

48. Sur les navires d'une longueur égale ou supérieure à 24 mètres, le réfectoire doit être séparé des postes de couchage.

49. Les dimensions et l'aménagement de chaque réfectoire doivent être suffisants pour qu'il puisse accueillir le nombre de personnes susceptibles de l'utiliser en même temps.

50. Sur les navires d'une longueur égale ou supérieure à 24 mètres, les pêcheurs doivent à tout moment avoir accès à un réfrigérateur d'un volume suffisant et avoir la possibilité de se préparer des boissons chaudes ou froides.

Installations sanitaires

51. Des installations sanitaires appropriées à l'utilisation du navire, qui comprennent des toilettes, lavabos, baignoires ou douches, doivent être

service of the vessel. These facilities shall meet at least minimum standards of health and hygiene and reasonable standards of quality.

52. The sanitary accommodation shall be such as to eliminate contamination of other spaces as far as practicable. The sanitary facilities used by women fishers shall allow for reasonable privacy.

53. Cold fresh water and hot fresh water shall be available to all fishers and other persons on board, in sufficient quantities to allow for proper hygiene. The competent authority may establish, after consultation, the minimum amount of water to be provided.

54. Where sanitary facilities are provided, they shall be fitted with ventilation to the open air, independent of any other part of the accommodation.

55. All surfaces in sanitary accommodation shall be such as to facilitate easy and effective cleaning. Floors shall have a non-slip deck covering.

56. On vessels of 24 metres in length and over, for all fishers who do not occupy rooms to which sanitary facilities are attached, there shall be provided at least one tub or shower or both, one toilet, and one washbasin for every four persons or fewer.

Laundry facilities

57. Amenities for washing and drying clothes shall be provided as necessary, taking into account the service of the vessel, to the extent not expressly provided otherwise.

58. For vessels of 24 metres in length and over, adequate facilities for washing, drying and ironing clothes shall be provided.

59. For vessels of 45 metres in length and over, adequate facilities for washing, drying and ironing clothes shall be provided in a compartment separate from sleeping rooms, mess rooms and toilets, and shall be adequately ventilated, heated and equipped with lines or other means for drying clothes.

Facilities for sick and injured fishers

60. Whenever necessary, a cabin shall be made available for a fisher who suffers illness or injury.

61. For vessels of 45 metres in length and over, there shall be a separate sick bay. The space shall be properly equipped and shall be maintained in a hygienic state.

prévues pour toutes les personnes à bord. Ces installations doivent correspondre aux normes minimales en matière de santé et d'hygiène et offrir un niveau de qualité raisonnable.

52. Les installations sanitaires doivent être conçues de manière à éliminer dans la mesure où cela est réalisable la contamination d'autres locaux. Les installations sanitaires utilisées par les pêcheuses doivent leur préserver un degré d'intimité raisonnable.

53. Tous les pêcheurs et toute autre personne à bord doivent avoir accès à de l'eau douce froide et chaude en quantité suffisante pour assurer une hygiène convenable. L'autorité compétente peut déterminer, après consultation, le volume d'eau minimal nécessaire.

54. Lorsque des installations sanitaires sont prévues, elles doivent être ventilées vers l'extérieur et situées à l'écart de tout local d'habitation.

55. Toutes les surfaces des installations sanitaires doivent être faciles à nettoyer correctement. Les sols doivent être recouverts d'un revêtement antidérapant.

56. Sur les navires d'une longueur égale ou supérieure à 24 mètres, tous les pêcheurs n'occupant pas un poste doté d'installations sanitaires doivent avoir accès au moins à une baignoire ou une douche, ou les deux, une toilette et un lavabo pour quatre personnes ou moins.

Buanderies

57. Dans la mesure où il n'en est pas expressément disposé autrement, des installations appropriées pour le lavage et le séchage des vêtements doivent être prévues selon les besoins, en tenant compte des conditions d'utilisation du navire.

58. Sur les navires d'une longueur égale ou supérieure à 24 mètres, des installations adéquates pour le lavage, le séchage et le repassage des vêtements doivent être prévues.

59. Sur les navires d'une longueur égale ou supérieure à 45 mètres, ces installations doivent être adéquates et situées dans des locaux séparés des postes de couchage, des réfectoires et des toilettes qui soient suffisamment ventilés, chauffés et pourvus de cordes à linge ou autres moyens de séchage.

Installations pour les pêcheurs malades ou blessés

60. Chaque fois que nécessaire, une cabine doit être mise à la disposition d'un pêcheur blessé ou malade.

61. Sur les navires d'une longueur égale ou supérieure à 45 mètres, une infirmerie séparée doit être prévue. Ce local doit être correctement équipé et maintenu dans un état hygiénique.

Other facilities

62. A place for hanging foul-weather gear and other personal protective equipment shall be provided outside of, but convenient to, sleeping rooms.

Bedding, mess utensils and miscellaneous provisions

63. Appropriate eating utensils, and bedding and other linen shall be provided to all fishers on board. However, the cost of the linen can be recovered as an operational cost if the collective agreement or the fisher's work agreement so provides.

Recreational facilities

64. For vessels of 24 metres in length and over, appropriate recreational facilities, amenities and services shall be provided for all fishers on board. Where appropriate, mess rooms may be used for recreational activities.

Communication facilities

65. All fishers on board shall be given reasonable access to communication facilities, to the extent practicable, at a reasonable cost and not exceeding the full cost to the fishing vessel owner.

Galley and food storage facilities

66. Cooking equipment shall be provided on board. To the extent not expressly provided otherwise, this equipment shall be fitted, where practicable, in a separate galley.

67. The galley, or cooking area where a separate galley is not provided, shall be of adequate size for the purpose, well lit and ventilated, and properly equipped and maintained.

68. For vessels of 24 metres in length and over, there shall be a separate galley.

69. The containers of butane or propane gas used for cooking purposes in a galley shall be kept on the open deck and in a shelter which is designed to protect them from external heat sources and external impact.

70. A suitable place for provisions of adequate capacity shall be provided which can be kept dry, cool and well ventilated in order to avoid deterioration of the stores and, to the extent not expressly provided otherwise, refrigerators or other low-temperature storage shall be used, where possible.

71. For vessels of 24 metres in length and over, a provisions storeroom and refrigerator and other low-temperature storage shall be used.

Autres installations

62. Un endroit approprié à l'extérieur des postes de couchage et aisément accessible à partir de ces derniers doit être prévu pour pendre les vêtements de gros temps et autre équipement de protection personnel.

Literie, vaisselle et couverts et fournitures diverses

63. Tous les pêcheurs à bord doivent avoir à leur disposition de la vaisselle, du linge de lit et autres linges appropriés. Toutefois, les frais de linge peuvent être recouvrés sous forme de coûts d'exploitation pour autant qu'une convention collective ou que l'accord d'engagement du pêcheur le prévoie.

Installations de loisirs

64. A bord des navires d'une longueur égale ou supérieure à 24 mètres, tous les pêcheurs doivent avoir accès à des installations, des équipements et des services de loisirs. Le cas échéant, les réfectoires peuvent être utilisés comme installations de loisirs.

Installations de communications

65. Dans la mesure du possible, tous les pêcheurs à bord du navire doivent avoir raisonnablement accès à des équipements pour effectuer leurs communications à un coût raisonnable n'excédant pas le coût total facturé à l'armateur à la pêche.

Cuisine et cambuse

66. Des équipements doivent être prévus pour la préparation des aliments. Dans la mesure où il n'en est pas expressément disposé autrement, ces équipements sont installés, si possible, dans une cuisine séparée.

67. La cuisine, ou coin cuisine lorsqu'il n'existe pas de cuisine séparée, doit être d'une dimension adéquate, être bien éclairée et ventilée et être correctement équipée et entretenue.

68. Les navires d'une longueur égale ou supérieure à 24 mètres doivent être équipés d'une cuisine séparée.

69. Les bouteilles de gaz butane ou propane utilisé à des fins de cuisine doivent être placées sur le pont découvert, dans un lieu abrité conçu pour les protéger contre les sources extérieures de chaleur et les chocs.

70. Un emplacement adéquat pour les provisions, d'un volume suffisant, doit être prévu et pouvoir être maintenu sec, frais et bien aéré pour éviter que les provisions ne se gâtent. Dans la mesure où il n'en est pas expressément disposé autrement, des réfrigérateurs ou autres moyens de stockage à basse température sont si possible utilisés.

71. Pour les navires d'une longueur égale ou supérieure à 24 mètres, une cambuse et un réfrigérateur ou autre local d'entreposage à basse température doivent être utilisés.

Food and potable water

72. Food and potable water shall be sufficient, having regard to the number of fishers, and the duration and nature of the voyage. In addition, they shall be suitable in respect of nutritional value, quality, quantity and variety, having regard as well to the fishers' religious requirements and cultural practices in relation to food.

73. The competent authority may establish requirements for the minimum standards and quantity of food and water to be carried on board.

Clean and habitable conditions

74. Accommodation shall be maintained in a clean and habitable condition and shall be kept free of goods and stores which are not the personal property of the occupants.

75. Galley and food storage facilities shall be maintained in a hygienic condition.

76. Waste shall be kept in closed, well-sealed containers and removed from food-handling areas whenever necessary.

Inspections by the skipper or under the authority of the skipper

77. For vessels of 24 metres in length and over, the competent authority shall require frequent inspections to be carried out, by or under the authority of the skipper, to ensure that:

(a) accommodation is clean, decently habitable and safe, and is maintained in a good state of repair;

(b) food and water supplies are sufficient; and

(c) galley and food storage spaces and equipment are hygienic and in a proper state of repair.

The results of such inspections, and the actions taken to address any deficiencies found, shall be recorded and available for review.

Variations

78. The competent authority, after consultation, may permit derogations from the provisions in this Annex to take into account, without discrimination, the interests of fishers having differing and distinctive religious and social practices, on condition that such derogations do not result in overall conditions less favourable than those which would result from the application of this Annex.

Nourriture et eau potable

72. L'avitaillement doit être suffisant compte tenu du nombre de pêcheurs à bord ainsi que de la durée et de la nature du voyage. Il doit être en outre d'une valeur nutritionnelle, d'une qualité, d'une quantité et d'une variété satisfaisantes eu égard également aux exigences de la religion des pêcheurs et à leurs habitudes culturelles en matière alimentaire.

73. L'autorité compétente peut établir des prescriptions concernant les normes minimales et la quantité de nourriture et d'eau devant être disponible à bord.

Conditions de salubrité et de propreté

74. Le logement des pêcheurs doit être maintenu dans un état de propreté et de salubrité et ne doit contenir ni bien ni marchandise qui ne soit pas la propriété personnelle des occupants.

75. La cuisine et les installations d'entreposage des aliments doivent être maintenues dans des conditions hygiéniques.

76. Les déchets doivent être gardés dans des conteneurs fermés et hermétiques qui sont retirés, quand il y a lieu, des espaces de manutention des vivres.

Inspections effectuées par le patron ou sous son autorité

77. Sur les navires d'une longueur égale ou supérieure à 24 mètres, l'autorité compétente doit exiger que des inspections fréquentes soient conduites par le patron ou sous son autorité pour assurer que:

a) les logements sont propres, décemment habitables, sûrs et maintenus en bon état;

b) les provisions d'eau et de nourriture sont suffisantes;

c) la cuisine, la cambuse et les équipements servant à l'entreposage de la nourriture sont hygiéniques et bien entretenus.

Les résultats de ces inspections ainsi que les mesures prises pour remédier à toute défaillance sont consignés et sont disponibles pour consultation.

Dérogations

78. L'autorité compétente peut, après consultation, permettre des dérogations aux dispositions de la présente annexe pour tenir compte, sans discrimination, des intérêts des pêcheurs ayant des pratiques religieuses et sociales différentes et particulières, sous réserve qu'il n'en résulte pas des conditions qui, dans l'ensemble, seraient moins favorables que celles qui auraient découlé de l'application de l'annexe.

No. 19A — Thursday, 16 June 2005
Nº 19A — Jeudi 16 juin 2005

 International Labour Conference

Record of Proceedings

Ninety-third Session, Geneva, 2005

19B

 Conférence internationale du Travail

Compte rendu des travaux

Quatre-vingt-treizième session, Genève, 2005

TEXT OF THE RECOMMENDATION CONCERNING
WORK IN THE FISHING SECTOR
SUBMITTED BY THE DRAFTING COMMITTEE

TEXTE DE LA RECOMMANDATION CONCERNANT
LE TRAVAIL DANS LE SECTEUR DE LA PÊCHE
PRÉSENTÉ PAR LE COMITÉ DE RÉDACTION

TEXT OF THE RECOMMENDATION CONCERNING WORK IN THE FISHING SECTOR

The General Conference of the International Labour Organization,

Having been convened at Geneva by the Governing Body of the International Labour Office, and having met in its 93rd Session on 31 May 2005, and

Taking into account the need to revise the Hours of Work (Fishing) Recommendation, 1920, and

Having decided upon the adoption of certain proposals with regard to work in the fishing sector, which is the fifth item on the agenda of the session, and

Having determined that these proposals shall take the form of a Recommendation supplementing the Work in Fishing Convention, 2005 (hereinafter referred to as "the Convention");

adopts this   day of June of the year two thousand and five the following Recommendation, which may be cited as the Work in Fishing Recommendation, 2005.

PART I. CONDITIONS FOR WORK ON BOARD FISHING VESSELS

Protection of young persons

1. Members should establish the requirements for the pre-sea training of persons between the ages of 16 and 18 working on board fishing vessels, taking into account international instruments concerning training for work on board fishing vessels, including occupational safety and health issues such as night work, hazardous tasks, work with dangerous machinery, manual handling and transport of heavy loads, work in high latitudes, work for excessive periods of time and other relevant issues identified after an assessment of the risks concerned.

2. The training of persons between the ages of 16 and 18 might be provided through participation in an apprenticeship or approved training programme, which should operate under established rules and be monitored by the competent authority, and should not interfere with the person's general education.

3. Members should take measures to ensure that the safety, lifesaving and survival equipment carried on board fishing vessels carrying persons under the age of 18 is appropriate for the size of such persons.

TEXTE DE LA RECOMMANDATION CONCERNANT LE TRAVAIL DANS LE SECTEUR DE LA PÊCHE

La Conférence générale de l'Organisation internationale du Travail,

Convoquée à Genève par le Conseil d'administration du Bureau international du Travail, et s'y étant réunie le 31 mai 2005, en sa quatre-vingt-treizième session;

Tenant compte de la nécessité de réviser la recommandation sur la durée du travail (pêche), 1920;

Après avoir décidé d'adopter diverses propositions relatives au travail dans le secteur de la pêche, question qui constitue le cinquième point à l'ordre du jour de la session;

Après avoir décidé que ces propositions prendraient la forme d'une recommandation complétant la convention sur le travail dans la pêche, 2005 (ci-après dénommée «la convention»),

adopte, ce   jour de juin deux mille cinq, la recommandation ci-après, qui sera dénommée Recommandation sur le travail dans la pêche, 2005.

PARTIE I. CONDITIONS DE TRAVAIL À BORD DES NAVIRES DE PÊCHE

Protection des adolescents

1. Les Membres devraient fixer les conditions requises en matière de formation préalable à l'embarquement des personnes âgées de 16 à 18 ans appelées à travailler à bord des navires de pêche, en prenant en considération les instruments internationaux relatifs à la formation au travail à bord de ces navires, notamment pour ce qui a trait aux questions de sécurité et de santé au travail telles que le travail de nuit, les tâches dangereuses, l'utilisation de machines dangereuses, la manutention et le transport de lourdes charges, le travail effectué sous des latitudes élevées, la durée excessive du travail et autres questions pertinentes recensées après évaluation des risques encourus.

2. La formation des personnes âgées de 16 à 18 ans pourrait être assurée par le biais de l'apprentissage ou de la participation à des programmes de formation approuvés, qui devraient être menés selon des règles établies sous la supervision des autorités compétentes et ne devraient pas nuire à la possibilité pour les personnes concernées de suivre les programmes de l'enseignement général.

3. Les Membres devraient prendre des mesures visant à garantir qu'à bord des navires de pêche qui embarquent des jeunes âgés de moins de 18 ans les équipements de sécurité, de sauvetage et de survie soient adaptés à leur taille.

4. The working hours of fishers under the age of 18 should not exceed eight hours per day and 40 hours per week, and they should not work overtime except where unavoidable for safety reasons.

5. Fishers under the age of 18 should be assured sufficient time for all meals and a break of at least one hour for the main meal of the day.

Medical examination

6. When prescribing the nature of the examination, Members should pay due regard to the age of the person to be examined and the nature of the duties to be performed.

7. The medical certificate should be signed by a medical practitioner approved by the competent authority.

8. Arrangements should be made to enable a person who, after examination, is determined to be unfit for work on board fishing vessels or certain types of fishing vessels, or for certain types of work on board, to apply for a further examination by a medical referee or referees who should be independent of any fishing vessel owner or of any organization of fishing vessel owners or fishers.

9. The competent authority should take into account international guidance on medical examination and certification of persons working at sea, such as the (ILO/WHO) *Guidelines for Conducting Pre-sea and Periodic Medical Fitness Examinations for Seafarers.*

10. For fishers exempted from the application of the provisions concerning medical examination in the Convention, the competent authority should take adequate measures to provide health surveillance for the purpose of occupational safety and health.

Competency and training

11. Members should:

(a) take into account generally accepted international standards concerning training and competencies of fishers in determining the competencies required for skippers, mates, engineers and other persons working on board fishing vessels;

(b) address the following issues, with regard to the vocational training of fishers: national planning and administration, including coordination; financing and training standards; training programmes, including pre-vocational training and also short courses for working fishers; methods of training; and international cooperation; and

(c) ensure that there is no discrimination with regard to access to training.

4. Les pêcheurs âgés de moins de 18 ans ne devraient pas travailler plus de huit heures par jour ni plus de quarante heures par semaine, et ne devraient pas effectuer d'heures supplémentaires à moins que cela ne soit inévitable pour des raisons de sécurité.

5. Les pêcheurs âgés de moins de 18 ans devraient être assurés qu'une pause suffisante leur soit accordée pour chacun des repas et bénéficier d'une pause d'au moins une heure pour prendre leur repas principal.

Examen médical

6. Aux fins de la détermination de la nature de l'examen, les Membres devraient tenir compte de l'âge de l'intéressé ainsi que de la nature du travail à effectuer.

7. Le certificat médical devrait être signé par du personnel médical agréé par l'autorité compétente.

8. Des dispositions devraient être prises pour permettre à toute personne qui, après avoir été examinée, est considérée comme inapte à travailler à bord d'un navire de pêche ou de certains types de navires de pêche, ou à effectuer certains types de tâches à bord, de demander à être examinée par un ou plusieurs arbitres médicaux indépendants de tout armateur à la pêche ou de toute organisation d'armateurs à la pêche ou de pêcheurs.

9. L'autorité compétente devrait tenir compte des directives internationales relatives à l'examen médical et au brevet d'aptitude physique des personnes travaillant en mer, telles que les *Directives relatives à la conduite des examens médicaux d'aptitude précédant l'embarquement et des examens médicaux périodiques des gens de mer* (OIT/OMS).

10. L'autorité compétente devrait prendre des mesures adéquates pour que les pêcheurs auxquels ne s'appliquent pas les dispositions relatives à l'examen médical prescrites dans la convention soient médicalement suivis aux fins de la santé et sécurité au travail.

Compétence et formation

11. Les Membres devraient:

a) prendre en compte les normes internationales généralement admises en matière de formation et de qualifications des pêcheurs en définissant les compétences requises pour exercer les fonctions de patron, d'officier de pont, de mécanicien et autres fonctions à bord d'un navire de pêche;

b) examiner les questions suivantes relatives à la formation professionnelle des pêcheurs: organisation et administration nationales, y compris la coordination; financement et normes de formation; programmes de formation, y compris la formation pré-professionnelle ainsi que les cours de courte durée destinés aux pêcheurs en activité; méthodes de formation; et coopération internationale;

c) s'assurer qu'il n'existe pas de discrimination en matière d'accès à la formation.

Part II. Conditions of Service

Record of service

12. At the end of each contract, a record of service in regard to that contract should be made available to the fisher concerned, or entered in the fisher's service book.

Special measures

13. For fishers excluded from the scope of the Convention, the competent authority should take measures to provide them with adequate protection with respect to their conditions of work and means of dispute settlement.

Payment of fishers

14. Fishers should have the right to advances against earnings under prescribed conditions.

15. For vessels of 24 metres in length and over, all fishers should be entitled to minimum payment in accordance with national laws, regulations or collective agreements.

Part III. Accomodation

16. When establishing requirements or guidance, the competent authority should take into account relevant international guidance on accommodation, food, and health and hygiene relating to persons working or living on board vessels, including the most recent editions of the (FAO/ILO/IMO) *Code of Safety for Fishermen and Fishing Vessels* and the (FAO/ILO/IMO) *Voluntary Guidelines for the Design, Construction and Equipment of Small Fishing Vessels.*

17. The competent authority should work with relevant organizations and agencies to develop and disseminate educational material and on-board information and guidance concerning safe and healthy accommodation and food on board fishing vessels.

18. Inspections of crew accommodation required by the competent authority should be carried out together with initial or periodic surveys or inspections for other purposes.

Design and construction

19. Adequate insulation should be provided for exposed decks over crew accommodation spaces, external bulkheads of sleeping rooms and mess rooms, machinery casings and boundary bulkheads of galleys and other

Partie II. Conditions de service

Relevé des états de service

12. A la fin de chaque contrat, un relevé des états de service concernant ce contrat devrait être mis à la disposition de chaque pêcheur concerné ou noté dans son livret de travail.

Mesures spéciales

13. Pour les pêcheurs exclus du champ d'application de la convention, l'autorité compétente devrait prendre des mesures prévoyant une protection adéquate en ce qui concerne leurs conditions de travail et des mécanismes de règlement des différends.

Paiement des pêcheurs

14. Les pêcheurs devraient avoir le droit au versement d'avances à valoir sur leurs gains dans des conditions déterminées.

15. Pour les navires d'une longueur égale ou supérieure à 24 mètres, tous les pêcheurs devraient avoir droit à un paiement minimal, conformément à la législation nationale ou aux conventions collectives.

Partie III. Logement

16. Lors de l'élaboration de prescriptions ou directives, l'autorité compétente devrait tenir compte des directives internationales applicables en matière de logement, d'alimentation, et de santé et d'hygiène concernant les personnes qui travaillent ou qui vivent à bord de navires, y compris l'édition la plus récente du *Recueil de règles de sécurité pour les pêcheurs et les navires de pêche* (FAO/OIT/OMI) ainsi que des *Directives facultatives pour la conception, la construction et l'équipement des navires de pêche de faibles dimensions* (FAO/OIT/OMI).

17. L'autorité compétente devrait travailler avec les organisations et agences pertinentes pour élaborer et diffuser des documents pédagogiques et des informations disponibles à bord du navire ainsi que des instructions sur ce qui constitue une alimentation et un logement sûrs et sains à bord des navires de pêche.

18. Les inspections du logement de l'équipage prescrites par l'autorité compétente devraient être entreprises conjointement aux enquêtes ou inspections initiales ou périodiques menées à d'autres fins.

Conception et construction

19. Une isolation adéquate devrait être fournie pour les ponts extérieurs recouvrant le logement de l'équipage, les parois extérieures des postes de couchage et réfectoires, les encaissements de machines et les

spaces in which heat is produced, and, as necessary, to prevent condensation or overheating in sleeping rooms, mess rooms, recreation rooms and passageways.

20. Protection should be provided from the heat effects of any steam or hot water service pipes. Main steam and exhaust pipes should not pass through crew accommodation or through passageways leading to crew accommodation. Where this cannot be avoided, pipes should be adequately insulated and encased.

21. Materials and furnishings used in accommodation spaces should be impervious to dampness, easy to keep clean and not likely to harbour vermin.

Noise and vibration

22. Noise levels for working and living spaces, which are established by the competent authority, should be in conformity with the guidelines of the International Labour Organization on exposure levels to ambient factors in the workplace and, where applicable, the specific protection recommended by the International Maritime Organization, together with any subsequent amending and supplementary instruments for acceptable noise levels on board ships.

23. The competent authority, in conjunction with the competent international bodies and with representatives of organizations of fishing vessel owners and fishers and taking into account, as appropriate, relevant international standards, should review on an ongoing basis the problem of vibration on board fishing vessels with the objective of improving the protection of fishers, as far as practicable, from the adverse effects of vibration.

(1) Such review should cover the effect of exposure to excessive vibration on the health and comfort of fishers and the measures to be prescribed or recommended to reduce vibration on fishing vessels to protect fishers.

(2) Measures to reduce vibration, or its effects, to be considered should include:

(a) instruction of fishers in the dangers to their health of prolonged exposure to vibration;

(b) provision of approved personal protective equipment to fishers where necessary; and

(c) assessment of risks and reduction of exposure in sleeping rooms, mess rooms, recreational accommodation and catering facilities and other fishers' accommodation by adopting measures in accordance with the guidance provided by the (ILO) *Code of practice on ambient factors in the workplace* and any subsequent revisions, taking into account the difference between exposure in the workplace and in the living space.

cloisons qui limitent les cuisines et les autres locaux dégageant de la chaleur et pour éviter, au besoin, toute condensation ou chaleur excessive, pour les postes de couchage, les réfectoires, les installations de loisirs et les coursives.

20. Une protection devrait être prévue pour calorifuger les canalisations de vapeur et d'eau chaude. Les tuyauteries principales de vapeur et d'échappement ne devraient pas passer par les logements de l'équipage ni par les coursives y conduisant. Lorsque cela ne peut être évité, les tuyauteries devraient être convenablement isolées et placées dans une gaine.

21. Les matériaux et fournitures utilisés dans le logement de l'équipage devraient être imperméables, faciles à nettoyer et ne pas être susceptibles d'abriter de la vermine.

Bruits et vibrations

22. Les niveaux de bruit établis par l'autorité compétente pour les postes de travail et les locaux d'habitation devraient être conformes aux directives de l'Organisation internationale du Travail relatives aux niveaux d'exposition aux facteurs ambiants sur le lieu de travail ainsi que, le cas échéant, aux normes de protection particulières recommandées par l'Organisation maritime internationale, et à tout instrument relatif aux niveaux de bruit acceptables à bord des navires adopté ultérieurement.

23. L'autorité compétente, conjointement avec les organismes internationaux compétents et les représentants des organisations d'armateurs à la pêche et de pêcheurs et compte tenu, selon le cas, des normes internationales pertinentes, devrait examiner de manière continue le problème des vibrations à bord des navires de pêche en vue d'améliorer, autant que possible, la protection des pêcheurs contre les effets néfastes de telles vibrations.

(1) Cet examen devrait porter sur les effets de l'exposition aux vibrations excessives sur la santé et le confort des pêcheurs et les mesures à prescrire ou à recommander pour réduire les vibrations sur les navires de pêche afin de protéger les pêcheurs.

(2) Les mesures à étudier pour réduire les vibrations ou leurs effets devraient comprendre:

a) la formation des pêcheurs aux risques que l'exposition prolongée aux vibrations présente pour leur santé;

b) la fourniture aux pêcheurs d'un équipement de protection individuelle agréé lorsque cela est nécessaire;

c) l'évaluation des risques et la réduction de l'exposition aux vibrations dans les postes de couchage, les salles à manger, les installations de loisirs et de restauration et autres locaux d'habitation pour les pêcheurs par des mesures conformes aux orientations données dans le *Recueil de directives pratiques sur les facteurs ambiants sur le lieu de travail* (OIT) et ses versions révisées ultérieures, en tenant compte des écarts entre l'exposition sur les lieux de travail et dans les locaux d'habitation.

Heating

24. The heating system should be capable of maintaining the temperature in crew accommodation at a satisfactory level, as established by the competent authority, under normal conditions of weather and climate likely to be met with on service, and should be designed so as not to endanger the health or safety of the fishers or the safety of the vessel.

Lighting

25. Methods of lighting should not endanger the health and safety of the fishers or the safety of the vessel.

Sleeping rooms

26. Each berth should be fitted with a comfortable mattress with a cushioned bottom or a combined mattress, including a spring bottom, or a spring mattress. The cushioning material used should be made of approved material. Berths should not be placed side by side in such a way that access to one berth can be obtained only over another. The lower berth in a double tier should not be less than 0.3 metres above the floor, and the upper berth should be fitted with a dust-proof bottom and placed approximately midway between the bottom of the lower berth and the lower side of the deck head beams. Berths should not be arranged in tiers of more than two. In the case of berths placed along the vessel's side, there should be only a single tier when a sidelight is situated above a berth.

27. Sleeping rooms should be fitted with curtains for the sidelights, as well as a mirror, small cabinets for toilet requisites, a book rack and a sufficient number of coat hooks.

28. As far as practicable, berthing of crew members should be so arranged that watches are separated and that no day worker shares a room with a watch-keeper.

29. On vessels of 24 metres in length and over, separate sleeping rooms for men and women should be provided.

Sanitary accommodation

30. Sanitary accommodation spaces should have:

(a) floors of approved durable material which can be easily cleaned, and which are impervious to dampness and properly drained;

Chauffage

24. Le système de chauffage devrait permettre de maintenir la température dans le logement de l'équipage à un niveau satisfaisant, établi par l'autorité compétente, dans les conditions normales de temps et de climat que le navire est susceptible de rencontrer en cours de navigation. Le système devrait être conçu de manière à ne pas constituer un risque pour la santé ou la sécurité de l'équipage, ni pour la sécurité du navire.

Eclairage

25. Les systèmes d'éclairage ne doivent pas mettre en péril la santé ou la sécurité des pêcheurs ni la sécurité du navire.

Postes de couchage

26. Toute couchette devrait être pourvue d'un matelas confortable muni d'un fond rembourré ou d'un matelas combiné, posé sur support élastique, ou d'un matelas à ressorts. Le rembourrage utilisé doit être d'un matériau approuvé. Les couchettes ne devraient pas être placées côte à côte d'une façon telle que l'on ne puisse accéder à l'une d'elles qu'en passant au-dessus d'une autre. Lorsque des couchettes sont superposées, la couchette inférieure ne devrait pas être placée à moins de 0,3 mètre au-dessus du plancher et la couchette supérieure devrait être équipée d'un fond imperméable à la poussière et disposée approximativement à mi-hauteur entre le fond de la couchette inférieure et le dessous des barrots du plafond. La superposition de plus de deux couchettes devrait être interdite. Dans le cas où des couchettes sont placées le long de la muraille du navire, il devrait être interdit de superposer des couchettes à l'endroit où un hublot est situé au-dessus d'une couchette.

27. Les postes de couchage devraient être équipés de rideaux aux hublots, d'un miroir, de petits placards pour les articles de toilette, d'une étagère à livres et d'un nombre suffisant de patères.

28. Dans la mesure du possible, les couchettes des membres de l'équipage devraient être réparties de façon à séparer les quarts et à éviter qu'un pêcheur de jour ne partage le même poste qu'un pêcheur prenant le quart.

29. Les navires d'une longueur égale ou supérieure à 24 mètres devraient être pourvus de postes de couchage séparés pour les hommes et pour les femmes.

Installations sanitaires

30. Les espaces destinés aux installations sanitaires devraient avoir:

a) des sols revêtus d'un matériau durable approuvé, facile à nettoyer et imperméable, et être pourvus d'un système efficace d'écoulement des eaux;

(b) bulkheads of steel or other approved material which should be watertight up to at least 0.23 metres above the level of the deck;

(c) sufficient lighting, heating and ventilation; and

(d) soil pipes and waste pipes of adequate dimensions which are constructed so as to minimize the risk of obstruction and to facilitate cleaning; such pipes should not pass through fresh water or drinking-water tanks, nor should they, if practicable, pass overhead in mess rooms or sleeping accommodation.

31. Toilets should be of an approved type and provided with an ample flush of water, available at all times and independently controllable. Where practicable, they should be situated convenient to, but separate from, sleeping rooms and washrooms. Where there is more than one toilet in a compartment, the toilets should be sufficiently screened to ensure privacy.

32. Separate sanitary facilities should be provided for women fishers.

Recreational facilities

33. Where recreational facilities are required, furnishings should include, as a minimum, a bookcase and facilities for reading, writing and, where practicable, games. Recreational facilities and services should be reviewed frequently to ensure that they are appropriate in the light of changes in the needs of fishers resulting from technical, operational and other developments. Consideration should also be given to including the following facilities at no cost to the fishers, where practicable:

(a) a smoking room;

(b) television viewing and the reception of radio broadcasts;

(c) projection of films or video films, the stock of which should be adequate for the duration of the voyage and, where necessary, changed at reasonable intervals;

(d) sports equipment including exercise equipment, table games, and deck games;

(e) a library containing vocational and other books, the stock of which should be adequate for the duration of the voyage and changed at reasonable intervals;

(f) facilities for recreational handicrafts; and

(g) electronic equipment such as radio, television, video recorder, DVD/CD player, personal computer and software, and cassette recorder/player.

b) des cloisons en acier ou en tout autre matériau approuvé qui soient étanches sur une hauteur d'au moins 0,23 mètre à partir du pont;

c) une ventilation, un éclairage et un chauffage suffisants;

d) des conduites d'évacuation des eaux des toilettes et des eaux usées de dimensions adéquates et installées de manière à réduire au minimum les risques d'obstruction et à en faciliter le nettoyage, et qui ne devraient pas traverser les réservoirs d'eau douce ou d'eau potable ni, si possible, passer sous les plafonds des réfectoires ou des postes de couchage.

31. Les toilettes devraient être d'un modèle approuvé et pourvues d'une chasse d'eau puissante, en état de fonctionner à tout moment et qui puisse être actionnée individuellement. Là où cela est possible, les toilettes devraient être situées en un endroit aisément accessible à partir des postes de couchage et des locaux affectés aux soins de propreté, mais devraient en être séparées. Si plusieurs toilettes sont installées dans un même local, elles devraient être suffisamment encloses pour préserver l'intimité.

32. Des installations sanitaires séparées devraient être prévues pour les pêcheuses.

Installations de loisirs

33. Là où des installations de loisirs sont prescrites, les équipements devraient au minimum inclure un meuble bibliothèque et des moyens nécessaires pour lire, écrire et, si possible, jouer. Les installations et services de loisirs devraient faire l'objet de réexamens fréquents afin qu'ils soient adaptés aux besoins des pêcheurs, compte tenu de l'évolution des techniques, des conditions d'exploitation ainsi que de tout autre développement. Lorsque cela est réalisable, il faudrait aussi envisager de fournir gratuitement aux pêcheurs:

a) un fumoir;

b) la possibilité de regarder la télévision et d'écouter la radio;

c) la possibilité de regarder des films ou des vidéos, dont le stock devrait être suffisant pour la durée du voyage et, si nécessaire, être renouvelé à des intervalles raisonnables;

d) des articles de sport, y compris du matériel de culture physique, des jeux de table et des jeux de pont;

e) une bibliothèque contenant des ouvrages de caractère professionnel ou autre, en quantité suffisante pour la durée du voyage, et dont le stock devrait être renouvelé à des intervalles raisonnables;

f) des moyens de réaliser des travaux d'artisanat pour se détendre;

g) des appareils électroniques tels que radios, télévisions, magnétoscopes, lecteurs de CD/DVD, ordinateurs, logiciels et magnétophones à cassettes.

Food

34. Fishers employed as cooks should be trained and qualified for their position on board.

PART IV. MEDICAL CARE, HEALTH PROTECTION AND SOCIAL SECURITY

Medical care on board

35. The competent authority should establish a list of medical supplies and equipment appropriate to the risks concerned that should be carried on fishing vessels; such list should include women's sanitary protection supplies together with discreet, environmentally friendly disposal units.

36. Fishing vessels carrying 100 or more fishers should have a qualified medical doctor on board.

37. Fishers should receive training in basic first aid in accordance with national laws and regulations, taking into account applicable international instruments.

38. A standard medical report form should be specially designed to facilitate the confidential exchange of medical and related information concerning individual fishers between the fishing vessel and the shore in cases of illness or injury.

39. For vessels of 24 metres in length and over, in addition to the provisions of Article 32 of the Convention, the following elements should be taken into account:

(a) when prescribing the medical equipment and supplies to be carried on board, the competent authority should take into account international recommendations in this field, such as those contained in the most recent editions of the (ILO/IMO/WHO) *International Medical Guide for Ships* and the (WHO) *Model List of Essential Medicines,* as well as advances in medical knowledge and approved methods of treatment;

(b) inspections of medical equipment and supplies should take place at intervals of no more than 12 months; the inspector should ensure that expiry dates and conditions of storage of all medicines are checked, the contents of the medicine chest are listed and conform to the medical guide used nationally, and medical supplies are labelled with generic names in addition to any brand names used, and with expiry dates and conditions of storage;

(c) the medical guide should explain how the contents of the medical equipment and supplies are to be used, and should be designed to enable persons other than a medical doctor to care for the sick or injured on board, both with and without medical advice by radio or

Nourriture

34. Les pêcheurs faisant office de cuisinier devraient être formés et compétents pour occuper ce poste à bord.

PARTIE IV. SOINS MÉDICAUX, PROTECTION DE LA SANTÉ ET SÉCURITÉ SOCIALE

Soins médicaux à bord

35. L'autorité compétente devrait établir une liste des fournitures médicales et du matériel médical qui devrait se trouver à bord des navires de pêche, compte tenu des risques encourus. Cette liste devrait inclure des produits de protection hygiénique pour les femmes et des récipients discrets non nuisibles pour l'environnement.

36. Un médecin qualifié devrait se trouver à bord des navires de pêche qui embarquent 100 pêcheurs ou plus.

37. Les pêcheurs devraient recevoir une formation de base aux premiers secours, conformément à la législation nationale et compte tenu des instruments internationaux pertinents.

38. Un formulaire de rapport médical type devrait être spécialement conçu pour faciliter l'échange confidentiel d'informations médicales et autres informations connexes concernant les pêcheurs entre le navire de pêche et la terre en cas de maladie ou d'accident.

39. Pour les navires d'une longueur égale ou supérieure à 24 mètres, en sus des dispositions de l'article 32 de la convention, les éléments suivants devraient être pris en compte:

a) en prescrivant le matériel médical et les fournitures médicales à conserver à bord, l'autorité compétente devrait tenir compte des recommandations internationales en la matière, telles que celles prévues dans l'édition la plus récente du *Guide médical international de bord* (OIT/OMI/OMS) et la *Liste modèle des médicaments essentiels* (OMS), ainsi que des progrès réalisés dans les connaissances médicales et les méthodes de traitement approuvées;

b) le matériel médical et les fournitures médicales devraient faire l'objet d'une inspection tous les douze mois au moins; l'inspecteur devrait s'assurer que les dates de péremption et les conditions de conservation de tous les médicaments sont vérifiées, que le contenu de la pharmacie de bord fait l'objet d'une liste et qu'il correspond au guide médical employé sur le plan national, que les fournitures médicales portent des étiquettes indiquant le nom générique outre le nom de marque, la date de péremption et les conditions de conservation;

c) le guide médical devrait expliquer le mode d'utilisation du matériel médical et des fournitures médicales et être conçu de façon à permettre à des personnes autres que des médecins de donner des soins aux malades et aux blessés à bord, avec ou sans consultation médicale par

satellite communication; the guide should be prepared taking into account international recommendations in this field, including those contained in the most recent editions of the (ILO/IMO/WHO) *International Medical Guide for Ships* and the (IMO) *Medical First Aid Guide for Use in Accidents Involving Dangerous Goods*; and

(d) medical advice provided by radio or satellite communication should be available free of charge to all vessels irrespective of the flag they fly.

Occupational safety and health

Research, dissemination of information and consultation

40. In order to contribute to the continuous improvement of safety and health of fishers, Members should have in place policies and programmes for the prevention of accidents on board fishing vessels which should provide for the gathering and dissemination of occupational health and safety materials, research and analysis, taking into consideration technological progress and knowledge in the field of occupational safety and health as well as of relevant international instruments.

41. The competent authority should take measures to ensure regular consultations on safety and health matters with the aim of ensuring that all concerned are kept reasonably informed of national, international and other developments in the field and on their possible application to fishing vessels flying the flag of the Member.

42. When ensuring that fishing vessel owners, skippers, fishers and other relevant persons receive sufficient and suitable guidance, training material, or other appropriate information, the competent authority should take into account relevant international standards, codes, guidance and other information. In so doing, the competent authority should keep abreast of and utilize international research and guidance concerning safety and health in the fishing sector, including relevant research in occupational safety and health in general which may be applicable to work on board fishing vessels.

43. Information concerning particular hazards should be brought to the attention of all fishers and other persons on board through official notices containing instructions or guidance, or other appropriate means.

44. Joint committees on occupational safety and health should be established:

(a) ashore; or

(b) on fishing vessels, where determined by the competent authority, after consultation, to be practicable in light of the number of fishers on board the vessel.

radio ou par satellite; le guide devrait être préparé en tenant compte des recommandations internationales en la matière, y compris celles figurant dans l'édition la plus récente du *Guide médical international de bord* (OIT/OMI/OMS) et du *Guide des soins médicaux d'urgence à donner en cas d'accidents dus à des marchandises dangereuses* (OMI);

d) les consultations médicales par radio ou par satellite devraient être assurées gratuitement à tous les navires quel que soit leur pavillon.

Sécurité et santé au travail

Recherche, diffusion d'informations et consultation

40. Afin de contribuer à l'amélioration continue de la sécurité et de la santé des pêcheurs, les Membres devraient mettre en place des politiques et des programmes de prévention des accidents à bord des navires de pêche prévoyant la collecte et la diffusion d'informations, de recherches et d'analyses sur la sécurité et la santé au travail, en tenant compte du progrès des techniques et des connaissances dans le domaine de la sécurité et de la santé au travail et des instruments internationaux pertinents.

41. L'autorité compétente devrait prendre des mesures propres à assurer la tenue de consultations régulières sur les questions de santé et de sécurité au travail, en vue de garantir que toutes les personnes concernées sont tenues convenablement informées des évolutions nationales et internationales ainsi que des autres progrès réalisés dans ce domaine, et de leur application possible aux navires de pêche battant le pavillon du Membre.

42. En veillant à ce que les armateurs à la pêche, les patrons, les pêcheurs et les autres personnes concernées reçoivent suffisamment de directives et de matériel de formation appropriés ainsi que toute autre information pertinente, l'autorité compétente devrait tenir compte des normes internationales, des recueils de directives, des orientations et de toutes autres informations utiles disponibles. Ce faisant, l'autorité compétente devrait se tenir au courant et faire usage des recherches et des orientations internationales en matière de santé et de sécurité dans le secteur de la pêche, y compris des recherches pertinentes dans le domaine de la santé et de la sécurité au travail en général qui pourraient être applicables au travail à bord des navires de pêche.

43. Les informations concernant les dangers particuliers devraient être portées à l'attention de tous les pêcheurs et d'autres personnes à bord au moyen de notices officielles contenant des instructions ou des directives ou d'autres moyens appropriés.

44. Des comités paritaires de santé et de sécurité au travail devraient être établis:

a) à terre; ou

b) sur les navires de pêche, si l'autorité compétente, après consultation, décide que cela est réalisable compte tenu du nombre de pêcheurs à bord.

Occupational safety and health management systems

45. When establishing methods and programmes concerning safety and health in the fishing sector, the competent authority should take into account any relevant international guidance concerning occupational safety and health management systems, including the *Guidelines on occupational safety and health management systems, ILO-OSH 2001*.

Risk evaluation

46. (1) Risk evaluation in relation to fishing should be conducted, as appropriate, with the participation of fishers or their representatives and should include:

(a) risk assessment and management;

(b) training, taking into consideration the relevant provisions of Chapter III of the International Convention on Standards of Training, Certification and Watchkeeping for Fishing Vessel Personnel, 1995 (STCW-F Convention) adopted by the IMO; and

(c) on-board instruction of fishers.

(2) To give effect to subparagraph (1)(a), Members, after consultation, should adopt laws, regulations or other measures requiring:

(a) the regular and active involvement of all fishers in improving safety and health by continually identifying hazards, assessing risks and taking action to address risks through safety management;

(b) an occupational safety and health management system that may include an occupational safety and health policy, provisions for fisher participation and provisions concerning organizing, planning, implementing and evaluating the system and taking action to improve the system; and

(c) a system for the purpose of assisting in the implementation of a safety and health policy and programme and providing fishers with a forum to influence safety and health matters; on-board prevention procedures should be designed so as to involve fishers in the identification of hazards and potential hazards and in the implementation of measures to reduce or eliminate such hazards.

(3) When developing the provisions referred to in subparagraph (1)(a), Members should take into account the relevant international instruments on risk assessment and management.

Technical specifications

47. Members should address the following, to the extent practicable and as appropriate to the conditions in the fishing sector:

Systèmes de gestion de la santé et de la sécurité au travail

45. Lors de l'élaboration de méthodes et de programmes relatifs à la santé et à la sécurité dans le secteur de la pêche, l'autorité compétente devrait prendre en considération toutes les directives internationales pertinentes concernant les systèmes de gestion de la santé et de la sécurité au travail, y compris les *Principes directeurs concernant les systèmes de gestion de la sécurité et de la santé au travail, ILO-OSH 2001*.

Evaluation des risques

46. (1) Des évaluations des risques concernant la pêche devraient être conduites, lorsque cela est approprié, avec la participation de pêcheurs ou de leurs représentants et devraient inclure:

a) l'évaluation et la gestion des risques;

b) la formation, en prenant en considération les dispositions pertinentes du chapitre III de la Convention internationale sur les normes de formation du personnel des navires de pêche, de délivrance des brevets et de veille, 1995, adoptée par l'OMI (convention STCW-F);

c) l'instruction des pêcheurs à bord.

(2) Pour donner effet aux dispositions de l'alinéa *a)* du sous-paragraphe (1), les Membres devraient adopter, après consultation, une législation ou d'autres mesures exigeant que:

a) tous les pêcheurs participent régulièrement et activement à l'amélioration de la santé et de la sécurité en répertoriant de façon permanente les dangers, en évaluant les risques et en prenant des mesures visant à les réduire grâce à la gestion de la sécurité;

b) un système de gestion de la santé et de la sécurité au travail soit mis en place, qui peut inclure une politique relative à la santé et à la sécurité au travail, des dispositions prévoyant la participation des pêcheurs et concernant l'organisation, la planification, l'application et l'évaluation de ce système ainsi que les mesures à prendre pour l'améliorer;

c) un système soit mis en place pour faciliter la mise en œuvre de la politique et du programme relatifs à la santé et à la sécurité au travail et donner aux pêcheurs un moyen d'expression publique leur permettant d'influer sur les questions de santé et de sécurité; les procédures de prévention à bord devraient être conçues de manière à associer les pêcheurs au repérage des dangers existants et potentiels et à la mise en œuvre de mesures propres à les atténuer ou à les éliminer.

(3) Lors de l'élaboration des dispositions mentionnées à l'alinéa *a)* du sous-paragraphe (1), les Membres devraient tenir compte des instruments internationaux pertinents se rapportant à l'évaluation et à la gestion des risques.

Spécifications techniques

47. Les Membres devraient, dans la mesure du possible et selon qu'il convient au secteur de la pêche, examiner les questions suivantes:

(a) seaworthiness and stability of fishing vessels;

(b) radio communications;

(c) temperature, ventilation and lighting of working areas;

(d) mitigation of the slipperiness of deck surfaces;

(e) machinery safety, including guarding of machinery;

(f) vessel familiarization for fishers and fisheries observers new to the vessel;

(g) personal protective equipment;

(h) fire-fighting and lifesaving;

(i) loading and unloading of the vessel;

(j) lifting gear;

(k) anchoring and mooring equipment;

(l) safety and health in living quarters;

(m) noise and vibration in work areas;

(n) ergonomics, including in relation to the layout of workstations and manual lifting and handling;

(o) equipment and procedures for the catching, handling, storage and processing of fish and other marine resources;

(p) vessel design, construction and modification relevant to occupational safety and health;

(q) navigation and vessel handling;

(r) hazardous materials used on board the vessel;

(s) safe means of access to and exit from fishing vessels in port;

(t) special safety and health requirements for young persons;

(u) prevention of fatigue; and

(v) other issues related to safety and health.

48. When developing laws, regulations or other measures concerning technical standards relating to safety and health on board fishing vessels, the competent authority should take into account the most recent edition of the (FAO/ILO/IMO) *Code of Safety for Fishermen and Fishing Vessels, Part A*.

Establishment of a list of occupational diseases

49. Members should establish a list of diseases known to arise out of exposure to dangerous substances or conditions in the fishing sector.

a) navigabilité et stabilité des navires de pêche;

b) communications par radio;

c) température, ventilation et éclairage des postes de travail;

d) atténuation du risque présenté par les ponts glissants;

e) sécurité d'utilisation des machines, y compris les dispositifs de protection;

f) familiarisation avec le navire des pêcheurs ou observateurs des pêches nouvellement embarqués;

g) équipement de protection individuelle;

h) sauvetage et lutte contre les incendies;

i) chargement et déchargement du navire;

j) appareaux de levage;

k) équipements de mouillage et d'amarrage;

l) santé et sécurité dans les locaux d'habitation;

m) bruits et vibrations dans les postes de travail;

n) ergonomie, y compris en ce qui concerne l'aménagement des postes de travail et la manutention et la manipulation des charges;

o) équipement et procédures pour la prise, la manipulation, le stockage et le traitement du poisson et des autres ressources marines;

p) conception et construction du navire et modifications touchant à la santé et à la sécurité au travail;

q) navigation et manœuvre du navire;

r) matériaux dangereux utilisés à bord;

s) sécurité des moyens d'accéder aux navires et d'en sortir dans les ports;

t) prescriptions spéciales en matière de santé et de sécurité applicables aux adolescents;

u) prévention de la fatigue;

v) autres questions liées à la santé et à la sécurité.

48. Lors de l'élaboration d'une législation ou d'autres mesures relatives aux normes techniques concernant la santé et la sécurité à bord des navires de pêche, l'autorité compétente devrait tenir compte de l'édition la plus récente du *Recueil de règles de sécurité pour les pêcheurs et les navires de pêche, Partie A* (FAO/OIT/OMI).

Etablissement d'une liste de maladies professionnelles

49. Les Membres devraient dresser la liste des maladies dont il est connu qu'elles résultent de l'exposition à des substances ou à des conditions dangereuses dans le secteur de la pêche.

Social security

50. For the purpose of extending social security protection progressively to all fishers, Members should maintain up-to-date information on the following:

(a) the percentage of fishers covered;

(b) the range of contingencies covered; and

(c) the level of benefits.

51. Every person protected under Article 34 of the Convention should have a right of appeal in the case of a refusal of the benefit or of an adverse determination as to the quality or quantity of the benefit.

52. The protections referred to in Articles 38 and 39 of the Convention should be granted throughout the contingency covered.

PART V. OTHER PROVISIONS

53. A Member, in its capacity as a coastal State, when granting licences for fishing in its exclusive economic zone, may require that fishing vessels comply with the standards of the Convention. If such licences are issued by coastal States, these States should take into account certificates or other valid documents stating that the vessel concerned has been inspected by the competent authority or on its behalf and has been found to be in compliance with the provisions of the Convention concerning work in the fishing sector.

Sécurité sociale

50. Aux fins d'étendre progressivement la sécurité sociale à tous les pêcheurs, les Membres devraient établir et tenir à jour des informations sur les points suivants:

a) le pourcentage de pêcheurs couverts;

b) l'éventail des éventualités couvertes;

c) le niveau des prestations.

51. Toute personne protégée en vertu de l'article 34 de la convention devrait avoir le droit de faire recours en cas de refus de la prestation ou d'une décision défavorable sur la qualité ou la quantité de celle-ci.

52. Les prestations visées aux articles 38 et 39 de la convention devraient être accordées pendant toute la durée de l'éventualité couverte.

PARTIE V. AUTRES DISPOSITIONS

53. Un Membre, en sa qualité d'Etat côtier, pourrait exiger que les navires de pêche respectent les normes énoncées dans la convention avant d'accorder l'autorisation de pêcher dans sa zone économique exclusive. Dans le cas où ces autorisations sont délivrées par les Etats côtiers, lesdits Etats devraient prendre en considération les certificats ou autres documents valides indiquant que le navire a été inspecté par l'autorité compétente ou en son nom et qu'il est conforme aux dispositions de la convention sur le travail dans le secteur de la pêche.

International Labour Conference

Record of Proceedings

Ninety-third Session, Geneva, 2005

20

Sixth item on the agenda: Promoting youth employment
(general discussion based on an integrated approach)

Report of the Committee on Youth Employment

1. The Committee on Youth Employment met for its first sitting on 31 May 2005. Initially, it consisted of 182 members (75 Government members, 53 Employer members, 54 Worker members). To achieve equality of voting strength, each Government member was allotted 954 votes, each Employer member 1,350 votes and each Worker member 1,325 votes. The composition of the Committee was modified six times during the session, and the number of votes attributed to each member was adjusted accordingly.[1]

2. The Committee elected its Officers as follows:

Chairperson:	Mr. M.L. Abdelmoumene (Government member, Algeria) at its first sitting.
Vice-Chairpersons:	Mr. P. Anderson (Employer member, Australia) and Ms. S. Burrow (Worker member, Australia) at its first sitting.
Reporter:	Ms. M.L.G. Imperial (Government member, Philippines) at its eighth sitting.

3. At its eighth sitting, the Committee appointed a Drafting Group to draw up a draft resolution and draft conclusions based on views expressed during the plenary discussions, for consideration by the Committee. The Drafting Group was composed as follows:

---

[1] The modifications were as follows:
(a) 1 June: 222 members (91 Government members with 612 votes each, 68 Employer members with 819 votes each and 63 Worker members with 884 votes each);
(b) 2 June: 227 members (103 Government members with 3,819 votes each, 57 Employer members with 6,901 votes each and 67 Worker members with 5,871 votes each);
(c) 3 June: 205 members (105 Government members with 33 votes each, 45 Employer members with 77 votes each and 55 Worker members with 63 votes each);
(d) 9 June: 148 members (112 Government members with 323 votes each, 19 Employer members with 1,904 votes each and 17 Worker members with 2,128 votes each);
(e) 10 June: 138 members (113 Government members with 156 votes each, 13 Employer members with 1,356 votes each and 12 Worker members with 1,469 votes each);
(f) 14 June: 139 members (115 Government members with 143 votes each, 13 Employer members with 1,265 votes each and 11 Worker members with 1,495 votes each).

Government members: Mr. P. Barker (New Zealand), Ms. O. Olanrewaju (Nigeria), Ms. M.S. Paysse (Uruguay), Mr. J.C. Sibbersen (Denmark) and Mr. G. Weltz (United States)

Employer members: Mr. P. Anderson (Australia), Ms. F. Awassi Atsimadja (Gabon), Ms. L. Horvatic (Croatia), Mr. D. Kelly (Canada) and Mr. V. Van Vuuren (South Africa)

Worker members: Ms. S. Burrow (Australia), Ms. Y. Ilesanmi (Nigeria), Mr. M. Lambert (Canada), Ms. J. Stephens (United Kingdom) and Ms. E. Toth Mucciacciaro (Croatia)

4. The Committee held 15 sittings.

5. The Committee had before it Report VI entitled *Youth: Pathways to decent work*, prepared by the Office on the sixth item on the agenda of the Conference: Promoting youth employment (general discussion based on an integrated approach).

Introduction

6. In his opening statement, the Chairperson emphasized the timeliness of the Committee's discussion on youth employment. He pointed to the international community's growing concern with employment of young people, as evidenced by the establishment of the United Nations Secretary-General's Youth Employment Network (YEN), the recent adoption of the United Nations General Assembly resolution on promoting youth employment, and the specific reference to decent and productive work for young women and men in the Millennium Development Goals (MDGs) of the United Nations. The discussion would provide an excellent opportunity for the tripartite constituents of the ILO to review not only the most effective strategies in the area of youth employment but also to assess the different tools at the disposal of member States in implementing such strategies, including through international labour standards and ILO policies, programmes and technical cooperation.

7. The representative of the Secretary-General of the Conference introduced the Office report entitled *Youth: Pathways to decent work* and outlined its main elements. She recalled that youth employment had been an item for general discussion at the International Labour Conference (ILC) in 1986, following the 1983 resolution concerning young people and the ILO's contribution to International Youth Year. Since then, the Office had implemented a number of initiatives, which provided the ILO with both knowledge and experience. A resolution concerning youth employment was adopted in 1998. The question of youth employment and training had also received significant attention in 2000 when the Conference held a general discussion on human resources training and development. The ILO was playing a leading international role in promoting the employment of young people in the framework of the YEN, was supporting lead countries on the development of national action plans on youth employment, and was preparing an analysis of those plans in order to evaluate progress made to date. The ILO was also committed to the MDGs of the United Nations, in particular to Goal 8, which set as a target the development and implementation of strategies for decent and productive work for youth, in collaboration with developing countries. Those activities were a reflection of the long-standing commitment of the ILO and its constituents to the creation of decent work for all young women and men, and were promoted through the Decent Work Agenda and its employment pillar, the Global Employment Agenda (GEA). Consistent with that commitment, Strategic Objective No. 2 of the ILO's Programme and Budget proposals for 2006-07 specified as an output that "ILO constituents have improved data, methodologies, best practice examples and technical support to develop and implement integrated, effective and inclusive policies and programmes to promote opportunities for young women and men to obtain decent and productive work." Lastly, the speaker stressed that clarity was sought on action required to ensure that international labour standards adequately addressed youth employment, as well as on the priorities for the ILO's policy, research, advocacy and technical assistance with regard to promoting decent and productive work for youth.

General discussion

8. The Worker Vice-Chairperson stressed the importance of the discussion on decent work for youth. She gave five examples of youth in various countries facing particular hardships or challenges, in order to demonstrate the wide diversity of youth employment problems. All the examples represented situations that were serious and warranted attention. However, some situations were more severe and permanent than others because they reflected disadvantage and discrimination perpetuated from one generation to another. The available evidence also clearly indicated that young girls, ethnic minorities and youth with disabilities were particularly disadvantaged in the labour market because they faced multiple forms of discrimination.

9. The Workers' group strongly endorsed the suggestion in the Office report that youth unemployment and underemployment imposed heavy and prolonged costs. For the individual young person, unemployment or poor quality work had drastic immediate implications, which also affected employment and income opportunities later in life. There were also profound social implications to lack of decent work, which influenced virtually all facets of life. For society as a whole, decent work deficits for youth meant that human and social capital were depleted and economic growth was forgone; public resources spent on education and training were not being utilized effectively; and the tax base was eroded as the cost of welfare rose.

10. The Workers' group was pleased with the Office report's recognition that the traditional notion of an orderly transition from school to work was a myth for the majority of young people. The dramatic erosion of traditional transition mechanisms highlighted the fact that analysis and policy prescriptions, which were based on life patterns or practices applicable in industrialized countries, might not be entirely transferable to other regions. Effective prescriptions for pathways to decent work for youth required a clear understanding of the particular root economic and labour market problems underlying decent work deficits in the different regions.

11. The Workers' group agreed with the Office report that faster economic growth and the provision of decent work for youth were important ingredients for promoting social stability and global security. It was universally recognized that decent work for youth could not be based on merely distributing the existing pool of good jobs more evenly: it was necessary to achieve a significant expansion of decent employment opportunities. That would require a considerable increase in aggregate demand in most countries through the reform of international policies to provide more policy space and increased international support for developing countries, as well as some increased flexibility within national monetary and fiscal policies. Such reforms constituted a necessary condition to produce pathways to decent work for youth, but would prove insufficient without an appropriate mixture of meso- and micro-level policies, including active labour market policies (ALMPs), industrial policies, wage policies and, most importantly, a renewed commitment to free education for all.

12. The speaker drew attention to the conclusions of the ILO Tripartite Meeting on Youth Employment: The Way Forward, held in October 2004. She believed that the conclusions

could be improved in four respects, namely by: focusing on policies that would reverse the increasing tendency for youth to be stuck in precarious, temporary, casual and other types of dead-end jobs; promoting policies that would reverse widening income disparities and overcome the tendency for young people to be stuck in low-paid jobs; elaborating international and national policies to extend the protection provided by the employment relationship and labour legislation to all young dependent workers who were currently denied that protection; and taking into account the conclusions of the Conference's general discussion on migration (2004), which stressed that migration under decent conditions could boost economic growth in both industrialized and developing countries.

13. Nevertheless, the Workers' group found the conclusions on youth employment from October 2004 to be balanced in two important respects. First, the conclusions recognized that improving the labour market position of youth would require action at both international and national levels and, in the national context, would involve a mix of policies at the macro, meso and micro levels. Second, the conclusions tried to reflect the needs of all regions and countries with vastly different labour market situations and, in that sense, they were generic conclusions that were broadly applicable to all countries.

14. The Workers' group suggested that the Committee endorse and adopt the conclusions, and use them as the generic first chapter of its own conclusions, which were applicable to all regions and all countries. A second chapter, based on the Committee's current discussions, would be more detailed and specific, and should focus more closely on those regions and countries that faced the greatest challenges in respect of youth employment, primarily developing countries. The content of the second chapter would need to: detail the policies required at international and national levels to boost aggregate demand in developing countries; describe in greater detail the economic policies required to enhance the employment intensity of economic growth in developing countries; and provide policy orientations to enhance productivity and decent work in the informal economy, and also to expand decent working opportunities through a renewed focus on infrastructure development and an extension of health, education and related services. Those two parts should constitute a practical implementation strategy for the ILO on decent work for youth.

15. Lastly, the Worker Vice-Chairperson stressed that, although ALMPs could provide solutions to youth employment problems in developing countries, the choice of policy prescriptions should be based on hard empirical evidence concerning their effectiveness. For example, the evidence suggested that one of the most important investments that governments could make was to ensure free universal education. Furthermore, in developing more detailed policies to promote pathways to decent work for youth, the Committee would need to focus on the implementation of labour legislation, improved labour inspection, effective utilization of tripartite dialogue, and the promotion of freedom of association and collective bargaining. The Workers' group intended to propose a major campaign to promote those standards that were most relevant to youth.

16. The Employer Vice-Chairperson recalled the importance of international social dialogue to promote youth employment, and stressed that the conclusions should provide leadership. Youth employment was of utmost importance to employers because they were the bedrock institution for employment promotion, and had a considerable role to play in shaping and influencing youth employment through an enabling environment.

17. He recalled that a great deal of work had already been done on the issue of youth employment, including: the adoption of five formal ILO resolutions between 1978 and 1998 and the ILO's ongoing focus through the GEA; the adoption of the United Nations Millennium Declaration in 2000; the YEN, which had provided guidance to countries on developing national action plans; and the tripartite discussion on youth employment in October 2004. Those efforts represented a substantial commitment by the international

community, yet were only a subset of more considerable work done on a daily basis at the national level, which included unilateral, bilateral, collective and tripartite initiatives in industrialized, transition and developing countries. However, changing circumstances required new analysis of the problem and potential solutions, and more emphasis on action to overcome the slow pace of translating policies into practical programmes and deliverable outcomes.

18. The speaker noted that more young people were in employment than a decade previously, as a result of global economic growth. And more young people were in education than a decade before. Yet much more was needed. Employment promotion had the potential to transform a society; youth employment promotion could transform a generation.

19. Therefore, solutions should be realistic. The global problem of youth employment might not be solved by the global economy but, without making globalization part of the solution at the national level, there would be no chance of meeting that challenge. Countries could not continue to depend on the international community to come to their aid and make policy decisions on their behalf at the national level. Lastly, investment, which was essential for job growth, occurred only in circumstances where it was safe and viable to invest, and where a solid human capital base existed.

20. Although shared principles and common experiences existed between countries, there was also great diversity in national capacities, experiences and circumstances, especially between developing and industrialized countries. Youth themselves varied in their needs and expectations. Consequently, there was no single policy approach.

21. The Employer Vice-Chairperson proposed the following key themes: broad support for policies aimed at reducing youth unemployment, improving education and creating an investment environment conducive to job growth; suitable preparation of jobseekers; entrepreneurship development; and strong public-private partnerships to develop lifelong learning and increase investment in people. He proposed a "back-to-basics" approach, focusing on: basic principles that governed economic growth; basic principles that governed employers' decisions to undertake investment; basic skills such as literacy among young people; basic principles on employability and vocational training; and basic principles concerning a regulatory framework that facilitated employment and removed barriers to entrepreneurship.

22. He underlined that youth employment was one dimension of broader employment promotion. The creation of employment opportunities depended on creating the conditions for a competitive private sector, an effective public sector, ALMPs, and a mature approach to migration. Globalization had the potential to create high-quality jobs for young people, but only if the right conditions existed at the national level. However, employment could not be created by legislation and regulation, and sometimes the impact of regulation could be counter-productive, especially for those on the margins of the labour market, such as youth. The speaker also joined the Workers' group in cautioning that youth employment must not be promoted at the expense of other groups, noting the need to promote overall employment growth.

23. The Employer Vice-Chairperson drew attention to the need to focus more on the supply side: what motivated young people? were they well informed? did they know about job opportunities and how to access them? In many countries, young people either had no access to proper education and training or had access to inadequate systems that did not prepare them for the labour market. Education, vocational training and apprenticeships were key to youth employability.

24. The Employers' group called for the following: creating an economic framework for investments and job creation for young people; emphasizing education and basic skills for young people; promoting relevant vocational education training for employable skills; and encouraging investment in entrepreneurship and small and medium-sized enterprise (SME) development. Those issues were a product of the collective learning experience, and were compatible with the YEN's "four Es" (employability, entrepreneurship, equal opportunities and employment generation).

25. The speaker concluded by noting the common ground between the tripartite partners. While governments were primarily responsible for creating the enabling environment for youth employment, employers had a specific role to play and contribution to make.

26. The Government members' interventions in the general discussion have been grouped according to theme rather than presented chronologically, to facilitate an understanding of the key issues, experiences and views expressed.

27. The Government member of Jamaica, speaking also on behalf of the Government members of Barbados, Suriname, and Trinidad and Tobago, drew attention to the crucial role of youth employment in small developing economies. The creativity of youth made small economies more competitive within the global economy. He stressed the significance of the social impact of lack of work for young people, including increased crime, violence and exposure to HIV/AIDS.

28. The Government member of the Democratic Republic of Congo emphasized that youth employment was one of the most important challenges in post-conflict countries where the generation of productive employment was the only way to fight against poverty. In that regard, a strong focus on youth was needed since the youth population in his country constituted a large proportion of the population, as well as approximately 80 per cent of the unemployed. Consequently, the Democratic Republic of Congo had prepared, with ILO support, a national programme for employment creation.

29. The Government member of Algeria noted that employment for young people was closely linked to the health of the economy of individual countries. Particular attention should be paid to specific sectors that created jobs. The economic growth rate in Algeria had a significant and observable impact on employment, particularly for youth.

30. The Government member of New Zealand agreed that the experiences of young people in developing countries differed greatly from those in developed countries and indicated his hope that commonalities could be found in the discussion. Pointing to the conclusions of the Tripartite Meeting on Youth Employment: The Way Forward (Geneva, October 2004), he supported the idea of the ILO playing a leading role in the promotion of youth employment. He encouraged the Committee to focus on four areas of discussion: first, how youth employment fitted with national decent work action plans; second, how to develop measurements to quantify progress; third, how to generate a tool kit of varying options that nations tackling youth employment could choose from; and, finally, the need for a synthesis of evaluations of country-level programmes focusing on youth employment.

31. The Government member of Côte d'Ivoire stated that youth unemployment was a waste of human resources, in particular in his country where more than 80 per cent of the unemployed were young people. Recent crises had worsened the situation, leaving many outside the production system when they should be contributing. He added that in his country, as in most developing countries, a special focus should be put on ensuring political and social stability and good governance, as the basis for sustainable development. It was equally important to discourage actions that would increase the economic dependency of developing countries.

32. The Government member of Nigeria, speaking on behalf of the Africa group, observed that youth unemployment was an immediate challenge in Africa, which faced serious problems such as armed conflicts, HIV/AIDS, the consequences of globalization, and international debt. She added that African countries needed international cooperation and support to reverse trends of stagnated growth and dwindling aid and to learn how to make globalization work positively in each country.

33. The Government member of South Africa endorsed the comments made on behalf of the Africa group and added that youth unemployment posed complex economic, social and moral policy issues. He described the negatively reinforcing problems of low growth rates leading to insufficient employment and, in turn, to diminished capacity by the State to deliver services and to govern, all potentially leading to political instability and civil strife. He emphasized that policy interventions focused on youth would fail if not undertaken in the context of measures to address the whole economy.

34. The Government member of the Islamic Republic of Iran reflected on the findings of the Office report and the continuing high levels of youth unemployment despite sustained national and international efforts. He called for global unity and coherence to ensure that globalization would secure the necessary conditions for improvements in employment for young people, noting the need for more equitable income distribution, trade rules that ensured fair benefits, and pro-employment growth policies, among other issues.

35. The Government member of Kenya observed that, given the high proportion of young people in Kenya's population – over 60 per cent – solving the youth unemployment problem was "50 per cent" of that country's development challenge.

36. The Government member of Egypt highlighted the particular importance of ALMPs. The first pillar of ALMPs was equality, which had been guaranteed by the Constitutions of all the member States. The second pillar, entrepreneurship, was difficult to promote in Egypt and in other developing countries, owing to limited credit access for youth to start their own businesses and to a shortage of business development services. Another important aspect of ALMPs for youth employment was the need to set in place incentive frameworks for investment, since jobs could not be created by legislation. Jobs were best created within booming markets, not just the labour market, but also the financial, technological and information markets. Finally, the speaker raised concern about the obsolete nature of many existing training curricula that were not enterprise-based and posed challenges for enhancing employability. Many governments lacked resources to update those curricula because World Trade Organization (WTO) regulations had put their economies in crisis.

37. The Government member of Ecuador added that a special unit had been created in the Ecuadorian Ministry of Labour to help young people find employment and create their own enterprises. The programme had already trained 1,000 young people and was expected to create 2,000 jobs. As with other countries, skills training and enterprise development were key issues in Ecuador.

38. The Government member of Nigeria, speaking on behalf of the Africa group, noted the positive lessons from countries such as Cameroon, Djibouti, Nigeria, Senegal, South Africa and Zambia, commenting particularly on the positive effect of integrating employment-intensive programmes for young people into national investment policies, and the value of integrating training, work experience and labour market services.

39. The Government member of Luxembourg, speaking on behalf of the Government members of the Committee Member States of the European Union (EU), expressed the EU's continuing support for the approach set out in the report of the World Commission on the Social Dimension of Globalization and the Decent Work Agenda. She stated that youth

employment should be incorporated into all social, employment and economic policies. She gave as an example the European Employment and Social Inclusion Strategies, and the European Youth Pact, noting that the latter incorporated a life-cycle approach to integrating issues of education, training and lifelong learning, social integration and balancing work and family life.

40. The Government member of Denmark introduced "flexicurity" as an effective labour market approach which helped his country balance the rights and social protection of individuals with the immediate and long-term needs of the labour market. The Danish social partners supported that model within an overall labour market strategy that ensured that everyone was able to access the labour market, and that enterprises could access workers with appropriate skills. Denmark's ALMP focused on education and lifelong learning, and on making sure that unemployed persons – particularly youth – found new employment as quickly as possible.

41. The Government member of Lebanon observed that the labour market was a market in knowledge, which was subject to rapid changes from day to day within the overall context of globalization and competitiveness. Youth had the right to work and to exploit the possible opportunities for them to work. At the same time, youth needed to be competitive. Human resources development, through relevant education and training answering the needs of today's society, was fundamental for improving productivity. In that regard, the speaker highlighted the need for a strategy; without one, even people with education and training might not be able to find jobs.

42. The Government member of Mexico stressed that the most important issue for his country was training and hoped that the discussion and conclusions of the Committee would emphasize best practices, specifically with regard to experiences in training young people and promoting an easier transition from education to employment.

43. The Government member of New Zealand observed that, despite the comparatively high education attendance levels in New Zealand, there still remained a significant number of young people who did not complete education and training. The Government aimed to tackle the issue by setting the goal that by 2007 all 15-19 year-olds would be either in employment, education or training. Some progress had already been made towards that goal – the share of young people who were not currently in employment, education or training was less than 9 per cent, down from 15 per cent two years previously.

44. The Government member of Jamaica, speaking also on behalf of the Government members of Barbados, Suriname, and Trinidad and Tobago, explained that education and training were essential for maximizing youth employment because they enabled a young person to be more employable, particularly to take full advantage of jobs generated in certain sectors of an expanding economy, and to access better jobs. He hoped that the ILO would raise support from the international agencies to help small developing economies create jobs on a sustainable basis and implement an adequate education and training system. Bilaterally, small countries should enter into strategic partnerships with other small countries and with industrialized countries. At the local level, partnership was needed between government, employers, trade unions and other community-based organizations. He drew attention to some areas of consensus – notably, the focus on employability through training and certification systems. At the same time, he stressed that training should focus not only on obtaining a job but also on making youth flexible and adaptable in light of constantly changing labour markets.

45. The Government member of the Libyan Arab Jamahiriya took pride in the young people of his country, who made up more than 50 per cent of the population. However, he said that strategies to ensure employment opportunities for them were critical, comprising the

development of microcredit, small and medium-sized enterprises and, most importantly, education and training, which were specific to different sector and employer requirements. He added that one of the challenges for his country and others in the developing world was the emigration of educated young people, and the need to ensure that decent jobs were available for them in their own countries.

46. The Government member of Kenya stated that the provision of basic universal education and vocational training was fundamental for tackling the youth employment challenge. At the same time, she pointed out that, while primary education was better than no education, it alone would not transform a pupil into a worker, as he or she would still be unable to gain access to reasonable work, let alone decent work. She emphasized the need to equip youth with basic, modern and marketable skills.

47. The Government member of India noted that the majority of youth entering the Indian labour market were illiterate, but that barriers to employment also existed for more educated young people, who lacked the technical and professional skills required by employers, resulting in higher unemployment among educated youth and inviting social unrest. He described India's employment creation programme, which included aspects of skills development, such as the introduction of a multiskilling and multi-entry system, but noted the need for a sustainable increase in current training efforts to adequately equip the labour force.

48. The Government member of Mozambique expressed support for statements made by the Government member of Nigeria on behalf of the Africa group. In the case of Mozambique, he stated that young people faced worse labour market outcomes, partly due to a lack of skills. That lack of skills was in part attributable to the inadequate capacity of technical and vocational institutions to meet the demand for skills, and the mismatch with skills demanded by the labour market. In addition, there was a lack of reliable information about changing skills needs, and a lack of resources to respond.

49. The Government member of Indonesia discussed her country's experience as a YEN lead country. The Government had established the national Indonesia Youth Employment Network (I-YEN) in 2003. The I-YEN was a collaborative effort involving a wide range of government agencies, employer associations, trade unions, and young people themselves. The I-YEN had launched the Indonesia Youth Employment Action Plan in August 2004 and had developed school programmes to promote entrepreneurship.

50. The Government member of Senegal described how more than half of the population was young and 65 per cent of the unemployed were below the age of 35 years in his country. As part of its participation as a lead country in the YEN, the Government had taken five youth employment measures. In 2001, it had earmarked US$20 million for a national fund which would be used to finance youth-focused initiatives, such as credit access for young people for starting small businesses, and which should lead to the creation of 12,500 jobs and to the formation of 2,300 micro-enterprises. Senegal had also developed a national agency for youth employment where young people could go to look for work and employers could go to seek workers, thus improving the match between supply and demand. The Government had established a national volunteer agency to promote citizenship awareness and provide training to young people, particularly in areas of agricultural production. National "tool centres" had also been created to train young people to become artisans, agricultural workers, etc. The 34 existing tool centres were expected to result in 10,000 jobs for young people. Lastly, the Government had established a national programme specific to youth.

51. The Government member of Canada expressed full support for the United Nations Millennium Development Goals, endorsed the ILO's leading role in the YEN and

encouraged the participation of other multilateral organizations in it. Her Government wished to continue working with the ILO through the YEN in order to help young people gain skills.

52. The Government member of the United Republic of Tanzania gave examples of how his Government was putting into practice the recommendations of the Youth Employment Summit (Mexico, 2004) and the directions of the YEN to address the MDGs, with a current focus on mapping the quantity and location of and the requirements, potential and prospects for decent work for young people, who made up over 60 per cent of the active population in the United Republic of Tanzania.

53. The Government member of China commented that, despite high economic growth of 9 per cent per annum in the past decade, youth unemployment remained unacceptably high. He explained that the Government would promote youth employment through the implementation of ALMPs, the establishment of a YEN office in China in May 2005 and a youth entrepreneurship programme implemented with the assistance of the ILO and the United Kingdom. China would be focusing on four areas for priority action: assistance to poor youth, particularly access to education; addressing rural-urban disparities; combining education with internship; and policies to support entrepreneurship.

54. The Government member of the United States pointed out that, as a follow-up to the elimination of child labour, there was a need to help young people become productive, empowered and engaged, which was not a simple task. He emphasized the immensity and diversity of the employment challenges facing youth, which indicated that there was no single solution. It was essential to identify the most disadvantaged youth for targeted programme intervention. The strategic approach adopted in the United States was based on four pillars: focus on alternative education and wider schooling; coordination of skills investment; concentration on the needs of the most disadvantaged youth; and accountability in attaining strategic outcomes.

55. The Government member of Ecuador stated that her Government gave priority to two issues that it considered to be the main pillars for a democratic and stable society: health and education. Education and training programmes were aimed at overcoming problems faced by young people, who made up almost one-third of the country's workforce. Nine per cent of young people between 18 and 30 years of age were unemployed or underemployed. The Committee's conclusions would be taken into account during a forthcoming law revision.

56. The Government member of the United Republic of Tanzania commented on the value of technical assistance received from the ILO in building approaches to facilitate the free movement of labour in East Africa, and called for further assistance in the areas of research, data and microcredit to enhance youth empowerment.

57. EU approaches, as described by the Government member of Luxembourg, incorporated complementary efforts towards job creation, school-to-work transition, working conditions and improved employability. She added that the EU had included youth employment in its development and external cooperation priorities.

58. The Government member of Norway shared the experiences of her country with policies for 16-24 year-olds. The five main elements were: the introduction of a statutory right for 16-21 year-olds to three years of upper secondary education, leading to vocational and higher education qualifications; apprenticeship training as part of the upper secondary entitlement, which included a subsidy for the on-the-job training element; a country-level follow-up service to reach young people who were neither working nor in school; the "youth guarantee" programme which offered places on labour market programmes to

young people under 20 years of age who were not in work or at school; and, finally, the public employment service, which provided placement assistance, job search skills and counselling.

59. The Government member of Japan reported on the Symposium on Globalization and the Future of Youth in Asia held in Tokyo in December 2004, which included the participation of 14 countries from the Asia region, and was assisted by the ILO. He noted the relevance of the Symposium conclusions – particularly those relating to the need of societies to support the voluntary contribution of young people by creating an enabling environment for young people – to the discussion and future conclusions of the Committee.

60. The Government member of Denmark noted that the Government had established a target for job creation and had had considerable success with its efforts to reduce youth unemployment. Currently, the unemployment rate for youth aged from 18 to 25 years was the same as that for the general population; however, for immigrant youth the rate was twice as high. Denmark used management by objectives to ensure that its policies were effective, and relied on the social partners to regulate a large part of the labour market through collective bargaining.

61. The Government member of Kenya recalled that, of the jobs available in her country, 94 per cent were in the informal economy, and that those jobs lacked most forms of protection and were short term at best. She also noted that 90 per cent of those employed in such jobs were young people, and that there was a real need to develop practical approaches for translating jobs in the informal economy into decent, sustainable jobs.

62. The Government member of Mozambique expressed similar points regarding his country, where only 5 per cent of the working population actually had a wage job and only 11 per cent worked in the formal sector. While secondary and tertiary sector activities had shown signs of recovery over recent years, he stated that the primary sector still constituted the main source of employment for youth, normally engaged in subsistence family businesses. In that regard, he asserted some gender differences in the youth labour market, where 59 per cent of young women stayed in the rural areas while young men actively sought work in the urban areas.

63. The Government member of the Netherlands shared the successful, concrete and action-oriented experience of the Netherlands, where the youth unemployment rate had fallen to 7.9 per cent in 2004. Some of the youth-specific programmes included the establishment of the Youth Unemployment Task Force, as well as a policy approach that emphasized the smooth transition from school to work.

64. The Government member of India shared some of the situations and experiences of India. He noted that there were 7 to 8 million young entrants to the labour market every year. Lack of basic skills, mismatch of skills with needs, lack of growth in the jobs available in the formal economy, the impact of structural adjustment on the recently hired and jobseekers, and the lack of financing for entrepreneurship all contributed to unemployment and employment in poor quality jobs for young people. India's Tenth Five-Year Plan included an objective to generate 50 million additional employment opportunities: 30 million through the normal economic growth process and 20 million through the implementation of special employment programmes. He stated that such special employment programmes had a sectoral focus, such as agriculture, construction, tourism, and information and communication technology sectors, as well as skills development, including targeted programmes for disadvantaged youths. The social partners were closely involved in that process with complementary roles.

65. He stressed that the Constitution of India aimed to achieve the central objective of international labour standards, which was to promote freely chosen productive employment. In the Indian context, where the informal economy formed a significant part of the overall economy, he noted the need to emphasize the promotion of SMEs, which were recognized for their tendency to be employment-intensive. With respect to the supply side of the labour market, he noted the need for a sustainable step up in the current training efforts to adequately equip the labour force.

66. The Government member of Tunisia acknowledged that employment was closely linked to economic growth, but that such linkage diverged from one country to another. He stated that some of the sources of such diversity might lie in the position of youth in the labour market, demographic factors and level of educational attainment. He particularly emphasized the importance of family planning and universal compulsory education. He noted that Tunisia had a successful policy experience in meeting employment and youth employment challenges through the implementation of programmes to provide employment to youth funded by the Tunisian Solidarity Fund and the National Employment Fund.

67. The Government member of Morocco emphasized that the youth employment challenge was a major preoccupation in Morocco. He explained that the declining trend in economic growth had worsened cyclical unemployment, exacerbated in recent years by large numbers of school leavers with degrees but without jobs. In view of such a situation, he described some of the efforts that had been made to tackle the consequences of youth unemployment and underemployment. He noted that such measures included the promotion of wage employment through the provision of training to boost the occupational skills of jobseekers, subsidized employment opportunities and incentives for youth entrepreneurship. He also touched on some of the targets of measures to promote employment, which included improved employability of youth in long-term unemployment, the expansion of direct employment opportunities and assistance in enterprise creation. On the demand side, he stated that some measures included assistance to businesses that were facing competitive pressures.

68. The Government member of Nigeria, speaking on behalf of the Africa group, cautioned that, in promoting youth employment, the Organization should not unwittingly encourage child labour and undermine the provisions of the Minimum Age Convention, 1973 (No. 138), and the Worst Forms of Child Labour Convention, 1999 (No. 182).

69. The Government member of the United Republic of Tanzania observed the particular transition issues faced by young people who had grown up as street children, orphans and other socially excluded groups.

70. The Government member of Canada agreed with the Worker and Employer Vice-Chairpersons, as well as with other Government members, in their commitment to elaborate a concrete action plan with clear orientations, specific objectives and deliverable outcomes. That suggestion was echoed by the Government member of South Africa. As reported by the Government member of Luxembourg, the EU called for a practical, action-oriented outcome with an action plan for global partnerships to exchange best practices and expertise.

71. The Government member of the Netherlands supported the view that the focus of the work of the Committee should be on developing countries. She supported the Employer Vice-Chairperson's call for "less talk and more action".

72. The Government member of India proposed an international skills development fund be established under the ILO umbrella for use by the developing countries to supplement

ongoing national efforts. He called for a more active role for the ILO in migration issues, particularly supporting the development of regional and global competency standards to facilitate the cross-border movement of skilled people, and for advocacy against restrictions to outsourcing.

73. The Government member of China proposed three objectives, which he hoped the Committee would achieve. As a first objective, he asked for a more appropriate direction for policy efforts with respect to youth employment. Secondly, he noted the need to achieve consensus on some of the issues, in order to put youth employment on a higher level. Thirdly, he emphasized the need for practical ways and methods to promote youth employment.

74. The Government members of South Africa and Nigeria, the latter speaking on behalf of the Africa group, both endorsed using the conclusions from the ILO Tripartite Meeting on Youth Employment: The Way Forward as the basis for discussion. The Government member of the Netherlands supported the Worker Vice-Chairperson's suggestion to adopt the conclusions of the Tripartite Meeting as Chapter 1 of the Committee's conclusions, also endorsing the Worker Vice-Chairperson's call to strengthen the conclusions in respect of precarious employment, income disparities, the employment relationship and migration.

75. The spokesperson for the International Young Christian Workers and the World Movement of Christian Workers made a statement concerning the vulnerable situation of young workers and the need to ensure that governments, workers and employers promoted decent and sustainable work through adherence to the principles of decent work and through their respective roles.

76. The Employer Vice-Chairperson, speaking in response to the opening statements of the Government members, was encouraged by the obvious commitment of the Government members to the search for solutions to the challenges of youth employment at both the national and international levels. He noted numerous synergies between the comments made by various Government members and the views of the Employers' group as reflected in his earlier statement. Specifically, he noted with appreciation the focus on youth employability by some Government members as well as the call by Government members for practical outcomes from the Committee. He expressed his appreciation for the fact that all Government members had recognized the need for economic growth and the need for relevant and up-to-date training as important components in the challenge of youth employment.

77. The Employer Vice-Chairperson noted other consistencies between the views of the Employers' group and Government members, namely the recognition that jobs would be created through enterprises and not through legislation, the recognition of the important role of entrepreneurship and ALMPs, the call for improvements in investment and productivity as factors affecting youth employment, the recognition of the importance of microcredit, and the call to improve literacy. The Employer Vice-Chairperson supported the requests of the Government members of New Zealand and the United States for the development and use of performance indicators and benchmarking to measure the progress of policies, and reiterated the need for the contribution of the Committee to be practical in nature. Finally, the Employer Vice-Chairperson acknowledged, as pointed out by the Government members of India and Kenya, that most youth worked in the informal economy in many countries.

78. The Worker Vice-Chairperson was also encouraged by the interventions of Government members so far. She reiterated her group's belief that a sustainable global economy depended on all ILO partners – governments, workers and employers – and the role each played in ensuring the functioning of a decent society. Governments, for example, had a

role in legislation, regulation and policy but also in the wise use of tax revenues, invested in creating the conditions for decent and functioning societies. Also, governments were employers and the public sector could provide a positive model and opportunities for labour market entry. Employers had a legitimate interest in profitable enterprises and, without that, economic growth might be constrained; however, she emphasized that employers also had a responsibility to those they employed. Finally, she noted that workers held the key to the global economy through their labour – which was not a commodity – and through the capital they held, as consumers, in their own right, and in the form of direct capital which was invested.

79. The Worker Vice-Chairperson reminded the Committee to be cautious in accepting conclusions based on an economic model promoting trade liberalization, a free market economy, deregulation, globalization and tax reform, as the only route towards economic growth and well-being. She pointed out that that model, a product of the Washington Consensus, had been called into question by leading academics and even the staff of the international financial institutions. She stressed that the Workers' group saw areas of convergent interest on many points, including the need for increased investment expenditure, both public and private, in many developing countries. She emphasized that there was shared responsibility for ensuring that succeeding generations would have the benefit of labour standards and decent work, and that workers would not accept measures which would reduce access to decent work. She indicated that the Workers' group was not opposed to globalization, but the process needed to be better governed to ensure that a much wider range of countries could benefit from the process. She emphasized that migration and investment policies should not conflict with international labour standards. She supported comments made by the Government member of Egypt on the need to reform multilateral cooperation arrangements such as those managed by the WTO. She referred to specific points of agreement with statements of individual Government members, noting, among others, Kenya's concern for formalizing the informal economy and Nigeria's call for increased investment in education.

80. The Worker Vice-Chairperson expressed agreement with numerous statements made by the Employers' group and Government members, but added that there still remained a need to reach consensus on what was to be the foundation for the remaining discussion within the Committee. She reiterated that the Workers' group would like to take the conclusions of the Tripartite Meeting on Youth Employment as the point of departure, especially given that they were reached through tripartite consultation and compromise, and focus the rest of the general part of the meeting on discussions of how to build practical solutions from there.

81. The Chairperson thanked the Employer and Worker Vice-Chairpersons and all Government members who had contributed to the opening discussion. He said that what had emerged from the discussion so far was the priority placed by governments, employers, workers and the international community at large on the issue of youth employment. He reminded the Committee that, in its report, the ILO called for an integrated approach and a plan for concrete action. The Chairperson then called on the Employer Vice-Chairperson to open the discussion of point 1 on the disadvantages faced by young people in the labour market and the consequences of their lack of access to decent work.

Points for discussion

Point 1. What are the major disadvantages faced by young people in the labour market? What are the consequences of their lack of access to decent work?

82. The Employer Vice-Chairperson pointed out that disadvantages in the labour market included both the disadvantages of those entering the labour market for the first time and of those already in the labour market. He interpreted the term "labour market" as referring to the formal economy only, noting that one of the policy objectives should be to facilitate movement from the informal to the formal economy. He added that the question referred to youth as "disadvantaged", without clarifying as compared with whom. For the purpose of the discussion, he would assume that that meant adults.

83. The speaker emphasized that disadvantages included barriers that employers faced in providing employment or high-quality employment. Those varied by region and country, with differences well described in the report, and related to both demand and supply.

84. On the demand side, he stressed the importance of paying attention to both disadvantages resulting from the lack of an enabling economic environment and those resulting from a poor-quality regulatory environment. An enabling economic environment would provide a proper framework to encourage investment, foster competitiveness and secure returns on investment, offer stability in the legal system and promote synergies between the public and private sectors. A high-quality regulatory environment would promote employment and entrepreneurship, would not unduly restrict migration and would support positive outcomes, specifically the employment of young people, through incentives for job creation and positive choices by young people. He emphasized that, without a strong commitment to creating the enabling economic environment and quality regulatory environment, barriers would result and young people would face disadvantages in the labour market.

85. For the Employers' group, private sector productivity and competitiveness were key to providing entry-level productive jobs for young people. The Employer Vice-Chairperson cautioned that youth employment policies must be sustainable and that expansionary policies, which created artificial demand, might be counter-productive. The speaker reiterated that promotion of youth employment could not be at the expense of other employment objectives; rather, creating jobs for youth should be part of a holistic employment strategy in which other areas of the labour market were adequately addressed.

86. The type of demand for sustainable jobs included areas such as part-time and temporary work, which had particular value for young people at entry level or those in an apprenticeship or vocational training.

87. On the supply side, the speaker criticized the lack of basic education and literacy, which was also a crucial element in dealing with child labour as it related to youth employment. He drew attention to the general trend of limited public expenditure on education and training despite the fact that they were essential for preparing young people for the labour market. He also lamented the poor link between many education systems and the needs of the labour market, in particular industry, and pointed to the need for efficient, knowledgeable and well-trained vocational trainers. Furthermore, young people needed to be equipped with broader life skills to enable them to search for a job, work and compete in the adult world, and to develop a sense of responsibility and adaptability.

88. The Employers' group also drew attention to the importance of ALMPs and labour market information (LMI), which were available to support youth employment. Often, the problem of lack of capacity to match supply with demand for skills could be addressed through ALMPs, especially for those disadvantaged in the labour market.

89. The speaker considered that in both developing and industrialized countries barriers to entrepreneurship development, such as lack of access to credit, disproportionately disadvantaged youth. It was important to develop a supportive social and physical infrastructure to help young entrepreneurs.

90. The speaker also recalled the advantages that young jobseekers had in the labour market: young people with a good education could offer enthusiasm, willingness to learn, adaptability, mobility, flexibility, faster skills acquisition and could be more realistic about their entry point into the labour market. Therefore, their disadvantaged position in the labour market resulted in a lack of real choice among both young jobseekers and employers and decreased productivity for enterprises. The costs spilled over to society as a whole with increased social welfare expenditures, decreased investment, migration of skilled workers and social unrest.

91. The Worker Vice-Chairperson recalled the observation by the ILO Director-General that the consequence of not meeting the challenge of youth unemployment and employment was a waste of a major part of the energy and skills of the best-educated generation. She drew attention to the seriousness of the labour market situation facing young people, where more than 200 million young people lived on less than US$1 a day, and roughly 460 million young people lived on less than US$2 a day. She further noted that during the ten years between 1993 and 2003, the global youth unemployment rate had risen from 11.7 per cent to 14.4 per cent, representing a 23 per cent increase. She cautioned that such a trend would continue and emphasized the need to place the pursuit of rapid and decent employment growth at the heart of international and national economic policy. This would require a stronger focus on expansionary economic policies.

92. She emphasized that finding a job was only one part of the problem for young people, and recounted examples of poor conditions of work faced by young employed people, even in industrialized countries. For many first-time jobseekers in developing countries work in export processing zones (EPZs) was the only source of employment in the formal economy. Yet the quality of employment in EPZs had been worsening over the years due to the lack of a strong protective environment for workers. Many more young people ended up working in the informal economy, where the picture was even worse.

93. As for the situation facing youth in industrialized countries, she noted a moderate decline in the youth unemployment rate, from 15.8 per cent in 1993 to 13.4 per cent in 2003, which was almost entirely attributed to youth withdrawing from the labour market by remaining in school for a longer duration. The change was minimal despite numerous factors which would have been favourable to young people, including demographic trends, better education and structural changes, growth in the services sector and information and communication technologies (ICT), increased policy attention and increased resources devoted to addressing youth labour market problems. She drew attention to Austria, Germany and Switzerland as exceptions to that trend. Their performance in terms of youth employment had been positive even though labour market institutions in those countries were often criticized as restrictive, indicating that labour market flexibility was less important than a smooth transition from education and training to work. On the quality of jobs available to youth in industrialized countries, she noted a strong tendency for youth to be in low-paid jobs and either to remain in that position in the medium term or to become unemployed again. She pointed out that youth wages had declined in most countries relative to adult wages in recent decades. However, this was not because adult wages were

growing rapidly. On the contrary, she noted that the wage share of national output had declined by about 5 percentage points between 1980 and 2002 for the OECD region as a whole. Hence, she concluded that labour costs had declined in most countries and could not be a cause of rising youth unemployment in developed countries.

94. With respect to developing countries, the Worker Vice-Chairperson described the seriousness of the situation facing youth and emphasized that such countries were in greatest need of assistance. She emphasized that, since the majority of youth in developing countries worked in the informal economy, without unemployment benefit systems, a large majority did not have the luxury of being unemployed. Hence, the worst problems concerned underemployment and the precariousness of work, in terms of long hours of work, extremely low pay or involvement in unpaid family work.

95. The Worker Vice-Chairperson called for special consideration of the specific situation faced by indigenous youth, in both developing and industrialized countries, who tended to face a higher risk of unemployment than non-indigenous youth.

96. In response to the Employers' group, the speaker cautioned that entrepreneurship too often left young people stuck in the informal economy as a result of either lack of access to credit or the high rate of default due to lack of knowledge or experience in managing a loan. She emphasized the importance of generating wage employment to make young people's employment sustainable.

97. Also in reply to the Employers' group, the Workers' group reminded the Committee that too narrow a focus on industry-specific training could be detrimental in some cases. Fields such as literature, arts, languages, culture and music provided the base for fast-growing sectors such as multimedia, tourism and trade, which most demanded the skills of the younger generation.

98. Lastly, the speaker cautioned that the consequences of too few opportunities for young people could be devastating both in economic terms and in terms of their right to decent work.

99. The Government member of Canada, speaking on behalf of a number of Government members of industrialized market economy countries (IMEC), supported the point raised by the Employers' group that young people faced disadvantages, but also had advantages – they brought a new way of thinking, an energy and enthusiasm, technological know-how and good working attitudes to the workplace.

100. A number of Government members noted that some young people were disadvantaged because of their status as indigenous persons, young immigrants, youth with disabilities, young parents or youth who were illiterate, situations that tended to exacerbate disadvantages already experienced by young people. The Government member of Jamaica stressed the importance of special interventions for young women.

101. Lack of relevant skills was a major disadvantage cited by Government members of both developed and developing countries. The Government member of Tunisia, in a point echoed by many other speakers, noted that some young people were highly skilled yet still lacked the opportunity to make use of their skills and training because their skills were not relevant to local labour needs. This often-cited "mismatch" was due to both inadequate connection between vocational training and demand and poor labour market information, as explained by the Government member of Peru.

102. Skills were a more acute problem for the significant number of young people who lacked even basic skills, a point noted by a number of Government members. Poor school

attendance and early drop-out rates were noted by the Government member of Uruguay and reiterated by other speakers. Programmes to reach school leavers and ensure that they reconnected with education or vocational training were described by the Government member of Sweden.

103. The Government member of Nigeria, speaking on behalf of the Africa group, agreed that education curricula were of limited relevance due to lack of consultation with enterprises or technological institutions. The problem was further compounded by the low level of training or the poor implementation of training programmes. Assistance to redesign education curricula of African countries would be of great advantage to them.

104. The Government members of Jamaica and Portugal raised the point that youth were often disadvantaged because employers required first-time jobseekers to have experience, which, by definition, they did not have. Furthermore, as cited by the Government member of Nigeria, among others, young people were often subject to a "last-in, first-out" challenge.

105. The existence of active conflicts and military occupation in some countries had an immediate and negative impact on employment possibilities for young people, as observed by the representative of the Palestinian Authority, echoed by the Government member of the Syrian Arab Republic. In all countries, the demands of families and family life also impacted on young people's prospects, often doubly so for women, as noted by the Government member of Uruguay, in relation to the experience of MERCOSUR and other Latin American countries.

106. The Government member of Nigeria, speaking on behalf of the Africa group, stated that there were important barriers to entrepreneurship development in the region, in particular the lack of financial resources and necessary skills. Young people felt poorly oriented to create new enterprises, their parents preferred them to be employed rather than taking the risk of creating something new on their own, there was a high rate of failure for new small enterprises, and they did not have access to loans or appropriate training.

107. A major disadvantage faced by young people in all countries related to the number and quality of jobs available to them. The Government member of Portugal noted that a critical problem was the lack of aggregate demand. The Government members of Jamaica and Uruguay commented on the poor quality of jobs available to labour market entrants.

108. The consequences of those disadvantages were manifested at a number of levels, affecting young people themselves, economic growth, social cohesion and stability. Government members shared the concern of the Workers' group that poor health and safety and increased precariousness of work led to economic insecurity for young people. Others commented on the potential for low self-esteem among young people who were unemployed or could not find good jobs. Alienation, the risk of long-term exclusion and the potential for young people to become vulnerable to drug addiction, unsafe work and exploitation were possible consequences described by the Government members of Jamaica, Sweden and Uruguay, among others. Another consequence of poor labour market information, noted by the Government member of Cameroon and other speakers, was the potential for unrealistic expectations by young people, who became "money seekers" rather than workers with a pride in their occupation, or who preferred higher status work to locally available work.

109. The Government member of Japan stressed that young people carried significant purchasing power and, therefore, the inability of countries to provide them with quality employment served as a significant threat to economic growth and to the global economy. The Government member of Portugal added that mismatches indicated that investments made in education and training were generating a suboptimal level of benefits and that the

workforce created was not being fully utilized, even though young workers could contribute considerably to increasing the competitiveness of a country. Other speakers commented on the potential for increased welfare costs, where such systems existed.

110. The Government member of Nigeria, speaking on behalf of the Africa group, underlined that 93 per cent of young people in Africa were working in the informal economy under unacceptable conditions – poor or no wages, difficult working hours and conditions, no social protection, and no right of freedom of association or collective bargaining. That low quality of work had led to social instability, crime, drug abuse, poverty and migration. The failure to access jobs in the formal economy was a danger for all, governments, employers' and workers' organizations, and society as a whole. The Government member of Jordan, on a point also noted by other speakers, commented that poor-quality jobs in terms of salary and working conditions resulted in dissatisfaction among young workers that affected their career choices and their behaviour. The Government member of Portugal concurred, stating that youth stuck in temporary employment under bad conditions had more difficulty attaining the stability in their lives needed to raise families, which could lead them to feel useless.

111. The Employer Vice-Chairperson expressed his satisfaction with the Government members' interventions which identified the disadvantages faced by youth and the barriers faced by employers and prospective employers. He welcomed the fact that youth were also identified as an asset and that challenges could be turned into advantages. He reiterated the importance of the dual roles of the public and private sectors to deal with that challenge, with governments having a role in investment in the infrastructure of learning, a role that was constrained in many developing countries by the poor availability of resources.

112. The Worker Vice-Chairperson emphasized that decent work deficits carried unacceptably high private costs for individuals and families, as well as social and economic costs. She referred to examples mentioned by Government members of the positive links between higher wages, increased aggregate demand and high levels of employment as evidence of the need to eliminate low-wage employment for youth. She commented on the value of wage employment as a secure step into the labour market for youth, and the success of measures to encourage that, such as the dual system of education with apprenticeship. She contrasted that with the high risk of failure associated with entrepreneurship. She supported steps taken to measure economic outcomes in terms of quality job creation. Quoting from paragraph 12 of the resolution concerning human resources training and development adopted by the ILC at its 88th Session, 2000, which stated that there was no universal model for investing in training, she urged employers to take more active responsibilities and commitment in providing training, jointly with workers and governments. She concluded by reminding the Committee that collective responsibility should be taken to ensure that a young person was not a dislocated person.

113. The Chairperson closed the discussion on point 1 and expressed his satisfaction with the various contributions that had been made, which covered a number of key points concerning access of young persons to decent work. He opened the floor to begin the discussion of point 2, which he considered to be crucial in laying the basis for the subsequent points for discussion.

Point 2. What are the components of the package of policies and programmes that encourage decent work for young people?

114. In his opening statement, the Employer Vice-Chairperson pointed out that there was a clear need for a wide array of national policies and programmes to meet the youth employment challenge, respecting the diversity of young people, of the economies in which they lived

and the differences between businesses that would seek to employ them. He recalled the back-to-basics propositions mentioned in his initial intervention, and added that, in effect, the disadvantages set out in the first point for discussion established the grounds for action to be taken.

115. He listed four categories of stakeholder interested in policies and programmes for young people (employers, youth, educators and governments), and proposed four specific actions for each stakeholder, calling that the "Employer's 16", a tool kit for practical youth employment initiatives.

116. With respect to employers, he proposed that they should:

- review job descriptions to see if they could be adapted to facilitate hiring of young people;

- ensure that their hiring processes recognized skills and capacity, not just qualifications and years of experience;

- participate also as educators and trainers to ensure that youth knew what business needed; and

- liaise and connect with young people and their organizations to obtain information about the source of labour that would be available to them and to inform youth of what employers expected.

117. As regards young people themselves, he urged them to:

- participate in basic learning, to develop essential skills of literacy, numeracy and where possible, technical know-how;

- actively look for work and job opportunities as soon as possible, even if only for work experience or basic part-time work, or a job that combined work with education;

- prepare themselves for responsibilities that accompanied employment in terms of assessing their willingness to learn and to adapt, to be reliable and productive; and

- develop skills that made them employable and attractive to employers.

118. Regarding educators, he proposed that they:

- fully integrate basic skills and qualities into students' education;

- provide career guidance and support to young people, including integrating career guidance and knowledge of industry into curricula;

- make education more flexible, through initiatives such as enhancing transferability of educational programmes and qualifications; and

- make education and training more relevant to business needs.

119. With respect to governments, he called on them to:

- support sustainable economic growth by adopting national policies and programmes, including regulatory frameworks, that would attract business investment and support competitive and productive enterprises;

- invest in basic education and development of employable skills for young people;

- support the development of the necessary physical and social infrastructure, including ALMPs that were relevant to industry and young people's needs, and which had measurable goals; and

- encourage the development of entrepreneurship and SMEs, which were a crucial part of all economies and accounted for much potential employment, in line with the recommendations set out in the report of the UNDP Commission on the Private Sector and Development, entitled *Unleashing entrepreneurship: Making business work for the poor* (2004).

120. To conclude, the Employer Vice-Chairperson emphasized the need to deal with underlying causes and not just symptoms, and to avoid short-term, quick-fix measures, which would not provide an appropriate return. He noted the necessary preconditions for investment and the establishment of competitive and productive enterprises, such as stable governance and legal institutions. He proposed that the 16 practical initiatives he had outlined should form the core framework of national policies and programmes for youth employment.

121. The Worker Vice-Chairperson indicated that simplistic solutions would not suffice when addressing the issue of youth employment. She stressed that in responding to that question the Workers' group would focus on policies to expand the quantity of employment, and would comment on employment quality issues and recommendations for ILO action under later points for discussion. She observed the consensus of the Committee participants that raising aggregate demand was the key to improving the labour market situation of young people. She drew attention to the Declaration on employment and poverty alleviation in Africa from the Third Extraordinary Summit of the African Union on Employment and Poverty Alleviation in Africa (Ouagadougou, September 2004), in which governments were called upon to make employment creation an explicit and central objective of economic and social policies. She noted that all organizations that had participated in drafting the background report for the Summit, which included the ILO, the World Bank and the International Monetary Fund, had agreed that youth employment must be addressed through an integrated approach. She stressed that macroeconomic policies were of key importance to determining outcomes of job creation; therefore, practical consideration should be given to creating an environment that fostered both public and private investment via macroeconomic policies. She advised, however, that governments should build an employment-impact assessment into the framework of macroeconomic policies, and noted that implementation of such an assessment would require the development of tools that effectively measured both the primary and secondary impacts of macroeconomic policies on employment.

122. The Worker Vice-Chairperson reiterated the need to reform international trade and financial policies and to improve the functioning of the rules and institutions that impacted on the global economy, for example, in rethinking policies on international debt payments. She suggested that the institutions governing the global market be addressed in the conclusions of the Committee. She hoped that the conclusions would also reflect the recommendations of the World Commission on the Social Dimension of Globalization to develop practical initiatives to increase the employment intensity of growth. She said that employment-intensive initiatives had mostly focused on improving physical infrastructure but could also be expanded to improving social infrastructure, and noted that independent evaluations of such programmes had found that a labour-based approach to increasing employment was both less costly than alternative approaches and also more efficient in terms of the impact on household income. She recommended, therefore, that employment-intensive investment strategies should be extended, both in terms of increasing the number of countries involved as well as of adapting the approach to less traditional sectors such as the health-care and education sectors which offered a large potential for rapid expansion.

123. In conclusion, she called for renewed attention to development in rural economies, including the establishment of agriculture processing industries, which offered large employment growth potential because of their relatively high employment elasticities, especially in low-income countries. Finally, she stated that a comprehensive policy promoting decent work would include ALMPs that would address, among other things, the improvement of the supply side of labour through training programmes and promotion of decent standards in human resources development, such as those encompassed in ILO Recommendation No. 195.

124. Government members, including those from the Islamic Republic of Iran and Italy, commented that, despite the large number of policies and programmes that had been developed and implemented, youth unemployment and underemployment persisted. That concern was taken up in interventions from the Government member of Canada, speaking on behalf of the Government members of a number of IMEC countries, the Government member of South Africa and others, who called for better evaluation and assessment of programmes against well-defined objectives, and support for programmes that had proven to be effective.

125. The Government member of Egypt proposed that four elements be included in any solutions to youth unemployment: political backing at the national and international levels; financial support by governments and the private sector; boosting entrepreneurship, taking into account the importance of technology; and involving youth in the shaping of solutions. The design of solutions should also take into consideration particular political and economic situations of different countries.

126. As many Government members had described barriers to young persons finding jobs, they equally emphasized the need for effective placement services, a point mentioned by the Government members of Italy and Mexico, and further elaborated by the Government member of Algeria, who described programmes that helped recent graduates find work by providing assistance with wage costs, and the recent expansion of employment services in his country.

127. Access to useful labour market information was another policy and programme element mentioned by a number of Government members. The Government member of Italy observed that young people in her country were very slow to join the labour market and lacked good information about work options, an issue that the Government member of Japan also addressed in describing the "vocational museum" approach to that issue. The Government member of France added that career orientation and information needed to be provided to young people in school, a point touched on by many speakers. Another aspect of labour market information was highlighted by the Government member of Jamaica, reflecting on CARICOM experience and the need for quality labour market information to signal skills needs so that training institutions could respond. Quality labour market information and the capacity for useful analysis were cited as a priority area for development by the Government member of Nigeria, speaking on behalf of the Africa group.

128. The need for skills training to be relevant to the job market was a common theme. The Government member of Nigeria spoke of the Africa group's emphasis on the need for the reform of education and training systems to make them more relevant, and their call to employers to assist directly in building that capacity. A comprehensive approach to building lifelong learning opportunities, including on-the-job training, was mentioned by the Government member of France, who emphasized that that would benefit youth but

would be useful throughout individuals' working lives. A number of Government members, including those of South Africa and some Caribbean countries, maintained the need for a comprehensive policy to act as a framework for initiatives within each country.

129. The Government member of Canada, speaking on behalf of a number of Government members of IMEC countries, introduced the issue of recognition of formal and non-formal learning as an important policy issue, a point that was also noted by other Government members, including the Government member of Jamaica.

130. Access to education at all levels was a key concern for many Government members. Recommended approaches included: ensuring universal, free access to basic education and, where possible, to higher levels of education; provision of student loans or work/study programmes to ensure access to post-secondary education; eliminating entry barriers to technical training and focusing instead on acquired competencies.

131. The different experiences of young women, of rural, isolated, excluded, at-risk and other marginalized groups of youth were recognized by many Government members, who emphasized that specialized programmes and policies addressing the needs of those young people would be required. Specialized programmes would also be required in specific circumstances, such as in the case of post-conflict countries where a range of integrated policies running from firearms control to training for ex-combatants would be required.

132. Most Government members supported entrepreneurship and self-employment as viable options for youth employment, but cautioned that policies and programmes must include adequate support, particularly mentoring and assistance with elements such as business planning and market analysis, which could most effectively be provided by successful employers. The Government member of South Africa added that small business development was also an important element in the policy mix, particularly in Africa where there was low economic growth, but he emphasized that support to small businesses had to be provided within a broader economic policy context and target youth employment specifically. He also mentioned worker cooperatives as another approach to employment development, a theme expanded on by the Government member of the Bolivarian Republic of Venezuela. Many Government members, including those of Algeria and the Islamic Republic of Iran, cited the centrality of access to credit for entrepreneurs.

133. The Government member of Nigeria, speaking on behalf of the Africa group, suggested that the necessary economic framework to achieve decent work for young people could be addressed in part through employment-centred macroeconomic policies, and that that could be supported through a redefinition of the MDGs to include a specific emphasis on employment.

134. The Government member of the Republic of Korea, among others, spoke of the need for a comprehensive approach to the development of national action plans for youth. Those plans could include a variety of strategies to increase overall demand and enhance employability.

135. A number of speakers also noted the need to ensure that basic anti-discrimination policies were in place, as a minimum, for ensuring that young people were able to find employment.

136. Finally, many Government members, including the Government member of Tunisia, endorsed the notion that young people should be directly involved in designing, delivering and evaluating policies and programmes for youth.

137. The Employer Vice-Chairperson summarized the main points that had emerged from the discussion, noting that the diversity of circumstances and the unevenness of problems implied context-specific solutions. He was encouraged that there already existed multitudes of policies and programmes aimed at reducing youth unemployment and underemployment through improving the process of transition from school to work as well as improving the economic environment for growth and competitiveness.

138. In pointing out some of the specific contributions made by the Government members of the Committee, he noted the efforts of Algeria and the Islamic Republic of Iran to provide job experience to unemployed youth and make available microcredit for young entrepreneurs. He also supported the view expressed by the Government member of the Republic of Korea that employment was ultimately created by enterprises and not by the government, and there was hence a need for a conducive framework for business development. He supported the need for special measures for youth with particular disadvantages and endorsed the call for the evaluation of policies and programmes. He agreed with the Government member of the Syrian Arab Republic on the benefit of reduced entry-level barriers to entrepreneurship.

139. The Worker Vice-Chairperson found that, despite the diversity of needs and experiences across countries and within countries, a consensus was emerging. She emphasized the importance of finding an integrated approach to addressing the youth employment challenge.

140. Highlighting some of the contributions made by the Government members of the Committee, the Worker Vice-Chairperson supported the views expressed by the Africa group, for a comprehensive package of policies for youth employment, at the macro, meso and micro levels. She recognized France's five-year plan on social cohesion and its efforts to combine formal training with on-the-job experience. She called for ILO support in replicating the South African model of cooperative development. Highlighting the contribution made by the Government member of Canada, she emphasized the need for multiple solutions, the importance of recognition and of a certification system of both formal and informal learning processes, and the need for a proactive reform of labour market policies. Noting the comment made by the Government member of the Bolivarian Republic of Venezuela, she emphasized the importance of quality in training.

Point 3. What are the respective roles of governments, employers' and workers' organizations in promoting pathways to decent work for young women and men?

141. The Employer Vice-Chairperson opened the discussion of this point by observing that the answer was in the question itself – all three partners must work collaboratively in their respective roles. Without their collaboration, the policies and programmes discussed earlier could not be achieved. He referred to the "Employer's 16" tool kit introduced under the second point for discussion and the roles described there. He added three additional points on the role of governments: the shaping of labour market policies, recognizing that for some governments that capacity was limited and needed to be built; the building of a regulatory system that supported employers not only to employ people but to "do business"; and the roles set out in the Human Resources Development Recommendation, 2004 (No. 195). In terms of the role of employers, he stated that they should work with governments to bring about a good environment for business creation; that they could and should act to improve education and vocational training as well as job creation; and that they could perform an important role in publicly advocating for solutions to the youth employment challenge.

142. The Worker Vice-Chairperson agreed that the social partners should ensure the participation of young people in policy development and implementation. She mentioned with pride that, with herself as an exception, the Worker representatives in the Drafting Group were under 30 years of age. In the opinion of the Workers' group, the role of governments had been well expressed by many examples to date. Governments had taken responsibility for action in finding first jobs for young people, for evaluating the results of that action, and for collecting and analysing data to discern trends and needs. Governments were providing universal access to education and training, developing systems of career counselling through job centres, promoting cooperatives, promoting a stable environment for public and private investment, encouraging land ownership and access to credit, and promoting decent work through legislation guaranteeing freedom of association, hours of work and safety. Governments and the social partners, bilaterally and in a tripartite approach, had roles to play in improving the match in supply and demand for labour and in improving conditions at the workplace. Other areas in which governments had a role, along with other partners at all levels, included migration policies and international aid and debt relief. Trade union roles included advocating a rights-based approach and reaching out to young people. In conclusion, she stressed that roles were not likely to be as structured and distinct as the Employers' group had suggested, but could be synchronized through tripartite discussion.

143. The majority of Government members agreed that governments bore the lead responsibility in areas related to education and training, with the Africa group emphasizing school curricula, the Government member of the Philippines and the Government member of Uruguay, speaking on behalf of the MERCOSUR countries, education, training and competency certification, the Government member of Portugal, a programme aimed at modernization and social cohesion, and other Government members calling for special training and programmes for those requiring them including, for example, the needs of ex-combatants, as identified by the Government member of the Democratic Republic of the Congo.

144. Labour market information, analysis and better matching of training content to labour market needs were accepted as a responsibility by many Government members. That was further elaborated by the Government members of Denmark and Sweden, the latter describing the level of quantitative and qualitative evaluation of the results of labour market policies undertaken by her Government, so that good results could be pursued and unintended consequences avoided.

145. The role of governments in creating a positive environment for business through effective regulation, legislation and tax regimes was noted by most Government members, including those speaking on behalf of the Africa and IMEC groups. That positive environment also included specific support to entrepreneurship and small business.

146. Most Government members referenced the need to include the social partners in designing policies and programmes, and many identified areas where employers' and workers' organizations could contribute in more depth: the Africa group asked for clarification on how employers would contribute, while the Government member of Canada summarized the views of some IMEC countries, indicating that employers' organizations could contribute to skills development, undertake research, provide opportunities for young people, provide resources to education systems, and provide friendly working environments for young people.

147. The role of social dialogue and collective bargaining as a way to involve the social partners was emphasized by the Government member of Uruguay, speaking on behalf of the Government members of MERCOSUR countries.

148. The Employer Vice-Chairperson expressed his appreciation for the contributions made by governments, particularly their willingness to assess the effectiveness of policies and programmes, and their acceptance of the need to provide macroeconomic and regulatory frameworks conducive to the development and growth of businesses and their capacity to create employment. Recognizing that each country had its own economic priorities, he appreciated the many areas of commonality that had been expressed in the summary statements made by a number of Government members that recognized the need for flexible systems that balanced protection with labour market needs, that supported entrepreneurship and reduced barriers, and that reduced transaction costs. He thanked governments for recognizing that laws did not themselves create jobs, but stressed that laws could create the stability and certainty needed for investment, and thus for job creation. He recalled the examples given, citing roles for governments, the social partners and young people themselves. Responding to the Government member of Nigeria's question, he asserted that employers would meet their responsibilities by working with governments to develop policies and programmes for youth.

149. The Worker Vice-Chairperson agreed with summaries made by some Government members of the roles of the tripartite partners. She appreciated the example given of Sweden's in-depth assessment of its active labour market programmes, and suggested that as an area for capacity building for other governments. She also welcomed the emphasis that the Government member of the Philippines had put on social dialogue, collective bargaining and freedom of association. She expressed her group's support to countries that suffered from armed conflicts. A major feature of ILO work should be to help countries emerging from conflict expand employment opportunities for ex-combatants. The Government member of Portugal had highlighted the critical need to focus on education, while the Government member of Denmark had emphasized the role that the social partners could play through social dialogue and collective bargaining. She welcomed the comprehensive statement made by the Government member of Canada but clarified that support from her group for approaches which balanced social protection with labour market needs would be based on the degree to which protection was realistically available. She noted that the Danish "flexi-security" model was based on a relatively high level of unemployment benefits and other social security payments. If that model was to be promoted in other countries, it would require similar levels of unemployment benefits and social security payments. In terms of simplification of business regulations, she noted that her group did not object to the simplification of bureaucratic procedures, but it would not accept any weakening of rights or protection.

Point 4. What is required to ensure that international labour standards address youth employment?

150. The Employer Vice-Chairperson stressed that international standards needed to facilitate the delivery of practical national policies. He suggested that the "Employer's 16" tool kit, delivered through constructive and active roles played by all tripartite stakeholders, could serve that objective. International standards must recognize and facilitate a conducive environment for economic activity and job creation, and should help address the issue of employability of young people, where quality of work was linked to capacity. The Declaration on Fundamental Principles and Rights at Work and its Follow-up, 1998 (ILO), was one of the most significant international means to ensure the rights of young people. Other standards relevant to youth existed, and there was no need for more standards. Instead, the focus should be on ensuring better use of the existing standards, through practical policy work, and monitoring their application. Since most youth were employed in the informal economy, international labour standards must be implemented in such a way as to facilitate the transition of SMEs from the informal to the formal economy. Lastly, given the diversity of national and local situations faced by the employers of youth,

international labour standards were most useful as a benchmark for business operations, without detailed prescriptions that risked being inappropriate.

151. The Worker Vice-Chairperson emphasized that the quality of jobs was as important as the quantity. The speaker stressed that all international labour standards were applicable to young workers and jobseekers and drew particular attention to: child labour,[2] forced labour,[3] the informal economy,[4] precariousness,[5] agriculture,[6] safety and health,[7] equality and non-discrimination,[8] wage policy,[9] working time,[10] freedom of association and collective bargaining,[11] and labour inspection,[12] as well as others which had been

---

[2] The Minimum Age Convention, 1973 (No. 138), the Minimum Age Recommendation, 1973 (No. 146), the Worst Forms of Child Labour Convention, 1999 (No. 182), and Worst Forms of Child Labour Recommendation, 1999 (No. 190).

[3] The Forced Labour Convention, 1930 (No. 29), the Forced Labour (Indirect Compulsion) Recommendation, 1930 (No. 35), and the Abolition of Forced Labour Convention, 1957 (No. 105).

[4] The Forced Labour Convention, 1930 (No. 29), the Abolition of Forced Labour Convention, 1957 (No. 105), the Freedom of Association and Protection of the Right to Organise Convention, 1948 (No. 87), the Right to Organise and Collective Bargaining Convention, 1949 (No. 98), the Equal Remuneration Convention, 1951 (No. 100), the Discrimination (Employment and Occupation) Convention, 1958 (No. 111), the Minimum Age Convention, 1973 (No. 138), and the Worst Forms of Child Labour Convention, 1999 (No. 182).

[5] The Private Employment Agencies Convention, 1997 (No. 181), the Private Employment Agencies Recommendation, 1997 (No. 188), the Part-Time Work Convention, 1994 (No. 175), and the Part-Time Work Recommendation, 1994 (No. 182).

[6] The Safety and Health in Agriculture Convention, 2001 (No. 184), and the Safety and Health in Agriculture Recommendation, 2001 (No. 192).

[7] The Occupational Safety and Health Convention, 1981 (No. 155), and its Protocol, and the Occupational Safety and Health Recommendation, 1981 (No. 164).

[8] The Equal Remuneration Convention, 1951 (No. 100), the Equal Remuneration Recommendation, 1951 (No. 90), the Discrimination (Employment and Occupation) Convention, 1958 (No. 111), the Discrimination (Employment and Occupation) Recommendation, 1958 (No. 111), the Vocational Rehabilitation and Employment (Disabled Persons) Convention, 1983 (No. 159), the Vocational Rehabilitation and Employment (Disabled Persons) Recommendation, 1983 (No. 168), the Migration for Employment Convention (Revised), 1949 (No. 97), the Migration for Employment Recommendation (Revised), 1949 (No. 86), the Migrant Workers (Supplementary Provisions) Convention, 1975 (No. 143), the Migrant Workers Recommendation, 1975 (No. 151), the Maternity Protection Convention, 2000 (No. 183), the Maternity Protection Recommendation, 2000 (No. 191), and the Indigenous and Tribal Peoples Convention, 1989 (No. 169).

[9] The Minimum Wage Fixing Convention, 1970 (No. 131), the Minimum Wage Fixing Recommendation, 1970 (No. 135), the Protection of Wages Convention, 1949 (No. 95), and the Protection of Wages Recommendation, 1949 (No. 85).

[10] The Hours of Work (Industry) Convention, 1919 (No. 1), and the Hours of Work (Commerce and Offices) Convention, 1930 (No. 30).

[11] The Freedom of Association and Protection of the Right to Organise Convention, 1948 (No. 87), and the Right to Organise and Collective Bargaining Convention, 1949 (No. 98).

[12] The Labour Inspection Convention, 1947 (No. 81), and its Protocol, and the Labour Inspection Recommendation, 1947 (No. 81).

mentioned in the report.[13] She hoped that the debate would lead to a renewed commitment to the promotion of employment through key instruments such as the Employment Policy Convention, 1964 (No. 122), to make employment creation a top priority of all national agendas. She drew particular attention to the importance of the universal rights of freedom of association and collective bargaining for young people, and called for an increase in labour inspections to eliminate abuses of those rights. Lastly, the Worker Vice-Chairperson proposed a promotional campaign for implementing ILO Conventions relevant to young people, based on 14 elements:

- the ILO should prepare a charter of young people's rights based on the relevant Conventions and Recommendations, to be distributed widely in as many languages as possible;

- the ILO should draw up guidelines on how governments can integrate the rights of young people into employment policy;

- trade unions and employers' organizations should prepare school training modules to educate young people on their rights and on the principles of industrial relations;

- the ILO should help to strengthen the capacity of workers' organizations to reach out to young people;

- the ILO should develop a list of key indicators for decent work for young people;

- the ILO should sponsor a global campaign called "You Have Rights" utilizing all media outlets that best attract the attention of young people;

- young people's rights should be promoted in the campaign for the extension of social protection;

- special attention should be paid to addressing the situation of young migrant workers within the ILO multilateral framework for all migrant workers;

- governments should organize tripartite national youth employment agencies that could elaborate employment promotion policies for young people and provide guidance on training possibilities and rights;

- governments should seek measures to ensure the protection of youth in minimum wage legislation;

- the ILO should develop guidelines summarizing best practices for youth employment policies at the national level;

- the ILO should strengthen the capacity of employers' and workers' organizations to participate in the formulation of employment promotion activities for young people;

- the ILO should investigate trends in employment of young people;

---

[13] The Unemployment Convention, 1919 (No. 2), the Night Work of Young Persons (Non-Industrial Occupations) Convention, 1946 (No. 79), Medical Examination of Young Persons (Non-Industrial Occupations) Convention, 1946 (No. 78), Employment Service Convention, 1948 (No. 88), the Human Resources Development Convention, 1975 (No. 142), the Labour Administration Convention, 1978 (No. 150), the Employment Promotion and Protection against Unemployment Convention, 1988 (No. 168), and the Night Work Convention, 1990 (No. 171).

- the ILO should consider developing new international labour standards to ensure that all workers, including youth, in triangular employment relationships are covered by social protection.

152. The Government member of the Netherlands, speaking on behalf of the Government members of the IMEC group, echoed the view of the Employers' group that there was no need for new labour standards targeted specifically at youth. Rather, the focus should be on better use and enforcement of current standards, particularly those included in the Declaration on Fundamental Principles and Rights at Work and its Follow-up, 1998 (ILO). An important means could be through national action plans. The Government member of Peru cautioned against creating new standards since the integration processes under way required strict compliance with labour legislation. She said that her country was in a position to strengthen its labour inspection system to improve compliance with national and international standards. The Government member of Nigeria, speaking on behalf of the Africa group, concurred and proposed enhancing the capacity of labour inspectors, as well as strengthening sanctions in cases of failure to comply with the law. The Government member of South Africa insisted on the urgency of strengthening law enforcement mechanisms for existing standards rather than focusing energy on developing new ones. The Government member of Mexico recalled that international labour standards were adopted by a tripartite body and hence their enforcement was a shared responsibility of the tripartite partners.

153. The Government member of the Syrian Arab Republic reminded governments of the need to remove barriers to employment creation. The Government member of Jamaica, speaking also on behalf of the Government members of the Bahamas, Barbados, Suriname, and Trinidad and Tobago, added that, although it was important to ensure that international labour standards were implemented, it was also important to revise some of them to reflect current changes in the world of work, such as the increasing prevalence of temporary employment. Any revision of standards should take youth into account. The Government member of Namibia considered that it was absolutely necessary to ensure that international labour standards could be adapted to different situations. The Government member of Nigeria, speaking on behalf of the Africa group, concurred, saying that international labour standards needed to be adapted to the specific situations and needs of small and medium-sized enterprises, and should be revised in order to include youth, particularly young people working in the informal sector. The Government member of the Netherlands, speaking on behalf of the Government members of the IMEC group, agreed on the need to improve working conditions in the informal economy and also suggested that standards-related activities be addressed in the sectors of the formal economy where young workers were numerous.

154. The Government member of Peru agreed with the Workers' group's proposal for a promotional campaign and suggested also promoting the creation of new enterprises. The Government members of France and Mexico both agreed that a campaign would be useful and added that it should encourage ratification of existing Conventions. The Government member of Namibia expounded on the importance of such a campaign, particularly in the informal economy: employers in his country were either ignorant or not well prepared because they did not comply with labour standards; and workers' representatives were not able to fulfil their role of monitoring compliance due to the fact that most workers were casual and did not belong to any trade union. The Government member of Nigeria, speaking on behalf of the Africa group, refined the proposal to include making human resources managers aware of the standards with which they needed to comply, and suggested that a campaign be directed at employers, particularly in the informal economy. The Government member of the Syrian Arab Republic hoped that a promotional campaign could heighten young people's awareness of their rights and labour standards and called on ministries of labour to undertake the responsibility for ensuring that national standards

included youth. The Government member of Jamaica, speaking also on behalf of the Government members of the Bahamas, Barbados, Suriname, and Trinidad and Tobago, also considered it necessary for governments to create awareness among the relevant national institutions of the importance of integrating youth employment in standards and policies. The Government member of the Netherlands, speaking on behalf of the Government members of the IMEC group, noted the importance of engaging the private sector in such a campaign. The Government member of Jamaica, speaking also on behalf of the Government members of the Bahamas, Barbados, Suriname, and Trinidad and Tobago proposed that the ILO elaborate a code of practice on youth employment similar to the one it had developed concerning gender issues.

155. The Employer Vice-Chairperson noted that consensus appeared to be emerging that there was no need to develop new labour standards concerning youth employment. Rather, it was necessary to make better use of existing standards through promotional activities, technical cooperation and the improvement of law enforcement mechanisms. He felt it had been generally accepted by the Committee that there was a need for some of those standards to be reviewed in order to be relevant to different situations. He reiterated that a rights-based approach did not fully serve the interests of young people, and employment rights were only part of the overall employment objective; therefore, the 14 issues proposed by the Workers' group had too narrow a focus. Furthermore, decent work indicators were not practical since there were different notions of decent work deficits, due to diversity of national experiences and circumstances. Concerning awareness-raising campaigns, he cautioned that such a task should not be the sole responsibility of the ILO but that it should be shared by multiple partners, especially at the national level.

156. The Worker Vice-Chairperson cited the Global Employment Agenda's declaration that decent work was desirable from both a social and economic perspective. Labour markets were socially embedded and improvements in the quality of employment were the best way to enhance productivity and foster economic growth. She expressed her concern at hearing words such as "flexible" and "adaptable" since standards were universal. She agreed that there was no need for further Conventions on youth employment. The focus should be about ensuring the ratification and implementation of existing Conventions, including strengthening labour inspection. Concerning decent work indicators, she stressed the need for empirical information in order to be able to undertake the right course of action.

Point 5. **What should be the priorities for the ILO's policy, research, advocacy and technical assistance with regard to promoting decent and productive work for youth?**

157. The Employer Vice-Chairperson, reflecting on the comparative advantage of the ILO, stressed its important role in bridging the gap between the work of international bodies and on-the-ground circumstances of employers' and workers' organizations and youth themselves, at the national level. In that regard, he suggested the ILO focus its policy efforts on barriers to access to employment, an appropriate environment for the creation of jobs for youth, employability issues and entrepreneurship development. Since a number of economies had a greater supply of labour than demand, initiatives to enhance capacity to secure self-employment were seen as an important mechanism for employment generation. As sustainability of such initiatives was paramount, there was a need to ensure that youth was provided with appropriate information and training about the nature of business undertakings. Finally, he noted that the policy work of the ILO should be constructively framed around the GEA, which was complementary to the "four Es" of the YEN.

158. Commenting on the issue of the ILO's knowledge-building on youth employment, the Employer Vice-Chairperson suggested that research be directed at examining the nature of the challenge in various economies, since information was a precondition for effective national policy. He argued that the research should be well designed, well targeted and supported by the social partners, to ensure its relevance. He noted the importance of information on: successes and failures in addressing youth employment; the means by which youth could access the labour market; identification of appropriate entry-level skills; and the feasibility of an international fund for skills development and training, as proposed by the World Bank.

159. While advocacy formed an important part of the work of the ILO, the Employer Vice-Chairperson stressed that it had to be in accord with, and supported by, the social partners. He reiterated the back-to-basics propositions of the Employers' group, emphasizing that the combined and collective pool of knowledge of the Committee members should be made well known and well understood by actors at the ground level. The focus of advocacy efforts should include job preparedness, practical ways to access the labour market, as well as promoting the advantages of employing young people.

160. With respect to technical assistance, the Employer Vice-Chairperson urged the ILO to work with the tripartite partners to advise on how to create an appropriate regulatory environment and economic policy framework, as well as structuring entrepreneurship activities and information. He suggested the development of a set of tools that could be used flexibly in formulating youth employment policy and programmes. Drawing on an example from Indonesia, a YEN lead country, he noted that such assistance could take the form of facilitating the building of networks and relationships between various stakeholders. He added that other forms of assistance could revolve around building and providing support to compile a knowledge base of good practice on youth employment, including education and skills acquisition. He commented on the Worker Vice-Chairperson's reference to a new international labour standard, reiterating the Employers' group's lack of support.

161. In conclusion, the Employers' group called for increasing partnerships with other international agencies, citing the YEN as an example. In such interagency relationships, the Employer Vice-Chairperson urged the ILO to undertake initiatives in coordinating such relationships in order to build a global network, as well as in sharing best practices on the policy activities related to youth employment.

162. The Worker Vice-Chairperson stated that paragraphs 7-10 of the conclusions of the Tripartite Meeting on Youth Employment: The Way Forward (October 2004), which addressed ILO action in the area of youth employment, constituted a solid basis for the conclusions of the Committee. She proposed a package of policies directed at assisting developing countries, where the challenge of youth employment was most severe. The package comprised ten components:

- Reforming the international policy framework to ensure more countries benefited from globalization.

- Placing employment and decent work at the centre of economic policies. She suggested the implementation of decent work would require the ILO to develop a package of indicators to assess decent work deficits. The ILO should develop an evaluation methodology to assess progress being made towards decent work.

- Enhancing the employment intensity of growth, particularly through employment-intensive infrastructure development programmes, noting the extensive work of the ILO in this area, as well as recent positive evaluations of programmes in Asia. She urged the ILO to expand that area of technical cooperation activities and to ensure adequate staffing.

- Expanding other employment-intensive private-sector initiatives including in tourism, culture and housing.

- Upgrading incomes and productivity in the agricultural sector, as well as developing upstream and downstream value-chains in primary-sector-based commodities. She argued that a similar sectoral approach could be adopted for expansion of private-sector activities to other sectors with potential for youth.

- Expanding of high-quality public services, including health care, education – especially in primary education in poor rural communities – and utilities.

- Increasing incomes and improving employment conditions and productivity in the informal economy. She recalled the pioneering energy and capacity of the ILO in the 1970s and the 1980s in the area of the informal economy, and called for further technical assistance and capacity building in that area.

- Adapting and expanding the use of ALMPs, which had been widely implemented in industrialized countries, to the needs and context of developing countries. While recognizing the cost of implementing such policies, the exchange of information and experiences could be useful for developing countries.

- Promoting collective bargaining, freedom of association, tripartite dialogue and labour legislation to ensure that work undertaken is decent.

- Carrying out well-funded and high-profile campaigns to promote international labour standards relevant to young people and adopting new international instruments to ensure all young workers receive legislative protection.

163. In conclusion, the Worker Vice-Chairperson emphasized the importance of involving youth in policy implementation, suggesting the use of online facilities as a forum for promotion and debate as well as face-to-face discussion through youth networks.

164. The Government member of Bahrain, remarking on the extensive reform programmes in the areas of labour markets, the economy and education and training in his country, noted that economic reform should seek to look for the value added in deregulating markets in order to enable the proper functioning of the private sector. He urged the ILO to support governments and employers' and workers' organizations in their efforts to enhance the employment options of young people.

165. The Government member of Canada, speaking also on behalf of the Government members of the following countries of the IMEC group: Australia, Denmark, Ireland, Italy, Japan, New Zealand, Portugal, Slovenia, Sweden, Switzerland, United Kingdom and the United States, suggested the ILO focus its efforts on working with other international organizations to ensure the provision of decent work for young people. She recommended that the ILO support the participation of young people in the discussions on the formulation of policies and programmes; develop tools to guide countries in their decent work programmes perhaps by promoting international exchanges of information on youth programmes; share and analyse best practices in the promotion of decent work; increase the capacity of the social partners to contribute to the promotion of decent work for young people; direct its technical assistance toward developing countries; design and implement a three-year knowledge-exchange strategy on youth employment, including peer evaluations of national action plans and the design of a virtual library on the ILO web site where best practices could be exchanged; establish and maintain a web forum for the exchange of

ideas and the development of lessons learned from promoting decent work for young people. She emphasized that all recommendations were subject to ILO budgetary constraints.

166. A number of Government members shared the experiences of particular initiatives in their own countries. The Government member of Japan supported the views expressed by the Government member of Canada, supplementing them with the experiences in his country. He noted the ILO role in organizing seminars for the purpose of promoting skills development. The Government member of Morocco shared the positive experience of his country in working with the ILO to support reforms in the textiles sector. The Government member of Luxembourg brought to the attention of the Committee the experience of the peer review programme of the European Employment Strategy, launched by the European Commission in 1999, and suggested the ILO serve as coordinator for a similar exchange of information on experiences in youth employment policies. He proposed that the ILO undertake a review of decent work for young people in order to assess and disseminate good practice and recommend instruments for promoting decent work. The Government member of Brazil, speaking also on behalf of the Government members of Argentina, Mexico, Paraguay, Peru, Uruguay and the Bolivarian Republic of Venezuela, noted that his Government had developed a national programme to help young people find employment, granting loans to young people and subsidies to companies willing to employ them. He emphasized that an evaluation had demonstrated that training was the most effective way to help young people enter the labour market.

167. The Government member of Nigeria, speaking on behalf of the Africa group, supported the Workers' group's proposals to review the conclusions of the Tripartite Meeting on Youth Employment: The Way Forward (October 2004) and to focus on the concerns of developing countries. Specifically, she drew attention to the adverse affects of debt repayments in developing countries and urged the ILO to link with other organizations to lend its voice to the cause of debt relief. She expressed the wish that the recommendations of the World Commission on the Social Dimension of Globalization be reflected in the conclusions of the Committee, given that they were of direct relevance. Specific proposals for ILO work included: evaluating the impact of economic and social reforms undertaken in developing countries on youth employment; assisting governments in mobilizing the necessary resources to offer safety nets to those affected by reforms; resuscitating the Jobs for Africa programme or initiating a programme of similar scope; engaging in technical cooperation that would lead to the enhancement of employability, entrepreneurship and sustainable self-employment; recommending monitoring and evaluation methods for technical cooperation programmes; undertaking a promotional and awareness campaign on international labour standards and rights; and establishing guidelines for the implementation of those standards.

168. The Government member of the Syrian Arab Republic stressed that the ILO should carry out technical cooperation programmes aimed at enabling governments and employers to: develop training programmes that met the needs of the labour market; provide technical assistance to governments on the modernization of law and the implementation of clear employment strategies; design information campaigns on international labour standards; promote social dialogue to increase awareness of the needs of the labour market; and stimulate donors to provide funds.

169. The Government member of Jamaica, speaking also on behalf of the Government members of the Bahamas, Barbados, Suriname, and Trinidad and Tobago, agreed with the Employers' group on the strategic position of the ILO with regard to youth employment. He emphasized that financial support would be crucial for Caribbean countries and, in that regard, the ILO was in a unique position to raise funds. He agreed with the Workers' group that ILO action should focus on developing countries. He recommended that the ILO:

concentrate on making progress by ensuring an effective implementation of programmes with the help of its constituents; promote the development of specific action plans aimed at ensuring the inclusion of youth in the labour market; help countries develop information systems on the labour market; carry out tripartite consultation on youth employment policies; promote the respect of core labour standards for all workers; raise awareness among young people on the importance of being represented by employers' and workers' organizations; provide technical assistance for the development of employment creation and skills training programmes and policies; and foster the creation of distance-learning institutions.

170. The Government member of the United Kingdom strongly supported the statement made by the Government member of Canada on behalf of the IMEC group. She informed the Committee that her Government would support the need for concrete action in the area of youth employment at the forthcoming summit of G8 countries and advocate the recommendation recently adopted by the African Commission to include a further 25 sub-Saharan countries in the YEN, urging the ILO and the governments of other G8 countries to do the same. She emphasized the value of a global peer exchange, which would allow countries to move beyond the sharing of good practice to that of best performance. She suggested that the ILO help countries develop data-collection systems not only on general employment but on youth employment in the informal economy, the level of education and training required by the labour market and the impact of HIV/AIDS, gender and armed conflict. With regard to the MDG review in September 2005, she stressed that the ILO was well positioned to undertake a global analysis of progress made.

171. The Government member of France suggested that the ILO advocate the integration of youth employment into national poverty reduction strategies. She emphasized the importance of exchanging best practices, in particular through a virtual library, peer review and the YEN.

172. The Government member of Tunisia supported the statements made by the Africa group and the Employer Vice-Chairperson that the ILO should advocate the advantages of employing young people. For that purpose, it should carry out research to establish good practices that could be adapted for countries in similar circumstances.

173. The Government member of Denmark, speaking also on behalf of the Government members of France, Norway, Portugal and Sweden, considered that ILO technical assistance should be targeted at developing countries to assist in the collection and dissemination of data, the design of youth employment action plans and the development of effective public employment services.

174. In summary, the Employer Vice-Chairperson acknowledged the contributions of Government members and recognized the limited financial capacity of the ILO. He reiterated the key areas for ILO action: expanding the knowledge base to inform policy-making; documenting country-level experiences and sharing best practices; technical assistance to increase employability; and on-the-ground activities with those directly involved in education and training. He stressed the important role of the YEN in developing national action plans on youth employment as well as its international advocacy role. In conclusion, he stated that ILO action should be relevant, realistic and capable of achieving practical outcomes.

175. The Worker Vice-Chairperson highlighted some important points raised by Government members regarding the role of the ILO: increased policy coherence in promoting decent work, including the need to involve the World Bank, International Monetary Fund (IMF) and WTO towards that end; tackling the underlying causes of poverty and youth unemployment in Africa, suggesting the re-establishment of ILO regional employment teams; improving labour market data on the informal economy, HIV/AIDS and gender disparities; advocating the involvement of the social partners in policy-making; and promoting the inclusion of youth employment in all development strategies.

Concluding comments

176. The Employer Vice-Chairperson emphasized the importance of the private sector in creating opportunities for young people in developing countries, again recalling the recommendations of the report of the UNDP Commission on the Private Sector and Development, entitled *Unleashing Entrepreneurship: Making Business Work for the Poor* (2004). He warned that the conclusions of the present discussion would not provide the full range of solutions, as policies continuously evolved and national circumstances differed; therefore, many issues needed further discussion and debate. He reiterated the Employers' group's objection to the development of indicators of decent work deficits due to the subjective nature of such measures.

177. The Worker Vice-Chairperson reminded the Committee of three key dimensions of the youth employment challenge – unemployment, underemployment and indecent work. She reiterated the need for a comprehensive, thorough and politically balanced strategy with a rights-based approach. She stressed the importance of focusing on developing countries and reminded the governments of developed countries of their dual responsibility – to tackle youth employment issues in their own countries and their responsibility towards developing countries. In response to concerns about the development of decent work indicators, she explained they would provide guidance on benchmarking progress.

Discussion on the draft conclusions on youth employment of the Drafting Group

178. At its ninth sitting, the Committee considered the draft conclusions. The Chairperson expressed his appreciation to the Drafting Group, with specific mention of the Chairperson of the Drafting Group – the Government member of Jamaica. He outlined the workplan and methods of work for the consideration of the draft conclusions.

Title

179. The Government member of Switzerland, speaking also on behalf of the Government members of Canada, Finland, France, Germany, the Netherlands, New Zealand, Norway, Portugal, Romania, Sweden and the United States, introduced an amendment to remove the words "rewarding and productive" after "decent" in the title and throughout the draft conclusions. Quoting from the ILO public web site definition:

> Decent work sums up the aspirations of people in their working lives. It involves opportunities for work that is productive and delivers a fair income, security in the workplace and social protection for families, better prospects for personal development and social integration, freedom for people to express their concerns, organize and participate in the decisions that affect their lives and equality of opportunity and treatment for all women and men.

"Decent work" was an inclusive phrase and should not be weakened with further qualification. She added that she had the agreement of all Government members for that amendment.

180. The Employer Vice-Chairperson did not support the amendment and felt disappointed that the discussion would start on this issue. The conclusions of the Tripartite Meeting on

Youth Employment: The Way Forward (October 2004) mentioned "decent and productive work" and Report VI, entitled *Youth: Pathways to decent work*, drew attention to United Nations Millennium Development Goal 8 that aimed to reach the target to "develop and implement strategies for decent and productive work for youth". That terminology, he emphasized, was agreed on in a tripartite debate and he feared that amending it would raise further complications. The Employers' group could leave "decent work" alone in the title of the draft conclusions and would agree to the deletion of the term "rewarding" throughout the draft report, however, they would not agree to delete the word "productive".

181. The Government member of France pointed out that the wording adopted by the Drafting Group was subject to discussion and review by the Committee.

182. The Worker Vice-Chairperson supported the amendment presented by the Government members. She mentioned that the Workers' group had not been comfortable with the qualification of the term "decent work" in the discussion that had led to the conclusions of the Tripartite Meeting on Youth Employment: The Way Forward (October 2004), and had also raised their concerns in the Drafting Group. She added that the concept of "decent work", agreed upon by all Members of the ILO, was sufficiently broad to cover a whole range of concepts and shared aspirations. Finally, she expressed concern over the term "rewarding", especially in view of the problems that it would pose in the French translation.

183. The Government members of Luxembourg (speaking also on behalf of the Government members of Austria, Belgium, Cyprus, Czech Republic, Estonia, Ireland, Italy, Slovakia, Slovenia and Spain), Nigeria (speaking on behalf of the Africa group), Tunisia, and Uruguay (speaking also on behalf of the Government members of Argentina, Brazil, Chile, Paraguay and the Bolivarian Republic of Venezuela) all spoke in favour of the amendment. The Government member of the Netherlands recalled that, as stated by the Government member of Switzerland when introducing the amendment, the entire Government group had already agreed to support it and now it also had the support of the Workers' group.

184. The Employer Vice-Chairperson indicated that his group would later suggest that the adjective "productive" remain in some parts of the text as in the conclusions of the Tripartite Meeting on Youth Employment: The Way Forward (October, 2004). The amendment was therefore adopted, causing a further amendment from the Worker members to fall.

Paragraph 1

185. The Employer Vice-Chairperson introduced an amendment to delete a reference to the appendix to the draft conclusions as well as the appendix itself. That would clarify the text because the appendix mentioned international labour standards that were relevant not only to youth employment but had broader application, and did not include all standards potentially relevant to youth. The Worker Vice-Chairperson responded that the appendix had been intended as a way to simplify the conclusions, so that each of the paragraphs of the text would not have to reference relevant instruments. As the conclusions defined the ILO plan of action, it was important to include references to the relevant standards. If they were not noted in the appendix, the Workers' group would seek to introduce references in the text to the international labour standards wherever relevant.

186. The Government member of Nigeria opposed the amendment on the grounds that the appendix included the most appropriate international labour standards and would serve as a reminder to all that they should be respected and enforced. The Government member of the

Netherlands agreed that the appendix was a useful means to avoid placing references throughout the text. The Employer Vice-Chairperson withdrew the amendment.

187. Paragraph 1 was adopted.

Paragraph 2

188. Introducing an amendment to add the words "for all" at the end of the paragraph, the Employer Vice-Chairperson explained that that addition would clarify that both poverty eradication and development, referred to in the sentence, applied to all, and equally that resolution of youth employment challenges would benefit society as a whole. The amendment was adopted following support from the Worker Vice-Chairperson and the Government member of Nigeria, speaking on behalf of the Africa group.

189. Paragraph 2 was adopted as amended.

Paragraph 3

190. The Government member of Spain proposed changing *calificaciones* to *cualificaciones* in the Spanish text, which was seconded. The Government member of Argentina proposed instead the word *competencias*. The amendment was adopted as subamended.

191. An amendment to remove the word "developed" in the reference to countries in the paragraph was proposed by the Government members of the Bahamas, Barbados, Jamaica, Suriname, and Trinidad and Tobago, in order to clarify that the existence of an ageing workforce was not limited to developed countries. Following the agreement of the Employer and Worker Vice-Chairpersons, the amendment was adopted.

192. The Government member of Jamaica, speaking also on behalf of the Government members of the Bahamas, Barbados, Suriname, and Trinidad and Tobago, sought to insert "in most developing countries with young workforces" after "challenge". The proposed amendment was intended to clarify that the demographic situation varied between countries. The Worker Vice-Chairperson suggested that the amendment be withdrawn, following the logic of the previously agreed amendment. The Employer Vice-Chairperson agreed, stating that no distinctions should be made between developed and developing countries, a sentiment echoed by the Government member of Nigeria. The amendment was withdrawn.

193. The Government member of Luxembourg introduced an amendment proposed by the Government members of the Committee Member States of the EU, in association with the Government members of Bulgaria and Romania, to replace the final sentence of the paragraph with "Policy-makers have to consider intergenerational issues and to recognize in this context a life-cycle approach." She explained that Government members were concerned that the existing sentence suggested competition between older and younger workers, and they wished to highlight intergenerational issues as well as the fact that workers had different needs at different stages of their lives. In supporting the amendment, the Worker Vice-Chairperson proposed a subamendment to add the sentence to the end of the paragraph rather than replacing the current final sentence as proposed. The Employer Vice-Chairperson supported the subamendment but asked for further clarification on the meaning of the life-cycle approach, as it was also mentioned later in the draft conclusions. The Government member of Luxembourg explained that a reference to "life cycle" in the paragraph was appropriate because the paragraph addressed challenges which would include the different needs of workers at different stages in their lives. The amendment was adopted as subamended.

194. Paragraph 3 was adopted as amended.

Paragraph 4

195. The Government member of Jamaica, speaking also on behalf of the Government members of the Bahamas, Barbados, Suriname, and Trinidad and Tobago, proposed replacing "and local" with "regional and international", to reflect the wide range of employment options available to young people. The Worker Vice-Chairperson agreed that youth were increasingly seeking regional and international prospects, but proposed a subamendment to retain the word "local". The Employer Vice-Chairperson agreed with the importance of the word "local" but was not clear on the intended meaning of "regional" – for his group that could refer to regions within a country as well as groupings of countries. The Government member of Jamaica clarified that the intent had been to refer to groupings of countries. The Worker Vice-Chairperson, recalling previous discussions on migration, thought the text would be too narrow without "regional and international" but insisted to keep "local" as well. The Employer Vice-Chairperson accepted the Worker members' subamendment. The amendment was adopted as subamended.

196. The Government member of Italy, seconded by the Government member of Luxembourg, proposed deleting after the word "employers" the words "of young workers". The aim of the proposed amendment was to clarify that the paragraph referred to all employers, not just to those who employed young workers. The Worker Vice-Chairperson supported the proposed amendment. The Employer Vice-Chairperson proposed a subamendment so that the line would read "governments, employers and young workers", in order to avoid possible confusion that the "employers" would refer to "young ... employers". The amendment was adopted as subamended.

197. The Government member of the United States, speaking also on behalf of the Government members of the Netherlands, Norway and Switzerland, proposed to place the final sentence as a separate paragraph, in order to give greater prominence to the sentence's reference to the Declaration on Fundamental Principles and Rights at Work and its Follow-up, 1998 (ILO). The Worker Vice-Chairperson asked that the proposed amendment be withdrawn, on the basis that the paragraph as written was intended to reflect both the diversity of situations facing youth and the indivisibility of rights for young people. The Employer Vice-Chairperson concurred that the two ideas should be linked in the same paragraph, and the amendment was withdrawn.

198. Paragraph 4 was adopted as amended.

Paragraph 5

199. An amendment proposed by the Government member of Tunisia to delete the paragraph was not seconded and fell.

200. The Government member of the United Republic of Tanzania, seconded by the Government member of Nigeria, proposed amending the first sentence so that it would state that "many young people are in education but only a few are employed in decent jobs ...". The Employer Vice-Chairperson asked that the amendment be withdrawn, emphasizing that many young persons were indeed in decent forms of employment, and noting that the remainder of the text referred to youth who were not in decent work. The Worker Vice-Chairperson, while recognizing that many young people were in fact unable to secure decent work, concurred with the Employers' group. The amendment was withdrawn.

201. The Worker Vice-Chairperson proposed an amendment to replace ", including permanent work as well as freely chosen part-time, temporary, casual or seasonal employment" with "with vastly different employment conditions, including permanent full-time, part-time as well as freely chosen casual, seasonal work", further subamending it to include the word "temporary." The intent of the proposed amendment, as subamended, was to recognize the range of types of work that might be sought by young people. The Employer Vice-Chairperson introduced a further subamendment to replace the words "freely chosen" with "mutually agreed" as he wanted to avoid an inference that workers could freely choose forms of employment not offered by their employers. He subsequently proposed the removal of the words "freely chosen". The Worker Vice-Chairperson agreed to the further subamendment. The amendment as further subamended was adopted.

202. The Employer Vice-Chairperson introduced an amendment to insert the following after the first sentence: "In many countries young people are able to compete with other workers and make successful transitions from education to the world of work. In developed countries, the ageing workforce also presents growing opportunities for young people." The objective was to show young people that there remained a sense of optimism about their prospects in the world of work. The new sentences provided a better balance between the positive and negative challenges that young people faced.

203. The Government member of the United States supported the proposed amendment, giving evidence from his own experience, noting that the statement reflected the sense of hope for a successful transfer of knowledge from older workers to younger workers. The Government members of Canada and the Netherlands also supported the amendment.

204. The Government member of Nigeria supported the first sentence but challenged the second sentence, stating that it repeated paragraph 3. The Government member of France questioned the underlying assumption that an ageing workforce would automatically result in more jobs for young people.

205. The Worker Vice-Chairperson proposed a subamendment to delete the words "compete with other workers" from the first sentence because the idea of competition did not belong in that paragraph. The Employer Vice-Chairperson agreed to the subamendment, as did the Government member of the Netherlands.

206. The Government member of Tunisia proposed an alternative subamendment that would substitute the word "replace" for the word "compete" which he felt to be too indicative of a sense of rivalry among workers. The Chairperson and others pointed out that that alternative subamendment would become moot if the first subamendment was accepted and consequently the Government member of Tunisia withdrew his subamendment.

207. The Government member of Zimbabwe introduced a subamendment to delete the words "in developed countries" from the second proposed sentence in light of earlier discussions on the same issue. The Worker Vice-Chairperson proposed replacing the word "developed" with "some" so that the second proposed sentence would read "in some countries, …". The Employer Vice-Chairperson agreed to the Worker members' proposal and the amendment as subamended was adopted.

208. Based on the previous discussion, the Employer Vice-Chairperson withdrew an amendment, as did the Government member of the Netherlands, speaking on behalf of the Government members of Australia, Canada, Norway and the United States.

209. The Government member of Australia, speaking also on behalf of the Government members of Canada, the Netherlands, Norway and the United States, introduced an amendment to add the following sentence after the second sentence "These forms of work

can provide entry points for young workers to the labour market and enhance their long-term employment prospects." That sentence was intended to provide a more balanced picture of the youth employment patterns which currently existed.

210. The Worker Vice-Chairperson opposed the amendment since it seemed to suggest that it was acceptable to discriminate against young workers by encouraging their participation in temporary and substandard working situations. The appropriate balance was evident without the amendment.

211. The Employer Vice-Chairperson endorsed the proposed amendment. The amendment reflected a common theme that he had noted in the Government members' interventions that alternatives to full-time permanent employment could help young people to get a foot in the labour market. The word "can" implied that the sentence was not meant to imply a universal tenet that held in all cases.

212. The Government member of the United Kingdom supported the proposed amendment. The Government member of the United States stated that alternative types of employment could offer a valuable pathway to a good career. The Government member of Algeria proposed a subamendment to replace the word "work" with "employment".

213. The Worker Vice-Chairperson stressed that few young people now entered the world of work with a sense of security, which had consequences. She proposed a subamendment to add "and which can sometimes" before "enhance" in order to emphasize that that was not always the case. She also proposed to add the following phrase to the end of the sentence: "but can often lead to young workers being caught in precarious employment".

214. The Employer Vice-Chairperson found the proposed subamendment from the Workers' group to be unacceptable because the negative aspects of youth employment were already addressed in the remainder of the paragraph. The Government member of Australia agreed with the Employers' group and added that the amendment had been proposed as a means to balance the negative points brought out in the latter sentences. Furthermore, "sometimes" and "can" were interchangeable so "sometimes" was not necessary.

215. The Worker Vice-Chairperson supported the subamendment proposed by the Government member of Algeria to replace "work" with "employment" and it was approved. She withdrew her subamendment and proposed an alternative subamendment to change the word "can" to "may", which the Committee accepted. The amendment was adopted as subamended.

216. The Employer Vice-Chairperson introduced an amendment to replace the words "trapped in" with the words "often with few other choices than". Other words used in that particular sentence already captured the idea of youth as being trapped in negative forms of work. In his view, the new wording proposed was more descriptive of the problem being identified, namely that, under some circumstances, young people did not have many choices. The word "trapped" was too harsh.

217. The Worker Vice-Chairperson was disappointed by that proposal since her group had already accepted that some positive aspects be added to the first part of the paragraph in order to achieve balance. Evidence showed that many young workers were indeed trapped as a consequence of poor working conditions and lack of security. The only way that she would accept the amendment was if it was subamended to replace the word "trapped" by the word "caught", as it was important that governments understood the seriousness of the issue of securing work for young people who had no choices.

218. The Government members of Denmark, the Netherlands and the United States, as well as of Côte d'Ivoire, speaking on behalf of the Africa group, did not accept the amendment. The word "trapped" described very clearly the situation of young workers in developing countries and the purpose of the paragraph was to portray positive and negative aspects of some kinds of work. It was balanced as it was. The Employer Vice-Chairperson withdrew the amendment.

219. Paragraph 5 was adopted as amended.

Paragraph 6

220. The Government member of the Bahamas, speaking also on behalf of the Government members of Barbados, Jamaica, Suriname, and Trinidad and Tobago, introduced an amendment to delete the words "in developing countries" after "there is significant regional variation in youth employment": that was true for both developed and developing countries. The amendment was adopted without discussion.

221. The Government member of Algeria, seconded by the Government member of Côte d'Ivoire, introduced an amendment to replace "the uneven impacts of globalization and the asymmetries in current global economic activity" with "the negative impacts of globalization and an inequitable distribution of the fruits of progress and development on a global scale". The amendment clarified the negative nature of the effects of globalization as well as the increased inequity among countries caused by globalization.

222. The Employer Vice-Chairperson could not support the proposed amendment because the text had already been widely debated in the Drafting Group and was already an acceptable compromise. Its purpose was to reflect the uneven impact of globalization, but it was important not to portray globalization as being only negative. Globalization was a reality that could also offer part of the solution to some problems. He proposed a subamendment to use the word "uneven" instead of "inequitable".

223. The Government member of Algeria agreed that globalization had both negative and positive effects, and proposed another subamendment to remove the word "negative".

224. The Worker Vice-Chairperson, despite her great sympathy for the Africa group, indicated that it might be difficult to replace the word "asymmetries" with "inequitable distribution". There had already been a discussion in the Drafting Group concerning the choice of that word and it had been impossible to reach consensus. The word "asymmetries" was a compromise and would be better to build a platform for work. The Government members of the Netherlands, Portugal and the United States supported the Workers' group.

225. The amendment was withdrawn.

226. The Government member of the Bahamas, speaking also on behalf of the Government members of Barbados, Jamaica, Suriname, and Trinidad and Tobago, introduced an amendment to replace the word "scourge" at the beginning of the third sentence, with the word "impact", which they considered to be less emotionally charged, more measurable and practical.

227. The Employer and Worker Vice-Chairpersons preferred to maintain the existing text and the proposed amendment was withdrawn.

228. The Government member of the Syrian Arab Republic, seconded by the Government member of Algeria, introduced an amendment to insert the words "and occupation" after

the word "conflict" in order to take into account the devastating effect that occupation could have on youth employment.

229. The Employer Vice-Chairperson did not support the amendment because it was important to remember that the conclusions should focus on youth employment. The amendment would detract from the discussion. The Government members of Canada, France and the Netherlands agreed with the Employers' group.

230. The Worker Vice-Chairperson understood very well that occupied territories could not grow because of the lack of independent and democratic government. She considered that the words "armed conflict" were strong enough and included the concept of occupation. She therefore could not support the proposed amendment. The amendment was withdrawn.

231. The Employer Vice-Chairperson introduced an amendment to delete "and the persistence of the informal economy" from the third sentence. In many countries the informal economy generated a large part of gross domestic product (GDP) and therefore reference to it in that context among other more problematic circumstances such as armed conflict, was not appropriate. It was better to address the informal economy in a separate paragraph.

232. The Worker Vice-Chairperson preferred that the text remain but she agreed that the Employers' group had made some valid points. Given the importance of the issue of the transition from the informal to the formal economy, it was important to ensure that that was dealt with elsewhere in the text if the amendment was adopted. The Government members of Côte d'Ivoire and Uruguay both preferred the original text, as governments had an interest in bringing the informal economy into the formal one. The Employer Vice-Chairperson assured the Workers' group that the reference to the informal economy would be addressed elsewhere. The amendment was adopted.

233. An amendment submitted by the Government members of the Bahamas, Barbados, Jamaica, Suriname, and Trinidad and Tobago fell as a consequence of other amendments being adopted.

234. The Worker Vice-Chairperson introduced an amendment to insert "and gender inequality" after "informal economy" in the second sentence, to acknowledge the untapped potential of the participation of women. The Employer Vice-Chairperson supported the amendment and stated that that issue was about investing in human capital, the potential for economic growth, sustainability of the economy and justice. The Government member of Canada supported the proposed amendment. The amendment was adopted.

235. The Government members of the Bahamas, Barbados, Suriname, and Trinidad and Tobago withdrew an amendment, as did the Employer Vice-Chairperson, as a consequence of other amendments being adopted.

236. Paragraph 6 was adopted as amended.

Paragraph 7

237. The Worker Vice-Chairperson introduced an amendment to insert "slow and jobless economic growth" after the words "linked to" in the first sentence. The amendment acknowledged the differences in the employment intensity of growth between countries. The Employer Vice-Chairperson did not support the amendment as the subsequent paragraph dealt with employment-intensive growth.

238. The Government member of Algeria supported the amendment, stating that slow economic growth was an obstacle to the creation of jobs, even in developed economies. He offered a

subamendment, changing the text to "slow economic growth which generates few jobs". The Workers' group supported that subamendment but further subamended it to "slow economic and employment growth". The Employer Vice-Chairperson agreed to the text as finally subamended. The amendment was adopted as subamended.

239. Paragraph 7 was adopted as amended.

Paragraph 8

240. The Worker Vice-Chairperson proposed replacing the words "entering and remaining in the labour market" with "securing and retaining decent work" to clarify that the issue being addressed was about staying in the labour force.

241. The Employer Vice-Chairperson thought that the amendment did not change the substance so he accepted it. The amendment was adopted.

242. Paragraph 8 was adopted as amended.

Paragraph 9

243. The Government member of Italy, seconded by the Government member of Luxembourg, proposed replacing "Whilst employment cannot be directly created by legislation or regulation, it is recognized that appropriate regulation can provide employment protection, particularly for young people." with "Whilst employment cannot be directly created but only incentivated by legislation or regulation, it is recognized that appropriate regulation can provide employment protection, which is a basic condition in order to create decent work, particularly for young people." The intent of the proposed amendment was to underline that policies could play a positive role in indirectly promoting employment and employment protection, which was an important factor in creating decent work.

244. The Employer Vice-Chairperson did not support the proposed amendment. The wording chosen by the Drafting Group was the result of a long discussion, and was taken directly from a previous discussion on youth employment. The Government member of the United States agreed with the Employers' group. The Government member of Australia also preferred the original text.

245. The Government member of Luxembourg, speaking also on behalf of the Government members of the Committee Member States of the EU, in association with the Government members of Bulgaria and Romania, supported the amendment. The Government member of Denmark added that ALMPs and other measures had an indirect effect in creating employment. The Government member of Argentina, speaking on behalf of the Government members of the MERCOSUR countries, also supported the amendment.

246. The Worker Vice-Chairperson suggested a subamendment to replace the word "incentivated" with "encouraged" and to replace "appropriate regulation" with "labour legislation based on international labour standards".

247. The Employer Vice-Chairperson appreciated the Workers' group's proposal but still thought the original draft text reflected the appropriate balance, and that a practical message was needed. Legislation and regulation did not create jobs, but they did have a role in protecting young workers. However, that point was more appropriately made in other paragraphs.

248. The Worker Vice-Chairperson disagreed with the view of the Employers' group, stating that numerous studies supported the view that legislation which protected workers could help productivity and economic growth.

249. The Employer Vice-Chairperson proposed an additional subamendment to add after "employment protection" the words "and underwrite increased productivity", which the Workers' group supported.

250. The Government member of Algeria proposed another subamendment to insert after "labour legislation" the words "and regulation", to which the Employers' group agreed. The amendment was adopted as subamended.

251. The Government member of Jamaica, on behalf of the Government members of the Bahamas, Barbados, Suriname, and Trinidad and Tobago, and the Government member of Tunisia proposed an amendment to delete the sentence "[Labour laws should apply to all young workers, including those in the informal economy and those currently lacking protection because of disguised employment relationship.]" since laws and regulations applied to all citizens, and the sentence did not add any value. The Employer Vice-Chairperson supported the amendment, stating that labour laws should apply to all young workers and that there was no reason to single out particular categories of young workers.

252. The Worker Vice-Chairperson agreed with the principle that labour laws should apply to all, but emphasized the need to recognize gaps in actual protection, particularly for young workers most at risk in the informal economy and those lacking protection due to disguised employment relationships, who were denied the protection of labour legislation and access to social security. The issue was prevalent in both developed and developing countries.

253. The Government member of the Netherlands asked that the text be retained to emphasize the notion that labour laws should apply to all young workers, including those in the informal economy. She pointed out that during the general discussion on Report V, entitled *The scope of the employment relationship*, at the 91st Session of the International Labour Conference in 2003, there had been no controversy over the concept of a disguised employment relationship. The Government member of Côte d'Ivoire, speaking on behalf of the Africa group, agreed and emphasized the need to highlight that laws and legislation should apply to all youth, including those who were currently not covered. The Government member of Algeria also agreed with keeping the original text.

254. The Government member of Jamaica defended the proposed amendment by reiterating that all laws always applied to all workers. He noted that some citizens might be under the perception that they had no recourse to law, but that was a matter of public education and better law enforcement. The Government member of Tunisia supported the amendment, noting that there was no need to discriminate between informal and formal employment.

255. The Employer Vice-Chairperson drew the attention of the Committee to two issues. First, the words "labour laws should apply to all young workers" would appear elsewhere in the conclusions so the sentence was not needed there. Second, with respect to the disguised employment relationship, the topic had grown out of the general discussion on Report V, entitled *The scope of the employment relationship*, at the 91st Session of the International Labour Conference in 2003, and the Governing Body of the ILO had subsequently resolved to discuss the matter further during the general discussion at the 95th Session of the International Labour Conference in 2006, with a view to developing a Recommendation. Hence, he concluded that the issue had not been resolved and that it was inappropriate to discuss it at that time. With regard to workers in the informal economy, he stated that there were some conceptual difficulties in that, by definition, the informal economy was informal due to the lack of coverage by labour legislation.

256. The Government member of Canada stated that the sentence should not be completely removed but could be reworded. The Government member of Luxembourg agreed.

257. The Worker Vice-Chairperson clarified that the sentence under consideration was a compromise text, and emphasized that the Committee should be prepared to recognize that unfortunately labour laws often did not cover workers in the informal economy, who were harassed, abused or unpaid, and workers in a disguised employment relationship who did not receive their rightful entitlements. She asked for withdrawal of the proposed amendment. The Government member of Uruguay concurred, stating that the sentence should be maintained since many workers had to resort to the informal economy as a source of employment.

258. The Government member of Jamaica proposed a rewording of the sentence to read "Labour laws do apply to all workers and should be supported by active public education and enforcement." The Chairperson ruled that procedurally it was not possible to subamend an amendment seeking to delete the entire sentence. The proposed amendment was withdrawn.

259. The Government member of Denmark, speaking also on behalf of the Government member of the United Kingdom, introduced an amendment to replace the bracketed text with "Labour laws and, where they exist, collective agreements should apply to all young workers, including those currently lacking protection because of disguised employment relationships. Efforts should be made to move those in the informal economy into the formal economy." The Government member of Algeria, and the Government member of Luxembourg, speaking on behalf of the Government members of the Committee Member States of the EU, in association with the Government members of Bulgaria and Romania, supported it.

260. The Employer Vice-Chairperson proposed a further subamendment, to place after "disguised employment" a footnote reading "As referenced in the conclusions of the ILO general discussion on the employment relationship [2003]". The Government member of Denmark agreed with that proposal. The Government member of Jamaica proposed a further subamendment to include a reference to active public education and enforcement, but withdrew it after observations that education and labour administration would be dealt with later in the text. The amendment, as subamended by the Government member of Denmark and the Employer members, was then adopted.

261. As a consequence of the preceding discussion, amendments proposed by the Employer members and the Government member of Algeria both fell, and the Employers' group and Workers' group each withdrew one amendment.

262. Paragraph 9 was adopted as amended.

Paragraph 10

263. The Government member of Jamaica, speaking also on behalf of the Government members of the Bahamas, Barbados, Suriname, and Trinidad and Tobago, proposed that the paragraph refer to "employment of" youth rather than "investment in" on the grounds that "investment" was too broad a term. The Employers' and Workers' groups preferred to retain "investment". The proposed amendment was withdrawn.

264. Paragraph 10 was adopted without amendment.

Paragraph 11

265. The Government member of Jamaica, speaking also on behalf of the Government members of the Bahamas, Barbados, Suriname, and Trinidad and Tobago, proposed that the words "investment in" be added after "undermines". The Employer Vice-Chairperson and the representative of the Worker Vice-Chairperson supported the amendment, and it was adopted.

266. The Government member of Italy suggested replacing the words "and are also associated" with "and may also be associated" so as not to suggest an automatic link. The amendment was supported by the Government member of Luxembourg, on behalf of the Government members of the Committee Member States of the EU, in association with the Government members of Bulgaria and Romania, along with the Employers' and Workers' groups. The amendment was adopted.

267. Paragraph 11 was adopted as amended.

Paragraph 12

268. The Government member of Algeria, seconded by the Government member of Nigeria, proposed deleting the word "uneven" from the first bullet point. The Employer Vice-Chairperson did not agree with the proposed amendment because the word had been agreed upon by the Drafting Group.

269. Following discussion, the Committee agreed to consider a new amendment incorporating that amendment with further changes. The Government member of the United Kingdom introduced a text developed by Government members, adding the words "which may have positive or negative consequences" to the opening sentence of the paragraph, removing the word "uneven" in the first bullet point, and removing the square brackets and the word "many" in the second bullet point. The Employer Vice-Chairperson supported the amendment, noting that it would allow for both positive and negative consequences in factors influencing youth employment.

270. The Government member of Nigeria, on behalf of the Africa group, supported the subamendment because it would simplify the future discussions concerning the paragraph. The representative of the Worker Vice-Chairperson also reluctantly supported the subamendment. She noted that the Workers' group would prefer specific reference to "uneven", but given the views expressed by the Government member of Nigeria, she was prepared to accept the subamendment in order to promote a consensus. The amendment was adopted as subamended. Consequently, eight further amendments relating to the first two bullet points fell, and a further one was withdrawn.

271. The Government member of Jamaica withdrew an amendment in light of the changed introductory sentence to the bullet points. The representative of the Worker Vice-Chairperson introduced an amendment to the seventh bullet point to change the word "workers" to "the protection of workers' rights", a change that the Employer Vice-Chairperson supported as it had no significance. The amendment was adopted.

272. Paragraph 12 was adopted as amended.

Paragraph 13

273. Paragraph 13 was adopted with acknowledgement of a grammatical amendment to the French text.

Paragraph 14

274. The representative of the Worker Vice-Chairperson introduced an amendment to replace in the first sentence the words "can be" with the word "is" because, based on her own experience as a young person, she could assert that the transition from education to work "is" problematic. The Employer Vice-Chairperson supported the amendment and it was adopted.

275. The Government member of Jamaica, speaking also on behalf of the Government members of the Bahamas, Barbados, Suriname, and Trinidad and Tobago, introduced an amendment to insert a new sentence "One concern is where young persons do not possess basic literacy skills that are necessary to access vocational training necessary and transition from a state of unemployability to employability." following the first sentence of the paragraph. The Employer Vice-Chairperson supported the concept, but suggested that it was already addressed in a later paragraph, a point the representative of the Worker Vice-Chairperson accepted.

276. The Government members of Jamaica, the Netherlands, Nigeria and the United States supported the amendment and agreed that the present paragraph dealt with challenges, the later one with policies. A subamendment proposed by the Employer Vice-Chairperson to address the point by inserting the words "such as basic literacy and numeracy skills" after the word "skills" in the fourth line of the paragraph was not accepted, but his further subamendment to add the words "and numeracy" after the word "literacy" in the first line of the new sentence was adopted, and the amendment was adopted as subamended.

277. The Employer Vice-Chairperson introduced an amendment to reorder the words in the second sentence to make it easier to understand. With the support of the representative of the Worker Vice-Chairperson, the amendment was adopted and consequently two further amendments to the sentence fell.

278. The Employer Vice-Chairperson introduced an amendment to replace the words "secure employment" with the words "sustainable employment opportunities" because employment must be sustainable. The representative of the Worker Vice-Chairperson proposed a subamendment to maintain the word "secure" before the proposed new text, as "sustainable" referred to the duration of employment and "secure" to other qualities. The Government member of Nigeria supported the proposed amendment as subamended, agreeing on the need for both sustainable and secure employment. The Employer Vice-Chairperson stated that as the Committee was not agreeing on an instrument, he would accept the subamendment. The amendment was adopted as subamended.

279. Three other amendments to the paragraph were withdrawn, and paragraph 14 was adopted as amended.

Paragraph 15

280. An amendment submitted by the Employer members was withdrawn as it conflicted with a previously adopted amendment, and paragraph 15 was adopted without amendment.

Paragraph 16

281. The representative of the Worker Vice-Chairperson proposed the insertion of the words "sexual harassment" after "discrimination" to reflect that additional obstacle faced by young women. The Employer Vice-Chairperson expressed his agreement and the amendment was adopted.

282. The Government member of Jamaica, speaking also on behalf of the Government members of the Bahamas, Barbados, Suriname, and Trinidad and Tobago, proposed inserting a new paragraph reading "In some cases young persons are denied access to employment opportunities for which they are fully qualified and competent solely on the basis of their youth." The Employer Vice-Chairperson did not support the amendment on the grounds that it highlighted only one of many grounds for discrimination and might suggest others were less important, that it presented employers negatively, and that a later paragraph addressed discriminatory barriers. The Worker Vice-Chairperson supported strengthening the reference to discrimination in the later paragraph if the proposed amendment was withdrawn.

283. The Government members of the Netherlands and the United States proposed subamendments, the first to place the text as a final sentence in paragraph 16, and the second to replace "youth" with "age" as a more inclusive term. Both subamendments were welcomed by the Government member of Jamaica. The Employer Vice-Chairperson expressed concern that the sentence could imply that employers deliberately denied access as a general state. The Government members of Jamaica and Nigeria observed that the new text clearly referred to "in some cases" and did not imply a general condition. The Employer Vice-Chairperson agreed with the consensus and the amendment as subamended was adopted.

284. Paragraph 16 was adopted as amended.

Paragraph 17

285. The Worker Vice-Chairperson explained that the amendment proposing to replace the words "and their organizations" with ", worker organizations" was intended as a clarification. The Employer Vice-Chairperson supported the amendment. Following a question from the Government member of Canada as to whether the change would imply that other "organizations of young persons" would not be involved in the development of policies and programmes, the Worker Vice-Chairperson stated that the paragraph referred to the participation of the social partners in tripartite processes, and was not intended to exclude the possibility of the partners inviting other organizations to participate in discussions. The amendment was adopted.

286. Paragraph 17 was adopted as amended.

Paragraph 18

287. Paragraph 18 was adopted without amendment.

Paragraph 19

288. The Employer members proposed an amendment to open the paragraph with the words "Although one size does not fit all," as that phrase had been used in the Committee's discussion and emphasized the message. The amendment was adopted.

289. An amendment proposed by the Government member of Côte d'Ivoire fell as it was not seconded.

290. The Government member of Luxembourg introduced an amendment proposed by the Government members of the Committee Member States of the EU, in association with the Government members of Bulgaria and Romania, to add the sentence "Youth employment should be considered in all social, employment and economic policies through a well-

balanced policy mix." between the first and second sentences, with the intention of strengthening the text and emphasizing that all policies were interrelated. The Employer Vice-Chairperson agreed that that was a helpful addition but suggested modifying it to refer to all relevant policies as potentially some policies would not affect youth employment. In agreeing to that subamendment, the Government member of Luxembourg stressed that the relevance of all policies to youth employment had been their intention but she would accept the subamendment. The amendment was adopted as subamended.

291. The Worker Vice-Chairperson explained that the intent of the proposed amendment to add the word "trade" to the description of the supportive policies was to reflect the Global Employment Agenda's recognition of the impact of trade policy, and the relationship between trade policy and employment outcomes. The Employer Vice-Chairperson indicated that his group did not accept the proposed amendment and would be concerned about entering into areas of policy outside the ILO's mandate. The Worker Vice-Chairperson reminded the Committee that the ILO Governing Body Committee on Employment and Social Policy had recently had a major discussion on trade policy, and that the intention of the proposed amendment was not prescriptive but served to identify an area for national policy, among others. Following comments from the Government members of Germany and Nigeria, the Employer Vice-Chairperson suggested a subamendment to add "national" to the word "trade", and the amendment was adopted as so subamended.

292. The Government member of Luxembourg, on behalf of the Government members of the Committee Member States of the EU, in association with the Government members of Bulgaria and Romania, proposed an amendment to insert ", with a full involvement of social partners," after the word "policies". She stated that the role of social partners was vital, especially in regard to training and wage policies.

293. The Worker Vice-Chairperson expressed her concern that the role for the social partners in the proposed amendment was specific to the EU and might not be appropriate in other countries. The Employer Vice-Chairperson suggested a subamendment to replace the words "a full" by "appropriate", a proposal supported by the Workers' group and the Government members of Luxembourg, New Zealand and Nigeria. The amendment was adopted as subamended, with an acknowledgement of the drafting point noted by the Government member of the United States.

294. The Government member of New Zealand, supported by the Government member of Canada, proposed an amendment to replace the words "which include an intergenerational approach" with "that aim to prevent cycles of disadvantage from being repeated across generations" in order to clarify the meaning of "an intergenerational approach". The amendment was supported by the Employers' and the Workers' groups, as well as by the Government member of Nigeria, and was adopted.

295. Paragraph 19 was adopted as amended.

New heading before paragraph 20

296. The Employer members proposed adding a new heading "Economic growth" before paragraph 20. They introduced the amendment by noting that such a heading would help readers navigate through the document. Following a discussion in which many members of the Committee expressed support for the principle of sub-headings but raised concerns about the practicality of seeking to reach agreement, the proposed amendment was withdrawn.

Paragraph 20

297. The Worker Vice-Chairperson proposed the insertion of a new sentence "Governments require greater policy autonomy and space to pursue expansionary macroeconomic policies and industrial policies designed to expand the manufacturing and service sectors of the economy." before the sentence starting "Social progress ...". She explained that that sentence was intended to reflect developing countries' views that they were constrained in their policy choices by external actors. She noted that there was a need to recognize that the governments of developing countries had the right to pursue their own economic and social objectives. The Employer Vice-Chairperson wished to hear Government members' positions on the amendment.

298. The Government members of Australia, Canada and France did not support the amendment on the basis that the conclusions should focus on practical policy issues for young people. The Government member of Nigeria supported the amendment by noting that most African countries needed some policy autonomy, particularly with respect to the Bretton Woods institutions, to effectively carry out their policy objectives, a view supported by the Government member of Argentina, on behalf of the Government members of the MERCOSUR countries and the Bolivarian Republic of Venezuela.

299. The Worker Vice-Chairperson clarified the amendment, noting that it stated that all governments had the right of self-determination.

300. The Government member of the Netherlands suggested a subamendment to delete the word "greater" between the words "require" and "policy autonomy". She noted that it would make the amendment neutral by indicating that it avoided the issue of more or less policy autonomy. The Worker Vice-Chairperson accepted the subamendment.

301. The Employer Vice-Chairperson expressed concern that the proposed amendment as subamended still gave particular focus to expansionary macroeconomic policy, which entailed risks that could have a counter-productive effect on the economy and on youth employment. The Employers' group did not support the amendment as subamended.

302. The Government members of Argentina and Jamaica supported the subamendment, stating that governments required some policy room and autonomy and had the right to accept risks.

303. The Worker Vice-Chairperson observed that the proposed amendment expressed the principle that every nation should have some level of autonomy to make such decisions.

304. In an attempt to reach a consensus, the Government member of Luxembourg, speaking on behalf of the Government members of the Committee Member States of the EU, in association with the Government members of Bulgaria and Romania, proposed a subamendment to replace the beginning of the amended text with "Governments should have space and ownership of their macroeconomic policies".

305. The Worker Vice-Chairperson supported that proposal with a further subamendment to replace the phrase "space and ownership of" in the subamendment and the words "macroeconomic policies and industry policies designed to expand the manufacturing and service sectors of the economy" in the original amendment, with the words "increased policy space to ensure ownership of their macroeconomic and industry policies, enabling them to expand their economies, including the manufacturing and service sectors".

306. The Employer Vice-Chairperson stated that the subamendment proposed by the Government member of Luxembourg offered a good solution and questioned whether the

Workers' members' subamendment satisfied the Government members. In response, the Government member of Nigeria reminded the Committee of a previous discussion on whether "policy space" needed to be qualified, and proposed to delete the word "increased"; the Government member of the Netherlands agreed.

307. The Worker Vice-Chairperson reluctantly agreed to remove the word "increased" so that the sentence would read "Governments should have policy space to ensure ownership of their macroeconomic and industrial policies, enabling them to expand their economies, including the manufacturing and services sectors." The Employer Vice-Chairperson accepted that formulation and the amendment was adopted as amended.

308. The Worker Vice-Chairperson introduced an amendment to replace "trade and foreign investment, should be harnessed to create high-quality jobs and training opportunities for young people" with "the rules and institutions governing international trade, finance and foreign direct investment should be reformed in order to promote decent work for youth".

309. The Employer Vice-Chairperson stated that he was prepared to consider an amendment to introduce the scope for improving the environment for international trade and foreign direct investment, but that needed to refer to policies. Therefore, he put forward a further subamendment to add before the word "globalization" the words "policies relating to" and after the word "should" to replace the words "be reformed" with the words "seek and, where required, be adapted to".

310. The Worker Vice-Chairperson suggested that the sentence be divided into two. After the word "hand" a full stop should be inserted, the comma and the word "and" should be deleted, and the new sentence would start with the words "Policies relating to". Second, the words "seek and, where required, be adapted to" should be replaced with "be reformed, wherever necessary,".

311. The Employer Vice-Chairperson put forward a proposal to combine his previous subamendment with the latter subamendment proposed by the Workers' group, to read "Social progress and economic growth should go hand in hand. Policies relating to globalization, including trade and foreign direct investment, should, wherever necessary, be reformed to create decent jobs for young people.", which ensured a balance of concepts. The Government member of Nigeria and the Worker Vice-Chairperson supported that proposal and the amendment, as subamended, was adopted. As a consequence, other proposed amendments to the paragraph fell.

312. The Worker Vice-Chairperson introduced an amendment to add "trade" to the list of policies (monetary and fiscal), noting that this amendment acknowledged the broader policy mix.

313. The Employer Vice-Chairperson agreed and proposed a subamendment to replace the word "must" with "should" in order to make the statement more directive than imperative, and to add "social security" to the list of policies so that the statement would read "monetary, fiscal, trade and social security policies".

314. The Worker Vice-Chairperson welcomed the additional focus on social security but asked the Employers' group to consider a further subamendment to move it to the end of the sentence so that it would read "employment generation and adequate social security". The Employer Vice-Chairperson clarified the intention to have the issue of social security addressed as a matter of policy attention and not as an outcome. The Government member of Denmark supported the subamendment proposed by the Employers' group, noting that "social security" should be added in connection with policies alone. The Government member of the Netherlands agreed.

315. The Worker Vice-Chairperson proposed an alternative subamendment to refer to social security in both places, in other words, with "policies" and also at the end of the sentence. The Employer Vice-Chairperson proposed that the end of the sentence read "… and social protection", to which the Worker Vice-Chairperson agreed. The amendment was adopted as subamended, and a subsequent amendment fell as a result.

316. Paragraph 20 was adopted as amended.

Paragraph 21

317. The Government member of Luxembourg introduced an amendment, on behalf of the Government members of the Committee Member States of the EU, in association with the Government members of Bulgaria and Romania, to replace "debt cancellation" with "debt relief", proposing a subamendment to change the text to "international debt relief, including debt cancellation". Debt relief could involve debt cancellation but could also cover areas such as extension of time frames for repayments or transfers to public investment. The Worker and Employer Vice-Chairpersons supported the amendment as subamended.

318. Although the Government member of Nigeria preferred "debt cancellation", she was willing to support the amendment. She added that in Africa debt repayments served to restrain governments from dealing with other problems, and noted her intention to address the matter in other forums. The Government member of Uruguay, also speaking on behalf of the Government members of Chile and the Bolivarian Republic of Venezuela, echoed the sentiments of the Government member of Nigeria. The amendment was adopted as subamended.

319. The Worker Vice-Chairperson introduced an amendment to include a reference to the recommendations of the World Commission on the Social Dimension of Globalization, an important ILO contribution, alongside the reference to the MDGs.

320. The Employer Vice-Chairperson noted that the amendment failed to recognize the fact that the recommendations of the Commission were not agreed to, in totality, by all the Commissioners who produced the report. He proposed a subamendment to change the text to "some of the recommendations" and delete "should be implemented" from the end of the sentence to be replaced with "in this regard". The Government members of Italy and Nigeria supported the amendment, as subamended.

321. The Government member of Denmark recalled that all of the relevant instruments specific to youth employment were listed in paragraph 1 and, therefore, did not support the proposed amendment. The Government members of Switzerland and the United Kingdom concurred.

322. The Worker Vice-Chairperson, emphasizing that the inclusion of the word "some" diluted the message, reluctantly agreed to the Employers' group's subamendment. The amendment was adopted as subamended.

323. The Government member of Luxembourg introduced an amendment on behalf of the Government members of the Committee Member States of the EU, in association with the Government members of Bulgaria and Romania, to replace the words "poverty reduction" with "poverty eradication". She emphasized that that served to strengthen the policy message concerning the fight against poverty. As there were no objections, the amendment was adopted.

324. The Government member of the United Republic of Tanzania, seconded by the Government member of Nigeria, proposed an amendment to insert the words "in September 2005" after "MDGs" to add clarity. The amendment was adopted.

325. The Government member of Luxembourg, on behalf of the Government members of the Committee Member States of the EU, in association with the Government members of Bulgaria and Romania, proposed an amendment to replace the words "work for young people" with "work for all with a focus on young people" at the end of the last sentence to make it more inclusive. The Government member of Algeria proposed a subamendment to add the word "decent" before the word "work". The amendment was adopted as subamended.

326. Paragraph 21 was adopted as amended.

Paragraph 22

327. The Worker Vice-Chairperson proposed an amendment to replace "A number of complementary policies are needed to enhance economic growth and high levels of employment." with "A range of complementary policies are needed to enhance the employment content of growth in order to achieve sustained rates of economic and productive employment growth." She subsequently proposed a subamendment to replace the words "in order to ... employment growth" by "while also increasing productivity".

328. The Government member of Luxembourg emphasized the need for well-balanced policies and to ensure employment rights and social protection. The Government member of Belgium pointed out the need to consider the quality of employment, as well as its productive aspect. To capture the Government members' views, the Worker Vice-Chairperson proposed to add "and ensuring adequate social protection" at the end of the sentence.

329. The Employer Vice-Chairperson supported the amendment with the change put forward by the Workers' group to capture the concerns of the Government members. The amendment was adopted as subamended. As a consequence, four subsequent amendments fell.

330. The Government member of Jamaica, speaking also on behalf of the Bahamas, Barbados, Suriname, and Trinidad and Tobago, introduced an amendment to insert the phrase "the quality of the" after "as well as" in the final sentence in order to capture a broader notion of labour supply. As there were no objections, the amendment was adopted.

331. The Employer Vice-Chairperson introduced an amendment to add the words "strengthen enterprises and" after the words "seek to", in order to identify one of the important objectives for policy development. He clarified that the intent was to ensure the sustainability of enterprises, and the amendment was therefore adopted.

332. The Employer Vice-Chairperson proposed adding a new sentence at the end of the paragraph, as follows: "Governments should review all policies to ensure they do not discriminate against the hiring of youth." The Worker Vice-Chairperson and the Government member of Algeria supported the amendment, which was adopted.

333. Paragraph 22 was adopted as amended.

Paragraph 23

334. The Employer Vice-Chairperson proposed replacing the word "jobs" with the word "work", on the basis that "work" was a more inclusive term. With the support of the Worker Vice-Chairperson, the amendment was adopted.

335. The Government member of Portugal introduced an amendment, on behalf of the Government members of the Committee Member States of the EU, in association with the Government members of Bulgaria and Romania, to replace the words "reduce poverty" with "eradicate poverty", for the same reasons as previously discussed. The amendment was adopted.

336. Paragraph 23 was adopted as amended.

Paragraph 24

337. The Employer Vice-Chairperson withdrew an amendment relating to headings. The Worker Vice-Chairperson withdrew an amendment to add "in the formal economy" after the words "to become entrepreneurs", having heard no support from the Employer Vice-Chairperson, the Government member of France or the Government member of the Netherlands. In doing so, she requested that the record take note of her statement that all parties should agree that government policies should encourage the creation of enterprises in the formal economy, and should not drive development of informal economy enterprises.

338. The Government member of Jamaica, speaking also on behalf of the Government members of the Bahamas, Barbados, Suriname, and Trinidad and Tobago, proposed adding the words "and venture capital" after the word "credit", to reflect that that was as important as credit for young entrepreneurs. The aim of the proposal was to address the most pertinent issue of helping young people to become entrepreneurs. In order to succeed, they would need access to credit and venture capital. The amendment was adopted.

339. The Government member of Jamaica withdrew an amendment relating to SMEs following discussion.

340. Paragraph 24 was adopted as amended.

Paragraph 25

341. The Employer Vice-Chairperson introduced an amendment to start the paragraph with the words "As stated in the 2004 UNDP report *Unleashing entrepreneurship: Making business work for the poor*", and in line 1 to replace "should" with "have to". The Worker Vice-Chairperson, noting that the paragraph was a quotation, proposed a subamendment deleting the second part of the proposed amendment. The amendment was adopted as subamended and, as a consequence, an amendment proposed by the Government member of Algeria fell.

342. Paragraph 25 was adopted as amended.

Paragraph 26

343. The Government member of Jamaica, speaking also on behalf of the Government members of the Bahamas, Barbados, Suriname, and Trinidad and Tobago, introduced an amendment to delete the words "including entrepreneurship" and the comma after the word "cooperatives". He explained that it was a grammatical question and in his view "entrepreneur" was included in the term "small enterprises". Neither the Employer nor Worker Vice-Chairpersons supported the amendment, stating that, in their view, the existing text reflected links among the three. The amendment was therefore rejected.

344. The Worker Vice-Chairperson introduced an amendment to insert the words "in the formal economy" after "enterprises", to illustrate the need for policies to support formation of enterprises in the formal economy and movement of workers from the informal to the formal economy. The Employer Vice-Chairperson did not support the amendment because he believed that policies did not have the ability to move workers from the informal to the formal sector. The Government member of Uruguay supported the amendment based on experience in her region where governments were making such efforts. The Government members of Denmark and the Netherlands did not support the amendment. The Government member of Algeria introduced a subamendment to use the words "legally existent" instead of the words "in the formal economy". The Employer Vice-Chairperson did not support the subamendment and offered a further subamendment that would add the words "and to assist young persons in the informal economy to move to the formal economy" following the word "enterprises". The amendment was adopted as subamended under the condition that the Office would edit the final text.

345. A further amendment relating to a heading was withdrawn by the Employers' group, and paragraph 26 was adopted as amended.

Paragraph 27

346. The Government member of Jamaica, speaking also on behalf of the Government members of the Bahamas, Barbados, Suriname, and Trinidad and Tobago, introduced an amendment to delete the two sentences "In developing countries, policies seeking to increase agricultural production, rural non-farm income … . The provision of adequate high-quality public services … and enabling environment for increased private investment and job growth.", explaining that those sentences were too prescriptive of policies that should be pursued. The Worker and Employer Vice-Chairpersons understood the concern that the list could be considered too exclusive. A subamendment to retain the sentences while changing "should" to "could" was adopted and the amendment was adopted as subamended.

347. The Worker Vice-Chairperson proposed adding ", tourism" after "manufacturing", as that was one of the sectors noted by the Committee as an area of potential employment for young people. The amendment was adopted. She withdrew an amendment and introduced a further amendment to insert the word "especially" after "services" in the phrase "public services in developing countries" to clarify that the phrase referred to both developed and developing countries. The amendment was supported by the Government members of Côte d'Ivoire and the Netherlands, and was adopted.

348. Paragraph 27 was adopted as amended.

Paragraph 28

349. The Worker Vice-Chairperson introduced an amendment to add the words "social protection" following "labour market". The Government member of Canada proposed a subamendment to insert the word "policies" so that the text would read "labour market and social protection policies and employment legislation …". The amendment as subamended was adopted, and in consequence a subsequent amendment fell.

350. The Government member of Canada, speaking also on behalf of the Government members of New Zealand, Norway, Switzerland and the United States, proposed that the words "based on" in the phrase "… legislation and regulations, based on international labour standards …" be replaced with "which take into account" to recognize that different countries would use the framework of international labour standards differently. After discussion, the amendment was adopted.

351. The Employer Vice-Chairperson proposed that two amendments dealing with reorganization of text in the paragraph be dealt with together. The amendments would increase ease of comprehension of the text. He proposed that the text in the second sentence following the words "employment of young persons" be deleted, and that the words "and recognizing collective bargaining, freedom of association, workplace safety, policies on wages and hours of work and other labour standards" be inserted into the first sentence after the words "social dialogue". The Worker Vice-Chairperson proposed a subamendment to use common ILO terminology, referring to "the right to collective bargaining and the promotion of freedom of association". The amendment was adopted as subamended. A further amendment was withdrawn by the Worker Vice-Chairperson.

352. Paragraph 28 was adopted as amended.

Paragraph 29

353. The Government member of Côte d'Ivoire, seconded by the Government member of Algeria, introduced an amendment to reflect that in some countries not all of the proposed mechanisms existed as yet. In place of the original text that "Governments and employers' and workers' organizations should jointly and regularly monitor the labour market and employment situation of young people", the text after "jointly" would read "establish labour market information and monitoring mechanisms to ensure a regular flow of information on the employment situation and specifically that of young people".

354. The Government members of France and the Netherlands supported the amendment. The Worker Vice-Chairperson proposed a subamendment that would insert "in consultation with" after "governments", which was further subamended by the Government member of the Netherlands to delete the word "jointly". The amendment was adopted as subamended.

355. The Employer Vice-Chairperson proposed an amendment adding "where appropriate" at the end of the last sentence, because some countries might already have effective policies. The Worker Vice-Chairperson subamended that to read "where necessary", and the amendment was adopted as subamended.

356. Paragraph 29 was adopted as amended.

Paragraph 30

357. After discussion, two amendments proposed by the Government member of Algeria, one by the Government member of Jamaica, and one by the Employer members were withdrawn.

358. The Employer Vice-Chairperson proposed adding "processes such as" after the word "through" in the phrase "… social and labour protection through well-resourced labour inspection …" in order to clarify that the examples given were not comprehensive. The amendment was adopted.

359. The Worker Vice-Chairperson proposed an amendment to replace "free organization of" with "right to organize" in the phrase "The free organization of informal economy workers and employers …" as the existing text use of "free" was not clear. The Employer Vice-Chairperson noted that the "right to organize" was not a phrase associated with employers' organizations, and that they understood "free" to include the free choice of individuals to join organizations. The Worker Vice-Chairperson introduced a subamendment to delete the word "free" in the original text. The amendment was adopted as subamended.

360. The Employer Vice-Chairperson proposed an amendment to insert "(including the removal of barriers to business entry)" after "regulatory changes". The amendment was adopted.

361. The Government member of Jamaica, speaking also on behalf of the Government members of the Bahamas, Barbados, Suriname, and Trinidad and Tobago, proposed an amendment to add "through incentives, such as management training, easy access to subsidized credit and simplified registration systems" to the final sentence following "enable young people in the informal economy to make the transition to the formal economy", to illustrate steps that could be undertaken. The Worker Vice-Chairperson proposed subamending the text to replace "easy" with "increased" and to delete "subsidized". The amendment was adopted as subamended.

362. Paragraph 30 was adopted as amended.

Paragraph 31

363. After discussion, the Government member of Jamaica withdrew an amendment.

364. The Worker Vice-Chairperson proposed an amendment to add the words "inclusive of quality public services" after the word "infrastructure", observing that without the quality element, public services would not support a good investment climate. The Employer Vice-Chairperson moved a subamendment to add ", recognition of property rights" at the end of the amendment since it was an important issue that had not yet been included in the conclusions. The amendment as subamended was adopted.

365. Paragraph 31 was adopted as amended.

Paragraph 32

366. The Employer Vice-Chairperson withdrew two amendments, and the Government member of Jamaica another.

367. The Employer Vice-Chairperson requested that two amendments relating to different paragraphs be dealt with together so that various changes intended to bring the text on training together would be considered at the same time. He proposed moving two sentences from paragraph 32 to paragraph 34 so that the two sentences from paragraph 32 – "Enterprises have a critical role to play in investment in training. A number of mechanisms used in combination to further investment to training and to guarantee access to training are required." – and the associated footnote reference to paragraph 12 of the resolution concerning human resources and development from the 88th Session of the International Labour Conference in 2000, would be placed in paragraph 34 between the sentences "A variety of initiatives … training to labour market needs." and "National policies should … and training opportunities." The Worker Vice-Chairperson suggested that the Office review whether paragraph 33 should be moved to before 32. The amendment was adopted as subamended.

368. The Worker Vice-Chairperson proposed inserting the words "in training and" following the words "further investment" and the amendment was adopted. The Government member of France, speaking on behalf of the Government members of the Committee Member States of the EU, in association with the Government members of Bulgaria and Romania, proposed adding the words "and vocational training" following "education" and that was adopted.

369. Paragraph 32 was adopted as amended and paragraphs 32 and 33 were reordered as suggested.

Paragraph 33

370. The Worker Vice-Chairperson noted a French language editorial point. The Government member of Portugal, speaking on behalf of the Government members of the Committee Member States of the EU, in association with the Government members of Bulgaria and Romania, introduced an amendment to replace "reducing" poverty with "eradicating". The amendment was adopted.

371. Paragraph 33 was adopted as amended.

Paragraph 34

372. The Worker Vice-Chairperson withdrew one amendment and paragraph 34 was adopted without amendment.

Paragraph 35

373. The Employer Vice Chairperson proposed adding the words "Public and private" and "can" so that the sentence would start "Public and private employment services can provide guidance …". The amendment was adopted.

374. The Government member of Jamaica, speaking on behalf of the Government members of the Bahamas, Barbados, Suriname, and Trinidad and Tobago proposed adding "career" after "provide" and "securing" after "finding" in the same sentence so it would read "… employment services can provide career guidance and … support young people in finding, securing and retaining jobs". The two amendments were adopted.

375. Paragraph 35 was adopted as amended.

Paragraphs 36, 37 and 38

376. Paragraphs 36, 37 and 38 were adopted without amendment.

Paragraph 39

377. The Employer Vice-Chairperson proposed deleting the words "and cross-cutting themes", as the reference was not clear. The Worker Vice-Chairperson stated that discrimination, decent work and social dialogue were understood as the cross-cutting themes of the Global Employment Agenda (GEA). On that basis, the Employer Vice-Chairperson subamended the proposal so that the section would read "the Global Employment Agenda including its ten core elements and cross-cutting themes" and that the footnote to the GEA should follow the word "themes". The amendment was adopted as subamended.

378. Paragraph 39 was adopted as amended.

Paragraph 40

379. The Government member of Jamaica, speaking on behalf of the Government members of the Bahamas, Barbados, Suriname, and Trinidad and Tobago, and the Government member of France, speaking on behalf of the Government members of the Committee Member States of the EU, in association with the Government members of Bulgaria and Romania, withdrew amendments calling for the deletion of the text "provided that there are adequate funds to support both the YEN and the promotion of decent, rewarding and productive work for youth".

380. The Government member of the Netherlands, speaking also on behalf of the Government members of Denmark, New Zealand, Sweden, Switzerland and the United States, introduced an amendment to replace the sentence "The ILO should consider proposing that the YEN be expanded …" with "The ILO should continue to promote the expansion of the YEN to include more countries, both developing and developed", inserting a full stop after "developed" and deleting the remaining text, replacing it with a new sentence reading "The ILO should ensure that it has the funds required to be a strong technical partner of the YEN." The speaker explained that the Government members sought two results with that amendment: that the ILO should promote the further expansion of the YEN and that the ILO should ensure it had the funds required to be a strong technical partner in the YEN. The Employer Vice-Chairperson suggested a subamendment to the last sentence of the proposed amendment, so that it would read "The ILO should ensure that it has the funds required to give effect to these conclusions and be a strong technical partner of YEN."

381. The Government member of France considered that the matter of funds did not fall under the mandate of the Committee, but rather under that of the Finance Committee.

382. The Government member of Jamaica, speaking also on behalf of the Government members of the Bahamas, Barbados, Suriname, and Trinidad and Tobago, proposed a subamendment to insert after the word "ILO" the words "through the full commitment of its constituent".

383. The Government member of the United Kingdom supported the original amendment and proposed a subamendment to insert after the word "developed" the words "as recommended by the report of the Commission for Africa". The Worker Vice-Chairperson could not agree with that subamendment because the report of the Commission for Africa focused only on one region whereas the amendment applied to countries around the world. The Government member of Nigeria agreed and the subamendment was withdrawn.

384. The Worker Vice-Chairperson supported the subamendment proposed by the Government member of Jamaica. The Government member of Nigeria agreed, as did the Employer Vice-Chairperson who stated that it did not change the amendment. The amendment was adopted as subamended by the Employer Vice-Chairperson and the Government member of Jamaica.

385. Paragraph 40 was adopted as amended.

Paragraph 41

386. The Government member of the United Republic of Tanzania, seconded by the Government members of the Netherlands and Nigeria, introduced an amendment to replace

the words "United Nations Millennium Declaration" with the words "United Nations Millennium Development Goals". The amendment was adopted.

387. The Government member of Nigeria, speaking on behalf of the Africa group, introduced an amendment to replace "[The ILO should play a role in promoting the resolution of the international debt problem and advocate increased resource flows into developing countries.]" with "The ILO should continue to play a leading role in sensitizing the international community to the social consequences of the debt problem and advocating increased resource flows into developing countries."

388. The Government member of the Netherlands, speaking on behalf of the Government members of IMEC present in the Committee, preferred to leave the text as it was and remove the brackets. There had been a lengthy discussion on the matter in the Drafting Group because the Government members of IMEC felt that it was not appropriate to include that issue in the conclusions. However, taking into account the importance of the problem, the Government members of IMEC were willing to accept the inclusion of the sentence as originally drafted. The Worker Vice-Chairperson supported the proposal. The Government member of Nigeria withdrew the amendment and the brackets were removed from the draft text.

389. Paragraph 41 was adopted as amended.

Paragraph 42

390. Paragraph 42 was adopted without amendment.

Paragraph 43

391. The Worker Vice-Chairperson withdrew an amendment and paragraph 43 was adopted without amendment.

Paragraph 44

392. The Employer Vice-Chairperson withdrew an amendment and paragraph 44 was adopted without amendment.

Paragraph 45

393. Paragraph 45 was adopted without amendment.

Paragraph 46

394. The Employer Vice-Chairperson introduced an amendment to delete in the first bullet point the words "aimed at young people" and to insert after the words "productive work" the words "for young people". The Worker Vice-Chairperson did not support the proposed amendment and preferred the text as it was because it made it clear that the campaign was to target young people, using their language and media outlets, rather than just being for their benefit. The amendment was withdrawn.

395. The Government member of Denmark, speaking on behalf of the Government members of the United Kingdom and the United States, introduced an amendment to replace, in the second bullet point, the words "workers and employers" with the words "the constituents of the ILO". The Government member of Portugal, speaking on behalf of the Government

members of the Committee Member States of the EU, in association with the Government members of Bulgaria and Romania, supported the amendment.

396. The Government member of Argentina proposed a subamendment to delete the words "workers and employers" since line 8 of the introductory sentence of the paragraph already mentioned that the ILO should undertake the actions listed in the bullet points in conjunction with its constituents. The Government member of Uruguay agreed and supported the subamendment.

397. The Employer Vice-Chairperson supported the amendment as originally proposed because he considered it appropriate to include governments. The Worker Vice-Chairperson also supported the original amendment.

398. The Government member of France proposed instead the phrase "working directly with its constituents to develop a set of instruments to help them promote".

399. The Government member of Denmark withdrew the proposed amendment in light of the observations made by the Government members of Argentina and Uruguay.

400. Paragraph 46 was adopted without amendment.

Paragraph 47

401. The Employer Vice-Chairperson proposed replacing the word "high" with "sustainable", which he felt to be a more logical choice in the context of the paragraph. The Worker Vice-Chairperson proposed a subamendment to combine the words to make the phrase "high and sustainable". The amendment was adopted as subamended.

402. Paragraph 47 was adopted as amended.

Paragraph 48

403. Paragraph 48 was adopted without amendment.

New paragraph between paragraphs 48 and 49

404. The Worker Vice-Chairperson proposed to insert a new paragraph after paragraph 48, which would read as follows:

> The Governing Body of the ILO should ensure that supervisory mechanisms adequately consider issues relevant to youth employment and rights issues. In particular, the Governing Body should request that the Committee on Legal Issues and International Labour Standards (LILS) consider the proposal to conduct a general survey to review the effect given to instruments related to the employment of young workers both in the States which have ratified one or more of these Conventions, and in those which have not.

405. The Employer Vice-Chairperson proposed a subamendment that would substitute the following text for the text proposed in the amendment:

> The ILO should give a cross-cutting youth dimension to all its work. In particular, it should seek age-disaggregated data relating to employment and the world of work and include specific sections addressing the youth dimension in its research, studies and reports, including those relating to international labour standards and the follow-up to the Declaration on Fundamental Principles and Rights at Work, as appropriate.

The Workers' group and the Government member of Algeria supported the amendment as subamended and it was adopted.

406. The new paragraph was adopted as amended.

Paragraph 50

407. The Worker Vice-Chairperson proposed to replace "on the use of the GEA" with "based on the GEA" and to insert a new sub-clause, which would add to the plan of action a request for the ILO to "organize periodic, regional youth employment technical meetings in order to build knowledge and exchange experiences among youth employment policy-makers and the social partners;". The Employer Vice-Chairperson noted the practical nature of the amendment and supported it, as did the Government member of Nigeria. The amendment was adopted.

408. The Employer Vice-Chairperson proposed to replace "support youth employment policies and programmes" with "effectively participate in the setting of policies and programmes in favour of youth employment". The idea of the clause was to increase the capacity of employers' and workers' organizations to participate in, and not just support, youth policies and programmes. The amendment was adopted without discussion.

409. Paragraph 50 was adopted as amended.

Paragraph 51

410. The Employer Vice-Chairperson proposed to replace the second sentence as follows:

   The ILO should support employers and workers and their respective organizations as appropriate, to:

   (i) review job descriptions to promote the hiring of youth, recognizing that young people bring positive attributes to work;

   (ii) recognize skills and productivity, not just qualifications or years of experience, to ensure that young workers have equal opportunities to other workers;

   (iii) help educate, train and mentor through investing in education and training, participating in training bodies and assisting school-to-work transition;

   (iv) work with industry partners, young people's networks and youth organizations to inform young people, schools, training bodies and employment agencies of both industry needs and expectations of young people;

   (v) to assist young people and employers of young people to:

   – develop, where opportunity exists, basic learning skills of literacy, numeracy and technological skills;

   – actively look for work and job opportunities, including entry-level work that combines employment with education or work experience;

   – prepare for the responsibilities of the world of work and career development by developing employability skills or upgrading skills through technical vocational training, and/or in the workplace.

411. The Employer Vice-Chairperson explained that the bullet points that followed were directed at specific organizations, therefore the preceding sentence needed to be reworded to improve the logic of the paragraph. He subamended the amendment to replace "as appropriate, to" with "as the case may be". The Worker Vice-Chairperson supported the amendment as subamended, noting that it improved the structure of the paragraph.

412. The Government member of France proposed a further subamendment to delete the phrase "where opportunities exist" in the first sub-point of sub-clause (v), to which the Employer Vice-Chairperson agreed. The amendment was adopted as subamended.

413. The Government member of Denmark, speaking on behalf of the Government members of the Committee Member States of the EU, in association with the Government members of Bulgaria and Romania, proposed to insert "In addition to the role of governments already noted," at the beginning of the second sentence. The amendment was adopted without debate.

414. Paragraph 51 was adopted as amended.

Paragraph 52

415. Paragraph 52 was adopted without amendment.

Appendix

416. The Worker Vice-Chairperson proposed an amendment to add "the Part-Time Work Convention, 1994 (No. 175)" after "(No. 189)". She pointed out that, within the context of rapid growth of part-time jobs, the Convention was particularly relevant for young people. The Employer Vice-Chairperson supported the amendment and it was adopted.

417. The appendix was adopted as amended.

Consideration and adoption of the report

418. The Committee considered its draft report at its 15th sitting. The Reporter introduced the draft report, with the annexed resolution and conclusions as amended by the Committee. She noted that the report faithfully reflected the richness of the discussion from the Employer and Worker Vice-Chairpersons, as well as the large number of Government members. Their wealth of experience, wisdom and goodwill had gone into making the discussion lively and productive.

419. The Committee unanimously adopted the report, subject to minor amendments and corrections to specific paragraphs submitted by some members.

420. The Secretary-General of the Conference, Mr. Juan Somavia, highlighted several important aspects recognized in the report and conclusions: the positive aspects young people brought to the labour market; the multiple pathways of young persons into employment; the value of an integrated approach to solving problems; the need to pay attention to both supply and demand issues; and the importance of adapting solutions to the unique economic and social conditions of each country. On the last point, he stressed the importance of building capacity to deliver differentiated solutions to accomplish the same objective.

421. The representative of the Worker Vice-Chairperson thanked the Chairperson for his strong leadership, patience and flexibility, which had been critical in making the Committee's deliberations a success. She thanked the Employer members for their cooperation and willingness to compromise on various issues to reach a consensus. She also thanked the Government members for engaging in serious and meaningful discussions. The Employer Vice-Chairperson expressed his group's gratitude to Government members for making laudable efforts in finding practical solutions on the issue of youth employment. He also

thanked the Workers' group for the understanding reached on a number of issues. Finally, he joined the Workers' group in thanking the Chairperson for his effective leadership. The Employer and Worker members thanked the Reporter, the secretariat, the interpreters and the translators, who had all played an essential role in bringing about the Committee's good results.

422. The Chairperson stated that it had been a great pleasure to work with the Committee members on the important and complex issue of youth employment. He had appreciated the open and frank discussions and the fact that there had been willingness to reach out to one another. The Committee had shown wisdom in striving for workable solutions. He congratulated the Employer Vice-Chairperson and the Worker Vice-Chairperson for their demonstrated leadership in negotiating to reach a consensus. He appreciated the efforts of the Government members in accommodating the views of the Employer and Worker members. He appreciated the supportive role and contribution of the secretariat. The Reporter, the interpreters and the translators all deserved praise for their hard and diligent work.

Geneva, 15 June 2005. *(Signed)* M.L. Abdelmoumene,
Chairperson.

M.L.G. Imperial,
Reporter.

Resolution concerning youth employment

The General Conference of the International Labour Organization, meeting in its 93rd Session, 2005,

Having undertaken a general discussion on the basis of Report VI, *Youth: Pathways to decent work*,

1. Adopts the following conclusions;

2. Invites the Governing Body to give due consideration to them in planning future action on youth employment and to request the Director-General to take them into account both when implementing the Programme and Budget for the 2006-07 biennium and allocating such other resources as may be available during the 2006-07 biennium.

Conclusions on promoting pathways to decent work for youth

1. In addressing the employment challenges faced by young women and men, it is important to recall the ILO Decent Work Agenda, the ILO Global Employment Agenda, the United Nations Millennium Declaration, the ILO Declaration of Philadelphia, the ILO Declaration on Fundamental Principles and Rights at Work and its Follow-up, the body of international labour standards relevant to work and young persons (see appendix), the conclusions of the Tripartite Meeting on Youth Employment: The Way Forward (Geneva, 13-15 October 2004), the World Commission report on the Social Dimension of Globalization and the ILO's participation in the inter-agency Youth Employment Network.

Issues and challenges

2. In all regions and countries, young women and men set out in life with dreams, hopes and aspirations. Yet everywhere young women and men face challenges in the labour market. If young people are to be given opportunities, then multiple pathways to decent employment are needed. Achieving decent work for young people is a critical element in poverty eradication and sustainable development, growth and welfare for all.

3. Young women and men bring numerous assets to the labour market: relevant and recent education and training; enthusiasm, hope and new ideas; willingness to learn and be taught; openness to new skills and technology; realistic expectations on entry to the labour market; mobility and adaptability; and represent a new generation to meet the challenge in countries with an ageing workforce. The challenge is to bring young people into employment without displacing other workers. Policy-makers have to consider intergenerational issues and recognize, in this context, a life-cycle approach.

4. Young people are employed and seek employment in diverse local, national, regional and international circumstances. This includes diversity between developing and developed economies, and within these economies. Governments, employers and young workers are not homogeneous groups; they have different needs, capacities and expectations. The ILO Declaration on Fundamental Principles and Rights at Work and its Follow-up is universal and applies to all workers, regardless of national circumstances and levels of development.

5. Many young people are in education or employed in decent jobs. In many countries, young people are able to make successful transitions from education to the world of work. In some countries, the ageing workforce also presents growing opportunities for young people. There are diverse forms of work in which young people can engage, with vastly different employment conditions, including permanent full-time or part-time work, as well as casual, temporary or seasonal work. These forms of employment may provide entry points for young workers to the labour market and enhance their long-term employment prospects. Unfortunately, there are also too many young workers who do not have access to decent work. A significant number of youth are underemployed, unemployed, seeking employment or between jobs, or working unacceptably long hours under informal, intermittent and insecure work arrangements, without the possibility of personal and professional development; working below their potential in low-paid, low-skilled jobs without prospects for career advancement; trapped in involuntary part-time, temporary, casual or seasonal employment; and frequently under poor and precarious conditions in the informal economy, both in rural and urban areas. Other young workers lack adequate incomes, access to education, training and lifelong learning, social protection, safe workplaces, security, representation and rights protected under international labour

standards, including freedom of association, collective bargaining and protection from harassment and discrimination.

6. Of the world's over 1 billion young people, 85 per cent live in developing countries with a high incidence of poverty and inadequate employment opportunities. There is significant regional variation in youth employment, with some countries facing greater challenges than others due in part to the uneven impacts of globalization and the asymmetries in current global economic activity. The scourge of HIV/AIDS, the weight of external debt, armed conflict, poor governance, unstable institutions and gender inequality compound weak economic growth and deter the public and private investment necessary to create jobs. Rapid population growth is expected to significantly increase the number of youth searching for decent work opportunities in most developing countries.

7. In developed economies, the challenge may be linked to slow economic and employment growth, the transition into employment, discrimination, social disadvantages, cyclical trends, and a number of structural factors. Variation in the youth employment challenge requires specific responses.

8. In too many instances, the labour market prospects for young people vary according to gender, age, ethnicity, education level, family background, health status and disability. Some groups are therefore more vulnerable and face particular disadvantage to securing and retaining decent work.

9. The regulatory environment for investment and enterprises and labour law should create an investment climate that fosters economic growth and decent employment of young persons. Whilst employment cannot be directly created but only encouraged by legislation or regulation, it is recognized that labour legislation and regulation based on international labour standards can provide employment protection and underwrite increased productivity, which are basic conditions in order to create decent work, particularly for young people. Labour laws and, where they exist, collective agreements, should apply to all young workers, including those currently lacking protection because of disguised employment relationships.[1] Efforts should be made to move those in the informal economy into the formal economy. The creation of an enabling environment, the pursuit of good governance and the sustainable existence of both physical and social infrastructure are necessary for the competitiveness of existing businesses and the start-up of new enterprises.

10. Investment in youth reaps benefits for individuals, communities and societies. Decent work for young people unleashes multiplier effects throughout the economy and society, boosting investment and consumer demand and ensuring more stable and cohesive social ties across generations, including sharing institutional workplace knowledge. It shifts young people from social dependence to self-sufficiency, helps them escape poverty and enables them to actively contribute to society.

11. Youth unemployment and underemployment impose heavy social and economic costs, resulting in the loss of opportunities for economic growth, erosion of the tax base which undermines investment in infrastructure and public services, increased welfare costs, and unutilized investment in education and training, and may also be associated with social instability and conflict, increased levels of poverty, crime and substance abuse.

---

[1] As referenced in the conclusions of the International Labour Conference's general discussion on the employment relationship (2003).

12. The youth employment challenge is bound to the general employment situation and, while it has its own dimensions, it is influenced by a number of general factors which may have positive or negative consequences, including:

    - the impact of globalization;
    - the impact of structural reforms in developing countries;
    - the level of, and fluctuation in, aggregate demand;
    - demographic trends;
    - the level of economic activity, public and private investment and sustainable growth;
    - the employment intensity of growth in developing countries;
    - an enabling regulatory environment for both enterprises and the protection of workers' rights;
    - entrepreneurship and enterprise creation options, including through cooperatives;
    - education and training outcomes;
    - the relationship between education and labour market needs; and
    - work experience and labour market services.

13. As new entrants to the labour market, some young workers lack the specific training or seniority that may buffer older workers from swings in market conditions; their employment is highly dependent on the state of the economy. During economic downturns, the practice of "last hired, first fired" and the lack of vacancies take a toll on young workers when they are less equipped to find new employment.

14. Whilst some young people transition effectively from education to work, the transition is problematic for too many others. One concern is when young persons do not possess basic literacy and numeracy skills that are necessary to access vocational training and transition from a state of unemployability to employability. Another concern is when, for protracted periods, young people are not in employment, education or training. In other instances, some young people do not complete schooling and/or have insufficient skills to gain secure and sustainable employment opportunities.

15. Failure to find a job may be linked to lack of relevant skills and training opportunities, to low demand for the skills in which young persons have trained, or to changing demand in the labour market. The mismatch that arises can lead to long periods of jobseeking, higher unemployment and sustained periods of lower skilled and precarious work. Lack of opportunities for work experience and entrepreneurial development, combined with the absence of adequate labour market information, vocational guidance and counselling, and poor job placement mechanisms, exacerbate the problem of getting a decent job.

16. Particular groups of young people face specific hardships due to discrimination and social exclusion, including those with disabilities, those affected by HIV/AIDS, indigenous youth, those involved in hazardous work, demobilized soldiers, ethnic minorities, migrants and other socially disadvantaged youth. In general, young women, in particular young women with children, are more prone to unemployment, discrimination, sexual harassment, underemployment and poor working conditions. In some cases, young persons

are denied access to employment opportunities for which they are fully qualified and competent solely on the basis of their age.

17. Governments and social partners are committed to addressing the youth employment challenge with the involvement of young women and men. Urgent action is required to enhance the involvement of young workers, workers' organizations and employers of young workers and their organizations in development, implementation and monitoring of youth labour market policies and programmes.

Policies and programmes for decent work for young people

18. The principles of the Employment Policy Convention, 1964 (No. 122), whereby "each Member shall declare and pursue, as a major goal, an active policy designed to promote full, productive and freely chosen employment", are fundamental to any employment policy directed at young people.

19. Although one size does not fit all, meeting the youth employment challenge calls for an integrated and coherent approach that combines macro- and microeconomic interventions and addresses both labour demand and supply and the quantity and quality of employment. Youth employment should be considered in all relevant social, employment and economic policies through a well-balanced policy mix. Supportive national trade, industry, training and wage policies, with appropriate involvement of the social partners, are also required to meet the youth employment challenge. The employment prospects of young people are inextricably linked to the general employment situation and can be especially vulnerable to fluctuations in economic conditions. Consequently, targeted interventions aimed at overcoming disadvantages, while promoting equality, social inclusion and an equitable society, are required. Policies and programmes that aim to prevent cycles of disadvantage from being repeated across generations are critical in achieving social inclusion and decent work for youth.

20. High and sustained economic growth is a necessary condition for the generation of employment, including quality employment for young people. This requires macroeconomic policy supportive of increased and sustainable employment growth through expanded investment, productive capacity and aggregate demand in conditions of economic and political stability. Governments should have policy space to ensure ownership of their macroeconomic and industrial policies enabling them to expand their economies including the manufacturing and services sectors. Social progress and economic growth should go hand in hand. Policies relating to globalization, including trade and foreign direct investment, should, wherever necessary, be reformed to create decent jobs for young people. Monetary, fiscal, trade and social security policies should be coherent with the overall objective of increased and sustainable economic growth, employment generation and social protection. Assessment of the likely employment implications of macroeconomic policy choices can better inform an adequate policy mix.

21. Placing economic growth and employment generation at the centre of national policy objectives calls for supportive and coherent national, regional and international policy frameworks. Reforms are required at the national and international levels to ensure developing countries have access to additional financial resources to promote economic development and decent work. International debt relief, including debt cancellation, and increased official development assistance (ODA) are important components of such reforms. In addition, some of the recommendations of the World Commission on the Social Dimension of Globalization are particularly relevant in this regard. National and international strategies to achieve the Millennium Development Goals (MDGs) should

combine economic growth, poverty eradication and social and employment objectives, including youth employment. The forthcoming review of the MDGs in September 2005 provides an excellent opportunity to assess the extent to which national, regional and international policies and strategies address the promotion of decent work for all with a focus on young people.

22. Increased and sustainable economic growth, while necessary, is not a sufficient condition for sustainable employment generation, particularly for young people. A range of complementary policies are needed to enhance the employment content of growth while also increasing productivity and ensuring adequate social protection. Policies should seek to strengthen enterprises and enhance labour demand as well as the quality of the labour supply. Governments should review all policies to ensure they do not discriminate against the hiring of youth.

23. In developing countries the employment intensity of growth must be increased. For example, employment-intensive investment in infrastructure has been shown to be an effective means to enhance sustainable decent work among low-income and low-skilled workers, as well as to create assets that enhance productivity and output. Such investment is a proven means to eradicate poverty, particularly when it is combined with training.

24. The development of entrepreneurship among young people is an important component of employment policies. Some young people have the potential to become entrepreneurs and create or join an enterprise. Some young people also have the potential to establish or join cooperatives. This potential should be actively nurtured through an enabling environment combining information on opportunities and risks faced by entrepreneurs and those involved in cooperatives, business development services directed particularly at young people, mentoring and financial services (including access to credit and venture capital) and simplifying registration (including business entry) procedures. Employers' organizations, together with governments, have an active role to play. The development of entrepreneurship and cooperatives should respect international labour standards. National legislation and policies concerning cooperatives should be in accordance with the Promotion of Cooperatives Recommendation, 2002 (No. 193).

25. As stated in the 2004 UNDP report *Unleashing entrepreneurship: Making business work for the poor*, developed country governments should:

> … foster a conducive international macroeconomic and policy environment to unleash the full potential of entrepreneurs in developing countries. A robust international economy provides markets for goods from developing country companies. In addition, increasing the flow of development aid and reforming the global trading system to provide fair economic opportunities to producers from developing countries are essential for promoting rapid growth in domestic private investment.

26. Policies for small enterprises, including entrepreneurship and cooperatives, should be reviewed for their relevance to young persons in different country circumstances. Policies to promote employment should also be reviewed to attract, inform and assist young persons in establishing or joining small enterprises, and to assist young persons in the informal economy to move to the formal economy. Small and medium-sized enterprises, including cooperatives, can be an engine of job creation and seedbeds for innovation and entrepreneurship. In some countries, many small and medium-sized enterprises are marginal and operate outside of the formal economy. The right to participate in employers' and workers' organizations by persons establishing or working in small businesses is important.

27. Tripartite dialogue can inform policies that target specific industries and sectors with strong potential for youth employment. In developing countries, policies seeking to

increase agricultural production, rural non-farm industries, manufacturing, tourism and technological capabilities could provide real prospects for raising both economic growth and decent employment for youth. The provision of adequate high-quality public services, especially in developing countries, in areas such as health care, education, utilities, power and water is required and will directly generate additional decent work for youth as well as providing an enabling environment for increased private investment and job growth. There is considerable scope to expand economic activity in key sectors through public and private initiatives which will also help economic and job growth. The development of skills relevant to technology, when coupled with education and vocational training, can open up new opportunities for young people.

28. Labour market and social protection policies and employment legislation and regulations, which take into account international labour standards and social dialogue and recognize the right to collective bargaining, and the promotion of freedom of association, workplace safety, policies on wages and hours of work and other labour standards, should ensure adequate protection of young workers and the improvement of their employment prospects. The regulatory environment for enterprises should create an investment climate that fosters economic growth and the decent employment of young persons.

29. Governments in consultation with employers' and workers' organizations should establish labour market information and monitoring mechanisms to ensure a regular flow of information on the employment situation, specifically of young people. In order to avoid precarious employment situations that deny workers basic rights, and ensure occupational safety and health protection, labour inspection and national labour administration systems should play a key role and need to be strengthened, where necessary.

30. Measures to address the working conditions of youth in the informal economy include small business management training, enhanced cooperation and organization of micro- and small enterprises and the full enforcement of social and labour protection through processes such as well-resourced labour inspection systems, labour courts and functioning tripartite institutions. The organization of informal economy workers and employers through their respective organizations is also important to achieving this objective. Emphasis should be placed on necessary regulatory changes (including the removal of barriers to business entry) to enable young people in the informal economy to make the transition into the formal economy through incentives, such as management training, increased access to credit and simplified registration systems.

31. An enabling environment for investment and enterprise creation is essential for growth and employment. This includes effective public and private investment in essential physical and social infrastructure, inclusive of quality public services, recognition of property rights, good governance, stable institutions, political stability, the rule of law including labour law, and a conducive legal framework for private investment, as advocated in the Job Creation in Small and Medium-Sized Enterprises Recommendation, 1998 (No. 189).

32. Access to universal, free, quality public primary and secondary education and investment in vocational training and lifelong learning are essential for individual and social enhancement and preparation for future working life. Education for all is an effective means of combating child labour and eradicating poverty.

33. Education, vocational training, core skills – including literacy and numeracy – labour market services and work experience and awareness of labour rights and occupational health and safety are essential components of a comprehensive policy to enhance the employability of young people. Education and vocational training policy should be broadly based, have a link to employment policy and should be responsive to the development of

core skills being used in workplaces. A key function of the education system should be the progressive development of employability skills among young people. [2]

34. Vocational education and lifelong training responsive to the evolving demand for skills in the labour market, along with apprenticeship schemes and other measures that combine training with work, are fundamental to improving youth employability. A variety of initiatives, including public and private partnerships, and appropriate incentives for individual and collective investments in human resources development, can ensure the continued relevance of vocational education and training to labour market needs. Enterprises have a critical role to play in investment in training. A number of mechanisms used in combination to further investment in training and to guarantee access are required. [3] National policies should aim to provide all young women and men with the broadest possible access to responsive vocational education and training opportunities. Such policies should be guided by the relevant provisions of the Human Resources Development Convention, 1975 (No. 142), and the Human Resources Development Recommendation, 2004 (No. 195). Education and training authorities should seek to:

- Integrate basic skills such as literacy, numeracy and, where possible, technological knowledge into education, equipping students with a foundation for the world of work.

- Incorporate career guidance and support, knowledge of industry along with industrial relations and essential labour issues, such as occupational safety and health, into the early years curricula.

- Foster career entry and career development, including the recognition of prior learning to facilitate transfer between educational programmes and through the transfer of relevant educational qualifications and credits.

- Make education more responsive to labour market needs by directly engaging educators with industry partners in the sector and encouraging student contact with industry. Programmes which, in the latter school years, combine learning with work or work experience can bring students and employers together.

---

[2] "Employability is defined broadly. It is a key outcome of education and training of high quality, as well as a range of other policies. It encompasses the skills, knowledge and competencies that enhance a worker's ability to secure and retain a job, progress at work and cope with change, secure another job if he/she so wishes or has been laid off, and enter more easily into the labour market at different periods of the life cycle. Individuals are most employable when they have broad-based education and training, basic and portable high-level skills, including teamwork, problem solving, information and communications technology (ICT) and communication and language skills, learning to learn skills, and competencies to protect themselves and their colleagues against occupational hazards and diseases. This combination of skills enables them to adapt to changes in the world of work. Employability also covers multiple skills that are essential to secure and retain decent work. Entrepreneurship can contribute to creating opportunities for employment and hence to employability. Employability is, however, not a function only of training – it requires a range of other instruments which results in the existence of jobs, the enhancement of quality jobs, and sustainable employment. Workers' employability can only be sustained in an economic environment that promotes job growth and rewards individual and collective investments in human resources training and development.", para. 9 of the resolution concerning human resources training and development, ILC, 88th Session, 2000.

[3] Para. 12 of the resolution concerning human resources training and development, ILC, 88th Session, 2000.

35. Public and private employment services can provide career guidance and counselling, impart up-to-date labour market information and support young people in finding, securing and retaining jobs. Where necessary, public employment services should be strengthened.

36. Taking into account relevant provisions of the Employment Policy (Supplementary Provisions) Recommendation, 1984 (No. 169), active labour market policies and programmes (ALMPs) can greatly facilitate initial employment as well as re-entry into employment. Labour market programmes could target youth, in particular disadvantaged young people, or mainstream programmes could be adapted to the needs of the individual. ALMPs are more likely to be effective when they are well targeted; meet the specific requirements of the intended beneficiaries, based on a careful analysis of the local employment situation; are linked to demand for real jobs; and include measures to improve the competencies, skills and sustainable employment opportunities of beneficiaries.

37. Social benefit programmes to support unemployed and underemployed youth should be established where they do not exist. Social benefit programmes should contribute to job search and labour market efficiency. However, public policy should assist young people to move into decent work or education as soon as possible.

38. Governments should take responsibility for the regular monitoring and evaluation of the performance of policies and programmes promoting decent work for young people. Assessing performance against established benchmarks is a proven method for moving forward. Knowledge about what works and what does not work, the relevance, effectiveness and efficiency of policies and programmes on youth employment should be compiled and disseminated widely and creatively. Tools which support employers, workers and governments to identify areas of work where there are gaps in the application of international labour standards are important and should be developed.

An ILO plan of action to promote pathways to decent work for youth

39. With regard to ILO work on youth employment, the Decent Work Agenda provides the paradigm, and the Global Employment Agenda, including its ten core elements and cross-cutting themes,[4] which include the "four Es"[5] of the Youth Employment Network (YEN), provide the policy pillars.

40. The ILO, in close collaboration with the social partners and relevant international agencies, should continue to play a leading role in the Youth Employment Network to promote decent work for young persons and to synchronize the work of the YEN with these conclusions. The ILO should continue to promote the expansion of the YEN to include more countries, both developing and developed. The ILO, through the full commitment of

---

[4] Promoting trade and investment for productive employment and market access for developing countries; promoting technological change for higher productivity, job creation and higher standards of living; promoting sustainable development for sustainable livelihoods; a call for policy integration to ensure macroeconomic policy for growth and employment; decent work through entrepreneurship; employability through improving knowledge and skills; active labour market policies for employment, security in change, equality, and poverty reduction; social protection as a productive factor; occupational safety and health – synergies between security and productivity; productive employment for poverty reduction and development.

[5] Employability, equal opportunities, entrepreneurship and employment creation.

its constituents, should ensure that it has the funds required to give effect to these conclusions and be a strong technical partner of the YEN.

41. The ILO should, with its tripartite constituents, strengthen partnerships with international financial institutions and United Nations organizations in order to give a central place to the promotion of youth employment in development policies and poverty reduction strategies, and in the forthcoming review of the United Nations Millennium Development Goals. This should include promotion of the ILO Decent Work Agenda and the Global Employment Agenda. The ILO should play a role in promoting the resolution of the international debt problem and advocate increased resource flows into developing countries.

42. The ILO plan of action, with particular focus on developing countries, is based on three pillars: building knowledge; advocacy; and technical assistance.

Building knowledge

43. In order to assist countries in developing their policies and programmes addressing the youth employment challenge, the ILO should expand knowledge on the nature and dimensions of youth employment, unemployment and underemployment. Particular emphasis should be placed on gathering factual data and empirical evidence on the effectiveness of country policies and programmes and in synthesizing the results of country studies and evaluations. This analysis should collect examples of where policy interventions have been successful and where they have not, and should extract lessons learned from such experiences. The ILO should facilitate global peer partnerships to promote better performance and disseminate and share best-practice experiences and models among its constituents, such as industry training and skills development, education linkages and human resources practices.

44. The ILO should develop a research agenda that includes the ILO strategy for evaluating the success of its youth-oriented technical cooperation projects, and use evaluation information to feed back into programme design. The ILO may draw on its experiences through evaluating its other youth-related efforts, for example the International Programme on the Elimination of Child Labour (IPEC).

45. The ILO should strengthen research and knowledge dissemination on the ten core elements covered in the ILO Global Employment Agenda and the relationship between these core elements and the achievement of decent work for youth, including a regularly updated web site and database, publications, newsletters and practical guides. The ILO should partner, as appropriate, with other international organizations in the gathering of information and empirical research.

Advocacy and the promotion of decent work for youth

46. The ILO should undertake a campaign to promote the conclusions of the general discussion on promoting pathways to decent work for youth. This campaign should include an international, regional and national focus which is developed in conjunction with the social partners. The campaign should have as its core objective the promotion and implementation of these conclusions with a specific focus on information for young people themselves, taking into account the specific needs and interests of young workers, including an appropriate focus on young women and other vulnerable groups. In conjunction with its constituents, the ILO should be responsible for:

- an international promotional campaign aimed at young people to promote decent work with a focus on employment creation, workers' rights and employability, as detailed in these conclusions;

- working directly with workers and employers in the development of tool kits which will assist governments and workers' and employers' organizations to promote awareness of their rights and responsibilities for decent work.

The ILO should target this campaign at young people through communication means that are most familiar to young people, including youth media and networks for students and other young people. The Committee on Employment and Social Policy of the Governing Body of the ILO should oversee the campaign.

47. The ILO should strengthen cooperation with multilateral institutions and other international organizations to promote policy coordination which makes the achievement of high and sustainable levels of employment growth a priority for all relevant international institutions. The ILO should also promote the strong emphasis on decent work for youth and the Global Employment Agenda in Poverty Reduction Strategy Papers, as well as decent work country programmes, YEN national action plans and other country-level activities undertaken by international financial institutions.

48. The ILO should promote good practice on policies and programmes for youth employment through tripartite meetings. This should include giving special attention to the gender dimension of the youth employment challenge, as well as the specific needs of young people affected by HIV/AIDS, and of those facing particular disadvantage due to disability, ethnic origin, labour migration and other specific circumstances.

49. The ILO should give a cross-cutting youth dimension to all its work. In particular, it should seek age-disaggregated data relating to employment and the world of work and include specific sections addressing the youth dimension in its research, studies and reports, including those relating to international labour standards and the follow-up to the ILO Declaration on Fundamental Principles and Rights at Work, as appropriate.

Technical assistance

50. The ILO should:

    (i) continue and intensify the provision of guidance and policy advice, particularly to developing countries, based on the Global Employment Agenda to promote decent work for youth;

    (ii) organize periodic, regional youth employment technical meetings in order to build knowledge and exchange experiences among youth employment policy-makers and the social partners;

    (iii) enhance the capacity of employers' and workers' organizations to effectively participate in the setting of policies and programmes in favour of youth employment, through its programme of technical cooperation, the International Training Centre of the ILO in Turin, and other means;

    (iv) strengthen the capacity of labour administration to promote the application of labour legislation at the workplace, for the benefit of all workers, including young women and men;

(v) assist developing countries in establishing and strengthening inspection services, public employment services, data-gathering and monitoring and evaluation systems on youth employment;

(vi) seek additional funding from donors to expand its programme of technical cooperation for the promotion of decent work for young women and men.

51. The ILO should maximize the comparative advantage of its tripartite structure in its activities to promote decent work for young persons. In addition to the role of governments already noted, the ILO should support employers and workers and their respective organizations, as the case may be, to:

(i) review job descriptions to promote the hiring of youth, recognizing that young people bring positive attributes to work;

(ii) recognize skills and productivity, not just qualifications or years of experience, to ensure that young workers have equal opportunities to other workers;

(iii) help educate, train and mentor through investing in education and training, participating in training bodies and assisting school-to-work transition;

(iv) work with industry partners, young people's networks and youth organizations to inform young people, schools, training bodies and employment agencies of both industry needs and expectations of young people;

(v) to assist young people and employers of young people to:

- develop basic learning skills of literacy, numeracy and technological skills;

- actively look for work and job opportunities, including entry-level work that combines employment with education or work experience;

- prepare for the responsibilities of the world of work and career development by developing employability skills or upgrading skills through technical vocational training, and/or in the workplace.

52. The ILO should support efforts to strengthen the capacity of workers' and employers' organizations to reach out and engage young workers and employers of young workers to ensure that their specific needs are taken into account in social dialogue processes, including collective bargaining.

Appendix

International labour standards relevant to work and young persons

In addition to the Conventions on fundamental principles and rights at work and their related Recommendations – the Freedom of Association and Protection of the Right to Organise Convention, 1948 (No. 87); the Right to Organise and Collective Bargaining Convention, 1949 (No. 98); the Forced Labour Convention, 1930 (No. 29); the Forced Labour (Indirect Compulsion) Recommendation, 1930 (No. 35); the Abolition of Forced Labour Convention, 1957 (No. 105); the Equal Remuneration Convention, 1951 (No. 100), and Recommendation, 1951 (No. 90); the Discrimination (Employment and Occupation) Convention, 1958 (No. 111), and Recommendation, 1958 (No. 111); the Minimum Age Convention, 1973 (No. 138), and Recommendation, 1973 (No. 146); the Worst Forms of Child Labour Convention, 1999 (No. 182), and Recommendation, 1999 (No. 190) – and to the priority Conventions on employment and labour inspection and their related Recommendations – the Employment Policy Convention, 1964 (No. 122), and Recommendation, 1964 (No. 122); the Employment Policy (Supplementary Provisions) Recommendation, 1984 (No. 169); the Labour Inspection Convention, 1947 (No. 81), and its Protocol of 1995; the Labour Inspection Recommendation, 1947 (No. 81); the Labour Inspection (Agriculture) Convention, 1969 (No. 129), and Recommendation, 1969 (No. 133) – these instruments include in particular: the Employment Service Convention, 1948 (No. 88), and Recommendation, 1948 (No. 83); the Labour Administration Convention, 1978 (No. 150), and Recommendation, 1978 (No. 158); the Private Employment Agencies Convention, 1997 (No. 181), and Recommendation, 1997 (No. 188); the Human Resources Development Convention, 1975 (No. 142), and Recommendation, 2004 (No. 195); the Job Creation in Small and Medium-Sized Enterprises Recommendation, 1998 (No. 189); the Part-Time Work Convention, 1994 (No. 175), and Recommendation, 1994 (No. 182); the Promotion of Cooperatives Recommendation, 2002 (No. 193); the Workers' Representatives Convention, 1971 (No. 135), and Recommendation, 1971 (No. 143); the Vocational Rehabilitation and Employment (Disabled Persons) Convention, 1983 (No. 159), and Recommendation, 1983 (No. 168); the Migration for Employment Convention (Revised), 1949 (No. 97), and Recommendation (Revised), 1949 (No. 86); the Migrant Workers (Supplementary Provisions) Convention, 1975 (No. 143), and the Migrant Workers Recommendation, 1975 (No. 151); the Indigenous and Tribal Peoples Convention, 1989 (No. 169); the Occupational Safety and Health Convention, 1981 (No. 155), and its Protocol of 2002; the Occupational Safety and Health Recommendation, 1981 (No. 164); the Safety and Health in Agriculture Convention, 2001 (No. 184), and Recommendation, 2001 (No. 192); the Maternity Protection Convention, 2000 (No. 183), and Recommendation, 2000 (No. 191); the Medical Examination of Young Persons (Industry) Convention, 1946 (No. 77); the Medical Examination of Young Persons (Non-Industrial Occupations) Convention, 1946 (No. 78); the Medical Examination of Young Persons Recommendation, 1946 (No. 79); the Protection of Wages Convention, 1949 (No. 95), and Recommendation, 1949 (No. 85); the Minimum Wage Fixing Convention, 1970 (No. 131), and Recommendation, 1970 (No. 135); the Social Security (Minimum Standards) Convention, 1952 (No. 102); the Employment Promotion and Protection against Unemployment Convention, 1988 (No. 168), and Recommendation, 1988 (No. 176); the Hours of Work (Industry) Convention, 1919 (No. 1), and the Hours of Work (Commerce and Offices) Convention, 1930 (No. 30); the Night Work Convention, 1990 (No. 171), and Recommendation, 1990 (No. 178).

CONTENTS

Page

*Sixth item on the agenda: Promoting youth employment
(general discussion based on an integrated approach)*

Report of the Committee on Youth Employment 1

Resolution concerning youth employment... 65

Conclusions on promoting pathways to decent work for youth... 66

International Labour Conference

Record of Proceedings

Ninety-third Session, Geneva, 2005

22

PART ONE

Third item on the agenda: Information and reports on the application of Conventions and Recommendations

Report of the Committee on the Application of Standards

Contents

	Page
PART ONE: General report	3
A. Introduction	3
B. General questions relating to international labour standards	10
C. Reports requested under article 19 of the Constitution: Hours of Work (Industry) Convention, 1919 (No. 1), and Hours of Work (Commerce and Offices) Convention, 1930 (No. 30)	20
D. Compliance with specific obligations	34

PART ONE

GENERAL REPORT

A. Introduction

1. In accordance with article 7 of the Standing Orders, the Conference set up a Committee to consider and report on item III on the agenda: "Information and reports on the application of Conventions and Recommendations". The Committee was composed of 205 members (125 Government members, 10 Employer members and 70 Worker members). It also included 8 Government deputy members, 77 Employer deputy members, and 164 Worker deputy members. In addition, 34 international non-governmental organizations were represented by observers. [1]

2. The Committee elected its Officers as follows:

   Chairperson: Mr. Sérgio Paixão Pardo (Government member, Brazil)

   Vice-Chairpersons: Mr. Edward E. Potter (Employer member, United States) and Mr. Luc Cortebeeck (Worker member, Belgium)

   Reporter: Ms. Carine Parra (Government member, France)

3. The Committee held 20 sittings.

4. In accordance with its terms of reference, the Committee considered the following: (i) information supplied under article 19 of the Constitution on the submission to the competent authorities of Conventions and Recommendations adopted by the Conference; (ii) reports supplied under articles 22 and 35 of the Constitution on the application of ratified Conventions; and (iii) reports requested by the Governing Body under article 19 of the Constitution on the Hours of Work (Industry) Convention, 1919 (No. 1), and the Hours of Work (Commerce and Offices) Convention, 1930 (No. 30). [2] The Committee was also called on by the Governing Body to hold a special sitting concerning the application by Myanmar of the Forced Labour Convention, 1930 (No. 29), in application of the resolution adopted by the Conference in 2000. [3]

Homage to Mr. Alfred Wisskirchen

5. The Employer members paid tribute to the work of Mr. Alfred Wisskirchen, who had retired from his role as Employer spokesperson after 22 years of the 35 years that he attended the ILO Conference. They underlined that he had participated in the work of this Committee with integrity, legal rigour and compassion. The Employer members saluted

---

[1] For changes in the composition of the Committee, refer to reports of the Selection Committee, *Provisional Records* Nos. 3 to 3J. For the list of international non-governmental organizations, see *Provisional Record* No. 2-1.

[2] Report III to the International Labour Conference – Part 1AI: Report of the Committee of Experts on the Application of Conventions and Recommendations; Part 1AII: Information document on ratifications and standards-related activities; Part 1B: Hours of work: From fixed to flexible?

[3] ILC, 88th Session (2000), *Provisional Records* Nos. 6-1 to 5.

him for his contribution to improve all aspects of the ILO supervisory machinery. The Worker members joined the Employer members in paying tribute to the work of Mr. Wisskirchen.

Work of the Committee

6. In accordance with its usual practice, the Committee began its work with a discussion on general aspects of the application of Conventions and Recommendations and the discharge by member States of standards-related obligations under the ILO Constitution. In this part of the general discussion, reference was made to Part One of the report of the Committee of Experts on the Application of Conventions and Recommendations and to the information document on ratifications and standards-related activities. During the first part of the general discussion, the Committee also considered its working methods with reference being made to a document submitted to the Committee for this purpose.[4] The second part of the general discussion dealt with the General Survey on *Hours of work: From fixed to flexible* carried out by the Committee of Experts. A summary of all aspects of the general discussion is set out in Part One of this report.

7. Following the general discussion, the Committee considered various cases concerning compliance with obligations to submit Conventions and Recommendations to the competent national authorities and to supply reports on the application of ratified Conventions. In this regard, reference was made to the Information note on the cases of serious failure by member States to respect their reporting or other standards-related obligations, submitted to the Committee by the secretariat for the first time this year. This note enumerated the principal difficulties encountered in fulfilling constitutional obligations and sought to identify some elements on which the technical assistance to help resolve these difficulties should focus.[5]

8. The Committee held a special sitting to consider the application of the Forced Labour Convention, 1930 (No. 29), by Myanmar. A summary of the information submitted by the Government, the discussion and conclusion is contained in Part Three of this report.

9. During its second week, the Committee considered 25[6] individual cases relating to the application of various Conventions. The examination of the individual cases was based principally on the observations contained in the Committee of Experts' report and the oral and written explanations provided by the governments concerned. As usual, the Committee also referred to its discussions in previous years, comments received from employers' and workers' organizations and, where appropriate, reports of other supervisory bodies of the ILO and other international organizations. Time restrictions once again required the Committee to select a limited number of individual cases among the Committee of Experts' observations. With reference to its examination of these cases, the Committee reiterates the importance it places on the role of the tripartite dialogue in its work and trusts that the governments of all those countries selected will make every effort to take the measures necessary to fulfil the obligations they have undertaken by ratifying Conventions. A summary of the information submitted by governments, the discussions,

---

[4] Work of the Committee on the Application of Standards, ILC, 93rd Session, C.App/D.1.

[5] ILC, 93rd Session, Committee on the Application of Standards, C.App/D.4.

[6] In one case, Bosnia and Herzegovina's Government did not attend in response to the Committee's invitation.

and conclusions of the examination of individual cases is contained in Part Two of this report.

10. To select the cases to be discussed in the second week, the Officers of the Committee submitted a draft list of the individual cases to be examined.[7]

11. The Worker members agreed with the adoption of the list of individual cases contained in document D.5. Once again, the adoption of the list had been the subject of important discussions within the Workers' group, as the criteria of rigour, equity and impartiality, which governed the work of the Conference Committee, the supervisory system and the ILO, were essential. The objective of the discussions on the list of individual cases was to seek solutions together to resolve problems of application. The proposed list contained 25 individual cases, which was a very limited number having regard to the Conference's schedule this year, which included the Governing Body elections. Of the 25 cases selected, 12 concerned freedom of association. A decrease in the number of cases relating to freedom of association would only be possible if determined actions were taken by the governments concerned. It should also be emphasized that the Committee of Experts had asked the Government of Sudan to provide to the Conference Committee information on the application of Convention No. 29 and the Government of Ecuador to provide information on the Medical Examination of Young Persons (Industry) Convention, 1946 (No. 77), and the Medical Examination of Young Persons (Non-Industrial Occupations) Convention, 1946 (No. 78).

12. The Worker members regretted that, because of time constraints, a certain number of cases could not be discussed. It was therefore important to urge governments to take the necessary measures to give effect to the respective Conventions. Particular attention should be given to the case of Pakistan with respect to the Freedom of Association and Protection of the Right to Organise Convention, 1948 (No. 87), on which it had not submitted a report this year. The Worker members also regretted that no case concerning the application of the Employment Policy Convention, 1964 (No. 122), for example that of Italy, had been chosen. Finally, they deeply regretted that the Committee could not discuss the application of Convention No. 29 by Japan. Even if the facts dated back over more than 60 years, the case was still relevant today. A discussion on the case had been requested in 2003. There was the risk that the categorical and systematic refusal to deal with this case would lead the supervisory system into an impasse. Therefore, as a definitive solution was desirable on this case, the Worker members proposed that an informal tripartite meeting be held, including all parties concerned, under the aegis of the Office. It was to be hoped that the Government and Employers of Japan would agree to collaborate to find an adequate solution.

13. The Employer members commended the Worker members on their efforts which enabled the Committee to adopt the list of individual cases as early as possible. This provided the governments concerned with adequate time to prepare. The Employer members would also have liked to see other cases on the list, in particular cases of progress. In addition, they commented on the statement by the Worker members concerning the application by Japan of Convention No. 29. The Conference Committee had discussed this case two years ago in the same context and the Committee of Experts had recognized that little could now be done concerning events that had occurred 60 years ago. In its two last observations, the Committee of Experts had made the point that it had no mandate to rule on the legal effect of bilateral and multilateral treaties that might have a bearing on the case. In the view of

---

[7] ILC, 93rd Session, Committee on the Application of Standards, C.App./D.5.

the Employer members, a discussion of the case of Japan in the Conference Committee would not be effective and would not have a tangible impact.

14. The Employer members also noted that once again nearly half of the individual cases selected for examination by the Conference Committee concerned the freedom of association Conventions. Many years ago, the Committee had adopted a system under which the cases mainly concerned freedom of association one year, and the following year was devoted to the examination of non-freedom of association cases. They suggested that the Committee might give some thought to a system of this type, which would make it possible to pay greater attention to cases of progress and to technical Conventions. They concluded by recommending the list of individual cases for adoption.

15. The Government member of the Republic of Korea indicated that, with regard to Convention No. 29, he shared the deep concerns and regrets expressed by the Worker members over the fact that the issue of so-called comfort women, involving sexual slavery by the Japanese military prior to and during the Second World War, had not been included in the individual cases for examination by the Committee. His Government considered this issue to be very important and hoped that, in the future, it would be taken up as an individual case in this forum. His delegation took note of the proposal presented by the Worker members that a tripartite meeting should be held to find an adequate solution for the issue.

16. The Government member of Japan stated that the discussion of specific cases should be conducted on the basis of the list agreed to by the Government, Employer and Worker members. His delegation believed that it was not appropriate to discuss a specific case in the course of the general discussion.

17. The Government member of Cuba stated that her delegation had for years been expressing serious concerns about the criteria for establishing the list of individual cases. Noting that the selection of cases in the list this year showed that an effort had been made to achieve a better regional balance, she thanked the Officers of the Committee. Nevertheless, she felt that the selection of cases still retained aspects of the previous politicized system under which developed countries which, according to the report of the Committee of Experts, had violated fundamental Conventions such as the Worst Forms of Child Labour Convention, 1999 (No. 182), were not included in the list. In conclusion, she stated that, while she appreciated the efforts made, she urged the Committee to continue to move forward so as to achieve more equity in the selection of individual cases.

18. The Government member of Zimbabwe recalled that his country had been continuously called before the Conference Committee for reasons related, not to the violation of the respective Convention, but to the political agendas of former colonial powers. He added that spending time refuting groundless claims by the purported representatives of the workers' movement took away from the time that could be gainfully spent on bettering the welfare of the workers in his and other countries. He therefore called for his country to be taken off the list of individual cases to be examined by the Conference Committee.

19. Following the general discussion on the draft list of individual cases to be examined, the Committee adopted the list (document D.5).

Working methods of the Committee

20. Referring to the establishment of the list of cases, the Worker members pointed out that the 2005 report of the Committee of Experts contained 774 observations and 1,419 direct requests, which meant more than 2,000 comments representing an increase of over 25 per cent in comparison to the previous year. The proposed list contained 25 cases, showing a

balance between Conventions and regions. The criteria used for the adoption of the list were the following: the nature of the comments of the Committee of Experts, in particular the presence of a "footnote"; the seriousness and persistence of cases of failure to apply the Conventions; the urgent and specific nature of the situation; and the possibility that the discussions would have a tangible impact on the situation. The additional elements proposed by the representative of the Secretary-General were also important. These were: the quality and significance of the replies provided by governments or the absence of any replies on their part; the comments submitted by workers' and employers' organizations; and the discussions held at previous sessions of the Conference Committee and its conclusions, in particular the existence of a special paragraph.

21. The Worker members pointed out that the approach of selecting certain cases rather than others had the result that the cases selected by the Committee consisted solely of violations of international labour standards. They were nevertheless of the view that certain cases of progress had to be mentioned as demonstrating through practical action adherence to the principles and standards of the ILO. This was the case, for example, of New Zealand on the application of Forced Labour Convention, 1930 (No. 29), or of the United Republic of Tanzania with respect to Freedom of Association and Protection of the Right to Organise Convention, 1948 (No. 87), and the Right to Organise and Collective Bargaining Convention, 1949 (No. 98). As emphasized by the representative of the Secretary-General, it was important to give greater visibility to the results achieved by the supervisory system. These cases of progress could inspire other countries to pursue dialogue and to believe that real changes were possible.

22. The Worker members also emphasized that the work of the Conference Committee formed part of the ILO's mandate and supported the work of other departments, particularly those involved in technical cooperation or in the promotion of standards. The discussion of the individual cases had to be held in this positive context of encouraging improvements in law and in practice relating to conditions of work and the life of men and women workers. In this regard, the Committee of Experts had also mentioned several cases of progress on the application of the Labour Inspection Convention, 1947 (No. 81). The application of this Convention was very important for the implementation of other Conventions ratified by a particular country. The Worker members also thanked the Committee of Experts for the general observation on the application of the Worst Forms of Child Labour Convention, 1999 (No. 182), on the sale and trafficking of children in West Africa. The Committee could discuss this issue when examining the case of Niger in relation to Convention No. 182.

23. With regard to the selection of individual cases, the Employer members were of the view that, in addition to the criteria set out in document D.1, other criteria could be taken into consideration, including the history of a case, whether or not the case involved technical Conventions not previously discussed or examined, whether the country concerned had ever appeared before the Committee, and any relevant cases of progress. These cases were important because they demonstrated that the supervisory bodies were reflecting on successful cases, which could help other countries to learn about implementation in law and practice. In addition, they would have liked to see more cases concerning technical Conventions, such as those on occupational safety and health, which involved issues of life and death, as well as a selection of countries that had never appeared before the Conference Committee. They pointed out that the selection of a case was not necessarily negative, but rather a process of dialogue to improve implementation in law and in practice. The selection of cases was based on criteria applied in the Committee's methods of work and, while there was always some level of imprecision, it was a sensible and honest process.

24. The Government member of the United States, speaking on behalf of the Government members of the Industrialized Market Economy Countries (IMEC), recalled that the Conference Committee had been debating for several years whether and how it should improve its methods of work, with the aim of making them more transparent, fairer and more efficient, and thus making the Committee more effective. As a consequence of this ongoing debate, some adjustments had been made and continued to be made. IMEC welcomed in particular the new practice of pausing after each individual case to allow the Chairperson sufficient time, in consultation with the Officers, to put forward a conclusion that accurately reflected the content and tone of the debate. IMEC also appreciated the efforts made this year to adopt the list of cases earlier than ever before. However, no major problems related to the methods of work of the Conference Committee had come to light and the Committee had come out in favour of its existing methods of work, including the system for selecting cases. The criteria and the process by which those criteria were applied were generally felt to be fair and just, although, as in any procedure, there might be room for improvement. IMEC continued to believe that the Committee's methods of work were sound, including the manner in which it selected cases for discussion. While the criteria listed in document D.1 could not guarantee a purely scientific list of cases, they did however lay the foundation for developing a list that was balanced and equitable and that engendered the confidence of the three groups. Nevertheless, IMEC had always supported efforts to promote genuine improvements in the ILO supervisory system and would continue to do so.

25. Regarding methods of work, the Government member of Italy welcomed the measures taken to improve transparency and objectivity. With respect to individual cases, he emphasized that the only reason for their being discussed in the Committee on the Application of Standards was to encourage compliance with international labour standards.

26. The Government member of Bahrain, speaking on behalf of the Government members of the Gulf Cooperation Council (Bahrain, Kuwait, Oman, Qatar, Saudi Arabia, United Arab Emirates and Yemen), expressed appreciation of the positive reaction of the Committee to the request to adopt the list of individual cases at the very beginning of the Committee's work so as to give governments more time to prepare their responses. He also commended the Committee's real willingness to review its working methods so as to ensure a tripartite balance, while pointing out the need to ensure that the Government group played a role in determining the criteria for selecting individual cases in cooperation with the Employers' and Workers' groups.

27. The Government member of India welcomed the efforts to reform the functioning of the Conference Committee, although there remained room for further improvement. He hoped that the criteria for the selection of cases would be more transparent and objective in the future so that there could be greater transparency in the supervisory system. The views of Governments and the Employer and Worker members from the countries concerned should be heard before the list was finalized. He believed that the appropriate forum to achieve a tripartite consensus on the selection of cases would be the Governing Body, which could take a decision at its March session. Finally, he stated that the discussion in the Conference Committee should take into account the socio-economic and cultural diversity of member States, and the conclusions adopted by the Committee should reflect the views of the constituents.

28. The Government member of Cuba expressed satisfaction at the diversity, clarity and sincerity that prevailed during the discussion of the methods of work of the Committee during its last session in June 2004. There were clear opinions expressed about the possibility of accepting or improving the methods of work, and there was consensus that the ILO was an institution of tripartite dialogue. He recalled that during the last meeting of the Committee, Cuba had presented ideas on behalf of a group of 18 countries (Algeria,

Belarus, Burundi, China, Cuba, Egypt, Ethiopia, India, Indonesia, Libyan Arab Jamahiriya, Malaysia, Myanmar, Pakistan, Syrian Arab Republic, Sudan, Venezuela, Viet Nam and Zimbabwe) on methods of work. The Movement of Non-Aligned Countries had endorsed this proposal. The methods of work were intended to provide more transparency and democracy in the Committee. He noted that, during the 91st Session of the Conference (June 2003), the members of the Movement of Non-Aligned Countries had expressed significant concern about the process agreed to by the Committee on cases of some developing countries. The treatment was selective and based on imprecise criteria. Some regional groups had also expressed similar concerns. As a result of these discussions, the Chairperson of the Committee on the Application of Standards in 2003 invited all of the members to prepare new proposals to be examined at the 92nd Session of the Conference.

29. In reply to the request, the group of 18 countries drafted a document suggesting some changes in the methods of work of the Committee. A document was presented to the Committee in 2004. Subsequently, the Ministerial Meeting of the Movement of Non-Aligned Countries endorsed this document and their proposals suggested, among others, that the Committee of Experts establish objective and transparent criteria that would provide a basis for the drawing up of the list of individual cases. The criteria should consider geographic balance and an equitable distribution of the fundamental and technical Conventions. It was further proposed to give enough time to member States to prepare their responses during the preparation of the list of individual cases. The list should be made available in March during the Governing Body and seek, among other things, to maintain the balance between the developed and developing countries. It was further suggested that sufficient time be given to the Chairperson of the Committee so that the deliberations could be adequately reflected in the Committee's conclusions. The objective of the document and its declarations was to support the improvement of the working methods of the Committee by looking for ways to promote greater transparency, objectivity and balance in the selection of individual cases. A total of 20 Governments (Algeria, Belarus, Burundi, China, Cuba, Egypt, Ethiopia, India, Indonesia, Libyan Arab Jamahiriya, Malaysia, Mauritania, Myanmar, Pakistan, Sudan, Syrian Arab Republic, Thailand, Venezuela, Viet Nam and Zimbabwe) expressed their recognition of the efforts made by the Office this year, especially under the guidance of the Department of International Labour Standards, to improve the methods of work of the Committee on the Application of Standards, which would strengthen its credibility. He expressed the hope that during the work of the 93rd Session of the Conference, the Committee would examine this question, and adopt tripartite methods, supported by new ideas of the Office, to find more appropriate ways of solving the problems that continued to preoccupy many Governments.

30. The Government member of the Bolivarian Republic of Venezuela expressed support for the statement of the Government of Cuba. She indicated the need to balance selection of individual cases to be examined. This stated selection must include developed and developing countries. Geographic distribution and diversity of Conventions examined should also be considered.

31. The Government member of Zimbabwe questioned the procedures used for the selection of the individual cases to be examined by the Conference Committee. Despite concerted efforts by his country to comply with the standards in question, his country had once again been called before the Committee this year. He therefore called for a review of the working methods of the Conference Committee, especially with regard to the criteria and reasons for the selection of individual cases. The continued abuse of the procedures would seriously impair the credibility of the ILO as a whole.

B. General questions relating to international labour standards

General aspects of the supervisory procedure

32. The Committee first of all noted the information presented by the representative of the Secretary-General concerning recent changes undergone by the International Labour Standards Department, as well as the vision and strategy for ILO standards proposed by her to the three groups of the Governing Body at its March 2005 session. She explained that the vision and strategy were organized around three major concepts: renewal, trust and visibility:

   (i) **"renewal"** which placed emphasis on a broad approach to the application of standards, which encompassed ratification, implementation, enforcement and influence. It relied on technical cooperation and assistance as important components to buttress social progress and international labour standards. In addition, a strong economic case had to be made for standards to support the ILO's traditional approach;

   (ii) **"trust"** which focused on a modernized, integrated and coherent supervisory system. The ILO supervisory system had to live up to the expectations raised by its status of being the most developed system at the international level. It should be and be seen as transparent, fair and effective;

   (iii) **"visibility"** which targeted an effective communication of the ILO standards message.

   She highlighted that the proposed vision and strategy was the framework within which the Department had been restructured. The Department has also developed a detailed plan of action to give effect to the proposed vision and strategy. She sincerely hoped that the Department, as it was now organized, would provide the best service possible to the supervisory bodies, including this Committee.

33. The Committee also noted the information presented by the representative of the Secretary-General concerning the mandate of the Committee and its working methods, information on the ratification and application of international labour standards, cases of progress, constitutional and other procedures, special procedures for freedom of association, policy regarding the revision of standards and the Global Report on forced and compulsory labour. She reported that, as of 31 May 2005, 7,312 ratifications had been registered, which constituted 92 new ratifications over the past year. She pointed out that 110 countries had ratified all eight ILO fundamental Conventions. On the obligation to submit reports, governments had submitted 64 per cent of the reports requested – a slight decrease over last year. Moreover, the Committee of Experts had expressed its deep concern regarding the fact that only 25 per cent of the reports requested had reached the Office by 1 September when they were due. She underlined that this was certainly an aspect which the Office needed to closely examine to determine what remedial steps were within its mandate to take.

34. In concluding, the representative of the Secretary-General conveyed her hopes as well as expectations from the Committee. She saw a tremendous synergy between the Committee of Experts, this tripartite Committee and the Office. She expected to see both firmness and fairness in ensuring that Members of the Organization honour the obligations which they had voluntarily assumed. She also expected understanding in the case of particular difficulties encountered by ILO Members as well as imaginative ways of resolving them. Moreover, she hoped to see how each of the tripartite groups individually approached the

various problems and issues before this Committee and how they worked together to reach a tripartite decision. Finally, she hoped that her colleagues and herself would be able to use what they had learned to enhance the vision and strategy to which she referred at the beginning of her statement, so that the Office's action with respect to the application of standards could be seen to be what it should be and was: an integral part of the action of the Organization as a whole.

35. The Committee welcomed Justice Robyn Layton, Chairperson of the Committee of Experts. She noted a number of changes in the composition of the Committee of Experts, including the retirement of Mr. Alburquerque, Mr. Bhagwati, Mr. Razafindralambo and Mr. Nwabueze, as well as the appointment of two new members, Mr. Cheadle and Ms. Nussberger. She pointed to the continuing decline of reports received as well as the late reporting of governments, both of which had a significant impact on the work of the secretariat in processing reports, which in turn affected the work of the Committee of Experts. On a positive note, however, there had been a significant increase in the number of observations made by employers' and workers' organizations which was essential to the good functioning and impact of the supervisory system.

36. The speaker also indicated that the Committee of Experts was continuing to review its working practices through its Subcommittee on Working Methods. The topics for discussion both in the Subcommittee and in plenary session concerned: logistics and the process of dealing with the increasing workload of additional reports, particularly now that there had been a large number of first reports requiring detailed analysis on the Worst Forms of Child Labour Convention, 1999 (No. 182), the interface of the work of the Committee of Experts with the secretariat in order to efficiently process the workload; the modification of the allocation of Conventions amongst the members of the Committee which allowed families of Conventions to be specially considered by both a member with a common law background as well as a member with civil law background; and continued efforts to improve the content, presentation, structure and comprehension of the Experts' report.

37. Moreover, in response to matters raised by this Committee, the Committee of Experts had adopted the following measures: (i) ensured in the report that there was clarity as to the member States, which had been the subject of footnotes. These were set out in paragraph 35 of the General Report and in footnotes 9 and 11; (ii) listed the cases of progress in which the Committee was able to express its satisfaction, or note with interest measures taken by particular countries. In total they had amounted to 320 for the year. She concluded by welcoming the participation of the two Vice-Chairpersons of this Committee to one of the plenary sessions of the Committee of Experts. The Experts regarded this collaboration as important for increasing the effectiveness of both committees in their respective supervisory roles.

38. The Employer members and the Worker members as well as all Government members who spoke welcomed the presence of the Chairperson of the Committee of Experts in the general discussion of the Conference Committee.

39. With regard to the General Report of the Committee of Experts, the Employer members laid out a number of suggestions for improvement. First, the cases of serious failure by member States to respect their reporting or other standards-related obligations should be dealt with in the same manner as special paragraphs since they constituted cases of "serious failures to report" and involved situations which undermined the whole supervisory process. The Committee of Experts could provide more in-depth analysis on why certain member States were not reporting, including better information on each country's specific circumstances and an overview of relevant developments over a period of years. Document D.4 represented a start in this analysis, but they believed it did not take

sufficiently into account questions of economic development and extraordinary natural catastrophes and war. Secondly, the Information Document on ratifications and standards-related activities contained valuable information on technical cooperation, but this should be enriched. It would be useful to know the context of the technical cooperation, how it related to comments of the Committee of Experts and the present Committee, and how it differentiated from technical cooperation under the Declaration on Fundamental Principles and Rights at Work.

40. Moreover, the Employer members felt that the Reader's Note at the beginning of the report could provide more detail and history on the Committee of Experts. This could include more information on the Committee of Experts' establishment in 1926 at the instigation of the present Committee, and the fact that this was done for a three-year trial period which had been extended to the present day. This fact underscored the close working relationship between the two Committees. Mentioning this might also correct the impression given in the last sentence of the second paragraph of the Reader's note that the Conference Committee was an ancillary body to the Committee of Experts. The Employer members added that the relevant elements of the briefing to the Conference Committee which had been given before this session could also be included in the Reader's note but that the briefing itself should continue because there would always be new members.

41. The Employer members believed that paragraph 37 of the Experts' report regarding the practical application of ILO Conventions through judicial and administrative decisions should be further developed. The Committee of Experts' report should be released as soon as possible after its adoption, preferably already by the end of February via the Internet. This would allow countries that might be selected for examination by this Committee to have enough time to prepare. In the view of the Employer members, the emphasis of the present Committee should be on the discussion of individual cases, and less emphasis should be placed on the general discussion and the General Surveys. With regard to the Subcommittee on Working Methods, it might consider holding a session with users of the report. This could also be done through regional consultations or a survey. Finally, the Employer members were of the view that Part III of the General Report dealing with collaboration with other international organizations went beyond the Experts' mandate and did not belong in the Committee of Experts' report. This section could be published elsewhere and it could provide more detail on the parties to collaboration and the time and place of collaboration.

42. The Worker members welcomed the good interaction and collaboration between the Committee of Experts and the Conference Committee which they considered to be essential. Despite their different roles, these two Committees shared the same objectives, and their smooth functioning continued to be vital to the success of the ILO supervisory system.

43. With regard to the changes made to the presentation of the report of the Committee of Experts, the Worker members were pleased to note that even more efforts had been made to make it more readable, particularly due to the inclusion of lists and annexes which gave a clearer indication of standards-related developments and the member States' implementation of their obligations. The footnotes concerning the countries that were obliged to provide full information to the Conference were also useful for identifying the cases to be discussed.

44. The Worker members pointed out that they had always advocated the cases of progress mentioned in the Committee of Experts' report. The governments concerned – particularly New Zealand in respect of Convention No. 29 and the United Republic of Tanzania in respect of the Freedom of Association and Protection of the Right to Organise Convention, 1948 (No. 87), and the Right to Organise and Collective Bargaining Convention, 1949

(No. 98), should be commended. The cases of progress could serve as models. It would be moreover interesting to know the criteria used by the Committee of Experts to express its satisfaction or interest about the measures taken by the governments and to have more information on this topic. It would also be useful to more clearly define what is meant by "progress" and to distinguish the cases of progress regarding the fundamental and priority Conventions from cases concerning other Conventions or from those referring to the obligation to supply reports.

45. The Worker members regretted the absence of information on the results obtained following the introduction of a new procedure requesting the United Nations and other specialized international organizations to provide information on the application of certain Conventions of common interest. With regard to the integrated approach, within the framework of which three topics had been already examined by a special Conference Committee, the Worker members were still not sure about the effective scope and added value of this approach in the fields which it intended to promote for the following two reasons. First, this approach had not yet led to concrete results. The conclusions adopted last year by the Conference by consensus on the subject of migrant workers referred to an action plan of the ILO to be established in partnership with other competent international organizations. The action plan included the elaboration of a non-binding multilateral framework for a rights-based approach to labour migration and the identification of actions to be undertaken with a view to a wider application of the relevant international labour standards. The ILO could ensure in this regard the better promotion of the Migration for Employment Convention (Revised), 1949 (No. 97), and the Migrant Workers (Supplementary Provisions) Convention, 1975 (No. 143), and the principles embodied by these instruments. Active promotional measures were expected in this field. Secondly, the integrated approach appeared to have the effect of stagnation in the adoption of the new Conventions and Recommendations. For some years now, no new Conventions had been adopted except in the maritime field. The twenty-first century was likely to become less "conventional" and more "promotional".

46. The Worker members noted with interest the strategic vision for standards presented by the representative of the Secretary-General and wished to reaffirm, along with the International Labour Standards Department, their confidence in a more modern and coherent supervisory system, and to make the message on standards more visible. Even if an economic argument could be used to support actions in favour of standards, the starting point of the Worker members' approach remained the full respect of social standards. The Worker members recalled the importance of international labour standards and noted with satisfaction that the Director-General had dedicated a part of his speech to standards-related activities at this session of the Conference.

47. The Government member of the United States, speaking on behalf of the IMEC countries noted the quality of the Conference Committee's work was dependent to a large extent on the quality of the annual report of the Committee of Experts. IMEC therefore appreciated the continuing efforts of the Committee of Experts to enhance the impact of its report and to make the report more readable and more accessible for all potential users. She noted that the Committee of Experts intended to consider further improvements in its working methods to enable it to manage its mounting workload. She emphasized that the Office itself was vitally important to the efficiency, effectiveness and integrity of the ILO supervisory system. She hoped that the recent organizational changes in the International Labour Standards Department, as well as the new vision and strategy for standards, would enable the Department to fulfil its mandate better and looked forward to working with the representative of the Secretary-General towards that goal. IMEC also called on the Director-General to ensure that the essential and ever-increasing work of the Department was among his highest priorities. The effectiveness of the Office in supporting the ILO supervisory system had a direct bearing on the credibility of the Organization as a whole.

48. Several speakers (Government members of Brazil, China, India, Italy, Lebanon, Portugal and Denmark, also speaking on behalf of the Government members of Iceland, Finland, Norway and Sweden, as well as Worker members of Brazil and Pakistan) commended the Committee of Experts for a clearer, user-friendly and comprehensive report which provided an overview of the problems encountered in the application of ratified Conventions and cases of progress. In this regard, the Government member of Italy emphasized the importance of the report of the Committee of Experts to the work of the Conference Committee. The complementary nature of these two Committees was essential for the efficient functioning of the supervisory system. The Government member of Denmark noted with particular interest that the Committee this year had taken due note of previous discussions in the Conference Committee on improvements in the presentation of its report and that changes were now being implemented. This remarkable accomplishment had been achieved through tripartite willingness and consensus supported by a competent staff. He noted that the improvement of standards and the effectiveness of the supervisory system was a continuing process. It was important for the supervisory system to be as effective as possible in the light of the high and increasing number of ratifications.

49. With regard to the content of the individual observations, the Employer members were of the view that the comments of the Experts needed to have a common and clear presentation. Some comments were cryptic, opaque and incomprehensible. They needed to be more consistent. A starting point would be a clear setting out of what a Convention called for. The comments should also make a clear distinction between allegations by third parties and the views of the Experts. Information requests should be consolidated. Along with individual observations, the content of direct requests corresponding to these observations should be published as well. This would put the comments in context and make them easier to understand. In this regard, the Worker member of Brazil emphasized the importance of not overly simplifying or reducing the amount of information. It was important not to fall into the trap of synthesizing too much, which could lead to the omission of information that was essential for an understanding of the issues.

50. The Government member of China said that her country was committed to the implementation of international labour standards and had started the process of ratification of the Discrimination (Employment and Occupation) Convention, 1958 (No. 111), and the Occupational Safety and Health Convention, 1981 (No. 155). She underlined that there existed good cooperation between her Government and the ILO on Convention No. 29 and the Abolition of Forced Labour Convention, 1957 (No. 105). Studies had been carried out on the practice in her country in relation to these Conventions and effective measures would be taken to ensure that they were given effect. She emphasized that her Government was intent on pursuing humanitarian policies, safeguarding the rights of workers and improving living conditions. However, her country was faced by great disparities between rural and urban areas and problems related to the globalization process. If all workers were to benefit from decent work, it would be necessary to adopt practical measures. Her country was therefore seeking to strengthen its cooperation with the ILO and other international organizations with a view to achieving economic and social progress.

51. The Government member of Bahrain, speaking on behalf of the Government members of the Gulf Cooperation Council, stated that the adoption of the Declaration on Fundamental Principles and Rights at Work and its Follow-up in 1998 had led to an increase in the number of fundamental Conventions ratified by the member States of the Council. This movement was part of a reform process to broaden the scope of political participation in the decision-making process. While welcoming the increasing number of ratifications, the Government member of Denmark pointed out that the high number of ratifications gave rise to a growing need for governments to receive consistent and reliable advice on the meaning and scope of the obligations that they assumed when ratifying ILO Conventions.

52. The Government member of the United States, speaking on behalf of the IMEC countries, and the Government member of Lebanon highlighted that due to the dramatic increase in the number of ratifications of ILO Conventions, especially the fundamental Conventions, the workload of the Committee of Experts had also increased dramatically. IMEC was therefore concerned about the current number of vacancies on the Committee of Experts and hoped that it would soon be operating at full capacity. Indeed, with due regard to budgetary considerations, it might be time to explore the possibility of increasing the maximum number of Experts, which had been maintained at 20 since the late 1970s. The Government member of Lebanon wondered whether the integrated approach would not place an undue burden on member States' reporting obligations. She also drew attention to the decrease in the number of Experts and wondered why the Governing Body had not made any nominations to the vacant posts, especially since the number of ratifications was continuing to increase. She hoped that the appointments would include Experts from the Arab region.

53. The Government member of Denmark welcomed the fact that the influence of international labour standards outside the ILO continued to increase and that there was a growing conviction in other international organizations that sustainable economic development could not take place without careful attention to the situation of the people in each country, particularly in economies undergoing the effects of globalization. The Worker member of Pakistan recalled that the workers in developing countries were facing major challenges due to globalization and economic deregulation, which were doing much to increase poverty, unemployment and social problems. The working people of the world therefore had great expectations of the ILO, which had a vital role to play in ensuring that national policies were in line with the requirements of social protection. The ILO, and particularly its supervisory system, was the social conscience of the world and the fundamental principles set out in its Conventions were of universal application. The Worker member of Pakistan made an appeal that certain industrialized countries ratify more Conventions.

54. The Worker member of India said that the community of workers throughout the world had the bitter experience of noting that most countries did not ratify ILO Conventions and that there was no effective mechanism to ensure that Conventions were duly ratified. Moreover, there was a major gap between ratification and actual implementation. Most countries did not have adequate laws to give effect to the ILO Conventions that they had ratified. In an era of exploitative globalization, retrograde reforms of current labour laws were being carried out in every country under the pretext of increasing competitiveness to the detriment of the working people. The processes of contract work, casual work and outsourcing were everywhere prevalent. When unemployment was the order of the day, the noble standards of the ILO were rapidly losing their relevance. It was necessary for the ILO to take this grim situation into account so that the ILO Conventions could be saved from the attacks of globalization.

55. The Worker member of France emphasized that standards-related activities were the soul of the ILO and it was on these activities that the visibility referred to by the representative of the Secretary-General should be based. Indeed, improving the effectiveness of standards-related activities would enhance the authority and pre-eminence of the ILO, as indicated by the World Commission on the Social Dimension of Globalization. The World Commission was of particular importance in view of the concerns, which were being heard increasingly broadly, particularly from the workers, concerning the direction taken by globalization, as financial and economic markets tended to prevail over labour standards. When labour inspectors were challenged in the exercise of their duties, and were even assassinated, as had been the case in France in 2004, the ILO was affected in a certain manner. Two things were important if standards-related activities were to be more effective: on the one hand, it was essential to insist on promoting the ratification of Conventions and, on the other, on the transposition of standards into national law.

Moreover, it was indispensable for States to attribute to their labour inspection services the means and the authority necessary to carry out their functions. In this regard, the Government member of Brazil pointed out that with the support of the International Labour Standards Department and the Social Dialogue Department a course had been held on international labour standards in MERCOSUR for labour inspectors with the participation of employer and worker representatives, to ensure that Conventions were not only ratified, but were applied in practice.

56. The Government member of Lebanon welcomed the Committee of Experts' efforts in improving its working methods. She wondered whether the Chairperson of the Committee of Experts could give further clarification on the procedures being considered within the Committee of Experts to enhance its supervisory work. Referring to the cooperation between the Committee of Experts and the other organizations of the United Nations system in the context of supervising the application of standards, she requested clarification on the manner in which information received from these organizations was being used and its impact on ILO standards-related activities. She once again called for a correction to be made to the term "representation" in the Arabic version of article 24 of the ILO Constitution and asked for the exact definition of the words "consensus" and "unanimity". She recalled that Lebanon lately had ratified the Working Environment (Air Pollution, Noise and Vibration) Convention, 1977 (No. 148), the Labour Administration Convention, 1978 (No. 150), and the Prevention of Major Industrial Accidents Convention, 1993 (No. 174), and that the Human Resources Development Recommendation, 2004 (No. 195), was going to be submitted to Parliament and that all obligations under articles 19 and 22 of the ILO Constitution had been complied with. Finally, the speaker, along with the Government member of Bahrain, speaking on behalf of the Government members of the Gulf Cooperation Council, emphasized the need for Arab Experts on standards-related issues in the field and at headquarters and for translation of the Committee of Experts' reports and report forms into Arabic.

Discussion on highlights and major trends in certain areas

57. The Worker members regretted that the 2005 report of the Committee of Experts did not contain any highlights or major trends in the application of international labour standards or more in-depth reviews of certain Conventions. It was hoped that the Committee of Experts would once more begin to carry out those specific reviews which were invaluable in so far as they focused attention on less visible Conventions. The effort put into preparing the general observation on the trafficking of children for labour exploitation in West Africa was much appreciated in this regard.

58. Concerning the general observation made by the Committee of Experts, it was important for governments to include in their next report information on: (1) the legislative measures adopted or envisaged to prohibit trafficking of children under 18 years of age for the purposes of economic and sexual exploitation by: (a) making any violation of this prohibition a criminal offence; and (b) imposing penal and other sanctions of an effectively dissuasive nature; (2) the measures adopted or envisaged to: (a) prevent such trafficking; and (b) formulate and implement programmes of action targeting multiple levels of society; (3) training, collaboration and awareness-raising for public officials on action to combat the trafficking of children; (4) statistics on the number of violations, investigations, prosecutions and convictions relating to the trafficking of children and the text of any court decisions in such cases; (5) the effective application of the principle of free and compulsory schooling for children, particularly for girls; and (6) the time-bound measures taken to prevent the engagement of children in trafficking, remove children from trafficking, protect the victims of trafficking and provide for their rehabilitation and social integration. The Worker members also emphasized the importance of international

cooperation in combating the transnational dimension of child labour. In this regard, they once again thanked the Committee of Experts for its general observation, which raised the issue of the international dimension of child labour and emphasized that in future this matter could be addressed in general observations on the application of other Conventions.

59. As a general matter, the Employer members believed that special surveys by the Committee of Experts should be the exception and not the rule. The General Survey method was the preferred approach. In the case of the special survey on the worst forms of child labour, the Employer members believed that this brief survey was appropriate in this case in that it provided a means for the Experts to provide information to governments on the content of their reports on the application of Convention No. 182 which was a very recent Convention.

Fulfilment of standards-related obligations

60. The Employer members noted that an astoundingly low number of reports were received on time and that a high number of first reports were received late. These failures hindered the work of this Committee and cast doubts about the level of commitment of a concerned government to meet its obligation to implement ratified Conventions in law and practice. They also expressed the concern that this Committee might be examining cases where the information was out of date.

61. On the subject of the submission of ILO Conventions and Recommendations to the competent authorities, the Employer members indicated that the purpose of this procedure was to ensure that newly adopted standards were rapidly brought to the attention of the authorities in member States, without prejudging whether or not a particular Convention should be ratified, which remained a matter of choice for the country concerned.

62. The Worker members expressed their concern over a series of shortcomings that continued to undermine the supervisory mechanism. One of the shortcomings concerned the obligation to submit instruments adopted by the Conference to the competent authorities – an obligation which formed the preliminary stage of the ratification and implementation of Conventions. In that connection, it was hoped that the memorandum concerning submission to the competent authorities, which had recently been revised by the Governing Body and which explained more clearly the obligations of the member States, would be widely circulated. The Office should launch a campaign in that respect, and personalized letters should be sent to the member States that had failed to comply with that obligation. It was regrettable that 14 member States had not submitted to the competent authorities the instruments adopted over the previous seven years.

63. The Worker members also regretted the fact that less than two-thirds of the reports requested from governments had been received. The Office should develop a more personalized approach for those countries failing to send reports and provide the Committee with more information on their situation. Furthermore, a growing number of governments did not respond to the comments made by the Committee of Experts: no response had been given to 444 comments concerning 49 countries, as opposed to 325 concerning 37 countries in the previous year. Further concern was expressed over the very high number of reports received late – one that was even more serious where first reports were involved. The 23 States that had not submitted first reports for several years should make a particular effort in that regard. Such delays adversely affected the progress of the work of the Committee of Experts and the present Committee and led to an unfortunate time-lag in the supervision of the application of standards. At the same time, a considerable increase in the number of observations communicated by the employers' and workers' organizations (533, as compared to 297 received last year) could be noted. This unprecedented high number proved the workers' confidence in the ILO in general and in

its standards in particular. The observations made by the social partners should be more widely used, since they constituted a necessary and useful supplement to the more legal conclusions reached by the Experts.

64. The Government member of Portugal indicated that the submission of texts to the competent authorities was of great importance, but raised difficulties due to the need for translation. The ILO Office in Geneva and the multidisciplinary teams should disseminate the new memorandum on submission. She took the opportunity to report that her Government had disseminated the instruments adopted between the 88th and 91st Sessions of the Conference and had examined them in consultation with the social partners. The information on unratified Conventions had in the past constituted an institutional problem, which was now resolved. She agreed with the statement by the Employer members that the cases of serious failure by member States to respect their reporting or other standards-related obligations were extremely important. In this respect, collaboration with other international organizations would facilitate supervision of the application of standards. As failure to submit reports on time interfered with the work of the Committee of Experts, it would be advisable to provide governments with assistance.

65. The Government member of Italy noted that this year his Government had sent all its reports and replied to all the comments within the required time period. He emphasized the need to send reports on time and to request assistance from the Office, where necessary. Furthermore, his Government had complied within the time limits with its obligation to submit to the competent authorities the instruments adopted at the 90th and 91st Sessions of the Conference.

66. The Government member of India stated that his Government had sent all the reports due for 2004 to the ILO and that in Part II of its report, the Committee of Experts had made some observations on the application of Conventions ratified by his country. It had also raised issues in requests addressed directly to the Government on the Abolition of Forced Labour Convention, 1957 (No. 105), the Indigenous and Tribal Populations Convention, 1957 (No. 107), and the Labour Statistics Convention, 1985 (No. 160). The information requested was being sought from the sources concerned and his Government was hoping to send a response to the ILO within the set deadlines. In addition, he wished to make some general observations regarding the necessity of evolving a holistic overview of all the reporting procedures and formats, whether under articles 19 and 22 of the Constitution or under the 1998 Declaration on Fundamental Principles and Rights at Work and its Follow-up. There was a need for simplification and avoidance of overlapping and repetition. The reporting procedures were in general burdensome and the questions in the report forms were not always user-friendly. In certain cases, data collection and recording under federal policy did not always conform to the requirements of ILO procedures.

67. The Worker member of France highlighted that the issue of allocating adequate resources to labour administrations was also related to the capacity of member States to fulfil their obligations, in particular with respect to reporting within the established deadlines. The decrease in the number of late reports was as essential to the supervisory system as the obligation to communicate reports to workers' and employers' organizations in accordance with article 23 of the ILO Constitution. The pressure exerted upon those member States, which were the most reticent in complying with standards, would be all the more effective, the greater the number that fulfilled their reporting obligations.

The reply of the Chairperson of the Committee of Experts

68. The Chairperson of the Committee of Experts expressed gratitude for the appreciation of the work of the Committee of Experts, which was making efforts to improve its methods of

work. She noted the suggestions made for further improvements and indicated that they would all be discussed, especially with regard to giving greater emphasis to cases of progress and providing further indications of the basis upon which progress was deemed to have been made. Concerning the question of the content of the observations and the call for them to be more consistent in their presentation, especially in relation to the level of detail provided, she said that it was necessary for the Committee of Experts to perform a balancing act to ensure that the comments were sufficiently detailed without being too burdensome. It was also necessary to take into consideration the fact that the report was already long. Concerning the question of the current membership of the Committee, due to the retirement of some of its members, she referred this issue to the representative of the Secretary-General. Finally, she said that her presence during the general discussion of the Conference Committee would undoubtedly enrich the discussions of the Committee of Experts.

The reply of the representative of the Secretary-General

69. The representative of the Secretary-General expressed her sincere thanks and gratitude to the members of the Committee for the very positive and constructive dialogue that had taken place. With reference to the suggestion concerning the term "automatic cases" in document D.4, the speaker indicated that the Office would propose for consideration to refer instead to "cases of serious failure by member States to respect their reporting and other standards-related obligations". In response to the questions by the Employer and Worker members on how to link the general factors set out in document D.4 with each particular situation of the countries concerned, she explained that the secretariat would identify the means to review more closely the reasons for such serious failures and would report back to the Committee at its session next year. As regards suggestions that the Office should adopt a more "personalized" approach to the treatment of the serious failures to fulfil reporting and other obligations, the speaker pointed out that the document D.4 already provided the beginning of the analysis which would enable the Office to focus technical assistance to countries where needs were clearly identifiable. The countries currently appearing on the list would be requested to identify such specific difficulties.

70. She further stated that the Office would take due note of the Employer members' suggestion that the Reader's note in the Committee of Experts' report should contain more information (in particular historical elements) and that the last sentence of the second paragraph should be revised. Regarding the hope expressed by the Worker members that the section on highlights and major trends that appeared in the 2004 General Report would be resumed next year, she indicated that the Committee of Experts had been duly informed of the discussions that had taken place last year in the Conference Committee. She had decided to provide for more time to reflect on these sections, and in particular on their contents and objectives. As regards the distinction between "consensus" and "unanimity", she explained that the Committee of Experts took its decisions by consensus, which meant that every member either agreed with the proposal or did not wish his or her disagreement to block the adoption of the proposal, in contrast to unanimity, which signified that every member agreed with a proposal. In response to the remark by the Employer members on paragraph 37, the speaker indicated that the Office, in collaboration with the Turin Centre, was proactively pursuing the training of judges to enable them to better take into account international labour standards, the supervisory system and other procedures. Regarding the Employer members' comments concerning collaboration with other international organizations addressed in the report, she recalled that the examination by the Committee of Experts of the European Code on Social Security was linked closely to the Social Security (Minimum Standards) Convention, 1952 (No. 102), and compliance with this Convention also implied compliance with the Code. The speaker also stressed the need for policy coherence within the UN system, taking into account, where appropriate, relevant international instruments.

71. With reference to the questions concerning the insufficient number of Experts, the speaker emphasized that the identification of candidates for the six current vacancies in the Committee of Experts would be one of the top priorities after the Conference, so that at its next session all of the vacancies would be filled. As for an increase in the number of Experts, a decision would have to be made by the Governing Body in this respect. Besides, a request was being prepared to the Officers of the Governing Body to add three extra days to the next session of the Committee of Experts.

72. In response to the Worker members' concerns about the integrated approach, the speaker observed that there were many aspects of the integrated approach which reinforced strong standards activities in the classical sense: for example, the need to ensure that each new standard harmoniously integrated into the existing corpus of standards as well as into the current economic and social context. With regard to a concern about "promotional instruments rather than conventional ones", she could only consider the standards activity in terms of *conventional* instruments, establishing clear rights and obligations (or recommending the establishment of such rights in the case of a Recommendation). Whatever the activity concerned, whether it was the adoption of a new standard or a promotional activity outside the area of standards, the effect must always be to contribute to a strong standards activity in the classical sense. In response to the comments concerning the Arabic translation of the ILO Constitution and in particular article 24, she indicated that these remarks would be transmitted to the competent services. Regarding the Employer members' proposal that the information document on ratifications and standards-related activities provide more detail on technical assistance, she responded that this proposal would be duly taken into account and stressed that an improved link between standards objectives and technical cooperation was a clear component of the Office's vision and strategy. Responding to the remarks by the Worker members, she emphasized that while the "rights" case for international labour standards was fundamental and could not be called into question, explaining the economic advantages of standards was a necessity today. Such arguments needed to be developed and made widely available. In terms of visibility, new tools needed to be developed to make standards accessible to the broadest audience possible, including the general public.

C. Reports requested under article 19 of the Constitution

Hours of Work (Industry) Convention, 1919 (No. 1), and Hours of Work (Commerce and Offices) Convention, 1930 (No. 30)

73. The Committee devoted part of its general discussion to the examination of the General Survey carried out by the Committee of Experts on the application of the Hours of Work (Industry) Convention, 1919 (No. 1), and the Hours of Work (Commerce and Offices) Convention, 1930 (No, 30). In accordance with the usual practice, this survey took into account information communicated by governments under article 19 of the Constitution, as well as the information communicated by member States which have ratified the instruments in their reports submitted under articles 22 and 35 of the Constitution and the comments received from employers' and workers' organizations to which the government reports were communicated in accordance with article 23, paragraph 2, of the ILO Constitution.

Opening remarks

74. The Employer members stated that the General Survey provided for a good basis of analysis and discussion on some aspects of working time, but by no means covered the entirety of issues relevant to this very complex matter. Further discussions on other important aspects of working time, such as holidays with pay, the organization of working time, night work, and weekly rest was required before a final diagnosis could be made by the Conference.

75. This observation raised the very important question as to how to deal with such a matter, and whether ILO guidance could be provided in this field. Already in 1967, the Committee of Experts had noted that several provisions of Conventions Nos. 1 and 30 were too restrictive in scope. It had also noticed an evolution towards more flexible approaches to methods of regulating working time at national level. As rightly indicated by the Committee of Experts in this year's survey, intensification of competition resulting from globalization, new information and communication technologies, new patterns of consumer demand for goods and services in the "24-hour economy", had a large impact on production methods and work organization. From the perspective of the enterprise, the drive to enhance use of capital, optimize labour costs, manage human resources in innovative ways, and respond to customer demands had resulted in new methods of flexible production and organization of working time. The Committee of Experts also noted that the profound demographic changes occurring in the modern world of work as reflected in the increasing entry of women into the paid labour market, the shift to dual-earner households, and the growing concern over the quality of working life had also shaped innovative arrangements concerning the duration and timing of work, which varied according to each worker's, and in some instances employer's, preferences and needs.

76. The Employer members expressed support for the approach taken by the OECD's Policy Brief *Clocking in and clocking out: Recent trends in working hours* to the effect that workers and employers should have considerable discretion to negotiate working time arrangements in a decentralized manner, although general rules were needed to structure this process to enforce certain minimum standards, for example concerning maximum hours of work related to health and safety aspects. They also drew attention to the World Bank's *World Development Report 2005*, according to which improvements in working conditions – including limitations to working time – in developed countries evolved gradually, hand in hand with more general economic progress and thus, attempting to apply the same or higher standards to countries at earlier stages of economic development and with weaker enforcement capacity often led to poor or even perverse results.

77. The Worker members expressed satisfaction for the fact that the General Survey of the Committee of Experts was an exhaustive, balanced and reliable report on the effects given to ILO instruments, as it was every year. The issue of working hours and the need for greater flexibility in working time was common to the entire industrialized and non-industrialized world. Wages and salaries, which were unavoidably linked to working hours, were of vital importance to the workers. At the European level, working hours were under the spotlight in the rediscussion of the Directive concerning certain aspects of the organization of working time.

78. The issue of working hours touched on two fundamental aspects of the human being: individual development through quality work which protects safety and health, but also guarantees the right to a social and civic life and to a balanced family life. It was therefore not an accident that the oldest ILO Convention concerned working hours. Limits on working hours and a working day of eight hours have always been one of the main claims of the worker movement since the nineteenth century. At its First Session in 1919, the ILC clearly declared itself in favour of retaining these two values by setting a double limit on

working time: eight hours a day and 48 hours a week. Eight hours a day for the sake of the worker's safety and health, 48 hours a week in order to lead a normal life. In 1930, Convention No. 30 extended these principles to the commercial and office sector.

79. The General Survey highlighted the fact that the long-term trend towards a reduction in weekly working hours had stopped in the last ten years. Moreover, this reduction in weekly working hours was accompanied by moves towards flexibility, which opened the door to even greater disparities. The concept of the working week was losing ground to the concept of an average calculated over a longer period, which led one to inquire whether the term working hours remained appropriate in absolute terms and if the trend to a reduction in this time was effective. In the industrialized countries, governments and employers were invoking the need for growth and competitiveness and becoming hostile to restrictions on working hours, at the same time contesting the need for social dialogue as a means of negotiation. Changes in family lifestyle and greater presence of women at the workplace, as well as decentralization of collective bargaining and growing individual relations between employers and workers were all having an impact on the notion of working hours. Unfortunately, the latter were now being considered only as an economic variable and the principles laid down in 1919 were being questioned.

80. The Worker members could not accept that these values be put into question. A worker without the legal protection of a limit of working hours was left defenceless before the laws of the market. International labour standards rightly sought to prevent the worker being considered as merchandise. The limit on working hours was a fundamental part of legal protection of workers and there was no question of making it a flexibility tool for economic performance. The Worker members fully agreed with the Committee of Experts that the minimal standards on working hours were a determining factor in the current environment. Technological, scientific, or cultural development would not change the basic reality that the worker's only wealth was his or her work. Consequently, labour law had to be a corrective right, which made a fundamental balance between the worker and the employer or rather, in current terms, between the worker and the person who held the wealth.

Hours of work: A multifaceted issue

81. A common thread in the interventions of all those who participated in the discussion was the cross-cutting and complex nature of working time issues. The Employer members stated that it was clear for them that the multifaceted topic of working time raised questions as to its suitability for international regulations. Although one could agree that there was a need for clear rules allowing for human working conditions with regard to protection against undue fatigue, reasonable leisure and opportunities for a personal life, it was also evident that work today was by nature very diverse and that therefore a "one size fits all" approach to working hours was simply not practical.

82. The Employer member of Denmark drew attention to some particular problems concerning local public employers in Denmark and most of Europe. These employers constituted major public service providers in services operating 24 hours a day, seven days a week. The main problem in relation to the General Survey was the unfortunate definition of the term "working hours" in Article 2 of Convention No. 30, which focused on the time during which the persons employed were at the disposal of the employer. This was a very unfortunate formulation because it totally ignored on-call duties and standby duties. Although the Committee of Experts had acknowledged this issue in pages 18-21 and 85-86 of the General Survey, it did not recognize the problems this created in modern public service where various kinds of on-call duties applied, for instance, for firefighters, nurses, doctors, etc. Stressing the need for a deeper understanding of the complexity of working

time and its consequences for public services, he regretted that issues, which were specific to different sectors, such as health care, were practically not addressed in the survey.

83. The Worker members took the view that in most countries, what was most important was not the methods by which working hours were regulated but the strictness with which they were applied in the different sectors. Law should not be confused with its effective application. For regulations on working time to become a reality, a labour inspectorate which was independent, in conformity with Convention No. 81, was required. More importantly, it was the application of the law or collective agreements to be guaranteed by the government and the judiciary, assisted by a well-equipped labour inspectorate and with the knowledge that workers would have access to the competent courts.

84. The Worker member of Bangladesh noted that in his country, in the formal sector the eight-hour day and 48-hour week were generally respected in accordance with national legislation, which allowed an additional 12 hours per week of overtime. In the informal sector, however, there was no compliance with the legal provisions. Moreover, the legislation on working time contained a provision giving the Government the possibility to derogate its provisions in whole or in part for a period of six months, which was extendable, and the Government also had the authority to completely waive limits on the hours of work for the same period. Account should be also taken of the insufficient coverage of the legislation concerning hours of work and of its weak enforcement, which, together with the very low wage level, had led to the situation where the workers were being forced to work up to 18 hours a day throughout the year, thus sacrificing personal leisure, family and social life and ignoring health and safety concerns, in order to earn some extra money to survive. For instance, in the garment sector, under the pressure of international competition, employers of some 4,000 factories employing millions of workers (90 per cent of which are women) started engaging workers for up to 16 hours per day in some cases, while workers were unable to protest for fear of losing their jobs.

85. The Worker member of Pakistan recalled that the regulation of working time had been a long struggle in the nineteenth and twentieth centuries. In the twenty-first century, new technologies led to new forms of working time, and with them, long hours of work, which were linked to occupational diseases and stress. The pressure of globalization had an effect on all workers, and especially those in EPZs, rural workers, workers in the informal economy and women. In this connection, the Worker member of the United Kingdom raised the issue of delivery lead times imposed on producers in developing countries by multinational retailers and brands, especially in the textile, garment and leather industry, and in the agricultural sector. He considered that there was a direct link between unreasonable lead times and excessive – and involuntary – overtime and emphasized that it was in these situations that women garment workers ended up working 72 hours without proper breaks – in some reported cases dying of exhaustion – or that workers worked through the night instead of spending time with their families, or that workers in EPZs clocked more than 100 hours in a single week. Multinational enterprises had to change these practices through strong national legislation, proper enforcement, strong international conventions that were fully implemented, and strong collective agreements on working time negotiated by independent trade unions.

86. The Worker member of Paraguay indicated that, as regards hours of work, there was much concern in Latin America and the Caribbean about the constant violation of workers' rights. At the present time, it was important to tackle so-called "rubbish" contracts, named as such due to the abuse that they involved. Such contracts did not take into account the eight-hour working day, nor social security, holidays or bonuses, and the wages were pitiful. The approach of some sectors of the employers and the governments in the region was that investment required flexibility which fell below the rights enshrined in labour laws, in the constitutions themselves and in ILO Conventions. The speaker expressed his

opposition to investments made in the name of modernization, whether in assembly plants or in public transport companies. Workers were obliged, in many cases, to work a 12- or 14-hour day as drivers and fare collectors, which gave rise to real abuse and violation of human rights.

87. The Worker member of South Africa pointed out that since the 1984 General Survey on working time, trends toward flexible working time had led to an increase in part-time employment, with the promise that more employment would be created. This promise had never materialized. Globalization, intensification of competition, increased diversification of customer demands and the feminization of the workforce had led to demands for increasing diversification of working time arrangements. The Worker member of Malawi noted that the actual level of working hours in each country was often pushed during peak seasons, as for example in the agricultural sector, where workers were sometimes exploited. These workers often worked 14-hour days without overtime compensation. The same situation could be found in the hotel industry. Multinational corporations had also taken advantage of such conditions. Given the importance of this issue, he wondered why efforts to address these problems were lacking. In this regard, he commended the efforts by the United Kingdom and South Africa to deal with the issue of working time in the context of developments in the world of work.

88. The Government member of Spain emphasized that working time was merely a productive resource while limitations on hours of work was a labour right which should already be considered an acquis. What should be discussed were maximum hours of work, not in terms of a maximum length of a 35-, 40-, 44- or 48-hour week, but solely as an upper limit. In the limit resided the right, which did not preclude that, as a second step, the quantity of such a limit could be fixed through collective bargaining or in parliament, depending on the circumstances. The determination of such a limit, which should be a humane limit, had nothing to do with the flexibility or rigidity of working conditions. Such a limit, as a condition of ensuring a quality of life for workers, their health and safety, constituted and should constitute a right, which was as necessary as it was undeniable. Another very different concept was the organization of work, as was the distribution of hours of work in the day, week or year. There it was appropriate to discuss "flexibility", which was of interest not only to the enterprise but also to the worker. The Government member of Lebanon commended the General Survey for its comprehensiveness and in-depth analysis of Conventions Nos. 1 and 30. She recalled that both Conventions had been ratified by Lebanon. The Lebanese Labour Code, which dated back to 1946, had provided for 48-hours maximum working week with no distinctions between the hours of work in industry and in offices. However, the actual hours of work in the public sector, the banking sector and in many enterprises in the public sector were less than 8 hours per day and 48 hours per week. Further exceptions for certain types of positions and jobs were also possible.

89. The Government member of Mexico stated that the integrated approach of the General Survey made it possible to grasp the complexity involved in regulating hours of work in the presence of new challenges stemming from the global economy, something which forced us to bear in mind that, as stated in paragraph 317 of the General Survey, "to reflect the 'human rights' perspective in the international regulation of hours of work, continues to be valid today". The speaker further indicated a number of inexact references to the legislation of her country and provided the correct information. Similarly, the Government member of Tunisia indicated that certain figures regarding working hours in his country were inaccurate and asked for the errors to be rectified.

Working time in modern labour market conditions: Search for balance between flexibility and workers' protection

90. Most of the members of the Committee who took part in the discussion addressed the problems related to working time regulation from a double perspective: on the one hand, the quest for flexibility, especially in a rapidly changing business environment, and on the other, the need for reconciliation of workers' welfare concerns with their work obligations.

91. The Employer member of the United Kingdom pointed out that flexible working time was essential for competitiveness, as it allowed employers to manage their workers and resources efficiently. Flexibility also allowed for job creation and quick adaptation to changing market conditions and fluctuating demand. Referring to the situation in the United Kingdom, he stressed that many flexible work patterns used in his country suited both employers and workers. United Kingdom employers had an excellent record in enabling workers to reconcile work and family life, which was demonstrated by the fact that the United Kingdom had the third highest employment rate for women across the European Union. The United Kingdom employers' experience with the EU's proposed changes to working time regulations highlighted the need for a very cautious approach to any idea of a new international instrument. It was essential to debate all the issues involved, such as opt-out, rest periods, night work, or paid holiday. These issues must be debated by social partners to avoid an instrument that defeats flexible working time patterns to the detriment of employers and workers.

92. The Worker members observed that admittedly working time regulations could not remain rigid or unchangeable, but added that recent developments in differentiated systems of working hours and working time organization showed that business needs for flexibility could be met in the framework of social dialogue. Therefore all normative work on these two instruments should be ring-fenced by all the necessary guarantees that protection of occupational safety and health and social and family life required. Thus, quality of life should be a just counterpart to any concession regarding flexibility to ensure a "win-win" situation. Furthermore, any revision of Conventions Nos. 1 and 30 which featured distribution of working hours should be based on the principle of solidarity, work distribution and on preserving the workers' quality of life. Discussions should be long-term and provide constructive responses to women's situation, given that their career path was fragmented by family requirements such as maternity, child care, parental care, etc. In addition, the discussion would be pointless if the intangible principle of decent pay were not included.

93. The Worker members further recalled that "working hours" were not defined in ILO Conventions. Nevertheless, they were described as "the time during which the worker is at the disposal of the employer". Despite everything, measuring working hours raised issues such as keeping the worker at disposal, which were far from settled. The discussion on the precise definition of working hours must remain open. For example, new forms of working time organization raise issues of integrating weekly rest periods and annual holidays into the equation, as the European Directive had shown. This progressive integration could lead to a new instrument, which would open several possibilities by allowing employers to respond to increased demand for flexibility and workers to take a more individual approach in order to better match professional with family needs.

94. The Employer member of South Africa referred to the South African Basic Conditions of Employment Act of 1997, which approached the issue of hours of work through a policy of "regulated flexibility". This Act was unique in combining effective protection with acknowledging that flexibility was best achieved through collective bargaining and social dialogue. Despite the pragmatic solutions offered by the Act, it had also shortcomings.

Sunday work continued to attract high premiums and was permitted only with an exemption, which was a problem in capital-intensive operations where continuous operations were justified and where shifts in customer demand and consumer preference required reorganization of weekly working time arrangements.

95. The Employer member of Colombia stated that the regulation of working hours aimed at protecting workers and enterprises from excessively long hours of work, which endangered the health and interfered with the personal development of workers. Nevertheless, the legislation needed to be sufficiently flexible to allow hours of work to be adapted to fluctuations in demand. The stricter the legislation concerning temporary employment and penalties for dismissal of a worker, the more important the need for flexibility was. There had always been a concern for maintaining a balance between labour (working time) and other human activities (time not worked), that is, the relationship between work and family life.

96. The Government member of India emphasized that in order to provide greater opportunities for employment and skills development to the workforce, flexibility of working hours with corresponding measures for providing optimal safety and health to the workers were very important, and national laws to ensure the above objectives should prevail at the workplace. The Government member of Lebanon regarded that Conventions Nos. 1 and 30 could be considered in certain respects as being flexible Conventions owing to the range of exceptions enumerated in their provisions. However, these exceptions may cause difficulties in implementation because of the lack of clarity and their ambiguous concepts. She also noted that there were some discrepancies between the provisions of the two Conventions and questioned whether these discrepancies were still justified.

97. The Worker member of Singapore stressed that the familiar catchphrase of flexibility denoted a one-way path which did not involve any benefits for workers. The latter were expected to work at all times without fixed rest days or fixed working hours in a day and without adequate advance notice, so as to plan their lives. On top of this, further forms of flexibility were introduced, such as part-time contracts and temporary work, which offered no job security at all, and provided low pay. Flexibility was not allowed for the benefit of workers so as to balance work and family, do community service or simply go back to school. This situation imposed a responsibility on governments to inject some sanity in working hours, to act as a fair referee, to pass laws and regulations and to enforce them, in order to protect people from exploitation and abuse. If governments adopted a laissez-faire attitude, and allowed the market to regulate itself, in a framework of poor economic conditions and high unemployment, workers would suffer. Echoing the same view, the Worker member of Kenya noted that workers had fallen into the trap of accepting flexibility through intimidation by employers. Flexibility should not be the subject of a Convention but rather regulated by domestic law. He stressed that reduced hours of work led to greater worker welfare and, by extension, greater productivity and social and economic development. Increased productivity, however, was not synonymous with more hours of work. The "choice" offered by some employers with regard to flexibility was not genuine as the bargaining position of employers and workers was not equal.

98. The Worker member of Brazil, referring to the excessively long working days in some sectors and the high number of accidents at the workplace related to long hours of work, emphasized that when talking about the health and lives of workers, one was not talking about goods, but rights. It was therefore dangerous to take only competitiveness into account, and economic considerations should not prevail over social ones. Any change must only be made with a view to improving quality of life and working conditions, subsequent to which the analysis and studies necessary in each country could be carried out. The Worker member of Cuba expressed the view that the flexibility of working time

was acceptable if guarantees were also included on incomes, health, the working day, personal time, holidays and weekly rest.

99. The Worker member of France indicated that a standard which would provide for flexible hours of work should be rejected, as it would weaken the central role of the ILO in the area of globalization. Similarly, the Worker member of India stated that fixed working time was preferable over flexible working hours in order to ensure that workers were not treated as a commodity. He opposed the flexibility of working hours introduced for the purpose of increasing the number of daily working hours in order to increase competitiveness and added value. He drew attention to the role of technological revolution and underlined the paradox that although new technologies allowing for increased production in less time could have led to reduced working hours and better working conditions and quality of life, workers instead were being retrenched.

100. The Worker member of Greece noted that in some parts of the world, work was synonymous with slavery. Since the end of the Second World War, productivity had increased exponentially, but poverty had increased at the same rate. New technologies had offered the hope of a better life for workers who would have more leisure time. But unemployment, precarious work, poverty and working time were increasing while a minority shared the wealth. In industrialized countries, especially in Europe, the struggle of the last half-century by the working movement had brought down working time to 40 hours a week and had gained paid holidays. But today, what the decision-makers were attempting to do on a worldwide scale was to reduce working conditions. He emphasized that the revision of a Convention to "legalize" socially regressive action could not be accepted and that the low number of ratifications for Convention No. 30 was not a sufficient argument for revision of the Convention.

Working time regulation and collective bargaining

101. A recurrent theme in the Committee's discussion was the crucial role of social dialogue and collective bargaining in matters of organization of working time. The Worker members recalled that in the light of a trend resulting from technological, economic and industrial development, some enterprises would like to give priority to decentralized social dialogue, which could go as far as replacing dialogue between partners by individual negotiations directly with workers subject to precarious work and the threat of unemployment. Consequently, any revision of Conventions Nos. 1 and 30 must ensure respect for the principle of collective bargaining. It was in this sense that in the Worker members' view, a legal system that allowed opting-out as in the United Kingdom was socially indefensible. All exceptions should be agreed to in social dialogue.

102. The Employer members reiterated that workers and employers should have considerable discretion to negotiate working time arrangements in a decentralized manner. They also acknowledged that flexibility was best achieved through collective bargaining and social dialogue.

103. The Government member of Greece underlined that encouraging social dialogue should be the main objective for all countries so that, through a collective bargaining procedure, an effective framework of working time organization would be achieved, which would meet workers' needs and facilitate the operation of undertakings. The ILO ought to play a leading role in this process in the light of recent international developments in the labour market, so that the "general standard" set out in the Conventions could be more widely accepted and characterized by legitimacy and effectiveness.

104. The Worker member of Australia underlined the importance of the ability of workers to influence the length and arrangement of their working time. The role of workers in

determining their working time arrangements underscored the importance of collective bargaining and strong trade unions. The Worker member of Singapore indicated that in order to ensure flexibility, but also fairness and long-term sustainability, strong trade unions, with freedom to negotiate and represent workers' interests effectively, were essential. In this sense, she found the suggestion made by the OECD policy brief cited in the General Survey to be particularly worrisome. According to the brief, workers and employers should have considerable discretion to negotiate working time arrangements in a decentralized manner. If by this the OECD was suggesting individual contracts, the impact would be serious as workers did not have the power to negotiate fair contracts on their own. The Worker member of France stated that decentralized collective bargaining at the enterprise level, often preferred to collective bargaining at the national sectoral level, did not prevent workers being pressured to accept to work more in order to ensure that the production was not re-located or subcontracted. This "blackmail" was more and more frequent, affected several sectors and did not concern industrialized countries only, as demonstrated by recent developments in the textile sector.

105. The Worker member of Panama stated that regulation in the domain of working time had, as its objective, the weakening of the regulatory function of the State within the framework of neoliberal ideology. It was unacceptable to allow that fundamental social issues be regulated by market laws and be flexible. The speaker also wondered which collective agreement could be applied in countries in which workers were still being killed for organizing unions and how a collective agreement could be negotiated if the workers were dismissed because of their desire to establish organizations. Without trade unions, collective bargaining did not exist. The Worker member of South Africa noted that basic principles on working time needed to be set forth in national legislation, so as to ensure coverage for domestic and agricultural workers. National legislation in this regard should be the outcome of a tripartite consultative process. Exceptions to working time standards should only be possible by agreement between employers and trade unions, and exceptions should be subject to a time limit.

Present-day relevance of Conventions Nos. 1 and 30

106. Some speakers referred in their comments to the continued relevance of the Conventions which were the subject of the General Survey. The Worker members fully agreed with the conclusions of the Committee of Experts, which stated that, even if Conventions Nos. 1 and 30 did not entirely reflect recent developments in work planning, they remained relevant. They observed that 85 years after the adoption of Convention No. 1, while globalization of the economy appeared to give the impression that the model of working relations was totally unsuitable for the needs of economic growth, it was striking that Convention No. 1 was still modern, and although it was designed to protect workers' health, it had flexibility built in, which was not intended at the outset.

107. The Employer members referred to their previous comments in previous paragraphs that several provisions of Conventions Nos. 1 and 30 were too restrictive to work well under modern realities.

108. The Worker member of Greece noted from other Worker member statements that the working day in developing countries was 12 hours, while in Europe the working week was around 40 hours on average. Conventions Nos. 1 and 30 were therefore still relevant. A Worker member of the United Kingdom stressed that the need to maintain a maximum 48-hour week was as compelling today as it was when Convention No. 1 was adopted. The speaker emphasized that long hours were a major health and safety issue. In the United Kingdom, hundreds of drivers at work died each year in road accidents when they lost concentration or fell asleep. Excessive hours caused heart disease, stress, fatigue and loss of concentration. The European Court of Justice had rejected the argument advanced by

the Government of the United Kingdom that hours of work was not a health and safety issue, making it clear that a maximum 48-hour week must be applied to all workers. It was important to remember what had been learnt in the first part of the twentieth century: people who work shorter hours are likely to be more productive, more efficient, safer and healthier. Only on that basis, a discussion on hours of work was likely to be productive.

109. The Worker member of Singapore affirmed that the core principles enunciated in Conventions Nos. 1 and 30 were still valid and relevant in ensuring sane and humane working hours for workers. Hence, one should not look immediately into revising the two Conventions. Further general discussions might be useful in order to examine some of the issues raised in the General Survey and in the debate without eroding the protection given to workers. The Government member of Lebanon stated that Conventions Nos. 1 and 30 were still relevant and flexible as they allowed certain exceptions. However, in her opinion, the Conventions read together could raise several problems in practice, due, for instance, to several differences which today could be difficult to understand and justify.

110. Some other speakers endorsed the Committee of Experts' conclusions that Conventions Nos. 1 and 30 no longer reflected modern realities and warranted revision. The Government member of Belgium noted that the needs of enterprises were not the same as in 1919 when Convention No. 1 was adopted. It was clear to the Government of Belgium that the Convention required revision and that a new instrument would be welcome which would allow enterprises, in return for the implementation of a strict framework and a guarantee of worker protection, to introduce the greater flexibility required by the current economy. The Government member of Canada indicated that, in the opinion of the Government, Conventions Nos. 1 and 30 were no longer relevant and that it was in favour of a more flexible approach on the matter. Nevertheless, the decision to formulate a new instrument should only be taken when more information was available on its scope and in the presence of a tripartite consensus.

111. The Government member of Portugal, while noting that Conventions Nos. 1 and 30 were still relevant in their objectives, pointed out that they did not match present day realities and had lost their universal applicability. The reason for the limited number of ratifications lay in the necessity of tackling the question of hours of work in a more flexible manner, with new forms of work organization. Therefore, the revision of these Conventions could lead to universal ratification and application. She concluded by emphasizing that regulating working time created a way to achieve decent work in the world.

112. The Worker member of Costa Rica stated that there was no need to revise Conventions Nos. 1 and 30 to achieve better productivity and efficiency. Daily working time of eight hours for six working days per week was not the result of a simple mathematical formula, but based on a guarantee of a dignified working life. It would also be preferable to revise the distribution of wealth. The Worker member of Senegal pointed out that Conventions Nos. 1 and 30 had been adopted in order to rein in the exploitative practices of employers. In spite of the inclusion of their provisions into national laws, these instruments had almost been rendered inadequate in response to current needs created by the rapid evolution of working time. Furthermore, the speaker considered that a better redefinition of the concept of working time could reconcile all the actors concerned and stressed the need for a clear method of computation of overtime work, especially with respect to certain categories of workers such as domestic workers, as a core element guaranteeing the respect of a maximum duration of hours of work.

Prospects for future ILO action

113. Many members of the Committee welcomed the idea of undertaking the revision of Conventions Nos. 1 and 30 and possibly drafting a single instrument on both working and

non-working time issues. Others expressed strong reservations or suggested cautiousness in planning any new standard-setting activities in this field.

114. The Employer members noted that the Committee of Experts was very clear as to the limits of its mandate and had stated that it could not dictate the way forward. However, the Committee of Experts did express its views on the matter. The ILO should consider innovative ways to provide guidance on the matter to member States – other than a normative approach. There was a need for a more flexible approach that took account of more modern forms of working time arrangements, such as part-time work, compressed workweeks, staggered hours, variable daily shift lengths, annualized working hours, flexitime and on-call work. Although the Committee of Experts did not go as far as to suggest the form the new instrument should take, they did make some practical suggestions as to its content. The Employer members believed that it was premature at that stage to decide whether the next step should be one which would take the ILO through a normative approach that would lead to the revision of the existing instruments. As highlighted by the General Survey, the ILO had already gone through that road and, through the years, the Committee had witnessed the shortcomings of the ILO Conventions on working time, particularly concerning their capacity to attract universal ratification.

115. The Worker members were open to an approach that proposed a single instrument which would cover the issue of working time in all its aspects, by reflecting on a much broader concept of working hours, which would include work, rest, holidays and leave, as well as career prospects. The directions sketched out by the Committee of Experts were in line with the Worker members' expectations, which could be summed up as: linking flexibility and safety; focusing the debate on quality; and basing flexibility on collective bargaining and intersectoral, sectoral and enterprise levels totally excluding any idea of exclusion clauses negotiated directly with workers. Effectively, such an important issue could only be efficiently regulated by the law. There was no place for soft law. However, the Worker members felt that it was too soon to approve of a revision process, as they sought guarantees to ensure that their concerns could be taken into account by governments and employers.

116. The Government member of Kenya supported the creation of a single instrument that would not only focus on flexibility but also on the length of working time, and which would address weekly rest, annual leave, and the various forms of the employment relationship affecting working time arrangements. The Government member of Austria underlined the importance of having a single instrument covering working time, as well as weekly rest and annual leave. In her view, such a new instrument had to be a binding Convention.

117. The Government member of India welcomed the proposed comprehensive review of the existing system of international regulation of working time which was in line with his country's consistent stand to give priority to revision and consolidation of already existing standards rather than setting new standards every year. While he supported the proposal to undertake a comprehensive review of standards relating to hours of work, he also considered that the welfare of the workers, as well as the specificities of the developing countries should be taken into account. The Government member of Namibia supported the suggestion by the Committee of Experts for the revision of Conventions Nos. 1 and 30 and to also review the instruments concerning weekly rest and holidays with pay. In connection with such a revision, serious consideration should be given to the informal sector, which had been rapidly expanding in Africa, being the main sector responsible for the creation of employment opportunities.

118. The Employer member of South Africa noted that the General Survey rightly highlighted the incompatibility of Conventions Nos. 1 and 30 with modern realities. The interface

between new forms of work and the appropriate regulation of working time was complex and needed further and comprehensive empirical study before the nature and form of any international regulation could be discussed meaningfully. At this stage, it was not feasible to conceive a single comprehensive instrument that would meet the criteria for modern standard setting. A prescriptive international instrument that was blind to the complexities of this issue risked affecting negatively levels of employment.

119. The Government member of Lebanon considered that it was essential to reflect before undertaking any revision and recalled that, if the process of revision was to be undertaken, the following important factors should be taken into account: the diverse needs of various member States; the necessary protection of workers; the existence of other Conventions concerning hours of work; Conventions concerning hours of work and that any comprehensive standard should come within the context of a promotional framework. The Government member of Lebanon also recalled that Conventions Nos. 1 and 30 did not address those persons who performed work outside their normal working hours, nor did Convention No. 1 make provision for labour inspections. She considered that these two themes should be recognized in any new instrument together with the new patterns of work. The Worker member of Bangladesh expressed serious concern about the nature, scope and definition of flexibility of the hours of work, which, under the pressure of international competition, could give way to new exploitation. The issue required thorough examination before any steps were taken towards the revision of the existing Conventions.

120. The Worker member of Cuba stated that, if a new instrument was adopted, it would not only have to account for the poor but ensure that they could aspire greater protection for health, safety and conditions of work, bearing in mind differences between developed and developing countries. The Worker member of Greece noted that the low number of ratifications for Convention No. 30 was not a sufficient argument for revision of the Convention. The revision of a Convention to "legalize" socially regressive action could not be accepted. As to regulating the problem of working hours through negotiated agreements, this assumed that workers and employers enjoyed the same possibilities of organization and action, which was not the case.

121. The Worker member of Tunisia stated that it was appropriate to consider revising the two Conventions to take into account modern technological developments, provided that such measures also dealt with the health and safety of workers, as well as training and the development of skills. Nonetheless, he pointed to the increasing use of subcontracting in employment, which was tantamount to trafficking of labour and which undermined labour rights. The use of subcontracting should be treated with the same seriousness as forced labour and child labour. Until this problem was dealt with, there could be no discussion of the revision of Conventions Nos. 1 and 30. The ratifications of Conventions Nos. 135 and 151 should also be promoted to bolster trade union protection.

122. The Worker member of Panama pointed out that what was sought through the revision of the Conventions was the intensification of, and regression to, new forms of slavery and exploitation involving workers all over the world. However, opposition to flexible working hours was clear. Behind all that logic lurked an ill-willed Machiavellism. Moreover, it was important to take into account the ethical aspect of the issue. The speaker wondered what sort of ethical and moral authority the Governments that had not ratified the Convention could have to request its revision. The revision of the Convention would create serious problems in individual companies. The speaker expressed his emphatic opposition to the revision of the Convention – a matter which should not have been raised in the first place.

123. The Worker member of Canada indicated that in an age where workers were expected to work more to make ends meet, it was vital that rights enshrined in Conventions Nos. 1 and 30 were not cut back. Replying to the Employer member of the United Kingdom, who believed that workers appreciated part-time work, he claimed the opposite was true. In his experience, most workers preferred a full-time job and he stated that the workers would always resist the goal of achieving prosperity through poverty. Finally, the Worker member of Kenya proposed that Conventions Nos. 1 and 30 should be included among the ILO fundamental Conventions, as a limit on working time was a human right.

Concluding observations

124. In their final remarks, the Employer members stated that they had listened attentively to the multi-faceted discussion of the General Survey. The interventions had raised important questions about the international regulation of working time. Workforces and worksites were by their nature different. As some speakers had noted, a "one size fits all" approach to working time was impractical. The Committee of Experts had recalled the many different arrangements of working time which now existed that had not been envisaged in Conventions Nos. 1 and 30. The instruments had failed to attract a significant number of ratifications. Working time standards were adequately provided for by national legislation and collective agreements, awards, and individual agreements.

125. The issue of comparative advantage that had been present in the elaboration of the two Conventions was still valid. This could be seen as some European countries struggled to overturn their 35-hour work week and were forced to cut "less pay and increased working time" deals. In view of this, the ILO should not seek to establish a new standard on working time.

126. The Employer members suggested that a proposal be put to the Governing Body to hold an expert meeting with a view to drafting a guidance document on working time, which should take into account these discussions and the General Survey. The results ought not be prejudged. There could additionally be Experts' meetings that might eventually lead to a Governing Body decision to have a general discussion on the subject of working time at a future International Labour Conference. As the long discussion on contract labour had shown, there should be a full debate on the issue before further action was taken.

127. In their closing statement, the Worker members indicated that they were not fooled by the strategy of contrasts adopted by the Employer members, which consisted in comparing two very different situations, that of South Africa (which seemed to be constructive but in which the debate on flexibility could not be conducted on an international level as, for reasons of national competitiveness it had to remain at the national level) and the somewhat exaggerated situation of the United Kingdom, and that they did not share their conclusions. They noted that the Employer members agreed to discuss certain issues in the debate on the flexibility of working time, such as health, safety, stress, and collective bargaining, but they did so by proposing another instrument, which would surely be promotional and therefore not binding. Furthermore, no suggestions to solve the problem of the low level of ratifications of Conventions Nos. 1 and 30 have been offered.

128. The Worker members proposed that the issues of working time should be studied more in-depth by collecting information on existing practices of flexibility in different sectors. The pragmatic attitude adopted by the Worker members did not mean that they had renounced the fundamental protection contained in ILO standards. It was appropriate to reaffirm the value of the standard-setting activities of the ILO, which aimed to correct the imbalance between employers and workers. The Worker members warned against forgetting the social battles and their *acquis*, such as limitations on hours of work. The issue could not be disassociated from other issues covered by ILO standards, which would be addressed in the International Labour Conference in 2006, such as the issue of the employment relationship. The objective of that discussion would be to establish principles to define the concept of "worker", entitled to protection by ILO standards. It was important to resolve

the legal issue raised by the fact that limitations on hours of work did not apply to workers with several jobs – an increasingly frequent situation due to the precariousness that often went along with flexibility. In addition, it would be appropriate to study the link between forced labour and work imposed on top of an ordinary working day. The issue of hours of work was also linked to respect for and promotion of collective bargaining with strong trade unions, whether on an inter-professional or sectoral level, as it was not adapted to the enterprise level or individual negotiation. Finally, the debate reaffirmed the goals of Convention No. 1, which were health, safety and protection of private life.

129. In the Worker members' view, accepting a pragmatic debate implied accepting to envisage not only the qualitative aspect but also the quantitative aspect, in particular evidence for the hours worked, the power of control of workers to monitor and the strengthening of labour inspection. Before they would be able to decide on any procedure, the Worker members wished to be assured that any action by the ILO would not result in a reduction of their rights, and that employers and governments would enter into a discussion with workers on an equal footing. The possibility of having a tripartite general discussion taking into account the realities, and in which every one would present their concerns, in a spirit of compromise respectful of workers' rights, appeared to be taking shape.

* * *

130. With respect to the General Survey on hours of work, the Chairperson of the Committee of Experts pointed out that the issue of hours of work was a fundamental concern and at the heart of all employment relationships. There were three particular factors which gave increasing prominence to its ongoing relevance and importance, namely: (i) the increased emphasis on the need to balance work and rest to take account of family responsibilities; (ii) the effects of globalization; and (iii) the desire for flexibility to promote efficiency and competition in the market place but, at the same time, ensure appropriate protection for the needs and preferences of workers. This General Survey highlighted a number of major features including the development, over the past 20 years, of a broad range of working time arrangements such as compressed work-weeks, staggered hours, variable daily shift lengths, annualized rather than weekly hours of work, flexitime, and on-call work. After reviewing country practices and taking account of comments about the impact of working time arrangements, the conclusions of the Committee of Experts were as follows: many of these new forms of working arrangements were likely to contravene the Conventions which were the subject of the General Survey; these Conventions could prevent the implementation of modern flexible working arrangements; and changes in work practices warranted revision of these Conventions. In the final paragraphs of the report, the Committee set out the elements which might require addressing in the event that ILO constituents concluded that a new instrument was required.

131. In her reply, the representative of the Secretary-General thanked the members of the Committee for the rich and varied discussion on this year's General Survey. She noted that the debate had brought forth strong views on the continued relevance of the two Conventions, the importance of balancing flexibility with protection of workers' safety, health, and family life, the importance of the role of a regulatory framework and collective bargaining, and the role of the social partners. She took due note of the suggestions and concerns of the Employer and Worker members as to the direction of any possible future ILO action in this area, and the fact that many governments supported the way forward as outlined in paragraph 332 of the General Survey. Referring to this Committee's message that the ILO should not consider a normative approach but should explore innovative ways to move ahead, she stated that the Office would prepare a document for the Governing Body which would summarize the views expressed during the discussion and leave it to the Governing Body to determine the appropriate course of action. She noted the proposals that such action could call for the holding of a tripartite meeting of experts on the topic of working time, with a view to preparing a guidance document, opening up the possibility of placing the question of a general discussion on the issue on the agenda of a future session of the International Labour Conference.

D. Compliance with specific obligations

132. The Employer members stated that document D.4 was partly a response to the suggestion made last November to the Committee of Experts by the Employers' group that a better analytical tool should be developed to understand why governments were not complying with their reporting obligations. This document was a first step in that it provided some history and background in relation to the reporting obligations and indicated the main reasons why governments did not submit the instruments adopted by the ILO to the competent authorities. They added that there was nothing wrong with the list of reasons mentioned, but that other significant reasons also needed to be taken into account such as economic difficulties and the resources available for the preparation of reports as well as the existence of the situation of war in the countries concerned. The main difficulty was that the failure by governments to submit reports in practice took on a far greater significance than violations which were currently mentioned in a special paragraph in the Committee's report on ratified Conventions. This was because the failure to report or to submit instruments to the competent authorities in effect undermined the effectiveness of the supervisory system.

133. The Worker members welcomed the opportunity to hold an exchange of views of the cases of serious failure by member States to respect their reporting or other standards-related obligations. In the first place, it had to be mentioned that these cases covered both the failure to meet the obligations established by the Constitution and the failure to meet standard-related obligations. Secondly, they often involved failure to supply reports or information in response to comments. These types of failure were just as important. Indeed, the failure to supply reports could be considered a deliberate strategy by countries to avoid an examination which would show failure to comply with Conventions, particularly fundamental Conventions. This attitude was unfair to those countries which complied with their commitments and had sent reports, which had submitted new instruments to the competent authorities or which had consulted with the social partners. Moreover, the reports submitted were sometimes very brief or prepared without consultation with the social partners. Thirdly, the cases of serious failure by member States to respect their reporting or other standards-related obligations were also subject to criteria that were quantitative in nature, such as the repeated failure to send reports without any justification to explain the delay.

134. The Worker members made some suggestions to improve the examination of the cases of serious failure by member States to respect their reporting or other standards-related obligations. Firstly, a distinction could be made for those countries, which could provide objective excuses or attenuating circumstances. Document D.4 presented by the Office contained an instructive list of the principal reasons for the failure of a member State to fulfil its obligations. Some of these reasons appeared to amount to insurmountable or attenuating circumstances. For example, the general situation of a country due to conflict or natural disasters could be mentioned. Moreover, institutional factors, such as the situation of the labour administration, or the possibility of mobilizing the social partners, or the languages of the countries, could also be accepted in the beginning. The use of such excuses could not, however, be tolerated over a long period of time, as the situation should improve progressively. As such, countries that were encountering difficulties should develop a strategy compliance with their obligations, which should be supported by technical assistance from the ILO. The obligation to submit instruments adopted by the ILO to the competent authorities should be based on the revised memorandum on submission. Moreover, the involvement of the social partners should be encouraged by promoting the ratification of the Tripartite Consultation (International Labour Standards) Convention, 1976 (No. 144). In conclusion, the Worker members stated that the current approach of the cases of serious failure by member States to respect their reporting or other standards-related obligations should be diversified. However, for those countries that did not comply with their obligations, it would be appropriate to re-establish the serious nature of their failure to send reports or to undertake tripartite consultations. In this case, it would be advisable to look into the possibility of including a special paragraph and an explicit reference in the final report of the Conference.

135. In examining individual cases relating to compliance by States with their obligations under or relating to international labour standards, the Committee applied the same working methods and criteria as last year.

136. In applying those methods, the Committee decided to invite all governments concerned by the comments in paragraphs 20 (failure to supply reports for the past two or more years on the application of ratified Conventions), 27 (failure to supply first reports on the application of ratified Conventions), 31 (failure to supply information in reply to comments made by the Committee of Experts), 61 (failure to submit instruments to the competent authorities), and 67 (failure to supply reports for the past five years on unratified Conventions and Recommendations) of the Committee of Experts' report to supply information to the Committee in two half-day sittings devoted to those cases.

Submission of Conventions and Recommendations to the competent authorities

137. In accordance with its terms of reference, the Committee considered the manner in which effect is given to article 19, paragraphs 5-7, of the ILO Constitution. These provisions require member States within 12, or exceptionally 18, months of the closing of each session of the Conference to submit the instruments adopted at that session to the authority or authorities within whose competence the matter lies, for the enactment of legislation or other action, and to inform the Director-General of the ILO of the measures taken to that end, with particulars of the authority or authorities regarded as competent.

138. The Committee noted from the report of the Committee of Experts (paragraph 53) that considerable efforts to fulfil the submission obligation had been made in certain States, namely: **Guatemala, Morocco, Nigeria** and **South Africa**.

139. In addition, the Committee was informed by various other States of measures taken to bring the instruments before the competent national authorities. It welcomed the progress achieved and expressed the hope that there would be further improvements in States that still experience difficulties in complying with their obligations.

Failure to submit

140. The Committee noted with regret that no indication was available that steps had been taken in accordance with article 19 of the Constitution to submit the instruments adopted by the Conference at the last seven sessions at least (from the 84th to the 90th Sessions) to the competent authorities, in the cases of **Afghanistan, Armenia, Cambodia, Haiti, Lao People's Democratic Republic, Sierra Leone, Solomon Islands, Somalia, Turkmenistan** and **Uzbekistan**.

Supply of reports on ratified Conventions

141. In Part B of its report (General questions relating to international labour standards), the Committee has considered the fulfilment by States of their obligation to report on the application of ratified Conventions. By the date of the 2004 meeting of the Committee of Experts, the percentage of reports received was 64.03 per cent, compared with 65.87 per cent for the 2003 meeting. Since then, further reports have been received, bringing the figure to 72.1 per cent (as compared with 72.6 per cent in June 2004, and 71.8 per cent in June 2003).

Failure to supply reports and information on the application of ratified Conventions

142. The Committee noted with regret that no reports on ratified Conventions had been supplied for the past two or more years by the following States: **Antigua and Barbuda, Armenia, Denmark** (Greenland), **Grenada, Iraq, Kiribati, Liberia, Paraguay, Solomon Islands, Tajikistan, United Republic of Tanzania – Zanzibar, The former Yugoslav Republic of Macedonia** and **Turkmenistan**.

143. The Committee also noted with regret that no first reports due on ratified Conventions had been supplied by the following countries: since 1992 – **Liberia** (Convention No. 133); since 1995 – **Armenia** (Convention No. 111), **Kyrgyzstan** (Convention No. 133); since 1996 – **Armenia** (Conventions Nos. 100, 122, 135, 151); since 1998 – **Armenia** (Convention No. 174), **Equatorial Guinea** (Conventions Nos. 68, 92); since 1999 – **Turkmenistan** (Conventions Nos. 29, 87, 98, 100, 105, 111); since 2001 – **Armenia** (Convention No. 176), **Kyrgyzstan** (Convention No. 105), **Tajikistan** (Convention No. 105); since 2002 – **Azerbaijan** (Conventions Nos. 81, 129), **Bosnia and Herzegovina** (Convention No. 105), **Gambia** (Conventions Nos. 29, 105, 138), **Saint Kitts and Nevis** (Conventions Nos. 87, 98, 100), **Saint Lucia** (Conventions Nos. 154, 158, 182); and since 2003 – **Bahamas** (Convention No. 147), **Bosnia and Herzegovina** (Convention No. 182), **Dominica** (Convention No. 182), **Equatorial Guinea** (Convention No. 182), **Gambia** (Convention No. 182), **Iraq** (Conventions Nos. 172, 182), **Kiribati** (Conventions Nos. 29, 105), **Paraguay** (Convention No. 182), **Serbia and Montenegro** (Conventions Nos. 24, 25, 27, 113, 114, 156) and **Uganda** (Convention No. 182). It stressed the special importance of first reports on which the Committee of Experts bases its first evaluation of compliance with ratified Conventions.

144. In this year's report, the Committee of Experts noted that 49 governments had not communicated replies to most or any of the observations and direct requests relating to Conventions on which reports were due for examination this year, involving a total of 444 cases (compared with 325 cases in December 2003). The Committee was informed that, since the meeting of the Committee of Experts, 22 of the governments concerned had sent replies, which would be examined by the Committee of Experts at its next session.

145. The Committee noted with regret that no information had yet been received regarding any or most of the observations and direct requests of the Committee of Experts to which replies were requested for the period ending 2004 from the following countries: **Afghanistan, Antigua and Barbuda, Azerbaijan, Belize, Bosnia and Herzegovina, Burundi, Cambodia, Cape Verde, Comoros, Côte d'Ivoire, Democratic Republic of the Congo, Denmark** (Greenland), **Djibouti, Georgia, Grenada, Guinea, Guyana, Iraq, Kazakhstan, Kyrgyzstan, Liberia, Libyan Arab Jamahiriya, Netherlands** (Aruba), **Pakistan, Paraguay, Saint Lucia, Sao Tome and Principe, Solomon Islands, Tajikistan, The former Yugoslav Republic of Macedonia, United Kingdom** (Montserrat), **Yemen** and **Zambia**.

146. The Committee noted the explanations provided by the governments of the following countries concerning difficulties encountered in discharging their obligations: **Afghanistan, Armenia, Bosnia and Herzegovina, Cambodia, Central African Republic, Chad, Côte d'Ivoire, Democratic Republic of the Congo, Denmark** (Greenland), **Djibouti, Guinea, Haiti, Iraq, Kiribati, Liberia, Netherlands** (Aruba), **Pakistan, Paraguay, Serbia and Montenegro, United Republic of Tanzania – Zanzibar, Uganda, United Kingdom** (Montserrat), **Yemen** and **Zambia**.

147. The Committee stressed that the obligation to transmit reports is the basis of the supervisory system. It requested the Director-General to adopt all possible measures to improve the situation and solve the problems referred to above as quickly as possible. It expressed the hope that the subregional offices would give all due attention in their work in the field to standards-related issues and in particular to the fulfilment of standards-related obligations. The Committee also bore in mind the reporting arrangements approved by the Governing Body in November 1993, which came into operation from 1996, and the modification of these procedures adopted in March 2002 which came into force in 2003.

Supply of reports on unratified Conventions and Recommendations

148. The Committee noted that 143 of the 272 article 19 reports requested on the Hours of Work (Industry) Convention, 1919 (No. 1), and the Hours of Work (Commerce and Offices) Convention, 1930 (No. 30), had been received at the time of the Committee of Experts' meeting, and a further four since, making 54 per cent in all.

149. The Committee noted with regret that over the past five years none of the reports on unratified Conventions and Recommendations, requested under article 19 of the Constitution, had been supplied by: **Afghanistan, Bosnia and Herzegovina, Congo, Democratic Republic of the Congo, Dominican Republic, Guinea, Guyana, Kazakhstan, Kyrgyzstan, Liberia, Sao Tome and Principe, Sierra Leone, Solomon Islands, Tajikistan, The former Yugoslav Republic of Macedonia, Togo, Turkmenistan, Uganda, Uzbekistan** and **Zambia**.

Communication of copies of reports to employers' and workers' organizations

150. Once again this year, the Committee did not have to apply the criterion: "The Government has failed during the past three years to indicate the representative organizations of employers and workers to which, in accordance with article 23(2) of the Constitution, copies of reports and information supplied to the ILO under articles 19 and 22 have been communicated."

Application of ratified Conventions

151. The Committee noted with particular interest the steps taken by a number of governments to ensure compliance with ratified Conventions. The Committee of Experts listed in paragraph 38 of its report new cases in which governments had made changes to their law and practice following comments it had made as to the degree of conformity of national legislation or practice with the provisions of a ratified Convention. There were 53 such cases, relating to 35 countries; 2,429 cases where the Committee has been led to express its satisfaction with progress achieved since the Committee of Experts began listing them in 1964. These results are tangible proof of the effectiveness of the supervisory system.

152. This year, the Committee of Experts listed in paragraph 40 of its report, cases in which measures ensuring better application of ratified Conventions had been noted with interest. It has noted 267 such instances in 103 countries.

153. At its present session, the Conference Committee was informed of other instances in which measures had recently been or were about to be taken by governments with a view to ensuring the implementation of ratified Conventions. While it is for the Committee of Experts to examine these measures, the present Committee welcomes them as fresh evidence of the efforts made by governments to comply with their international obligations and to act upon the comments of the supervisory bodies.

Specific indications

154. The Government members of **Afghanistan, Armenia, Barbados, Bosnia and Herzegovina, Cambodia, Central African Republic, Chad, Côte d'Ivoire, Democratic Republic of the Congo, Denmark** (Greenland), **Djibouti, Dominican Republic, Guinea, Haiti, Iraq, Kiribati, Liberia, Netherlands** (Aruba), **Pakistan, Paraguay, Serbia and Montenegro, United Republic of Tanzania – Zanzibar, Uganda, United Kingdom** (Montserrat), **Yemen** and **Zambia** have promised to fulfil their reporting obligations as soon as possible. The Government member of Pakistan indicated that it was in the process of amending some of its labour legislation, including the Industrial Relations Ordinance, 2002.

Cases of progress

155. The Committee noted with satisfaction that in a number of cases – including some involving basic human rights – governments have introduced changes in their law and practice in order to eliminate divergences previously discussed by the Committee. It considers the highlighting of these cases a positive example to encourage governments to positively respond to comments of the supervisory bodies.

Special sitting concerning the application by Myanmar of the Forced Labour Convention, 1930 (No. 29)

156. The Committee held a special sitting concerning the application by Myanmar of Convention No. 29, in conformity with the resolution adopted by the Conference in 2000. A full record of the sitting appears in Part Three of the report.

Special cases

157. The Committee considered it appropriate to draw the attention of the Conference to its discussion of the cases mentioned in the following paragraphs, a full record of which appears as Part Two of this report.

158. As regards the application by **Belarus of the Freedom of Association and Protection of the Right to Organise Convention, 1948 (No. 87),** the Committee took note of the written information supplied by the Government, the statement made by the Government representative, the Deputy Minister of Labour, and the discussion that took place thereafter. The Committee noted from the comments of the Committee of Experts that the Commission of Inquiry submitted its report to the Governing Body at its 291st Session in November 2004. The Committee recalled that the conclusions and recommendations of the Commission of Inquiry concerned the application of rules and regulations relating to the activities of trade unions and other public associations in a manner amounting to a

condition of previous authorization for the formation of unions and with an impact uniquely upon those unions outside of the traditional trade union federation or which oppose it, contrary to Article 2 of the Convention; the non-conformity of the law on mass activities, and its application, with Article 3 of the Convention and of Presidential Decree No. 8 on measures for receiving and using foreign gratuitous aid with Articles 5 and 6 of the Convention. The Committee, like the Committee of Experts, further noted with deep concern the information concerning proposed amendments to the law on trade unions aimed at substantially increasing the requirements for trade union registration at various levels. The Committee noted the Government's indication according to which it had adopted an appropriate plan of action to give effect to the recommendations of the Commission of Inquiry and that it had submitted to all interested parties an Explanatory Letter on the norms and provisions of international and domestic legislation. The Government also indicated that the recommendations of the Commission of Inquiry were published in a magazine of the Ministry of Labour, which was sent to almost all enterprises in the country. It also referred to an experts' council established to review the labour legislation, which included in its composition the Federation of Trade Unions of Belarus (FPB) and the Congress of Democratic Trade Unions (CDTU). The Committee expressed its grave concern at the serious discrepancies between the law and practice on the one hand and the provisions of the Convention on the other, which it considered seriously threatened the survival of any form of an independent trade union movement in Belarus. It deplored the fact that no real concrete and tangible measures had yet been taken to resolve the vital matters raised by the Committee of Experts and the Commission of Inquiry, including as regards a number of recommendations made by the latter that were to have been implemented by 1 June 2005. It urged the Government to take the necessary measures immediately to ensure that full freedom of association was ensured in law and in practice so that workers could freely form and join organizations of their own choosing and carry out their activities without interference by the public authorities and to ensure that independent trade unions were not the subject of harassment and intimidation. Furthermore, the Committee supported the recommendation made by the Commission of Inquiry that the presidential administration issue instructions to the Prosecutor-General, the Minister of Justice and court administrators, that any complaints of external interference made by trade unions should be thoroughly investigated, and considered that such steps aimed at ensuring truly effective guarantees for the rights enshrined in the Convention would further benefit from the Government's implementation of the recommendations made by the United Nations Special Rapporteur on the independence of judges and lawyers. The Committee requested the Government to provide a full report on all measures taken to implement the recommendations of the Commission of Inquiry for examination by the Committee of Experts at its next meeting. The Committee further urged the Government to accept a mission from the Office to assist in the drafting of the legislative amendments requested by the Commission of Inquiry and to evaluate the measures taken by the Government to implement fully the Commission's recommendations. The Committee decided to include its conclusions in a special paragraph of its general report.

159. As regards the application by **Myanmar of the Freedom of Association and Protection of the Right to Organise Convention, 1948 (No. 87),** the Committee took note of the statement made by the Government representative and the detailed discussion that followed. The Committee recalled that it had discussed this serious case on many occasions over more than 20 years, and that since 1996 its conclusions had been included in a special paragraph for continued failure to implement the Convention. The Committee deplored the fact that, despite these continued efforts of dialogue between this Committee and the Government, there was still absolutely no progress made in adopting a legislative framework that would allow for the establishment of free and independent trade union organizations. Moreover, the Committee noted with grave concern from the Committee of Experts' comments that the report supplied by the Government contained none of the information requested by this present Committee, relevant draft laws were not provided,

nor did the Government reply to the comments made by the ICFTU. The Committee could only condemn the absence of any meaningful dialogue with the Government in this respect and trusted that its future reports would provide all requested information. The Committee took note of the statement made by the Government, which referred once again to the need to await the promulgation of the Constitution before a legislative framework for the recognition of freedom of association could be established. The Government also indicated that the National Convention had agreed that laws to protect the rights of workers and to create job opportunities should also be enacted. Recalling that fundamental divergences existed between the national legislation and practice and the Convention since the Government had ratified the Convention 50 years ago, the Committee once again urged the Government in the strongest terms to adopt immediately the necessary measures and mechanisms to guarantee to all workers and employers the right to establish and join organizations of their own choosing, as well the right of these organizations to exercise their activities and formulate their programmes, and to affiliate with federations, confederations and international organizations, without interference from the public authorities. It further urged the Government to repeal Orders Nos. 2/88 and 6/88, as well as the Unlawful Association Act, so that they could not be applied in a manner that would infringe upon the rights of workers' and employers' organizations. The Committee was obliged once again to stress that respect for civil liberties was essential for the exercise of freedom of association and firmly expected the Government to take positive steps urgently, with full and genuine participation of all sectors of society regardless of their political views, to amend the legislation and the Constitution to ensure full conformity with the Convention. It further requested the Government to take all measures to ensure that workers and employers could exercise their freedom of association rights in a climate of complete freedom and security, free from violence and threats. The Committee urged the Government to ensure the immediate release of all workers detained for attempting to exercise trade union activities and to ensure that no worker was sanctioned for having contact with a workers' organization. The Committee urged the Government to communicate all relevant draft laws as well as a detailed report on the concrete measures adopted to ensure improved conformity with the Convention, including a response to the serious matters raised by the ICFTU, for examination by the Committee of Experts this year. The Committee recalled all of its conclusions in the case concerning the application of Convention No. 29 in Myanmar as regards the ILO's presence in the country. The Committee considered that, given that the persistence of forced labour could not be disassociated from the prevailing situation of a complete absence of freedom of association, the functions of the Liaison Officer should include assistance to the Government to fully implement its obligations under Convention No. 87. The Committee firmly hoped that it would be in a position to note significant progress on all these matters at its next session. The Committee decided to include its conclusions in a special paragraph of its report. It also decided to mention this case as a case of continued failure to implement the Convention.

Continued failure to implement

160. The Committee recalls that its working methods provide for the listing of cases of continued failure over several years to eliminate serious deficiencies, previously discussed, in the application of ratified Conventions. This year the Committee noted with great concern that there had been continued failure over several years to eliminate serious discrepancies in the application by **Myanmar of the Freedom of Association and Protection of the Right to Organise Convention, 1948 (No. 87).**

161. The government of the country to which reference is made in paragraph 159 is invited to supply the relevant reports and information to enable the Committee to follow up the abovementioned matter at the next session of the Conference.

Participation in the work of the Committee

162. The Committee wished to express its gratitude to the 69 governments which collaborated by providing information on the situation in their countries and participating in the discussions of their individual cases.

163. The Committee regretted that, despite the invitations, the governments of the following States failed to take part in the discussions concerning their countries' fulfilment of their constitutional obligations to report: **Azerbaijan, Bahamas, Belize, Burundi, Cape Verde, Congo, Georgia, Kazakhstan, Kyrgyzstan, Libyan Arab Jamahiriya, Tajikistan, Togo** and **Uzbekistan**. It decided to mention the cases of these States in the appropriate paragraphs of its report and to inform them in accordance with the usual practice.

164. The Committee noted that the Permanent Mission of Bosnia and Herzegovina to the United Nations Office in Geneva had indicated in a letter dated 10 June 2005 that, for reasons of force majeur, the delegation of Bosnia and Herzegovina regretted that it would be unable to attend the meeting of the Conference Committee on the Application of Standards on 11 June 2005. Information was appended to the letter summarizing briefly the action taken by the Government to comply with its constitutional and standards-related reporting obligations and the assistance requested from the Office. All the above information was reflected in document D.13 submitted to the Committee. The Committee regretted that **Bosnia and Herzegovina** did not participate in the discussion of individual cases on the application by **Bosnia and Herzegovina of the Freedom of Association and Protection of the Right to Organise Convention, 1948 (No. 87),** although the Government delegation was accredited to the Conference. The Worker members expressed their indignation at the attitude of the Government of Bosnia and Herzegovina in relation to both the Committee and the ILO. It should be recalled that this was the third year that this case had been examined by the ILO supervisory bodies. Despite the observations made by the Committee of Experts in 2003, 2004 and 2005, the Government had not replied. The information contained in document D.13 did not provide any new elements. As this was a case of repeated failure to cooperate with the ILO supervisory system, they called for it to be included in a special mention of the Committee's report. The Employer members expressed the belief that there was little the Committee could do in relation to this case in view of the absence of the Government representative before the Committee. In its report, the Committee would have to confine itself to expressing regret at the failure of the Government to appear before the Committee to discuss the problems relating to its application of Convention No. 87 and to note that by this omission the Government was undermining the ILO's supervisory system.

165. The Committee noted with regret that the governments of the States which were not represented at the Conference, namely **Antigua and Barbuda, Comoros, Dominica, Equatorial Guinea, Gambia, Grenada, Guyana, Lao People's Democratic Republic, Saint Kitts and Nevis, Saint Lucia, Sao Tome and Principe, Sierra Leone, Solomon Islands, Somalia, The former Yugoslav Republic of Macedonia** and **Turkmenistan**, were unable to participate in the Committee's examination of the cases relating to them. It decided to mention these countries in the appropriate paragraphs of this report and to inform the governments, in accordance with the usual practice.

Geneva, 14 June 2005.

(Signed) Mr. Sérgio Paixão Pardo,
Chairperson.

Ms. Carine Parra,
Reporter.

No. 22 – Thursday, 16 June 2005

International Labour Conference

Record of Proceedings
Ninety-third Session, Geneva, 2005

22 PART TWO

Third item on the agenda: Information and reports on the application of Conventions and Recommendations

Report of the Committee on the Application of Standards

Contents

	Page
PART TWO: Observations and information concerning particular countries	3
I. Observations and information concerning reports on ratified Conventions (articles 22 and 35 of the Constitution)	3
A. General observations and information concerning certain countries	3

        a) Failure to supply reports for the past two years or more on the application of ratified Conventions

        b) Failure to supply first reports on the application of ratified Conventions

        c) Failure to supply information in reply to comments made by the Committee of Experts

        d) Written information received up to the end of the meeting of the Committee on the Application of Standards

	Page
B. Observations and information on the application of Conventions	8
Convention No. 29: Forced Labour, 1930	8
– MAURITANIA, MYANMAR (see Part Three), SUDAN	
Convention No. 77: Medical Examination of Young Persons (Industry), 1946 and Convention No. 78: Medical Examination of Young Persons (Non-Industrial Occupations), 1946	14
– ECUADOR	
Convention No. 81: Labour Inspection, 1947	15
– ROMANIA	
Convention No. 87: Freedom of Association and Protection of the Right to Organise, 1948	17
– ARGENTINA, BELARUS, BOSNIA AND HERZEGOVINA, BURUNDI, COLOMBIA, GUATEMALA, MYANMAR, PANAMA, RUSSIAN FEDERATION, SWAZILAND, TURKEY, BOLIVARIAN REPUBLIC OF VENEZUELA	
Convention No. 95: Protection of Wages, 1949	50
– ISLAMIC REPUBLIC OF IRAN	
Convention No. 98: Right to Organise and Collective Bargaining, 1949	52
– AUSTRALIA, ZIMBABWE	
Convention No. 102: Social Security (Minimum Standards), 1952	59
– PERU	

Convention No. 111: Discrimination (Employment and Occupation), 1958 62
– SAUDI ARABIA

Convention No. 144: Tripartite Consultation (International Labour Standards), 1976   63
– NEPAL, UNITED STATES

Convention No. 182: Worst Forms of Child Labour, 1999 67
– NIGER, QATAR

Appendix I. Table of reports received on ratified Conventions
(articles 22 and 35 of the Constitution) 73

Appendix II. Statistical table of reports received on ratified Convention
(article 22 of the Constitution) 77

II. Submission to the competent authorities of the Conventions and
Recommendations adopted by the International Labour Conference
(article 19 of the Constitution) 79

Observations and Information

(a) Failure to submit instruments to the competent authorities

(b) Information received

III. Reports on unratified Conventions and on Recommendations
(article 19 of the Constitution) 80

(a) Failure to supply reports on unratified Conventions and on Recommendations
for the past five years

(b) Information received

(c) Reports received on unratified Conventions Nos. 1 and 30 as of 16 June 2005

Index by countries to observations and information contained in the report 82

PART TWO

OBSERVATIONS AND INFORMATION CONCERNING PARTICULAR COUNTRIES
I. OBSERVATIONS AND INFORMATION CONCERNING REPORTS ON RATIFIED CONVENTIONS (ARTICLES 22 AND 35 OF THE CONSTITUTION)

A. General Observations and Information concerning Certain Countries

(a) Discussion of cases of serious failure by member States to respect their reporting or other standards-related obligations

The Employer members stated that document D.4 was partly a response to the suggestion made last November to the Committee of Experts by the Employers' group that a better analytical tool should be developed to understand why governments were not complying with their reporting obligations. This document was a first step in that it provided some history and background in relation to the reporting obligations and indicated the main reasons why governments did not submit the instruments adopted by the ILO to the competent authorities. They added that there was nothing wrong with the list of reasons mentioned, but that other significant reasons also needed to be taken into account, such as economic difficulties and the resources available for the preparation of reports, as well as the existence of the situation of war in the countries concerned. The main difficulty was that the failure by governments to submit reports in practice took on a far greater significance than violations which were currently mentioned in a special paragraph in the Committee's report on ratified Conventions. This was because the failure to report or to submit instruments to the competent authorities in effect undermined the effectiveness of the supervisory system.

The Worker members welcomed the opportunity to hold an exchange of views on the so-called "automatic cases", which tended at present to be treated in automatic pilot mode, which lead to certain perhaps undesired consequences. In the first place, it had to be mentioned that these cases covered both the failure to meet the obligations established by the Constitution and the failure to meet standards-related obligations. Secondly, they often involved failure to supply reports or information in response to comments. These types of failure were just as important. Indeed, the failure to supply reports could be considered a deliberate strategy by countries to avoid an examination which would show failure to comply with Conventions, particularly fundamental Conventions. This attitude was unfair to those countries which complied with their commitments and had sent reports, which had submitted new instruments to the competent authorities or which had consulted the social partners. Moreover, the reports submitted were sometimes very brief or prepared without consultation with the social partners. Thirdly, the "automatic cases" were also subject to criteria that were quantitative in nature, such as the repeated failure to send reports without any justification to explain the delay.

The Worker members made some suggestions to improve the examination of so-called "automatic cases". Firstly, a distinction could be made for those countries which could provide objective excuses or attenuating circumstances. Document D.4 presented by the Office contained an instructive list of the principal reasons for the failure of member States to fulfil their obligations. Some of these reasons appeared to amount to insurmountable or attenuating circumstances. For example, the general situation of a country due to conflict or natural disasters could be mentioned. Moreover, institutional factors, such as the situation of the labour administration, or the possibility of mobilizing the social partners, or the languages of the countries, could also be accepted in the beginning. The use of such excuses could not, however, be tolerated over a long period of time, as the situation should improve progressively. As such, countries that were encountering difficulties should develop a strategy for compliance with their obligations, which should be supported by technical assistance from the ILO. The obligation to submit instruments adopted by the ILO to the competent authorities should be based on the revised Memorandum concerning submission. Moreover, the involvement of the social partners should be encouraged by promoting the ratification of Convention No. 144. In conclusion, the Worker members stated that the current approach to "automatic cases" should be diversified. However, for those countries that did not comply with their obligations, it would be appropriate to re-establish the serious nature of their failure to send reports or to undertake tripartite consultations. In this case, it would be advisable to look into the possibility of including an automatic special paragraph and an explicit reference in the final report of the Conference. The new terminology used to refer to "automatic cases" namely "cases of serious failure by member States to respect their reporting or other standards-related obligations" was perhaps longer, but it was certainly clearer.

A Government representative of Afghanistan accepted with great pleasure the invitation to address the Conference Committee, which had a key role to play in promoting social justice throughout the world, by facilitating dialogue between governments and social partners. Sadly, for many years his country had been unable to send a delegation to meet the Committee. Hence, it was particularly auspicious to be able to share good news with the Committee's members. Since 2002, the International Labour Office had been working in Kabul. In that time, the ILO had sought to establish decent working conditions for all women and men by providing technical assistance to the social partners.

Since the ILO Liaison Office had been opened in the spring of 2003, several practical activities in support of the international labour Conventions ratified by Afghanistan had been commenced. Employment service centres had been established in Kabul and in several provinces. The Employment Services Centre Project which, amongst other activities, assisted jobseekers in gaining access to vocational training and employment, was funded by the German Government, with technical assistance provided by the ILO. In the near future, labour market surveys would be conducted and would provide information that would shape his country's national employment policy. The survey data would also help to identify training and employment-generation needs. In view of the success of current activities, he sincerely hoped that other ILO programmes would begin, such as an IPEC programme to combat child labour.

In May this year, the first tripartite workshop on issues relating to international labour standards had been held in Kabul. The workshop was hosted by the Ministry of Labour and Social Affairs, with the assistance of international labour standards specialists from Geneva and New Delhi. During the tripartite meeting, a joint report on the application of ratified Conventions had been produced, which had been forwarded to the International Labour Office for submission to the Committee of Experts. This report was testimony to his country's commitment to fruitful dialogue with both the Conference Committee and the Committee of Experts.

Following the parliamentary elections scheduled later in the year, it was the intention of the Afghan authorities, in close consultation with the social partners, to submit to the National Assembly the instruments adopted by the Conference since 1985. It was also intended to give priority to the ratification of fundamental Conventions relating to minimum age and child labour. The 1987 Labour Code was currently being amended so as to ensure that Afghan legislation fully complied with international labour standards. He called upon the Committee to recognize the progress made by Afghanistan in providing a tripartite report on the application of Conventions. It was the intention of his Government, together with representatives from employers' and workers' organizations, to continue to work in collaboration with the International Labour Office in the field of international labour standards.

A Government representative of Denmark regretted that Greenland had not met the deadline this year for responding to the comments made by the Committee of Experts regarding the three Conventions in question. He assured the Committee that Denmark had made every effort to ensure that Greenland met its reporting obligations in full and in due time. Putting the issue in perspective, he recalled that Greenland was the world's largest island, but had a population of fewer than 60,000 inhabitants. Accordingly, Greenland's administration was extremely small, which meant that it was vulnerable and sensitive to even small changes in staff. He had been informed that the person previously responsible for ILO reports had left for another job. This meant that Greenland had to rebuild the very special competence needed to respond to ILO report forms. At the same time, it had been emphasized that Greenland recognized the importance of ILO instruments and would catch up on the missing reports as soon as possible.

Finally, he reminded the Committee of the fact that the Home Rule Authority in Greenland had full autonomy in the area of social and labour policy. The Danish Government could therefore neither instruct the Home Rule Authority in this area nor fulfil the reporting obligations on behalf of Greenland. He assured the Committee that Greenland was fully aware of its reporting responsibilities. The Home Rule Authority was actively examining the issues raised by the Committee of Experts and would endeavour to respond as soon as possible.

A Government representative of Liberia conveyed the greetings of the National Transitional Government and the people of Liberia. As a founding member of the ILO, Liberia had always endeavoured to play a meaningful role in upholding and promoting its principles. However, its activities within the ILO had been hindered due to the civil crisis which had torn the entire country. He thanked the United Nations and the international community, which had played a very commendable role in helping to restore stability in his country. Due to the prolonged crisis in Liberia, it had been very difficult to make any substantial reports on ratified Conventions. However, he provided a brief overview of the current efforts being made concerning the application of certain Conventions as peace and stability steadily returned to Liberia.

Following the ratification of Convention No. 182, Liberia had been making great efforts to ensure its effective implementation. Immediately following its ratification, the Ministry of Labour had embarked upon vigorous consultations with the tripartite stakeholders, as required by the Convention, to formulate a plan of action for its implementation. Following the holding of the National Tripartite Conference in Monrovia in December 2002, a commission had been established to handle all child labour cases in the country, namely the National Commission on Child Labour (NACOMAL), which was composed of representatives of the Government, workers and employers, as well as child advocacy groups and civil society organizations. The Commission was currently engaged in efforts to create the necessary awareness of the danger and implications of child labour in the country. It was also making efforts to negotiate with IPEC and other sympathetic organizations for assistance with its programmes. Considering the urgency of the matter, officials of the Commission were represented on his delegation to meet the IPEC Director.

He added that Convention No. 144, ratified by Liberia in 2003, was considered very meaningful for the country's labour administration in view of its potential to enhance and solidify the relationship between the tripartite partners. A national tripartite consultative group was being established for the implementation of the Convention.

In an effort to fully apply Convention No. 111, an Act had been submitted to the National Legislature to amend the existing labour laws of Liberia, which contained clauses that were quite discriminatory and gave employers undue advantages over workers, for example in relation to arbitrary dismissal. Adoption of the amendment to this provision was expected very soon. He added that Conventions Nos. 138 and 142 had been submitted to the National Legislature for ratification and a Bill to ban trafficking in persons for adoption into law. This Act would deter persons engaged in the business of violating other people's free movement in the country and would make it a felony for anyone to engage in the trafficking of persons.

Finally, he emphasized the tremendous efforts made by his Government to combat the spread of the killer HIV/AIDS in Liberia. His Government had engaged in sensitizing the labour force on control methods and had entered into a partnership with UNFPA under the project entitled, *HIV/AIDS in the workplace*. The project covered three countries and its extension to cover the rest of the countries was under negotiation so that the entire labour sector could benefit from this programme.

In conclusion, he said that reports on the other Conventions as requested by the Committee of Experts would be available by 15 September 2005.

A Government representative of Kiribati stated that the failure of his country to submit reports was due to administrative problems and he assured the Committee that his Government would make every effort to submit its reports on time. However, certain problems, such as lack of capacity and staff training did exist. Therefore, he reiterated the request for ILO technical assistance made by his Government at the Second South-East Asia and Pacific Subregional Tripartite Forum on Decent Work, held in Melbourne in April 2005.

A Government representative of Paraguay, with reference to paragraphs 20, 27 and 31 of the General Report of the Committee of Experts, stated that it attributed great transcendence to the ILO and its standard-setting function, guidance and technical assistance. His Government recognized the positive and constructive comments made by the Committee of Experts concerning national laws and regulations. He regretted that, despite the efforts made by the competent authorities to reply to these comments, they had not been able to do so and the information was overdue. He reaffirmed the will of the authorities of his country to fulfil its obligations relating to the ILO in conformity with international labour standards, and undertook to make every effort to submit the reports due and the information requested as soon as possible.

The Employer member of Iraq emphasized that his country was going through an extraordinary situation, but that it was nevertheless making progress towards democracy and compliance with its international commitments. Iraq had prepared a draft Labour Code in cooperation with the ILO Regional Office for Arab States, which would soon be submitted for examination to the National Assembly. The recent elections had helped to strengthen human rights in the country and had restored many of the freedoms of the population, including the right to establish trade unions and the right to strike. He hoped that the ILO would provide the technical assistance necessary for his country to build up its capacities and respond to the requirements of today.

A Government representative of the United Republic of Tanzania spoke on behalf of the Government of Zanzibar and indicated that the issues at hand were to do with the reports on Conventions Nos. 58, 81 and 86. The Government of the United Republic of Tanzania recognized the importance of accurate reporting on the ILO Conventions which it had ratified. In the absence of the Government representative of Zanzibar, he indicated that the Government was working closely with the ILO Office to submit the said reports by 15 September 2005. He concluded that both the Governments of the United Republic of Tanzania and of Zanzibar were engaged in changing their labour legislation and that information on these developments would be included in the reports submitted to the Office.

The Worker members emphasized that the obligation to submit reports was a key element of the ILO supervisory system. Failure to meet this obligation for two years or more gave the countries concerned an unjustified advantage as it prevented the Committee from examining their national law and practice in relation to the ratified Conventions. They recalled that only a few governments had spoken concerning their failure to meet their reporting obligations, while other countries had been either absent or not accredited to the Conference. Certain considerations, such as situations of crisis or conflict, the lack of personnel or resources, or restructuring had been invoked as an excuse. The Worker members called upon the Committee to urge these countries to respect their commitments and to invite them to request ILO technical assistance to this end.

The Employer members said that it was noteworthy that there had been greater participation by Governments in the discussion than in previous years. Evidently, if a government was not even accredited to the Conference or registered with the Committee, this was a clear signal that there was indeed a problem. They called for the Committee of Experts in future to provide more specific information on the reasons why governments were not fulfilling their reporting obligations. Fulfilling reporting obligations was fundamental because it was the basis of the work of this Committee and of the supervisory system. Without reporting, the supervisory system would fail before it even started. If governments did not supply information, it was difficult to assess whether they were complying with the requirements of ratified Conventions. They concluded that one of the reasons could be the lack of in-depth analysis by countries before ratifying a Convention and they called on the Office to provide appropriate assistance in this regard.

The Committee noted the information supplied and the explanations provided by the Government representatives who had taken the floor. The Committee recalled the fundamental importance of submitting reports on the application of ratified Conventions, not only for their actual communication, but also of doing so within the prescribed time limits, for the proper functioning of the supervisory system. The Committee expressed concern that the Governments of Antigua and Barbuda, Armenia, Denmark (Greenland), Grenada, Iraq, Kiribati, Liberia, Paraguay, Solomon Islands, Tajikistan, United Republic of Tanzania (Zanzibar), Turkmenistan and The former Yugoslav Republic of Macedonia, had not yet submitted reports on the application of ratified Conventions, and urged them to do so as soon as possible. The Committee decided to mention these cases in the appropriate section of its General Report. The Committee noted the member States which had taken the floor and explained the difficulties encountered, and those which had expressed their willingness to comply with their obligations. The Committee noted the member States which had requested ILO technical assistance and asked the Office to give effect to these requests.

(b) Failure to supply first reports on the application of ratified Conventions

The Worker members emphasized that first reports were of particular importance because they provided the basis on which the Committee of Experts carried out its first evaluation of the application of a ratified Convention, on the one hand, and helped the Government to avoid, from the beginning, problems of interpretation concerning the application of Conventions. They added that first reports were essential for the supervisory system and requested the member States concerned to make a particular effort to fulfil their obligations in this regard.

The Employer members said that the provision of the first report on the application of ratified Conventions was one of the first indications of whether a country was interested in applying them and that, once the decision to ratify a Convention had been taken, countries should be capable of sending the first report. Failure to provide the first report constituted a contradiction by a State which ratified a Convention but then did not submit information, or represented in the very least a lack of care at the time of ratification of Conventions. In their view, the failure to send the first report was a matter of particular concern.

A Government representative of Armenia explained that her statement would cover all the paragraphs of the Committee of Experts' report concerning reporting obligations. She said that, although Armenia had been a Member of the ILO since 1992, due to socio-economic crisis and a painful transitional period of substantive institutional changes and structural and legal reforms, it had only been able to start cooperation with the ILO and to take steps towards the fulfilment of its reporting obligations as of 2004. For example, a special unit responsible for relations with the ILO, including reporting obligations, had been created within the Ministry of Labour and Social Issues and regular dialogue had been established with the social partners on the dissemination of practical knowledge about the principles and rights enshrined in ILO Conventions and other documents adopted by the International Labour Conference. She added that Armenia had signed a technical cooperation programme with the ILO and had ratified 13 new Conventions. All these steps showed the seriousness of her Government's commitment towards the ILO.

With reference to reporting obligations and the submission of Conventions and Recommendations to the competent authorities, she indicated that certain difficulties of a technical nature existed, such as the timely and accurate translation of documents into the national language and the lack of reporting skills of the staff involved. Her Government had requested technical assistance from the ILO to overcome these difficulties and she hoped for a positive response in this regard. She concluded by assuring the Committee that her Government was committed to fulfilling its obligations and overcoming delays.

A Government representative of Chad indicated that his Government had taken note of the comments made by the Committee of Experts on Conventions Nos. 132 and 182 and emphasized that his Government's reports had been submitted to the ILO last April.

A Government representative of the Bahamas stated that the report on Convention No. 147 was forthcoming and should be submitted within ten days. The Bahamas remained committed to ensuring that the reports due and replies to the comments of the Committee of Experts were submitted on a timely basis.

A Government representative of Kiribati indicated that the explanations given in his previous statement applied to this paragraph of the Committee of Experts' report. However, his Government would still need technical assistance on this matter.

A Government representative of Paraguay referred to his previous statement concerning the failure to supply reports for the past two years or more on the application of ratified Conventions.

A Government representative of Serbia and Montenegro recalled that her country had joined the ILO in 2000 and had since then ratified 69 ILO Conventions. She added that her Government had immediately started to report on the application of Conventions and had sent 25 reports so far. As was indicated in document D.3, a report had also been submitted on Convention No. 102. Six reports were still pending, but the Government was in the process of preparing them and they would be submitted as soon as possible. She indicated that the delay was due to the internal constitutional transformation that took place in 2003 and the fact that a large number of reports had to be prepared in a short period of time. She explained that the transformation had resulted in a substantial decentralization, following which labour matters had been fully transferred from the federal level to the level of the two states. Some time would be needed to organize the new administrative structures, but the newly established communication structures should enable the respective governments to proceed with reporting more expeditiously. She hoped that in the near future her Government would be able to submit the reports required by the ILO.

A Government representative of Uganda stated that the report on Convention No. 182 was under preparation. She added that a lot of progress had been made on this Convention following ratification and cooperation with IPEC. As this first report on Convention No. 182 needed to be comprehensive and detailed, her Government was making every effort to complete it on time while ensuring the necessary quality. The report would be submitted, along with the other reports due, between 1 June and 1 September 2005.

The Employer members indicated that the failure to supply the first report was often related to Convention No. 182, which had recently been ratified by a large number of countries. It was a paradoxical situation for a country to ratify a Convention and then immediately fail to provide a report. In response to the allegations by some countries of special circumstances as a justification for this situation, it was important to point out that the Office was ready to provide the necessary technical assistance and that such assistance should be given priority.

The Worker members observed that only eight Governments had replied, in the Committee, with respect to their failure to submit first reports on the application of ratified Conventions. Moreover, they had often given the same reasons for justifying this failure. It was unacceptable that certain first reports had been due for several years, which constituted a very serious failure. They called upon the Office to contact the member States concerned to determine the specific reasons for this failure and invited the latter to request the technical assistance of the Office, where necessary.

The Committee noted the information and explanations provided by the Government representatives who took the floor. The Committee reiterated the crucial importance of providing first reports on the application of ratified Conventions, and noted in particular the major impact in this respect of Convention No. 182, the most ratified of the fundamental Conventions in recent years.

The Committee decided to mention the following cases in the appropriate section of the General Report: in particular since 1992 – Liberia (Convention No. 133), since 1995 – Armenia (Convention No. 111), Kyrgyzstan (Convention No. 133); since 1996 – Armenia (Conventions Nos. 100, 122, 135, 151); since 1998 – Armenia (Convention No. 174), Equatorial Guinea (Conventions Nos. 68, 92); since 1999 – Turkmenistan (Conventions Nos. 29, 87, 98, 100, 105, 111); since 2001 – Armenia (Convention No. 176), Kyrgyzstan (Convention No. 105), Tajikistan (Convention No. 105); since 2002 – Azerbaijan (Conventions Nos. 81, 129), Bosnia and Herzegovina (Convention No. 105), Gambia (Conventions Nos. 29, 105, 138), Saint Kitts and Nevis (Conventions Nos. 87, 98, 100), Saint Lucia (Conventions Nos. 154, 158, 182); and since 2003 – Bahamas (Convention No. 147), Bosnia and Herzegovina (Convention No. 182), Dominica (Convention No. 182), Gambia (Convention No. 182), Equatorial Guinea (Convention No. 182), Iraq (Conventions Nos. 172, 182), Kiribati (Conventions Nos. 29, 105), Paraguay (Convention No. 182), Serbia and Montenegro (Conventions Nos. 24, 25, 27, 113, 114, 156), Uganda (Convention No. 182).

The Committee noted with concern that few countries had provided explanations and requested the Office to contact the countries listed. The Committee noted the countries which had requested assistance and asked the Office to give effect to these requests.

(c) Failure to supply information in reply to comments made by the Committee of Experts

The Worker members observed that incomplete or unclear reports, or the late submission of the reports due, seriously hampered the work of the Conference Committee and of the Committee of Experts. Governments had to take the comments formulated by the Committee of Experts seriously and fulfil their obligations. The number of governments which failed to reply to requests made by the Committee of Experts was constantly increasing. This year, in 444 cases (covering 49 countries), the governments had not replied to the comments of the Committee of Experts, while last year this number was 325 (covering 37 countries). The attitude of these governments was unacceptable. The Worker members indicated that they had discussed the case of Pakistan with respect to Conventions No. 87 and 98 and the consequences for the workers in that country. As in the other cases, this situation was unacceptable in the opinion of the Worker members.

The Employer members said that at times the reports supplied by States were difficult to understand or the information provided was incomplete. The obligation to submit reports with additional information was part of the process covered by the general obligation to supply reports. There had been no improvements this year, as 49 countries, compared with 37 in 2004, had not provided the additional information requested. This was serious because such information made it possible to determine whether the case was serious. Without relevant and clear information, the entire process would fall apart, which also constituted a failure in relation to countries which regularly submitted their reports within the prescribed time limits.

A Government representative of Barbados regretted that her country had been unable to meet all of its reporting obligations, particularly since it was committed to the principles of the ILO and usually submitted fully detailed and timely reports. She assured the Committee that of those listed in the General Report, the reports on Conventions Nos. 63 and 81 had already been submitted. The report on Convention No. 118 was also ready and available for submission to the Committee. A simplified report on Convention No. 105 had also been submitted. However, there were outstanding comments in respect of this Convention relating to the observations made by the Committee of Experts. She added that there were also outstanding reports on Conventions Nos. 108 and 147. She explained that in each of these cases the difficulty in submitting the outstanding reports and comments had arisen because her Government had not yet received the comments from all of the social partners. She assured the Committee that reports on the remaining Conventions would be submitted to the Committee shortly.

A Government representative of Cambodia indicated that, as a result of the technical assistance provided by the Office, Cambodia had made progress the previous year. Hence, the reports for the year 2004 had already been sent. With regard to the reports for 2005, they had not yet been prepared because of the changes within the Ministry of Labour. In July 2004, the Government of Cambodia had been restructured and a new Ministry of Labour had been created, combining a part of the former Ministry of Social Affairs and the Ministry of Education. He added that his Government was ready to prepare the reports for 2005. However, because the staff of the different services had changed posts due to the restructuring, the staff that were competent in the field of labour had not yet taken up their functions, in particular those related to the drafting of ILO reports. He hoped that the new Ministry of Labour and Vocational Training would fulfil its reporting obligations.

A Government representative of Côte d'Ivoire indicated that his Government took due note of the information contained in paragraph 31 of the report of the Committee of Experts concerning failure to supply information in reply to the comments made on Conventions Nos. 81 and 129. He stated that his Government had not been able to send a reply within the established deadlines. The reports had been prepared, but the annexes were still missing. He indicated that his Government sincerely regretted this situation and was committed to fulfilling its obligations after the Conference. Moreover, he undertook to ensure that such delays did not occur again in the future.

A Government representative of the Democratic Republic of the Congo expressed his Government's regret at not having fulfilled its obligations. Concerning the failure to supply information in response to the comments made by the Committee of Experts, he indicated that the normal operation of the public service of the State had been paralysed due to the difficulties encountered by the country as a result of the war. These difficulties had caused a delay in the submission of the reports concerning Conventions Nos. 81, 87, 98, 100, 102 and 150. However, the Government undertook to submit these reports to the employers' and workers' organizations and to supply them to the ILO not later than 1 September 2005. Concerning the reports requested under article 19 of the Constitution, his Government had found it inappropriate to send these reports without having first submitted them to the employers' and workers' organizations. To date, the reports concerning Conventions Nos. 1 and 30 on working time, Convention No. 122 on employment policy, Convention No. 142 on human resources development, Recommendation No. 69 on medical care and Recommendation No. 189 on job creation in small and medium-sized enterprises had been prepared. He added that his Government's failure to supply reports could be explained, among other reasons, by the fact that the Minister of Labour and Social Insurance had not received some correspondence. In conclusion, he stated that in order to facilitate the work of the Committee of Experts, his Government was determined to supply the reports requested within the time limits established.

A Government representative of Denmark referred to his previous statement and recalled Greenland's limited population and small administration. He said that Greenland deeply respected the ILO's instruments. He added that over the past 20-30 years Greenland had obtained increased autonomy on social and labour law issues. This meant that Greenland had sometimes been led to question commitments assumed by Denmark on its behalf. Moreover, the Government of Denmark could not instruct the Home Rule Authority in Greenland or fulfil the reporting obligations on its behalf. In 2003, his country had received important and systematic assistance from the ILO Office, which had helped it to determine precisely which Conventions should be considered as having been ratified by Greenland. He noted that this assistance would help Greenland to fulfil its reporting obligations, including the obligation to reply to the comments from the Committee of Experts.

A Government representative of Djibouti indicated that Conventions Nos. 111, 138 and 182 had been ratified the previous year, which meant that Djibouti had ratified the eight fundamental Conventions. With regard to the failure to submit information in reply to the comments of the Committee of Experts, Djibouti had ratified a fairly large number of Conventions (68) which had overloaded the labour services responsible for preparing reports. Moreover, several of these Conventions had no relevance to the economic activities in the country. The Government was therefore thinking about the possibility of denouncing certain Conventions. He requested the technical assistance of the ILO in relation to this matter.

A Government representative of Haiti indicated that information concerning Conventions Nos. 14, 24, 25, 29, 77, 78, 81, 87, 98, 100 and 106 would be sent to the Office.

A Government representative of Guinea indicated that, with regard to the issue of the failure to submit instruments to the competent authorities, the Government had submitted Conventions adopted by the ILO to the Parliament for ratification. Conventions Nos. 156 and 159, as well as Conventions Nos. 138 and 182 on child labour, could be mentioned as examples. With regard to the failure to supply reports for the past two years or more on the application of ratified Conventions, he indicated that Guinea had ratified 58 Conventions and thus had become one of 110 member States that had ratified all the fundamental Conventions, the principles of which were contained in the ILO Declaration. He took due note of the information provided and undertook to supply the necessary reports. Finally, concerning failure to supply information in reply to comments made by the Committee of Experts, he said that almost all the reports had been sent in accordance with the schedule prepared by the Government in collaboration with the international labour standards specialist. Thus, reports on Conventions Nos. 87, 95, 98, 113, 117, 122, 133, 139 and 140 had been supplied, as well as those concerning Conventions Nos. 135, 150 and 151. Reports on Conventions Nos. 3, 16, 100, 144, 149, 152 and 159 would be sent.

He recognized that the reports had not been prepared within the established time limits and said that in future this situation would change. Moreover, the reports that had not yet been sent would be supplied to the ILO. The Government was making efforts to fulfil its obligations. For example, a new Labour Code had been adopted which was more flexible. Furthermore, the reports were always sent to workers' and employers' organizations, in conformity with article 23 of the Constitution. Measures had also been taken with regard to child labour, and in particular the Government was collaborating with ILO/IPEC. Finally, he indicated that the reports would be sent by the end of 2005 at the latest and requested technical assistance from the ILO.

A Government representative of the Netherlands said that he appreciated being given the opportunity to explain the situation in Aruba in more detail before the Committee. He thanked the Committee of Experts for its transparency and good work. He said that the Labour Department of Aruba had undergone a major reorganization in June 2004. This reorganization had come with many changes in different functions and unfortunately had interfered with the day-to-day operation of the Department. He added that at the moment the Government of Aruba was busy responding to observations made by the Committee of Experts, as stated in the General Report, paragraph 31. He apologized for that delay and hoped that the necessary information would be submitted within the next three months.

A Government representative of Pakistan said that his country had sent reports on most of the Conventions ratified. He regretted that replies to some of the comments of the Committee of Experts had not been sent as they required certain information from different stakeholders, such as provincial governments and federal ministries. He said that the matter had already been referred to them. Some of the required information had been received, although a few had yet to respond. He noted that replies would be provided to the Committee in the near future. He informed the Committee that his Government was in the process of amending some of its labour laws, including the Industrial Relations Ordinance, 2002, which had been referred to in the comments under Conventions Nos. 87 and 98. He reiterated the importance and respect attached by his Government to the work of the Conference Committee.

A Government representative of Paraguay referred to his previous statement on failure to supply reports for the past two years or more on the application of ratified Conventions.

A Government representative of the United Kingdom apologized on behalf of Montserrat for its failure to fully respond to the requests for reports under article 22 of the ILO Constitution. She assured the Committee that this was not due to a lack of commitment on the part of the Government of Montserrat to fulfil its obligations as a Member of the ILO, but due to a question of capacity. She said that unfortunately the reality of the situation was that Montserrat was an extremely small autonomous island with limited human and financial resources. While this was not an excuse, it had to be recognized that heavy reporting schedules could place a considerable burden on even the largest administrations. Her Government had been working with the Government of Montserrat to help it address the capacity issue. In December 2004, in conjunction with the ILO Caribbean Office, her Government had held a workshop for a number of Caribbean-based territories, including Montserrat, with the specific aim of reviewing ILO reporting requirements and other standards-related activities. She was pleased to report that, following the workshop, the Government of Montserrat was making progress. A Human Rights Reporting Committee had been established which was considering ways to ensure that all future human rights reports, including those that covered ILO Conventions, were completed on time and that all outstanding ILO reports were submitted as soon as possible.

A Government representative of Yemen recalled that his country had ratified 29 Conventions, which demonstrated its readiness to fulfil its commitments in relation to the ILO and its instruments. He indicated that a copy of the new draft Labour Code had been sent to the Office for technical comments and that his country intended to consider these comments when assessing whether its legislation was in accordance with the obligations of the Conventions it had ratified. It was still awaiting a response from the ILO. He said that in the past his country had been able to submit its reports within the established time limits due to the technical assistance received. However, it had now encountered certain difficulties and required assistance, but he regretted to note that there had been a reduction in the rate of technical assistance to countries in his region in recent years. He therefore called for the volume of assistance provided in the region to be strengthened. In conclusion, he reaffirmed his Government's commitment to the ILO's principles and standards.

A Government representative of Zambia expressed deep sadness at the failure of his country to provide timely responses to the requests for information and the comments of the Committee of Experts. He assured the Conference Committee that this failure was not deliberate and was not intended to undermine the valuable work of the supervisory system. The reason lay with the long drawn-out process of the restructuring of the Ministry of Labour, during the course of which the staff experienced in attending to the reporting requirements of the ILO had taken early retirement. Nevertheless, he assured the Committee that in future all the reports and information required by the supervisory bodies would be attended to promptly. Some of the reports that were overdue had already been dispatched and the others would be prepared and sent off as soon as possible. With a view to resolving the problem of lack of capacity, approaches had been made to the ILO to provide training for the new administrative officers responsible for ILO reporting procedures.

The Worker members, while thanking the Governments concerned for their replies, stated that they had heard almost the same reasons as in the past for their failure to send replies to the comments made by the Committee of Experts. Despite the opportunity afforded to them, several Governments had not taken the floor on this subject. Considering the importance of the obligation to submit reports, the Worker members emphasized that governments had to be urged to comply with these requirements.

The Worker member of Pakistan said that he had listened to the statement by the Government representative and wished to draw his attention to the importance of submitting the reports due on Conventions Nos. 87, 98 and 100. He recalled that the Committee of Experts had requested the Government to amend the Industrial Relations Ordinance, 2002, to bring it into conformity with its international obligations under ILO Conventions. He therefore urged the Government to amend its legislation in the near future so that trade union rights were restored to workers, who were at particular risk in the current process of liberalization and privatization. He hoped that the commitment made by the Government representative would be put into effect in the near future through strong action to amend the legislation that infringed the basic rights of freedom of association and collective bargaining.

The Employer members indicated that the explanations provided by Governments were similar to those which had been advanced for many years, namely war, administrative problems, the need for ILO technical assistance. Some speakers had referred to the issue of the ratification of many Conventions in a relatively short period of time, and others to the restructuring of the labour administration. Still others had undertaken to supply the reports in the near future. They emphasized the relevance and importance of supplying reports, which was part of and affected not only the work of the Conference Committee, but of the entire process of supervising the application of international labour standards.

The Committee took due note of the information and explanations provided by the Government representatives who took the floor. It noted with concern the large number of countries which had not replied to the comments on several Conventions. The Committee emphasized the great importance, for the continuation of dialogue, of providing clear, relevant and full information. It reiterated that this was part of the constitutional obligation to supply reports. It urged Governments to request the assistance of the ILO to overcome any difficulties they might face and asked the Office to give effect to such requests.

The Committee urged the Governments concerned, and particularly, Afghanistan, Antigua and Barbuda, Azerbaijan, Belize, Bosnia and Herzegovina, Burundi, Cape Verde, Cambodia, Comoros, Côte d'Ivoire, Democratic Republic of the Congo, Denmark (Greenland), Djibouti, Georgia, Grenada, Guinea, Guyana, Iraq, Kazakhstan, Kyrgyzstan, Liberia, Libyan Arab Jamahiriya, Netherlands (Aruba), Pakistan, Paraguay, Saint Lucia, Sao Tome and Principe, Solomon Islands, Tajikistan, The former Yugoslav Republic of Macedonia, United Kingdom (Montserrat), Yemen, Zambia, to make every effort to provide the requested information as soon as possible. The Committee decided to mention these cases in the appropriate section of its General Report.

(d) Written information received up to the end of the meeting of the Committee on the Application of Standards [1]

Botswana. Since the meeting of the Committee of Experts, the Government has sent replies to most of the Committee's comments.

Cameroon. Since the meeting of the Committee of Experts, the Government has sent reports on unratified Conventions, unratified Protocols and Recommendations.

Chad. Since the meeting of the Committee of Experts, the Government has sent replies to most of the Committee's comments.

Cyprus. Since the meeting of the Committee of Experts, the Government has sent replies to all of the Committee's comments.

Denmark. Since the meeting of the Committee of Experts, the Government has sent replies to most of the Committee's comments.

Djibouti. The ratification of Convention No. 182, adopted at the 87th Session of the Conference.

France (French Southern and Antarctic Territories). Since the meeting of the Committee of Experts, the Government has sent replies to all of the Committee's comments.

France (Guadeloupe). Since the meeting of the Committee of Experts, the Government has sent replies to most of the Committee's comments.

France (Martinique). Since the meeting of the Committee of Experts, the Government has sent replies to all of the Committee's comments.

France (Réunion). Since the meeting of the Committee of Experts, the Government has sent replies to all of the Committee's comments.

France (St. Pierre and Miquelon). Since the meeting of the Committee of Experts, the Government has sent replies to all of the Committee's comments.

Haiti. Since the meeting of the Committee of Experts, the Government has sent the reports due concerning the application of ratified Conventions.

Kyrgyzstan. Since the meeting of the Committee of Experts, the Government has sent the first report on Convention No. 81.

Latvia. The instruments adopted by the Conference at the last ten sessions (from the 81st to the 91st Sessions) have been submitted, on 4 June 2004, to the Parliament of the Republic of Latvia.

Lesotho. Since the meeting of the Committee of Experts, the Government has sent the first reports on Conventions Nos. 105 and 150 and replies to most of the Committee's comments.

Madagascar. Since the meeting of the Committee of Experts, the Government has sent the first report on Convention No. 182.

Mali. Since the meeting of the Committee of Experts, the Government has sent reports on unratified Conventions, unratified Protocols and Recommendations.

Mongolia. Since the meeting of the Committee of Experts, the Government has sent reports on unratified Conventions, unratified Protocols and Recommendations.

Mozambique. Since the meeting of the Committee of Experts, the Government has sent replies to most of the Committee's comments.

Netherlands (Netherlands Antilles). Since the meeting of the Committee of Experts, the Government has sent replies to all of the Committee's comments.

Niger. Since the meeting of the Committee of Experts, the Government has sent replies to all of the Committee's comments.

Pakistan. Since the meeting of the Committee of Experts, the Government has sent the first reports on Conventions Nos. 100 and 182.

Saint Vincent and the Grenadines. Since the meeting of the Committee of Experts, the Government has sent reports on unratified Conventions, unratified Protocols and Recommendations.

Sao Tome and Principe. The ratifications of Conventions Nos. 182 and 184, adopted at the 87th and the 89th Sessions of the Conference (1999 and 2001, respectively), were registered on 4 May 2005.

Serbia and Montenegro. Since the meeting of the Committee of Experts, the Government has sent replies to most of the Committee's comments.

Seychelles. Since the meeting of the Committee of Experts, the Government has sent replies to most of the Committee's comments.

Slovakia. Since the meeting of the Committee of Experts, the Government has sent reports on unratified Conventions, unratified Protocols and Recommendations.

Somalia. Since the meeting of the Committee of Experts, the Government has sent all of the reports due concerning the application of ratified Conventions.

Sweden. Since the meeting of the Committee of Experts, the Government has sent replies to all of the Committee's comments.

Trinidad and Tobago. Since the meeting of the Committee of Experts, the Government has sent replies to most of the Committee's comments.

United Kingdom (Isle of Man). Since the meeting of the Committee of Experts, the Government has sent replies to all of the Committee's comments.

Zambia. Since the meeting of the Committee of Experts, the Government has sent the first report on Convention No. 182.

---

[1] The list of the reports received is to be found in Part Two of the Report: Appendix I.

B. Observations and information on the application of Conventions

Convention No. 29: Forced Labour, 1930

MAURITANIA (ratification: 1961). **A Government representative** stated that the inclusion of this case in the list of cases to be examined by the current session of the Committee was seen by his country as a constructive step, motivated by the intention to draw up an inventory of progress made in implementing the recommendations of the Committee of Experts, in particular following the direct contacts mission of May 2004.

The Government representative presented the measures taken by his Government since then: (1) the adoption of a draft Labour Code elaborated with the assistance of the ILO and the entry into force of the Labour Code on 16 July 2004; (2) the extension of the definition of forced labour provided in article 5 of the draft Labour Code to forced labour which did not result from the non-execution of an employment contract, in conformity with the formula proposed by the Committee of Experts; (3) the criminalization of forced labour through the Act of 17 July 2003 and by virtue of sections 5 and 435 of the new Labour Code. The penalties provided for also applied to aggravated acts of violence or threats of violence exercised by a person in order to ensure another person's services, or take the product of his or her activity. According to the Labour Code, the aggravated violence extended to violence against freedom of movement, freedom of work, the free disposal of one's goods and the free exercise of parental responsibilities (penalties foreseen: five to ten years of forced labour, fines, loss of civil and political rights); (4) the repeal of the provisions of the Labour Code concerning the administration and direction of trade unions, which were discriminatory vis-à-vis foreigners, by virtue of section 273 of the new Labour Code, which allowed foreigners to undertake such functions if they complied with certain conditions, in conformity with Convention No. 87; (5) the repeal of the Ordinance of 1962, which delegated certain powers to the local chiefs concerning the maintenance of public order, by virtue of the Act of 27 January 2005. It should be noted that this Ordinance had not been replaced and that its provisions which had been considered contrary to Article 2 of the Convention no longer existed; (6) the establishment of the list of services which were considered to be essential for the population by Order No 566/MFPT/MFPE adopted by the Ministers of the Interior and Employment. This list excluded henceforth the postal service and public transport.

The Government representative also presented the various measures taken by his Government in order to improve the living conditions of workers, promote standards and consolidate the rule of law: (1) initiation on 4 July 2004, of the first free collective negotiations organized in more than 20 years with the participation of the employers and the five trade union confederations, negotiations which had led in particular to an increase of the inter-professional guaranteed minimum wage (SMIG) by more than 365 per cent; (2) the elaboration of a technical cooperation programme to promote the ILO Declaration on Fundamental Principles and Rights at Work; (3) the implementation of programmes to fight against poverty, with encouraging results, which led to believe that the objectives set in the areas of health, education and housing would be attained by 2015; (4) the creation of an inter-ministerial structure aimed, in the first place, to introduce the organs responsible for the law's implementation to international labour standards in the area of forced labour (two seminars held in Nouakchott and Kiffa) and then, in the second place, awareness-raising among the populations, especially in the disadvantaged areas, with the support of the United States Embassy in Mauritania; (5) the national programme for good governance contained a component on "promotion of human rights and reinforcement of civil society's capacity". The Lutheran World Federation had been associated with this programme. The Government had recognized three human rights associations: the Mauritanian Human Rights Association, the think tank on economic and social development and SOS-Esclaves.

The Government was about to approve a national plan for the promotion and protection of human rights, elaborated with the assistance of the United Nations High Commissioner for Human Rights. The plan included sections on the most vulnerable groups and on the partnership between the Government and civil society. With regard to the second section, the Government had solicited the assistance of the ILO and the UNDP.

The Employer members recalled that Convention No. 29 required the suppression of forced labour in all forms, that the illegal exaction of forced labour be a punishable offence, and that penalties imposed by law were adequate and strictly enforced. Mauritania had adopted a first Decree to abolish slavery in 1905; the 1963 Labour Code prohibited forced labour and imposed relevant penal sanctions. As noted by the Committee of Experts, however, the Labour Code provisions only applied to employers and workers in a formal employment relationship. In 1980, the Government had adopted a declaration abolishing slavery, and in 1981, it had adopted an ordinance abolishing slavery and providing for compensation to former slave-owners. From 1990 to 2000, the Government had repeatedly insisted that forced labour no longer existed in the country.

They noted that previous comments of the Committee of Experts had held that slavery persisted in Mauritania, citing information from the report of the Working Group on Slavery of the United Nations Sub-Commission on Prevention of Discrimination and Protection of Minorities. The Committee of Experts' current comments cited the observations in the report of the direct contacts mission of May 2004, which had noted that the Government considered the practice of forced labour "entirely exceptional and, in any case, not more developed than that in certain major cities in the industrialized world". The direct contacts mission had also noted the views of the Free Confederation of Mauritanian Workers (CLTM), which held that "situations of forced labour are widespread in Mauritania". The Employer members also noted that the direct contacts mission concluded that further research and investigation into the continued existence of forced labour was needed, and they therefore urged the Government to cooperate with such further investigations in order to determine the extent to which forced labour persisted.

The Employer members also noted the amended Labour Code of 2004, which abolished forced labour in any labour relationship, not just where it was governed by an employment contract. In addition, Act No. 2003-025 of 17 July 2003 regarding trafficking of persons made such acts punishable by imprisonment. They noted the Government representative's position that this legislation was also intended to prohibit violence in connection with the freedom of movement.

In view of the above, and in light of the conclusions of the direct contacts mission, it appeared that while progress had been made with regard to legislative measures prohibiting forced labour, more information was needed regarding penal sanctions for violations of this legislation. They urged the Government to provide information on the jurisdictions competent to receive complaints and the penalties imposed under the Labour Code and the Act on trafficking of persons, including the number of complaints lodged and the respective court decisions.

They commended the Government on action taken to combat poverty through economic and social means. This notwithstanding, the Employer members saw this matter as a problem of the application and enforcement by the Government of relevant national legislation. As a result, they urged the Government to improve the application and enforcement of national legislation, including the consistent enforcement of penalties for any offences relating to forced labour. Finally, as the direct contacts mission had noted, there was no enforcement mechanism for labour legislation, and resources allocated to the labour inspectorate were scarce. They wished to reinforce that allocation of additional resources for the labour inspectorate was only one of a number of mechanisms by which national legislation could be more effectively enforced. In conclusion, they urged the Government to acknowledge the problems of forced labour that still existed and to establish, with the ILO, an information and awareness-raising campaign to sensitize all elements of the population to the issue, including those who were most susceptible of being victims.

The Worker members recalled that this Committee had been examining this case since 1982 and raised a question regarding the evolution of the situation in the past 25 years. Despite numerous references by the Committee of Experts to the issue of persons descended from former slaves who were obliged to work for a person who claimed the status of being their "master", and the persistence of this phenomenon described in the report by the organization SOS-Slavery, the Government had not yet provided a response on the concrete cases nor indicated whether investigations had been conducted in these particular cases. The Government continued to minimize, and even to deny, the forced labour practices and to present them, as for the direct contacts mission of 2004, as entirely exceptional and not more developed than in certain major cities in the industrialized world. It was paradoxical that the Government denied the existence of slave-like practices and at the same time pursued amendments of its legislation aimed at the prohibition of such practices, thus following the demands formulated by the Committee of Experts requesting the extension of the prohibition of forced labour to any labour relationship, the imposition of sanctions in conformity with the Convention, the repeal of provisions allowing the village chiefs to requisition labour and the establishment of a complete list of essential services in which such practice was authorized. In this regard, the Worker members noted with interest and satisfaction the adoption of the new Labour Code, which had extended the scope of prohibition of forced labour to any labour relationship, even where it was not derived from an employment contract, the introduction of penal sanctions under the Act of 2003 punishing trafficking in persons, the establishment of the complete list of essential services and the repeal of the text allowing the requisitioning of persons. They observed, however, that those legislative changes had not yet been followed by practical results, and that measures still had to be taken to make them operational. In fact, the application of the new laws was likely to create confusion in a situation where the principle of the prohibition of forced labour and the sanctions applicable in case of violation were provided for in the two different legislative texts. Besides, the Labour Code contained no reference to persons working at their former "master's" home and deprived of the freedom to move and to work anywhere else. As specified in the report of the direct contacts mission, the exercise of the right of appeal was therefore decisive. As it was explained in the report of SOS-Slavery, there was collusion between the "masters" and the judicial system. The "master's" descendants constituted the overwhelming majority of the leading class of the country, including the army administration, judicial staff and police forces. The direct contacts mission indicated that there was no labour law enforcement machinery because of the scarce resources allocated to the labour inspectorate. At the same time, strict application of economic, social and educational measures allowing for the reintegration and indemnification of the victims appeared necessary. The Worker members praised the legal progress achieved and wished that it were followed by practical results, and that the Government would be expressly requested to assume the obligations in regard to the integration in one and the same text of the provisions prohibiting forced labour and imposing sanctions, the preparation of detailed reports on the forced labour cases, competent jurisdictions and sanctions imposed, the organization of the information campaign on slavery, the elaboration of the social and economic action plan against poverty and the vestiges thereof, the ratification and application of Convention No. 144 on tripartite consultations and the guarantee of freedom of expression for trade unions and civil society. Besides, while having noted the success of the direct contacts mission, the Worker members proposed a new mission of this kind in order to assist the Government in putting its obligations into practice and to assess the needs for technical assistance. They stated that they would be happy to see slavery definitively eradicated before the 25th anniversary of the first examination of this case by this Committee.

A Worker member of Mauritania stated that significant progress had been made and that ILO technical assistance had accompanied that process. Forced labour was related to the problem of poverty and was a scourge that developing countries must fight against. The way that SOS-Slavery had presented the problem of slavery in Mauritania was biased; it was an exaggerated and sensational account. The speaker also refuted the statements alleging that there was no freedom of association in the country. Similarly, it was not possible to assert that freedom of movement was restricted in the country. The direct contacts mission had not been able to find any instances thereof.

Another Worker member of Mauritania stated that his country had once again been included in the list of cases because the Government continued to deny the existence of slavery, and yet slavery existed and was practised in all its forms. That year, three people, including one journalist, had been imprisoned for around two months, accused of having helped a slave escape from his masters. The case was still pending before the court. Such action demonstrated the severity of the practice. Thousands of people were kept as slaves, yet the Government's arguments always referred to measures taken to combat poverty or illiteracy. Such measures were not, however, of any benefit to slaves, given their position, since they were the property of their masters. Today, their freedom, emancipation and promotion must be secured by means of specific policies and awareness campaigns.

The provisions of the new Labour Code were confusing, very general, and did not form a suitable regulatory basis for dealing with cases of forced labour or slavery. Similarly, penalties were not imposed upon offenders, and no judgements had ever been made in favour of slaves, despite the number of complaints filed in connection with the practice of forced labour. All the above demonstrated the Government's lack of commitment to eradicating slavery and improving the conditions of victims with a view to their integration into the working society of the country.

The Government had recently recognized a number of trade union organizations and human rights associations, including SOS-Slavery. Although such action was courageous, the fundamental issue was that of the effective eradication of slavery through the adoption of specific measures. The Government should firstly acknowledge the existence of that phenomenon and reaffirm its commitment to taking economic, social and legal measures.

The speaker said that his organization, the CLTM, endorsed the recommendations of the ILO direct contacts mission, and assured the Government of its cooperation in eliminating the scourge in question, in the belief that the promotion of social dialogue and the creation of a permanent cooperation framework would be very positive in terms of human rights. Finally, he emphasized that the CLTM, his organization, was a trade union organization that was free and independent of political parties and the Government.

The Employer member of Mauritania said he was surprised to see Mauritania on the list of individual cases. Things had to be seen as they were; the case had to be tackled objectively and one should be wary of NGOs and political parties that used the situation to fulfil certain political objectives. Slavery no longer existed in Mauritania and the Government had set up appropriate structures to eradicate inequality and combat poverty. The information given by the Government was objective and true. Given the above, the speaker felt that Mauritania had been cited due to the valuable and substantial progress made.

The Worker member of the Central African Republic reminded those present at the meeting that despite the emergence of new forms of forced labour, one must not forget those forms which, although considered to be "old", were still very much in existence given the fact that the descendants of slaves were slaves today. Despite the uncertainty as to its scale, the phenomenon really existed, and subjected the many people affected in the various regions of the country to all types of incredible, but real, abuse. The information available did not clarify whether penalties for carrying out those practices were actually imposed, and there was no evidence of any conviction in that respect. The Government only provided very general responses. However, it formulated precise allegations against a trade union organization accused of using that issue for political means, contrary to the principle set forth in Convention No. 87 of non-interference in trade union activities aimed at defending workers' rights, including those of slaves, and therefore a solution should have been found in social dialogue and not in confrontation. The speaker observed that it was high time the Government provided precise statistics on the number of workers used as slaves, on the penalties imposed and on the practical reinsertion measures in place. In conclusion, the speaker recalled the need for proper dialogue on the issue of forced labour. The trade union organizations strongly hoped that such dialogue would very soon commence and that the Government would make efforts to ensure that, in its next report, the Committee of Experts would be able to note real progress in that area.

The Government member of France stated that it would be useful to know what this Committee still expected of the Mauritanian Government, which had received a direct contacts mission, as had been requested by the Committee in 2002 and 2003, and which had also put into effect the essence of the mission's recommendations.

The previous observations of the Committee of Experts concerned three points. Previously, forced labour was not sanctioned severely enough; the prevailing provisions in the Labour Code dealing with this matter assumed the existence of a labour contract, which was rare in cases of forced labour, and the sole penalties provided for were fines. The only means of applying heavier penalties was through other penal provisions. The Committee of Experts moreover criticized the too frequent use of the right to requisition staff and the extensive list of services considered as essential. On all of these points, the new legislation brought about considerable progress. The list of essential services had been revised, and more importantly, the new Labour Code had defined forced labour as a crime in itself, subject to ten years' imprisonment. It was necessary to continue to draw upon the ongoing work of the ILO and UNDP.

The case of Mauritania could turn out to be a case of progress in its legislative developments. But there also, the problem was the aftermath of slavery. Convention No. 29 could not solve the situations of poverty and cultural alienation experienced by the descendants of former slaves, even if they were free. The speaker stated that the ILO should develop better instruments to regulate the informal economy and to provide support for descendants of slaves with a view to ensuring their economic, social and cultural integration.

The Government member of Finland, speaking also on behalf of the Government members of Denmark, Iceland, Norway and Sweden, noted that while the Government appeared to consider the problem of slavery as marginal, the information sources cited in the Committee of Experts' report confirmed that slavery was a reality in Mauritania, the extent of which was unknown. She feared that the victims of this heinous practice were often vulnerable individuals belonging to economically weak groups, such as women and children. Nothing could justify slavery and it was a crime against the fundamental human right of personal freedom and integrity. It affected both individual dignity and psychological development and often led to deplorable social situations. She noted the Government's efforts in this matter, but it appeared that these measures had not been enough. She therefore requested the Government to give full effect in law and practice to the points raised by the Committee of Experts, to ensure that employers' and workers' organizations as well as NGOs were involved in this process, to avail itself of ILO technical assistance, and to provide a detailed reply to all questions raised in the report of the Committee of Experts.

The Government representative wished to answer certain questions that had been raised during the discussion. As regards the reference of the Employer members to the Ordinance of 1981, he explained that it had been adopted in the particular context of the adaptation of national legislation to Islamic law. The point was not to fill a legal void but to provide the moral authority for the prohibition of slavery as foreseen in the Labour Code.

As regards the definition of forced labour, reference should be made to Convention No. 29. Forced labour should not be confused with the problem of poverty. The existing legal gaps had been filled and if Mauritanians who lived in conditions of poverty and insecurity represented about 40 per cent of the population, not all of them were descendants of slaves. It was not easy to eradicate situations of poverty and vulnerability which resulted from social status, and the Government in recent years had proactively implemented a programme of action in economic, social and cultural domains that was especially aimed at descendents of slaves. It was not true that the Mauritanian Government had not or was not undertaking efforts or measures targeting descendants of slaves. For example, it had organized ambitious programmes in the cities, particularly to provide accommodation, as well as in rural areas. It was worth noting that descendants of slaves were represented at the management level in public office, the armed forces, the police, public service, etc.

Concerning the question of application of appropriate penalties provided in the legislation, all the courts were competent to examine cases and accordingly apply appropriate penalties. In this regard, the Government had been committed to provide precise and exhaustive information on the cases mentioned in the report of SOS-Slavery. Moreover, it had not been proved that these allegations were correct.

As for the necessity to strengthen labour inspection, Mauritania had indeed limited resources common to a developing country, and international assistance for the strengthening of labour inspection would be welcome.

The speaker was surprised that the Worker members had referred to the existing contradiction between legislation and national practice. The Committee of Experts in its comments had requested to change the legislation. These changes had been made and due to the amendments to the Labour Code, Mauritania now had effective legal provisions to deal with all situations of forced labour. At the same time, the Government had taken a number of measures to combat, in practice, the problem of poverty as well as in the areas of schooling, education and health. The Government has done its utmost despite the limited resources it disposed of as a less developed country. There was no proof that in Mauritania anyone was compelled to work.

As regards the sensitization campaign requested by a number of speakers, the Government representative considered that this campaign had already started with the assistance of the ILO within the framework of the action plan to promote human rights, which included important information, communication and education measures, and that had to be approved shortly by the Government. In addition, in the past few years five workshops had been organized on the issue of domestic work of girls.

Finally, as regards the imprisonment of a journalist, the speaker indicated that the facts mentioned were not accurate. The Government was ready to accept all the positive and constructive actions which might help to eliminate the existing shortcomings.

The Employer members thanked the Government representative for his reply to the discussion. They indicated that the conclusions should reflect the positive measures taken by the Government in connection with the amendment to the Labour Code that had extended the scope of the provision regarding the prohibition of forced labour. They noted that forced labour had been made an offence under the amended Labour Code, and that the penalties for this offence had been included in the Act regarding the trafficking of persons. The Employer members therefore noted the progress made by the Government in bringing its national legislation into compliance with the Convention. Nevertheless, they emphasized the need for additional information on the jurisdictions competent to receive complaints and on the penalties imposed under the Labour Code and the Act regarding the trafficking of persons, as had been requested by the Committee of Experts.

The Employer members observed that, in the face of conflicting information received from the Government, on the one hand, and from the workers' organizations, on the other hand, it was unclear how widespread the persistence of the problem of forced labour was. They considered that further research and investigation on the continued existence of forced labour and the magnitude of the problem was necessary, which could entail a direct contacts mission.

The Employer members expressed their very serious concern with the persistence of the allegations of forced labour and urged the Government to adopt the necessary measures to eradicate all practices of forced labour in all of its forms, placing particular emphasis on the enforcement of the national legislation, including the penalties for the exaction of forced labour. Referring also to the Committee of Experts' comments concerning the absence of an enforcement mechanism for labour legislations and the scarce resources allocated to the labour inspectorate, which had been noted by the direct contacts mission in 2004, the Employer members considered it necessary to reflect in the conclusions that the allocation of additional resources was only one of a number of mechanisms by which the legislation could be more effectively enforced. Finally, the Employer members urged the Government to institute, with the assistance of the ILO, an information and awareness-raising campaign to sensitize all elements of the population to the serious problem of forced labour.

The Worker members favourably welcomed the progress made in legislation and appreciated the contribution made by the direct contacts mission. They had hoped to examine the effects in practice and requested the Government to undertake a series of concrete legal steps, namely, the abrogation of the powers of village chiefs, the introduction of sanctions in the new Labour Code, and the provision of reports on cases brought before justice. They also asked for policy measures in the form of an information campaign aimed at the whole population, and a plan of action against poverty and the repercussions of slavery and to promote freedom for civil society. They also invited the Government to make international commitments, in particular, the ratification of Convention No. 144 on tripartite consultation. In a positive spirit, the Worker members proposed the organization of a new direct contacts mission in order to determine in a definitive manner whether or not slavery existed in Mauritania, and to put into effect the commitments and the technical cooperation mentioned earlier.

The Committee took note of the information given by the Government representative and the discussion that had ensued. The Committee recalled that the present case had been discussed in the same Committee in the past, notably in 2002 and 2003. In that regard, the Committee noted that the Government had accepted the visit of the direct contacts mission, which had taken place in May 2004. The Committee took note of all the information set out in the report of the Committee of Experts, in particular that concerning the new Labour Code, adopted in July 2004, which provided for the prohibition of forced labour – a prohibition that covered any type of work, even that not subject to an employment contract – and the imposition of penal sanctions.

The Committee took note of the information given by the Government representative concerning the adoption of the new Labour Code; the penalization of forced labour under the law prohibiting trafficking in persons; the adoption of the decree laying down the list of essential service establishments; the increase in the interprofessional minimum wage; the programmes to combat poverty, especially the technical cooperation programme devised in conjunction with the ILO for the promotion of the ILO Declaration on Fundamental Principles and Rights at Work; and the creation of an inter-ministerial structure which aimed to make those responsible more aware of the application of labour standards, including those on forced labour. The Committee also took note of the statement by the Government representative concerning the recognition of human rights associations involved in activities that focused on issues related to forced labour.

The Committee indicated with some concern that in its report the direct contacts mission referred to allegations, made by certain workers' organizations, that some forced labour practices continued to exist – practices that were the vestiges of legally abolished slavery.

The Committee noted the Committee of Experts' concern about the possible effects, in practice, of the fact that the general prohibition on forced labour was provided for in the Labour Code, while penalties were provided for in a specific law punishing another crime, namely the law prohibiting trafficking of persons of 2003.

The Committee trusted that the legislative measures adopted would produce rapid practical results that would bring an end to the vestiges of slavery and that the Government would be able to provide information on legal actions taken in various jurisdictions, by virtue of section 5 of the Labour Code, and on the penalties imposed.

The Committee, having noted the progress made by the Government in the field of legislation, invited it to submit an exhaustive and detailed report that:

(1) responded to all the comments made by the Committee of Experts;

(2) contained full information on the competent jurisdictions to receive complaints and the penalties imposed;

(3) contained all elements relating to the awareness campaign;

(4) provided information on the consultations held with the social partners.

The Committee invited the Government to continue to avail itself to the technical cooperation of the ILO and other donors, which should include an awareness campaign on forced labour.

The Committee, having taken into account the conflicting information on the persistence of the practices of forced labour and slavery, decided that the Office undertake a fact-finding mission. That mission should review the effective application of national legislation.

(MYANMAR (ratification: 1955). See Part Three.)

SUDAN (ratification: 1957). **A Government representative** stated that he was the Chairperson of the Committee for the Eradication of Abduction of Women and Children (CEAWC), which reported to the Presidency of the Republic and thus in a position to report on the details of the case. He was pleased to report that the CEAWC was dealing with 14,000 reported abduction cases, of which 11,000 had been successfully resolved through laborious documentation, tracing, retrieval, and reunification measures. Over US$3 million had been spent on these efforts, two-thirds of which the Sudanese Government had provided in the period from March 2004 to March 2005, due to the slow flow of donor funds. The Government had committed to funding the resolution of the remaining 3,000 abduction cases, of which many were not abduction cases in the strict sense, as the persons affected, with the knowledge of international agencies, had requested not to be transferred back to their place of origin. The cooperation of the CEAWC with the Dinka Chiefs Committee (DCC) underlined the peace-building perspective of the work of CEAWC.

Because of government funding, the CEAWC had been able to process more than 7,500 cases last year alone. This showed that Sudan was serious about addressing the problem of abductions. Indeed, these efforts had been recognized by the international community, such as in the 61st Session of the United Nations Commission on Humans Rights, which had adopted a resolution (E/CN.4/RES/2005/82) welcoming the efforts of the Government of Sudan to combat the abduction of persons, in particular the work of the CEAWC, and the Deputy Special Representative of the UN Secretary-General for Sudan, who in a letter of 11 May 2005 had noted that many abducted persons had returned home.

With regard to the comment of the ICFTU contesting the position that the Government had taken at the 2004 session of the ILC, namely that all abductions in Sudan had stopped, the Government representative reconfirmed that indeed all abductions had ceased. He noted that the Dinka Chiefs Committee (DCC), which had been a major complainant in the abduction cases, was now an integral part of the CEAWC (four out of the six top positions were held by Dinka) and could testify to the fact that the abductions had stopped.

On the one hand, the UN Commission on Human Rights had in many of its resolutions endorsed CEAWC course of action in not pressing penal sanctions, as long as abductors were cooperating with CEAWC. For example, resolution No. 2002/16 referred to «bringing to justice the perpetrators who are not wishing to cooperate».

In view of the above progress, the case of Sudan should not have appeared on this Committee's list and should be considered closed. If not, this Committee would face the unprecedented situation of pursuing a case in which the local communities affected and the concerned UN organizations had noted progress.

Another Government representative (Minister of Labour and Administrative Reform) pointed out that the progress that had been made could not have been possible without the participation of the tribal groups concerned – the Dinka, the Messiria, the Rezigat and others. He regretted that the Committee of Experts' report was based on old and erroneous information, and he was surprised that the case had resurfaced after it had been shelved the previous year. Moreover, he pointed out that the United Nations agencies referred to the problem of abductions, whereas this Committee spoke of slavery, a term his Government totally rejected.

He announced that the Government and the Sudanese People's Liberation Movement (SPLM) had ended the conflict in the Southern Sudan, Blue Nile and Nuba Mountain regions, which was the underlying cause of the abductions. The historic agreement signed by the Government and the SPLM on 9 January 2005 in Nairobi would seal this peace. A constitutional commission had been established to draft an interim Constitution, which would go to Parliament and the National Liberation Council of the SPLM for endorsement next week. The interim Constitution would include a bill of rights banning slavery. He thanked the participants of a recent donors' conference in Norway, in particular Norway and the EU Member States, the United States, and the African and Arab countries, for their support of the peace process. Next year, the Sudanese ILO delegation would include SPLM members.

In light of the above, he called for the case to be closed. He reminded the Committee that his delegation was against a direct contacts mission and would reject any proposal to establish one. He also stated that any attempt to link this case with the situation in the Darfur region was unacceptable, as that particular case had a different dimension and was being addressed by the Government, the United Nations and the African Union. He voiced his concern about members that tried to use this weak case for their own political reasons. There was a need for this Committee to review its functions so as to prevent a double standard. The ILO should concentrate on the positive developments in the case and provide technical assistance, especially in the areas of demobilization and resettlement of refugees and displaced persons.

The Worker members regretted that the Committee had to examine once again the application of Convention No. 29 by Sudan. During the last session of the Conference, the Committee expressed its deep concern with the continuing reports of abductions and forced labour practices and requested the Government to take effective and quick measures to bring to an end these practices. The Worker members noted both the positive and negative elements in the Committee of Experts' observation following the Government's report submitted in October 2004, as well as the comments transmitted by the international bodies, international workers' organizations and NGOs. After the conclusion of the three peace protocols in May 2004, one of which contained provisions concerning human rights and the rights of the child, and the liberation of more than 1,000 abducted persons, they praised the conclusion this year of a comprehensive peace agreement in the North-South conflict. Unfortunately, these developments did not bring a solution to the grave problems of the application of Convention No. 29.

According to the Government, abductions had been stopped completely. Indeed, the Committee for the Eradication of Abduction of Women and Children (CEAWC) had not registered new cases of abductions for two years. However, this fact was not entirely convincing, since the CEAWC had no capacity to collect information and to conduct investigations. For the Darfur region, in particular, all the available reports issued either by the NGOs or by the international bodies, including the latest report of the United Nations International Commission of Inquiry on Darfur, revealed numerous cases of abductions and sex slavery. The Commission of Inquiry assumed, in particular, that cases of rape and other forms of sexual violence were committed on a large scale in Darfur by the Janjaweed militia and by the regular army soldiers.

The CEAWC recognized that 14,000 persons had been abducted. It provided assistance in the retrieval of 2,628 victims between 1999 and May 2004. Thus, about 10,000 abducted persons were still waiting to be identified and reunited with their families. However, according to the information communicated by UNICEF, the retrieval operations by the CEAWC had been suspended since March 2005.

Besides, the Government had been requested on many occasions to ensure that the appropriate penal sanctions were effectively applied to perpetrators. The CEAWC confirmed that the best way to eradicate the abductions was to institute legal proceedings. During the last session of the Conference, the Minister of Labour stated before this Committee that the Government provided for financial means allowing the CEAWC to resort to legal action, while making it clear that these procedures were too long and susceptible of becoming harmful to the victims themselves. Today, the first legal action against those responsible for abductions was still awaited. The Government should at least accelerate the judicial procedures and ensure better protection for the victims.

The Worker members observed that the Government reiterated all the time its condemnation of all forms of slavery and confirmed its commitment to cooperate with the international organizations to eradicate the phenomenon of abductions. Consequently, they once again proposed a direct contacts mission in order to assess the real situation on the spot and to evaluate the country's needs in technical assistance, even if they noted from the statement of the Government representative that the Government would not accept such a proposal.

The Employer members expressed their surprise that the Government appeared defensive in this case; they thought they would welcome the opportunity to provide information which was not available to the Committee and to highlight the positive developments in the matter. They recalled that Convention No. 29 required each ratifying member State to undertake to suppress the use of forced or compulsory labour in all its forms within the shortest possible period, and that for the purposes of this Convention the term "forced or compulsory labour" should mean all work or service which was exacted from any person under the menace of any penalty and for which the said person had not offered himself voluntarily. They noted that the Government had not stated that forced labour had been abolished. The fact that there were 3,500 cases remedied in the past year indicated that there was still a problem, which was not likely to disappear very soon. This made it difficult to agree with the Government's position that the case was closed.

There was not enough information available to evaluate if abductions had indeed ceased in the Sudan. The Government had mentioned that it had submitted a report to the ILO, but the Employer members were not aware of any document submitted to the Committee, as was the usual practice. As a result the Government should ensure that any relevant information was submitted to the Committee of Experts.

The Employer members were also surprised by the total rejection of a direct contacts mission, especially in light of recent developments in the Sudan. The peace agreement and opening of society would appear to call for greater engagement with the ILO. Such a mission would allow for a greater understanding of the details of prosecutions of cases of abductions. In conclusion, the Employer members agreed that there had been some tangible positive steps in this case. However, much of the information was unverifiable, so it was not possible to say that forced labour had been abolished in the country.

The Worker member of Sudan stated that the accusations of slavery and forced labour were not just an insult to the Government but to the Sudanese people and trade unions who, he recalled, had overthrown two military governments through popular uprisings and strikes. The case had been first discussed in 1984 following the publication of a book by two Sudanese scholars. The Government had always maintained that the main reason behind abductions was the 50-year civil war which had recently ended. After discussions with the international community, the CEAWC was established with international financial support which had not yet been received. Nevertheless, with its own meagre resources, the Government had resolved 75 per cent of the cases of abductions and had, through tedious negotiations, concluded a peace accord. Yet, none of these positive developments was reflected in the report of the Committee of Experts, even though they were commended by the UN Commission on Human Rights. This case was being inappropriately linked to the Darfur situation, which was miserable but which would be overcome without foreign intervention. The Committee should seek to make available the technical assistance that had been mentioned in the conclusions of this case last year. It was time for this Committee to steer away from political issues and concentrate on the application of international labour standards, an important issue for workers in Africa and the underdeveloped South.

The Employer member of Sudan emphasized that Sudan had made progress but the Committee of Experts had not noted this in its report. He cited, in particular, the conclusion of a global peace accord which included, at the same time, the drafting of an interim Constitution guaranteeing human rights and commitment to the revision of national laws with a view to ensuring their conformity with the peace agreement and the interim Constitution. Social dialogue had been strengthened in Sudan and had become an essential instrument in dealing with important issues facing the country. The international community appreciated and encouraged this progress.

The speaker stated that the abductions were linked to the civil war. Thanks to the peace agreement, these had ceased and several hundreds of people had been returned to their place of origin. But new challenges appeared on the horizon concerning the creation of opportunities for decent work, and guarantees of the rights of the child and human rights. He hoped that the Committee would take note of these developments with a view to supporting them and he invited the ILO to provide Sudan with the assistance necessary to reinforce trade union organizations and to promote social dialogue.

The Government member of Luxembourg, speaking on behalf of the European Union, as well as of Albania, Bosnia and Herzegovina, Bulgaria, Canada, Croatia, Norway, Romania, Serbia and Montenegro, Switzerland, The former Yugoslav Republic of Macedonia, Turkey and Ukraine, expressed the European Union's grave concern with the situation that was the subject of the Committee of Experts' observations and strongly condemned the continuing slave-like practices of abduction, trafficking and forced labour in Sudan, which impacted especially on women and children. The speaker also noted with deep concern the convergence of allegations and a broad consensus among the United Nations bodies, the representative organizations of workers and non-governmental organizations concerning the continuing existence and scope of the practices of abduction and the exaction of forced labour, which constituted a gross violation of Convention No. 29, since victims were forced to perform work for which they had not offered themselves voluntarily, under extremely harsh conditions and combined with ill-treatment which might include torture and death.

The speaker recalled that, in 2004, this Committee invited the Government to take effective and quick measures to punish those responsible for the violations. She urged the Government to take the necessary measures to ensure that legal proceedings were instituted against perpetrators and penal sanctions were imposed, thus putting an end to impunity, which should be a high priority.

The speaker pointed out that the European Union was committed to supporting the restoration of peace and development in Sudan and backed the efforts undertaken by the African Union in this regard. The European Union welcomed the Comprehensive Peace Agreement (CPA) signed in January 2005 in the North-South conflict, but remained deeply concerned about the continuing violence against the civilian population in Darfur. She expressed the hope that the upcoming peace talks in Abuja would be successful, and that the full implementation of the CPA would be achieved and positive developments in the crisis in Darfur would take place. Given the gravity of the situation, she urged the Government to take immediate and effective action to eradicate all forms of forced labour.

The Government member of Nigeria expressed her dissatisfaction with the mode of the selection of individual cases and pointed out that the original list of individual cases had been altered to the disadvantage of the African region.

A point of order was raised by the Worker member of France.

The Chairperson ruled on the motion by calling on the speaker to stick to the point of the discussion.

The Government member of Nigeria continued by stating that Sudan had been going through the throes of war, which had been of great concern to the African region, and she considered the Sudanese case to be the result of the conflict. She was happy to note that the situation had been brought to an end. Referring to the information provided by the Government representative to the Committee concerning the activities of the CEAWC, the speaker observed that international organizations like UNICEF had provided some assistance in order to complement the Government's efforts in this area and had acknowledged these efforts. She suggested that, since the war had come to an end and the Government had shown convincing evidence of its commitment to eliminate abductions, this Committee should reconsider its stand on the case. She also recommended to remove this case from the list of individual cases and to provide assistance to the Government to effectively deal with the matter.

The Worker member of Cuba stated that the report of the Committee of Experts highlighted the complexity of the case of Sudan. There was no doubt as to the gravity of the situation described, although references to its causes were few. Meanwhile, as acknowledged by the Committee, the Government had taken positive steps and renewed its commitment to resolving the problem of forced labour. Efforts should be made to understand the enormous challenges faced by the Government in effectively carrying out its responsibilities. Recently, there had been news of a peace agreement in an armed conflict that had affected the country since 1955. The peace agreement would undoubtedly play an important part in the future development of the country, yet a significant amount of time and effort would be needed before it produced successful results in practice.

For all the aforementioned reasons, the speaker requested that the Committee recommend the provision of technical cooperation from the ILO and the international community, in order to enable the Sudanese Government to make greater progress in resolving the problems identified in the present forum – problems that it had to commit itself to dealing with. It was important to take into account that the war had ended, which meant that there would be a favourable climate for the normal application of laws and for the improved fulfilment of the Government's obligations. The present Committee should also be careful to take into consideration the information provided by the Sudanese Worker member, the progress made to date, and the renewed commitments of the Government. The speaker hoped that legislation in Sudan would be rigorously applied, ensuring full compliance with Convention No. 29.

The Government member of South Africa noted that a number of international organizations and governments had taken it upon themselves to ensure that the Government and the people of Sudan were given much-needed support. He pointed out that in situations where war, poverty and suffering reigned, ILO Conventions would remain very hard to implement. However, it appeared that the Government had made great progress. The speaker called upon governments and organizations from all over the world to respond positively to the appeal of the Sudanese Government on behalf of the Sudanese people. He pointed out that, in this spirit, ILO technical assistance would play a very important role in addressing the current issue and emphasized the importance of dialogue.

The Worker member of Brazil said that she had read very carefully the report of the Committee on Experts and the report on the field activities of the Committee for the Eradication of Abduction of Women and Children, which had managed to resolve 75 per cent of cases. She had also read the report by the Government of Sudan, which highlighted the Government's efforts to retrieve abducted persons and bring an end to the phenomenon of abduction in the region of conflict. Moreover, she had studied with special attention the observations of the ICFTU based on the reports of the US Department of State.

The speaker felt that the present Committee should ask itself why it had insisted, for 16 consecutive years, on bringing Sudan before the Committee, why it had tried to impose sanctions on Sudan on the pretext of forced labour, when all those present at the meeting knew that there was a civil war in the south of the country and that the Government, following the protocols, had signed a peace agreement in January of that year. The Committee should also ask itself what the real technical reason was for saying that there was forced labour in a region when what really existed there was war. The answer to those questions was very simple and was well illustrated in the account published in the United States press by a member of the United States mission to Sudan – an account that clearly highlighted the existence of vast oil reserves in southern Sudan and in the region of south Darfur. That, and that alone, was why the US Department of State was really interested in imposing sanctions on Sudan, thus justifying other well-known serious consequences, and also explained the continued existence of armed conflict in the region.

Consequently, the speaker ended her statement by urging the Committee not to commit any further acts of injustice against a long-suffering African country that had been exploited and punished by war. While acts of injustice were repeatedly committed against certain countries by imposing sanctions, the superpowers not only enslaved other nations, but also promoted war and military occupation in order to take away their wealth.

The Worker member of the Libyan Arab Jamahiriya stated that trade union organizations, such as the Trade Union Confederation of Coastal and Saharan Countries and the Organization of African Trade Union Unity, regularly visited Sudan and were therefore more familiar with the realities of the country. The civil war had lasted more than 50 years and he was pleased with the peace accord that had been signed at the beginning of this year as well as with the will shown by the Government to ensure stability in the country. The report of the Government indicated that abductions had ceased and that the Government was ready to examine previous cases, a development which deserved support and encouragement so that the Government could maintain the process of peace and stability which it had begun.

In conclusion, he stated that the Committee, because it was neutral and just, should appreciate the efforts made by the Government of Sudan and provide it with the necessary support instead of systematically placing it on the list of individual cases as had been done in the past 16 years.

The Government member of Egypt pointed out that according to reports of certain international organizations, the efforts made by Sudan had borne fruit. Despite economic problems and geographic challenges, Sudan manifested a political will to combat the scourge of forced labour through the CEAWC. She stated that donor countries had contributed to the financing of CEAWC projects and she invited the Office to provide the Government with technical assistance to overcome further difficulties.

In conclusion, she underlined that Sudan had made progress and she hoped that the donor countries would increase their aid so that this country could fight forced labour even better. She invited the Committee to take note of the efforts made by Sudan in light of the particular conditions it faced.

The Worker member of Senegal noted that the case of the violation of Convention No. 29 by Sudan was again before the Committee and that the information contained in the report of the Committee of Experts contested statements made by the Government. This Committee should therefore objectively evaluate the facts. Indeed corroborating sources, notably the report of the United Nations International Commission of Inquiry on Darfur of 2005, indicated that the practice of abductions, trafficking, forced labour and sexual slavery affected thousands of women and children in the regions where there was armed conflict. Despite the commitment by the CEAWC to prosecute those responsible and the funds that had been attributed towards this goal, no legal action had been undertaken against perpetrators. The efforts of the Government in this regard were spotty. Slavery continued to be a reality in Sudan where thousands of people still awaited their liberation and where new abductions still took place. While the global peace accord signed by the Government and the SPLM in January 2005 was a positive development and contributed to a new environment, it would not automatically lead to the end of abductions and violations of human rights, as the events in Darfur had shown. Thus while different perspectives persisted, standards had to continue to apply and this Committee had to remain loyal to its values no matter what happened. A refusal to accept a mission by the ILO signified that the Government refused to cooperate, and the Committee should thus maintain the course, even if this might not please all.

The Government member of the Libyan Arab Jamahiriya stated that thanks to projects which the Government of Sudan had implemented with the international community, the Government had succeeded in resolving several hundreds of cases of abductions and forced labour. He recalled that these efforts had been recognized by the Commission on Human Rights in April 2005, but in contrast, they had not been mentioned in the report of the Committee of Experts. In view of this progress, he requested that Sudan be removed from the list of individual cases.

The Government member of Cuba said that the peace efforts that had been made with the support and participation of a regional mechanism, had made it possible to entertain the hope that the prolonged conflict which had caused the people of Sudan unspeakable suffering, including the types of violations referred to in the Committee of Experts' report, would be brought to an end. The peace agreements should facilitate the establishment of a government of national unity, under which it would be the responsibility of all parties to jointly guarantee an end to all forced labour practices. This opportunity to be in control of the situation should encourage the implementation of legislative, administrative and penal measures to put an end to the impunity of those guilty of such acts. The eradication of all forms of forced labour and the promotion and dissemination of international labour standards would not only justify the existence of the ILO, but would contribute greatly to the consolidation of peace and national reconstruction in a prosperous society. The ILO should be ready to respond positively to the request for technical assistance for the adoption of new legislation and other measures.

The Government member of the Syrian Arab Republic stated that Sudan had experienced a civil war that had lasted for over half a century and had devastated the country, in particular economically and socially. Despite this difficult situation, the Government had made considerable efforts to establish peace and stability in the country, which would result in the economic and social stability that was necessary to improve conditions of work. Taking into account, in particular, the Government's efforts to apply international labour standards and to remedy the situations caused by the war, he hoped that the ILO would provide his country with the material and technical assistance necessary to help to overcome the difficulties that it was facing.

The Government representative was pleased to hear from all the comments made that the elements presented in his report to the Conference Committee had been generally accepted. However, one correction should be made with regard to certain figures mentioned during the discussion. The true figures were 3,500 and 7,500 abducted persons who the CEAWC had been able to retrieve and who had rejoined their families. These figures did not refer to prosecutions of those responsible for the abductions. Since the commencement of the activities of the CEAWC in 1999, and following the cessation of hostilities, the total of 11,000 abducted persons had been retrieved and some were reunited with their families.

He stated that he did not wish to make any comments on the allegations made by some of the Worker members. Many United Nations agencies had visited Darfur and had confirmed the situation as explained by the Government. They had agreed that the CEAWC was effective in dealing with the matter. Nevertheless, he believed that Darfur was of no relevance to the case that was being discussed by the Committee.

He affirmed that, with respect to the measures taken concerning abductions, his Government would continue to use traditional methods, such as tribal conciliation meetings, rather than undertaking legal action to prosecute those responsible for the abductions. This was the wish of the tribes and the Dinka Chiefs Committee. He added that even the United Nations had accepted this approach.

In conclusion, he emphasized that there was no forced labour in his country, although abductions had occurred. Those who had been abducted had stayed with their abductors until payments were made and arrangements were made for their reunification with their families. However, he insisted that the case was now closed as there were no more abductions. In view of the formation of a government of national unity, including those who were previously opponents, it was necessary to focus on development and recovery.

The Worker members said that the discussion on the case of Sudan had been marked by great differences of opinion between the members of the Committee, and even within the Workers' group. In this respect, they indicated that the ICFTU and WCL delegates disassociated themselves from the views expressed by some of their Worker colleagues. Diverging views and ideologies had always been respected in the Workers' group. It was, therefore, necessary for this rule to be respected by all and for all official reports describing certain undeniable facts to be taken into consideration. It was important to remember that tripartism, the underlying principle of the ILO, was based on free thinking and independence of opinion.

The Worker members proposed that a direct contacts mission should visit the country to obtain more information on the current situation and thereby clear up any misunderstandings. Such a mission could assess the need for technical assistance. They called on the Government to organize such a mission, which would also reinforce its position. Nevertheless, in the event that the Government did not accept a direct contacts mission, the Committee would be bound to adopt strong conclusions, which would have to describe this as a case of continued failure. They also requested that the case be included in a special paragraph of the Committee's report.

The Employer members said that of all the cases examined by the Committee, this was one of the most serious and had been examined on many occasions. The real question was whether forced labour had been abolished in practice in the country. Clearly, while the Government was making some effort, as it had indicated to the Committee, the measures taken needed to be reinforced.

The Employer members wished to recall that the work of the Conference Committee needed to be based essentially on facts rather than representations. Moreover, they recalled that in long-standing cases, such as the present one, it was not at all unusual for the conditions prevailing in a country to be the subject of independent verification. Indeed, if the Government wanted this case to be closed, as it claimed, it should welcome such independent verification. If other United Nations agencies were visiting the country, the ILO should be able to do so too.

They nevertheless expressed the belief that a certain sensitivity was required in a case in which there had been a certain amount of progress over the past two years. The progress made should be recognized and the financial and other support provided by the international community should be reinforced. As they imagined that the Government representative had no authority to do anything other than reject a proposal for a direct contacts mission, an effort could be made to find an alternative solution. Sudan was, after all, a poor war-scarred developing country. The Government should be requested to provide a detailed report containing full and specific information on all the matters raised by the Committee of Experts. The ILO should also enter into discussions with the Government with a view to the establishment of a credible fact-finding process. If the Government believed that the case was closed, it should be prepared to demonstrate that it was closed. However, they indicated that if the Government was not prepared to agree to a fact-finding exercise this year, the attitude of the Employer members would change next year.

The Committee took note of the information supplied by the Government and of the discussion which ensued. The Committee noted that this case had been discussed in this Committee over a period of years. The Committee noted the report of the Committee of Experts that the situations concerned constituted gross violations of the Convention, since the victims were forced to perform work for which they had not offered themselves voluntarily, under extremely harsh conditions and combined with ill-treatment which might include torture and death.

The Committee took note of the information provided by the Government according to which it had dealt through traditional means with 11,000 out of the 14,000 cases of abduction which had cost more than 3 million dollars, two-thirds of which was contributed to by the Government. The Government further indicated that over the last 12 months about 7,500 persons were retrieved compared with 3,500 from 1999 to 2004. The Government referred to the end of the civil war and the fact that the practice of abduction no longer existed. The Government requested technical assistance in the area of demobilization and reinsertion.

The Committee observed the convergence of allegations and the broad consensus among the United Nations bodies, the representative organizations of workers and non-governmental organizations concerning the continuing existence and scope of the practices of abduction and the exaction of forced labour.

The Committee noted that while there had been positive and tangible steps, including the conclusion of the Comprehensive Peace Agreement, it was of the view that there was no verifiable evidence that forced labour had been abolished.

The Committee invited the Government to avail itself of the technical assistance of the ILO and other donors to enable it to eradicate the practices identified by the Committee of Experts and to bring the perpetrators to justice.

The Committee considered that only an independent verification of the situation in the country would enable it to determine that forced labour in the country had ended. The Committee therefore decided that, in the framework of the ILO technical assistance, a full investigation of the facts be undertaken and requested the Government to provide the ILO with all the necessary assistance.

The Committee requested the Government to provide detailed information on all the issues on an urgent basis in its next report to the Committee of Experts and expressed the firm hope that the full application of the Convention, in law and in practice, could be noted in the near future.

C. 77

Convention No. 77: Medical Examination of Young Persons (Industry) Convention, 1946 and Convention No. 78: Medical Examination of Young Persons (Non-Industrial Occupations) Convention, 1946

ECUADOR (ratification: 1975). **A Government representative** (Minister for Labour and Employment) stated that his Government's presence at the Committee was an indication of its keen interest in ensuring compliance with the Conventions. The current constitutional Government wanted to resolve the problems deriving from the application of ILO standards, which had existed for a number of years. Indeed, as a demonstration of its desire to address that situation, another Government representative was also in attendance at the present Committee.

Another Government representative stated that, as a member of the National Congress and chairman of the Labour and Social Committee, he was extremely interested and very much predisposed to bring Ecuadorian legislation into conformity with the content of the international labour Conventions. A Labour Code reform bill had been drafted, based upon the observations of the Committee of Experts for Conventions Nos. 77 and 78. The legislative bill defined "industrial undertakings" and "non-industrial undertakings" and determined the obligatory nature of the medical examination of young persons, the periodicity of such examinations until the age of 21, and the carrying out of those examinations free of charge. The Health and Hygiene Unit of the Ministry of Labour and Employment was authorized to issue the medical certificates and could also suggest physical and professional rehabilitation measures in the event that the examinations revealed any disability. The new legislation required that employers kept the original certificates so that they could be made available to labour inspectors. Labour inspectors had to carry out the necessary visits to verify compliance with the standards. Copies of the documents pending before the National Congress in relation to the aforementioned Labour Code reform bill had been submitted to the Office.

As regards the work of young persons, and within the framework of the fight against child labour, another Labour Code reform bill had been introduced in order to ensure a minimum working age of 15, the limit of the working day, maximum loads carried, bans on working in certain activities in case of violation of the labour rights of young people, and the corresponding administrative and legal claims required under the international labour Conventions. Copies of the documents pending before the National Congress in that respect had also been submitted to the Office.

The Employer members noted that this case had been identified with a footnote by the Committee of Experts, indicating that they had lost patience with the Government of Ecuador. They recalled that the purpose of Conventions Nos. 77 and 78 was to prevent the employment of children and young persons under the age of 18 unless they had been found fit through medical examination for the employment in question, in industrial undertakings and in non-industrial occupations respectively. These instruments were clearly important for the protection of children.

They recalled that since Ecuador had ratified the Conventions 29 years ago, it had not adopted legislation to give effect to them. The Committee of Experts had made previous requests for legislative measures to be taken in 1995 and 2001. A Labour Code had been adopted in 1997 which prohibited the employment of young persons under the age of 18 in industries or occupations deemed to be dangerous. In 2002, the Committee of Experts had commented on the Government's stated intention to introduce regulations which would reflect the definition of "industrial undertakings", as set out by Conventions Nos. 77 and 78. This year's report provided no indication if this had happened. In 2003, the Committee of Experts had pointed out that, while recognizing the Government's efforts to give effect to Conventions Nos. 138 and 182, such steps did not necessarily address the issues raised by Conventions Nos. 77 and 78. There was no indication in this year's report that the Government had responded to the detailed requests for information made by the Committee of Experts in 2002 and 2003.

It was no doubt worrying that no progress had been made in this case for so long, and it revealed the need for this Committee to consider a broader range of Conventions. Technical cases like this one were important and deserved regular consideration. The Employer members emphasized that the failure to implement the Conventions and to provide information meant that this Committee could not assess how serious the problem of young persons working in industrial undertakings actually was. They were interested to know if there were any practical measures in place addressing this matter, especially in the informal sector, despite the lack of legislation. They also hoped that the Experts would consider what steps, if any, labour inspectors should take in view of Article 7 of both instruments, which required employers to file and keep available to labour inspectors either the medical certificate for fitness for employment or the work permit or workbook showing that there were no medical objections to the employment as may be prescribed by national laws or regulations. They also wished to receive more information on the situation on the ground, especially in the informal economy. Finally, they wished to know if the Experts had considered this case in light of the fact that in Ecuador's legal system, ILO Conventions were directly applicable as law, an element which might shift the focus of the case to more practical questions.

In conclusion, the Employer members stated that the Committee should assess whether or not the Government of Ecuador had supplied the requested full particulars to this year's Conference. The information supplied by the Government today was welcome, but its late arrival caused problems for the effective and transparent tripartite discussion in this Committee. They hoped to have the benefit of the Government's information in the next report of the Committee of Experts.

The Worker members indicated that they had been very careful and patient, perhaps too much so, in respect of the violations of Conventions Nos. 77 and 78, which Ecuador had ratified 30 years ago. It was pitiful that, after all this time, there had been no step forward. The topic of the violation of the respect for health and safety at work was of concern, especially when talking about the health and quality of life of workers, and this subject was all the more serious when it concerned young workers.

The Worker members emphasized that in Ecuador and in the majority of Latin American countries, every day large contingents of children entered the labour market in risky jobs and receiving wages much lower than those of ordinary workers. The number of child workers in Ecuador was impressive. Some estimates referred to 1,200,000 child workers. In view of such figures, it was crucial that the Government adopt urgent measures to conform to the Conventions under discussion. Common sense dictated that it was logical to perform a medical examination on children before they began work, and during and after a job as well. In this sense, section 141 of the Labour Code of 1997 required medical examinations of persons under 21 years of age who worked in mines or quarries.

In spite of the observations of the Committee of Experts over all these years, the Government of Ecuador, or successive governments, had not taken note of these comments, without explaining why there were requirements for medical examinations for certain jobs and not others. Without doubting the good intentions of the Government representatives, the Worker members wanted more precise information with regard to the timeframe in which legislation that would deal with this shameful situation would come into force. The Government should be more concrete and present detailed information on its draft legislation, in addition to seeking the technical advice of the ILO.

The Worker member of Ecuador expressed his concern at the outrage provoked by the Government of Ecuador and the 29-year delay in taking legislative action to give effect to the provisions of the Conventions. This situation put at risk the health and life of the workers, who lacked coverage by any legal instrument implementing the objectives of the Convention and were subject to employers who were not really obliged to respect it, even though there was partial legislation such as the Labour Code and the Children and Young Person's Code which governed certain activities.

With respect to Article 1(3) of Convention No. 77, he stated that if the competent authority defined the line of division which separated industry from agriculture on one hand, and commerce and other non-industrial occupations on the other, it was clear that after 49 years of existence, a revision of the Convention and/or a revision of legislation was necessary, in view of the fact that the agricultural sector underwent a permanent evolution toward large agro-industrial enterprises, which appeared and created great risks in developing countries which did not make the health of workers a priority but rather focused on reducing production costs. For example, in Ecuador, the banana and flower industry reached important production levels for export, and, as a consequence, the workforce found itself without protection, because the majority of workers were youths, in many cases children, who were not subject to medical examinations either before or after recruitment. Moreover, because of the growing poverty in the country, around 1,200,000 children worked, which, when compared to the 900,000 persons working in the formal sector, indicated that more children worked than adults.

The speaker stated that there was neither the political will nor the resources necessary to provide protection for workers. Indeed, there were technical and scientific studies which demonstrated the serious health problems from which workers suffered, such as skin cancer and respiratory and pulmonary ailments. Indiscriminate fumigation and the lack of control over the use of chemicals engendered congenital deformations, not only in workers, but also on bordering plantations and populations. The use of discarded plastic materials sprayed with chemicals by workers was an irresponsible act against workers and their families. Therefore, the responsibility of the State in the protection of the health of workers was large, and it should provide for the examination of workers before entering employment in order to prevent chronic illnesses and to protect public health. This situation was all the more difficult to control given that almost all banana and flower plantations used contract labour or hourly workers, with a high incidence of minors, and which did not allow trade union activity so as to exercise more control. At the slightest indication of organizing a trade union, workers were fired or subject to intimidation. For example, on the property of the greatest banana exporter in Ecuador, criminal acts had been perpetrated against workers for the sole reason of having wanted to organize.

To conclude, the speaker expressed his confidence that the current Government would adopt all measures necessary to apply the two Conventions in question, and make amendments where necessary, in the briefest time possible, so as to conform to the standards ratified by Ecuador.

The **Employer member of Ecuador** said it was worrying that his country had not incorporated the content of Conventions Nos. 77 and 78 into its legislation, despite having ratified them a long time ago. Conventions were not only to be adopted and signed, they should also be complied with. He made it clear that the assertion that the formal sector in Ecuador mistreated child workers was not true. Employers in the formal economy contracted workers of statutory age, who joined companies in full possession of their rights. He regretted that Ecuador had not submitted information on those Conventions to the Committee of Experts. Employers would be vigilant to ensure that the ILO Conventions were incorporated into the legislation of their country. Ratified Conventions had to be observed in practice.

A **Government representative** (Minister for Labour and Employment) stated that the fact that the current Government of his country had come to power only three weeks ago did not relieve it of the responsibility to ensure compliance with ILO Conventions. He wished to express his Government's keen interest in incorporating the content of international labour standards into Ecuadorian legislation. It might have seemed as if Ecuador lacked the authority and the legislation to ensure the respect of the most fundamental human rights. He pointed out that such an assumption was a grave misunderstanding, since Ecuador had specific regulations on the protection of human rights, within a constitutional framework that monitored the observance of those regulations. Human rights and the protection thereof were not the responsibility of one State, but the entire international community. There were regulations covering pre-employment, periodic and retirement medical examinations, as well as those assessing aptitude for work. There were basic standards, like Convention No. 182, the Children and Young Persons Code, the Labour Code (with its reforms that had already been presented to Parliament) and specific protective regulations, such as Decision No. 584 and the Regulations on the Health and Safety of Workers. Such a body of legislation supported the activities of the Ministry of Labour.

The speaker regretted that compliance with the relevant Conventions had not been achieved in the past 29 years, together with the consequent inconvenience caused to the international community. For that reason, he requested that his Government be granted the opportunity to rectify this situation and that faith once more be had in a Government that was democratic and therefore respectful of human rights. The information requested by the Committee of Experts would be presented in that spirit and the Government stood ready to receive ILO technical assistance. The Committee of Experts would then be able to examine the legal context of his country and would see that young people were in fact legally protected. The law governing those issues was being discussed for a second time, after which it would undoubtedly be immediately approved, published and brought into effect.

Another Government representative said that he shared the unease that had just been expressed. There were, however, indications that the matter would be resolved. He felt that a logistical deficiency had occurred of which he had not been aware. In his capacity as chairman of the Labour and Social Committee of the National Congress since 2003, he made a commitment to tackle that situation in such a way as to end incompliance with the ILO Conventions. There was still time, until September 2005, to submit the relevant information to the Committee of Experts, and he was very much predisposed to deal with those issues in Parliament before the end of the year.

The **Employer members** thanked the Government representatives for the information provided and noted the apology made by the Minister of Labour and Employment. They were of the view that, if needed, the Government should avail itself of ILO technical assistance to implement Conventions Nos. 77 and 78 in national legislation. The protection of youth in employment was fundamental to the economic development and growth of a country. They noted the Government's offer to accept a mission to Ecuador. It was also important to be constructive rather than critical in this case. The Employer members insisted that the Government provide the Experts with draft legislation intended to give effect to Conventions Nos. 77 and 78 and a timetable for its full implementation, in time so that the Experts could consider this information at their meeting in November 2005. Given the information provided by the Minister on the situation in his country, they also felt that the Government should confirm to the Experts the involvement of labour inspectors with regard to Article 7 of both Conventions. The Committee would benefit from the Experts' assessment of practical steps taken on the ground in different sectors, both in the formal and informal economy. In conclusion, they stated that it was time for progress to be made and for this Committee to have a full factual and legal understanding of the case.

The **Worker members** stated that the situation of children workers in Ecuador called for in-depth consideration and certainly in relation to other Conventions like Nos. 138 and 182, which clearly were related with those under consideration in this Committee. The Committee must consider the data submitted by the Government, and the latter should supply a more detailed information on the draft law, request the technical assistance of the ILO and to provide to this Committee detailed information on the legislation and measures to avoid the violation of the Conventions under consideration and to protect the children who had to be integrated in the labour market.

The **Committee noted the information provided by the Government representative, Minister of Labour, and the discussion that ensued. The Committee noted the information contained in the report of the Committee of Experts according to which, 29 years after ratification and despite repeated requests from the Experts, the Government had not yet adopted legislative measures to give effect to the provisions of the two Conventions.**

The Committee noted the information provided by the Government representative. A Bill to amend the Labour Code which, according to the Government representative, was based on the comments that the Committee of Experts had been making for years, had been submitted to the National Congress. The Government indicated that it had furnished a copy of the Bill to the Office and that, if necessary, it would request assistance from the Office in order to bring the legislation into conformity with the Convention. The Committee noted the regret expressed by the Government concerning the serious delay in responding to the long-standing comments of the Committee of Experts. It expressed the hope that this Bill would be adopted without delay to give effect to the provisions of these two Conventions. Moreover, the Committee requested the Government to adopt the necessary measures in collaboration with the most representative organizations of employers and workers concerned, in order to guarantee the dissemination of information to all persons concerning the requirement for the medical examination of minors under 18 years of age before their admission to employment so as to ensure the implementation of the Conventions in law and in practice. The Committee requested in particular that measures be taken requiring the employer to keep available for labour inspectors either the medical certificate for fitness for employment, or the work permit, or the work book showing that there were no medical objections to employment. It requested the Government to submit information, for review by the Committee of Experts, on the results of the work of labour inspectors in this regard.

Noting that the Government was open to availing itself of ILO technical assistance, the Committee decided that a technical advisory mission should be undertaken to the country to evaluate the situation of compliance with the Conventions in law and in practice. The Committee insisted that the Government provide, in its next report, detailed information on all the issues raised by the Committee of Experts, including on any progress made concerning the adoption of the Bill to amend the Labour Code and the timetable for its adoption. It also requested the Government to report on the practical steps taken in order to apply the Conventions with the social partners and to indicate the results achieved in its next report.

Convention No. 81: Labour Inspection, 1947 [and Protocol, 1995]

ROMANIA (ratification: 1973). A **Government representative** explained that section 256 of the Labour Code, which provided for a special law to regulate the functioning and organization of the labour inspectorate, should not be understood in the sense of repealing existing legislation. Such special law regulated the organization and functioning of the labour inspectorate within the general framework of Labour Code. Both Act No. 108/1999 on Labour Inspection and the respective Regulation approved by Government Decision No. 767/1999 had been drafted in accordance with the provisions of Convention No. 81, so there was no need to repeal these texts.

The speaker indicated that Articles 13 and 17 of Convention No. 81 concerning the powers of labour inspectors were implemented by Act No. 108/1999 on Labour Inspection, which provided for compulsory measures in order to remedy any deficiencies found, including the application of penalties, taking out of service any technical equipment in case of imminent danger of accident, as well as informing the prosecutor of cases considered as criminal offences. Statistical information on the exercise by labour inspectors of their powers to initiate legal proceedings could be found in the Annual Report of the Labour Inspectorate that would be transmitted to the ILO in the near future.

Since the Labour Code did not provide for penalties applicable to employers for the non-observance of the provisions on hours of work and rest periods, the Labour Inspectorate had initiated proposals to amend and supplement it in this respect. The Government was discussing the amendments to the Labour Code with the representative trade unions and employers' organizations. The texts of the amendments would be communicated to the ILO after approval by the competent authorities.

The speaker further indicated that confidentiality of the source of complaints was ensured by the Law on Labour Inspection, and any case of infringement was punishable with appropriate penalties and could be brought before the Discipline Commission of the Territorial Labour Inspectorate. Provisions concerning confidentiality would be also included in the Statute of the labour inspector, the adoption of which was scheduled for 2005. However, she noted that in the records of the Labour Inspectorate there were no registered complaints related to non-compliance by labour inspectors with the provisions on confidentiality of the source of complaints.

Concerning the application of adequate penalties in the sense of Article 18 of the Convention, the speaker indicated that, in order to take into account inflation, the amount of financial penalties set by the legislation had been increased in 2002 by Government Decision No. 238/2002, a copy of which would be transmitted to the ILO in the near future, together with the other documents requested by the Committee of Experts.

As regards the training of labour inspectors, which was carried out within the framework of a national programme for professional training, the speaker mentioned two projects implemented with the assistance of the Ministry of Labour and Social Affairs of Spain, as well as the training programme planned at the National Institute of Administration on applying labour legislation.

Finally, the speaker pointed out that the Government was determined to pursue its efforts to improve the legislative framework in compliance with the provisions of ILO standards.

The Worker members recalled that, since 2003, Romania had a Labour Code which provided that, in order to put into operation its provisions relating to the organization and functioning of the labour inspectorate, a special law should be adopted to that effect. In this regard, Convention No. 81 provided that officials of the labour inspectorate had to be impartial, while exercising their functions under the supervision of a central authority, to be adequately trained, to be assured of stability of employment to guarantee their independence, and lastly, to be sufficient in number. Besides, the labour inspectors must benefit from the reimbursement of any professional expenses connected with the performance of their duties, in order to have the highest possible autonomy. In this regard, it followed from the Committee of Experts' report that the system of the reimbursement of their professional travel expenses was under revision, but that more information was required on this matter. The Committee of Experts also noted that the Government was undertaking measures to strengthen the administrative capacity of the labour inspectorate, the scope of these measures was not yet known and their conformity with Convention No. 81 and coherence with other applicable legislative texts should be examined. The Worker members also stated that they had been informed about a draft law aiming, inter alia, at the definition of the status of labour inspectors and hoped that the Government would keep the Committee of Experts informed on this point. The functioning of the labour inspectorate in its relationship with the complainants, as well as the putting into operation of the balanced policy of sanctions, constituted another important aspect of the legal framework of labour inspection. Thus, the Committee of Experts noted that the policy of sanctions in relation to the offences in the field of hours of work and rest periods was far from being transparent and requested clear and tangible information on the existing policy of sanctions. The Worker members supported this request and considered that it was an important question in the sense that the clear and non-equivocal policy of sanctions brought progress and social peace and contributed to the legal security of the complainants. This policy must be also really dissuasive in the sense that it should involve sanctions that were higher than any profit gained by perpetrators. The Government had to take these considerations into account in the course of the adaptation of its legislation.

In addition, the Worker members noted that, according to the Committee of Experts, the guarantees of confidentiality of complaints filed by the workers, particularly in the field of hours of work, were insufficient. However, the absence of the real guarantee of confidentiality opened the way to pressure or reprisals against potential complainants, which, in addition to the burden of proof borne by the workers, made their position even more difficult. These circumstances made the means at the workers' disposal to defend their rights purely theoretical, and the Government should provide information on the risks encountered by the workers who filed a complaint.

In conclusion, the Worker members wished that, in the nearest future, the Government, after having announced many reforms but having communicated little information as to their content, would furnish to the Committee of Experts the indications on the nature and the scope of the reforms envisaged.

The Employer members recalled that Convention No. 81 had been a subject of discussion in the present Committee in 1988. The Report of the Committee of Experts made reference to the enactment, in 2003, of the Labour Code, in which it was provided that a special law would govern the creation and organization of the labour inspectorate. The enactment of the said Code would not have repealed previous provisions relating to that subject, and labour inspection methods were being revised in accordance with European Union directives. Further clarification was required in order to adequately establish the legal texts that governed the organization and operations of the labour inspectorate.

With regard to Articles 13 and 17 of the Convention, relating to the powers of inspectors to take specific steps in serious and urgent cases, and to the liability to legal proceedings of persons who violated the provisions, such powers were provided for in other regulatory provisions. It was, therefore, a case of establishing whether the inspectors applied in practice the powers bestowed upon them by the Convention. That was difficult to establish, since the Government had not submitted an annual general report on labour inspection activities, as required under Articles 20 and 21 of the Convention.

As regards the provisions of Article 15(c) of the Convention, relating to confidentiality of the source of complaints, the Committee had requested that the Government provide it with information on how such confidentiality was guaranteed. Another aspect concerned Article 18 of the Convention, relating to adequate penalties for violations of legal provisions enforceable by inspectors and for obstructing inspectors in the performance of their duties. From the Report, the fact also emerged that the level of financial penalties was not adjusted to take into account inflation. The Committee of Experts would consider it regrettable if employers preferred to pay fines because they found them more economical than taking often costly occupational safety and health measures or paying workers' salaries on time. In the Employers' view, that economic assessment by the Committee of Experts ignored other mechanisms put at the disposal of inspectors by the Convention, such as the power to warn and advise, or even the powers provided for in Article 13, paragraphs 1, 2 and 3, which were as follows:

– to take steps with a view to remedying defects observed in plant, layout or working methods which they may have reasonable cause to believe constitute a threat to the health and safety of the workers;

– to order alterations to the installation or plant, to be carried out within a specified time limit, to secure compliance with the legal provisions relating to the health or safety of the workers;

to adopt measures with immediate executory force in the event of imminent danger to the health or safety of the workers.

As regards Article 11, paragraph 2, of the Convention, relating to the arrangements to reimburse to labour inspectors any travelling and incidental expenses which may be necessary for the performance of their duties, the Employer members indicated that it was a matter of determining whether the amount of funds assigned to labour inspectors was enough to fulfil that purpose.

The Employer members noted that the Committee had noted with interest the detailed information received concerning the various measures adopted, which covered the training, the number of inspectors, procedural manuals, good practice guides for employers, etc.

Finally, the Employer members emphasized that the aforementioned information did not substitute or entirely cover the content of the annual general report specified in Article 21 of the Convention, and it was therefore hoped that the Government would be able to submit that report as soon as possible, in compliance with Article 20 of the Convention.

The Worker member of Romania stated that the need for the active labour inspection, which would have at its disposal adequate resources and powers, had always been advocated by the Romanian trade unions.

The existing problems seemed to result from the fact that the Labour Code adopted in 2003 provided for the adoption of a special law on the organization of the labour inspection, without repealing the old legislation in this field.

The legislation gave to the labour inspectorate the powers of supervision, command and pursuit and provided for a wide scope of sanctions. However, it might be noted that in practice the inspections resulted in simple notifications deprived of any force, even in case of multiple offences. Judicial complications led to the impunity of perpetrators. Due to the small amount of fines, the employers preferred to pay fines rather than to undertake changes and necessary costly reorganizations, while the non-respect of the confidentiality of the source of complaints by the inspectors exposed the workers to reprisals. Besides, under the pressure of the international financial institutions and foreign investors, the Government revealed the intention to abridge the Labour Code in an unacceptable way. The speaker, therefore, requested the Government to take appropriate measures to bring the legislation into conformity with the Convention and to assess the necessity of the technical assistance to harmonize or amend the Labour Code.

The Government representative, in response to questions raised by the Worker member of Romania regarding the confidentiality of sources of complaints to labour inspectors, stated that her Government would soon adopt measures to clarify this situation. She noted that the registry of the labour inspectorate contained no complaints regarding the confidentiality of complainants. This document, along with others requested by the Committee of Experts, would be transmitted soon.

The Worker members thanked the Government for the explanations it had given, particularly those relating to the efforts made to train inspectors in cooperation with another European Union country. They encouraged the Government not to reform the Labour Code under pressure from international financial institutions, but to do so in the light of ILO international labour standards, and reiterated their hope that the Government would provide the Committee of Experts, before its next session, with useful information regarding the scope and nature of the envisaged legislative reform. They particularly insisted on the need for a guarantee that the travelling expenses of inspectors would be adequately reimbursed, and also emphasized the questions of complaint confidentiality and the establishment of a transparent and dissuasive sanctions policy. The Committee of Experts should, in that respect, examine the conformity of both the Labour Code and the related draft amendments with ILO standards. If the Government did not provide the required information without delay, a technical assistance mission should be proposed.

The Employer members highlighted the positive aspects mentioned by the Committee of Experts. They requested that the Government take steps to clarify the legislative situation and that it submit an annual inspection report containing all the elements provided for in Articles 20 and 21 of the Convention, as well as all the other information requested by the Committee of Experts. If need be, the country could ask the Office for technical assistance to help bring itself into conformity with the Convention.

The Committee noted the information provided orally by the Government and the discussion that followed. The Committee noted that the issues raised by the Committee of Experts related to the shortcomings of a legislative. structural and logistical nature, which are hindering the proper operation of the Labour Inspectorate.

The Committee noted the statements made by the Government representative concerning the efforts made by his country to strengthen labour inspection by increasing the numbers of staff and undertaking training programmes for inspectors in the context of European and bilateral cooperation. According to the Government, following the adoption of a new Labour Code in February 2003, tripartite consultations had been held with a view to the amendment of the legislation, through the establishment of appropriate supervisory mechanisms, including methods for the determination and adjustment of financial penalties. The envisaged changes should improve compliance with legal provisions, particularly in relation to the use of overtime hours, weekly rest, night work and child labour. According to the Government, the level of the penalties applicable for violations of the labour legislation in general had been readjusted taking into account monetary inflation, under Decision No. 238 of 2002. A copy of this Decision and of certain texts respecting the travel expenses of labour inspectors would be provided to the Office in the near future. The Committee also noted the Government's commitment to provide detailed information in its next report to the Committee of Experts and to inform the Office of the outcome of the tripartite consultations held with a view to strengthening the inspection system, as well as on the draft of the statute of the labour inspector.

The Committee encouraged the Government to pursue its efforts to strengthen the numbers and quality of human resources in the labour inspection services. It also requested it to take the necessary measures rapidly to bring the legislation into conformity with the Convention and to provide the relevant information requested by the Committee of Experts, as well as information on the nature and scope of application of the envisaged reforms. The Committee emphasized in particular that measures should be taken so that inspectors could discharge their functions effectively, as envisaged in Article 13 of the Convention, in the event of danger to the health or safety of the workers. It also requested the Government to ensure that, in accordance with Article 17 and 18, violations of the legal provisions enforceable by the labour inspector gave rise to legal proceedings against those responsible and that the penalties applicable were set in manner that remained dissuasive despite monetary fluctuations and that they were effectively applied.

The Committee drew the Government's attention to the importance of the principle of the confidentiality of sources of complaints, as set out in Article 15 (c) of the Convention, to ensure the protection of workers against any risk of reprisal by the employer. It further emphasized that the climate of confidence necessary for the collaboration of workers in inspection activities required strict respect for this principle by inspectors: it emphasized that it was the responsibility of the Government to ensure compliance with this principle and requested it to keep the Office informed of the progress achieved in this respect.

The Committee also reminded the Government of the need to take measures to ensure that an annual report was published and communicated to the ILO by the central labour inspection authority, in accordance with Article 20, and that it contained the information required by each of the clauses of Article 21, if possible in the manner set out in Recommendation No. 81, which supplemented the Convention. The Committee emphasized that the publication of a report of this nature was intended to provide visibility to the operation of the inspection system and to allow for its evaluation with a view to its improvement, taking into account in particular the views of the social partners. The Committee requested the Government to envisage, if necessary, having recourse to the technical assistance of the Office for the implementation of the relevant provisions of the Convention.

Convention No. 87: Freedom of Association and Protection of the Rights to Organise, 1948

ARGENTINA (ratification: 1960). **A Government representative** noted that the Committee of Experts in its observation of 2004 had expressed the hope that the dialogue initiated by the Government in 2003 would be reflected in the near future by the full implementation of some strictly normative aspects of Act No. 23551 on trade union associations which had been the subject of comments in previous years.

The speaker announced that her Government had presented on 6 May 2005 its detailed reply to the comments of ICFTU and the Argentine Workers' Central (CTA).

She recalled that, on examination of Act No. 23551, the Committee of Experts had, in 1989, expressed satisfaction at its promulgation, given that it was the result of a full social and political consensus and that it replaced that markedly anti-union standard set by the dictatorship which governed Argentina from 1976 to 1983. The satisfaction expressed by the Committee of Experts was corroborated by the attitude of the Government which began, in May 1984, a complete process of consultation with the ILO, culminating in the report produced by the direct contact mission led by the late. Nicolas Valticos, with the proposal to bring the new legislation into line with the principles of Convention No. 87. Valticos's mission provided the groundwork for the pillars of the future law on union associations, whose parameters were respected by legislators in developing and implementing the new normative regime.

Since the beginning of the legislative process, there had been a genuine intention to adapt the law to ILO principles making it compatible with the specificities and complexities of the country, in particular of the union movement.

Act No. 23551 followed the pattern in which the Argentine union movement had developed throughout the second half of the twentieth century in which the establishment and functioning of all trade union associations was guaranteed. There were 2,716 first-level union associations registered in Argentina, of which 1,380 (more than 50 per cent) had trade union status. In addition, of the total union associations with union status, 55 per cent or exactly 731 had requested and negotiated their union status.

As to the second-level associations, 92 federations were registered in Argentina, of which 74 had trade union status. More than 80 per cent of second-level entities had trade union status.

In addition, there were 14 trade union third-level associations in Argentina and more than 40 per cent of the six confederations also had union status.

In Argentina, the number of public and private salaried workers totalled 9,100,000 men and women, with on average one first-level union association for every 3,350 salaried workers.

In the same way, according to data provided by the respective union associations, there were some 3,750,000 affiliated workers at the first-level, i.e. more than 40 per cent of salaried workers belonged to a union. If trade union associations of the higher level were also included, this figure would rise to 6,250,000 members or over 65 per cent.

The data provided spoke for itself and showed that men and women workers in Argentina freely enjoyed and exercised their inalienable rights to form the associations which they found appropriate and could join if they wished.

Similarly, national practice demonstrated that Argentine legislation relating to trade union associations guaranteed free and full exercise of freedom of association, whose primary purpose was social dialogue, especially the collective negotiation of employment contracts.

Argentina could claim a high level of achievements in collective bargaining. From 1988 to date 1,169 collective agreement had been concluded, 406 of which were current. Collective agreements at the enterprise level concluded in this period numbered 763, or 65 per cent of the total. Since 1988, 97 collective agreements a year had been concluded on average.

The speaker pointed to the sustained economic growth recorded in Argentina in the last biennium, with support for economic, social and labour policies closely linking growth, employment and distribution of wealth, as well as direct measures by the Ministry of Labour, Employment and Social Security to promote collective bargaining. Collective bargaining had recorded unprecedented unheard of development. In 2004, so many collective contracts and wage agreements had been concluded that the figures recorded during the 1990s had been doubled.

The speaker stated that the data provided demonstrated clearly that in Argentina freedom of association was not only a recognized legal right but also a right that was fully exercised to an extent that it placed the country in the leading ranks of the countries of the world that were more advanced in social dialogue, unionization and collective bargaining.

Legislation did not impede the exercise of obtaining trade union status for registered union associations in the full exercise of freedom of association which prevailed in the country. A total of 197 union associations had obtained union status in keeping with the process stipulated by Act No. 23551 and its associated decree. This meant that, on average, over the 16 years in which Act No. 23551 had been in force, a union was granted union status every month.

The previous trend had been accelerated by the development of an administrative policy which used the comparison mechanism for representation established in section 28 of Act No. 23551, which was only brought into action to check that there was no imbalance between the personal and territorial limits of the registered association requesting union status and those of the association which already had union status.

The consensus between the two most representative trade unions in the public sector (UPCN and ATE) was incorporated by the Ministry of Labour in Resolution No. 255 dated 22 October 2003, which allowed competition between already formed unions and new associations which claimed legitimate representation in the public sector. The principle of pluralistic representation was therefore integrated into the public sector.

All the above demonstrated that the will of the social players in the

C. 87

public sector in two unions, one an affiliate of the CGT and the other of the CTA, through dialogue and consensus, was indispensable in order to incorporate changes to the representation of the workers, tailored to the dynamics of the separate sectors.

Regarding the legislative processing of commercial trade unions and those in the trade or professional categories, the speaker recalled that points (a) and (b) of section 4 of Act No. 23551 explicitly guaranteed and promoted the right of workers to form trade union associations that they considered to be appropriate and to join or leave the same, as provided for in Convention No. 87. In addition, section 10 of the same Act considered trade union associations similar to those set up for workers in the same activity or related activities, such as those intended for workers in the same trade, profession or category even though they broke down into distinct activities or workers who offered services within the same enterprise. Three union specifics taken into account for incorporation under Article 2 of Convention No. 87 recognized the right of workers to form organizations that they deemed appropriate: (a) vertical trade unions which grouped workers in the same branch, industry or economic activity; (b) horizontal trade unions which grouped workers in a same trade or profession, even if they divided into branches or distinct sectors; and (c) enterprise-level trade unions.

National legislation (section 23 of Act No. 23551) regulating trade union legislation allowed all trade union associations without distinction to: (a) represent on request the individual rights of their members; (b) promote the setting-up of cooperative and mutual societies, the improvement of labour, social security and social insurance legislation; and promote general education and occupational training of its workers; (c) set membership payments; and (d) hold assemblies and meetings without prior authorization and also to represent collective interests whenever an association with union status was not present in a particular activity or profession.

Registered first-level associations, in affiliating with a second-level organization were provided with all the rights of first-level associations with trade union status as long as the management adhered to and integrated into a first-level association.

Decree No. 757/01 of 2001 established that trade union organizations with registration had the right to defend and represent before the State and before employers, the individual interests of their members on identical terms to the clauses contained in section 22 of Decree No. 467/88, regulated by Act No. 23551.

Tax law had established that all trade unions, without distinction, were subject to exemption from payment of taxes for regular profits and were not obliged to pay other national taxes, such as, for example, a tax on personal wealth or on assumed minimum earnings.

Section 47 of Act No. 23551 featured a highly protective clause on universal coverage, which gave each worker or trade union – without distinction – who was prevented or obstructed in the exercise of their legally guaranteed rights of freedom of association, the protection of these rights before a competent court, in conformity with fast-track proceedings, for which the law had ordained the immediate halting of all anti-union activity. Jurisprudence had determined that the criterion for interpretation of rights of freedom of association must be wide ranging, even if the provisions of Section No. 23551 were not self-contained, but rather derived from article 14bis of the national Constitution.

The speaker maintained that all legislation which regulated the exercise of fundamental rights could always be improved. It had to be acknowledged that national law and practice together with democracy had allowed Argentine workers to enjoy the full exercise of their rights of freedom of association. The Government had always been receptive to carrying out technical cooperation activities with the ILO, which would result in advances in the way designated to improvements in national legislation. Currently, there was a constructive process in hand in Argentina, the foundation of which was social dialogue. This way, which progressed according to consensus, had already recorded significant institutional achievements which reflected the plurality of the separate social actors. Such achievements were borne out by official participation of the CTA, all the social and labour organs of MERCOSUR, the consultation provided for Convention No. 144, the round-table dialogue on the promotion of decent work in which the worker delegation had taken part at the 90th, 91st, 92nd and 93rd Sessions of the Conference.

In 2004, the Government had convened and re-established the functioning of the National Council for Employment, Productivity and Minimum Wages, after years of inactivity, which was attended by both employers' and workers' organizations. The CTA began, in September 2004, the application formalities for union status within deadlines, applying the procedures laid down in Act No. 23551.

The speaker noted that, as indicated by the Committee of Experts in its observation of 2004, her Government had to present its comments on the questions raised before September, in the context of the regular reporting cycle.

In conclusion, the Government representative reaffirmed the political will to bring about social and employment changes but this will would not be sufficient if it were not accompanied by a search for consensus. In order for the legislative changes to be viable and fruitful, they had to be carried out through comprehensive social dialogue and constructive participatory consensus.

The Employer members expressed doubts with regard to the appropriateness, as a basis for discussion before the Conference Committee, of the observation of the Committee of Experts concerning the application of Convention No. 87 by Argentina, given that the brevity of the observation made it difficult to understand the substance of the case. Although technically the presence of an observation in the report of the Committee of Experts meant that the Conference Committee could hold a discussion on this case, this particular observation was included in the report merely because of comments made by the ICFTU and the CTA without any indication as to the position of the Committee of Experts in relation to these comments.

The Employer members suggested that the Committee of Experts needed to reconsider the timing of observations made on the basis of comments sent by employers' and workers' organizations, so as to avoid comments which were so limited in scope that the Committee could hardly find any basis for discussion. The practice was that, if comments were made by employers' and workers' organizations, an observation would be included in the report of the Committee of Experts regardless of whether the Government had answered or not. But, if these comments were simply referred to without any corresponding analysis by the Committee of Experts, then they were not very useful for the work of the Conference Committee. This Committee was not a complaints-based body such as, for instance, the Committee on Freedom of Association. Its mandate was not to examine complaints but to verify whether a country had given effect to a ratified Convention in law and in practice. The introduction of observations in the report of the Committee of Experts, based solely on external comments without any finding by the Committee of Experts, created a possibility of manipulation of the system; it ensured that, if an organization made a complaint, the case would be included in the report and therefore could also be found on the list of cases to be discussed before the Conference Committee. However, the criterion for including cases on the list should not be whether trade unions were active or passive in specific countries. Inclusion in the report of the Committee of Experts should not be automatic every time there was a comment from an employers' or workers' organization, unless the Committee of Experts had something to say on it. Otherwise, it might be better to leave such comments out of the report and address them in the framework of the regular reporting cycle when the Government's report was examined. As to the failure of the Government to reply to the comments by the ICFTU and the CTA, which had been noted with regret by the Committee of Experts, the Employer members would have liked to know the date on which the deadline for providing such a reply had expired, as this element would have enabled them to ascertain the Government's commitment to the supervisory mechanism.

In conclusion, the Employer members emphasized that what mattered was not the number of observations included in the report of the Committee of Experts but their quality. The legislative problems which were the subject matter of the observation under discussion were completely unknown to the majority of the members of the Conference Committee who were not familiar with Argentine law. There was not enough information on the context and no findings as to the facts by the Committee of Experts. The Employer members therefore noted with regret the Committee's inability to properly discuss and give consideration to this case and stated that the conclusions on this case should be appropriately limited.

The Worker members asserted that after careful consideration they approved the inclusion of this case as an individual case. They considered that the respect of every worker's right to join a trade union of his own choice in conformity with the principles set forth by Convention No. 87 was neither a concession to neo-liberalism nor a return of authoritarian interference into trade union activities. The aim was to adapt trade union law to the particular context of Argentina. For over 15 years, several contradictions between Argentine legislation and the Convention had been pointed out, including by the Committee on Freedom of Association, as noted by this present Committee in 1998.

While recognizing the merits of Act No. 23551, the Committee of Experts had criticized the following sections of this Act: section 28, which required an association, in order to contest the trade union status of an association, to have a "considerably higher" number of members (*'personería gremial'*); section 21 of implementing Decree No. 467, which qualified this term: as well as sections 29, 30, 38(5), 48 and 52 of the Act. In response to the criticism raised over the years, successive Governments had initially promised measures and had then invoked lack of consensus, with no concrete results. In 1998, the Conference Committee concluded that "Act No. 23551 contained conditions for granting trade union status (*'personería gremial'*) which were not compatible with the Convention" and deplored that "the Government did not provide any additional elements in response to the questions raised for number of years". A technical assistance mission carried out the following year did not result in any definite conclusion. Likewise, an additional mission in 2001 did not contribute an adequate response.

The current situation was characterized by the problems of actual relevance concerning trade union status (*'personería gremial"*), namely anti-unionism and considerable discrimination in collective bargaining and in the protection of trade unionists. Moreover, the situation could turn into a trade union monopoly, which would be unacceptable from the point of view of the Convention in so far as it would not correspond to freedom of choice of workers but would be rather imposed by law.

Given these facts, the Worker members declared that they were obliged to consider this case as one characterizing the continuous lack of implementation and that they were expecting evidence of real political will on the part of the Government to reach a durable solution on the substantive issues raised in the observation of 2003.

A Worker member of Argentina reported that the Committee of Experts had insisted on the incompatibility of the Act on trade union associations with Convention No. 87 for 15 years. Since the adoption of the Act of 1988, four technical assistance missions had been carried out in the country without positive results.

In its report for 2000, the Government explicitly recognized the incompatibility of the law with the Convention. For its part, the Committee of Experts had reiterated on several occasions the necessity to bring the national legislation into conforming with the Convention. Nevertheless, the Government had not taken concrete action to date. In effect, for example, since the mission which took place in 2001 in the country, with the aim of lending technical assistance to a tripartite commission, three decrees had been promulgated which did not meet requirements for compliance. Moreover, one of them, which referred to the possibility of self-financing of registered trade unions, was repealed 30 days after its promulgation.

The speaker stressed that in Argentina two classes of trade unions existed – those which had trade union status and consequently all rights and benefits, and registered trade unions which enjoyed more limited rights.

The sections of the Act criticized by the Committee of Experts referred mostly to the dispute system of " trade union status" classification by a registered trade union against a trade union already holding trade union status.

The Act demanded that the requesting union have a considerably higher number of members; as a minimum, it should exceed the previous organization's paying membership by 10 per cent. Such organizations, which contested union status and which were registered, lacked the most fundamental rights, unlike organizations with trade union status. In effect, these latter enjoyed the right to special protection of their representatives, the right to representation in a dispute, especially the right to strike, and the right to deduct membership contributions from workers' wages.

The Committee of Experts and the present Committee had both raised objections to the section which referred to the awarding of union status for commercial, office, professional or first-level trade unions if a trade union type of activity already existed, since the Act demanded so many requirements that it was practically impossible to incorporate. In this way, the Ministry of Labour recently denied union status to the union of managerial staff of the Banco Provincia of Buenos Aires since the Asociacion Bancaria previously existed with trade union status. The Committee on Freedom of Association had examined a similar situation which affected the trade union of the Lockhead company which had applied for trade union status.

As far as collective representation in the case of conflict was concerned, the Committee of Experts had considered that associations with trade union status were given an advantage compared to other organizations in matters of representation of collective interests that were different from collective bargaining. Among these collective interests was primarily the right to strike which was denied to registered-only organizations. For example, in a recent case examined by the Committee on Freedom of Association, which concerned the Workers' Union of commercial employees of Jujuy in which a member of a trade union without union status was fired as a result of strike action, reintegration was not considered possible because the trade union lacked union status. Moreover, when a registered organization had recourse to strike action, the Ministry of Labour initiated the conciliation process with the main union in the conflict setting aside the organization that was at the origin of the conflict.

On the other hand, the possibility of deducting union dues and other contributions was only granted to entities with trade union status. The Committee on Freedom of Association had examined the question in case No. 2050 and had requested that the Government take measures in a manner that did not discriminate against organizations that were registered only. The speaker noted that special protections granted to the trade union representatives in conformity with Conventions Nos. 87, 98, and 135 were only extended in Argentine law to the representatives of organizations that had trade union status. There were innumerable legal examples that demonstrated that representatives of simply registered organizations did not enjoy employment stability and as a consequence could be dismissed.

All of this led to the conclusion that trade union protection in national legislation was not sufficient, contrary to the assertions of the Government. In effect, the special protection established in Convention No. 98 was not a preventive mechanism, but rather provided judicial recourse that could be activated after the dismissal had taken place or for another anti-union act. In this manner it violated the principle of equality between the organizations. The anti-discriminatory arrangements in the Act did not create special protection , rather the opposite, as noted by the Government in 2002. In effect, the Committee of Experts had identified this type of general protection as insufficient.

The speaker noted that the privileges granted to organizations with union Status should not be confused with a system of representative trade unions accepted by the supervisory organs of the ILO. In effect, this set of rules only affected collective bargaining.

The so-called "Argentine model" created real privileges that went beyond collective bargaining to the benefit of certain organizations and, consequently, with discrimination against other organizations. It has to be noted that the Government unjustifiably delayed the recognition procedure for more than six months, adding reasons not grounded in the law. Moreover, in previous meetings of this Committee, the Worker members had referred to the violation of the human rights of certain trade union leaders. In effect, the trade union leaders were tried on numerous occasions simply because they had participated in various strikes and conflicts. In this sense, in conjunction with the National Human Rights Secretary, draft legislation was prepared that the Executive never submitted to the Parliament. In reality, one found more than 4,000 workers and trade union leaders who risked legal action.

Before adopting any conclusions, it had to be noted that the technical assistance missions obtained insufficient results, due to the continued breaches by the Government. The speaker concluded that the Government must be urgently requested to bring its legislation into line with Convention No. 87 and commit itself in the near future and communicate the results obtained at the next session of the Committee of Experts.

Another Worker member of Argentina, speaking on behalf of the General Labour Confederation of Argentina (CGTRA), said that the current Act, in keeping with the spirit and the letter of Convention No. 87, established the principle of "the most representative union" and its respective privileges in conformity with international practices. This Act had consolidated and continued to consolidate the representative unions that had managed to carry on during the worst crises by establishing a broad and efficient social network and dealing with the effects of the decline of the current economic and political model. This Act and its regulatory Decree, through the resulting implementation structures, enabled the current unions, which had been strengthened and organized under the Trade Union Act, to consolidate the rights of employed and unemployed workers and their families, during the terrible crisis that had recently affected the country. This was why strong support for these institutions was important. This Act enabled union unity, allowed unequivocal representation and effective action, and encouraged political pluralism in the union movement. There were no privileged trade unions, but trade unions that cared for the needs of workers.

The Act was based on the existence of free, strong and democratic trade unions organized by the workers themselves according to the principle of freedom, which granted more powers to the most representative unions at the federal, branch, trade and enterprise levels. Representativity was what made it possible to grant trade union status to a registered organization, which gave it collective bargaining and conflict resolution capacity. Any organization could request trade union status, and only in the event that another organization with trade union status already existed at the federal, branch, trade, occupation or enterprise level, would a process to compare representativity be undertaken as provided by the same Act.

The Argentine trade union system guaranteed the unequivocal will of the workers to form trade unions within a context of freedom, while strengthening the effectiveness of trade union action and avoiding fragmentation of this strength, which was the result of workers' unity. Indeed, the unity of trade unions was compatible with the right to trade union plurality and therefore respected freedom of association under the terms and scope of the Convention.

The speaker emphasized that freedom of association should not be defined out of context, but should respond to the social situation and labour relations in the country. Negotiation by workers constituted one of the main elements of freedom of association. In the context of the critical economic situation, Argentine law guaranteed the development of sufficient organizational and negotiation capacities, in conformity with the concepts established in Convention No. 87. The concept of freedom of association took precedence over that of individual freedoms; it was neither an end in itself, nor was it an individual freedom, but an instrument for workers as a group to contribute to the protection of their common interests.

The current Act responded to existing balances in labour relations, as it was respectful of the democratic principles of trade unions and guaranteed the fulfilment of workers as a group. Freedom of association existed in Argentina because there were no restrictions to the right to form workers' organizations or obtain legal status. Neither were there limitations to trade unions or federations, nor obstacles to international affiliation. There was no obligation to belong to a central, nor were there obstacles to free and democratic internal organization independent of the Government and employers. There were no obstacles to the creation of internal movements within organizations, which guaranteed the plurality within and the strength of their external expression. The Act prohibited the suspension or dissolution of a union by administrative authority and thus provided for protection from and punishment of trade union persecution. Furthermore, the Act had proved to be effective in the face of dictatorships, the most extreme neo-liberal policies, and profound crises that had affected the country. On the other hand, even in the event that Parliament agreed to amend the law, there were no guarantees that an excessively rigorous application of the law, not validated by the situation, would ensure better protection for the workers. A discussion of these issues was always possible in the context of democracy and the framework established by the national Constitution.

The Argentine trade union system had the ability and opportunity to help the millions of workers who were unemployed as a result of the crisis, by taking on the responsibility of applying the laws of mutual solidarity between those who had work and those who had lost their jobs. This would not have been possible without the existence of strong trade unions which were the result of the model that had been challenged by some sectors. Thus, the present trade union movement was able to create a system to address the specific needs of unemployed workers and their families so that none of the workers that had lost their jobs and had a trade were deprived of its services. The current model ensured the protection of employment, gave hope to those who had lost their jobs, and provided an active presence in the face of poverty, unemployment, marginalization and the needs of the unemployed.

The Worker member of Italy stated that in the context of globalization it was extremely important that the principle of freedom of association could be defined in a comprehensive way in legislation and fully implemented in practice. The speaker pointed out that the full implementation of this right not only could give further possibilities to workers by making them more responsible and develop the effectiveness of key ILO principles, such as tripartism, social dialogue, industrial relations and collective bargaining, but could also improve the quality of response to the challenges that a country like Argentina was facing. There could be no alternative to such an approach.

The existing limitations to the right to organize did not make negotiations with employers easier. On the contrary, fair legislation that provided the possibility for all workers to establish an organization of their own choosing would create a background of wider participation and responsibility. The Argentinian Government, which had ratified Convention No. 87, should therefore take adequate steps to amend its legislation with a view to eliminating the restrictions that the Committee of Experts had identified over the past few years, and after four technical assistance missions, in particular to review the concept of "considerably higher" number of members, as compared to other organizations, for acquiring trade union status; to repeal provisions permitting only associations with trade union status to benefit from the check-off of trade union dues; and to revise provisions giving trade union protection only to the organizations with trade union status.

The speaker recalled that in Italy trade union membership not only was still high but continued to grow, despite new forms of work, the precariousness of the labour market and increased unemployment. There were three major trade union confederations and a number of small trade unions, all of them benefiting from the same rights and duties, taking part in collective bargaining and industrial relations and having the right to check-off, even though their membership was less than that of the majority union. Each elected trade union representative both from the big and the small organizations had the right to be protected in the same way and no trade union status was required for a union to be able to negotiate with the employers. Similar rights should be granted to Argentinian workers.

Progress could never come from limitations, but from dialogue and the widest acceptance of ILO instruments. There was an urgent need to create conditions for legislative changes, which would pave the way for sound and inclusive industrial relations and collective bargaining at the company and sectoral level, and for a broad and consistent social dialogue and tripartite consultations for the improvement of workers' life.

The Worker member of Brazil wished to express her opposition to the inclusion of Argentina in the list of countries that did not respect freedom of association. Including Argentina in the list demonstrated that the present Committee sought to condemn those countries whose governments wished to maintain a sovereign development policy.

After having survived one of the bloodiest dictatorships in Latin America, Argentine workers had had to face the lengthy liquidation of their country by a submissive government that had sold its own nation and that maintained a close relationship with the United States. During that period, the Argentine Government had not been questioned before the present Committee. Now that Argentina had a democratic government that wanted to get the country's economic development back on track, now that the country was beginning to adopt a different approach to the problem of debt, and now that it was limiting the activities of the big multinationals and preventing other large companies from reducing rights and hampering the trade union organization of workers, Argentina appeared on the list of countries that did not respect freedom of association.

It was not for the ILO to try to divide Argentine workers. That had nothing to do with freedom of association. The Argentine trade union movement had a long and historical tradition of fighting for workers' rights and of unitary trade union organization. Democracy and freedom of association meant the plurality of ideas within a single organization, without the imposition of any exclusivity or hegemony. In Argentina, only recently, both CGTs had merged to form a single CGT, representing 90 per cent of Argentine workers. Such action had been an important step towards consolidating democracy and freedom of association in the country and should be welcomed enthusiastically by the present Committee.

The Worker member of Spain stated that discrimination and special treatment were not based on any objective system of measuring representation, but simply on the basis of "I arrived first" and "I was already here". Therefore, the trade union that had already been established could collect trade union dues through check-off facilities, a right that was denied to new trade unions. The trade union that had already been established could protect its representatives, while new trade unions could not, even if they had the same number of members. The trade union that had already been established could call a strike, manage it and negotiate it, while new trade unions could not. Finally, the speaker requested that the Committee recommend in its conclusions something more than a technical assistance mission, since it was a not a case of whether the Argentine Government had the knowledge or technical capacity to bring Argentine legislation into line with ILO standards, but a problem regarding the political will to end trade union discrimination.

The Worker member of Norway recalled that during five previous sessions of the ILC the fact that the Government of Argentina had not brought its legislation in line with Convention No. 87 had been lamented. During the ILC in the year 2000, the Government finally had acknowledged the substance of the comments of the Committee of Experts and admitted that Argentine law was in conflict with Convention No. 87. The Nordic workers had waited patiently for the Government to fulfil its promise to remedy this situation, but this had been in vain. Act 23551 gave certain unions privileges not given to others. New unions needed 10 per cent more dues-paying members than already established unions in order to be registered as trade union organizations. A simple majority was not enough. Those unions which were not registered as trade unions were considered associations, with few of the benefits of registered unions. Only registered trade unions were allowed to represent workers in a conflict, engage in collective bargaining, demand legal protection for their members and use the check-off system to collect dues. Only registered unions were allowed to strike.

She further noted that the economic reality of Argentina had changed considerably since the Constitution of Argentina established the practice of recognizing only one national union central. Especially in the last decade of economic crisis, employer-worker relations had become much more complex. Workers' rights were threatened to an unprecedented degree. In this regard, she recalled that the CTA had been founded in 1991. However, because of Argentine law, it was not recognized as a trade union organization until 1997. Despite the fact that the CTA had more than a million members, it was not invited to participate in the ILO Conference until 2003. It was still not allowed to register sectoral unions as trade union organizations. Because it was a new organization without the privileges given by law to established organizations, only 57 of its member organizations were registered as trade unions while 180 were regarded as associations. There had been cases where shop stewards in these associations had been fired for exercising their right to union activity because they did not have the legal protection granted to shop stewards in registered unions.

She concluded by stating that the workers of Argentina deserved the right to be represented by the trade union of their choice. The CTA was a democratic and representative trade union organization. She requested the Government of Argentina to facilitate a change in the law in order to bring it into line with the Convention it had ratified in 1960.

The Worker member of Uruguay, after emphasizing the good work carried out by Mr. Gernigon (the recently retired, former head of the Freedom of Association Branch and who had been ever attentive to workers' needs), stated that he was quite familiar with the Argentine trade union movement, since Uruguay was a neighbouring country and the movement was a long-standing one. He was therefore well aware of its unitary vocation. At present, workers in Argentina had more than one choice as regards trade unions, a situation that he would not comment on. However, that did not mean that both Centrals could not work and contribute jointly with respect to issues that were very important to workers in the region, when participating in the Confederation of Central Unions of the Southern Cone (*Coordinadora de Centrales Sindicales del Cono Sur*). They did the same institutionally in the Consultative Economic and Social Forum, amongst others.

The failure of Argentine legislation to adapt fully to Convention No. 87 had for years been a subject of discussion in the Committee. The different Governments had not listened to the Committee's recommendations, despite a number of ILO technical missions carried out in Buenos Aires.

The speaker said that he had noted the Argentine Government's willingness to bring its legislation into line with the Convention, but emphasized that the Government must not continue to prolong that process, and that it must promise, before the Committee, and in conjunction with the trade unions, to report the following year that the country had brought itself into conformity with Convention No. 87.

The Government representative welcomed the comments made by the spokesperson for the Worker members, who had acknowledged the importance of Act No. 23551, a product of Argentina's recently recovered democracy and of the strength of the Argentine trade union movement. She reaffirmed that her country had submitted a report on Convention No. 87 in 2003 and that it would do so again in September 2005.

As regards the observations made by the ICFTU and the CTA, referred to by the Committee of Experts at its 75th Session, the speaker reiterated that her Government had submitted its comments in writing to the International Labour Standards Department in May 2005. Consequently, her Government did not owe any reports relating to the issue under examination. She made it clear that Act No. 23551 conferred important rights on registered associations and that section 23 thereof granted a registered association the right to set its membership fee and to receive that fee from its members. That right guaranteed the growth and patrimonial development of trade unions.

The speaker reaffirmed that in Argentina the right to strike was enshrined in article 14bis of the National Constitution and that it was not subject to any restriction in the text of Act No. 23551, indeed all trade union associations were entitled to exercise that right. With regard to the cases that had been cited, she indicated that her Government had submitted its reports as required. As she had said before, Argentine legislation could indeed be improved, within a context of political freedom and democracy. Consequently, she reiterated her country's commitment to carrying out ILO technical cooperation activities, with the active participation of the social partners, in order to achieve the necessary consensus between those who were the true protagonists of freedom of association.

Within that context, she reiterated her desire to find, in social dialogue and consensus, in fulfilment of the mandate set forth in ILO Convention No. 144, the instrument needed to ensure the legitimacy of the regulatory changes that deserved to be made.

The **Employer members** stated that four elements should be reflected in the conclusions. First, the Government should provide a timely report to the Committee of Experts so that the information could be subject to complete review; secondly, the Committee should insist that the Government implement Convention No. 87 in law and practice; thirdly, the Government should follow up on its stated willingness to accept technical assistance by the Office; and finally, the Committee of Experts should provide a comprehensive and complete examination of the matter in their next report.

The **Worker members** stated that as a result of the discussion and the information received over the years, they thought they had a precise and exhaustive idea of the problems relating to freedom of association in Argentina. Although all the parties recognized the importance, originality and historical role of the Argentine trade union movement, the fact remained that Argentine legislation did not fulfil all the requirements set forth in Convention No. 87. It was the Government's task to ensure the application, in law and in practice, of all the provisions of that Convention. The Worker members hoped that the Government would not delay in taking all the necessary steps to find appropriate solutions to the problems under discussion, with ILO mediation if necessary, and that the report to be submitted to the Committee of Experts at its next session would show evidence to that effect.

The Committee took note of the information provided by the Government representative and the discussion that followed. The Committee noted from the observation of the Committee of Experts that for several years it had been requesting the Government to amend certain provisions of Act No. 23551 of 1988 on trade union associations and the corresponding Decree, which contained requirements as regards the granting of trade union status to trade union associations, the requirements to contest trade union status and the benefits which associations with trade union status enjoyed over those that were simply registered. The Committee noted that the Government had already sent its reply to the comments of the International Confederation of Free Trade Unions (ICFTU) and the Central of Argentine Workers (CTA) on the application of the Convention which set out the abovementioned legislative questions and certain acts of anti-union repression.

The Committee took note of the statements of the Government according to which trade union legislation, which had respected the guidelines of ILO technical assistance in 1984, had guaranteed the majority of trade union rights set forth in the Convention, as shown by the high number of trade union associations, the rate of unionization (more than 65 per cent), and the number of sectoral and enterprise-level collective agreements (1,169). The Committee noted that, according to the Government, a great majority of the registered organizations enjoyed trade union status and that each month a new union was accorded this status. The Committee noted that the Government was open and receptive for the carrying out of technical cooperation with the ILO to improve national legislation, on the understanding that the right path was broad social dialogue and the participative construction of consensus. The Committee hoped that this information would be examined by the Committee of Experts at its next meeting.

The Committee hoped that the dialogue between the Government and all the social partners, with technical assistance by the ILO, would translate into amendments of the legislation permitting the full application of the provisions of the Convention in national law and practice.

The Committee requested the Government to provide in its next report information on all outstanding issues, so that the Committee of Experts would dispose of all the elements for a complete examination of the situation in the country.

BELARUS (ratification: 1956). The Government communicated the following written information:

The Commission of Inquiry regarding Belarus' observance of the Freedom of Association and Protection of the Right to Organise Convention, 1948 (No. 87), and the Right to Organise and Collective Bargaining Convention, 1949 (No. 98), was appointed by the Governing Body of the International Labour Organization at its 288th Session in November 2003. The Government of Belarus gave every support to the Commission to accomplish its task. All the necessary information, meetings and consultations were provided. The Commission issued its report in July 2004. The report contains recommendations for the Government of Belarus concerning improvements of the national legislation in the field of freedom of association and protection of trade union rights. The deadline for the implementation of some recommendations was fixed for 1 June 2005. In November 2004, the Government of Belarus officially stated that everything that would be undertaken by the Government to fulfil the Commission's recommendations would be carried out within the framework of the law, in strict conformity with its competence, principles of division of power and non-interference of the State in the internal business of trade unions. In order to implement the recommendations of the Commission, the Government of the Republic of Belarus has taken the following steps:

1. According to the requirement of the Commission its recommendations have been published in the magazine of the Ministry of Labour and Social Protection of the Republic of Belarus named *Labour Safety and Social Protection*, which is distributed in all Belarusian enterprises and organizations.

2. The Government has adopted the appropriate plan of action. The copy of the plan has been forwarded to the International Labour Office.

The actions stipulated by the plan will be carried out in three basic directions:

– Further improvements of the national legislation and law enforcement on creation and registration of trade unions; realization by trade unions of their authorized activity (recommendations Nos. 1, 2, 3, 6, 9 and 10).

– Perfection of the mechanisms of protection of the rights of trade unions and prevention of discrimination in the sphere of labour relations owing to membership of the workers in trade unions (recommendations Nos. 4, 5, 7 and 8).

– Development of social partnership and social dialogue (recommendations Nos. 11 and 12).

3. In line with the recommendations, the Government has developed the draft Law of the Republic of Belarus "On associations of the employers" aimed at the further development of the system of social partnership. The draft Law has already been studied by the ILO and has received a positive reaction. Also in line with the recommendations, the Government is working out the new draft Law of the Republic of Belarus "On trade unions". At this stage the provisions of the draft are discussed at the level of experts of the Ministry of Labour in close cooperation with the wide range of interested state agencies, trade unions and employers.

4. In line with the recommendations, the Government has established an expert council on development of the social and labour legislation aimed at maintaining the constant dialogue and interaction between the authorities, trade unions (including representatives of the Federation of Trade Unions of Belarus and the Belarusian Congress of Democratic Trade Unions), employers, NGOs, scientists, and the Ministry of Labour of Belarus. The Council provides a wide forum for exchange of the views and proposals on the development of the national labour legislation, role of the State, trade unions and employers in the system of social partnership.

5. In line with the recommendations, the Ministry of Labour of Belarus has prepared and submitted to all interested parties (enterprises, trade unions, state agencies) the Explanatory Letter with interpretation of the norms and provisions of the international and domestic legislation determining principles of interaction between social partners and non-interference by the employers and trade unions in the internal affairs of each other.

6. In line with the recommendations, during the period of January-April 2005, the State Labour Inspection has examined the number of enterprises employing more than 2 million workers in total on the subject of law enforcement practice in conclusion of fixed-term labour contracts. More than 1,000 infringements of labour legislations were found and 226 entrepreneurs were penalized (fines, management responsibility etc.). The inspection, however, did not discover any facts of anti-trade union discrimination on those enterprises.

7. Now the Ministry of Labour of Belarus, in cooperation with the ILO, is preparing joint seminars within the framework of implementation of the recommendations of the Commission.

For the implementation of some recommendations the Government urgently needs technical and expert assistance from the International Labour Office, namely, in the field of trade union registration, regulation of trade union mass actions, regulation of external financial assistance, building up education and awareness tools. The Government of Belarus remains committed to continue to cooperate with the ILO in perfection of the system of socio-economic relations in Belarus and in further fulfilment of the recommendations of the Commission of Inquiry.

In addition, before the Committee, a **Government representative** emphasized the importance of the cooperation between her Government and the ILO Commission of Inquiry appointed under article 26 of the ILO Constitution to examine the observance by the Government of the Republic of Belarus of Conventions Nos. 87 and 98, in order to gain a proper understanding of the present case. Although the Government had

C. 87

not considered it necessary to appoint the Commission of Inquiry, once it had been established it had demonstrated its willingness to cooperate with the Commission, for example by providing all necessary information on the law and practice concerning freedom of association and hosting the mission of the Commission to Belarus in April 2004. During its mission, the Commission had met government officials, trade unions and employers' organizations without any interference from the Government. It had then conducted formal hearings in Geneva at which the Government had been represented by officials of the Ministry of Labour and Social Protection and the Ministry of Justice of Belarus. The Commission had expressed its appreciation to the Government of Belarus for the full cooperation it had provided in respect of all aspects of the Commission's work and for its cordial and open attitude.

The Government had studied carefully the report entitled "Trade union rights in Belarus" prepared by the Commission of Inquiry and the recommendations contained therein. In its letter to the Director-General, as well as at the 291st Session of the Governing Body in November 2004, the Government had expressed its willingness to fulfil the Commission's recommendations, in the light of the situation of Belarus and its sovereign interests.

The Commission's recommendations included 12 points and covered various issues. Several recommendations, including the deadline for their implementation, needed to be adapted to the particular situation of Belarus. To do so, the Government had adopted a Plan of Action, under which the process of implementation of the Commission's recommendations would involve all the social partners and other concerned parties. The Plan aimed at further improvement of the national legislation and practice on the establishment and registration of trade unions and the exercise of their activities, improvement of the mechanisms of protection of trade union rights and protection against acts of anti-union discrimination, and the development of tripartism and social dialogue. The practical implementation of this Plan was to be carried out on the basis of a list of concrete measures to be taken within the first six months of 2005. This first stage of the implementation process had been already carried out and the Government was presently working on the second stage of this process. The recommendations of the Commission had been published in the Journal of the Ministry of Labour and Social Protection, *Social and Labour Protection*, and could be found on numerous web sites, including the ILO web site.

The Commission had further recommended taking measures to prevent acts of interference by employers in the activities of trade unions, in particular by issuing clear instructions to enterprise managers. In this regard, the Ministry of Labour and Social Protection had sent a letter to all concerned parties in which it had explained that the relevant national legislation and international standards on social partnership prohibited all acts of interference by social partners in the each other's internal affairs.

The Commission of Inquiry had raised the issue of the use of fixed-term contracts, which were a significant trend in many countries. The legislation of Belarus also provided for the possibility to conclude fixed-term contracts. The main legislative acts in this area were the Labour Code and Presidential Decree No. 29 of 26 July 1999 on additional measures to improve labour relations, to strengthen labour and managerial discipline. The Labour Code laid down the conditions for conclusion of fixed-term labour contracts and set their maximum length at five years. Decree No. 29 granted the employer the right to conclude contracts with workers for a minimum term of not less then one year and provided for additional guarantees for employees with whom the contracts had been concluded, such as additional paid holidays and increased wage rates. The Labour Inspectorate, with the participation of trade unions, carried out regular inspections to supervise the use of fixed-term contracts. During the period of January-April 2005, the Labour Inspectorate had examined the application of labour legislation concerning the use of fixed-term contracts in enterprises employing, in total, over 2 million workers. A number of violations had been found, fines had been imposed on 226 employers, and administrative sanctions had been taken against 210 employers. However, in general, it appeared that contracts were concluded in accordance with the legislation in force. She added that workers employed on fixed-term contracts enjoyed the same rights as those employed under indefinite labour agreements, i.e. the right to organize and to collective bargaining and the right to strike. No cases of discrimination in the use of fixed-term contracts had been found. As anti-union discrimination was prohibited under section 14 of the Labour Code, any decision by an employer to conclude a fixed-term contract with an employee based on his or her trade union membership would be illegal.

The recommendations of the Commission of Inquiry paid close attention to the question of the registration of trade unions. The Plan of Action provided for the improvement of the legislation, including the relevant provisions of the law on trade unions. The Government was already working on a concept to make changes to this law. To this effect, the Ministry of Justice had analysed the application of legislation on trade union registration. In particular, all cases of refusal to register primary trade union organizations had been examined. According to the information made available by the Ministry of Justice, as of 1 January 2005, some 20,195 primary trade unions were registered, compared with 1,031 in 2004. The complaints addressed to the ILO mentioned 43 cases of denial of registration of primary trade unions. However, according to the analyses of the Ministry of Justice, in ten cases the primary trade unions had not applied for registration and in six cases, the organizations were duly registered. In only eight cases, the primary organizations, following a denial of registration, had reapplied for the registration, and in only nine cases denial of registration had been appealed in court. However, practice showed that if a decision to deny registration was not based on the legislation, recourse to the courts brought positive results, as illustrated by the registration of a primary trade union of the Belarusian Free Trade Union at the "Alforma" enterprise.

The Government of Belarus was ready to review the situation and take measures relating to any well-founded complaints of violation of trade union rights. However, it could only act within the scope of its competence and could not overturn judicial decisions or bypass the legislation in force.

The Commission of Inquiry had requested the Government to undertake a thorough review of its industrial relations system. To accomplish this task, a special Council of Experts, composed of representatives of the Government, trade unions, employers' organizations, NGOs and academics, had been established by the Ministry of Labour and Social Protection. Trade union members of this Council were represented by the Federation of Trade Unions of Belarus and the Belarusian Congress of Democratic Trade Unions.

She noted that the Plan of Action and the list of measures to be taken had been submitted to the ILO. The Government had been informing the ILO of the steps taken to implement the recommendations. All further information in this respect would be provided to the Committee on Freedom of Association. In order to give effect to the recommendations of the Commission of Inquiry, the Government was counting on the ILO's technical assistance and consultations had been held with the Office for this purpose, and particularly for the organization of three seminars on international experience on the establishment and registration of trade unions, mechanisms to protect trade union rights and the development of social dialogue. Such seminars would allow a better understanding of the tasks before the Government and the determination of the best approach to be taken to implement the recommendations. The proposal to conduct the seminars had been made by the Belarusian delegation during the Governing Body session in March 2005. Although the possibility of organizing seminars in May 2005 had been discussed, unfortunately, due to the circumstances beyond its control, their organization before the Conference had not been possible. The Government had received a communication from the Office emphasizing the need to discuss this question during the Conference.

In conclusion, she said that her Government had difficult and complex issues to solve, but that concrete steps had already been taken to implement the recommendations of the Commission of the Inquiry. Certain recommendations had already been implemented. Others, which were more complex, including those of legislative nature, needed more effort.

The Worker members said that the Committee of Experts' report recounted the history of the case of Belarus from November 2003, when a Commission of Inquiry had been established by the Governing Body. They emphasized that this was the tenth anniversary of the complaint submitted to the ILO in 1995 by the ICFTU, the WCL, the Free Trade Union of Belarus and the Congress of Democratic Unions of Belarus concerning serious restrictions on the right to strike, the suspension of trade unions by presidential ordinance, serious acts of anti-union discrimination and the arrest and detention of trade union members. On several occasions the Committee on Freedom of Association had examined cases on this subject and the Government had adopted an "empty chair" policy in 1996 and 2002. Despite making occasional progress, Belarus had been the subject of comments by the Committee in 2000, 2001 and 2002, following which the Governing Body had decided to establish a Commission of Inquiry, which had formulated 12 very explicit recommendations.

The Worker members noted the Government's statement that it had adopted a plan of action. The details of this plan, however, should have been revealed much earlier to the parties concerned, with a view to its examination by the Committee. The Government claimed it was establishing a council of experts composed of the Ministry of Labour, trade unions and NGOs, but there was no indication of any measures taken to guarantee that it was of a balanced composition. The Worker members emphasized that the Government alone was responsible for bringing the national legislation into conformity with international labour standards and that in no case could the ILO share this responsibility. They were sceptical about the official information provided.

The Worker members recalled the recommendations made and assistance offered by ILO bodies for several years, to which the Government still had not replied or acted upon. They therefore considered that the comments of the Committee of Experts were still valid, despite the text presented to the Committee by the Government. They also referred to the conclusions of the ILO European Regional Meeting in February 2005 and the position of the European Commission, which might envisage reconsidering the aid allocated to the country in view of the flagrant violations of ILO standards on freedom of association.

In conclusion, the Worker members stated that the situation was too serious for them to be satisfied with promises of action or future requests for assistance. The exercise of any form of independent trade union activity in Belarus was in real danger. They demanded action demonstrating the political will to respect ILO standards and requested the Committee to adopt conclusions which reflected the gravity of the case.

The Employer members thanked the Government representative for the information provided and recalled that the Committee had been discussing the case for over ten years. They indicated that, after listening to the Government representative, they remained somewhat sceptical of the Government's will to give full effect to the Convention at any time in the future. The Government representative had said that measures would be taken in the light of national conditions and bearing in mind its sovereignty. They therefore reminded the Government that almost half a century ago when it ratified the Convention it had made its decisions concerning the issues of sovereignty involved. The Government representative had also stated that some of the recommendations of the Commission of Inquiry would have to be adapted in the light of national conditions. In this respect, the Employer members recalled that the Convention concerned fundamental workplace standards and the very basic and fundamental issue of freedom of association and the right to organize. Although providing a list of the planned activities, set out in a Plan of Action, the Government representative had indicated that their implementation would take longer than envisaged by the Commission of Inquiry. Moreover, although it had been reported that measures were envisaged to prevent interference by enterprises in trade union activities, the Government representative had made no mention of the issue of interference by the Government, on which the Committee of Experts had expressed deep concern.

The Employer members noted that the Government representative had referred to the development of a concept in relation to this case. However, they emphasized that, in view of all the action taken on the case by various ILO bodies, the concept of what needed to be done should now be fairly clear. The real form of assistance that was required by the Government from the ILO was technical assistance for the drafting of legislation to give effect to the Convention, so that effective measures could be taken to overcome the discrepancies highlighted by the Committee of Experts.

The Worker member of Belarus, on behalf of the Federation of Trade Unions of Belarus (FPB), the largest trade union centre in the country, noted that trade union pluralism existed in Belarus, as illustrated by the existence of about 40 trade unions which were either united into two trade union centres or functioned autonomously, and that this fact explained the diversion in the views on the issues discussed by the Conference Committee. He regretted that neither the observations of the Committee of Experts, nor the previous conclusions of the Conference Committee had taken into account the information which was regularly provided by his organization to the ILO, and which testified to the substantive changes undergone by the trade union movement in Belarus during the past few years. For instance, currently no law on labour and social issues could be adopted without consultations with trade unions. The rights of trade unions in the field of monitoring the application of labour legislation were also increased. He underlined that this process involved not only the FPB, but also other trade unions. The tripartite National Council for Labour and Social Issues held regular meetings three to four times per year. The government working group was headed by the First Deputy Prime Minister. This fact testified to the influence trade unions had and to the seriousness with which the Government considered the ILO principle of tripartism. The tripartite General Agreement dealing with the issues of labour, social and economic interests of workers and providing for the protection of trade union activists was an example of promotion of social partnership in the country. In the last six months, about 400 trade unions had been established in the private sector of the economy, mainly in small enterprises, where relations between workers and employers were not always good. All of the abovementioned accomplishments were due to the hard work of trade unions, especially the FPB.

However, he was not completely satisfied with the statement of the Government representative. He understood that, although the process of changing the legislation was by nature a slow one, he considered that the Government was moving too slowly. He also expressed his reservations as concerned the issue of fixed-term labour contracts. The gaps in the legislation on contractual forms of employment allowed employers to act in an arbitrary fashion. The fact that there were no massive violations in the use of this type of employment was only due to the fact that the legislation was supplemented by the abovementioned General Agreement. However, this Agreement was not an act of legislation but rather of a recommendatory nature. He called on the Government to adopt a legislative act, the draft of which was prepared by the unions at the beginning of this year.

The speaker welcomed the Plan of Action adopted by the Government to implement the recommendations of the ILO Commission of Inquiry and thought that this would contribute to the improvement of social and labour legislation, particularly because this process would involve the active participation of trade unions. Establishment of the Council on the questions of improvement of social and labour legislation was another important step, and the active participation of trade unions in this body would make the work on the amendment of legislation on establishment and functioning of trade unions even more productive. He concluded by stressing the need for ILO technical assistance in implementing the Plan of Action.

The Government member of the United States indicated that the 2004 observation had confirmed and expanded upon the concerns that the Committee of Experts and the Conference Committee had been raising for many years. These concerns included requirements of law that affected uniquely those unions that were outside the structures of the FPB or opposed its leadership. These requirements gave rise to apprehensions that they were being applied intentionally to suppress independent unions, in flagrant violation of the provisions of the Convention. The Commission of Inquiry documented numerous examples of this and the experts noted with deep concern reports from the Congress of Democratic Trade Unions that proposed amendments to the Law on Trade Unions would further strengthen what was a de facto state-controlled trade union monopoly in Belarus.

The Commission of Inquiry had made 12 very specific recommendations to the Government of Belarus, most of which should have been implemented by the time this Conference had convened, but were not. The speaker called upon the Government of Belarus to implement all of the Commission of Inquiry recommendations in full and without further delay. The recent election of the Government of Belarus to a regular seat on the ILO Governing Body made it all the more imperative that the Government demonstrated by its actions that it was committed to the principles the ILO stood for. Among these principles, none was more fundamental than the right of workers and employers to establish democratic organizations of their own choosing, free from the interference of governments and government-dominated organizations enjoying virtual monopoly status under laws that contravened ratified ILO Conventions.

The speaker noted that the ILO, with support from her Government and others, was attempting to ensure that independent trade unionism in Belarus survived a sustained assault by the Government of Belarus, which was well-documented in the report of the Commission of Inquiry. The Committee of Experts had warned that the survival of any form of independent trade union movement in Belarus was truly at risk. She stressed that eveything possible should be done to ensure that this warning did not come true. The workers of Belarus deserved no less than workers everywhere: trade unions that spoke for them, were accountable to them, and were free from government interference.

The Government member of Cuba expressed surprise at the inclusion of Belarus in the list of countries because of the short period of time since the presentation of the report of the Commission of Inquiry and the Government's reply. Instead, progress in the application of the Plan of Action by the Government should be evaluated depending on what was contained in its next report. The Government had not had sufficient time to take all legislative and administrative action to apply the Plan of Action, whose objective was the restructuring of the entire system of labour and social relations in the country. In addition, account should be taken of the written information supplied by the Government to the Conference Committee. The draft Law on Employers' Organizations had been forwarded to the ILO for comments. Also, the Labour Inspectorate had visited enterprises employing in total more than 2 million workers and recorded more than 1,000 violations, sanctioned 226 enterprises, but had not found any anti-union activities. Account should be taken of the fact that the Government fully supported the Commission of Inquiry. However, the time allowed for compliance with recommendations was not enough. The Government had requested ILO technical assistance. Such technical assistance would facilitate application of the measures contained in the Plan of Action.

The Government member of Luxembourg, speaking on behalf of the Member States of the European Union, as well as Bulgaria and Romania as countries in the accession process; Turkey and Croatia as candidate countries; Bosnia and Herzegovina and Serbia and Montenegro, countries of the process of stabilization and association and potential candidates; Norway, EFTA country member of the European Economic Area; as well as Ukraine and Switzerland; recalled that in its statement during the 291st Session of the Governing Body (November 2004), the European Union had expressed serious concern about the situation in Belarus as regards adherence to democratic principles, human rights and respect for the rule of law, as well as the non-fulfilment of its international commitments. The European Union had called upon the Government of Belarus to fully implement all 12 recommendations made by the Commission of Inquiry without delay and within the deadlines set in the report.

The EU remained deeply concerned by the observations of the Committee of Experts following the conclusions of the Commission of Inquiry. The Committee of Experts stated that the survival of any form of an independent trade union movement in Belarus was truly at risk.

The EU was closely monitoring the situation in Belarus, where the lack of progress could result in the temporary withdrawal of benefits under the Generalised System of Preferences. In this context, the EU was deeply concerned by the findings of the report of the investigation carried out by the European Commission, which highlighted serious and systematic violations of the most basic principles of freedom of association in Belarus. These findings were consistent with the conclusions of the Commission of Inquiry and the observations of the Committee of Experts.

The EU further noted the Government's information concerning steps taken or envisaged including the reference to a Plan of Action with a view to implementing the recommendations of the Commission of Inquiry. The EU expected the Government of Belarus to fully implement the conclusions of the Commission of Inquiry and to give full effect in law and in practice to all the points raised by the Committee of

Experts on the application of the Convention. The EU called for a meaningful and constructive dialogue between the ILO and the Government of Belarus in order to guarantee the full implementation of the recommendations of the Commission. These were essential, not only for the protection of workers and their rights, but also for the development of democracy.

The Government member of the Russian Federation considered that the Government of Belarus had made efforts to resolve the problems raised by the Commission of Inquiry and the Committee of Experts. As concerned the most important but very complex issue of legislation, the work was being carried out, but needed a certain amount of time. In this connection, all the relevant technical assistance from the Office would be of great importance. He emphasized the willingness of the Government of Belarus to cooperate with the ILO and considered that the situation was developing in the right direction and that adequate solutions would be soon found.

An observer of the International Confederation of Free Trade Unions (ICFTU) and President of the Belarusian Congress of Democratic Trade Unions (CDTU)) stated that the list of violations of trade union rights in Belarus continued to grow and included the denial of registration of about 30 independent trade unions, the requirements of legal address and of 10 per cent minimum membership to establish a trade union, harassment, detentions, dismissals and transfers of trade union leaders and union members and the continuing denial of the CDTU's right to participate in the meetings of the National Council for Labour and Social Issues. As far as freedom of association was concerned, the situation in Belarus had considerably worsened. Eight members of trade unions who had testified before the Commission of Inquiry had been fired. The acts of pressure exerted on trade unions and their members to leave their unions intensified as hundreds of persons had been called in by the local authorities and threatened with non-renewal of their labour contracts and reprisals by the police. During these meetings, explicit reference had been made to the Presidential Instructions. The registration of the Radio and Electronics, Automobile and Agricultural Machinery Workers' Union had been denied, as was the registration of a trade union in Mogilev due to a problem with the legal address. The State mass media, the only media that existed in the country, treated the independent trade unions as "enemies of the people" and "traitors sponsored by western bosses". He doubted that the Government would implement the recommendations of the Commission of Inquiry, as was already demonstrated by the continuous refusal of the Government to implement recommendations of other ILO supervisory bodies. He considered that the Plan of Action was a clear attempt by the Government to evade its responsibilities as no Plan of Action could replace the good will needed to ensure respect for trade union rights in Belarus.

The Government member of Myanmar congratulated the Government of Belarus for its efforts in cooperating with the Commission of Inquiry and for adopting an appropriate National Plan of Action. His Government was encouraged to learn that the Government of Belarus had developed a draft law on associations of the employers. His Government also noted the commitment of the Government of Belarus to implement the recommendations of the Commission of Inquiry and to cooperate with the ILO. The ongoing constructive engagement between the Government of Belarus and the ILO was therefore supported.

The Government member of China noted that the Government of Belarus was taking positive steps to give effect to the recommendations of the Commission of Inquiry and had made progress in this respect. The Government had also reiterated its willingness to cooperate with the ILO. What was needed at this stage was the provision of technical support by the ILO and the international community to the Government. Such help would enable the Government and the social partners to jointly put the Plan of Action into practice so as to implement the Convention.

The Government representative explained that her Government had approached the Office with a request to hold three seminars on international experience with the establishment and registration of trade unions, mechanisms to protect trade union rights and the development of social dialogue. Such seminars would provide additional knowledge on freedom of association principles and would allow a better understanding of the tasks before the Government and the determination of the best approach to be taken to implement the recommendations of the Commission of Inquiry. She emphasized that her Government fully understood its responsibility to implement the recommendations of the Commission of Inquiry. The Plan of Action was based on the list of concrete measures to be taken in this respect. Its first stage had been already carried out and the Government was currently working on its second stage. The Government maintained contacts with the ILO and would continue to provide further information to the Committee on Freedom of Association. In line with Recommendation No. 12, the Government had established an expert council on the development of social and labour legislation. Trade union members of this Council were represented by the Federation of Trade Unions of Belarus and the Belarusian Congress of Democratic Trade Unions.

In regard to the concern expressed over the adaptation of the implementation of the Commission's recommendations to the reality of Belarus, she stated that in Belarus, as in many other countries, the principle of separation of power prevented the Government from acting outside of the scope of its competence.

With respect to the question of anti-union discrimination, although her Government understood the need to improve the machinery of protection against acts of anti-union discrimination, currently all workers who felt themselves victims of discrimination, in accordance with section 14 of the Labour Code, had the right to appeal to courts.

Social dialogue was recognized in Belarus. The Government, workers' and employers' organizations cooperated and worked together in the Committee on Improvement of Labour Legislation and the National Council on Social and Labour Issues. She pointed out that the Belarusian Congress of Democratic Trade Unions (CDTU) along with the Federation of Trade Unions of Belarus (FPB) were both members of the National Council, despite the fact that the FPB was a much larger organization, and explained that if the membership of the Council was to be determined by the number of members, the CDTU would not be able to become the member of the Council.

The Government representative pointed out the achievement of the Government in the sphere of social protection and employment policy. She concluded by stating that freedom of association was guaranteed by the Constitution and recognized by other legislative acts. Her Government was open to dialogue and ready to accept ILO assistance in order to improve the situation. It had already adopted a certain number of measures and would continue to do so.

The Worker members remarked that the Government had presented the situation in terms that brought its credibility into question. For instance, it had accepted to review labour legislation in cooperation with the ILO, but only on condition that the recommendations made to it be congruent with its policies. Over the last ten years in Belarus, independent trade unionism had gradually disappeared. Currently, the Government had put a Plan of Action into operation, but without stipulating its content. It claimed that it was fighting precariousness of jobs through extension of fixed-term contracts, but the reality completely negated these claims. It had made no reply on the non-respect of the immunity of persons who had provided information to the Commission of Inquiry; nor on the number of trade unions that had nonetheless obtained their registration without having to enter the structures of the FPB. It had also made no response to the fact that the Congress of Democratic Trade Unions had not been invited to sit with the Group of Experts on legislative reforms, despite having announced the setting up of this latter to the ILO Governing Body six months ago. The Worker members had asked that the conclusions reflect the fact that this case constituted a continuing failure to implement the Convention and that an impartial evaluation of the situation was required, in conformity with each of the points raised in the report of the EU.

The Employer members maintained the scepticism they had expressed in their opening remarks as to the real prospects of resolving this case rapidly. They recalled that the Government had ratified the Convention 49 years ago and expressed the wish that the Government would resolve all problems at hand before the 50th anniversary of the ratification. The Plan of Action announced by the Government representative was reminiscent of similar plans announced in the past and the Committee should not be prepared to accept another delay. The momentum should be maintained for the swift adoption of measures for the full implementation of the Convention. In this regard, the Employer members took note of the Government representative's statement that her country needed technical assistance from the ILO on advice in drafting the statutory provisions necessary to bring the law into line with the Convention. The Employer members agreed with the Worker members that this case was serious and indeed, a special case, given that the institution of a Commission of Inquiry was a rare event which occurred only in serious circumstances. The Employer members considered that the Government should be given credit for its intention to address several issues. Thus, the case should be included in a special paragraph in the Committee's report but should not be referred to as a case of continuous failure to implement the Convention.

The Committee took note of the written information supplied by the Government, the statement made by the Government representative, the Deputy Minister of Labour, and the discussion that took place thereafter. The Committee noted from the comments of the Committee of Experts that the Commission of Inquiry submitted its report to the Governing Body at its 291st Session in November 2004. The Committee recalls that the conclusions and recommendations of the Commission of Inquiry concerned the application of rules and regulations relating to the activities of trade unions and other public associations in a manner amounting to a condition of previous authorization for the formation of unions and with an impact uniquely upon those unions outside of the traditional trade union federation or which oppose it, contrary to Article 2 of the Convention; the non-conformity of the law on mass activities, and its application, with Article 3 of the Convention and of Presidential Decree No. 8 on measures for receiving and using foreign free aid with Articles 5 and 6 of the Convention. The Committee, like the Committee of Experts, further notes with deep concern the information concerning proposed amendments to the law on trade unions aimed at substantially increasing the requirements for trade union registration at various levels.

The Committee noted the Government's indication according to which it has adopted an appropriate plan of action to give effect to the recommendations of the Commission of Inquiry and

that it has submitted to all interested parties an Explanatory Letter on the norms and provisions of international and domestic legislation. The Government also indicated that the recommendations of the Commission of Inquiry were published in a magazine of the Ministry of Labour, which is sent to almost all enterprises in the country. It also referred to an experts' council established to review the labour legislation, which included in its composition the Federation of Trade Unions of Belarus (FPB) and the Congress of Democratic Trade Unions (CDTU).

The Committee expressed its grave concern at the serious discrepancies between the law and practice on the one hand and the provisions of the Convention on the other, which it considered seriously threatened the survival of any form of an independent trade union movement in Belarus. It deplored the fact that no real concrete and tangible measures had yet been taken to resolve the vital matters raised by the Committee of Experts and the Commission of Inquiry, including as regards a number of recommendations made by the latter that were to have been implemented by 1 June 2005. It urged the Government to take the necessary measures immediately to ensure that full freedom of association was ensured in law and in practice so that workers could freely form and join organizations of their own choosing and carry out their activities without interference by the public authorities and to ensure that independent trade unions were not the subject of harassment and intimidation. Furthermore, the Committee supported the recommendation made by the Commission of Inquiry that the presidential administration issue instructions to the Prosecutor-General, the Minister of Justice and court administrators, that any complaints of external interference made by trade unions should be thoroughly investigated, and considered that such steps aimed at ensuring truly effective guarantees for the rights enshrined in the Convention would further benefit from the Government's implementation of the recommendations made by the United Nations Special Rapporteur on the independence of judges and lawyers. The Committee requested the Government to provide a full report on all measures taken to implement the recommendations of the Commission of Inquiry for examination by the Committee of Experts at its next meeting.

The Committee further urged the Government to accept a mission from the Office to assist in the drafting of the legislative amendments requested by the Commission of Inquiry and to evaluate the measures taken by the Government to implement fully the Commission's recommendations.

The Committee decided to include its conclusions in a special paragraph of its general report.

BOSNIA AND HERZEGOVINA (ratification: 1993). The Permanent Mission of Bosnia and Herzegovina to the United Nations Office in Geneva, in a letter dated 10 June 2005 and signed by the Ambassador Jadranka Kalmeta, communicated the following information:

Because of force-majeure, the delegation of Bosnia and Herzegovina regrets to be unable to assist at the meeting of the Committee on the Application of Standards on 11 June.

Due to this, we attach the NON PAPER prepared by the delegation of the Government of Bosnia and Herzegovina.

We take this opportunity to express our renewed gratitude to the ILO, in particular, to the Regional Office in Budapest and the Office in Sarajevo. We hope that the ILO will maintain its support and valuable assistance to enable Bosnia and Herzegovina to fulfil its obligations towards this Organization.

Non paper

Suffering from the heavy consequences of the recent military conflict and going through the process of reforms in nearly every sphere, Bosnia and Herzegovina is facing at present numerous challenges.

The new Law of 15 March 2003 concerning the Ministries and other administrative bodies of Bosnia and Herzegovina designated the Ministry of Civil Affairs as the body ensuring coordination between the entities of the country (which together with the cantons of the Federation of Bosnia and Herzegovina have full authority in this area), taking the responsibility particularly for the areas of work, employment, social protection, health and pension system. With regard to the ILO, the Ministry has the following priorities:

(1) provision of reports on the ratified Conventions;
(2) provision of reports on the non-ratified Conventions;
(3) complaints and observations submitted to the ILO concerning non-observance by Bosnia and Herzegovina of ratified Conventions, including:
 (a) the case of Aluminium-Mostar;
 (b) the case of Ljubija;
 (c) the case of the Confederation of Independent Trade Unions of Bosnia and Herzegovina;
 (d) the case of the employers of the Serb Republic of Bosnia and of the Confederation of Employers of the Federation of Bosnia and Herzegovina;
 (e) the case of the Associated Workers' Trade Union;
(4) payment of contribution.

To fulfil its obligations towards the ILO, the Government has taken the following measures:

The case of the Confederation of Independent Trade Unions of Bosnia and Herzegovina

In May 2005, the Government, by way of the Ministry of Civil Affairs and the Ministry of Justice, requested special assistance from the ILO with a view to resolving this issue (modification of the legislation to allow the registration of the Confederation at the state level) and expertise on the part of the ILO. Last month, an agreement between the Confederation of Independent Trade Unions of Bosnia and Herzegovina and the Trade Union of the Serb Republic of Bosnia has created the Trade Union Confederation at the national level. Progress has been made in the elaboration of the legislation concerning social dialogue and social partners at the national level.

The case of the employers of the Serb Republic of Bosnia and of the Confederation of Employers of the Federation of Bosnia and Herzegovina

With regard to the complaint made by the employers' organizations of the two entities, the Government stated that these organizations have the right to obtain state registration. Pursuant to this, an Association of the Employers of Bosnia and Herzegovina was established. The Government considers this case to be resolved. The ILO and the Committee on the Application of Standards will be informed of the latest developments in writing.

Conclusion

– The authorities of Bosnia and Herzegovina in liaison with the ILO office in Sarajevo undertake considerable efforts to prepare reports on ratified Conventions. It is a great pleasure to inform you that with the help of the ILO office in Sarajevo 13 reports have been prepared and will be sent to the ILO in the near future. Preparation of other reports is under way.
– Aware of its obligations, Bosnia and Herzegovina prepares the necessary documents and translations for the responsible state bodies. We hope that the report of the next session of the Conference would mention Bosnia and Herzegovina among States fully complying with their obligations.
– With regard to the complaints concerning violation of the Conventions by Bosnia and Herzegovina, it will request replies from the constituent entities on what has been accomplished in the cases of Aluminium and Ljubija and inform the ILO in writing.
– The case of the employers' organizations being resolved, Bosnia and Herzegovina with the help of the ILO will try to resolve the problem of registration of the Confederation of Independent Trade Unions by modifying the legislation. It will provide all the necessary assistance in order that the Confederation applies, together with the Association of the Trade Unions of the Serb Republic of Bosnia, the decision to establish the Trade Union Confederation at the national level.
– We take this opportunity to once again express our gratitude to the ILO and in particular the Regional Office for Europe in Budapest and the office in Sarajevo. We hope that the ILO will continue to provide valuable assistance enabling Bosnia and Herzegovina to fulfil its obligations to the ILO.

The Chairperson noted that the Permanent Mission of Bosnia and Herzegovina to the United Nations Office in Geneva had indicated in a letter dated 10 June 2005 that, for reasons of force majeur, the delegation of Bosnia and Herzegovina regretted that it would be unable to attend the meeting of the Conference Committee on the Application of Standards on 11 June 2005. Information was appended to the letter summarizing briefly the action taken by the Government of Bosnia and Herzegovina in order to comply with its constitutional and standards-related reporting obligations and the assistance requested from the Office.

The Worker members expressed their indignation at the attitude of the Government of Bosnia and Herzegovina in relation to both the Committee and the ILO. It should be recalled that this was the third year that this case had been examined by the ILO supervisory bodies. Three complaints had been submitted to the Committee on Freedom of Association since 2002. These complaints were from both employers' and workers' organizations, the last of which had been submitted by the Confederation of Free Trade Unions of Bosnia and Herzegovina. The first complaint had been made to the Committee on Freedom of Association in 2002, which had adopted conclusions in 2003 requesting the Committee of Experts to examine the case, taking into account its legal implications. Nevertheless, despite the observations made by the Committee of Experts in 2003, 2004 and 2005, the Government had not replied. Once again today, the Government had not appeared. However, it had provided some information, which was contained in a written document submitted to the Conference Committee but this information did not provide any new elements. The Government said that it was ready to accept ILO technical assistance, but it was difficult to see the value of such assistance when the Government showed no willingness to cooperate. This situation was unacceptable and the Government needed to be aware of this. As the Government had not shown up, there appeared to be a problem of procedure. However, taking into account the deceitful attitude of the Government and its absence, despite its registration at the Conference, the Worker members proposed that the Committee should note that it had received written information from the Government, but that they had brought no new elements to the case. Furthermore, as this was a case of repeated failure to cooperate with the ILO supervisory system, they called for it to be included in a special paragraph of the Committee's report as a case of continued failure to comply with standards-related obligations.

The **Employer members** considered that there was little the Committee could do in relation to this case in view of the absence of the Government representative. In its report, the Committee would have to confine itself to expressing regret at the failure of the Government to appear before the Committee to discuss the problems relating to its application of the Convention and to note that by this absence it was undermining the ILO's supervisory system.

BURUNDI (ratification: 1993). **A Government representative** first recalled his country's attachment to the international labour Conventions which it had ratified, particularly Convention No. 87. He provided details in answer to the points raised by the Committee of Experts in its observations.

Regarding the principles laid down in Article 2 of Convention No. 87, in particular the right of workers without distinction of any kind – including public servants – to form organizations of their choice and to affiliate to them, several provisions in Act No. 1/018 of 20 October 2004, guaranteed this right. Section 37 of that Act did not forbid magistrates to form associations but simply stipulated that the exercise of the right to strike could be regulated for certain professional categories, while laying down, naturally, that union rights were not recognized for members of the armed forces and security forces. Under section 33 of Act No. 1/001 of 29 February 2000 on the reform of the statute of magistrate, magistrates had the right to freedom of association, including the right to strike as set out in relevant regulations. It was true that the Ministry of Justice had considered that the registration of the Union of Magistrates of Burundi (SYMABU) was not valid because section 14 of the Labour Code excluded magistrates from its field of application. However, a regulatory text on freedom of association of magistrates was being studied. In the same way, the validity of the registration of all public sector trade unions which had been registered with the Ministry of Labour and Social Security was currently being studied by an ad hoc committee.

Regarding the right of minors to freedom of association, it could be noted that, even if, according to the Labour Code, minors needed parental authorization for this, in practice this obligation was not taken into account.

Regarding the provisions relating to the election of trade union leaders which were contrary to Article 3 of the Convention, the Government would undertake to study a modification of section 275 of the Labour Code as requested by the Committee of Experts.

Regarding the right to strike, the provisions for application of the Labour Code relating to the modalities of exercise of this right had not yet been taken. The Committee of Experts' proposals which sought amendment of section 213 of the Code, were being studied with the social partners.

For the revision of the Labour Code, a consultant hired by the National Council for the fight against AIDS would contribute to the integration of HIV/AIDS into this instrument. A tripartite workshop to validate this integration was planned for the near future. The Government and the workers' trade unions would doubtless want other provisions of the Labour Code (including those relating to section 213) to be revised. This undertaking would require financial and technical assistance from the ILO if it were to be completed rapidly.

The **Worker members** observed that Burundi had ratified the Convention in 1993 and that the Committee of Experts had been making observations on this country since 1999, observations which concerned, on the one hand, the fact that the Government did not regularly send reports and, on the other hand, the fact that it did not reply to questions concerning the following points: (1) the legal and practical obstacles to the exercise of the right to organize by magistrates; (2) the right of minors under the age of 18 to organize freely and without conditions; (3) the right of organizations to elect their representatives in full freedom and to organize their activities freely. On this last point, the Worker members recalled that unfortunately interference in the internal affairs of trade unions represented a permanent temptation for many Governments. However, by virtue of the Convention, trade unions were free to determine their statutes and procedures and although doubts might eventually arise as to the legality of these statutes or procedures, it pertained to the judicial instances to decide, and never to the Government. The inconsistency between section 271 of the Labour Code and the Convention hardly disguised the real intentions of the Burundi authorities to control the trade union movement. These intentions were nevertheless showing through in the current paralysis of the National Labour Council. The Worker members therefore requested that, in its conclusions, the Committee invite the Government to urgently rectify these problems which had been revealed a long time ago, to guarantee in practice the exercise of freedom of association without obstacles and to communicate officially the measures taken in this sense.

The **Employer members** noted that this was the first time that the Committee discussed this case after Burundi's ratification of the Convention in 1993. With regard to the right to organize of magistrates, it was necessary to clarify whether magistrates were public employees, which was not the case in all countries. The Employer members were surprised that the Committee of Experts did not examine the issue of the right of minors to organize within the broader context of Conventions Nos. 138 and 182, also ratified by Burundi. With regard to section 275(3) of the Labour Code which excludes persons sentenced to more than six months' imprisonment with no suspension from holding trade union office, they stated that a unionist with a criminal record might in fact not be fit to hold office. Recalling the Committee of Experts' comment regarding the requirement established by the Labour Code to have worked for one year in an occupation to stand for trade union office, the Employer members recalled their position that the only legitimate criteria was that the individual was fit and qualified. Concerning the question of authorizing a strike, it was not clear whether the Committee of Experts criticized the legislation in force as it did not state whether a simple majority was considered as reasonable. Basic democratic principles would suggest that a substantial number of affected workers should have an opportunity to vote on action which in the short-term led to loss of wages and benefits.

The **Government member of Cuba** pointed to the information provided by the Government on the draft regulation under consideration on freedom of association for magistrates, as well as the willingness to modify certain sections of the Labour Code criticized by the Committee of Experts to bring them into conformity with the Convention. The speaker emphasized that the development of new legislation or the modification of the Labour Code should be the product of consultations, which could be difficult to successfully conclude. The request by the Government for technical assistance should be taken into account given the current revision of the Labour Code, the situation of public service workers and the development of regulations for freedom of association for magistrates.

An observer of the ICFTU indicated that the greatest difficulty for a government claiming to be democratic was to accept differences of opinion and contradiction among its partners, and to respond through negotiation, since to negotiate was to recognize a conflict of interests and to want to solve it democratically. The principle underlying Convention No. 87 was that freedom of association was indispensable to a democracy. Freedom of association meant freedom of organization, freedom to elect representative members of trade unions and freedom to affiliate. Therefore, it was inadmissible that the Minister of Labour and Social Security of the Republic of Burundi should attempt to replace the leaders and members of the Trade Union Confederation of Burundi (COSYBU) on the pretext that the mandate of its leaders had expired, to decide on how the organization should be administered, using as an argument an erroneous interpretation of Article 8, paragraph 1, of Convention No. 87. It was worth recalling that the legality in question under this Article was that which stemmed from respect of national legislation and trade union organization statutes, and by imprisoning the president and treasurer of COSYBU, it was the Government that was flouting legality. The speaker, therefore, invited the Committee to take urgent action in the face of this grave infringement of union freedoms.

The **Government representative** declared that his Government would certainly take into consideration all the comments made by the Committee, while adding that he made a rule of being open to dialogue. Regarding the incidents to which the ICFTU had referred, he reported that the appropriate legal bodies had been informed of the allegations concerning the imprisonment of the President and Treasurer of COSYBU. The Government was willing to strictly respect its international commitments, but it should not be forgotten that the country had just experienced ten years of war, on top of which an economic embargo that had practically amounted to a total blockade, could be added.

The **Worker members** stated that the discussion had shown the pertinence of the Committee of Experts' observation. The credibility of the Government was called into question, as it continued to proclaim its legality while at the same time trying to silence the trade union movement. The Worker members expected the Government to abstain in the future from any interference in the administration and activities of trade unions. The Worker members requested that the Committee, in its conclusions, asked the Government to provide a detailed report on the legislation concerned and its application in practice, in particular concerning trade union independence.

The **Employer members** stated that the Government should provide a comprehensive report on the outstanding issues, which would enable the Committee of Experts to make a full assessment of the situation.

The Committee took note of the statement made by the Government representative, as well as the discussion that took place thereafter. The Committee recalled that this case concerned, among others, the right to organize of magistrates and the right of employers' and workers' organizations to elect their representatives in full freedom and to organize their administration and activities without interference from the public authorities.

The Committee noted the information provided by the Government according to which the Labour Code was undergoing a process of revision. It further noted that draft regulations on the right to organize of magistrates were being studied and an evaluation was being carried out by an ad hoc committee of the situation of all unions with respect to the labour legislation and the legisla-

tion on the public service. Finally, the Government requested the technical assistance of the Office in order to rapidly conclude the work on the revision of the Labour Code.

The Committee noted with concern the information provided about governmental interference in the internal activities of the Confederation of Burundi Trade Unions (COSYBU) and the detention of its president and treasurer in September of last year.

The Committee expressed the firm hope that the revision of the Labour Code would be completed in the near future and would include full consultation with the social partners. It urged the Government to take the necessary steps to ensure that workers' organizations could carry out their activities without interference by the public authorities. Noting the Government's request for technical assistance, the Committee hoped that, with the assistance of the Office, the Government would be in a position to supply a detailed report to the Committee of Experts on the concrete measures taken to bring its law and practice into full conformity with the Convention.

The Worker members wished to draw the Committee's attention to important information concerning some recent developments; in fact, since 2 June 2005, Pierre Claver Hayasandi had been prohibited from leaving the country, and his passport had been confiscated. Even though he had managed to reach Geneva, he did not know what awaited him on his return to Burundi. The Office should investigate this delicate case and make strict recommendations to the Government. It could also make recommendations with a view to the reinstatement of the 1 May holiday.

The Government member of Cuba requested information on the procedure followed, in so far as it was not common practice in the present Committee to accept new statements after the adoption of the conclusions.

The Chairperson indicated that there had been no change to the usual procedure, but that he had accepted the statement of the Worker members in view of its exceptional nature.

COLOMBIA (ratification: 1976). A Government representative of Colombia expressed acknowledgement of the valuable cooperation and support received from the ILO, and through it, from the countries which had collaborated in the cooperation programme. International cooperation needed to continue to be a fundamental tool in the relationship between the ILO and Colombia, as reflected in the good results of the Technical Cooperation Programme. His country had always analysed with respect the observations made by the Committee of Experts with a view to the progressive harmonization of the national legislation with the ILO Conventions that it had ratified.

With reference to the situation of violence in his country, he stated that it had been affecting society for a number of decades and that his Government, which shared the general concern, had set the goal of reducing violence. Unfortunately, this moment had not yet arrived and it had not been possible to overcome the problem, although he could announce a sustained trend of a decrease in violence. In 2002, nearly 29,000 homicides had been recorded; in 2004, there were 20,000, which amounted to a decrease of 30.61 per cent. In the specific case of labour union leaders, whereas in 2002, unfortunately 205 had been murdered, in 2004 the number of murdered trade unionists had been 89, representing a reduction of 56.58 per cent. If this trend for the reduction of violence continued, by the end of the present year, there would be 15,000 homicides, representing a reduction of nearly 50 per cent in relation to the year when the present Government took office.

The direct contacts mission which visited the country in 2000 had indicated that the Colombian State was not implementing in any form a policy to exterminate any group of society. It was illegal armed groups and drug traffickers who were responsible for the murders, kidnappings and threats against trade unionists, mayors, journalists, religious leaders, councillors, indigenous peoples, teachers, soldiers, judges, business people, traders and various personalities in national public life. In some cases, even though they were minimal, officials of the current State, acting on an individual basis, had committed abuses. In such cases, the Government had sought to clarify the facts and impose appropriate penalties. The violent death of even one person was enough for the Government to pursue its action to strengthen state measures to guarantee the life of its citizens including, very specially, trade union leaders and members.

The efforts made by the current Government to protect vulnerable groups were not confined to the democratic security policy, but also included the Protection Programme, under the responsibility of the Ministry of the Interior and Justice. He indicated in this respect that over 70 per cent of the nearly 40 million dollars from the national budget for the period 2002-04 had been allocated for the protection of trade union leaders.

According to the report of the National Prosecutor's Office for the period 2002-04 on cases currently under investigation for offences of homicide, in which the victim was associated with a labour union, there had been 36 preventive detentions, 21 charges, four sentences and 131 investigations, which amounted to significant progress in comparison with ten years ago.

To this needed to be added the effort made by the Government to respond, in an increasingly broad, detailed and appropriate manner, to the allegations made to the Committee on Freedom of Association, as recognized by trade union groups themselves. Between 1993 and 2003, these allegations had been related almost exclusively to the murder of trade unionists. Now, the new allegations covered other types of attitudes relating to the exercise of trade union rights, which constituted progress.

He said that it would be an enormous mistake not to acknowledge the problem, just as it would be an enormous mistake to ignore the efforts and achievements that were little by little being made by his country in this respect. He therefore considered that Colombia could be deemed to be a country of progress, even though certain problems persisted, which were in the process of being resolved. If a solution were to be found, three simultaneous elements were required, namely, time, resources and political will. And he reaffirmed the political will of the Government.

With regard to the efforts to combat impunity, he said that there were already detainees and four persons had been convicted. A new system of bringing criminal charges had recently been established in the country, with emphasis on oral procedures and which, combined with the strengthening of the National Prosecutor's Office, would ensure that investigations were more efficient and more effective.

He then referred to the process of legislative amendment, which was a time-taking process, and to the differences between the national legislation and Convention No. 87. He said that the process of legislative reform had taken time and had merited its acknowledgement by the Committee of Experts. At the beginning of the 1990s, a high number of amendments had been made to the legislation and the country had been acknowledged to be a case of notable progress, as indicated in the 1994 General Survey of the Committee of Experts. In its report in 2001, the Committee of Experts had noted with satisfaction the measures taken by Colombia, which had taken into account ten comments made by the Committee of Experts. Of those, there were now currently three, which was lower than average for the countries mentioned in the report.

He indicated in this respect that he challenged the comments relating to the prohibition upon federations and confederations calling strikes. The Government had explained that the Colombian system of freedom of association, the right to organize and collective bargaining was structured around enterprise unions, to which all the inherent attributions of freedom of association and the rights deriving from Convention No. 87 had been granted. His Government considered that this system was entirely valid, was not in violation of Convention No. 87 and permitted better levels of negotiation and social dialogue. His country did not admit that such a limitation constituted a denial of freedom of association and the right to organize.

Secondly, the Committee of Experts had made comments concerning the prohibition of strikes in services the interruption of which could endanger the life, safety or health of the whole or part of the population, and the possibility to dismiss trade union leaders who had intervened or participated in an illegal strike. He recalled that the right to strike was enshrined in the Constitution of his country, with the sole exception of essential public services. Under the Colombian legal system, the concept of public service related to those services provided by the State directly or through private entities, regularly or continuously, to cater for the needs of the population and in which the public interest was implicit.

With regard to the possibility envisaged in the law to dismiss workers who participated in collective stoppages which had been declared unlawful, he emphasized that the legislation established requirements and procedures that had to be complied with by workers and employers before calling a strike. Whenever reference was made to an unlawful strike, this did not constitute any limitation on the right to strike, but referred to situations in which the clearly established requirements had not been complied with and which could not therefore receive legal recognition, as they did not *stricto sensu* fit the concept of a strike.

He added that all the efforts referred to had to be accompanied by the generation of more jobs. In this respect, he indicated that the growth rate of the economy in recent years had been around 4 per cent, which had resulted in the creation of more jobs and a decrease in the unemployment rate over the past two years.

He emphasized the role played by the ILO in promoting social dialogue and expressed gratitude to the Office for its contribution in this field. He called upon trade union leaders and employers to join together in endeavouring to take advantage of the legal areas available to them under the Constitution and to leave aside all types of pressure, both internal and external, intended to polarize relations between them. He added that it was not desirable for a multiplicity of organizations which were not representative of workers to be ruining the reputation of Colombia.

In conclusion, he called for social dialogue to become a crucial instrument through which the ILO and the countries which had demonstrated their concern at the situation in Colombia could contribute in a positive manner to the continuation of the Technical Cooperation Programme approved by the Governing Body in March 2005. He recalled that his country needed time and resources to make progress and he hoped that, encouraged by the results achieved, the international community would provide assistance through the ILO.

The Employer members thanked the Government representative of Colombia for the information provided. They pointed out that the case of Colombia was taking place in a context of civil war and all-pervasive violence which was affecting everyone throughout society, including the Government, employers' organizations and trade unions. The Committee of Experts had indicated on numerous occasions that employer's organizations and trade unions could only operate effectively in a climate of peace and respect for fundamental human rights. However, the problems in Colombia were of a very deep-rooted societal nature. They were placed in perspective by the fact that the financing provided by the drug cartels to the FARC and the paramilitary was even higher than the national budget. The Committee was therefore faced with a conundrum: there could not be any freedom of association in a climate of violence. However, this did not mean that freedom of association would end the violence. Even if the provisions of the labour law met the requirements of Convention No. 87, this was not going to solve the societal issues at stake. This was true for all the three issues relating to freedom of association and the right to strike which were currently being examined by the Conference Committee. Nevertheless, the Employer members emphasized that the violence in Colombia remained unacceptable and undermined the right to freedom of association. If such violence was to be ended, it was important for democratic institutions to be strengthened, and the Government was making efforts to this end.

They noted, in this context, that the issues raised by the Committee of Experts mainly related to the right to strike and that there was no need to deal with them in detail as the Employer's position in this regard was very well-known and had been clearly indicated in the context of the application of Convention No. 87 by Guatemala.

In conclusion, the Employer members believed that the Committee should draw the following conclusions on this case. Firstly, it was fundamental for freedom of association in the country that the Government did everything to end the violence. Secondly, the ILO technical cooperation programme, which had resulted in some progress, should be continued and enhanced. There was, however, a need for more information to be provided on the tangible results achieved through this Technical Cooperation Programme, which they would comment on further in their conclusion to the discussion of the case.

The Worker members indicated that in Colombia approximately 5 per cent of the active population was affiliated to a trade union and less than 1 per cent was covered by a collective agreement. This situation was the result of laws, measures and practices that were hostile to the right to organize. The percentages had been plummeting in recent years for the following reasons: firstly, the legal guarantees that permitted the exercise of freedom of association and collective bargaining were still not in conformity with Convention No. 87, as frequently emphasized by the Committee of Experts; secondly, the decisions of the three powers flouted the provisions of this Convention. Finally, in practice, a series of factors gave rise to the enormous difficulty of implementing the Convention.

They recalled that the Committee of Experts emphasized four issues in its report. These included the prohibition on the calling of strikes by federations and confederations; the prohibition of strikes in services which were not necessarily essential in the strict sense of the term, particularly as in case of the workers of ECOPETROL; the discretion of the Minister of Social Protection to refer a dispute to arbitration when a strike exceeded a period longer than one year; and the procedures for registering trade unions and the excessive use made by the authorities of their powers to evaluate subscriptions. They reminded the Government firmly of the need to put into practice its proposal made to the Conference Committee the previous year, namely to discuss this matter with the ILO to find a solution. However, another year had gone by and nothing had been done. They further recalled that the Committee had asked the Government in its conclusions of 2004 to supply information on the points to which it had not replied in its report.

The Worker members recalled in the first place the statements made by the Worker members at the Committee's previous session according to which the rights of workers, in particular trade union rights, which were guaranteed by the national legislation were not respected in the context of the merger, liquidation or restructuring of public or private services. Workers' organizations were generally informed of the restructuring on the day it took place. Workers and trade union leaders were dismissed summarily and there was no prior consultation with the unions. The new entities created after such mergers or restructuring usually hired the same persons, but without collective agreements, which were not renewed, and based on arrangements under which the implementation of the provisions of Convention No. 87 was impossible, as the recruitment of workers was carried out by temporary employment agencies or more often through *associated labour cooperatives*. And yet, it was an enshrined ILO principle, contained in Recommendation No. 193, that cooperatives should not be established or used for the purposes of undermining labour legislation, establishing disguised employment relations or violating the rights of workers through the establishment of pseudo-cooperatives. A large number of enterprises and institutions had undergone this process, including TELECOM, Bancafé and other enterprises related to the social security system, including hospitals. What made the situation even more serious was that it did not consist of a few isolated events. The combination of these practices amounted to an intent to eliminate freedom of association and the related rights. In a clearly planned manner and in response to agreements signed with the World Bank and the IMF, the same scenario was repeated time and again: trade unions were not consulted, measures were adopted on a de facto basis and the powers were used to achieve this end, based on a total denial of trade union rights.

The Worker members added that policies to promote flexible labour rights in recent years had led to a sharp increase in unemployment and employment in the informal economy. To address this situation, the CGT had sought authorization at its congress to proceed with the direct affiliation of workers, but this had been categorically denied. The Worker members emphasized the aggravation of violence, with 174 cases of murders or death threats against trade union leaders between January and April 2004, as well as searches of union premises, arbitrary detentions and kidnappings. This figure had risen to 214 over the same period in 2005, to which the deaths of at least another three trade union leaders should be added, bringing the total number of murders this year to 19. The arbitrary detention of trade unionists, which was on the rise, demonstrated that trade union activities were being criminalized while the murderers of trade unionists remained free. Although there were programmes to protect trade unionists, they needed to be combined with action to identify the perpetrators of threats against unionists. The Worker members denounced the silence of the Government on these cases and the lack of action to investigate them and punish those responsible.

The Worker members also referred to the solidarity missions that had been undertaken by ORIT and the international occupational federations which had tried to visit Colombia, without success, as entry into the country had been refused. They therefore requested explanations from the Government on this subject. Other missions had been able to visit the Colombian authorities, and meet the President, who had confirmed the willingness to enter into dialogue, but who, paradoxically, had insisted on the need for more participative trade unions which were less demanding. Yet, the very essence of trade unions was to ensure the protection of workers' rights through the organization of their activities and the formulation of their programmes of action, which were principally based on the advancement of their claims. They also expressed astonishment that the authorities should give voice to criteria concerning the type of trade union movement that they wished to see, which constituted interference in matters that were normally the sole responsibility of trade unions.

In conclusion, the Worker members emphasized the gravity and continued deterioration in the situation with regard to freedom of association and the right to organize in Colombia. The problems raised by the Committee of Experts in relation to the incompatibility of national law and practice with the provisions of the Convention and the persistence of a climate of violence were aggravated by specific events which demonstrated that the authorities did not support social dialogue and did not really wish to have trade unions, or only trade unions which were essentially participative. Such a situation was the antithesis of decent work and a denial of international law. It could only give rise to higher levels of under employment, unemployment, social exclusion, poverty and violence. And it had to be recognized that violence, in all its forms, and without wishing to justify it in any way, was deeply rooted in the absence of social justice. Freedom of association was a pillar of decent work and social justice. Laws and practices which ran counter to it would only sow the seeds of injustice and strengthen the vicious circle of violence.

A Worker member of Colombia said that trade unionists in his country were concerned by the actions of the Government and the employers to diminish the influence of ILO standards and its supervisory bodies. With regard to violations of trade union rights in his country, he said that the three trade union federations had provided information to the ILO Governing Body and the Committee on Freedom of Association. Although the Constitution of Colombia provided that duly ratified international labour Conventions formed part of internal law, the destruction of Colombian trade unionism was continuing. He referred to various events which violated trade union rights: (1) the dismissal of 3,400 workers from Banco Cafetero with a view to putting an end to the trade union and collective bargaining; (2) the declaration of the strike by workers at ECOPETROL as being unlawful and the subsequent dismissal of 247 workers; and (3) the dismissal of workers from state institutions (such as TELECOM, the Social Insurance Institute, hospitals, etc.) in which trade unions were in operation and collective labour agreements had been negotiated, only for them to be hired on temporary contracts for the provision of services, administrative or civil law contracts, or through cooperatives or other arrangements.

With regard to the violation of human rights, he added that trade union leaders and activists in the CUT continued to suffer various types of aggression. In 2004, 17 leaders and 71 trade union members had been assassinated, while in 2005, two leaders and 17 members had been murdered. This showed the continued policy to exterminate trade union members of CUT. The sector which had been most affected by acts of violence was education and, to a lesser extent, health workers. Nevertheless, death threats were on the increase for all trade unionists, as could be seen in the municipal enterprises of Cali. Finally, he indicated that the situation in Colombia continued to be very serious and called for the State to be urged to punish acts that violated freedom of association and the right to organize and for the necessary measures to be taken to prevent anti-union activities. He called upon the Government to give effect to the recommendations made by the ILO supervisory bodies, particularly those of the Committee on Freedom of Association. He urged the Government to strengthen the programme of protection for trade union leaders and requested the ILO to maintain and improve the Technical Cooperation Programme with Colombia. He also urged the ILO to organize a tripartite mission to Colombia as soon as possible. Finally, he called for the case of Colombia to be included in a special paragraph of the Committee's report.

Another Worker member of Colombia said that for years both the Committee of Experts and the Conference Committee had been urging the Government to take measures to bring the labour legislation and practice into full conformity with the Conventions on freedom of association. The discrepancies concerned the following provisions: the prohibition of the right to strike for federations and confederations (section 417 (i) of the Labour Code); the prohibition on strikes in non-essential service sectors (section 450 of the Labour Code); the power of the Minister of Social Protection to submit a dispute to arbitration in the event a strike lasting longer than a certain period (section 448, paragraph 4, of the Labour Code); the dismissal of trade union leaders for participating in strikes (section 450 of the Labour Code); declaring a strike illegal by the administrative rather than by the judicial or independent authorities; the denial of the right to collective bargaining for public servants and at the branch level; and the difficulties in the process of trade union registration.

He considered that the above facts were evidence of the persistence of violations of the right to freedom of association despite the Government of Colombia's repeated commitments to take measures to ensure that workers enjoyed the right to freedom of association and collective bargaining. The political and legal arguments to justify restrictions on freedom of association put forward by the Government and employers were evidence of a strategy to eliminate trade unionism in Colombia, the motto of which appeared to be "labour relations without trade unions or collective bargaining".

He stated that it was obvious that the creation of trade unions was being restricted. During the 1990s, an average of 88 trade unions had been established every year, compared with 104 in 2000 and 2001, 11 in 2003 and 6 in 2004. Some 40,000 trade union affiliates had been lost in the public and private sectors during the two-and-a-half year period of President Uribe's Government. Out of a total working population of 18 million people, fewer than 80,000 workers a year were covered by collective agreements. Employers used bribes to sign agreements with non-unionized workers and the Government simulated the liquidation of enterprises with a view to eliminating unions, collective bargaining and the immunity of union leaders. There were other acts that violated freedom of association, such as the case of the Agrarian Fund, TELECOM, Bancafé and Adpostal. The direct withdrawal by the administrative authorities of the legal authorization for trade unions to operate at the request of employers was an anti-union practice by the Government and the employers which supported it.

The prohibition of the right to strike was another violation in Colombia as in the case of the strike by the USO trade union in ECOPETROL, the purpose of which was to defend the national heritage and national sovereignty, but which was declared illegal by the Government, leading to the dismissal of 248 workers, including 26 trade union leaders, and the failure to comply with the court ruling previously agreed to by the parties. He therefore called for the case to be included in a special paragraph of the Committee's report.

Another Worker member of Colombia expressed his disappointment at the contrast between the expressions of good will provided by the Government representative and the situation in practice, particularly since the possibility of the way ever being open for trade union activities in his country was increasingly distant. Speaking of freedom of association in Colombia was like speaking of something exotic, because this fundamental right that was inherent to democracy was denied. He said that the ritual of the Conference Committee, which had now been repeated for over 20 years in this case, had not resulted in a way being found to resolve a conflict affecting an economically active population of 22 million people, of whom 4 million were without employment, 10 million were in the informal economy and the great majority had no stable work.

Trade unionism in his country was brutally affected on two sides: firstly, the practice of grave violations of Conventions Nos. 87, 98, 151 and 154, inter alia, affected the stability of trade unionism through murders, forced exiles, threats and intimidation. He referred to the incident in Arauca where three trade union leaders had been assassinated. He drew the Committee's attention to the fact that, for the neo-liberals and advocates of capitalist globalization, the best trade union was one which did not exist.

Moreover, the imposition of labour cooperatives, as practised in the private and public sectors, temporary contracts, subcontracting, the hiring of parallel staff on civil contracts and the constant challenges to an appropriate relationship between capital and labour all provided grounds demonstrating the urgency of reactivating the Ministry of Labour, which had now been merged with the Ministry of Health under the title of Ministry of Social Protection, and which had been converted into a new menace for trade unionism. It could not be understood that in his country there was no longer a Ministry of Labour to guarantee proper relations between capital and labour. For example, situations had occurred in which the Minister of Communication herself had convened workers in hotels to place them under pressure so that they would accept voluntary retirement plans, thereby denying collective bargaining.

He affirmed that his country needed a Ministry of Labour that was serious, dynamic, respectful of national and international standards, with the strengthening of labour inspection to prevent unlawful measures against workers.

He expressed deep concern with regard to freedom of association and the workers employed by TELECOM, whose enterprise had not only been militarized, but who had been dismissed and their trade union abolished, and whose entitlement to retirement pensions had even been denied by the instructions of the Ministry of the Interior. Around 2,000 workers were at risk of losing the benefits of over 25 years' service for the State. The new TELECOM refused to comply with the orders issued by judges in his country who favoured the workers, especially mothers who were heads of families and the disabled. He called for the Labour Code, the Constitution and ILO Conventions and Recommendations to be complied with. Finally, he said that the workers and trade unions in his country were calling for assistance so that they could merely continue to exist.

The Government member of Luxembourg, speaking on behalf of the European Union (EU) and for the Government members of Bosnia and Herzegovina, Bulgaria, Croatia, The former Yugoslav Republic of Macedonia, Norway, Romania, Serbia and Montenegro, Switzerland, Turkey and Ukraine, supported Colombia's efforts to bring about justice, social advancement and national reconciliation and to fight against impunity and human rights violations. In this context, she welcomed the recent ratification by Colombia of the Worst Forms of Child Labour Convention, 1999 (No. 182). However, she pointed out that the situation of trade union rights in Colombia had been the subject of comments by the Committee of Experts for many years and had been before the Conference Committee a number of times. It had also been the subject of numerous complaints examined by the Committee on Freedom of Association. She indicated that while the EU recognized the Government's efforts to increase protective measures aimed at ensuring the security of trade union leaders and trade union premises, it nevertheless expressed grave concern at the continuous high levels of violence and the climate of impunity, in which such acts of violence continued to occur. As the United Nations Commission of Human Rights had recently noted, trade unionists continued to be among the most targeted groups. She stated that the EU strongly condemned the murders and kidnappings of trade unionists and other vulnerable groups, mainly perpetrated in 2004 by illegal armed groups. The EU expected the Government to secure the right to life and security and to address the issue of impunity, which continued to be a major obstacle to the exercise of trade union rights in Colombia. She called upon the Government to make full use of the advisory services and technical assistance of the ILO in order to strengthen democracy and enhance the rule of law in the country, in accordance with the intention expressed at the highest level of the Colombian State during previous meetings of the Government Body.

Finally, the speaker stated that the EU regretted that the lack of progress with regard to certain legislation impeded the full exercise and development of trade union activities. The EU remained concerned, among other matters, at the prohibition of strike action in a wide range of sectors which were not essential services, but which were nevertheless defined as such under Colombian law. The speaker emphasized the importance of social dialogue and called on the Government of Colombia to take resolute action to bring its national law and practice into line with the requirements of the Convention.

The Worker member of France referred to a meeting held on 16 September 2004 between the President of Colombia, Mr. Uribe, and a trade union delegation headed by the General Secretaries of the ICFTU and the WCL, Mr. Guy Ryder and Mr. Willis Thys, in which she had participated representing her trade union organization *Force ouvrière*. During this meeting, President Uribe had indicated that, in his opinion, Colombian trade unionism was too assertive and not sufficiently participative, or in other words trade unions did not have an entrepreneurial attitude. According to the President, Colombian trade unionism had to change because trade unions were using archaic methods which were bound to disappear in the modern world. In this regard, she indicated that President Uribe's attitude was a matter of grave concern. Indeed, the principle of non-interference by the public authorities in freedom of association was the basis of Convention No. 87. However, it seemed that Mr. Uribe, in contrast, considered that it was normal for a President to define the nature of trade unionism in his country. This attitude did not seem to him to be a violation of Convention No. 87.

By way of illustration, she cited the following passages of a letter sent by the President of Colombia to the President of the enterprise ECOPETROL: "By the present letter, I would like to express warm thanks and congratulations to you as President of ECOPETROL and to all the directors and workers of the enterprise for having completed the process of negotiation with USO ... This process, with the full support of the law and constitutional guarantees, is an example for the whole country. In Colombia we need to create a culture of participative rather than assertive trade unionism."

The fact that the Convention No 87 was violated by the President himself explained the present situation in Colombia, particularly with regard to the adoption of legislative provisions and legal procedures. These were systematically intended to bring an end to a certain type of trade unionism, namely "assertive" trade unionism. This was the case with the policy to promote a particular type of cooperative, which not only denied power to workers in the enterprise, but were also accompanied by the prohibition of the right to organize. It was also the case with the policy to promote "union contracts", which were intended to transform trade unions into temporary work agencies and to bring an end rapidly to their role of representing workers. It was also the case of all the economic reforms which had seriously weakened or put an end to the right of collective bargaining, such as the pensions reform. Unfortunately, this policy had already borne fruit. Between 2001 and 2004, the number of trade unions created annually had dropped from 140 to six. The numbers spoke for themselves. This policy of the denigration of free trade unions was accompanied by precise vocabulary used in the public speeches by President Uribe. Indeed, he systematically tried to associate free trade unions, or "assertive" unions, with rebellion and guerrilla warfare.

With regard to the assassination on 4 August 2004 of three trade unionists by the armed forces in the region of Arauca, President Uribe had indicated during the meeting on 16 September 2004 that the victims had been members of the guerrilla forces. It even appeared that the Public Prosecutor's Office had recognized that they were trade unionists. The will of the President to bring an end to free trade unionism explained the general climate of violence towards trade unions. Furthermore, this policy was supported by the employers. In this regard, the speaker indicated that during the meeting on 16 September 2004 with the Vice-President of the National Association of Industries (ANDI), Mr. Echavarria, he had expressed the same point of view as President Uribe, indicating that Colombian trade unions were too "assertive" and not sufficiently "participative". This showed that in Colombia the political and economic powers only accepted social dialogue on condition that the social partners were obedient and discreet. They were not prepared to breathe life into the basic principles of democracy.

The intimidation of Colombian trade unionists was so serious that it even went beyond the borders of Colombia. Trade unionists who had also participated in the meeting of 16 September 2004 had been identified by the Government and were now being prevented from carrying out their international trade union activities freely. On 3 November 2004, the trade unionists Victor Baez, Secretary-General of ORIT-ICFTU, Rodolfo Benitez, Secretary-General of UNI America, Antonio Rodriguez, Secretary-General of ITF America, and Cameron Duncan, Secretary-General of ISP America, had been turned back at Bogotá airport. It could therefore be concluded that their names were on a blacklist. This situation was of grave concern. The speaker added that she had not returned to Colombia since September 2004 and feared to do so. As she had participated in the meeting with President Uribe, she supposed that her name was also on a blacklist. The intimidation had nothing to do with the war that was being waged in Colombia. The mere fact of being a free trade unionist supporting free trade unionism in Colombia raised fears for her safety.

Everyone was entitled to their personal opinion on what trade unions should be in their country. Some might even desire in their innermost selves that trade unions were less assertive. However, it was recognized that interference by the public authorities in trade union activities was a violation of Convention No. 87. The definition of what trade unions should be was a task that was the responsibility of the workers and the workers alone. Any vision to the contrary could lead, as in the case of Colombia and elsewhere, to the worst abuses and atrocities. In conclusion, she called on the Committee to convey this message with as much clarity and firmness as possible to the Government of Colombia.

The Government member of the United States said that, in its observation, the Committee of Experts had noted with grave concern the persistent climate of violence in Colombia and the situation of impunity that contributed to it, which prevented the free and effective exercise of trade union rights guaranteed in Convention No. 87. Her Government shared this concern and she pointed out that, although the number of murders had declined, the level of violence and threats of violence was still too high, while the number of convictions of the perpetrators of these acts was unacceptably low.

She added that freedom of association was critical if Colombia were to move successfully towards peace, social justice, reconciliation and democracy. While acknowledging the steps that the Government had taken, she emphasized that the Committee of Experts and the Committee on Freedom of Association had often recalled that workers' and employers' organizations could only exercise their activities effectively in a climate free of violence and the threat of violence. She, therefore, urged the Government to continue to take full advantage of the ILO's Technical Cooperation Programme for Colombia to reinforce protection measures for trade unionists. She called upon the Government to make greater efforts to investigate and prosecute those responsible for the violence that had claimed so many lives. Finally, she encouraged the Government to move forward with the labour law reforms recommended by the Committee of Experts so as to bring the country's laws fully in line with the provisions of the Convention.

The Worker member of Chile referred to various violations of Convention No. 87. The strike that had been called in April 2004 by the trade union USO had been declared illegal by the Minister of Social Protection under the pretext that the oil industry was an essential public service. Declaring the strike illegal had led to the dismissal of 247 union members, under section 450 of the Labour Code. In the case of 106 of these workers, whose reintegration had been ordered by a voluntary arbitration tribunal, a new trial had been initiated. Furthermore, over 1,000 disciplinary procedures had been set in motion to punish workers for exercising their right to strike. He also referred to the administrative decision which had led to the closure of Bancafé and the hospitals and clinics of state social enterprises. He emphasized that such arbitrary action without consultation had led to the destruction of two large union organizations and the violation of labour rights and collective agreements.

He said that union persecution was demonstrated by the discovery in August 2004 of "Operation Dragon", when a lieutenant colonel of the Colombian army, military registry No. 7217167, was arrested and found in possession of documents on the activities of SINTRAEMCALI and information on operation dragon plans for the extra-judicial assassination of the president of the union, Luis Hernandez Monroy, its legal adviser Berenice Celeyta and the leader Alexander Lopez, among others. It was also planned to infiltrate the union and create another enterprise-controlled union.

He added that 270 rural workers belonging to the rural workers' federation FENSUAGRO had been imprisoned and concluded by saying that violations of freedom of association in Colombia had increased in gravity and by asserting the right of workers in full freedom to establish organizations, elect their representatives, determine their programmes and save their own lives.

The Government member of Canada thanked the Government representative of Colombia for the additional information provided. However, he said that, despite the Government's efforts to improve security, and despite its acknowledgement in the London and Cartagena Declarations of the need to protect and guarantee the right to life and freedom of expression, the situation remained very serious. Trade unionists continued to disappear and continued to be threatened and assassinated. They were also facing other forms of violence, including, harassment, abductions and forced exile, as well as illegal searches and arbitrary detentions. Unfortunately, the perpetrators of these crimes were rarely brought to justice and his Government would look out for any positive results of the measures recently taken by the Government to end impunity. He urged the Government to take additional and concrete steps to end impunity in the country, to ensure that adequate resources were provided for the protection of trade unionists, and to work with the ILO through its Technical Cooperation Programme to pursue constructive social dialogue as a means of achieving social stability, respect for freedom of association and collective bargaining rights.

The Worker member of Venezuela said that the Committee had been examining the case of Colombia for many years and that each year the situation grew worse for the workers of the country. This year once again it was necessary to take note of very serious violations. For example, ECOPETROL had dismissed 247 trade unionists because they had opposed the policy of privatization and greater flexibility in the enterprise. TELECOM had been closed and mass dismissals had been undertaken in the Banco Cafetero. The postal administration and audiovisual companies had also been closed. These measures had been taken with the clear intention of making employment more flexible and less regular, through the imposition of so-called workers' cooperatives with the view to abolishing collective agreements and destroying trade unions. She also referred to acts of violence against trade union leaders and members. Between 1 January 2005 and the month of April, 16 unionized workers had been murdered, 123 had suffered death threats, 12 had been the victims of attempts upon their life, four had been kidnapped, 40 had been held under arbitrary detention and six had been forcibly displaced. The violence was reducing the level of unionization, as the workers were afraid to establish or join trade unions. She also referred to a plan to eliminate the trade union leaders of SINTRAEMCALI for having opposed the policy of greater flexibility and deregulation that was being imposed upon enterprises in the sector. Finally, she said that the Government needed to be called upon to guarantee the rights of organization, collective bargaining and strike and to put an end to the climate of violence against trade union leaders and members, and to the impunity enjoyed by those responsible for such violence. The Government should also be urged to take the necessary measures to reform the legislation and bring it into conformity with the Conventions on freedom of association and collective bargaining.

The Employer member of Colombia said that he had requested the floor because of a remark by the Worker member of France since she had given a false account of a meeting of the group of trade unionists which had visited the country in September 2004. He therefore wished the Committee to hear directly from the actors involved. He said that Colombia was experiencing a very difficult situation, a long-standing situation of generalized violence and that Colombian enterprises wished to build an inclusive society in a constructive and positive manner. The entrepreneurial sector was contributing to this and was even providing additional resources. For example, 3.34 per cent of the income from sales were allocated to activities of a social nature. Employers promoted family compensation funds. Economic, social and political indicators, as well as action to combat drug trafficking, showed that progress was possible at the institutional level. This was where the private sector wanted resources to be managed in an effective and transparent manner. The recent policies to restructure public entities had been supported by the employers. He stated that he was a member of the Board of the Colombian Social Security Institute, which was of tripartite composition. He indicated that the Institute was losing 250 million dollars a year and that it was clear that dialogue was needed within the Board to find a solution. The position of the union had been intransigent and it had refused any change. It had to be taken into consideration that in a public entity, not only the workers were to be taken into account, but also the millions of insured persons. In relation to the reference to pensions, he said that there were no funds and that currently an estimated 12.5 per cent of the budget went on pensions. In other words, the pay-as-you-go system had collapsed. He asserted that, as a result, there was no policy specifically targeting the workers of the Pensions Institute, but a need to restructure the State. He indicated that 50 state enterprises had been undergoing renovation in various ways, which reflected the restructuring of the public sector in which employers and workers had been invited to participate. However, he said that the workers had never attended the meetings. The Dialogue Commission, which should operate every month and offered a space for dialogue, was not being used as the attitude of the unions was confrontational and not constructive. He said that both he and the National Association of Industries (ANDI) wished to build, through social dialogue and technical cooperation, a society with a better distribution of wealth. Statements by ANDI on the labour chapter of the free trade agreement had appeared in a Colombian newspaper. ANDI had indicated that, with or without the free trade agreement, it was necessary to move forward to change the cooperative system, the legal definition of the concept of essential public services and to modify the collective labour system in areas in which rights were being used in an abusive manner.

The Government member of Peru emphasized the efforts made by the Government of Colombia to reduce the violence and congratulated the Government members who had acknowledged this, in particular the Government representative who spoke on behalf of the European Union. He stated that his country had also gone through a process of internal violence which had been the result of terrorist movements, and he was aware that these actions affected various social sectors, including the trade union movement. He indicated that it was necessary to avoid excesses in the fight against violence. He requested this forum to acknowledge the efforts made by the Government and the people of Colombia and to ask the international community to continue to support this process, which was of particular value for the security of the countries in the region. He hoped that the Government, employers and workers could, through social dialogue and with the technical support of the ILO, create a space for tripartite dialogue similar to that existing in his country. In conclusion, he emphasized that in a climate of violence there could be no real democracy, and without democracy there could not be real respect for workers' rights.

The Worker member of the United Kingdom called for an end to the politicization which was weakening the authority of the Conference Committee. He reaffirmed that the comprehensive campaign to destroy the trade union movement in Colombia was extremely grave, with 94 more murders of trade unionists in 2004, which was more than in the rest of the world combined. Since 2002, there had been a 65 per cent increase in the total number of violations of the human rights of trade unionists, in the form of murders, disappearances, death threats, arbitrary detention and forcible displacement, and an 800 per cent increase in violations against women trade unionists. Yet, some members of the Conference Committee were still claiming that the situation was improving. He added that trade unionists were even harassed when they travelled outside Colombia and that the current regime was refusing to implement the United Nations recommendation demanding an end to the holding of military intelligence files on trade unionists.

He said that it was incredible that a government could arbitrarily detain dozens of trade unionists each year, yet remain unable to break the impunity with which state forces and their paramilitary allies murdered trade unionists. Moreover, detained trade unionists were commonly accused of rebellion and, even though they were eventually released for lack of evidence, the accusation alone served to place them on the death list of the paramilitaries. It had been said by the Employers' group of the Governing Body, in the case of the failure of Myanmar to comply with its obligations under Convention No. 29, that the prevailing impunity was an indication of its tolerance of the gross violation of forced labour, and that any State which lacked the means to punish such crimes was in violation of the principles defended by the ILO. It was absolutely clear that the very same principles should apply to cases of murder in Colombia. He said that delegations from the trade union movement in his country visited Colombia regularly and had been provided by the Vice-President with a list of 13 cases in which it was claimed that the perpetrators had been sentenced and imprisoned. Yet, even in these 13 cases, out of the total of 791 murders of trade unionists between 1999 and 2004, in at least three cases the information provided had been inaccurate or economical with the truth. Indeed, the Government representative had now referred to only four convictions. Focusing on three specific cases, he outlined the inconsistencies in the information provided by the Government and undertook to provide the Office with the related documentation. He said that he could only conclude that, in attempting to suggest that the issue of impunity was being dealt with, the Government was not providing accurate information. He further cited a putative tripartite agreement referred to by the Government of Colombia in a recent discussion in the Governing Body as proof of the progress reached in terms of social dialogue, which had, in fact, been repudiated by the trade unions. He had also received information that the Government had revested to the National Treasury $83,000 unspent from the ILO fund – which the Governing Body had not been told. He expressed concern that the Conference Committee was being prevented from reaching appropriate decisions regarding the case of Colombia, not only by the political and economic interests involved, but also by the lack of verifiable and accurate information. Yet, the ILO's supervisory bodies had the right to expect member States to provide truthful information, which was the underlying reason why a tripartite high-level mission to Colombia was required.

He urged the Committee to adopt conclusions which reflected the continuing deterioration in the situation and that the continued violations of Conventions Nos. 87 and 98 were indeed destroying the Colombian trade union movement. If the Committee failed to do so, it would be encouraging further repression, rather than fulfilling its essential role of defending the fundamental right of all workers whatsoever to join and establish organizations of their own choosing for the defence of their interests, including through free collective bargaining.

The Government member of Brazil indicated that his Government was following with great attention developments in Colombia with respect to freedom of association and had taken due note of the statement made by the Government representative. His Government considered that the Conference Committee should support the measures that had been taken with a view to encouraging and strengthening social dialogue in Colombia. It should also take into account the results achieved by the Technical Cooperation Programme concluded between the Government of Colombia and the ILO. He hoped that the Government of Colombia would follow up the measures that had been proposed to improve labour relations in the country.

The Government member of Mexico thanked the Government representative of Colombia for the information provided, which demonstrated the Government's constructive attitude and its cooperation to guarantee the trade union rights provided for in Convention No. 87. The results described might not be up to the expectations of the Committee, but it should be recognized that they indicated that progress was gradually being made. The situation made it difficult to punish the perpetrators of violent acts against trade unionists and violence was affecting all sectors of society. She encouraged the Government, employers and workers of Colombia to strengthen their dialogue and cooperation so as to continue implementing the special Technical Cooperation Programme for the country.

The Government member of China said that the information provided by the Government representative showed that Colombia was indeed making efforts to protect trade union rights. Action was therefore being taken and progress was being made. However, although a gradual improvement was being achieved in the effort to solve the problem, all sides agreed that there was still a long way to go. She noted that the ILO and the Government were engaged in cooperation and hoped that it would be effective in achieving a solution to the problem. She called upon all sides to adopt a practical attitude to enhancing the implementation of the Convention in Colombia and to achieve a settlement of the important issues at stake.

A Government representative said that his comments in reply to the previous speakers could be divided into three parts: (1) there was agreement on important points; (2) there were differences of information; and (3) there were differences of opinion. With regard to the areas of agreement, he felt that employers, workers, most governments and the Government of Colombia all agreed that the ILO programme of technical cooperation had been functioning and that it should continue to do so. He asserted that they should agree to implement the Governing Body's decision of March 2005 and to seek the necessary resources. He pointed out that there had been agreement in so far as governments, as well as employers and workers, had all made reference to violence, and had indicated that the violence was the result of subversive groups and the drug trafficking that had placed the country in this situation. They had also all agreed that even one death was unacceptable. They agreed on the fact that this unacceptable violence, which was inexplicable due to its complexity, made union activities difficult. He added that it was also a difficult situation for employers who ran the risk of being kidnapped and assassinated. There was a situation of generalized violence and the labour situation had to be understood in this context. They had also agreed on the need to combat impunity.

With regard to the second point, differences of information, he recalled the assertion that Bancafé was a solid enterprise. This, however, was wrong, as the Government had already provided it with 612 million dollars, of which 55 million were intended for pensions. Moreover, they were not in agreement on statistics. The workers had said that unemployment had increased, while the Government had indicated that unemployment in 2001 was 20 per cent and had fallen to 12 per cent last month. Government figures showed a clear fall in unemployment. He also referred to other indicators and said that he was offering the data supplied by the Government to the workers so they could examine them, noting that the data had been compiled by independent entities. Nor was there agreement that, as claimed by the workers, the number of collective agreements was falling, as 491 collective agreements had been concluded in 2000, 433 in 2001 and over 400 in 2004. In other words, the average number of collective agreements concluded had not changed. There had not been agreement on the statement that the health care system was not functioning, as last year had witnessed the greatest increase in health coverage for the underprivileged sector of the population. He regretted to hear statements claiming that justice was rarely impartial. He pointed out that many judges were union members and he could not accept the assertion that they were being manipulated. With regard to TELECOM, he said that the Government had no means to support it and that TELECOM did not have sufficient capital. He recalled that many European countries had been obliged to privatize public enterprises and that the President of Colombia had not taken a decision to liquidate TELECOM, but had decided to maintain the enterprise under efficient management. Reference had been made to the dismissal of workers, but nothing had been said about the 70 million dollars provided in compensation and other benefits. It had been said that credit was not available for farmers, but the amount of funds available for microcredit had increased to 2.1 billion dollars. The Government was said to have prohibited the access of trade union members, but Mr. Carlos Rodriguez, who was in the room, did not mention that he had called from the airport because of the difficulties encountered and that after a few hours his group had been able to go through, had been received by the Government and that their visas had even been extended to 30 days. One group of workers had decided to return to their respective countries, but that was a voluntary decision. As for the death of trade union members, he indicated that the workers had not mentioned that the Arauca investigation had been transferred from a military to a civilian court.

Finally, the speaker said that he could not accept the fact that a tripartite forum used adjectives with reference to interventions and that Mr. Uribe had been called a fascist and a liar, or the State an assassin. This was not acceptable behaviour in the ILO for employers or for workers. The discussion should be of a predominantly technical nature and he was concerned about such statements, which were loaded with hate and political interest. He refused to respond to such accusations, except to deny them.

On behalf of his Government, he called upon employers and workers to understand that the situation of the Colombian people was difficult, but that progress was being made. There had been some encouraging results, which showed not that the problems had been resolved, but that efforts were continuously being made. He indicated that, earlier in the day, he had held a meeting with the Chairperson of the Committee on Freedom of Association and that he had invited him to come to Colombia and meet with the various sectors of Colombian society and all the actors involved in the issue of impunity. He emphasized that both problems and achievements should be recognized. It was necessary to be careful, because there was a risk that, in seeking to punish Colombia, decisions might be taken which could then be used for political purposes, which would not benefit the people of Colombia. He called for the Technical Cooperation Programme to be continued so as to strengthen social dialogue and help reduce violence.

Another Government representative (Vice-Minister of Social Protection) stated the importance of collaboration and cooperation between all instances of the Organization and the Government of Colombia. The Government had invited the Chairperson of the Committee on Freedom of Association to visit the country and meet with the Executive Branch, judges, supervisory bodies, workers' and employers' organizations and to get in touch with public opinion. His Government would provide all the necessary information to explain and find a solution to the problems. Collaboration was necessary in order to ensure greater transparency.

The speaker stated that his Government was ready to extend the invitation to the spokespersons for the Worker and Employer members of this Committee, if their visit would contribute to the better understanding of the situation and to finding solutions.

The Worker members took note of the Government's proposals for a visit to take place in Colombia to take full cognizance of the actual situation in the country. They agreed that the problems of the country went well beyond those mentioned by the Committee of Experts in its observation, as witnessed by the obstacles encountered by workers' organizations when they sought to have the most fundamental rights of their members respected.

The Worker members suggested that the Conference Committee decide in favour of a high-level tripartite mission to Colombia, which would include among its members the two Vice-Chairpersons of the Conference Committee and whose mandate would be the application of the Convention and technical cooperation.

The Employer members observed that the problem of violence was central to this difficult case and putting an end to it was essential for the resolution of the case. They noted that the Government was facing difficulties in addressing this problem comprehensively.

The Employer members took note of the proposal made by the Government representative to invite the Chairperson of the Committee on Freedom of Association and the Vice-Chairpersons of the Conference Committee to visit the country. They saw this as a positive step that should be commended. They wanted to draw attention, however, to the need to recognize that the mandate and purpose of the Committee on Freedom of Association was different from that of the Conference Committee. The mandate of the Conference Committee was limited to the implementation of the Convention in law and in practice. The Committee on Freedom of Association had a broader mandate which was not limited to the terms of the Convention.

The Employer members concluded by noting that the visit would include contacts with the social partners and monitoring bodies, and would place emphasis on the implementation of the Convention in law and in practice with particular focus on the ILO special Technical Cooperation Programme for Colombia.

The Committee took note of the oral information provided by the Minister of Social Protection and the discussion that followed. The Committee observed with great concern that the pending problems were extremely serious and related in particular to murders of trade union leaders and members, other acts of violence against trade unionists and the situation of impunity enjoyed by the perpetrators. The Committee observed that the acts of violence also affected other sectors and groups including the employers, in particular through abductions. The Committee noted that the Committee on Freedom of Association had examined serious complaints concerning murders and acts of violence against trade unionists. The Committee condemned once again in the strongest terms all these acts of violence in the context of the dramatic situation of violence experienced by the country and indicated to the Government that it had the obligation to take all necessary measures urgently in order to put an end to violence and guarantee the security of persons.

The Committee took note of the Government's statements according to which the number of murders of trade unionists and acts of violence had decreased and the authorities had adopted measures for the protection of trade unionists and trade union premises. The Committee also noted the information contained in the report of the Attorney-General on indictments, detentions and sentences in relation to murders as well as on the new system of incrimination to increase the effectiveness of the investigations in the framework of the fight against impunity.

The Committee recalled that the organizations of workers and employers could exercise their activities in a free and meaningful manner only in a climate that was free from violence and once again urged the Government to guarantee the right to life and security, and to reinforce urgently the necessary institutions to put an end to the inadmissible situation of impunity which constituted a great obstacle to the exercise of the rights guaranteed by the Convention. The Committee requested the reinforcement of the protection measures for trade unionists and of the ILO Technical Cooperation Programme. The Committee observed more generally that the climate which reigned in the country endangered the exercise of trade union activities and other human rights and that this situation was unacceptable. The Committee noted that the Government had invited the Chairperson of the Committee on Freedom of Association to meet with the social actors and the competent authorities in Colombia.

With regard to the requested legal reforms, the Committee took note of the Government's statements on the legal questions raised by the Committee of Experts. The Committee took note of the Government's statements according to which time was needed to move ahead in the process of adjusting the labour legislation and the tripartite labour negotiation.

The Committee took note of the information and allegations of the Worker members in relation to: the failure to respect trade union rights in the context of a large number of restructurings, privatizations, or mergers, particularly in the pubic sector among others; mass dismissals; other anti-union dismissals; the recourse to cooperatives which constituted hidden employment relationships and deprived workers of freedom of association and collective bargaining; the increasing recourse to collective accords with non-unionized workers and the slowness, complexity, malfunctioning, and partiality of judicial processes. The Committee requested the Government to communicate information to the Committee of Experts on all the above points.

The Committee requested the Government to send a detailed report to the Committee of Experts, so that it could examine the developments at its next meeting, including the reply to the comments presented by trade union organizations with regard to the acts of violence, to obstacles to the registration of trade unions and to the provisions mentioned by the Committee of Experts. The Committee requested the Government to report on the number of cases of murders which had come to an end before the judicial instances and in which it had been possible to identify those responsible and punish those guilty so that the serious situation of impunity could be contained.

The Committee expressed the firm hope that in the very near future real progress would be observed in particular in order to overcome all obstacles to the full exercise of freedom of association with a view to allowing trade union organizations to exercise the rights guaranteed by the Convention in a climate of full security, free from threats and fear. The Committee underlined the importance of having these objectives met through social dialogue and agreement and recalled that the technical assistance of the Office was at the Government's disposal. The Committee requested the Government and the social actors to reactivate social dialogue without delay. The Committee urged the Government to take measures in this respect urgently.

The Committee, noting that the Government had extended its invitation to the Chairperson of the Committee on Freedom of Association and the Employer and Worker Vice-Chairpersons of the Committee on the Application of Standards, decided that a high-level tripartite visit should take place led by the Chairperson of the Committee on Freedom of Association accompanied by the spokespersons of the Employer and Worker groups of the Committee. The visit that should take place would include meetings with the Government, the organizations of workers and employers, the competent organs of Colombia in the area of investigation and supervision, and would place particular emphasis on all questions relative to the application of Convention No. 87 in law and in practice and to the ILO special Technical Cooperation programme for Colombia.

GUATEMALA (ratification: 1952). A Government representative (Minister of Labour and Social Security) declared his firm conviction that the mechanisms of control on the application of international standards that the ILO had put in place created an important mechanism for cooperation for the country. The observations of the Committee of Experts were objective, sincere and useful in order to strengthen the institutional regime, the governance and the democracy of Guatemala. The correct utilization of the observations of the Committee of Experts permitted the Government and the social partners to position themselves so that they do not lose sight of the true sense of international labour legislation.

The speaker recalled that Guatemala has faced significant obstacles in its history of confrontation and ideological intolerance. The advances that have been presented in the observations of the Committee of Experts seem small, but in Guatemala constituted true progress if one takes into account the profound problems that have to be confronted by means of effective social dialogue. In order to continue advancing, there was a need to count on the support of the Committee, the Conference, the Employers, and principally the trade unions.

In relation to the observations of the Committee of Experts, the speaker enthusiastically expressed the recognition of the sincere political will of the Government to collaborate with the ILO during the direct contacts mission conducted in 2004 and the positive assessment of the commitments made by the Government. With this sentiment the Government representative stated that his Government has promoted the integration and the function of the Tripartite Commission of International Affairs, which has met and worked in uninterrupted form from 2004 to the present and has obtained advances in the consultation and agreement for the creation of a mechanism of "immediate intervention" in order to examine the complaints within the competence of the Committee on Freedom of Association and the observations on the application of international conventions, that will begin to function soon. The complaints that are not sent directly to the ILO, except in the instance of problems of national interpretation, can be resolved in the country. Likewise, the Government analysed with the employers and trade unions the necessary legal reforms to overcome the problems that they had with the reforms of 2003, in particular the existence in the national penal legislation of provisions against freedom of association principles. The Government looked to address the aspects indicated by the Committee of Experts in relation to ILO Conventions Nos. 87 and 98, the eligibility requirements for becoming a trade union leader, the legal criteria to establish the necessary votes to call a strike and the legal definition of essential services in relation to the exercise of the right to strike. In this respect, the Tripartite Commission has arrived at a consensus to undertake the legal reforms necessary that permit adaptation of the Labour Code to the relevant international standards on discrimination in employment and occupation. In this sense, the Government has presented a proposal to Congress for its approval. Many of the problems identified by the Committee of Experts have been resolved through laws that have amended problematic provisions, as in the case of Government Decree 700/2003.

In relation to the commitments made before the direct contacts mission, the Government representative stated that his Government has met all of those and noted concrete advances in the approval of initiatives for legal reform that the Tripartite Commission had accepted and requested the assistance of the Office, in order to organize the first national seminar on labour rights and freedom of association.

With respect to the competence of labour inspection regarding trade union rights of civil servants, the labour inspection is competent to hear complaints of violations of trade union rights of public employees and act as a mediator, as has been affirmed in various rulings of the Tribunal of Conflict of Jurisdiction of the Supreme Court of Guatemala. The mechanism to deal with this was actually being used to obtain an alternative solution to collective conflicts between public sector workers and their employers.

With regard to the creation of trade unions in industry, the speaker noted that it was only a problem of interpretation of the applicable legislation, and that section 215 of the Labour Code, that did not violate any principle of freedom of association by providing that in order to form and industry trade union, at the branch level, workers can establish unions at the enterprise level so long as they were all of a similar nature. If a union movement did not have a sufficient number of members to establish an industry trade union they could then establish an enterprise union where they could group with a variety of enterprises of the same nature, and where they needed only 20 workers. If today no such union has been established, this was because the trade union movement was not as yet sufficiently developed.

With respect to the imbalance between trade unions and solidarist associations, the speaker noted the operational deficiencies in tabulating the real number of active trade unions and their affiliates. The Government has worked to overcome these deficiencies in a project to systemize the labour register, but it would take time to complete this project due to the lack of funds. The speaker requested the support of the Office in finalizing this project. The indicator of the number of solidarist associations and their affiliates was a result of a unilateral declaration of these associations although there were no objective elements to confirms that there was in practice violation of trade union rights.

The speaker recognized the existence of certain institutional weaknesses in Guatemala for this type of crime. The acts of violence have diminished considerably and the Government supported the interventions of the authorities to complete their investigations quickly and effectively. The speaker noted that the Government was considering a protection mechanism recommended by the direct contacts mission in 2004. In closing, the speaker observed that the Committee of Experts had recognized the efforts of the Government by listing the country among those who had made progress. He requested that the case of Guatemala should not be mentioned in a special paragraph since this would not contribute to the strengthening of national institutions.

The Worker members indicated that, although the information presented by the Government of Guatemala tended to show progress, the reality refuted these assertions. The changes mentioned by the Committee of Experts in its report should be greeted with caution, taking into account the new facts which reinforced the concerns raised by the many elements that demonstrated the persistence of the violation of Convention No. 87 in Guatemala. While, according to the report of the Committee of Experts, the labour inspectorate would have the power to impose sanctions in case of violation of trade union rights, in fact the Constitutional Court had restricted this power in August 2004 and the labour inspectorate was often not on the side of the workers during social conflicts. On this point, further information on the staff of the labour inspectorate, the sanctions imposed in case of freedom of association violations and their effective application would be necessary. The Worker members underlined that Act No. 35 of 1996, known as the anti-strike act, still prohibited workers in public services from striking under penalty of imprisonment. This was sufficient to demonstrate that the restrictions of the Guatemalan workers' rights had not yet been lifted.

The Worker members protested against the assertion of the Government that "civil society" organizations tended to show little respect for the institutional means for addressing labour disputes, an assertion which tended, in their view, to discredit the social partners when these claimed the application of the rights and procedures to which they themselves were submitted.

The Worker members underlined that the rule imposing a requirement to be of Guatemalan nationality and working in the enterprise or sector concerned in order to be elected as trade union leader, remained in force although it had been found contrary to Convention No. 87, just like the rule imposing a requirement of 50 per cent plus one of the workers in the sector in order to be able to establish an industry trade union, a fact which created interminable delays or even refusals of trade unions' registration. This situation was in contrast to the assertions of the Government which claimed that the situation had gotten back to normal and attributed the length of the delays to the workers, on the grounds that they "had failed to present documents", an assertion which demonstrated by the way that, in reality, the situation had not yet returned to normal. Moreover, with regard to the «maquila» sector, the Government had mentioned the existence of two trade union organizations, which were really few in relation to the number of enterprises in this sector.

The Worker members also underlined that the confusion which endured on the subject of registration of trade union organizations in the taxation register, on which the Committee on Freedom of Association had already pronounced itself, appeared to allow the carrying out of controls over trade unions at any time. Moreover, the obstacles in the area of collective agreements remained numerous in practice: pressure on trade unionists, arbitrary dismissals of trade unionists, etc., as well as problems already raised with regard to the judicial power such as corruption, influence peddling, lack of vocational training, partiality, unexpected interventions by the Constitutional Court paralysing the action of the Labour Ministry. The Worker members noted a certain incoherence in this respect between the Guatemalan authorities, which had recognized the existence of a structural problem in the administration of justice as a whole, and the comments of the Committee of Experts which gave the impression that the changes made would guarantee an immediate handling of the problems relative to freedom of association. They also raised the incoherence between the announcement of the acquittal of Mr. Rigoberto Dueñas and the new charges brought against him by justice due to an appeal lodged in the Appeals Court, despite the conclusions of the Committee on Freedom of Association, the direct contacts mission and the messages of support by employers rallied in the Coordination Committee of agricultural, commercial, industrial and financial associations (CACIF).

The Worker members stated that the principle "in dubio, pro operario", according to which the most favourable legal rule should apply to workers in case of doubt, was largely refuted in practice as it was more common to decide a case on the basis of often biased legal precedents in contempt of the legislative prerogatives of Congress. They denounced the tendency to systematically take away labour conflicts from the competence of the Labour Ministry in order to bring them before the penal courts so as to prosecute and reprimand trade union leaders by reason of their social action.

The Worker members denounced the persistence of several facts: (i) the climate of violence and the acts which impeded the free exercise of freedom of association as illustrated by the numbers provided by the Government: 42 acts of violence in 2002-03 for example; (ii) the impunity which surrounded the acts of violence committed against trade unionists; and (iii) the persistence of threats and harassment against trade union leaders as demonstrated by the recent repression of the demonstration against the adoption of the free trade treaty, which had been adopted without consultations with the social partners despite its decisive impact on employment. They also denounced the acts of unauthorized entry into the trade union premises of several trade unions on 9, 10 and 11 May 2005, which had not given rise to any investigation, as well as the violence faced by workers in the informal economy, like Julio Rolando Raquel, secretary-general of a trade union, murdered at the end of 2004 without any legal proceedings having been instituted against the perpetrators of this act, an example which was unfortunately part of a very long list.

Finally, the Worker members differentiated themselves in relation to the assessment of the Committee of Experts which was too optimistic in their view, considering that: one could not talk of progress as long as trade unionists were being murdered, harassed or threatened; repression was being aggravated; so many cases (12) remained pending before the Committee on Freedom of Association; so many problems of application of Conventions Nos. 87 and 98 remained in practice.

The Employer members thanked the Government for providing complete and comprehensive information and noted that the ILO's 2004 direct contact mission was successful. They welcomed that the Government extended the mandate of the mission to Convention No. 87. The number of issues dealt with by the Committee of Experts had decreased but a number of problems remained. The Government worked towards solving them through the National Tripartite Committee. It was a central principle of the Convention that freedom of association could only be realized in an atmosphere free from violence and intimidation. The cases of violence against trade unionists, including cases of murder, were entirely unacceptable. While the Government established a Special Public Prosecutor, the results achieved were mixed and there was no information available to determine whether the measures taken were adequate. The Labour Code's requirement that trade union leaders be of Guatemalan origin was not in accordance with the Convention. Regarding the need to have "50 per cent plus one" of those working in an enterprise as a requirement to form an industry trade union, the Employer members stated that that percentage was too high. However, it was unclear on how the rule worked in practice in terms of the ability of smaller unions to engage collective bargaining. As to the right to strike, the position of the Employer members was well known. Due to the different situations from country to country, no single approach could exist in respect to the quorum required to call for a strike. Similarly, concerning essential services in which compulsory arbitration could be imposed, no «one-size- fits-all» approach was possible, as a given service may be essential in one country, but not in another, depending on the respective levels of development. In conclusion, the remaining problems went beyond questions of interpretation and the Government needed to do more to ensure the application of the Convention in law and practice. Further ILO assistance would facilitate the resolution of the outstanding issues.

The Worker member of Guatemala noted that while it was true that the situation in his country was examined in the past because of the persistent failure of the Government to apply ratified ILO Conventions, it was necessary to pursue, perseverance was required to ensure that pending issues were settled. Fifty years after ratifying Convention No. 87, Guatemala continued to prevent the forming of new trade unions in the country, when not seeking to eliminate those that already existed, as had been the case in the National Center of books and didactic texts «José de Ipiña Ibarra» of the Ministry of Education (CENALTEX) company or in certain communes of Retahuleu, Tecun Human etc.

The speaker mentioned hurdles put in the way of trade unions in the country, even after they had been recognized and legalized by the Ministry of Labour: Leaders threatened, intimidated, persecuted or dismissed. Although, after the direct contact mission's visit the Government decided to free trade unionist Rigoberto Duenas, none of the charges against him actually being sustainable, a high court decided to take legal action against him, completely ignoring the information provided to the Committee of Experts. Secondly, the Committee of Experts received information according to which «the Labour Inspectorate was granted certain jurisdiction in the system of sanctions provided in case of non-respect of trade union freedoms», once it was ascertained that such sanctions had in fact been taken. The Constitutional Court had declare this jurisdiction to be unconstitutional, thereby creating a gap in the applicable law as a result of the disappearance of the jurisdictional body authorized to impose fines.

The speaker pointed out that the workers were the target of various acts of aggression – 122 were recorded in 2004, 68 to date in 2005, of which 12 in recent weeks: The judiciary had shown little diligence – 90 per cent of cases were filed and forgotten. Though in many previous cases, investigations had been opened, as had been the case following the death of trade unionist Julio Raquel, whose own wife has identified the culprits, the Public Prosecutor had not been diligent in any respect. This demonstrated an absence of judicial capacity and an absence of political will by the Government to act

The speaker mentioned that the Government had put obstacles to the opening of the Office of the UN High Commissioner for Human Rights, which demonstrated the lack of will on behalf of the Government to put in place the conditions required for the effective application fo human rights and freedom of association in the country.

The Labour Code clearly provided for the reintegration within 24 hours of a worker who had been dismissed for having formed a trade union, which showed that the problem at the centre of violations of these rights lay in the lack of will by the State to have them respected.- Thus workers had to wait light years for a court to pass verdict on their case, while others charged with other offences were provided with immunity from prosecution by the labour tribunals.

The clauses in section 390 and 430 of the Guatemalan Penal Code considered as penal all labour conflicts involving the workers. At the same time, when a worker pressed charges for flagrant abuses of his rights by an employer, the competent authorities remained silent. If, on the other hand, an employer pressed false charges against a worker, as was the case with the Maria de Lourdes agricultural enterprise, measures were immediately taken against the workers. Many men and women workers in this enterprise had been dismissed for having helped to form a trade union.

In the last two years, Government policy on workers' demonstrations consisted in accusing union leaders of terrorism. The President of the Republic had publicly threatened to imprison leaders at demonstrations. Several cases had confirmed this stance. A demonstration by the pilots' union had led to the imprisonment of 30 union leaders; a demonstration by the street traders' union had led to the imprisonment of 11 union leaders; another demonstration had led to the death of a child; another ended with the eviction of farmers in the Retahuleu district, with several deaths and many incarcerations. During demonstrations against the free trade agreement, thanks to the solidarity shown by the Prosecution for Human Rights, it had been possible to free all the leaders after the police had surrounded the offices where they were meeting and putting them in jail.

In conclusion, the speaker appealed to the solidarity of government and workers around the world, as well as to the ILO, to give Guatemalans the opportunity to live in dignity and obtain justice.

The Employer member of Guatemala expressed satisfaction with the progress noted by the report of the Committee of Experts and by the present Committee itself as being due to the merit of the national authorities and the employers. Progress on Conventions No. 98 and 129 had been clearly emphasized, and there had been positive comments on Convention No. 87. The direct contact mission of May 20045 noted a reduction in violence as well as a real will to submit various issues related to legal reform to tripartite discussion. The Congress of the Republic could then incorporate the national tripartite agreements into national legislation.

In Guatemala, the current climate was favourable to positive and concrete steps being taken to bring national legislation into conformity with international labour Conventions. The Constitutional Court had even recently recognized the competence of the judicial system to take sanctions against non-respect of freedom of association principles. This did not mean to say tha a legal void had existed prior to this regarding the imposition of sanctions, but that the courts could henceforth impose them.

In his opinion, some trade union organizations were taking part in tripartite dialogue while others preferred using the complaints procedure at national level. Events were currently leaning towards some legal issues – which, nevertheless, did not concern constitutional reform of the regulation of the right to strike, on which Convention No. 87 said nothing – being resolved by social dialogue. The ILO should show confidence in the process currently underway in Guatemala. In any case, the exercise of trade union rights had to conform to the law. No illegal practices could be allowed under the cover of freedom association.

The Government member of Norway, speaking also on behalf of the Governments of Denmark, Finland, Iceland and Sweden, noted the information supplied to the direct contact mission by the Special Public Prosecutor's Office, indicating a significant decrease in physical violence, while the number of cases involving threats and coercion had increased considerably. According to the Government, all cases relating to murder and other offences were still at the stage of investigation. This situation was of grave concern. Criminal proceedings were extremely slow and impunity was the norm in cases concerning trade unionists. The Nordic countries emphasized that trade union rights could only be exercised in an atmosphere which is free from violence and coercion. As requested by the Committee of Experts, the Government should be asked to provide information on any offences against trade unionists reported to the Special Prosecutor's Office. It was hoped that the Government would make every effort to ensure full respect for trade union members' human rights and that concrete progress on the above-mentioned point could be noted in the near future.

The Worker member of Panama denounced the violence and aggression shown by the Guatemalan authorities towards the trade union movement. He said that, in a letter addressed to the Vice-President of the Republic of Guatemala, he had condemned 122 acts of aggression committed in 2004 and 68 recorded to date in 2005 (of which 12 had taken place in recent weeks). In Guatemala, illegal armed groups and secret wings of the security services (CIACS) were acting in concert with thee security forces and were partly linked to organized crime and certain employers' organisations. The Prosecutor for Human Rights had condemned both the impunity that CIACS enjoyed and its collusion with the military intelligence services and organized crime. The UN Verification Mission to Guatemala had also declared the situation alarming. CIACS had been blamed in complaints lodged concerning human rights abuses, but no judicial proceedings had been initiated to allow investigations to be opened on these crimes and to find the guilty parties.

As regarded the situation concerning trade unionist Rigoberto Duenas, the speaker was confident that a final solution would soon be found to obtain his release. The Government of Guatemala seemed not to have the political will to address illegal acts against freedom of association and it had to be requested to provide information of complaints that had been lodged.

The Worker member of Costa Rica stated that a purely juridical analysis could not explain the Guatemalan problem. As regarded the trade union situation, the Government had shown itself to be unable to deal with complaints concerning illegal dismissals or violation of collective agreements. Joining other speakers in condemning the situation, he referred to the rigid attitude of the legal system which passed laws contrary to workers' rights and which benefited solidarist associations. The speaker also recalled that legal procedures related to the Mi Terra and El Tesoro estates, to the municipality of Livington and the El Anco estate had been ongoing for many years without producing concrete results. The workers members finally expressed his solidarity with unionist Rigoberto Duenas.

The Government member of El Salvador expressed her understanding of the situation in Guatemala and referred to the statement made by the Government representative. The efforts made by the Government of Guatemala to overcome the difficulties highlighted in the Committee of Experts' observations should be praised. The Office should support such efforts.

The Worker member of Norway recalled that the Committee had asked the Government to rectify breaches of the Convention for many years, and yet, workers in Guatemala continued to be victims of serious violations of labour rights, including the right to strike. It was disturbing to see that the direct contact mission found that threats and use of coercion against workers were increasing considerably. The Government's promises to remedy anti-union practices were thus put in question. The fact that only one per cent of workers in Guatemala were organized was due to the climate of fear that prevailed in the country. Unionists risked losing their jobs and even their life. When a demonstration took place following the Government's approval of the free trade agreement with the United States, which had been concluded without consulting civil society, the armed police and soldiers surrounded the office of a trade union which took part in the demonstration. In May 2005, unknown perpetrators broke into the offices of several trade union organizations. Only information about the organizations was stolen, while valuable equipment was left untouched. Such incidents increased the fear among trade unionists, preventing them from carrying out their democratic trade union rights. The Committee of Experts still listed severe restrictions of freedom of association contrary to the Convention, including section 241 of the Labour Code, regarding the number of workers needed at a workplace to be allowed to call a strike. The same applied to the imposition of compulsory arbitration in cases of public sector strikes of services which are not essential according to the ILO. Despite many promises by the Government to amend the labour laws and the pledges made to the direct contact mission, few measures had been taken. No legal strikes took place in 2004 and the harassment of workers continued, both in the private and public sector. Only if the Labour Code and section 390 of the Penal Code were changed, would the Government's commitment be credible. Finally, the ILO should consider more serious measures to change the situation.

The Government representative reaffirmed the will to continue the efforts recognized by the Committee of Experts and the direct contact mission. His Government intended to continue the fight against corruption. The situation regarding trade unionist Rigoberto Dueñas was being examined by the penal justice system and was not being treated as a case of trade union persecution. The delegation at the present session of the Conference was testimony to the openness to dialogue of his Government since it also included a magistrate of the Supreme Court of Justice and various members of the Congress of the Republic.

The Worker members stated that, considering the elements contained in the Committee of Experts' report together with the situation prevailing in the country, it was unthinkable to conclude that progress had been made in this case. In their view, all the elements mentioned in the discussion showed that the problems persisted and to some extent even worsened.

The Worker members therefore asked that the Committee, in its conclusions, ask the Government to provide a detailed report containing precise answers to all the questions raised by the Committee of Experts regarding the application of Convention No. 87. The Government should also be asked to take, as a matter of urgency, all necessary measures to guarantee the exercise of freedom of association, adopting legislation and ensuring practice in accordance with the Convention.

While recognizing that the technical assistance demanded by the Government could be useful, the Worker members asked that the Government would be requested to provide, in its next report: (1) an assessment of the measures taken by the national tripartite committee, the Special Prosecutor's Office and the labour inspectorate; (2) statistical information indicating the number of registered trade unions and solidarist associations, as well as (3) information on the follow-up measures taken to the related conclusions of the Committee of Freedom of Association.

The Employer members concluded that, while the situation was improving, it was not yet perfect. The Committee of Experts should undertake a full assessment of the situation and the information requested by the Workers members would be useful for that purpose.

The Committee took note of the oral information provided by the Government representative and the discussion that followed. The Committee noted with concern that the pending problems related to acts of violence against trade unionists, excessive delays in criminal proceedings and the impunity which often prevailed, as well as restrictions in law or in practice to the establishment, functioning and free exercise of the activities of trade unions, as well as penal sanctions for such activities. The Committee took note of the comments presented to the Committee of Experts by various trade union organizations. The Committee also took note of the results of a direct contacts mission carried out in May 2004 and the commitments undertaken by the Government.

The Committee took note of the statements of the Government representative according to which Guatemala was supporting all the actions of the competent authorities in order to conclude the criminal investigations on acts of violence against trade unionists in a prompt and effective manner. The Committee took note that, according to the Government, certain questions raised by the Committee of Experts constituted problems of legal interpretation which could be overcome through the application of the legal rule which was most favourable to the workers. In particular, according to the Government, the problem relative to Decree No. 700-2003 on essential services had been overcome by virtue of subsequent laws.

The Committee underlined that trade union rights could only be exercised in a climate that is free from violence and threats of any kind and requested the Government to make all efforts to guarantee the exercise of trade union rights in a climate of full security for trade unionists and to improve the administrating of justice and avoid impunity. The Committee requested the Government to take the necessary measures to bring the legislation and practice into full conformity with the provisions of the Convention, and to communicate a complete report containing all pending questions, to the Committee of Experts this year. The Committee requested the Government to send concrete information on the number of inspections, the sanctions imposed in cases of violations of trade union rights in all sectors including the *maquila***, attaching statistics and numbers of trade unions and solidarist associations, as well as on the result of the criminal investigations of the Special Public Prosecutor's Office. The Committee expressed the hope that in the very near future it would be in a position to observe progress in relation to the pending problems and recalled that the technical assistance of the ILO was at the disposal of the Government.**

MYANMAR (ratification: 1955). **A government representative** stated that in Myanmar, workers were always regarded as one of the major driving forces for development. Their essential role was always recognized, their social welfare was always looked after and their rights were always protected in accordance with the law by successive Myanmar governments. Both the State Constitutions of 1947 and 1974 had contained relevant provisions with regard to the role of workers in Myanmar society and their rights. He recalled that there had been labour unions under the parliamentary democracy, which had lasted from 1948 to 1962, and workers' organizations under the socialist economic system, which had lasted from 1962 to 1988. It was well known that the second Constitution of 1974 had ceased to exist in 1988 in accordance with the wishes of the people.

The current Myanmar Government had been striving to establish a modern, developed and democratic state in accordance with the aspirations of its people. In this respect, Myanmar had adopted a seven-step Road Map, the first step of which was the reconvening of the National Convention. This process, which had started in 1993 and had been interrupted in 1996, was to lay down the basic principles for drafting a new state Constitution. During its sessions between 1993 and 1996, the National Convention had laid down basic principles, including basic principles concerning workers. The resumed session of the National Convention, which had started on 20 May 2004, had conducted clarifications and deliberations on basic principles for the social sector, including the rights of workers and their social welfare rights. The deliberations also had dealt with the basic principle of forming workers' organizations. In the process of drafting a new state Constitution, these basic principles would provide a framework for drafting detailed provisions relating to these aforementioned matters. At its most recent session, starting on 17 February 2005, the National Convention had adopted some detailed basic principles for the social sector to be contained in the Union legislative list. These basic principles, among other things, included matters related to the rights of workers, i.e. hours of work, rest periods, holidays, occupational safety, labour disputes, social security and labour organizations. The National Convention had also agreed that laws to protect the rights of workers and to create job opportunities should also be enacted. The delegates attending the National Convention had also shared the view that an Occupational Safety Act and Occupational Hazard Act should be included in the Union legislative list. He concluded by stating that appropriate workers' organizations would emerge once Myanmar had its new Constitution.

The Worker members stated that it was more than embarrassing that this case was this year again before the Committee. Last year the Committee had decided to include the conclusions once again in a special paragraph on continued failure to apply the Convention. It appeared from the report of the Committee of Experts that the Government of Myanmar was not at all prepared to adopt any of the changes requested and had not sent any of the requested information, particularly on the concrete means adopted to ensure improved conformity with the Convention.

They recalled that the legislation and military decrees that this Committee had examined over the years were still in force and they prohibited trade union organization and allowed for the punishment of those who tried to establish any form of democratic organization. This legislation included Order No. 2/88, issued by the SLORC on 18 September 1988, the date of the military coup, which prohibited any activity by five persons or more, such as "gathering, walking or marching in procession, chanting slogans, delivering speeches regardless of whether the act is with the intention of creating disturbances or committing crime or not". Other repressive legislation included the 1908 Unlawful Association Act, which provided for imprisonment of no less than two years for members of unlawful associations or persons taking part in unlawful meetings, and Order No. 6/88, known as the "Law on the formation of associations and organizations", which required organizations to apply for permission to operate and provided that unauthorized organizations would not be permitted to be formed or continue to exist and pursue activities. This Order also provided for five years' imprisonment for persons who violated it, and up to three years' imprisonment for persons found guilty of being members of, or aiding and abetting or using the paraphernalia of unauthorized organizations.

The Worker members noted that the Government had reported once again that there were several associations of workers in the country. They recalled that the Committee on Freedom of Association had found that such associations were not a substitute for free and independent trade unions and that they had none of the attribute characteristics of free and independent workers' organizations. The legitimate trade union organization – the Federation of Trade Unions-Burma (FTUB) – was impeded from existing freely, and workers were not allowed to form and join unions of their choice. On the contrary, they were persecuted or arbitrarily arrested. Moreover, the Secretary-General of the FTUB, Mr. Maung Maung, had been repeatedly accused of terrorism before this Committee, even recently. The FTUB was obliged under existing law to operate in a clandestine manner, yet despite this obstacle it had succeeded in organizing workers on a large scale inside the country, both in the agricultural and in the industrial and service sector.

The Worker members recalled the case of Mr. Myo Aung Thant, who was condemned to life imprisonment for trade union activities, and of his wife Aye Ma, who, after having spent seven years in the terrible Insein Jail on similar charges, was now not even allowed to write to her husband. They informed the Committee that on 21 May, they had been informed by the Seafarers Union of Burma (SUB) that one of its leaders, Mr. Koe Moe Naung, had been arrested on 19 May at his residence in Ranong at the border between Thailand and Myanmar by two unidentified men, brought to the village-based Light Infantry Regiment 431 and tortured to death during interrogation. Mr. Koe Moe was a trade union leader who was organizing Burmese fishermen and migrant workers from Myanmar in the Ranong province.

Moreover, gatherings on the occasion of 1 May had been repressed, as well as other gatherings to protest against working conditions. For those who were not obliged to perform forced labour, the average salary in Myanmar was US$4-5 a month, and working time was 48 hours per week, plus 12 to 15 hours of overtime, which would be paid at US$ 0.02 per hour if only companies were able to pay. In fact, due to strict bank regulations made after the 2003 bank crisis, companies could not withdraw more than 200,000 Kyats (approximately US$200) per week. Under such conditions, most of the time salaries as well as overtime could not be paid.

The junta claimed that this situation was due to economic sanctions. This was not true. The economy was in the hands of the junta, who drained all the profits; already 49 per cent of the national budget and 30 per cent of the GDP was allocated to the military.

The Government repeatedly declared that Myanmar was a country in transition and that the issue of freedom of association was going to be examined by the National Convention, responsible for elaborating the new Constitution. For more than 16 years now, the military Government of Myanmar had been promising to adopt a new Constitution in which the issue of freedom of association would be addressed, but nothing had happened. The new National Convention had been deeply criticized as unrepresentative and undemocratic, not only by the democratic Burmese organizations and the National League for Democracy, but also by governments and parliaments from all over the world, including many in the region itself and by many members of the ASEAN.

In conclusion, in view of the above, the Worker members asked for a special paragraph on the continued failure to apply the Convention. They urged the Government of Myanmar to put into practice, immediately and without any further delay, the conclusions of the Committee on Freedom of Association and of the Committee of Experts.

The Employer members stated that the Government of Myanmar no longer had any credibility before this Committee. It had promised for more than a decade to resolve the problems in this case through the adoption of a new Constitution. The Committee of Experts had asked for detailed information, but none had been received. The case had been discussed since 1991 and had repeatedly been the object of a special paragraph as a case of continuous failure to implement the Convention. What was clear was that there were no free and independent trade unions in Myanmar. The Government did not deny this. All trade union activities constituted punishable offences under the law. The Committee of Experts and the Committee on Freedom of Association had consistently stated that workers' welfare associations were not substitutes for free and independent trade unions. The Employer members were not against such associations, but noted that these associations did not satisfy the requirements of Convention No. 87. They urged the Government to take a positive step in this case and to elaborate a Constitution and law that would allow workers and employers to enjoy freedom of association. The Employer members agreed with the Worker members that this case be included in a special paragraph.

A representative of the International Confederation of Free Trade Unions (ICFTU) stated that the Myanmar regime presented the physical release of Mr. Shwe Mahn as a step forward, but this person, as well as Messrs. Nai Min Kyi, Aye Myint and Myo Aung Thant should never have been arrested at all.

While the ILO and the international community called for democratic changes, the Myanmar regime referred to the so-called National Convention as a step forward, though the people of Myanmar considered it unrepresentative and undemocratic.

The speaker recalled that more than 150 workers of the Simmaliek dockyard had been killed in 1974 during a general strike organized in protest against the bad economic situation and against the setting up by the regime of the "Workers Councils". Moreover, in a meeting held in July 2004 in the Shwe Pyi Tha industrial zone, the current regime had established the "Workers Supervision Committee", in defiance of the right to organize freely without any interference from the Government or employers. This meeting was held after the 92nd Session of the ILC, which had adopted a special paragraph on the situation of denial of freedom of association in Myanmar. The speaker considered this as a proof that there was no political will to comply with the Convention. He also put forward a number of concrete examples where the military authorities had forcibly moved the 1 May gatherings to other locations, arrested trade union leaders and intervened in labour disputes, which had led to chaos, both for the workers and the employers.

The speaker observed that, though the Director-General of the Department of Labour and his office had been to a certain extent responsive to the needs of the workers in certain cases, he at the same time had been very abusive towards the ILO and the ICFTU in the course of the press conference of 15 March 2005, where he had accused the ILO of "arbitrary pressure put on Myanmar".

The speaker considered that, as compared to ten years ago, the workers of Myanmar had become much more aware of their basic rights, thanks to the ILO and the ICFTU. They had started practicing their rights either by going to the civil courts, to the Labour Department or to the ILO Liaison Office. This should be encouraged.

The speaker concluded by saying that freedom of association and the right of workers to establish independent trade unions was denied by the Myanmar regime, and he called upon the ILO and the Committee members to use all available means at their disposal to help the workers of Myanmar to gain their right to associate freely and independently, in accordance with ILO standards.

The Government member of Luxembourg, speaking on behalf of governments of Member States of the European Union, as well as of Bosnia and Herzegovina, Bulgaria, Croatia, The former Yugoslav Republic of Macedonia, Norway, Romania, Turkey, Serbia and Montenegro, Switzerland, and Ukraine stated that this Committee had discussed this case on many occasions and included its conclusions in a special paragraph of its report for several years, having listed the case as one of continued failure to implement the Convention.

The speaker pointed out that there had been no progress with respect to the adoption of a legislative framework allowing the establishment of free and independent organizations.

The European Union noted with particular regret that, despite the pressing demand of the Committee last year, the Myanmar authorities did not provide the required information on concrete measures adopted. She noted with concern that, in addition to the total absence of a legislative framework guaranteeing the right to organize, there existed legislation containing restrictions on freedom of association or provisions which could be applied in a manner that seriously impaired the right to organize.

The European Union urged the Myanmar authorities to take all the necessary measures to ensure that workers and employers could fully exercise the rights guaranteed by the Convention in a climate of full security and in the absence of threats or fears, and that no one could be sanctioned for contacts with workers' and employers' organizations or with the ILO. The Myanmar authorities should provide a detailed reply on the serious matters raised in the Committee of Experts' report and by the ICFTU.

The **Government member of Cuba** stated that, taking into account the internal situation of Myanmar, which had been largely discussed in this Committee, cooperation, constructive dialogue and technical assistance were the most appropriate means which could facilitate for the Government of Myanmar the resolution of the complex problems related to Convention No.87.

The speaker requested the Government of Myanmar, also in the spirit of cooperation, to provide the Committee of Experts with detailed information on the application of the Convention, so that it could make a comprehensive analysis of the problems encountered and the solutions proposed.

The **Government member of the United States** stated that once again this year the Committee of Experts had noted a total lack of progress towards creating a legislative framework under which free and independent workers' organizations could be established in Myanmar. She referred to the Government's statement before the Committee last year that the national convention had held deliberations on basic principles for the social sector, including the rights of workers, which would provide such a framework. However, the National Convention did not include representatives of the democratic opposition and ethnic minority groups, and therefore any constitution, referendum or election emerging from the deliberation of this unrepresentative body would be seriously flawed and would not constitute meaningful steps toward national reconciliation and the establishment of democracy. The speaker pointed out that, as in the case of Convention No. 29, the Government had demonstrated its disregard for obligations that it freely assumed 50 years ago when these two Conventions were ratified. It was no surprise that citizens of Myanmar who believed in human rights and advocated the right of workers to organize confronted enormous risks, including arrest and imprisonment, such as a Nobel Peace laureate Aung San Suu Kyi, who had spent the majority of the past 17 years under detention and still remained under house arrest and was virtually incommunicado. She called upon the Myanmar authorities to immediately and unconditionally release Ms. Aung San Suu Kyi together with all other political prisoners.

The speaker emphasized that strong and independent workers' organizations could provide significant help to the authorities to eradicate forced labour if the Government were genuinely committed to doing so. However, ILO attempts to engage the Government on this matter had been rebuffed, and freedom from forced labour, like freedom of association, continued to be systematically violated, both in law and in practice. The Government should demonstrate, in this matter as in the matter of forced labour, that it was prepared to take action to meet its ILO obligations. As soon as the Government would do that, she was confident that the ILO would be ready to help.

Another Government representative stated that the National Convention brought together all political parties and ethnic groups of the country, including the 17 national groups that had ceased armed struggle and had joined the peace process. Of 1,086 delegates, 633 were of national ethnic groups. Workers, peasants and all other economic sectors were represented as well. Concerning allegations made against the Department of Labour, she affirmed that the rights and welfare of workers would be provided for by the Department until the new Constitution was in force. Her Government did not have information on allegations concerning specific workers who no longer resided in the territory of Myanmar.

The **Worker members** thanked the Employer members and the Governments that had supported their position on this case. It was clear from the Committee of Experts' report, from the information provided by the Worker members and the Secretary-General of the Federation of Trade Unions-Burma, and by the Employer members that the situation in Myanmar was getting worse and that Convention No. 87 was gravely violated. They noted that on 29 June, the Nobel Prize laureate Aung San Suu Kyi would celebrate her 60th birthday under house arrest. They asked the Committee to adopt once again a special paragraph on continuous failure to implement Convention No. 87 and urged the Government to urgently comply with the Convention and with the requests of this Committee and the Committee on Freedom of Association.

The **Employer members** thanked the Government member of Cuba for suggesting ILO technical assistance in this case. This might be an appropriate way forward. In this respect, they wished that two paragraphs from the conclusion of the Special Sitting on Myanmar and the Forced Labour Convention, 1930 (No. 29), be included in the conclusions to this case. The first paragraph could be adapted as follows: *The ILO's presence in Myanmar should be strengthened to enhance its capacity to carry out all its various functions, and the Government should issue the necessary visas without delay. These functions should include assistance to the Government to implement completely its obligations under Convention No. 87.* The other paragraph to be included would read: *The freedom of movement of the Liaison Officer a.i. as recognized by the Understanding and necessary to the discharge of his functions should be fully respected.*

The Committee took note of the statement made by the Government representative and the detailed discussion that followed. The Committee recalled that it had discussed this serious case on many occasions over more than 20 years, and that since 1996 its conclusions had been included in a special paragraph for continued failure to implement the Convention. The Committee deplored the fact that, despite these continued efforts of dialogue between this Committee and the Government, there was still absolutely no progress made in adopting a legislative framework that would allow for the establishment of free and independent trade union organizations. Moreover, the Committee noted with grave concern from the Committee of Experts' comments that the report supplied by the Government contained none of the information requested by this present Committee, relevant draft laws were not provided, nor did the Government reply to the comments made by the ICFTU. The Committee could only condemn the absence of any meaningful dialogue with the Government in this respect and trusted that its future reports would provide all requested information.

The Committee took note of the statement made by the Government, which referred once again to the need to await the promulgation of the Constitution before a legislative framework for the recognition of freedom of association could be established. The Government also indicated that the National Convention had agreed that laws to protect the rights of workers and to create job opportunities should also be enacted.

Recalling that fundamental divergences existed between the national legislation and practice and the Convention since the Government had ratified the Convention 50 years ago, the Committee once again urged the Government in the strongest terms to adopt immediately the necessary measures and mechanisms to guarantee to all workers and employers the right to establish and join organizations of their own choosing, as well the right of these organizations to exercise their activities and formulate their programmes, and to affiliate with federations, confederations and international organizations, without interference from the public authorities. It further urged the Government to repeal Orders Nos. 2/88 and 6/88, as well as the Unlawful Association Act, so that they could not be applied in a manner that would infringe upon the rights of workers' and employers' organizations.

The Committee was obliged once again to stress that respect for civil liberties was essential for the exercise of freedom of association and firmly expected the Government to take positive steps urgently, with full and genuine participation of all sectors of society regardless of their political views, to amend the legislation and the Constitution to ensure full conformity with the Convention. It further requested the Government to take all measures to ensure that workers and employers could exercise their freedom of association rights in a climate of complete freedom and security, free from violence and threats. The Committee urged the Government to ensure the immediate release of all workers detained for attempting to exercise trade union activities and to ensure that no worker was sanctioned for having contact with a workers' organization. The Committee urged the Government to communicate all relevant draft laws as well as a detailed report on the concrete measures adopted to ensure improved conformity with the Convention, including a response to the serious matters raised by the ICFTU, for examination by the Committee of Experts this year.

The Committee recalled all of its conclusions in the case concerning the application of Convention No. 29 in Myanmar as regards the ILO's presence in the country. The Committee considered that, given that the persistence of forced labour could not be disassociated from the prevailing situation of a complete absence of freedom of association, the functions of the Liaison Officer should include assistance to the Government to fully implement its obligations under Convention No. 87.

The Committee firmly hoped that it would be in a position to note significant progress on all these matters at its next session.

The Committee decided to include its conclusions in a special paragraph of its report. It also decided to mention this case as a case of continued failure to implement the Convention.

The Workers members were of the opinion that if the tasks of the Liaison Officer were to include also a support to the Government of Myanmar for the implementation of Convention No. 87, the Liaison Office should be appropriately reinforced and adequate resources and means should be provided. This would be necessary so as not to weaken the already difficult work of the Liaison Officer on Convention No. 29. For this reason, the Worker members would have preferred the inclusion in the conclusion of the two paragraphs of the conclusions of the Special Sitting on Convention No. 29, concerning the need to strengthen the ILO Liaison Office. The Employer members associated themselves with the statement made by the Worker members.

PANAMA (ratification: 1958). A **Government representative** (Vice-Minister for Labour and Social Development) stated that his Government had yet to deal with several unresolved cases before the Committee on Freedom of Association (CFA) of violation of Conventions Nos. 87 and 98 – cases which it had inherited from previous governments. One of those, Case No. 1931, involved issues addressed in the comments of the Committee of Experts. Case No. 1931 had originated in a complaint against the Government of Panama submitted to the Committee on Freedom of Association by the International Organisation of Employers (IOE) and the National Council of Private Enterprise (CONEP) on 12 June 1997. In the complaint, the plaintiffs had claimed that the legislation in force restricted the rights of employers and their organizations, in violation of ILO Conventions Nos. 87 and 98, which formed part of the fundamental rights of workers. On the basis of the 318th Report of the Committee on Freedom of Association of the Governing Body, in its definitive report on Case No. 1931, it was evident that it had declared itself in favour of the requests of the IOE and CONEP, supporting the call for the reform of the Labour Code in the following areas: (a) the immediate closure of an enterprise in the event of a strike (paragraph 1 of articles 493 and 497 of the Labour Code). Employers complained that these provisions adversely affected the basic needs of enterprises, particularly as regards the maintenance of installations, accident prevention and the rights of employers and managerial staff to enter work premises and carry out their duties; (b) ensuring it was possible – it was considered an obligation – for workers to unilaterally submit collective disputes to arbitration (section 2 of article 452 of the Labour Code); (c) limiting the number of party representatives (delegates and advisers) in the collective bargaining process, which involved interference in the autonomy of free will, since that was an issue to be determined by the parties involved in that process (paragraph 3 of article 427 of the Labour Code); (d) the penalty of withdrawal from the collective agreement of a party and the failure to respond to a list of demands (paragraph 2 of article 510 of the Labour Code); (e) the payment of wages during ten days of strike. The Committee on Freedom of Association considered that the legislation should be amended so that payment of the wages corresponding to the days of strike would not be imposed by the legislation, but would be a matter subject to collective bargaining by the parties. The Committee on Freedom of Association had also requested that the withdrawal from conciliation by one of the parties would not give rise to disproportionate penalties and that the failure to respond to a list of demands would not result in unbalanced penalties.

Finally, still in relation to Case No. 1931, the ILO had reminded the Government that it stood ready to provide all the assistance necessary, so that Panamanian legislation could be brought more adequately into line with the ratified Conventions on freedom of association and collective bargaining.

The speaker said that his Government had been informing the ILO for a number of years that it would be impossible to carry out the Labour Code reforms requested by the Committee on Freedom of Association, due to the lack of consensus between the social partners (workers and employers), despite the efforts made in that regard by his Government. ILO technical cooperation had been used since 2002 to train the social partners on Conventions Nos. 87 and 98 with a view to increasing awareness of the scope of their provisions, however no significant progress had been made.

With regard to Case No. 1931, his Government pointed out the need for ILO technical advice, within the framework of international technical cooperation, in order to find consensual solutions that would enable national legislation to be brought into line with Conventions Nos. 87 and 98. His Government, in conjunction with the social partners, would shortly discuss when would be the most appropriate time to try to resolve the problem of Case No. 1931. It should be taken into account that the Government was in the midst of a process of state modernization and legislative reform.

The Government had furnished a good deal of information on the cases pending before the Committee on Freedom of Association. The speaker indicated that in the Labour Committee of the National Assembly proposals were under discussion involving the provisions mentioned by the Committee of Experts relating to the rights of civil servants and minimum services.

The **Worker members** recalled that, in 2003, this Committee had already had the opportunity to discuss this case due to the persistence of the observations of the Committee of Experts on the application of Convention No. 87 by Panama. The imposition of conditions on the establishment of trade union organizations, notably those for civil servants, the restriction of trade union activities in certain sectors or in relation to realities on the ground, and the restriction for certain sectors with regard to affiliation with a confederation: these were all elements of freedom of association which were in jeopardy. The report of the Committee of Experts had identified other questions to which no response had been received, such as problems of imposed arbitration; limits on the number of organizations by enterprise or by province; the imposition of a minimum number of members for the establishment of an employers' or workers' organization; the nationality requirement to serve on the executive organs of a trade union; the interpretation of the notion of essential services and interference in industrial disputes, especially strikes. The recognition by the Government of these problems and their appeal for ILO technical assistance were, in view of the declarations that had been made by the Government in 2003, but mild progress which had to be confirmed by a demonstration of concrete and real will to address the problems, which for the most part dated back to 1958, the year Panama ratified Convention No. 87. In spite of the resolution of certain problems in the application of this instrument, fundamental questions persisted which successive governments denied, either by claiming the superiority of domestic legislation or practice over provisions of the Convention, or by requesting technical assistance by the Office, along the lines of what had been done again by the Government representative today. In conclusion, the Worker members stated that the credibility of the Committee was in question and that it could no longer accept that, after all these years, it had still not received effective and concrete responses. In view of this, they reiterated their appeal to the Government to provide, at the next session of the Conference, a report indicating concrete measures taken with a view to bringing national law and practice into line with the Convention.

The **Employer members** stated that it was as if nothing had changed since this Committee had examined this case in 2003. The comments of the Employer members in 2003 could be exactly reproduced in extenso here. Further, all of the issues raised in 2003 were still of great concern. In particular, the fact that provisions of the Labour Code allowed for the closure of an enterprise during a strike was not an issue related to the right to strike, rather it was a massive interference in the running of an enterprise and in the collective bargaining process. They were surprised that the Committee of Experts had not addressed an issue raised in the 2003 discussion of this case, namely, the payment of wages during a strike. The requirement to pay wages during a strike was not appropriate and interfered with the process of collective bargaining and the management of an enterprise. In addition, the Government had indicated that it would welcome the technical assistance of the ILO. It would thus be in a position to provide a full report to the Committee of Experts next year, the preparation of which should include both social partners.

They concluded by noting that the last time this case had been discussed, the Government had claimed that no action could be taken because an election was imminent. This year, the Government had stated that progress had not been made because it was a new Government. There was no more room for excuses from the Government for not addressing these serious violations of the requirements of Convention No. 87.

The **Employer member of Panama** stated that following several years of excuses from the Government – the latest being the election campaign – for not bringing Panamanian legislation into line with Convention No. 87, the new Government found itself in a situation that it had inherited from the past. It was essential that, as of now, the Government respected the Conventions it had ratified, in this case Convention No. 87, placing emphasis on consultation with the social partners. Another matter of concern was the conditions imposed on the notion of consensus in the expression "consensual formula" as this could not justify the non-respect of obligations arising from Conventions Nos. 87 and 98. With confidence in the new Government, it was hoped that it would soon set a date for an ILO technical assistance mission, with a view to bringing Panamanian legislation into line with Convention No. 87.

The **Worker member of Panama,** indicating his full agreement with the report of the Committee of Experts with regard to the complaints made by the National Council of Organized Workers (CONATO), stated that it was at least suspicious that the employers of his country had intervened in this international forum for the application of Convention No. 87. These were the same employers who promoted and put into practice policies and measures which impeded the same Convention they were invoking. This had led to the situation in which the subcontracting of workers in his country had already turned into a new attack against trade union organization and collective bargaining and human rights, to the detriment of the dignity of Panamanian workers.

The speaker stated that the international community should be aware that every day, trade union organization was a clandestine activity, despite being recognized by the Constitution and in the law. In fact, today there had been lay-offs in an enterprise for the sole crime of wanting to organize to defend against abuses which some unscrupulous employers inflicted on workers.

In view of these examples, the speaker wished to state clearly that the workers of his country and the entire trade union movement were not ready to accept any labour reform which included a retreat from articles 491.1, 493.1 and 497. These were the only articles which guaranteed workers that employers would not violate or circumvent their right to organize, to collectively bargain and to strike.

He indicated his concern about the rightward drift of this international organization. Free enterprise should not be confused with freedom of association, as was the case in the Committee on Freedom of Association Case No. 1931, which had been filed by private enterprises in his country. He underlined the seriousness of stripping workers of their legitimate right to work, and thus their contribution to the growth of the enterprise through their personal effort, and he emphasized that the negation of the right to strike, to establish trade unions and to collectively bargain of public servants constituted a real outrage to the state workers which this Committee could not accept. He concluded with the hope that there would be prompt pronouncement of this Committee in this respect.

Following a point of order raised by the **Employer member of Panama** during the intervention of the **Worker member of Panama**, the **Chairperson** asked the speakers to limit their speeches to the case at hand.

The **Worker member of Costa Rica**, having expressed his full support for the statement made by the trade union representative of Panama, said that it was utterly paradoxical that in the Committee on the Application of Standards – which should watch over the principles and values, both moral and legal, of freedom of association – someone should dare to maintain a position which ultimately aimed to weaken that very freedom of association. That is what really lay behind the actions of the Panamanian business sector, which with the excuse of invoking compliance with Convention No. 87, sought to open a discussion to "revise" the laws of its country, with a clear objective to revoke laws that protected the exercise of freedom of association and the right to strike. For such employers, it was impossible to accept the democratic principle that when the majority of workers in an enterprise, organized in the form of a trade union, decided to call a strike, that strike would take place and the enterprise must cease its activities. This was a guarantee under Panamanian law which the employers, invoking Convention No. 87, wished to annul.

The speaker said that that law should be defended absolutely by the present Committee. Those powerful groups should not be allowed to get away with what they wanted. The representative of the Government of Panama should himself be the first to defend the right to strike, enshrined in the country's laws. No one in the present Committee had the right to demand less freedom of association. That would be a contradiction in terms. He hoped that the present Committee would take a firm stand to prevent the restriction of freedom of association and the right to strike in Panama.

The Worker member of Paraguay expressed his agreement with the Committee of Expert's report concerning complaints presented by the National Council of Organized Workers (CONATO). Workers' rights continued to be violated in a situation in which groups of extremely powerful employers did not respect the national laws or ILO Conventions. They continued to strangle workers through their failure to pay salaries, bonuses or leave.

He pointed out that with respect to the protection of human rights and respect for labour legislation, governments in many cases ratified ILO Conventions just to forget later that they were in force. This led to the violation of these rights, including the right to strike and the right to collective bargaining provided by Conventions Nos. 87 and 98. It was important to take this fact into account and adopt appropriate measures to guarantee the application of the above Conventions in practice and respect for human rights, which was also respect for the life of workers and their families.

The Government member of the Dominican Republic endorsed the statement by the Government representative of Panama in that the Committee should recognize the efforts that the new Government had been making in relation to Convention No. 87 concerning freedom of association, through its request for technical assistance to solve the problems that had arisen, in consultation and dialogue with the social partners. The statements made by the Government representative therefore appeared to reflect the existence of a culture of dialogue.

The Government member of El Salvador considered that it was important to implement the request by the Government of Panama for technical assistance from the ILO Subregional Office so as to ensure a better application of the Convention, in the context of dialogue and consultation with the social partners, and to achieve agreement among them. She expressed solidarity with the Government of Panama in its ongoing efforts to solve these problems.

The Government representative, having considered the observations made by the Worker members and the Employer members, reiterated the content of his speech, expressing his confidence in tripartism, consensus and the observance of international law.

The Worker members stated that, in the absence of the reply and actions on the part of the Government regarding the shortcoming identified over a number of years, they reiterated their request to the Government to supply, to the next session of the Conference, a report indicating concrete measures taken with a view to bringing the national legislation and practice into conformity with the Convention, particularly with regard to the conditions governing the establishment of trade union organizations, restrictions of trade union activities in certain sectors or in relation to realities on the ground, as well as restrictions for certain sectors as regards the affiliation to a confederation. They also wished that the Government would reply to the problems which had existed for many years, like compulsory arbitration, the limitation of the number of organizations by enterprise or by province, the imposition of a minimum number of members required for the establishment of an organization of employers and workers, the nationality requirement to become a member of an organization's executive organs, the interpretation of the notion of essential services, and also the interference in labour disputes, particularly in the case of a strike. The Worker members also requested the Government to accept effective technical assistance of the ILO, with a view to assessing the situation and to searching the unequivocal solutions to the problems raised.

The Employer members noted that the Government had accepted meaningful ILO technical assistance in this matter. In this regard, this assistance should also include the evaluation of the Bill mentioned by the Government representative to ensure that it addressed all matters in this case. They also noted that the Government had indicated it would involve the social partners in the preparation of the next report to the Committee of Experts.

The Committee took note of the oral statement given by the Government representative and the discussion that followed. The Committee observed that for a number of years the Committee of Experts had highlighted serious problems regarding the application of the Convention both in national law and in practice. The problems in question related to the existence of legal obstacles to establishing workers' and employers' organizations, to the trade union monopoly imposed by law in public institutions, to the requirement that one must be Panamanian in order to form part of the executive board of a trade union, to the possibility of imposing compulsory arbitration in cases of collective disputes, to the ban on the affiliation of public service federations to union centrals that encompassed private sector organizations and to legislative interference in the activities of workers' and employers' organizations. The Committee had also asked the Government to submit to the Committee of Experts a copy of the draft law on export processing zones. The Committee took note of the comments made before the Committee of Experts by a workers' organization and an employers' organization.

The Committee took note of the statement by the Government representative, according to which technical assistance from the ILO was needed in order to find consensual solutions to the problems set out by the Committee of Experts in relation to Conventions Nos. 87 and 98.

The Committee regretted that the technical assistance it had proposed in its 2003 review of the case had not yet materialized and that no significant progress had been recorded as regards the application of the Convention, but it noted that the Government had agreed to accept a technical assistance mission and that it stood ready to resolve the pending problems through dialogue with the social partners.

The Committee strongly hoped that the Government would take the necessary steps, with ILO technical assistance and in close cooperation with the social partners, to ensure that workers' and employers' organizations could fully enjoy the rights and guarantees enshrined in the Convention without any interference from the public authorities.

The Committee condemned the lack of progress over recent years and urged the Government to submit to the Committee of Experts, before the next meeting, a report containing detailed and precise information on the measures taken, including copies of any draft laws that had been drawn up or new legislation that had been adopted. The Committee requested that the social partners be fully involved in the drafting of the said report and hoped to be able to examine all the information the following year. The Committee also hoped that in the very near future it would be able to see significant and specific progress and that the technical assistance mission would be able to examine the draft law referred to by the Government.

RUSSIAN FEDERATION (ratification: 1956). **A Government representative** stated that important and complex questions should be examined in a retrospective manner. The Labour Code of the Russian Federation was adopted over two years ago. The work on the Code was carried out in an open and democratic manner, in close cooperation with the social partners. The Labour Code had set up new labour relations, which had been formed after the transition from a centrally-planned to a market economy. In conditions of the social and economic changes, the Government of the Russian Federation and representatives of workers' and employers' organizations had reached social consensus and agreed that the new Labour Code was a crucial document for the development of the country. For the first time, the Labour Code laid down the principle of tripartite cooperation and developed further the fundamental provisions of the Russian Constitution. The Code had been drafted with the help of ILO experts, who had prepared numerous recommendations, most of which had been accepted and incorporated. With the help of the ILO, new social dialogue institutions had been developed; they included tripartite and bipartite bodies and mechanisms. All this work had been carried out by the Tripartite Commission on Social and Labour Relations, by reaching mutually acceptable solutions. To supplement the Labour Code, additional legislative acts had been adopted in consultation with the social partners. Twenty-one sections of the Labour Code dealt with the issue of settlement of labour disputes. The Code also regulated other issues in the field of labour, such as wages, employment and social protection. Because labour relations were constantly changing due to varying economic conditions, the work to improve the Labour Code was an ongoing process. By the decision of the Government and the State Duma, a tripartite working group had been established to analyse the practice and to prepare draft amendments to the Code. The Government's aim, as demonstrated by the ratification of all eight fundamental Conventions of the ILO, was to embody international standards in the national legislation.

With respect to the observations of the Committee of Experts, and more particularly to the quorum required for a strike ballot, section 410 was in conformity with international law, in particular with article 8(1)(d) of the International Covenant on Economic, Social and Cultural Rights. At the same time, the question of reducing down to 50 per cent the number of delegates needed to decide on strike action was being presently discussed by the working group on the improvement of the Labour Code. Concerning restrictions imposed on the right to strike of certain categories of workers, the Labour Code provided for an exhaustive list of cases where a strike was prohibited. These included workers employed in the sectors of the economy relating to defence and the security of the population. These restrictions were formulated on the basis of article 17 of the Constitution, which provided that the exercise of individual rights and freedoms should not violate the rights and freedoms of other persons. This approach was in conformity with article 8(1)(c) and (2) of the International Covenant on Economic, Social and Cultural Rights. On 1 February 2005, a new Law on State Civil Service had come into effect. This law had revoked the provision previously contained in section 11 of the Law on State Service, which had contained restrictions on the right to strike for state service employees. Section 410 of the Code, which provided for a requirement to indicate a possible duration of the strike, did not restrict in any way the right of workers to take strike action, as it did not provide for any time limits imposed on strikes. In fact, in order to extend the duration of strikes, no additional action was needed. After the entry into force of the Labour Code, and in particular section 413, restrictions on strike action provided for in other previously adopted legislative acts, which contradicted section 413 of the Code, no longer applied.

In respect of workers whose right to strike was restricted by the legislation in force, the Government representative pointed out that these workers enjoyed the right to organize and to settle their labour disputes in court. The current legislation provided for a limited list of undertakings where minimum services had to be ensured during a strike. These included organizations responsible for the safety and health of the population. Minimum services were determined in consultation with trade unions, and only if consensus was not reached, the executive body had the responsibility to draw up such a list, taking into account the interests, safety and health of the population. The workers had the right to appeal this decision in court. Furthermore, pointing out to the recent developments, he explained that four centres responsible for settling collective labour disputes had been set up in the Russian Federation. It was intended that their decisions as to establishing the lists of minimum services would be final.

He also explained the interpretation to be given to section 11 of the Labour Code and pointed out that this section did not refer to the restrictions as regards the application of labour legislation to such categories of workers as women, youth and workers with family responsibilities but, on the contrary, referred to the additional guarantees provided for by the Russian legislation. More specifically, it concerned the prohibition of work in unhealthy and dangerous conditions for pregnant women and persons under 18 years old.

Finally, he stressed that the issue of improving labour legislation was the sphere of competence of the social partners and that this work was carried out in the framework of bodies established on a tripartite basis and included examination of the application of labour standards in practice.

The Employer members noted that this was the first time that a case concerning this country was being discussed in the post-Cold War context. The issue of trade union monopoly which had been a long-standing problem in the country was no longer in question and a much broader right to organize was now available. As to the substance of the issue under discussion, the Employer members considered that, as the right to strike was not explicitly mentioned in the Convention, its application could be subject only to a general appreciation, although the Committee of Experts had made specific comments in this respect. In the Employer members' view, the Government should be commended for indicating that they were in the process of resolving the issues raised in the observation of the Committee of Experts. With regard to the requirement of organizing a ballot in order for a strike to be authorized, the Employer members considered that such a requirement was in line with the fundamental need to safeguard the democratic rights of trade union members. It was appropriate, therefore, that a strike ballot should involve the majority of the workers in a workplace. Although a requirement for all workers to vote would have been too high, the two-thirds requirement of the Labour Code did not seem excessive. The Employer members further wished to emphasize that the precedents of the Committee on Freedom of Association had no bearing on the question of whether a requirement to indicate the duration of a strike was in conformity with the Convention, given that the Committee on Freedom of Association was not limited to the language of the Convention. The same was true with regard to the question of essential services which should vary depending on the circumstances of each country. Where a general prohibition of strikes existed, however, appropriate alternatives involving recourse to a third party should be available to permit to overcome the impasse in negotiations.

The Worker members recalled that the case concerned the application of Articles 2 and 3 of Convention No. 87 which had been severely and negatively impacted by several provisions of the Labour Code of 1995 on which the Committee of Experts had widely commented. They had taken note of the modifications to this legislation which had been announced by the Government and would observe its effects in practice before pronouncing themselves in this respect.

The Worker members observed that: (1) although the right to strike was in fact enshrined in the Labour Code, in practice recourse to strike action was subject to conditions such as two-thirds of workers concerned being present at the general assembly and a quorum of 50 per cent of voters required, making strikes practically impossible at the sector or intersectoral level; (2) by requiring trade union organizations to stipulate the duration of the strike, the law prejudiced the rights of these organizations to carry out activities without interference from the public authorities; (3) the executive authorities of the State did not constitute an independent body which had the trust of all parties for deciding a dispute over the establishment of a minimal service, as the Convention foresaw; (4) the ban on strike action for all railway employees as well as for many other categories of state employees (public servants exercising authority in the name of the State) greatly exceeded the limits generally allowed for this restriction; (5) where strike action was prohibited it was essential that collective conflicts could be resolved by an independent body and not by the Government.

The Worker members also remarked that, generally speaking, these criticisms had already been made in 2003 and even in 2001 and the Conference Committee awaited not just a small step by the Government but a plausible demonstration of its genuine will to follow up quickly on the measures recommended by the Conference Committee and by the Committee of Experts.

The Worker member of the Russian Federation speaking on behalf of the Federation of Independent Trade Unions of Russia, the largest trade union in the country, recalled that trade union pluralism existed in the Russian Federation and that this fact explained different interpretations given to various legislative provisions. The right to strike was an inalienable right of workers and trade unions, which represented their social and economic interests. The strike was the most radical measure to which trade unions had recourse only in exceptional cases. The strike was not an end in itself but a response to flagrant and persistent violations of workers' rights and interests. If employers fully complied with the agreements concluded with trade unions through collective bargaining, and if the Government and the supervisory bodies rigorously controlled the application of labour and other legislation, workers would have no reason to have recourse to such an extreme measure to defend their interests. As the opposite was often taking place, labour legislation needed to contain provisions which would allow workers, without any excessive restrictions or prohibitions, to fully exercise their inalienable right to strike.

The Committee of Experts had presented its observations on the application of the Convention by the Russian Federation on more than one occasion. Two years ago, the Committee of Experts had made similar observations, to which the Government had not provided a response in a timely manner.

He agreed with the Committee of Experts, which considered that the list of professions where the right to strike was restricted was excessively broad. He also considered that the disputes which could lead to strike action should be settled by courts which were, by their nature and according to the Constitution, independent bodies, and not by the Government, as provided by the legislation. Moreover, the quorum required for a strike ballot might have been in fact lowered to a reasonable level. He further questioned the requirement to notify the duration of the strike, which should be allowed to last as long as its goals had not been reached and the dispute not resolved.

Other points, not raised by the Committee of Experts, but which were nevertheless problematic to trade unions, concerned the absence of a right granted to national sectoral trade unions to call a general strike on enterprises of a given sector. The strike was a prerogative of an enterprise trade union. That meant that workers of the same economic sector could not express their solidarity with other workers trying to solve an industrial dispute with their employer. In law as in practice, a strike at a large corporation belonging to the same owner but regrouping enterprises of various sectors of the economy would be impossible. That explained the fact that a large number of strikes in the country had been declared illegal. The speaker finally expressed his satisfaction with the fact that the Committee of Experts was constantly reminding the Government of its responsibility to bring legislation into conformity with the Conventions it had ratified. A complete application of international labour standards was beneficial to all – the Government, employers, and above all, to workers.

The Worker member of Romania said that this case had been examined by the Committee on Freedom of Association in 2003 and 2004. In this respect, it could be considered a flagrant violation of the Convention which was a fundamental ILO Convention.

Section 11 of the Labour Code of the Russian Federation envisaged restrictions on the right to strike for certain persons, including persons with two jobs, persons with family responsibilities, women, young persons and civil servants. The Government imposed other restrictions on the right to strike for holders of a contract under civil law, who were excluded from the scope of application of the Labour Code. These restrictions constituted a violation of Article 2 of the Convention, which provided that workers and employers, without distinction whatsoever, should have the right to establish and to join organizations of their own choosing.

Section 410 of the Labour Code required that at least two-thirds of the workers be present at the meeting in which the decision to call a strike was being decided and that the decision be adopted by at least half of the delegates present. Furthermore, section 410 of the Labour Code required workers' organizations to notify the Government of the planned duration of the strike, which constituted a violation of their right to organize without interference by the public authorities.

Section 412 of the Labour Code contained an exhaustive list of organizations and enterprises in which a minimum service had to be assured in the event of a strike. The disagreements concerning the establishment of a minimum service were regulated by an executive body of the Russian Federation under section 412 of the above Labour Code. However, in accordance with ILO practice, these disagreements had to be regulated by an independent body. By virtue of section 413 of the above Labour Code, the right to strike was prohibited for certain activities in the productive sector as well as for essential services, for which decisions concerning collective conflicts were taken by the Government. However, in the event of restrictions or limitations on the right to strike, which deprived workers of an important means of protection, workers should benefit from conciliation, mediation and arbitration measures.

Taking into consideration that this was the second time that this case was being discussed in this Committee, the Government should take all the necessary measures to bring its legislation into conformity with the Convention.

The Employer member of the Russian Federation stated that the work on the amendment of the Labour Code was presently under way and carried out by the special working group created by the State Duma. Several provisions had already been amended but sections 412 and 413 had not yet been discussed. Since the work on the amendment of the Labour Code was not yet concluded, it was premature to examine this piece of legislation. He finally pointed out that the Employer members considered that the provisions of the Convention did not contain any reference to the right to strike and therefore did not confer such a right.

Another Government representative (Deputy Minister of Health and Social Development) concluded by stating that her Government was prepared to cooperate further with the ILO on the issues discussed and to report on the progress made in this respect. She stressed once again that the efforts were being made to amend the Labour Code and that the work in this respect was carried out in consultation with the social partners.

The Employer members took note of the Government's last indication that it was committed to studying appropriate amendments to the legislation so as to bring it in line with the Convention. It was however often the case that governments set up commissions working on legislative reform over long periods of time. They therefore wished to ask the Government to ensure that the working group would constitute an effective process that would lead to concrete improvements of the situation in a short period of time.

The Worker members emphasized that the consistent practice of adopting a number of measures of a limited scope shortly before the Conference, did not reflect positively on the States concerned. They requested that, in its report, the Committee call on the Government to rapidly take measures to ensure that the provisions of the Labour Code, which had been criticized for such a long time, be finally brought into conformity with the Convention, and also to request the Government to provide information on the measures adopted in the next session of the Conference.

The Committee took note of the statement made by the Government representative and of the detailed discussion that followed. The Committee recalled that the comments made by the Committee of Experts referred to the rights of employers' and workers' organizations to organize their administration and activities without interference by the public authorities.

The Committee took note of the Government's statement, according to which the Labour Code had been the subject of extensive consultations with the social partners and that a tripartite working party of the Duma would examine the effectiveness of the provisions in the Labour Code with a view to possible modifications; the working party was currently discussing certain reforms to the provisions mentioned by the Committee of Experts.

The Committee requested the Government to take all measures necessary for the process under way to be carried out in an efficient and rapid manner in order to bring national legislation and practice into conformity with the Convention in the near future. The Committee requested the Government to send before the next meeting of the Committee of Experts a detailed report containing full information on progress made in this respect.

SWAZILAND (ratification: 1978). **A Government representative** said that his country was listed among the 25 countries whose delegates had been invited to supply information to the Conference Committee. In this respect, he expressed deep concern at the still unclear method of listing countries for discussion concerning the application of ratified Conventions adopted by the ILO. He recalled the statements made by certain delegates during the general discussion and called for a more fair and transparent system so that countries could be selected on the basis of scientific criteria that would render the process more just and clear to all delegations. In view of all the positive steps that had been taken to give effect to Convention No. 87, his Government had expected that at least a case of progress would have been recorded with respect to Swaziland.

He emphasized that, while Swaziland had appeared before the Committee on a number of occasions, the country had obviously taken significant steps to implement the Convention in practice, in consultation with the social partners and with the assistance of the ILO. As such, Swaziland had been able to build the necessary confidence with regard to freedom of association and the right to organize. However, he indicated that most of the allegations made in the Committee of Experts' observation were based on incorrect facts and a mistaken assessment of the situation, and should therefore be challenged.

Firstly, with respect to the comments of the Committee of Experts relating to the alleged death of a trade unionist during a protest march organized by Swazi labour federations on the occasion of a meeting of the Commonwealth countries in Mbabane in August 2003, he admitted that there had been an instance where violence had ensued during the protest, but he strongly denied that a trade unionist had died on that occasion. He explained that an agreement had been reached between the authorities and the organizers of the action with respect to the designated areas where it could be held, due to security reasons related to the presence of the Heads of State attending the Commonwealth meeting. Although the protest action had started peacefully, a confrontation had occurred when an attempt had been made to leave the designated area. However, he affirmed that no trade unionist had died and no such death had been reported by the media or by the leadership of the trade unions. His Government aligned itself fully with the view expressed by the Committee of Experts that, whenever a trade unionist died in a protest action, a commission of inquiry should be set up, and he invited the ILO, ICFTU and SFTU to take part in such a commission so that the country's name could be cleared.

Secondly, with respect to the exclusion of prison service staff from the scope of the Industrial Relations Act, he indicated that the prison service consisted of 1,300 employees. He assured the Committee that his Government had not remained indifferent to the comments made by the Committee of Experts on this issue in the past and that it had undertaken a critical analysis of the prison service in order to assess how best compliance with the obligations under the Convention could be achieved. Nevertheless, his Government had come to the conclusion that, in the context of Swaziland, as in the case of many other small developing countries, the prison service should in fact be considered as an "armed force" and did not therefore fall within the scope of the Act, in the same way as the police service and the army. Moreover, it should be noted that the staff in the prison service had not been disadvantaged in respect of wages and conditions of employment, especially when compared to other civil servants belonging to the Swaziland National Association of Civil Servants (SNACS), the Swaziland National Association of Teachers (SNAT) and the Swaziland National Nurses Association (SNA), because the outcome of the negotiations undertaken by these associations had to be applied to the entire civil service.

Thirdly, with respect to the application of section 40(13) of the Industrial Relations Act respecting charges against trade union leaders, he indicated that this section had been amended by the Industrial Relations Amendment Act, No. 8, of 2000, with the full participation of the social partners and in consultation with the ILO. Legal charges against trade union leaders could now only be brought in cases of criminal activities, and malicious and grossly negligent acts. This should therefore no longer be an issue and he wondered why it was still being raised by the Committee of Experts.

Fourthly, turning to the points raised in the Committee of Experts' observation with respect to the process and outcome of the drafting of the Constitution, he stated that the process had benefited from assistance from the Commonwealth and the European Union, and that the draft text would be reviewed by both Houses of Parliament in August 2005. He firmly believed that the draft Constitution would comply with the country's international obligations under the Convention. Part IV on fundamental rights and freedoms provided for: (a) freedom of conscience, expression and of peaceful assembly and association and movement; and (b) respect for the rights of workers. It was clear that a conscious decision had been taken to protect these rights in line with the Decent Work Agenda. The draft text of the Constitution would be made available to the Office and could be consulted on the Government's web site www.gov.sz .

Fifthly, he referred to the comments of the Committee of Experts on the length of time taken in attempting to settle a dispute before an organization could embark on a lawful strike action. He was pleased to report that his Government had relied on tripartite dialogue and ILO technical assistance to amend the Industrial Relations Act. The amendment would enter into force in August 2005. One of the highlights of the amendment was that it sought to cut drastically the dispute resolution period by encouraging the direct reporting of disputes to the Conciliation, Mediation and Arbitration Commission. He expressed the belief that reasonable flexibility should be afforded to the social partners to engage in meaningful dialogue and resolve their disputes amicably. If the tripartite partners still felt that the Act did not comply with the obligations concerning strike action, his Government would be pleased to work with them and the ILO to rectify the situation.

Finally, with respect to the allegations made concerning a Bill to regulate internal security, he stated that there was no record of such a Bill, although a proposal had been submitted in the past but had been abandoned four years ago. No such Bill was currently being discussed in Parliament.

In conclusion, he said that his Government was willing to work with the ILO to achieve the full compliance of its law and practice with the obligations under Convention No. 87.

The Worker members thanked the Government representative for his intervention and the information provided. The Committee was examining the case of Swaziland for the eighth time in 10 years. On several occasions, the Government had committed itself to achieve progress. However, even though some progress had indeed been achieved, the situation was very different in practice. The adoption in 2000 of the Industrial Relations Act had appeared to be a positive step. However, despite the adoption of the Act, the Government was still making use of laws on the state of emergency against workers and their organizations, namely the Public Order Act, 1963, and section 12 of the Decree of 1973 on trade union rights, which had repealed the Declaration of Rights and was contrary to all civil freedoms. Since 1973, the current Government of Swaziland had been running the country through the use of force, impunity, the lack of social dialogue, denial of the authority of the law, ignoring dissidents, brutality against citizens engaged in peaceful demonstrations and failure to respect the judicial authorities.

Once again, the Committee of Experts had referred to several serious violations of Convention No. 87. In the first place, the national legislation did not afford prison personnel the right to organize. In this respect, the Committee of Experts recalled that, under the terms of Article 2 of the Convention, workers, without distinction whatsoever, had the right to establish and join organizations of their own choosing without previous authorization. Once again, the Government had indicated that it planned to include the prison services within the scope of the Industrial Relations Act. Nevertheless, in view of its record, it was difficult to believe that it would keep its promise.

Secondly, the Committee of Experts had once again raised the issue of the length of the compulsory procedure for the settlement of disputes envisaged before strike action could be taken, which was too long and particularly intricate. A procedure of this nature was in violation of Article 3 of the Convention and was intended to discourage any strike action. It was clear that such provisions were unacceptable as they were in violation of fundamental freedoms. The Government had once again indicated that it was planning to reduce the length of the procedure. However, once more, in view of its record, it was difficult to believe that it would keep its promises.

In the third place, with regard to the possibility envisaged in the Industrial Relations Act to take civil action against federations, trade unions and individuals who participated in protest actions, the Worker members said that such a procedure was a violation of their rights and might expose them to costs which would have the effect of dissuading them from exercising their trade union rights. In this respect, the Government had indicated that the issue of legal action had not arisen. However, it had not provided information on the application of the law in this regard.

Fourthly, the Committee of Experts had once again indicated that the Public Order Act, 1963, and section 12 of the 1973 Decree, abolishing trade union rights, still appeared to be in force. It had requested the Government to keep it informed of the procedure for the drafting of a national Constitution which would accord with international standards and would guarantee respect for trade union rights, and repeal the above Decree. However, the Government had not provided information on this subject.

In the fifth place, according to the information provided to the Office by the ICFTU, the police had dispersed a demonstration in August 2003, making use of violence, and a trade unionist had been killed. In this respect, the Committee of Experts had recalled that freedom of assembly was one of the fundamental trade union rights and that the authorities should refrain from any action likely to restrict this right. It had also called for the holding of an independent judicial inquiry into the case of a participant in the union demonstration who had been killed during the demonstration. It was to be hoped that the Government representative would propose the holding of such an inquiry.

The Committee of Experts had also requested the Government in its observation concerning Convention No. 98 to adopt specific provisions setting out sufficiently effective and dissuasive sanctions to protect workers' organizations against acts of interference by employers or their organizations.

With a view to ensuring the implementation of Convention No. 87, the legislation prohibiting the right to organize of prison staff, the procedure for the settlement of disputes and the 1973 Decree on the rights of organizations needed to be amended or repealed. The fundamental problem in the case of Swaziland was the 1973 Decree on the rights of organizations. This problem was all the more important as the process of the adoption of the Constitution seemed to have been suspended.

In conclusion, the Worker members requested the Government to allow civil society and trade union federations to participate in the drafting of the new Constitution. Furthermore, the draft Constitution should be submitted to the Committee of Experts or, in view of the tight deadline, it would be desirable for an ILO mission to visit the country to provide advice on the draft text. This would make it possible to establish a framework for social dialogue.

The Employer members, after thanking the Government representative for the information provided, emphasized that free speech was a fundamental element of freedom of association. They therefore urged the Government to ensure that the restrictions that were currently placed on free speech were lifted. Referring to the process of the development of the Constitution, which had been under way for several years now, they noted that Decree No. 4 discouraged group submissions, thereby undermining any proper process of consultation. It was of great importance that the provisions of the Constitution were aligned with the obligations set out in the Convention. For this purpose, it would be very valuable if the draft of the Constitution could be analysed by the Committee of Experts and therefore the Government should provide the text of the Constitution once it had been finalized. The paradox in the present case was that the basis for social dialogue appeared to be in place but not used in practice. The Employer members, therefore, urged the Government to build on this platform with the technical assistance of the ILO.

The Worker member of Swaziland responded to the statement by the Government representative, by stating that in Swaziland there was a disregard for the rule of law, extravagance in the face of poverty, a major HIV/AIDS problem, lack of democracy, officially-sponsored violence and poor governance. There was also an attempt to vilify the spokespersons of organizations which had access to the international media.

Swaziland had been ruled by emergency decree for 33 years, there were no political parties, all power was invested in the head of state, and there was no separation of powers.

There had been gross violations of Convention Nos. 87 and 98, arrests of labour leaders and even the death of a young girl at a demonstration. Amnesty International had also reported deaths in prison cells. It was only under great pressure that the Government had acceded to the new Labour Law in 2000. However, there had been no significant improvement in practice, implementation or enforcement. The country had a record of ratifying human rights related conventions and treaties, but was one of the worst violators of these instruments.

The speaker noted that this was the eighth time that Swaziland had appeared before the Conference Committee since 1996 for flagrant disregard and violation of Conventions Nos. 87 and 98 that it had ratified in 1978. The Conference Committee and the Committee of Experts had urged that Swaziland conform with the letter of these Conventions by allowing the police and prison staff to form and join associations of their choice; shortening the process for allowing a lawful strike; addressing section 40(13) of the Industrial Relations Act, making unions liable for losses suffered, if the loss happened during a legal protest; and refraining from use of the public order decrees of 1963 and 1973. The Government was also called on to lay the Security Bill before the Committee of Experts before it passed into law. However, the spirit of the Bill had been incorporated into the Constitution Bill to be shortly adopted by Parliament. The Constitution Bill limited freedom of expression and association, as well as denying a role to political parties in the governance of the country. All powers would be vested in the King.

The speaker therefore demanded that the Government allow police and prison staff freedom of association and collective bargaining rights; shorten the dispute process; remove the liability clause from the Industrial Relations Act, 2000; repeal sections 11, 12 and 13 of the 1973 Decree; repeal the 1963 Public Order Act; repeal section 4 of Decree No. 2 of 1996; engage in social dialogue and allow civil society to participate before finalizing the Constitution Bill; lay the Constitution document before the Committee of Experts to ensure conformity with Conventions; and provide a progress report to the Governing Body in November 2005.

The speaker stated that the people of Swaziland looked to the Committee to deliver human rights, social justice and human dignity.

The Government member of Namibia thanked the Government representative for the information supplied on the comments of the Committee of Experts. It was noteworthy that positive steps have been taken by the Government of Swaziland to give effect to the comments of the Committee of Experts and to adopt legislative amendments that would be in conformity with the provisions of the Convention. The speaker commended the Government for its willingness to cooperate with the social partners and the ILO on this specific subject.

The Government member of Nigeria recalled that the Government representative of Swaziland in his response informed the Conference Committee that his country was prepared to set up a commission of inquiry, if there were sufficient facts that a trade unionist had lost his life during the noted protest. This was enough evidence that the Government of Swaziland was prepared to work with the ILO in implementing the provisions of the Convention, and with regard to the protection of the lives of trade unionists in that country. Based on the intervention of the Government representative it was clear that there was not only the political will for implementation of the provisions of the Convention, but also to listen to the ILO on issues that pertained to the fundamental rights of trade unionists. The speaker requested that the Conference Committee encourage the Government in its continued efforts to amend and improve other areas that had yet to be worked on.

The Government member of Cuba highlighted the measures taken by the Government and invited it to report whether prison staff enjoyed the right to freely associate in trade unions, bearing in mind that if they were armed forces or police personnel they could be excluded from the application of the Convention. Finally, the speaker pointed out that the Government could take advantage of ILO technical assistance.

The Government member of South Africa welcomed the Government of Swaziland's proposed and apparent improvements mentioned by the Government representative. The speaker stated that the Government had requested technical assistance and further noted that it should be provided to the Government. He called on the Government to engage in social dialogue with its social partners.

The Government representative thanked all speakers for their contributions, which would be taken into consideration as far as they related to the Convention. The future Constitution was in line with Swaziland's international obligations. He reiterated that the Internal Security Bill was no longer pursued and that the Government was encouraged by the assistance provided by the ILO and other countries with a view to promoting social dialogue. They would continue to work towards full application of the Convention.

The Worker members stated that this Committee turned back to the violations of freedom of association in Swaziland almost in every session and that as long as the Committee of Experts would indicate that these serious violations remained, the Committee would not have a choice but to discuss the case once again, and insist that the Government bring its legislation and practice into conformity with the Convention. They recalled that what was expected of the Government was to modify the law prohibiting the right to organize for prison staff; reform the procedure required for strike action to be taken, which was too long and onerous; abrogate the Decree of 1973, which suppressed trade union rights. They also considered that the draft new Constitution should be submitted to consultations with the social partners, or analysed by the Committee of Experts, with regard to its conformity with international labour standards before its adoption.

The Worker members envisaged the dispatch of a high-level mission with the participation of experts, a mission which could bring to light information on the death of a person during the protest of 2003. They specified that a refusal to accept such a mission would justify, in their view, the inclusion of this case in a special paragraph of the report, as a case of continued failure to implement the Convention.

The Employer members recalled that it was of fundamental importance that the Government fully implement social dialogue and address the discrepancies between the Convention and its law and practice as noted in the observation of the Committee of Experts. The Employer members had the impression that the Government had not been totally transparent in terms of the information provided to the Conference Committee and the Committee of Experts and emphasized in this respect the need for the Government to provide a detailed report to the Committee of Experts on the action taken in respect of the discrepancies noted with regard to the implementation of the Convention. The Employer members associated themselves with the proposal made by the Worker members for a high-level mission aimed at establishing a social dialogue framework in the country and examining the possible impact of the new Constitution on the implementation of the Convention in law and in practice. They doubted that the Government representative had authority to agree to a mission today, but urged the Government to agree to such a high-level mission before next year.

The Committee took note of the statement made by the Government representative, as well as the discussion that followed. The Committee recalled that this case had been discussed on numerous occasions over the past ten years. The Committee observed that the comments of the Committee of Experts referred to the right to organize of prison staff and various aspects of the right of employers' and workers' organizations to organize their activities without government interference.

The Committee noted the statement made by the Government that no deaths had occurred during the protest action referred to in the Committee of Experts' report. With regard to the right to organize of prison staff, the Government had indicated that it was reviewing the matter and hoped that it would soon be resolved. With regard to the constitutional process, the Government had stated that Parliament was currently debating the question and the Constitution would be made available to the Committee of Experts once it was promulgated. Finally, the Government had stated that the internal security Bill had been abandoned four years ago and was no longer an issue.

The Committee noted with regret that the 1963 Public Order Act and the 1973 Decree on the rights of organization, upon which the Committee of Experts had been commenting for many years, were still in force and invoked by the Government. Moreover, the Committee noted the serious concerns raised in respect of the Decree which prohibited any involvement by civil society in the drafting process of the new Constitution and its content.

The Committee recalled that social dialogue was a fundamental aspect of the full implementation of the Convention. It urged the Government to hold full and meaningful consultations with the most representative employers' and workers' organizations, and civil society as a whole, on the draft Constitution and to ensure that none of its articles would have the effect of contravening the Convention, and that its adoption would result in the effective repeal of the 1973 Decree and of Decrees Nos. 11, 12 and 13 adopted under the terms of that Decree. It further requested the Government to take the necessary measures to eliminate the remaining discrepancies between the law and practice and the Convention. The Committee requested the Government to provide detailed information in its next report to the Committee of Experts on all the measures taken in this regard and to provide a copy of the Constitution so that the Committee of Experts could examine its conformity with the Convention. The Committee also urged the Government to accept a high-level mission to establish a meaningful framework for social dialogue and to review once again the impact of the Constitution on the rights embodied in the Convention.

TURKEY (ratification: 1993). A Government representative recalled, in the first place, that this year the Committee of Experts had expressed satisfaction and interest at a number of the measures taken by his country for the implementation of Convention No. 87. In this respect, several legislative amendments had been formulated with the active participation of the social partners. The Committee of Experts had also raised a number of points on which it had requested further information on the implementation of the Convention, to which he wished to respond.

With regard to the "trial period" required for public servants and the scope of Act No. 4688, he indicated that the Act had been amended, based on social dialogue, by Act No. 5198. At a recent meeting of the Tripartite Consultation Board, it had been decided that work would be continued on the new draft, including the removal of the trial period and enlarging the scope of the Act with regard to the categories entitled to the right to organize. He added that the allegation that public employees, who were increasingly recruited under fixed-term contracts, were excluded from the scope of Act No. 4688, was misleading. Fixed-term employees had the same union rights as their counterparts in the private sector. Furthermore, it was intended to remove some of the restrictions now contained in section 15 of the Act so as to limit exceptions to positions of trust in so far as possible.

On the subject of the criteria used by the Ministry of Labour to determine the branch of activity into which an establishment fell, and criticism that this might hinder the right of workers to join unions of their choice, he wished to make a clarification. With a view to preventing disputes, Act No. 2821 envisaged careful demarcation of branches of activity, taking into account international standards. In the exceptional case of an inter-union dispute as to demarcation, the Ministry of Labour was responsible for making a determination at the request of the parties, and its decision could be appealed to the courts. The determination of branches of activity in his country was based on objective criteria with a view to maintaining a sound and effective collective bargaining system in which workers were free to join any union established in the respective branch of activity. With reference to the case of Dok Gem-Is, he indicated that a jurisdictional dispute had led to a transfer of competence between two unions, with the workers remaining free to join other unions in the branch or to establish a new union.

In response to the request for information by the Committee of Experts on the proposed merger of certain branches, he indicated that the purpose was once again to rationalize the organizational structure in accordance with international standards and to remove unnecessary overlapping. For example, sugar and food, as well as road, railway, sea and air transport, which were listed as separate branches under the existing system, would be merged, based on objective criteria, such as the organizational structure of international trade union secretariats. Past indictments had no adverse impact on the right to organize of workers, who are once again free to join organizations of their own choosing. The proposed modification, which was intended to combine a few branches with a view to clarifying the nature and scope of industrial unions, had been classified by the Committee of Experts as "not in itself incompatible with the Convention".

With regard to the comment by the Committee of Experts that several provisions of Acts Nos. 2821, 2822 and 4688 unduly regulated internal union matters and might therefore give rise to undue interference by the public authorities, he emphasized that the procedures envisaged did not hinder the independence of organizations, but were intended to serve as guidelines for the democratic functions of unions, transparency in their activities and the protection of the rights of their members.

Turning to the observation by the Committee of Experts that section 10 of Act No. 4688 empowered the Ministry and union members to apply to the courts for the removal of union officers who were in breach of the provisions on union elections, he said that the final decision lay with the courts and the provisions were in practice invoked most frequently by trade union members. The purpose was again to protect the rights of union members and safeguard union democracy. Nevertheless, the Tripartite Consultation Board had decided to examine the matter further.

Turning to the comment of the Committee of Experts that the restriction set out in Act No. 4688 had been maintained concerning the suspension of the term of a union officer during her or his candidacy in local or general elections and would be terminated in the event of failure in such elections, he said that the criticism was based on a misunderstanding. The duties of such officers were, in practice, terminated in the event that they were elected, rather than if they failed to be elected. The relevant provision was based on a constitutional provision and the Committee of Academics was seeking an appropriate solution.

With reference to the comment by the Committee of Experts that section 35 of Act No. 4688 made no mention of strike action in the public sector, he indicated that workers engaged under employment contracts in the public sector enjoyed the same right to strike as workers in the private sector. Nevertheless, he recalled that the right of public servants to strike under the terms of the Convention had not been resolved in the context of the ILO. Even so, in accordance with the views of the Committee of Experts that the right to strike in the public sector should only be limited in the case of public servants engaged in the administration of the State, the Government was launching a reform intended to define "public servants" in the narrow sense and to distinguish them carefully from other public employees. Taking into account the comments of the Committee of Experts, the issue of the right to strike of other public employees would be addressed, although a constitutional amendment would be required. He undertook to keep the ILO informed of progress in this regard.

Concerning the restrictions contained in Act No. 2822 on the right to strike, he emphasized that the draft Bill to amend section 29 of Act No. 2822 had made significant progress in deleting certain occupations or services in which strike action was not currently allowed, including lignite-fed power plants, banking and public notary services and urban land, road, rail and sea transport. The removal of the restriction on the right to strike in the production, refining and distribution of natural gas, town gas and petroleum was also being debated by the Committee of Academics. In this case, the right to strike had been given priority and expanded through its extension to workers in establishments where it had formerly been prohibited.

With reference to limitations on strike picketing, he said that the removal of certain restrictions, such as the prohibition on providing places of shelter for picketers in front of and around the plants concerned, was included in the Government's reform agenda.

Turning to the comment by the Committee of Experts that there was an excessively long waiting period before a strike could be called, he indicated that the time periods envisaged were maximum ceilings intended to provide some flexibility for the parties. The draft legislation envisaged a simpler and more flexible mediation process which would shorten the period for a union to call a strike.

On the subject of the prohibition of strikes for political purposes, workplace occupations, general and sympathy strikes, he noted that these restrictions emanated from article 54 of the Constitution. He added that the lawfulness of some of the categories of industrial action referred to by the Committee of Experts, including secondary boycotts, general strikes and workplace occupations, was controversial among academics and was not shared by all legal systems.

Referring to the comment that Act No. 2822 provided for heavy sanctions for participation in unlawful strikes, he indicated that the records did not include information on any trade unionists indicted for such activities. However, work was being carried out by the Committee of Academics on this issue, which would be taken up by the Tripartite Consultation Board. With regard to the application of section 312 of the Penal Code to trade unionists in the legitimate exercise of their activities, he said that section 59 of Act No. 2821 clearly specified the penal sanctions applicable for contraventions of the Act. So far, the Ministry of Labour was not aware of any trials or indictments of trade unionists under this provision. The issue of how collective agreements could be concluded in establishments covered by strike bans was still a disputed issue.

On the subject of the lawsuit against DISK, he indicated that the requirement of ten years' active employment to be able to establish a union, as set out in the Constitution, had been repealed by a constitutional amendment. The Committee of Academics had also decided to amend Act No. 2821 in this respect. He indicated that no lawsuit had been brought against DISK officers by the Ministry on those grounds, but only for their removal from office due to the failure to meet the requirement concerning active employment.

In conclusion, he re-emphasized that, as noted with satisfaction by the Committee of Experts, his country had made significant progress in bringing its legislation into conformity with ILO standards. In this connection, he welcomed the ILO's pioneering role in contributing to his country's effort to accede to the European Union. The comments of the Committee of Experts had therefore been bringing its efforts in guiding its labour legislation into line with European Union standards and Turkey was determined to maintain its sincere efforts to achieve that goal.

The Worker members thanked the Government for the detailed information provided which should be examined by the Committee of Experts. The context of this case was a positive one. Turkey had undertaken serious reform efforts and had made significant progress in respect to international and European standards regarding human rights and the rule of law. While most of the positive changes occurred in legislation and a gap remained between the law and its implementation in practice, the Government had a remarkable record, which gave rise to expectations. The Worker members recognized the work done by the Government regarding the issues under discussion in the Committee, but stressed that much more needed to be done. One could not ignore the shortcomings with regard to the application of Convention No. 87. Violation of basic trade union rights had a long and appalling record in Turkey. Many of the violations in law were the heritage of the military rule of the 1980s and the ILO had criticized the situation in Turkey many times in the past 25 years, even before the country had ratified Conventions Nos. 87 and 98. The Worker members regretted that the Government followed a delaying tactic with regard to addressing the serious shortcomings in the trade union and industrial relations legislation. That was striking, as the Government had been able to act very quickly on other issues in the past two years, for instance regarding the implementation of the European *aquis* in the field of social policy or the reforms to bring the army under democratic control. It was therefore difficult to accept that the Government was unable for decades to amend the legislation in question on points which were clear and on which the ILO had sent many technical assistance missions. The Worker members explained this as an indication of a lack of political will on the part of the Government and the low priority given to this issue so far.

The Worker members stressed that the fact that this case had not been before the Committee since 1997 did not mean that all issues had been resolved. In its report, the Committee of Experts had expressed satisfaction only in connection with just just one specific point, i.e. the repeal of a provision imposing compulsory arbitration in export processing zones. Recalling that the Committee of Experts also noted with interest six planned amendments to Acts Nos. 2821 and 2822, the Worker members insisted that these were, in fact, only potential improvements, as the draft bills concerned had not yet been adopted. It was unusual that the Committee of Experts would draw such firm conclusions on the basis of draft legislation. Attention should also be paid to the fact that, according to the Committee of Experts, some deficient provisions had been repealed but reintroduced elsewhere. In addition, the Committee of Experts continued to raise concerns over a number of issues: (1) the right to organize of certain categories of public servants; (2) the determination by the Government of the branches of industry which were the basis for organizing industrial-level unions; (3) several provisions pertaining to the internal functioning of unions; (4) the removal of trade union executive bodies in case of non-respect of government requirements regarding the internal functioning of trade unions; and (5) the right to strike in the public service and outside the public sector.

The far-reaching restrictions of the right to organize, including the right to strike, of public employees were a very serious issue. A key problem was the definition of public employee, which was much wider than provided for under the Convention, which allowed restrictions of the right to strike only for public employees who exercised authority in the name of the State and for those working in essential services in the strict sense of the term. The studies regarding the definition of public employee announced by the Government would, of course, take time, but they should not be turned into another excuse to continue long-standing violations of fundamental trade union freedoms. The Worker members urged the Government to confirm that it intended to amend the legislation in question in the near future in order to bring it into line with the Convention.

The issue of definition of branches was highly important for workers to exercise their right to form and join unions of their own choosing. On the basis of the present legislation, workers could simply have their union taken away from them. In this regard, the Worker members regretted that the Government had not commented on the conclusions and recommendations of the Governing Body regarding Case No. 2126 of the Committee on Freedom of Association to which the Committee of Experts had referred in its report.

There were very many ways in which the public authorities could interfere in the internal affairs of trade unions on the basis of the legislation in force which contained many unnecessary and detailed prescriptions of how trade unions should operate. These provisions brought to mind the years of military dictatorship, when trade unions were seen as dangerous and subversive organizations. The national Constitution written by the regime at that time contained numerous anti-trade union provisions. Most of them had been repealed, but, regrettably, many survived in the legislation, which was based on these constitutional provisions. Against this background, the Government's argument that these legislative provisions were intended to further the democratic functioning of trade unions was rejected as absurd. The Worker members urged the Government to amend as quickly as possible the legislation in question. They also urged for an end to the practice of public prosecutors in Turkey to open cases against trade unions which allegedly had violated these laws, including the lawsuit against DISK under section 54 of the Trade Unions Act mentioned by the Committee of Experts. Fortunately, DISK had recently been acquitted.

The Worker members also stressed that the problems in Turkey regarding the application of the Convention were not restricted to legal matters but also concerned violations in practice. Such violations occurred regularly, as evidenced by the many observations by trade union organizations and the cases of the Committee on Freedom of Association to which the Committee of Experts had referred in its observation. As a small but telling example, the Worker members stated that Turkish workers could change union membership only through an act of a public notary for a fee of 40 euros. This practice should be abolished as soon as possible. Further, with reference to the Committee of Experts' comments regarding restrictions on freedom of association in the four south-eastern provinces of the country, the Worker members highlighted a lawsuit under way against EGITIM-SEN, a teacher's union, for alleged breaches of the Constitution and the Trade Unions Act which might very well lead to closure of the union. The Committee of Experts should look into this matter and the Conference Committee should discuss the issue after they had given their opinion.

In conclusion, there were certain improvements, which were welcomed. However, these improvements were modest and practically all of them still had to materialize in so far as they were only contained in draft legislation. The Government had been extremely slow in addressing the deficiencies in trade union and industrial relations legislation, which was a matter of political priority and will. The Worker members urged the Government to make a firm commitment that it would indeed act without delay, and in the way recommended and requested by the Committee of Experts. They also requested the Government to do whatever was in its competence to end the opening of new court cases based on anti-union articles of the Constitution which had already been repealed, and still existing legislation based upon these, but now under review. The Committee should highlight both progress and backwardness of Turkish trade union and industrial relations legislation and encourage the Government to bring this legislation into line with the Convention, with the same determination as that displayed in the reforms made in other areas in the process of Turkey's bid for EU membership.

The Employer members thanked the Government for the information it had provided, some of which was new and would have to be examined by the Committee of Experts before the Employer members could comment on it, due to its complexity. The report of the Committee of Experts provided some positive indications with regard to this case. In paragraph 38 of its report, the Committee of Experts had listed Turkey among the countries where progress had been achieved, thus expressing its satisfaction at the adoption of certain measures by this country. Moreover, in its observation the Committee of Experts had noted with interest certain other measures which were in the process of adoption with regard to ten significant points. Several provisions had been enacted and others considered. A Committee of Academics had been set up to prepare draft legislation.

Nevertheless, the Committee of Experts had clearly noted difficulties in relation to other points. In this respect, the Employer members emphasized that although the Government had been taking significant steps to bring its law into conformity with the Convention, it was important to take further steps in this direction. They noted as a positive sign the fact that the Government seemed to have the political will and to clearly understand the steps needed to remedy the situation. The outstanding issues were detailed and complex as shown both by the observation of the Committee of Experts and the Government's response. The Conference Committee did not have the ability to resolve these issues directly and needed the assistance of the Committee of Experts in this respect. The Employer members considered that the level of nuance and detail involved in the full implementation of the Convention was astounding and wondered whether this reflected appropriately the initial purpose of the Convention.

The Employer members concluded by noting that this was a continued case of progress in the implementation of the Convention, as indeed the Committee of Experts had also noted, and that the Government should provide details in its report to the Committee of Experts so as to explain the situation in the country and enable the Conference Committee to return to this case in the future.

The Worker member of Turkey stated that noteworthy improvements had been made in bringing the law into conformity with the Convention. Certain remaining obstacles to the full implementation of the Convention were going to be removed with the adoption of the two draft bills, while the social partners had been involved in consultations to harmonize the labour legislation in accordance with ILO and EU standards. Nevertheless, certain concerns remained. While originally the Government had amended section 37 of the Trade Unions Act No. 2821 – which concerned the suspension of trade union mandates in case trade union officers ran for office in local or general elections and the termination of their mandates upon election – later on the amendment had been withdrawn and section 37 remained unchanged in the draft bill. In addition to this, Act No. 3984 prohibited trade unions from establishing their own television and radio channels despite the fact that the audio and visual media were the most effective methods to ensure that the voices of trade unionists were heard. Furthermore, in 2003, a strike at the Pasabahce Glassware Factory had been postponed twice on the basis of section 33 of Act No. 2822 which provided for a 60-day postponement in case of threat to public health and national security. The speaker expressed doubts about whether a strike at a glassware factory could constitute a threat to national security. In addition to this, a new effective system for the resolution of collective disputes was necessary given that under the current system, the right to strike could not be exercised before the expiration of a five-month period which included a mediation stage beginning 30 days after the opening of negotiations. As for the case of EGITIM-SEN mentioned by the Worker members in their opening statement, he wished to specify that it was necessary to wait for the comments of the Committee of Experts on this matter, which concerned the national Constitution and the independence of the judiciary, before any discussion could take place on whether there was a violation of the Convention. The speaker concluded by urging the Government to adopt the legislative amendments as soon as possible in accordance with its stated commitment.

The Employer member of Turkey stated that over the last 20 years improvements had been made in Turkey, as recognized by the Committee of Experts. The Ministry of Labour and Social Security and the social partners had signed a Protocol in 2001 with a view to modernizing the labour legislation. A Committee of Academics had been established to prepare a draft Trade Unions Act, and a draft Collective Labour Agreement, Strike and Lockout Act. While the drafts prepared balanced the interests of the social partners, the Committee of Experts had found that some aspects were incompatible with ILO criteria. Unfortunately, the texts on which the Committee of Experts had commented were not the latest version of the drafts. As they stood at present, the texts did no longer contain a strike prohibition for banks and public notaries; the prohibition of unions' television and radio stations;

the conditions of being of Turkish nationality and having at least ten years of employment for eligibility to stand for trade union office; the possibility that Governors send observers to the general assemblies of trade unions; the requirement to obtain permission to invite foreign trade unionists to Turkey or to travel abroad. The Committee of Academics established by the social partners and the Government had always taken the comments of the Committee of Experts into account. The Conference Committee should request the Government to supply the latest version of the draft legislation. Section 312 of the Penal Code had been amended and did no longer relate to trade union activities. In conclusion, the situation in Turkey was not serious. There was a tripartite agreement to further develop the current draft legislation and it was expected that a major reform of collective labour law would be approved during the coming legislative period.

The Government member of Cuba stated that the explanations offered by the Government were meant to clarify certain issues raised by the Committee of Experts and recalled with satisfaction the amendments made to Act No. 4688 and important modifications to Acts Nos. 2821 and 2822. The Government had provided further examples of collaboration when it submitted new legislative projects for consultation.

The Worker member of Pakistan took note of the positive developments in Turkey with regard to the fundamental right to freedom of association, to the effect that the Government had prepared draft bills to modify Acts Nos. 2821 and 2822 in order to bring its law and practice into conformity with the comments made by the Committee of Experts in its observation. The speaker emphasized that the Government needed to do more in order to fully bring its legislation in line with the Convention and urged the Government to rectify the situation as soon as possible.

The Government representative thanked the members of the Committee for their valuable contributions to the discussion. Over the past 20 years there had been discussions and criticisms made about the legislation of Turkey and he noted with satisfaction that these criticisms had been allayed during the last five years as the Committee of Experts had indicated. With regard to concerns expressed about the pace of the legislative reform, he wished to assure the Committee that the current Government was determined to bring about change. A three-member Committee of Academics, all experts in their field, had been established to take up the revision of the laws on freedom of association and collective bargaining. The Committee of Academics had finalized its proposals which would be discussed among the social partners from 16 to 18 June 2005 in order to be given final form. The proposals would then be taken up for tripartite consultations in September 2005. The legislative process was based entirely on tripartite social dialogue.

As for the specific issues raised during the discussion, the speaker pointed out that the reason why the adoption of the draft bills amending Acts Nos. 2821 and 2822 had been deferred was that, in the meantime, new laws had been adopted, namely, the Associations Act and the Penal Code, the provisions of which had to be studied carefully in order to harmonize them with the text of the two draft bills. For instance, the new Associations Act had repealed the previous requirement that a Government observer be present during the general assemblies of associations. The Penal Code provided for sanctions against acts of anti-union discrimination which went as far as imprisonment. However, the process of examination and harmonization of the texts required time. The Committee of Academics would give due consideration to this issue upon its return to Turkey.

With regard to the issue of suspension of trade union mandates in case of participation in elections at the local or national levels, the speaker specified that trade union leaders could return to their trade union posts in case they lost the local or general elections. In case they were elected, the Committee of Academics had initially proposed that trade union leaders could maintain both posts (in the trade union and in Parliament) except for officers of public service unions who could maintain only one post. However, when the Committee of Academics had completed the draft, it became clear that the provision was incompatible with the national Constitution and therefore had to be lifted. The Committee of Academics was contemplating ways to remedy this situation.

As for the comments made by the Worker members with regard to the need to appear before a notary in order to join or resign from a trade union, the speaker indicated that this provision had been introduced in 1971 in order to avoid inter-union disputes on the recognition of representativeness for collective bargaining purposes. However, the Committee of Academics was aware of the difficulties that this provision raised and its modification or repeal was possible. With respect to the mediation process, the speaker specified that it lasted for 15 days and applied in case there was no agreement between the parties after 30 days of negotiations. The Committee of Academics was planning to eliminate one step in the procedure for the resolution of disputes in order to streamline it.

With regard to the case of EGITIM-SEN, the speaker noted that, as this case had not been examined by the Committee of Experts, it would be better to wait for comments before discussing it before the Conference Committee. Nevertheless, he wished to specify that this case related to the constitution of EGITIM-SEN, which provided as one of the trade union's purposes the provision of education in one's mother tongue. By "education" the provision of formal basic education was referred to and not the right to use one's own language freely in the media or through the provision of private education, which was henceforth guaranteed in Turkey in conformity with EU criteria. Because of these provisions, the Governor's office, which was the competent authority for the registration of trade unions and for granting them legal personality, had requested the trade union to make corrections to its constitution. However, no changes had been made and the judicial authorities had become involved. The Supreme Court had rendered a decision to dissolve the trade union as it had not brought its constitution into conformity with the law. The Ministry of Labour had maintained a flexible and tolerant stance with regard to this issue and had given the trade union extra time to correct its constitution. It would continue to do its utmost to see that EGITIM-SEN was revived and that the necessary changes were made to its constitution. The speaker further specified that the administrative authorities did not have the power to dissolve trade unions and that this competence rested exclusively with the courts.

The Worker members regretted again the practice of repealing certain provisions, while reintroducing them elsewhere, and the opening of court cases against trade unions based on legislation which the Government intended to repeal. In response to the Government's indication that all changes to labour legislation had been based on social dialogue, they stated that even where legislative measures would be taken based on tripartite consultation, it did not necessarily seem that they would be in line with the Conventions. It was up to the Committee of Experts. The Conference Committee should urge the Government to demonstrate its concrete political will to bring about change by adopting the proposed legislation in the very near future and to report on this achievement in its next report to the Committee of Experts.

The Employer members expressed appreciation for the detailed reply of the Government representative. They asked the Government to provide a complete report to the Committee of Experts on all the points raised and to include therein any draft legislation or proposals that might address the observations relating to the implementation of the Convention.

The Committee took note of the oral information provided by the Government representative and of the ensuing discussion. The Committee noted with interest that, according to the report of the Committee of Experts, a provision had been introduced into the legislation to bring it into greater conformity with the Convention in one specific area. Nonetheless, the Committee noted with concern that there was still a certain number of descrepancies between the legislation and the Convention regarding the rights of workers and employers without any distinction to form organizations that they deemed appropriate and to affiliate themselves with these organizations and to the right of workers' organizations to draw up their statutes and rules, to freely elect their representatives and organize their activities without interference by the authorities in the public and private sectors. The Committee noted that different workers' organizations had presented comments on the application of the Convention.

The Committee took note of the Government's statements according to which its objective was to eliminate the different divergences between the Act on public employees' trade unions, the Trade Unions Act and the Collective Labour Agreements, Strike and Lockout Act through draft laws. The Committee also took note of the explanations provided by the Government on the legislation in force.

The Committee expressed its concern at the legal action taken to dissolve DISK. The Committee urged the Government to take the steps necessary to withdraw the legal action taken and to take steps to avoid legal cases based on legislation that was in the process of being amended and which was not in conformity with the Convention.

The Committee also requested the Government to communicate all relevant information on the dissolution of EGITIM-SEN so that the Committee of Experts could examine this matter in full knowledge of the facts. While taking note with interest of the different draft laws under preparation to bring the law into conformity with the Convention, the Committee requested the Government to spare no efforts to ensure that such draft laws were rapidly adopted taking into account the comments of the Committee of Experts so that they could be examined on the occasion of the next report.

The Committee requested the Government to provide in its next report to the Committee of Experts detailed and complete information on all pending issues including all the topics raised by the Committee, the latest draft laws and whatever text was adopted, and expressed the hope that it could take note in the near future of major progress, specifically that the legislation and national practice would be brought into full conformity with the Convention.

BOLIVARIAN REPUBLIC OF VENEZUELA (ratification: 1982). A Government representative noted that once again his Government was appearing before the Committee to provide information on the situation with regard to the application of Convention No. 87, as it had repeatedly done since 1991, when Hugo Chavez took office as President and initiated sustained and rapid changes in the political, social and economic fields intended to combat poverty, injustice and exclusion and to promote forms of direct and indirect participation by the population in public affairs.

In the period between 1999 and 2004, some 410 trade union organizations had been established on average every year, compared with the period between 1994 and 1998 when the number of trade union organizations registered had only reached 229. Moreover, in 2003, a total of 535 collective agreements had been deposited, with the number rising to 834 in 2004. He said that these figures were available on the web site of the Ministry of Labour.

He maintained that, despite the clear intention of his Government to provide information, the Bolivarian Republic of Venezuela had once again been included in the list of cases to be examined by the Committee, which bore witness to the continuation of significant political interest which, far from seeking social progress, had more to do with the past era of privilege and prerogative.

He said that his Government had agreed to receive two direct contacts missions in only a few years, the first in May 2002 and the second in October 2004. With regard to the reform of the Basic Labour Act, the first draft formulated by the Ministry of Labour had taken on board all of the recommendations of the Committee of Experts, which dated from 1991. This draft text had already been approved at its first reading by the National Assembly and established a system of trade union elections which accorded the possibility for organizations to accept voluntarily the technical assistance and support of the National Electoral Board. This text had been supported by five trade union confederations (UNT, CTV, CUTV, CGT and CODESA) after a dialogue and consultation meeting convened by the Ministry of Labour in November 2004. He added that a more recent version of the draft text, which he described as being of a more progressive nature, increased the number of trade union leaders covered by trade union protection, strengthened the special protection measures and explicitly envisaged the re-election of trade union leaders, as had been occurring in practice.

In view of the great importance of the reform for the country as a whole, the National Assembly had informed the Supreme Court of Justice of the need to extend the period originally set to reform the legislation prior to December 2004. This was justified by the need to extend the consultations with the social partners, particularly at the request of employers' associations, and especially FEDECAMARAS which, since October 2004, and in letters sent by its President on 4 and 23 May this year, had requested the broadening of consultations. On 23 May 2005 a delegation of FEDECARAMAS which included among others Mr. Alexis Garridosoto, member of the employers' delegation to this 93rd Session of the Conference, had met with the President of the subcommittee for labour and trade union complaints of the National Parliament. The representatives of FEDEINDUSTRIA, CONFAGAN and EMPREVEN had also petitioned for the same reason. The request for broader consultations was based on the decision to undertake an overall reform of the labour legislation, instead of the piecemeal reform originally planned, which was to have been limited to aspects related to freedom of association and collective bargaining. He added that, while dialogue was going ahead, the National Assembly was also making progress in the reform of social security legislation, and particularly the laws respecting occupational safety and health and employment insurance. The Occupational Safety and Health Act had been adopted the previous day.

He indicated that, in relation to the alleged refusal to recognize the Executive Committee of the CTV, the Social Appeals Chamber of the Supreme Court of Justice had ruled in June 2004 that those who claimed to be the leaders of the Confederation were not trade union leaders and had ruled that the CTV did not fulfil the condition of being the majority or most representative trade union organization. The action leading to this judicial ruling had not been initiated by the Government, but by persons who considered themselves to be members of the Executive Committee of the CTV. In January 2005, the National Electoral Council had declared the CTV election to be void on the grounds of the absence of reports confirming the results as well as the issuing of reports by a non-existent electoral committee, among other electoral irregularities, as a result of which the Executive Committee was neither elected, legal nor statutory. Despite these rulings, the Ministry of Labour had convened the CTV as an institution. This was a de facto approach which had enabled it to attend various labour and social dialogue forums. Various minutes produced during the meetings and the corresponding invitations to social dialogue, confirmed this situation of openness by the Government in this regard.

He indicated that, on the subject of dialogue with the social partners, the report of the Committee of Experts showed its limitations by minimizing the impact of the consultations held on such subjects as minimum wages, stability of employment, labour reform and other sectoral matters. In previous years, these consultations, which the Government had never failed to carry out, had taken place in a context marked by polarization and the use of trade union representation as an instrument for the promotion of political partisan, including personal, projects which had nothing to do with the interests of the nation and the majority of the population.

It was clear that employers affiliated to FEDECAMARAS, for example, in the automobile, chemical, pharmaceutical and textile branches, were participating in the tripartite sectoral social dialogue forums.

Since October 2004, when it had obtained 70 per cent support in the popular vote, the Government had called upon those actors which where excluding themselves from social dialogue. Since that date, the conviction had grown that democratic social dialogue could not exclude any sector. He referred in detail to the various meetings held with employers' and workers' organizations over the past eight months, including one concerning the composition of the delegation to the 93rd Session of the International Labour Conference. Even the President of FEDECAMARAS had been present at some of those meetings.

The numerous working meetings held with trade union organizations had been supplemented by consultations carried out by the Ministry of Labour in the context of the Andean Community and the ILO on combating child labour, labour migration and occupational safety and health, among other subjects.

With regard to the concerns expressed by the IOE and the ICFTU, he indicated that his Government had provided detailed information to both the Governing Body and the Committee on Freedom of Association and had indicated its position on the conclusions and recommendations adopted by the Committee on Freedom of Association, which in his view went beyond the scope of its competence and mandate, and in other cases contained inaccuracies or mistaken evaluations of the events which had occurred. In accordance with the recommendations of various regional groups, including that of Latin America and the Caribbean (GRULAC), he considered that it was necessary to avoid duplication in the use of ILO procedures, which gave rise to unnecessary costs and could lead to contradictory outcomes or conclusions. He therefore considered that the information requested was already available to the ILO.

In conclusion, he said that his Government had achieved sustained progress in the matters under examination and that it was therefore important to allow it and help it to continue its work, as it had been doing with all the social partners, in accordance with the recommendations made by the Committee of Experts. It was the responsibility of the Committee of Experts to verify and evaluate the progress achieved in the Bolivarian Republic of Venezuela over the rest of 2005.

The Employer members expressed appreciation of the presence of the Government representative and the moderate tone adopted in the discussion. The heart of the present case, in their view, concerned the application of Article 3 of the Convention, which provided that "workers' and employers' organisations shall have the right to draw up their constitutions and rules, to elect their representatives in full freedom, to organise their administration and activities and to formulate their programmes", and that "the public authorities shall refrain from any interference which would restrict this right or impede the lawful exercise thereof". However, the Employer members did not believe that the Government understood the meaning of this provision.

They recalled that the present case concerned the interference by the Government in the activities of representative organizations of employers and workers and, in particular, the national employers' organization FEDECAMARAS. The interference by the Government had even affected the work of the present Conference through its meddling in the composition of the Employers' group. Although the Government representative had expressed approval of the direct contacts mission, referred to also in the comments of the Committee of Experts, he had given no indication of any intention by the Government to strengthen bipartite or tripartite dialogue in the country. The CTV, a workers' organization and FEDECAMARAS, the sole national representative employers' organization, were both excluded from the social dialogue forum in the country and the Government was failing to respect the criteria of representativeness. With regard to the reforms to the labour legislation, the Employer members understood that, while some 50 laws had been adopted on workplace matters, none of them had been formulated in consultation with representative organizations of the social partners. The serious nature of the situation was illustrated by the fact that the former President of FEDECAMARAS had been placed under arrest and was now in exile. In view of the gravity of the situation, the IOE had found it necessary to intervene in the context of cases brought before the Committee on Freedom of Association. The Government representative claimed that the Government was prepared to provide further information and called for the progress achieved to be acknowledged. What the Employer members wished to see was concrete action demonstrating the will of the Government to comply with its obligations under the Convention. Expertise was clearly required if the situation was to be improved. The Employer members therefore proposed that the Government should consider inviting the Chairperson of the Committee on Freedom of Association to visit the country, verify the national situation and provide assistance in the modification of the employment legislation to bring it into conformity with the requirements of the Convention. Alternatively, the Government could accept the visit of a tripartite mission for the same purpose. The Employer members emphasized that the time for fact-finding was now over. Action was needed, and it was needed now.

The Worker members thanked the Government representative for the replies provided orally and those colleagues in the Workers' group who had refrained from intervening on the case in view of its geopolitical implications and the choices made concerning social matters and development.

The last discussion by the Committee of the case concerning the application of Convention No. 87 by the Bolivarian Republic of Venezuela had taken place in a climate of political and social instability, marked in particular by an attempted coup d'état, which had given rise to major tension in the world of work. The Workers' group had then taken note of the draft reform of the law that was intended to respond to the multiple issues relating to violations of the Convention raised previously. They had also expressed their concern relating to the cases examined by the Committee on Freedom of Association and had requested the Government not to interfere in the internal affairs of workers' and employers' organizations. In addition, they had requested the Government to recognize the Executive Committee of the Confederation of Workers of Venezuela (CTV). A return to dialogue with the social partners had therefore been requested.

With regard to the observation made by the Committee of Experts this year, it should be noted with interest that the direct contacts mission requested by the Conference Committee had taken place in October 2004, and had shown that the Government had submitted a Bill to amend the Basic Labour Act to the National Assembly, accompanied by a schedule for its adoption.

Once adopted, the Bill would resolve a series of important obstacles which had been hindering the application of Convention No. 87 for over ten years. The Committee of Experts had therefore included this case in the list of cases of progress, although it had not noted it "with interest". Although progress had been achieved in relation to the legislation, it had to be noted that, with respect to the refusal to recognize the Executive Committee of the CTV and also with regard to social dialogue with the social partners, no tangible and convincing progress had been made, despite the Government's commitment to give effect to the points raised in the discussion in 2004.

The Worker members called for the Convention to be given effect in law and in practice. They therefore hoped that in its next report the Government would provide detailed information on the progress achieved in this regard.

A Worker member of the Bolivarian Republic of Venezuela said that since 1999 the trade union movement in the Bolivarian Republic of Venezuela had been providing evidence to the ILO Conference that the Government of the Bolivarian Republic of Venezuela was systematically violating Conventions Nos. 87 and 98. For five consecutive years, the various ILO supervisory bodies had concluded, in special paragraphs and through two direct contacts missions, that the Bolivarian Republic of Venezuela did not afford the necessary guarantees for the exercise of freedom of association, and he considered that the Committee should be firm in this case. He recalled that the Committee on Freedom of Association had received over 50 complaints on this subject. Despite the repeated requests for the Government to remedy these violations, the Venezuelan authorities had ignored the recommendations of the ILO supervisory bodies. In his view, this was illustrated by several facts. The Government representative had given assurances to the Committee that trade union elections would not continue to be managed by the State, but this commitment had not been fulfilled. On the contrary, the National Electoral Council had declared the Executive Committee of the CTV illegal. The Government representative had assured the Committee that the CTV and its Executive Committee would be recognized, but had not given effect to this undertaking. He had also promised to renew social dialogue with all the social partners but, as noted by the direct contacts mission in 2004, this had not occurred. It had not even been possible to organize a tripartite meeting during the direct contacts mission. He called for the report of the mission to be distributed to the members of the Committee. In view of the repeated violations of Conventions, he requested the Committee to take appropriate measures to resolve the situation, which constituted a violation of freedom of association in the Bolivarian Republic of Venezuela, and to reestablish social dialogue. He concluded by saying that if the problems could be discussed by all the parties, this would benefit his country.

Another Worker member of the Bolivarian Republic of Venezuela said that the National Union of Venezuelan Workers (UNT) had been created in response to the position taken by those who had led the trade union movement for over 40 years and who had later formed an alliance with the employers, which had even led to a coup d'état in April 2002. She added that the dictatorship headed by the employers' leadership had been short-lived. The people had been mobilized, returning to Venezuela the leading role of participatory democracy. An ICFTU mission which had visited the country in August 2004 had witnessed the freedom and massive participation of the people in the referendum of confirmation.

She asserted that the UNT was a central organization that was independent of the Government, employers and political parties, and was composed of many former members of the CTV who had distanced themselves from that union following its alliance with FEDECAMARAS. She added that the UNT would hold elections to elect its leaders and its various bodies at the end of October this year. Asserting that it had been registered in accordance with all the requirements, she felt that the direct contacts mission which had visited her country in 2004 had shown bias and misinformation, as its report had referred to the UNT as being "recognized, despite having an unelected Executive Committee". She indicated that the legitimacy of the UNT came from its participation in the negotiation of collective agreements and in large enterprises in the public and private sectors, where it had taken over in most cases from the CTV. She made reference to the repeated statement in the Committee's report that the CTV was the most representative central organization based on the fact that it had represented 68.73 per cent of union members in 2001. She indicated, however, that these figures had surely been obtained from the data of the National Electoral Council and did not take into account the new trade union situation. She indicated that trade union elections were being organized in the normal manner and that the National Electoral Council only took action at the demand of workers' organizations which so requested and that an example of this was provided by the elections of FETRACONSTRUCCION, a federation led by Manuel Cora who had just concluded his electoral campaign without the supervision of the National Electoral Council.

In relation to the legislative reforms, she indicated that in her country, in addition to the Basic Labour Act, several laws were being examined, including laws respecting occupational social security schemes, the working environment, housing, health and workers' participation in enterprise management.

She said that, following the coup d'état, four workers, other than the CTV leaders, had been convened on the Presidential Commission for National Dialogue and that she had participated in that dialogue. Together with employers from the pharmaceutical sector, who were members of FEDECAMARAS, and the Government, they had succeeded in formulating policies to balance employment and increase the production of generic drugs.

She added that the Venezuelan citizens and in particular the workers, had demanded that the Government put an end to impunity and that the organs of the state (Judiciary, Attorney General of the Republic) acted in accordance with the law in order to avoid hidden agents who acted against the interests of the Venezuelan people.

She emphasized that the UNT was working to consolidate dialogue, whereas the CTV and FEDECAMARAS were carrying out a boycott as part of their subversive plans, but that they had agreed to enter into dialogue now that the coup d'état had failed. The sabotage of the oil industry and the coup d'état had caused deaths, as well as economic and structural losses. She expressed her opposition to a complaint submitted by FEDECAMARAS and thanked the Worker members of Colombia, Cuba and the Bolivarian Republic of Venezuela, among others, for their support.

The Government member of Cuba thanked the Government representative for the information provided and said that the Government of the Bolivarian Republic of Venezuela had taken on the responsibility of reforming the labour legislation, as recommended by the Committee of Experts, and that these reforms had already been approved in their first reading. The increase in the number of collective agreements, the establishment of new trade unions and the free exercise of the right to strike were evidence that Convention No. 87 was being applied in the Bolivarian Republic of Venezuela.

He said that the Supreme Court of Justice had indicated that it was impossible to legally determine that the CTV was the most representative trade union, and that the National Electoral Council had voided the CTV's elections on the grounds of lack of transparency. Nevertheless, the Government had continued to invite it to tripartite dialogue forums, at both the national and international levels. FEDECAMARAS had also participated in the various dialogue forums.

The Government of the Bolivarian Republic of Venezuela had also accepted the two direct contacts missions, thus opening the door for technical cooperation. He recalled that the report of the Committee of Experts had noted the progress made. He asserted that this case was a clear indication that political criteria were continuing to prevail in the inclusion of the case of the Bolivarian Republic of Venezuela in the Committee's debates, as the country had already adopted the necessary measures to give effect to the Convention. He therefore considered that this case should no longer be included in the list of cases to be examined by the Conference Committee in future.

The Government member of the United States noted that, in reviewing this case again this year, the Committee of Experts had benefited greatly from the report of the direct contacts mission that had visited the Bolivarian Republic of Venezuela in October 2004. According to the mission's report, the Government had submitted a number of amendments to the Basic Labour Act which would have the effect of bringing it more closely into line with Convention No. 87. This was a welcome development and demonstrated the value of such missions and the important role they played in the ILO's supervisory system. Too often, governments viewed such missions as punitive in nature and refused to cooperate with them. As this case made clear, however, direct contacts missions were of a constructive nature, and governments would be well advised to receive them and cooperate fully with them when the supervisory bodies so recommended.

Unfortunately, the rest of the information in the report of the Committee of Experts was not so encouraging. The report referred to the violation of the right of the CTV to elect its representatives in full freedom and to organize its activities, discrimination by the authorities against the CTV's Executive Committee, and the Government's refusal to engage in meaningful social dialogue with the CTV and FEDECAMARAS. According to the Committee of Experts, practices such as these violated the freedom of choice of Venezuelan workers and employers. The Committee of Experts rightly pointed out that equality of treatment between organizations had to be ensured if the principle of free choice enshrined in the Convention was to be upheld.

The Government member of the Islamic Republic of Iran said that, following a series of crises in recent years, the reforms made by the Bolivarian Republic of Venezuela in the fields of the economy and legislation were an indication of its good intentions and of the determination of the Government to overcome the obstacles that it was facing. Undoubtedly, the economic and legislative reforms that were being carried out would create appropriate conditions for the achievement of democracy and the promotion of tripartism, the right to organize, freedom of association and collective bargaining. ILO technical cooperation and assistance would be an effective tool to accelerate the positive action taken by the Government with a view to removing the obstacles to the full application of Conventions Nos. 87 and 98.

The Government member of Panama said that he had listened very carefully to the Government representative of the Bolivarian Republic of Venezuela and that emphasis should be placed on the efforts made by the country to give effect to the provisions of Convention No. 87. He also emphasized the willingness of the Government to collaborate in providing information on the progress achieved, in the form of the Basic Labour Act, which was currently undergoing its first reading in Parliament. In his view, as a result of the outcome of the two direct contacts missions, it would now be sufficient to return to the usual mechanism of supplying reports to supervise the application of the Convention.

The Government member of Paraguay, speaking on behalf of MERCOSUR, said that the Government had shown positive signs of its willingness to give effect to the provisions of the Convention. He considered some of the signals of the extension of social dialogue to be encouraging, such as the inclusion of the CTV in the ILO delegation, the consultation of the CTV regarding the documents under discussion in the Andean region and the participation of the CTV in the national dialogue forums established to discuss these issues.

It was important to emphasize that the comments made in previous years by the Committee of Experts with a view to advancing legislative reform in respect of freedom of association had been included by the Government in the Bill which was being examined by the National Assembly, and which had been the subject of tripartite debate and consultation. He recalled that the Government had accepted visits by two direct contacts missions, which had observed the situation in the country and endorsed the Government's actions as being in harmony with ILO objectives, principles and standards.

The Government member of Egypt said that she had listened with interest to the Government representative, who had described the positive measures taken to improve the rights and freedoms of trade unions set out in the new draft Labour Code. She called on the Committee to take into consideration the efforts made by the Government and to provide it with the necessary technical support and assistance.

The Government member of China thanked the Government representative for the information provided and said that she had listened with great interest to the discussion concerning the implementation of the Convention. She noted that the Government had made remarkable achievements in reforming its legislation and in promoting social dialogue. These successes demonstrated the Government's willingness to cooperate with the social partners. The achievements of the Government needed to be acknowledged and she hoped that the ILO would provide technical support to assist developing countries such as the Bolivarian Republic of Venezuela to improve their social and labour situation.

The Government representative thanked most of those who had participated in the discussion for recognizing that his country had made progress in giving effect to its democratic commitment to achieve greater participation and inclusive social dialogue, with particular emphasis on the representativity of the major actors. Social dialogue was now no longer a monopoly for those who had been able to make their voices heard in the past. Organized workers and employers, who had not been heard for decades, were now participating in the development of public policies which took into account their needs and interests.

The two direct contacts missions sent by the ILO had given rise to a dynamic of meetings and forums in which all the social partners had participated, including representatives of FEDECAMARAS and the CTV, on subjects which included labour policy. Nevertheless, to those who were now calling for social dialogue, he wished to say that back home they were attending meetings in which such burning topics were being discussed as wages and food programmes for workers, labour reforms, labour immobility, etc. His Government, which sought coherence between promises and practice, invited the Executive Committee of the CTV, for example, to progress from words to action and to enter into collaboration and to ensure coherence between what they asserted and did in the country and what they denounced in Geneva. For example, it would have been important that Mr Cora appear at the social dialogue meetings convened by the Ministry of Labour, which he never attended, instead of using this scenario in order to misinform the public on what really happened. On the subject of trade union elections, he emphasized that the National Electoral Council, which had been so heavily criticized, was an independent and autonomous body which commanded the respect of the executive, legislative and judicial authorities, and of the Comptroller General's Office of the Republic and the other organs of popular power. In his country, there was no discrimination against trade unions and none of them received preferential treatment. It was necessary to overcome the conflictual political situation affecting the country. Nevertheless, his Government, which had recognized all the social partners, needed to take into account the fact that it governed in the interests of everyone and did not renounce its duty to govern for the majority, and particularly of those categories which had up to now been excluded from citizen's participation as well as the just distribution of the petroleum income and the rest of the country's wealth, thus overcoming the injustices of the post. Social dialogue needed to be inclusive, participative and an agent of transformation.

The reform of the Basic Labour Act, which had been formulated with the technical assistance of the ILO Standards Department, was currently being examined by the National Assembly with the participation of FEDECAMARAS. This reform would have to be the subject of consultation with the workers and of their approval. Finally, he emphasized that his Government would continue to endeavour to follow up the recommendations made by the Office when these were relevant. It was all the more convinced that it was necessary to make progress in legislative reform towards a model of society which established a new value for the relationship between capital and labour in which labour would be appreciated from the point of view of solidarity and cooperation on the basis of the wealth it generated, so as to achieve the wealth's just distribution. This reform, which had been debated for two years, and which included the most recent standards on occupational safety and health within a context of social dialogue, was now nearly complete. It should not be forgotten that the previous legislation had required six years' discussion. His Government undertook to transmit to the Office in due time the outcome of a process which would benefit the great majority of workers in the Bolivarian Republic of Venezuela. He confirmed that the Government would remain within the regular supervisory mechanism through the presentation of the steps and progress made during the rest of the year, to the Committee of Experts.

The Employer members thanked the Government representative for his reply. They expressed a certain surprise at the moderation of the position expressed by the Worker members in the discussion of this case, particularly in view of the reference made by the Committee of Experts to the comments of the ICFTU and the IOE, as well as the detention order issued against the President of the CTV and the measures taken against leaders and members of employers' and workers' organizations. Such a situation would normally be condemned outright by the Workers' group, as a result of the violation of the fundamental principle of free and independent organizations. Yet, few complaints had been heard with regard to the failings of the consultation in process undertaken by the Government and its failure to implement Convention No. 87. The Employer members wished to put on record their condemnation of the arbitrary measures adopted against members of workers' and employers' organizations. Indeed, the current President of FEDECAMARAS could not leave the country without the permission of the authorities, which was a clear violation of the principles of freedom of association.

In view of the importance of the case, the Employer members wished to take the unusual step of proposing a set of conclusions for the Committee. They noted in this respect that changes and amendments to the conclusions proposed by the Chairperson always seemed to come from the Worker members. In a democratic body, they felt that the Employer members should be able to contribute in the same way. Their proposed conclusions were as follows:

The Committee noted the oral information provided by the Government representative and the discussion that followed. The Committee noted with deep concern that the problems raised by the Committee of Experts referred to questions relating to the basic right of workers and employers to form organizations of their own choosing, the right of these organizations to elect their representatives in full freedom, to draw up their rules without interference by the authorities and to organize their activities.

The Committee also noted the emphasis placed in the report of the direct contacts mission on the fact that for years the Executive Committee of the CTV had not been recognized in law by the Government and in practice had only been recognized for very limited purposes. The Committee noted that the current situation had prevented the Executive Committee from the normal exercise of its rights and had seriously prejudiced it. The Committee also noted that the CTV Executive Committee, which was the product of an election process, was only recognized in practice by the Government for very limited purposes, while having the Executive Body of the UNT central organization was recognized, despite not having an Executive Body adopted through an electoral process.

The Committee considered that the above situation, and in particular the excessive delay by the National Electoral Council, had gravely prejudiced the Executive Committee of the CTV and its member organizations, thereby violating the right of this organization to elect it representatives in full freedom and to organize its activities, as recognized in Article 3 of the Convention, as well as the principles of due process. The Committee once again urged the Government to recognize the Executive Committee of the CTV for all purposes immediately.

The Committee once again urged the Government to renew dialogue with the social partners. The Committee noted that, according to the report of the direct contacts mission, the executive bodies of the CTV and FEDECAMARAS had not participated in social dialogue in the broadest sense of the term, particularly in sectoral dialogue.

The Committee also noted that, according to the report of the direct contacts mission, in response to the availability for dialogue demonstrated unequivocally by the central and regional executive bodies of FEDERCAMARAS (the sole confederation of employers in the country and which was at the highest level of representativeness) and the Executive Committee of the CTV, the Minister of Labour had not given indications of wishing to promote or intensify bipartite or tripartite dialogue on a solid basis with these bodies: in practice, such dialogue had practically not existed for years and only took place in an episodic manner.

The Committee noted with regret that the information contained in the report of the direct contacts mission showed that representatives of the three minority workers' confederations did participate in social dialogue forums, alongside a workers' confederation which had a provisional executive board, and that on the employers side three less representative organizations participated which were not members of the employers' confederation FEDECAMARAS.

The Committee considered that strict criteria of representativeness were not respected in those sectoral dialogue forums and that the executive boards of the central organizations CTV and FEDECAMARAS were excluded from such forums, and therefore suffered discrimination.

The Committee further noted that, according to the report of the direct contacts mission, effective consultations between the Government and the executive bodies of the CTV and FEDECAMARAS on labour issues had been limited and had been of an exceptional nature. The Committee also urged the Government, without delay, to convene periodically the National Tripartite Commission and to examine in this context, together with the social partners, the laws and the order which had been adopted without tripartite consultation.

The Committee emphasized the importance of the Government and the most representative organizations of employers and workers engaging in in-depth dialogue on matters of common interest. The Committee requested the Government to keep it informed of any form of social dialogue with the CTV and FEDECAMARAS and their member organizations and to ensure equality of treatment between organizations.

The Committee deeply deplored the arrest of officials of employers' and workers' organizations and emphasized that the arrest of these officials for reasons linked to actions relating to legitimate demands was a serious restriction of their rights and a violation of freedom of association, and it requested the Government to respect this principle. The Committee urged the Government to terminate immediately the judicial proceedings against the President of FEDECAMARAS, Mr. Carlos Fernandez, and that the detention order against the President of the CTV, Mr. Carlos Ortega, be lifted. It requested the Government to provide information on the detention orders issued against six trade union leaders or members of UNAPETROL and that the restrictions on the movement of the current President fo FEDECARAMAS, Mrs Albis Munõz be lifted.

The Committee urged the Government to initiate contacts with the members of UNAPETROL in order to find a solution to the problem of registering the union. It also requested the Government to initiate negotiations with the most representative workers' confederations to find a solution to the dismissal of 18,000 workers from the PDVSA enterprise and to institute an independent investigation without delay into instances of alleged acts of violence against trade unionists.

The Committee requested the Government to give effect to the recommendations of the Committee on Freedom of Association so as to secure the full application of Convention No. 87. The Committee requested the Government to accept a high-level tripartite mission, which would include a meeting with the Government and with employers' and workers' organizations, placing particular emphasis on all matters relating to the application of Convention No. 87 in law and practice.

The Worker members, in response to the conclusions proposed by the Employer members, noted that it was not the usual practice of the Committee for a group to propose conclusions in place of the Chairperson. It was for the Chairperson alone to propose the conclusions and for the groups to make comments, as appropriate.

They said that the case of the Bolivarian Republic of Venezuela had been dealt with by the Committee on several occasions in recent years and that real and tangible progress, albeit insufficient, had been noted. They added that the Government was not solely responsible for the climate of division and antagonism that the country was experiencing, considering that it had made real efforts, even if much remained to be done, particularly with regard to social dialogue. They called upon the Government to continue to seek ILO technical assistance to resolve the issues raised in relation to the application of the Convention.

The Committee took note of the statement made by the Government representative and of the discussion that followed. The Committee observed with concern that the problems raised by the Committee of Experts, which also reflected the comments made by the International Confederation of Trade Unions (ICFTU) and the International Organization of Employers (IOE), included: legal restrictions upon the right of workers and employers to form organizations of their own choosing; the right of these organizations to draw up their rules and elect their officers freely and the right to organize their activities, without interference by the public authorities; the refusal to recognize the executive committee of the CTV; the exclusion of certain workers' and employers' organizations in social dialogue to the disadvantage of the Confederation of Workers of Venezuela (CTV) and FEDECAMARAS; the detention order of leaders, in particular Mr. Carlos Fernández; and restrictions of movement on Ms. Albis Muñoz. The Committee further noted the results of the direct contacts mission that took place in October 2004.

The Committee took note of the statement of the Government representative according to which a draft law adopted in the first reading of the National Assembly had been the subject of consultations and the Government expected its adoption in the near future. It also noted that the Government had included FEDECAMARAS and the CTV in the framework of inclusive dialogue without exclusion of any social partners. Moreover, the Government pointed out

that the National Electoral Council had declared the electoral process of the CTV null and void and that the Government had already replied to the Committee on Freedom of Association on the questions raised by the ICFTU and the IOE.

Noting that the Bill submitted to the National Assembly aimed at resolving problems of a legislative nature and mentioned by the Committee of Experts had still not been adopted in the second reading, the Committee requested the Government to take measures to accelerate its passing and to carry out full and meaningful consultations with the most representative workers' and employers' organizations. The Committee observed insufficiencies in the social dialogue and the need for progress to be made in this respect.

The Committee underlined the importance of full respect for Article 3 of the Convention and that the public authorities should not interfere in the elections and activities of workers' and employers' organizations. It took note of the Government's statement that recourse to the National Electoral Council was optional for occupational organizations and urged the Government to fully respect this commitment.

The Committee invited the Government to lift immediately the restrictions on the freedom of movement imposed on the leaders of FEDECAMARAS, Mr. Carlos Fernández and Ms. Albis Muñoz.

The Committee requested the Government to send a complete and detailed report to the Committee of Experts on all the pending questions for examination at its next meeting and hoped that it would be able to note the progress awaited and, concretely, that the national law and practice would be brought into full conformity with the Convention.

The Committee invited the Government to request a high-level technical assistance of the Office for the abovementioned objectives, with particular emphasis on questions concerning interference with the autonomy of workers' and employers' organizations.

The Employer members referred to their previous statements. In the face of the persistence of the problems which remained pending without being resolved, they could anticipate that it would be eventually necessary to discuss the situation in the Bolivarian Republic of Venezuela again the following year. The Employer members would prefer to send a high-level Governing Body tripartite mission to visit the country in order to find solutions conducive to the full application of the Convention and make progress in the sense of the conclusions which had been agreed upon.

The Government representative spoke on the obstacles that the Employer members' spokesperson had generated during the debate, interfering with the right of workers and governments, who certainly constituted the majority, to have their own opinion. Such obstacles affected the methods of work and the constructive spirit which had prevailed in the debate until then.

Moreover, he objected to the statement made by the Employer members' spokesperson that Venezuela should be included in the list of individual cases for examination by the Conference Committee the coming year, which demonstrated the negative predisposition of this spokesperson who wanted to turn the Conference Committee against his country.

With regard to the individual persons mentioned in the conclusions, these were found in the position of defendant through the autonomous and independent decisions of the Judiciary, in accordance with due process without any interference by the Government authorities. The Judicial proceedings had been instituted as a consequence of the presumed activities of the abovementioned persons, a small group of people, during the events of 2002 and 2003 against the national Constitution and laws. These persons had approved the decree for the dissolution of all public powers in the Government's seat, while the constitutionally legitimate President had been abducted in the midst of a coup d'état.

In any way, the Presidency of FEDECAMARAS had been designated by the Government as the main delegate of the Venezuelan Employers' delegation which had attended the present 93rd session of the Conference and had been able to get out of the country any time this had been necessary with the due judicial authorization, without any effect on her personal or professional life.

Moreover, the speaker was once again pleased to note the cooperation and high level technical assistance provided by the regional Office of the ILO in Lima. In this case, the technical assistance or cooperation in question, of a regional nature, should serve in order to follow up to the joint declaration of the five trade union confederations of November 2004, with regard to the regime of trade union elections.

The Government requested that this declaration be recorded in the provisional records.

Convention No. 95: Protection of Wages, 1949

ISLAMIC REPUBLIC OF IRAN (ratification: 1972). A **Government representative** pointed out that since ratification of the Convention, this was the first time that the Conference Committee discussed its application by the Islamic Republic of Iran, which demonstrated the Government's continued commitment to fulfil its obligations concerning the protection of wages of the labour force, as well as its reporting obligations. The Government's economic policies and structures had not created a dynamic for job creation and unemployment was high.

The Government, therefore, had intensified its efforts and had developed, with ILO assistance, an employment strategy. A better environment for enterprise creation and private investment needed to be established. Sectoral policies relating to minimum wages, productivity, training, social security, labour market regulation and tripartism and social dialogue formed a good foundation to build a functioning labour market. However, these polices could still be significantly improved and the Government was determined to rectify the situation. While the public sector played a dominant role, particularly in urban areas, a process of privatization was ongoing. Minimum wages were constantly revised in the light of inflation and enforced through labour inspection.

Over recent years, the textile industry had been facing serious problems due to a number of factors, such as globalization and competition. Some factories incurred heavy losses and were forced to cease operations. In turn, workers filed wage claims with the Ministry of Labour some of which could be settled by the Ministry through social dialogue. The Government had taken urgent measures, designed to redress the losses incurred on account of non-payment of wages. More than half of the workers affected had been compensated on the basis of early retirement legislation. The remaining workers had been paid three months pay for each year of service. In comparison, most countries only provided for up to one months' pay as severance payment. Other measures taken included: (1) some US$100,000 of financial credits for the implementation of structural adjustment in the textile industry; (2) US$230 million low interest loans in foreign currency for equipment renovation; (3) payment of unemployment benefits to job-seekers who had not been paid; and (4) measures to promote entrepreneurship. The Government would supply the necessary statistical information and documentation, as well as information on the results achieved, to the ILO within the next three months. Further, the Government would appreciate technical cooperation with respect to resolving the wage crisis.

The **Employer members** emphasized that during the last ten years the Conference Committee had examined in a regular manner the individual cases related to the grave situation of wage arrears and the inability of governments to deal with regular payments in line with Article 12, paragraph 1, of the Convention. As the Committee of Experts had noted in its General Survey of 2003, it had become a worrying and persistent phenomenon, particularly in countries making the transition to a market economy. The case of the Islamic Republic of Iran was different because it was not a country in transition and the problems affected a specific sector, the textile sector, where there was a consistent delay in wage payments.

The Committee of Experts had presented observations on this issue, with respect to the Islamic Republic of Iran, on two occasions, but this was the first time that the Committee had examined this case.

The Government provided information on the system of remedies for the legal protection of wages in the Islamic Republic of Iran and had provided information as to the actual situation of employment in certain textile factories. Despite this, the main problem was the lack of detailed information in order to understand the complete background and the level of compliance, in practice, with the Convention. In particular, it was important to consider statistical information that allowed an adequate evaluation of the real dimension of the problem, the number of workers affected, the amounts of wages due, and the inspections and sanctions imposed for lack of compliance.

The Employer members' organizations underlined, on repeated occasions, the importance of the Convention, which dealt with one of the essential questions of the labour relationship. The payment of wages profoundly affected the living conditions of workers, at times for prolonged periods. It could also have perverse effects on the functioning of the economy, incrementally leading to social instability, affecting the informal economy, and worsening the conditions of life, including situations of unfair competition. Despite this, there existed factors that could permit a better understanding of the causes of this situation. In certain situations, a specific sector could be confronted with the obligation to modernize the productive structure, with the consequent immediate implications for employment. On other occasions, the lack of liquidity for reasons of a circumstantial fall in demand impeded short-term capital, preventing the payment of wages. Nonetheless, nothing justified failing to pay wages. To alleviate the circumstances, legislation, through what was stipulated in Article 11 of the Convention, established a system of protection especially to deal with wage claims as opposed to other privileged creditors. In some cases the establishment of an inclusive system of collective security allowed crisis situations to be addressed.

With regard to the information provided by the Government, it was impossible to know the real dimension of the problem in the textile sector and other sectors that experienced or could have experienced delays in wage payments. The practical reality of the prevailing legal arrangements was also unknown. As a consequence, the Government needed to prepare more detailed information on these questions and indicate the socio-economic context, the difficulties faced by sectors affected by these delays or non-payment in order to better understand the circumstances in this situation, and it was also possible that some cases required technical assistance from the ILO.

The **Worker members** noted that the Government representative had not denied the serious shortcomings in the implementation of the Convention as indicated by the ICFTU and the WCL. Unfortunately, her answer had not provided a clear picture of the scale, nature and extent of the problems identified in the observation of the Committee of Experts. Although the problems were especially visible in the textile sector, in reality they touched upon a broad range of economic activity in both the public and private sectors, from the oil and shoe industry to telecommunications and hospitals. The Worker members hoped that the information that the Government had promised to submit to the Committee of Experts would cover the full scale of the problem. The Worker members considered that it was unfortunate that the Government representative had not referred to the allegations of police brutality against protesting workers, workplace arrests, abductions and disappearances. The Government representative had also not clearly indicated the measures taken or envisaged so as to ensure the improved implementation of the Convention. Reference had only been made to the available instruments, not to their actual use or contribution to the protection of the workers concerned.

In conclusion, the Worker members had four points to make. Firstly, they supported the request made by the Committee of Experts for the provision of detailed information by the Government. Secondly, they suggested that the Committee of Experts recommend to the Government to give social dialogue an important place in the efforts to solve the problems identified. Thirdly, they noted that this was a case in which the Government could benefit from the technical assistance of the ILO. Fourthly, they observed that the effective protection of wages was very difficult, if not impossible, without free and independent trade unions. Therefore, the Government could be well advised to ratify Conventions Nos. 87 and 98 as soon as possible in order to create the best possible conditions for real trade union activity, also in the framework of resolving the problem at hand.

The Worker member of the Islamic Republic of Iran stated that abusive pay practices and non-payment of wages were affecting a considerable number of countries, including the Islamic Republic of Iran. The Committee of Expert's view that non-payment of wages was part of a vicious circle affecting the national economy as a whole had been highlighted. The workers affected by non-application of the Convention comprised four categories.

Firstly, the workers who are working in factories and units which are currently operating, but their wages are not being paid because of the so-called cash flow problem that units are facing.

Secondly, the workers of factories whose units are undergoing restructuring. Under this category, either the whole or a large percentage of them are covered by unemployment benefit. They receive 85 per cent of their salary on the basis of their last 24 months' average pay. The remaining 15 per cent is paid by the employer along with the other benefits as per the collective agreement signed by the trade union of that unit. In such cases, the unpaid wages comprise 15% per cent wage and other related annual benefits.

Thirdly, as per the early retirement provisions of the Hard and Hazardous Jobs Act, workers with 20 consecutive, or 25 non-consecutive, years of service in these jobs can retire. Under section 24, of the Labour Law a retiring worker is eligible for retirement benefits. After retirement, the worker receives a pension from social security organization, but the employer, on its part, delays the payment of retirement benefit, which also varies from a few months to a year, or sometimes longer.

Fourthly, under the Renovation and Restructuring Industries Act, a worker with 25 years of service can retire with 30 days' pay. The social security contribution for the remaining five years is equally shared by the employer and the Government. In this case, the employer must agree and consent to the retirement of the worker. This right is abused by the employer, who dictates his terms to the worker, and agrees to his retirement on the condition that the worker does not press for payment of the retirement benefit, waiting to receive it after a few months or up to two years.

The majority of the non-payment of wages takes place in the first two groups of workers.

The speaker stated that the situation was much more serious than presented by the Committee of Experts. Further, a clarification was necessary regarding unpaid unemployment benefits and pensions, which concerned workers of factories undergoing restructuring programmes. In these cases, workers received 85 per cent of their average salaries in the form of unemployment benefits and the remaining 15 per cent from the employer. Non-payment of benefits could occur because each stage of the restructuring programme had to be approved by the Supreme Labour Council, and the Social Security Organization abstained from the payment of unemployment benefits unless it had received a letter extending the programme from the Ministry of Labour. Where restructuring programmes did not exist, workers suffered because they could not receive unemployment benefits and could not avail themselves of other social security benefits, including health benefits.

The speaker gave a detailed account of many situations in which the non-payment of wages had serious consequences for the workers concerned and their families. Workers were no longer able to pay back their housing loans, financial difficulties led to the break up of families, and even several cases of suicide were known. Where factory units had cash flow problems, provincial authorities as well as the Ministry of Labour provided assistance. While appreciating the efforts made by the Government, the speaker called for a change in the Government's attitude regarding the issue of non-payment of wages. He urged an increased allocation of the budget to the Workers Support Fund, which was currently far from sufficient. Recalling that the Convention called for means to redress the injury caused, including through fair compensation for losses incurred on account of delayed payment, the Government should adopt legislation requiring the payment of interest if wages arrears exceeded three months. Further, a tripartite committee should be established to follow-up the matter and the ILO should provide technical assistance. It was hoped that the Government would provide the information requested by the Committee of Experts and that progress could be noted soon.

The Government member of Canada welcomed the Islamic Republic of Iran's cooperation with the Organization, including its hosting of several visiting ILO delegations, as well as the signature of a Memorandum of Understanding with the ILO. It urged the Government to strengthen its commitment by permitting the ILO to reopen its Office in Teheran.

However, application of the Convention continued to be very problematic. Abusive pay practices and the non-payment of wages affected the national economy in its entirety which could have disastrous social and financial consequences. Unpaid workers and their families were deprived of their means of subsistence. They needed to have an effective recourse. In addition, workers put their safety at risk when they took to the street to claim their rights. In addition, he noted that the Labour Code's legal remedies for the recovery of unpaid wages and the settlement of wage claims were appreciated, but confirmation that wages and all arrears were indeed paid was necessary.

The speaker urged the Government to take immediate and concrete measures to eliminate the problem of unpaid wages, especially in the textile sector. The Government should provide the Committee of Experts current and detailed data on the employment situation in the textile industry and possibly other sectors where regular payment of wages was an issue, to enable an analysis of the situation.

In conclusion, ILO Conventions had minimal impact when human rights were not respected in practice. The Government of Canada remained extremely preoccupied by the situation of human rights in the Islamic Republic of Iran, including problems such as the independence of the judiciary, arbitrary detention, freedom of expression, treatment of women and treatment of persons belonging to religious and ethnic minorities. Only when these basic human rights were respected would Iranian workers enjoy the full rights they were entitled to.

Another Government representative wished to provide information in connection with certain questions raised. After the Islamic revolution, 250,000 small and medium-sized enterprises had been established in the Islamic Republic of Iran. However, in recent years, many industries faced tremendous challenges due to the negative consequences of globalization, without being in a position to profit from its benefits due to insufficient policies and inappropriate managerial practices. Low productivity, lack of appropriate machinery and high production costs prevented Iranian industries from competing in the global markets and deprived the workers of a decent livelihood. For instance, in the textile sector, low productivity and dated machinery had plunged the industry into bankruptcy with the total number of workers laid off amounting to 35,000. In order to support the industry, the Government had provided amounts equivalent to US$72 million for the industry's adjustment; 112 million in contributions for exports; 230 million in the form of low interest rate bank loans for renovation of machinery and equipment. In addition to this, 140,000 laid-off persons were receiving unemployment benefits in 2004. The minimum wage was being determined every year on the basis of tripartite consultations and in connection with the annual inflation rate. For the year 2005, the minimum wage amounted to approximately US$140. A series of other allowances were also paid to workers, as well as children and housing allowances.

In conclusion, the speaker reiterated that the Government had done its utmost to end the crisis in connection with the different entitlements of workers. Many deferred allowances had been paid while the textile industries had been renovated and had resumed their activities. Unemployed people were receiving their benefits. With regard to workers' demonstrations for the payment of their wages, efforts were being made to avoid the intervention of military forces. The Government had devised macroeconomic plans and a series of key strategies to promote employment, targeting an 8 per cent rate of growth so as to decrease unemployment to 7 per cent. Moreover, vast efforts were made in the area of vocational training and microcredit. A new initiative entailed the co-payment of workers' salaries by the Government and the employer at a rate of 50 per cent for each side. The Government representative indicated that a statistically detailed report would be submitted on all the above issues to the Committee of Experts in the forthcoming months.

The Employer members emphasized the need to fully apply the Convention in law and in practice. They requested the Government to provide detailed information, in particular statistical data, to allow a full picture to be drawn on the delayed payment or the non-payment of wages in specific sectors, the number of workers affected and the amount of wages due. They also asked for information relative to the effective implementation of the legislation in force and the socio-economic context, as well as the difficulties faced by the sectors in which the delays or non-payment occurred. They reiterated that the Office should provide appropriate technical assistance to the Government.

The Worker members recalled the four points they had raised during their initial intervention and emphasized that the Government should provide a detailed and specific reply to all points brought up during the discussion in its report to the Committee of Experts.

The Committee noted the oral explanations given by the Government representative and the ensuing discussion.

The Committee observed that the situation related to the application of the principle set out in Article 12, paragraph 1, of the Convention dealing with the payment of wages at regular intervals, particularly in the textile industry where a very high number of workers were reported to receive their wages with several months' delay. According to the comments of the ICFTU and the WCL, the situation prevailing throughout the country was dramatic and the growing unrest among Iranian workers was often met with violence on the part of the authorities.

The Committee took careful note of the information supplied by the Government representatives concerning the problems experienced by the national economy, such as the high unemployment rate, low productivity and inadequate private investment, and the efforts made by the Government for devising a new employment strategy, accelerating privatization and improving the business environment in the country. It noted, in particular, the information concerning the crisis in the textile industry in recent years which had led a large number of enterprises to file for bankruptcy or undergo restructuring.

The Committee also noted that, according to the indications provided by the Government, certain steps had been taken such as the implementation of a structural programme for the textile sector and the granting of loans for the modernization of textile factories and equipment. The Committee further noted the Government's indication that full statistical information would be submitted to the Office within three months.

The Committee stressed the importance that it attached to the Convention which related to a fundamental workers' right affecting their day-to-day life and that of their families. While mindful of the financial difficulties experienced by various sectors of the national economy, such as the textile sector, the Committee reminded the Government that the delayed payment of wages or the accumulation of wage arrears clearly contravened the letter and the spirit of the Convention and risked rendering the application of most of its other provisions meaningless.

The Committee reiterated that the problems of delayed payment or non-payment of wages called for sustained efforts, open and continuous dialogue with the social partners, and a wide range of measures, both at the legislative level and in practice, in order to ensure an effective supervision of national laws through labour inspection. The Government should provide information on the mechanisms in place to provide effective settlement of wage arrears. The Committee requested the Government to take all necessary measures to ensure that workers who claimed payment for unpaid wages were not the subject of abusive treatment and violence.

The Committee urged the Government to take all necessary steps to find viable solutions to the wage crisis faced by various sectors of economic activity, including but not limited to the textile industry, in accordance with the principles set forth in the Convention. It also asked the Government to prepare for the next session of the Committee of Experts a detailed report containing concrete information on the measures taken to ensure the application of the Convention in practice. Such information should include all relevant data including, for instance, the sectors, type of establishments and number of workers affected and the amount of accumulated wage arrears, the average length of the delay in the payment of wages, the number of inspections made, infringements observed and penalties imposed, workers' claims accepted and rejected and any time schedule for the settlement of outstanding wage arrears as well as a detailed description of the relevant legal remedies in the Labour Code and information on how these had been applied in the present circumstances.

The Committee expressed the hope that the Government would spare no effort to improve national laws and practices aiming at protecting wage earners from abusive pay conditions and that it would soon put an end to the persistent problems of non-payment of wages.

Finally, the Committee welcomed the Government's readiness to rectify the existing situation and to accept technical assistance from the Office.

Convention No. 98: Right to Organise and Collective Bargaining, 1949

AUSTRALIA (ratification: 1973). A Government representative said that since 1998 the Committee of Experts had published a number of comments on Australia's federal workplace relations legislation and the implementation of the Convention, which had been the subject of ongoing dialogue between the Government and the Committee of Experts. Given the lengthy consideration by the Government of the issues raised by the Committee of Experts, it was disappointing that more progress had not been made towards resolving them. He added that the comments of the Committee of Experts related to detailed technical issues regarding the interpretation of Australia's federal workplace relations legislation and the scope of the Convention. The Committee of Experts considered that Article 4 imposed an unqualified obligation to promote collective bargaining at the expense of all other forms of bargaining. He said that his Government did not agree with that view. Article 4 required measures for the encouragement and promotion of collective bargaining to be taken "where necessary" and such measures were to be "appropriate to national conditions". He emphasized, in this regard, that collective bargaining had been the norm in Australia for more than a century and continued to be so. The Workplace Relations Act did not give primacy to individual bargaining over collective bargaining, but provided for additional machinery to facilitate individual bargaining as an alternative to collective bargaining where the parties so wished. Under the Act, individual agreement making, like collective agreement making, was at the top of an award safety net of minimum wages and conditions negotiated through a process involving collective bargaining. Access to individual bargaining provided the parties with another choice. He indicated that there was nothing in the Convention to suggest that this was inappropriate. The promotion of collective bargaining did not entail restricting the availability of individual bargaining. It should be noted in this respect that Australian employees were predominantly covered by collective agreements, with 20 per cent of all Australian employees relying on the award safety net, 40.9 per cent being covered by collective agreements, and 39.1 per cent being covered by individual agreements. He added that Australia's system of conciliation and arbitration had a well-established and substantial element of collective bargaining, supported by several features. Firstly, participation in the formal system set up by the Act was voluntary, which meant that workers, employers and their representative organizations were free to negotiate and make agreements outside the formal system. Secondly, the Australian industrial relations system had been and continued to be predominantly based on collective bargaining. Thirdly, the system continued to provide machinery for the negotiation of collective agreements. Fourthly, Australia had mature, sophisticated and well-resourced trade unions and employers' organizations able to inform members of their rights and obligations and to represent these members in collective bargaining or individual bargaining with equal facility. Finally, an employee who chose to bargain individually could arrange to be represented by a bargaining agent, such as a trade union, during negotiations. He concluded that, as collective bargaining was the historical norm in Australia, the availability of individual agreements as a choice among several forms of bargaining instruments could not reasonably be considered to contravene the Convention. Accordingly, in the language of Article 4 of the Convention, the Act was consistent with Australian "national conditions" and Australia was not in breach of the Convention.

He added that the ongoing criticism by the Committee of Experts of individual workplace agreements illustrated its particular interpretation of the Convention and its opposition to individual bargaining arrangements. In its observation, the Committee of Experts had considered that the provisions of the Workplace Relations Act concerning individual agreements and collective certified agreements might operate to create disincentives for workers to join trade unions. In making this observation, the Committee of Experts had mistakenly believed that collective bargaining could only take place with union involvement. Under the provisions of the Workplace Relations Act, collective bargaining could and did take place between employers and their employees, whether or not they were union members, and whether or not unions were involved. Many of the comments of the Committee of Experts in relation to individual agreements implied that the latter were inherently anti-union. Specifically, the Committee of Experts considered that the offer and acceptance of individual agreements was an act of anti-union discrimination, in breach of Article 1 of the Convention. He emphasized that this was not the case. The parties might choose to enter into individual agreements and be active members of a trade union. Individuals could also make use of a trade union as their bargaining agent in negotiating an individual agreement.

As reflected in Australia's various reports to the ILO, the Workplace Relations Act provided protection against acts of anti-union discrimination. Account needed to be taken of the overlap between freedom of association provisions and the provisions of section 170CK of the Workplace Relations Act, which prohibited termination of employment on the grounds of trade union membership. Although the Committee of Experts considered that termination due to refusal to negotiate an individual agreement was not covered by the freedom of association provisions, he emphasized that this was not the case. While there was no express reference to this situation in the Act, the freedom of association provisions prohibited discriminatory action on the grounds that an employee was entitled to the benefit of an industrial instrument. Terminating the employment of an employee for refusing to negotiate an individual agreement was a breach of these provisions, the remedies for which included reinstatement and the payment of compensation. The freedom of association provisions also provided protection against dismissal or otherwise being prejudiced for engaging in union activities, consistent with Article 1. In conclusion, the Workplace Relations Act provided protection against anti-union discrimination through extensive provisions in accordance with Article 1 of the Convention.

He added that certain comments made by the Committee of Experts took little account of the context in which developments had occurred.

One example was the reference made to the Container Terminals Case before the Australian Industrial Relations Commission (AIRC). The Committee of Experts had failed to explain that this was an unfair dismissal case involving a trade union official who had frequently absented himself from work. In this case, the AIRC had ordered the reinstatement of the employee in question. The Committee of Experts had also considered that the absence of protected action in pursuit of a multi-employer agreement amounted to anti-union discrimination. Once again, this was not the case. Agreements were not reached only as a result of industrial action. Where parties, including employers, could take protected action, they could still avail themselves of other remedies under the Workplace Relations Act if they considered they were discriminated against in relation to the negotiation of a multiple business agreement.

He reiterated that the Workplace Relations Act did not give primacy to individual bargaining over collective bargaining. It simply provided additional machinery to facilitate individual bargaining as an alternative to collective bargaining where that was what the parties wanted. His Government considered that individual workplace agreements played an important role in providing workplace flexibility and a greater range of agreement options for employers and employees. He called upon the Committee of Experts to reconsider its opposition to individual agreements in the light of the information provided and the arguments advanced concerning the interpretation of the Convention. He recognized that the matters raised by the Committee of Experts reflected the difficulties inherent in understanding the technical complexity of Australia's workplace relations framework, which was unique. His Government therefore stood ready to work with the ILO with a view to resolving outstanding issues by helping it understand Australia's industrial arrangements.

The Employer members thanked the Government representative for the information provided. They indicated that there were a number of aspects to the case. The first concerned what the Committee of Experts considered to be a lack of protection against the dismissal of certain categories of workers under section 170CK of the Workplace Relations Act, 1996. However, the Employer members considered that some of the comments made by the Committee of Experts on this issue needed to be further clarified before the matter could be pursued. They indicated that the heart of the case related to Article 4 of the Convention which, in the view of the Committee of Experts, appeared to overlap to a certain extent with Articles 1 and 2 of the Convention. However, it was the belief of the Employer members, based on the preparatory work for the Convention, that Articles 1, 2 and 3 of the Convention addressed the issue of the protection of the right to organize and protection against acts of anti-union discrimination, while Article 4 was more closely related to the promotion of voluntary negotiation. The terms of Article 4, which provided that "measures appropriate to national conditions shall be taken, where necessary, to encourage and promote the full development and utilization of machinery for voluntary negotiation between employers or employers' organizations and workers' organizations, with a view to the regulation of terms and conditions of employment by means of collective agreements", offered a dual flexibility. This was based on measures that were both "appropriate to national conditions" and which were to be adopted "where necessary". This requirement meant that there had to be effective recognition of the right to collective bargaining, but as long as such recognition existed, it did not exclude individual or other types of bargaining, nor did it specify the level at which bargaining should take place. This provision was designed to be adapted to a broad variety of national situations in which bargaining took place at different levels and in different forms. In the view of the Employer members, the Committee of Experts was endeavouring, through its reading of Article 4, to impose a very narrow meaning on what was essentially a very flexible clause.

The Worker members thanked the Government representative for the information provided. The case of Australia was very clear.

In the first place, the Committee of Experts had noted that the Workplace Relations Act, 1996, did not seem to offer sufficient protection from acts of anti-union discrimination against workers who refused to negotiate an Australian workplace agreement and insisted that their conditions of work should be regulated by collective agreements. This discrimination could take place at the time of recruitment, during employment or in relation to dismissal and was contrary to Convention No. 98, particularly Article 1 (anti-union discrimination) and Article 4 (obstacles to collective bargaining). Firstly, with regard to discrimination at the time of recruitment, the Australian courts had found that there was no discrimination in a case in which an employer had made a job offer conditional upon the signature by the future employee of an Australian workplace agreement on the grounds that in that case there was no pre-existing relationship between the parties concerned. In this respect, the Committee of Experts had recalled that the protection provided for in the Convention covered both the time of recruitment and the period of employment, including cessation of the employment contract. With regard to discrimination during employment, the courts had once again found no anti-union discrimination in a case in which employees had been required to sign an Australian workplace agreement in order to receive a wage increase, thereby giving up their right to collective bargaining. The Committee of Experts recalled, in this regard, that Article 1 of Convention No 98 covered all acts which "otherwise" prejudiced a worker in any manner, and not only in relation to dismissal. With regard to discrimination in relation to termination of employment, the Workplace Relations Act, 1996, prohibited the dismissal of workers who refused to negotiate an Australian workplace agreement. However, broad categories of workers were excluded from the scope of the Act, and particularly, employees on contracts of employment for a specified period of time or a specified task, employees on probation or engaged on an occasional basis.

Secondly, the Committee of Experts had pointed out that the Workplace Relations Act, 1996, did not provide protection against anti-union discrimination in the case of the negotiation of multiple enterprise agreements. In this respect, the Government admitted that the provisions of the Act were intended to facilitate the negotiation of agreements at the enterprise or workplace level. The parties were nevertheless free to negotiate and conclude agreements covering several enterprises outside the formal system, if they so wished. However, according to the Committee of Experts, the choice of the level of negotiation should be for the partners themselves to decide and the parties were best placed to decide on the most appropriate level of negotiation.

Thirdly, the Workplace Relations Act, 1996, allowed an employer to conclude an agreement with one or more workers' organizations, where each organization had at least one member employed in the enterprise. The employers could therefore choose the union with which they wished to negotiate. In this respect, the Committee of Experts concluded that this procedure enabled employers to interfere in the functioning of trade unions, which was contrary to Article 2 of Convention No. 98.

Fourthly, the Workplace Relations Act, 1996, provided that an individual employment contract excluded the application of a subsequent collective agreement, even where the latter was more favourable to the worker. The Committee of Experts considered this to constitute anti-union discrimination.

Fifthly, certain provisions of the Workplace Relations Act, 1996, allowed workers to be represented by trade unions, but employers could easily avoid this by unilaterally modifying the scope and object of negotiations or by simply stating that they no longer wished to seek an agreement. In the view of the Committee of Experts, under the terms of this Act, a request for trade union representation could lead to the partial or total abandonment of negotiations, which implied that the Act dissuaded workers from seeking such representation. On the other hand, an employer could directly conclude agreements with its employees without going through trade unions. On this point, the Committee of Experts had recalled that effective protection needed to be provided for the right to trade union representation and that negotiations with non-unionized workers could take place only where there was no representative trade union in the enterprise.

Sixthly, the Workplace Relations Act, 1996, provided for the deduction of remuneration in the event of a strike. In this respect, the Committee of Experts felt that, even if it was not contrary to the Convention to deduct remuneration for strike days, it was incompatible with the Convention for the Act to impose such deductions in all cases. Indeed, in a system of voluntary collective bargaining, the parties should be able to negotiate on this point.

Seventhly, the Workplace Relations Act, 1996, provided that a new employer could choose the organization with which he or she wished to negotiate. The Act provided that any agreement could be applied for three years, during which period collective agreements were not applicable. According to the Committee of Experts, such agreements should only be concluded in special circumstances and should not last as long as regular collective agreements, which could not exceed three years.

The Worker members indicated that the Committee of Experts' observations were overwhelming. The Government should accept the recommendations of the Committee of Experts and amend the Workplace Relations Act, 1996. They urged the Government to provide a report containing detailed information on the measures taken to amend the Act and to request the Office's advice before adopting any new provisions.

The Worker member of France commended the work of the Committee of Experts, the conclusions of which were once again complete and precise, and allowed an understanding of the spirit and letter of the Australian labour legislation. With regard to the substance of the issue, it was disturbing to note that the provisions of the Workplace Relations Act, 1996, in practice violated the rights of workers to organize and bargain collectively. The Act had to be amended, especially considering the current economic situation, as it seriously challenged the mandate of the ILO. The discussion on the General Survey on hours of work had demonstrated the danger of using a flexible notion or concept in respect of labour standards. In that debate it had been recalled that, taking into account recent experience, especially in Europe, the promotion, at the request of certain employers and governments, of negotiation at the local, or even individual, level, commonly referred to as the "opt-out" clause, weakened the ability of workers to defend their rights. The promotion of negotiation at the enterprise or individual level, to the detriment of sectoral collective agreements, encouraged a form of blackmail in a context of increasing unemployment and precarity. It was not infrequent to hear an employer say: "either accept my conditions, or I will subcontract the work or delocalize the enterprise". The consequences of the Australian labour legislation on the workers concerned, however, went even further. Indeed, it grouped together a wide range of conditions, resulting in the de facto denial of the right of workers to organize. This was the case when, in law, the promise of a job or pay rise was dependent on the employee renouncing her or his right to collective bargaining, which could then be used by the employer and interpreted as the worker having forever renounced the right to engage in union activities. According to the Government, nothing was compulsory. But what freedom did an employee have when isolated in the labour market and considered to be a simple commodity? According to information on the Australian workplace agreement provided to employees by employment agencies, workers could choose their work schedule. However, to what extent did an employee on her or his own have any choice other than to accept?

The Preamble of the ILO Constitution of 1919, recalled in the General Survey on hours of work, stated that "the regulation of the hours of work" was among the measures urgently required to improve conditions of labour. But for regulations to effectively take into account the needs of workers, they had to provide for collective bargaining. Collective bargaining, however, could only exist if workers were guaranteed freedom of association. The Australian Workplace Relations Act did exactly the opposite. This was the case when, under the Act, a collective action by workers to negotiate a sectoral agreement covering several enterprises was considered illegal. The Government had indicated that workers were free to negotiate sectoral collective agreements, but any action to demand such agreements could be considered illegal. This was a one-way concept of freedom. He concluded by urging the Government to recognize the legal basis of the comments of the Committee of Experts and the Conference Committee.

The Worker member of the United Kingdom recalled the discussion by the Committee in 1996 of a very similar case concerning the application of Articles 1 and 4 of the Convention by his own country, where trade unionists had been subject to inducements and pressures to relinquish the protection of collective agreements in favour of the total lack of protection provided by individual contracts. In that same year, the Australian Government had adopted its infamous Workplace Relations Act, constituting an import from his country that should have been immediately turned back. He recalled that in 1996 the Committee of Experts had noted that an amendment to the legislation in the United Kingdom prevented industrial tribunals from redressing situations in which employees who refused to give up the right to collective negotiation had been deprived of a pay rise and therefore raised significant problems of compatibility with the principles of freedom of association. The Committee on Freedom of Association had commented that such a provision could hardly be said to constitute a measure to encourage voluntary negotiation with a view to the regulation of terms and conditions of employment by means of collective agreements, as provided in Article 4 of the Convention. The Committee of Experts had concluded that section 13 of the United Kingdom Trade Union and Labour Relations Act, 1992, was likely to result in a situation wherein collective bargaining would be easily and effectively discouraged and that the Act failed to protect the right of a union member to make use of the union's essential services, such as collective bargaining.

In that year, the Conference Committee had noted the insufficiency of the protection afforded by the legislation to workers against acts of anti-union discrimination. It had called upon the Government to re-examine the situation so that its law and practice gave unambiguous effect to the principles contained in the Convention, and particularly to guarantee respect for the protection against acts of anti-union discrimination and to promote collective bargaining.

The 1992 Act in the United Kingdom had been amended in 1999 to make it clear that action short of dismissal on grounds of union membership or activities did include acts of omission. Yet in 2002, the European Court of Human Rights had found in the Wilson/Palmer case that trade union law in the United Kingdom was still not compatible with Article 11 of the European Convention on Human Rights on freedom of association. In particular, the European Court had found that workers had the right not to be bribed by employers not to be union members, not to access the services of a union or not to be collectively represented by a union through collective bargaining. It had also ruled that union members should be free from discrimination on grounds that they made use of union services, including collective bargaining. The Employment Relations Act, 2004, had revised the law in the United Kingdom in the light of that judgement and in compliance with it.

He said that he had drawn attention to the 1996 discussion of the case of the United Kingdom for the very simple reason that all three of the ILO's key supervisory mechanisms had been here before and made their views very clear on precisely the matters that were now being discussed. The law and practice in Australia was therefore explicitly and knowingly in violation of Convention No. 98 and constituted a determined attempt to destroy the right to collective bargaining in the country, which gave true grounds for nightmares.

The Worker member of Australia said that it gave her no pleasure to represent the Australian workers, who were now being forced to watch the systematic dismantling of a civilized industrial relations system in which employees had rights. It was a shocking reality to know that this was a deliberate act by the Government of a democratic nation and to witness its impact on the lives of Australian workers. There was no pretence that Australian laws promoted collective bargaining, even when an overwhelming majority of employees had expressed the desire to stand up for each other and bargain collectively. Instead, it was the employer who decided whether bargaining would occur or an employee would be forced to sign an individual contract.

It was no exaggeration to state that there was no right to bargain collectively in Australia. It was now legal for the employer to make it a precondition of employment that an employee sign an individual contract. The effect was to prevent employees being covered by a collective agreement for up to three years. As noted by the Committee of Experts, such situations could amount to anti-union discrimination, contrary to Article 1 of the Convention, and could not be said to encourage and promote voluntary collective bargaining, as required under Article 4. Indeed, there was no question that Australian legislation was in violation of Convention No. 98, as it permitted employers to make the obtaining of a job, the obtaining of a benefit of employment, and the continuation of a job, dependent upon employees abandoning their right to bargain collectively. This was not an unintended consequence of Australian legislation. It was Government policy that individual bargaining should prevail over collective bargaining to the exclusion of collective agreements.

It was difficult to believe that a Government in a democratic nation could be so determined to dismantle collective bargaining. Nevertheless, it threatened universities and technical colleges with loss of funding unless they ignored the fact that their employees were organized and offered them individual contracts. The same was true for state government projects and private sector infrastructure projects which involved national Government financing. The Government did not prohibit collective agreements in universities, but insisted that every collective contract must contain a clause giving precedence to individual bargaining. It did the same within its own departments. The outcomes were becoming very clear as wages and conditions were driven down. All of these cases were in violation of Convention No. 98, because they failed to encourage collective bargaining, actively discouraged collective bargaining and restricted the autonomy of the parties to reach agreements independently and without interference by government. Moreover, where the parties at the workplace opted to conclude a collective agreement, they were constrained in what they could agree to. The law placed restrictions on both the content of agreements and the levels at which agreements could be pursued. In addition, a decision of the High Court last year has the effect that a number of other provisions have been determined to be outside the scope of lawful bargaining, including the voluntary agreement of employers to payroll deductions of union fees.

If the right to Collectively Bargain is not guaranteed as an unenforceable right, then Freedom of Association and the Right to Organize is similarly fictitious.

With respect to activities to advance the interests of members, the Australian laws are very restrictive.

For example, it has been found that, (once an employer has successfully signed all the employees onto individual agreements), a union no longer enjoys the statutory right to visit employees in the workplace, in order to hold discussions with the employees, regardless of union membership at that workplace. (ALDI Foods v NUW)

And, at the same time that the High Court decision last year limited the matters which may be included in an enforceable collective contract, it also limited the matters about which workers may take industrial action with immunity.

Multi-employer agreements were effectively subject to prior approval, as they could only be enforced if they met a public interest test. Australian law prohibited employers and employees from freely negotiating matters which, in the opinion of the Committee of Experts, should be left to the parties. For example, it was prohibited to negotiate strike pay and a law was currently before Parliament to prohibit the inclusion in collective contracts of provisions governing the right of entry of unions into workplaces.

Recent examples were provided highlighting cases where employees were dismissed for refusing individual contracts that reduced their pay significantly, workers who hold a formal ballot in support of collective bargaining and whose employer refused and began discriminating against union members. Recent academic research highlighting the impacts was mentioned.

For over a century, Australian labour law had been based on the assumption that the Government's powers were limited to settling industrial disputes through an independent process of conciliation and arbitration. Yet, the Government was now set upon shifting the very constitutional basis upon which it legislated. As the power of corporations prevailed, labour was coming to be defined through its relationship with the corporation and was being left with no independent status or dignity. The Government's recent announcements showed that it had no regard for its obligations under the Conventions that it had ratified and even intended to deny those obligations even further at a time when, paradoxically, it had sought and obtained membership of the ILO Governing Body. She could only conclude that it was high time to call the Government of Australia to account.

The Employer member of Australia expressed his total and strong support for all the statements made on behalf of the Government of Australia. He recalled that, as had already been pointed out, Article 4 of the Convention was subject to two important qualifications which were contained in the words "where necessary" and "appropriate to national conditions". It was clear that Article 4 required certain measures to be taken only where necessary or when appropriate to national conditions. In this respect, it was important to note that the Australian system of industrial relations was a hybrid system of bargaining and compulsory conciliation and arbitration. The whole system encouraged and promoted collective agreements between employers and employers' organizations and workers' organizations, while at the same allowing other forms of agreement, including individual agreements.

He emphasized that Article 4 of the Convention did not require the encouragement and promotion of one form of agreement to the exclusion of other forms of agreement, as the Committee of Experts appeared to believe. If Article 4 had so required, it was reasonable to expect that this would have been stated, in clear terms. In fact, an examination of the preparatory work carried out for this Convention showed that the flexibility provided for in Article 4 was intended and deliberate, and that there was no basis for the restrictive approach adopted by the Committee of Experts. The words "where necessary" had been added to the Office draft following a proposal made by the Australian Government; the words "appropriate to national conditions" had been added by a working party of the Conference Committee that drafted the Convention. He added that the Reporter of that Committee had said, in presenting his report to the members of the Conference, that "Articles 3 and 4 were drafted in terms designed to take account of the widely divergent conditions in various countries". In this respect, he reiterated his statement that the Australian system, taken as a whole, did indeed encourage and promote certain forms of collective agreement, while allowing other forms of agreement. There was no requirement in Article 4 to exclude these other forms of agreement, nor was there a requirement for every provision in the legislation to encourage and promote a certain form of agreement.

Finally, with respect to "Greenfield agreements", he pointed out that these related to a special form of collective agreement, which was common in the building industry, where a project might well start with a very small workforce, which could grow quickly to a large workforce, and then disappear with the completion of the project after a relatively short period of time. He asserted that the Committee of Experts' had constructed hypothetical argument that these agreements may be made for a period of three years, and that this potentially prejudiced the workers' choice of a bargaining agent for a considerable period of time. However, the Committee of Experts had ignored the fact that such an agreement could only be made with one or more organizations of employees entitled to represent the interests of the workers whose employment was likely to be subject to the agreement. They had also ignored the benefits to all concerned of the stability of such agreements. It was therefore difficult to understand how it could be argued that the legislative provisions did not comply with Article 4 of Convention No.98.

With regard to the comment of the Committee of Experts concerning the freedom of choice of the level of bargaining, he indicated that the possibility of industrial action to force the adoption of a particular waiver of bargaining would make nonsense of the concept of freedom of choice.

In conclusion, he reiterated his support for the statement made by the Australian Government, in particular with respect to the Committee of Experts' comments related to anti-union discrimination. It was clear from the Government's statement that the legislation did provide adequate protection in this respect, as required by Article 1 of the Convention.

The Worker member of Pakistan took note with appreciation of the observation made by the Committee of Experts on the application by Australia of Convention No. 98, concerning the obstacles faced in implementing the principles and basic right of collective bargaining and the need to amend the Workplace Relations Act, 1996. He questioned the interpretation made by the Employer members of Conventions Nos. 87 and 98, especially as it had been clearly stated by the Committee of Experts that the national legislation of Australia was in conflict with the Convention.

Coming from Pakistan, he had great respect for a country such as Australia, which was well advanced in terms of its democratic, social and economic development. He emphasized that, under the Convention, the Government should also respect the right of employers to freedom of association, and that Article 2 of Convention No. 98 clearly stated that "workers' and employers' organizations shall enjoy adequate protection against any acts of interference by each other or each other's agents or members in their establishment, functioning or administration". This meant that employers should not impose conditions on workers with respect to their right to bargain collectively. He added that many lacunae existed in the Workplace Relations Act which denied the right to collective bargaining to newly recruited workers and workers on probationary contracts, which amounted to an anti-union attitude.

Referring to Article 1 of Convention No. 98, he stated that the legislation in Australia constituted a disincentive to becoming a union member, that it did not protect workers against anti-union discrimination and that it did not promote collective bargaining. He hoped that the Government would bring its law and practice into conformity with the Convention, and would refer in this regard to the case of the United Kingdom, which had also been the subject of a discussion by the Committee.

The Worker member of New Zealand stated that he had followed with great concern the application of the Australian Workplace Relations Act, 1996, which was having the same negative impact on workers as the highly criticized Employment Contracts Act of 1991 in New Zealand, and which was perhaps even worse than the New Zealand legislation. The ILO had rightfully questioned the Workplace Relations Act because it was not in conformity with the provisions of Convention No. 98 and it undermined trade union activity and organization on several levels. It also severely deterred, rather than promoted collective bargaining, from the very beginning of a worker's career. In addition, collective membership and support was effectively denied in favour of individualized arrangements by forcing employees into the individualized Australian workplace agreement. The Workplace Relations Act, therefore, had a considerable impact in preventing collectivization and unionization.

This was illustrated by the fact that state sector employers, who were well aware of the possibilities under the existing legislation, had reportedly forced workers to declare that they would not join a union. In his view, this was effectively asking workers to contract out of fundamental human rights and he expressed concern that these cases might only be the tip of the iceberg, as workers might be too afraid to speak up.

He said that it was no coincidence that, despite the criticism, the Government had not taken any remedial action, since it was well aware of the impact of its policies. In his view, the Government was disregarding workers' rights in its desperation to destroy any form of political opposition, including Australian organized labour. The Government was very well aware that trade union membership in New Zealand had been decimated to the point that within a decade several long-standing unions had collapsed and overall union density had shrunk from 56 per cent to 21 per cent of New Zealand's wage and salary earners. The Government also knew that terms and conditions of employment for many workers previously covered by collective agreements had greatly deteriorated. Pay increases, penal rates, overtime rates – in fact genuine negotiations had become something of the past in New Zealand. More importantly, workers, especially non-unionized workers, had become less confident in themselves at negotiating with employers on a range of issues, whether or not they were included in collective agreements. Unions had become more narrow in their focus, moving away from being involved in wider employment and social issues on behalf of workers, in favour of being simple bargaining agents concerned with trying to survive by negotiating employment agreements in a hostile environment.

He emphasized that under this kind of legislation, decent work was impossible and tripartism and social dialogue would be a thing of the past, with workers becoming more vulnerable. The policies mentioned were the antithesis of the ILO's decent work programme and had to be challenged if the ILO was to be serious about decent work. Recalling that employment equity had suffered, as the New Zealand task force on Pay and Employment Equity (PAEE) had discovered that discretionary pay systems and an absence of collective bargaining fostered pay and employment inequity, he said that this would also be the immediate and ongoing impact of the implementation of the Workplace Relations Act in Australia. Moreover, he felt that even if more favourable legislation were to be adopted, as had been the case in New Zealand in 2001, significant damage would already have been done to the union movement in particular, and to workplace relations in general. Employers and workers would not easily embark once again on a constructive relationship based on mutual respect and an ability to engage in social dialogue.

Australia should be made to realize that this type of law was unacceptable to the ILO. However, the Australian Government appeared to have a different view, as it believed that the current Workplace Relations Act did not go far enough in denying workers' collective rights and it was drawing up new legislation. The Australian Government had also recently stated to the Governing Body that its record on Convention No. 98 was of no consequence to it, nor was it a source of embarrassment.

He concluded that this situation could not continue. It was time that the Australian Government was brought into touch with real democracy and fundamental rights. The Conference Committee should act decisively, and he urged the Australian Government to amend the Act immediately so that it complied with the requirements of Convention No. 98.

The Government representative thanked all those who had contributed to the discussion, although he indicated that he did not share all the views expressed during the debate. Moreover, a number of the statements made had been inaccurate and had gone beyond the scope of the comments made by the Committee of Experts. He reaffirmed the willingness of his Government to work with the Committee of Experts to help in gaining an understanding of the Australian industrial relations system and in resolving the issues raised in its comments.

The Employer members noted the divergent views expressed by members of the Committee. One of the issues that had been raised during the discussion concerned the protection afforded to certain categories of workers from dismissal on the basis of trade union activities. The Employer members recalled that two types of protection were provided by Australian legislation in relation to trade union membership, depending on the category of worker. The protection provided for under section 170CK of the Workplace Relations Act, 1996, applied to a wide range of trade union activities. The expression employed by the Committee of Experts in this respect, namely, that the sections "do not seem to provide adequate protection against anti-union discrimination", betrayed a certain caution. In the view of the Employer members, the Australian legislation afforded effective protection for the right to collective bargaining. They also considered that Article 4 of the

Convention was an intentionally flexible provision and that nothing in it could be interpreted as limiting the type of agreement to be concluded or the level of bargaining. It would, therefore, be necessary for the members of the Committee to find common ground in a context of differing views.

The Worker members indicated that divergent legal views had been expressed in the discussions on the case of Australia. Some members were of the opinion that there was a violation of Convention No. 98, while others thought that it was a question of a difference of interpretation of the Convention. The Government representative had stated that the Workplace Relations Act, 1996, did not hinder the organization of collective bargaining. It was, therefore, important to recall that Convention No. 98 provided for the promotion of free collective bargaining, which was not the case in Australia. Referring to the comments of the Committee of Experts, the Worker members called on the Government to supply a report containing detailed information on the measures taken to amend the Workplace Relations Act, 1996, and to request the opinion of the Office before adopting new legal provisions.

The Committee noted the statement by the Government representative and the debate that followed. The Committee recalled that the Committee of Experts had been making comments for several years on certain provisions of the Workplace Relations Act, particularly in relation to the exclusion from the scope of application of the Act of certain categories of workers, the limitations on the scope of union activities covered by protection against anti-union discrimination and the relationship between individual contracts and collective agreements.

The Committee noted the Government's statement that there was an extensive system of collective bargaining and that individual negotiation was not given priority over collective bargaining, but that the system offered an alternative for both employees and employers. The Committee also noted the Government's statement concerning the complexity of the situation and its wish to continue a constructive dialogue with the Committee of Experts.

The Committee requested the Government to provide a detailed report to the Committee of Experts on all elements relating to the application of the Convention, in both law and practice, including the discussion held in the present Committee, taking into account all matters relating to the impact of the legislation on the effective recognition of the right to collective bargaining, and the measures adopted or envisaged by the Government. The Committee also requested the Government to provide copies of all draft laws that might relate to the application of the Convention. The Committee requested the Committee of Experts to examine the elements of the debate on this case. The Government should consider requesting the advice of the Office in this respect.

ZIMBABWE (ratification: 1998). The Government communicated the following written information:
1.1. The Government of Zimbabwe confirms that it commenced a review of its labour legislation and that the Bill has since been approved by Cabinet and published as H.B. 1/2005. It will be tabled for debate before Parliament, during the 1st Session of the 6th Parliament of Zimbabwe, which resumes in June 2005.
1.2. The Government confirms further that all legislative amendments it undertook to include at the 92nd Session of the Conference have been incorporated into the Bill. These in particular are:
  (i)   Repeal of section 22 of the Labour Act, Chapter 28.01, which permitted the fixing of maximum wages by the Minister or at all.
  (ii) The repeal of sections 25(2)(b), 79(2)(b) and 81(1)(b) of the Labour Act, Chapter 28.01, which permitted the authorities not to register collective bargaining agreements which were deemed not to be equitable to consumers and the public generally.
1.3. The Government confirms that it is up to date with all correspondence relating to the reports by the International Confederation of Free Trade Unions.
2. The Government notes that the Committee of Experts also suggests that sections 25(2)(c), 79(2)(c) and 81(1)(c) of the Labour Act, Chapter 28.01, which permits the authorities not to register a collective bargaining agreement "which has become unreasonable or unfair having regard to the respective rights of the parties ...", be repealed for want of compliance with Convention No. 98.
It is noted that the Convention specifically recognizes two grounds by the authorities for declining to register collective bargaining agreements, viz.:
  (i)   a procedural flaw in the collective bargaining agreement; or
  (ii) inconsistency with general labour legislation minimum standards.
Stricto senso there may be no room for declining to register on grounds of unfairness or reasonableness with respect to the rights of the parties.
The Convention being supreme and binding, Zimbabwe has no hesitation in amending its laws accordingly so as to be in keeping with the wording of the Convention.
3. The Government also notes that the Committee of Experts is not comfortable with section 25(1) of the Labour Act, which generally provides that an agreement reached by more than 50 per cent of the employees at a workplace is binding regardless of the position of the other unionized employees.

It is felt that this section does not recognize the provisions of Article 4 of the Convention which requires "measures ... to encourage and promote the full development and utilization of machinery for voluntary negotiations between employers or employers' organizations and workers' organizations ...".
Section 25(1) of the Labour Act ensures majority rule at the workplace. It is a cornerstone of democracy in all practice that the voice of the majority prevails. The proposal by the Committee of Experts implies that the concept of majority rule does not apply in collective bargaining. The Government is of the strong view that section 25(1) is consistent with universal democratic practice, which Convention No. 98 recognizes.
In the circumstances, Zimbabwe stands further guided by the Committee of Experts on the point in the light of this explanation.
4. Finally, the Government appreciates the Committee of Experts' observation that the issue of prison staff is a constitutional question as explained by the Government at the 92nd Session of the Conference.
5. The Government observes with deep concern that, notwithstanding substantial compliance with Convention No. 98, it continues to be listed with respect to the same Convention. It has appeared before this Committee consecutively since 2002 in circumstances which do not meet the selection criteria for listing Members before this Committee.
At all previous Zimbabwe appearances, discussions have degenerated into political discourse. Convention No. 98 is used as a smokescreen to demonize Zimbabwe because of the unpopularity of Zimbabwe's domestic policies in the circles of some former colonial powers.
6. Zimbabwe also does not lose sight of the Nicodemus circumstances under which it was eventually listed through the agency of errant and dubious unionists at this 93rd Session and warns the ILO against the inevitable impairment of its credibility as a transparent and objective international organization.
In view of the foregoing and given the known selection criteria for listing Members, Zimbabwe urges Officers of the Committee to objectively consider its case.

In addition, before the Committee, a Government representative stated that his Government had prepared and made available its response to the observations of the Committee of Experts. He reiterated that Zimbabwe had fully undertaken the process of implementation of all commitments it had made at the previous session of the Conference Committee. It had tabled a Bill amending the Labour Relations Act with a view to repealing sections 22, 25(2)(b), 79(2)(b) and 81(1)(b). This Bill was due for debate in Parliament this June. All social partners had participated in drafting the Bill and the draft was made public. Furthermore, to implement the observations of the Committee of Experts, the Government had now agreed to repeal sections 25(2)(c), 79(2)(c) and 81(1)(c) of the Labour Relations Act, which subjected collective agreements to ministerial approval on the grounds that the agreement was deemed unreasonable or unfair with regard to the rights of the parties. As the Bill was still before Parliament, it was not too late to include these amendments.

With regard to section 25(1) of the Labour Relations Act, which provided for the binding nature of collective agreements approved by more than 50 per cent of employees at a workplace regardless of the views of a unionized minority, and with regard to the statement made by the Government last year before the Conference Committee to the effect that employment council codes took precedence over workers' council codes and hence gave precedence to unionized agreements, the Committee of Experts had correctly pointed out that codes of conduct did not regulate all issues covered by collective agreements. Although his Government questioned whether by disregarding the views of the majority at the workplace, shop-floor democracy was not discarded, it nevertheless would abide by the decision of the Committee of Experts.

With regard to the request of the Committee of Experts to reply to the ICFTU comments, the Government representative indicated that his Government did not deal directly with the ICFTU as the latter was not an ILO body. As for the specific alleged violations of the freedom of association brought by individuals or the ICFTU, the Government had provided its response. These matters were for the Committee on Freedom of Association to examine and not the Conference Committee.

On the issue of prison staff, the speaker explained that any guarantee of the exercise of the rights afforded by the Convention was premised upon the prison service being deemed not to be a military force under the Constitution. But until the Constitution was amended, this situation would remain unchanged. Social partners were very aware of this fact.

The Government representative expressed his bewilderment at the fact that Zimbabwe had to appear before the Conference Committee for the fourth time as the questions at issue were of a legislative nature and mostly related to the interpretation of several provisions, and no problems with the practical application of the Convention were raised. There were no discernible criteria to justify the discussions of Zimbabwe before the Conference Committee for over four years. In his Government's opinion, his country was called before the Conference Committee at the demand of some former colonial powers who were openly agitating for regime change in the country following a successful land reform programme. But there could be other appropriate forums to talk of other concerns, which were not covered by Convention No. 98. The Conference Committee should focus on the issues raised by the Committee of Experts. His Government once again called for a review of the working methods of the Conference Committee.

The Employer members thanked the Government for the information provided and assured the Government that the case had not been selected on the basis of any political consideration. This was rather a case involving tangible progress, which was one of the criteria for selection provided for under the Committee's methods of work. Zimbabwe had recently ratified the Convention and the Committee of Experts had already noted some legislative reforms with satisfaction. Nevertheless, some problems remained. Sections 25, 79 and 81 of the Labour Code needed to be amended and, according to the Government, such amendments were under way. While the Bill concerned was already finalized, there was still time to include amendments to common subsection (c) of these sections, as requested by the Committee of Experts. The requirement to submit collective bargaining agreements to the Ministry for approval was an interference with the ability of workers and employers to determine the conditions of employment independently from the Government. The Government did not provide information on section 22 which constituted a serious constraint on the subject matter and scope of collective bargaining and, therefore, needed to be removed. Regarding section 25(1), the Government should clarify whether a union was required to cover a certain percentage of the employees in order to be able to bargain collectively. In conclusion, the Government had already addressed a number of problems, but it was crucial that the remaining points would be properly addressed. The Government should supply a comprehensive report to the Committee of Experts on all the outstanding issues and should take advantage of technical assistance provided by the ILO in order to remove all legislative provisions that interfered with collective bargaining in accordance with the Convention.

The Worker members noted that the application of the Convention in Zimbabwe had been under discussion by the Conference Committee, the Committee on Freedom of Association and the Committee of Experts for several years. In 2003, the Conference had asked the Government to accept a direct contacts mission and to inform the Committee of Experts. In 2004, the Conference had revealed that the Government had not accepted this direct contacts mission, invoking the fact that such a move could not be undertaken for strictly legal reasons, while in its 2003 conclusions the Conference had referred to violations of the Convention in practice and in law. The Worker members considered that the attitude of the Government demonstrated clearly that it did not wish to give up interfering with collective negotiations, and that it sought to retain the possibility of signing direct agreements with workers, even where unions existed. The Government had declared that it had decided to repeal the ministerial approval as a prerequisite to collective agreements and the setting of minimum wages. In doing so, it nevertheless revealed that this reform had been decided by itself alone, without discussion between the social partners and that in addition it reserved the right to put the matter before Parliament. But, in a truly democratic state, aware of its credibility, a draft law had to be submitted to Parliament and run the risk of being opposed. The Government had not taken the opportunity offered to it to take up social dialogue again. At present, it was happy to repeat its promises of 2003 and 2004, without even mentioning a timetable for these reforms. The Government admitted that the Convention took priority over domestic law and announced that it would modify sections 25(2)(b), 79(2)(b) and 81(1)(b) of the Labour Relations Act, without any concrete measure actually backing up these declarations, and it had still not modified section 22 of the Labour Relations Act in order to ensure that a trade union could undertake collective bargaining, even if it represented less than 50 per cent of wage earners. For the Worker members such an obstacle clearly showed the Government's intention of continuing to exercise control over collective bargaining and, more generally, to deny the fundamental principles of freedom of association.

A Worker member of Zimbabwe stated that it was sad to note that the Zimbabwe Congress of Trade Unions (ZCTU) had come back with the same concerns that it had raised at last year's session of the Committee. The Government's continued anti-trade union attitude was evident in the fact that provisions of the Labour Relations Act requiring collective bargaining agreements to be submitted for ministerial approval and to be published as statutory instruments in order for them to be in force, as well as provisions fixing maximum wages were still in force. The Government had stated in 2004 that it would address these issues by reforming legislation in consultation with the social partners. In fact, the Government had published Labour Act Amendment Bill H.B. 1 of 2005 without consulting the social partners on its substance. The Bill did not address some of the abovementioned issues of concern to the ZCTU, nor did it address the use of the Public Order and Security Act (POSA) by police and security agencies to arrest trade unionists because of their trade union activities. Furthermore, public service employees were removed from the ambit of the Labour Relations Act and were placed under the scope of the Public Service Act, which did not allow public service employees to join trade unions or to collectively bargain. At the last session of the Committee, the ZCTU had also raised the issue of prison service employees, who did not enjoy the right to collective bargaining. The Government had indicated that it would rectify this through a constitutional amendment, yet the amendment pending before the current Parliament did not address this concern. Tripartism was not implemented seriously in the country. While the Government had asked the social partners for submissions on the amendment of the Labour Relations Act, the submissions of the workers had just been shelved. The tripartite system lacked a governing statute and relied on the will of the Government to be convened. The speaker concluded by pointing to further problems in the application of the Convention. He noted that a tripartite event to mark the World Health and Safety Day, attended by government officials, employers, ILO representatives and national social security authority officials, had been disrupted by the police, who had arrested only ZCTU members. Furthermore, the POSA had been used to attack the informal economy, which had been developed by trade unions as a poverty-reduction strategy. The POSA and the Access to Information and Protection of Privacy Act (No. 5 of 2002) were also used to attack trade unions. He urged the Government to commit itself to respecting the Convention.

Another Worker member of Zimbabwe stated that he was the Third Vice-President of the Zimbabwe Congress of Trade Unions (ZCTU). He could confirm that the Government had tabled the Labour Act Amendment Bill H.B. 1 which addressed the concerns raised during last year's session of this Committee. In this regard, he found the listing of Zimbabwe in the individual cases before this Committee counterproductive. He wished to state for the record that the case had not been put on the list by the ZCTU or any regional trade union association, but rather by persons with ulterior political motives. It was not appropriate for this Committee to address political developments in Zimbabwe, as this was better left for the persons directly involved. He stated that the ZCTU was pleased with the legislative progress that had been made in this case, and felt that these developments should be applauded. He was of the view that this forum was not the place to address internal disputes within the ZCTU or to resolve issues of persons who had fallen out of favour with the ZCTU.

The Employer member of Zimbabwe recalled that last year the employers had urged the Committee to give the Government time to address the issues that had been raised. He wished to report, from the employers' perspective, on the progress that had been made over the past 12 months. The speaker noted with satisfaction the positive tenor of the Committee of Experts' report and expressed surprise that the Conference Committee had included Zimbabwe again in the list of individual cases. He recalled the steps that had been taken previously to promote the concept of social dialogue by ensuring maximum participation by employers in the process of law reform and acknowledged the assistance Zimbabwe had received from the ILO through the ILO/SWISS Project, which continued to bring the social partners together in spite of the differences that existed. The employers' efforts undertaken on the bipartite and tripartite level had contributed to the publication by the Government, in January 2005, of the Labour Act Amendment Bill H.B. 1 of 2005, which sought to address most of the points raised by this Committee in 2004. The Bill proposed to repeal section 22 of the Labour Relations Act, which permitted the fixing of maximum wages by the minister, as well as sections 25(2)(b), 79(2)(b) and 81(l)(b), which permitted the authorities not to register collective agreements which were deemed not to be equitable to consumers and the public generally. These provisions of the Bill seemed to respond to the Committee of Experts' concerns with a view to ensuring compliance with the Convention. However, as regards section 25(1) of the Labour Relations Act, while having noted the Committee's concern that where a union had not managed to recruit 50 per cent of the workers at a workplace, representatives of non-unionized workers would be able to negotiate directly with the employer, even if a trade union existed at the enterprise, the speaker believed that this section promoted the concept of majority rule at the workplace. He therefore considered that workers were sufficiently protected. The speaker recalled that Zimbabwe had been appearing before this Committee on allegations of failure to comply with the Convention for the fourth consecutive year. Although it had been a learning experience, which had resulted in significant improvements to the labour legislation, each appearance had generated the kind of publicity that the country could well do without. He called on the Committee to give Zimbabwe and its social partners a chance to make progress on the case.

The Government member of Malawi stated that it had not been appropriate to put Zimbabwe on the list of individual cases. He had heard allegations that it originally had not been on the list, but had somehow been placed there at the last minute. He stated that this Committee's credibility rested on its objectivity and fairness. He noted from the Committee of Experts' report that Zimbabwe was cooperating with the ILO. This development needed to be encouraged instead of condemned. Social dialogue, especially as set out in Convention No. 144, could play an important role. He suggested that before a case went before this Committee, it should first be discussed in a tripartite setting at the national and regional levels. It was not clear whether this case had ever been discussed at these levels. He concluded by stating that it was important to promote the application of Convention No. 98. It was also important for this Committee to act openly and objectively.

The Government member of China stated that he had listened carefully to the response by the Government and to the discussion. It was clear from the Committee of Experts' report that Zimbabwe was amending the laws which had been the subject of concern. The Government representative had mentioned further actions which would be taken in this regard. The Government appeared to be making progress and needed more time. His delegation supported the efforts of the Zimbabwe Government and he urged the ILO to provide relevant technical cooperation.

The Government member of Canada expressed his concern regarding the fact that the Government had failed to follow up its stated intentions to adopt legislation in response to the questions raised by the Committee of Experts. Even though the legal framework had evolved, it was regrettable that the exercise of the right to collective bargaining, which included the right of workers to freely choose their representatives and the right of those representatives to perform their duties without interference, had become increasingly difficult. Moreover, those rights could not be fully exercised without respect for human rights, and there was reason to be deeply concerned by the recent upsurge in human rights violations in Zimbabwe. The speaker encouraged the Government of Zimbabwe to take the necessary steps to guarantee the right to collective bargaining of workers' organizations.

The Government member of Kenya stated that his Government had carefully studied the Committee of Experts' report and the response by the Government regarding conformity with the Convention. He noted that, during the last four years, Zimbabwe had been appearing before this Committee to provide information on the progress made with regard to issues raised by the ZCTU. In its reply, the Government had indicated efforts undertaken to redress the situation by carrying out legislative reform: a Bill had been brought before the Cabinet committee and would be promulgated in June 2005. The speaker wished to commend the Government for this legislative reform, which proved its willingness to cooperate with the ILO in addressing the concerns raised, and expressed the view that the Committee of Experts should allow the Government to complete this reform, in order to guarantee full compliance with the Convention. He also suggested that, taking into account the country's circumstances, the ILO should consider and offer technical assistance to Zimbabwe, in order to enable it to complete the review process and to bring legislation into line with the principles of the Convention.

The Government member of Cuba stated that, after having studied the most recent report of the Committee of Experts, he had been able to note that, in the case of Zimbabwe, there had been recognition of progress made in the reform of labour legislation. The speaker therefore wondered why Zimbabwe had been included in the list. He felt that it was not technically relevant to discuss such a case in the present Committee. The report of the Committee of Experts was not unfavourable towards Zimbabwe and had taken note of the progress made in a process in which perfection could not be aspired to over night. The issue in question and the request for the improvement of certain aspects of the country's labour legislation and its practical application could have been addressed in the next reporting cycle. The speaker indicated that the logical conclusion to all the above was that the inclusion of Zimbabwe in the list of countries appearing before the present Committee could be attributed to the same political reasons that had been repeatedly referred to as a negative element affecting the credibility of the Committee. He wished to express his firm belief that singling out Zimbabwe in the present Committee would not help the country to improve social dialogue. Finally, he expressed his hope that the conclusions would contain an offer of ILO technical assistance, which would contribute and be an effective support to the improvement of the reform process currently under way in Zimbabwe with the support of its Government.

The Government member of Nigeria stated that there was an evident need to talk about transparency in the establishment of the list of individual cases before this Committee. She recalled that her Government had stated last year before this Committee that it believed that the aim of the individual cases was not punitive, but rather to ensure that the social partners coexisted in a harmonious industrial relations environment and that ratified ILO standards were enshrined in national legislation. All the parties concerned should be encouraged to engage in social dialogue to resolve the issues at hand, and this Committee must be seen to be supporting this. The speaker pointed out that, during the last year, the Government of Zimbabwe had made remarkable progress in regard to the Committee of Experts' concerns and had responded positively by elaborating the Labour Act Amendment Bill H.B. 1 of 2005. The Government had indicated its willingness to amend the law with a view to bringing it into conformity with the Convention, and therefore should be collectively encouraged to do more, especially through ILO technical assistance, and to continue along this progressive path.

The Government member of Luxembourg, speaking on behalf of Governments of the Member States of the European Union, as well as of Bosnia and Herzegovina, Bulgaria, Croatia, The former Yugoslav Republic of Macedonia, Norway, Romania, Serbia and Montenegro, Switzerland, Turkey, Ukraine and the United States stated that the European Union was alarmed at the situation in Zimbabwe, given the news on constant politically motivated violence, restrictions on the freedom of opinion, expression, association and assembly. Independent trade unions were an important element of civil society, and in this context the European Union expressed its concern at the inability of independent organizations in Zimbabwe to operate without fear of harassment or intimidation. The speaker recalled that this case had been the subject of comments by the Committee of Experts for many years, and in recent years it had also been before this Committee. The European Union shared the regret of the Committee of Experts that the Government had not made sufficient efforts to amend the Labour Relations Act in order to meet the requirements of the Convention. However, it noted that the Government would table new legislation, which might aim at resolving some of the issues previously raised. The speaker urged the Government to bring the legislation into conformity with the Convention and to create an environment in which the right to collective bargaining could be assured.

The Government member of South Africa noted that the first paragraph of the Committee of Experts' observation on this case indicated that the Government of Zimbabwe was engaged in a process to respond to the issues that had been raised in this Committee the previous year. From what he had noted in the case, he was happy with the progress made. This raised the question of why Zimbabwe had nonetheless been selected for the list of individual cases, which appeared to be almost exclusively composed of developing countries. Where clear criteria did not exist, it was inevitable that those affected would question the method of selecting cases. The case was a clear example of the lack of transparency in the working methods of the Committee. He further noted that without social dialogue, the problems in this case would not be easy to solve. He called on the Committee to assist Zimbabwe's efforts in this case and to take every opportunity to promote relevant social dialogue.

During the speaker's intervention, the **Chairperson** recalled that statements should focus on the case at hand, and not on the working methods of the Committee, which had been the subject of a previous debate.

The Government member of Namibia expressed his surprise at the inclusion of Zimbabwe on the list of individual cases, as his Government had done the previous year, and stated that this fact raised serious questions about the working methods of the Committee. It was clear from the Committee of Experts' report that the Government of Zimbabwe was in the process of adopting legislative amendments in order to ensure conformity with the Convention. The speaker considered that the Government had been making progress and wished to congratulate it for its sustained efforts, positive actions and concrete steps to address the Committee of Experts' concerns. He stated that the Government must be given appropriate time to conclude the adoption of amendments.

The Government representative thanked the governments that had taken the floor in his country's support. With regard to the issues raised by the Worker members, he indicated that he had responded to them in his written reply to the Committee. The Worker members had also questioned the political will of the Government to resolve this case. He took great exception to this statement, and recalled that Zimbabwe had joined the ILO and had ratified ILO Conventions voluntarily. There could be no question about the political will of his Government to engage with the ILO. With regard to the question of the participation of the social partners in the drafting of the Labour Act Amendment Bill, he pointed out that the employers in Zimbabwe had participated in consultations, but the trade unions had refused, based on the advice of their foreign handlers who did not want to support the ZANU-PF Government. He recalled that this Bill, which addressed the problems raised by the Committee, was already on the Parliament's agenda and would most likely be debated in a few days. The speaker appealed to Zimbabwean workers to address any problems they had directly to the Government, and not seek international forums to do so. With regard to the intervention of the Government member of Canada, he questioned his capacity to provide solutions in this matter, given his distance from the country.

With regard to comments on Zimbabwe's informal economy, he stated that trade union claims of having established a flourishing informal economy were not true. The Government had allowed the informal economy to develop in the 1990s following an economic adjustment programme. While it had brought some economic relief, the informal economy had also allowed illegal activities to flourish, and its massive size was now causing serious infrastructure and public health problems. For these reasons, the recent police actions were necessary. Now the Government was building a new infrastructure to support the informal economy and people were returning to their activities. The support for the Government was clear from every election.

The Employer members expressed their appreciation for the information provided by the Government representative, which mentioned draft legislation that would soon be debated by Parliament. The Government should supply copies of these texts to the ILO. Turning to the question of the transparency in the process of selecting individual cases for this Committee, which had been raised by numerous delegations, the Employer members noted that the selection of a particular case was often due to a lack of certainty by members as to what was really happening in the country concerned. The Committee had always been ruled by a double credo: to trust, but also to verify. When the Committee selected an individual case for examination, it was often done to seek and verify information about what was happening on the ground. The best way to respond to a case was to provide complete and accurate information on the situation in question; if this was done, the case might disappear from the list. In this respect, they urged the Government to consider accepting a direct contacts mission to verify that the legislative measures under way in Zimbabwe indeed furthered the application of the Convention.

The Worker members regretted having to make the following statement prior to the drawing of conclusions on the case. They distanced themselves from the comments made by a Worker member of Zimbabwe, the Third Vice-President of the Zimbabwe Congress of Trade Unions (ZCTU), which was a purely honorific title. The ZCTU was represented at that meeting by its General Secretary, and its Chairperson. The latter was present as a member of the ICFTU, since the Government had refused to appoint him as a worker representative, which undermined the principles defended by the ILO. In that regard, the status of the above mentioned Worker member was the subject of a complaint pending before the Credentials Committee. The Committee should also know that Government representatives of Zimbabwe had, on this very day, both inside and outside the meeting room, exerted unacceptable pressure on the workers of Zimbabwe. Finally, the Worker members wished to highlight that they were aware that violations to the Convention existed in every country, as demonstrated by the examination of Australia's application of the Convention this year.

With regard to the case under examination, the Worker members emphasized the continuous lack of will shown by the Government, which would not take constructive steps to align its legislation with the Convention. In its 2003 conclusions, the present Committee had been accommodating and had proposed a direct contacts mission with a view to following in situ the planned legislative revision process. The Government had rejected that mission, which it considered as interference. The Worker members wondered what the new legislative changes were worth in a climate of permanent intimidation, and thus proposed a new direct contacts mission with a view to ensuring that the envisaged changes would comply with the Convention, both in law and practice.

The Worker members wished to point out that, for the sake of the serenity of the discussion, they had limited the number of their statements. That had not been case as far as the Government representatives were concerned. The discussion had therefore been imbalanced and that was regrettable.

The Committee took note of the written statement made by the Government and the oral information provided by the Government representative, the Minister of Public Service, Labour and Social Welfare, and of the debate that followed. The Committee noted with concern that the problems raised by the Committee of Experts referred to: the legal requirement that collective agreements be submitted for ministerial approval in order to guarantee that said provisions were equitable to consumers, to the general public or to any party to the collective agreement; the Minister's power to fix a maximum wage and the maximum amount that may be payable by way of benefits, allowances, bonuses or increments by statutory instrument prevailing over any collective agreement; the legal provisions under which, if workers' committees (including non-unionized workers) concluded a collective agreement with the employer, that agreement must be approved by the trade union and more than 50 per cent of the workers; and the constitutional provisions depriving prison staff of the rights guaranteed by the Convention. The Committee also noted that the International Confederation of Free Trade Unions (ICFTU) had submitted comments to the Committee of Experts and that two cases concerning Zimbabwe were currently pending before the Committee on Freedom of Association.

The Committee noted that the Government had informed the Committee of Experts that the provisions concerning the ministerial approval of collective agreements would be amended, although not in all cases provided for in the legislation, and that measures were being taken to repeal the provision giving the Minister the power to fix a maximum wage and the maximum amount that may be payable by way of certain benefits. The Committee noted the statement by the Government representative that, in keeping with this undertaking, the Bill to amend sections 22, 25(2)(b), 79(2)(b) and 81(1)(b) was due to be debated in Parliament this month. Consideration would also be given to amending other provisions mentioned by the Committee of Experts.

The Committee recalled the importance that it attached to the principle that the rights guaranteed by the Convention be applied in national law and practice and emphasized the importance of full social dialogue, as well as extensive consultation with employers' and workers' organizations on all legislation affecting them. Effective guarantees for this principle implied full respect for the independence of employers' and workers' organizations.

The Committee urged the Government to take all necessary measures to bring the law and practice into full conformity with the Convention, and expressed its hope that, in the very near future, it would be in a position to note concrete progress in connection with all the pending issues. The Committee requested the Government to submit a clear and comprehensive report to the Committee of Experts, with information on all the problems mentioned, a copy of the draft or the legislation adopted, and a full reply to the comments made by the ICFTU on the application of the Convention.

Taking into account the statement made by the Government representative to the effect that there was a certain degree of misunderstanding in the Committee with respect to the situation in the country, the Committee, in a fully constructive spirit, felt that a direct contacts mission could provide greater clarity on the situation, in particular on the ongoing legislative process.

The Government representative indicated that this was not the first occasion on which the present case had been discussed by the Committee and the Government wished to reaffirm its position, as stated previously, that it was not prepared to accept a direct contacts mission now.

The Worker members emphasized that the statement by the Government representative was regrettable as they had made every possible effort to approach the case in a positive manner and to demonstrate that a direct contacts mission was necessary. However, in view of the Government's attitude and its refusal to cooperate, the Worker members requested the inclusion of a special paragraph in the report of the Committee.

The Employer members noted that the Government representative had indicated that his country was not prepared to receive a direct contacts mission for now. As they believed that this was an indication that the Government representative did not have the authority to accept such a mission at this moment, and since the most important consideration was the ability to verify the situation at the national level and the action that was being taken, they proposed that consideration could also be given to the sending of a high-level ILO technical assistance mission to the country as an alternative. That would give the Government the opportunity before the Committee next met to accept one of these two alternatives as a means of demonstrating its good faith and willingness to participate in the verification process. The Employer members could not therefore at this stage support the proposal made by the Worker members for the Committee's conclusions on this case to be placed in a special paragraph of its report. However, they urged the Government to give serious consideration to agreeing to some type of meaningful verification arrangement involving the ILO.

Convention No. 102: Social Security (Minimum Standards), 1952

PERU (ratification: 1961). A Government representative (Vice-Minister of Labour) referred to the points made by the Committee of Experts in its observations of 2004 and in addition presented a detailed and extensive written report indicating progress made. He was pleased that the Conference Committee had focused on questions of social security and had not confined itself to Conventions on freedom of association.

I. Health-care scheme

The speaker pointed out that in cases of home visits those affiliated to Health Care Providers (EPS) were entitled from September 2005 to the additional "Doctor at Home" service in the framework of the Contractual Plan with EPS in all contractual plans signed up to by insurance-takers.

As to the changes brought about in the departments of Amazonas, Apurimac, Madre de Dios, Huancalevica, Huánuco, Moquegua and Pasco on applications for membership of the EPS system, the speaker said that 84 per cent of the total number of regular and potential members had been covered in enterprises related to the EPS system at a rate of 4.69 enrolments on average in 2004, including in the abovementioned departments.

In the sample available on "Health care services in enterprises related to EPS plans for departments by type of establishment", in December 2004, one clinic was registered in December 2004 in the Huánuco department, compared with what had been reported in May 2004.

According to available data, health care establishments were operating in the departments of Madre de Dios, Huancavelica and Moquegua. Patients were accepted when their clinical condition warranted it.

The documents sought by the Committee of Experts had been ordered by the Health Care Providers Supervisory Authority and would be appended to the note to be presented on the application of Convention No. 102 in September 2005.

The speaker stated that the participation of affiliated members in the administration of individual institutions could affect the constitutional rights to freedom of operation and ownership of the private establishments taking over from the EPS. Convention No. 102 was based on the assumption that service provision to the public was provided by the State. Consequently, it was logical that contributors played a part in administration. However, in private sector participatory schemes in the services of the public service, the role of the State had changed from one of service provider to one of regulation and administration. Convention No. 102 could be interpreted in the sense that member participation could be carried out by publicly regulated bodies.

II. Pension system
Private pensions system

The speaker referred to the need to have pensions representing at least 40 per cent of the reference salary, recalling that the private pensions system (SPP) was an individual capitalization scheme in that the pension paid out was in direct relation to the amount paid in by the worker during his/her working life, the yield generated by investments and the no-claims bonus if applicable. In this respect, the pensions administered by SPP could not be set in advance.

The speaker provided an estimate based on certain acceptable assumptions: a contribution tax of 8 per cent, a pension of 460 soles, an annual profits tax of 5 per cent at age 65, and 14 annual payments. From the above, it could be deduced that a member contributing for 30 years, i.e. starting as from 35 years old, at a pension level of 460 soles (approximately US$141) would, at the age of 65, receive a payment of 52.4 per cent for men and 50.8 per cent for women. On the other hand, if the worker contributed for 40 years, the payment would be 95.3 per cent for a man and 92.3 per cent for a woman.

The approved minimum pension scheme was a complementary scheme and did not replace state action. The minimum pension represented a guarantee offered by the State to those workers who, in compliance with age and contribution requirements, could not attain a pension that was equal to or greater than the minimum pension established by the SNP.

However, according to the provisions of the Supreme Decree No. 100-2002-EF, those workers who had collected a retirement pension under the modalities of the retirement plan and whose account had expired, had no subsequent claim to the minimum pension. The Supervisory Authority had requested the Ministry of Economy and Finance to evaluate the possibility of financing extraordinary pensions for those workers affiliated to the SPP who could not collect the minimum pension because they were collecting a retirement pension at the time Act No. 27617 came into force, and who currently were receiving a pension that was lower than the minimum pension; and for those workers who did not collect a pension due to the fact that the funds of the Cuenta Individual de Capitalización (CIC) had been exhausted.

The retirement plan could be revoked. Contributors could change to whatever other types of pension they chose: Family Trust Annuity (in new soles or dollars), Provisional Annuity with Deferred Trust Annuity (in new soles or dollars), or complementary products or services within the basic modalities. The SPP guaranteed full cover complemented by an environment which, with appropriate information provided, allowed the contributor to opt for other conditions.

The speaker explained that when a worker went below the security threshold for invalidity and survivor's coverage, he/she could receive a pension under a life annuity trust. In the case where the contributor could not be covered by SPP, a pension was paid out from his/her CIC funds and from the no-claims bonus. The insured person could join the retirement programme and later on opt for an annuity trust, which would ensure coverage until death.

The speaker advised that CIC fund management was handled by AFP, which collected a fee for its services. The AFP could collect commissions as a function of the type of pension fund. In the case of voluntary contributions, the amount of commission collected by the AFP for withdrawal of the abovementioned contributions, could be replaced by an amount sufficient to cover the balance of the Voluntary Fund or the balance of the Voluntary Fund of Legal Persons. They established modifications to the current account with respect to permanent benefits in an administration whose results could be achieved by those members of SPP. AFP could supply programmes that reduced the fees for the service benefits so that it adequately compensated the fidelity and future membership of an affiliated member in the pension fund.

The private system also featured a minimum pension so that the State could subsidize the pension adequately for affiliated members that fulfilled the requirements of age and contributions. The minimum pension was financed directly from funds in the Public Treasury.

In relation to the calculation of the total security costs charged to protected wage earners, the speaker insisted that contributors in the private system were obligated to contribute individual costs at a rate of 8 per cent of monthly remuneration. These contributions were allowed to accumulate to finance retirement benefits since the private pension system was a direct function of the early individual contributions made by workers during their working life.

III. The pension system administered by the ONP

The speaker also stated that part of the pension amount was reduced for those who had 15 years of membership, as stipulated in Decree No. 19990, for those affiliated since December 1992 and 60 years of age and who had completed the required number of contributions. Nevertheless, with regard to the application of Convention No. 102, the ONP had provided answers regarding the qualification costs in terms of the impact of the plan for the National Pension System in terms of the actuarial costs.

In conclusion, the speaker stated that the ILO should deal with the real challenge and contribute to the modernization of the social security system.

The Employer members expressed the view that the case under examination was one of real progress. The Committee of Experts had been looking at this question for many years and the Conference Committee had discussed it on two occasions in 1997 and 2002. More questions were raised at that time, however, than answers given by the Government. The Employer members noted that much more information was at the disposal of the Committee this time. With regard to the issue of medical care, they noted that there seemed to be no violations of the Convention. The Government had provided information with regard to the duty to ensure house visits both in its reply to the Committee of Experts and orally before the Conference Committee. With regard to the issue of individual insurance providers, in particular the duty to ensure the participation in the management of protected persons (Article 72 of the Convention), the Employer members considered that, although the legislation did not provide for such participation, there were supervision and control mechanisms such as, for instance, the need to obtain the approval of the Ministry of Health and to submit health plans to the public authorities in order to be able to carry out their activities. Also, the Committee of Experts pointed out that such mechanism procedures did provide some guarantee for the rights of insured persons. Because of this, the Employer members considered that the provisions of the Convention might be excessively restrictive in this respect.

With regard to the issue of private pension systems, an issue which concerned many other Latin American countries, the Employer members noted with satisfaction that the Committee of Experts accepted that both public and private systems fell within the terms of the Convention. This allowed minimum standards of social security to be guaranteed in different ways.

With regard to other issues raised in the Committee of Experts' observation, the Employer members noted that the Government had reported on various areas of progress. Concerning the minimum rate of 40 per cent of the reference wage applying to the old-age benefit, the Employer members took note of the Government representative's statement which contained figures actually higher than 40 per cent. The Committee of Experts had moreover noted progress in the public pensions level which had risen by 86 per cent between December 1997 and September 2004. The Employer members stated that they disagreed with the Committee of Experts on the issue of the distribution of the costs of fund administration. The observation of the Committee of Experts seemed to imply that the costs should be obligatorily shared between the employers and workers. However, the Convention did not indicate that there was an obligation of equal contributions except in serious situations. In Peru, the employers made voluntary contributions. The Convention only required to prevent serious situations. Moreover, the reported drop in the costs of fund administration in 2002 was a further sign of progress.

Another area of progress was the duty to include a representative of the protected pensions in the management of the public pensions system. Act No. 27617 provided that two representatives of pensioners would be appointed to the Board of the Consolidated Reserve Fund. However, the system was quite complicated and the Employer members agreed with the Committee of Experts that further information was needed in order to establish its conformity with the Convention. The Employer members trusted that the Government would provide this information as it had done in the past.

The Worker members indicated that since the introduction of the new health and pensions system in 1997, the Government had not adopted the necessary measures to apply the Convention. Neither had it presented on this occasion the information necessary to evaluate the conformity of the legislation with the Convention. With regard to the private health system, the observations of the Committee of Experts spoke for themselves and were conclusive with respect to the lack of information by the Government on the measures adopted or foreseen to guarantee the participation of the protected persons in the administration of the health providers.

With regard to the private pensions system, the Government had provided neither statistical information to allow an evaluation of the amount of the benefits, nor information on the measures taken to guarantee that the worker who had opted for programmed retirement would receive the pay and old age and invalidity benefits for the whole duration of the contingency, once the capital accumulated in his individual account had been used up; nor information on the costs, administrative expenses and amount of commissions in favour of private pension fund administrators (AFP).

All this information was necessary in order to evaluate whether Article 71, paragraph 1, of the Convention was applied. By virtue of this Article, "the cost of the benefits provided in compliance with this Convention and the cost of the administration of such benefits shall be borne collectively by way of insurance contributions or taxation or both in a manner which avoids hardship to persons of small means and takes into account the economic situation of the Member and of the classes of persons protected".

The Government had also not communicated actuarial studies and calculations with regard to the financial equilibrium of the public and private institutions required by Article 71, paragraph 3, and Article 72, paragraph 2, of the Convention nor provided information on the measures foreseen to guarantee the participation of the protected workers in the private pensions system administration.

Even more worrying was the fact that the majority of Peruvians were excluded from the health and pensions coverage. Although the Committee of Experts referred to some of Peru's poorest departments, the speaker stated that the problem was national. According to ILO data, in 2000, approximately 60 per cent of the economically active population worked in the informal economy and 7 per cent was unemployed. These percentages had not changed in reality.

The Conference Committee and the Worker members in particular, had firmly supported that the States should protect the weaker segments of the population. It was impossible for a worker to contribute to a private system due to his modest income. Only society could protect workers through systems of intergenerational solidarity. Without the necessary social protection it was impossible to contribute to the creation of the conditions for attaining decent work. Whatever the nature of the system, public or private, the principles of the Convention should be observed with regard to the participation of the protected persons in the administration, financing and functioning of the systems. The State should for its part take on the responsibility of the social security systems so that the benefits would be duly paid.

The Worker members concluded by reiterating that the Government had not provided the requested information to the Committee of Experts and that the system of social security benefits was not in compliance with the requirements of the Convention.

The Worker member of Peru stated that the private pensions system in Peru did not guarantee an adequate pension since the workers' income was low. Increases discussed by the Congress in the draft law on the operational application of the system which in fact were obligatory, had affected the free choice of workers.

The participation of the workers in the supervision of the health insurance providers and the private pension fund administrators (AFP) were very important since these entities were being financed with the funds of the insured. Unfortunately, in reality workers did not have the right to participate in the AFP since the member representing the workers to the Board of Directors had not been elected by them.

The Employer member of Chile stated that the capitalization systems were a response to the important demographic changes which had taken place in the world. In fact, the life expectancies had increased at the same time as the rate of birth had decreased. The ratio between active and passive workers had dropped considerably. In some cases, a single active worker had to cover a passive worker rendering impossible the financing of the intergenerational system and leading progressively to the adoption of a system of defined contributions in which the pension depended on the amount of the contributions made and the eventual profit. Pensions should be rendered profitable through a diversification of the investments.

With regard to unemployment and the informal economy and its relation to coverage, the speaker considered that these important issues should be addressed by public policies and were not the responsibility of the welfare system. Therefore, the pension system had to be based on three pillars so that the State could take on the responsibility for covering those who were unemployed or worked in the informal economy or did not contribute to the private pensions system. The coverage systems should be improved, giving better incentives for hedging to private pension fund administrators (AFP).

The speaker shared the concerns expressed with regard to the need for strict and technical supervision of the AFP.

The Worker member of Paraguay stated that the reform of the health and pension system was adopted without consultation or agreement on the part of workers' organizations, thus giving rise to a system that excluded the majority of workers. The new system did not respond to the real social security needs of workers. The public and private social security systems should be improved by taking into account the particular circumstances of workers in the informal economy and unemployed workers, who should also be covered. Finally, the speaker insisted that the Government should respond to all of the questions raised by the Committee of Experts.

The Worker member of Chile indicated that the fragmenting and inadequate information provided by the Government had not allowed the Committee of Experts to make observations which would be comprehensible to all. As for the Government's statements relative to the dependency of pensions on the accumulated capital in the individual capitalization accounts, the speaker underlined that only workers made contributions, at the rate of 10 per cent of their salary, in order to finance the old-age benefits. Moreover, the costs of fund administration should be deducted from the contribution of the worker, which was contrary to the Convention. As a consequence, the majority of workers did not manage to cover the minimum pension. In fact, approximately 76 per cent of those affiliated to the system did not have sufficient funds to finance the minimum pension and for this reason, the Government should promise to cover 40 per cent of the pension.

The speaker added that the Government violated the Convention with regard to the tripartite social security contribution as only workers made contributions in the private system. The system did not provide for the contribution of the employer or the administrators themselves of the pension funds. It also did not provide for the granting of reduced pensions to workers after 15 years of contribution. Moreover, a serious risk existed that the mishandling by the pension funds administrators would cause considerable losses in the individual capitalization accounts so that workers could not count on the accumulated funds at the end of their lives, when they were most in need of them. The system had already suffered losses during various periods.

The speaker regretted that the Government had not referred to the comments presented by the World Confederation of Labour (WCL) and urged the Government to respect its commitments and modify the legislation in order to bring it into conformity with the provisions of the Convention.

A **Government representative** insisted that the public system that existed was insolvent and that it was necessary to find an alternative that gave opportunities to the private sector. In fact, any worker could opt between the public system and an individual account in a private system. An important modification to the social security system had been accepted: employers were in charge of health, while workers were in charge of their pensions.

The private pension system did not violate Convention No. 102. The Government had provided information that contained detailed answers on the administrative costs of the private system. It had requested cooperation and would do so in the future.

The AFP had reduced administrative costs and the private system was more competitive. The AFP had given complete information and was subject to close scrutiny by a pension fund administrator. All of the expenditures and investments that affected the AFP were made public.

In response to the statement by the Employer member from Chile, the speaker declared that the protection of workers was part of government policy. The reduction of underemployment and those employed in the informal economy were priority issues to strengthen the social security system. In Congress, debates had taken place regarding methods of exiting the private system and moving to the public system, and therefore it could not be said that the public system no longer existed. The private system of pensions had been the subject of modifications to improve it. Minimum pensions had been established, coverage improved, and enhanced profitability indicators had been found in AFP. The workers retained a real alternative in the private pension system. His Government believed that this system complied with the Convention, with regard to both health benefits and old-age benefits.

The Employer members stated that the information and statistics provided by the Government in this case pointed to positive developments which indicated that private and public social security systems could coexist. The problems that had arisen in practice were undoubtedly due to the fact that the basic reform of the social security system had only begun ten years ago, that the country suffered from a high unemployment rate and a large number of workers were active in the informal economy. Nonetheless, the information in this case did not lead to the conclusion that there was a violation of Convention No. 102. The President of the International Federation of Pension Funds Administrators had provided this Committee with his expert opinion on the benefits of private social security systems and the urgent need for private and public systems to coexist. The ILO should assist the Government in ensuring that private and public systems can co-exist in this development. Furthermore, the Government should supply information on supervision procedures in the private system.

The Worker members considered that public schemes constituted a pillar of the pension and health-care systems. As indicated by the Committee of Experts, a certain level prescribed by the Convention must be guaranteed, regardless of the type of system selected. The Worker members therefore requested the following: that the Government should give particular attention to all the aspects mentioned and communicate detailed information on the measures taken in response to the Experts' questions and concerns, given the lack of protection of the majority of the population; that the ILO should provide technical assistance in order to guarantee the compliance of the national legislation and practice with the Convention; that the Committee of Experts should formulate a detailed comment taking into account all the elements of the discussion and the information submitted by the Government; and that the Government should supply information allowing the assessment of the scheme introduced more than 15 years ago.

The Committee noted the oral and written information provided by the Government representative and the discussion that followed. The Committee nonetheless observed that, since the introduction in 1997 of the new, mostly private health and pension systems, the Government had not adopted all measures necessary to give effect to various provisions of the Convention, nor had it provided the necessary information to evaluate these systems with the Convention. With regard to the private health-carte scheme, the Committee hoped that, the Government would provide the information requested by the Committee of Experts on the measures adopted or foreseen to guarantee the participation of protected persons in the administration of the Health Care Providers (EPS) scheme.

With regard to the private pensions system, the Committee also hoped that the Government would provide information, including statistics, which would permit the evaluation of the amount of benefits, as well as the measures adopted or foreseen to guarantee a worker who had opted for programmed retirement the payment of old-age and invalidity benefits throughout the duration of the contingency. The Committee also hoped that the Government would provide information on the costs, administration charges and the rate of commissions charged to workers affiliated with private pension fund administrators (AFP).

Finally, with regard to the private and public pensions systems, the Committee hoped that the Government would communicate actuarial calculations and studies on the equal financing of public and private institutions, and indicate the measures it envisages to take to guarantee the participation of protected persons in the administration of the private pensions system. The Committee therefore urged the Government to take the necessary measures to give effect to the provisions of the Convention and to provide in its next report all information requested by the Committee of Experts, so that it may be examined with the information provided by the Government in this Committee. The Committee suggested that the

C. 111

Government have recourse to technical assistance from the ILO to resolve pending problems of application of the Convention.

Convention No. 111: Discrimination (Employment and Occupation), 1958

SAUDI ARABIA (ratification: 1978). **A Government representative** assured the Committee of his country's commitment to comply with the ILO Conventions that it had ratified and that it was also envisaging the ratification of other Conventions. He described his country's cooperation with the ILO and mentioned, as an example, the technical assistance provided in the framework of the draft Labour Code, which had later been discussed in the Consultation Council before being submitted to the Council of Ministers. Various ILO technical missions had visited his country. He indicated that national laws and regulations were not discriminatory, and that the issues raised by the Committee of Experts could be the result of a problem in the supervision of their implementation. The Constitution of Saudi Arabia guaranteed human dignity, equality and justice, and prohibited any form of injustice.

His country regularly examined its legal texts with a view to improving them through reforms in all fields. Moreover, a number of reforms had been adopted which were beneficial to both Saudi nationals and foreign nationals. Examples included reforms for the promotion of women's rights in the fields of education, training and employment, while other measures were planned. In Saudi Arabia, there were 2,200,000 women students in higher education representing 50 per cent of all students while, in higher education women represented even 58 per cent of the students; 26 technical training facilities for women had been constructed and there was a plan to open 15 others. Women represented 24 per cent of physicians and 53 per cent of nurses. There were over 429,000 women working in 2004, a figure which would reach 847,000 in 2009, and 253,000 women were working in the public sector, representing 34 per cent of public servants as a whole. Moreover, national legislation guaranteed equality between men and women in respect of both rights and obligations. His Government had taken a number of measures intended to reinforce the labour inspection system so as to guarantee the application of the Conventions that had been ratified. Measures had also been taken to guarantee the rights of migrant workers and prohibit their inhumane treatment. While certain migrant workers could believe that their wages had been reduced upon arrival in the Kingdom, this was due to the fact that intermediate agencies in the country of origin of these workers were giving them misleading information about their wages and the nature of the work to be done. Consultations had been held with their countries of origin with a view to finding more appropriate solutions to the problems which arose. Measures had also been taken to prevent the confiscation of migrant workers' passports and to guarantee their freedom of movement in the country. To reinforce the application of these measures, the Ministry of Labour had established an administrative body responsible for the protection of migrant workers. In the same context the Minister of Labour had recently taken a decision concerning the prohibition of all form of human trafficking, including the sale of persons, non-compliance with contract obligations and inhumane treatment.

In conclusion, he emphasized that his Government was requesting the Office to send a technical assistance mission from the International Labour Standards Department to address the issues raised in the comments of the Committee of Experts concerning this Convention and the other Conventions ratified by his country.

The Worker members thanked the Government representative for the information provided and welcomed the Government's commitment to implement the Convention. They welcomed the statistics on the participation of women in employment and vocational training and the Government's request for technical assistance. They stated that the case of Saudi Arabia was mainly a case of allegations, requests and question marks. Despite the Government's good intentions, it had not provided much information on the issues raised by the ICFTU, and they supported the request made by the Committee of Experts to the Government to provide full and detailed information on this matter as quickly as possible. On a few points however, they wished to go beyond the questions and requests for information made by the Committee of Experts.

First, with respect to discrimination against migrant workers, the Committee of Experts had expressed concern at the effects of the foreign labour sponsorship system on migrant workers. Despite the seriousness of the allegations made, the Government's reaction to these allegations was not very convincing. According to the Government, there was no basis for discrimination in any form in the law and it was unaware of the alleged reduction of wages. The Government also claimed that, if these practices existed at all, they were isolated incidents and mainly caused by the malfunctioning and malpractices of mediating offices in sending countries. The concern of the Committee of Experts related to the fact that the legislation regulating the labour sponsoring system gave disproportionate powers to employers over migrant workers, which could lead to discrimination on the basis of race and national extraction with respect to their conditions of work. The Worker members called for the Committee's conclusions on the case to request the Government to clarify in its next report whether the present legislation and special regulations in practice afforded sufficient protection to migrant workers. If this was not the case, the Government would need to bring its legislation in line with the Convention.

Second, with regard to the adoption and implementation of a national policy to promote equality of opportunity and treatment, as required by Article 2 of the Convention, the Worker members referred to the comments of the Committee of Experts and urged the Government to take measures to address these gaps in the relevant legislation in line with the Committee of Experts' observations. They indicated that they wished to see this clearly reflected in the Committee's conclusions on this case.

Third, they referred to the comments made by the Committee of Experts with respect to discrimination against migrant workers on the basis of sex with particular reference to migrant domestic workers. The allegations included references to shortcomings in law and practice, in particular the fact that the Labour Code did not protect domestic workers. While this had not been denied by the Government, its position seemed to be that such protection by the law was not necessary as domestic workers were sufficiently protected by the habit of Saudi Arabians to treat them as members of their families. However, even if this was true, it would still be unacceptable for the Convention not to be implemented in law. The Worker members would have liked the Committee of Experts to be more precise and firm in its reaction to the Government's position. There was not a single indication in the report that legal measures to protect migrant domestic workers were indeed in place and the Government representative had not provided any information in this regard. It should therefore be clearly stated in the conclusions that such measures should be included in the relevant legislation, unless of course the Government could provide assurances that this was all a misunderstanding and that the relevant legal provisions did indeed already exist. In such a case, the Government was urged to make the relevant legal texts available to the Committee of Experts as soon as possible.

Fourth, with regard to section 160 of the Labour Code, even if this provision did not result in de facto segregation on the basis of sex, which was questionable, the section should still be repealed. Saudi Arabia had to implement the Convention in practice as well as in law. The legislation should be brought into line with the Convention. The Committee's conclusions should therefore encourage the Government to repeal section 160 of the Labour Code.

Finally, the Worker members recalled that Article 3(a) of the Convention provided that each country for which the Convention was in force had to undertake, by methods appropriate to national conditions and practice, to seek the cooperation of employers' and workers' organizations and other appropriate bodies in promoting the acceptance and observance of the national policy to promote equality of opportunity and treatment in respect of employment and occupation. They requested the Government to explain in its next report the manner in which this Article was implemented and called upon the Government to seek the contribution of organized labour and business in Saudi Arabia in collecting the information to be supplied to the ILO.

The Employer members thanked the Government representative for attending the discussion of this case by the Committee and referred to the last occasion on which it had been examined by the Committee in 1993. The focus of the discussion on that occasion had been on the issue of equality of opportunity and treatment of men and women workers, particularly in view of the provisions of section 160 of the 1969 Labour Code, which proclaimed that in no case should men and women intermingle at the workplace. They recalled that 12 years had since elapsed, but the situation was still essentially the same, despite the fact that occupational segregation was in violation of the basic principles set out in the Convention. The second aspect of the discussion in 1993 had concerned the access of women to vocational education and training.

With regard to the comments made by the Committee of Experts this year, the Employer members noted the indication that other matters were being raised in a request addressed directly to the Government. They suggested that in future it would be useful if the Committee of Experts could give some indication of the subjects covered by such direct requests. One aspect raised in the comments of the Committee of Experts concerned discrimination against migrant workers, particularly on grounds of race, sex, religion and national extraction. In this respect, the Committee of Experts had placed emphasis on the difficulties faced by migrant workers in gaining access to the courts so as to be able to enforce the rights that were legally recognized. Paragraph 7 of the observation by the Committee of Experts was of particular importance. It drew attention to the obligation of the Government, under Article 2 of the Convention, to declare and pursue a national policy designed to promote equality of treatment in respect of employment and occupation by methods appropriate to national conditions and practice, with a view to eliminating any discrimination on the grounds of race, colour, sex, religion, political opinion, national extraction or social origin. In this regard, the Employer members emphasized that much clearly remained to be done to give effect to this provision. They therefore proposed that the Government request the technical assistance of the ILO, which could be very helpful to the Government in establishing laws and regulations as a basis for a credible policy of non-discrimination in employment and occupation.

The Government representative thanked the Employer and Worker members for their comments and indicated that they would be taken into consideration. He recalled that the ILO had been created to safeguard the rights of employers and workers. In response to the comments made, he indicated that no restrictions were placed on the employment opportunities of migrant workers, who benefited from all the facilities available to workers of Saudi nationality. If they were seeking work, they could make use of temporary work agencies with a view to entering a new employment relationship. Employers of migrant workers did not have a hold over them and they were free to seek alternative employment. He said that his Government had devoted considerable attention to issues relating to domestic workers and that contacts and cooperation had been established between the Ministry of Labour and the authorities of the major sending countries. A new department had been established within the Ministry to look after the welfare of migrant workers and an emergency telephone line had been established for women domestic workers. Through these channels, migrant workers in Saudi Arabia could seek help, as well as assistance in finding alternative employment. In response to the comments made concerning section 160 of the Labour Code, he noted that its provisions were based on the societal culture in the country. He emphasized that men and women workers enjoyed exactly the same rights and freedoms, but that the work was performed in two different places. Finally, he re-emphasized that many training opportunities were being developed for women, including the establishment of 26 technical schools.

The **Worker members** thanked the Government representative for the additional information provided. However, this information had not removed their concerns, which they hoped would be reflected in the Committee's conclusions. Moreover, the conclusions should make the link between the matters that were of concern and the areas on which the proposed technical commission would focus. They emphasized that it was not enough for the Government to make promises, or just to say that the practices that were the subject of the comments of the Committee of Experts were a product of the national culture. The ratification of a Convention was an act of free will by a country and if the Committee of Experts demonstrated that the national legislation was not in accordance with the requirements of the Convention, the Government should amend its legislation as rapidly as possible to bring it into line in accordance with the recommendations of the ILO supervisory bodies.

The Committee noted the statement made by the Government representative of Saudi Arabia as well as the ensuing discussion. It noted that the observation of the Committee of Experts discussed by the Committee dealt with serious allegations made by the International Confederation of Free Trade Union (ICFTU) of substantial discrimination against men and women migrant workers on the basis of race, religion and sex, as well as occupational segregation on the basis of sex and the access of women to vocational training, education and particular occupations.

The Committee noted the information provided by the Government representative concerning a new draft Labour Code which was currently being examined. The Government had referred to the measures undertaken by it to improve the access to employment, education and training of women with a view to increasing their participation in the labour market. Statistics had been provided on the participation of women in the labour market, as well as information concerning the measures taken to protect domestic workers. The Government had reiterated its commitment to dialogue and its openness to ILO technical assistance.

The Committee noted the efforts made by the Government to promote and protect the rights of male and female migrant workers. It noted however that the practical impact of those efforts remained unclear, and that considerable problems appeared to exist in the application of the Convention in law and practice with regard to the situation of migrant workers. The Committee therefore emphasized the importance of carrying out a more detailed examination of the situation of men and women migrant workers with a view to determining the situation in practice, as requested by the Committee of Experts. The Committee invited the Government, as recommended by the Committee of Experts, to declare and pursue a national equality policy which covered all workers, including migrant workers, with a view to eliminating discrimination against them on all the grounds listed in the Convention. The Committee emphasized that such a policy had to include effective mechanisms to address existing discrimination, including remedies accessible to men and women migrant workers. In doing so, the Government should fully consult with and involve employers' and workers' organizations, as well as other appropriate bodies, in accordance with Article 3(a) of the Convention. The Committee also requested the Government to take the necessary measures to bring its legislation into line with the Convention so as to provide effective protection for migrant workers against discrimination, in particular measures to deal with the problems of domestic workers and of workers who required special protection against the effects of the foreign labour sponsorship system.

The Committee welcomed the efforts to promote women's access to vocational training and education in various disciplines and hoped that further progress would be possible in the future. However, the Committee continued to be concerned that women continued to be excluded from certain jobs and occupations. It requested the Government to take effective measures to promote and ensure the equal access of women to employment and all occupations.

The Committee noted, as indicated by the Committee of Experts, that section 160 of the Labour Code could result in occupational segregation by sex. The Committee hoped that the new Labour Code, which was currently under review would take into account fully the requirements of the comments of the Convention and the Committee of Experts, and the above section would be repealed.

The Committee welcomed the Government's request for a technical assistance mission and considered that this assistance should include all the points raised by the Committee of Experts and the Conference Committee concerning the effective application of the Convention in law and practice.

Convention No. 144: Tripartite Consultation (International Labour Standards), 1976

NEPAL (ratification: 1995). A **Government representative** stated that by ratifying the Convention Nepal had accepted tripartite cooperation as a basis for the formulation of laws and policies and decision-making regarding the application of international labour standards. The benefit of such consultations for economic development and social justice was fully recognized. Tripartite cooperation had been undertaken on many issues, such as occupational safety and health, elimination of bonded labour and child labour, or the issue of HIV/AIDS. Tripartite consultations were pursued in the formulation of labour migration policy and the preparation of a decent work action plan. The institutional mechanism for tripartite consultation was the Central Labour Advisory Board, which could make recommendations to the Government on labour matters. The Government, in cooperation with the Board, had organized the second Labour Conference in Kathmandu in January 2005, where a declaration was adopted containing a commitment of achieving labour relations that would be a cornerstone for successful nation-building.

The workers' and employers' representatives on the Central Labour Advisory Board were nominated by their respective organizations. In addition to the formally nominated representatives, additional participants took part in the meetings and expressed their views, a practice which was believed to be in conformity with Article 3 of the Convention. A permanent secretariat for the Board had been established in the Ministry of Labour and Transport Management, but the social partners had sought no direct administrative support. In fact, workers' and employers' organizations had developed facilities to carry out the activities envisaged by the Convention. Social partners were involved in all training and workshops regarding labour matters organized by the Ministry, except in-house training for Ministry staff.

The Government was aware that the obligation of consultation under Article 5(1)(d) of the Convention went beyond the communication of reports. It was established practice to circulate draft reports in advance of meetings to discuss in detail reports on Conventions, questionnaires, or proposals for submission and to incorporate the comments made by the social partners. The documents were only sent to the ILO when all the social partners agreed, and copies were forwarded to workers' and employers' organizations. No annual report pursuant to Article 6 of the Convention had been prepared in the last three years. The Ministry would prepare such a report as and when all social partners deemed it necessary. Finally, the Government would convey to the ILO any future developments with regard to the application of the Convention in practice.

The **Worker members** expressed their strong concern at the situation prevailing in Nepal, its repercussions for the Nepali trade union movement, and on civil society in the country. It was the responsibility of the Conference Committee not only to assess whether the legislation was in conformity with this Convention, which was ratified by Nepal in 1996, but also to establish how it functioned in practice.

The Worker members noted with great concern the number of issues on which the Committee of Experts requested detailed and updated information from the Government as to how it implemented essential provisions of the Convention.

With regard to effective tripartite consultations, the Committee requested that the Government describe in detail the nature and form of the relevant procedures and to indicate whether the necessary consultations had taken place, as required under Article 2 of the Convention.

The Government was also invited to describe how worker and employer representatives on consultative bodies were chosen and how the Government ensured that they were represented on an equal footing, as required under Article 3 of the Convention.

With regard to administrative support and training, requests were made of the Government to report on any financial means allocated for training of participants in procedures covered by Article 4 of the Convention.

With regard to tripartite consultations required by the Convention, the Committee acknowledged that consultations had been held concerning the possible ratification of Conventions Nos. 87 and 105, and particularly expressed its thanks to the ILO Kathmandu Office for the assistance it provided.

However, the Committee also noted that in certain cases reports required under article 22 of the ILO Constitution, were simply commu-

C. 144

nicated to the social partners rather than consulting with them as required under Article 5, paragraph 1(d), of Convention No. 144, which appeared to be in breach of the Convention.

Finally, as concerns the operation of the consultative procedures, the Committee requested that the Government indicate the scope and outcome of any consultations held with representative organizations as it related to the production of an annual report on the working of procedures covered by the Convention.

The Worker members expressed concern at the paradoxical situation prevailing in Nepal, where the Government had supposedly put in place various bodies and mechanisms designed to fulfil the requirements laid down by the Convention and then had replaced consultations with the social partners with legal appeals filed by lawyers of these social partners against arbitrary detentions, decrees banning public gatherings and demonstrations, lack of registration of trade union organizations and other breaches of fundamental rights at work.

The Worker members noted that when the King had assumed direct executive powers in February 2005 and had declared a state of emergency, hundreds of citizens had been arbitrarily detained, including nearly two dozen trade union activists, trade union offices were monitored, searched and at times closed down, union meetings had been forbidden and rallies had been banned, while registration of several union organizations had been refused. Several union leaders had been jailed in the last three months, some of them women, and often held in appalling conditions. Six of them remained in detention.

A number of basic constitutional rights were suspended, starting with trade union rights, but also included the right to freedom of expression and assembly; the right to information; the right to property; the right to privacy; and the right to constitutional remedy. Press censorship was imposed and so was the generalized practice of preventive detention, applied, amongst many others, to leaders of journalists' trade unions.

Tensions between the King and civil society parties continued to run high. In April 2005 the King lifted the state of emergency, which was due to expire. However, many basic citizens' rights including freedom of the press and freedom of assembly remained suspended.

Many of these events had been directly witnessed by the international union movement as they had unfolded during the meeting of the Executive Board of the Asian and Pacific Organization of the International Confederation of Free Trade Unions (ICFTU) in Kathmandu. The President of the ICFTU-affiliated Nepal Trade Union Congress (NTUC), Laxman Basnet, who was also a member of the ILO Governing Body, had had to meet the ICFTU Executive clandestinely. He then had had to leave the country, in order to escape arrest.

Throughout these tragic events, the ILO Office in Kathmandu had played a remarkable role in assisting Nepal's social partners and had intervened on their behalf with the authorities. The Kathmandu ILO Office and its Director deserved to be congratulated by the Committee.

Beyond these events, however, the ILO deserved recognition for many other achievements in Nepal, such as its long-standing efforts to promote social dialogue and training as well as other work aimed, among other things, at securing ratification by Nepal of Convention No. 169 on indigenous and tribal peoples. Many observers had noted that ratification of this important instrument could contribute significantly to helping the country to overcome the dramatic internal armed conflict, which had cost hundreds of workers their lives.

With continued technical support from the ILO, the concept and approaches of social dialogue had been well taken and adopted by the ILO constituents in the country. A series of dialogues had been concluded and a bipartite core group had been formed to discuss a seven-point agenda, which included social security and labour flexibility among others. A 19-point guideline to reform the existing labour legislation had been developed and agreed between the employers and the workers.

However, it was highly regrettable that government interference in trade union affairs put these positive developments under threat. The unions had faced difficulties in registering their affiliates and had complained about being barred from access to the Department of Labour.

Trade unions had warned the Government that they might withdraw from the ongoing bipartite social dialogue on labour law reform if the Government did not cease to interfere in union activities. There were strong reasons to believe that the Government was trying to eliminate the entire trade union movement in the country because it saw unions as a threat to direct rule by the King.

And finally, with regard to the issue of tripartite consultations, the Government had forwarded the credentials of its delegates to the 93rd Session of the Conference without due consultation of the social partners. The country's three national federations had not been properly consulted regarding their representatives to this Conference.

The Worker members welcomed the lifting of the emergency in Nepal and urged the Government to respect the fundamental rights of freedom of association to make effective tripartite consultation meaningful since it was a sine qua non for tripartite consultation. They welcomed the intervention of the ILO Director-General for the concern expressed about the security of Mr Basnet, Worker Member of the ILO Governing Body. They hoped for a rapid end to civil strife in the interest of peace and security – social progress of Nepal nation. In these efforts, the Government should seek the cooperation of the trade union movement by developing social dialogue and strengthening tripartism in the country. The Worker members believed that the Government should be strongly urged by the Committee to respond to all the questions raised in detail by the Committee of Experts concerning implementation of the Convention. A further request was also made to take full advantage of ILO technical assistance with a view, not only to overcoming problems in the implementation of this Convention, but also to lifting any obstacles that might prevent it from ratifying other ILO fundamental Conventions. This included Convention No. 87, and with the continued cooperation of the ILO to enable it to ratify, Convention No. 169.

The Employer members recalled that Nepal had ratified the Convention in 1995 and welcomed the undertaking by the Government of Nepal to promote tripartite consultations for the first time. This case was examined by the Conference Committee for the first time.

The language of the Convention, with regard to the choice of consultation mechanism was flexible, but the procedures should, however, be determined after consultation with the most representative organizations. The Employer members further highlighted that the employers' and workers' organizations were not bound by the final decision or the position adopted by the Government and noted the Government's indication to the effect that representatives of employers and workers were freely chosen by their organizations, and that it had set up a permanent secretariat at the Central Labour Advisory Board in 2004. They emphasized, however, that it had to be clear that this structure was responsible for the procedures referred to in the Convention and further questioned whether the Government of Nepal consulted the most representative organizations when compiling information and preparing reports to be forwarded to the ILO. Finally, the Employer members urged the Government to apply procedures that would ensure effective consultations.

An observer of the International Confederation of Free Trade Unions (ICFTU) stated that in the absence of freedom of association in the country no real tripartism was possible. The Government had banned all kinds of trade union activities and the unions of public employees, teachers and the press had been attacked recently. At the same time, fake unions had been set up and submitted for accreditation at the present session of the Conference. In this regard, a case was pending before the Credentials Committee. Further, changes in the Labour Law had been made without consultation, as well as changes in the press legislation. Due to the state of emergency, many peaceful workers had been killed.

The Government member of Pakistan recalled the vital importance of the Convention for the social partners. The Government was making extensive efforts to implement tripartite consultations at all levels and had made various efforts to ensure effective consultations on all matters covered by the Convention. A permanent Central Labour Advisory Board had been established. The Government had made it a tradition to consult workers' and employers' representatives before drawing up replies to the report dealing with ILO Conventions. The speaker expressed the hope that the Government would not only continue its efforts to have extensive consultations under the terms of the Convention but also provide in time information on the steps taken to hold such consultations in the framework of the Convention.

The Government representative emphasized that the political situation in the country was very difficult as the Government had to fight Maoist terrorism. It was in these circumstances that the Government had to declare the state of emergency, which had suspended several legislative acts implementing Conventions ratified by Nepal. This radical measure had to be taken in order to ensure the security and therefore the freedoms of Nepal's citizens. However, the state of emergency had ended and many of the suspended rights had been restored. There were no more restrictions imposed on the freedom of assembly. The Government was not interfering in trade union activities and was fully aware of the importance of social partnership. As regards the tripartite representation in this Conference, the Government indicated that all questions in this respect were duly replied to in the Credentials Committee.

The Worker members stated that, while ensuring security in the country was a legitimate concern of the Government, the respect of the right to freedom of association was equally an important matter. The situation with respect to freedom of association was serious and the Government was requested to rectify the situation as a matter of urgency and engage in a meaningful social dialogue. This would be a crucial contribution towards achieving peace and social progress in Nepal.

The Employer members stated that the Government should fully respond on the issues raised by the Committee of Experts with regard to the procedures for effective tripartite consultations and take full advantage of technical assistance to continue to strengthen the social dialogue process which appeared to have commenced. The Employer members finally took note of the comments made by the Worker members on the positive role of the ILO Office in Kathmandu in helping the Government reinforce social dialogue, and recommended the strengthening of the role of technical assistance in this respect.

The Committee took note of the statement by the Government representative and of the discussion that ensued. The Government representative had supplied information on the tripartite meetings that had taken place in Nepal and the matters that had been discussed. According to the Government representative, the social

partners were able to participate freely in the consultations and all the meetings held by the authorities were open to all social partners.

The Committee, noting the exceptional circumstances of the country, called for social dialogue and expressed the view that Convention No. 144 could contribute to the restoration of democracy and to the process of peace building. The Committee was of the view that the consultations that had taken place in the Central Labour Advisory Committee seemed to be insufficient. The Committee noted that the Office could contribute, through technical assistance, to promoting a sincere and constructive social dialogue among all the parties concerned within the scope of Convention No. 144. The Committee invited the Government to take all appropriate measures to promote tripartite dialogue on international labour standards. It also requested the Government to supply a report for the next session of the Committee of Experts on the progress achieved in guaranteeing effective tripartite consultation in a manner satisfactory to all the parties concerned, including information on the functioning of the procedures provided for in the Convention. The Government was also requested to note the deep concern expressed in the Conference Committee at the present situation pertaining to the respect of fundamental rights in the country and its impact on the exercise of tripartite consultations.

UNITED STATES (ratification: 1988). A Government representative stated that the United States took its obligations under ratified Conventions very seriously. She pointed out that the United States had ratified Convention No. 144 in 1988 and since then had submitted eight reports under article 22 of the ILO Constitution, describing the mechanism for tripartite consultations on ILO matters and supplying details and documentation on the wide range of consultations held.

She recalled that tripartite arrangements had been established in 1975 when the United States was contemplating withdrawal from the ILO. There had been tripartite consultation at the highest level on the decision to withdraw and, during the period of withdrawal, on whether and when to return. The mechanism was a Cabinet Level Committee that included the President of the AFL-CIO and a representative from the United States Chamber of Commerce. Upon rejoining the ILO in February 1980, the United States formalized the Cabinet Level Committee as a federal advisory committee called the President's Committee on the ILO. This structure was established on the basis of consultation with, and agreement of, the representative worker and employer organizations, and ensured that those organizations would be able to act in full independence. In fact, it was significant in terms of Convention No. 144 that the United States business community itself had decided that the United States Council for International Business would replace the Chamber of Commerce on the new tripartite committee.

The President's Committee was the pinnacle of the tripartite mechanism and provided for consultation at the highest level. More continual consultation occurred through a staff-level consultative group and in the Tripartite Advisory Panel on International Labour Standards (TAPILS) that was created specifically to examine the legal feasibility of ratifying selected ILO Conventions. One of the first conventions that TAPILS had examined was Convention No. 144. After an extensive review, TAPILS had unanimously concluded and reported to the President's Committee that existing United States practice gave full effect to the Convention. The framework for tripartite consultations had not changed since. The nature of the procedures had been modified somewhat over the years, however, to meet the needs and preferences of the members, and, especially, to take advantage of modern technology. As for the scope of tripartite consultations, the function of the President's Committee was to consult on all matters relating to United States participation in the ILO. Consultations therefore covered a broad spectrum, surpassing the five topics required under Article 5(1) of Convention No. 144.

The speaker pointed out that this was the first time that the Committee of Experts had expressed any concern at all about United States application of the Convention. The question, she noted, was whether tripartite consultations in the United States were effective. In studying the observation, the Government had looked carefully at the most recent General Survey on Convention No. 144 (2000) in order to better understand how the Committee of Experts had interpreted this aspect of the Convention. She noted that, firstly, the Committee of Experts had found that Convention No. 144 was a very flexible, promotional instrument that did not lay out precise requirements as to methods of application, but instead provided wide latitude for adopting procedures that were suited to national conditions and practice. Secondly, the purpose of consultations was to assist the Government in reaching a decision for which it alone had responsibility. The Convention did not require either negotiation or agreement. Third, consultations should not be merely a token gesture. Fourth, consultations did not have to be initiated solely by the Government. And, fifth, the Convention did not require an annual meeting, or for that matter, any meetings at all. Consultations could be based either on an exchange of communications or on discussions within tripartite bodies. Furthermore, although the Convention indicated that consultation should be undertaken at least once a year, it did not require annual consultations on every point in Article 5(1).

Turning to the factual issues of the case, she stated that there had indeed not been a meeting of the President's Committee since May 2000. In fact, since the United States ratified Convention No. 144 in 1988, the President's Committee had met on only six occasions. This was because the President's Committee only met when warranted by ILO-related issues that required a decision at the highest level. The Secretary of Labor would not call a meeting of the President's Committee as a token gesture. Nor would the Secretary call a meeting unless the attendance of the Presidents of the AFL-CIO and the United States Council for International Business was assured. As a consequence, most ILO consultations were held less formally.

The observation also indicated that the TAPILS did not meet during the reporting period. She announced that the Panel had met last month to begin reviewing Convention No. 185 on Seafarers' Identity Documents. With regard to Convention No. 111, progress had been slow. On the basis of a finding by TAPILS that United States law and practice were in full conformity with its provisions, Convention No. 111 had been forwarded by the President in May 1998 to the United States Senate with a request for advice and consent to ratification. Since then, Convention No. 111 had consistently been on a list of treaties that the Executive Branch considered to deserve priority attention. The Senate, however, while apparently not disinclined to consider the Convention, had given precedence to treaties having a direct bearing on national security.

With regard to the Committee of Experts' observation that for the first time since 1991, the Government had not convened a full meeting of the consultative group in preparation of the 2004 ILO Conference, she pointed out that the Department of Labor had in fact scheduled its usual full pre-Conference briefing but learned subsequently that a significant portion of the delegation, particularly from the AFL-CIO, could not attend. Consequently, the meeting had to be rescheduled at a time that could include the AFL-CIO, closer to the opening of the Conference, with more limited attendance. In the 25 years since the United States rejoined the ILO, this had been the first and only time the Department of Labour had failed to organize a full tripartite pre-Conference meeting. This year, the Government had again hosted a full tripartite meeting in preparation of the 2005 ILO Conference.

Finally, in regard to the complaint filed with the Credentials Committee at the 2004 ILO Conference on behalf of the AFL-CIO, she stated that there had not been a drastic change in the number of non-government delegation members financed by the United States Government last year and the issue had been discussed on several occasions in the tripartite Consultative Group. The temporary reduction had been strictly the result of budgetary, rather than political, reasons. This year, her Government had once again financed the same number of worker and employer representatives that it had, on average, funded for the past 17 years.

In conclusion, she believed that United States tripartite consultations on ILO matters were effective and well within the letter and spirit of Convention No. 144. Her Government would continue without fail to provide full details on United States implementation of this priority Convention. The United States Government looked to the tripartite partners to provide their constructive input toward continuing to make tripartite consultation in the United States a dynamic and meaningful process.

The Worker members recalled that Convention No. 144 set forth the obligation for ratifying States to establish, in accordance with national practice, effective tripartite consultations with respect to the matters concerning the activities of the ILO. To contravene these provisions or to interpret this instrument in a restrictive manner imperilled the credibility of trade unions as well as the efficiency of ILO standards in that this Convention created the framework enabling the realization of Conventions Nos. 87 and 98. For the past three years, the Government had not convoked the President's Committee or the Tripartite Advisory Panel on International Labour Standards (TAPILS), the bodies intended to implement Convention No. 144. The AFL-CIO was forced to make a complaint to the Credentials Committee at the 92nd Session of the International Labour Conference due to the fact that the Government had attributed insufficient resources to allow for the participation and functioning of the workers' delegation in all of the Conference's activities. The observation of the Committee of Experts had established that the Government had clearly ceased to be active in the tripartite process and had taken no action toward further ratifications of ILO standards. The structures for tripartite consultations existed but their functioning remained purely virtual. The reason for this attitude by the Government appeared to be based on the principle that no Convention should be ratified if doing so would imply modifications of national legislation. This led to the conclusion that it was pointless to convoke the competent bodies and amounted to the United States Government refusing to recognize the usefulness of ILO standards as instruments for the improvement of labour law. Indeed, such a practice, if not fought energetically, risked leading to a dangerous jurisprudence which would authorize every State which would need to adapt its legislation to ratify a Convention to refuse to set into motion the ratification procedures. In conclusion, the Worker members considered that, in view of the United States' role on the international stage, it was urgent that the Government provide a constructive example and reactivate as soon as possible the competent bodies responsible for tripartite consultation.

The Employer members pointed out that Convention No. 144 was an instrument of high value for the social partners, and that the discussion of this case showed that the ILO supervisory system allowed to establish a dialogue with all the member States which had ratified the

Conventions regardless of their level of development. It also brings out the fact that there is no negative connotation in inviting a government to provide information to the Conference. The Committee had to assess the manner in which the United States applied in practice the provisions of Convention No. 144. In this regard, the Committee of Experts referred to Article 2, paragraph 1, of the Convention, which provided for the establishment of procedures ensuring effective consultations between representatives of the government, employers and workers on the matters concerning the activities of the ILO.

Concerning, first of all, the procedures: the International Labour Conference intended to allow certain flexibility on the manner in which the consultations had to be conducted. Besides, Article 2, paragraph 2, expressly provided that the procedures should "be determined in each country in accordance with national practice". This approach presumed that different methods could be adopted by different countries, including the use of technologies that allowed for consultations to take place even without having to meet in person, for example, through video-conference on the internet.

Concerning, secondly, the specific activities referred to in Article 5 of the Convention, it should be made clear that the scope of application of the Convention had been perfectly defined. Other questions, such as those raised by the Credentials Committee in 2004, were therefore excluded from the scope of application of the Convention.

The Employer members took note that specific bodies had been created in the United States, with the sole goal to conduct consultations with the employers and workers. Regarding the workers' wish that these bodies have their meetings on a more regular basis, it should be pointed out that Convention No. 144 was silent about the frequency of the consultations and therefore, no legal parameter existed to make an assessment on the application of the Convention. In her intervention, the Government representative provided detailed information on the procedures and meetings recently organized by the Government in order to give effect to the Convention. The Employer members consequently stated that they associated themselves with the Committee of Experts' demand and encouraged the Government to continue to report on the latest measures taken on the application of the Convention. They hoped that this information would be reflected in the future report by the Committee of Experts.

The Worker member of the United States noted that the ratification of Convention No. 144 was important because it institutionalized a more effective and pragmatic process for tripartite consultation with the purpose, among other things, of increasing the number of ratifications by the United States. In the 55-year period from 1934, when the United States joined the ILO, until 1988, the United States ratified only five Conventions, all in the maritime family. It was not until the ratification of Convention No. 144 in 1988 that the United States, for the first time in the history of its membership in the ILO, began to consider in a much more serious way the ratification of selected ILO Conventions. From 1990 until 2001, the United States had ratified another five Conventions, including two of the ILO fundamental Conventions, Conventions Nos. 105 and 182. So in only 11 years, the United States had ratified as many Conventions as it had in the first 52 years of its membership in the ILO. He noted that the Government representative had conceded that not a single meeting of the President's Committee had been convened since May 2000, in over five years or since the current Administration had been in office. By way of defence, she had recalled that the President's Committee had not met from 1990 to 1996. He noted that during this period three important Conventions had been ratified, which stood in stark contrast to the current Administration, which had yet to ratify a Convention over which it had any responsibility.

He also noted that not a single meeting of TAPILS had been held since this Administration took office until last month. While he was pleased that the review process for the ratification of Convention No. 185 on seafarer's identity documents had begun, he emphasized that with the exception of this very recent development, the tripartite process, especially as it is related to future ratification of ILO Conventions, had virtually ground to a halt. Furthermore, the process of Senate ratification of Convention No. 111 had languished so long that the Department of Labour had felt compelled to update the TAPILS law and practice report that had been originally submitted to the Senate in 1988. The fact that the mere drafting of this update took years was a clear indication that the ratification of Convention No. 111 was not seen as an urgent matter by the Administration. The AFL-CIO had met with key Senators and their staff on a number of occasions. But the current Administration's party was in the majority in the Senate, and had not yet taken any steps to further ratification.

The speaker stated that he was encouraged by the words of the Government representative but would like to see more action. Specifically, he would like to see the convening of a President's Committee meeting so that TAPILS could be given new guidance on possible ratifications and a renewed mandate to push ahead with its work. He would like to see the Administration actively lobbying Congress for the ratification of Convention No. 111. He also would like to see the Administration support the activities of the International Labour Affairs Bureau of the Department of Labour (ILAB). Among other things, ILAB was the United States Government's primary point of contact with the ILO, and it did all the reporting and provided extra-budgetary funding for the ILO's field programmes. Sadly, every year it had been in office, this Administration had proposed to drastically reduce funding for ILAB. The repeated effort to virtually de-fund ILAB out of existence could not be reconciled with the statement that the United States took its membership in the ILO and its obligations under ratified Conventions seriously.

He concluded by stating that the United States Government had an important and timely opportunity to demonstrate to the world its commitment to the multilateral system and to the ILO in particular. It was time to get the tripartite consultative process in the United States moving again and to improve its ratification record. The AFL-CIO would do its part to bear the responsibility of tripartism. The onus of responsibility rested on the shoulders of the Administration, which up until recently had not shown a good record in this matter.

The Worker member of India stated that this case was a clear violation of Convention No. 144. For the first time since 1991, the United States Government had not convened a full consultative group in 2004 in preparation for the Conference. Only such a group could ensure effective and meaningful participation of all the social partners in the Conference. This lack of this preparation was a violation of democratic norms and was unbecoming for a country which never failed to project itself as the champion of democracy. He also noted the case before the Credentials Committee in 2004 in which the United States had not fully funded travel and subsistence expenses for the worker delegation to the Conference. He urged the Government to learn from countries which were not as rich and powerful as the United States but which would hardly think of not treating all parties in a delegation equally and not paying for relevant expenses. He urged the Government to address the comments of the Committee of Experts and to fully implement Convention No. 144.

The Government member of Cuba stated that the strengthening of tripartism and social dialogue was one of the strategic objectives of the ILO and that compliance with that principle therefore deserved special attention in its supervisory bodies, such as the present Committee. It was clear that greater attention should be focused on Governments that had only ratified a small number of Conventions. It would thus be advisable that the ILO, within the framework of the promotion of fundamental rights at work, also promoted in that country the ratification of other Conventions, such as Convention No. 87 on freedom of association, which formed the basis of the Convention under examination.

The Worker member of Pakistan stated that the United States, in its role as the leader of the developed world and as one of the states of chief industrial importance in the Governing Body, should play an exemplary role not only in the ratification of ILO Conventions but in their implementation in letter and spirit. He shared the concerns of the AFL-CIO and urged the Government to give effect to the recommendations of the Committee of Experts to ensure effective consultation in a manner that satisfied all parties concerned, and to follow up on the recommendations made by the Credentials Committee regarding a complaint made against the United States at the 92nd Session of the Conference in 2004. With regard to the Government representative's position that there were no specific procedures for consultation laid down in Convention No. 144, he pointed out that the Tripartite Consultation (Activities of the International Labour Organization) Recommendation, 1976 (No. 152), provided specific guidance on the implementation of the Convention, notably on the holding of yearly consultations (paragraph 7) and the issuance of an annual report on the workings of the procedures (paragraph 9). He concluded by noting that the United States often pressed for the ratification and implementation of fundamental Conventions in other countries. In the light of this, the United States should take the lead in ratifying and implementing such Conventions itself.

The Worker member of Singapore noted that Convention No. 144 upheld the core ILO principle of social dialogue. While the Convention allowed for some flexibility on how tripartite consultation should be carried out, there had to be at least regular discussions or meetings. There also had to be some agreement on the form of consultation that should take place. Otherwise, one party might understand «consultation» as an email exchange, whereas the other party might think otherwise. From the facts in this case, it appeared that the agreed form of consultation was a regular meeting. No other modes of consultation had been agreed upon.

She stated that the failure of the United States, a major world power, to comply with this Convention could send a wrong signal to the rest of the world. Already many voices pointed to the low ratification rate of ILO Conventions by the United States, and some countries had even used this as a justification for not ratifying. She hoped that the Government's refusal to convene a full meeting of the consultative group was not an indication of its lack of interest in international labour standards. She called on the Government to convene meetings as required, to conduct meaningful consultations with the social partners and to ratify more Conventions.

The Worker member of Cuba associated himself with the intervention of the Worker member of the United States. He considered it advisable that the statement of the Worker spokesperson would be duly taken into account in the conclusions, which should conform to the discussion and reflect the interests of the Workers' group and those of the workers of the world.

The Government representative stated that she had listened carefully and had taken note of the discussion. She recalled that there was regular tripartite consultation with the United States social partners before ILO Governing Body and Conference sessions. Her Government would continue to report fully on the application of Convention No. 144 and would respond to the questions raised in this discussion in its next report to the Committee of Experts.

The Worker members observed that, in view of its place in the world, the United States should behave in an exemplary manner. They urged the Government to reactivate the bodies competent in the field of tripartite consultations. They took note of the information provided by the Government representative to the effect that the consultations relating to the ratification of Conventions Nos. 111 and 185, which had been suspended, were resumed. These consultations had to be pursued with respect to Convention No. 144, and not only on an informal basis, which had been promised by the Government. The recourse to technology in no case could replace the dynamics of contacts between the Government and the social partners. The Government must take up the initiative and act more efficiently than during the past few years. It must give a basic impulse to the tripartism and thus show its good will, particularly by ratifying the new Conventions.

The Employer members stated that they had noted with interest the response of the Government according to which consultations were held in a manner satisfactory to the three parties, and that an appeal had been made to the employers and workers to also take initiatives in this domain. They hoped that the Government would continue to provide information on the measures taken and those that it envisaged taking to hold consultations in the framework of Convention No. 144.

The Committee noted the statement made by the Government representative and the discussion that followed. The Committee noted that, in accordance with the Convention and the comments made by the Committee of Experts in its observation, the Government and the social partners should establish procedures to ensure effective consultations.

The Committee noted the information provided by the Government on the background and implementation of the Convention, including the schedule of the meeting of the President's Committee and the Tripartite Advisory Panel on International Labour Standards (TAPILS), in particular the meeting held by TAPILS in May 2005 on Convention No. 185. The Committee noted the information relating to the procedure relating to the ratification of Convention No. 111, which was being examined by the Senate. The Committee also noted the information on the meetings held by the consultative group to prepare for the Conference. The Committee noted the importance that the Government attached to social dialogue and the holding in practice of the tripartite consultation required by the Convention.

The Committee hoped that the consultations concerning the ratification of Conventions Nos. 111 and 185 would be concluded in the near future. The Committee requested the Government to take all the appropriate measures to promote tripartite dialogue on international labour standards. The Committee hoped that the Government would provide information in its next report on the progress made to guarantee the holding in practice of tripartite consultations in a manner that was satisfactory for all the parties concerned.

Convention No. 182: Worst Forms of Child Labour, 1999

NIGER (ratification: 2000). **A Government representative,** Minister of the Public Service and Labour) expressed her surprise at the fact that her country once again had been included into the list of individual cases, whereas the matters of the Committee of Experts' concern in this case did not relate exclusively to her country, but could be found in the majority of the poor countries with important informal sectors. Niger had decisively placed itself within the process of eradication of human rights violations, proved by the ratification of the eight fundamental ILO Conventions, by the study on the identification of obstacles to the implementation of the ILO Declaration on the Fundamental Principles and Rights at Work of 1998 and by the collaboration with IPEC and the programme of support to the implementation of the Declaration. The Government had to face ancient practices related essentially to the consequences of poverty. In this regard, Niger had elaborated a strategy of poverty reduction which had integrated the various dimensions of the subjects examined in the present case. Even if the goal had not yet been attained, the considerable efforts undertaken by the Government had brought the results, and Niger counted on the increased support and cooperation of the ILO and on international solidarity, in order to resolutely lead this fight. The problems of application of Convention No. 182 in the context of a developing country had been thus described. As regards more particularly the measures taken to prohibit and eliminate the sale and trafficking of children, the speaker asserted that Niger was not a country involved in the sale or trafficking of children, and that public authorities were not aware of such practices. Concerning the measures taken to combat forced labour of which children are the victims, it should be recalled that begging was connected with the cultural and educative practices aiming at developing humility and compassion in adults. However, the competent bodies were considering appropriate measures to respond to the risks which stemmed from these practices caused by poverty. Concerning the programmes of action aimed at combating child labour, Niger had launched a new IPEC programme and would furnish information on the implementation of the whole set of programmes from which it benefited. As regards the application of sanctions, the speaker indicated that the judges had received no complaints and therefore had not had an opportunity to impose sanctions. Even if the Government had made a particular effort in law enforcement, economic reality still would not allow the effective application of standards, and the emphasis had been made more particularly on the awareness-raising and sensitivization campaigns. In conclusion, the speaker pointed out that her Government continued to undertake important efforts for the children's schooling, but they remained dependent on the limited financial possibilities of the country and were affected by the strong demographic growth. It was therefore impossible to fix a deadline on which the objective of the complete schooling of all the children could be attained.

The Employer members noted that this was the first examination by this Committee of a case dealing with the worst forms of child labour under Convention No. 182; up to now, such matters had been dealt with under the Forced Labour Convention, 1930 (No. 29). The high ratification rate of Convention No. 182 indicated that there was a clear international consensus on the importance of eliminating the worst forms of child labour.

Turning to the specific elements of the case, the Employer members noted that the Government had not responded to a request for information by the Committee of Experts on penalties against the worst forms of child labour. While laws clearly existed which prohibited begging by children, trafficking of children, and certain types of work for persons under the age of 18, more information was needed on the application of these penalties for the offences in practice, and on how many children were affected by such practices. The Government should provide the necessary information on the application and enforcement of the penalties for the offences.

They noted that this case also dealt with trafficking of children and with the custom of placing children under the tutelage of spiritual guides, who often compelled them to beg. This custom caused even greater difficulties in an urban environment than in a rural one. Finally, the case dealt with hazardous work. The Employers shared the concern of the Committee of Experts on this matter. Nonetheless, they were surprised that the Experts had not raised the issue that work which should be prohibited under Article 3(d) of the Convention should, under its Article 4(1), be determined by national laws or regulations or by the competent authority, after consultation with the organizations of employers and workers concerned, taking into consideration relevant international standards, in particular paragraphs 3 and 4 of the Worst Forms of Child Labour Recommendation, 1999 (No. 190). The procedure for the determination of the types of work to be prohibited should not be neglected.

They concluded by noting that this case related to poverty. The worst forms of child labour resulted in children not receiving an education, which, as the Government representative had pointed out, risked creating a lost generation in the country. For this reason, the lack of education played an important role in the application of Convention No. 182.

The Worker members thanked the Government of Niger for the submission of its first report on the application of Convention No. 182. The Committee of Experts referred to its comments on child labour formulated earlier under Convention No. 29. These comments concerned, first of all, the sale and trafficking of children, with regard to which the Committee, while having noted the legislation in force, requested the Government to take urgent measures concerning its application in practice, since the sale and trafficking of children was one of the worst forms of child labour. These comments also concerned children entrusted to a spiritual guide who required them to beg in exchange for his services. On this point, since the Government's will to eradicate these practices had been already expressed in 2004, the Worker members requested the Government to provide information on putting this will into practice. Lastly, these comments concerned child labour in mines, which, according to certain estimates referred to by the Committee of Experts, employed up to 250,000 children in revolting conditions.

The Worker members observed that the information supplied by the Government in its report and provided orally to this Committee contained no reference to the fundamental problem of the work of children in mines. They associated themselves with the Committee of Experts' requests to insist that the Government take urgent measures with a view to prohibiting children under 18 years of age from underground work in mines, in accordance with the ILO Conventions, and to break the silence in this regard by providing information in extenso on the situation of children working in mines.

The Worker member of the United Kingdom welcomed the remarkable ratification rate of Convention No. 182, which since 1999 had become the most rapidly ratified Convention in the history of the ILO. Universal ratification remained an achievable aim provided that the campaign was pursued. The Convention had refocused international and national attention on child labour and had also led to a phenomenal leap in the level of ratification of Convention No. 138. As wholly complementary Conventions he urged all Members which had ratified Convention No. 182, but not yet Convention No. 138, to examine as a priority and through tripartite consultation the advantages that ratification of Convention No. 138 would bring to their national strategies for

C. 182

the elimination of child labour, where necessary seeking the technical assistance of the ILO, and to proceed to ratification without delay. These two fundamental human rights Conventions, alongside Convention No. 29, were cornerstones of decent work and of sustainable national development policies.

The case of Niger, which demonstrated a degree of political will by the Government through its relationship with the IPEC, also recalled the urgent need for action because the challenges to be met in Niger, as in other West African countries, involved very great and grave suffering of children damaged by trafficking and slavery, including sexual slavery, forced begging, and hazardous work in mines and quarries. What was important was for that political will to be sustained, rather than denying the existence of trafficking. He therefore expressed concern at the detention of two leading anti-slavery activists, Ilguilas Weila and Alasanne Biga of the NGO Timidra, a partner of Anti-Slavery International, in what appeared to be an attempt to silence outspoken critics of slavery in Niger. Both had twice been denied bail. He called on the Government to either release them or to ensure that their trial was open, impartial, and held soon in a public court.

He welcomed the general observation of the Committee of Experts in relation to trafficking and the request to all governments which had ratified the Convention to supply information on key elements of its application, namely legislation, measures to prevent trafficking, programme development, training and awareness raising, the collection of statistical data, time-bound measures for prevention, removal, rehabilitation and reintegration, effective monitoring and international cooperation. In this context, he welcomed the development of the West Africa subregional LUTRENA programme, as combating trafficking required extensive cross-border and international cooperation.

He emphasized in particular the relationship between the elimination of child labour, including its worst forms, and free, compulsory, universal, accessible and formal basic education, provided as a quality public service for all children. He said that at the heart of every community should be a good school. In this respect, he shared the view of the Committee of Experts that explaining child labour and trafficking for child labour simply as a consequence of poverty was too simplistic. Child labour was both a cause and consequence of poverty. It acted as a brake on the human development of the individual child and on the human resources of the nation. Every child out of school, every trafficked child, diminished the ability of national economies to meet sustainably the challenges of the global economy. All too often, child labour turned the child into an unemployed adult, lacking the transferable skills and education required in the formal labour market. It therefore contributed a loss of valuable human resources. He expressed the view that child labour would never be eliminated without the provision of universal education, but equally universal education would never be achieved without the elimination of child labour. It was not poverty alone that denied children access to school, but rather social injustice and inequality. Making education a key public priority was indeed possible, even when countries were not rich. It was a far better investment than weapons of war. In this respect, there was a need for global solidarity, as foreseen in the Convention and the Recommendation, as well as for a just and equitable global economic and trading system. Nevertheless, levels of literacy were higher in certain poor countries than in some far richer industrialized countries because they had chosen equity over greed. Another common feature of such countries was the comparatively high social status of women. He recalled, in this respect, that 2005 was to have been the year in which all countries would reach the interim Millennium Development Goal of equal school enrolment of girls and boys. Unfortunately, this had been a miserable failure, even though evidence showed the exponential social and economic benefits of the education of the girl child. He emphasized that access to education was not just a matter of provision, although experience showed that even the poorest parents would send their child to school if it was free and accessible. It was also a matter of empowerment. Empowered communities, through social mobilization, could overcome the democratic deficit and demand that their governments meet their needs as citizens for equal legal protection, decent work for adults and schools for their children.

In conclusion, he said that the elimination of child labour, including its worst forms, was not just a poverty issue. It was an issue of education, gender, class, discrimination, the labour market, exploitation, decent work for adults, social justice, crime, equity, development, tripartism, democracy and, above all, fundamental human rights. Conventions Nos. 138 and 182 were indivisibly linked with all other fundamental human rights at work proclaimed by the ILO and were the most significant normative tools available for the elimination of all forms of child labour. He therefore thanked the Committee of Experts for the sense of urgency that it had injected into the general observation on Convention No. 182, especially with regard to trafficking. In welcoming and supporting the general observation, he called for no longer wasting entire generations of children and also for the universal ratification and implementation of Conventions Nos. 138 and 182. In so doing, an important contribution would be made to «making poverty history» by making every child, boy or girl, a school-going child.

The Worker member of Niger recalled that child labour and forced labour were considered by workers' organizations in Niger as a scourge which destroyed decent work and gave rise to economic insecurity, which was the reason for their commitment to the IPEC programme. He emphasized that the ratification of Conventions Nos. 29 and 182 was an act of political will by Niger, which was being reinforced and encouraged by the ILO through its technical cooperation programmes. He hoped this political will would continue and be reinforced by action taken in practice.

He indicated that, in Africa in general and in Niger in particular, child labour was more an issue of underdevelopment than of culture and its eradication requested measures to combat poverty and promote good economic governance. That poverty was perpetuated by the international financial institutions (the IMF and the World Bank) through the structural adjustment programmes imposed on the State. He called for assistance to be provided to Niger to combat poverty which was the surest means of ensuring the schooling of children in Niger so as to prepare for their future and that of their country.

Finally, he emphasized that slavery and forced labour, which were vile and unlawful practices in the informal economy, could not be resolved solely by law. He called on the ILO to design a technical cooperation programme with Niger for the elimination of this scourge with the participation of all the national partners.

The Government member of the United States emphasized that international cooperation and assistance – by both the ILO and the international community at large – were critical to achieving the elimination of the worst forms of child labour in Niger. As her country had ratified Convention No. 182, it was obliged under Article 8 to assist Niger and other countries in their efforts to secure a better, brighter future for their children. Consequently, her Government was currently sponsoring a project in Niger targeting some 18,000 children aged between 6 and 18 years with the aim of reducing their engagement in the worst forms of child labour by increasing their participation in appropriate education programmes. The project was helping the Government of Niger to develop a national action plan aimed at reducing child labour, improving school quality and improving access to education. In addition, her Government was working with ILO/IPEC to develop a project to remove children from gold, salt, stone and mineral mining in Niger and in a neighbouring country. The project would also put in place a structure to prevent child labour in mining beyond the life of the project.

In conclusion, she hoped that projects like these would help the Government of Niger to achieve the full application of Convention No. 182 in law and, more importantly, in practice, within the shortest possible period.

The Employer member of Niger said that his country was poor and disadvantaged and that this should be taken into account. He emphasized that there was no trafficking in children in his country. He acknowledged the existence of work by young persons which, according to him, was limited to small mining enterprises. He added that these children did not go to school for reasons of poverty and were therefore obliged to work to meet their daily needs. He indicated that 6 million children were of school age, but one-third of them did not go to school for the above reasons.

The Worker member of Senegal emphasized that the Government of Niger had been called for the second time in two years to appear before the Committee on the issue of the violation of ratified Conventions. Last year, the Committee had examined Convention No. 29, and today the discussion was devoted to Convention No. 182.

In 2004, the members of the Committee had discussed the persistence of forced labour in the country, despite the measures taken by the Government to solve the situation with the help of the labour inspection services, the ILO/IPEC programme and collaboration with NGOs.

In 2001, a study carried out by the ILO had proposed certain measures to combat forced labour, such as the strengthening of the legal arsenal, the organization of information activities, awareness campaigns and the education of the population on its rights and obligations, and the development of the conditions for access to means of subsistence through freely chosen employment. The report also described the working conditions of children in mines and quarries. In this regard, it was important to emphasize that a little less than a half of workers in mines were children and that in certain quarries the number could reach 50 per cent. These activities were arduous and dangerous and involved risks for children. Although the Government had ratified Conventions Nos. 138 and 182, which set the minimum age of 18 years for admission to hazardous work, the national legislation did not seem to prohibit this type of child labour.

The information contained in the observation made by the Committee of Experts confirmed the existence of the problem of trafficking in girls for the purpose of labour exploitation, for domestic work and for sexual exploitation. This information also confirmed that boys were victims of trafficking for the purpose of labour exploitation.

It was important to emphasize that, contrary to other countries, the Government of Niger was ready to cooperate. However, in accordance with the principles shared by all the members of the Committee, no transaction would be permitted. The Committee had to give explicit and formal directives to the Government to encourage it to take necessary measures to ensure the application of the Convention in law and practice. For example, the Government could adopt a plan of action for ten years to reinforce the rights of the child and to ensure that they attended school. Cooperation with the ILO/IPEC programme could contribute to the achievement of this aim. Moreover, the programme could include measures for social reintegration as well as a poverty eradication plan. Finally, he called for Iiguilas Weila and Alasanne Biga to be freed.

The Government member of Cuba said that the Committee should bear in mind that Niger was one of the poorest countries in the world and that, despite this fact, the Committee of Experts had nevertheless noted that a number of legislative measures had been taken by the Government and specific programmes were being implemented with the technical assistance of the ILO and other international organizations. This demonstrated the Government's interest in finding solutions. She emphasized that Niger genuinely needed international cooperation and referred to the economic crisis and the lack of infrastructure and human resources, following years of exploitation and pillage. She indicated that Cuba, a country with scarce resources but great will, which was subjected to an economic blockade had, for example, sent a medical team to Niger and urged the Committee to call for international assistance and cooperation with a view to solving the problems in question. In this respect, she endorsed the request made by the Government representative of Niger and stated that international solidarity was also a principle of humanism.

The Employer member of the United States said that, as one of the drafting members of Convention No. 182, it was gratifying for him to be in this Committee and to witness the substantial and rapid rate of ratification and implementation of the Convention. He was pleased to see that Niger had ratified Convention No. 182, and that the country had not done this without recognizing that some key difficulties existed with respect to its implementation. He emphasized that this was, however, the whole idea behind the Convention, namely to bring attention and action to these issues and to support action. He recalled that Convention No. 182 referred to the worst forms of child labour, and that it was generally recognized that, while the whole issue of child labour should be addressed, this would have to be done in stages. He noted that work done by children that did not affect their health or personal development or interfere with their schooling was generally regarded as positive, and contributed to the child's development and the welfare of families. It provided skills and experience and contributed to children becoming useful and productive members of society in their adult life.

He emphasized that there were 300 million child labourers and that Convention No. 182 did not address all of those. The worst forms of child labour were well known. They related to labour which interfered with education and development and which was mentally, socially or morally dangerous and harmful to children. In his view there was no debate in Niger on these issues or on issues of slavery or trafficking. Referring to Article 4 of the Convention, he pointed out that for the determination of the types of work referred to in Article 3(d) which were harmful to the health, safety or morals of children, the relevant paragraphs of Recommendation No. 190 should be taken into account. The reason for this specific reference was because there was an understanding that not all situations of child labour could be defined in the Convention. Moreover, the Convention provided for tripartite consultation to determine these types of work.

However, the most important provision of Convention No. 182 was Article 8. It was unique in providing that member States should take appropriate steps to assist one another in giving effect to the provisions of this Convention through enhanced international cooperation and assistance. As this case was one of the first cases on Convention No. 182 discussed by the Conference Committee, the Committee should reflect on whether and how it should congratulate, condemn or support the countries concerned. It was impossible to address the situation of all 300 million child labourers straightaway, but it was important to work together to help a few of them already.

The Government representative said that she had taken due note of all the interventions. She emphasized that neither the worst forms of child labour nor trafficking in children existed in Niger. With regard to child labour and begging, she indicated that her country had made every effort to combat this scourge and was committed for that purpose to eliminating illiteracy. She added that education was provided at the primary and secondary school levels but, because of poverty, the primary concern of children was not going to school, but rather to meet their daily needs. She said that her country had been making considerable efforts to eliminate this scourge and had requested assistance from the international community. She considered that education was the best means of eliminating the worst forms of child labour and called for international solidarity in this respect.

The Employer members thanked the Government representative for the information provided. They indicated that they were uncertain whether the Government of Niger was or was not in denial of the existence of problems in the implementation of the Convention. There was clearly a need for technical assistance by the ILO to assess in practice the actual situation, as indicated by the Committee of Experts in its observation. They recalled the statement by the Employer member of Niger indicating that 50 per cent of the population was below 15 years of age and stated that Niger was clearly facing huge problems, especially considering the extensive poverty that prevailed in the country. It was, therefore, essential and critical that other countries which had ratified Convention No. 182, and which had the means to help, ensured that they provided assistance to Niger, particularly to give effect to its obligations under Article 7 of the Convention, to take measures to ensure access to free basic education and, wherever possible and appropriate, vocational training for all children removed from the worst forms of child labour. In addition, there was a need for changes in the legislation, although the Employer members cautioned that this would not be sufficient in itself. The implementation of the Convention in practice would require an effective labour inspection system and enforcement mechanisms. The Employer members had serious doubts that such mechanisms existed in law and in practice in Niger.

The Worker members encouraged the Government to continue its efforts to eliminate child labour, in particular with the technical assistance of the ILO. The Government should pay particular attention to the problem of child labour in mines when adopting legislative measures and developing programmes of action. Moreover, it was important for trade unions to be more closely associated with the elimination of this problem. It was to be hoped that the next report by the Government would provide detailed information on the measures taken with regard to child labour in mines.

The Worker members expressed their concern at the action taken against anti-slavery activists and their firm conviction that, in combating slavery, dialogue would lead to solutions being found.

Concerning the general observation made by the Committee of Experts, it was important for governments to include in their next reports information on: (1) the legislative measures adopted or envisaged to prohibit trafficking of children under 18 years of age for the purposes of economic and sexual exploitation by (*i*) making any violation of this prohibition a criminal offence and (*ii*) imposing penal and other sanctions of an effectively dissuasive nature; (2) the measures adopted or envisaged to (*i*) prevent such trafficking and (*ii*) formulate and implement programmes of action targeting multiple levels of society; (3) training, collaboration and awareness-raising for public officials on action to combat the trafficking of children; (4) statistics on the number of violations, investigations, prosecutions and convictions relating to the trafficking of children and the text of any court decisions in such cases; (5) the effective application of the principle of free and compulsory schooling for children, particularly for girls; and (6) the time-bound measures taken to prevent the engagement of children in trafficking, remove children from trafficking, protect the victims of trafficking and provide for their rehabilitation and social integration.

The Worker members also emphasized the importance of combating the transnational dimension of child labour. In this regard, they once again thanked the Committee of Experts for its general observation, which raised the issue of the international dimension of child labour and emphasized that in future this matter could be addressed in general observations on the application of other Conventions.

The Committee noted the information provided by the Government representative and the discussion that ensued. The Committee noted the information contained in the report of the Committee of Experts relating to the use of children in begging, in hazardous work, in mines and quarries, and the sale and trafficking of children in Niger for purposes of economic and sexual exploitation.

The Committee took note of the information provided by the Government highlighting the issues of poverty and the limits of its education system, as well as the Government's view that the sale and trafficking of children did not exist in Niger. The Committee also took note of the Government's request for ILO technical assistance.

The Committee shared the concern of the Committee of Experts with regard to the vulnerability of children who begged in the streets, as well as those performing hazardous work in mines and quarries. The Committee emphasized the seriousness of such violations of Convention No. 182. In this regard, the Committee noted that various action programmes had already been undertaken in collaboration with ILO/IPEC and other governments to remove children from such situations. The Committee further noted that the Government of Niger had expressed its willingness to continue its efforts to eradicate such situations with the technical assistance and cooperation of the ILO.

The Committee stressed that the use of children in begging and in hazardous work in mines and quarries constituted one of the worst forms of child labour and that the Government was obliged to take, by virtue of Article 1 of the Convention, immediate and effective measures to secure the prohibition and the elimination of the worst forms of child labour as a matter of urgency. The Committee requested the Government to indicate the effective and time-bound measures taken to remove child beggars under 18 years old from the streets as well as children under 18 working in hazardous conditions in mines and quarries. It also requested the Government to provide additional information on the measures taken to provide for the rehabilitation and social integration of these children, in conformity with Article 7, paragraph 2, of the Convention.

While noting of the Government's commitment to implement the Convention, the Committee underlined the importance of free and compulsory schooling to preventing the worst forms of child labour. The Committee urged the Government to take the necessary measures without delay to ensure access to free basic education for both boys and girls, especially in rural or particularly disadvantaged areas.

Concerning the issue of the sale and trafficking of children, and the Government's indication that such a practice did not exist in Niger, the Committee decided that an ILO fact-finding mission be undertaken to the country. This fact-finding mission should also

examine all the issues raised in the comments of the Committee of Experts and in this Committee.

The Committee called on ILO member States to provide assistance to the Government of Niger in line with Article 8 of the Convention, with special priority on facilitating free basic education as provided in Article 7. The Committee requested the Government to undertake efforts to apply the Convention in cooperation with the social partners and to report in detail on the results achieved in its next report to the Committee of Experts.

The Worker members stated that all underground work was hazardous and should be prohibited for persons under 18 years of age.

The Employer members stated that it is not up to the Conference Committee to indicate whether, with respect to Convention No. 182, underground work should be qualified as hazardous or not.

QATAR (ratification: 2000). The Government communicated the following written information:

Law No. 22 of the year 2005 on the prohibition of bringing in, employing, training and involving children in camel racing

I, Tameem Bin Hamad Al-Thani, Vice-Emir of the State of Qatar,

After examination of the provisional amended statute, namely Articles (22), (23), (34), and (51), and Law No. (1) of the year 1994 concerning juveniles, and Law No. (7) of the year 1999 concerning regulation of the Ministry of Civil Service Affairs and Housing and determination of its competence,

And Labour Law No. (14) of the year 2004,

And Decree No. (54) of the year 1995 allowing the affiliation of the State of Qatar to the Convention on the Rights of the Child,

And Decree No. (29) of 2001 on ratification of the Convention concerning the prohibition and immediate action for the elimination of the worst forms of child labour (No. 182) and the 1999 urgent procedures to eliminate it,

And the proposition of the Minister of Civil Service Affairs and Housing,

And the draft Law submitted by the Council of Ministers,

And after consultation with the Consultative Council,

We decided the following law:

Article (1)

Is considered a child, according to the provisions of this law, a person who is less than 18 years old.

Article (2)

It is prohibited to bring in, employ, train or involve children in camel racing.

Article (3)

Officers of the Labour Department, Ministry of Civil Service Affairs and Housing, who will be the object of the Attorney-General's decision, by mutual agreement with the Minister of Civil Service Affairs and Housing, will have the capacity of judicial investigation commissioners in order to determine and prove crimes which are contrary to the provisions of this law and related decisions.

Article (4)

Anyone who breaches the provision of Article (2) of this law will be imprisoned for no less than three years and no more than ten years and fined a minimum of fifty thousand QR and nor more than two hundred thousand QR, without precluding any more severe punishment stated by other laws.

Article (5)

The Minister of Civil Service Affairs and Housing will issue the necessary decisions to enforce the provisions of this law.

Article (6)

All competent authorities shall enforce this law which must be implemented from the date of its publication in the *Official Journal*.

Tameem Bin Al-Thani,
Vice Emir of the State of Qatar

Issued at the Emiri Diwan
On 23 May 2005

In addtion, before the Committee, a Government representative stated that Qatar had ratified the Convention less than one year after its adoption and since then the Government had always cooperated with the Committee of Experts and had provided the necessary information. The Government would also fully reply to the observation under discussion in the Committee. Two years ago an institute for the protection of children and women had been established which provided an institutional framework for the protection of children's rights. The High Council for Family Affairs was also involved in such matters and numerous seminars and workshops had been organized. With regard to the participation of children as jockeys in camel racing, the Government informed the Committee that Law No. 22 had been promulgated on 23 May 2005, which prohibited the bringing in, involving or participation of children as jockeys and/or other involvement of persons below the age of 18 in camel races, as well as the training of persons under the age of 18 for such a purpose. The Law provided for sanctions of fines up to 200,000 rials and of imprisonment between three to ten years. The Labour Inspectorate was responsible for supervising the Law's application and was cooperating with the public prosecutor in order to ensure strict implementation and enforcement of this legislation. The Government representative further stated that a light robot had been developed to replace children as camel jockeys and had already been successfully tested. Children had previously participated in camel racing as a hobby always with the authorization of their parents while the High Council for Family Affairs was making every effort to integrate the children concerned in the educational system.

The Employer members emphasized the particular significance of the Convention which sought to protect the most vulnerable members of society, the children. In adopting this Convention, the ILO had recognized that this issue was a priority, not only at the national, but also at the international level. The Convention was intended to address a particularly abhorrent situation, and was adopted for this reason unanimously and quickly by the ILO. Underlying the entire Convention was a recognition of the urgency of the matter. Although the Convention was adopted in 1999, the issues it sought to redress had been present for far too many years, and had been discussed far too often in consideration of other Conventions, and especially Convention No. 29. The adoption of Convention No. 182 had reflected the inadequacies of existing instruments to address certain circumstances, a great urgency to eliminate the worst forms of child labour and a frustration at the lack of progress in eliminating the worst forms of child labour under the other instruments.

The Employer members noted, in this connection, that they remained frustrated at the fact that the issues which had given rise to this case, i.e., the trafficking of children for the purposes of, and the use of children in, the camel racing industry, continued to exist. They agreed with the Committee of Experts that the issue of trafficking and forced labour of children and the use of children as camel jockeys, could be examined more specifically and appropriately under this Convention especially because of the need for immediate and effective steps. The Convention was to address the worst forms of child labour in distinction to the other forms of child labour, which might be beneficial and adequate for the development of children, for which Convention No. 138 provided a framework. Convention No. 182 was a clear and unequivocal call to action for member States to take immediate and comprehensive steps, as a matter of urgency.

The Employer members considered that the fact that this case was being commented upon and further information was being sought by the Committee of Experts was evidence that children's involvement in camel racing continued. In addition, the comments of the Government, as noted by the Committee of Experts, had indicated that while certain measures appeared to be taken, they were not effective. The Committee of Experts had commented on the concept of the worst forms of child labour as applying to those under the age of 18. Article 3 of the Convention set out the types of work which constituted the worst forms of child labour. These could be distinguished into two categories. The first group was found in Articles 3(a) through (c) and included forms of slavery or practices similar to slavery, such as the sale and trafficking of children; forced or compulsory labour; the use, procuring or offering of a child for prostitution; the use, and procuring or offering of a child for illicit activities, in particular for the production and trafficking of drugs. For purposes of this case, the Committee of Experts had commented, and the Employers agreed, that the sale and trafficking of children, and forced or compulsory labour for the purposes of camel jockeying fell within Article 3(a) of the Convention. Thus, the Convention required trafficking in children to be immediately eliminated and prohibited. According to the observation of the Committee of Experts, no evidence had been provided and the Employer members assumed that the Government had failed to do so.

The second category of worst forms of child labour were found in Article 3(d) which referred to "work which by its nature or the circumstances in which it is carried out, is likely to harm the health, safety or morals of children". Work which fell under Article 3(d) required that the Government in consultation with employers' and workers' organizations, develop a list of the types of work in accordance with national laws, which were also the worst forms of child labour. The Government should take immediate measures to develop the list, in consultation with the social partners, and then take immediate and effective measures to prohibit and eliminate these worst forms of child labour. In other words, the determination of the worst forms of child labour under Article 3(d) did not require less immediacy or urgency, but simply an additional step. Regrettably, in its comments, the Committee of Experts had failed to recognize this unique feature of Article 3(d), as described in Article 4. There was also no indication by the Committee of Experts or by the Government that such a consultation had taken place or a list prepared. The Employer members, therefore, encouraged the Government to consult with the social partners immediately for this purpose.

The Employer members considered that camel racing was inherently dangerous to the health and safety of children, and did not foresee any circumstances where camel racing would not be considered as a worst form of child labour in accordance with Article 3(d). It was not clear from the comments of the Committee of Experts that the Government shared this view. Therefore, the Employer members asked the Government to clarify its position on this issue.

Article 7 of the Convention, required that governments take steps to ensure effective implementation and enforcement, including through the provision of penal sanctions. While there was an indication in the report of the Committee of Experts that section 193 of the National Penal Code criminalized trafficking of persons, which should be noted as a positive element, unfortunately, there was neither evidence that the measure was effective, nor that penalties had been applied. The Employer members encouraged the Government to ensure the effective implementation and enforcement of the national penal law and to provide the necessary information on the penal sanctions that had been imposed in practice. Absent of such information, the Employer members would remain sceptical that such a measure was being enforced against an activity whose primary purpose was the entertainment of the wealthy social élite.

The Employer members further observed that by asking for additional information on camel jockeys under the age of 18, the Committee of Experts suggested that there might be circumstances where the Government believed that camel jockeying by children was not a violation of the Convention. In this respect, the Employer members requested the Government to provide clear information that under no circumstances were children under the age of 18, working as camel jockeys, and to take effective measures to this end.

In addition, the Committee of Experts commented on measures put in place that might differentiate between children that were nationals and those that were non-nationals involved in camel racing. Such a distinction based on nationality would not be appropriate nor in compliance with the Convention which was clear in that the worst forms of child labour were to be addressed, regardless of nationality or any other distinction.

Finally, the Committee of Experts had stated that camel jockeying was likely to harm the health and safety of children and therefore fell under Article 3(d) of the Convention. While the Employer members agreed with the underlying sentiment of the Committee of Experts, they took exception, with regard to the approach of determining what circumstances fell within Article 3(d). In so doing, the Committee of Experts had exceeded its mandate and failed to consider Article 4 of the Convention according to which the list of circumstances that would fall under Article 3(d) should be determined by the national governments, after consultation with employers' and workers' organizations and periodically examined and revised in consultation with these social partners.

The Convention recognized that there were root causes underlying the circumstances of the worst forms of child labour, and particularly the problem of trafficking of children, was recognized as one which took place, not only within countries but also between them. It was not just a national problem but also an international one. Accordingly, the Convention required member States to take steps to assist one another through enhanced international cooperation and assistance. Regrettably, in this case, there was no indication of any cooperative efforts between countries. Given the requirement for immediate measures to be taken, there should be information on such cooperative measures. The Employer members requested the Government to provide any information on cooperative measures taken directly or through the Gulf Cooperation Council. The Government was reminded that technical cooperation was available to it, to assist it in giving effect to the Convention.

The Committee of Experts had observed that there were cases of children being trafficked for the purposes of camel racing and had invited the Government to redouble its efforts to improve the situation. In the view of the Employer members, the trafficking of children should be immediately prohibited and eliminated as a matter of urgency. The implementation of the Convention was not a matter of degree, but a "black and white" issue. As long as there were still reported cases of trafficking, as observed by the Committee of Experts, there was evidence that any measures taken to date had not been effective, as required by the Convention. The circumstances of children engaged in camel jockeying had been discussed in this Committee far too often, and it was the Employer members' intention to remind and encourage governments to implement this fundamental Convention. They wished to remind the Government of the technical assistance available through the ILO and strongly encouraged it to seek such assistance. They further noted that the Government had ratified the Convention in 2000, shortly after its adoption. The time had now come to ensure full compliance with the Convention.

The Employer members thanked the Government for its efforts to respond to the observation of the Committee of Experts in a timely manner and for the information contained in the response, which indicated that a new law, Law No. 22, had been adopted on 23 May 2005 to the effect that "it is prohibited to bring in, employ, train or involve children in camel racing". The Employer members commended the Government for the clear and broad scope of this prohibition. They asked the Government to confirm that the Law applied to all children under 18, both Qatari and non-Qatari, without distinction. They also noted that section 6 of Law No. 22 provided that the Law "shall be enforced from the date of its publication in the official journal" and asked the Government to confirm that the Law had been published and was in force.

Finally, with regard to the general observation made by the Committee of Experts, the Employer members noted, that due to the fact that this was a new Convention and its requirements were urgent and a priority, it might be of assistance to the Conference Committee to deviate from its mandate and provide comments in relation to the understanding of the Convention. As for the comment related to activities in West Africa, since the trafficking of children was not confined to one region, they believed such comments were not of assistance as they could detract from the recognition that this was an international issue.

The Worker members noted that the Committee had discussed for several years the suffering of children trafficked to the Gulf region for forced labour exploitation as camel jockeys. This exploitation violated at least three Conventions (Nos. 29, 138 and 182), involving boys sometimes less than 10 years old in trafficking, forced labour and employment and hazardous work below the minimum age.

Qatar had ratified Convention No. 182 but not Convention No. 138. While welcoming recent legislative developments in the county, the Worker members suggested that for a coherent national strategy to eliminate child labour, Qatar should also ratify Convention No. 138.

As regards trafficking, there was no doubt that numerous young children had been trafficked to the Gulf, including Qatar. In reply to the Government's claim that they were there with their families, the Worker members had hoped that the denial stage had been passed as a barrier to resolution of the problem. The annual United States report on trafficking in persons of June 2005 stated that: "Qatar is a destination for men and women trafficked for the purpose of labour exploitation and young boys trafficked for the purpose of exploitation as camel jockeys. Children trafficked for exploitation as camel jockeys come primarily from South Asia and Sudan. Most no longer remember where they come from."

The report also noted that "the Government of Qatar does not fully comply with the minimum standards for the elimination of trafficking and is not making significant efforts to do so. During the rating period, the Government failed to show evidence of significant efforts to combat identified severe forms of trafficking on the three fronts of prosecution, protection and prevention. A 2003 National Action Plan remains unimplemented. The Government of Qatar does not collect statistics on persons trafficked into the country. According to diplomatic sources and NGOs, there have been no rescues of the estimated 75 to 250 child camel jockeys, nor prosecutions of the traffickers. The Government provides no shelter for trafficking victims; instead it detains and punishes trafficking victims for immigration violence."

As regards hazardous work, there were severe risks of injury and even death, psychological trauma and abuse. On immediate prohibition and elimination, Qatari law prohibited employment in hazardous work for Qatari children under 18, but a non-Qatari worker required the approval of the Department of Labour and a work permit, which was insufficient. The prohibition should apply to all children, regardless of their nationality. Trafficked workers were undocumented; therefore, much more evidence was required to prove that Qatar was immune to the problem.

The denial that trafficking existed was at odds with the Qatari penal code, section 193 of which made liable to ten years' imprisonment any person found guilty of importing, exporting, selling, taking possession of or disposing of a person, which sounded remarkably like a description of trafficking.

The Worker members questioned the formulation used by the Committee of Experts in its observation in noting that the Government should provide information on the measures taken to ensure that non-Qatari camel jockeys under 18 years of age did not perform their work under circumstances detrimental to their health and safety. A similar formulation was also used for similar violations in the United Arab Emirates. But, the Conference Committee's conclusions in 2003 on the UAE case stipulated that camel jockeying was "intrinsically hazardous" and therefore should not be performed by any person under 18 years of age. It seemed that the Government of Qatar had understood the hazardous nature of camel jockeying and the Worker members welcomed the issuing of Law No. 22, which specifically referred to Convention No. 182 and stated that a child was a person under 18 years of age, and also forbade the employment, training or involvement of children in camel racing. It did not refer to different rules for non-Qatari children. It did provide for judicial investigation to determine and prove crimes in violation of the Law, a minimum of three years' imprisonment and a fine of between 50,000 and 200,000 Qatari rials. The Ministry of Civil Affairs and Housing would issue the necessary decisions to enforce the Law and ensure that all competent authorities would implement it.

The Worker members wanted to know how the Government intended to identify violations of the Law, what measures it was taking to rehabilitate, repatriate and compensate child camel jockeys, and ensure that psychiatric and medical care, counselling and education were provided. Measures on tracing families were also important. They asked if legislation that prohibited and punished the employment of children of any nationality under the age of 18 in other types of hazardous work were being taken as a matter of priority. Statistics on prosecutions for violations, successful convictions and sentences passed, broken down by year, were also required. A report should also be made on any measures of cooperation between Qatar, other Gulf States and countries of origin of child victims and on steps taken to harmonize legislation on camel racing in the Gulf countries.

The Government representative thanked all members of the Committee for their contributions. His delegation had already met with senior ILO officials and had requested technical assistance with a view to solving remaining problems. The Committee of Experts had commented on Qatar for the first time under this Convention, and the Government would provide all information requested in time. The issue had been brought to the attention of all levels of Government. The Government representative also confirmed that Law No. 22 applied to all children, irrespective of their nationality. Further, the Law prohibited the bringing-in of children, which meant that trafficking was also covered. He reiterated that the Labour Inspectorate was competent to ensure compliance with this legislation and that harsh sanctions could be imposed for violations. There was also international cooperation with other countries in the region to address the problem of trafficking. In addition, the Government was studying the possibility of ratifying Convention No. 138. The labour legislation already prohibited the employment of persons under the age of 18, irrespective of nationality, in work likely to harm health, safety or morals. Finally, it was stated that the United States report on trafficking of persons had been issued before the promulgation of Law No. 22 and that the United States Government through its Ambassador to Qatar had paid tribute to the Law as an important effort to eliminate trafficking. The Government was committed to continued cooperation with the ILO and other partners on this matter.

The Employer members were encouraged by the measures taken by the Government as evidenced in the adoption of Law No. 22. However, they remained sceptical as to the effective implementation of the Convention given the urgency with which the Government should address this issue. They, therefore, called on the Government to give details on the penalties imposed under the Law, on efforts to harmonize the legislation on camel racing throughout the Gulf countries as well as to reply to the Committee of Experts concerning measures taken to implement the Convention in law and in practice. The Employer members also called on the Government to engage immediately in social dialogue in order to develop a list of the worst forms of child labour and to provide information to the Committee in this regard. They took note of the Government representative's assurances that Law No. 22 was being implemented and had entered into force and waited for the Committee of Experts to review its conformity with the Convention. They called on the Government to continue to participate in international cooperation efforts to bring its law and practice into conformity with the Convention and to provide information to the effect that Law No. 22 applied to all children regardless of nationality. They finally urged the Government to avail itself of the technical assistance of the ILO and to use such assistance on a priority and urgent basis in conformity with the terms of the Convention. The Employer members finally reiterated the priority that they attached to this Convention.

The Worker members noted a brief but informative discussion. The challenge was the effective implementation of the new Law and recognition by the Government that it was not immune from the trafficking problem. The Worker members asked that the Committee recommend the Government to identify violations of the Law, inter alia, by carrying out regular unannounced inspections to identify, release and rehabilitate any child being used as a jockey and ensure that those responsible for trafficking and using under age jockeys were prosecuted. Measures must be taken to rehabilitate, repatriate and compensate child camel jockeys, and ensure that the children concerned were provided with psychiatric and medical care, counselling and education. The Government should also ensure that family tracing was carried out before repatriation and that services were in place to care for the child if no family were found. The Government should introduce legislation through tripartite cooperation to prohibit and punish the employment of children of any nationality under 18 years of age in other types of hazardous work, as a matter of priority. The Government was invited to seek technical assistance from the ILO. Finally, the Worker members requested the Government to provide to the Committee of Experts information on these points and on any other measures of cooperation passed between Qatar, other Gulf States and the countries of origin of the child victims and on steps taken to harmonize legislation on camel racing in the Gulf countries.

The Committee noted the written and oral information provided by the Government representative and the discussion that ensued. The Committee noted the information contained in the report of the Committee of Experts relating to the sale and trafficking of children under 18 years into Qatar for work as camel jockeys and the hazardous nature of this activity.

In this regard, the Committee noted the information provided by the Government representative that Law No. 22 of May 2005 prohibited the trafficking of children under 18 to Qatar to work in camel racing. The Government also pointed out that by virtue of article 4 of this recently enacted Law, whoever violated the prohibition on the trafficking of children to work as camel jockeys was liable to between three and ten years imprisonment and a fine, and that article 2 of the recently enacted Law No. 22 of 2005 prohibited the employment, training and use of children in camel racing, and that by virtue of article 1 of the Law, a child was a person under 18 years of age.

The Committee also noted the intent expressed by the Government representative to combat child trafficking for labour exploitation. This intent was reported to be reflected in concrete measures, including the purchase and use of robots to replace the use of children as camel jockeys. The Committee further noted that the Government of Qatar had expressed its willingness to continue its efforts to eradicate such situations with the technical assistance of the ILO. The Committee also noted that the Government was considering the ratification of Convention No. 138.

While welcoming the recent measures taken, the Committee urged that children should no longer continue to be victims of trafficking for the purpose of labour exploitation, and that those responsible would be punished. The Committee emphasized that, in accordance with Article 3(a) of the Convention, the sale and trafficking of children for labour exploitation, including camel racing, constituted one of the worst forms of child labour and that the Government was obliged, by virtue of Article 1 of the Convention, to take immediate and effective measures to secure the prohibition and elimination of the worst forms of child labour as a matter of urgency. In this regard, the Committee urged the Government to take the necessary measures to ensure that unannounced inspections were carried out by the labour inspectorate and that persons, regardless of their nationality, who trafficked in children to work as camel jockeys, were prosecuted and sufficiently effective and dissuasive penalties were imposed.

The Committee expressed its concern about the inherently hazardous nature of this activity. The Committee asked the Government to take necessary measures to ensure also that Qatari or non-Qatari children under 18 years of age did not perform any work under the circumstances that were likely to be detrimental to their health, safety or morals. The Committee recalled that Convention No. 182 had to be applied without distinction as to nationality. The Committee also invited the Government to take steps to develop social dialogue on the implementation of the Convention, in particular, concerning the determination of types of hazardous work, in accordance with Articles 3(d) and 4(1) of the Convention.

Noting that the Government was prepared to avail itself of ILO technical assistance, the Committee decided that a technical advisory mission should be undertaken to the country to evaluate the situation of compliance with the Convention in law and practice.

The Committee requested the Government to provide detailed information in its next report to the Committee of Experts on measures taken to implement Convention No. 182 and in, particular, the implementation in practice of the Penal Code and the new Law, including the number of infringements reported, investigations, prosecutions, convictions and penal sanctions applied. The Committee also requested the Government to provide detailed information on the effective and time-bound measures taken to prevent trafficking and to remove former child victims of trafficking from hazardous work and to provide for their rehabilitation and social integration, in conformity with Article 7(2) of the Convention. These measures should include the repatriation, family reunification and support for former child victims of trafficking.

Finally, the Committee requested the Government to provide information on the steps taken to harmonize the legislation on camel racing in the Gulf region.

Appendix I. Table of reports received on ratified Conventions
(articles 22 and 35 of the Constitution)

Reports received as of 16 June 2005

The table published in the Report of the Committee of Experts, page 497, should be brought up to date in the following manner:

Note: First reports are indicated in parentheses.
Paragraph numbers indicate a modification in the lists of countries mentioned in Part One (General Report) of the Report of the Committee of Experts.

Barbados — 16 reports requested
(Paragraph 31)
- 11 reports received: Conventions Nos. 29, 63, 81, 98, 101, 105, 111, 118, 135, 144, 182
- 5 reports not received: Conventions Nos. 22, 74, 108, 138, 147

Belgium — 22 reports requested
- 21 reports received: Conventions Nos. 8, 9, 16, 22, 23, 29, 53, 55, 68, 69, 73, 74, 81, 92, 105, 129, 138, 147, 151, 154, (182)
- 1 report not received: Convention No. 56

Botswana — 11 reports requested
(Paragraph 31)
- 7 reports received: Conventions Nos. 14, 29, 87, 98, 105, 144, 151
- 4 reports not received: Conventions Nos. 111, 138, 173, 182

Central African Republic — 16 reports requested
(Paragraph 31)
- 15 reports received: Conventions Nos. 14, 18, 29, 41, 62, 81, 87, 95, 98, 101, 105, 118, 119, 138, 182
- 1 report not received: Convention No. 117

Chad — 11 reports requested
(Paragraphs 27 and 31)
- All reports received: Conventions Nos. 14, 26, 29, 41, 81, 87, 105, (132), 135, 151, (182)

Chile — 14 reports requested
- All reports received: Conventions Nos. 8, 9, 16, 22, 29, 63, 103, 105, 115, 135, 138, 140, 151, 182

China — 8 reports requested
- All reports received: Conventions Nos. 16, 22, 23, 138, (150), (167), 170, (182)

Cyprus — 17 reports requested
(Paragraph 31)
- All reports received: Conventions Nos. 16, 23, 29, 81, 92, 105, 111, 135, 138, 142, 147, 150, 151, 154, 160, 171, (182)

Denmark — 30 reports requested
(Paragraph 31)
- 24 reports received: Conventions Nos. 8, 16, 29, 73, 81, 92, 105, 111, 119, 120, 122, 129, 134, 135, 138, 139, 144, 147, 149, 151, 160, 163, 169, 182
- 6 reports not received: Conventions Nos. 9, 52, 53, 108, 142, 150

Dominica — 14 reports requested
(Paragraph 31)
- 8 reports received: Conventions Nos. 8, 14, 22, 29, 81, 105, 111, 138
- 6 reports not received: Conventions Nos. 16, 100, 108, (144), (169), (182)

France — 30 reports requested

- All reports received: Conventions Nos. 8, 9, 16, 22, 23, 29, 53, 55, 56, 63, 68, 69, 71, 73, 74, 81, 82, 92, 105, 108, 129, 133, 134, 135, 138, 142, 145, 146, 147, 182

France - French Guiana — 28 reports requested

- All reports received: Conventions Nos. 8, 9, 16, 22, 23, 29, 53, 55, 56, 58, 68, 69, 71, 73, 74, 81, 92, 105, 108, 112, 113, 125, 129, 133, 135, 145, 146, 147

France - French Southern and Antarctic Territories — 20 reports requested
(Paragraph 31)

- All reports received: Conventions Nos. 8, 9, 16, 22, 23, 53, 58, 68, 69, 73, 74, 87, 92, 98, 108, 111, 133, 134, 146, 147

France - Guadeloupe — 28 reports requested
(Paragraph 31)

- All reports received: Conventions Nos. 8, 9, 16, 22, 23, 29, 53, 55, 56, 58, 68, 69, 71, 73, 74, 81, 92, 105, 108, 112, 113, 125, 129, 133, 135, 145, 146, 147

France - Martinique — 28 reports requested
(Paragraph 31)

- All reports received: Conventions Nos. 8, 9, 16, 22, 23, 29, 53, 55, 56, 58, 68, 69, 71, 73, 74, 81, 92, 105, 108, 112, 113, 125, 129, 133, 135, 145, 146, 147

France - Réunion — 28 reports requested
(Paragraph 31)

- All reports received: Conventions Nos. 8, 9, 16, 22, 23, 29, 53, 55, 56, 58, 68, 69, 71, 73, 74, 81, 92, 105, 108, 112, 113, 125, 129, 133, 135, 145, 146, 147

France - St. Pierre and Miquelon — 21 reports requested
(Paragraph 31)

- All reports received: Conventions Nos. 9, 16, 22, 23, 29, 53, 55, 56, 58, 63, 69, 71, 73, 81, 105, 108, 125, 129, 145, 146, 147

Ghana — 29 reports requested
(Paragraph 31)

- 22 reports received: Conventions Nos. 1, 8, 14, 22, 29, 30, 69, 74, 87, 89, 94, 98, 100, 103, 106, 107, 108, 111, 149, 150, 151, 182
- 7 reports not received: Conventions Nos. 16, 23, 58, 81, 92, 105, 117

Guinea — 32 reports requested

- 17 reports received: Conventions Nos. 3, 14, 16, 29, 62, 95, 105, 113, 117, 122, 135, 139, 142, 150, 151, 152, 159
- 15 reports not received: Conventions Nos. 10, 26, 33, 81, 87, 94, 111, 118, 119, 120, 121, 133, 134, 140, 144

Haiti — 18 reports requested
(Paragraphs 20 and 31)

- 11 reports received: Conventions Nos. 14, 24, 25, 29, 81, 87, 98, 100, 105, 106, 111
- 7 reports not received: Conventions Nos. 1, 19, 30, 77, 78, 90, 107

Iceland — 7 reports requested

- All reports received: Conventions Nos. 29, 105, 108, 111, 138, 147, 182

Kyrgyzstan — 43 reports requested

- 4 reports received: Conventions Nos. (81), 87, 95, 100
- 39 reports not received: Conventions Nos. 11, 14, 16, 23, 27, 29, 32, 45, 47, 52, 69, 73, 77, 78, 79, 90, 92, 98, 103, (105), 106, 108, 111, 113, 115, 119, 120, 122, 124, 126, (133), 134, 138, 142, 147, 148, 149, 159, 160

Lesotho — 11 reports requested
(Paragraphs 27 and 31)

- 8 reports received: Conventions Nos. 87, 98, 100, (105), 111, 144, (150), (155)
- 3 reports not received: Conventions Nos. 45, 135, 167

Madagascar
18 reports requested

(Paragraph 27)
- 16 reports received: Conventions Nos. 81, 87, 88, (97), 98, 100, 111, 117, 119, 120, 122, 127, 129, 144, 159, (182)
- 2 reports not received: Conventions Nos. 13, 173

Malta
20 reports requested

- All reports received: Conventions Nos. 2, 13, 45, (53), 62, (74), 87, 88, 96, 98, 100, 111, 119, 127, 135, 136, (147), 148, 159, (180)

Netherlands - Netherlands Antilles
8 reports requested

(Paragraph 31)
- All reports received: Conventions Nos. 14, 29, 87, 88, 101, 106, 122, 172

Niger
13 reports requested

(Paragraph 31)
- All reports received: Conventions Nos. 6, 13, 14, 87, 98, 100, 102, 111, 119, 135, 142, 148, 154

Pakistan
17 reports requested

(Paragraph 27)
- 9 reports received: Conventions Nos. 1, 14, 45, 81, 89, (100), 106, 159, (182)
- 8 reports not received: Conventions Nos. 18, 87, 96, 98, 105, 107, 111, 144

Panama
13 reports requested

- All reports received: Conventions Nos. 13, 45, 87, 88, 98, 100, 111, 119, 120, 122, 127, 159, 181

Saint Vincent and the Grenadines
6 reports requested

- All reports received: Conventions Nos. 87, 98, 100, 101, 111, (180)

Serbia and Montenegro
43 reports requested

(Paragraph 31)
- 25 reports received: Conventions Nos. (12), (14), (19), 29, (32), (81), 87, (89), (90), (97), (98), 100, (102), (106), (111), (121), 122, 129, (132), 135, 138, (140), (142), (143), (158)
- 18 reports not received: Conventions Nos. (11), (13), (24), (25), (27), (45), (88), (113), (114), 119, (136), (139), (148), (155), (156), (159), (161), (162)

Seychelles
7 reports requested

(Paragraph 31)
- 6 reports received: Conventions Nos. 87, 98, 100, 111, 148, 151
- 1 report not received: Convention No. 2

Slovakia
29 reports requested

- All reports received: Conventions Nos. 13, 29, 34, 45, 87, 88, 98, 100, 102, 105, 111, 115, 120, 122, 128, 130, 136, 139, 144, 148, 155, (156), 159, 161, 167, (171), 173, 176, (184)

Slovenia
23 reports requested

- All reports received: Conventions Nos. 13, 45, 87, 88, 98, 100, 111, 119, 122, 135, 136, 138, 139, 140, 142, 148, 155, 159, 161, 162, (173), (175), (182)

Somalia
5 reports requested

(Paragraph 20)
- All reports received: Conventions Nos. 29, 45, 84, 105, 111

Swaziland
17 reports requested

- 15 reports received: Conventions Nos. 11, 14, 45, 81, 87, 89, 98, 100, 101, 105, 111, 131, (138), 144, (182)
- 2 reports not received: Conventions Nos. 29, 96

Sweden
26 reports requested

(Paragraph 31)
- All reports received: Conventions Nos. 13, 87, 88, 98, 100, 111, 115, 119, 120, 122, 128, 135, 139, 144, 148, 151, 154, 155, 159, 161, 162, 167, 170, 174, (175), 176

United Republic of Tanzania - Tanganyika   3 reports requested

- 1 report received: Convention No. 101
- 2 reports not received: Conventions Nos. 45, 88

Trinidad and Tobago   8 reports requested
(Paragraph 31)
- All reports received: Conventions Nos. 29, 87, 98, 100, 105, 111, 144, 159

Turkey   16 reports requested

- All reports received: Conventions Nos. 45, 87, 88, 96, 98, 100, 102, 111, 115, 119, 122, 127, 135, 144, 151, 159

United Kingdom   12 reports requested

- All reports received: Conventions Nos. 2, 87, 98, 100, 111, 115, 120, 122, 135, 144, 148, 151

United Kingdom - Anguilla   10 reports requested

- All reports received: Conventions Nos. 14, 29, 58, 82, 87, 98, 101, 105, 140, 148

United Kingdom - Falkland Islands (Malvinas)   7 reports requested

- All reports received: Conventions Nos. 14, 29, 45, 82, 87, 98, 105

United Kingdom - Isle of Man   5 reports requested
(Paragraph 31)
- All reports received: Conventions Nos. 2, 87, 98, 122, 151

Zambia   19 reports requested
(Paragraph 27)
- 5 reports received: Conventions Nos. 100, 111, 135, 148, (182)
- 14 reports not received: Conventions Nos. 87, 98, 105, 117, 122, 136, 141, 144, 149, 151, 154, 159, 173, 176

Grand Total

A total of 2,569 reports (article 22) were requested,
of which 1,852 reports (72.09 per cent) were received.

A total of 331 reports (article 35) were requested,
of which 303 reports (91.54 per cent) were received.

Appendix II. Statistical table of reports received on ratified Conventions as of 16 June 2005

(article 22 of the Constitution)

Conference year	Reports requested	Reports received at the date requested		Reports received in time for the session of the Committee of Experts		Reports received in time for the session of the Conference	
1932	447	-		406	90.8%	423	94.6%
1933	522	-		435	83.3%	453	86.7%
1934	601	-		508	84.5%	544	90.5%
1935	630	-		584	92.7%	620	98.4%
1936	662	-		577	87.2%	604	91.2%
1937	702	-		580	82.6%	634	90.3%
1938	748	-		616	82.4%	635	84.9%
1939	766	-		588	76.8%	-	
1944	583	-		251	43.1%	314	53.9%
1945	725	-		351	48.4%	523	72.2%
1946	731	-		370	50.6%	578	79.1%
1947	763	-		581	76.1%	666	87.3%
1948	799	-		521	65.2%	648	81.1%
1949	806	134	16.6%	666	82.6%	695	86.2%
1950	831	253	30.4%	597	71.8%	666	80.1%
1951	907	288	31.7%	507	77.7%	761	83.9%
1952	981	268	27.3%	743	75.7%	826	84.2%
1953	1026	212	20.6%	840	75.7%	917	89.3%
1954	1175	268	22.8%	1077	91.7%	1119	95.2%
1955	1234	283	22.9%	1063	86.1%	1170	94.8%
1956	1333	332	24.9%	1234	92.5%	1283	96.2%
1957	1418	210	14.7%	1295	91.3%	1349	95.1%
1958	1558	340	21.8%	1484	95.2%	1509	96.8%

As a result of a decision by the Governing Body, detailed reports were requested as from 1959 until 1976 only on certain Conventions.

Conference year	Reports requested	Reports received at the date requested		Reports received in time for the session of the Committee of Experts		Reports received in time for the session of the Conference	
1959	995	200	20.4%	864	86.8%	902	90.6%
1960	1100	256	23.2%	838	76.1%	963	87.4%
1961	1362	243	18.1%	1090	80.0%	1142	83.8%
1962	1309	200	15.5%	1059	80.9%	1121	85.6%
1963	1624	280	17.2%	1314	80.9%	1430	88.0%
1964	1495	213	14.2%	1268	84.8%	1356	90.7%
1965	1700	282	16.6%	1444	84.9%	1527	89.8%
1966	1562	245	16.3%	1330	85.1%	1395	89.3%
1967	1883	323	17.4%	1551	84.5%	1643	89.6%
1968	1647	281	17.1%	1409	85.5%	1470	89.1%
1969	1821	249	13.4%	1501	82.4%	1601	87.9%
1970	1894	360	18.9%	1463	77.0%	1549	81.6%
1971	1992	237	11.8%	1504	75.5%	1707	85.6%
1972	2025	297	14.6%	1572	77.6%	1753	86.5%
1973	2048	300	14.6%	1521	74.3%	1691	82.5%
1974	2189	370	16.5%	1854	84.6%	1958	89.4%
1975	2034	301	14.8%	1663	81.7%	1764	86.7%
1976	2200	292	13.2%	1831	83.0%	1914	87.0%

Conference year	Reports requested	Reports received at the date requested		Reports received in time for the session of the Committee of Experts		Reports received in time for the session of the Conference	
\multicolumn{8}{	c	}{As a result of a decision by the Governing Body (November 1976), detailed reports were requested as from 1977 until 1994, according to certain criteria, at yearly, two-yearly or four-yearly intervals.}
1977	1529	215	14.0%	1120	73.2%	1328	87.0%
1978	1701	251	14.7%	1289	75.7%	1391	81.7%
1979	1593	234	14.7%	1270	79.8%	1376	86.4%
1980	1581	168	10.6%	1302	82.2%	1437	90.8%
1981	1543	127	8.1%	1210	78.4%	1340	86.7%
1982	1695	332	19.4%	1382	81.4%	1493	88.0%
1983	1737	236	13.5%	1388	79.9%	1558	89.6%
1984	1669	189	11.3%	1286	77.0%	1412	84.6%
1985	1666	189	11.3%	1312	78.7%	1471	88.2%
1986	1752	207	11.8%	1388	79.2%	1529	87.3%
1987	1793	171	9.5%	1408	78.4%	1542	86.0%
1988	1636	149	9.0%	1230	75.9%	1384	84.4%
1989	1719	196	11.4%	1256	73.0%	1409	81.9%
1990	1958	192	9.8%	1409	71.9%	1639	83.7%
1991	2010	271	13.4%	1411	69.9%	1544	76.8%
1992	1824	313	17.1%	1194	65.4%	1384	75.8%
1993	1906	471	24.7%	1233	64.6%	1473	77.2%
1994	2290	370	16.1%	1573	68.7%	1879	82.0%
\multicolumn{8}{	c	}{As a result of a decision by the Governing Body (November 1993), detailed reports on only five Conventions were exceptionally requested in 1995.}
1995	1252	479	38.2%	824	65.8%	988	78.9%
\multicolumn{8}{	c	}{As a result of a decision by the Governing Body (November 1993), reports are henceforth requested, according to certain criteria, at yearly, two-yearly or five-yearly intervals.}
1996	1806	362	20.5%	1145	63.3%	1413	78.2%
1997	1927	553	28.7%	1211	62.8%	1438	74.6%
1998	2036	463	22.7%	1264	62.1%	1455	71.4%
1999	2288	520	22.7%	1406	61.4%	1641	71.7%
2000	2550	740	29.0%	1798	70.5%	1952	76.6%
2001	2313	598	25.9%	1513	65.4%	1672	72.2%
2002	2368	600	25.3%	1529	64.5%	1701	71.8%
2003	2344	568	24.2%	1544	65.9%	1701	72.6%
2004	2569	659	25.6%	1645	64.0%	1852	72.1%

II. SUBMISSION TO THE COMPETENT AUTHORITIES OF THE CONVENTIONS AND RECOMMENDATIONS ADOPTED BY THE INTERNATIONAL LABOUR CONFERENCE (ARTICLE 19 OF THE CONSTITUTION)

Observations and Information

(a) Failure to submit instruments to the competent authorities

The Employer members said that the obligation to submit instruments adopted by the International Labour Conference to the competent authorities arose from the ILO Constitution and that the term "competent authorities" normally referred to the legislature. This obligation involved two important elements. The first was the obligation to inform employers and workers, which derived from the ILO Constitution, and to consult them, in the case of countries that had ratified Convention No. 144. The second was the obligation to inform the competent authorities, sometimes accompanied by proposals in which governments expressed their views, it being understood that this did not imply the obligation to ratify a Convention or accept a Recommendation. They could even submit a Convention to the competent authorities and recommend that the Convention that was being submitted not be ratified, and compliance with this obligation therefore should not pose any problems. They urged governments to comply with this obligation and, if necessary, to request ILO technical assistance.

The Worker members emphasized that the obligation to submit instruments to the competent authorities constituted one of the fundamental mechanisms of the ILO system. It helped in strengthening relations between the ILO and national authorities, promoting the ratification of Conventions and in stimulating the tripartite dialogue at the national level. It was important for the Committee of Experts to explain the nature of this obligation and the means by which it was to be fulfilled. They emphasized that submission did not involve the obligation by governments to propose the ratification of the Conventions or the acceptance of the Recommendations under consideration. They expressed their concern at the great backlog built up by certain countries and the resulting difficulties in making it up. They hoped that the Committee would urge the governments of Member states to comply with this obligation and remind them of the possibility of having recourse to technical assistance for this purpose.

A Government representative of Cambodia said that the new Ministry of Labour, with the technical assistance of the ILO, would make every effort to submit to the competent authorities the instruments adopted from the 82nd to the 91st Sessions of the Conference.

The Employer members regretted that only one Government representative had provided information of any sort to explain its failure to submit instruments to the competent authorities. It was therefore necessary to reiterate the fact that submission did not imply ratification, but was an obligation that member States could and had to comply with and they therefore urged them to do so.

The Worker members indicated that the procedure in question should not give rise to problems in countries with a democratic system. It was clear that ILO instruments had to be submitted to the competent authorities. While noting the work of the Governing Body in revising the Memorandum concerning the obligation of submission, they hoped that the Memorandum would be widely distributed and, in particular, used to improve the situation and ensure that ILO instruments were submitted to the competent authorities.

The Committee noted the information and verbal explanations provided by the sole Government representative to have taken the floor. The Committee regretted that the countries listed, namely, Afghanistan, Armenia, Cambodia, Haiti, Lao People's Democratic Republic, Sierra Leone, Solomon Islands, Somalia, Turkmenistan and Uzbekistan, had not sent any information in this respect and urged them to supply reports in the near future containing information on the submission of Conventions, Recommendations and Protocols to the competent authorities. The Committee expressed deep concern at the delays and failures to submit instruments, and at the increase in the number of such cases, as these were obligations derived from the Constitution and were essential for the effectiveness of standards-related activities. In this respect, the Committee reiterated that the ILO could provide technical assistance to contribute to compliance with this obligation. The Committee decided to mention all the above cases in the appropriate section of the General Report.

(b) Information received

Djibouti. The ratification of Convention No. 182, adopted at the 87th Session of the Conference (1999), was registered on 28 February 2005.

Latvia. The instruments adopted by the Conference at the last ten sessions (from the 81st to the 91st Sessions) have been submitted, on 4 June 2004, to the Parliament of the Republic of Latvia.

Sao Tome and Principe. The ratifications of Conventions Nos. 182 and 184, adopted at the 87th and the 89th Sessions of the Conference (1999 and 2001, respectively), were registered on 4 May 2005.

III. REPORTS ON UNRATIFIED CONVENTIONS, RECOMMENDATIONS
(ARTICLE 19 OF THE CONSTITUTION)

(a) Failure to supply reports on unratified Conventions, on Recommendations and on Protocols for the past five years

The Worker members recalled that article 19 of the ILO Constitution established the obligation for member States to supply reports on unratified Conventions and Recommendations. These reports served as a basis for the drafting of general surveys and gave an overview of the obstacles that might prevent States from ratifying Conventions. The reports also showed whether standards were still adapted to the economic and social situation. This year, in the context of the General Survey, governments had had to supply reports concerning Conventions Nos. 1 and 30 on hours of work. In this regard, it was regrettable that only 52.57 per cent of the reports requested had been supplied. The Worker members emphasized that over the past five years too many countries had not fulfilled the obligation to supply reports on unratified Conventions and on Recommendations and urged the governments concerned to comply with article 19 of the ILO Constitution.

The Employer members said that the supply of reports on unratified Conventions was of great importance for the Committee of Experts to be able to prepare general surveys and examine the extent to which national law and practice were in accordance with the instruments concerned. They emphasized that cases of failure to submit reports in the last five years on unratified Conventions and on Recommendations should not give rise to problems in practice. They urged governments to comply with their obligations or, where appropriate, to explain the reasons why they had not been able to do so.

A Government representative of the Congo assured the Conference Committee of the commitment of his Government to comply with its constitutional obligations. In this respect, the Congo had ratified all the fundamental Conventions and last year reports on Conventions Nos. 13, 14, 26, 29, 81, 87, 89, 95, 98, 100, 105, 111, 119, 138, 144, 149, 150, 152 and 182 had been sent to the Office, thereby complying with the provisions of article 22 of the ILO Constitution. With regard to the supply of reports on unratified Conventions and on Recommendations, his country took due note of the comments made by the Committee of Experts. While indicating that his Government would take all the necessary measures as rapidly as possible to resolve this situation, he noted that one of the reasons for the failure to comply with this obligation was the change of government in his country.

A Government representative of the Dominican Republic invited the secretariat to take a careful look at the reasons for including the Dominican Republic on the list of countries which for the past five years had not submitted any of the reports requested for the preparation of the General Survey. He indicated that his country had ratified Convention No. 122, which had been the subject of the General Survey the previous year, and which indicated that the information provided by his Government had been examined by the Committee of Experts in the context of articles 19 and 22 of the ILO Constitution. Furthermore, information on his country had been included on 54 occasions in the General Survey of 2003 on the protection of wages. It would therefore be presumptuous to consider that his country had not met its obligations under article 19 of the Constitution. He asserted that his country complied with its obligations related to reporting and submission and responded to the Office's other requests, which was why he was surprised that his country had been included in the group of countries listed for non-compliance. Finally, he emphasized the importance of the ratification of the ILO's fundamental Conventions and their full implementation by the authorities and social partners.

A Government representative of Uganda stated that it was regrettable that his Government had not been able to supply the reports requested. He added that his Government had sought technical clarifications and guidance from the Office with respect to its obligations regarding the submission of these reports. The situation had now been settled, and his Government would, in the course of the first week of July 2005, supply reports on Convention No. 81, the Protocol of 1995 to Convention No. 81, Recommendations Nos. 81 and 82, Convention No. 129 and Recommendation No. 133.

A Government representative of Zambia referred to his previous statement in which he had deeply regretted that his Government had encountered difficulties in fulfilling its obligations to submit reports on time. He recalled that this was due to the restructuring of the Ministry of Labour, which had taken much longer than expected, and which had resulted in the early retirement of those officials who had been responsible for reporting to the ILO. However, the Ministry was now taking the necessary steps, with the assistance of the local ILO Office, to prepare these reports as soon as possible, and it would start training the new officials in the very near future.

The Worker members regretted that the statements made by Government representatives had not provided much new information on the reasons for their failure to supply reports. The Committee should therefore urge governments to comply fully with this obligation established by the ILO Constitution, thereby allowing the Committee of Experts to prepare complete general surveys.

The Employer members thanked the representatives of the four Governments which had presented additional information, but pointed out that this information had not provided any further significant elements. In one case, reference had been made to a change of government, in another to the restructuring of the Ministry of Labour, in a third to an error in relation to the receipt of the reports, and in another to the need for ILO technical assistance. They urged member States to collaborate in complying with this basic obligation and, where appropriate, to explain any difficulties encountered and the reasons for their failures to comply, as this would help to determine how attuned the instruments were to the situation at the national level.

The representative of the Secretary-General, in response to the statement by the Government member of the Dominican Republic, said that following a verification of the relevant files she could confirm that none of the reports due from his country for the past five years on unratified Conventions and on Recommendations had been received by the Office. She added that, with a view to the preparation of general surveys that were as complete as possible, in cases where it was not supplied directly by the government, the Office endeavoured to find information that was available on the countries concerned. She indicated that the Office was prepared to discuss with the Government any difficulties that it was encountering in this regard.

The Committee noted the information and explanations provided by the Government representatives who had taken the floor. The Committee emphasized the importance that it attached to the constitutional obligation of supplying reports on unratified Conventions and on Recommendations. Such reports made it possible to evaluate the situation more fully in the context of the general surveys prepared by the Committee of Experts. The Committee urged all member States to comply with their obligations in this respect and expressed the firm hope that the Governments of Afghanistan, Bosnia and Herzegovina, Congo, Democratic Republic of the Congo, Dominican Republic, Guinea, Guyana, Kazakhstan, Kyrgyzstan, Liberia, Sao Tome and Principe, Sierra Leone, Solomon Islands, Tajikistan, The former Yugoslav Republic of Macedonia, Togo, Turkmenistan, Uganda, Uzbekistan and Zambia would comply in future with their obligations under article 19 of the Constitution. The Committee reaffirmed the availability of the Office to provide technical assistance to help in complying with these obligations. The Committee decided to mention these cases in the appropriate section of its General Report.

The Worker members indicated that the present situation was a matter of concern as it involved serious breaches of constitutional obligations. Governments needed to make all possible efforts to fulfil their obligations. They called for a discussion to be held on the methods of work relating to cases of serious failure of member States to respect their obligations to supply reports and other standards-related obligations so as to prepare for the next session of the Committee on this issue.

The Employer members agreed with the Worker members that the failure of member States to respect their reporting or other standards-related obligations constituted a serious failure in the system in general. It was necessary to improve the procedures followed by the Conference Committee concerning these cases and for the Committee of Experts to provide fuller information, on a country-by-country basis, on why such failures in reporting were occurring, as well as on cases in which assistance was being provided. In their view, it would not be possible to solve these problems until the underlying reasons for non-compliance with reporting and other obligations were known and understood.

The representative of the Secretary-General, in response to the discussion, indicated that the Office had taken note of the suggestions made by the Employer and Worker members. The Office would examine once again the information made available to the Conference Committee with a view to providing it with much fuller information next year. The countries concerned would be asked to provide explanations on the specific reasons which had prevented them from fulfilling their obligations, whether they were of an institutional, political or other nature, so that technical assistance could be provided to help overcome such obstacles. It was to be hoped that this process could be undertaken in consultation with the Officers of the Committee and that the information provided would allow the Conference Committee to engage in a fuller discussion of the important issues arising out of cases of serious failure by member States to respect their reporting or other standards-related obligations.

(b) Information received

Since the meeting of the Committee of Experts, reports on unratified Conventions and on Recommendations have subsequently been received from the following countries: Cameroon, Mali, Mongolia, Slovakia and St. Vincent and the Grenadines.

(c) Reports received on unratified Conventions Nos. 1 and 30 as of 16 June 2005

In addition to the reports listed in Appendix VII on page 135 of the Report of the Committee of Experts (Report III, Part 1B), reports have subsequently been received from the following countries: Barbados, Mongolia, Slovakia and Trinidad and Tobago.

INDEX BY COUNTRIES TO OBSERVATIONS AND INFORMATION CONTAINED IN THE REPORT

Afghanistan
   Part One: General report, paras. 140, 145, 149
   Part Two: I A (c)
   Part Two: II (a)
   Part Two: III (a)

Antigua and Barbuda
   Part One: General report, paras. 142, 145, 165
   Part Two: I A (a), (c)

Argentina
   Part Two: I B, No. 87

Armenia
   Part One: General report, paras. 140, 142, 143
   Part Two: I A (a), (b)
   Part Two: II (a)

Australia
   Part Two: I B, No. 98

Azerbaijan
   Part One: General report, paras. 143, 145, 163
   Part Two: I A (b), (c)

Bahamas
   Part One: General report, paras. 143, 163
   Part Two: I A (b)

Belarus
   Part Two: I B, No. 87

Bosnia and Herzegovina
   Part One: General report, paras. 143, 145, 149, 164
   Part Two: I A (b), (c)
   Part Two: I B, No. 87
   Part Two: III (a)

Burundi
   Part One: General report, paras. 145, 163
   Part Two: I A (c)
   Part Two: I B, No. 87

Cambodia
   Part One: General report, paras. 140, 145
   Part Two: I A (c)
   Part Two: II (a)

Cape Verde
   Part One: General report, paras. 145, 163
   Part Two: I A (c)

Colombia
   Part Two: I B, No. 87
   Part One: General report, paras. 145, 163

Belize
   Part One: General report, para. 158
   Part Two: I A (c)

Comoros
   Part One: General report, paras. 145, 165
   Part Two: I A (c)

Congo
   Part One: General report, paras. 149, 163
   Part Two: III (a)

CÙte d'Ivoire
   Part One: General report, para. 145
   Part Two: I A (c)

Democratic Republic of the Congo
   Part One: General report, paras. 145, 149
   Part Two: I A (c)
   Part Two: III (a)

Denmark (Greenland)
   Part One: General report, paras. 142, 145
   Part Two: I A (a), (c)

Djibouti
   Part One: General report, para. 145
   Part Two: I A (c)

Dominica
   Part One: General report, paras. 143, 165
   Part Two: I A (b)

Dominican Republic
   Part One: General report, para. 149
   Part Two: III (a)

Ecuador
   Part Two: I B, Nos. 77, 78

Equatorial Guinea
   Part One: General report, paras. 143, 165
   Part Two: I A (b)

Gambia
   Part One: General report, paras. 143, 165
   Part Two: I A (b)

Georgia
   Part One: General report, paras. 145, 163
   Part Two: I A (c)

Grenada
   Part One: General report, paras. 142, 145, 165
   Part Two: I A (a), (c)

Guatemala
   Part Two: I B, No. 87

Guinea
   Part One: General report, paras. 145, 149
   Part Two: I A (c)
   Part Two: III (a)

Guyana
   Part One: General report, paras. 145, 149, 165
   Part Two: I A (c)
   Part Two: III (a)

Haiti
   Part One: General report, para. 140
   Part Two: II (a)

Islamic Republic of Iran
   Part Two: I B, No. 95

Iraq
   Part One: General report, paras. 142, 143, 145
   Part Two: I A (a), (b), (c)

Kazakhstan
   Part One: General report, paras. 145, 149, 163
   Part Two: I A (c)
   Part Two: III (a)

Kiribati
    Part One: General report, paras. 142, 143
    Part Two: I A (a), (b)

Kyrgyzstan
    Part One: General report, paras. 143, 145, 149, 163
    Part Two: I A (b), (c)
    Part Two: III (a)

Lao People's Democratic Republic
    Part One: General report, paras. 140, 165
    Part Two: II (a)

Liberia
    Part One: General report, paras. 142, 143, 145, 149
    Part Two: I A (a), (b), (c)
    Part Two: III (a)

Libyan Arab Jamahiriya
    Part One: General report, paras. 145, 163
    Part Two: I A (c)

Mauritania
    Part Two: I B, No. 29

Myanmar
    Part One: General report, paras. 156, 159, 160
    Part Two: I B, No. 87
    Part Three: No. 29

Nepal
    Part Two: I B, No. 144

Netherlands (Aruba)
    Part One: General report, para. 145
    Part Two: I A (c)

Niger
    Part Two: I B, No. 182

Pakistan
    Part One: General report, para. 145
    Part Two: I A (c)

Panama
    Part Two: I B, No. 87

Paraguay
    Part One: General report, paras. 142, 143, 145
    Part Two: I A (a), (b), (c)

Peru
    Part Two: I B, No. 102

Qatar
    Part Two: I B, No. 182

Romania
    Part Two: I B, No. 81

Russian Federation
    Part Two: I B, No. 87

Saint Kitts and Nevis
    Part One: General report, paras. 143, 165
    Part Two: I A (b)
Saint Lucia
    Part One: General report, paras. 143, 145, 165
    Part Two: I A (b), (c)

Sao Tome and Principe
    Part One: General report, paras. 145, 149, 165
    Part Two: I A (c)
    Part Two: III (a)

Saudi Arabia
    Part Two: I B, No. 111

Serbia and Montenegro
    Part One: General report, para. 143
    Part Two: I A (b)

Sierra Leone
    Part One: General report, paras. 140, 149, 165
    Part Two: II (a)
    Part Two: III (a)

Solomon Islands
    Part One: General report, paras. 140, 142, 145, 149, 165
    Part Two: I A (a), (c)
    Part Two: II (a)
    Part Two: III (a)

Somalia
    Part One: General report, paras. 140, 165
    Part Two: II (a)

Sudan
    Part Two: I B, No. 29

Swaziland
    Part Two: I B, No. 87

Tajikistan
    Part One: General report, paras. 142, 143, 145, 149, 163
    Part Two: I A (a), (b), (c)
    Part Two: III (a)

United Republic of Tanzania - Zanzibar
    Part One: General report, para. 142
    Part Two: I A (a)

The former Yugoslav Republic of Macedonia
    Part One: General report, paras. 142, 145, 149, 165
    Part Two: I A (a), (c)
    Part Two: III (a)

Togo
    Part One: General report, paras. 149, 163
    Part Two: III (a)

Turkey
    Part Two: I B, No. 87

Turkmenistan
    Part One: General report, paras. 140, 142, 143, 149, 165
    Part Two: I A (a), (b)
    Part Two: II (a)
    Part Two: III (a)

Uganda
    Part One: General report, paras. 143, 149
    Part Two: I A (b)
    Part Two: III (a)

United Kingdom (Montserrat)
    Part One: General report, para. 145
    Part Two: I A (c)

United States
    Part Two: I B, No. 144

Uzbekistan
    Part One: General report, paras. 140, 149, 163
    Part Two: II (a)
    Part Two: III (a)

Bolivarian Republic of Venezuela
    Part Two: I B, No. 87

Yemen
    Part One: General report, para. 145
    Part Two: I A (c)

Zambia
    Part One: General report, paras. 145, 149
    Part Two: I A (c)
    Part Two: III (a)

Zimbabwe
    Part Two: I B, No. 98

No. 22 — Thursday, 16 June 2005

International Labour Conference

Provisional Record **22**
PART
Ninety-third Session, Geneva, 2005 THREE

THIRD PART

Special sitting to examine developments concerning the question of the observance by the Government of Myanmar of the Forced Labour Convention, 1930 (No. 29)

CONTENTS

	Page
A. Record of the discussion in the Committee on the Application of Standards...	2
B. Observation of the Committee of Experts on the Application of Conventions and Recommendations on the observance of the Forced Labour Convention, 1930 (No. 29) by Myanmar, ...	10
Document D.6	14
C. Report of the Director-General	14
I. Brief summary of developments since June 2004	14
II. Latest developments since March 2005	15
D. Report of the Liaison Officer a.i.	21
I. Activities of the Liaison Officer a.i. since March 2005	21
II. Developments on the concrete steps identified by the very High-Level Team (vHLT) and the Governing Body	21
III. Developments on specific allegations	22
Document D.7	26
E. Developments concerning the question of the observance by the Government of Myanmar of the Forced Labour Convention, 1930 (No. 29)	26
1. Document GB.291/5/1	26
2. Document GB.291/5/1(Add.)	45
3. Document GB.291/5/2	47
4. Document GB.292/7/1	55
5. Document GB.292/7/2	59
6. Document GB.292/7/2(Add.)	71
7. Document GB.292/7/3	75
8. Conclusions of the Governing Body at its 292nd Session (March 2005)	87

22 Part 3/1

A. RECORD OF THE DISCUSSION IN THE COMMITTEE ON THE APPLICATION OF STANDARDS

A Government representative of Myanmar indicated that, in their determination to eliminate forced labour and to continue Myanmar's cooperation with the ILO, the authorities in his country had taken significant actions in response to the conclusions and the aide-mémoire of the very High-Level Team (vHLT) which had visited Myanmar in February. The vHLT had been received by the Prime Minister of the Union of Myanmar on behalf of the State Peace and Development Council (SPDC) on 22 February 2005. The Prime Minister, in his letter of 10 March 2005 to the vHLT, had reiterated Myanmar's commitment to the elimination of the vestiges of forced labour in close cooperation with the ILO.

Turning to the case of U. Shwe Mahn, he recalled that U. Shwe Mahn had originally been sentenced to death for high treason, a sentence which had later been commuted to life imprisonment and then again reduced to five years' imprisonment. Hardly any nation would release someone who had committed such a serious crime. But the Myanmar authorities had released him, as requested by the Governing Body, to show the Myanmar authorities' willingness to further build confidence and as a sign of positive cooperation with the ILO. As such, this was a major concession on the part of the Myanmar Government. A focal point in the armed forces for dealing with Convention No. 29, headed by Deputy Adjutant-General Colonel Khin Soe and assisted by seven General Staff Officers Grade-1, had been established on 1 March 2005. Colonel Khin Soe and two members of the focal point had met with the ILO Liaison Officer a.i. on 12 May at the Department of Labour at the latter's request. There could be further meetings between them as and when necessary.

Indeed, the Minister for Labour had already informed the Director-General of the ILO of the aforementioned actions and had given such assurances by his letter dated 21 May 2005. He had also emphasized Myanmar's readiness to consider a new approach for the elimination of forced labour and to begin discussions at an appropriate time and level to be determined between the two sides. The Government of Myanmar had fully cooperated with the ILO Liaison Officer a.i. in dealing with the complaints related to requisitions of labour. All 50 cases in 2004 and further eight cases in 2005 reported by the ILO Liaison Officer a.i. had been disposed of.

Turning to three cases of complaints for exacting forced labour which were mentioned in the report of the Liaison Officer a.i. of June 2005 (Document No. C.App./D.6), the speaker noted that this document reported that there had been no further developments regarding the Toungup and Hinthada cases and that in the Aunglan case, the complainants had withdrawn the case under duress. Actually, in the Toungup case, actions had been taken against those responsible and the case had already been closed. In the Hinthada instance, the complaints against the head of the Village Peace and Development Council (VPDC) had been rejected by the Township Court as there was no evidence of forced labour. Then the head of VPDC, in his personal capacity, had lodged charges against the complainants for false complaints and defamation against him. The complainants had been found guilty and were fined accordingly. They had since been released after settling the fine. As for the Aunglan case, the Field Observation Team (FOT) had filed a report that Nga-pyin village road had been reconstructed annually by the villagers on a voluntary basis and there had been no forced labour nor forced cash contribution. In fact, U Win Lwin, the person who had died accidentally when a mound of laterite had collapsed on him, was the major beneficiary of the road since he was the sole owner of a motor vehicle in the village. His relatives had been deceived by a third person that had told them that they could receive financial compensation. Later on, they had withdrawn the complaint with their full consent. There had been no undue pressure from the authorities to force them to withdraw the case. In recent times, the authorities had encountered an increasing number of false complaints. They were ready to discuss with the ILO at an appropriate time and level to find a solution to this problem.

The ILO Liaison Officer a.i. had been accorded the same freedom of movement accorded to diplomats and UN personnel within the established procedures. The Liaison Officer a.i. had mentioned in his report that he was able to freely undertake travel in line with the previously established practice, and that he could visit parts of Mon State and southern Kayin State from 18 to 20 May at a very short notice. The above-mentioned actions of the Myanmar Government clearly testified to its political will and the commitment to eliminate forced labour in the country and its willingness to continue its cooperation with the ILO.

The speaker protested against the participation in the Committee by Mr. Maung Maung, who in his Government's view was a civil servant turned traitor, a criminal, a fugitive from justice and a terrorist. Myanmar had been put under constant pressure on the issue of forced labour by the ILO based on false, distorted and exaggerated information provided by him. He concluded by stating that his Government was firmly committed to the eradication of forced labour in the country.

The Worker members stated that once again the situation in Burma/Myanmar had worsened. Forced labour continued to rage with even greater brutality and the Government demonstrated its bad faith, as established by numerous sources, to mention only two, which would not raise any doubt: the report of the Committee of Experts and documents Nos. 6 and 7 prepared by the Office concerning recent developments.

The Committee of Experts had once again examined the follow-up given to the following recommendations of the Commission of Inquiry of 1998: (1) a legislative recommendation to modify the basic laws of 1907 and 1908, so as to bring them into conformity with Convention No. 29 by abolishing any possibility of requisitioning labour; (2) an administrative recommendation to ensure that, in practice, no forced labour could be imposed by the army, nor by other authorities; and (3) a judicial recommendation to apply effective criminal sanctions in cases of forced labour.

The report of the Committee of Experts was implacable: the laws were still not amended or modified in spite of 30 years of promises. The Orders left the laws unchanged and proved to be inefficient. At the very least, they had to be accompanied by concrete measures which would ensure that, in practice, no labour could be imposed. To that effect, the Committee of Experts recommended four types of action: (1) that specific and concrete instructions be issued to the civilian and military authorities. However, if they were in fact issued, they did not provide for or indicate the various forms of prohibited labour; (2) that publicity was given to the Orders. However, although they had been translated into all dialects, apparently they had not been distributed or displayed in ethnic areas, where the prevalence of forced labour appeared to be the highest; (3) the need to budget adequate means to hire free wage labour for public activities which were based on forced labour. In its latest report, the Government provided no information on this subject; and (4) that monitoring machinery be established. The Committee of Experts observed that the Convention 29 Implementation Committee, as well as field observation teams, lacked credibility. The allegations of forced labour were examined by the very same authorities that imposed the forced labour – the administration and the army – and were therefore systematically rejected. The cases brought before the courts were systematically rejected and declared not receivable. For the first time, the complaints were brought before the courts, but none of the six complaints lodged in 2004 had been declared receivable. Even worse, following their contacts with the ILO Liaison Officer a.i., certain victims had been arrested or imprisoned for alleged defamation.

The observation of the Committee of Experts was to a large extent corroborated by the recent information provided by the Liaison Officer a.i. and the ICFTU, as well as by the specifics concerning the places, the factual dates and the names of implicated army officers. Thus, the ICFTU already had numerous incidents of forced labour and recruitment recounted by the victims to be included in its next report: other documents provided by the NGO mentioned other cases of exactions suffered by civilians and ethnic minorities. The political context had deteriorated. The Government had changed faces but not policy. The permanent representative of the Government in Geneva could not continue to carry out his functions and Aung San Suu Kyi was still strictly assigned to her residence where she was virtually held incommunicado.

The total lack of cooperation with the ILO had been demonstrated on several occasions: the vHLT had not been received at the appropriate level and the Liaison Officer a.i. did not dispose of the initially accepted freedom of movement. Certainly, two or three positive facts could be noted: the liberation of U. Shwe Mahn, who nevertheless remained convicted of terrorism and high treason; the fact that the Supreme Court had declared that the contacts with the ILO had not constituted an offence; several proceedings instituted against several guilty persons – civilians – and not military ones, who were mainly responsible for forced labour.

After reviewing the case of Myanmar once again, the conclusion stayed clear; the sentiment was that, unfortunately, forced labour was "far from being a practice on the way to extinction", that the Government was not at all disposed to eliminate forced labour in the country and that moreover, henceforth, proceedings would be instituted against those complainants who submitted a complaint based on motives found to be groundless.

The Worker members protested against the accusations brought by the Government against the persons who strove for freedom of association and freedom of speech – a familiar method in the history of infamous governments.

The Worker members quoted from the 2004 Conference Committee conclusion that "the Governing Body at its next session should be ready to draw the appropriate conclusions, including reactivation and review of the measures and action taken including those regarding foreign direct investment, called for in the resolution of the International Labour Conference of 2000, unless there was a clear change in the situation in the meantime".

The Worker members observed that the Governing Body had discussed Burma and Convention No. 29 in November 2004 and March 2005, and, given the absence of any significant change, drew the appropriate conclusions. If anything, the situation had deteriorated both politically and in regard to the Government's cooperation with the ILO.

The Worker members pointed out that the development of a new Constitution lacked credibility inside the country and within the international community, as the National League for Democracy (NLD) was still barred from participating and its leader remained under house arrest. They understood that there had been no access to her for many months and there were growing concerns about her health.

A number of ethnic areas such as Shan State and Arakan State had experienced new suppression, arrests and turmoil. The International Confederation of Free Trade Unions (ICFTU) had documented an increase in forced labour in these areas. The discussion was not about the degree to which the Government was cooperating with the ILO, but about what the ILO could do on behalf of victims of forced labour. They said that the ineffectiveness of actions over many years had condemned many people to fundamental human rights abuses.

Quoting the Director-General's document, the worker members pointed out that a broad majority of Governing Body members were of the opinion that the reactivation of the measures to be taken under article 33 of the ILO Constitution in accordance with the 2000 Conference resolution would be fully justified. The vHLT was obliged to abort its mission after only two days having failed to secure meetings at the highest level.

The Governing Body of March 2005 attempted to ascertain what few positive developments had taken place and they accepted that some were not unimportant. However, forced labour was still being exacted with absolute impunity, not a single military official having been prosecuted. In addition, most of the concrete steps outlined in the aide-memoire of the vHLT had not been implemented. The ILO's patience had almost run out. The March Governing Body agreed to a reactivation of the measures under article 33 and this was acted on by the Director-General in April. The reactivation was carried out in a 'soft' manner in the hope of positive developments with regard to the strengthening of the ILO presence among others.

But, even given the belated release of U. Shwe Mahn and his apparent good health, he still remained guilty of high treason for simply providing information on forced labour to the ILO and his association with the Federation of Trade Unions-Burma (FTUB). This could not be allowed to stand. Furthermore, there had been more negative developments over the past few weeks: the strengthening of the ILO presence was being hampered by visa refusal for an additional staff member and of the Liaison Officer a.i. freedom of movement was severely restricted. He now had to submit an itinerary 14 days in advance.

Finally, and most insidious of all, the Liaison Officer a.i. had been informed that "false complaints of forced labour were placing a great drain on government resources and undermining the dignity of the State ... and that legal action would be taken against complainants or their representatives who lodged false complaints". The ILO had directed the Liaison Officer a.i. to suspend contacts in view of the seriousness of this development.

Referring to the report of the Liaison Officer a.i. it appeared that not a single case of forced labour that he had brought to the attention of the authorities since March 2005 had been found to be valid. Those who had provided the information to the Liaison Officer a.i. were now liable to prosecution under the new policy. They sought assurances that this would not happen.

The Worker members found it ominous that the notion of voluntary labour had crept back into the response of the Implementation Committee to explain away the allegations.

The Worker members were of the opinion that the Government had quite deliberately set out to undermine the ILO presence and neutralize the ability of the Liaison Officer a.i. to receive complaints or even talk to people.

In view of the foregoing, the Worker members presented a number of proposals. The constituents should give particular attention to ensuring that no direct foreign investment, imports or exports, grants, loans or credits should be made to state or military-owned enterprises, including those operated by international private equity funds, would contribute directly or indirectly to the perpetuation or extension of forced or compulsory labour. Several States and organizations had already taken steps along these lines. Secondly, the Worker members proposed that the constituents should report regularly on the above-mentioned issue in time for the November Governing Body to allow the situation to be assessed and a plan of action to be undertaken by the ILO.

The Worker members called on the Conference Committee to request the Director-General to invite all international organizations referred to in the 2000 resolution to reconsider any cooperation with the Government and to assess and report on any forms of material and financial assistance extended to the country which could affect directly or indirectly the practice of forced labour. The request applied to international and regional financial institutions, multilateral development agencies, and international lending agencies.

The Worker members also proposed that the Director-General be invited to renew the ILO's request to the ECOSOC that it place on the agenda of its July 2006 session, an item concerning Myanmar's consistent failure to implement the recommendations contained in the report of the ILO Commission of Inquiry.

The Worker members further proposed that the Committee share the view of the vHLT and the Governing Body with regard to the necessity to further strengthen the Liaison Office, insisting on the importance of its field capacity, and that the Liaison Office concentrate on reinforcing policy dialogue with national authorities, including members of the State Peace and Development Council (SPDC) and the military at all levels, taking advantage of the authorities' commitment to "constructive cooperation with the ILO", as expressed in the Minister of Labour's letter of 21 May 2005.

Finally, the Worker members proposed that ILO monitoring activities on forced labour be further developed, especially with respect to ethnic areas. The Worker members called on the Government to guarantee the complete freedom of movement of the Liaison Officer a.i. and issue visas without further delay for additional staff. They demanded that the Government completely exonerate those convicted of high treason because of their contact with the ILO and the FTUB, as well as an end to the new policy of prosecuting those considered to be providing false information regarding forced labour to the ILO.

The ILO's credibility was at stake and it must continue to compel the Government to live up to its obligations under Convention No. 29, as well as to demonstrate to all those affected by forced labour that the international community, led by the ILO, actively supported their expectations for a better life.

The Employer members shared the concerns of the Worker members in relation to this long-standing and troublesome case. They observed that the Conference Committee's mandate to examine the measures taken to implement the Commission of Inquiry's recommendations and to apply Convention No. 29 by Myanmar was straight forward. As a fundamental matter, there was a gross failure by the Government of Myanmar to meet the international obligations that it had voluntarily undertaken 50 years ago to eliminate forced labour.

The Employer members considered that the fact that the Government's failure to implement Convention No. 29 was so obvious, rendered incomprehensible its failure to remedy the situation. The legal authority for the exaction of forced labour continued to be in place, as the Village Act and the Towns Act continued to confer broad authority on local authorities to requisition labour in violation of Convention No. 29. Noting that the Government representative had spoken of constraints in this respect, the Employer members observed that the only constraint they could identify was a lack of political will. Besides failing to revoke the Village and Towns Acts, no other concrete action had been taken to immediately bring to an end the exaction of forced labour in practice, in particular by the military, as called for by the Commission of Inquiry and the Committee of Experts. In paragraph 6 of its observation, which highlighted the heart of the matter, the Committee of Experts had identified four areas in which action should be taken by the Government to achieve this outcome, namely issuing specific and concrete instructions to civilian and military authorities to end the practice of forced labour, ensuring that the prohibition of forced labour be given wide publicity, providing budgeting of adequate means for the replacement of forced labour and ensuring the enforcement of the prohibition of forced labour. As the Government had never said that it could not put a stop to forced labour, it was obvious to the Employer members that it simply lacked the will to do so.

The Employer members observed that in contrast to previous years, when the Government used to take some small steps just before the Conference, the situation this year involved a regression in the Government's attitude and backsliding from the previous state. Following a discussion at the November 2004 Governing Body, a vHLT had arrived in Yangon only to find out that it would be unable to meet with the highest authorities in Myanmar even though the Government had been aware of the vHLT's terms of reference. Moreover, the Conference Committee had now been informed that the ILO Liaison a.i. Officer had limited freedom of movement. The fact that the Governing Body had decided to transmit the 2000 resolution adopted by the Conference under article 33 of the ILO Constitution, to the ILO member States and international organizations for appropriate action, indicated that it had lost its "wait-and-see" attitude and was losing patience.

The Employer members considered that the begrudging attitude of the Government to the release of prisoners and its minimalist proposal for a "new approach" hardly inspired any confidence. In their view, the bottom line was not the "process" but the achievement of substantive outcomes in the elimination of forced labour. It was now time for concrete action. Anything else was a travesty of international justice and the rights of forced labourers in Myanmar. The Employer members concluded by inviting the Myanmar Government to do the right thing by effectively eliminating forced labour.

The Government member of Luxembourg, speaking on behalf of the Member States of the European Union, as well as Bulgaria and Romania as countries in the accession process; Turkey and Croatia as candidate countries; Albania, the former Yugoslav Republic of Macedonia, Bosnia and Herzegovina and Serbia and Montenegro as countries of the Stabilisation and Association Agreement and potential candidate countries; Norway as a member of the European Free Trade Association (EFTA) and of the European Economic Area; and Switzerland and Liechtenstein as members of EFTA, observed that no convincing steps had been taken by the authorities in Burma/Myanmar as a follow-up to the aide-mémoire of the vHLT who had visited the country in February 2005 as well as the letter of the Director-General of the ILO. This ran against the request made by the March 2005 session of the Governing Body for the Burma/Myanmar authorities to take urgent and well-defined steps to eradicate forced labour, and the European Union's request for these steps to be implemented "well before the June 2005 International Labour Conference". The European Union shared the Committee of Experts' grave concern at the lack of implementation by the authorities in Burma/Myanmar of the 1998 recommendations of the Commission of Inquiry suggesting that legislation be brought into line with Convention No. 29, that the local authorities, especially the military, no longer impose forced or compulsory labour, and that those imposing forced labour be brought to justice. Although these recommendations were made seven years ago and were still valid, no significant and sustained action had been taken for their implementation.

Although the European Union continued to believe in the value of the Joint Plan of Action, designed to eradicate forced labour, they shared the concerns of the vHLT with regard to its future as recent actions by the Burma/Myanmar authorities had called into question their commitment to this Plan of Action. The authorities' persistent policy of unnecessary delay indicated a lack of will which was further reflected in the fact that the authorities had still not created an environment in which victims of forced labour could be assured that they would not suffer retaliation for their cooperation with the ILO. In this respect, the European Union called for assurances from the Burma/Myanmar authorities at the highest level that no action would be taken against any person who lodged a complaint on forced labour.

The European Union and the other delegations noted that in spite of the Burma/Myanmar authorities' repeated assurances of good intentions, in practice forced labour continued to be exacted on a very broad scale in many parts of the country, in particular by the military, and sometimes in circumstances of severe cruelty and brutality as had been noted by the Committee of Experts. While changes could not occur overnight, the ILO had been considering this issue for nine years, the Commission of Inquiry had provided a set of recommendations, High and very High-Level Teams had visited the country, and an aide-mémoire containing concrete steps to facilitate the effective eradication of forced labour had been presented to the authorities, and even a Joint Plan of Action had been elaborated. A period of nine years seemed to be more than adequate for the Burma/Myanmar authorities to have brought their practices into line with the ILO recommendations. Despite this, the measures taken had been insignificant to address effectively the continuous practice of forced labour in the country.

Although the European Union and the other delegations welcomed the release of U. Shwe Mahn, they also considered that neither he nor the other two persons should have been charged in the first place, simply for having contacts with the ILO, and that the charges against all three persons involved should be lifted altogether. Moreover, although they welcomed the fact that the Liaison Officer a.i. had been able to meet with the Foreign Minister and had been promised "interaction" with the military focal point, they considered that convincing evidence of a substantive change in political will, approach and corresponding action by the authorities was still lacking. They continued to believe that the ILO should have access to the authorities at the highest level on a regular basis.

The European Union had therefore come to the following conclusions. First, the European Union asked for measures under article 33 of the ILO Constitution to be revisited with a view to their reinforcement, considering that a wait-and-see approach was no longer acceptable when forced labour was continuing, and in some cases leading even to the death of those involved. Second, the European Union demanded that the authorities in Burma/Myanmar took immediate and concrete steps to eradicate forced labour, as outlined in the report of the Commission of Inquiry in 1998 and in the aide-mémoire of the vHLT in February 2005, and further asked for an explicit reference in the proposed draft Constitution banning the practice of forced labour, in line with Myanmar's commitments to the ILO. Third, the European Union strongly supported maintaining and reinforcing the ILO's presence in Burma/Myanmar to achieve this goal. The implementation of a facilitator mechanism, as outlined in the Joint Plan of Action would be a step in the right direction.

The Government member of the United States pointed out that once again, the reports before the Conference Committee presented a mixed picture of developments concerning the Government of Myanmar's observance of Convention No. 29. The Government representative indicated that in February 2005, the authorities had informed the ILO Liaison Officer a.i. that a township court had convicted and sentenced four local officials under section 374 of the Penal Code in three separate trials. Though the Government of the United States could not confirm that the officials were serving their sentences, this was the first time that a complaint had been lodged under this section of the Penal Code. She recalled that one of the Commission of Inquiry's recommendations was that penalties under this section be strictly enforced. Three trials in one court did not constitute strict enforcement in a country where forced labour was as widespread as it was in Myanmar, but she indicated that the Government of the United States did not discount this development. And, although U. Shwe Mahn should never have been imprisoned, his release in April and the meeting of the Liaison Officer a.i. with the army focal point for forced labour in May were steps in the right direction.

But these steps were overshadowed by the many other indications that the Government's stated commitment to eliminate forced labour was mere rhetoric. The vHLT had not been received at the appropriate level in Rangoon and had to cut short its visit. The Government had not approved the ILO's request to send another official to Myanmar to assist the Liaison Officer a.i. The Convention 29 Implementation Committee's response to the numerous complaints of forced labour submitted to it by the Liaison Officer a.i. had been inadequate, and in April, the Government had informed the Liaison Officer a.i. that legal action would be taken against so-called "false complaints", a development that struck at the heart of the Plan of Action to which the Government had once said it was committed. None of the three recommendations of the Commission of Inquiry had been carried out. Moreover, all the available evidence indicated that the use of forced labour, particularly by the army, continued unabated and was sometimes accompanied by acts of extreme violence.

Finally, the Government representative stated that under these circumstances, the Minister of Labour's offer to the Director-General to consider a new approach for the elimination of forced labour appeared to be little more that a delaying tactic. She considered that the authorities had had an opportunity to discuss a new approach when the vHLT visited Rangoon in February, but had declined to do so. The Government needed to demonstrate by its deeds that its commitment to the Plan of Action was genuine and that it was prepared to create the conditions under which the Plan could be implemented. It should comply fully with the suggestions made by the vHLT in its aide-memoire. The time was long past when the ILO could be satisfied with discussions of a new approach for the elimination of forced labour in the absence of evidence that the Government was prepared to carry them out. The Government representative therefore repeated her strong plea to demand action instead of promises for the sake of Myanmar's workers and workers everywhere.

The Worker member of Singapore expressed regret at the fact that the issue of forced labour in Myanmar had been under discussion for 11 years without much progress, which demonstrated the Government's contempt for the ILO supervisory mechanism. The feeble explanations given each time in order to obfuscate and divert attention from the real issues had generated growing frustration. The Conference Committee should no longer maintain a "wait-and-see" attitude while Burmese people were being forced into bondage and tortured if they refused to do so and while children were being forced into the army. The Conference Committee should not forget that each of the complaints of forced labour received by the Liaison Officer a.i. and the thousands of documented complaints by the ICFTU, FTUB and other human rights organizations represented human lives which had been subjected to the cruellest form of deprivation, i.e., of one's freedom to decide whether or not to work.

The speaker emphasized that, according to the Liaison Officer a.i., the worst forms of this cruel treatment had taken place against the ethnic minorities primarily in the remote border areas where there was heavy military presence. The Asia Forum for Human Rights and Development (Forum-Asia) had reported the continued persistence of forced labour, extortions and exactions concerning the Rohyngia Muslims in the Northern Rakhine State. They were forced to do sentry duty and erect gates and bamboo fences around the hamlets of Maungdaw purportedly to protect the villagers, but they had to provide their own construction materials, such as bamboo and wooden poles and were also required to maintain the gate and fences. Two hundred fifty Rohyngia Muslim villagers in Maungdaw were forced to build a model village with houses for those resettled from other parts of Burma. In the words of one Rohyngia villager from the Gaw Yah Khar Li Village Tract in Maungdaw Township, "we are living like slaves inside our own country. We have no rights there. They can confiscate our land any time. They can use us as labour whenever they want". The speaker deplored this situation and emphasized that the Burmese Government should be made to stop this.

The speaker further noted with grave concern the intimidation and harassment conducted against those who complained of forced labour including through the applicable legal processes, noting that the ability to complain without fear of persecution was absolutely essential to preserve the integrity of the system. Three forced labour complaints had been rejected by the courts purportedly because of lack of evidence. The speaker found it appalling that two of the three dismissed complainants had been prosecuted for defamation and imprisoned for six months. She further took note of the grave concerns raised by the Liaison Officer a.i. in his report with regard to his meeting with the Director-General of the Department of Labour on 26 April 2005 during which the latter had again stressed that legal action would be taken against those who lodged false complaints. Furthermore, on 9 March 2004, three persons had been convicted of high treason including on the basis of contacts with the ILO Liaison Officer a.i. Although the Court had decided that such contacts were legal, it nevertheless seemed to imply that the ILO was some kind of an illegal or clandestine body for which a special ruling was necessary. This undermined the very basis for having a Liaison Office. In addition to this, there had not been a single conviction under section 374 of the Penal Code, despite numerous complaints of forced labour. Moreover, specific complaints brought to the attention of the Convention 29 Implementation Committee had been systematically denied. Finally, the Liaison Officer a.i. had indicated in his report that two individuals had been arrested after returning to their village following a visit to him in Yangon to lodge a complaint. This demonstrated the systematic failure to investigate forced labour cases and raised serious doubts about the credibility of the system. The speaker concluded by urging the Government to stop the persecution of minorities through the use of forced labour, the forced recruitment of child soldiers and the harassment against those filing complaints of forced labour. She called for a strengthening of the ILO's presence in Myanmar and supported the suggestion of the Liaison Officer a.i. to second an ILO official to Yangon.

The Government member of Australia expressed strong support for the role played by both the vHLT and the ILO Liaison Officer a.i. in Yangon, in assisting the Myanmar authorities to observe Convention No. 29, and further supported the Office's expansion to provide greater technical cooperation, calling upon the Myanmar Government to take the simple step of granting a visa allowing an additional ILO staff member to join the Liaison Office. Noting that the elimination of forced labour practices throughout the country should be given high priority based on the firm commitment of the Government, the speaker deeply regretted the circumstances which prevented the vHLT from successfully completing its mandate and again called upon Myanmar to cooperate fully with the ILO so as to demonstrate its commitment to eliminating forced labour. Critical to this would be urgent action on all the four points set out in the vHLT's aide-mémoire of 23 February 2005. The speaker further commended the decision to release U. Shwe Mahn but also expressed disappointment at the fact that he continued to be impugned. Noting the Government's willingness to consider a new approach to the elimination of forced labour, he urged it to move quickly to engage the ILO at a senior level to ensure that this commitment was translated into concrete action. He noted that despite commitments made, the Conference Committee still awaited real results and should therefore recommend to the Governing Body to closely consider progress in the Government's new approach at its meeting in November 2005.

He further noted the establishment of a focal point on forced labour in the military to address the serious problems of requisition of labour by the Tatmadaw, and urged the Myanmar Government to ensure its full and effective cooperation. A critical first step in this respect would be to establish clear protocols for cooperation with the Liaison Officer a.i. and this could only be achieved through regular and open contacts. He further called on the Government of Myanmar to take genuine steps to ensure that Myanmar citizens could cooperate with the ILO with full confidence that they would not face retribution for doing so. The principle of unfettered access to the Liaison Officer a.i. and any facilitator was central to cooperation between the ILO and Myanmar and was a key requirement for the future implementation of the Plan of Action.

The Government representative concluded by emphasizing his country's deep concern over the situation in Myanmar. The Government had failed to address the troubling issues raised in the ILO and other international fora regarding forced labour and had failed to meet its international obligations in this respect. His country remained particularly concerned about the lack of concrete progress made toward political reform and national reconciliation in Myanmar, and the continued detention of political prisoners including Aung San Suu Kyi.

The Worker member of Italy pointed out that the military Government representative failed to address fundamental problems such as a highly centralized decision making structure, severe restrictions on private commercial activity, disproportionate military spending (49.9 per cent of public expenditure) to create the largest army in Southeast Asia. The country ranked 142 in the corruption ranking of 145 countries. Myanmar was the leading producer of methamphetamine and second producer of opium. The garment and textile industry was the conduit for money-laundering and clandestine export of narcotics. Business could not be carried out without the involvement of the junta under a 1989 law. The monopoly of economic production was in the hands of the Union of Myanmar Economic Holdings and its branch, Myanmar Economic Corporation. European Union foreign direct investment represented 30.37 per cent of total FDI, mostly in the oil and gas sector, the major funding instrument of the military regime. The EU's share of garment imports from Myanmar was about 66 per cent. Five ASEAN countries had invested some US$3.9 billion as of March 2004, representing 51.08 per cent of total FDI.

The speaker said that 15 years of constructive engagement and threats of political sanctions had failed to bring about even a single democratic reform aimed at ending forced labour. The fact that discussion on violations of Convention No. 29 were still ongoing demonstrated the Government's uncompromising attitude. Only coordinated international action could bring effective change. It was time for ILO constituents, international financial institutions, including the ADB, the Greater Mekong Subregion and the related Trade and Investment Flagship Programme to take effective measures. But international organizations and NGOs which had any dealings with the junta should also reconsider their cooperation. Governments, employers and workers should review their relations with Myanmar and take suitable steps, including recourse to the International Court of Justice, to fight against the continuation or extension of forced labour. The speaker appealed to them to ensure that no foreign direct or indirect investment, imports or exports, grants, loans or credits that could lead to the continuation or extension of forced labour be made to the regime. She also appealed to governments and the European Union to implement Article XX of the GATT, which referred to measures relating to the protection of human health and products of prison labour. Finally, she appealed to governments and enterprises to contribute to the changes necessary to bring democratic development and a stable economy.

The Government member of Canada expressed his country's grave concern at the lack of improvement in Burma's situation which remained extremely serious. He thanked the vHLT, the ILO Liaison Officer a.i. and the Office for their efforts in trying to engage the Burmese authorities and regretted the lack of cooperation by the authorities who prevented the vHLT from successfully completing its mission. The speaker welcomed the release of U. Shwe Mahn and noted that the Labour Minister's letter of 21 May 2005 to the ILO Director-General had indicated that Burma was ready to consider a new approach for the elimination of forced labour. Nevertheless, the absence of any significant improvement, and in particular the authorities' failure to imple-

22 Part 3/5

ment the measures recommended by the Commission of Inquiry and the aide-mémoire of the vHLT, was deeply disappointing. His country had watched with growing unease the unfavourable developments that had been unfolding in Burma and had made clear on many occasions that Aung San Suu Kyi and other leaders of the democratic movement should be liberated immediately and unconditionally while noting that the current National Convention process lacked any credibility. His country remained concerned about human rights violations, which were being perpetrated throughout the country, particularly in situations of conflict, including in addition to forced labour, extra-judicial executions, torture, rape, internal displacement and destruction of villages and livelihoods.

He concluded by calling on the Burmese authorities: (1) to take immediate and effective measures to eliminate forced labour as outlined in the report of the Commission of Inquiry of 1998 and in the aide-mémoire of the vHLT of February 2005; (2) to facilitate the addition of an ILO staff member to the Liaison Office; (3) to reinstate the freedom of movement necessary for the Liaison Officer a.i. to effectively fulfil his mandate; (4) to permit the establishment of a facilitator mechanism and ensure that no action be taken against any person who made a complaint concerning forced labour; (5) to undertake a dialogue with the ILO at the highest level to develop a new approach for the elimination of forced labour. The speaker finally indicated that in the absence of concrete results in the eradication of forced labour, his country supported strengthening the implementation of the measures enumerated in the 2000 resolution of the Conference.

The Worker member of the Netherland drew the Committee's attention to the role of the OECD Guidelines for Multinational Enterprises in the context of the implementation of the 2000 resolution of the Conference and the reporting thereon. The 2004 decision of the OECD Investment Committee to limit the scope of application of the Guidelines to FDI and FDI-related trade had considerably restricted the use of the Guidelines for this purpose. This was a fact even in countries such as the Netherlands where the Government had previously suggested that trade unions should address all economic relations of enterprises under the OECD Guidelines. As the ILO was stepping up its efforts to ensure implementation of the 2000 resolution, it was important also to review the role of these Guidelines. The speaker recalled that the National Contact Points set up by OECD member States had the task of promoting better awareness of the OECD Guidelines. In the context of Burma, this could mean giving more publicity to the reviewed economic relations of a given government with Burma. The Contact Points should also draw attention to the fact that, under the Guidelines, enterprises should make a contribution to the elimination of forced labour and should respect established government policies, for instance, as in the case of the Netherlands, a policy of discouragement of economic relations. The National Contact Points should seek the support of employers' organizations for such an awareness-raising campaign, while the trade unions should play a role in such an effort at the enterprise, national and international levels, including through the European Works Councils. The Trade Union Advisory Committee of the OECD had held two workshops in 2005 to draw the attention of European Works Councils to the OECD Guidelines. In cases of FDI and FDI-related trade, where enterprises refused to take the action demanded by the 2000 Conference Resolution and the OECD Guidelines, trade unions would continue to bring complaints to the National Contact Points. In the past, several such complaints had led to changes in the behaviour of companies. Where cases were outside the scope of the OECD Guidelines, the Government should open an alternative way for addressing them. In the Netherlands, efforts were being made to address the continued timber import from Burma by Dutch enterprises. Following appeals by the Netherlands Burma Center, some firms had agreed to stop their imports, while four enterprises had not, i.e. Worldwood, Bruijnzeel, Boogaerdt, and Van der Stadt.

The Government member of Indonesia, speaking on behalf of the Government members of the Association of South-East Asian Nations (ASEAN) countries, expressed appreciation to the ILO for its continuing support and cooperation with the Government of Myanmar in its effort to eliminate the practice of forced labour in the country. The ASEAN countries acknowledged the importance of the ILO presence in Myanmar and the role played by the Liaison Officer a.i. in assisting the Myanmar authorities in the observance of Convention No. 29. The commitment of the Government of Myanmar to observe the Convention and to eliminate the practice of forced labour in the country was welcomed. The positive developments as contained in the letter dated 21 May 2005 from the Minister of Labour of Myanmar to the Director-General were noted with interest, in particular the Government's readiness to consider a new approach in addressing the issue, the freedom of movement extended to the Liaison Officer a.i., the release of U. Shwe Mahn, in response to the aide-mémoire presented by the vHLT and the conclusions adopted by the Governing Body in March 2005, as well as the recent meeting of the Liaison Officer a.i. with the Ministry of Labour and the Army focal point, in compliance with ILO's request. It was important to continue the process of dialogue and cooperation rather than to adopt alternative measures. In this regard, the Government of Myanmar had expressed its willingness to continue to cooperate with the ILO. The ASEAN countries therefore called on the Myanmar Government and the ILO to continue their dialogue, while the Conference Committee should continue to play a constructive role in this matter.

The Government member of New Zealand recalled that her country had repeatedly called for immediate action by the Government of Myanmar to cease the deplorable practice of forced labour, to empower the victims of forced labour, and to set in place clear and tangible measures to punish perpetrators. However, she observed with deep concern and frustration that once more there had been little tangible improvement. She deeply regretted that the patience of the international community continued to be tried, that the small concessions made by the Government had not gone far enough, and most significantly, that these direct violations of the human rights of Myanmar's people continued to go unaddressed by their Government.

Concerning cooperation with the ILO, particularly through the resident presence in Yangon, which was an essential element of the Government of Myanmar's response to this serious situation, she remained concerned that the Liaison Officer a.i. had not regained the full range of freedom of movement granted to him previously and did not understand why it had not been possible for the Government to remove administrative barriers to the strengthening of the Liaison office. She looked forward to a credible explanation and corrective action in this regard. The international community required concrete evidence of the commitment of the Government of Myanmar to end forced labour. She took note of the meeting of the Liaison Officer a.i. with the military focal point and looked forward to more such meetings so that identifiable progress could be achieved. She also noted with interest the release of U. Shwe Mahn and trusted he would not suffer further harassment for carrying out his legitimate peaceful political activities.

The Government representative expressed concern, however, at the report of intimidation of those coming forward to the Liaison Officer a.i. with complaints of forced labour. She wished to express her country's support for the Plan of Action and noted that its implementation would depend on the establishment of the necessary political environment whereby complaints could be received by the Facilitator without fear of retribution. The fact that such conditions did not yet exist, and that the ILO Office had as a consequence been placed in an extremely difficult situation as outlined in the Report of the Director-General, should be of deep concern to the Conference Committee. She also noted that her country looked forward with interest to learning details of the "new approach" mentioned by the Government in their letter to the Director-General of 21 May 2005 and urged that this approach be based on the policy of zero tolerance to the use of forced labour and an immediate end to the culture of impunity.

She concluded by observing that although the ILO, through special sittings of the Conference Committee and discussions at the Governing Body, had registered time and again its deep concerns at the situation in Myanmar, the Government of Myanmar did not seem to have registered fully the seriousness of these concerns or share them. The time for concrete and credible action was well and truly overdue.

The Worker member of Japan stated that despite the promises of the Government, forced labour was being widely practised in Myanmar, as pointed out by the Committee of Experts. Political and financial support given by some countries to the Government of Burma through the Asian Development Bank (ADB) projects was one reason for the survival of the military regime and forced labour in Burma. Foreign investment in Burma had increased since the 2000 Conference resolution on Myanmar, with one-third of it being concentrated in the oil and gas sector. The ADB was involved in supporting the military regime through its Program of Economic Cooperation in the Greater Mekong Subregion (GMS Program) launched in 1992. In November 2001, the 10th Greater Mekong Sub-Region Ministerial Conference adopted a strategic framework for an integrated and prosperous Mekong subregion, identifying flagship programmes in areas such as transport and economic corridors, telecommunications and energy interchanges, and cross-border trade and investment. These programmes played an important role in encouraging ASEAN countries and multinational companies to invest in the energy sector in Burma. ADB had provided US$887 million in these projects, which included the Mawlamyine deep-sea port project and the Mawlamyine road section project in Burma. It was very regrettable that such financial and political support assisted the military regime to survive and thus forced labour continued to exist. Not only all ILO Members but also the ADB was responsible to eradicate forced labour in Burma. The speaker urged governments and employers to cease giving any advantages to the military regime of Burma.

The Government member of India noted that since the March 2005 session of the Governing Body the Liaison Officer a.i. had been able to visit certain parts of Mon State and southern Kayin State and had met with the Minister for Labour. He further took note of the assurances of continuing cooperation with the ILO provided by the Government of Myanmar and the new approach for the elimination of forced labour mentioned by the Minister of Labour in his letter dated 21 May 2005 to the ILO Director-General. The speaker noted that his country viewed these new developments positively and considered that the Government of Myanmar needed to be encouraged in its efforts to eliminate forced labour. He expressed the hope that the discussion before the Conference Committee would be constructive in helping the Government of Myanmar to move in the direction of further cooperation with the ILO.

The Worker member of the Republic of Korea raised the issue of the Shwe Natural Gas Project in Arakan State, in which Daewoo International and the Korea Gas Corporation were involved. Great concern had been expressed about these projects and their possible serious effect on local people, both in Arakan and Chin States, particularly with the increase in deployment of the armed forces under the pretext of guarding the pipeline. Forced relocation, forced labour, summary executions, torture and other human rights violations were claimed to have taken place, in relation to Unlocal and Total corporations. These claims seemed to be well founded, according to Nyi Nyi Lwin, who participated in the workshop on "What are the problems in the Shwe Natural Gas Project?", held in Seoul. Local fishermen entering the Shwe field were deprived of their ships and tortured. In addition, local inhabitants were drafted forcibly to cut down forests to build the Daewoo International Project Office. He requested the Government to ensure that measures would be taken to prevent the cases of Total and Unlocal being repeated. He called for the postponement of the extraction of the Shwe natural gas field until the time when the people of Western Burma could participate directly in decisions about the use of their resources and related infrastructure development without fearing persecution, including forced labour. He also called on the Government to provide more detailed information on the Shwe Natural Gas Project and to monitor it more closely. Finally, he also urged the Government of the Republic of Korea to suspend the Project and provide information to the Committee, taking all necessary measures in line with the Conference resolution of 2000 on the Shwe Natural Gas Project calling on constituents, the UN and other multilateral agencies to review relations with Myanmar and cease any relations that might aid the military junta to abet forced labour.

The Government member of Belarus declared that his country followed with attention developments in the situation of Myanmar, as appeared in the documents presented by the ILO and the information provided by the Government representative of Myanmar. Belarus took note of the progress which had taken place in the short period of time since the Governing Body's session of March 2005. He took note of positive dynamic, which demonstrated that a constructive dialogue with the authorities was taking place. Numerous facts attested to it: the extension of the dialogue between the ILO representative and the authorities and the confirmation of his freedom of movement in the country; the liberation of U. Shwe Mahn; the follow-up given to 56 complaints concerning forced labour, out of 58 in total; and the continuing progress in various directions provided for in the Plan of Action. The Government of Myanmar demonstrated by its deeds its engagement to fight sincerely the problem of forced labour in the country, the phenomenon which, according to the document "Alliance against forced labour in the world", today concerned more than 12 million individuals in all corners of the world. The speaker pointed out that progress in this domain would only be possible through constructive dialogue and cooperation with the ILO. The eradication of forced labour needed time and history had taught that when complex problems, especially social ones, were solved by force, the innocent population was the first to suffer and, in the end, the objectives were not reached.

The Worker member of Pakistan recalled that the issue of forced labour in Myanmar had been under discussion in the ILO since 1964 and that there was now urgency in making progress in eliminating this practice in the country. Forced labour was a violation of fundamental human rights and dignity, as emphasized by the 2005 Global Report under the Declaration of Fundamental Principles and Rights at Work. The Government of Myanmar had not yet amended the provisions of the Towns Act and the Village Act, which allowed for the exaction of forced labour, as requested by the Commission of Inquiry. The Government's argument that amendments could not be made due to the absence of a legislative body was devoid of truth, as it in fact recently had made legislative changes in other areas. He also urged the Government to implement all other recommendations of the Commission of Inquiry and the vHLT.

The Government member of the Russian Federation stated that the Russian Federation, like other participants in this discussion, was unconditionally devoted to the goal of eradicating forced labour in Myanmar. Energetic efforts undertaken by the Office to that end deserved to be commended. In fact, there had been recently some positive developments, such as the release of the third person originally convicted of high treason. Many members of the Committee had not considered these developments sufficient. The most effective way to achieve progress in this case was to continue dialogue with the Myanmar authorities, to preserve and develop the existing mechanisms of cooperation between the ILO and the Government of this country.

An observer representing the World Organization Against Torture stated that her organization was alarmed by the continued use of forced labour against hundreds of thousands of people in Myanmar, often associated with torture and other types of physical and psychological abuse. The Committee of Experts had been stressing its concern about the use of forced labour in Myanmar and the existence of legislation in contradiction with Convention No. 29 since 1964. However, no substantive measures had been taken by the Government to ban forced labour. As was noted by the ILO Director-General in his 2005 Global Report, still today there existed no political will in Myanmar to take strong measures against military and local authorities that benefited economically from forced labour.

The speaker emphasized that forced labour was always cruel, inhuman and degrading and as such it could be considered as an act of torture. In Myanmar, it was often accompanied by other forms of torture, including enforced displacement, rape, as well as food and health care deprivation or other ill-treatment resulting in death. Where resistance to forced labour was raised, further ill-treatment, detentions and extra-judicial executions followed. Furthermore, forced labour frequently entailed sexual exploitation, child labour, human minesweeping, the extortion and forced eviction of civilians, and extremely harsh labour conditions. Recent reports from the field spoke of government officers who had forced civilians to risk their lives by performing sentry duties, and a military commander who had beaten a civilian to death in Shan State for refusing to provide his vehicle for forced labour. Forum-Asia had provided evidence of renewed use of forced labour in the Northern Arakan State in construction work, harvesting, portering and other duties for the military. The enforced enrolment of children in the army, with the threat of imprisonment, was also a common practice throughout the country. She recalled that torture in Myanmar was by no means restricted to its direct association with forced labour and was often exerted upon pro-democracy activists, monks, or women in the form of sexual abuse.

She concluded by urging that all necessary measures be taken in order to ensure the compliance by Myanmar with the absolute interdiction of forced labour and other human rights abuses associated with it, and that concrete and energetic measures would be taken by the International Labour Conference to ensure the full implementation of Convention No. 29 and of the provisions of the June 2000 resolution.

The Government member of Japan said that it was clear from the discussion so far that many members were far from satisfied with the situation of forced labour in Myanmar. The question that therefore faced this Committee was whether to pursue punitive options or to further impress upon the Government of Myanmar the need to engage in dialogue and cooperation with the ILO. After long and agonizing consideration, his delegation had decided that the best way forward was to further encourage the Myanmar authorities to engage in dialogue with the international community. A number of positive steps had been noticed in this case, including the release of U. Shwe Mahn, who, in his view, could not be guilty of treason for having had contacts with the ILO, and the establishment of a focal point in the military for dealings with the ILO. Undoubtedly these positive steps needed to be further elaborated.

All positive steps that had been taken in Myanmar were due to the pursuance of dialogue between the international community and Myanmar. This should not be underestimated or undermined. The ILO was, and would be, an important contact in the country. As an outcome, it was important to ensure an improvement in the situation in the country, not just a demonstration of political will.

At the same time, excuses could not be made for the Myanmar Government. It was regrettable that improvement only occurred under pressure from the international community. His Government was not advocating a continuation of a "wait-and-see" attitude. To the contrary, he urged the Myanmar Government to take the concrete steps of facilitating contacts between the focal point in the armed forces on Convention No. 29 and the ILO at the appropriate high level, and ensuring full freedom of movement for the Liaison Officer a.i.. He also called for Members to use every multilateral and bilateral meeting at which Myanmar was present to remind the Government of its obligations. The situation should be further examined at the subsequent Governing Body session.

The Worker member of Germany recalled that the Governing Body had for years been dealing with the case of forced labour in Myanmar – an endless tragedy in which hundreds of thousands of people were subject to compulsory labour in road building and other infrastructure projects and services for the military, abduction of children by military forces, and, most recently, prosecution for having had contacts with the ILO. For years the Government of Myanmar had issued assurances that it was eliminating forced labour and cooperating with the ILO. Yet, she wondered why, if this were the case, instances of forced labour continued to be reported, no action had been documented by the Government in response to such complaints, no legal action had been taken against authorities that had used forced labour, the Liaison Officer a.i. was denied freedom of movement in the country, the vHLT had not been able to complete its mission, and the ILO had been disparaged at a press conference held by the authorities in Yangon. Patience was at an end in this case, and the credibility of the ILO and its Members was at stake. The ILO had already outlined a possible framework of action in its resolution of the International Labour Conference in 2000, and it was time to take such measures in collaboration with other international organizations.

The Government member of Cuba said that the question of the application of Convention No. 29 by the Government of Myanmar had been closely followed by her delegation since the adoption of the Conference resolution in 2000. Since that date, some joint action had been taken by the ILO and the Government of Myanmar – action which, according to the report, had yielded positive results. The presence of the ILO Liaison Officer a.i., who had been granted the same status as diplomats and United Nations personnel, had been an important factor in furthering dialogue and cooperation.

The speaker took note of the recent meeting between the Minister for Labour and the ILO Liaison Officer a.i., as well as the meeting held between the ILO Liaison Officer a.i. and the army focal point, both of which provided a good example of the Government's willingness to enter into dialogue and cooperation. She indicated that she considered in a positive light the letter dated 21 May 2005 from the Minister for Labour to the ILO Director-General. In considering the possibility of continued constructive dialogue and cooperation with the Government of Myanmar, her Government felt that coercive measures relating to trade and international investment were not suitable mechanisms for achieving progress in any country and, on the contrary, such measures created even greater difficulties for the people one wanted to protect.

Finally, the speaker encouraged the Government of Myanmar and the ILO to find, within the framework of a mutual commitment to constructive cooperation, solutions to the complex problems under discussion.

The Government member of the Republic of Korea said that his delegation had carefully considered the recent developments reported by the representative of the Government of Myanmar. His delegation had perceived the establishment of a focal point in the armed forces, the subsequent meetings between the focal point and the ILO Liaison Officer a.i., and the release of U. Shwe Mahn as positive developments. The ILO needed to maintain a solid presence and active engagement in Myanmar. At the same time, he associated himself with the concerns expressed by other delegations regarding the current situation in Myanmar and requested that the country demonstrate its political will to eliminate forced labour, with immediate and concrete actions. He urged the Myanmar Government to make clear at the highest level its intention to eliminate forced labour.

The Government member of China stated that the instances of progress which had been cited by the Government representative of Myanmar fully demonstrated its commitment to eradicating forced labour. These positive steps had been the result of cooperation and dialogue between the ILO and Myanmar. This dialogue and cooperation should be encouraged and confrontation should be avoided. Her delegation agreed with the statement made by the Government member of Indonesia who had spoken on behalf of ASEAN. She hoped the ILO and the Government of Myanmar would strengthen their cooperation.

A representative of the International Confederation of Free Trade Unions (ICFTU), speaking with the authorization of the Officers of the Committee observed that, since the last special sitting at the 2004 Conference, the political and social situation of the Burmese people had worsened. After the internal coup which had destituted General Kyn Nyunt and most of the military intelligence, the repressive situation all over the country had worsened dramatically, particularly in ethnic areas and along the borders, where there was an increase of violence from the army. The Nobel Peace Prize winner Aung San Suu Kyi remained under house arrest and totally incommunicado; U. Shwe Mahn, though finally released at the request of the ILO, was still accused of high treason by the Minister of Labour in his recent letter to the Director-General of the ILO.

During the last few months, there had been evidence of hundreds of cases of forced labour, not only in the border areas, where the army used forced labourers as porters and minesweepers, but throughout the country. He pointed to one case where the chairperson of the State Peace and Development Council (SPDC) of Myawaddi township in Karen State gave instructions obliging six villages and more than 2,000 people to implement the summer rice cultivation. Forced labour was also used in the construction of the India-Burma border trade road in Chin State. The army also used the labour of prisoners for road construction.

Moreover, during the last Governing Body session in March, the junta had organized a press conference in Yangon where the ILO was accused of exerting one-sided pressure on Myanmar by siding with expatriate destructionists, and during which the exaction of forced labour in Myanmar was presented as a cultural tradition of this country.

The speaker was very concerned by the number of persons who had come to the Liaison Officer a.i. to report on cases of forced labour that had been subsequently arrested and detained, and the fact that the vast majority of cases raised by the Liaison Officer a.i. had been declared false. The Committee should therefore take immediate steps to develop a mechanism enabling the victims of forced labour to seek and obtain redress, with full guarantees of security against reprisals, thus contributing to the fight against impunity. The speaker also urged both the Governments and the Employers to follow up the decisions of last November's Governing Body session, as regards the foreign direct investments in all their forms, in order to stop immediately any private investment and any other economic dealings with the regime, which might contribute to its stability and perpetuate forced labour. Moreover, the ILO's field capacity should be strengthened, in order to attain full freedom of movement and access to the people outside Yangon. The speaker urged the Committee to take the necessary measures which would allow the ILO, its constituents and other international organizations to force the junta to respect the fundamental human right not to be subjected to forced labour.

The Worker member of Australia stated that this case was a matter of political will – the choice to stand up for a people oppressed and abused by forced labour in a nation without democratic rights or a rule of law that met any test of judicial fairness. She referred to the report of Earth Rights International, which contained further disturbing information on prisoner porters, forced farming, sexual slavery, food theft and harassment of local leaders and villages, which seemed unbelievable in the twenty-first century.

The speaker emphasized that the Myanmar regime was well-known to the Governments, Employers and Workers of this Committee. This regime had tested their diplomacy to the limits and now mocked the Committee: not only had it enslaved its citizens in forced labour, but it held its democratic leader imprisoned. Despite this, its representative presented another set of excuses for some of the worst crimes against humanity and another set of false promises. While U. Shwe Mahn had been released, though he was guilty of no crime except standing up for his people's rights, another union organizer, with the Burmese Seaman's Union, Moe Naung, had been murdered for doing his job, and there was information of at least one more case of a trade unionist's murder.

Though the Workers and the Employers in this Committee stood together on this matter, the Governments' support was needed. The speaker urged the Governments to scale up their efforts to end trade and foreign direct investment, and called on the international financial institutions, including regional banks, to withdraw loans, grants and banking services from Myanmar, in order to make further economic and diplomatic relationships with this regime conditional on both the end of forced labour, and more broadly, on genuine democratic process.

The speaker thanked the Governments of the European Union, United States, Canada, New Zealand, India, Japan, the Republic of Korea and Australia for their commitment, but expressed the hope to see all the Governments in the Asia-Pacific region take a stand on the side of humanity and human rights, and to take the strongest possible stand against this regime. This would be especially important in 2006 when ASEAN and other governments would begin negotiations on a potentially significant trading bloc. Trade was not acceptable with a nation guilty of some of the worst violations of human and worker rights. In this regard she expressed her disappointment with the statement of the Indonesian Government, since the Indonesian Parliament had recently issued a resolution urging the Government to boycott the ASEAN meeting if military-ruled Myanmar took the rotating chair; the resolution also stated that the struggle of the people of Myanmar to improve the democratic process in the country should be supported also by South-East Asian companies, including those from Indonesia.

While the speaker was aware of concerns expressed by the Governments of Singapore, Malaysia and the Philippines on this matter, she urged these Governments to take a stronger stand and called on the majority in the Committee to take the strongest possible measures under article 33 of the ILO Constitution.

The Government member of Ukraine stated that his delegation aligned itself with the statement made by the Government member of Luxembourg, who had spoken on behalf of the European Union.

The Government member of the Libyan Arab Jamahiriya emphasized that the important matter under discussion should be examined in the light of the application of the Convention. The Government of Myanmar must take into account the observations made and take all necessary measures to implement the ILO resolutions.

The Government representative of Myanmar recalled that in his previous interventions at the Governing Body, he had expressed his fear that the discussion of this case would become politicized by some nations. He regretted that these fears had come true. Many speakers had touched on political matters which were not related to Convention No. 29. He strongly objected to this.

The Employer members expressed their disappointment with the closing statement of the Government representative of Myanmar. They had expected him to indicate what Myanmar would do as a positive response to the discussion of this case. Instead, he had simply confirmed their view that there was no political will to solve the problem. The matter that had been discussed was a correct legal policy question, which the vast majority of interventions had addressed. The issues at hand were relatively simple. The Employers were looking for an indication that Myanmar would amend or revoke the Village and Towns Acts, and widely publicize the prohibition of forced labour. Yet, the Government had not addressed these issues, which was extremely disappointing.

The Worker members recalled that this Committee had a long tradition of objectively reviewing the facts. The facts in this case were clear: there was no evidence that practices of forced labour in Myanmar were diminishing. Forced labour continued to be exacted on the population by the military rulers of the country. The picture set forth in documents D.6 and D7 was not positive, as it indicated that cooperation with the ILO was restrained. The lack of response by the Government to this case called the authority of this Committee into question. The facts of this case could not be ignored for political or economic reasons.

The Worker members also said that they were extremely disappointed with the statements made by the representative of the Government of Myanmar regarding a situation that was, to all intents and purposes, clear. It would therefore be counter-productive to continue waiting, since the Government would take no concrete measures. Like the Employer members and most of the Governments, the Worker members asked the Government to take action without delay. They also requested that their concrete proposals be considered in the conclusions. Their proposals, which were not punitive measures, aimed to direct the economy and the labour situation in Myanmar towards the observance of ILO standards. It was therefore appropriate to reactivate the measures taken under article 33 of the Constitution.

After taking note of the information from the Government representative, the Committee noted with grave concern the observation of the Committee of Experts which examined the measures taken by the Government to give effect to the recommendations of the Commission of Inquiry. The Committee of Experts had once again pointed out in its observation that the recommendations of the Commission of Inquiry had still not been implemented. The Committee of Experts and the vast majority of speakers in the Committee had expressed its strongest condemnation and urged the Government to demonstrate its stated determination to eliminate forced labour and to take the necessary measures to ensure compliance with the Convention. The extent of forced labour had not significantly changed in most areas, including ethnic areas, and its worst forms – including forced labour for the army and forced recruitment of child soldiers – continued.

In this regard, the Committee had taken note of the latest developments reported by the Director-General as well as by the Liaison Officer ad interim. The Committee welcomed the release of the third person in the high treason case, but regretted that he was not exonerated of the charges. The Committee could only deplore the fact that the Government had failed to demonstrate sufficient commitment to the elimination of forced labour, as reflected both by its treatment of the very High-Level Team (vHLT), and by its response to the concrete steps recommended by the vHLT and by the Governing Body. The Committee was alarmed in particular by the Government's stated intention to prosecute people it accuses of lodging false complaints of forced labour, and by the apparent intimidation of complainants.

In the view of the Committee, recent developments had further confirmed the conclusions of the Governing Body at its March 2005 session that the "wait-and-see" attitude that prevailed among most members since 2001 had lost its raison d'être and could not continue. The Committee's general view was that Governments, Employers and Workers, as well as other international organizations, should now activate and intensify the review of their relations with Myanmar that they were called upon to make under the 2000 resolution, and to urgently take the appropriate actions, including as regards foreign direct investment in all its various forms, relations with State- or military-owned enterprises in Myanmar. In accordance with the conclusions of the Governing Body in March, the present conclusions should be transmitted to all those to whom the 2000 resolution was addressed. The results of such reviews should be fully reported to the Director-General so that the Governing Body could have a complete picture in November. As regards the Economic and Social Council (ECOSOC), it should be requested to reactivate its consideration of the item placed on its agenda in 2001 in this regard, and Members in ECOSOC should be ready to support such a move.

The Committee noted that a number of serious issues, some of which were already identified by the vHLT in its aide-mémoire, needed to be urgently resolved:

1. The Government should give clear assurances that no action would be taken against persons lodging complaints of forced labour, or their representatives, in order that the Liaison Officer a.i. could fully continue to accept and channel such complaints to the competent authorities, and urgent discussions should be undertaken with a view to making available the safeguards and protection built into the Facilitator mechanism.

2. A number of serious allegations of forced labour that were still outstanding, including those concerning the army, should be resolved in a credible manner.

3. The ILO's presence in Myanmar should be strengthened to enhance its capacity to carry out all its various functions, and the Government should issue the necessary visas without delay.

4. The freedom of movement of the Liaison Officer a.i. as recognized by the Understanding and necessary to the discharge of his functions should be fully respected.

The Committee was of the view that the test of the real commitment of the authorities was and still remained their willingness to urgently discuss the outstanding issues at the highest level and to commit to a substantive policy dialogue that can finally address the forced labour problem. This commitment should moreover be reflected in changes to the law as well as in any future Constitution. Depending on developments in this regard, the general view was that the Governing Body at its next session should not limit itself to reviewing the steps taken under the 2000 resolution, but should also be ready to consider further steps.

B. OBSERVATION OF THE COMMITTEE OF EXPERTS ON THE APPLICATION OF CONVENTIONS AND RECOMMENDATIONS ON THE OBSERVANCE OF THE FORCED LABOUR CONVENTION, 1930 (NO. 29) BY MYANMAR

Myanmar (ratification: 1955)

1. The Committee notes the Government's report and the comments by the International Confederation of Free Trade Unions (ICFTU) contained in communications dated 14 June, 31 August, 1 September, 7 October and 10 November 2004. These comments, which are accompanied by many documents reporting the persistence of the use of forced labour in Myanmar, have been forwarded to the Government for any comments which it wishes to make in this respect. The Committee also notes the documents submitted to the Governing Body at its 289th and 291st Sessions (March and November 2004) on developments concerning the question of the observance by the Government of Myanmar of Convention No. 29, as well as the discussions in the Governing Body during these sessions and in the Conference Committee on the Application of Standards in June 2004.

2. Once again this year, the Committee is examining the measures adopted by the Government to give effect to the recommendations of the Commission of Inquiry appointed by the Governing Body in March 1997 following a complaint submitted in June 1996 under article 26 of the Constitution. In the report that it published in July 1998, the Commission of Inquiry concluded that the Convention was violated in national law and in practice in a widespread and systematic manner, and it adopted the following recommendations:

(a) that the relevant legislative texts, in particular the Village Act and the Towns Act, be brought into line with the Convention;

(b) that in actual practice, no more forced or compulsory labour be imposed by the authorities, in particular the military; and

(c) that the penalties which may be imposed under section 374 of the Penal Code for the exaction of forced or compulsory labour be strictly enforced.

Amendment of the legislation, paragraph 539(a) of the report of the Commission of Inquiry

Brief history

3. The Committee has previously set out the history of this situation in detail in earlier observations. In brief, the Committee recalls that, in its report, the Commission of Inquiry urged the Government to take the necessary steps to ensure that the Towns Act, 1907, and the Village Act, 1908, which confer broad powers upon the local authorities to requisition labour, in violation of the Convention, were without further delay brought into conformity with the Convention. In summary, under particular sections of these acts, non-voluntary work or services may be exacted from any person residing in a village tract or in a town ward, and failure to comply with a requisition made under the legislation is punishable with penal sanctions. The Commission of Inquiry found that these Acts therefore provide for the exaction of "forced or compulsory labour" within the definition of Article 2, paragraph 1, of the Convention.

4. In its observation in 2001, the Committee noted that although the Village Act and the Towns Act still needed to be amended, an "Order directing not to exercise powers under certain provisions of the Towns Act, 1907, and the Village Act, 1908", Order No. 1/99, as modified by an "Order Supplementing Order No. 1/99", dated 27 October 2000, could provide a statutory basis for ensuring compliance with the Convention in practice, if bona fide effect was given by the local authorities and by civilian and military officers empowered to requisition or assist with requisition, under the Acts. In effect, the Order provides for the possibility of requisitioning labour in exceptional circumstances, where such work or service is important and of direct interest for the community and in the event of an emergency posing an imminent danger to the general public and the community, and in circumstances where it is impossible to obtain voluntary labour by the offer of the usual rates of wages. It also provides for the possibility of issuing directives which may set aside the restrictions on powers of requisitioning. In this respect, the Committee indicated that a bona fide application of this Order involved the adoption of the measures indicated by both the Commission of Inquiry in paragraph 539(b) of its report and by the Committee of Experts in its previous comments (regarding specific instructions and the budgeting of adequate means to hire free wage labour for the public activities which are today based on forced and unpaid labour).

5. The Committee observes that, as set out in the paragraphs below, the measures requested have not been adopted or have only been adopted partially and that the exaction of forced labour persists on a broad scale. It appears that the orders have not been effective and that it has therefore become more imperative to take action without delay for the amendment or repeal of the Towns and Village Acts with a view to the elimination of the legislative basis for the exaction of forced labour and the incompatibility of these texts with the Convention. The Committee notes that, in his intervention in the Conference Committee on the Application of Standards in June 2004, the Government representative of Myanmar stated that, with regard to the "amendment of the Village Act and the Towns Act (...) his Government had been exploring ways and means to modify certain of their provisions" and had consulted with various parties in this respect. Recalling that the Commission of Inquiry recommended that these amendments should be done without further delay and completed at the very latest by 1 May 1999, the Committee of Experts hopes that the Government will finally take the necessary measures to amend in the very near future the provisions in question of the Towns Act, 1907, and the Village Act, 1908, as it has been promising to do for over 30 years.

Measures to bring an end to the exaction of forced labour in practice (paragraph 539(b) of the report of the Commission of Inquiry) and available information on existing practices

6. The Committee recalls that, in its recommendations, the Commission of Inquiry emphasized that, besides amending the legislation, concrete action needed to be taken immediately to bring to an end the exaction of forced labour in practice, in particular by the military. In its previous observations, the Committee of Experts identified four areas in which measures should be taken by the Government to achieve this outcome: issuing specific and concrete instructions to the civilian and military authorities; ensuring that the prohibition of forced labour is given wide publicity; providing for the budgeting of adequate means for the replacement of forced or unpaid labour; and ensuring the enforcement of the prohibition of forced labour.

7. Specific and concrete instructions. In its previous observations, the Committee drew the Government's attention to the fact that, in the absence of specific and concrete instructions enabling the civilian and military authorities to identify the various forms and manners of exaction of forced labour, it would be difficult to bring an end to forced labour in practice. The Committee observed that, although "explanations", "instructions" and "directives" had been given at offices of the Peace and Development Councils at various levels and the offices of the General Administration Department, the Department of Justice and the police forces and township courts, and despite the guidance provided by the field observation teams during their visits in the country, the Government had supplied no details on the contents of the explanations, instructions, directives or guidance, nor had it provided the text of any instruction or directive containing details of the tasks for which the requisitioning of labour is prohibited or the manner in which the same tasks are to be performed without resorting to forced labour.

8. The Committee notes that, in its latest report, the Government states that it has made every effort to ensure the prohibition of the use of forced labour under Order No. 1/99 and its Supplementing Order. The Government also provides three documents intended to support its contentions (Instructions No. 1/2004, dated 19 August 2004, of the Department of General Administration, in Burmese; the Directive issued by the Supreme Court to all states and divisional judges, all district judges and all township judges, by letter dated 2 November 2000 and letter No. 1002(3)/202/G4 "to prevent illicit summon on the requisition of forced labour", signed by the director-general of the police force, which had already been provided to the ILO). The Committee observes that none of these documents would enable the authorities concerned to identify practices which constitute forced labour.

9. The Committee also notes from the Government's last report, and the intervention of the Government representative in the Conference Committee on the Application of Standards in June 2004, the reference to the holding of information workshops on the implementation of Convention No. 29 in various regions of the country during the course of 2004. The Committee considers that such workshops do not appear to have had the desired effect and that, until effective measures have been taken to enable the civilian and military authorities to identify the various forms and manners of exaction of forced labour that should be prohibited, it will not be possible to bring an end to forced labour in practice.

10. In conclusion on this point, the information provided by the Government shows once again that clear and effectively conveyed instructions are still required to indicate to all the representatives of the authorities, including the members of the armed forces, the kinds of practices that constitute forced labour and for which the requisitioning

of labour is prohibited, and the manner in which the same tasks are henceforth to be performed. In a previous observation, the Committee enumerated a number of tasks and practices which are closely related with the exaction of forced labour, namely:

- portering for the military (or other military/paramilitary groups, for military campaigns or regular patrols);
- construction or repair of military camps/facilities;
- other support for camps (guides, messengers, cooks, cleaners, etc.);
- income-generation by individuals or groups (including work in army-owned agricultural and industrial projects);
- national or local infrastructure projects (including roads, railways, dams, etc.);
- cleaning/beautification of rural or urban areas;
- the supply of materials or provisions of any kind, which must be prohibited in the same way as demands for money (except where due to the State or to a municipal authority under the relevant legislation) since in practice, demands by the military for money or services are often interchangeable.The Committee once again requests that these matters be addressed urgently.

11. *Publicity given to orders.* The Committee noted previously, from the information provided by the Government, that measures continued to be taken in order to make the prohibition of forced labour contained in Order No. 1/99 and its Supplementing Order widely known by all the authorities concerned and the general public. It noted that these measures included conveying information through bulletins and pamphlets, distributing copies of orders translated into ethnic languages, and the work of field observation teams.

12. In its last report, the Government reaffirms that copies of Order No. 1/99 and its Supplementing Order have been widely distributed throughout the country. The Committee understands, from the information provided by the Government, which appears to be confirmed by the Liaison Officer a.i., that the translation of the Orders into the four Chin dialects has been completed. In this respect, the Committee notes that, according to the Liaison Officer a.i., "although all the translations have been completed, he has yet to see these translations posted in any ethnic area that he has visited, or to meet anyone in these areas who has seen these translations, and he is therefore yet to be convinced that they have been widely distributed by the authorities" (document GB.289/8, submitted to the 289th Session of the Governing Body in March 2004, paragraph 10).

13. The Committee hopes that the Government will provide copies of the instructions issued to the armed forces and information on the meetings, workshops and seminars organized for the dissemination of these instructions in the armed forces. It once again hopes that measures will be taken to ensure that the texts, duly translated, are distributed and displayed in ethnic areas, which are those where the prevalence of forced labour practices appear to be the highest.

14. *Budgeting of adequate means.* In its recommendations, the Commission of Inquiry emphasized the need to budget for adequate means to hire free wage labour for the public activities which are today based on forced and unpaid labour. In its report, the High-level Team (2001) stated that it had received no information allowing it to conclude that the authorities had indeed provided for any real substitute for the cost-free forced labour imposed to support the military or public works projects.

15. In its previous observations, the Committee pursued the matter and sought to obtain concrete evidence that adequate means are budgeted to hire voluntary paid labour. The Government in response has reiterated its previous statements according to which there is always a budget allotment for each and every project, with allocations which include the cost of material and labour. The Committee observed, however, that in practice forced labour continued to be imposed in many parts of the country, in particular in those areas with a heavy presence of the army, and that the budgetary allocations that may exist were not adequate to make recourse to forced labour unnecessary. The Government has not provided any information on this subject in its latest report. The Committee once again asks that adequate means be budgeted for the civilian and the military authorities to allow them to carry out their tasks without using forced labour and that the next report indicate the measures taken in this regard.

16. *Monitoring machinery.* With regard to the measures taken by the Government to ensure the enforcement of the prohibition of forced labour, the Committee notes the information provided by the Government representative to the Conference Committee on the Application of Standards in June 2004. It notes that these measures include the establishment of seven field observation teams empowered to carry out investigations into allegations of the use of forced labour, the findings of which are submitted to the Convention 29 Implementation Committee. With regard to the activities of the Implementation Committee, the Committee of Experts notes, according to the information contained in the document submitted to the Governing Body in November 2004 (GB.291/5/2, paragraph 13), that "recent experience of the Liaison Officer a.i. has shown that specific complaints of forced labour brought to the attention of the Convention 29 Implementation Committee are systematically denied, and cases brought directly before the courts are rejected. The picture which emerges is of a response by the authorities to complaints of forced labour that is lacking in credibility. This is all the more concerning given the types of cases involved. While a number of the allegations which have been raised with the authorities are extremely serious cases involving the army often in remote areas, others relate to comparatively minor cases of forced labour imposed by local officials in central Myanmar. Action on these latter cases should be more straightforward because of both the location and nature of the offences involved. The fact that the authorities have not taken steps to deal with these latter cases must raise serious doubts as to the possibility of making significant progress in those areas under the control of the army, where all the indications are that the forced labour situation is far more serious in both form and extent".

17. The Committee also notes that, in the view of the Liaison Officer a.i., "the mechanism put in place by the authorities for addressing forced labour allegations, that of sending an ad hoc team composed of senior government officials to the region to conduct an investigation, is not well suited to dealing with the increasing numbers of cases" (GB.291/5/1, paragraph 12). The Liaison Officer a.i. indicates that allegations of forced labour tend to be investigated internally by the General Administration Department. Cases concerning the army (that is, cases of forced recruitment, or forced labour allegedly imposed by the army) are referred by the Convention 29 Implementation Committee to the representative of the Ministry of Defence. These cases are also investigated internally by the army. The Committee of Experts notes that, "of the 38 cases referred to the Convention 29 Implementation Committee, responses have been received in 18 cases. In all these cases, the allegation that forced labour was involved was rejected. In the six cases where individuals complained directly to the court, three cases were rejected on the grounds that there was no prima facie evidence of forced labour (…)".

18. The Committee observes, as does the Liaison Officer a.i., that the assessments made by the field observation teams and the Convention 29 Implementation Committee appear to lack credibility, particularly as the ILO continues to receive trustworthy evidence that this practice continues to be widespread. The Committee once again expresses the hope that the Government will take the necessary measures to develop a credible, fair and more effective procedure for investigating allegations of forced labour, in particular those involving the army, and that it will cooperate more closely in future with the Liaison Officer.

Information available on actual practice

19. The Committee notes that the Liaison Officer a.i.'s general evaluation of the forced labour situation, on the basis of all the information available to him is that "although there have been some improvements since the Commission of Inquiry, the practice remains widespread throughout the country, and is particularly serious in border areas where there is a large presence of the army" (report of the Liaison Officer a.i., document GB.291/5/1, paragraph 9). The Committee further notes that at the time of his report (22 October 2004), the Liaison Officer a.i. had received a total of 72 complaints in 2004, and that interventions had been made with the authorities on 38 cases. Of these 38 cases, 18 concerned various forms of forced labour (other than forced recruitment); 13 concerned forced recruitment of minors into the armed forces; one case concerned alleged harassment of a complainant; and six were direct complaints by individuals to Myanmar courts under section 374 of the Penal Code, copies of which had been communicated to the Liaison Officer a.i. by the complainants.

Recent information

20. In communications dated 14 June, 31 August, 1 September and 7 October 2004, the ICFTU forwarded many documents to the ILO bearing witness to the persistence of the systematic use of forced labour by the military authorities on a very broad scale. The cases of forced labour described in these documents occurred in many areas of Myanmar (the States of Chin, Kachin, Kayin, Mon, Rakhine and Shan and the Ayeyarwady, Magway, Bago, Sagaing, Tenasserim and Yangon Divisions) during the period between September 2003 and September 2004, and are supported by precise information referring to the locations and dates of the reported facts and the army units and the names of the officers involved.

21. The documents provided include a report by the Federation of Trade Unions of Burma (FTUB) of over 100 pages in length entitled "Forced labour in Burma (Myanmar): Forced labour after 2003 Inter-

national Labour Conference". This report contains dozens of testimonies by victims of forced labour for the military. The witnesses were mostly used as porters (of arms, munitions, wood, supplies, etc.), on construction or maintenance sites of roads or bridges, or exploited in labour camps and paddy fields controlled by the army. The experiences of the witnesses included:

- being requisitioned as a consequence of a military order directed to village heads in rural areas to provide villagers for unpaid labour for portering, working on construction sites and the maintenance of military camps (many provided copies of labour requisition orders);
- being forced to participate in military training programmes, doing sentry duty or acting as guides;
- being forced by military chiefs to comply with a system of enforced labour rotation whereby each family in a village must provide a certain number of family members each day, under the menace of reprisals or a fine. The requisitioned workers have to equip themselves with their own tools and provide the food necessary for their own subsistence for the duration of their work, which is mostly unknown.

In addition, witnesses report that the types of ill-treatment suffered include:

- being deprived of food;
- being systematically beaten when they collapsed through exhaustion or sought permission to rest;
- in the most serious cases, reporting that porters incapable of walking due to a wound or extreme fatigue were purely and simply assassinated;
- mutilations and violent deaths occurring during mine-clearing operations, with the persons equipped only with rakes.

The military are also said to commit other acts of violence, including: murders, rapes, torture, pillage, the intentional burning of habitations, the destruction of plantations and consumer goods, forced expropriations and expulsions, as well as confiscating and extorting money and goods under the pretext of various types of taxation.

22. The ICFTU also forwarded a document prepared by the Asian Legal Resource Centre, an NGO with general consultative status with the United Nations Economic and Social Council, and which is based in Hong Kong, reporting two cases of forced labour imposed upon civilians by the authorities. The document illustrates the manner in which the authorities endeavour to turn against those who refuse to comply with requisition orders. The first case concerns two inhabitants of Henzada (old name for Hinthada) Township, Ayeyarwady Division, who in July 2003 refused to perform sentry duty at the Buddhist monastery of Oatpone village. They were sentenced respectively to one month and six months of imprisonment under the Penal Code for intentional failure to furnish assistance to a public servant in the execution of his public duty (section 187) and the threat of injury to any public servant (section 189). They filed a case under section 374 of the Penal Code (penalizing the imposition of unlawful compulsory labour), but both complainants were dismissed by the Henzada Township Court. The authorities filed a counter-complaint for defamation (sections 499 and 500 of the Penal Code) and the two complainants were both subsequently sentenced to six months' imprisonment on 7 October 2004. The second case concerns an inhabitant of Kawmhu Township, Yangon Division, who in April 2004 brought a complaint against the local authorities under section 374 of the Penal Code, and who had previously been threatened with legal action for failing to comply with instructions to work on a road in the neighbourhood. The local authorities then organized other villagers to depose that no one had been coerced to undertake the road construction and that the work in question had been carried out voluntarily. The ICFTU expresses the fear that the case may be decided against the complainant, in the same way as in the first case.

23. The other documents provided by the ICFTU include:

- three other reports by the FTUB, entitled: "State-induced violence and poverty in Burma", dated June 2004; "Impact of US sanctions on the textile and garment industry in Burma" and "All-round impact of promotion of tourism on the entire community of Ngwe Saung area in Ayeyarwady Division, Burma", both dated 2004, and the testimony of a child soldier, dated 2 January 2004;
- articles by various press agencies and human rights defence organizations reporting dozens of cases of forced labour, including the use of around 250 villagers from the Muslim minority in Rohingya in Maungdaw Township, Arakan State, to build houses for 130 families of Buddhist settlers from the centre of the country, and the requisitioning of 500 other villagers in June 2004 to build a bridge under the orders of the NaSaKa (border security forces). These articles refer to other cases of the exploitation of ethnic minorities by the authorities, such as the forced labour exacted from Naga villagers for the construction of tourist accommodation for the Naga New Year celebrations in Layshee (Sagaing Division) and the exploitation for the purposes of tourism of certain Salons (also called Mokens), forced to perform traditional dances (Tenasserim Division). Other cases reported include the abduction of civilians for use as human shields during a military operation carried out against the armed groups in southern Mon State and northern Tenasserim Division during the period December 2003-January 2004 and the rape of women villagers in southern Ye Township (Mon State) during the same period;
- the authentic translation of the ruling in Criminal Regular Trial No. 111/2003 of the Yangon Northern District Court of 28 November 2003 sentencing nine persons to death for high treason, based on evidence for the charges which included alleged contacts between a number of them and the ILO and having received or communicated information relating to the activities of the Organization;
- the authentic translation of the ruling of the Supreme Court in the same case, reducing the sentences of the accused to transportation for life for five of them and, for the four others, to three years' imprisonment with rigorous labour (case No. 457/2003, Nay Win, Shwe Mann, Naing Tun and others v. Union of Myanmar). The ILO subsequently received, on 21 October 2004, the authentic translation of the ruling issued on 14 October 2004 by the Supreme Court on the application for special appeal in the same case. The sentences of the four accused who had been convicted on appeal to three years' imprisonment with rigorous labour were reduced to two years' imprisonment with rigorous labour, while that of Shwe Mann, convicted on appeal to transportation for life, was reduced to five years' imprisonment with rigorous labour. Moreover, the Supreme Court found that references to contacts with the ILO contained in the ruling of the Yangon Northern District Court should be deleted from the judgement, as the Supreme Court indicated that "communication and cooperation with the ILO does not amount to an offence under the existing laws of Myanmar";
- the second preliminary report of the Ad Hoc Commission on the Depayin Massacre, dated May 2004; and
- two documents prepared by the Federation of Trade Unions Kawthoolei (FTUK) reporting dozens of other cases of forced labour, including two interviews with victims of forced labour dated 19 June 2004.

24. The Committee notes the new allegations of the forced recruitment of children by the armed forces contained in the documents supplied by the ICFTU and the report on the activities of the Liaison Officer a.i. submitted to the Governing Body in November 2004 (document GB.291/5/1). Among the cases brought to the attention of the Liaison Officer a.i., is one of a young person of 15 years of age who, according to the allegations, was recruited into the army and then escaped, before being arrested and convicted by a court martial to four years' imprisonment for desertion.

25. The Committee recalls in this respect that it previously requested the Government to provide information on any investigation that may have been undertaken to ascertain that in practice no person under 18 is recruited into the armed forces and that it hoped that the Government, with the assistance of the ILO, would make every effort to carry out a thorough assessment of the extent of this practice and would take the necessary action to put an end to it.

26. With regard to programmes of military training and service, the Government indicates in its last report that it has established a Committee for Prevention against Recruitment of Minors, headed by the Secretary (2) of the State Peace and Development Council. While noting this information, the Committee observes, from a reading of the many documents in the file, that the recruitment of children to serve in army units is still current and that certain young persons have been convicted by military courts to sentences of imprisonment for desertion. The Committee urges the Government to bring an end to these practices and to enter into full and complete collaboration with the Liaison Officer a.i. in dealing with complaints that are brought to his attention, and to ensure that young persons who are victims of such abuses cannot in future be convicted by military courts.

27. In conclusion on this subject, the Committee notes that forced and compulsory labour continues to be prevalent in many areas of the country, and particularly in the border areas inhabited by ethnic minorities, in which there is a strong military presence. It notes with concern the many documents brought to its attention by the ICFTU and the cases followed by the Liaison Officer a.i., that demonstrate forcefully that the exaction of forced labour is far from disappearing in practice. It notes the Government's statement concerning its determination to eliminate forced labour in the country; however, the Committee considers that this determination has not so far led to the

achievement of the expected results. The Committee trusts that the Government, in keeping with its expressed intention, will significantly increase its efforts to bring a definitive end to forced labour, and urges the Government to pursue its cooperation with the ILO for this purpose. The Committee hopes that the Government will reply in detail concerning all the cases of forced labour reported by the ICFTU.

Imposition of the penalties established by the Penal Code in cases of the illegal exaction of forced or compulsory labour

28. The Committee recalls that in its report the Commission of Inquiry urged the Government to take the necessary measures to ensure that the penalties established under section 374 of the Penal Code for the exaction of forced or compulsory labour be strictly enforced, in conformity with Article 25 of the Convention. In the view of the Commission of Inquiry, this would require thorough investigation, prosecution and adequate punishment of those found guilty.

29. The Committee notes from the report submitted by the Liaison Officer a.i. to the Governing Body in November 2004 (document GB.291/5/1, paragraph 13 and Appendix II) that, for the first time, cases have been brought to the courts of Myanmar under section 374 of the Penal Code concerning the illegal exaction of forced labour. However, it notes that none of the six cases brought during the course of 2004 led to the initiation of proceedings, nor even to recognition of a situation of forced labour. In three cases, the courts rejected the cases on the grounds that there was no prima facie evidence of forced labour. Further, in two of the three cases which have been completed, the complainants were even sentenced to six months' imprisonment for defamation and these persons had already been imprisoned for refusing to carry out the forced labour. The three other cases were still ongoing at the time of the report (22 October 2004). Furthermore, the Liaison Officer a.i. indicates in his report that "two individuals were arrested after returning to their village following a visit to him in Yangon. During the visit, one of the individuals provided details on a direct complaint he had made to a court under section 374 of the Penal Code, concerning forced labour in Kawhmu Township (Yangon Division)" (document GB.291/5/1, paragraph 17).

30. The Committee notes that, although for the first time cases have been brought under section 374 of the Penal Code by individuals claiming to be victims of the exaction of forced labour, none of these cases has yet been found receivable. It notes that the fact that certain victims have been arrested after contacting the Liaison Officer a.i., or convicted to a sentence of imprisonment for defamation after bringing a case under section 374 of the Penal Code, creates a climate of fear which is likely to dissuade victims from turning to the courts. It hopes that the Government will make every effort to ensure that the victims of forced labour are in practice able to avail themselves of the provisions of section 374 of the Penal Code without risking prosecution for defamation and that they can freely contact the Liaison Officer a.i. without running the risk of being arrested or interrogated by the police forces. It hopes that the Government will provide information in its next report on the progress achieved in this field.

Joint Plan of Action

31. In its last observation, the Committee noted with interest that a Joint Plan of Action for the Elimination of Forced Labour Practices in Myanmar had been agreed upon on 27 May 2003 between the ILO and the Government. Although the Joint Plan of Action was welcomed by the Conference Committee on the Application of Standards during the discussion at the 91st Session of the International Labour Conference, the Conference Committee also observed that its debate was taking place in the context of recent events, and the resulting climate of uncertainty and fear, which "called seriously into question the will and ability of the authorities to make significant progress in the elimination of forced labour". The Committee of Experts notes that the situation has scarcely improved since then, particularly in the view of the fact that three persons have been convicted for high treason on grounds which include contacts with the ILO. Although the Supreme Court ruling on a special appeal commuted the death sentence which had been imposed on these persons in November 2003 by a court in Myanmar to sentences of imprisonment of two and five years and acknowledged the legality of contacts with the ILO, the Committee notes that the Workers' group, the Employers' group and many Government members of the Governing Body expressed regret at the continued detention of the persons concerned and called for their immediate release or pardon. The situation of these persons is a matter of great concern to the Committee. The Committee regrets that, under these conditions, the Joint Plan of Action cannot be implemented as envisaged. It notes the decision of the Governing Body to field a very high-level mission to evaluate the attitude of the authorities and assess their determination to continue their cooperation with the ILO (GB.291/5, Conclusions).

Concluding comments

32. The Committee notes once again with grave concern, that the recommendations of the Commission of Inquiry have still not been implemented: the provisions of the Towns Act, 1907, and the Village Act, 1908, allowing requisition of labour in violation of the Convention, have not been repealed; forced labour continues to be exacted in many areas of the country, in circumstances of severe cruelty and brutality; and no person responsible for the exaction of forced labour has been prosecuted or convicted under the relevant provisions of the Penal Code. The Committee expresses its strongest condemnation and urges the Government to demonstrate its expressed determination to eliminate forced labour and to take the necessary measures to ensure compliance with the Convention.

Document D.6

C. Report of the Director-General

I. Brief summary of developments since June 2004

1. In the conclusions it adopted last year at the close of the special sitting concerning the application by Myanmar of the Forced Labour Convention, 1930 (No. 29), the Committee on the Application of Standards, inter alia, noted that the measures taken by the Government had not brought about significant progress in actual practice and forced labour continued to be exacted in many parts of the country. It further noted its grave concern at the convictions of three persons for high treason, including on grounds of contacts with the ILO, and agreed with the Governing Body that this situation clearly was not one in which the Plan of Action could be credibly implemented. The Committee also noted with appreciation the continued cooperation extended to the Liaison Officer by the Government and the freedom of movement that he enjoyed. As regards the increasing numbers of individual complaints of forced labour being received by the Liaison Officer, this demonstrated the usefulness of the ILO presence. The Committee had to note with concern, however, that the response so far was inadequate and this cast serious doubt on the willingness of the authorities to take the concrete steps necessary to ensure the elimination of forced labour in practice. The following brief overview of the main developments since its last session should be of interest to the Committee.

2. At its 291st Session (November 2004), the Governing Body had before it two reports from the Liaison Officer a.i., on his activities and a report from the Director-General.[1] The Governing Body was gravely concerned by developments in the situation and the continued impunity of those who exact forced labour. While the recent judgement of the Supreme Court in the high treason case did answer the fundamental question of the legality of contacts with the ILO, the Governing Body regretted the continued detention of the persons concerned when their guilt had not been established, and called for their immediate release. While a broad majority were of the opinion that the reactivation of the measures to be taken under article 33 and in accordance with the Conference resolution of 2000 would be fully justified, it was nevertheless felt that the sudden replacement of the previous interlocutors of the Organization following changes among the Myanmar leadership justified an evaluation of the current attitude of the authorities and their determination to effectively address the continuing practice of forced labour. The Director-General was therefore requested to field a "very high-level team" to make such a determination, and report the results to the next session of the Governing Body so that it would then be able to determine the necessary consequences on the basis of full knowledge either as regards further action by the Organization under article 33, or for the implementation of the joint Plan of Action. In addition, the Office was requested to provide further information for the next session on the actions taken on the basis of the 2000 resolution.

3. Accordingly, the Director-General constituted a very High-Level Team (vHLT) comprising Sir Ninian Stephen (former Governor-General of Australia); Ms. Ruth Dreifuss (former President of the Swiss Confederation); and Mr. Eui-yong Chung (former Chairperson of the Governing Body, Member of the National Assembly of the Republic of

---

[1] Docs. GB.291/5/1, GB.291/5/1(Add.) and GB.291/5/2.

Korea, and Chairperson of the Foreign Relations Committee of the Uri Party). The vHLT arrived in Myanmar on 21 February. On 23 February, having failed to secure the necessary meetings at the highest level in order to complete its mandate, and having had discussions and making its views known to the Minister for Labour and the Prime Minister, the vHLT decided to depart the country. It handed over to the Minister for Foreign Affairs a statement to this effect, attached to which was an informal aide-mémoire setting out the main concrete steps on which it believed progress should be made. It insisted that despite its early departure, the door was still open for further developments.

4. The 292nd Session (March 2005) of the Governing Body had before it three reports: (i) a report on further action taken pursuant to the 2000 resolution of the International Labour Conference; (ii) a report from the Liaison Officer a.i., on his activities together with an addendum setting out the latest developments; and (iii) the report of the very High-Level Team.[2] In its consensus conclusions, the Governing Body noted that the most largely shared sentiment was one of condemnation over the failure of the highest authorities to take advantage of the unique opportunity that the visit of the vHLT represented to resume a credible dialogue on the issues of concern, and also the feelings of grave concern over the general situation that this revealed. Although there were indications from the Prime Minister and comments from the Myanmar Ambassador alleging that the necessary political will existed, the credibility of this message and the usefulness of the ILO's present approach was cast into grave doubt by other indications, including the attitude towards the vHLT. Although some concrete developments appeared to go in the right direction, in particular the prosecutions and punishment of authorities responsible for having recourse to forced labour as well as the establishment of a focal point in the army, in the circumstances the overall assessment fell far short of the Governing Body's expectations. The Governing Body noted the growing feeling that the "wait-and-see" attitude that prevailed among members since 2001 appeared to have lost its *raison d'être* and could not continue. It therefore unanimously agreed to transmit its conclusions to all those to whom the 2000 resolution was addressed – including relevant agencies – with a view to them taking the appropriate action. At the same time, it noted that the ILO was not closing the door to a resumption of positive dialogue with the Myanmar authorities and that any concrete developments should be taken objectively into account by members when deciding on the action they would take. Progress with regard to the strengthening of the ILO presence as well as the other items covered by the vHLT's aide-mémoire, including the immediate release of U Shwe Mahn, should be a concrete test in this regard.

II. Latest developments since March 2005

5. In accordance with the conclusions of the Governing Body in March 2005, the Director-General wrote on 21 April to the governments of member States of the ILO, to international organizations, and to the United Nations Economic and Social Council (ECOSOC), drawing their attention to these conclusions. These letters are reproduced in Appendix I. At the same time, the Director-General wrote to the Minister for Labour of Myanmar. This letter, and the reply from the Minister, are reproduced in Appendices II and III, respectively.

6. In parallel with the discussions between the Liaison Officer a.i., and the authorities in Yangon (reported in detail in Part B below), relevant discussions also took place between the Office and the Permanent Representative of Myanmar in Geneva. Certain developments and comments made in Yangon, in particular by the Director-General of the

---

[2] Docs. GB.292/7/1, GB.292/7/2, GB.292/7/2(Add.) and GB.292/7/3, respectively.

Department of Labour in his meeting with the Liaison Officer a.i., on 26 April,[3] touched on matters which were fundamental to the effectiveness of the ILO presence and gave rise to serious concerns on the part of the Office. These concerns were made known to the Myanmar authorities, and the Office highlighted the need, in view of the nature of the issues involved, for clarification at the earliest occasion and at the appropriate level. The vHLT office made it clear in this regard that, as suggested on the occasion of the vHLT's visit, it was ready to carry out a joint in-depth review of the Plan of Action, including in particular the facilitator mechanism, in the light of recent experiences, and that it would be important for the authorities to indicate their readiness to conduct such a review at the earliest opportunity and at the appropriate level. It underlined the fact that, pending such a review, it was inherent to the very *raison d'être* of the ILO presence, and to its status, that it was able to have any contacts for any purpose consistent with its mandate, including with alleged victims of forced labour or their representatives, and that no action should be taken against those concerned. It also underlined that the International Labour Conference should receive appropriate assurances on this vital point. At the same time, relevant instructions were given to the Liaison Officer a.i., in particular as regards the implications for continued processing of specific allegations of forced labour pending the necessary assurances.

7. A subsequent reply from the Minister for Labour to the Director-General's letter of 21 April, as well as a meeting between the Minister for Labour and the Liaison Officer a.i., while still containing a number of concerning elements, appears at the same time to indicate a willingness to have the necessary discussions at the required level in order to address these matters.

---

[3] See para. 12 of the report of the Liaison Officer a.i.

Appendix I

(a) Letter dated 21 April from the Director-General to the member States of the ILO

Dear Sir,

I have the honour to draw your attention to the agreed conclusions reached by the Governing Body of the ILO at its 292nd Session (March 2005) concerning the question of the observance by Myanmar of the Forced Labour Convention, 1930 (No. 29), which are attached.

These conclusions have to be considered in the framework of the resolution concerning this question adopted by the International Labour Conference at its 88th Session (June 2000), and to the letter addressed to your Government in this regard on 8 December 2000. I have attached both herewith for ease of reference.

Under operative paragraph 1(b) of this resolution, the Organization's constituents are called upon to undertake a review of their relations with Myanmar and to report back at appropriate intervals to the ILO Governing Body. The Governing Body's abovementioned conclusions convey the growing feeling that the "wait-and-see" attitude which has prevailed among most Members since 2001 "appears to have lost its *raison d'être* and cannot continue".

At the same time, the conclusions make it clear that Members, in carrying out the review they are called upon to make, and reaching their conclusions, are expected to take objectively into account any development that may take place in Myanmar from now on as regards the four points raised by the very High-Level Team's aide-mémoire (GB.292/7/3, Appendix III(b), also attached).

The Office for its part is to report on any developments to the Committee on the Application of Standards of the International Labour Conference in June. A full report on action taken by the Organization's constituents will be prepared for the November session of the Governing Body. These reports will include any relevant information you may wish to provide.

May I also request that you bring the contents of this letter to the attention of the employers' and workers' organizations of your country so that they may take any appropriate action and inform me either directly or through you.

Yours faithfully,

(Signed) Juan Somavia

(b) Letter dated 21 April from the Director-General to international organizations [4]

Dear Sir,

You will recall that in my letter dated 8 December 2000 I transmitted to you for appropriate action the resolution adopted by the International Labour Conference at its 88th Session (June 2000) concerning the question of the observance by Myanmar of the Forced Labour Convention, 1930 (No. 29). A copy of this resolution is attached for easy reference.

In the framework of that resolution, the Governing Body of the ILO reviewed the situation at its 292nd Session (March 2005) and agreed conclusions, which are attached.

The Office for its part is to report on any developments to the Committee on the Application of Standards of the International Labour Conference in June. A full report on action taken by the Organization's constituents will be prepared for the November session of the Governing Body. These reports will include any relevant information you may wish to provide.

Yours sincerely,

(Signed) Juan Somavia

---

[4] Sent to all international organizations to which the 2000 resolution was addressed, and also sent to ECOSOC, *mutatis mutandis*.

Appendix II

Letter dated 21 April from the Director-General to the Myanmar Minister for Labour

Dear Minister,

As you are aware, the Governing Body at its March session agreed conclusions concerning the observance by your country of the Forced Labour Convention, 1930 (No. 29), which are attached herewith.

As provided for in these conclusions, I have now apprised the Organization's constituents and relevant international organizations of these conclusions. Copies of sample letters are attached. In this framework, it is of the greatest importance that the Myanmar authorities provide a clear indication of their willingness to give positive consideration to the outstanding issues. These include the strengthening of the ILO's presence as well as the other items covered by the vHLT's aide-mémoire, as well as the immediate release of Shwe Mahn – which could then be reported to the International Labour Conference in June.

It is therefore urgent that you could pursue the necessary consultations in Yangon with the Liaison Officer a.i., it being understood that parallel consultations can take place in Geneva as appropriate.

Yours sincerely,

(Signed) Juan Somavia

Appendix III

Letter dated 21 May from the Myanmar Minister for Labour to the Director-General

Excellency,

I am pleased to inform you that the Government of the Union of Myanmar gives due consideration to the items covered by aide-mémoire of vHLT. The developments on these issues have already been mentioned in the "Memorandum on Myanmar's Compliance of ILO Convention 29 and Her cooperation with ILO" issued by the Ministry of Labour. I would like to inform you on further developments.

In recent days, discussions and exchange of views on matters concerning the elimination of forced labour in Myanmar took place in parallel both in Yangon and Geneva.

Upon the request of the ILO Liaison Officer a.i., I myself met with the ILO Liaison Officer a.i. on May 9, 2005 at the Minister's Office. The Government's position on elimination of forced labour and other related matters were made known to the ILO Liaison Officer a.i. and discussions were conducted in a very frank manner.

Myanmar Government took into serious consideration on the persistent requests by the Governing Body to release Shwe Mann, who committed a crime of high treason. He has already been released from the prison on 18 May 2005.

The Army Focal Team Leader Colonel Khin Soe and two members of his team met with the ILO Liaison Officer a.i. on May 12, 2005 at the Department of Labour. The meeting was in compliance to a request by the ILO Liaison Officer a.i.

Concerning the freedom of movement of the ILO Liaison Officer a.i., it has been clearly stated in the terms of Understanding for the appointment of an ILO Liaison Officer that the freedom of movement accorded to diplomats and UN personnel with the established procedures will be extended to the ILO Liaison Officer. Recently, the Myanmar authorities allowed the ILO Liaison Officer a.i. to travel to Kayin State at an extremely short notice.

In a spirit of cooperation with the ILO, Myanmar is ready to consider a new approach for the elimination of forced labour to be discussed at an appropriate time and level to be determined between the two sides.

I would like to assure you that Myanmar looks forward to constructive cooperation with the International Labour Organization based on mutual trust and interest.

Yours sincerely,

(Signed) U Thaung

D. Report of the Liaison Officer a.i.

I. Activities of the Liaison Officer a.i. since March 2005

1. The Liaison Officer a.i., had a number of meetings with the authorities. On 9 May he met with the Minister for Labour. He met with the Director-General of the Department of Labour on 8 and 26 April, and 12 and 17 May. He also had meetings with officials from the Department of General Administration (Ministry of Home Affairs) and the Ministry of Foreign Affairs. On 12 May he met for the first time with Col. Khin Soe (the Vice-Adjutant General) who was designated on 1 March as the army focal point with the ILO.

2. In addition to these meetings with the authorities, the Liaison Officer a.i., also met in Yangon and in Bangkok with members of the diplomatic community, representatives of United Nations agencies, and representatives of non-governmental organizations.

3. From 18 to 20 May, the Liaison Officer a.i., visited parts of Mon State and southern Kayin State. [5] This trip was conducted independently of the authorities. In line with the previously established practice, he informed the authorities shortly before his departure of his plans. Some of the places that he visited were restricted areas, but where there were no significant security concerns. He was able to freely visit all areas that he wished to. [6]

II. Developments on the concrete steps identified by the very High-Level Team (vHLT) and the Governing Body

4. *The release of U Shwe Mahn.* U Shwe Mahn, one of three persons originally convicted of high treason including on grounds of contact with the ILO, was released from prison on 29 April. [7] The Liaison Officer a.i., has been able to confirm that U Shwe Mahn is well and has returned home to his family. The Minister for Labour indicated to the Liaison Officer a.i., in their meeting on 9 May that although U Shwe Mahn was a convicted terrorist against whom there was conclusive evidence, the authorities had nevertheless set him free on the request of the ILO. This was a positive gesture to demonstrate the commitment of the Myanmar side to continuing its cooperation with the ILO.

5. *The strengthening of the ILO presence.* As indicated to the Governing Body in March, [8] it was decided that in the first instance this step would take the form of the secondment of an ILO official to Yangon to assist the interim Liaison Officer. The necessary approvals from the authorities have been pending since 24 January. In the meeting on 9 May, the Minister for Labour indicated that this matter was still under review by the higher authorities. If the

---

[5] He travelled by road from Yangon to Mawlamyine (Moulmein), the capital of Mon State, and from there to Kyain-seikgyi town in southern Kayin State.

[6] He was informed, however, that this arrangement was to be seen as an exception, and it was underlined that in general he would be expected, like all diplomats and UN officials, to apply for permission for travel 14 days in advance. See para. 6 below.

[7] The other two persons had been released on 4 January. See GB.292/7/2, para. 7.

[8] Doc. GB.292/7/2, para. 3.

ILO presence was found to be of mutual benefit, a positive response could be given on this point. If not, the viability of the ILO presence could be called into question.

6. *A renewed commitment to the freedom of movement of the Liaison Officer a.i.* As reported above, the Liaison Officer a.i., was able to freely undertake travel in line with the previously established practice. At the same time, however, the Minister for Labour indicated to the Liaison Officer in their meeting that the ILO could not be excepted from the general requirement that all diplomats and UN international staff apply for travel authorization by submitting a detailed itinerary to the Protocol Department 14 days in advance. In his meeting with the Liaison Officer a.i., on 17 May, the Director-General of the Department of Labour reaffirmed that the authorities regarded this trip as an exception and that it should not be seen as establishing a precedent.

7. *Credible solutions to the forced labour cases in Toungup and Hinthada.* No further developments have taken place in this regard, and the authorities have declined to discuss this matter further.

8. *The appointment of a high-level focal point in the army.* As reported to the Governing Body in March,[9] this important step was taken on 1 March, with the appointment of a team of eight senior military officers, headed by the Vice-Adjutant General. The Liaison Officer a.i., had a meeting with the Vice-Adjutant General on 12 May, and was able to brief him on his work and hear about the mandate and activities of the focal point. Following these discussions, the Liaison Officer a.i., requested a further meeting before the International Labour Conference during which some specific issues could be raised. A meeting was scheduled to take place on 26 May, but the Liaison Officer a.i., was subsequently informed that the Vice-Adjutant General had been called away from Yangon to deal with an urgent matter.

9. *The issuance of a public order to army units not to requisition labour.* The authorities indicated that, as stated in their "Memorandum" of March 2005,[10] a number of (secret) orders were issued by the Ministry of Defence and the army at various levels instructing all members of the armed forces to abide by the orders prohibiting forced labour. The Liaison Officer a.i., has suggested to the authorities that if this is the case, then a relatively straightforward first step could be to declassify these orders.

10. *Reconfirmation of the commitment of the authorities to the joint Plan of Action.* The Liaison Officer a.i., has raised this matter in various discussions with the authorities. The authorities pointed out that it was the ILO that had decided to suspend the implementation of the joint Plan of Action. However, there were indications, including from the Minister for Labour, that it could be possible to have detailed discussions on this matter at the appropriate level.

III. Developments on specific allegations

11. Since the finalization of his report to the March session of the Governing Body, on 18 February, the Liaison Officer a.i., has made interventions on a further five cases reported to him:

---

[9] Doc. GB.292/7/2(Add.), para. 3.

[10] ibid.

- *Intervention dated 2 March.* According to the allegation, labour was requisitioned by the authorities in Aunglan township (Magway Division) in November and December 2004 for the construction of a local road, and one villager was killed in an accident while being forced to quarry rocks as part of this project. This allegation was made to the ILO by a close relative of the individual who was killed, with the support of an additional 15 villagers who indicated that they were also forced to contribute labour for the project. In total, one person from each of the 280 households in the village was ordered by the local authorities to do the work. Any family who failed to contribute labour was fined. The family of the worker killed did not receive any support or compensation from the authorities. (Further details on the follow-up to this case are provided below.)

- *Intervention dated 10 March.* According to the allegation, hundreds of local people were requisitioned by the authorities in Katha township (Sagaing Division) in 2004 and again in 2005 for the construction of a local road. This allegation was made to the ILO by an individual from the area who had to participate in this project. Those who were forced to participate received no payment, and had to supply their own tools and rations. Compulsory cash contributions were also collected to cover the cost of materials for the construction of bridges. Any household that could not contribute a worker had to pay a fine.

- *Intervention dated 11 March.* This intervention concerned the alleged forced recruitment of a minor into the army. According to the information received, in November 2004 a meeting was held between an army officer and village leaders in Thongwa township (Yangon Division) at which a 17-year-old boy was selected by the elders (along with several other boys) and ordered to accompany the officer to a recruitment centre, where he was recruited against his will.

- *Interventions dated 21 April.* These interventions, addressed to the newly-appointed army focal point, concerned two cases of forced recruitment into the army. In both cases, documentary evidence of the date of birth was provided, indicating that the boys were aged 14 and 16 at the time of recruitment.

12. In a development of sufficient seriousness to be immediately brought to the attention of headquarters, the Liaison Officer a.i., was informed during his meeting with the Director-General of the Department of Labour on 26 April that false complaints of forced labour were placing a great drain on Government resources and undermined the dignity of the State, and that it was therefore necessary to "take measures as a deterrent against false complaints being lodged". It was indicated that legal action would now be taken, under certain specified sections of the Penal Code,[11] against complainants or their representatives who lodged "false complaints". Preparations were under way to do so in certain recent cases. In the light of this, the Liaison Officer a.i., was instructed by ILO headquarters to temporarily suspend dealing with new allegations of forced labour, while clarifications were sought from the Myanmar authorities. In his meeting with the Minister for Labour on 9 May, the Liaison Officer a.i., was informed that the authorities had evidence that false complaints of forced labour were being systematically made to the ILO by politically-motivated individuals. The Minister had referred such cases to the competent authorities for legal action to be taken, although he could not say whether such action would be taken or not. He gave assurances that the authorities had no intention to punish complainants.

---

[11] The sections of the Penal Code were identified as: 182b (giving false information with intent to cause a public servant to use his lawful power to the injury or annoyance of any person), 420 (cheating and dishonesty), 468 (forgery for the purpose of cheating) and 499 (defamation).

13. In letters dated 15 March, 18 April, 4 May, 9 May and 18 May, the Convention 29 Implementation Committee responded to a number of the forced labour cases raised by the Liaison Officer a.i.:

- As regards the allegation of forced labour for road construction in Ramree township (Rakhine State), [12] it was indicated that funds allocated to the project had been systematically disbursed to workers, and that no forced labour was used. However, the township Chairman and the Deputy Superintendent of Police were reprimanded for "shortcomings in complying with Order Supplementing Order 1/99".

- As regards the allegation of forced labour cultivating land previously confiscated by an army battalion in Putao township (Kachin State), [13] it was found that the allegation was untrue, and furthermore that any rice purchased by the battalion from farmers was paid for at more than reasonable rates.

- As regards the allegation of forced labour imposed by the army for road construction in Thandaung township (Kayin State), during which a 15-year-old boy stepped on a landmine and lost his leg, it was found that the incident had taken place, but that the villagers were contributing their labour of their own free will when the boy stepped on an insurgent-laid mine.

- As regards the allegation of forced labour for the construction of a road in Katha township (Sagaing Division), [14] it was found that no forced labour or compulsory contributions were demanded, and that the road in question was constructed voluntarily by the local people on their own arrangement.

- As regards three allegations of forced recruitment of children into the armed forces, [15] in two cases it was found that the individuals were over the age of 18 and had been voluntarily recruited. The findings as regards age were inconsistent with documentary evidence of date of birth, copies of which were provided to the authorities in each case. In the third case, it was indicated that the individual had gone absent without leave and been declared a deserter. No response was given concerning the evidence presented that he was only 14 at the time of recruitment.

---

[12] See doc. GB.291/5/1, para. 14.

[13] See doc. GB.292/7/2, para. 14.

[14] See para. 11 above.

[15] See para. 11 above (intervention dated 11 Mar.); doc. GB.292/7/2, para. 13 (intervention dated 15 Feb.); and doc. GB.291/5/1, para. 14 (intervention dated 13 Sep.).

14. *The allegation of forced labour in Aunglan township.* As regards the allegation of forced labour for the construction of a road in Aunglan township (Magway Division), during which one villager was killed, the authorities indicated that investigations had found the allegation to be false as no forced labour had been used and the individual had been killed while willingly contributing his labour.[16] Legal action would be taken against "unscrupulous third parties" who had persuaded the family to make this false complaint. The Liaison Officer a.i., then received a letter from the brother of the deceased, withdrawing the complaint.[17] The Liaison Officer a.i., also received other information according to which pressure was put on the local people to deny that there had been forced labour, and that the family of the deceased was intimidated by the field observation team and signed the letter withdrawing the complaint under duress.

---

[16] See para. 11 above. The initial response was provided in a letter dated 18 April from the Convention 29 Implementation Committee. In the letter, it was indicated that a field observation team had been dispatched to investigate, and it had been found that no forced labour, compulsory contributions or fines were imposed, and that the individual who had died had been contributing labour willingly at the time. Further clarification was provided by the Director-General of the Department of Labour in his meeting with the Liaison Officer a.i., on 26 April. It was indicated that because of the seriousness of the allegation a second field observation team had been dispatched to the area from 5 to 7 April. This investigation had confirmed that no forced labour had occurred, although 7 family members of the deceased had continued to insist that there had been forced labour. Once these persons had been investigated further, however, it had been found that they had made a false complaint because of their grief, because of a certain grudge against the local authorities, and because some "unscrupulous third parties" had taken advantage of the situation.

17 This letter was dated 7 April, the same day that the second field observation team completed its investigation.

INTERNATIONAL LABOUR OFFICE

GB.291/5/1
291st Session

Governing Body

Geneva, November 2004

Document D.7

E. Developments concerning the question of the observance by the Government of Myanmar of the Forced Labour Convention, 1930 (No. 29)

Report of the Liaison Officer a.i.

I. Background

1. At its special sitting in June 2004, the Committee on the Application of Standards of the International Labour Conference had before it, inter alia, three documents setting out the developments over the previous year.[1] At the end of its discussion, the Committee adopted the following conclusions:

    After taking note of the information provided by the Government representative, the Committee noted with deep concern the observation of the Committee of Experts which examined the measures taken by the Government to give effect to the recommendations of the Commission of Inquiry. The Committee of Experts had noted in its observation that the three main recommendations of the Commission of Inquiry were still to be implemented. In spite of the Government's assurances of its good intentions, the measures taken had not brought about significant progress in actual practice and forced labour continued to be exacted in many parts of the country. No person responsible for imposing forced labour had ever been prosecuted or sentenced under the relevant provision of the Penal Code. In view of the slowness of progress, the Committee of Experts had expressed the hope that the process of dialogue and cooperation which had developed between the ILO and the Government could offer a real chance of bringing about more rapid and concrete progress, in particular through the implementation of the Plan of Action.

    In this regard the Committee had to note its grave concern at the fact that three persons had been convicted of high treason, including on grounds of contacts with the ILO. The Committee was further deeply concerned that, although on appeal the Supreme Court had commuted the death sentences, it had failed to bring clarity on this crucial point, despite the

---

[1] ILC, 92nd Session (Geneva, 2004), Committee on the Application of Standards, documents C.App./D.5, C.App./D.5(Add.) and C.App./D.5(Add.2). Relevant sections concerning developments in the elimination of forced labour following the 289th Session (March 2004) of the Governing Body are reproduced in Appendix III.

earlier assurances of the Government that contacts with the ILO could not be considered illegal in Myanmar. The Committee also expressed its concern at the freedom of association issues raised by the Supreme Court's findings. It joined the Governing Body in endorsing the recommendations put forward by the informal facilitator as regards the grounds for convicting the three persons and the need to release them. It agreed that this situation clearly was not one in which the Plan of Action could be credibly implemented.

The Committee had also taken note of the information provided by the Liaison Officer ad interim on his activities. It noted with appreciation the continued cooperation extended to the Liaison Officer by the Government and the freedom of movement that he enjoyed. It considered the fact that individuals were lodging complaints concerning forced labour with the Liaison Officer in increasing numbers, demonstrating the usefulness of the ILO presence. However, the Committee had to note with concern that the response to the individual allegations so far raised was inadequate and that to date not a single one of these allegations had been verified by the authorities nor had anyone so far been prosecuted for illegally imposing forced labour. This cast serious doubt on the willingness of the authorities to take the concrete steps necessary to ensure the elimination of forced labour in practice.

In that respect, reference was made to the fact that certain forms of forced labour referred to by the Commission of Inquiry, such as work on infrastructure projects, using forced labour, forced recruitment of children and even the use of persons as minesweepers were still in use. The dissemination of information in relevant languages also left much to be desired.

The Committee took due note of the assurances provided by the Government representative that a further review by the Supreme Court would take place which would, inter alia, clarify the question of the legality of contacts with the ILO. The Committee was of the opinion that the Government now had a final opportunity to give practical effect to these assurances and to the recommendations of the informal facilitator. It noted that the Governing Body at its next session should be ready to draw the appropriate conclusions, including reactivation and review of the measures and action taken including those regarding foreign direct investment, called for in the resolution of the International Labour Conference of 2000, unless there was a clear change in the situation in the meantime.

Finally, the Committee recalled that the Government would have to supply a detailed report for examination by the Committee of Experts at its next session on all the steps taken to ensure compliance with the Convention in law and in practice.

2. Mr. Richard Horsey continued to act as interim ILO Liaison Officer.

II. Activities of the Liaison Officer a.i.

3. The Liaison Officer a.i. had a number of meetings with the authorities in which he gave his advice on the forced labour situation and on the steps which in his view were needed to achieve the elimination of the practice, and in which he discussed specific complaints he had received and his concerns relating to these. He met with the Convention 29 Implementation Committee on 3 September. He also had a series of meetings with the Director-General of the Department of Labour on 1 July, 24 August, 6 September and 1 October, as well as meetings with the Director-General of the Department of General Administration (Home Affairs) on 8, 17 and 30 September and 22 October. In addition, he met with the Director-General of the International Organizations and Economic Department of the Ministry of Foreign Affairs on 8 September. Despite a number of requests, the Liaison Officer a.i. has not so far been able to meet with the Minister for Labour. Since 18 September the Minister has been assigned the additional portfolio of Minister at the Prime Minister's Office, requiring him to be absent from Yangon for extended periods. On 19 October, the Prime Minister was replaced in a significant reshuffle within the ruling State Peace and Development Council (SPDC).[2]

4. In addition to these meetings with the authorities, the Liaison Officer a.i. also met with members of the diplomatic community, as well as with representatives of United Nations agencies, the International Committee of the Red Cross, and international non-governmental organizations in Yangon and Bangkok. He also had the opportunity to have discussions with a number of ethnic-nationality political parties.

5. From 28 to 29 July the Liaison Officer a.i. accompanied, in an observer capacity, a field observation team to Kawhmu in Yangon Division.[3] The team's activities consisted of holding an information workshop on forced labour, attended by around 100 local and regional officials. From 13 to 17 September the Liaison Officer a.i. visited Toungup township in Rakhine State, together with the Informal Facilitator, Mr. Léon de Riedmatten. The authorities chose not to participate in this visit, and it was therefore conducted independently.

III. Developments in the high treason case

6. On 4 August the defence lawyer in the case lodged a further "special appeal" to the Supreme Court on behalf of eight of the nine persons in the case, including the three with an ILO connection.[4]

7. On 23 September the Supreme Court accepted the case for special appeal. The Special Appellate Bench of the Supreme Court issued its judgement on 14 October. The judgement was transmitted to the ILO by the authorities the same day, and an official translation was received on 20 October. The salient points of the judgement, based on an examination of both texts, are as follows:[5]

   – With regard to the question of contacts with the ILO, the Court stated that since Myanmar was a member of the United Nations and other international organizations such as the ILO, and was cooperating with them, any person was free to communicate or cooperate with such organizations. Therefore, communication or cooperation with the ILO does not amount to an offence under the existing laws of Myanmar. Upon reviewing the original court judgement, the Court ordered that the text concerning contacts with the ILO, which was irrelevant to the case, be deleted from the original judgement.

   – The convictions of Nai Min Kyi and U Aye Myint under section 123 of the Penal Code (encouraging, harbouring or comforting persons guilty of high treason) were upheld on the grounds that they had sent incorrect information about Myanmar to

---

[2] The new Prime Minister is Lt. Gen. Soe Win, formerly Secretary-1 of the SPDC. Lt. Gen. Thein Sein was promoted from Secretary-2 to replace Lt. Gen. Soe Win as Secretary-1.

[3] This is a township where a number of complaints concerning forced labour have been lodged with the court (see paras. 15 and 17 below).

[4] The ninth person, together with three of the others, had also appealed through the officer-in-charge of the prison. The Special Appellate Bench of the Supreme Court considered both appeals concurrently.

[5] The full text of the judgement can be made available by the Office.

illegal organizations abroad, but their sentences were reduced from three years' imprisonment with hard labour to two years' imprisonment with hard labour. [6]

– The conviction of U Shwe Mahn for high treason was altered to section 123 of the Penal Code (encouraging, harbouring or comforting persons guilty of high treason) on the grounds that he abetted other appellants who had committed high treason and that he had communicated with individuals in Thailand (namely, Maung Maung and Zarni Thwe) who were members of illegal organizations opposing the Myanmar government. His sentence was reduced from life imprisonment to five years' imprisonment with hard labour. [7]

8. On 18 October Mr. Kari Tapiola wrote on behalf of the Director-General of the ILO to the Myanmar Minister for Labour. This letter is reproduced in Appendix I.

IV. Developments in the forced labour situation

Overview

9. On the basis of all the information available to him, the Liaison Officer a.i.'s general evaluation of the forced labour situation continues to be, as presented previously to the Governing Body, [8] that although there have been some improvements since the Commission of Inquiry, the practice remains widespread throughout the country, and is particularly serious in border areas where there is a large presence of the army.

10. The Liaison Officer a.i. continues to receive significant numbers of complaints directly from individuals alleging they have been subjected to forced labour, or from representatives of such persons. Often these individuals are in fact complaining on behalf of a larger group of persons or community subjected to forced labour. There have now been a total of 72 such complaints in 2004, and interventions have been made with the authorities on 38 of these cases. [9] Of these 38 cases, 18 concerned various forms of forced labour (other than forced recruitment), 13 concerned forced recruitment of minors into the armed forces, one case concerned alleged harassment of a complainant and six were direct complaints by individuals to Myanmar courts under section 374 of the Penal Code, copies

---

[6] The decision of the Supreme Court in the first appeal that the pre-trial detention period was to be deducted from the prison terms still stands.

[7] The Court also ruled that the pre-trial detention period was to be deducted from the prison term. Of the other six persons in the case, none of whom had an ILO connection, four had their convictions for high treason upheld and remain sentenced to life imprisonment. The two other persons had their sentences under section 123 of the Penal Code reduced from three to two years' imprisonment.

[8] See GB.286/6 (Mar. 2003), para. 7; GB.288/5 (Nov. 2003), para. 8; and GB.289/8 (Mar. 2004), para. 10.

[9] Of the remaining 34 cases, 18 were considered to be outside the mandate of the Liaison Officer, in eight cases of forced recruitment interventions had already been made by another agency, one case concerned an allegation already raised with the authorities in 2003, six cases were pending and one complaint directly to the court under section 374 of the Penal Code, copied to the Liaison Officer, was subsequently withdrawn.

of which had been communicated to the Liaison Officer by the complainants. (A list of all these cases is provided in Appendix II.)

11. In cases of alleged forced recruitment of minors, the Liaison Officer a.i. has written to the Convention 29 Implementation Committee with the details of the allegation, requesting that the Committee take urgent action to verify this information in order that, if it is confirmed, the individuals in question can be returned to the care of their parents and an investigation carried out into the circumstances of their recruitment so that any person found to have acted illegally can be prosecuted. In other cases of alleged forced labour, the Liaison Officer a.i. has written to the Convention 29 Implementation Committee providing details of the allegation and recommending that, in line with the Committee's procedures, a field observation team (FOT) be sent to the area in question to investigate the allegation, and expressing his readiness to accompany this FOT in an observer capacity. In cases of direct complaints to a court under section 374 of the Penal Code, he has written to the Convention 29 Implementation Committee indicating that he has been made aware of the complaint, that he would remain in contact with the complainant during the complaint procedure, and requesting the Committee to keep him informed of any developments.

12. In the view of the Liaison Officer a.i., the mechanism put in place by the authorities for addressing forced labour allegations, that of sending an ad hoc team composed of senior Government officials to the region to conduct an investigation, is not well-suited to dealing with the increasing numbers of cases.[10] Indeed, as the number of allegations has increased, they have tended to be investigated internally by the General Administration Department; the Liaison Officer a.i. has not been invited to observe any such investigations, nor is he aware of any safeguards to avoid potential conflicts of interest. Cases concerning the army (that is, cases of forced recruitment, or cases of forced labour allegedly imposed by the army) have been referred by the Committee to the representative of the Ministry of Defence. These cases are investigated internally by the army, with only a short response on the findings being reported by the Committee, despite requests from the Liaison Officer a.i. for detailed written reports of all investigations. The role of FOTs has been limited largely to conducting information-dissemination workshops.[11] The Liaison Officer a.i. believes that such activities can play an important role in raising awareness of the prohibition of forced labour among local officials, but only in a context where action is being taken against those who violate this prohibition.

13. To date, of the 38 cases referred to the Convention 29 Implementation Committee, responses have been received in 18 cases.[12] In all these cases, the allegation that forced labour was involved was rejected. In the six cases where individuals complained directly to the court, three cases were rejected on the grounds that there was no prima facie evidence of forced labour, and in three cases the trials are still ongoing. More disturbingly, in two of

---

[10] The former Liaison Officer had already expressed certain concerns relating to the FOT mechanism in a letter to the authorities dated 16 November 2003 (see GB.288/5/1, para. 2). While many of the specific concerns were subsequently addressed, the more fundamental step of reviewing the composition of such teams was not taken.

[11] FOTs have visited a number of areas, mostly to hold information-dissemination workshops, but also on certain occasions to investigate allegations of forced labour. These areas include, in July, Kawhmu in Yangon Division (accompanied by the Liaison Officer a.i. in an observer capacity), Myeik in Tanintharyi Division and Pyapon in Ayeyawaddy Division and, in August, northern Rakhine State and Kayin State.

[12] Verbal responses have also been received in a further four cases (written responses are pending). The remaining cases on which responses have not been received mostly concern the army.

the cases that were rejected, the complainants were prosecuted for defamation and imprisoned for six months each. [13]

Details of cases

14. Details of 23 cases on which interventions were made in 2004 have already been presented to the Governing Body and the Committee on the Application of Standards of the International Labour Conference. [14] Details on new cases are provided below:

– *Intervention dated 28 May.* According to the allegation, a 13-year-old boy was detained by two men while walking in Yangon, and taken against his will to an army recruitment centre where he was forced to enlist under the threat of being imprisoned if he refused. Subsequently, he took an opportunity to run away and return to his family. He was advised by his family to turn himself in and seek a formal discharge because of his young age, rather than risk being treated as a deserter. However, after taking this advice and turning himself in to his battalion, he was sentenced to six months' imprisonment, after which he was ordered to continue his military service. [15] Supporting documentary information was provided, including, inter alia, the judgement of the court martial, as well as the boy's birth certificate, student card and family list. The Liaison Officer a.i. urged the Implementation Committee to take the necessary steps to verify this information, in order that if it was confirmed a review of the boy's conviction could take place with a view to ensuring his release from prison and his formal discharge from the army, as well as the prosecution of any officials found to have acted illegally.

– *Intervention dated 6 July.* The intervention concerned four allegations of forced labour that were received from individuals from different villages in Bago township (in Bago Division). In the first case, it was alleged that villagers were being requisitioned by the local authorities to construct a road embankment. In the second case, it was alleged that for the past year villagers had been required by the authorities to provide ten persons at all times, on a rotation basis, for sentry duty. In the third case, villagers from the same village were being requisitioned by the local authorities to clear 500 acres of land for the establishment of a teak plantation. In each of these cases, every household in the village had been given a quota of work to complete, and were threatened with arrest if they did not do so. In the fourth case, it was alleged that the township authorities requisitioned villagers from a number of villages in the area to work on the construction of barracks and other buildings for four new artillery battalions. A total of 30,000 bamboo poles also had to be provided by the villagers for the construction. To cover other construction costs, villagers also had to provide compulsory cash contributions in addition to their labour. Vehicles and their drivers were also requisitioned for transporting materials.

– *Intervention dated 8 July.* According to an allegation received from a number of alleged victims, labour had been requisitioned for at least three years by Military Operations Command No. 5 based in Toungup (Rakhine State), for the cultivation of its farm land. According to the information provided, the land in question had been

---

[13] See paras. 16 and 21 below.

[14] See doc. C.App./D.5 (ILC, 2004), paras. 9-17 (reproduced in Appendix III) and doc. GB.289/8, paras. 15, 16 and 18.

[15] The Liaison Officer a.i. subsequently learned that the individual was sent back to his battalion from military detention on 23 September.

previously confiscated from farmers for the establishment of this military command, after which farmers were required to continue cultivating the land on behalf of the military, using their own cattle and tools.

- *Intervention dated 9 July.* According to an allegation from an alleged victim in Hinthada township (Ayeyawaddy Division), the township authorities had given instructions to the local authorities to provide round-the-clock sentries to guard an unoccupied monastery. Since then, more than one year ago, the local authorities had been requisitioning three to four villagers on a rotation basis to perform this duty.[16]

- *Intervention dated 23 July.* According to an allegation from persons living in Maungdaw township (Rakhine State), labour was being requisitioned by the authorities on a large scale from several villages in the northern part of the township for the construction of a number of bridges. Muslim villagers were particularly affected, but Rakhine Buddhist villagers were also being requisitioned. In addition to labour, the villagers were also required to provide gravel for the construction. Approximately 45 persons per village had to work on these projects each day. The allegation pointed out that the timing of the work at the end of the planting season meant that the impact on individuals was particularly great, as this was the most critical time for work in their own fields or, in the case of landless labourers, the time when they were able to earn the most from casual agricultural labour.

- *Intervention dated 13 September.* According to the allegation, a 14-year-old boy was detained while walking in Yangon and forced to enlist under threat of imprisonment. After completing basic military training, the boy was assigned to a battalion and a few months later suffered a gunshot wound at the front line as well as a serious bout of malaria. He was not permitted to leave the army and after treatment he was returned to his unit. Feeling he had no other options, he went absent without leave. Supporting documentary information was provided, including a copy of the boy's family list which established his identity and age. The Liaison Officer a.i. urged the Implementation Committee to take the necessary steps to verify this information, in order that if it was confirmed the boy could be given a formal discharge from the army and assurances that no action would be taken against him; an urgent investigation should then be carried out into the circumstances of his recruitment so that any person found to have acted illegally could be prosecuted.

- *Intervention dated 12 October.* According to an allegation from persons living in Ramree township (Rakhine State), labour was being requisitioned by the authorities from 40 villages in the area for the repair of a road. The villagers had been forced to work on the repair of this road every year for several years; the most recent incident began in July and was ongoing at the time the complaint was made in early October. The timing of this latest incident placed a particular burden on villagers as it was the peak agricultural period. Vehicle owners also had their vehicles requisitioned for the project, without compensation. Villagers were threatened by the police that action would be taken against them if they did not provide their labour. One student had been prosecuted by the local authorities during a previous incident in March for allegedly refusing to work on the project.

15. The Liaison Officer a.i. was also informed by individuals of four additional complaints they had made directly to Myanmar courts under section 374 of the Penal Code (which concerns the illegal imposition of forced labour). There have now been a total of six complaints of this kind. The details of the four new cases are as follows. One case

---

[16] This case has also been the subject of a direct complaint to the courts under section 374 of the Penal Code (see para. 16 below).

concerned an individual who claimed that he had been requisitioned for a road construction project in Kawhmu township (Yangon Division); this project had also been the subject of the two previous complaints of this kind. All three trials were still ongoing at the time that this report was finalized.

16. The three other new cases concerned individuals who claimed that they had been requisitioned for sentry duty in Hinthada township (Ayeyawaddy Division).[17] Two of the individuals refused to do this work, and as a result were prosecuted and sentenced by the township court to prison terms of several months. After their release from prison at the end of their sentences, the two individuals lodged complaints under section 374 of the Penal Code against the official who had requisitioned them for the work. Included with the complaints were the original trial documents which, the complainants argued, established beyond doubt that the demand for them to do the sentry work constituted forced labour. According to court documents provided to the Liaison Officer a.i., the township court (presided over by the same judge that had originally sentenced the individuals for refusing to do the work) dismissed the case following a police investigation, on the grounds that there were no indications that coercion or forced labour was involved. This finding was seemingly contradicted by the earlier decision of the same court to sentence the two individuals to prison terms for failing to carry out the work. The complainants subsequently tried, unsuccessfully, to lodge the complaint with a higher court. Furthermore, the official accused of requisitioning the labour then lodged a counter-suit against the two individuals for defamation; this case was accepted by the court and the two individuals were subsequently found guilty (again, by the same judge) and given six-month prison terms on 7 October. The third individual who lodged a complaint concerning this alleged forced labour incident submitted in support of his complaint a written summons from the local authorities indicating that he had a final opportunity to provide labour or face legal action. The township court also rejected this case on the grounds that there was no prima facie evidence of forced labour.

Action by the authorities against complainants

17. The Liaison Officer a.i. has received information according to which two individuals were arrested after returning to their village following a visit to him in Yangon. During the visit, one of the individuals provided details on a direct complaint he had made to a court under section 374 of the Penal Code, concerning forced labour in Kawhmu township (Yangon Division). According to the information, which was received from one of these individuals, the two were arrested by the police at their respective homes the evening they returned, and interrogated, inter alia, about their visit to the ILO. They were held in the police lock-up overnight and released the following afternoon. The two persons also submitted a complaint on this matter directly to the Minister for Home Affairs. In a letter dated 7 July, the Liaison Officer a.i. urged the Convention 29 Implementation Committee to ensure that this incident was fully investigated as a matter of urgency and that he was kept informed of the results. He underlined that it would clearly be a matter of great concern if contacts with the Office of the ILO Liaison Officer could give rise to such action on the part of the police, all the more so in the light of the recent high treason case and of the repeated assurances given at all levels and on various occasions by the authorities. It might also cast serious doubt on the possibility to effectively implement the Formal Understanding on the Facilitator, which contained a specific provision that no action should be taken against complainants. In addition, he pointed out that this matter could also reflect badly on the complaint procedure under section 374 of the Penal Code given that this was one of the

---

[17] All three cases concerned sentry duty at an unoccupied monastery (see also para. 14 above).

first such complaints ever to be lodged and as such would no doubt be followed with particular interest. No response has been received from the authorities. [18]

18. The Liaison Officer a.i. was also informed of another incident of this kind. According to this information, three persons from Toungup township (Rakhine State) were detained and interrogated by the local authorities on suspicion of having provided information to the ILO concerning an incident of forced labour in the area which was the subject of an intervention by the Liaison Officer a.i. [19] At the end of their interrogation, the three persons were allegedly required to sign their names on blank sheets of paper, and were warned that they would shortly be arrested and interrogated further. On 19 August the Liaison Officer a.i. wrote to the Convention 29 Implementation Committee expressing similar concerns as in the previous case. [20] He indicated that, because of these concerns, and the possibility that further action might be taken against these persons, he had invited the informal facilitator, Mr. Léon de Riedmatten, to join him on a visit to the area. He also urged the Committee to participate in this visit, in order that the realities of the situation could be fully and credibly assessed. However, no member of the authorities was available.

19. Accordingly, the Liaison Officer a.i. and Mr. Léon de Riedmatten visited Toungup township from 13 to 17 September. During the visit, they were able to have detailed discussions with local people, including the three persons against whom action had allegedly been taken, as well as with members of the local authorities. They were also able to visit the location where the alleged forced labour had taken place. As a result of these visits and discussions, they are of the view that the essential facts of the situation are not in doubt, and that the allegations concerning both the original forced labour incidents and the action taken against the three individuals were accurate. The seriousness of the forced labour incidents was reinforced, both in terms of their scale and the harshness of the conditions, as was the fact that these incidents had occurred on the orders of the army. In addition, events which occurred in the area during their visit gave rise to further concerns over the safety of the persons met during the visit. On their return to Yangon on 17 September, the Liaison Officer a.i. and Mr. Léon de Riedmatten met with the Secretary of the Convention 29 Implementation Committee [21] to give details on the outcome of the visit and to express their serious concerns.

20. When after one month no response had been received from the authorities, the Liaison Officer wrote to the Convention 29 Implementation Committee on 22 October underlining the seriousness of this case and restating the recommendations of the informal facilitator. These were that the authorities should: (i) take the necessary steps to ensure that there is no retaliation against the three persons suspected of having provided information to the ILO on this case, or any other individual met during the visit; (ii) ensure that the villagers in this area are not subject to forced labour in the future; and (iii) ensure that compulsory contributions in cash or in kind are not required from villagers for projects of this nature. The letter also underlined that, in addition to these recommendations of the informal facilitator concerning the future, it was imperative that there be a thorough investigation of

---

[18] However, following the initial incident the complainant has faced no further problems.

[19] See doc. C.App./D.5. (ILC, 2004), para. 11 (reproduced in Appendix III).

[20] See para. 17 above.

[21] That is, U Myat Ko, Director-General of the General Administration Department.

the forced labour incidents which had taken place, in order that those responsible could be held accountable. [22]

21. The Liaison Officer a.i. is also deeply concerned at the fact that two individuals who made complaints to a court were subsequently found guilty of defamation and imprisoned. [23] This is all the more concerning as these two individuals had already served prison sentences for refusing to perform forced labour. On 8 October the Liaison Officer a.i. wrote to the Convention 29 Implementation Committee expressing his concerns and recommending: (a) that he be able to urgently meet with the two persons, preferably at his office rather than in a place of detention; and (b) that, in view of the prima facie evidence that forced labour had occurred, an urgent investigation be conducted into the events in Hinthada and in particular into the conduct of the township court in these two cases, as well as a third related case, [24] in order that the apparent contradictions in the court's actions could be credibly resolved. At the time this report was finalized, the Liaison Officer a.i. had not received a response to the concerns he had expressed. However, information had been received from the authorities according to which the two individuals had been released. Any further details will be reported to the Governing Body.

Responses received from the authorities

22. In letters to the Liaison Officer a.i. dated 30 July and 9, 27 and 31 August, the authorities presented their findings on a number of allegations of forced labour that he had raised.

    – As regards the allegation of forced labour for road-widening projects in Chin State, [25] the authorities indicated that the projects had been carried out by the Public Works Department using machinery. No members of the public had been involved, although in one case members of local community organizations had happily contributed labour and, in another case where a retaining wall had to be built, local churchgoers participated happily in the work and contributed money voluntarily for the project. These findings contradicted the assertions of the local people engaged in these projects that the Liaison Officer a.i. had spoken to, and the photographs that he had submitted showing local people engaged in the work.

    – As regards the allegation of forced labour in Naukmee village in Bogale township (Ayeyawaddy Division) for road projects, [26] the authorities indicated that the work had been organized by local leaders, for community benefit. In a response to the authorities dated 30 September, the Liaison Officer a.i. pointed out that the information provided appeared to indicate that forced labour in the sense of Convention No. 29 had occurred since the nature and scale of the work would put it beyond the scope of the exception in the Convention concerning minor communal service.

---

[22] The Liaison Officer a.i. has received information from the area according to which no further action has been taken against the three persons suspected of having provided information to the ILO in this case.

[23] See para. 16 above.

[24] See para. 16 above.

[25] See doc. C.App./D.5 (ILC, 2004), para. 16 (reproduced in Appendix III).

[26] ibid., para. 10 (reproduced in Appendix III).

- As regards the allegation of forced labour for guard duty and land clearing in Pantanaw township (Ayeyawaddy Division),[27] the authorities indicated that the work in question had been organized and agreed by the local community in order to obtain funds for community projects, and did not therefore constitute forced labour.

- As regards the two allegations of forced labour in Bogale township (Ayeyawaddy Division),[28] the authorities indicated that in the first case the work was organized by community elders with the willing participation of villagers. In the second case, the authorities found that village chairmen had agreed to provide the township chairman with funds for the project, and that when the villagers were informed of this decision, they had freely donated the necessary funds. However, since it was found that the funds were not sufficient for the project (constructing government offices), they were instead used for a school and to provide a new zinc roof for the township office of the Union Solidarity and Development Association (USDA).[29]

- As regards the allegation of forced labour in Maungdaw township (Rakhine State),[30] the authorities indicated that a field observation team had investigated the matter and found that a budget had been allocated for the project under the control of the NaSaKa border security force, who subcontracted the work to a private contractor. Workers were paid and there was no forced labour.

23. In a further letter to the Liaison Officer a.i. dated 31 August, the authorities presented their findings on four allegations of forced recruitment that he had raised.[31] It was confirmed that the four individuals were serving in army battalions as alleged. The authorities indicated that, according to the records kept at the time of recruitment, all four individuals had been over the age of 18 when recruited. Furthermore, two of the individuals had been interviewed and had expressed a wish to continue military service; the third individual had subsequently gone absent without leave, and the fourth was serving a sentence in a military prison for desertion. In a response to the authorities dated 30 September, the Liaison Officer a.i. pointed out that the ages of the four individuals recorded at recruitment were contradicted by documentary evidence (including birth registration documents, student cards, household lists and identity papers) that was provided to the authorities with the original allegations. This situation inevitably raised doubts as to whether the recruitment had been genuinely voluntary, particularly given the young age at which the individuals were alleged to have been recruited. In the case of the fourth individual, who had now been sent from military prison back to his battalion, no information had been provided as to whether his recruitment was found to have been voluntary. An urgent investigation should therefore be conducted into all these cases and appropriate action taken.

24. On 3 September the Liaison Officer a.i. met with the Convention 29 Implementation Committee. He was briefed on the work of the Committee, including information dissemination activities in various parts of the country, as well as the action it had taken to investigate specific allegations of forced labour that he had transmitted. As regards the forced recruitment of children, the Committee noted that, in addition to setting up in January a High-level Committee for the Prevention of the Recruitment of Child Soldiers, it

---

[27] ibid., para. 12 (reproduced in Appendix III).

[28] ibid., paras. 13 and 14 (reproduced in Appendix III).

[29] The USDA is a government-sponsored mass organization.

[30] See para. 14 above.

[31] ibid., para. 17 (reproduced in Appendix III) and para. 14 above.

was working in consultation with UNICEF on ways to address the issue.[32] The Committee underlined that the authorities were doing all that they could to implement their part of the joint Plan of Action on forced labour, even if the ILO was not prepared to go ahead with the Plan at this time. In the Committee's view, this demonstrated the strong political will of the authorities to eliminating forced labour. The Liaison Officer a.i. recalled that a key concern of the ILO was the three persons convicted of high treason, which had been discussed in detail at the previous meeting. He recalled that it was vital for there to be judicial clarity on the question of the legality of contacts with the ILO, and that it was important that this be translated into concrete steps in the case of the three individuals. As regards developments on the elimination of forced labour, the large number of individual complaints that he had received and transmitted to the authorities was extremely significant. These cases provided an opportunity to the authorities to give a concrete demonstration of their stated political will to eliminate forced labour. In contrast, a lack of credible action in these cases would tend to give the impression that the authorities were not serious in addressing this problem. In this regard, he was concerned that all the responses that he had received so far stated that the allegations had been found to be untrue. None of the cases of direct complaints by individuals to the courts had so far been found in the complainants' favour. To date, no official in Myanmar had been found guilty of imposing forced labour, even though it was recognized that the practice continued. Even more concerning was the fact that in some cases action had been taken by the authorities against complainants. The Liaison Officer a.i. urged the Committee to investigate these cases as a matter of priority. He noted that the current state of affairs would inevitably cast doubt on the credibility of the Committee and its work, and on the political will of the authorities to seriously address the problem.

Yangon, 22 October 2004.

---

[32] This included developing an action plan to address child recruitment, and the establishment of a Directorate for Military Strength to enforce recruitment procedures. The Committee for the Prevention of the Recruitment of Child Soldiers has so far met three times. At its last meeting on 5 October, Lt. Gen. Thein Sein (its Chairman), in comments reported in the state press, noted that in Myanmar "there are laws, rules, orders and directives that protect the rights of the children. Forced labour is also prohibited as Myanmar people are noble-minded". He went on to add that "groups with negative views ... are also making false statements on narcotic drugs, human trafficking and forced labour with the intention of tarnishing the dignity of the State among international communities" (*New light of Myanmar*, 6 Oct. 2004).

Appendix I

Letter dated 18 October from Mr. Tapiola to the Myanmar Minister for Labour

Dear Minister,

On behalf of the Director-General who is now absent from Geneva, I wish to thank the authorities for the copy of the new Supreme Court judgment in the High Treason case. At first sight, it appears to contain elements of interest regarding the rights of Myanmar citizens to freely communicate with the ILO.

We shall study carefully the judgement as soon as a full official translation is available, in the light of the discussions at the International Labour Conference and the Informal Facilitator's report. We shall examine the specific grounds on which the sentences still maintain the continued imprisonment of the three persons concerned although for a shorter period. In the meanwhile, I do wish to express that their early release remains a possibility and should be given urgent consideration.

At the same time, I must express serious concern about certain other developments which have been reported to the Convention 29 Implementation Committee. It is my hope that these matters can be speedily clarified, as they will have to be reported and are liable to affect the Governing Body debate.

This is also why I trust that you can have an early opportunity to have a discussion with the ILO Liaison Officer ad interim.

Yours sincerely,

(Signed) Kari Tapiola.

Appendix II

Cases on which interventions have been made (2004)

Case type	Location	Intervened	Response	Details of response from the authorities
Forced recruitment	Hlaingthaya township, Yangon Division	26/01/2004	23/02/2004	The child in question was released from army back to the care of his parents on 5/2/2004, but recruitment was found to have been voluntary.
Forced labour	Twante township, Yangon Division	28/01/2004	05/05/2004	Implementation Committee found the allegation to be unfounded, but the district chairman was removed from his post for "being a burden to the people".
Forced recruitment	Hlaingthaya township, Yangon Division	29/01/2004	17/02/2004	The child in question was released from army back to the care of his parents on 5/2/2004, but recruitment was found to have been voluntary.
Forced labour	Thandaung township, Kayin State	24/02/2004	None to date	
Forced recruitment	Twante township, Yangon Division	11/03/2004	26/05/2004	Found to have been voluntarily recruited when over the age of 18.
Forced labour	Bogale township, Ayeyawaddy Division	12/03/2004	09/08/2004	Work found to have been jointly organized by community elders and local authorities. Response ambiguous as to whether this could have nevertheless involved forced labour.
Forced recruitment	Insein township, Yangon Division	18/03/2004	26/05/2004	Individual not found to be serving in the battalion mentioned in the allegation.
Forced recruitment	North Okkalapa township, Yangon Division	18/03/2004	26/05/2004	Found to have been over the age of 18 when recruited and currently imprisoned for desertion. No indication given as to whether the recruitment was found to have been voluntary.
Forced recruitment	Thakehta township, Yangon Division	18/03/2004	26/05/2004	Found to have been voluntarily recruited when over the age of 18.
Forced labour	Toungup township, Rakhine State	07/04/2004	None to date	
Forced labour	Toungup township, Rakhine State	07/04/2004	None to date	
Forced recruitment	Khayan township, Yangon Division	08/04/2004	None to date	
Forced labour	Bogale township, Ayeyawaddy Division	09/04/2004	31/08/2004	Found to have been community development work carried out collectively by the villagers.
Forced labour	Bogale township, Ayeyawaddy Division	09/04/2004	31/08/2004	It was found that no forced labour was involved in the project, and that voluntary cash donations had been received but had been insufficient for the project, so the funds had been used for construction of a school building and roof of the USDA office.
Forced labour	Pantanaw township, Ayeyawaddy Division	09/04/2004	27/08/2004	Work found to have been carried out willingly by villagers after the majority had agreed to do this work for free in return for a donation of funds to village community projects.
Forced recruitment	Hlaingthaya township, Yangon Division	23/04/2004	26/05/2004	Found to have been voluntarily recruited when over the age of 18.
Forced labour	Monywa township, Sagaing Division	29/04/2004	None to date	(Verbal response indicated that the allegation was unfounded.)
Forced recruitment	Hlaingthaya township, Yangon Division	30/04/2004	31/08/2004	Found to have been recruited when over the age of 18, and to have been absent without leave since 4 June 2004.

Case type	Location	Intervened	Response	Details of response from the authorities
Forced recruitment	Thingangyun township, Yangon Division	30/04/2004	31/08/2004	Found to have been voluntarily recruited when over the age of 18.
Forced recruitment	Twante township, Yangon Division	30/04/2004	31/08/2004	Found to have been voluntarily recruited when over the age of 18.
Section 374 complaint [1]	Kawhmu township, Yangon Division	04/05/2004	sub judice	
Forced labour	Falam district, Chin State	20/05/2004	30/07/2004	No forced labour found to have been involved.
Section 374 complaint [1]	Kawhmu township, Yangon Division	26/05/2004	sub judice	
Forced recruitment	Shwepyitha township, Yangon Division	28/05/2004	31/08/2004	Found to have been recruited when over the age of 18. No indication given as to whether the recruitment was found to have been voluntary. Arrested for desertion and given six-month sentence in a military prison. Returned to his battalion on 23 September.
Forced labour	Bago township, Bago Division	06/07/2004	None to date	(Verbal response indicated that the allegation was unfounded.)
Forced labour	Bago township, Bago Division	06/07/2004	None to date	(Verbal response indicated that the allegation was unfounded.)
Forced labour	Bago township, Bago Division	06/07/2004	None to date	(Verbal response indicated that the allegation was unfounded.)
Forced labour	Bago township, Bago Division	06/07/2004	None to date	
Other [2]	Kawhmu township, Yangon Division	07/07/2004	None to date	
Forced labour	Toungup township, Rakhine State	08/07/2004	None to date	
Forced labour	Hinthada township, Ayeyawaddy Division	09/07/2004	None to date	
Section 374 complaint [1]	Hinthada township, Ayeyawaddy Division	22/07/2004	—	Case rejected by court on the grounds that there was no prima facie evidence of forced labour. Complainant subsequently sentenced to 6-month prison term for defamation on 7/10/2004.
Forced labour	Maungdaw township, Rakhine State	23/07/2004	31/08/2004	Official investigation (by FOT) found that the allegations of forced labour on the bridge projects were not true.
Section 374 complaint [1]	Hinthada township, Ayeyawaddy Division	06/08/2004	—	Case rejected by court on the grounds that there was no prima facie evidence of forced labour. Complainant subsequently sentenced to 6-month prison term for defamation on 7/10/2004.
Section 374 complaint [1]	Kawhmu township, Yangon Division	09/08/2004	sub judice	
Forced recruitment	Kyimindine township, Yangon Division	13/09/2004	None to date	
Section 374 complaint [1]	Hinthada township, Ayeyawaddy Division	01/10/2004	—	Case rejected by court on the grounds that there was no prima facie evidence of forced labour.
Forced labour	Ramree township, Rakhine State	12/10/2004	None to date	

[1] In this table, "374 complaint" refers to a direct complaint to a Myanmar court under section 374 of the Penal Code concerning the illegal imposition of forced labour. [2] This was a case of alleged harassment and arrest by the police following the visit of two persons to the ILO in connection with an allegation of forced labour.

Appendix III

Extract from document C.App./D.5, Committee on the Application of Standards, ILC, 92nd Session (June 2004) [1]

[...]

Activities of the Liaison Officer a.i.

5. On 9 April the Liaison Officer a.i. met with the Minister for Labour in order to discuss the outcome of the Governing Body debate and the steps which could be envisaged to give effect to the Governing Body's conclusions. The Liaison Officer a.i. had further meetings with the Minister on 7 and 24 May, together with the informal facilitator Mr. de Riedmatten.

6. In a meeting on 29 April with the Director-General of the Myanmar Department of Labour, the Liaison Officer a.i. had the opportunity to discuss matters relating to the practical elimination of forced labour. A meeting on 5 May with the Convention 29 Implementation Committee provided the opportunity to have more detailed discussions in this regard, as set out in paragraphs 18-20 below. In a subsequent meeting on 18 May with the Director-General of the Department of Labour, the Liaison Officer a.i. was able to reiterate some of the comments and concerns that he had expressed in the meeting with the Convention 29 Implementation Committee.

7. In addition to these meetings with the authorities, the Liaison Officer a.i. also had the opportunity to have discussions with the diplomatic community in Yangon and Bangkok, as well as with representatives of United Nations agencies, international non-governmental organizations and the International Committee of the Red Cross.

8. From 10 to 15 May, the Liaison Officer a.i. travelled to Chin State. [2] This trip was conducted independently of the authorities. The Liaison Officer a.i. was able to travel to all areas that he wished without any restrictions or escort, and was able to meet freely with a range of persons, as well as with members of the Chin State Peace and Development Council including its Secretary.

Developments on specific allegations

9. Since the finalization of his report to the 289th Session of the Governing Body in March, the Liaison Officer a.i. has received a considerable number of additional complaints, mostly from alleged victims or their representatives, concerning incidents of forced labour. This brings the total number of complaints received so far in 2004 to 40. The Liaison Officer a.i. has now transmitted 21 of these cases to the Convention 29 Implementation Committee for investigation and action. [3] In two further cases, the individuals who presented allegations to the Liaison Officer a.i. had also lodged direct complaints with a Myanmar court under section 374 of the Penal Code. This is the

---

[1] See ILC, 92nd Session (Geneva, 2004), *Provisional Record* No. 24, Part 3, section D, *Latest developments since the 289th Session of the Governing Body (Mar. 2004)*.

[2] He travelled from Mandalay to Chin State via Kalemyo, returning to Mandalay via Gangaw. In Chin State he visited the townships of Tiddim, Falam and Hakha.

[3] Of the remaining cases, five were rejected on the grounds that they were not sufficiently precise or credible for action to be taken, five cases were judged not to fall within the mandate of the Liaison Officer, seven cases of forced recruitment had already been the subject of interventions by another agency, and two cases were sub judice as the complainants had made direct complaints to a court under section 374 of the Penal Code (see below).

first time that a complaint has been lodged under this section of the Penal Code.[4] In these cases, the Liaison Officer a.i. wrote to the Convention 29 Implementation Committee informing it that he had received copies of the complaints and underlining that, particularly as these were the first complaints of this kind and as such could be expected to generate considerable interest, it was important for the credibility of the process that they be handled in a fully transparent manner. He indicated that he would remain in contact with the complainants throughout the case and asked that he be kept informed of developments.

10. On 12 March the Liaison Officer a.i. transmitted to the Convention 29 Implementation Committee an allegation of forced labour that he had received from an individual from Naukmee village in Bogale township (Ayeyawaddy Division). This individual alleged that they had very recently been forced by the local authorities to participate in the upgrading of a village access road along with hundreds of other villagers from several villages in the area. The individual also alleged that forced labour had been imposed for a number of other projects in the recent past.

11. On 7 April the Liaison Officer a.i. transmitted to the Convention 29 Implementation Committee an allegation of forced labour that he had received from a number of individuals from Toungup township (Rakhine State). These individuals alleged that an army battalion had very recently forced them and around 800 other villagers from several villages in the area to work under difficult conditions on the construction of embankments as part of a land reclamation project. The Liaison Officer a.i. also received a separate allegation containing similar information concerning the same project.

12. On 9 April the Liaison Officer a.i. transmitted to the Convention 29 Implementation Committee three further allegations of forced labour that he had received. The first of these allegations was made by three individuals from Pantanaw township (Ayeyawaddy Division). These individuals alleged that villagers from one village tract in the area were currently being forced by the local authorities to carry out guard duty at a local official's house and at a nearby fish-breeding project being implemented by the local authorities. They also had to work clearing land for a football field.

13. The second allegation transmitted to the Committee on 9 April was made by an individual from Magu village tract in Bogale township (Ayeyawaddy Division). According to this allegation, two villagers were required by the local authorities at all times for general duties at the village tract office. Villagers carried out this duty on a rotation basis, and anyone who failed to be present was subject to a fine. Villagers were also forced to participate in other projects, such as constructing embankments and widening the access road. Copies of two orders from the local authorities requisitioning such labour were provided.

14. The third allegation transmitted to the Committee on 9 April was made by an individual from Ama village tract in Bogale township (Ayeyawaddy Division). According to this allegation, one person from each household had been forced by the local authorities for the previous three weeks to participate in the construction of 13 government offices as part of a project to upgrade Ama to a sub-township.

15. On 29 April the Liaison Officer a.i. transmitted to the Convention 29 Implementation Committee an allegation of forced labour that he had received from an individual from Monywa township (Sagaing Division). According to this allegation, villagers from five villages were being forced to work on the resurfacing with rocks of a five-mile section of road. In addition to the labour the villagers had to provide the rock chippings, which entailed financial costs.

16. On 20 May the Liaison Officer a.i. transmitted to the Convention 29 Implementation Committee a case of forced labour that had come to his attention during his recent visit to Chin State, including photographs he had taken showing the nature and scope of the work. The Liaison Officer a.i. had found that work was under way at the time of his visit to Tiddim and Falam towns to widen the main road passing through these towns. The households along these roads were required to carry out this work, which included considerable excavation of the steep hill into which the road

---

[4] Section 374 of the Penal Code makes forced labour a criminal offence, in the following terms: "Whoever unlawfully compels any person to labour against the will of that person shall [be] punished with imprisonment of either description for a term which may extend to one year, or with fine, or with both".

was cut, as well as the construction of a high retaining wall and surfacing of the newly widened section with rock.

17. In letters dated 11 and 18 March, and 8, 23 and 30 April, the Liaison Officer a.i. transmitted to the Convention 29 Implementation Committee nine detailed allegations concerning forced recruitment into the army. Information concerning the alleged circumstances of the recruitment, together with copies of identification documents of the boys, was provided to the Committee. Seven of these allegations concerned the forcible recruitment of boys between the ages of 13 and 16. The Liaison Officer a.i. requested the Committee to ensure that urgent action was taken to verify these allegations in order that, if they were confirmed, these children could be returned to the care of their families as soon as possible and an urgent investigation then carried out into the circumstances of their recruitment so that any person found to have acted illegally could be prosecuted. Of the remaining two cases, one concerned a 15-year-old boy who it was alleged was forcibly recruited into the army, but then ran away after two months and resumed his education. He was subsequently arrested and sentenced by court martial to four years' imprisonment for desertion. The Liaison Officer a.i. requested the Committee to ensure that an urgent investigation was carried out in order that, if the information was confirmed, the court martial verdict would be reviewed and the individual released as appropriate. The other case concerned a 13-year-old boy who it was alleged was recruited into the military against his will. A few months later, after completing basic training and being posted to a battalion, he was allowed a home visit and subsequently did not return to his battalion. He was therefore now facing the possibility of being arrested and court-martialled for desertion. The Liaison Officer a.i. requested the Committee to ensure that urgent action was taken to verify this information in order that, if it was confirmed, the individual could be given a formal discharge from the military and assurances that no action would be taken against him. In both of these cases, the Liaison Officer a.i. also requested the Committee, if the information was confirmed, to ensure that investigations were carried out into the circumstances of recruitment so that any person found to have acted illegally could be prosecuted.

18. *Meeting with the Convention 29 Implementation Committee.* On 5 May the Liaison Officer a.i. met with the Implementation Committee and was briefed on the recent work of the Committee and the action taken in light of the various allegations, as detailed below. The Liaison Officer a.i. thanked the Committee for the information on its work and for the cooperation that he had received. The Liaison Officer a.i. noted the increasing number of allegations he was receiving from individuals, as well as the first complaint under section 374 of the Penal Code. This demonstrated not only a degree of confidence in the ILO, but also showed that complainants had a degree of confidence that the authorities would take action in cases of forced labour. It was important that the Committee continue to take concrete and credible action in response to allegations. In this regard, the Liaison Officer a.i. noted that most of the allegations transmitted in the last few months were still under investigation, and he was still awaiting written reports on those investigations that had been completed. So far, none of the allegations that had been brought to the attention of the Committee had been found by the Committee to be correct, and the Committee had not found any cases of forced labour through its field observation teams.[5] The Liaison Officer a.i. was aware that in some cases forced labour practices had been stopped and administrative action had been taken against local officials as a result of allegations that he had transmitted. However, if the official position of the Committee continued to be that the allegations were unfounded, this would inevitably cast doubt on the credibility of the Committee and its work, particularly given the increasing number of allegations. These comments and concerns were reiterated by the Liaison Officer a.i. in a letter to the Committee following the meeting, and in subsequent meetings with the Minister for Labour and the Director-General of the Department of Labour.

19. *Detailed responses to allegations.* During the Implementation Committee meeting, the representative of the Ministry of Defence provided information on action that had been taken with regard to allegations concerning the military. He indicated that the allegation of forced labour in Thandaung township (Kayin State) transmitted by the Liaison Officer a.i. after his visit to the area[6]

---

[5] No new visits by field observation teams had taken place since the last meeting with the Committee on 29 January. However, in a letter dated 26 May the Director-General of the Department of Labour (who serves as Joint Secretary of the Implementation Committee) indicated that he had held a two-day workshop for 120 participants, including a number of senior officials, on "Raising awareness of ILO Convention 29" in Myeik township, Tanintharyi Division.

[6] This allegation was transmitted to the Committee on 24 February. See GB.289/8, para. 18.

was still under investigation. As regards the nine allegations of forced recruitment, investigations had been completed in four cases. In three cases, the information transmitted by the Liaison Officer a.i. had been confirmed. However, no information was provided on any action that had been taken to return these boys to their families or to investigate the circumstances of their recruitment. In the fourth case, the investigation had found that the information was incorrect as no person fitting the description in the allegation had been located in the battalion mentioned. The other five cases were still under investigation. The representative of the Ministry of Defence then gave some details on the recruitment procedure used by the military. He underlined that all soldiers were recruited voluntarily and had to be over the age of 18. In 2003, 75 recruits had been rejected as they had been found to be under age. If information was subsequently received that recruitment procedures had been violated and a recruit had not been voluntarily recruited or was under age, the case was investigated and the recruit discharged as appropriate. As a result of such investigations, there had been 68 discharges in 2002, and 12 discharges in 2003. Officials found to have violated recruitment procedures had action taken against them. There had been 17 such cases in 2002 and five in 2003.

(a) The Committee then provided information on action that had been taken on allegations concerning local authorities. As regards the allegation of forced labour in Twante township (Yangon Division), [7] the Committee indicated that this allegation was unfounded, but that the district chairman had nevertheless been removed from his post for "being a burden to the people". This was confirmed in a letter from the Director-General of the Department of General Administration received that day. The remaining allegations were still under investigation.

(b) On 26 May the Liaison Officer a.i. received information from the Ministry of Defence, transmitted in a letter from the Department of Labour. According to this information, investigations had been carried out into five allegations of forced recruitment transmitted by the Liaison Officer a.i. In one case, it was found that the person was not serving in the battalion alleged, and in the other four cases the information in the allegations was confirmed, except as regards the dates of birth of the persons concerned, which in all cases were such that the persons would have been 18 or over at the time of recruitment. [8] In three cases the information indicated that after interviewing the persons and confirming that they were voluntary recruits it had been learned that their parents "had been persuaded to make false allegations". In the fourth case it was indicated that the person was serving a sentence for desertion. The Liaison Officer a.i. notes that he saw original identification documents (such as birth certificates and family registration lists) showing the age of the individuals in all these cases, and that copies of these were transmitted to the authorities together with the allegations. The evidence received thus contradicts the assertions of the authorities.

---

[7] This allegation was transmitted to the Committee on 28 January. See GB.289/8, para. 15.

[8] There were also some slight discrepancies in the dates of recruitment. Four of the five cases were those that the representative of the Ministry of Defence had provided information on in the Implementation Committee, although there were further discrepancies between his statement and the letter concerning the ages of the persons concerned.

INTERNATIONAL LABOUR OFFICE	GB.291/5/1(Add.)
	291st Session
Governing Body	Geneva, November 2004

FIFTH ITEM ON THE AGENDA

Developments concerning the question of the observance by the Government of Myanmar of the Forced Labour Convention, 1930 (No. 29)

Addendum

1. Since the finalization of document GB.291/5/1 additional developments have taken place which may be of interest to the Governing Body.

2. In letters from the Convention 29 Implementation Committee dated 25 October, the Liaison Officer a.i. received some further responses to allegations that he had raised with the Committee. As regards the allegation that forced labour was used for the construction of a road in Monywa township,[1] it was indicated that this had been arranged by the local authorities at the request of the Buddhist abbot, that villagers had participated willingly, and that no forced labour was involved. As regards the allegations of forced labour on three projects in Bago township,[2] in one case it was found that no forced labour or compulsory contributions had been involved. In the second case, which concerned alleged sentry duty, it was found that the duty had not constituted forced labour as it had merely taken the form of an instruction to villagers to exercise vigilance while going about their normal activities. In the third case, which concerned work at a government teak plantation, it was found that villagers were not satisfied with the wages they were receiving and had stopped work. No forced labour had been imposed.

3. In addition, the Liaison Officer a.i. was able to have a meeting with the Convention 29 Implementation Committee on 4 November, in which some additional information was provided. The Committee indicated that the Myanmar authorities were still strongly in favour of the implementation of the Plan of Action, which in their view demonstrated the continued commitment to cooperating with the ILO. The Director-General of the Supreme Court then gave some clarifications concerning the case in Hinthada township.[3] According to the information provided, the two individuals who had been convicted and imprisoned

---

[1] See doc. C.App./D.5 (ILC, 2004), para. 15 (reproduced in GB.291/5/1, Appendix III).

[2] See GB.291/5/1, para. 14.

[3] See GB.291/5/1, paras. 14 and 17.

for defamation had now been released on payment of a fine. He added that if they were not satisfied with the conviction, they could apply to the court for a revision. The Liaison Officer a.i. pointed out that it would be understandable if the individuals were reluctant to do so, having been twice imprisoned by the court in attempting to assert their rights, and he reiterated his request that the competent authorities initiate a full investigation of this case. The representative of the Ministry of Defence gave a verbal update on investigations of forced labour allegations that concerned the army. As regards the allegation of forced labour in Thandaung township,[4] the concerned authorities had indicated that workers were paid at prevailing rates and had willingly performed the work. As regards an allegation of forced labour for the construction of army facilities in Bago township,[5] it was found that the villagers had been paid and fed and had taken part willingly, being very happy to have this employment. As regards the serious incident of forced labour in Toungup township,[6] it was found that preliminary work on the project had been carried out by the personnel of the battalions concerned, but these units did not have sufficient manpower for the construction of earth dams. Therefore, 1,400 villagers from five nearby villages had been assigned this work in February and March 2004, as had been stated in the allegation. This project could potentially reclaim nearly 1,000 acres of land, and it was found that due to this the villagers had participated willingly, and had given their signatures to attest to this. These responses have not so far been communicated formally in writing to the Liaison Officer a.i., and the comments of the new Minister for Labour (reported below) suggest that the matter may still be open.

4. On 5 November it was announced that the Myanmar Ministers for Labour and Home Affairs "had been permitted to retire". The Minister for Science and Technology, U Thaung, was appointed concurrently as Minister for Labour. A regional military commander, Maj-Gen Maung Oo, was appointed Minister for Home Affairs.

5. The Liaison Officer a.i. had a meeting with the new Minister for Labour, U Thaung, on 10 November. The Minister reiterated the commitment of his Government to cooperating with the ILO on the elimination of forced labour and indicated that the rules, regulations and laws concerning forced labour would be strictly enforced. The Liaison Officer a.i. underlined the significance in particular of the Toungup case, and the fact that the response given in the meeting with the Convention 29 Implementation Committee was not credible. The Minister undertook to look into this case further. He gave assurances that if it was true, then it would be regarded as a very serious matter and action would certainly be taken against those responsible.

Yangon, 11 November 2004.

---

[4] See GB.289/8, para. 18.

[5] See GB.291/5/1, para. 14.

[6] See GB.291/5/1, paras. 18-20.

INTERNATIONAL LABOUR OFFICE	GB.291/5/2
Governing Body	291st Session Geneva, November 2004

FIFTH ITEM ON THE AGENDA

Developments concerning the question of the observance by the Government of Myanmar of the Forced Labour Convention, 1930 (No. 29)

Report of the Director-General

I. Background to the present report

1. In the conclusions adopted following the discussion at its special sitting in June 2004, the Committee on the Application of Standards of the International Labour Conference noted, inter alia, that "the Governing Body at its next session should be ready to draw the appropriate conclusions, including reactivation and review of the measures and action taken including those regarding foreign direct investment, called for in the resolution of the International Labour Conference of 2000, unless there was a clear change in the situation in the meantime".

2. The following report is aimed at assisting the Governing Body to review the situation in the light of all relevant developments since the measures were first activated at the end of 2000, and draw the appropriate conclusions.

II. Brief history of developments

Developments leading up to the 2000 resolution of the International Labour Conference

3. Following a complaint in June 1996 under article 26 of the Constitution, a Commission of Inquiry was established in 1997 to examine the observance by the Government of Myanmar of the Forced Labour Convention, 1930 (No. 29). The authorities did not permit the Commission of Inquiry to visit Myanmar, and the Commission therefore had to take testimony in neighbouring countries from refugees and others who had recently left Myanmar. In its report issued in July 1998, the Commission of Inquiry found that the Convention had been violated in law, as well as in actual practice in a widespread and systematic manner. It recommended that the relevant legislative texts be brought into line with the Convention, that in actual practice no more forced labour be imposed by the

authorities, in particular the military, and that the penalties which may be imposed under section 374 of the Penal Code for the exaction of forced labour be strictly enforced.

4. The main response of the Government limited itself to issuing an order (Order 1/99 of May 1999) temporarily suspending the power to requisition labour under the Village and Towns Acts. This was however only a partial measure and without real effect. In view of the Government's failure to take the necessary action to implement the recommendations of the Commission of Inquiry, the International Labour Conference adopted at its 87th Session (June 1999) a resolution on the widespread use of forced labour in Myanmar.[1] Subsequently, at its 88th Session (June 2000) the International Labour Conference adopted a resolution under article 33 of the Constitution on measures to secure the compliance of Myanmar with the recommendations of the Commission of Inquiry. This resolution approved the following measures, which took effect on 30 November 2000:

(a) to decide that the question of the implementation of the Commission of Inquiry's recommendations and of the application of Convention No. 29 by Myanmar should be discussed at future sessions of the International Labour Conference, at a sitting of the Committee on the Application of Standards specially set aside for the purpose, so long as this Member has not been shown to have fulfilled its obligations;

(b) to recommend to the Organization's constituents as a whole – governments, employers and workers – that they: (i) review, in the light of the conclusions of the Commission of Inquiry, the relations that they may have with the member State concerned and take appropriate measures to ensure that the said Member cannot take advantage of such relations to perpetuate or extend the system of forced or compulsory labour referred to by the Commission of Inquiry, and to contribute as far as possible to the implementation of its recommendations; and (ii) report back in due course and at appropriate intervals to the Governing Body;

(c) as regards international organizations, to invite the Director-General: (i) to inform the international organizations referred to in article 12, paragraph 1, of the Constitution of the Member's failure to comply; (ii) to call on the relevant bodies of these organizations to reconsider, within their terms of reference and in the light of the conclusions of the Commission of Inquiry, any cooperation they may be engaged in with the Member concerned and, if appropriate, to cease as soon as possible any activity that could have the effect of directly or indirectly abetting the practice of forced or compulsory labour;

(d) regarding the United Nations specifically, to invite the Director-General to request the Economic and Social Council (ECOSOC) to place an item on the agenda of its July 2001 session concerning the failure of Myanmar to implement the recommendations contained in the report of the Commission of Inquiry and seeking the adoption of recommendations directed by ECOSOC or by the General Assembly, or by both, to governments and to other specialized agencies and including requests similar to those proposed in paragraphs (b) and (c) above;

---

[1] This resolution, inter alia, prevented the Government of Myanmar from receiving any technical cooperation or assistance from the ILO, other than direct assistance to implement immediately the recommendations of the Commission of Inquiry, or receiving any invitation to attend meetings, symposia and seminars organized by the ILO, except such meetings that have the sole purpose of securing immediate and full compliance with the said recommendations, until such time as it had implemented the recommendations of the Commission of Inquiry. The only meetings the Government is invited to are the International Labour Conference and the specific sessions of the Governing Body where the issue of Myanmar is discussed

(e) to invite the Director-General to submit to the Governing Body, in the appropriate manner and at suitable intervals, a periodic report on the outcome of the measures set out in paragraphs (c) and (d) above, and to inform the international organizations concerned of any developments in the implementation by Myanmar of the recommendations of the Commission of Inquiry.

5. In parallel to these developments, there had been an exchange of correspondence between the Director-General and the Myanmar authorities,[2] which led to two ILO technical cooperation missions visiting Yangon, in May and October 2000, to provide assistance to the authorities for the immediate implementation of the recommendations of the Commission of Inquiry.[3] These missions resulted in the adoption of an additional order supplementing Order 1/99, which prohibited forced labour in more clear terms, covering all authorities including the army.

Developments following the adoption of the 2000 resolution

6. In accordance with the 2000 resolution, the Director-General wrote to member States in December 2000, and through them to employers' and workers' organizations, bringing their attention to the relevant paragraph of the resolution and requesting that they inform him of any action taken or envisaged in this regard. In accordance with the resolution, the Director-General also wrote to international organizations, as well as setting in motion the procedures necessary to have the matter placed on the agenda of the July 2001 session of the United Nations Economic and Social Council (ECOSOC).

7. The initial responses received by the Director-General were summarized in an interim report to the March 2001 session of the Governing Body.[4] The replies from the Organization's constituents indicated that in general they had adopted what was then described as a "wait-and-see" approach, in the light of the ongoing dialogue which was taking place between the ILO and the Myanmar authorities and which seemed to have the potential of achieving positive results. This approach appeared to receive some additional justification when agreement was reached on the visit to Myanmar in September and October 2001 of a High-level Team (HLT) appointed by the ILO to assess in full independence and freedom of movement the realities of the forced labour situation. This in turn led to the appointment of an ILO Liaison Officer in Myanmar in May 2002, and in May 2003 to agreement on a joint Plan of Action to address forced labour, including in particular the establishment of a Facilitator mechanism to address specific complaints regarding forced labour. Both of these steps were key recommendations of the HLT.

8. However, the momentum in the process of dialogue and cooperation slowed in part due to uncertainties following the crackdown on the National League for Democracy (NLD) around the time of the completion of the draft Plan. It did not prove possible to go ahead with the implementation of the joint Plan of Action, and there were increasingly calls toreturn to the application of the measures adopted under the 2000 resolution.[5] The hopes

---

[2] See ILC, 88th Session, 2000, *Provisional Record* No. 4, Annex II.

[3] For the reports of these missions, see ILC, 88th Session, 2000, *Provisional Record* No. 8 and GB.279/6/1 (November 2000).

[4] GB.280/6 (March 2001).

[5] These calls were made in the debates in the Governing Body at its 286th Session (March 2003), 288th Session (November 2003) and 289th Session (March 2004), and were reflected in the

of proceeding with the Plan were further damaged in March 2004 by the discovery of a court case in which three people were convicted of high treason including on the basis of contacts and cooperation with the ILO.

9. The fact that no formal request has been made for updated information on action taken under the 2000 resolution does not, however, mean that no further action was taken directly or indirectly on the basis of this resolution. It is difficult to have a comprehensive picture of developments, but the Office is aware of some subsequent actions, a number of which have been widely publicized. *United States:* [6] In addition to sanctions already imposed on Myanmar in recent years, on 28 July 2003 the United States Congress enacted the "Burmese Freedom and Democracy Act". Section 2 on findings specifically cites the Director-General's call for all ILO constituents to review their relations with the regime to ensure they do not directly or indirectly contribute to forced labour. [7] *European Union:* Since 1997, the Council of the EU has been denying Myanmar access to generalized tariff preferences since it has not been proven that the practice of forced labour has been brought to an end. It has also renewed, on a biannual basis, its Common Position on Myanmar first adopted in 1996 in which it deplores the practice of forced labour. The European Parliament also adopted several resolutions condemning, inter alia, the use of forced labour, the latest dated 16 September 2004. *International organizations:* As regards international organizations other than the EU, the main developments relate to ECOSOC [8] and the OECD. [9] *Non-state entities :* It is more difficult to assess action taken by non-state entities and as regards disinvestment. The Office has however collected some information in this regard. International and national workers' organizations, together with NGOs and

conclusions adopted at those sessions. Similar calls were also made in the Committee on the Application of Standards at the 92nd Session (June 2004) of the International Labour Conference.

[6] Some other member States are known to have taken measures against Myanmar, but the ILO is not aware of a link with the 2000 resolution.

[7] The Act provides, inter alia, for a one-year ban on imports from Myanmar (section 3). It also contains a reporting obligation on trade sanctions covering bilateral and multilateral measures undertaken by the United States and other governments and the extent to which they were effective in improving conditions in the country. On 10 July 2004, the import restrictions were renewed for an additional year. The US House of Representatives and Senate subsequently adopted, on 13 and 21 September respectively, a joint bipartisan resolution urging the United Nations Security Council to take action on the situation in Myanmar. The House of Representatives resolution explicitly refers to the use of forced labour. See also, as regards the impact of the Act, "Developments in Burma" (House of Representatives, Committee on International Relations, Joint Hearings, 25 March 2004, Serial No. 108-123).

[8] After consideration of an item entitled: "Measures to be taken for the implementation by Myanmar of the recommendations of the ILO Commission of Inquiry on forced labour", ECOSOC adopted without discussion on 25 July 2001 a resolution (2001/20) in this regard. In its resolution, ECOSOC took note of the ILC 2000 resolution as well as the developments which took place in 2001 within the ILC. ECOSOC also requested the Secretary-General to keep it informed of further developments. At its following substantive session in October 2002, ECOSOC was orally informed of developments and since then, no further discussion has taken place.

[9] In 2001 the OECD's Trade Union Advisory Committee raised the issue of forced labour in Myanmar and tabled a letter which noted the adoption of the ILC 2000 resolution and asked the Committee on International Investment and Multinational Enterprises to explain the OECD guidelines and discuss how they could be used to contribute to the elimination of forced labour in Myanmar. The response from the Committee indicated that primary responsibility was accorded to national contact points in addressing such inquiries. Subsequently, a number of national contact points took multinational activity in Myanmar into consideration and some issued recommendations to companies in this regard (see OECD Guidelines for Multinational Enterprises: 2002 report by the chair of the annual meeting of the National Contact Points).

networks, have been organizing boycott and disinvestment campaigns targeting companies doing business in Myanmar, using in particular the ILC 2000 resolution. This has undoubtedly had an impact on the climate for foreign investment in Myanmar, and a number of companies have withdrawn from the country as a result of these campaigns.

III. Overview of the current situation

Developments in the high treason case

10. As regards the first concern expressed by the Governing Body in its March conclusions, the new judgement makes clear that contacts with the ILO as an international organization of which Myanmar is a Member are legal. As pointed out to the Minister for Labour by the Office as soon as the first judgement came to the Director-General's attention, such clarification was essential from the viewpoint of the continued presence of the ILO in the country. It should be noted, however, that despite the recommendation of the informal facilitator for the release of the three individuals, the conviction of the three individuals has been maintained on grounds that seem to have shifted, and they have to serve a (reduced) prison sentence. The second concern of the Governing Body, relating to freedom of association ramifications, is unfortunately not remedied by the new judgement.

Situation in actual practice

11. The situation of forced labour in Myanmar, as described in detail in the recent reports of the Liaison Officer a.i., remains of grave concern. While there is general agreement that some improvements in the situation have occurred in central parts of Myanmar, forced labour continues to be imposed in all the various forms identified by the Commission of Inquiry, in particular in remote areas under the authority of the army, of which the Liaison Officer a.i. had first-hand evidence.

Situation in law

12. It seems clear that whatever the deficiencies of the Orders prohibiting forced labour, the problem of the continued prevalence of forced labour is not due to the form and content of these Orders. Nor is the problem primarily related to lack of knowledge of the Orders, as they have been widely (if unevenly) disseminated, and the remarkable fact is that the population seems more and more ready to use this legal remedy. Rather, the problem is one of effectively implementing the prohibition contained in the Orders. So far, no one has been punished under section 374 of the Penal Code for imposing forced labour. Recent disturbing developments indicate that, on the contrary, people can be punished as a result of lodging complaints regarding forced labour. This tends to give further support to the HLT's findings concerning the existing legal avenues and the need to look for alternative channels such as the Facilitator.

Follow-up to allegations

13. The recent experience of the Liaison Officer a.i. has shown that specific complaints of forced labour brought to the attention of the Convention 29 Implementation Committee are systematically denied, and cases brought directly before the courts are rejected. The picture which emerges is of a response by the authorities to complaints of forced labour that is lacking in credibility. This is all the more concerning given the types of cases involved. While a number of the allegations which have been raised with the authorities are extremely serious cases involving the army in often remote areas, others relate to comparatively minor cases of forced labour imposed by local officials in central Myanmar. Action on these latter cases should be more straightforward because of both the location and nature of the offences involved. The fact that the authorities have not taken steps to deal with these latter cases must raise serious doubts as to the possibility of making significant progress in those areas under the control of the army, where all the indications are that the forced labour situation is far more serious in both form and extent. Two of the cases reported by the Liaison Officer a.i. shed a particularly clear light on this situation.

14. The first case concerns the situation in Hinthada township.[10] This case involved three separate complaints from individuals to the court under section 374 of the Penal Code, all concerning the same incident of forced labour. The township in question is close to Yangon, and the incident appears at first sight to have involved a relatively minor case of forced labour imposed by local officials.[11] This case should therefore have been relatively straightforward to resolve. The reason that the case is such a serious one is due to the failure of the authorities to deal in a credible way with the complaint. This has resulted in a situation where not only were two individuals imprisoned for refusing to perform forced labour, but when this situation came to light through a subsequent complaint to the court on their part, the court failed to respond credibly to the complaint,[12] and furthermore found the two persons guilty of defamation and imprisoned them for a second time (although they have now been released).

15. The second case concerns an incident of forced labour in Toungup township, a remote part of the country.[13] This is an extremely important case, as it contains a number of elements which highlight both the serious nature of the forced labour problem, and the difficult steps needed to effectively address this problem. First, the work was required for an economic project (a land reclamation scheme) initiated by the army, and the orders to requisition villagers came from the army. Second, the case is serious because of the large numbers of villagers involved and the harsh conditions under which they were forced to work, and because of the harassment subsequently faced by the complainants. Third, a joint visit to the region by the Liaison Officer a.i. and the informal facilitator was able to confirm the essential facts of the situation. Solving cases such as this requires a capacity and willingness on the part of the central authorities to enforce the law with respect to the army. The attitude that they will adopt in this case will be a significant test of their continued commitment.

IV. Options available to the Governing Body

16. The framework given by the Committee on the Application of Standards[14] was mainly concerned with the high treason case, on which there have been important developments. However, there is a widespread feeling, strengthened by the situation described above, that

---

[10] See GB.291/5/1, paras. 16 and 20.

[11] That is, sentry duty at an (unoccupied) monastery.

[12] The complainants subsequently tried to lodge the case with a higher court, without success.

[13] The case in question involved the requisitioning of several hundred villagers by the village-level authorities, under orders from the army. These villagers, including old women, had to work for several days at a time under very harsh conditions in a mangrove swamp, building an earth dam as part of an army land-reclamation project. See GB.291/5/1, paras. 18-20.

[14] See paragraph 1 above.

it is difficult to maintain a "wait-and-see" approach. It seems therefore appropriate to place the problem in a broader perspective. This requires assessing recent developments in the light of the assumptions which the Governing Body has consistently been guided by, which are based on the HLT's analysis of the situation and whose continued relevance is confirmed by the above developments.

17. As the HLT noted, forced labour is deeply rooted in the historical, political and military situation of the country. The fact that Myanmar has a large army which adopts a self-reliance strategy for its forces in the field is a major current obstacle to the elimination of the practice. Nevertheless, the HLT was of the opinion that forced labour could be eliminated if there was a real commitment from the authorities to do so, and that this in turn could bring about a change in the attitude of the international community. The HLT felt that this commitment could in particular express itself through the various steps which it recommended, that is, a permanent presence of the ILO and a form of Ombudsman mechanism to help overcome the lack of institutional remedies for victims, one of the main obstacles that the HLT identified.

18. Indeed, the fact that agreement was reached on the appointment of a Liaison Officer in Myanmar as well as on the Facilitator mechanism was an indication of a certain commitment by the authorities. The question which must now be asked, taking in particular into account the treatment of allegations, is whether this commitment continues. Some relevant indications were also given by the Minister for Home Affairs when he stated in a meeting with the informal facilitator in September that instructions had recently been given to the regional commanders by the senior leadership, including Senior General Than Shwe himself, to stop using forced labour. It remains to be seen, however, what could be the impact of the recent leadership changes in relation to the commitment of the authorities on the forced labour issue. If there is a continued commitment on the part of the authorities to eliminating forced labour, then the lack of progress on individual cases must in any case raise doubts about the institutional ability to implement such a commitment, in particular vis-à-vis the army. An important test in this regard will be the action taken with respect to the Toungup case. This case reinforces the need for a renewed examination of the root causes of the problem and of the role of the army.

19. The seriousness of the current situation as reflected in the report of the Liaison Officer a.i. cannot be in any doubt. The question before the Governing Body is what type of action is best suited to bringing a verifiable improvement in that situation. It seems useful to review as objectively as possible the various options that one may think of, it being understood that they may be mutually exclusive.

20. One option would be to now move ahead with the implementation of the Plan of Action. There was a general feeling before the high treason case came to light, in the more positive general context which prevailed at the beginning of the year, that it would be useful and desirable to go ahead with the Plan. This would certainly not have been possible without clarity being brought to the question of the legality of contacts with the ILO. It could now be argued that the positive developments in the high treason case in this regard have removed the main obstacle to the implementation of the Plan of Action. Indeed, it is very clear with regard to the main element of the Plan, the Facilitator, that there is a real demand for such a mechanism among the population in all parts of the country. It is also clear that the ILO's concern that there be appropriate guarantees protecting complainants from retaliation was also valid. The fact that there have been cases of retaliation against people who complained to the Liaison Officer a.i., and that there have been no credible outcomes when victims have complained directly to the courts, demonstrates the need for the kind of institutional guarantees that the Facilitator mechanism contains. The recent case in Toungup in which the informal facilitator generously accepted to be involved, demonstrated very clearly both the great potential value of the mechanism, but also its limitations. While the Facilitator mechanism is vital in giving an avenue of legal remedy for victims, with appropriate guarantees, it cannot directly address the root causes of the problem, in particular with regard to the army. In serious cases such as in Toungup, where an informal solution is impossible and may not in any case be appropriate, the willingness and capacity on the part of the authorities to take the necessary action, in particular as regards the army, is a sine qua non. Should this willingness be clearly confirmed, then the ILO could examine with the authorities how the Organization could help them to translate that willingness into practice and address the root causes of the problem even more directly and on a broader basis than the existing Plan of Action.

21. A second option would be for the Governing Body to reactivate consideration by governments and other relevant entities of the action that they have been called upon to take under the 2000 resolution. This has been repeatedly raised in the Governing Body. The Governing Body could thus decide to instruct the Director-General to write to the constituents as a signal that they should draw the appropriate consequences of the fact that the momentum which had been gained and which justified the "wait-and-see" approach has stopped. This could take the form of a request, following up on his letter of December 2000, for details on subsequent action taken with regard to the resolution. The Director-General would report to the Governing Body on the responses received.

22. One important point to consider would be the impact this move may have on the continued ILO presence and, reciprocally, what could be the impact of a continued ILO presence on the attitude of the constituents towards reactivating their consideration of the action to be taken on the basis of the resolution. The experience gained so far from this presence has been invaluable, in particular the possibility to have first-hand information on the realities of forced labour which was not previously available. It has allowed for a degree of greater mutual understanding and confidence between the ILO and the Myanmar authorities. Support for such a presence has come from many quarters, and there have also been calls to expand it. While a reactivation of the measures might not necessarily have automatic consequences for the presence, it would undoubtedly have an impact on the context in which the Liaison Officer can meaningfully discharge his functions, which presumes engagement and cooperation with the authorities. If, for instance, a situation was created where the ILO presence functioned in a way which was of more benefit to the authorities than to the victims of forced labour, this might have consequences for the possibility of continuing a meaningful presence.

23. It must be recognized at the same time that important elements of information for deciding on the appropriate course of action to choose may still be missing. This relates to the continued willingness of the authorities at different levels, and particularly at the highest level, not only to maintain cooperation with the ILO, but to take the action necessary to solve the serious problems identified in this report. This is particularly relevant given the recent changes in the senior leadership of Myanmar. As indicated above, the authorities' reaction to the Toungup case will provide an important first indication, but which may need to be complemented by a first-hand assessment at the highest level. If evidence of such a commitment is forthcoming, then discussions will be needed to identify ways to translate it into concrete steps to remedy the root causes of the forced labour problem. Again it will be crucial to assess from the highest levels of authority, particularly the army, their readiness and determination to take these steps.

Geneva, 3 November 2004.

 INTERNATIONAL LABOUR OFFICE

Governing Body

GB.292/7/1
292nd Session

Geneva, March 2005

SEVENTH ITEM ON THE AGENDA

Developments concerning the question of the observance by the Government of Myanmar of the Forced Labour Convention, 1930 (No. 29)

Further action taken pursuant to the resolution of the International Labour Conference regarding forced labour in Myanmar

1. The resolution adopted in 2000 under article 33 of the Constitution by the International Labour Conference called on the Organization's constituents to "review, in the light of the conclusions of the Commission of Inquiry, the relations that they may have with [Myanmar] and take appropriate measures to ensure that [Myanmar] cannot take advantage of such relations to perpetuate or extend the system of forced or compulsory labour referred to by the Commission of Inquiry, and to contribute as far as possible to the implementation of its recommendations". A similar call was made to international organizations. The resolution invited the Director-General to report to the Governing Body on the outcome of the measures undertaken by the member States and international organizations.

2. The initial responses received by the Director-General from the constituents and international organizations were summarized in an interim report to the March 2001 session of the Governing Body.[1] Later that year negotiations between the Office and the Government of Myanmar led into the visit of the High-level Team and subsequent negotiations for, first, the understanding on a liaison officer and then the different elements of a joint Plan of Action. The Office has continued to monitor developments without, however, specifically approaching the constituents and international organizations.

3. In his report concerning Myanmar to the November 2004 session of the Governing Body,[2] the Director-General noted that, although no formal request had been made to the

---

[1] GB.280/6.

[2] GB.291/5/2.

constituents for updated information on action taken under the 2000 resolution, this did not mean that no further action had been taken directly or indirectly on the basis of the resolution. While it was difficult to have a comprehensive picture, the Director-General indicated some subsequent actions of which the Office was aware. In the conclusions on this item at its November 2004 session, the Governing Body requested the Office to provide further information for its March 2005 session on the actions taken on the basis of the 2000 resolution, to complement that already provided. The Office therefore requested the assistance of all field offices in obtaining information on action taken by governments or non-state entities, including employers' and workers' organizations and bodies at all levels, and by NGOs and civil society actors more generally.

4. The present paper reflects responses to that request, along with other information obtained concerning action referring specifically to either the 2000 International Labour Conference resolution or the problem of forced labour in Myanmar. However, it cannot be exhaustive. Moreover, it does not cover a variety of actions taken by governments, trade unions, business or intergovernmental or non-governmental organizations in relation to Myanmar which do not ostensibly fall within the remit of the 2000 resolution.

5. As intimated in November, certain governments have acted individually as well as through international organizations to which they belong. In the United States, in accordance with the 2003 Burmese Freedom and Democracy Act, import restrictions have been renewed annually (most recently in July 2004); assets of members of that Government's regime in the United States have been frozen and their travel banned; the award of funds by international financial institutions to which the United States belongs is opposed; and there is regular reporting by the State Department on the effect of trade sanctions on the country. Specific reference is made in the legislation to forced labour and the ILO. There is also information as to legislative or administrative measures taken by some individual states of the United States (California, Massachusetts, New York, Vermont) concerning particular business disinvestment.

6. The Government of Japan has withheld new economic cooperation with Myanmar, except for humanitarian assistance impacting directly on poor living conditions. Following the events of May 2003, it suspended all economic cooperation for several months. The Government of Australia is reported to have deferred its recurring human rights training programme and frozen certain agricultural assistance. The United Kingdom has called on UK companies to review investments in Myanmar; and it has frozen certain assets. Canada imposed in 2003 tighter restrictions on visas and travel and on exports to Myanmar. In October 2003, Switzerland extended the measures first taken in October 2000, by tightening its arms embargo and extending financial and travel restrictions.

7. Among workers' organizations, the International Confederation of Free Trade Unions (ICFTU) has led an active campaign with Global Union Federations and many national workers' organizations to promote the implementation of the 2000 International Labour Conference resolution. Since 2001, it has targeted the withdrawal of multinational companies from Myanmar. This has been done by contacting them directly, citing the 2000 International Labour Conference resolution, and publishing an updated list of those doing business there. The ICFTU has, together with the European Trade Union Confederation, presented arguments to institutions of the European Union, to international financial institutions, and to countries in the Asia-Pacific region and elsewhere. Trade unions in several countries have campaigned for individual companies to cease activities in Myanmar, or for individual governments to adopt sanctions similar to those described above.

8. As regards measures taken by employers' organizations in relation to follow-up to the 2000 resolution or concerning forced labour in Myanmar, no specific information is

available. In respect of multinational businesses, as mentioned in the November 2004 paper to the Governing Body, the campaigns run by trade unions as well as by various non-governmental organizations (for instance Burma Campaign, Actions Birmanie, Clean Clothes Campaign, Earth Rights International), have in some cases referred directly to the resolution. One such campaign, endorsed recently by the Prime Minister of the United Kingdom, has focused on tourism. As one object of a trade union-led campaign, the only major long haul airline service to Yangon (Lauda Air) has been singled out.

9. Where disinvestment action by individual companies has followed, this has often been as the result of a broader campaign in the context of human rights issues and corporate social responsibility. In one reported case (the American Apparel and Footwear Association), a 2003 call for a ban on imports of textiles, apparel and footwear from Myanmar cited the ILO resolution as one of its justifications. In another, the Triumph International garment manufacturer announced in January 2002 the closure of its manufacturing site in Myanmar, following a campaign which had drawn attention to forced labour in the country. In December 2004, an oil company (Unocal) is reported to have reached agreement to settle a human rights lawsuit in California (United States), in which forced labour in the construction of the Yadana pipeline was alleged. The company was said to have agreed to compensate 14 Burmese villagers.

10. In the United Nations, further to the information provided in November 2004, the Special Rapporteur on Myanmar referred in August 2004 to the special sitting of the Committee on the Application of Standards of the 2004 International Labour Conference, noting that agreement on implementation of the joint Plan of Action was not yet possible. More recently, the General Assembly adopted a resolution,[3] noting the conclusions of the 2004 International Labour Conference Application Committee and asking the Government of Myanmar, among other things, to take immediate action to implement the recommendations of the Commission of Inquiry concerning Convention No. 29.

11. Action taken in the OECD context was included in the November paper. Among the international financial institutions, neither the Asian Development Bank nor the World Bank has provided any new lending to Myanmar since 1987. Most recent news from ASEAN is that in May 2004, labour ministers noted with satisfaction the pledge made by Myanmar for continued cooperation with the ILO in their efforts to abolish forced labour practices. They expressed their optimism as to the removal of obstacles to implementation of the joint Plan of Action.

12. On the other hand, in the European Union, as well as the measures indicated in November to deny Myanmar access to generalized tariff preferences and renew the Common Position on Myanmar deploring the practice of forced labour, reference is made by the European Council in this context to the failure of the Myanmar authorities "to take action to eradicate the use of forced labour in accordance with the recommendations of the International Labour Organization's High-level Team Report of 2001". The aim has been to tighten the measures already taken by, for instance, extending the scope of the visa ban and asset freeze; maintaining the arms embargo; and adding a prohibition on making financial loans or credits available to, and acquiring or extend participation in, listed Myanmar state-owned enterprises.

13. The European Parliament has adopted several resolutions condemning the lack of democratic process, human rights abuses in general and the use of forced labour in particular, the latest dated 16 September 2004. Resolutions adopted in 2002 and 2003 expressly refer to the ILO in terms of urging the Government of Myanmar to authorize the

Geneva, 18 February 2005.

[3] A/RES/59/263, 23 Dec. 2004.

opening of an ILO Liaison Office (11 April 2002) and giving access to the ILO without limit to areas of the country where the use of forced labour was reported (13 March 2003).

INTERNATIONAL LABOUR OFFICE

Governing Body

GB.292/7/2
292nd Session

Geneva, March 2005

SEVENTH ITEM ON THE AGENDA

Developments concerning the question of the observance by the Government of Myanmar of the Forced Labour Convention, 1930 (No. 29)

Report of the Liaison Officer a.i.

I. Background

1. Following discussion of the item at its 291st Session (November 2004), the Governing Body adopted the following conclusions:

   The Governing Body, having heard the explanations provided by the Permanent Representative of Myanmar, Ambassador Mya Than, proceeded to examine in detail the information and analysis provided in the documents which was supplemented during the debate, notably on the part of the Workers. It seems overall that the Governing Body remains gravely concerned by developments in the situation and the continued impunity of those who exact forced labour. More particularly, as regards the high treason judgement discussed at the previous session, as well as by the Committee on the Application of Standards of the International Labour Conference, the Workers' group, the Employers' group and many Governments, while recognizing that the judgement by the Supreme Court did answer the fundamental question of the legality of the contacts with the ILO, expressed regret at the continued detention of the persons concerned when their guilt had not been established, and called for their immediate release or pardon. In the circumstances, the Workers' group, the Employers' group, and a number of Governments were of the opinion that reactivation of the measures to be taken under article 33 and in accordance with the Conference resolution of 2000 would be fully justified. Furthermore, the Workers' group insisted that the strength of the ILO presence, whose importance and contribution were recognized and welcomed by the whole of the Governing Body, should be reinforced for the eradication of the problem.

   At the end of the debate, a number of speakers did however consider that the problems identified in the reports as well as the sudden replacement of the previous interlocutors of the Organization following the changes which had occurred among the leadership of the Myanmar Government justified an evaluation of the current attitude of the authorities and their determination to effectively address the continuing practice of forced labour. The attitude that they will adopt, which does not yet seem clearly defined, about the very alarming cases identified in the documents before the Governing Body, constitutes a real test of this determination.

   This is why the Governing Body requests the Director-General to field a very high-level mission to evaluate the attitude of the authorities and assess their determination to continue their cooperation with the ILO, the modalities of which must make it possible to address the root causes of the problems described in the reports. The Director-General will have to ensure that the conditions of such a mission and the credentials of those charged with conducting it, as well as the position of its interlocutors at the highest political level, are such that it is able to meet these objectives and ensure the intervention has the required visibility. The Director-General will report on the results of this mission to the next session of the Governing Body. The Governing Body will then be able to determine the necessary consequences on the basis of full knowledge either as regards further action by the Organization under article 33, including as regards foreign direct investment, or for the implementation of the Plan of Action. In addition, the Office has been requested to provide further information for the next session on the actions taken on the basis of the 2000 resolution, to complement that provided in the report of the Director-General.

2. Mr. Richard Horsey continued to act as interim ILO Liaison Officer. The present report summarizes his activities since November 2004. Information concerning the visit of the very high-level team to Yangon as well as the information requested by the Governing Body on actions taken on the basis of the 2000 resolution will be reported separately.[1]

3. As regards the question of strengthening the office of the Liaison Officer, it was decided that in the first instance this would take the form of a secondment of an ILO official to Yangon to assist the interim Liaison Officer. This was conveyed to the authorities in Yangon on 24 January, but at the time this report was finalized the necessary approvals were still pending.

II. Activities of the Liaison Officer a.i.

4. The Liaison Officer a.i. had a number of meetings with the authorities, both to discuss the general forced labour situation and specific complaints that he had received and communicated to the authorities.[2] On 11 February 2005 he met with the Deputy Minister for Labour. He also had a series of meetings with the Director-General of the Department of Labour on 14 December, 20 January, 8 and 9 February, as well as meetings with the Director-General and Deputy Director-General of the Department of General Administration (Home Affairs) on 16 December, 26 January and 17 February.

5. In addition to these meetings with the authorities, the Liaison Officer a.i. also met with members of the diplomatic community and with representatives of United Nations agencies, the International Committee of the Red Cross, international non-governmental organizations and the international business community. He also met with representatives of the National League for Democracy.

6. From 13 to 20 January, the Liaison Officer a.i. visited northern Sagaing Division, in the remote north-west of the country.[3] He took advantage of a government-organized trip to a new year festival in order to join a charter flight to the area (there is no regular access by air to the region). This festival brought together Naga villagers from a wide geographical area and therefore also represented a good opportunity to gain an overview of the situation in the area. On 16 January, following the festival, the Liaison Officer a.i. planned to travel south by river and road and visit a number of towns and villages en route. This onward travel was to be conducted independently of the authorities. However, he was informed

---

[1] See GB.292/7/3 and GB.292/7/1, respectively.

[2] In some cases, these meetings were also concerned with the modalities for the visit of the very high-level team.

[3] He travelled from Yangon to Hkamti by plane, then on to Lahe (where the Naga festival was held) by road. On his return, he travelled from Lahe to Hkamti by road, then from Hkamti to Tamanthi, Homalin, Mingin and Monywa by boat. He returned from Mandalay to Yangon by plane.

that his travel by road was not permitted and that he could only proceed by boat. This had the effect of considerably limiting the places that he was able to visit. Such a restriction was not in conformity with the understanding on the freedom of movement of the Liaison Officer a.i..

III. Developments in the high treason case

7. On 3 January 2005, two of the persons whose convictions had an ILO connection, Nai Min Kyi and U Aye Myint, were released from prison as part of a wider release of more than 5,000 prisoners coinciding with Myanmar's Independence Day.[4] The Liaison Officer a.i. has had the opportunity to meet with both of these individuals and can report that they are both fine. The third person whose conviction had an ILO connection, U Shwe Mahn, remains in prison.

IV. Developments in the forced labour situation

Overview

8. On the basis of all the information available to him, the Liaison Officer a.i.'s general evaluation of the forced labour situation continues to be, as presented previously to the Governing Body,[5] that although there have been some improvements since the Commission of Inquiry, the practice remains widespread throughout the country, and is particularly serious in border areas where there is a large presence of the army. One significant recent development which should be noted, however, is the prison sentences handed down to four local officials for imposing forced labour, and a number of other prosecutions initiated by the authorities concerning specific cases raised by the Liaison Officer a.i.[6] In his view, these developments can contribute significantly to changing the climate of impunity surrounding officials who continue to impose forced labour, and thus to reducing the prevalence of the practice. It is vital, however, that similar steps are also taken with regard to the military, which continues to be responsible for the majority of forced labour. If the recent trend continues, and is extended to the army, it can represent the beginnings of a credible response to the problem.

9. The Liaison Officer a.i. is continuing to receive complaints from individuals alleging they have been subjected to forced labour, or from representatives of such persons. Often these individuals are in fact complaining on behalf of a larger group of persons or a community subjected to forced labour. In 2004, there were a total of 80 such complaints, and interventions were made with the authorities on 46 of these cases.[7] Of these 46 cases, 26

---

[4] One other person in the case, whose conviction did not have an ILO connection, was also released at the same time.

[5] See GB.286/6 (Mar. 2003), para. 7; GB.288/5 (Nov. 2003), para. 8; GB.289/8 (Mar. 2004), para. 10; and GB.291/5/1 (Nov. 2004), para. 9.

[6] See para. 14 below.

[7] Of the remaining 34 cases, 20 were considered to be outside the mandate of the Liaison Officer, in nine cases of forced recruitment interventions had already been made by another agency, one case concerned an allegation already raised with the authorities in 2003, three cases were pending and one complaint directly to the court under section 374 of the Penal Code, copied to the Liaison Officer, was subsequently withdrawn.

concerned various forms of forced labour (other than forced recruitment), 13 concerned forced recruitment of minors into the armed forces, [8] one case concerned alleged harassment of a complainant (who has now successfully prosecuted local officials for imposing forced labour) and six were direct complaints by individuals to Myanmar courts under section 374 of the Penal Code, copies of which had been communicated to the Liaison Officer a.i. by the complainants. So far in 2005, the Liaison Officer a.i. has received a further 14 cases, and interventions have so far been made on six of these cases, as detailed below (a list of all these cases is appended).

10. In cases of alleged forced recruitment of minors, the Liaison Officer a.i. has written to the Convention 29 Implementation Committee with the details of the allegation, requesting that the Committee take urgent action to verify this information in order that, if it is confirmed, the individual in question can be returned to the care of their parents and an investigation carried out into the circumstances of their recruitment so that any person found to have acted illegally can be prosecuted. In other cases of alleged forced labour, the Liaison Officer a.i. has written to the Convention 29 Implementation Committee providing details of the allegation and recommending that, in line with the Committee's procedures, a field observation team (FOT) be sent to the area in question to investigate the allegation, and expressing his readiness to accompany this FOT in an observer capacity.

11. Of the 46 cases transmitted to the Convention 29 Implementation Committee in 2004, responses have been received in 36 cases. [9] In five cases, the authorities have upheld the allegations (partly or in full) and have initiated criminal prosecutions against the officials involved. In 25 cases, the allegation that forced labour was involved was rejected. In the six cases where individuals complained directly to the court, three cases went to trial and resulted in the officials concerned being sentenced to prison terms. (As reported previously, the other three cases were rejected on the grounds that there was no prima facie evidence of forced labour.)

12. As indicated in an earlier report, [10] the Liaison Officer a.i. considers that the mechanism put in place by the authorities for addressing forced labour allegations, that of sending an ad-hoc team composed of senior government officials to the region to conduct an investigation, is not well-suited to dealing with the increasing numbers of cases. As the number of allegations has increased, they have tended to be investigated internally by the General Administration Department or the Ministry of Defence. He has always underlined, however, that the credibility of the investigation mechanism would be ultimately judged by its results. It is therefore encouraging that, notwithstanding the abovementioned concerns, this mechanism has begun to produce results in the form of prosecutions of officials implicated in the imposition of forced labour, as detailed below.

---

[8] As regards this question, on 4 Feb. the *New Light of Myanmar* reported, in a front-page item headlined "Myanmar still facing unjust accusations of child soldiers as only slanders and falsehoods reach UN" that the Committee for Prevention of Recruitment of Minors for Armed Forces, established in Jan. 2004, had met the previous day. The Chairman of the Committee, Lt. Gen Thein Sein, was reported as stating in his opening remarks that "conspirators are framing the Tatmadaw for the alleged forced recruitment of juvenile soldiers for the front lines and trying to raise the matter at the United Nations for the global body to take action against Myanmar. Thus, the Committee will have to pay attention to refuting the matter".

[9] Verbal responses have also been received in a further two cases.

[10] See GB.291/5/1 (Nov. 2004), para. 12.

Details of cases

13. Details of 33 cases on which interventions were made in 2004 have already been presented to the Governing Body and the Committee on the Application of Standards of the International Labour Conference.[11] Details on new cases in December 2004 and in 2005 on which the Liaison Officer a.i. made interventions are provided below:

- *Intervention dated 7 December 2004.* The intervention concerned four allegations of forced labour that were received from individuals from different townships in Sagaing Division. In the first case, it was alleged that Tamu district Forestry Department had ordered the heads of two village tracts to provide villagers to work on a teak plantation project. One person from each household in the villages concerned was requisitioned to carry out this work (a total of more than 200 people), and anyone who refused was fined. In the second case, according to the information received from a number of alleged victims, several hundred villagers in Kalewa township were forced to do work on the road from Kalewa to Mawlaik, and several people who did not participate were detained and fined. In the third case, it was alleged that a number of people in Tamu town were ordered by a police officer to perform all-night sentry duty for several consecutive nights. Any person who was unable to perform this duty was required to hire a substitute at their own expense. In the fourth case, it was alleged that several hundred villagers from a number of villages in Homalin township were requisitioned by the township chairman, through their village heads, to work on the repair of a number of bridges on the road from Homalin to Hkamti. Villagers received no payment and had to provide their own food. Any person who failed to take part was liable to a fine.

- *Intervention dated 8 December.* According to the allegation made by three individuals from the area, people from a number of villages in Toungup township (Rakhine State) were required to collect large quantities of firewood for the army's Military Operations Command No. 5, for use in brick kilns it was operating as an income-generation project.[12] No compensation was provided, and any household that could not collect its quota had to pay a fine.

- *Intervention dated 9 December.* According to the allegation from a number of individuals concerned, labour was being requisitioned on a large scale from many villages in Kyaikto township (Mon State) to clear land for a new road through the township. In addition to labour, villagers had to provide the necessary tools, and arrange their own transport to the work site (which in many cases meant walking for several hours in the dark to and from the work site). Villagers who were unable to perform these duties were liable to a fine.

- *Intervention dated 10 December.* According to the allegation from individuals concerned, the township chairman and police chief of Tabayin township (Sagaing Division) requisitioned residents of the town to repair an irrigation canal and plant trees along the approach road to the town. These instructions were given in the evening by loudspeaker. Anyone who failed to take part was fined.

- *Intervention dated 22 December.* According to the allegation, the army's Infantry Battalion 46 was confiscating land from villagers in Putao township (Kachin State), and then forcing these villagers to continue cultivating the land on behalf of the battalion, for which they would receive only a limited proportion of the final crop.

---

[11] See C.App./D.5 (ILC, 2004), paras. 9-17; GB.289/8, paras. 15, 16 and 18; and GB.291/5/1, paras. 14-16.

[12] This is the third allegation that has been received concerning this particular army unit. See below, as well as GB.291/5/1, para. 14 and C.App./D.5. (ILC, 2004), para. 11.

This allegation was made by 20 individuals concerned, on behalf of 102 affected persons.

- *Intervention dated 2 February 2005.* According to the allegation, a village-tract chairman in Myaing township (Magway Division) forced villagers to dig 350 three-foot-deep pits along the sides of a new road project in preparation for the planting of trees. This work had to be completed on the day the order was given. Any family that was unable to provide a worker was fined.

- *Intervention dated 3 February.* According to the allegation, a number of villagers in Thandaung township (Kayin State) were forced by soldiers of Light Infantry Battalion 439 to do repair work on the road from Bawgaligyi to Busakee. While carrying out this work, one 15-year-old boy stepped on a landmine and lost his leg.

- *Intervention dated 4 February.* According to the allegation, the police and village-tract authorities in Mawlamyinegyun township (Ayeyawaddy Division) forced villagers to cultivate police land as part of an income-generation project for police staff welfare funds. This practice has been ongoing since 2000. Villagers are also required to provide their own tools and bring their own food, as well as contribute cash to the police funds.

- *Intervention dated 15 February.* This intervention concerned two alleged cases of forced recruitment of children into the army. In the first case it was alleged that a boy now aged 15 had been kidnapped off the street in Yangon by an army sergeant in 2002 at the age of 12 and had been recruited against his will into the army. After undergoing basic military training he was assigned to an army battalion and sent on a number of military operations during which he contracted malaria. The second case concerned a boy from Yangon who was allegedly recruited against his will in January 2005 at the age of 15. According to the allegation, he was currently undergoing basic military training.

- *Intervention dated 18 February.* According to the allegation, extensive forced labour was being used by the army in Pyinmana and Lewe townships (Mandalay Division) for the construction of camps and facilities for army Battalions 603, 604, 605 and an air defence battalion. At least 14 villages in the area had to provide 200 workers each, on a daily basis, for this work. In addition to labour, each village had to provide roofing and construction materials and transport for the project.

Responses received from the authorities

14. In letters to the Liaison Officer a.i. dated 1 and 17 February, the authorities presented their findings on a number of allegations of forced labour that he had raised.

    - As regards three complaints of forced labour lodged directly with the township court in Kawhmu (Yangon Division),[13] the authorities indicated that the three separate trials had now concluded and the accused local officials had been found guilty under section 374 of the Myanmar Penal Code.[14] Three of these officials had been sentenced to eight-month prison terms, and a fourth, who was found guilty on two separate counts, was sentenced to a 16-month prison term.

---

[13] See C.App./D.5 (ILC, 2004), para. 9.

[14] Section 374 of the Penal Code concerns the illegal imposition of forced labour and provides for a prison term which may extend to one year, or a fine, or both.

- As regards the allegation of forced labour imposed by the army for a land reclamation project in Toungup township (Rakhine State),[15] the authorities indicated that an investigation had found that some village-tract officials were guilty of imposing forced labour, extortion and abuse of power, and (legal) action was being taken against them. No indication was given of any findings regarding the army unit (Military Operations Command No. 5) implicated in the allegation.

- As regards the allegation of forced labour on a teak plantation in Tamu (Sagaing Division),[16] it was indicated that sufficient funds had been allocated to the project, and that a Forestry Department official had temporarily misappropriated these funds, which were subsequently disbursed to the workers. The official concerned would be prosecuted for misappropriation of funds. The response was unclear as to whether the workers had been initially forced to work on the project, or had been freely hired and then not paid.

- As regards the allegation of forced labour for the road from Kalewa to Mawlaik (Sagaing Division),[17] it was found that the village-tract chairman had requisitioned 120 villagers for this work on three occasions. He had also fined seven people for failing to do the work. This was a violation of Order No. 1/99, and he was being prosecuted.

- As regards the allegation of forced labour imposed by the police for sentry duty in Tamu town,[18] an investigation found no basis to the claims, and no further action would be taken.

- As regards the allegation of forced labour for the repair of bridges on the road from Homalin to Hkamti (Sagaing Division),[19] it was found that these projects were the responsibility of the Public Works Department. This department had hired a private contractor to carry out the work. Villagers had been freely hired to work on these projects, but had agreed to donate their wages towards the cost of a new roof for the local school. No further action would be taken.

- As regards the allegation of forced labour imposed by the army in Toungup township (Rakhine State) for the collection of firewood,[20] an investigation had found that Military Operations Command No. 5 had arranged to purchase the wood through the village-tract chairman. Instead of hiring woodcutters to do this, however, the chairman had forced the villagers to do so. Therefore, (legal) action was being taken against him.

- As regards the allegation of forced labour for a road construction project in Kyaikto township (Mon State),[21] it was indicated that the villagers had participated willingly in this project and that a considerable amount of money had been disbursed to them in labour charges. It was therefore concluded that the allegation was not true. The Liaison Officer a.i. has confirmed from another source that, following an on-the-spot

---

[15] See C.App./D.5 (ILC, 2004), para. 11.

[16] See para. 13 above.

[17] ibid.

[18] ibid.

[19] ibid.

[20] ibid.

[21] ibid.

investigation by the authorities (during which the villagers reportedly confirmed to the investigators that they had been forced to work on the project), a significant amount of money was distributed to the villages concerned by way of compensation.

Yangon, 18 February 2005.

Appendix

Cases on which interventions have been made (2004-05)

Case type	Location	Intervened	Response	Details of response from the authorities
Forced recruitment	Hlaingthaya township, Yangon Division	26/01/2004	23/02/2004	The child in question was released from the army back to the care of his parents on 5/2/2004, but recruitment was found to have been voluntary.
Forced labour	Twante township, Yangon Division	28/01/2004	05/05/2004	The Convention 29 Implementation Committee found the allegation to be unfounded but the district chairman was removed from his post for "being a burden to the people".
Forced recruitment	Hlaingthaya township, Yangon Division	29/01/2004	17/02/2004	The child in question was released from the army back to the care of his parents on 5/2/2004, but recruitment was found to have been voluntary.
Forced labour	Thandaung township, Kayin State	24/02/2004	None to date	[Verbal response from the Convention 29 Implementation Committee, according to which work was voluntary and paid at prevailing rates.]
Forced recruitment	Twante township, Yangon Division	11/03/2004	26/05/2004	Found to have been voluntarily recruited when over the age of 18.
Forced labour	Bogale township, Ayeyawaddy Division	12/03/2004	09/08/2004	Work found to have been jointly organized by community elders and local authorities. Response ambiguous as to whether this could have nevertheless involved forced labour.
Forced recruitment	Insein township, Yangon Division	18/03/2004	26/05/2004	Individual not found to be serving in the battalion mentioned in the allegation.
Forced recruitment	North Okkalapa township, Yangon Division	18/03/2004	26/05/2004	Found to have been over the age of 18 when recruited and currently imprisoned for desertion. No indication given as to whether the recruitment was found to have been voluntary.
Forced recruitment	Thakehta township, Yangon Division	18/03/2004	26/05/2004	Found to have been voluntarily recruited when over the age of 18.
Forced labour	Toungup township, Rakhine State	07/04/2004	17/02/2005	[See following.]
Forced labour	Toungup township, Rakhine State	07/04/2004	17/02/2005	Found that local officials had requisitioned labour and money from villagers and abused their powers. Instruction had been given to take action against these officials. No indication of findings regarding the army unit implicated in the allegation.
Forced recruitment	Khayan township, Yangon Division	08/04/2004	None to date	

22 Part 3/67

Case type	Location	Intervened	Response	Details of response from the authorities
Forced labour	Bogale township, Ayeyawaddy Division	09/04/2004	31/08/2004	Found to have been community development work carried out collectively by the villagers.
Forced labour	Bogale township, Ayeyawaddy Division	09/04/2004	31/08/2004	It was found that no forced labour was involved in the project, and that voluntary cash donations had been received but had been insufficient for the project, so the funds had been used for construction of a school building and roof of the USDA office.
Forced labour	Pantanaw township, Ayeyawaddy Division	09/04/2004	27/08/2004	Work found to have been carried out willingly by villagers after the majority had agreed to do this work for free in return for a donation of funds to village community projects.
Forced recruitment	Hlaingthaya township, Yangon Division	23/04/2004	26/05/2004	Found to have been voluntarily recruited when over the age of 18.
Forced labour	Monywa township, Sagaing Division	29/04/2004	25/10/2004	Found that at the request of the Buddhist Abbot, the authorities arranged the upgrading of the road, and villagers took pert willingly in providing their labour to produce rock chippings for the project. No forced labour found to have been involved.
Forced recruitment	Hlaingthaya township, Yangon Division	30/04/2004	31/08/2004	Found to have been recruited when over the age of 18, and to have been absent without leave since 4 June 2004.
Forced recruitment	Thingangyun township, Yangon Division	30/04/2004	31/08/2004	Found to have been voluntarily recruited when over the age of 18.
Forced recruitment	Twante township, Yangon Division	30/04/2004	31/08/2004	Found to have been voluntarily recruited when over the age of 18.
§374 complaint	Kawhmu township, Yangon Division	04/05/2004	01/02/2005	Two accused sentenced to 16-month and eight-month prison terms, respectively.
Forced labour	Falam district, Chin State	20/05/2004	30/07/2004	No forced labour found to have been involved.
§374 complaint	Kawhmu township, Yangon Division	26/05/2004	01/02/2005	Two accused sentenced to 16-month and eight-month prison terms, respectively.
Forced recruitment	Shwepyitha township, Yangon Division	28/05/2004	31/08/2004	Found to have been recruited when over the age of 18. No indication given as to whether the recruitment was found to have been voluntary. Arrested for desertion and given 6-month sentence in a military prison. Returned to his battalion on 23 September.
Forced labour	Bago township, Bago Division	06/07/2004	25/10/2004	No forced labour or compulsory contributions found to have been imposed for the project.
Forced labour	Bago township, Bago Division	06/07/2004	25/10/2004	Sentry duty had been requested of villagers for a long time, but only during the day, and only required being watchful when going about normal household work. It did not therefore constitute forced labour, and there were no compulsory contributions.

Case type	Location	Intervened	Response	Details of response from the authorities
Forced labour	Bago township, Bago Division	06/07/2004	25/10/2004	Workers were paid on government teak plantation, but were not satisfied with the wages and stopped work. No forced labour or compulsory contributions were found to have been involved.
Forced labour	Bago township, Bago Division	06/07/2004	None to date	[Verbal response in the Implementation Committee according to which villagers had been paid and fed and worked willingly.]
Other	Kawhmu township, Yangon Division	07/07/2004	None to date	[Alleged harassment of a complainant, who has now successfully brought a prosecution against local officials for imposing forced labour.]
Forced labour	Toungup township, Rakhine State	08/07/2004	None to date	
Forced labour	Hinthada township, Ayeyawaddy Division	09/07/2004	None to date	
§374 complaint	Hinthada township, Ayeyawaddy Division	22/07/2004	31/08/2004	Case rejected by court on the grounds that there was no prima facie evidence of forced labour. Complainant then found guilty of defamation and imprisoned for six months, but subsequently released.
Forced labour	Maungdaw township, Rakhine State	23/07/2004	31/08/2004	Official investigation (by FOT) found that the allegations of forced labour on the bridge projects were not true.
§374 complaint	Hinthada township, Ayeyawaddy Division	06/08/2004	31/08/2004	Case rejected by court on the grounds that there was no prima facie evidence of forced labour. Complainant then found guilty of defamation and imprisoned for 6 months, but subsequently released.
§374 complaint	Kawhmu township, Yangon Division	09/08/2004	01/02/2005	Accused sentenced to an 8-month prison term.
Forced recruitment	Kyimindine township, Yangon Division	13/09/2004	None to date	
§374 complaint	Hinthada township, Ayeyawaddy Division	01/10/2004	–	Case rejected by court on the grounds that there was no prima facie evidence of forced labour.
Forced labour	Ramree township, Rakhine State	12/10/2004	None to date	
Forced labour	Tamu township, Sagaing Division	07/12/2004	17/02/2005	It was found that a Forestry Department official temporarily misappropriated pay for workers, who were later paid. He would be prosecuted for misappropriation. Response unclear as to whether workers were forced, or hired but then not paid.
Forced labour	Kalewa township, Sagaing Division	07/12/2004	17/02/2005	Local official found to have requisitioned 120 people on three occasions, and fined seven people for failing to work. This was a violation of Order No. 1/99 and the official would be prosecuted.
Forced labour	Tamu township, Sagaing Division	07/12/2004	17/02/2005	It was found that the allegation was unfounded and no further action would be taken.
Forced labour	Homalin township, Sagaing	07/12/2004	17/02/2005	Project found to have been the responsibility of the Public Works Department, who had hired a private

Case type	Location	Intervened	Response	Details of response from the authorities
	Division			contractor. Workers were hired voluntarily and had agreed that their pay be donated for a new roof for the school. No further action would be taken.
Forced labour	Toungup township, Rakhine State	08/12/2004	17/02/2005	It was found that the army unit concerned had paid a local official to provide firewood. This official had not hired woodcutters but had instead forced villagers to cut the wood. Accordingly, action was being taken against the official.
Forced labour	Kyaikto township, Mon State	09/12/2004	17/02/2005	It was found that villagers had participated willingly in the project, and over 2.7 million kyat in labour fees had been disbursed to the workers in 22 villages. No forced labour found to have been involved.
Forced labour	Tabayin township, Sagaing Division	10/12/2004	None to date	
Forced labour	Putao township Kachin State	22/12/2004	None to date	
Forced labour	Myaing township, Magway Division	02/02/2005	None to date	
Forced labour	Thandaung township, Kayin State	03/02/2005	None to date	
Forced labour	Mawlamyinegyun township, Ayeyawaddy Division	04/02/2005	None to date	
Forced recruitment	Insein township, Yangon Division	15/02/2005	None to date	
Forced recruitment	Hlaingthaya township, Yangon Division	15/02/2005	None to date	
Forced labour	Yamethin district, Mandalay Division	18/02/2005	None to date	

INTERNATIONAL LABOUR OFFICE GB.292/7/2(Add.)
292nd Session

Governing Body Geneva, March 2005

SEVENTH ITEM ON THE AGENDA

Developments concerning the question of the observance by the Government of Myanmar of the Forced Labour Convention, 1930 (No. 29)

Report of the Liaison Officer a.i.

Addendum

1. Since the finalization of document GB.292/7/2, a number of additional developments have taken place which may be of interest to the Governing Body.

Developments following the visit of the vHLT

2. The Myanmar Prime Minister, Lt. Gen. Soe Win, wrote to Sir Ninian Stephen on 10 March. This letter is reproduced in the appendix.

3. In a meeting with the Liaison Officer a.i. on 11 March, the Director-General of the Department of Labour reinforced the fact that there had been close cooperation between the Government of Myanmar and the Liaison Officer a.i. on individual cases, which had resulted in a number of prosecutions. He also indicated that the Office of the Commander-in-Chief (army), had ordered the creation of a focal point in the army to facilitate cooperation with the ILO on cases concerning the military. The focal point was to be the Vice-Adjutant General, Col. Khin Soe, assisted by seven grade-1 staff officers.[1] These elements were contained in a 56-page "Memorandum on Myanmar's compliance of ILO Convention 29 and her cooperation with ILO" which he provided to the Liaison Officer a.i. at the end of the meeting.[2] The Memorandum also contained a detailed account of the history of relations between the ILO and Myanmar and the views of the authorities on the various developments that had taken place. These latter details formed the basis of a

---

[1] It was indicated that this order from the Office of Vice-Senior General Maung Aye was transmitted in letter ref. 865/18-ka/003 dated 1 March 2005. Grade-1 staff officers normally have the rank of lieutenant colonel.

[2] Copies of this Memorandum can be made available by the Office.

Government press conference held on 15 March concerning "the arbitrary pressure put on Myanmar by ILO", which was reported at length in the state press the following day.[3]

Developments concerning allegations raised by the Liaison Officer a.i.

4. In letters to the Liaison Officer a.i., dated 21 February and 7, 9 and 11 March, the authorities provided further details as regards action taken on cases of forced labour that he had raised:

– As regards the allegation of forced labour on a teak plantation in Tamu (Sagaing Division), on which the authorities had already instituted proceedings against a Forestry Department official,[4] it was indicated that on 18 February the court had found the official guilty under section 409 of the Penal Code (misappropriation of funds) and sentenced him to a two-year prison term.

– As regards the allegation of forced labour for the road from Kalewa to Mawlaik (Sagaing Division), on which the authorities had also instituted separate proceedings against a local official,[5] it was indicated that also on 18 February the court had found this official guilty under section 374 of the Penal Code (illegal requisition of labour) and sentenced him to an eight-month prison term.

– As regards the allegation of forced labour imposed by the army for a land reclamation project in Toungup township (Rakhine State), on which the authorities had already stated that action was being taken against civilian officials found to have been involved,[6] it was indicated that two local officials had been found guilty and sentenced to six-month prison terms by the township court on 28 February. No information was provided regarding any action against the army unit implicated in the allegation.

– As regards the allegation of forced labour imposed by the same army unit in Toungup township (Rakhine State) for the collection of firewood, on which the authorities had already stated that action was being taken against local officials found to have been responsible,[7] it was indicated that two local officials had been found guilty in a separate case and also sentenced to six-month prison terms on 28 February. Again, no information was provided regarding any action against the army unit implicated in the allegation.

– As regards the allegation of forced labour imposed by the police and local authorities in Mawlamyinegyun township (Ayeyawady Division) for the cultivation of police land,[8] it was indicated that although the investigation found the incident did not

---

[3] See *New Light of Myanmar*, 16 March 2005, "Big nations of west bloc use ILO as political forum to put pressure on Myanmar in order to install their puppet government in power", pp. 6, 7, 10, 11, 13, 14, 15 and 16. (Copies of the article are on file and can be made available by the Office.)

[4] See GB.292/7/2, paras. 13 and 14.

[5] ibid.

[6] See GB.292/7/2, para. 14.

[7] See GB.292/7/2, paras. 13 and 14.

[8] See GB.292/7/2, para. 13.

amount to forced labour, three police officers and two local officials were responsible for certain wrongdoings, and administrative action was being taken against them.

5. With regard to his intervention dated 15 February concerning the alleged forced recruitment of a boy in January 2005,[9] the Liaison Officer a.i. can report that the boy was released on 28 February and is back in the care of his family.

6. On 14 March, the Liaison Officer a.i. wrote to Col. Khin Soe, the newly-designated focal point in the army, requesting a meeting. He also transmitted to Col. Khin Soe two allegations of forced recruitment of minors that he had just received. He can report that the two children concerned were released back into the care of their families the following day.

Yangon, 16 March 2005.

---

[9] See GB.292/7/2, paras. 13 and 14.

Appendix

Letter dated 10 March from the Myanmar Prime Minister to Sir Ninian Stephen

Dear Sir Ninian,

I have the honour of writing to you in reference to the visit of the very High-Level Team (vHLT) that you headed to Myanmar during the fourth week of February of this year.

I was given the duty of receiving the vHLT as the leadership was engaged with the National Convention that had been recently reconvened. As you may be aware the Convention is the first and most crucial step of the seven point Road Map for a transition to democracy in Myanmar. The success or failure of the National Convention will determine the future of my country. I cannot but stress the importance that we attach to the process.

I appreciated the opportunity of meeting with your goodself and the eminent members of the team. In the course of the meeting I explained to you the socio-economic situation and the progress that country had achieved. I also took the opportunity to underline the process of cooperation between Myanmar and the ILO on the issue of forced labour. We have stated on several occasions in the past that we are committed to the elimination of the vestiges of forced labour in close cooperation with ILO. I wish to reassure you that we are against forced labor and are committed to this principle.

Myanmar has cooperated with the United Nations and its Specialized Agencies in the past and will continue to do so also in the future. In like manner Myanmar intends to continue its cooperation with the ILO.

As regards the aide memoire presented to the Honourable Minister for Foreign Affairs by the vHLT, we are willing to give it careful consideration.

I avail myself of this opportunity to convey to you, Sir Ninian, the assurances of my highest consideration.

I remain,

Yours sincerely,

(Signed) Lt. Gen. Soe Win

cc: Her Excellency Mme Ruth Dreifuss, member of the vHLT
  The Honourable Eui-yong Chung, member of the vHLT
  His Excellency Mr. Juan Somavia, Director-General of the Office of the ILO

INTERNATIONAL LABOUR OFFICE	GB.292/7/3
Governing Body	292nd Session Geneva, March 2005

SEVENTH ITEM ON THE AGENDA

Developments concerning the question of the observance by the Government of Myanmar of the Forced Labour Convention, 1930 (No. 29)

Report of the very High-Level Team

I. Establishment and mandate of the very High-Level Team

1. In the conclusions it adopted after the discussions at its 291st Session (November 2004), the Governing Body, inter alia, requested the Director-General to field a very high-level mission to Myanmar, in the following terms:

> … At the end of the debate, a number of speakers did however consider that the problems identified in the reports as well as the sudden replacement of the previous interlocutors of the Organization following the changes which had occurred among the leadership of the Myanmar Government justified an evaluation of the current attitude of the authorities and their determination to effectively address the continuing practice of forced labour. The attitude that they will adopt, which does not yet seem clearly defined, about the very alarming cases identified in the documents before the Governing Body, constitutes a real test of this determination.
>
> This is why the Governing Body requests the Director-General to field a very high-level mission to evaluate the attitude of the authorities and assess their determination to continue their cooperation with the ILO, the modalities of which must make it possible to address the root causes of the problems described in the reports. The Director-General will have to ensure that the conditions of such a mission and the credentials of those charged with conducting it, as well as the position of its interlocutors at the highest political level, are such that it is able to meet these objectives and ensure the intervention has the required visibility. The Director-General will report on the results of this mission to the next session of the Governing Body. The Governing Body will then be able to determine the necessary consequences on the basis of full knowledge either as regards further action by the Organization under article 33, including as regards foreign direct investment, or for the implementation of the Plan of Action. …

2. Accordingly, the Director-General constituted a very High-Level Team (vHLT) to fulfil the mandate defined in these conclusions, as follows:

- The Right Honourable Sir Ninian Stephen, former Governor-General of Australia, who chaired the previous High-Level Team in 2001;

- Her Excellency Madame Ruth Dreifuss, former President of the Swiss Confederation;

- The Honourable Eui-yong Chung, former Chairperson of the Governing Body of the ILO, Member of the National Assembly of the Republic of Korea and Chairperson of the Foreign Relations Committee of the Uri Party.

3. The composition of the vHLT and the dates when it was ready to visit Myanmar (21-25 February 2005) were communicated to the Myanmar authorities by the Director-General. All precautions were taken to ensure that the modalities for the visit would be such that the vHLT would be able to successfully complete its mandate, and it was on the understanding that the Myanmar authorities had understood and agreed with this essential point that the vHLT agreed to finalize its arrangements. Full details of the relevant exchange of correspondence and discussions are provided in Appendix I.

II. Programme of meetings

4. The members of the vHLT and their support staff met in Bangkok on 20 and 21 February 2005 for pre-departure discussions.[1] They then proceeded to Yangon on the evening of 21 February.

5. On arrival at the airport in Yangon, the vHLT was provided by the Deputy Minister for Labour with a programme of meetings that had been arranged for it by the authorities. This programme (reproduced in Appendix II) no longer included a meeting with State Peace and Development Council (SPDC) Secretary-1, the explanation being that he was busy with the National Convention, although the vHLT was informed verbally that it could expect a meeting with the Prime Minister the next day.[2] The vHLT's expectation was that this programme would be discussed and finalized as a matter of priority in the meetings it would have the following day.

6. The following morning (22 February) the vHLT met with the Minister for Labour. Sir Ninian Stephen first presented an overview of the background to the visit and the mandate of the team. Mr. Chung, as former Chairperson of the Governing Body, was then able to explain the critical importance of the visit in the light of the previous debates in the Governing Body on this issue. He underlined the positive gesture towards maintaining the ongoing dialogue with the authorities that the decision to appoint the vHLT represented on the part of the Governing Body, as well as the potential risks if this gesture was not

---

[1] The support staff were as follows: Mr. Francis Maupain (Special Adviser to the ILO Director-General), who acted as the vHLT's Executive Secretary, together with Mr. Richard Horsey (ILO Liaison Officer a.i. in Yangon) and Mr. Léon de Riedmatten (who for several years has been the informal facilitator between the ILO and the authorities). The ILO Executive Director for Standards and Fundamental Principles and Rights at Work, Mr. Kari Tapiola, was in Bangkok on other matters, and was also able to participate in these pre-departure discussions.

[2] Myanmar is ruled by a military council, the SPDC, and all policy is decided at this level (rather than by ministers) in particular by its two senior leaders, Senior General Than Shwe (SPDC Chairman, Commander-in-Chief of the armed forces, and Minister for Defence) and Vice-Senior General Maung Aye (SPDC Vice-Chairman and Army Commander). The Prime Minister is the fourth-ranking member of the SPDC, with authority over civilian/government matters, but not military matters. This was not the case for the former Prime Minister, who before his removal had been involved in the ILO process and who had authority to some extent over the military.

responded to as expected with a meeting at the highest political level. Madame Dreifuss then elaborated on the concrete points (subsequently provided to the Minister for Foreign Affairs – see below) which would need to be addressed by the vHLT, provided a meeting at the highest level was granted, as well as some explanations of how these points were relevant in the vHLT's view to the resolution of the issue. The Minister for his part explained that the agreement by the authorities to receive the vHLT should be seen as a positive indication of their commitment. He indicated that contribution of labour was an age-old tradition in Myanmar, and that misunderstandings over forced labour often arose because of this. He also asserted that certain groups were giving false information to the media, to the ILO and to the United Nations concerning such matters. He nevertheless recognized that certain incidents of forced labour could arise when village heads exceeded their authority. He underlined that all cases of forced labour, including in his view those raised by the Liaison Officer a.i., occurred at this level. When he received information in this regard an investigation was conducted and those responsible prosecuted as appropriate. He noted that most of the cases raised by the Liaison Officer a.i. had now been disposed of. As regards a meeting with the senior leadership of the SPDC, the Minister indicated that Senior General Than Shwe was very busy with the National Convention and that Vice-Senior General Maung Aye was not in the capital. The vHLT reiterated the critical need for such a meeting, which it had already made clear prior to commencing its visit, and the extremely difficult position that it would be in should assurances in this regard not be given.

7. That afternoon, the vHLT had the opportunity to meet with the Prime Minister. The Prime Minister began by giving a very detailed presentation on the socio-economic and political situation in the country and the progress that had been made in this regard over the last 15 years. He then noted that on matters raised by the ILO there had also been progress in his view. The people of Myanmar were allowed a great degree of freedom and had a strong community spirit, which also extended to their participation in construction of roads and other projects. This gave rise to certain misunderstandings and allegations. So too did the negative views of certain small groups inside and outside the country. Nevertheless, he realized that these age-old practices could not necessarily be transposed to the modern age. It was also possible that some village heads abused their authority, and legal action was taken in such cases. The members of the vHLT then gave an overview similar to that which they had presented to the Minister for Labour that morning. They also again underlined the need for a meeting with the senior leadership. Disturbing reports indicated that the army was responsible for some very serious cases of forced labour, and it was necessary to have discussions with those having authority over the military. This was why their mandate called so explicitly for such a senior-level meeting. The Prime Minister took note of all these points, but did not give any specific responses either to the question of a senior-level meeting, or as regards the concrete steps outlined by the vHLT.

8. The following morning (23 February), having received no further indications regarding a meeting with the senior leadership, the vHLT decided that there was no point in continuing with the remaining meetings at the technical level and therefore cut short its visit. An unfortunate consequence of this was that the other contacts which the vHLT had planned to have also had to be cancelled. The vHLT requested another meeting with the Minister for Labour to explain the position, but he had already departed Yangon. It decided therefore to keep its meeting with the Minister for Foreign Affairs that morning, and to take advantage of that opportunity to explain to him, and through him to the highest authorities, the reasons for its decision, without going into any technical discussions. At the end of that meeting, having given the necessary clarifications, it handed over the prepared statement that it would issue that afternoon on departing the country. Attached to this statement the vHLT provided an informal aide-memoire setting out the main concrete steps on which it believed progress should be made. The vHLT also insisted that despite its early departure the door was still open for further developments. The Minister responded to these points but was not in a position to provide any of the reassurances sought. As regards the Plan of Action, he was ready to facilitate discussions between the ILO and the Ministry of Labour, whose competence it was. He also gave assurances that if at any time the Liaison Officer a.i. had issues that he wished to raise, his Directors-General were available for discussions.

9. At the request of the vHLT, the Liaison Officer a.i., who remained in Yangon, held a briefing for the diplomatic community and the press that afternoon concerning its early departure, at which the statement and aide-memoire were distributed. These are reproduced in Appendix III.

III. Conclusions

10. Although the vHLT regrettably had to cut short its visit to Yangon it is nevertheless in a position to contribute some significant clarifications to the Governing Body's consideration of the issue.

11. The main achievements of this visit may indeed be the fact that on the one hand it has allowed information to pass to the top level of the hierarchy and on the other hand has allowed the vHLT to pass back to the Governing Body a direct and independent assessment of the attitude of the authorities based on its experience over two days.

12. First, the decision of the vHLT to cut short its meetings at the technical level in the absence of any concrete commitments to have a meeting at the highest political level has undoubtedly managed to reach the senior leadership, despite the general reluctance on the part of the technical level to pass on negative news to that level. It is thus reasonable to think that even without having seen the vHLT, the senior leadership are now at least aware of the concrete points which according to the ILO require urgent attention if there is to be credible progress towards eradication of forced labour.

13. Second, beyond the assurance that the authorities are fully committed to the eradication of forced labour and that the ILO should take the word of the Ministry of Labour and of the Prime Minister as a fully reliable and sufficient expression of the commitment of the SPDC, the vHLT was disturbed by some eloquent silences or omissions:

- No direct reference was made to the implementation of the Plan of Action, except by the Minister for Foreign Affairs, although he then pointed out that this matter fell within the competence of the Ministry of Labour. Nothing was said about the Facilitator mechanism despite repeated reference to it by the vHLT itself.

- Behind the resurgence of the traditional theme about the lack of understanding on the part of the international community for the cultural dimension of practices which had nothing to do with forced labour, and the emphasis on the fact that the only real cases of forced labour were now credibly taken care of for the first time through criminal proceedings against village heads under section 374 of the Penal Code, the vHLT felt there was an implicit message that the Plan of Action may now have become unnecessary.

- There was no direct answer to the repeated plea made by the vHLT about the need to address cases involving the military, which was the justification for its insistence to have access to the top level of leadership and which was the object of specific proposals attached to the statement communicated to the Minister for Foreign Affairs (that is, issuance of an executive instruction to all military units, and the establishment of a focal point within the army).

14. These are fundamental questions to which a credible answer can come only from the highest authorities, as it is only at this level that the Government and military chains of command are integrated. There is still time before the discussion in the Governing Body for the authorities to correct any misinterpretation which may have occurred because of the circumstances within which the mission took place (which was the main reason cited at the start of the mission for the difficulty of finalizing the programme as the vHLT wished). This is why the vHLT was careful to leave a door open in the statement they issued upon departure, and to give a chance to the authorities to show in the few weeks to come that they are indeed interested in having a meaningful and bona fide dialogue on these issues.

15. It is obviously not for the vHLT to make any suggestions as regards the course of action which the Governing Body may wish to take depending on what may happen between now and its discussion. All that it wishes to say to both parties as an independent team is its conviction as a result of this visit that a bona fide and meaningful dialogue at the required level of decision-making could bring positive results. In the view of the vHLT this has been borne out by the remarkable achievements which have been made possible by the ILO presence, which certainly needs to be further strengthened, and to which the vHLT wishes to pay tribute in concluding this report.

Bangkok, 25 February 2005.   *(Signed)*   Ninian Stephen,

Ruth Dreifuss,

Eui-yong Chung.

Appendix I

Exchange of correspondence and discussions on the modalities for the vHLT's visit

1. In a letter dated 12 January 2005 to the Myanmar Minister for Labour, the Director-General informed the Myanmar authorities of the composition of the vHLT and the dates when it was ready to visit Myanmar (21-25 February), and underlined the need for appropriate modalities for the efficient discharge of its mandate to be agreed upon. The reply from the Minister for Labour dated 24 January welcomed the visit of the vHLT and the proposed dates, but gave rise to uncertainties as regards the modalities for the visit. For this reason and to ensure that all precautions had been taken to avoid potential misunderstandings, the Director-General wrote again to the Minister for Labour on 4 February and at the same time discussions were initiated in Yangon between the ILO Liaison Officer a.i. and the Myanmar authorities on the detailed modalities for the visit. Copies of the relevant correspondence are provided herewith.

2. The exchange of letters between the Director-General and the Minister for Labour and the discussions that the Liaison Officer a.i. had with the Ministry of Labour did not result in a clear indication that a meeting between the vHLT and the senior leadership of the State Peace and Development Council (SPDC) would be possible. Informal indications were given in these meetings, however, which suggested that the authorities understood the critical need for a meeting with the senior SPDC leadership in order for the vHLT to successfully discharge its mandate, and that the possibility for such a meeting remained open. The draft programme proposed by the authorities prior to the arrival of the vHLT included a meeting with Secretary-1 of the SPDC, but did not make mention of a meeting with the senior leadership.

3. Given the short time remaining before the proposed visit, the Liaison Officer a.i. wrote to the Minister for Labour on 10 February, confirming that the various meetings proposed at the technical level, as well as with SPDC Secretary-1, were considered by the vHLT to be important and valuable, but that a meeting with the senior leadership – namely, Senior General Than Shwe or Vice-Senior General Maung Aye – was seen by the vHLT as critical to its mandate. The letter also noted that unless clear indications were urgently received concerning the possibility of such a meeting, the vHLT might have to draw the conclusion that it was not possible to fulfil its mandate on the basis of the proposed programme.

4. The Liaison Officer a.i. reiterated these points in a meeting with the Deputy Minister for Labour on 11 February, and he warned that if the vHLT was not able to receive some assurances in this regard, it might have to make the difficult decision not to proceed with its visit. The Deputy Minister replied that there was a strong likelihood that the Prime Minister would meet with the vHLT, but that he was not in a position at that stage to give similar assurances as regards the meeting with the senior leadership. He did however explain that this was not because such a meeting was being ruled out, but rather because certain internal and external constraints made it difficult to give a firm commitment to such a meeting in advance.

5. In the circumstances, and in view of the time constraints, the International Labour Office agreed with the members of the vHLT that it should inform the Myanmar authorities that they were prepared to have the necessary formalities and arrangements for their visit completed, but only on the understanding that a satisfactory programme would be finalized as soon as possible on the vHLT's arrival in Yangon. It was on this understanding that visas were being requested. The Liaison Officer a.i. sent a *note verbale* to the authorities on 15 February to this effect (also reproduced herewith). At the same time, he passed a verbal message to the authorities that if the vHLT's understanding was incorrect, it was extremely important that it should be informed of this prior to commencing its mission in order to avoid a potentially more embarrassing situation.

(a) Letter dated 12 January 2005 from the Director-General to the Myanmar Minister for Labour

Dear Minister,

As you are aware, the Governing Body of the ILO at its last session in November 2004 adopted important conclusions concerning the situation of Myanmar, the full text of which is attached for ease of reference.

I have the honour to advise you that, as I was requested by the Governing Body, I have now constituted a very High-Level Team to fulfil the mandate defined in these conclusions, and whose objective is to a large extent to follow up on a previous HLT which successfully visited Myanmar in 2001 and was received by His Excellency Senior General Than Shwe and his colleagues of the State Peace and Development Council (SPDC).

The composition of this very High-Level Team is designed to ensure the highest possible degree of integrity, continuity and credibility in the discharge of the above mandate. It is as follows:

- The Right Honourable Sir Ninian Stephen, KG, AK, GCMG, GCVO, KBE, PC, former Governor-General of Australia, who chaired the former HLT in 2001;

- Her Excellency Madame Ruth Dreifuss, former President of the Swiss Confederation;

- The Honourable Eui-yong Chung, former Chairperson of the Governing Body of the ILO, Member of the National Assembly of the Republic of Korea and Chairperson of the Foreign Relations Committee of the Uri Party.

The very High-Level Team will be ready to visit Myanmar during the week of 21-25 February 2005 it being understood that appropriate modalities for the efficient discharge of its mandate will have been agreed well ahead between the Myanmar authorities and the ILO.

I am glad to inform you in that respect that my colleagues stand ready both in Yangon and in Geneva to undertake the necessary consultations for that purpose at the earliest convenience of the Myanmar authorities.

I trust that in view of the extreme importance of this visit for the future cooperation between Myanmar and the ILO and indeed with the international community at large, you will no doubt wish to bring the contents of this letter to Senior General Than Shwe's personal attention.

Yours sincerely,

(Signed) Juan Somavia.

(b) Letter dated 24 January 2005 from the Myanmar Minister for Labour to the Director-General

Excellency,

I would like to acknowledge the receipt of your letter dated 12 January 2005 concerning the visit of the ILO very High-Level Team to be headed by the Right Honourable Sir Ninian Stephen, former Governor-General of Australia.

I am pleased to inform you that we welcome the visit of the very High-Level Team during the week of 21-25 February. It will be a busiest time for all of us because the National Convention will be in session at the time. Despite this situation, we assure you for all possible arrangement for the activities of very High-Level Team. It is my pleasure to inform you that the Chief Justice, Attorney-General and the ministers from the ministries concerned will be available to have separate meetings for constructive dialogue.

Freedom of contact will be granted with the exception of the meeting with the persons who are under detention or have been put under restraint according to the existing law.

The members of the very High-Level Team will be granted the privileges accorded to the personnel from the UN organizations as in the case of previous ILO missions to Myanmar.

I am looking forward to the fruitful cooperation between Myanmar and ILO.

Yours sincerely,

(Signed) U Thaung.

(c) Letter dated 4 February 2005 from the Director-General to the Myanmar Minister for Labour

Dear Minister,

Thank you for your letter dated 24 January 2005 in reply to my letter of 12 January 2005 concerning the visit of a very High-Level Team.

I note that the dates for the visit are acceptable to the authorities despite some inconvenience it may create and I wish to thank you for that.

As regards other modalities, I would first like to remind you that the recognition of the freedom of contacts which is mentioned in your letter is essential to enable each mission to discharge its specific mandate. The nature of such contacts of course varies with the specific object of the mission. In the present case, the mandate given by the Governing Body does not call for the same type of contacts as the previous one. However, it must be clear that it is ultimately for the members of the very High-Level Team to determine what contacts may be relevant to the effective discharge of the mandate entrusted to them by the Governing Body, and to approach the authorities for that purpose as appropriate. The contents of your letter seem to fully allow for this.

The most critical aspect of the modalities now is to agree on a programme which enables the very high-level mission to discharge the mandate of the Governing Body. While of course discussions at the technical level such as those indicated in your letter are necessary and welcome, the said mandate implies that the very High-Level Team will meet the senior leadership. It is with that understanding that the members of the very High-Level Team have accepted to participate. The Office is ready to discuss urgently a programme that meets this requirement.

Yours sincerely,

(Signed) Juan Somavia.

(d) Note verbale *dated 15 February 2005 from the Office of the Liaison Officer to the Minister for Labour*

The Office of the ILO Liaison Officer presents its compliments to the Minister for Labour of Myanmar and has the honour to convey to His Excellency the following information.

The Office of the ILO Liaison Officer has been instructed by ILO headquarters in Geneva to inform His Excellency the Minister for Labour, and through him the State Peace and Development Council, that following consultations with the members of the very High-Level Team and on the basis of the indications provided through the Liaison Officer as regards the tentative programme of their visit and the prospects for a meeting at the highest level, they have agreed to have the necessary formalities and arrangements for their visit completed. These steps are being taken, however, on the understanding that the tentative programme will be adjusted, complemented and finalized as appropriate as soon as possible upon their arrival in Yangon.

It is on this understanding that the necessary visas are being urgently requested, in the case of Sir Ninian Stephen and His Excellency Eui-yong Chung through the Myanmar embassies in their respective countries, and through the Permanent Mission of Myanmar in Geneva for Her Excellency Madame Ruth Dreifuss and for Mr. Francis Maupain, who is to accompany the vHLT as its Executive Secretary.

The Office of the ILO Liaison Officer avails itself of this opportunity to renew to the Minister for Labour of Myanmar the assurances of its highest consideration.

Appendix II

Programme of meetings arranged by the authorities and provided to the vHLT on its arrival in Yangon

[Note that this was not the programme of meetings that actually took place, as explained in the main text of this report.]

Monday, 21 February

18:45 Arrival at Yangon International Airport
(H.E. Deputy Minister for Labour will meet the team at the airport)

Tuesday, 22 February

10:00 Call on H.E. U Thaung (Minister for Science and Technology and Labour)

16:00 Call on H.E. Maj. Gen. Maung Oo (Minister for Home Affairs)

19:30 Dinner to be hosted by H.E. the Minister for Labour

Wednesday, 23 February

11:30 Call on H.E. U Nyan Win (Minister for Foreign Affairs)

15:00 Call on H.E. U Aung Toe (Chief Justice)

Thursday, 24 February

10:00 Meeting with Implementation Committee

p.m. —

Friday, 25 February

a.m. —

p.m. —

19:45 Departure from Yangon
(H.E. the Deputy Minister for Labour will see the team off at the airport)

Appendix III

(a) Statement by the ILO very High-Level Team at the close of its visit to Myanmar

The mandate which had been entrusted to the vHLT by the Governing Body of the ILO at its 291st Session (November 2004) was to evaluate the attitude of the Myanmar authorities at the highest level to the elimination of forced labour and assess their determination to continue their cooperation with the ILO in this regard. Its composition had been established accordingly. The Myanmar authorities were fully aware of these terms of reference before the mission departed for Yangon. However, the mission was informed on its arrival that for various reasons linked to the National Convention the programme did not include the meetings that would have enabled it to successfully complete its mandate as it understood it.

Under the circumstances, and after having discussions and making its views known to the Minister for Labour and to the Prime Minister, the mission decided that there would be no point at this stage to have more in-depth discussions at the technical level on the concrete steps outlined in those meetings which in the mission's view could contribute to alleviating recent concerns expressed in the Governing Body.

The vHLT will submit its report to the next session of the ILO Governing Body in March.

Yangon, 23 February 2005.

(Signed) Sir Ninian Stephen
on behalf of the vHLT.

(b) Aide-memoire

Additional concrete steps considered by the mission to be important for the effective eradication of forced labour

- Issuing a public executive instruction from the competent SPDC level to give effect to the provision in Order Supplementing Order 1/99 that the Ministry of Defence should issue further directives to all units under its command not to requisition forced labour, and giving adequate publicity to same.

- Reconfirmation of the commitment of the authorities to the terms of the joint Plan of Action on forced labour, including identification of the Facilitator, together with the appointment of a high-level focal point in the army to deal with allegations that concern the army.

- Renewing the commitment of the authorities to the freedom of movement of the ILO Liaison Officer.

- Taking additional measures that could build confidence vis-à-vis the people of Myanmar as regards the possibilities to lodge complaints regarding forced labour. Such measures should include extending the amnesty which was granted to the two persons in the high-treason case to the third person whose conviction had an ILO dimension, as well as credible solutions to the serious forced labour cases identified by the ILO Governing Body in November 2004.

292nd Session of the Governing Body of the International Labour Office
(March 2005)

SEVENTH ITEM ON THE AGENDA

Developments concerning the question of the observance by the Government of Myanmar of the Forced Labour Convention, 1930 (No. 29)

Conclusions

1. The easiest and most pleasant part of my task is to convey on our joint behalf our sincere gratitude to the members of the very High-Level Team (vHLT) for having accepted a very difficult assignment and for their dedication in discharging it scrupulously both in letter and spirit. Now comes a much more painful and difficult task, and I am indebted to my colleagues the Officers for having given me their support and advice.

2. In drawing the conclusions of the present debate it is important to recall the conclusions reached by the Governing Body at its previous session, which set the parameters for our present consideration of the matter. Following recent leadership changes, the main preoccupation of the Governing Body in establishing the vHLT was to have an objective basis to evaluate the attitude and the real will of the authorities at the highest level, and their determination to continue their effective cooperation on the outstanding issues; this evaluation would then enable the Governing Body to draw the appropriate consequences in full knowledge of the facts, including as regards action under article 33.

3. In that framework, after hearing the message from the Ambassador, Mr. Nyunt Maung Shein, we have had a broad debate.

4. The most largely shared sentiment was one of condemnation over the failure of the highest authorities to take advantage of the unique opportunity that the visit of the vHLT represented to resume a credible dialogue on the issues of concern, and also the feelings of grave concern over the general situation that this reveals.

5. Indeed, the Prime Minister's indications to the Members of the vHLT as well as the comments of the Ambassador allege that the necessary political will exists. However, the attitude towards the vHLT, along with the press conference held in Yangon on 15 March and even some of the remarks made this morning by the Ambassador of Myanmar, casts into grave doubt the credibility of this message and the usefulness of the ILO approach.

6. Apart from the assurances and indications, there are the facts. Some of them seem to a number of us to go in the right direction, in particular the prosecutions and punishment of authorities responsible for having recourse to forced labour and the establishment of a focal point in the army on the initiative of the Vice-Senior General.

7. But in the circumstances the overall assessment falls far short of our expectations. And this is the reason why, according to the Workers' proposal, joined by certain Governments, the Governing Body has no other choice but to ask the Office to take a certain number of formal steps to strengthen the measures under the resolution of June 2000, but also at the same time to strengthen the Liaison Office.

8. Other Government members and the Employers, while sharing the same sense of condemnation of the actions of the authorities, were in view of the closeness of the International Labour Conference starting 31 May inclined to test, for the last time, the true will of the authorities to cooperate with the ILO, before resuming the examination of these measures and taking a decision on them. Other Governments limited themselves to calling for an urgent restarting of an effective and meaningful dialogue, without reference to specific measures.

9. In the treatment of this particularly difficult case, the solidarity of all the groups has always given strength to the position of the ILO. It is the view of my colleagues and myself that this strength should be maintained. Three considerations may help us.

    – First, the question is not strictly speaking for us to adopt new measures under article 33. These measures have already been taken under the resolution adopted by the Conference in 2000, which is binding on the Governing Body and the other organs of the ILO as long as it has not been modified. These measures clearly remain in force with regard to all constituents and others to whom the resolution is addressed.

    – The next question is whether it is time for members to resume their consideration of the action which they have been and still are called upon to take under the resolution of June 2000. This question arises because most of them have suspended their action since the beginning of 2001 as a result of the progress which seemed to be under way at the time, and which resulted in certain concrete developments in particular through the ILO presence. At this stage, and on the basis of the information at our disposal, the growing feeling is that the "wait-and-see" attitude that prevailed among most members, following the initiation of meaningful dialogue since 2001, appears to have lost its raison d'être and cannot continue.

    – A third consideration is that under the resolution the ILO cannot prejudge the action which each individual member may find it appropriate to take as a result of their review; the only thing which is expected from all of them is to report at suitable intervals to explain what they have done and why.

10. At the same time it is clear that the ILO is not closing the door to the resumption of a positive dialogue with the Myanmar authorities in line with the views wisely expressed by the vHLT and a large number of those who took the floor during the debate; it is clear in particular that the existence of such dialogue and the concrete results it could produce should be taken objectively into account by members when deciding the outcome of their review. The extent to which progress will be achieved with regard to the strengthening of the ILO presence as well as the other items covered by the vHLT's aide-mémoire, including the immediate release of Shwe Mahn, should be a concrete test in this regard.

11. In the light of these considerations, the conclusions that myself and my colleagues think the Governing Body could unanimously agree on taking is to transmit to all those to whom the 2000 resolution was addressed – including relevant agencies – the results of our deliberations reflected in the present conclusions, with a view to them taking the appropriate action resulting from the above considerations.

12. The Officers of the Governing Body are mandated to closely follow any developments. These developments will be the subject of a document before the Committee on the Application of Standards of the International Labour Conference in June.

No. 22 — Thursday, 16 June 2005

AUTHENTIC TEXTS OF INSTRUMENTS ADOPTED BY THE CONFERENCE

Recommendation 196

RECOMMENDATION CONCERNING WORK IN THE FISHING SECTOR[1]

The General Conference of the International Labour Organization,

Having been convened at Geneva by the Governing Body of the International Labour Office, and having met in its 93rd Session on 31 May 2005, and

Taking into account the need to revise the Hours of Work (Fishing) Recommendation, 1920, and

Having decided upon the adoption of certain proposals with regard to work in the fishing sector, which is the fifth item on the agenda of the session, and

Having determined that these proposals shall take the form of a Recommendation supplementing the Work in Fishing Convention, 2005 (hereinafter referred to as "the Convention");

adopts this sixteenth day of June of the year two thousand and five the following Recommendation, which may be cited as the Work in Fishing Recommendation, 2005.

PART I. CONDITIONS FOR WORK ON BOARD
FISHING VESSELS

Protection of young persons

1. Members should establish the requirements for the pre-sea training of persons between the ages of 16 and 18 working on board fishing vessels, taking into account international instruments concerning training for work on board fishing vessels, including occupational safety and health issues such as night work, hazardous tasks, work with dangerous machinery, manual handling and transport of heavy loads, work in high latitudes, work for excessive periods of time and other relevant issues identified after an assessment of the risks concerned.

2. The training of persons between the ages of 16 and 18 might be provided through participation in an apprenticeship or approved training programme, which should operate under established rules and be monitored

---

[1] The proposed Convention to which this Recommendation refers was not adopted by the Conference owing to the lack of a quorum. The Conference asked the Governing Body to place on the agenda of the 96th Session of the Conference (2007) an item concerning work in the fishing sector, based on the report of the Committee on the Fishing Sector of the 93rd Session. This Recommendation will be reviewed by the Conference during the examination of the item placed on its agenda.

Recommandation 196
RECOMMANDATION CONCERNANT LE TRAVAIL DANS LE SECTEUR DE LA PÊCHE[1]

La Conférence générale de l'Organisation internationale du Travail,

Convoquée à Genève par le Conseil d'administration du Bureau international du Travail, et s'y étant réunie le 31 mai 2005, en sa quatre-vingt-treizième session;

Tenant compte de la nécessité de réviser la recommandation sur la durée du travail (pêche), 1920;

Après avoir décidé d'adopter diverses propositions relatives au travail dans le secteur de la pêche, question qui constitue le cinquième point à l'ordre du jour de la session;

Après avoir décidé que ces propositions prendraient la forme d'une recommandation complétant la convention sur le travail dans la pêche, 2005 (ci-après dénommée «la convention»),

adopte, ce seizième jour de juin deux mille cinq, la recommandation ci-après, qui sera dénommée Recommandation sur le travail dans la pêche, 2005.

PARTIE I. CONDITIONS DE TRAVAIL À BORD DES NAVIRES DE PÊCHE

Protection des adolescents

1. Les Membres devraient fixer les conditions requises en matière de formation préalable à l'embarquement des personnes âgées de 16 à 18 ans appelées à travailler à bord des navires de pêche, en prenant en considération les instruments internationaux relatifs à la formation au travail à bord de ces navires, notamment pour ce qui a trait aux questions de sécurité et de santé au travail telles que le travail de nuit, les tâches dangereuses, l'utilisation de machines dangereuses, la manutention et le transport de lourdes charges, le travail effectué sous des latitudes élevées, la durée excessive du travail et autres questions pertinentes recensées après évaluation des risques encourus.

2. La formation des personnes âgées de 16 à 18 ans pourrait être assurée par le biais de l'apprentissage ou de la participation à des programmes de formation approuvés, qui devraient être menés selon des

---

[1] Le projet de convention auquel se réfère la présente recommandation n'a pas été adopté par la Conférence faute de quorum. la Conférence a demandé au Conseil d'administration d'inscrire à l'ordre du jour de la 96e session de la Conférence (2007) une question relative au travail dans le secteur de la pêche sur la base du rapport élaboré par la Commission du secteur de la pêche lors de la 93e session. La présente recommandation sera revue par la Conférence à l'occasion de l'examen de la question inscrite à son ordre du jour.

by the competent authority, and should not interfere with the person's general education.

3. Members should take measures to ensure that the safety, lifesaving and survival equipment carried on board fishing vessels carrying persons under the age of 18 is appropriate for the size of such persons.

4. The working hours of fishers under the age of 18 should not exceed eight hours per day and 40 hours per week, and they should not work overtime except where unavoidable for safety reasons.

5. Fishers under the age of 18 should be assured sufficient time for all meals and a break of at least one hour for the main meal of the day.

Medical examination

6. When prescribing the nature of the examination, Members should pay due regard to the age of the person to be examined and the nature of the duties to be performed.

7. The medical certificate should be signed by a medical practitioner approved by the competent authority.

8. Arrangements should be made to enable a person who, after examination, is determined to be unfit for work on board fishing vessels or certain types of fishing vessels, or for certain types of work on board, to apply for a further examination by a medical referee or referees who should be independent of any fishing vessel owner or of any organization of fishing vessel owners or fishers.

9. The competent authority should take into account international guidance on medical examination and certification of persons working at sea, such as the (ILO/WHO) *Guidelines for Conducting Pre-sea and Periodic Medical Fitness Examinations for Seafarers*.

10. For fishers exempted from the application of the provisions concerning medical examination in the Convention, the competent authority should take adequate measures to provide health surveillance for the purpose of occupational safety and health.

Competency and training

11. Members should:
(a) take into account generally accepted international standards concerning training and competencies of fishers in determining the competencies required for skippers, mates, engineers and other persons working on board fishing vessels;
(b) address the following issues, with regard to the vocational training of fishers: national planning and administration, including coordination;

règles établies sous la supervision des autorités compétentes et ne devraient pas nuire à la possibilité pour les personnes concernées de suivre les programmes de l'enseignement général.

3. Les Membres devraient prendre des mesures visant à garantir qu'à bord des navires de pêche qui embarquent des jeunes âgés de moins de 18 ans les équipements de sécurité, de sauvetage et de survie soient adaptés à leur taille.

4. Les pêcheurs âgés de moins de 18 ans ne devraient pas travailler plus de huit heures par jour ni plus de quarante heures par semaine, et ne devraient pas effectuer d'heures supplémentaires à moins que cela ne soit inévitable pour des raisons de sécurité.

5. Les pêcheurs âgés de moins de 18 ans devraient être assurés qu'une pause suffisante leur soit accordée pour chacun des repas et bénéficier d'une pause d'au moins une heure pour prendre leur repas principal.

Examen médical

6. Aux fins de la détermination de la nature de l'examen, les Membres devraient tenir compte de l'âge de l'intéressé ainsi que de la nature du travail à effectuer.

7. Le certificat médical devrait être signé par du personnel médical agréé par l'autorité compétente.

8. Des dispositions devraient être prises pour permettre à toute personne qui, après avoir été examinée, est considérée comme inapte à travailler à bord d'un navire de pêche ou de certains types de navires de pêche, ou à effectuer certains types de tâches à bord, de demander à être examinée par un ou plusieurs arbitres médicaux indépendants de tout armateur à la pêche ou de toute organisation d'armateurs à la pêche ou de pêcheurs.

9. L'autorité compétente devrait tenir compte des directives internationales relatives à l'examen médical et au brevet d'aptitude physique des personnes travaillant en mer, telles que les *Directives relatives à la conduite des examens médicaux d'aptitude précédant l'embarquement et des examens médicaux périodiques des gens de mer* (OIT/OMS).

10. L'autorité compétente devrait prendre des mesures adéquates pour que les pêcheurs auxquels ne s'appliquent pas les dispositions relatives à l'examen médical prescrites dans la convention soient médicalement suivis aux fins de la santé et sécurité au travail.

Compétence et formation

11. Les Membres devraient:

a) prendre en compte les normes internationales généralement admises en matière de formation et de qualifications des pêcheurs en définissant les compétences requises pour exercer les fonctions de patron, d'officier de pont, de mécanicien et autres fonctions à bord d'un navire de pêche;

b) examiner les questions suivantes relatives à la formation professionnelle des pêcheurs: organisation et administration

financing and training standards; training programmes, including pre-vocational training and also short courses for working fishers; methods of training; and international cooperation; and

(c) ensure that there is no discrimination with regard to access to training.

PART II. CONDITIONS OF SERVICE

Record of service

12. At the end of each contract, a record of service in regard to that contract should be made available to the fisher concerned, or entered in the fisher's service book.

Special measures

13. For fishers excluded from the scope of the Convention, the competent authority should take measures to provide them with adequate protection with respect to their conditions of work and means of dispute settlement.

Payment of fishers

14. Fishers should have the right to advances against earnings under prescribed conditions.

15. For vessels of 24 metres in length and over, all fishers should be entitled to minimum payment in accordance with national laws, regulations or collective agreements.

PART III. ACCOMODATION

16. When establishing requirements or guidance, the competent authority should take into account relevant international guidance on accommodation, food, and health and hygiene relating to persons working or living on board vessels, including the most recent editions of the (FAO/ILO/IMO) *Code of Safety for Fishermen and Fishing Vessels* and the (FAO/ILO/IMO) *Voluntary Guidelines for the Design, Construction and Equipment of Small Fishing Vessels.*

17. The competent authority should work with relevant organizations and agencies to develop and disseminate educational material and on-board information and guidance concerning safe and healthy accommodation and food on board fishing vessels.

nationales, y compris la coordination; financement et normes de formation; programmes de formation, y compris la formation pré-professionnelle ainsi que les cours de courte durée destinés aux pêcheurs en activité; méthodes de formation; et coopération internationale;

c) s'assurer qu'il n'existe pas de discrimination en matière d'accès à la formation.

PARTIE II. CONDITIONS DE SERVICE

Relevé des états de service

12. A la fin de chaque contrat, un relevé des états de service concernant ce contrat devrait être mis à la disposition de chaque pêcheur concerné ou noté dans son livret de travail.

Mesures spéciales

13. Pour les pêcheurs exclus du champ d'application de la convention, l'autorité compétente devrait prendre des mesures prévoyant une protection adéquate en ce qui concerne leurs conditions de travail et des mécanismes de règlement des différends.

Paiement des pêcheurs

14. Les pêcheurs devraient avoir le droit au versement d'avances à valoir sur leurs gains dans des conditions déterminées.

15. Pour les navires d'une longueur égale ou supérieure à 24 mètres, tous les pêcheurs devraient avoir droit à un paiement minimal, conformément à la législation nationale ou aux conventions collectives.

PARTIE III. LOGEMENT

16. Lors de l'élaboration de prescriptions ou directives, l'autorité compétente devrait tenir compte des directives internationales applicables en matière de logement, d'alimentation, et de santé et d'hygiène concernant les personnes qui travaillent ou qui vivent à bord de navires, y compris l'édition la plus récente du *Recueil de règles de sécurité pour les pêcheurs et les navires de pêche* (FAO/OIT/OMI) ainsi que des *Directives facultatives pour la conception, la construction et l'équipement des navires de pêche de faibles dimensions* (FAO/OIT/OMI).

17. L'autorité compétente devrait travailler avec les organisations et agences pertinentes pour élaborer et diffuser des documents pédagogiques et des informations disponibles à bord du navire ainsi que des instructions sur ce qui constitue une alimentation et un logement sûrs et sains à bord des navires de pêche.

18. Inspections of crew accommodation required by the competent authority should be carried out together with initial or periodic surveys or inspections for other purposes.

Design and construction

19. Adequate insulation should be provided for exposed decks over crew accommodation spaces, external bulkheads of sleeping rooms and mess rooms, machinery casings and boundary bulkheads of galleys and other spaces in which heat is produced, and, as necessary, to prevent condensation or overheating in sleeping rooms, mess rooms, recreation rooms and passageways.

20. Protection should be provided from the heat effects of any steam or hot water service pipes. Main steam and exhaust pipes should not pass through crew accommodation or through passageways leading to crew accommodation. Where this cannot be avoided, pipes should be adequately insulated and encased.

21. Materials and furnishings used in accommodation spaces should be impervious to dampness, easy to keep clean and not likely to harbour vermin.

Noise and vibration

22. Noise levels for working and living spaces, which are established by the competent authority, should be in conformity with the guidelines of the International Labour Organization on exposure levels to ambient factors in the workplace and, where applicable, the specific protection recommended by the International Maritime Organization, together with any subsequent amending and supplementary instruments for acceptable noise levels on board ships.

23. The competent authority, in conjunction with the competent international bodies and with representatives of organizations of fishing vessel owners and fishers and taking into account, as appropriate, relevant international standards, should review on an ongoing basis the problem of vibration on board fishing vessels with the objective of improving the protection of fishers, as far as practicable, from the adverse effects of vibration.

(1) Such review should cover the effect of exposure to excessive vibration on the health and comfort of fishers and the measures to be prescribed or recommended to reduce vibration on fishing vessels to protect fishers.

(2) Measures to reduce vibration, or its effects, to be considered should include:

(a) instruction of fishers in the dangers to their health of prolonged exposure to vibration;

18. Les inspections du logement de l'équipage prescrites par l'autorité compétente devraient être entreprises conjointement aux enquêtes ou inspections initiales ou périodiques menées à d'autres fins.

Conception et construction

19. Une isolation adéquate devrait être fournie pour les ponts extérieurs recouvrant le logement de l'équipage, les parois extérieures des postes de couchage et réfectoires, les encaissements de machines et les cloisons qui limitent les cuisines et les autres locaux dégageant de la chaleur et pour éviter, au besoin, toute condensation ou chaleur excessive pour les postes de couchage, les réfectoires, les installations de loisirs et les coursives.

20. Une protection devrait être prévue pour calorifuger les canalisations de vapeur et d'eau chaude. Les tuyauteries principales de vapeur et d'échappement ne devraient pas passer par les logements de l'équipage ni par les coursives y conduisant. Lorsque cela ne peut être évité, les tuyauteries devraient être convenablement isolées et placées dans une gaine.

21. Les matériaux et fournitures utilisés dans le logement de l'équipage devraient être imperméables, faciles à nettoyer et ne pas être susceptibles d'abriter de la vermine.

Bruits et vibrations

22. Les niveaux de bruit établis par l'autorité compétente pour les postes de travail et les locaux d'habitation devraient être conformes aux directives de l'Organisation internationale du Travail relatives aux niveaux d'exposition aux facteurs ambiants sur le lieu de travail ainsi que, le cas échéant, aux normes de protection particulières recommandées par l'Organisation maritime internationale, et à tout instrument relatif aux niveaux de bruit acceptables à bord des navires adopté ultérieurement.

23. L'autorité compétente, conjointement avec les organismes internationaux compétents et les représentants des organisations d'armateurs à la pêche et de pêcheurs et compte tenu, selon le cas, des normes internationales pertinentes, devrait examiner de manière continue le problème des vibrations à bord des navires de pêche en vue d'améliorer, autant que possible, la protection des pêcheurs contre les effets néfastes de telles vibrations.

(1) Cet examen devrait porter sur les effets de l'exposition aux vibrations excessives sur la santé et le confort des pêcheurs et les mesures à prescrire ou à recommander pour réduire les vibrations sur les navires de pêche afin de protéger les pêcheurs.

(2) Les mesures à étudier pour réduire les vibrations ou leurs effets devraient comprendre:

a) la formation des pêcheurs aux risques que l'exposition prolongée aux vibrations présente pour leur santé;

(b) provision of approved personal protective equipment to fishers where necessary; and

(c) assessment of risks and reduction of exposure in sleeping rooms, mess rooms, recreational accommodation and catering facilities and other fishers' accommodation by adopting measures in accordance with the guidance provided by the (ILO) *Code of practice on ambient factors in the workplace* and any subsequent revisions, taking into account the difference between exposure in the workplace and in the living space.

Heating

24. The heating system should be capable of maintaining the temperature in crew accommodation at a satisfactory level, as established by the competent authority, under normal conditions of weather and climate likely to be met with on service, and should be designed so as not to endanger the health or safety of the fishers or the safety of the vessel.

Lighting

25. Methods of lighting should not endanger the health and safety of the fishers or the safety of the vessel.

Sleeping rooms

26. Each berth should be fitted with a comfortable mattress with a cushioned bottom or a combined mattress, including a spring bottom, or a spring mattress. The cushioning material used should be made of approved material. Berths should not be placed side by side in such a way that access to one berth can be obtained only over another. The lower berth in a double tier should not be less than 0.3 metres above the floor, and the upper berth should be fitted with a dust-proof bottom and placed approximately midway between the bottom of the lower berth and the lower side of the deck head beams. Berths should not be arranged in tiers of more than two. In the case of berths placed along the vessel's side, there should be only a single tier when a sidelight is situated above a berth.

27. Sleeping rooms should be fitted with curtains for the sidelights, as well as a mirror, small cabinets for toilet requisites, a book rack and a sufficient number of coat hooks.

28. As far as practicable, berthing of crew members should be so arranged that watches are separated and that no day worker shares a room with a watch-keeper.

b) la fourniture aux pêcheurs d'un équipement de protection individuelle agréé lorsque cela est nécessaire;

c) l'évaluation des risques et la réduction de l'exposition aux vibrations dans les postes de couchage, les salles à manger, les installations de loisirs et de restauration et autres locaux d'habitation pour les pêcheurs par des mesures conformes aux orientations données dans le *Recueil de directives pratiques sur les facteurs ambiants sur le lieu de travail* (OIT) et ses versions révisées ultérieures, en tenant compte des écarts entre l'exposition sur les lieux de travail et dans les locaux d'habitation.

Chauffage

24. Le système de chauffage devrait permettre de maintenir la température dans le logement de l'équipage à un niveau satisfaisant, établi par l'autorité compétente, dans les conditions normales de temps et de climat que le navire est susceptible de rencontrer en cours de navigation. Le système devrait être conçu de manière à ne pas constituer un risque pour la santé ou la sécurité de l'équipage, ni pour la sécurité du navire.

Eclairage

25. Les systèmes d'éclairage ne doivent pas mettre en péril la santé ou la sécurité des pêcheurs ni la sécurité du navire.

Postes de couchage

26. Toute couchette devrait être pourvue d'un matelas confortable muni d'un fond rembourré ou d'un matelas combiné, posé sur support élastique, ou d'un matelas à ressorts. Le rembourrage utilisé doit être d'un matériau approuvé. Les couchettes ne devraient pas être placées côte à côte d'une façon telle que l'on ne puisse accéder à l'une d'elles qu'en passant au-dessus d'une autre. Lorsque des couchettes sont superposées, la couchette inférieure ne devrait pas être placée à moins de 0,3 mètre au-dessus du plancher et la couchette supérieure devrait être équipée d'un fond imperméable à la poussière et disposée approximativement à mi-hauteur entre le fond de la couchette inférieure et le dessous des barrots du plafond. La superposition de plus de deux couchettes devrait être interdite. Dans le cas où des couchettes sont placées le long de la muraille du navire, il devrait être interdit de superposer des couchettes à l'endroit où un hublot est situé au-dessus d'une couchette.

27. Les postes de couchage devraient être équipés de rideaux aux hublots, d'un miroir, de petits placards pour les articles de toilette, d'une étagère à livres et d'un nombre suffisant de patères.

28. Dans la mesure du possible, les couchettes des membres de l'équipage devraient être réparties de façon à séparer les quarts et à éviter qu'un pêcheur de jour ne partage le même poste qu'un pêcheur prenant le quart.

29. On vessels of 24 metres in length and over, separate sleeping rooms for men and women should be provided.

Sanitary accommodation

30. Sanitary accommodation spaces should have:

(a) floors of approved durable material which can be easily cleaned, and which are impervious to dampness and properly drained;

(b) bulkheads of steel or other approved material which should be watertight up to at least 0.23 metres above the level of the deck;

(c) sufficient lighting, heating and ventilation; and

(d) soil pipes and waste pipes of adequate dimensions which are constructed so as to minimize the risk of obstruction and to facilitate cleaning; such pipes should not pass through fresh water or drinking-water tanks, nor should they, if practicable, pass overhead in mess rooms or sleeping accommodation.

31. Toilets should be of an approved type and provided with an ample flush of water, available at all times and independently controllable. Where practicable, they should be situated convenient to, but separate from, sleeping rooms and washrooms. Where there is more than one toilet in a compartment, the toilets should be sufficiently screened to ensure privacy.

32. Separate sanitary facilities should be provided for women fishers.

Recreational facilities

33. Where recreational facilities are required, furnishings should include, as a minimum, a bookcase and facilities for reading, writing and, where practicable, games. Recreational facilities and services should be reviewed frequently to ensure that they are appropriate in the light of changes in the needs of fishers resulting from technical, operational and other developments. Consideration should also be given to including the following facilities at no cost to the fishers, where practicable:

(a) a smoking room;

(b) television viewing and the reception of radio broadcasts;

(c) projection of films or video films, the stock of which should be adequate for the duration of the voyage and, where necessary, changed at reasonable intervals;

29. Les navires d'une longueur égale ou supérieure à 24 mètres devraient être pourvus de postes de couchage séparés pour les hommes et pour les femmes.

Installations sanitaires

30. Les espaces destinés aux installations sanitaires devraient avoir:

a) des sols revêtus d'un matériau durable approuvé, facile à nettoyer et imperméable, et être pourvus d'un système efficace d'écoulement des eaux;

b) des cloisons en acier ou en tout autre matériau approuvé qui soient étanches sur une hauteur d'au moins 0,23 mètre à partir du pont;

c) une ventilation, un éclairage et un chauffage suffisants;

d) des conduites d'évacuation des eaux des toilettes et des eaux usées de dimensions adéquates et installées de manière à réduire au minimum les risques d'obstruction et à en faciliter le nettoyage, et qui ne devraient pas traverser les réservoirs d'eau douce ou d'eau potable ni, si possible, passer sous les plafonds des réfectoires ou des postes de couchage.

31. Les toilettes devraient être d'un modèle approuvé et pourvues d'une chasse d'eau puissante, en état de fonctionner à tout moment et qui puisse être actionnée individuellement. Là où cela est possible, les toilettes devraient être situées en un endroit aisément accessible à partir des postes de couchage et des locaux affectés aux soins de propreté, mais devraient en être séparées. Si plusieurs toilettes sont installées dans un même local, elles devraient être suffisamment encloses pour préserver l'intimité.

32. Des installations sanitaires séparées devraient être prévues pour les pêcheuses.

Installations de loisirs

33. Là où des installations de loisirs sont prescrites, les équipements devraient au minimum inclure un meuble bibliothèque et des moyens nécessaires pour lire, écrire et, si possible, jouer. Les installations et services de loisirs devraient faire l'objet de réexamens fréquents afin qu'ils soient adaptés aux besoins des pêcheurs, compte tenu de l'évolution des techniques, des conditions d'exploitation ainsi que de tout autre développement. Lorsque cela est réalisable, il faudrait aussi envisager de fournir gratuitement aux pêcheurs:

a) un fumoir;

b) la possibilité de regarder la télévision et d'écouter la radio;

c) la possibilité de regarder des films ou des vidéos, dont le stock devrait être suffisant pour la durée du voyage et, si nécessaire, être renouvelé à des intervalles raisonnables;

(d) sports equipment including exercise equipment, table games, and deck games;

(e) a library containing vocational and other books, the stock of which should be adequate for the duration of the voyage and changed at reasonable intervals;

(f) facilities for recreational handicrafts; and

(g) electronic equipment such as radio, television, video recorder, DVD/CD player, personal computer and software, and cassette recorder/player.

Food

34. Fishers employed as cooks should be trained and qualified for their position on board.

PART IV.   MEDICAL CARE, HEALTH PROTECTION AND SOCIAL SECURITY

Medical care on board

35. The competent authority should establish a list of medical supplies and equipment appropriate to the risks concerned that should be carried on fishing vessels; such list should include women's sanitary protection supplies together with discreet, environmentally friendly disposal units.

36. Fishing vessels carrying 100 or more fishers should have a qualified medical doctor on board.

37. Fishers should receive training in basic first aid in accordance with national laws and regulations, taking into account applicable international instruments.

38. A standard medical report form should be specially designed to facilitate the confidential exchange of medical and related information concerning individual fishers between the fishing vessel and the shore in cases of illness or injury.

39. For vessels of 24 metres in length and over, in addition to the provisions of Article 32 of the Convention, the following elements should be taken into account:

(a) when prescribing the medical equipment and supplies to be carried on board, the competent authority should take into account international recommendations in this field, such as those contained in the most recent editions of the (ILO/IMO/WHO) *International Medical Guide for Ships* and the (WHO) *Model List of Essential Medicines*, as well as advances in medical knowledge and approved methods of treatment;

(b) inspections of medical equipment and supplies should take place at intervals of no more than 12 months; the inspector should ensure that

d) des articles de sport, y compris du matériel de culture physique, des jeux de table et des jeux de pont;

e) une bibliothèque contenant des ouvrages de caractère professionnel ou autre, en quantité suffisante pour la durée du voyage, et dont le stock devrait être renouvelé à des intervalles raisonnables;

f) des moyens de réaliser des travaux d'artisanat pour se détendre;

g) des appareils électroniques tels que radios, télévisions, magnétoscopes, lecteurs de CD/DVD, ordinateurs, logiciels et magnétophones à cassettes.

Nourriture

34. Les pêcheurs faisant office de cuisinier devraient être formés et compétents pour occuper ce poste à bord.

PARTIE IV. SOINS MÉDICAUX, PROTECTION DE LA SANTÉ ET SÉCURITÉ SOCIALE

Soins médicaux à bord

35. L'autorité compétente devrait établir une liste des fournitures médicales et du matériel médical qui devrait se trouver à bord des navires de pêche, compte tenu des risques encourus. Cette liste devrait inclure des produits de protection hygiénique pour les femmes et des récipients discrets non nuisibles pour l'environnement.

36. Un médecin qualifié devrait se trouver à bord des navires de pêche qui embarquent 100 pêcheurs ou plus.

37. Les pêcheurs devraient recevoir une formation de base aux premiers secours, conformément à la législation nationale et compte tenu des instruments internationaux pertinents.

38. Un formulaire de rapport médical type devrait être spécialement conçu pour faciliter l'échange confidentiel d'informations médicales et autres informations connexes concernant les pêcheurs entre le navire de pêche et la terre en cas de maladie ou d'accident.

39. Pour les navires d'une longueur égale ou supérieure à 24 mètres, en sus des dispositions de l'article 32 de la convention, les éléments suivants devraient être pris en compte:

a) en prescrivant le matériel médical et les fournitures médicales à conserver à bord, l'autorité compétente devrait tenir compte des recommandations internationales en la matière, telles que celles prévues dans l'édition la plus récente du *Guide médical international de bord* (OIT/OMI/OMS) et la *Liste modèle des médicaments essentiels* (OMS), ainsi que des progrès réalisés dans les connaissances médicales et les méthodes de traitement approuvées;

b) le matériel médical et les fournitures médicales devraient faire l'objet d'une inspection tous les douze mois au moins; l'inspecteur devrait

expiry dates and conditions of storage of all medicines are checked, the contents of the medicine chest are listed and conform to the medical guide used nationally, and medical supplies are labelled with generic names in addition to any brand names used, and with expiry dates and conditions of storage;

(c) the medical guide should explain how the contents of the medical equipment and supplies are to be used, and should be designed to enable persons other than a medical doctor to care for the sick or injured on board, both with and without medical advice by radio or satellite communication; the guide should be prepared taking into account international recommendations in this field, including those contained in the most recent editions of the (ILO/IMO/WHO) *International Medical Guide for Ships* and the (IMO) *Medical First Aid Guide for Use in Accidents Involving Dangerous Goods*; and

(d) medical advice provided by radio or satellite communication should be available free of charge to all vessels irrespective of the flag they fly.

Occupational safety and health

Research, dissemination of information and consultation

40. In order to contribute to the continuous improvement of safety and health of fishers, Members should have in place policies and programmes for the prevention of accidents on board fishing vessels which should provide for the gathering and dissemination of occupational health and safety materials, research and analysis, taking into consideration technological progress and knowledge in the field of occupational safety and health as well as of relevant international instruments.

41. The competent authority should take measures to ensure regular consultations on safety and health matters with the aim of ensuring that all concerned are kept reasonably informed of national, international and other developments in the field and on their possible application to fishing vessels flying the flag of the Member.

42. When ensuring that fishing vessel owners, skippers, fishers and other relevant persons receive sufficient and suitable guidance, training material, or other appropriate information, the competent authority should take into account relevant international standards, codes, guidance and other information. In so doing, the competent authority should keep abreast of and utilize international research and guidance concerning safety and health in the fishing sector, including relevant research in occupational safety and health in general which may be applicable to work on board fishing vessels.

s'assurer que les dates de péremption et les conditions de conservation de tous les médicaments sont vérifiées, que le contenu de la pharmacie de bord fait l'objet d'une liste et qu'il correspond au guide médical employé sur le plan national, que les fournitures médicales portent des étiquettes indiquant le nom générique outre le nom de marque, la date de péremption et les conditions de conservation;

c) le guide médical devrait expliquer le mode d'utilisation du matériel médical et des fournitures médicales et être conçu de façon à permettre à des personnes autres que des médecins de donner des soins aux malades et aux blessés à bord, avec ou sans consultation médicale par radio ou par satellite; le guide devrait être préparé en tenant compte des recommandations internationales en la matière, y compris celles figurant dans l'édition la plus récente du *Guide médical international de bord* (OIT/OMI/OMS) et du *Guide des soins médicaux d'urgence à donner en cas d'accidents dus à des marchandises dangereuses* (OMI);

d) les consultations médicales par radio ou par satellite devraient être assurées gratuitement à tous les navires quel que soit leur pavillon.

Sécurité et santé au travail

Recherche, diffusion d'informations et consultation

40. Afin de contribuer à l'amélioration continue de la sécurité et de la santé des pêcheurs, les Membres devraient mettre en place des politiques et des programmes de prévention des accidents à bord des navires de pêche prévoyant la collecte et la diffusion d'informations, de recherches et d'analyses sur la sécurité et la santé au travail, en tenant compte du progrès des techniques et des connaissances dans le domaine de la sécurité et de la santé au travail et des instruments internationaux pertinents.

41. L'autorité compétente devrait prendre des mesures propres à assurer la tenue de consultations régulières sur les questions de santé et de sécurité au travail, en vue de garantir que toutes les personnes concernées sont tenues convenablement informées des évolutions nationales et internationales ainsi que des autres progrès réalisés dans ce domaine, et de leur application possible aux navires de pêche battant le pavillon du Membre.

42. En veillant à ce que les armateurs à la pêche, les patrons, les pêcheurs et les autres personnes concernées reçoivent suffisamment de directives et de matériel de formation appropriés ainsi que toute autre information pertinente, l'autorité compétente devrait tenir compte des normes internationales, des recueils de directives, des orientations et de toutes autres informations utiles disponibles. Ce faisant, l'autorité compétente devrait se tenir au courant et faire usage des recherches et des orientations internationales en matière de santé et de sécurité dans le secteur de la pêche, y compris des recherches pertinentes dans le domaine de la santé et de la sécurité au travail en général qui pourraient être applicables au travail à bord des navires de pêche.

43. Information concerning particular hazards should be brought to the attention of all fishers and other persons on board through official notices containing instructions or guidance, or other appropriate means.

44. Joint committees on occupational safety and health should be established:

(a) ashore; or

(b) on fishing vessels, where determined by the competent authority, after consultation, to be practicable in light of the number of fishers on board the vessel.

Occupational safety and health management systems

45. When establishing methods and programmes concerning safety and health in the fishing sector, the competent authority should take into account any relevant international guidance concerning occupational safety and health management systems, including the *Guidelines on occupational safety and health management systems, ILO-OSH 2001*.

Risk evaluation

46. (1) Risk evaluation in relation to fishing should be conducted, as appropriate, with the participation of fishers or their representatives and should include:

(a) risk assessment and management;

(b) training, taking into consideration the relevant provisions of Chapter III of the International Convention on Standards of Training, Certification and Watchkeeping for Fishing Vessel Personnel, 1995 (STCW-F Convention) adopted by the IMO; and

(c) on-board instruction of fishers.

(2) To give effect to subparagraph (1)(a), Members, after consultation, should adopt laws, regulations or other measures requiring:

(a) the regular and active involvement of all fishers in improving safety and health by continually identifying hazards, assessing risks and taking action to address risks through safety management;

(b) an occupational safety and health management system that may include an occupational safety and health policy, provisions for fisher participation and provisions concerning organizing, planning, implementing and evaluating the system and taking action to improve the system; and

(c) a system for the purpose of assisting in the implementation of a safety and health policy and programme and providing fishers with a forum to

43. Les informations concernant les dangers particuliers devraient être portées à l'attention de tous les pêcheurs et d'autres personnes à bord au moyen de notices officielles contenant des instructions ou des directives ou d'autres moyens appropriés.

44. Des comités paritaires de santé et de sécurité au travail devraient être établis:

a) à terre; ou

b) sur les navires de pêche, si l'autorité compétente, après consultation, décide que cela est réalisable compte tenu du nombre de pêcheurs à bord.

Systèmes de gestion de la santé et de la sécurité au travail

45. Lors de l'élaboration de méthodes et de programmes relatifs à la santé et à la sécurité dans le secteur de la pêche, l'autorité compétente devrait prendre en considération toutes les directives internationales pertinentes concernant les systèmes de gestion de la santé et de la sécurité au travail, y compris les *Principes directeurs concernant les systèmes de gestion de la sécurité et de la santé au travail, ILO-OSH 2001*.

Evaluation des risques

46. (1) Des évaluations des risques concernant la pêche devraient être conduites, lorsque cela est approprié, avec la participation de pêcheurs ou de leurs représentants et devraient inclure:

a) l'évaluation et la gestion des risques;

b) la formation, en prenant en considération les dispositions pertinentes du chapitre III de la Convention internationale sur les normes de formation du personnel des navires de pêche, de délivrance des brevets et de veille, 1995, adoptée par l'OMI (convention STCW-F);

c) l'instruction des pêcheurs à bord.

(2) Pour donner effet aux dispositions de l'alinéa *a)* du sous-paragraphe (1), les Membres devraient adopter, après consultation, une législation ou d'autres mesures exigeant que:

a) tous les pêcheurs participent régulièrement et activement à l'amélioration de la santé et de la sécurité en répertoriant de façon permanente les dangers, en évaluant les risques et en prenant des mesures visant à les réduire grâce à la gestion de la sécurité;

b) un système de gestion de la santé et de la sécurité au travail soit mis en place, qui peut inclure une politique relative à la santé et à la sécurité au travail, des dispositions prévoyant la participation des pêcheurs et concernant l'organisation, la planification, l'application et l'évaluation de ce système ainsi que les mesures à prendre pour l'améliorer;

c) un système soit mis en place pour faciliter la mise en œuvre de la politique et du programme relatifs à la santé et à la sécurité au travail et

influence safety and health matters; on-board prevention procedures should be designed so as to involve fishers in the identification of hazards and potential hazards and in the implementation of measures to reduce or eliminate such hazards.

(3) When developing the provisions referred to in subparagraph (1)(a), Members should take into account the relevant international instruments on risk assessment and management.

Technical specifications

47. Members should address the following, to the extent practicable and as appropriate to the conditions in the fishing sector:

(a) seaworthiness and stability of fishing vessels;

(b) radio communications;

(c) temperature, ventilation and lighting of working areas;

(d) mitigation of the slipperiness of deck surfaces;

(e) machinery safety, including guarding of machinery;

(f) vessel familiarization for fishers and fisheries observers new to the vessel;

(g) personal protective equipment;

(h) fire-fighting and lifesaving;

(i) loading and unloading of the vessel;

(j) lifting gear;

(k) anchoring and mooring equipment;

(l) safety and health in living quarters;

(m) noise and vibration in work areas;

(n) ergonomics, including in relation to the layout of workstations and manual lifting and handling;

(o) equipment and procedures for the catching, handling, storage and processing of fish and other marine resources;

(p) vessel design, construction and modification relevant to occupational safety and health;

(q) navigation and vessel handling;

(r) hazardous materials used on board the vessel;

(s) safe means of access to and exit from fishing vessels in port;

(t) special safety and health requirements for young persons;

donner aux pêcheurs un moyen d'expression publique leur permettant d'influer sur les questions de santé et de sécurité; les procédures de prévention à bord devraient être conçues de manière à associer les pêcheurs au repérage des dangers existants et potentiels et à la mise en œuvre de mesures propres à les atténuer ou à les éliminer.

(3) Lors de l'élaboration des dispositions mentionnées à l'alinéa *a)* du sous-paragraphe (1), les Membres devraient tenir compte des instruments internationaux pertinents se rapportant à l'évaluation et à la gestion des risques.

Spécifications techniques

47. Les Membres devraient, dans la mesure du possible et selon qu'il convient au secteur de la pêche, examiner les questions suivantes:

a) navigabilité et stabilité des navires de pêche;

b) communications par radio;

c) température, ventilation et éclairage des postes de travail;

d) atténuation du risque présenté par les ponts glissants;

e) sécurité d'utilisation des machines, y compris les dispositifs de protection;

f) familiarisation avec le navire des pêcheurs ou observateurs des pêches nouvellement embarqués;

g) équipement de protection individuelle;

h) sauvetage et lutte contre les incendies;

i) chargement et déchargement du navire;

j) appareaux de levage;

k) équipements de mouillage et d'amarrage;

l) santé et sécurité dans les locaux d'habitation;

m) bruits et vibrations dans les postes de travail;

n) ergonomie, y compris en ce qui concerne l'aménagement des postes de travail et la manutention et la manipulation des charges;

o) équipement et procédures pour la prise, la manipulation, le stockage et le traitement du poisson et des autres ressources marines;

p) conception et construction du navire et modifications touchant à la santé et à la sécurité au travail;

q) navigation et manœuvre du navire;

r) matériaux dangereux utilisés à bord;

s) sécurité des moyens d'accéder aux navires et d'en sortir dans les ports;

t) prescriptions spéciales en matière de santé et de sécurité applicables aux adolescents;

(u) prevention of fatigue; and

(v) other issues related to safety and health.

48. When developing laws, regulations or other measures concerning technical standards relating to safety and health on board fishing vessels, the competent authority should take into account the most recent edition of the (FAO/ILO/IMO) *Code of Safety for Fishermen and Fishing Vessels, Part A*.

Establishment of a list of occupational diseases

49. Members should establish a list of diseases known to arise out of exposure to dangerous substances or conditions in the fishing sector.

Social security

50. For the purpose of extending social security protection progressively to all fishers, Members should maintain up-to-date information on the following:

(a) the percentage of fishers covered;

(b) the range of contingencies covered; and

(c) the level of benefits.

51. Every person protected under Article 34 of the Convention should have a right of appeal in the case of a refusal of the benefit or of an adverse determination as to the quality or quantity of the benefit.

52. The protections referred to in Articles 38 and 39 of the Convention should be granted throughout the contingency covered.

PART V. OTHER PROVISIONS

53. A Member, in its capacity as a coastal State, when granting licences for fishing in its exclusive economic zone, may require that fishing vessels comply with the standards of the Convention. If such licences are issued by coastal States, these States should take into account certificates or other valid documents stating that the vessel concerned has been inspected by the competent authority or on its behalf and has been found to be in compliance with the provisions of the Convention concerning work in the fishing sector.

u) prévention de la fatigue;

v) autres questions liées à la santé et à la sécurité.

48. Lors de l'élaboration d'une législation ou d'autres mesures relatives aux normes techniques concernant la santé et la sécurité à bord des navires de pêche, l'autorité compétente devrait tenir compte de l'édition la plus récente du *Recueil de règles de sécurité pour les pêcheurs et les navires de pêche, Partie A* (FAO/OIT/OMI).

Etablissement d'une liste de maladies professionnelles

49. Les Membres devraient dresser la liste des maladies dont il est connu qu'elles résultent de l'exposition à des substances ou à des conditions dangereuses dans le secteur de la pêche.

Sécurité sociale

50. Aux fins d'étendre progressivement la sécurité sociale à tous les pêcheurs, les Membres devraient établir et tenir à jour des informations sur les points suivants:

a) le pourcentage de pêcheurs couverts;

b) l'éventail des éventualités couvertes;

c) le niveau des prestations.

51. Toute personne protégée en vertu de l'article 34 de la convention devrait avoir le droit de faire recours en cas de refus de la prestation ou d'une décision défavorable sur la qualité ou la quantité de celle-ci.

52. Les prestations visées aux articles 38 et 39 de la convention devraient être accordées pendant toute la durée de l'éventualité couverte.

PARTIE V. AUTRES DISPOSITIONS

53. Un Membre, en sa qualité d'Etat côtier, pourrait exiger que les navires de pêche respectent les normes énoncées dans la convention avant d'accorder l'autorisation de pêcher dans sa zone économique exclusive. Dans le cas où ces autorisations sont délivrées par les Etats côtiers, lesdits Etats devraient prendre en considération les certificats ou autres documents valides indiquant que le navire a été inspecté par l'autorité compétente ou en son nom et qu'il est conforme aux dispositions de la convention sur le travail dans le secteur de la pêche.

The foregoing is the authentic text of the Recommendation duly adopted by the General Conference of the International Labour Organization during its Ninety-third Session which was held at Geneva and declared closed on the sixteenth day of June 2005.

IN FAITH WHEREOF we have appended our signatures this twentieth day of June 2005.

Le texte qui précède est le texte authentique de la recommandation dûment adoptée par la Conférence générale de l'Organisation internationale du Travail dans sa quatre-vingt-treizième session qui s'est tenue à Genève et qui a été déclarée close le seizième jour de juin 2005.

EN FOI DE QUOI ont apposé leurs signatures, ce vingtième jour de juin 2005:

The President of the Conference,
Le Président de la Conférence,

The Director-General of the International Labour Office,
Le Directeur général du Bureau international du Travail,

RESOLUTIONS ADOPTED BY THE CONFERENCE

Resolutions adopted by the International Labour Conference at its 93rd Session

(Geneva, June 2005)

I

Resolution concerning youth employment [1]

Resolution concerning youth employment

The General Conference of the International Labour Organization, meeting in its 93rd Session, 2005,

Having undertaken a general discussion on the basis of Report VI, *Youth: Pathways to decent work*,

1. Adopts the following conclusions;

2. Invites the Governing Body to give due consideration to them in planning future action on youth employment and to request the Director-General to take them into account both when implementing the Programme and Budget for the 2006-07 biennium and allocating such other resources as may be available during the 2006-07 biennium.

Conclusions on promoting pathways to decent work for youth

1. In addressing the employment challenges faced by young women and men, it is important to recall the ILO Decent Work Agenda, the ILO Global Employment Agenda, the United Nations Millennium Declaration, the ILO Declaration of Philadelphia, the ILO Declaration on Fundamental Principles and Rights at Work and its Follow-up, the body of international labour standards relevant to work and young persons (see appendix), the conclusions of the Tripartite Meeting on Youth Employment: The Way Forward (Geneva, 13-15 October 2004), the World Commission report on the Social Dimension of Globalization and the ILO's participation in the inter-agency Youth Employment Network.

Issues and challenges

2. In all regions and countries, young women and men set out in life with dreams, hopes and aspirations. Yet everywhere young women and men face challenges in the labour market. If young people are to be given opportunities, then multiple pathways to decent employment are needed. Achieving decent work for young people is a critical element in poverty eradication and sustainable development, growth and welfare for all.

3. Young women and men bring numerous assets to the labour market: relevant and recent education and training; enthusiasm, hope and new ideas; willingness to learn and be taught; openness to new skills and technology; realistic expectations on entry to the labour market; mobility and adaptability; and represent a new generation to meet the challenge in countries with an ageing workforce. The challenge is to bring young people into employment without

---

[1] Adopted on 15 June 2005.

displacing other workers. Policy-makers have to consider intergenerational issues and recognize, in this context, a life-cycle approach.

4. Young people are employed and seek employment in diverse local, national, regional and international circumstances. This includes diversity between developing and developed economies, and within these economies. Governments, employers and young workers are not homogeneous groups; they have different needs, capacities and expectations. The ILO Declaration on Fundamental Principles and Rights at Work and its Follow-up is universal and applies to all workers, regardless of national circumstances and levels of development.

5. Many young people are in education or employed in decent jobs. In many countries, young people are able to make successful transitions from education to the world of work. In some countries, the ageing workforce also presents growing opportunities for young people. There are diverse forms of work in which young people can engage, with vastly different employment conditions, including permanent full-time or part-time work, as well as casual, temporary or seasonal work. These forms of employment may provide entry points for young workers to the labour market and enhance their long-term employment prospects. Unfortunately, there are also too many young workers who do not have access to decent work. A significant number of youth are underemployed, unemployed, seeking employment or between jobs, or working unacceptably long hours under informal, intermittent and insecure work arrangements, without the possibility of personal and professional development; working below their potential in low-paid, low-skilled jobs without prospects for career advancement; trapped in involuntary part-time, temporary, casual or seasonal employment; and frequently under poor and precarious conditions in the informal economy, both in rural and urban areas. Other young workers lack adequate incomes, access to education, training and lifelong learning, social protection, safe workplaces, security, representation and rights protected under international labour standards, including freedom of association, collective bargaining and protection from harassment and discrimination.

6. Of the world's over 1 billion young people, 85 per cent live in developing countries with a high incidence of poverty and inadequate employment opportunities. There is significant regional variation in youth employment, with some countries facing greater challenges than others due in part to the uneven impacts of globalization and the asymmetries in current global economic activity. The scourge of HIV/AIDS, the weight of external debt, armed conflict, poor governance, unstable institutions and gender inequality compound weak economic growth and deter the public and private investment necessary to create jobs. Rapid population growth is expected to significantly increase the number of youth searching for decent work opportunities in most developing countries.

7. In developed economies, the challenge may be linked to slow economic and employment growth, the transition into employment, discrimination, social disadvantages, cyclical trends, and a number of structural factors. Variation in the youth employment challenge requires specific responses.

8. In too many instances, the labour market prospects for young people vary according to gender, age, ethnicity, education level, family background, health status and disability. Some groups are therefore more vulnerable and face particular disadvantage to securing and retaining decent work.

9. The regulatory environment for investment and enterprises and labour law should create an investment climate that fosters economic growth and decent employment of young persons. Whilst employment cannot be directly created but only encouraged by legislation or regulation, it is recognized that labour legislation and regulation based on international labour standards can provide employment protection and underwrite increased productivity, which are basic conditions in order to create decent work, particularly for young people. Labour laws and, where they exist, collective agreements, should apply to all young

workers, including those currently lacking protection because of disguised employment relationships.[1] Efforts should be made to move those in the informal economy into the formal economy. The creation of an enabling environment, the pursuit of good governance and the sustainable existence of both physical and social infrastructure are necessary for the competitiveness of existing businesses and the start-up of new enterprises.

10. Investment in youth reaps benefits for individuals, communities and societies. Decent work for young people unleashes multiplier effects throughout the economy and society, boosting investment and consumer demand and ensuring more stable and cohesive social ties across generations, including sharing institutional workplace knowledge. It shifts young people from social dependence to self-sufficiency, helps them escape poverty and enables them to actively contribute to society.

11. Youth unemployment and underemployment impose heavy social and economic costs, resulting in the loss of opportunities for economic growth, erosion of the tax base which undermines investment in infrastructure and public services, increased welfare costs, and unutilized investment in education and training, and may also be associated with social instability and conflict, increased levels of poverty, crime and substance abuse.

12. The youth employment challenge is bound to the general employment situation and, while it has its own dimensions, it is influenced by a number of general factors which may have positive or negative consequences, including:
– the impact of globalization;
– the impact of structural reforms in developing countries;
– the level of, and fluctuation in, aggregate demand;
– demographic trends;
– the level of economic activity, public and private investment and sustainable growth;
– the employment intensity of growth in developing countries;
– an enabling regulatory environment for both enterprises and the protection of workers' rights;
– entrepreneurship and enterprise creation options, including through cooperatives;
– education and training outcomes;
– the relationship between education and labour market needs; and
– work experience and labour market services.

13. As new entrants to the labour market, some young workers lack the specific training or seniority that may buffer older workers from swings in market conditions; their employment is highly dependent on the state of the economy. During economic downturns, the practice of "last hired, first fired" and the lack of vacancies take a toll on young workers when they are less equipped to find new employment.

14. Whilst some young people transition effectively from education to work, the transition is problematic for too many others. One concern is when young persons do not possess basic literacy and numeracy skills that are necessary to access vocational training and transition from a state of unemployability to employability. Another concern is when, for protracted periods, young people are not in employment, education or training. In other instances, some young people do not complete schooling and/or have insufficient skills to gain secure and sustainable employment opportunities.

15. Failure to find a job may be linked to lack of relevant skills and training opportunities, to low demand for the skills in which young persons have

---

[1] As referenced in the conclusions of the International Labour Conference's general discussion on the employment relationship (2003).

trained, or to changing demand in the labour market. The mismatch that arises can lead to long periods of jobseeking, higher unemployment and sustained periods of lower skilled and precarious work. Lack of opportunities for work experience and entrepreneurial development, combined with the absence of adequate labour market information, vocational guidance and counselling, and poor job placement mechanisms, exacerbate the problem of getting a decent job.

16. Particular groups of young people face specific hardships due to discrimination and social exclusion, including those with disabilities, those affected by HIV/AIDS, indigenous youth, those involved in hazardous work, demobilized soldiers, ethnic minorities, migrants and other socially disadvantaged youth. In general, young women, in particular young women with children, are more prone to unemployment, discrimination, sexual harassment, underemployment and poor working conditions. In some cases, young persons are denied access to employment opportunities for which they are fully qualified and competent solely on the basis of their age.

17. Governments and social partners are committed to addressing the youth employment challenge with the involvement of young women and men. Urgent action is required to enhance the involvement of young workers, workers' organizations and employers of young workers and their organizations in development, implementation and monitoring of youth labour market policies and programmes.

Policies and programmes for decent work for young people

18. The principles of the Employment Policy Convention, 1964 (No. 122), whereby "each Member shall declare and pursue, as a major goal, an active policy designed to promote full, productive and freely chosen employment", are fundamental to any employment policy directed at young people.

19. Although one size does not fit all, meeting the youth employment challenge calls for an integrated and coherent approach that combines macro- and microeconomic interventions and addresses both labour demand and supply and the quantity and quality of employment. Youth employment should be considered in all relevant social, employment and economic policies through a well-balanced policy mix. Supportive national trade, industry, training and wage policies, with appropriate involvement of the social partners, are also required to meet the youth employment challenge. The employment prospects of young people are inextricably linked to the general employment situation and can be especially vulnerable to fluctuations in economic conditions. Consequently, targeted interventions aimed at overcoming disadvantages, while promoting equality, social inclusion and an equitable society, are required. Policies and programmes that aim to prevent cycles of disadvantage from being repeated across generations are critical in achieving social inclusion and decent work for youth.

20. High and sustained economic growth is a necessary condition for the generation of employment, including quality employment for young people. This requires macroeconomic policy supportive of increased and sustainable employment growth through expanded investment, productive capacity and aggregate demand in conditions of economic and political stability. Governments should have policy space to ensure ownership of their macroeconomic and industrial policies enabling them to expand their economies including the manufacturing and services sectors. Social progress and economic growth should go hand in hand. Policies relating to globalization, including trade and foreign direct investment, should, wherever necessary, be reformed to create decent jobs for young people. Monetary, fiscal, trade and social security policies should be coherent with the overall objective of increased and sustainable economic growth, employment generation and social protection. Assessment of

the likely employment implications of macroeconomic policy choices can better inform an adequate policy mix.

21. Placing economic growth and employment generation at the centre of national policy objectives calls for supportive and coherent national, regional and international policy frameworks. Reforms are required at the national and international levels to ensure developing countries have access to additional financial resources to promote economic development and decent work. International debt relief, including debt cancellation, and increased official development assistance (ODA) are important components of such reforms. In addition, some of the recommendations of the World Commission on the Social Dimension of Globalization are particularly relevant in this regard. National and international strategies to achieve the Millennium Development Goals (MDGs) should combine economic growth, poverty eradication and social and employment objectives, including youth employment. The forthcoming review of the MDGs in September 2005 provides an excellent opportunity to assess the extent to which national, regional and international policies and strategies address the promotion of decent work for all with a focus on young people.

22. Increased and sustainable economic growth, while necessary, is not a sufficient condition for sustainable employment generation, particularly for young people. A range of complementary policies are needed to enhance the employment content of growth while also increasing productivity and ensuring adequate social protection. Policies should seek to strengthen enterprises and enhance labour demand as well as the quality of the labour supply. Governments should review all policies to ensure they do not discriminate against the hiring of youth.

23. In developing countries the employment intensity of growth must be increased. For example, employment-intensive investment in infrastructure has been shown to be an effective means to enhance sustainable decent work among low-income and low-skilled workers, as well as to create assets that enhance productivity and output. Such investment is a proven means to eradicate poverty, particularly when it is combined with training.

24. The development of entrepreneurship among young people is an important component of employment policies. Some young people have the potential to become entrepreneurs and create or join an enterprise. Some young people also have the potential to establish or join cooperatives. This potential should be actively nurtured through an enabling environment combining information on opportunities and risks faced by entrepreneurs and those involved in cooperatives, business development services directed particularly at young people, mentoring and financial services (including access to credit and venture capital) and simplifying registration (including business entry) procedures. Employers' organizations, together with governments, have an active role to play. The development of entrepreneurship and cooperatives should respect international labour standards. National legislation and policies concerning cooperatives should be in accordance with the Promotion of Cooperatives Recommendation, 2002 (No. 193).

25. As stated in the 2004 UNDP report *Unleashing entrepreneurship: Making business work for the poor*, developed country governments should:

> ... foster a conducive international macroeconomic and policy environment to unleash the full potential of entrepreneurs in developing countries. A robust international economy provides markets for goods from developing country companies. In addition, increasing the flow of development aid and reforming the global trading system to provide fair economic opportunities to producers from developing countries are essential for promoting rapid growth in domestic private investment.

26. Policies for small enterprises, including entrepreneurship and cooperatives, should be reviewed for their relevance to young persons in different country circumstances. Policies to promote employment should also be reviewed to attract, inform and assist young persons in establishing or joining small enterprises, and to assist young persons in the informal economy to move

to the formal economy. Small and medium-sized enterprises, including cooperatives, can be an engine of job creation and seedbeds for innovation and entrepreneurship. In some countries, many small and medium-sized enterprises are marginal and operate outside of the formal economy. The right to participate in employers' and workers' organizations by persons establishing or working in small businesses is important.

27. Tripartite dialogue can inform policies that target specific industries and sectors with strong potential for youth employment. In developing countries, policies seeking to increase agricultural production, rural non-farm industries, manufacturing, tourism and technological capabilities could provide real prospects for raising both economic growth and decent employment for youth. The provision of adequate high-quality public services, especially in developing countries, in areas such as health care, education, utilities, power and water is required and will directly generate additional decent work for youth as well as providing an enabling environment for increased private investment and job growth. There is considerable scope to expand economic activity in key sectors through public and private initiatives which will also help economic and job growth. The development of skills relevant to technology, when coupled with education and vocational training, can open up new opportunities for young people.

28. Labour market and social protection policies and employment legislation and regulations, which take into account international labour standards and social dialogue and recognize the right to collective bargaining, and the promotion of freedom of association, workplace safety, policies on wages and hours of work and other labour standards, should ensure adequate protection of young workers and the improvement of their employment prospects. The regulatory environment for enterprises should create an investment climate that fosters economic growth and the decent employment of young persons.

29. Governments in consultation with employers' and workers' organizations should establish labour market information and monitoring mechanisms to ensure a regular flow of information on the employment situation, specifically of young people. In order to avoid precarious employment situations that deny workers basic rights, and ensure occupational safety and health protection, labour inspection and national labour administration systems should play a key role and need to be strengthened, where necessary.

30. Measures to address the working conditions of youth in the informal economy include small business management training, enhanced cooperation and organization of micro- and small enterprises and the full enforcement of social and labour protection through processes such as well-resourced labour inspection systems, labour courts and functioning tripartite institutions. The organization of informal economy workers and employers through their respective organizations is also important to achieving this objective. Emphasis should be placed on necessary regulatory changes (including the removal of barriers to business entry) to enable young people in the informal economy to make the transition into the formal economy through incentives, such as management training, increased access to credit and simplified registration systems.

31. An enabling environment for investment and enterprise creation is essential for growth and employment. This includes effective public and private investment in essential physical and social infrastructure, inclusive of quality public services, recognition of property rights, good governance, stable institutions, political stability, the rule of law including labour law, and a conducive legal framework for private investment, as advocated in the Job Creation in Small and Medium-Sized Enterprises Recommendation, 1998 (No. 189).

32. Access to universal, free, quality public primary and secondary education and investment in vocational training and lifelong learning are essential for individual and social enhancement and preparation for future

working life. Education for all is an effective means of combating child labour and eradicating poverty.

33. Education, vocational training, core skills – including literacy and numeracy – labour market services and work experience and awareness of labour rights and occupational health and safety are essential components of a comprehensive policy to enhance the employability of young people. Education and vocational training policy should be broadly based, have a link to employment policy and should be responsive to the development of core skills being used in workplaces. A key function of the education system should be the progressive development of employability skills among young people. [1]

34. Vocational education and lifelong training responsive to the evolving demand for skills in the labour market, along with apprenticeship schemes and other measures that combine training with work, are fundamental to improving youth employability. A variety of initiatives, including public and private partnerships, and appropriate incentives for individual and collective investments in human resources development, can ensure the continued relevance of vocational education and training to labour market needs. Enterprises have a critical role to play in investment in training. A number of mechanisms used in combination to further investment in training and to guarantee access are required. [2] National policies should aim to provide all young women and men with the broadest possible access to responsive vocational education and training opportunities. Such policies should be guided by the relevant provisions of the Human Resources Development Convention, 1975 (No. 142), and the Human Resources Development Recommendation, 2004 (No. 195). Education and training authorities should seek to:

- Integrate basic skills such as literacy, numeracy and, where possible, technological knowledge into education, equipping students with a foundation for the world of work.

- Incorporate career guidance and support, knowledge of industry along with industrial relations and essential labour issues, such as occupational safety and health, into the early years curricula.

- Foster career entry and career development, including the recognition of prior learning to facilitate transfer between educational programmes and through the transfer of relevant educational qualifications and credits.

---

[1] "Employability is defined broadly. It is a key outcome of education and training of high quality, as well as a range of other policies. It encompasses the skills, knowledge and competencies that enhance a worker's ability to secure and retain a job, progress at work and cope with change, secure another job if he/she so wishes or has been laid off, and enter more easily into the labour market at different periods of the life cycle. Individuals are most employable when they have broad-based education and training, basic and portable high-level skills, including teamwork, problem solving, information and communications technology (ICT) and communication and language skills, learning to learn skills, and competencies to protect themselves and their colleagues against occupational hazards and diseases. This combination of skills enables them to adapt to changes in the world of work. Employability also covers multiple skills that are essential to secure and retain decent work. Entrepreneurship can contribute to creating opportunities for employment and hence to employability. Employability is, however, not a function only of training – it requires a range of other instruments which results in the existence of jobs, the enhancement of quality jobs, and sustainable employment. Workers' employability can only be sustained in an economic environment that promotes job growth and rewards individual and collective investments in human resources training and development.", para. 9 of the resolution concerning human resources training and development, ILC, 88th Session, 2000.

[2] Para. 12 of the resolution concerning human resources training and development, ILC, 88th Session, 2000.

- Make education more responsive to labour market needs by directly engaging educators with industry partners in the sector and encouraging student contact with industry. Programmes which, in the latter school years, combine learning with work or work experience can bring students and employers together.

35. Public and private employment services can provide career guidance and counselling, impart up-to-date labour market information and support young people in finding, securing and retaining jobs. Where necessary, public employment services should be strengthened.

36. Taking into account relevant provisions of the Employment Policy (Supplementary Provisions) Recommendation, 1984 (No. 169), active labour market policies and programmes (ALMPs) can greatly facilitate initial employment as well as re-entry into employment. Labour market programmes could target youth, in particular disadvantaged young people, or mainstream programmes could be adapted to the needs of the individual. ALMPs are more likely to be effective when they are well targeted; meet the specific requirements of the intended beneficiaries, based on a careful analysis of the local employment situation; are linked to demand for real jobs; and include measures to improve the competencies, skills and sustainable employment opportunities of beneficiaries.

37. Social benefit programmes to support unemployed and underemployed youth should be established where they do not exist. Social benefit programmes should contribute to job search and labour market efficiency. However, public policy should assist young people to move into decent work or education as soon as possible.

38. Governments should take responsibility for the regular monitoring and evaluation of the performance of policies and programmes promoting decent work for young people. Assessing performance against established benchmarks is a proven method for moving forward. Knowledge about what works and what does not work, the relevance, effectiveness and efficiency of policies and programmes on youth employment should be compiled and disseminated widely and creatively. Tools which support employers, workers and governments to identify areas of work where there are gaps in the application of international labour standards are important and should be developed.

An ILO plan of action to promote pathways to decent work for youth

39. With regard to ILO work on youth employment, the Decent Work Agenda provides the paradigm, and the Global Employment Agenda, including its ten core elements and cross-cutting themes,[1] which include the "four Es"[2] of the Youth Employment Network (YEN), provide the policy pillars.

40. The ILO, in close collaboration with the social partners and relevant international agencies, should continue to play a leading role in the Youth Employment Network to promote decent work for young persons and to synchronize the work of the YEN with these conclusions. The ILO should

---

[1] Promoting trade and investment for productive employment and market access for developing countries; promoting technological change for higher productivity, job creation and higher standards of living; promoting sustainable development for sustainable livelihoods; a call for policy integration to ensure macroeconomic policy for growth and employment; decent work through entrepreneurship; employability through improving knowledge and skills; active labour market policies for employment, security in change, equality, and poverty reduction; social protection as a productive factor; occupational safety and health – synergies between security and productivity; productive employment for poverty reduction and development.

[2] Employability, equal opportunities, entrepreneurship and employment creation.

continue to promote the expansion of the YEN to include more countries, both developing and developed. The ILO, through the full commitment of its constituents, should ensure that it has the funds required to give effect to these conclusions and be a strong technical partner of the YEN.

41. The ILO should, with its tripartite constituents, strengthen partnerships with international financial institutions and United Nations organizations in order to give a central place to the promotion of youth employment in development policies and poverty reduction strategies, and in the forthcoming review of the United Nations Millennium Development Goals. This should include promotion of the ILO Decent Work Agenda and the Global Employment Agenda. The ILO should play a role in promoting the resolution of the international debt problem and advocate increased resource flows into developing countries.

42. The ILO plan of action, with particular focus on developing countries, is based on three pillars: building knowledge; advocacy; and technical assistance.

Building knowledge

43. In order to assist countries in developing their policies and programmes addressing the youth employment challenge, the ILO should expand knowledge on the nature and dimensions of youth employment, unemployment and underemployment. Particular emphasis should be placed on gathering factual data and empirical evidence on the effectiveness of country policies and programmes and in synthesizing the results of country studies and evaluations. This analysis should collect examples of where policy interventions have been successful and where they have not, and should extract lessons learned from such experiences. The ILO should facilitate global peer partnerships to promote better performance and disseminate and share best-practice experiences and models among its constituents, such as industry training and skills development, education linkages and human resources practices.

44. The ILO should develop a research agenda that includes the ILO strategy for evaluating the success of its youth-oriented technical cooperation projects, and use evaluation information to feed back into programme design. The ILO may draw on its experiences through evaluating its other youth-related efforts, for example the International Programme on the Elimination of Child Labour (IPEC).

45. The ILO should strengthen research and knowledge dissemination on the ten core elements covered in the ILO Global Employment Agenda and the relationship between these core elements and the achievement of decent work for youth, including a regularly updated web site and database, publications, newsletters and practical guides. The ILO should partner, as appropriate, with other international organizations in the gathering of information and empirical research.

Advocacy and the promotion of decent work for youth

46. The ILO should undertake a campaign to promote the conclusions of the general discussion on promoting pathways to decent work for youth. This campaign should include an international, regional and national focus which is developed in conjunction with the social partners. The campaign should have as its core objective the promotion and implementation of these conclusions with a specific focus on information for young people themselves, taking into account the specific needs and interests of young workers, including an appropriate focus on young women and other vulnerable groups. In conjunction with its constituents, the ILO should be responsible for:
– an international promotional campaign aimed at young people to promote decent work with a focus on employment creation, workers' rights and employability, as detailed in these conclusions;

- working directly with workers and employers in the development of tool kits which will assist governments and workers' and employers' organizations to promote awareness of their rights and responsibilities for decent work.

The ILO should target this campaign at young people through communication means that are most familiar to young people, including youth media and networks for students and other young people. The Committee on Employment and Social Policy of the Governing Body of the ILO should oversee the campaign.

47. The ILO should strengthen cooperation with multilateral institutions and other international organizations to promote policy coordination which makes the achievement of high and sustainable levels of employment growth a priority for all relevant international institutions. The ILO should also promote the strong emphasis on decent work for youth and the Global Employment Agenda in Poverty Reduction Strategy Papers, as well as decent work country programmes, YEN national action plans and other country-level activities undertaken by international financial institutions.

48. The ILO should promote good practice on policies and programmes for youth employment through tripartite meetings. This should include giving special attention to the gender dimension of the youth employment challenge, as well as the specific needs of young people affected by HIV/AIDS, and of those facing particular disadvantage due to disability, ethnic origin, labour migration and other specific circumstances.

49. The ILO should give a cross-cutting youth dimension to all its work. In particular, it should seek age-disaggregated data relating to employment and the world of work and include specific sections addressing the youth dimension in its research, studies and reports, including those relating to international labour standards and the follow-up to the ILO Declaration on Fundamental Principles and Rights at Work, as appropriate.

Technical assistance

50. The ILO should:
(i) continue and intensify the provision of guidance and policy advice, particularly to developing countries, based on the Global Employment Agenda to promote decent work for youth;
(ii) organize periodic, regional youth employment technical meetings in order to build knowledge and exchange experiences among youth employment policy-makers and the social partners;
(iii) enhance the capacity of employers' and workers' organizations to effectively participate in the setting of policies and programmes in favour of youth employment, through its programme of technical cooperation, the International Training Centre of the ILO in Turin, and other means;
(iv) strengthen the capacity of labour administration to promote the application of labour legislation at the workplace, for the benefit of all workers, including young women and men;
(v) assist developing countries in establishing and strengthening inspection services, public employment services, data-gathering and monitoring and evaluation systems on youth employment;
(vi) seek additional funding from donors to expand its programme of technical cooperation for the promotion of decent work for young women and men.

51. The ILO should maximize the comparative advantage of its tripartite structure in its activities to promote decent work for young persons. In addition to the role of governments already noted, the ILO should support employers and workers and their respective organizations, as the case may be, to:
(i) review job descriptions to promote the hiring of youth, recognizing that young people bring positive attributes to work;

(ii) recognize skills and productivity, not just qualifications or years of experience, to ensure that young workers have equal opportunities to other workers;

(iii) help educate, train and mentor through investing in education and training, participating in training bodies and assisting school-to-work transition;

(iv) work with industry partners, young people's networks and youth organizations to inform young people, schools, training bodies and employment agencies of both industry needs and expectations of young people;

(v) to assist young people and employers of young people to:
- develop basic learning skills of literacy, numeracy and technological skills;
- actively look for work and job opportunities, including entry-level work that combines employment with education or work experience;
- prepare for the responsibilities of the world of work and career development by developing employability skills or upgrading skills through technical vocational training, and/or in the workplace.

52. The ILO should support efforts to strengthen the capacity of workers' and employers' organizations to reach out and engage young workers and employers of young workers to ensure that their specific needs are taken into account in social dialogue processes, including collective bargaining.

Appendix

International labour standards relevant to work and young persons

In addition to the Conventions on fundamental principles and rights at work and their related Recommendations – the Freedom of Association and Protection of the Right to Organise Convention, 1948 (No. 87); the Right to Organise and Collective Bargaining Convention, 1949 (No. 98); the Forced Labour Convention, 1930 (No. 29); the Forced Labour (Indirect Compulsion) Recommendation, 1930 (No. 35); the Abolition of Forced Labour Convention, 1957 (No. 105); the Equal Remuneration Convention, 1951 (No. 100), and Recommendation, 1951 (No. 90); the Discrimination (Employment and Occupation) Convention, 1958 (No. 111), and Recommendation, 1958 (No. 111); the Minimum Age Convention, 1973 (No. 138), and Recommendation, 1973 (No. 146); the Worst Forms of Child Labour Convention, 1999 (No. 182), and Recommendation, 1999 (No. 190) – and to the priority Conventions on employment and labour inspection and their related Recommendations – the Employment Policy Convention, 1964 (No. 122), and Recommendation, 1964 (No. 122); the Employment Policy (Supplementary Provisions) Recommendation, 1984 (No. 169); the Labour Inspection Convention, 1947 (No. 81), and its Protocol of 1995; the Labour Inspection Recommendation, 1947 (No. 81); the Labour Inspection (Agriculture) Convention, 1969 (No. 129), and Recommendation, 1969 (No. 133) – these instruments include in particular: the Employment Service Convention, 1948 (No. 88), and Recommendation, 1948 (No. 83); the Labour Administration Convention, 1978 (No. 150), and Recommendation, 1978 (No. 158); the Private Employment Agencies Convention, 1997 (No. 181), and Recommendation, 1997 (No. 188); the Human Resources Development Convention, 1975 (No. 142), and Recommendation, 2004 (No. 195); the Job Creation in Small and Medium-Sized Enterprises Recommendation, 1998 (No. 189); the Part-Time Work Convention, 1994 (No. 175), and Recommendation, 1994 (No. 182); the Promotion of Cooperatives Recommendation, 2002 (No. 193); the Workers' Representatives Convention, 1971 (No. 135), and Recommendation, 1971 (No. 143); the Vocational Rehabilitation and Employment (Disabled Persons) Convention, 1983 (No. 159), and Recommendation, 1983 (No. 168); the Migration for

Employment Convention (Revised), 1949 (No. 97), and Recommendation (Revised), 1949 (No. 86); the Migrant Workers (Supplementary Provisions) Convention, 1975 (No. 143), and the Migrant Workers Recommendation, 1975 (No. 151); the Indigenous and Tribal Peoples Convention, 1989 (No. 169); the Occupational Safety and Health Convention, 1981 (No. 155), and its Protocol of 2002; the Occupational Safety and Health Recommendation, 1981 (No. 164); the Safety and Health in Agriculture Convention, 2001 (No. 184), and Recommendation, 2001 (No. 192); the Maternity Protection Convention, 2000 (No. 183), and Recommendation, 2000 (No. 191); the Medical Examination of Young Persons (Industry) Convention, 1946 (No. 77); the Medical Examination of Young Persons (Non-Industrial Occupations) Convention, 1946 (No. 78); the Medical Examination of Young Persons Recommendation, 1946 (No. 79); the Protection of Wages Convention, 1949 (No. 95), and Recommendation, 1949 (No. 85); the Minimum Wage Fixing Convention, 1970 (No. 131), and Recommendation, 1970 (No. 135); the Social Security (Minimum Standards) Convention, 1952 (No. 102); the Employment Promotion and Protection against Unemployment Convention, 1988 (No. 168), and Recommendation, 1988 (No. 176); the Hours of Work (Industry) Convention, 1919 (No. 1), and the Hours of Work (Commerce and Offices) Convention, 1930 (No. 30); the Night Work Convention, 1990 (No. 171), and Recommendation, 1990 (No. 178).

II

Resolution to place on the agenda of the next ordinary session of the Conference an item entitled "Occupational safety and health" [1]

The General Conference of the International Labour Organization,

Having adopted the report of the Committee appointed to consider the fourth item on the agenda,

Having in particular approved as general conclusions, with a view to the consultation of Governments, proposals for a Convention and a Recommendation concerning occupational safety and health,

Decides that an item entitled "Occupational safety and health" shall be included in the agenda of its next ordinary session for second discussion with a view to the adoption of a Convention and Recommendation.

III

Resolution concerning the flag of the International Labour Organization [1]

The General Conference of the International Labour Organization,

Mindful of the necessity to allow the Organization to be given the visibility it might need,

Noting that other international organizations of the United Nations system have adopted, through their competent organs, flags carrying their respective emblems,

Considering that the emblem, approved by the Director-General in Instruction No. 325 of 1 September 1967, is universally recognized as the International Labour Organization's logo,

Noting that the Governing Body of the International Labour Office has adopted the code and the regulations for the use of the flag of the International

---

[1] Adopted on 15 June 2005.

Labour Organization under the reservation that they come into force after the adoption of this resolution,

1. decides that a flag of the International Labour Organization is adopted which bears the emblem symbolizing tripartism and approved by the Director-General in Instruction No. 325 of 1 September 1967;
2. takes note of the code and regulations for the use of the flag of the International Labour Organization adopted by the Governing Body.

(a) Flag code of the International Labour Organization

1. Design of flag

The flag of the International Labour Organization shall be the official emblem of the International Labour Organization centred on a United Nations blue background, as approved by the Director-General on 1 September 1967. Such emblem shall appear in white on both sides of the flag except where otherwise prescribed by the regulations. The flag shall be made in such sizes as may, from time to time, be prescribed by the regulations.

2. Dignity of flag

The flag shall not be subjected to any indignity.

3. Flag protocol

1. The flag of the International Labour Organization shall not be subordinated to any other flag.
2. The manner in which the flag of the International Labour Organization may be flown, in relation to any other flag, shall be prescribed in the regulations.

4. Use of flag by the International Labour Organization

1. The flag shall be flown:
(a) from all buildings, offices and other property occupied by the International Labour Organization;
(b) from any official residence when such residence has been so designated by regulation;

2. The flag shall be used by any unit acting on behalf of the International Labour Organization such as any committee or commission or other entity established by the International Labour Organization, in such circumstances not covered in this code as may become necessary in the interests of the International Labour Organization.

5. Use of flag generally

The flag may be used in accordance with this flag code by governments, organizations and individuals to demonstrate support of the International Labour Organization and to further its principles and purposes. The manner and circumstances of display shall conform, in so far as appropriate, to the laws and customs applicable to the display of the national flag of the country in which the display is made.

6. Prohibition

The flag shall not be used in any manner inconsistent with this code or its regulations. On no account shall the flag or a replica thereof be used for commercial purposes or in direct association with an article of merchandise. The

Director-General, subject to the approval of the Officers of the Governing Body, may deviate from this principle in special circumstances, such as the celebration of an anniversary of the Organization.

7. *Mourning*

The Director-General shall prescribe by regulation or otherwise the cases in which the flag shall be flown at half mast as a sign of mourning.

8. *Manufacture and sale of flag*

1. The flag may be manufactured for commercial purposes only upon written consent of the Director-General.
2. Such consent shall be subject to the following condition:

The manufacturer shall ensure that every purchaser of the flag receives a copy of this code and the regulations for implementing it and is informed of the conditions, set out in this code and its regulations, on which the flag may be used.

9. *Violation*

Any violation of this flag code and its regulations shall be punished in accordance with the laws of the country in which it takes place.

10. *Regulations and amendments*

The Governing Body, upon the Director-General's proposal, is empowered to make or revise the regulations for implementing this code and to amend the code, as appropriate.

(b) *Regulations for the use of the flag of the International Labour Organization*

These regulations are issued in pursuance of article 10 of the International Labour Organization flag code.

I. DIMENSIONS OF FLAG

1. In pursuance to article 1 of the flag code the proportions of the International Labour Organization flag shall be:

(a) hoist (width) of the International Labour Organization flag – 2;
   fly (length) of the International Labour Organization flag – 3;
or
(b) hoist (width) of the International Labour Organization flag – 3;
   fly (length) of the International Labour Organization flag – 5;
or
(c) the same proportions as those of the national flag of any country in which the International Labour Organization flag is flown.

2. The emblem shall in all cases be one-half of the hoist of the International Labour Organization flag and entirely centred.

II. FLAG PROTOCOL

The International Labour Organization flag may be displayed as follows:

1. *General provisions*

(a) The International Labour Organization flag may be displayed alone or with one or more other flags.

(b) When the International Labour Organization flag is displayed with one or more other flags, all the flags must be displayed on the same level and be of approximately equal size.

(c) On no account may any flag displayed with the International Labour Organization flag be displayed on a higher level than the International Labour Organization flag or be larger than it.

(d) The International Labour Organization flag may be displayed on either side of any other flag without being deemed to be subordinated to any such flag within the meaning of article 3, paragraph 1, of the International Labour Organization flag code.

(e) The International Labour Organization flag should normally only be displayed on a building or flagstaff from sunrise to sunset. The International Labour Organization flag may also be displayed at night in exceptional cases.

(f) The International Labour Organization flag should never be used as drapery of any sort, never festooned, drawn back, nor up, in folds, but always allowed to fall free.

2. *Closed circle of flags*

Other than in a circle of the flags of the United Nations and other specialized agencies, the International Labour Organization flag should not, in principle, be made part of a circle of flags. When flags are placed in a circle, the flags, other than the International Labour Organization flag, should be displayed in the French alphabetical order of the countries represented reading clockwise. The International Labour Organization flag should always be displayed on the flagpole in the centre of the circle of flags or in an appropriate adjoining area.

3. *Line, cluster or semicircle of flags*

In line, cluster or semicircle groupings all flags other than the International Labour Organization flag shall be displayed in the French alphabetical order of the countries represented starting from the left. In such cases, the International Labour Organization flag should either be displayed separately in an appropriate area or in the centre of the line, cluster or semicircle or, in cases where two International Labour Organization flags are available, at both ends of the line, cluster or semicircle.

4. *National flag of the country in which the International Labour Organization flag is displayed*

(a) The national flag of the country should appear in its normal position according to the French alphabetical order of the countries.

(b) When the country concerned wishes to make a special display of its national flag, the flags should be arranged in a line, cluster or semicircle and the national flag placed at each end of the line, cluster or semicircle separated from the grouping by an interval of not less than one-fifth of the total length of the line.

III. USE OF FLAG GENERALLY

1. Under article 5 of the International Labour Organization flag code, the International Labour Organization flag may be used to demonstrate the support

of the International Labour Organization and to further its principles and purposes.

2. It is considered especially appropriate that the International Labour Organization flag should be displayed on the following occasions:

(a) on the national day of the country in which the flag is displayed;

(b) on the occasion of any official event, particularly in honour of the International Labour Organization; and

(c) on the occasion of any official event which might or is desired to be related in some way to the International Labour Organization.

IV. Prohibitions

1. In accordance with article 6 of the International Labour Organization flag code, on no account shall the International Labour Organization flag or replica thereof be used for commercial purposes or in direct association with an article of merchandise.

2. Furthermore, neither the International Labour Organization flag nor any replica thereof shall be stamped, engraved or otherwise affixed on any stationery, books, magazines, periodicals or other publications of any nature whatsoever in a manner such as could imply that any such stationery, books, magazines, periodicals or other publications were published by or on behalf of the International Labour Organization unless such is in fact the case or in a manner such as has the effect of advertising a commercial product.

3. Subject to the provisions of paragraph 2 of this section, and with the exception of articles manufactured for presentation or sale to participants in the various meetings of the International Labour Organization, neither the International Labour Organization flag nor any replica thereof should be affixed in any manner on any article of any kind. Subject to the same exceptions, the International Labour Organization flag should not be reproduced on articles made of cloth, leather, material, synthetic material, etc. The International Labour Organization flag may be manufactured in the form of a lapel button.

4. Subject to the special cases mentioned in paragraphs 2 and 3, no mark, insignia, letter, word, figure, design, picture or drawing of any nature shall ever be placed upon or attached to the International Labour Organization flag or placed upon any replica thereof.

V. Mourning

1. In accordance with article 7 of the International Labour Organization flag code, whenever the Director-General of the International Labour Office proclaims that the International Labour Organization is in official mourning, the International Labour Organization flag, wherever displayed, shall mark such an event by being flown at half mast during the period of official mourning.

2. Heads of offices and heads of International Labour Organization missions away from headquarters are authorized by the Director-General to lower the International Labour Organization flag to half mast in cases where they wish to follow official mourning in the country in which such offices or missions have their headquarters.

3. The International Labour Organization flag when displayed at half mast should first be hoisted to the peak for an instant and then lowered to the half-mast position. The flag should again be raised to the peak before it is lowered for the day. By "half mast" is meant lowering the flag to one-half the distance between the top and bottom of the mast.

4. Crepe streamers may be affixed to flagstaffs flying the International Labour Organization flag in a funeral procession only by order of the Director-General of the International Labour Office.

5. When the International Labour Organization flag is used to cover a casket, it should not be lowered into the grave or allowed to touch the ground.

IV

Resolution concerning the adoption of the Programme and Budget for 2006-07 and the allocation of the budget of income among member States [1]

The General Conference of the International Labour Organization,

In virtue of the Financial Regulations, adopts for the 70th financial period, ending 31 December 2007, the budget of expenditure of the International Labour Organization amounting to US$594,310,000 and the budget of income amounting to US$594,310,000, which, at the budget rate of exchange of 1.25 Swiss francs to the US dollar, amounts to 742,887,500 Swiss francs, and resolves that the budget of income, denominated in Swiss francs, shall be allocated among member States in accordance with the scale of contributions recommended by the Finance Committee of Government Representatives.

V

Resolution concerning the arrears of contributions of Armenia [2]

The General Conference of the International Labour Organization,

Having regard to paragraph 7 of article 10 of the Financial Regulations,

Accepts the arrangement proposed by the Government of Armenia for the settlement of its arrears of contributions due for the period 1992-2004 to the effect that:

(a) in 2005, the Government of Armenia will pay in full its contribution for the year 2005;

(b) in subsequent years, the Government of Armenia will continue to pay its current contribution in full in the year for which it is due;

(c) the Government of Armenia will settle arrears that have accumulated up to and including 31 December 2004, amounting to 1,935,666 Swiss francs, by payment, beginning in 2005, of 20 annual instalments in accordance with the following schedule:

Years		Annual instalment (in Swiss francs)	Total
2005-08	4 years	48 000	192 000
2009-12	4 years	72 000	288 000
2013-16	4 years	96 000	384 000
2017-20	4 years	120 000	480 000
2021-23	3 years	144 000	432 000
2024	1 year	159 666	159 666
Total			1 935 666

---

[1] Adopted on 15 June 2005 by 415 votes in favour, with 7 against and 2 abstentions.
[2] Adopted on 6 June 2005.

Decides that Armenia shall be permitted to vote, in accordance with paragraph 4 of article 13 of the Constitution of the International Labour Organization, after the conclusion of the present business.

VI

Resolution concerning the arrears of contributions of the Republic of Moldova [1]

The General Conference of the International Labour Organization,

Having regard to paragraph 7 of article 10 of the Financial Regulations,

Accepts the arrangement proposed by the Government of the Republic of Moldova for the settlement of its arrears of contributions due for the period 1992-2004 to the effect that:

(a) the payment of 3,548 Swiss francs made by the Government of the Republic of Moldova in April 2005 will be applied against its full contribution for the year 2005;

(b) in subsequent years, the Government of the Republic of Moldova will continue to pay its current contribution in full in the year for which it is due;

(c) the Government of the Republic of Moldova will settle arrears that have accumulated up to and including 31 December 2004, amounting to 2,729,346 Swiss francs, by payment, beginning in 2006, of first instalment of 136,473 Swiss francs and 19 annual instalments of 136,467 Swiss francs;

Decides that the Republic of Moldova shall be permitted to vote, in accordance with paragraph 4 of article 13 of the Constitution of the International Labour Organization, after the conclusion of the present business.

VII

Resolution concerning the arrears of contributions of Togo [2]

The General Conference of the International Labour Organization,

Having regard to paragraph 7 of article 10 of the Financial Regulations,

Accepts the arrangement proposed by the Government of Togo for the settlement of its arrears of contributions due for the period 1992-2004 to the effect that:

(a) in 2005, the Government of Togo will pay in full its contribution for the year 2005;

(b) in subsequent years, the Government of Togo will continue to pay its current contribution in full in the year for which it is due;

(c) the Government of Togo will settle arrears that have accumulated up to and including 31 December 2004, amounting to 213,453 Swiss francs, by payment, beginning in 2006, of seven annual instalments of 27,924 Swiss francs and one final instalment of 17,985 Swiss francs.

Decides that Togo shall be permitted to vote, in accordance with paragraph 4 of article 13 of the Constitution of the International Labour Organization, after the conclusion of the present business.

---

[1] Adopted on 6 June 2005.
[2] Adopted on 15 June 2005.

VIII

Resolution concerning the arrears of contributions of Georgia [1]

The General Conference of the International Labour Organization,

Having regard to paragraph 7 of article 10 of the Financial Regulations,

Accepts the arrangement proposed by the Government of Georgia for the settlement of its arrears of contributions due for the period 1993-2004 to the effect that:

(a) in 2005, the Government of Georgia will pay in full its contribution for the year 2005;

(b) in subsequent years, the Government of Georgia will continue to pay its current contribution in full in the year for which it is due;

(c) the Government of Georgia will settle arrears that have accumulated up to and including 31 December 2004, amounting to 3,071,902 Swiss francs, by payment, beginning in 2006, of 14 annual instalments in accordance with the following schedule:

Years	Amount (in Swiss francs)
2006	46 079
2007	61 438
2008	61 438
2009	61 438
2010	61 438
2011	122 876
2012	153 595
2013	153 595
2014	307 190
2015	368 628
2016	368 628
2017	430 066
2018	430 066
2019	445 427
Total	3 071 902

Decides that Georgia shall be permitted to vote, in accordance with paragraph 4 of article 13 of the Constitution of the International Labour Organization, after the conclusion of the present business.

IX

Resolution concerning the arrears of contributions of Iraq [1]

The General Conference of the International Labour Organization,

Having regard to paragraph 7 of article 10 of the Financial Regulations,

---

[1] Adopted on 15 June 2005.

Accepts the arrangement proposed by the Government of Iraq for the settlement of its arrears of contributions due for the period 1988-2004 to the effect that:

(a) in 2005, the Government of Iraq will pay in full its contribution for the year 2005;

(b) in subsequent years, the Government of Iraq will continue to pay its current contribution in full in the year for which it is due;

(c) the Government of Iraq will settle arrears that have accumulated up to and including 31 December 2004, amounting to 6,127,793 Swiss francs, by payment, beginning in 2005, of 19 annual instalments of 306,390 Swiss francs and a final instalment of 306,383 Swiss francs,

Decides that Iraq shall be permitted to vote, in accordance with paragraph 4 of article 13 of the Constitution of the International Labour Organization, after the conclusion of the present business.

X

Resolution concerning the composition of the Administrative Tribunal of the International Labour Organization [1]

The General Conference of the International Labour Organization,

Decides, in accordance with article III of the Statute of the Administrative Tribunal of the International Labour Organization, to renew the term of office of Ms. Geneviève Gaudron for three years,

Expresses its appreciation to Ms. Flerida Ruth P. Romero for her contribution over the last five years to the work of the Administrative Tribunal of the International Labour Organization.

XI

Resolution concerning the assessment of contributions of new member States [1]

The General Conference of the International Labour Organization,

Decides, in accordance with the established practice of harmonizing the rates of assessment of ILO member States with their rates of assessment in the United Nations, that the contribution of Samoa to the ILO budget for the period of its membership in the Organization in 2005 be based on an annual assessment rate of 0.001 per cent.

XII

Resolution concerning the scale of assessments of contributions to the budget for 2006 [1]

The General Conference of the International Labour Organization,

Decides, in accordance with article 9, paragraph 2, of the Financial Regulations, to adopt the draft scale of assessments for the year 2006 based on the scale adopted by the United Nations General Assembly in December 2003 as set out in column 3 of Appendix III to this document.

---

[1] Adopted on 13 June 2005.

RESOLUTIONS

CONTENTS

		Page
I.	Resolution concerning youth employment	1
II.	Resolution to place on the agenda of the next ordinary session of the Conference an item entitled "Occupational safety and health"	12
III.	Resolution concerning the flag of the International Labour Organization	12
IV.	Resolution concerning the adoption of the Programme and Budget for 2006-07 and the allocation of the budget of income among member States	17
V.	Resolution concerning the arrears of contributions of Armenia	17
VI.	Resolution concerning the arrears of contributions of the Republic of Moldova	18
VII.	Resolution concerning the arrears of contributions of Togo	18
VIII.	Resolution concerning the arrears of contributions of Georgia	19
IX.	Resolution concerning the arrears of contributions of Iraq	19
X.	Resolution concerning the composition of the Administrative Tribunal of the International Labour Organization	20
XI.	Resolution concerning the assessment of contributions of new member States	20
XII.	Resolution concerning the scale of assessments of contributions to the budget for 2006	20